P9-CFF-601

Connect™ Accounting

Instructors...

 Want to **streamline** lesson planning, student progress reporting, and assignment grading? (Less time planning means more time teaching...)

Need to **collect data and generate reports** required by accreditation organizations, such as AACSB and AICPA? (Say goodbye to manually tracking student learning outcomes...)

Want an **instant view** of student or class performance relative to learning objectives? (No more wondering if students understand...)

With **McGraw-Hill *Connect*™ Accounting,**

INSTRUCTORS GET

- The ability to **post assignments** and other communication between students and instructors.

- Simple **assignment management**, allowing you to spend more time teaching.

- **Auto-graded homework.**

- **Customized course gradebook** where grades are automatically posted.

- **Online testing capability**.

- A **progress-tracking** function that allows you to easily assign materials that conform to AACSB and AICPA standards.

Q Want an online, **searchable version** of your textbook?

Wish your textbook could be available online while you're doing your homework?

A *Connect*™ **Plus Accounting eBook**

If your instructor has chosen to use *Connect*™ *Plus Accounting*, you have an affordable and searchable online version of your book integrated with your other online homework tools.

Connect™ **Plus Accounting eBook offers features like:**

- topic search
- adjustable text size
- jump to page number
- print by section

Q Want to get more **value** from your textbook purchase?

Think learning accounting should be a little bit more **interesting**?

A **Check out the companion website for this textbook www.mhhe.com/phillips3e**

We put it there for you. Go online for test tips and practice problems whenever you study. The companion website for this book includes **quizzes, PowerPoints, and Internet activities** to help you study. Get more from your textbook—use the Online Learning Center.

fundamentals of
FINANCIAL ACCOUNTING
www.mhhe.com/phillips3e

Third Edition

FRED PHILLIPS
University of Saskatchewan

ROBERT LIBBY
Cornell University

PATRICIA A. LIBBY
Ithaca College

McGraw-Hill Irwin

McGraw-Hill Irwin

FUNDAMENTALS OF FINANCIAL ACCOUNTING

Published by McGraw-Hill/Irwin, a business unit of The McGraw-Hill Companies, Inc., 1221 Avenue of the Americas, New York, NY, 10020. Copyright © 2011, 2008, 2006 by The McGraw-Hill Companies, Inc. All rights reserved. No part of this publication may be reproduced or distributed in any form or by any means, or stored in a database or retrieval system, without the prior written consent of The McGraw-Hill Companies, Inc., including, but not limited to, in any network or other electronic storage or transmission, or broadcast for distance learning.

Some ancillaries, including electronic and print components, may not be available to customers outside the United States.

This book is printed on acid-free paper.

1 2 3 4 5 6 7 8 9 0 DOW/DOW 1 0 9 8 7 6 5 4 3 2 1 0

ISBN   978-0-07-352710-9
MHID   0-07-352710-6

Vice president and editor-in-chief: *Brent Gordon*
Editorial director: *Stewart Mattson*
Publisher: *Tim Vertovec*
Director of development: *Ann Torbert*
Senior sponsoring editor: *Dana Woo*
Senior development editor: *Kimberly D. Hooker*
Vice president and director of marketing: *Robin J. Zwettler*
Marketing director: *Sankha Basu*
Marketing manager: *Kathleen Klehr*
Vice president of editing, design and production: *Sesha Bolisetty*
Manager of photo, design & publishing tools: *Mary Conzachi*
Lead production supervisor: *Carol A. Bielski*
Cover and interior designer: *Matt Diamond*
Senior photo research coordinator: *Jeremy Cheshareck*
Photo researcher: *Editorial Image, LLC*
Senior media project manager: *Allison Souter*
Typeface: *10.5/12 Goudy*
Compositor: *Laserwords Private Limited*
Printer: *R. R. Donnelley*

Library of Congress Cataloging-in-Publication Data

Phillips, Fred.
    Fundamentals of financial accounting / Fred Phillips, Robert Libby,
Patricia A. Libby.—3rd ed.
        p. cm.
    Includes index.
    ISBN-13: 978-0-07-352710-9 (alk. paper)
    ISBN-10: 0-07-352710-6 (alk. paper)
    1. Accounting. I. Libby, Robert. II. Libby, Patricia A. III. Title.
HF5636.P545 2011
657—dc22

                                                        2009042931

Dedication

I dedicate this book to the best teachers I've ever had:
my Mom and Dad, Barb, Harrison, and Daniel

FRED PHILLIPS

Jenni, John, and Emma Rose Drago, Herman and Doris Hargenrater,
Laura Libby, Oscar and Selma Libby

PATRICIA AND ROBERT LIBBY

Meet the Authors

Fred Phillips

Fred Phillips is a professor and the George C. Baxter Chartered Accountants of Saskatchewan Scholar at the University of Saskatchewan, where he teaches introductory financial accounting. He also has taught introductory accounting at the University of Texas at Austin and the University of Manitoba. Fred has an undergraduate accounting degree, a professional accounting designation, and a PhD from the University of Texas at Austin. He previously worked as an audit manager at KPMG.

Fred's main interest is accounting education. He has won 11 teaching awards, including three national case-writing competitions. Recently, Fred won the 2007 Alpha Kappa Psi Outstanding Professor award at the University of Texas at Austin, and in 2006, he was awarded the title Master Teacher at the University of Saskatchewan. He has published instructional cases and numerous articles in journals such as *Issues in Accounting Education, Journal of Accounting Research,* and *Organizational Behavior and Human Decision Processes*. He received the American Accounting Association's Outstanding Research in Accounting Education Award in 2006 and 2007 for his articles. Fred is a past associate editor of *Issues in Accounting Education,* and a current member of the Teaching, Curriculum, & Learning and Two-Year College sections of the American Accounting Association. In his spare time, he likes to work out, play video games, and drink iced cappuccinos.

Robert Libby

Robert Libby is the David A. Thomas Professor of Accounting at Cornell University, where he teaches the introductory financial accounting course. He previously taught at the University of Illinois, Pennsylvania State University, the University of Texas at Austin, the University of Chicago, and the University of Michigan. He received his BS from Pennsylvania State University and his MAS and PhD from the University of Illinois; he also is a CPA.

Bob is a widely published author specializing in behavioral accounting. He was selected as the AAA Outstanding Educator in 2000 and received the AAA Outstanding Service Award in 2006. His prior text, *Accounting and Human Information Processing* (Prentice Hall, 1981), was awarded the AICPA/AAA Notable Contributions to the Accounting

Literature Award. He received this award again in 1996 for a paper. He has published numerous articles in *The Accounting Review*, *Journal of Accounting Research*, *Accounting, Organizations, and Society*; and other accounting journals. He has held a variety of offices in the American Accounting Association and is a member of the American Institute of CPAs and the editorial boards of *The Accounting Review*, *Accounting, Organizations, and Society*, *Journal of Accounting Literature*, and *Journal of Behavioral Decision Making*.

Patricia A. Libby

Patricia Libby is associate professor of accounting and coordinator of the financial accounting course at Ithaca College, as well as faculty advisor to Beta Alpha Psi, Ithaca College Accounting Association, and Ithaca College National Association of Black Accountants. She previously taught graduate and undergraduate financial accounting at Eastern Michigan University and the University of Texas at Austin. Before entering academe, she was an auditor with Price Waterhouse (now PricewaterhouseCoopers) and a financial administrator at the University of Chicago. She received her BS from Pennsylvania State University, her MBA from DePaul University, and her PhD from the University of Michigan; she also is a CPA.

Pat conducts research on using cases in the introductory course and other parts of the accounting curriculum. She has published articles in *The Accounting Review*, *Issues in Accounting Education*, and *The Michigan CPA*. She has also conducted seminars nationwide on active learning strategies, including cooperative learning methods.

Focused on Financial Accounting in the Context of Real Business

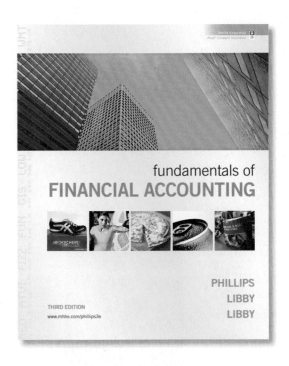

fundamentals of
FINANCIAL ACCOUNTING

PHILLIPS
LIBBY
LIBBY

THIRD EDITION
www.mhhe.com/phillips3e

> *The text is extremely well written with enough details to explain the topics and not too much to confuse students.*
>
> –Laurie Dahlin, *Worcester State College*

> *Students should find the use of companies from their generation, as examples, interesting.*
>
> –Diane Marker, *University of Toledo*

The second edition of Phillips/Libby/Libby *Fundamentals of Financial Accounting* was a great success, thanks to the ideas and direction provided by a dedicated panel of reviewers, many students, and a host of talented contributors. It was named **"Revision of the Year"** across all of McGraw-Hill's business and economics textbooks.

The third edition furthers our commitment to providing the best accounting textbook for teaching and learning financial accounting. With its innovative student-centered approach, unique and interactive pedagogical tools, and compelling instructor and student resources, no other text presents financial accounting in such a clear and student-friendly manner. The keys to its success:

ENGAGING WRITING. *Fundamentals of Financial Accounting* introduces students to financial accounting using an appropriate mix of conversational wording, clear and concise presentations, and everyday examples. It does this without ever sacrificing its rigor or the concepts that are important to grasping financial accounting. Students can feel comfortable as they are introduced to the world of financial accounting.

RELEVANT FOCUS COMPANIES. Each chapter of *Fundamentals of Financial Accounting* makes financial accounting come alive by using a real company whose products and services are popular with students. Students learn financial accounting concepts through the use of examples from such companies as **American Eagle** (clothing), **Activision** (video games), **Skechers** (shoes), and **Under Armour** (sportswear).

THE POWER OF REINFORCEMENT. Several tools help reinforce the concepts discussed in the text. Coach's Tips and You Should Know are innovative and student-friendly pedagogical features that appear in the margins to reinforce concepts in the text as well as offer helpful insight.

> *This book is an easy and informative book. It contains many examples that would appeal to students which in turn makes them more likely to read. . . . Your problems are outstanding and it makes it so helpful when you include similar problems to allow the professor to be able to go through one and assign another that is almost identical, but uses different numbers. Overall, it is one of the best books I have seen or reviewed. The authors have done an outstanding job with this text! . . . It beats out all other books I have seen thus far.*
>
> –Stephen Benner, *Eastern Illinois University*

Dedicated to Student Motivation and Success

The accounting world is encountering new challenges and *Fundamentals of Financial Accounting* aims to help you and your students take them in stride. You will find some important changes in the third edition that will give your students the tools and information necessary to help them succeed. Based on the feedback and advice from several financial accounting faculty, the most significant of those changes include:

- The **entrepreneurial focus company in Chapter 1** has been **extended through Chapters 2, 3, and 4,** allowing students to see how a business plan (Chapter 1) leads to actual financing and investing decisions (Chapter 2), operating activities (Chapter 3), and adjustments made prior to evaluating the financial results (Chapter 4). Students emerge from the first four chapters with a solid understanding of how the accounting process plays a pivotal role in business.

- Anticipating a greater emphasis on **International Financial Reporting Standards** (IFRS) in the United States and recognizing its presence in more than 100 countries worldwide, we have integrated selected IFRS topics in appropriate chapters at a level suitable for introductory financial accounting. We summarize these topics at the end of the last chapter in the book (in chapter supplement 13B) and we tie this summary to specific references in each chapter. To support discussions and analyses involving IFRS, we have introduced more than 20 questions and exercises in **end-of-chapter assignments** that specifically focus on IFRS.

> *The authors did a great job of* **explaining the importance of financial reporting** *in the world economy—from the smallest business to the largest.*
>
> –Tim Mills, *Eastern Illinois University*

- To further engage students and provide instructors material for in-class discussion, we integrate Spotlight features in each chapter, focusing on business decisions, ethics, internal controls, financial reporting, and the world (IFRS). Key Spotlights are supported by 4-minute videos that are scripted specifically for this textbook.

> *[Chapter 2] provides* **exceptionally clear steps for analyzing accounting transactions.** *I particularly like the fact that the chapter focuses on transactions that impact only the balance sheet, leaving for later transactions that impact the income statement. I believe this approach will enable students to more readily* **grasp a concept** *that confuses many.*
>
> –Lisa Thornton, *Truckee Meadows Community College*

> *Phillips/Libby/Libby 3e* **introduces all of the financial statements** *in the first chapter, then utilizes debits and credits combined with increases and decreases for transactions affecting the balance sheet, and then* **reinforces the methodology** *when presenting the transactions affecting the income statement in Chapter 3. This area is the toughest for students and requires the most practice. Phillips understands this and* **expertly navigates** *through the two statements and demonstrates how the two interconnect and depend upon each other, setting the stage for an easier adjustment and closing process ahead.*
>
> –Margaret Costello Lambert, *Oakland Community College*

Real Companies Bring Accounting Concepts to Life

> *Conversational style and excellent use of feature companies to engage students and foster their understanding of difficult concepts and topics.*
>
> —Matthew Muller, *Adirondack Community College and University at Albany*

> *The Cedar Fair example [Chapter 9] is one that I think students will clearly understand. In fact, I think the introductory discussion is probably the best I've ever seen at helping students begin to understand the issue of [the] long-term asset decision [and] about whether to expand or not and the why of the decision.*
>
> —Gary Adna Ames, *BYU-Idaho*

Not all students learn financial accounting with ease. With so many distractions these days, it is difficult to keep both majors and non-majors focused on the big picture. The authors of *Fundamentals of Financial Accounting* understand the challenges instructors face and the need for a financial accounting text that is relevant, easy to read, and current.

Fundamentals of Financial Accounting responds by using **carefully chosen focus companies that students not only recognize but are familiar with because they have visited or used their products.** From companies like the local pizza restaurant to the world's most familiar businesses, each chapter features the business and accounting concepts underlying prominent companies such as Walmart, Activision, Cedar Fair, American Eagle, National Beverage, Under Armour, and General Mills.

Through crisp, clear, and engaging writing, the financial decisions these companies make and the financial statements they use come alive for students and they are able to see the big picture of how accounting relates to the real world—their world.

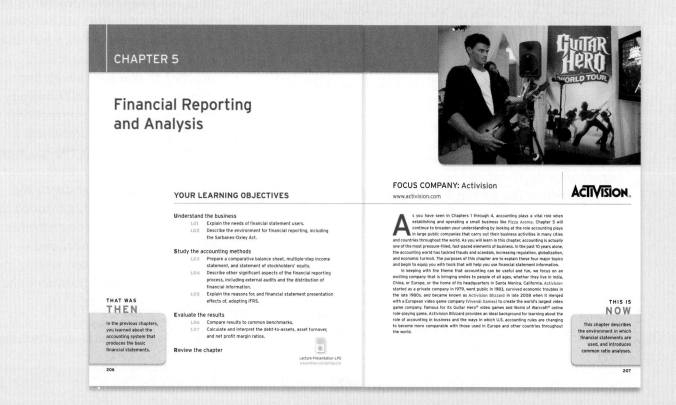

From **Concepts** to **Comprehension**— Reinforcement Is Key

Whether you're presenting, discussing, or problem solving, you want materials that will motivate students and hold their interest. Motivating today's students requires materials that connect them with the workplace and encourage them to think about course topics before, during, and after class. *Fundamentals of Financial Accounting* offers students many tools to help reinforce the concepts discussed throughout the text.

(c) Obtain Loan from Bank Pizza Aroma borrows $20,000 from a bank, depositing those funds in its bank account and signing a formal agreement to repay the loan in two years.

Picture

Receives

Gives

Name

- Pizza Aroma has received $20,000 cash.
- Pizza Aroma gave a note, payable to the bank for $20,000.

COACH'S TIP

Notes payable are like accounts payable except that they (a) charge interest, (b) can be outstanding for long periods (more than one year), and (c) are documented using formal documents called notes.

Analyze

	Assets	=	Liabilities	+	Stockholders' Equity
(c) Cash	+20,000	=	Note Payable		+20,000

Coach's Tips

Every student needs encouragement and Coach's Tips are just one way *Fundamentals of Financial Accounting* fulfills that need. Coach's Tips appear throughout the text and in selected end-of-chapter problems to offer tips, advice, and suggestions.

How's it going?
Self-Study Practice

Research shows that students learn best when they are actively engaged in the learning process. This active learning feature engages the student, provides interactivity, and promotes efficient learning. These quizzes ask students to pause at strategic points throughout each chapter to ensure they understand key points before moving ahead.

How's it going?   Self-Study Practice

The following transactions are typical operating activities for Florida Flippers, a scuba diving and instruction company. Indicate the amount of expense, if any, that should be recognized in June for each activity.

Operating Activity	Amount of Expense Incurred in June
1. In June, Florida Flippers paid $6,000 cash for insurance for July–December.	
2. In June, Florida Flippers paid $4,000 in wages to employees who worked in June.	
3. In June, Florida Flippers used $2,400 of electricity, to be paid in July.	

After you have finished, check your answers with the solution in the margin.

> *I really liked the discussions on **fraud, SOX and IFRS**. These are important topics which really must be addressed. [Chapter 5] does a **great job in addressing timely topics**—why financial statements have failed in the past and how we are addressing weaknesses of the statements, and what to anticipate in the future. **Your discussion on IFRS was great.***
>
> —Linda K. Whitten, *Skyline College*

Videos Put the Spotlight on Issues in Financial Accounting

NEW!

Spotlight Features

Each chapter includes Spotlight features focusing on business decisions, ethics, internal controls, financial reporting, and the world (IFRS). These features are designed to further engage students and provide instructors with material for in-class discussion.

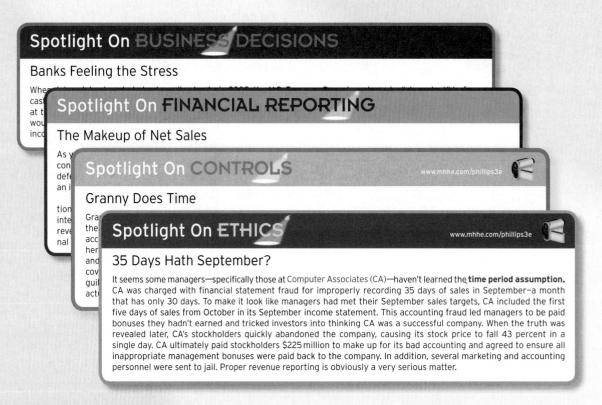

Spotlight On BUSINESS DECISIONS

Banks Feeling the Stress

Spotlight On FINANCIAL REPORTING

The Makeup of Net Sales

Spotlight On CONTROLS   www.mhhe.com/phillips3e

Granny Does Time

Spotlight On ETHICS   www.mhhe.com/phillips3e

35 Days Hath September?

It seems some managers—specifically those at Computer Associates (CA)—haven't learned the **time period assumption.** CA was charged with financial statement fraud for improperly recording 35 days of sales in September–a month that has only 30 days. To make it look like managers had met their September sales targets, CA included the first five days of sales from October in its September income statement. This accounting fraud led managers to be paid bonuses they hadn't earned and tricked investors into thinking CA was a successful company. When the truth was revealed later, CA's stockholders quickly abandoned the company, causing its stock price to fall 43 percent in a single day. CA ultimately paid stockholders $225 million to make up for its bad accounting and agreed to ensure all inappropriate management bonuses were paid back to the company. In addition, several marketing and accounting personnel were sent to jail. Proper revenue reporting is obviously a very serious matter.

- **Spotlight on Business Decisions**—helps students develop strong decision-making skills by illustrating the relevance of accounting in real-world decision making and the lessons learned from the global economic crisis.

- **Spotlight on Financial Reporting**—connects chapter topics with real-world disclosures provided in the financial statements of our focus companies and other contrast companies.

- **Spotlight on Controls**—highlights applications of internal control principles in the workplace.

- **Spotlight on Ethics**—emphasizes ethical issues faced in business and the importance of acting responsibly.

Videos

NEW!

Selected Spotlight on Ethics and Financial Reporting features are brought to life in 4-5 minute newsmagazine-style videos, which are available on the text Online Learning Center www.mhhe.com/phillips3e. These investigative videos written by Fred Phillips tie to specific topics in *Fundamentals of Financial Accounting*. Bring business and accounting into your classroom in a way that is sure to engage students and get them talking about the stories in your textbook.

Chapter	Video Title	Video Description
Chapter 3 (page 99)	Time Is Money	In 2000-01, Computer Associates violated the time period assumption in order to present a picture of smooth, steady growth. This video illustrates the effect of shifting sales from one period to another and asks students to discuss its impact.
Chapter 4 (page 169)	Anatomy of a Business Failure	Circuit City once was a leading electronics retailer. But, as this video demonstrates, the company's financial problems led to a free-fall in the company's stock price. This video walks students through the series of events that ultimately ended when Circuit City liquidated in January 2009.
Chapter 6 (page 268)	Granny Does Time	After twelve years of honest bookkeeping, a grandmother begins embezzling from her employer by writing checks to herself, recording them as inventory purchases, and then destroying them when preparing the bank reconciliation. This is a must-see video for future business owners and financial advisers because it underscores the importance of internal controls over cash and inventory.
Chapter 7 (page 320)	Dodging Bullets	Body armor made by DHB Industries in 2004-05 for the U.S. Marines and local police departments did not meet quality standards. Knowing the impact of an inventory writedown, DHB tried to conceal its problems. By telling these events, this video invites students to consider how fraudulent actions may put innocent people in harm's way.
Chapter 8 (page 371)	Resetting the Clock	This video describes how a credit manager at MCI used his knowledge of the allowance method to avoid recording $70 million in bad debts. The video shows students how small initial missteps led the credit manager to redirect his genuine ambition into criminal actions, which ended in a prison sentence and personal ruin.
Chapter 9 (page 404)	Simple Violations, Serious Consequences	This video describes how the simple act of capitalizing expenses enabled WorldCom to mislead financial statement users. Students are invited to consider the judgment inherent in many seemingly simple accounting decisions.

I thought the coverage on fraud and SOX was very good. Also, the inclusion of GAAP vs. IFRS. This is the first textbook that I have read that covers this very important issue. The information presented was easy to read and understand.

–Victoria White, *Ivy Tech Community College of Indiana–Evansville*

Practice and Review Materials

To effectively evaluate and guide student success with the appropriate feedback, you need homework & test materials that are **easy to use** and tied to the chapter discussions.

> *It was very readable throughout making it more likely that students will pick it up and use it. Features like the Homework Helper section also make sure to point out helpful tips and clarifications.*
>
> –Amy Bentley,
> *Tallahassee Community College*

Each chapter of *Fundamentals of Financial Accounting* is followed by an extensive variety of end-of-chapter material that applies and integrates topics presented in the chapter. We have retained many of the popular items from prior editions and added new types of end-of-chapter materials including a Homework Helper, multiple-perspective discussion questions, comprehensive problems, and continuing cases.

Chapter Summary

Each chapter concludes with an end-of-chapter summary, organized by chapter learning objective, that revisits the learning objectives from the beginning of the chapter.

Key Terms

Includes key terms, definitions, and page references. Full definitions for all key terms are found in the back of the text.

Homework Helper

Immediately precedes each chapter's homework materials, highlighting subtleties discussed in the chapter and providing practice advice so that students can avoid common pitfalls when completing homework.

NEW!

HOMEWORK HELPER

Account Name	Description
Revenues	
Sales	Arise from delivering products in the ordinary course of business
Service Revenues	Arise from providing services in the ordinary course of business
Rental Revenues	Amounts earned by renting out company property
Interest Revenues	Amounts earned on savings and loans to others
Dividend Revenues	Dividends earned from investing in other companies
Fees Earned	Fees that the company charges its customers
Expenses	
Cost of Goods Sold	Cost of products sold in the ordinary course of business
Repairs & Maintenance Expense	Cost of routine maintenance and upkeep of buildings/equipment
Advertising Expense	Cost of advertising services obtained during the period
Depreciation Expense	Cost of plant and equipment used up during the period
Insurance Expense	Cost of insurance coverage for the current period
Salaries and Wages Expense	Cost of employees' salaries and wages for the period
Rent Expense	Cost of rent for the period
Supplies Expense	Cost of supplies used up during the period
Delivery Expense	Cost of freight to deliver goods to customers
Utilities Expense	Cost of power, light, heat, Internet, and telephone for the period
Amortization Expense	Cost of intangible assets used up or expired during the period
Interest Expense	Interest charged on outstanding debts owed during the period
Income Tax Expense	Taxes charged on net income reported for the period

Alternative terms
- Net income also can be called net earnings.
- Prepaid Rent and Prepaid Insurance can be called Prepaid Expenses, which is reported as a current asset on the balance sheet.

Helpful reminders
- To properly understand why Prepaid Expenses is an asset and Unearned Revenue is a liability, emphasize the first word (prepaid and unearned).
- If the trial balance doesn't balance, look at the difference between total debits and total credits. If it is . . .
  - **The same as** one of your T-account balances, you probably forgot to include the account

Build Confidence and Success

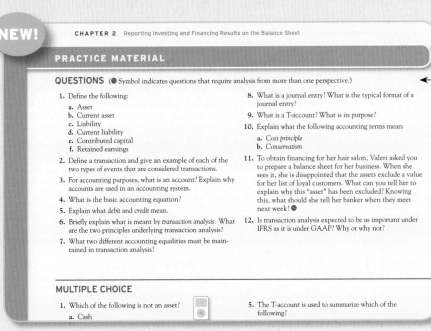

CHAPTER 2 Reporting Investing and Financing Results on the Balance Sheet

PRACTICE MATERIAL

QUESTIONS (● Symbol indicates questions that require analysis from more than one perspective.)

1. Define the following:
   a. Asset
   b. Current asset
   c. Liability
   d. Current liability
   e. Contributed capital
   f. Retained earnings
2. Define a transaction and give an example of each of the two types of events that are considered transactions.
3. For accounting purposes, what is an account? Explain why accounts are used in an accounting system.
4. What is the basic accounting equation?
5. Explain what *debit* and *credit* mean.
6. Briefly explain what is meant by *transaction analysis*. What are the two principles underlying transaction analysis?
7. What two different accounting equalities must be maintained in transaction analysis?

8. What is a journal entry? What is the typical format of a journal entry?
9. What is a T-account? What is its purpose?
10. Explain what the following accounting terms mean:
    a. *Cost principle*
    b. *Conservatism*
11. To obtain financing for her hair salon, Valeri asked you to prepare a balance sheet for her business. When she sees it, she is disappointed that the assets exclude a value for her list of loyal customers. What can you tell her to explain why this "asset" has been excluded? Knowing this, what should she tell her banker when they meet next week? ●
12. Is transaction analysis expected to be as important under IFRS as it is under GAAP? Why or why not?

MULTIPLE CHOICE

1. Which of the following is not an asset?
   a. Cash

5. The T-account is used to summarize which of the following?

Multi-perspective Discussion Questions

Each chapter includes 10-20 questions that ask students to explain and discuss terms and concepts presented in the chapter. Selected questions, denoted with an icon, are designed to help students begin developing critical thinking skills. These questions are ideal for sparking debate at the beginning of class or when transitioning between or reviewing topics.

Multiple-Choice Questions

Each chapter includes 10 multiple-choice questions that let students practice basic concepts. Solutions for these questions are provided in the back of the text.

Mini-Exercises

These assignments illustrate and apply a single learning objective from the chapter.

Exercises

These additional assignments illustrate and apply single and multiple learning objectives from the chapter.

Problems (Coached, Set A, and Set B)

Each chapter includes three problem sets to help students develop decision-making skills. Coached problems include question-specific tips to assist students who need a little help getting started. Sets A and B are similar problems but without the coaching.

Comprehensive Problems

Selected chapters include problems that cover topics from earlier chapters to refresh, reinforce, and build an integrative understanding of the course material. These are a great resource for helping students stay up-to-date throughout the course.

Skills Development Cases

Each chapter offers cases designed to help students develop analytical, critical thinking, and technology skills. These cases are ideal for individual assignments, class discussions, and group projects.

Continuing Case

In Chapter 1, students are introduced to Nicole's Getaway Spa (NGS). In each chapter, the continuing case feature extends this case and requires students to apply topics from the current chapter.

CONTINUING CASE

NEW!

CC1 Financial Statements for a Business Plan

Nicole Mackisey is thinking of forming her own spa business, Nicole's Getaway Spa (NGS). Nicole expects that she and two family members will each contribute $10,000 to the business and receive 1,000 shares each. Nicole forecasts the following amounts for the first year of operations, ending December 31, 2010: Cash on hand and in the bank, $2,150; amounts due from customers from spa treatments, $1,780; building and equipment, $70,000; amounts owed to beauty supply outlets for spa equipment, $4,660; notes payable to a local bank for $38,870. Cash dividends of $2,000 will be paid to the stockholders during the year. Nicole also forecasts that first year sales revenues will be $40,000; wages will be $24,000; the cost of supplies used up will be $7,000; selling and administrative expenses will be $5,000; and income taxes will be $1,600.

Required:

1. Based on Nicole's estimates, prepare a (forecasted) income statement for Nicole's Getaway Spa for the year ended December 31, 2010.
2. Prepare a (forecasted) statement of retained earnings for Nicole's Getaway Spa for the year ended December 31, 2010.
3. Prepare a (forecasted) balance sheet for Nicole's Getaway Spa at December 31, 2010.

Photo Courtesy of Apple.®

iPod Downloadable Content

Fundamentals of Financial Accounting is a media-integrated textbook that provides students with portable educational contents—just right for those students who want to study when and where it's most convenient for them. Students have the option to download content for review and study to their Apple® iPods and most other MP3 and MP4 devices. iPod icons appear throughout the text, pointing students to chapter-specific audio lecture presentations slides, course-related videos, and multiple-choice practice questions.

The following icons appear throughout the chapter and end of chapter. All iPod content can be downloaded to **iPod**, **Zune**, or **MP3 devices** (audio and visual depending on your device). Refer to the Online Learning Center, www.mhhe.com/phillips3e, to download content and to access Excel templates.

Lecture Presentation–LP1
www.mhhe.com/phillips3e

Lecture Presentation slides allow for study before and after class.

Video–1.1
www.mhhe.com/phillips3e

Topical videos are directly related to the chapter discussions.

Quiz 1
www.mhhe.com/phillips3e

Multiple-choice quizzes provide additional practice.

www.mhhe.com/phillips3e

Excel templates are tied to selected end-of-chapter assignments designated with this icon.

What's New in the Third Edition?

In response to the feedback and guidance from numerous financial accounting faculty, *Fundamentals of Financial Accounting*, 3e includes several important new changes, including new chapter openers, 140 **new** end-of-chapter assignments, and refinements and updates to over 400 remaining questions, exercises, problems, and cases. Several new features are introduced in this edition, including Spotlight features (see page x), Homework Helper, multi-perspective discussion questions, continuing cases, comprehensive problems, and questions, exercises, and problems that specifically relate to IFRS, the global economic crisis, and XBRL.

CHAPTER 1
Focus Company: Pizza Aroma, Inc.

- Revised conceptual framework discussion
- Introduction of IFRS
- New ethical conduct discussion

CHAPTER 2
New Focus Company: Pizza Aroma, Inc.

- New visuals to demonstrate transaction analysis steps
- IFRS spotlight on transaction analysis and the role of principles versus rules
- New discussion of surviving the credit crisis with a strong balance sheet
- Introduction of the current ratio

CHAPTER 3
New Focus Company: Pizza Aroma, Inc.

- New visual to demonstrate operating cycle transactions
- New Spotlight on Ethics video explaining Computer Associates's violation of the time period assumption

CHAPTER 4
New Focus Company: Pizza Aroma, Inc.

- New visuals to illustrate the analyses required in making adjustments
- New Spotlight on Financial Reporting video depicting Circuit City's slide into bankruptcy

CHAPTER 5
Focus Company: Activision Blizzard

- New Spotlight on Business Decisions explaining accounting's role in the Treasury Department's stress test for banks

- New Self-Study Practice on financial statement articulation
- New Spotlight on Financial Reporting introducing XBRL
- New section on financial statement presentation under GAAP and IFRS
- New financial statement analyses, including two U.S. companies and one European competitor
- New section explaining how transactions affect ratios

CHAPTER 6
Focus Company: Walmart

- New section and visuals applying control principles to cash transactions
- Revised Spotlight on Controls focusing on granny fraud video
- Inventory purchasing moved to Chapter 7

CHAPTER 7
New Focus Company: American Eagle Outfitters

- New chapter opener
- 2 new Self-Study Practice features
- New visuals to demonstrate and contrast inventory costing methods
- New Spotlight on IFRS and Spotlight on Ethics (with video) describing an inventory valuation fraud at DHB Industries
- Three chapter supplements are included to demonstrate inventory costing in a perpetual system (A), explain inventory error effects (B), and contrast inventory recording under periodic and perpetual systems (C).

CHAPTER 8
Focus Company: Skechers

- New Spotlight on Business Decisions depicting the significance of bad debts to Target's decision to grant credit to individual consumers during difficult economic times

- Percentage of sales moved from chapter supplement to body of chapter
- New Spotlights on using an aging schedule to focus collection efforts and on comparing stated credit terms to turnover analyses
- New video to support Spotlight discussing a credit manager's accounting fraud at MCI

CHAPTER 9
Focus Company: Cedar Fair

- Partial year depreciation is now integrated into the chapter
- 2 new Spotlights discussing IFRS's accounting for component costs, R&D, and fair value

CHAPTER 10
Focus Company: General Mills

- New section highlighting the vital role of liabilities in financing a business
- New visuals and discussion of payroll, new visuals to demonstrate bond amortization
- New Spotlight on bond pricing
- New Spotlight on IFRS thresholds for recording contingent liabilities
- New section on the quick ratio
- New Spotlight on surviving a financial crunch

CHAPTER 11
New Focus Company: National Beverage

- New Spotlights on dividend cuts and choosing between stock dividends and stock splits
- New Spotlight on preferred stock classification

CHAPTER 12
New Focus Company: Under Armour

- New Spotlights contrasting cash flows and net income for W. T. Grant and Lehman Brothers
- New Spotlight contrasting classification of dividends and interest under GAAP and IFRS

- New illustrations contrasting indirect and direct methods using Under Armour's financials
- Detailed discussion of direct method moved to last topic in chapter body

CHAPTER 13
New Focus Company: Lowe's

- More prominent placement for vertical analysis
- New Spotlight comparing Lowe's GAAP accounting policies with the IFRS accounting policies of Europe's largest home improvement retailer (Kingfisher)

APPENDIX A
New Focus Company: The Home Depot

We selected Home Depot as the new focus company because its operations are familiar to students, its financial statements are relatively straightforward, and it reveals the impact of a financial downturn (while still reporting a profit, which helps to avoid potentially confusing ratios).

APPENDIX B
New Focus Company: Lowe's

We selected Lowe's as the new focus company because in terms of operations, geography, and size, Lowe's is a close competitor to The Home Depot.

APPENDIX C

New graphic to show the power of compounding and new section demonstrating present value computations using Excel

APPENDIX D
New Focus Company: Washington Post

The introduction and appendix outline are presented in the body of the text, while the detailed discussions and illustrations are available for download from the textbook's Online Learning Center **www.mhhe.com/phillips3e**

Leading Technology Extends
Learning Beyond the Classroom

McGraw-Hill Connect Accounting
LESS MANAGING. MORE TEACHING. GREATER LEARNING.

McGRAW-HILL *CONNECT ACCOUNTING* FEATURES

Connect Accounting offers a number of powerful tools and features to make managing assignments easier, so faculty can spend more time teaching. With *Connect Accounting* students can engage with their coursework anytime and anywhere, making the learning process more accessible and efficient. *Connect Accounting* offers you the features described below.

Simple assignment management

With *Connect Accounting*, creating assignments is easier than ever, so you can spend more time teaching and less time managing. The assignment management function enables you to:

- Create and deliver assignments easily with selectable end-of-chapter questions and test bank items.
- Streamline lesson planning, student progress reporting, and assignment grading to make classroom management more efficient than ever.
- Go paperless with the eBook and online submission and grading of student assignments.

Smart grading

When it comes to studying, time is precious. *Connect Accounting* helps students learn more efficiently by providing feedback and practice material when they need it, where they need it. When it comes to teaching, your time also is precious. The grading function enables you to:

- Have assignments scored automatically, giving students immediate feedback on their work and side-by-side comparisons with correct answers.

▶ **McGraw-Hill *Connect Accounting*** is an online assignment and assessment solution that connects students with the tools and resources they'll need to achieve success.

▶ **McGraw-Hill *Connect Accounting*** helps prepare students for their future by enabling faster learning, more efficient studying, and higher retention of knowledge.

Instructor Library

The *Connect Accounting* Instructor Library is your repository for additional resources to improve student engagement in and out of class. You can select and use any asset that enhances your lecture. The *Connect Accounting* Instructor Library includes:

- eBook
- PowerPoint files
- Videos

Student Study Center

The *Connect Accounting* Student Study Center is the place for students to access additional resources. The Student Study Center:

- Offers students quick access to lectures, practice materials, eBooks, and more.
- Provides instant practice material and study questions, easily accessible on the go.
- Gives students access to the Personal Learning Plan described below.

Personal Learning Plan

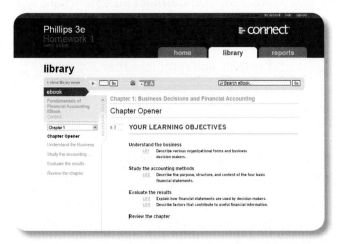

The Personal Learning Plan (PLP) connects each student to the learning resources needed for success in the course. For each chapter, students:

- Take a practice test to initiate the Personal Learning Plan.
- Immediately upon completing the practice test, see how their performance compares to chapter learning objectives or content by sections within chapters.
- Receive a Personal Learning Plan that recommends specific readings from the text, supplemental study material, and practice work that will improve their understanding and mastery of each learning objective.

Diagnostic and adaptive learning of concepts: LearnSmart

Students want to make the best use of their study time. The LearnSmart adaptive self-study technology within *Connect Accounting* provides students with a seamless combination of practice, assessment, and remediation for every concept in the textbook. LearnSmart's intelligent software adapts to every student response and automatically delivers concepts that advance the student's understanding while reducing time devoted to the concepts already mastered. The result for every student is the fastest path to mastery of the chapter concepts.

LearnSmart

- Applies an intelligent concept engine to identify the relationships between concepts and to serve new concepts to each student only when he or she is ready.

- Adapts automatically to each student, so students spend less time on the topics they understand and more practice time on those they have yet to master.
- Provides continual reinforcement and remediation, but gives only as much guidance as students need.
- Integrates diagnostics as part of the learning experience.
- Enables you to assess which concepts students have efficiently learned on their own, thus freeing class time for more applications and discussion.

Student progress tracking

Connect Accounting keeps instructors informed about how each student, section, and class is performing, allowing for more productive use of lecture and office hours. The progress-tracking function enables you to:

- View scored work immediately and track individual or group performance with assignment and grade reports.
- Access an instant view of student or class performance relative to learning objectives.
- Collect data and generate reports required by many accreditation organizations, such as AACSB and AICPA.

Lecture capture

Increase the attention paid to lecture discussion by decreasing the attention paid to note taking. For an additional charge Lecture Capture offers new ways for students to focus on the in-class discussion, knowing they can revisit important topics later. For more information on lecture capture capabilities in *Connect Accounting,* see the discussion of Tegrity, on this page.

McGraw-Hill Connect Plus Accounting

McGraw-Hill reinvents the textbook learning experience for the modern student with *Connect Plus Accounting.*
A seamless integration of an eBook and *Connect Accounting, Connect Accounting Plus Accounting* provides all of the *Connect Accounting* features plus the following:

- An integrated eBook, allowing for anytime, anywhere access to the textbook.

- Dynamic links between the problems or questions you assign to your students and the location in the eBook where that problem or question is covered.
- A powerful search function to pinpoint and connect key concepts in a snap.

In short, *Connect Accounting* offers you and your students powerful tools and features that optimize your time and energies, enabling you to focus on course content, teaching, and student learning. *Connect Accounting* also offers a wealth of content resources for both instructors and students. This state-of-the-art, thoroughly tested system supports you in preparing students for the world that awaits.

For more information about Connect, go to **www.mcgrawhill connect.com**, or contact your local McGraw-Hill sales representative.

Tegrity Campus: Lectures 24/7

Tegrity Campus is a service that makes class time available 24/7 by automatically capturing every lecture. With a simple one-click start-and-stop process, you capture all computer screens and corresponding audio in a format that is easily searchable, frame by frame. Students can replay any part of any class with easy-to-use browser-based viewing on a PC, Mac, or iPod, or other mobile device.

Educators know that the more students can see, hear, and experience class resources, the better they learn. In fact, studies prove it. Tegrity Campus's unique search feature helps students efficiently find what they need, when they need it, across an entire semester of class recordings. Help turn your students' study time into learning moments immediately supported by your lecture. With Tegrity Campus, you also increase intent listening and class participation by easing students' concerns about note-taking. Lecture Capture will make it more likely you will see students' faces, not the tops of their heads.

To learn more about Tegrity watch a 2-minute Flash demo at **http://tegritycampus.mhhe.com**.

CourseSmart
Learn Smart. Choose Smart.

 CourseSmart is a new way for faculty to find and review eTextbooks. It's also a great option for students who are interested in accessing their course materials digitally and saving money.

CourseSmart offers thousands of the most commonly adopted textbooks across hundreds of courses from a wide variety of higher education publishers. It is the only place for faculty to review and compare the full text of a textbook online, providing immediate access without the environmental impact of requesting a print exam copy.

With the CourseSmart eTextbook, students can save up to 45 percent off the cost of a print book, reduce their impact on the environment, and access powerful Web tools for learning. CourseSmart is an online eTextbook, which means users access and view their textbook online when connected to the Internet. Students can also print sections of the book for maximum portability. CourseSmart eTextbooks are available in one standard online reader with full text search, notes and highlighting, and email tools for sharing notes between classmates. For more information on CourseSmart, go to **http://www.coursesmart.com**.

Tools to Support Teaching

☑ Instructor CD-ROM

ISBN 00726967-5

Access to the instructor's key text ancillary materials at your finger tips. You can find all of the instructor ancillaries available on one convenient CD-ROM: PowerPoint slides, Solutions Manual, Instructor's Resource Manual, Test Bank and Computerized Test Bank, Solutions to Excel templates, text exhibits, and more.

☑ Presentation Slides

Prepared by Susan Galbreath at David Lipscomb University, Jon Booker and Charles Caldwell at Tennessee Technological University, and author Fred Phillips. Completely customized PowerPoint presentations for use in your classroom. Available on the Instructor CD-ROM.

NEW! ☑ Synchrosummaries

Prepared by Fred Phillips, these are a synchronized set of ready-to-use instructor presentation slides and student class notes. For instructors, this package minimizes prep time, simplifies co-ordination, and contributes to consistency across multiple instructors. For students, the partially completed class notes provide structure while still requiring them to attend to the most important points in the instructor's presentation. Students have a reason to attend class, but now it is to think rather than just frantically copy every word on the slides.

NEW! ☑ Animated PowerPoint exhibits and exercises

These aren't the typical set of PowerPoint slides that accompany most textbooks. These slides allow you to present key chapter topics and build solutions to popular end-of-chapter exercises one step at a time. Walk students through each stage in the thinking process.

☑ Solutions Manual

Prepared by Fred Phillips. Provides solutions to end-of-chapter questions, mini-exercises, exercises, problems, and cases. Available on the Instructor CD-ROM and text Web site.

☑ Test Bank

Prepared by Darlene Coarts, at the University of Northern Iowa. Available on the Instructor CD-ROM and password protected Instructor site, this comprehensive Test Bank includes more than 1,500 true/false, multiple choice, problems, and matching questions, each tagged by learning objective, topic area, difficulty level, and AACSB, Bloom's, and AICPA categories.

☑ Instructor's Resource Manual

Prepared by Jeannie Folk at College of DuPage. Includes overviews of chapter topics and resources to help you prepare for class. It describes the ready-to-use resources that support the text (including synchrosummaries) and presents other enrichment resources, including innovative active learning exercises that you can use in class. This manual is a must-read for any instructor interested in improving teaching evaluations. Available on the Instructor CD-ROM and text Web site.

☑ Instructor Excel Templates

Solutions to the student Excel Templates used to solve selected end-of-chapter exercises and problems. These assignments are designated by the Excel icon. Available on the text Web site.

☑ EZ Test

ISBN 0077269047

McGraw-Hill's EZ Test is a flexible and easy-to-use electronic testing program that allows instructors to create tests from book-specific items. EZ Test accommodates a wide range of question types and allows instructors to add their own questions. Multiple versions of the test can be created and any test can be exported for use with course management systems such as BlackBoard/WebCT. EZ Test Online is a new service that gives instructors a place to easily administer EZ Test-created exams and quizzes online. The program is available for Windows and Macintosh environments.

ASSURANCE OF LEARNING READY

Many educational institutions today are focused on the notion of *assurance of learning*, an important element of some accreditation standards. *Fundamentals of Financial Accounting* is designed specifically to support your assurance of learning initiatives with a simple, yet powerful solution.

Each test bank question for *Fundamentals of Financial Accounting* maps to a specific chapter learning objective listed in the text. You can use our test bank software, EZ Test and EZ Test Online, or *Connect Accounting* to easily query for learning outcomes/objectives that directly relate to the learning objectives for your course. You can then use the reporting features of EZ Test or *Connect Accounting* to aggregate student results in a similar fashion, making the collection and presentation of assurance of learning data simple and easy.

AACSB STATEMENT

The McGraw-Hill Companies is a proud corporate member of AACSB International. Understanding the importance and value of AACSB accreditation, *Fundamentals of Financial Accounting* recognizes the  curricula guidelines detailed in the AACSB standards for business accreditation by connecting selected questions in the test bank to the six general knowledge and skill guidelines in the AACSB standards.

The statements contained in *Fundamentals of Financial Accounting* are provided only as a guide for the users of this textbook. The AACSB leaves content coverage and assessment within the purview of individual schools, the mission of the school, and the faculty. While *Fundamentals of Financial Accounting* and the teaching package make no claim of any specific AACSB qualification or evaluation, within the Test Bank to accompany *Fundamentals of Financial Accounting* we have labeled selected questions according to the six general knowledge and skill areas.

Tools to Support Learning

☑ Online Learning Center

www.mhhe.com/phillips3e
The Online Learning Center includes multiple choice quizzes, Excel templates, PowerPoint presentations, and iPod downloadable content.

☑ Student PowerPoint Presentations

Selected presentation slides reproduced in student version. Presentation Slides are located on the text's Online Learning Center.

☑ Check Figures

Prepared by J. Lowell Mooney at Georgia Southern University. This tool provides answers to select problems and cases. Check Figures are located on the text's Online Learning Center.

☑ Study Guide

ISBN: 0077269691
Prepared by Jeannie Folk at College of DuPage. An outstanding learning tool, this guide gives students a deeper understanding of the course material and reinforces, step by step, what they are learning in the main text.

☑ Working Papers

ISBN: 0077269705
Prepared by Earl Godfrey at Gardner-Webb University. Working Papers are provided to assist you in solving complex text assignments. The Working Papers are available both in print and as Excel spreadsheets.

☑ Excel Templates

Available on the Online Learning Center www.mhhe.com/phillips3e. These templates are tied to selected end-of-chapter material. These assignments are designated by the Excel icon.

☑ Financial Accounting Video Library

Created to stimulate classroom discussion and illustrate key concepts in financial accounting. These videos are available on the Online Learning Center.

☑ McGraw-Hill's Connect Accounting

See page xvii.

☑ Personal Learning Plan

See page xviii.

☑ LearnSmart

See page xviii.

McGraw-Hill Customer Care Contact Information

At McGraw-Hill, we understand that getting the most from new technology can be challenging. That's why our services don't stop after you purchase our products. You can e-mail our Product Specialists 24 hours a day to get product training online. Or you can search our knowledge bank of Frequently Asked Questions on our support Web site. For Customer Support, call **800-331-5094**, e-mail **hmsupport@mcgraw-hill.com**, or visit **www.mhhe.com/support**. One of our Technical Support Analysts will be able to assist you in a timely fashion.

Acknowledgements

We are deeply indebted to the following individuals who helped develop, critique, and shape the extensive ancillary package:

Jeannie Folk, College of DuPage; Darlene Coarts, University of Northern Iowa; Janice Fergusson, University of South Carolina; Earl H. Godfrey, Gardner-Webb University; J. Lowell Mooney, Georgia Southern University; Jon A. Booker, Tennessee Technological University; Charles W. Caldwell, Tennessee Technological University; Susan C. Galbreath, David Lipscomb University; James Aitken, Central Michigan University; Catherine Plante, University of New Hampshire; Debra L. Schmidt, Cerritos College; LuAnn Bean, Florida Institute of Technology; Jane Wiese, Valencia Community College; Kimberly Temme, Maryville University of Saint Louis; Brandy Mackintosh, University of Saskatchewan; and Jack Terry, ComSource Associates, Inc.

We also received invaluable input and support from present and former colleagues and students, in particular Jocelyn Allard, Anders Bergstrom, Shari Boyd, Kara Chase, Shana M. Clor, Nicole Dewan, Erin Ferguson, Aaron Ferrara, Robin Harrington, Lee Harris, Blair Healy, Candice Heidt, Devon Hennig, Carrie Hordichuk, Lorraine Hurst, Jennifer Johnson, Nancy Kirzinger, Paul Knepper, Deborah Loran, Nicole Mackisey, Diana Mark, Roger Martin, Jason Matshes, Jennifer Millard, Kimberley Olfert, Ryan Olson, David Pooler, Jessica Pothier, Nick Purich, Emery Salahub, Bailey Schergevitch, Marie Tait, and Kory Wickenhauser.

Last, we thank the extraordinary efforts of a talented group of individuals at McGraw-Hill/Irwin who made all of this come together. We would especially like to thank our editorial director, Stewart Mattson; Tim Vertovec, our publisher; Dana Woo, our senior sponsoring editor; Kimberly Hooker, our senior developmental editor; Kathleen Klehr, our marketing manager; Mary Conzachi, our lead project manager; Matt Diamond, our designer; Carol Bielski, our production supervisor; Allison Souter, our media producer; Jeremy Cheshareck, our photo research coordinator; David Tietz, our photo researcher; and Marcy Lunetta, our permissions researcher.

We also want to recognize the valuable input of all those who helped guide our developmental decisions for the past three editions.

Editorial Review Board

Gary Adna Ames, *Brigham Young University-Idaho*
Gilda Agacer, *Monmouth University*
Peter Aghimien, *Indiana University-South Bend*
James Aitken, *Central Michigan University*

Frank Aquilino, *Montclair State University*
Timothy Baker, *California State University-Fresno*
Laurie Barfitt, *Delta State University*
Ira Bates, *Florida A & M University*
Benjamin Bean, *Utah Valley State College*
Deborah Beard, *Southeast Missouri State University*
John Bedient, *Albion College*
Linda Bell, *William Jewell College*
Judy Benish, *Fox Valley Technical College*
Steve Benner, *Eastern Illinois University*
Amy Bentley, *Tallahassee Community College*
Joseph Berlinski, *Prairie State College*
George Bernard, *Seminole Community College*
Chris Bjornson, *Indiana University Southeast*
Cynthia Bolt, *Citadel School of Business Administration*
David Bojarsky, *California State University-Long Beach*
Amy Bourne, *Oregon State University*
Bruce Bradford, *Fairfield University*
Robert Braun, *Southeastern Louisiana University*
Linda Bressler, *University of Houston-Downtown*
Alison Brock, *Imperial Valley College*
Helen Brubeck, *San Jose State University*
Myra Bruegger, *Southeastern Community College*
Gene Bryson, *University of Alabama-Huntsville*
Tracy Bundy, *University of Louisiana-Lafayette*
Esther Bunn, *Stephen F. Austin State University*
Christy Burge, *University of Louisville*
Ron Burrows, *University of Dayton*
Julia Camp, *Providence College*
Michael Campbell, *Montana State University-Billings*
Elizabeth Cannata, *Johnson and Wales University*
Jeannette Carlisle, *Lone Star College North Harris*
Janet Cassagio, *Nassau Community College*
Betty Chavis, *California State University-Fullerton*
Bea Chiang, *The College of New Jersey*
Linda Christiansen, *Indiana University Southeast*
Anne Clem, *Iowa State University*
Darlene Coarts, *University of Northern Iowa*
Jay Cohen, *Oakton Community College*
Norman Colter, *University of New Mexico-Albuquerque*
Debora Constable, *Georgia Perimeter College*
Robert Conway, *University of Wisconsin-Platteville*
John Cooper, *Wentworth Institute of Technology*
Anthony Copa, *Anoka-Ramsey Community College*
Meg Costello Lambert, *Oakland Community College*

Sue Counte, *Saint Louis Community College-Meramec-Kirkwood*
Rich Criscione, *Moorehead State University*
John Critchett, *Madonna University*
Marcia Croteau, *University Maryland-Baltimore County*
Stephen Crow, *California State University Sacramento*
Kathy Crusto-Way, *Tarrant Community College*
Karl Dahlberg, *Rutgers University*
Laurie Dahlin, *Worcester State College*
David Davis, *Tallahassee Community College*
Jan Kyle Davison, *Jefferson Davis Community College*
David Deeds, *University of Northern Iowa*
John E. Delaney, *Southwestern University*
Jamie Doran, *Muhlenberg College*
Norris Dorsey, *California State University, Northridge*
Joanne Duke, *San Francisco State University*
Jeff Edwards, *Portland Community College*
Craig R. Ehlen, *University of Southern Indiana*
Susan Eldridge, *University of Nebraska at Omaha*
Steven Ernest, *Baton Rouge Community College*
Janice Fergusson, *University of South Carolina*
Linda Flaming, *Monmouth University*
Lou Fowler, *Missouri Western State University*
Harlan Fuller, *Illinois State University*
Lisa Gillespie, *Loyola University-Chicago*
Mark Gleason, *Metropolitan State University*
Mariana Grau-Nathan, *Houston Community College*
Barbara Gregorio, *Nassau Community College*
Tony Greig, *Purdue University*
Ronald Guidry, *University of Louisiana-Monroe*
Geoffrey Gurka, *Mesa State College*
Abo-El-Yazeed Habib, *Minnesota State University*
Laurie Hagberg, *Trident Technical College*
Heidi Hansel, *Kirkwood Community College*
Coby Harmon, *University of California-Santa Barbara*
Betty S. Harper, *Middle Tennessee State University*
Phillip Harper, *Middle Tennessee State University*
Candice S. Heino, *Anoka Ramsey Community College*
George Heyman, *Oakton Community College*
Anita Hope, *Tarrant County College*
Robert Hurt, *California Polytechnic Pomona*
Laura Ilcisin, *University of Nebraska-Omaha*
Sharon Jackson, *Sanford University*
Shondra Johnson, *Bradley University*
Derek Johnston, *Colorado State University*
David Juriga, *Saint Louis Community College at Forest Park*

John Karayan, *California Polytechnic Pomona*
Ann Kelley, *Providence College*
Ann Kelly, *Georgia Southern University*
Janice Kerber, *Durham Tech Community College*
Tim Kizirian, *California State University-Chico*
April Klein, *New York University*
Janice L. Klimek, *Central Missouri State University*
Christine Kloezeman, *Glendale Community College*
Trevor Knox, *Muhlenberg College*
Mark Kohlbeck, *Florida Atlantic University*
Dennis L. Kovach, *Community College of Allegheny*
Cynthia Krom, *Marist College*
Terrie Kroshus, *Inver Hills Community College*
Christy Land, *Catawba Valley Community College*
Phillips Landers, *Pennsylvania College of Technology*
Joe Larkin, *Saint Josephs University*
Laurie Larson, *Valencia Community College*
Daniel Law, *Gonzaga University*
G. Suzzane Lay, *Mesa State College*
Ron Lazer, *University of Houston-Houston*
Chuo-Hsuan Lee, *SUNY Plattsburgh*
Xu Li, *University of Texas, Dallas*
Betsy Lin, *Montclair State University*
Joseph Lipari, *Montclair State University*
Chao-Shin Liu, *University of Notre Dame*
Julie Lockhart, *Western Washington University*
Claudia Lubaski, *Lorain County Community College*
Joseph Lupino, *Saint Mary's College of California*
Mostafa Maksy, *Northeastern Illinois University*
Diane Marker, *University of Toledo*
Angie Martin, *Tarrant County College*
James Martin, *Washburn University*
Peter Martino, *Johnson & Wales University*
Dawn Massey, *Fairfield University*
Christian Mastilak, *Xavier University*
Maureen McBeth, *College of DuPage*
Florence McGovern, *Bergen Community College*
Noel McKeon, *Florida Community College*
Chris McNamara, *Finger Lakes Community College*
Kevin McNelis, *New Mexico State University*
Barbara Merino, *University of North Texas*
Tony Mifsud, *Catawba Valley Community College*
Paul Mihalek, *Central Connecticut State University*
Paulette Miller, *Collin County Community College*
Tim Mills, *Eastern Illinois University*

Susan Minke, *Indiana University/Purdue University-Ft Wayne*

Birendra Mishra, *University of California, Riverside*

Syed M. Moiz, *Marian College*

Dennis Moore, *Worcester State College*

Charles Moores, *University of Nevada, Las Vegas*

Arabian Morgan, *Orange Coast College*

Judy Morse, *Providence College*

Michelle Moshier, *University at Albany*

Gerald Motl, *Xavier University*

Matt Muller, *Adirondack Community College*

Johnna Murray, *University of Missouri-St. Louis*

Brian Nagle, *Duquesne University*

Presha Neidermeyer, *West Virginia University*

Barbara Norris, *Johnson & Wales University*

Adel M. Novin, *Clayton College & State University*

Thomas Nunamaker, *Washington State University*

Ron O'Brien, *Fayetteville Technical Community College*

Emeka Ofobike, *University of Akron*

Janet O'Tousa, *University of Notre Dame*

Jo-Ann Pacenta, *Pennsylvania College of Technology*

Susanna Pendergast, *Western Illinois University*

Viola Persia, *Stony Brook University*

Jan Pitera, *Broome Community College*

Duane Ponko, *Indiana University of Pennsylvania*

Todd Pull, *Georgia Perimeter College*

Mary Prater, *Clemson University*

Elizabeth Rabe, *Bacone College*

Kris Raman, *University of Northern Texas*

Rama Ramamurthy, *Ohio State University*

Richard Rand, *Tennessee Tech University*

Alan Ransom, *Cypress College*

Tommy Raulston, *Midwestern State University*

Donald Raux, *Siena College*

Aaron Reeves, *Saint Louis Community College-Forest Park*

Patrick Reihing, *Nassau Community College*

Gayle Richardson, *Bakersfield College*

Joanne Rockness, *University of North Carolina-Wilmington*

Carol Rogers, *Central New Mexico Community College*

Mark Ross, *Western Kentucky University*

Eric Rothenburg, *Kingsborough Community College*

Ann Rowell, *Central Piedmont Community College*

John Rude, *Bloomsburg University of Pennsylvania*

Karen Russom, *North Harris College*

Huldah A. Ryan, *Iona College*

Amy Santos, *Manatee Community College*

Marguerite Savage, *Elgin Community College*

Albert Schepanski, *University of Iowa*

Arnie Schneider, *Georgia Institute of Technology*

Henry Schulman, *Grossmont College*

Ann E. Selk, *University Wisconsin-Green Bay*

Gabrielle Serrano, *Elgin Community College*

Ted Skekel, *University of Texas-San Antonio*

John Smigla, *Robert Morris University*

Talitha Smith, *Auburn University*

Virginia Smith, *Saint Mary's College of California*

Karen Sneary, *Northwestern Oklahoma*

Nancy Snow, *University of Toledo*

Barb Squires, *Corning Community College*

James Stekelberg, *Clackamas Community College*

Dennis Stovall, *Grand Valley State University*

Stephen Strand, *Southern Maine Community College*

Arlene Strawn, *Tallahassee Community College*

Gloria Stuart, *Georgia Southern University*

Aida Sy, *Baruch College*

Albert Taccone, *Cuyamaca College*

Robert Taylor, *Mayland Community College*

Steve Teeter, *Utah Valley State*

Denise Teixeira, *Chemeketa Community College*

Lisa Thornton, *Truckee Meadows Community College*

Michael Ulinski, *Pace University*

Stacy Wade, *Western Kentucky University*

Robin Wagner, *San Francisco State University*

Suzanne Ward, *University of Louisiana*

Nancy Weatherholt, *University of Missouri-Kansas City*

Andrea Weickgenannt, *Northern Kentucky University*

Cheryl Westen, *Western Illinois University*

Vicki White, *Ivy Tech Community College of Indiana-Evansville*

Linda Whitten, *Skyline College*

Jane Wiese, *Valencia Community College*

Satina Williams, *Marist College*

Darryl Woolley, *University of Idaho*

Christian Wurst, *Temple University*

Michael Yampuler, *University of Houston-Houston*

Kathryn Yarbrough, *University North Carolina-Charlotte*

Myung-Ho Yoon, *Northeastern Illinois University*

Gregory Yost, *University of West Florida*

Lin Zheng, *Georgia College State University*

Ping Zhou, *Baruch College*

Advice on Using Your Textbook

What does it take to do well in your Financial Accounting course? Our research finds that the way you read and use your textbook can have a major impact on your course performance.* The following graphic summarizes our primary findings, which suggest four things you can do to improve your chances of earning a good grade.

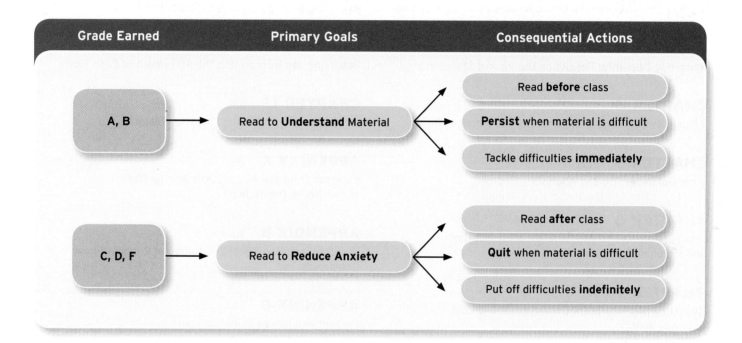

Grade Earned	Primary Goals	Consequential Actions
A, B	Read to **Understand** Material	Read **before** class; **Persist** when material is difficult; Tackle difficulties **immediately**
C, D, F	Read to **Reduce Anxiety**	Read **after** class; **Quit** when material is difficult; Put off difficulties **indefinitely**

1. **Read the chapters to learn rather than just to get through them.** Learning doesn't miraculously occur just because your eyes have skimmed all the assigned lines of the textbook. You have to think and focus while reading to sink the material into your understanding and memory. Use the text's learning objectives to focus on what's really important in the chapters.

2. **Don't be discouraged if you initially find some material challenging to learn.** At one time or another, both the best and weakest students describe themselves as "confused" and "having a good grasp of the material," "anxious" and "confident," and "overwhelmed" and "comfortable." The simple fact is that, for anyone, learning new material can be challenging and initially confusing. Success does not depend as much on whether you become confused as it does on what you do when you become confused.

3. **Clear up confusion as it arises.** A key difference between the most and least successful students is how they respond to difficulty and confusion. When successful students are confused or unsure, they immediately try to enhance their understanding through rereading, self-testing, and seeking outside help if necessary. In contrast, unsuccessful students try to reduce anxiety by delaying further reading or by resorting to memorizing without understanding. Aim to clear up confusion when it arises because accounting in particular is a subject for which your understanding of later material depends on your understanding of earlier material.

4. **Think of reading as the initial stage of studying.** Abandon the idea that "studying" only occurs during the final hours before an exam. By initially reading with the same intensity that occurs when later reviewing for an exam, you can create extra time for practicing exercises and problems. This combination of concentrated reading and extensive practice is likely to contribute to better learning and superior exam scores.

* B.J. Phillips, and F. Phillips, "Sink or Skim: Textbook Reading Behaviors of Introductory Accounting Students," *Issues in Accounting Education* 22 (February 2007), pp. 21–44.

BRIEF CONTENTS

CONTENTS

CHAPTER 10

Reporting and Interpreting Liabilities   450

GENERAL MILLS   451

CHAPTER 11

Reporting and Interpreting Stockholders' Equity   504

NATIONAL BEVERAGE CORP.   505

CHAPTER 12

Reporting and Interpreting the Statement of Cash Flows   552

UNDER ARMOUR   553

CHAPTER 13

Measuring and Evaluating Financial Performance   610

LOWE'S   611

APPENDIX A

Excerpts from the Fiscal 2008 Annual Report of The Home Depot Inc.   A.1

APPENDIX B

Excerpts from the Fiscal 2008 Annual Report of Lowe's Companies, Inc.   B.1

APPENDIX C

Present and Future Value Concepts   C.1

fundamentals of
FINANCIAL ACCOUNTING

www.mhhe.com/phillips3e

CHAPTER 1

Business Decisions and Financial Accounting

YOUR LEARNING OBJECTIVES

Understand the business

LO1   Describe various organizational forms and business decision makers.

Study the accounting methods

LO2   Describe the purpose, structure, and content of the four basic financial statements.

Evaluate the results

LO3   Explain how financial statements are used by decision makers.

LO4   Describe factors that contribute to useful financial information.

Review the chapter

THAT WAS
THEN

If you think accounting is far removed from your personal life, you might be in for a surprise. Your ordinary life experiences, especially as a student, actually prepare you well to learn accounting.

Lecture Presentation-LP1
www.mhhe.com/phillips3e

FOCUS COMPANY: Pizza Aroma, Ithaca, NY

Welcome to the world of business and financial accounting. One of our goals for this book is to help you see the role that accounting plays in helping people turn their good ideas into successful businesses. The founder of FedEx first introduced his ideas about a nationwide transportation business in a college essay. With the help of accounting, FedEx has become a multibillion dollar business. Perhaps the only thing stopping you from doing this is that you don't feel you know what's involved in starting and running a business. We're here to help with that.

Another important goal for us is to explain topics in ways that you can relate to. We want you to see that your personal life experiences help you to learn accounting. Often, we will explain topics in the context of a real business. For example, in the first four chapters, you will learn the steps that one person took to start his own business and turn his dream into reality. By reading about his experiences, you'll gain a realistic understanding of how accounting is a key part of all businesses. So, let's get started.

About two decades ago, Mauricio Rosa brought his young family from El Salvador to America to build a better life. While working in several New York pizza restaurants, he perfected a gourmet pizza concept. Thinking gourmet pizza would be a great addition to the local restaurant scene, Mauricio decided to start his own pizza business. Although eager to get started, Mauricio had several questions and decisions to consider. He contacted Laurie Hensley, a local CPA (certified public accountant) to ask her advice. As you will read in this chapter, Laurie met with Mauricio in June to help him understand what's involved in starting a business and monitoring its success. He eventually started a business, called Pizza Aroma, which actually exists—at 128 S. Cayuga St. in Ithaca, NY.

THIS IS NOW

This chapter focuses on the key financial reports that business people rely on when evaluating a company's performance.

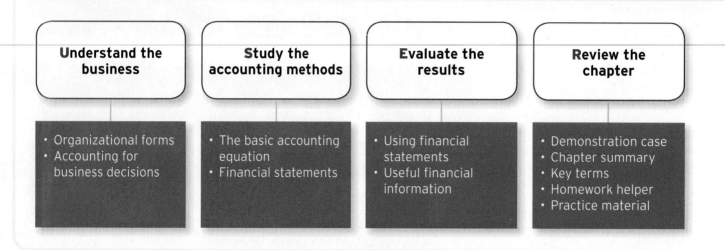

Understand the business	Study the accounting methods	Evaluate the results	Review the chapter
• Organizational forms • Accounting for business decisions	• The basic accounting equation • Financial statements	• Using financial statements • Useful financial information	• Demonstration case • Chapter summary • Key terms • Homework helper • Practice material

Understand the Business

 "Mauricio, we should start by talking about how you want to organize your business."

"Well, I'm opening a gourmet pizza restaurant. What else do I need to know?"

Learning Objective 1
Describe various organizational forms and business decision makers.

Video 1.1
www.mhhe.com/phillips3e

ORGANIZATIONAL FORMS

Laurie outlined three primary ways businesses can be organized. While other business forms exist, such as limited liability companies, BizStats.com reports that the following three are the most common: sole proprietorship, partnership, and corporation.

Sole Proprietorship

This is a form of business owned (and usually operated) by one individual. It is the easiest form of business to start because it doesn't require any special legal maneuvers. Just get a business license and you're good to go. A sole proprietorship is considered a part of the owner's life, with all profits (or losses) becoming part of the taxable income of the owner, and the owner being personally liable for all debts of the business.

Partnership

A partnership is similar to a sole proprietorship, except that profits, taxes, and legal liability are the responsibility of two or more owners instead of just one. It is slightly more expensive to form than a sole proprietorship because a lawyer typically is needed to draw up a partnership agreement, which describes how profits are shared between partners and how that would change if new partners are added or existing partners leave.

The key advantage of a partnership over a sole proprietorship is that it typically has more resources available to it, which can fuel the business's growth.

Corporation

Unlike sole proprietorships and partnerships, a corporation is a separate entity from both a legal and accounting perspective. This means that a corporation, not its owners, is legally responsible for its own taxes and debts. Thus, owners cannot lose more than their investment in the corporation, which is a major advantage to the owners. Two disadvantages of incorporation are that the legal fees for creating a corporation can be high and income taxes must be paid by both the corporation and its owners.

Corporations can raise large amounts of money for growth because they divide ownership of the corporation into shares that can be sold to new owners. A share of the corporation's ownership is indicated on a legal document called a stock certificate. The owners of a company's stock (stockholders) can buy and sell stock privately or publicly on a stock exchange if the company has legally registered to do so. Most corporations start out as private companies and will apply to become public companies ("go public") if they need a lot of financing, which they obtain from selling new stock certificates to investors. Some big-name corporations, like Cargill and Chick-Fil-A, haven't gone public because they get enough financing from private sources, but many that you are familiar with (and most examples in this book) are public companies.

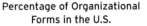

Percentage of Organizational Forms in the U.S.

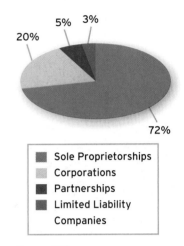

3%
5%
20%
72%

- Sole Proprietorships
- Corporations
- Partnerships
- Limited Liability Companies

Source: BizStats.com.

"I'm interested in limiting my legal liability and getting some financing by selling ownership shares to investors, so I will create a private corporation called Pizza Aroma, Inc. What's next?"

ACCOUNTING FOR BUSINESS DECISIONS

Most companies exist to earn profits for their stockholders. They earn profits by selling goods or services to customers for more than they cost to produce. Mauricio's company will be successful if it is able to make pizzas at a cost of $2 and sell them for $9. To know just how successful his company is, Mauricio will need to establish and maintain a good system of financial recordkeeping—an accounting system. **Accounting** is an information system designed by an organization to capture (analyze, record, and summarize) the activities affecting its financial condition and performance and then report the results to decision makers, both inside and outside the organization. It's such a key part of business that business people typically talk about their companies using accounting terms, which is why they often call it the "language of business."

Every organization needs accountants to assist in reporting financial information for decision making and to help its owners understand the financial effects of those business decisions. Mauricio can get this help in one of two ways. He can hire an accountant to work as an employee of his business (a **private accountant**) or he can contract with someone like Laurie who provides advice to a variety of businesses (a **public accountant**). Because Mauricio's business is small, he doesn't yet need a full-time accountant. Instead, he agrees that Pizza Aroma will pay fees to Laurie for basic services. She'll help him to set up an accounting system and advise him on key business decisions.[1]

YOU SHOULD KNOW

Accounting: A system of analyzing, recording, and summarizing the results of a business's activities and then reporting the results to decision makers.

"How will an accounting system help me run my business?"

---

[1]The chapter supplement on page 20 describes the wide variety of accounting career choices available.

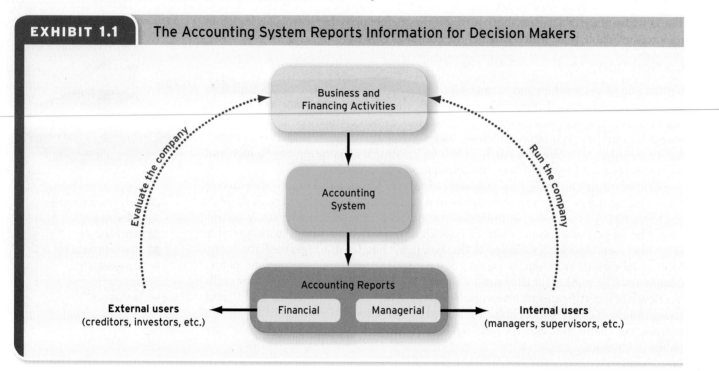

EXHIBIT 1.1 | The Accounting System Reports Information for Decision Makers

The main goal of an accounting system is to capture information about the business and financing activities of a company so that it can be reported to decision makers, both inside and outside the business. Exhibit 1.1 illustrates this role and shows that this information can be presented in two kinds of reports. **Managerial accounting reports** include detailed financial plans and continually updated reports about the operating performance of the company. These reports are made available only to the company's employees (internal users) so that they can make business decisions related to production, marketing, human resources, and finance. For example, managerial accounting reports are needed when determining whether to build, buy, or rent a building; whether to continue or discontinue making particular products; how much to pay employees; and how much to borrow. As manager of a restaurant, Mauricio will regularly need managerial accounting reports to monitor the quantity of supplies on hand, evaluate the various costs associated with making and selling his gourmet pizza, and assess the productivity of his employees.

 "Others outside your business will need financial information about your restaurant. For example, where will the money come from to start your business?"

"My wife and I will probably contribute $30,000 from personal savings. But I'll still need to ask the bank for a $20,000 loan to buy equipment. What will the bank want to know?"

YOU SHOULD KNOW

Financial statements:
Accounting reports that summarize the financial results of business and financing activities.

Laurie described **financial accounting reports,** called **financial statements,** which are prepared periodically to provide information to people not employed by the business. These external financial statement users aren't given access to detailed internal records of the company, so they rely extensively on the financial statements. Creditors and investors are the two primary external user groups, but other external users also find the information helpful.

- **Creditors**—anyone to whom money is owed.
  - **Banks** use financial statements to evaluate the risk that they will not be repaid the money they've loaned to a company. Because banks are taking a risk when they loan money to a company, they want periodic financial reports from the company so they can keep an eye on how it is doing and intervene if it looks like the company will have trouble repaying the loan.
  - **Suppliers** also want to be sure a business can pay them for the goods or services they deliver. They usually check the business's credit standing and may also ask for its financial statements before entering into significant business relationships.
- **Investors**
  - **Stockholders** are a major external user group. Both existing and future stockholders rely on financial statements to evaluate whether the company is financially secure and likely to be a profitable investment.
- **Other external users**
  - Certain **customers** use financial statements to judge the company's ability to provide service on its products and honor warranties.
  - Various local, state, and federal **governments** also collect taxes based on information used to prepare the financial statements.

In Pizza Aroma's case, the bank will be the main external user. Mauricio will be expected to prepare financial statements to obtain the loan and then regularly provide updated financial reports until the loan is repaid. If the company's stock is ever sold to other investors, these stockholders will rely on financial statements to estimate the value of their shares and determine whether to buy, sell, or hold Pizza Aroma stock.

While Mauricio understood everything Laurie had told him up to this point, he had another major concern.

"I want to sound intelligent when I talk to my banker, but I don't know much about accounting."

 "This is a common concern for new business owners, so let's start with the most basic thing you need to know about accounting."

Study the Accounting Methods

THE BASIC ACCOUNTING EQUATION

One of the central concepts to understanding financial reports is that **what a company owns must equal what a company owes to its creditors and stockholders**. In accounting, there are special names for what a company owns and what a company owes to creditors and stockholders, as shown below.

Learning Objective 2
Describe the purpose, structure, and content of the four basic financial statements.

Resources Owned . . .	=	Resources Owed . . .	
by the **company**		to **creditors**	to **stockholders**
Assets	**=**	**Liabilities**	**+** **Stockholders' Equity**

YOU SHOULD KNOW

The **basic accounting equation**
is A = L + SE. **Separate entity
assumption:** The financial
reports of a business are
assumed to include the results
of only that business's activities.

The relationship between assets (A), liabilities (L), and stockholders' equity (SE) is known as the **basic accounting equation.** The business itself, not the stockholders who own the business, is viewed as owning the assets and owing the liabilities. This is called the **separate entity assumption,** which requires that a business's financial reports include only the activities of the business and not those of its stockholders.

The elements of the basic accounting equation are fundamental to reading and understanding financial statements, so let's look at each in detail.

Assets

An **asset** is an economic resource presently controlled by the company; it has measurable value and is expected to benefit the company by producing cash inflows or reducing cash outflows in the future. For Pizza Aroma, assets include things like cash, supplies, cookware, and equipment such as tables, chairs, and pizza ovens.

Liabilities

Liabilities are measurable amounts that the company owes to creditors. If Pizza Aroma borrows from a bank, it would owe a liability called a Note Payable. This particular name is used because banks require borrowers to sign a legal document called a *note,* which describes details about the company's promise to repay the bank. Pizza Aroma is likely to also owe suppliers for ingredients and other supplies delivered to Pizza Aroma. When a company buys goods from another company, it usually does so on credit by promising to pay for them at a later date. The amount owed is called an Account Payable because purchases made using credit are said to be "on account." Pizza Aroma could also owe wages to employees (Wages Payable) and taxes to governments (Taxes Payable). From a legal perspective, creditors have priority over stockholders. Thus, if a company goes out of business, liabilities must be paid before any amounts are paid to stockholders.

Stockholders' Equity

Stockholders' equity represents the owners' claims on the business. These claims arise for two reasons.

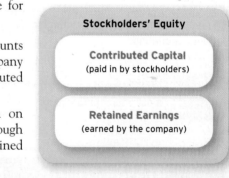

1. First, the owners have a claim on amounts they contributed directly to the company in exchange for its stock (Contributed Capital).

2. Second, the owners have a claim on amounts the company has earned through profitable business operations (Retained Earnings).

The second item listed above is particularly important because a business can survive only if it is profitable. It will be profitable if the total amount earned from selling goods and services is greater than the costs incurred to generate those sales. Theoretically, these profits belong to the company's owners, so they increase stockholders' equity. Through these profits, owners can get more money back from the company than they paid in (a return on their investment).

Given the importance of a company's profits, accounting systems separately track the two components of profit: revenues and expenses.

Revenues   Revenues are earned by selling goods or services to customers. For Pizza Aroma, revenues are measured at the amount the company charges its customers for pizza.

Expenses   Expenses are all costs of doing business that are necessary to earn revenues. For Pizza Aroma, these include advertising, utilities, rent, wages, insurance, repairs, and supplies used in making pizza. Expenses are said to be incurred to generate revenues. The word *incurred* means that the activities giving rise to a cost (e.g., running an ad, using electricity) have occurred in the period in which the related revenues have been generated.

Net Income   Although *profit* is used in casual conversation, the preferred term in accounting is *net income*. Net income is calculated as revenues minus expenses. For Pizza Aroma to be profitable, its revenues must be greater than its expenses. (If revenues are less than expenses, the company would have a net loss, but for now we'll be optimistic and assume that Pizza Aroma is going to earn a profit.) **By generating net income, a company increases its stockholders' equity,** as illustrated below. This net income can be left in the company to accumulate (with earnings that have been retained from prior years) or it can be paid out to the company's stockholders for their own personal use (called *dividends*).

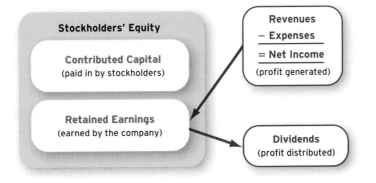

Dividends   A company's profits are accumulated in Retained Earnings until a decision is made to distribute them to stockholders in what is called a dividend. The simplest type of dividend, and the most common for a small business like Pizza Aroma, is a dividend paid in cash. **Dividends are not an expense incurred to generate earnings.** Rather, dividends are a distribution of earnings. They are determined at the discretion of the company's stockholders. If Mauricio wanted, he could choose to leave all the profits in Pizza Aroma by never declaring a dividend.

"Okay, I think I get it, but can you tell me how all those items relate to each other and where they are reported in the financial statements?"

FINANCIAL STATEMENTS

Assets, liabilities, stockholders' equity, revenues, expenses, and dividends appear in different reports that collectively are called financial statements. The term *financial statements* refers to four accounting reports, typically prepared in the following order:

1. **Income Statement**
2. **Statement of Retained Earnings**
3. **Balance Sheet**
4. **Statement of Cash Flows**

   Financial statements can be prepared at any time during the year, although they are most commonly prepared monthly, every three months (quarterly reports), and at the end of the year (annual reports). Companies are allowed to choose a calendar or fiscal year-end. A calendar year is a 12-month period ending on December 31, and a fiscal year is a 12-month period ending on a day other than December 31. The toy maker Mattel uses a calendar year-end because this is the start of its slow business period. Fewer toys are sold in January through May than in the first three weeks of December.

The only U.S. professional sports team operating as a public company—Green Bay Packers, Inc.—has chosen a fiscal year-end of March 31, the month after the season wraps up with the Pro Bowl.

The Income Statement

YOU SHOULD KNOW

Income statement: Reports the amount of revenues less expenses for a period of time.
Unit of measure assumption: Results of business activities should be reported in an appropriate monetary unit, which in the United States is the U.S. dollar.

The first financial statement prepared is the **income statement** (also called the statement of operations). Laurie gives Mauricio Exhibit 1.2 to show what Pizza Aroma's income statement might look like for the month ended September 30, assuming he is able to open his restaurant on September 1. The heading of the income statement identifies who, what, and when: the name of the business, the title of the report, and the time period covered by the financial statement. Larger businesses with thousands or millions of dollars in revenues and expenses add a fourth line under the date to indicate if the numbers reported are rounded to the nearest thousand or million. For international companies, this fourth line also reports the currency used in the report. An international company based in the United States, like Papa John's, will translate any foreign currency into U.S. dollars—basically assuming all its business was done in U.S. dollars. This is the **unit of measure assumption.** We see it in the reporting currency used in other countries: Nestlé (Swiss franc), Lego (Danish kronen), and Adidas (euro).

EXHIBIT 1.2 | **Income Statement**

PIZZA AROMA

		Explanation
PIZZA AROMA, INC. **Income Statement** **For the Month Ended September 30, 2010**		Who: Name of the business What: Title of the statement When: Accounting period
Revenues		
Pizza Revenue	$11,000	Revenue earned from the sale and delivery of pizza to customers
Total Revenues	11,000	**Total amount earned during September**
Expenses		
Supplies Expense	4,000	Cost of pizza ingredients used-up in September
Wages Expense	2,000	Cost of employee wages for work done in September
Rent Expense	1,500	Cost of rent for the month of September
Utilities Expense	600	Cost of utilities used in September
Insurance Expense	300	Cost of insurance coverage for September
Advertising Expense	100	Cost of advertising done in September
Income Tax Expense	500	Cost of taxes on September's income
Total Expenses	9,000	**Total expenses incurred in September to generate revenues**
Net Income	$ 2,000	**Difference between total revenues and total expenses**

YOU SHOULD KNOW

Accounts: Accumulate and report the effects of each different business activity.

Notice that an income statement for Pizza Aroma would have three major captions—revenues, expenses, and net income—corresponding to the equation for the income statement (Revenues − Expenses = Net Income). Individual types of revenues and expenses would be reported under the revenue and expense headings. These **accounts,** as they are called, are typical for most businesses, whether small or big. Notice that each major caption has a subtotal, and the bottom line amount for net income has a double underline to highlight it. Finally, a dollar sign appears at the top and bottom of the column of numbers.

When listing the accounts on the income statement, revenues are on top, usually with the largest, most relevant revenue listed first. Then expenses are subtracted, again from largest to smallest, except that Income Tax Expense is the last expense listed. Net Income is the difference between total revenues and total expenses.

"So, does the $2,000 of Net Income mean I'll have that much more cash?"

 "No. Net income is a measure of how much better off your business is, not how much cash you made."

Laurie's point is one of the key ideas of the income statement. It's quite common for a business to provide goods or services to customers in one month, but not collect cash from them until a later month. Similarly, expenses for the current month's activities may actually be paid in a different month. You'll have a chance to learn this in more detail later, but it's worth trying to understand from the beginning that revenues don't necessarily equal cash coming in during the month and expenses don't always equal cash going out during the month.

Mauricio seemed disappointed to see only $2,000 of projected net income for the first month. Laurie reassured him that it's typical for new businesses like Pizza Aroma to initially struggle to generate a profit because they have lots of expenses related to advertising and employee training but relatively little revenues because they haven't yet built a loyal customer base.[2] Pizza Aroma's net income will likely increase in the future after the business becomes well known. By selling more pizza, revenues will increase without a major increase in expenses, except for the cost of ingredients and supplies that will be used in making the additional pizzas. Expenses like employee wages and rent will likely not increase all that much.

"I guess that's not so bad. It does make me want to watch my expenses and try to boost my pizza sales quickly. What about the amount Pizza Aroma owes to the bank? Should we talk about the balance sheet?"

 "Before we look at that, I want to show you the next statement that connects the income statement to the balance sheet, so you'll understand the relationships between the reports."

The Statement of Retained Earnings

Pizza Aroma will report a **statement of retained earnings**, as shown in Exhibit 1.3. A more comprehensive statement of stockholders' equity that explains changes in all stockholders' equity accounts is provided by large corporations. But for Pizza Aroma, most changes in stockholders' equity relate to generating and distributing earnings, so a statement of retained earnings is just as good as a full-blown statement of stockholders' equity. The heading in Exhibit 1.3 identifies the name of the company, the title of the report, and the accounting period. The statement starts with the Retained Earnings balance at the beginning of the period. Remember that retained earnings are the profits that have accumulated in the company over time. Because this is a new business, there aren't any accumulated profits yet so the beginning balance is $0. Next, the statement adds Net Income and subtracts any Dividends for the current period, to arrive at Retained

> **YOU SHOULD KNOW**
>
> **Statement of retained earnings:** Reports the way that net income and the distribution of dividends affected the financial position of the company during the period.

---

[2]In fact, 50 percent of all new businesses fail or close within the first six years of opening. Not many start out with a positive net income in the first month. For more information on small business failures, see Brian Headd, "Redefining Business Success: Distinguishing between Closure and Failures," *Small Business Economics*, 21: 51–61, 2003.

EXHIBIT 1.3	Statement of Retained Earnings	

PIZZA AROMA, INC. Statement of Retained Earnings For the Month Ended September 30, 2010		Explanation
		Who: Name of the business What: Title of the statement When: Accounting period
Retained Earnings, September 1, 2010	$ 0	Last period's ending Retained Earnings balance
Add: Net Income	2,000	Reported on the income statement (Exhibit 1.2)
Subtract: Dividends	(1,000)	Distributions to stockholders in the current period
Retained Earnings, September 30, 2010	$1,000	This period's ending Retained Earnings balance

Earnings at the end of the period.[3] Again, a dollar sign is used at the top and bottom of the column of numbers and a double underline appears at the bottom.

The Balance Sheet

YOU SHOULD KNOW

Balance sheet: Reports the amount of assets, liabilities, and stockholders' equity of a business at a point in time.

The next financial report is the **balance sheet**. It is also known as the statement of financial position. The balance sheet's purpose is to report the amount of a business's assets, liabilities, and stockholders' equity at a specific point in time. Exhibit 1.4 presents Pizza Aroma's projected balance sheet. Think of the balance sheet as a picture or screen capture of Pizza Aroma's resources and claims to resources at the end of the day on September 30, 2010.

EXHIBIT 1.4	Balance Sheet	

PIZZA AROMA, INC. Balance Sheet At September 30, 2010		Explanation
		Who: Name of the business What: Title of the statement When: Point in time
Assets		**Resources controlled by the company**
Cash	$14,000	Amount of cash on hand and in the business's bank account
Accounts Receivable	1,000	Pizza Aroma's right to collect from customers for prior credit sales
Supplies	3,000	Amount of food and paper supplies on hand
Equipment	40,000	Cost of ovens, tables, etc.
Total Assets	$58,000	**Total amount of the company's resources**
Liabilities and Stockholders' Equity		**Claims on the company's resources**
Liabilities		Creditors' claims on the company's resources
Accounts Payable	$ 7,000	Amount owed to suppliers for prior credit purchases (on account)
Note Payable	20,000	Amount of loan owed to the bank (for promissory note)
Total Liabilities	27,000	Total claims on the resources by creditors
Stockholders' Equity		Stockholders' claims on the company's resources
Contributed Capital	30,000	Amount stockholders contributed for company stock
Retained Earnings	1,000	Total earnings retained in the business (Exhibit 1.3)
Total Stockholders' Equity	31,000	Total claims on the company's resources by stockholders
Total Liabilities and Stockholders' Equity	$58,000	**Total claims on the company's resources**

---

[3]For companies that have a net loss (expenses exceed revenues), the statement of retained earnings would subtract the net loss rather than add net income.

Notice again that the heading specifically identifies the name of the company and title of the statement. Unlike the other financial reports, the balance sheet is presented for a point in time (at September 30, 2010). The assets are listed in order of how soon they are to be used or turned into cash. Likewise, liabilities are listed in order of how soon each is to be paid or settled.

The balance sheet first lists the assets of the business, which for Pizza Aroma total $58,000. The second section lists the business's liabilities and stockholders' equity balances, also totaling $58,000. The balance sheet "balances" because the resources equal the claims to the resources. The basic accounting equation (also called the balance sheet equation) reflects the business's financial position at September 30, 2010:

Assets	=	Liabilities	+	Stockholders' Equity
$58,000	=	$27,000	+	$31,000

Cash is the first asset reported on the balance sheet. The $14,000 would represent the total amount of cash on hand and in Pizza Aroma's bank account. The $1,000 reported as Accounts Receivable would represent Pizza Aroma's right to collect from customers for sales made on credit. Pizza Aroma intends to allow local colleges to buy pizza for college events on account by running a tab that Pizza Aroma sends as a bill when the deliveries are made. The $3,000 reported for Supplies indicates the cost of pizza supplies that are expected to remain on hand at September 30, 2010. The same is true for the $40,000 of Equipment. According to the **cost principle** of accounting, assets are initially reported on the balance sheet based on their original cost to the company.

Under liabilities, the $7,000 of Accounts Payable is the amount that Laurie expects Pizza Aroma will owe suppliers for food and paper supplies purchased on account. The Note Payable is the written promise to repay the loan from the bank. As with all liabilities, these are financial obligations of the business arising from past business activities.

Finally, within stockholders' equity, Contributed Capital reflects the dollar amount of the company's stock that will be given when Mauricio and his wife contribute $30,000 to the company. Retained Earnings reports the earnings expected to be retained in the company as of September 30, 2010. It matches the ending amount of Retained Earnings on the statement of retained earnings (Exhibit 1.3).

> **COACH'S TIP**
>
> Any account name containing *receivable* is an asset and any containing *payable* is a liability.

"Besides monitoring my revenues and expenses, it looks like I need to make sure I have enough assets to pay my liabilities."

"Sharp observation! Your creditors are most interested in your ability to pay cash to them in the future. However, not all assets can be easily turned into cash and not all revenues and expenses are received or paid in cash. So, there is one more important financial statement."

The Statement of Cash Flows

Pizza Aroma's projected income statement (back in Exhibit 1.2) shows a positive net income of $2,000. However, net income is not necessarily equal to cash because revenues are reported when earned and expenses when incurred regardless of when cash is received or paid. The fourth financial report of interest to external users, then, is the **statement of cash flows**. It includes only those activities that result in cash changing hands. Exhibit 1.5 shows Pizza Aroma's projected statement of cash flows for the month ended September 30, 2010.

> **YOU SHOULD KNOW**
>
> **Statement of cash flows:** Reports the operating, investing, and financing activities that caused increases and decreases in cash during the period.

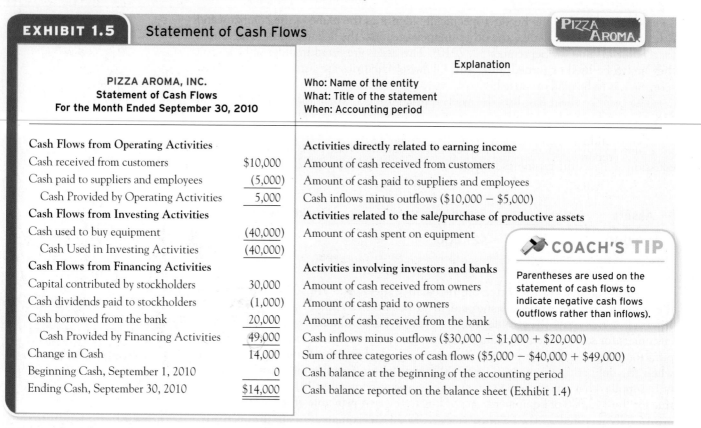

EXHIBIT 1.5 | Statement of Cash Flows

PIZZA AROMA, INC. Statement of Cash Flows For the Month Ended September 30, 2010		Explanation
		Who: Name of the entity
		What: Title of the statement
		When: Accounting period
Cash Flows from Operating Activities		Activities directly related to earning income
Cash received from customers	$10,000	Amount of cash received from customers
Cash paid to suppliers and employees	(5,000)	Amount of cash paid to suppliers and employees
Cash Provided by Operating Activities	5,000	Cash inflows minus outflows ($10,000 − $5,000)
Cash Flows from Investing Activities		Activities related to the sale/purchase of productive assets
Cash used to buy equipment	(40,000)	Amount of cash spent on equipment
Cash Used in Investing Activities	(40,000)	
Cash Flows from Financing Activities		Activities involving investors and banks
Capital contributed by stockholders	30,000	Amount of cash received from owners
Cash dividends paid to stockholders	(1,000)	Amount of cash paid to owners
Cash borrowed from the bank	20,000	Amount of cash received from the bank
Cash Provided by Financing Activities	49,000	Cash inflows minus outflows ($30,000 − $1,000 + $20,000)
Change in Cash	14,000	Sum of three categories of cash flows ($5,000 − $40,000 + $49,000)
Beginning Cash, September 1, 2010	0	Cash balance at the beginning of the accounting period
Ending Cash, September 30, 2010	$14,000	Cash balance reported on the balance sheet (Exhibit 1.4)

COACH'S TIP

Parentheses are used on the statement of cash flows to indicate negative cash flows (outflows rather than inflows).

The statement of cash flows is divided into three types of activities:

1. **Operating:** These activities are directly related to running the business to earn profit. They include buying supplies, making pizza, serving food to customers, cleaning the store, buying advertising, renting a building, repairing ovens, and obtaining insurance coverage.

2. **Investing:** These activities involve buying and selling productive resources with long lives (such as buildings, land, equipment, and tools), purchasing investments, and lending to others. As Exhibit 1.5 shows, Pizza Aroma expects to purchase equipment for $40,000 cash.

3. **Financing:** Any borrowing from banks, repaying bank loans, receiving contributions from stockholders, or paying dividends to stockholders are considered financing activities.

Pizza Aroma's statement of cash flows is typical of a new start-up business or a business in expansion. The negative number for investing cash flows occurs because the company needs to buy a significant amount of equipment. The bank will be interested in watching how the cash flows reported on this statement change in the future to assess Pizza Aroma's ability to make cash payments on the loan.

Notes to the Financial Statements

The four basic financial statements are not complete without notes to help financial statement users understand how the amounts were derived and what other information may affect their decisions. We'll talk about notes in more detail in later chapters.

"How does the whole picture fit together?"

Relationships among the Financial Statements

Exhibit 1.6 shows how the four basic financial statements connect to one another. The arrows show that:

 Net Income, from the income statement, is a component in determining ending Retained Earnings on the statement of retained earnings.

 Ending Retained Earnings from the statement of retained earnings is then reported on the balance sheet.

 The Cash on the balance sheet is equal to the ending Cash reported on the statement of cash flows.

EXHIBIT 1.6 Relationships among the Financial Statements

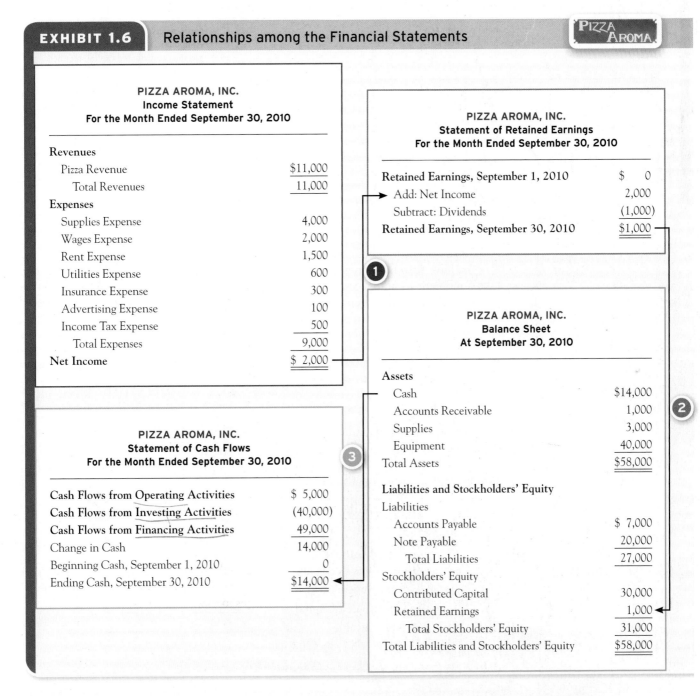

PIZZA AROMA, INC.
Income Statement
For the Month Ended September 30, 2010

Revenues	
Pizza Revenue	$11,000
Total Revenues	11,000
Expenses	
Supplies Expense	4,000
Wages Expense	2,000
Rent Expense	1,500
Utilities Expense	600
Insurance Expense	300
Advertising Expense	100
Income Tax Expense	500
Total Expenses	9,000
Net Income	$ 2,000

PIZZA AROMA, INC.
Statement of Retained Earnings
For the Month Ended September 30, 2010

Retained Earnings, September 1, 2010	$ 0
Add: Net Income	2,000
Subtract: Dividends	(1,000)
Retained Earnings, September 30, 2010	$1,000

PIZZA AROMA, INC.
Balance Sheet
At September 30, 2010

Assets	
Cash	$14,000
Accounts Receivable	1,000
Supplies	3,000
Equipment	40,000
Total Assets	$58,000
Liabilities and Stockholders' Equity	
Liabilities	
Accounts Payable	$ 7,000
Note Payable	20,000
Total Liabilities	27,000
Stockholders' Equity	
Contributed Capital	30,000
Retained Earnings	1,000
Total Stockholders' Equity	31,000
Total Liabilities and Stockholders' Equity	$58,000

PIZZA AROMA, INC.
Statement of Cash Flows
For the Month Ended September 30, 2010

Cash Flows from Operating Activities	$ 5,000
Cash Flows from Investing Activities	(40,000)
Cash Flows from Financing Activities	49,000
Change in Cash	14,000
Beginning Cash, September 1, 2010	0
Ending Cash, September 30, 2010	$14,000

EXHIBIT 1.7	Summary of Four Basic Financial Statements

Financial Statement	Purpose: To report . . .	Structure	Examples of Content
Income Statement	The financial performance of the business *during the current accounting period.*	Revenues − Expenses = Net Income	Sales revenue, wages expense, supplies expense, rent expense
Statement of Retained Earnings	The accumulation of earnings retained in the business *during the current accounting period* with that of prior periods.	Beginning Retained Earnings + Net Income (this period) − Dividends (this period) = Ending Retained Earnings	Net income is from the income statement. Dividends are amounts distributed this period.
Balance Sheet	The financial position of a business *at a point in time.*	Liabilities Assets = + Stockholders' Equity	Cash, receivables, supplies, equipment, accounts payable, notes payable, contributed capital, retained earnings
Statement of Cash Flows	Activities that caused increases and decreases in cash *during the current accounting period.*	+/ − Cash Flows from Operating Activities +/ − Cash Flows from Investing Activities +/ − Cash Flows from Financing Activities = Change in Cash + Beginning Cash = Ending Cash	Cash collected from customers, cash paid to suppliers, cash paid for equipment, cash borrowed from banks, cash received from selling stock

A summary of the four basic financial statements is presented in Exhibit 1.7.

You have seen lots of new and important material in this section. Before moving on, take a moment to practice what you've read. This is the best way to make sure you've paid enough attention when reading about how business activities are reported in financial statements.

How's it going?   Self-Study Practice

In the space provided, indicate: (1) the type of account (A = asset, L = liability, SE = stockholders' equity, R = revenue, E = expense), and (2) whether it is reported on the income statement (I/S), statement of retained earnings (SRE), balance sheet (B/S), or statement of cash flows (SCF).

Account Title	Type	Statement
1. Land	A	B/S
2. Wages Expense	E	I/S
3. Accounts Receivable	A	B/S
4. Rent Revenue	R	I/S
5. Contributed Capital	SE	B/S
6. Note Payable	L	B/S

After you have finished, check your answers with the solution in the margin.

Solution to Self-Study Practice

	Type	Statement
1.	A	B/S
2.	E	I/S
3.	A	B/S
4.	R	I/S
5.	SE	B/S
6.	L	B/S

"So, you've just seen how your financial statements should look in one month and how they relate. Are you feeling okay with all this?"

"It actually makes me anxious to get started. What will my external users look for?"

Evaluate the Results

USING FINANCIAL STATEMENTS

Learning Objective 3
Explain how financial statements are used by decision makers.

The financial statements are a key source of information when external users, like creditors and investors, make decisions concerning a company. As you will see throughout this course, the amounts reported in the financial statements can be used to calculate percentages and ratios that reveal important insights about a company's performance. For now, however, let's consider how creditors and investors might gain valuable information simply by reading the dollar amounts reported in each financial statement.

- Creditors are mainly interested in assessing:
  1. **Is the company generating enough cash to make payments on its loan?** Answers to this question will come from the statement of cash flows. In particular, creditors would be interested in seeing whether operating activities are producing positive cash flows. Pizza Aroma's expected net inflow of $5,000 cash from operating activities is very good for a new business.
  2. **Does the company have enough assets to cover its liabilities?** Answers to this question will come from comparing assets and liabilities reported on the balance sheet. Pizza Aroma is expected to own slightly more than twice what it owes to creditors at September 30 (total assets of $58,000 versus total liabilities of $27,000). With $14,000 in Cash, Pizza Aroma would be able to immediately pay all of its Accounts Payable and part of its Note Payable if needed.
- **Investors expect a return on their contributions to a company.** The return may be immediate (through dividends) or long-term (through selling stock certificates at a price higher than their original cost). Dividends and higher stock prices are more likely if a company is profitable. As a result, investors look closely at the income statement (and statement of retained earnings) for information about the company's ability to generate profits (and distribute dividends).

"I've heard a lot about 'cooking the books.' How do users know the information they're getting is useful and can be trusted?"

USEFUL FINANCIAL INFORMATION

Learning Objective 4
Describe factors that contribute to useful financial information.

Laurie indicated that businesses must apply accounting principles in an ethical business environment.

Generally Accepted Accounting Principles

As it turns out, the system of financial statement reporting in use today has a long history—all the way back to a publication in 1494 by an Italian monk and mathematician, Luca Pacioli. Currently, the Financial Accounting Standards Board (FASB) has

YOU SHOULD KNOW

Generally Accepted Accounting Principles (GAAP): Rules of accounting created by the Financial Accounting Standards Board for use in the United States.

the primary responsibility for setting the underlying rules of accounting in the U.S. As a group, these rules are called **Generally Accepted Accounting Principles,** or **GAAP** for short (pronounced like the name of the clothing store).

The accounting rules in the United States are similar, for the most part, to those used elsewhere in the world, but some important differences exist. The FASB is working alongside the International Accounting Standards Board (IASB) to eliminate these differences so that investors can more easily compare the financial statements of companies from different countries. Throughout this course, we'll use a pullout feature called Spotlight on the World to alert you to important differences.

YOU SHOULD KNOW

International Financial Reporting Standards (IFRS): Rules of accounting created by the International Accounting Standards Board for international use.

Spotlight On THE WORLD

The accounting rules developed by the IASB are called **International Financial Reporting Standards**, or **IFRS** for short. As the map indicates, accounting bodies in many countries already require or permit the use of IFRS (dark green), or plan to converge with IFRS in the near future (blue). The plans for converging U.S. GAAP with IFRS are discussed in Chapter 5.

The main goal of GAAP and IFRS is to ensure companies produce financial information that is useful to present and potential investors, lenders, and other creditors in making decisions in their capacity as capital providers. For financial information to be judged useful, it must possess two fundamental characteristics: relevance and faithful representation. Information is relevant if it makes a difference in decision making and it is a faithful representation if it fully depicts the economic substance of business activities. The usefulness of financial information is enhanced when it is (i) comparable (to prior periods and other companies), (ii) verifiable, (iii) timely, and (iv) understandable. To achieve these broad objectives, the FASB and IASB have developed a framework that outlines the financial elements to be measured and reported as well as various concepts for measuring and reporting financial information. Laurie summarized these elements and concepts for Mauricio, highlighting in red the concepts briefly introduced already (see Exhibit 1.8). (The remaining concepts will be introduced in later chapters and all will be reviewed in the final chapter.)

EXHIBIT 1.8	**Key Concepts for External Financial Reporting**

Objective of External Financial Reporting
To provide useful financial information to external users for decision making
- It must be relevant and a faithful representation of the business
- It is more useful if it is comparable, verifiable, timely, and understandable

Elements to Be Measured and Reported
- Assets, Liabilities, Stockholders' Equity, Revenues, Expenses, Dividends

Concepts for Measuring and Reporting Information
- **Assumptions:** Unit of Measure, Separate Entity, Going Concern, Time Period
- **Principles:** Cost, Revenue Recognition, Matching, Full Disclosure
- **Exceptions:** Cost-Benefit, Materiality, Industry Practices

"Who is responsible for ensuring that businesses follow GAAP?"

Laurie told Mauricio that a company's managers have primary responsibility for following GAAP. To provide additional assurance, some private companies and all public companies hire independent auditors to scrutinize their financial records. Following rules approved by the Public Company Accounting Oversight Board (PCAOB) and other accounting bodies, these auditors report whether, beyond reasonable doubt, the financial statements represent what they claim to represent and whether they comply with GAAP. In a sense, GAAP are to auditors and accountants what the criminal code is to lawyers and the public. The Securities and Exchange Commission (SEC) is the government agency that oversees stock exchanges and financial reporting by public companies in the U.S.

 "Overall, users expect information that is truthful, and this assumes that the company is following strong ethical business and accounting practices."

Ethical Conduct

Ethics refers to the standards of conduct for judging right from wrong, honest from dishonest, and fair from unfair. Intentional financial misreporting is both unethical and illegal. As you will see throughout this course, some accounting and business issues have clear answers that are either right or wrong. However, many situations require accountants, auditors, and managers to weigh the pros and cons of alternatives before making final decisions. To help ensure these decisions are made in a professional and ethical manner, the American Institute of Certified Public Accountants (AICPA) requires that all its members adhere to a **Code of Professional Conduct.**

Mauricio's concern about "cooking the books" likely stems from hearing about several high-profile accounting frauds that occurred a few years ago involving Enron, WorldCom (now owned by Verizon), Global Crossing, and Xerox. In response to these frauds, the U.S. Congress stepped into the crisis to create the **Sarbanes-Oxley Act.** The Act requires top managers of public companies to sign a report certifying their responsibilities for the financial statements, maintain an audited system of **internal controls** to ensure accuracy in the accounting reports, and maintain an independent committee to oversee top management and ensure that they cooperate with auditors. As a result of the act, corporate executives now face severe consequences—20 years in prison and $5 million in fines—if they are found guilty of committing accounting fraud.

> **YOU SHOULD KNOW**
>
> **Sarbanes-Oxley Act (SOX):** A set of laws established to strengthen corporate reporting in the United States.

Spotlight On ETHICS

Accounting Scandals

Accounting scandals are driven by greed and the fear of personal or business failure. Initially, some people may appear to benefit from fraudulent reporting. In the long run, however, fraud harms most individuals and organizations. When it is uncovered, the corporation's stock price drops dramatically. In one case involving MicroStrategy, the stock price dropped 65 percent in a single day of trading, from $243 to $86 per share. Creditors are also harmed by fraud. As a result of a fraud at WorldCom, creditors recovered only 42 percent of what they were owed. They lost $36 billion. Innocent employees also are harmed by fraud. At Enron, 5,600 employees lost their jobs and many lost all of their retirement savings. The auditing firm of Arthur Andersen, which once employed 28,000 people, went out of business after becoming entangled in the WorldCom and Enron frauds.

Ethical conduct is just as important for small private businesses as it is for large public companies. Laurie's advice to Mauricio and to all managers is to strive to create an ethical environment and establish a strong system of checks and controls inside the company. Do not tolerate blatant acts of fraud, such as employees making up false expenses for reimbursement, punching in a time card belonging to a fellow employee who will be late for work, or copying someone's ideas and claiming them as his or her own. Also be aware that not all ethical dilemmas are clear-cut. Some situations will require you to weigh one moral principle (e.g., honesty) against another (e.g., loyalty). Advise your employees that, when faced with an ethical dilemma, they should follow a three-step process:

1. **Identify who will benefit from the situation** (often the manager or employee) and the harm it could cause others (other employees, the company's reputation, owners, creditors, and the public in general).

2. **Identify the alternative courses of action.**

3. **Choose the alternative that is the most ethical**—and that you would be proud to have reported in the news.

Often, there is no one right answer to ethical dilemmas and hard choices will need to be made. In the end, however, following strong ethical practices is a key factor in business success and in ensuring good financial reporting.

Epilogue for Pizza Aroma

Mauricio got going quickly and, in August, created a corporation called Pizza Aroma, Inc. Things didn't turn out exactly as he had planned, but his dream-turned-business has been successful. Pizza Aroma has received the "Best Pizza" award several years in a row in the *Ithaca Times* readers' poll.

The next three chapters will take you step by step through the financing, investing, and operating decisions that occurred at Pizza Aroma during its first month of business. We will look at the way accountants collect data about business activities and process it to construct the financial statements. The key to success in this course is to **practice** the skills that are presented in this text. It is very difficult to learn accounting without doing the assignments and keeping up with the reading.

SUPPLEMENT 1A: ACCOUNTING CAREERS

Even during difficult economic times, accounting positions are abundant. According to the U.S. Department of Labor's most recent projections, over 20,000 new accounting jobs are expected to be added each year through 2016. Exhibit 1S.1 summarizes the career opportunities available in private and public accounting. Accountants employed by a single organization are in private accounting. Accountants who charge fees for services to a variety of organizations, like Laurie, are in public accounting. Accounting graduates often start their careers in public accounting firms and then at some point move into private accounting within business, governmental organizations such as the Internal Revenue Service (IRS) and Federal Bureau of Investigation (FBI), or not-for-profit organizations (NPOs). Many become top managers of large companies. Some even enter academia to teach and conduct research.

Accountants may pursue a variety of certifications, including the CPA (Certified Public Accountant), CFE (Certified Fraud Examiner), CMA (Certified Management Accountant), CIA (Certified Internal Auditor), CFM (Certified Financial Manager), Cr. FA (Certified Forensic Accountant), and CFA (Chartered Financial Analyst), among others. For additional information on accounting careers, certifications, salaries, and opportunities, visit www.aicpa.org, www.collegegrad.com, and www.imanet.org.

EXHIBIT 1S.1 Overview of Career Choices in Accounting

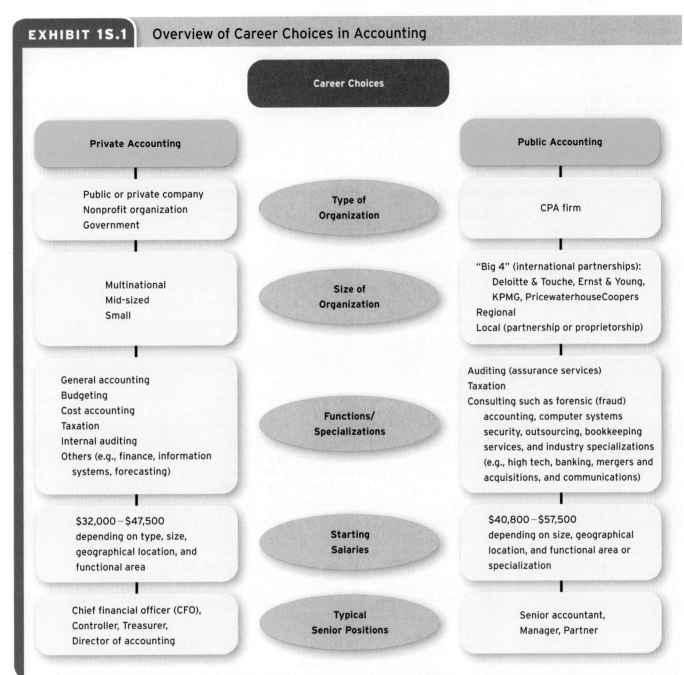

Private Accounting		Public Accounting
Public or private company Nonprofit organization Government	**Type of Organization**	CPA firm

Multinational
Mid-sized
Small
	Size of Organization	"Big 4" (international partnerships):
		  Deloitte & Touche, Ernst & Young,
		  KPMG, PricewaterhouseCoopers
		Regional
		Local (partnership or proprietorship)

General accounting
Budgeting
Cost accounting
Taxation
Internal auditing
Others (e.g., finance, information
  systems, forecasting)
	Functions/ Specializations	Auditing (assurance services)
		Taxation
		Consulting such as forensic (fraud)
		  accounting, computer systems
		  security, outsourcing, bookkeeping
		  services, and industry specializations
		  (e.g., high tech, banking, mergers and
		  acquisitions, and communications)

$32,000–$47,500 depending on type, size, geographical location, and functional area	**Starting Salaries**	$40,800–$57,500 depending on size, geographical location, and functional area or specialization
Chief financial officer (CFO), Controller, Treasurer, Director of accounting	**Typical Senior Positions**	Senior accountant, Manager, Partner

Source: 2008 Robert Half *Salary Guide*. www.collegegrad.com/careers/all.shtml.

REVIEW THE CHAPTER

DEMONSTRATION CASE

The introductory case presented here reviews the items reported on the income statement, statement of retained earnings, and balance sheet, using the financial statements of Under Armour, Inc.—a public company founded in 1996 by a former University of Maryland football player to develop, market, and distribute athletic apparel and gear. Following is a list of items and amounts (in thousands of U.S. dollars) adapted from Under Armour, Inc.'s financial statements for the quarter ended September 30, 2008.

UNDER ARMOUR

eXcel

www.mhhe.com/phillips3e

Accounts Payable	$129,724	Other Expenses	$ 1,736
Accounts Receivable	151,086	Other Liabilities	10,425
Cash	40,152	Property and Equipment	70,645
Contributed Capital	176,330	Retained Earnings, September 30, 2008	143,445
Dividends	0	Retained Earnings, July 1, 2008	117,782
General and Administrative Expenses	71,788	Sales Revenues	231,946
Income Tax Expense	19,080	Total Assets	474,886
Inventories	163,612	Total Expenses	206,283
Net Income	25,663	Total Liabilities	155,111
Notes Payable	14,962	Total Liabilities and Stockholders' Equity	474,886
Operating Expenses	113,679	Total Revenues	231,946
Other Assets	49,391	Total Stockholders' Equity	319,775

Required:

1. Prepare an Income Statement, Statement of Retained Earnings, and a Balance Sheet for the quarter, following the formats in Exhibits 1.2, 1.3, and 1.4.
2. Describe the content of these three statements.
3. Name the other statement that Under Armour would include in its financial statements.
4. Did financing for Under Armour's assets come primarily from liabilities or stockholders' equity?
5. Explain why Under Armour would subject its statements to an independent audit.

Suggested Solution

1. The first step to reach a solution is to distinguish accounts as belonging to the income statement (revenues and expenses), statement of retained earnings (retained earnings and dividends), and balance sheet (assets, liabilities, and stockholders' equity). Organize the accounts in proper format and follow the flow from one to another (as shown by the following arrows).

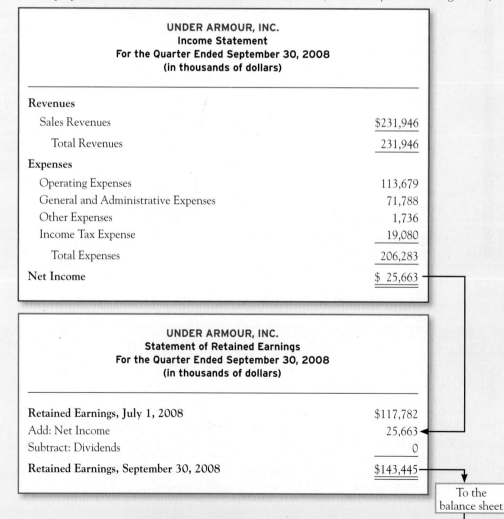

UNDER ARMOUR, INC.
Income Statement
For the Quarter Ended September 30, 2008
(in thousands of dollars)

Revenues	
Sales Revenues	$231,946
Total Revenues	231,946
Expenses	
Operating Expenses	113,679
General and Administrative Expenses	71,788
Other Expenses	1,736
Income Tax Expense	19,080
Total Expenses	206,283
Net Income	$ 25,663

UNDER ARMOUR, INC.
Statement of Retained Earnings
For the Quarter Ended September 30, 2008
(in thousands of dollars)

Retained Earnings, July 1, 2008	$117,782
Add: Net Income	25,663
Subtract: Dividends	0
Retained Earnings, September 30, 2008	$143,445

To the balance sheet

UNDER ARMOUR, INC.
Balance Sheet
At September 30, 2008
(in thousands of dollars)

Assets	
Cash	$ 40,152
Accounts Receivable	151,086
Inventories	163,612
Property and Equipment	70,645
Other Assets	49,391
Total Assets	**$474,886**
Liabilities	
Accounts Payable	$129,724
Notes Payable	14,962
Other Liabilities	10,425
Total Liabilities	155,111
Stockholders' Equity	
Contributed Capital	176,330
Retained Earnings	143,445
Total Stockholders' Equity	319,775
Total Liabilities and Stockholders' Equity	**$474,886**

From the statement of retained earnings

2. The income statement reports the most common measure of financial performance for a business: net income (revenues minus expenses during the accounting period). The statement of retained earnings links the net income number from the income statement to the end-of-period retained earnings balance on the balance sheet. The balance sheet reports the amount of assets, liabilities, and stockholders' equity of a business at a point in time.

3. Under Armour would also present a statement of cash flows.

4. The balance sheet indicates that financing for Under Armour's assets is provided primarily from stockholders' equity ($319,775) rather than liabilities ($155,111).

5. Like all public companies, Under Armour will subject its financial statements to an audit because it is required by the SEC to have an independent audit. Also, an audit will give users greater confidence in the accuracy of financial statement information because the people who audited the statements are required to meet professional standards of ethics and competence.

CHAPTER SUMMARY

Describe various organizational forms and business decision makers. p. 4   **LO1**

*   Sole proprietorships are owned by one individual, are relatively inexpensive to form, and are not treated legally as separate from their owners. Thus, all profits or losses become part of the taxable income to the owner who is also responsible personally for all debts of the business.

*   Partnerships are businesses legally similar to proprietorships, but with two or more owners.

*   Corporations are separate legal entities (thus, corporations pay taxes) that issue shares of stock to investors (stockholders) and are more costly to establish. Stockholders cannot be held liable for more than their investment in the corporation. Private corporations issue stock to a few individuals while public corporations issue stock in the stock market.

*   Business decision makers include creditors (banks, suppliers), investors (stockholders), customers, governments, and other external users.

LO2 **Describe the purpose, structure, and content of the four basic financial statements. p. 7**

- The *income statement* reports the net amount that a business earned (net income) over a period of time by subtracting the costs of running the business (expenses) from the total amount earned (revenues).
- The *statement of retained earnings* explains changes in the retained earnings account over a period of time by considering increases (from net income) and decreases (from dividends to stockholders).
- The *balance sheet* reports what the business owns (reported as assets) at a particular point in time and how much of the financing for these assets came from creditors (reported as liabilities) and stockholders (reported as stockholders' equity).
- The *statement of cash flows* explains changes in the cash account over a period of time by reporting inflows and outflows of cash from the business's operating, investing, and financing activities.

LO3 **Explain how financial statements are used by decision makers. p. 17**

- Creditors are mainly interested in assessing whether the company: (1) is generating enough cash to make payments on its loan, and (2) has enough assets to cover its liabilities. Answers to these questions are indicated by the statement of cash flows and the balance sheet.
- Investors look closely at the income statement for information about a company's ability to generate profits, and at the statement of retained earnings for information about a company's dividend distributions.

LO4 **Describe factors that contribute to useful financial information. p. 17**

- Companies generate useful financial information by applying Generally Accepted Accounting Principles (GAAP) or International Financial Reporting Standards (IFRS) in an ethical business environment.
- To be useful, information must be relevant and a faithful representation of reality. Information is more useful when it is comparable, verifiable, timely, and understandable.

KEY TERMS

Accounting p. 5
Accounts p. 10
Balance Sheet p. 12
Basic Accounting Equation p. 8
Financial Statements p. 6

Generally Accepted Accounting
  Principles (GAAP) p. 18
Income Statement p. 10
International Financial Reporting
  Standards (IFRS) p. 18

Sarbanes-Oxley Act (SOX) p. 19
Separate Entity Assumption p. 8
Statement of Cash Flows p. 13
Statement of Retained Earnings p. 11
Unit of Measure Assumption p. 10

See complete definitions in the glossary in the back of this text.

HOMEWORK HELPER

Alternative terms
- The balance sheet also can be called the statement of financial position.
- The income statement also can be called the statement of operations.
- Net Income also can be called Net Earnings.

Helpful reminders
- The balance in each account is reported once and only once in either the balance sheet, income statement, or statement of retained earnings.

Frequent mistakes
- Dividends are not expenses. Dividends relate to distributing (not generating) earnings. Consequently, a company's dividends are reported on its statement of retained earnings (not its income statement).

PRACTICE MATERIAL

QUESTIONS (⊖ Symbol indicates questions that require analysis from more than one perspective.)

1. Define *accounting*.

2. Valeri is opening a hair salon but she does not know what business form it should take. What can you tell her about the advantages and disadvantages of operating as a sole proprietorship versus a corporation? ⊖

3. Briefly distinguish financial accounting from managerial accounting.

4. The accounting process generates financial reports for both internal and external users. Describe some of the specific groups of internal and external users.

5. Explain what the separate entity assumption means when it says a business is treated as separate from its owners for accounting purposes.

6. List the three main types of business activities on the statement of cash flows and give an example of each.

7. What information should be included in the heading of each of the four primary financial statements?

8. What are the purposes of (*a*) the balance sheet, (*b*) the income statement, (*c*) the statement of retained earnings, and (*d*) the statement of cash flows?

9. Explain why the income statement, statement of retained earnings, and statement of cash flows would be dated "For the Year Ended December 31, 2009," whereas the balance sheet would be dated "At December 31, 2009."

10. Briefly explain the difference between *net income* and *net loss*.

11. Describe the basic accounting equation that provides the structure for the balance sheet. Define the three major components reported on the balance sheet.

12. Describe the equation that provides the structure for the income statement. Explain the three major items reported on the income statement.

13. Describe the equation that provides the structure for the statement of retained earnings. Explain the four major items reported on the statement of retained earnings.

14. Describe the equation that provides the structure for the statement of cash flows. Explain the three major types of activities reported on the statement.

15. Briefly describe the organization that is responsible for developing accounting measurement rules (generally accepted accounting principles) in the United States.

16. What is the main goal for accounting rules in the United States and around the world? What characteristics must financial information possess to reach that goal?

17. Briefly define what an ethical dilemma is and describe the steps to consider when evaluating ethical dilemmas.

18. In what ways might accounting frauds be similar to cases of academic dishonesty?

MULTIPLE CHOICE

1. Which of the following is *not* one of the four basic financial statements?

    a. The balance sheet
    b. The audit report
    c. The income statement
    d. The statement of cash flows

Quiz 1
www.mhhe.com/phillips3e

2. Which of the following is true regarding the income statement?

    a. The income statement is sometimes called the statement of operations.
    b. The income statement reports revenues, expenses, and liabilities.
    c. The income statement only reports revenue for which cash was received at the point of sale.
    d. The income statement reports the financial position of a business at a particular point in time.

3. Which of the following is false regarding the balance sheet?

    a. The accounts shown on a balance sheet represent the basic accounting equation for a particular business.
    b. The retained earnings balance shown on the balance sheet must agree with the ending retained earnings balance shown on the statement of retained earnings.

    c. The balance sheet summarizes the net changes in specific account balances over a period of time.
    d. The balance sheet reports the amount of assets, liabilities, and stockholders' equity of a business at a point in time.

4. Which of the following regarding retained earnings is false?

    a. Retained earnings is increased by net income.
    b. Retained earnings is a component of stockholders' equity on the balance sheet.
    c. Retained earnings is an asset on the balance sheet.
    d. Retained earnings represents earnings not distributed to stockholders in the form of dividends.

5. Which of the following is not one of the items required to be shown in the heading of a financial statement?

    a. The financial statement preparer's name.
    b. The title of the financial statement.
    c. The financial reporting date or period.
    d. The name of the business entity.

6. Which of the following statements regarding the statement of cash flows is false?

    a. The statement of cash flows separates cash inflows and outflows into three major categories: operating, investing, and financing.

b. The ending cash balance shown on the statement of cash flows must agree with the amount shown on the balance sheet at the end of the same period.

c. The total increase or decrease in cash shown on the statement of cash flows must agree with the "bottom line" (net income or net loss) reported on the income statement.

d. The statement of cash flows covers a period of time.

7. Which of the following regarding GAAP is true?

  a. GAAP is an abbreviation for generally applied accounting principles.

  b. Changes in GAAP always affect the amount of income reported by a company.

  c. GAAP is the abbreviation for generally accepted accounting principles.

  d. Changes to GAAP must be approved by the Senate Finance Committee.

8. Which of the following is true?

  a. FASB creates SEC.

  b. GAAP creates FASB.

  c. SEC creates CPA.

  d. FASB creates GAAP.

9. Which of the following would *not* be a goal of external users reading a company's financial statements?

  a. Understanding the current financial state of the company.

  b. Assessing the company's contribution to social and environmental policies.

  c. Predicting the company's future financial performance.

  d. Evaluating the company's ability to generate cash from sales.

10. Which of the following is not required by the Sarbanes-Oxley Act?

  a. Top managers of public companies must sign a report certifying their responsibilities for the financial statements.

  b. Public companies must maintain an audited system of internal control to ensure accuracy in accounting reports.

  c. Public companies must maintain an independent committee to meet with the company's independent auditors.

  d. Top managers of public companies must be members of the American Institute of Certified Public Accountants.

> For answers to the Multiple-Choice Questions **see page Q1** located in the last section of the book.

MINI-EXERCISES

LO4   M1-1 Identifying Definitions with Abbreviations

The following is a list of important abbreviations used in the chapter. These abbreviations also are used widely in business. For each abbreviation, give the full designation. The first one is an example.

Abbreviation	Full Designation
1. CPA	Certified Public Accountant
2. GAAP	_____
3. FASB	_____
4. SEC	_____
5. IFRS	_____

LO1, 2, 4   M1-2 Matching Definitions with Terms or Abbreviations

Match each definition with its related term or abbreviation by entering the appropriate letter in the space provided.

Term or Abbreviation	Definition
___ 1. SEC	A. A system that collects and processes financial information about an organization and reports that information to decision makers.
___ 2. Investing activities	
___ 3. Private company	B. Measurement of information about a business in the monetary unit (dollars or other national currency).
___ 4. Corporation	
___ 5. Accounting	C. An unincorporated business owned by two or more persons.
___ 6. Partnership	
___ 7. FASB	D. A company that sells shares of its stock privately and is not required to release its financial statements to the public.
___ 8. Financing activities	
___ 9. Unit of measure	

____ 10. GAAP

____ 11. Public company

____ 12. Operating activities

E. An incorporated business that issues shares of stock as evidence of ownership.

F. Buying and selling productive resources with long lives.

G. Transactions with lenders (borrowing and repaying cash) and stockholders (selling company stock and paying dividends).

H. Activities directly related to running the business to earn profit.

I. Securities and Exchange Commission.

J. Financial Accounting Standards Board.

K. A company that has its stock bought and sold by investors on established stock exchanges.

L. Generally accepted accounting principles.

M1-3 Matching Definitions with Terms

LO2, 4

Match each definition with its related term by entering the appropriate letter in the space provided.

Term	Definition
____ 1. Relevance	A. The financial reports of a business are assumed to include the results of only that business's activities.
____ 2. Faithful Representation	
____ 3. Comparability	B. The resources owned by a business.
____ 4. Separate Entity	C. Financial information that can be compared across businesses because similar accounting methods have been applied.
____ 5. Assets	
____ 6. Liabilities	
____ 7. Stockholders' Equity	D. The total amounts invested and reinvested in the business by its owners.
____ 8. Revenues	E. The costs of business necessary to earn revenues.
____ 9. Expenses	F. A feature of financial information that allows it to influence a decision.
____ 10. Unit of Measure	
	G. Earned by selling goods or services to customers.
	H. The amounts owed by the business.
	I. Financial information that depicts the economic substance of business activities.
	J. The assumption that states that results of business activities should be reported in an appropriate monetary unit.

M1-4 Matching Financial Statement Items to Balance Sheet and Income Statement Categories

LO2

According to its annual report, "Procter & Gamble markets a broad range of laundry, cleaning, paper, beauty care, health care, food and beverage products in more than 140 countries around the world, with leading brands including Tide, Ariel, Crest, Crisco, Vicks and Max Factor." The following are items taken from its recent balance sheet and income statement. Mark each item in the following list with letters to indicate whether it would be reported as an <u>A</u>sset, <u>L</u>iability, or <u>S</u>tockholders' Equity account on the balance sheet or a <u>R</u>evenue or <u>E</u>xpense account on the income statement.

_L_ 1. Accounts Payable

_A_ 2. Accounts Receivable

_A_ 3. Cash

_E_ 4. Income Tax Expense

_E_ 5. Selling and Administrative Expenses

_R_ 6. Sales Revenue

_L_ 7. Notes Payable

_SE_ 8. Retained Earnings

LO2   **M1-5   Matching Financial Statement Items to Balance Sheet and Income Statement Categories**

Mark each item in the following list with letters to indicate whether it would be reported as an Asset, Liability, or Stockholders' Equity account on the balance sheet or a Revenue or Expense account on the income statement.

____ 1. Accounts Receivable   ____ 5. Cash

____ 2. Sales Revenue   ____ 6. Advertising Expense

____ 3. Equipment   ____ 7. Accounts Payable

____ 4. Supplies Expense   ____ 8. Retained Earnings

LO2   **M1-6   Matching Financial Statement Items to Balance Sheet and Income Statement Categories**

Tootsie Roll Industries

Tootsie Roll Industries manufactures and sells more than 60 million Tootsie Rolls and 20 million Tootsie Roll Pops each day. The following items were listed on Tootsie Roll's recent income statement and balance sheet. Mark each item from the balance sheet as an Asset, Liability, or Stockholders' Equity and each item from the income statement as a Revenue or Expense.

____ 1. Accounts Receivable   ____ 6. Sales Revenue

____ 2. Selling and Administrative Expenses ____ 7. Notes Payable

____ 3. Cash   ____ 8. Retained Earnings

____ 4. Machinery   ____ 9. Accounts Payable

____ 5. Promotion and Advertising Expenses

LO2   **M1-7   Matching Financial Statement Items to Balance Sheet and Income Statement Categories**

GENERAL MILLS

General Mills is a manufacturer of food products, such as Lucky Charms cereal, Pillsbury crescent rolls, and Jolly Green Giant vegetables. The following items were presented in the company's financial statements. Mark each item from the balance sheet as an Asset, Liability, or Stockholders' Equity and each item from the income statement as a Revenue or Expense.

_L_ 1. Accounts Payable   _A_ 6. Cash

_SE_ 2. Contributed Capital   _SE_ 7. Retained Earnings

_A_ 3. Equipment   _E_ 8. Selling and Administrative Expenses

_A_ 4. Accounts Receivable   _R_ 9. Sales Revenue

_L_ 5. Notes Payable   _A_ 10. Supplies

LO2   **M1-8   Matching Financial Statement Items to Balance Sheet and Income Statement Categories**

Microsoft Corporation

Microsoft Corporation manufactures home entertainment devices like Xbox®, creates software like Word®, and operates networks like MSN Hotmail®. The following items were presented in the company's financial statements. Mark each item from the balance sheet as an Asset, Liability, or Stockholders' Equity and each item from the income statement as a Revenue or Expense.

____ 1. Accounts Payable   ____ 6. Contributed Capital

____ 2. Cash   ____ 7. Accounts Receivable

____ 3. Retained Earnings   ____ 8. Sales Revenue

____ 4. Property and Equipment   ____ 9. Selling and Administrative Expenses

____ 5. Notes Payable   ____ 10. Promotion Expense

LO2   **M1-9   Matching Financial Statement Items to the Four Basic Financial Statements**

Match each element with its financial statement by entering the appropriate letter in the space provided.

Element	Financial Statement
_D_ 1. Cash Flows from Financing Activities	A. Balance Sheet
_B_ 2. Expenses	B. Income Statement
_D_ 3. Cash Flows from Investing Activities	C. Statement of Retained Earnings
_A_ 4. Assets	D. Statement of Cash Flows
_C_ 5. Dividends	
_B_ 6. Revenues	
_D_ 7. Cash Flows from Operating Activities	
_A_ 8. Liabilities	

M1-10 Matching Financial Statement Items to the Four Basic Financial Statements

LO2

Prior to being acquired in November 2007 by Luxottica Group—an Italian eyeware company—Oakley, Inc., reported the following items in its financial statements. Indicate whether these items would have appeared on the balance sheet (B/S), income statement (I/S), statement of retained earnings (SRE), or statement of cash flows (SCF).

_____ 1. Dividends   _____ 5. Cash Flows from Operating Activities

_____ 2. Total Stockholders' Equity   _____ 6. Total Liabilities

_____ 3. Sales Revenue   _____ 7. Net Income

_____ 4. Total Assets   _____ 8. Cash Flows from Financing Activities

M1-11 Reporting Amounts on the Statement of Cash Flows

LO2

Learning which items belong in each cash flow statement category is an important first step in understanding their meaning. Use a letter to mark each item in the following list as a cash flow from <u>O</u>perating, <u>I</u>nvesting, or <u>F</u>inancing activities. **Put parentheses around the letter if it is a cash _outflow_ and use no parentheses if it's an _inflow_.**

_(F)_ 1. Cash paid for dividends   _(O)_ 4. Cash paid to suppliers and employees

_O_ 2. Cash collected from customers   _(I)_ 5. Cash paid to purchase equipment

_F_ 3. Cash received when signing a note   _F_ 6. Cash received from issuing stock

M1-12 Reporting Amounts on the Statement of Cash Flows

LO2

Learning which items belong in each category of the statement of cash flows is an important first step in understanding their meaning. Use a letter to mark each item in the following list as a cash flow from <u>O</u>perating, <u>I</u>nvesting, or <u>F</u>inancing activities. **Put parentheses around the letter if it is a cash _outflow_ and use no parentheses if it's an _inflow_.**

_____ 1. Cash paid to purchase equipment   _____ 4. Cash paid for dividends

_____ 2. Cash collected from customers   _____ 5. Cash paid to suppliers and employees

_____ 3. Cash received from selling equipment   _____ 6. Cash received from issuing stock

M1-13 Preparing a Statement of Retained Earnings

LO2

Stone Culture Corporation was organized on January 1, 2009. For its first two years of operations, it reported the following:

Net Income for 2009	$36,000	Dividends for 2010	$ 20,000
Net Income for 2010	45,000	Total assets at the end of 2009	125,000
Dividends for 2009	15,000	Total assets at the end of 2010	242,000

On the basis of the data given, prepare a statement of retained earnings for 2009 (its first year of operations) and 2010.

M1-14 Preparing an Income Statement, Statement of Retained Earnings, and Balance Sheet

LO2, 3

The following information was reported in the December 31, 2007, financial statements of Southwest Airlines, Inc. (listed alphabetically, amounts in millions).

Accounts Payable	$1,731	Other Assets	$ 2,581
Accounts Receivable	845	Other Liabilities	3,107
Aircraft Fuel Expense	2,536	Other Operating Expenses	2,145
Cash	2,213	Other Revenue	336
Contributed Capital	2,153	Property and Equipment	10,874
Dividends	14	Repairs and Maintenance Expense	616
Income Tax Expense	413	Retained Earnings (as of December 31, 2007)	4,788
Interest Expense	69	Salaries Expense	3,213
Landing Fees Expense	560	Supplies	259
Notes Payable	4,993	Ticket Revenues	9,861

1. Prepare an income statement for the year ended December 31, 2007.
2. Prepare a statement of retained earnings for the year ended December 31, 2007.
   TIP: Assume the balance in retained earnings was $4,157 (million) at January 1, 2007.
3. Prepare a balance sheet at December 31, 2007.
4. Using the balance sheet, indicate whether the total assets of Southwest Airlines at the end of the year were financed primarily by liabilities or stockholders' equity.

EXERCISES

LO2   **E1-1** **Reporting Amounts on the Four Basic Financial Statements**

Using the following table and the equations underlying each of the four basic financial statements, show (a) that the balance sheet is in balance, (b) that net income is properly calculated, (c) what caused changes in the retained earnings account, and (d) what caused changes in the cash account.

Assets	$18,200	Beginning Retained Earnings	$3,500
Liabilities	13,750	Ending Retained Earnings	4,300
Stockholders' Equity	4,450	Cash Flows from Operating Activities	1,600
Revenue	10,500	Cash Flows from Investing Activities	(1,000)
Expenses	9,200	Cash Flows from Financing Activities	(900)
Net Income	1,300	Beginning Cash	1,000
Dividends	500	Ending Cash	700

LO2   **E1-2** **Reporting Amounts on the Four Basic Financial Statements**

Using the following table and the equations underlying each of the four basic financial statements, show (a) that the balance sheet is in balance, (b) that net income is properly calculated, (c) what caused changes in the retained earnings account, and (d) what caused changes in the cash account.

Assets	$79,500	Beginning Retained Earnings	$20,500
Liabilities	18,500	Ending Retained Earnings	28,750
Stockholders' Equity	61,000	Cash Flows from Operating Activities	15,700
Revenue	32,100	Cash Flows from Investing Activities	(7,200)
Expenses	18,950	Cash Flows from Financing Activities	(5,300)
Net Income	13,150	Beginning Cash	3,200
Dividends	4,900	Ending Cash	6,400

LO2, 3   **E1-3** **Preparing a Balance Sheet**

DSW, Inc.   DSW, Inc., is a designer shoe warehouse, selling some of the most luxurious and fashionable shoes at prices that people can actually afford. Its balance sheet, at November 1, 2008, contained the following (listed alphabetically, amounts in thousands).

Accounts Payable	$136,405	Other Liabilities	$ 79,148
Accounts Receivable	11,888	Property, Plant, and Equipment	233,631
Cash	45,570	Retained Earnings	179,538
Contributed Capital	291,248	Total Assets	785,383
Notes Payable	99,044	Total Liabilities and Stockholders' Equity	?
Other Assets	494,294		

Required:

1. Prepare the balance sheet as of November 1, solving for the missing amount.
2. As of November 1, did most of the financing for assets come from creditors or stockholders?

E1-4 Completing a Balance Sheet and Inferring Net Income

LO2, 3

Ken Young and Kim Sherwood organized Reader Direct as a corporation; each contributed $49,000 cash to start the business and received 4,000 shares of stock. The store completed its first year of operations on December 31, 2009. On that date, the following financial items for the year were determined: December 31, 2009, cash on hand and in the bank, $47,500; December 31, 2009, amounts due from customers from sales of books, $26,900; property and equipment, $48,000; December 31, 2009, amounts owed to publishers for books purchased, $8,000; one-year note payable to a local bank for $2,850. No dividends were declared or paid to the stockholders during the year.

Required:

1. Complete the following balance sheet at December 31, 2009.

Assets		Liabilities and Stockholders' Equity	
Cash	$_____	**Liabilities**	
Accounts Receivable	_____	Accounts Payable	$_____
Property and Equipment	_____	Note Payable	_____
		Total Liabilities	_____
		Stockholders' Equity	
		Contributed Capital	_____
		Retained Earnings	13,550
		Total Stockholders' Equity	_____
Total Assets	$_____	Total Liabilities and Stockholders' Equity	$_____

2. Using the retained earnings equation and an opening balance of $0, work backwards to compute the amount of net income for the year ended December 31, 2009.
3. As of December 31, 2009, did most of the financing for assets come from creditors or stockholders?
4. Assuming that Reader Direct generates net income of $3,000 and pays dividends of $2,000 in 2010, what would be the ending Retained Earnings balance at December 31, 2010?

E1-5 Labeling and Classifying Business Transactions

LO2

The following items relate to business transactions involving K·Swiss Inc.

K·Swiss Inc.

a. Coins and currency
b. Amounts K·Swiss owes to suppliers of watches
c. Amounts K·Swiss can collect from customers
d. Amounts owed to bank for loan to buy building
e. Property on which buildings will be built

      f.   Amounts distributed from profits to stockholders
      g.   Amounts earned by K·Swiss by selling watches
      h.   Unused paper in K·Swiss head office
      i.   Cost of paper used up during month
      j.   Amounts contributed to K·Swiss by stockholders

Required:

1. Identify an appropriate label (account name) for each item as it would be reported in the company's financial statements.
2. Classify each item as an asset (A), liability (L), stockholders' equity (SE), revenue (R), or expense (E).

LO2, 3

Regal Entertainment Group

E1-6   Preparing an Income Statement and Inferring Missing Values

Regal Entertainment Group operates movie theaters and food concession counters throughout the United States. Its income statement for the quarter ended June 26, 2008, reported the following (listed alphabetically, amounts in thousands):

Admissions Revenues	$455,700	Net Income	?
Concessions Expenses	25,500	Other Expenses	$233,800
Concessions Revenues	188,900	Other Revenues	31,200
Film Rental Expenses	247,000	Rent Expense	90,000
General and Administrative Expenses	65,700	Total Expenses	?

Required:

1. Solve for the missing amounts and prepare an income statement for the quarter ended June 26, 2008.
   TIP: First put the items in the order they would appear on the income statement and then solve for the missing values.
2. What is Regal's main source of revenue and biggest expense?

LO2

E1-7   Preparing an Income Statement

Home Realty, Incorporated, has been operating for three years and is owned by three investors. J. Doe owns 60 percent of the total outstanding stock of 9,000 shares and is the managing executive in charge. On December 31, 2009, the following financial items for the entire year were determined: sales revenue, $166,000; selling expenses, $97,000; interest expense, $6,300; promotion and advertising expenses, $9,025; and income tax expense, $18,500. Also during the year, the company declared and paid the owners dividends amounting to $12,000. Prepare the company's income statement.

LO2

E1-8   Inferring Values Using the Income Statement and Balance Sheet Equations

Review the chapter explanations of the income statement and the balance sheet equations. Apply these equations in each of the following independent cases to compute the two missing amounts for each case. Assume that it is the end of the first full year of operations for the company.
    TIP: First identify the numerical relations among the columns using the balance sheet and income statement equations. Then compute the missing amounts.

Independent Cases	Total Revenues	Total Expenses	Net Income (Loss)	Total Assets	Total Liabilities	Stockholders' Equity
A	$100,000	$82,000	$	$150,000	$70,000	$
B		80,000	12,000	112,000		60,000
C	80,000	86,000		104,000	26,000	
D	50,000		13,000		22,000	77,000
E		81,000	(6,000)		73,000	28,000

E1-9 Preparing an Income Statement and Balance Sheet   LO2, 3

Five individuals organized Miami Clay Corporation on January 1, 2009. At the end of January 31, 2009, the following monthly financial data are available:

Total Revenues	$131,000
Operating Expenses	90,500
Cash	30,800
Accounts Receivable	25,300
Supplies	40,700
Accounts Payable	25,700
Contributed Capital	30,600

No dividends were declared or paid during January.

Required:

1. Complete the following income statement and balance sheet for the month of January.

MIAMI CLAY CORPORATION
Income Statement
For the Month Ended January 31, 2009

Total Revenues	$_____
Operating Expenses	_____
Net Income	$_____

MIAMI CLAY CORPORATION
Balance Sheet
At January 31, 2009

Assets
Cash	$30,800
Accounts Receivable	25,300
Supplies	40,700
Total Assets	$96,800

Liabilities
Accounts Payable	$_____
Total Liabilities	_____

Stockholders' Equity
Contributed Capital	_____
Retained Earnings	_____
Total Stockholders' Equity	_____
Total Liabilities and Stockholders' Equity	$_____

2. Discuss whether Miami Clay Corporation will be able to pay its liabilities. Consider the relationship between total assets and total liabilities.

LO2, 3   **E1-10 Analyzing and Interpreting an Income Statement**

Three individuals organized Pest Away Corporation on January 1, 2009, to provide insect exter-
mination services. The company paid dividends of $10,000 during the year. At the end of 2009,
the following income statement was prepared:

PEST AWAY CORPORATION
Income Statement
For the Year Ended December 31, 2009

Revenues		
Service Revenue	$192,000	
Sales Revenue	24,000	
Total Revenues		$216,000
Expenses		
Supplies Expense	$ 76,000	
Salaries and Wages Expense	33,000	
Advertising Expense	22,000	
Other Expenses	46,000	
Total Expenses		177,000
Net Income		$ 39,000

Required:

1. What was the amount of average monthly revenue?
2. What was the average amount of monthly salaries and wages expense?
3. Explain why advertising is reported as an expense.
4. Explain why the dividends are not reported as an expense.
5. Can you determine how much cash the company had on December 31, 2009? Answer yes or
   no, and explain your reasoning.

LO2   **E1-11 Matching Cash Flow Statement Items to Business Activity Categories**

Tech Data Corporation

Tech Data Corporation is a leading distributor of computer peripherals and network solutions and
recently was ranked by *Fortune* as the second most admired company in its industry category. The
following items were taken from its recent cash flow statement. Mark each item in the following
list with a letter to indicate whether it is a cash flow from Operating, Investing, or Financing
activities. **Put parentheses around the letter if it is a cash *outflow* and use no parentheses if it's
an *inflow*.**

_____ 1. Cash paid to suppliers and employees

_____ 2. Cash received from customers

_____ 3. Cash received from borrowing long-term debt

_____ 4. Cash received from issuing stock

_____ 5. Cash paid to purchase equipment

LO2   **E1-12 Matching Cash Flow Statement Items to Business Activity Categories**

Coca-Cola Company

The Coca-Cola Company is one of the world's leading manufacturers, marketers, and distributors
of nonalcoholic beverage concentrates and syrups, producing more than 300 beverage brands.
Mark each item in the following list with a letter to indicate whether it is a cash flow from
Operating, Investing, or Financing activities. **Put parentheses around the letter if it is a cash
outflow and use no parentheses if it's an *inflow*.**

_____ 1. Purchases of equipment

_____ 2. Cash received from customers

_____ 3. Cash received from issuing stock

_____ 4. Cash paid to suppliers and employees

_____ 5. Cash paid on notes payable

_____ 6. Cash received from selling equipment

COACHED PROBLEMS

CP1-1 Preparing an Income Statement, Statement of Retained Earnings, and Balance Sheet   LO2

Assume that you are the president of Nuclear Company. At the end of the first year of operations (December 31, 2009), the following financial data for the company are available:

Cash	$12,000
Accounts Receivable	59,500
Supplies	8,000
Equipment	36,000
Accounts Payable	30,297
Notes Payable	1,470
Sales Revenue	88,000
Operating Expenses	57,200
Other Expenses	8,850
Contributed Capital	61,983
Dividends	200

Required:

1. Prepare an income statement for the year ended December 31, 2009.
    TIP: Begin by classifying each account as asset, liability, stockholders' equity, revenue, or expense. Each account is reported on only one financial statement.
2. Prepare a statement of retained earnings for the year ended December 31, 2009.
    TIP: Because this is the first year of operations, the beginning balance in Retained Earnings will be zero.
3. Prepare a balance sheet at December 31, 2009.
    TIP: The balance sheet includes the ending balance from the statement of retained earnings.

CP1-2 Interpreting the Financial Statements   LO3

Refer to CP1-1.

Required:

1. Evaluate whether the company was profitable.
2. Evaluate whether the company could have paid a greater amount for dividends.
3. Evaluate whether the company is financed mainly by creditors or stockholders.
4. Determine the amount of cash increase or decrease that would be shown in the statement of cash flows.

CP1-3 Reporting Amounts on the Four Basic Financial Statements (Challenging Problem)   LO2

Life Time Fitness, Inc., reported the following information for the nine-month period ended September 30, 2008. Items are listed alphabetically, and are in thousands of dollars.   Life Time Fitness

Accounts Payable	$ 102,665	Other Assets	$117,108
Accounts Receivable	5,318	Other Liabilities	86,234
Cash (December 31, 2007)	5,354	Retained Earnings (January 1, 2008)	199,890
Cash (September 30, 2008)	7,119	Gym Revenues	575,667
Contributed Capital	381,728	Gym Operating Expenses	350,835
Supplies	14,739	Advertising and Marketing Expense	23,608
Notes Payable	647,120	General and Administrative Expense	83,207
Rent and Other Expenses Payable	119,482	Interest and Other Expenses	20,316
Property and Equipment	1,451,641	Income Tax Expense	38,895

Other cash flow information:	
Cash received from issuing common stock	$ 9,061
Cash paid to purchase equipment	354,255
Cash paid to suppliers and employees	472,265
Repayments of borrowings	13,043
Cash received from customers	574,824
Cash received from borrowings	95,558
Cash received from sale of long-term assets	161,885
Dividends paid to stockholders	0

Required:

Prepare the four basic financial statements for the nine months ended September 30, 2008.

TIP: Prepare the four statements in the following order:

a. Income statement
b. Statement of retained earnings
c. Balance sheet
d. Statement of cash flows

GROUP A PROBLEMS

L02

PA1-1 Preparing an Income Statement, Statement of Retained Earnings, and Balance Sheet

eXcel

www.mhhe.com/phillips3e

Assume that you are the president of High Power Corporation. At the end of the first year of operations (December 31, 2010), the following financial data for the company are available:

Cash	$13,300
Accounts Receivable	9,550
Supplies	5,000
Equipment	86,000
Accounts Payable	32,087
Notes Payable	1,160
Sales Revenue	91,000
Operating Expenses	58,700
Other Expenses	8,850
Contributed Capital	59,103
Dividends	1,950

Required:

1. Prepare an income statement for the year ended December 31, 2010.
2. Prepare a statement of retained earnings for the year ended December 31, 2010.
3. Prepare a balance sheet at December 31, 2010.

L03   PA1-2 Interpreting the Financial Statements

Refer to PA1-1.

Required:

1. Evaluate whether the company was profitable.
2. Evaluate whether the company could have paid a greater amount for dividends.
3. Evaluate whether the company is financed mainly by creditors or stockholders.
4. Determine the amount of cash increase or decrease that would be shown in the statement of cash flows.

PA1-3 Reporting Amounts on the Four Basic Financial Statements

LO2

The following information for the year ended December 31, 2006, was reported by OSI Restaurant Partners, Inc., the company that owns and operates Outback Steakhouse and Carrabba's Italian Grill restaurants. Amounts are in millions of dollars.

OSI Restaurant Partners, Inc.

Accounts Payable	$ 166	Dividends	$ 39
Wages and Taxes Payable	120	Other Liabilities	517
Cash (balance on January 1, 2006)	84	Other Revenues	21
Cash (balance on December 31, 2006)	94	Property, Fixtures and Equipment	1,549
Food and Supplies Expense	1,415	Restaurant Sales Revenue	3,920
General and Administrative Expenses	235	Utilities and Other Expenses	1,104
Food and Supply Inventories	87	Wages Expense	1,087
Notes Payable	235	Retained Earnings, January 1, 2006	1,074
Other Assets	529	Contributed Capital	86

Other cash flow information:	
Cash paid to purchase equipment	$ 384
Cash paid to suppliers and employees	2,578
Cash received from customers	2,946
Cash received from bank borrowings	375
Repayments of bank borrowings	294
Cash received from sale of fixtures and equipment	32
Other cash outflows used for financing activities	62
Other cash outflows used for investing activities	2
Common stock issued to owners	16
Dividends paid in cash	39

Required:

Prepare the four basic financial statements for 2006.

GROUP B PROBLEMS

PB1-1 Preparing an Income Statement and Balance Sheet

LO2

Assume that you are the president of APEC Aerospace Corporation. At the end of the first year of operations (December 31, 2009), the following financial data for the company are available:

Cash	$13,900
Accounts Receivable	9,500
Supplies	9,000
Equipment	86,000
Accounts Payable	30,277
Notes Payable	1,220
Sales Revenue	94,000
Operating Expenses	60,000
Other Expenses	8,850
Contributed Capital	62,853
Dividends	1,100

Required:

1. Prepare an income statement for the year ended December 31, 2009.
2. Prepare a statement of retained earnings for the year ended December 31, 2009.
3. Prepare a balance sheet at December 31, 2009.

LO3 ~~PB1-2~~ **Interpreting the Financial Statements**

Refer to PB1-1.

Required:

1. Evaluate whether the company was profitable.
2. Evaluate whether the company could have paid a greater amount for dividends.
3. Evaluate whether the company is financed mainly by creditors or stockholders.
4. Determine the amount of cash increase or decrease that would be shown in the statement of cash flows.

LO2 **PB1-3 Reporting Amounts on the Four Basic Financial Statements**

The Cheesecake Factory Incorporated reported the following information for the fiscal year ended January 2, 2007. Amounts are in thousands of dollars.

Accounts Payable	$ 45,570	Other Assets	$ 186,453
Accounts Receivable	11,639	Other Liabilities	126,012
Wages and Other Expenses Payable	117,226	Other Revenues	8,171
Cash (balance on January 3, 2006)	31,052	Retained Earnings (beginning)	440,510
Cash (balance on January 2, 2007)	44,790	Prepaid Rent	43,870
Food and Supplies Expense	333,528	Property and Equipment	732,204
General and Administrative Expenses	72,751	Restaurant Sales Revenue	1,315,325
Food and Supply Inventories	20,775	Utilities and Other Expenses	414,978
Notes Payable	39,381	Wages Expense	420,957
Contributed Capital	239,744	Dividends	49,994

Other cash flow information:	
Additional investments by stockholders	$ 33,555
Cash paid to purchase equipment	243,211
Cash paid to suppliers and employees	1,123,353
Repayments of borrowings	170,242
Cash received from customers	1,276,008
Cash received from borrowings	175,000
Cash received from sale of long-term assets	115,975
Dividends paid in cash	49,994

Required:

Prepare the four basic financial statements for the fiscal year ended January 2, 2007.

SKILLS DEVELOPMENT CASES

LO1, 2, 3 **S1-1 Finding Financial Information**

Refer to the financial statements of The Home Depot in Appendix A at the end of this book, or download the annual report from the *Cases* section of the text's Web site at www.mhhe.com/phillips3e.

Required:

1. What is the amount of net income for the year ended February 1, 2009?
2. What amount of sales revenue was earned for the year ended February 1, 2009?
3. How much inventory does the company have on February 1, 2009?
4. How much does The Home Depot have in cash on February 1, 2009?
5. The Home Depot's stock is traded on the New York Stock Exchange under the symbol HD. What kind of company does this make The Home Depot?

S1-2 Comparing Financial Information

LO1, 2, 3

Lowe's

Refer to the financial statements of The Home Depot in Appendix A and Lowe's in Appendix B at the end of this book, or download the annual reports from the *Cases* section of the text's Web site at www.mhhe.com/phillips3e.

Required:

1. Was Lowe's net income for the year ended January 30, 2009, greater (or less) than The Home Depot's?
2. Was Lowe's sales revenue for the year ended January 30, 2009, greater (or less) than The Home Depot's?
3. Did Lowe's have more (or less) inventories than The Home Depot at the end of January 2009?
4. Did Lowe's have more (or less) cash than The Home Depot at the end of January 2009?
5. Is Lowe's the same type of business organization as The Home Depot?
6. On an overall basis, was Lowe's or The Home Depot more successful in the 2008 fiscal year?

S1-3 Internet-Based Team Research: Examining an Annual Report

LO1, 2, 3

Reuters

As a team, select an industry to analyze. Reuters provides lists of industries and their makeup at www.reuters.com/finance/industries. Each group member should access the annual report (or Form 10-K filed with the SEC) for one publicly traded company in the industry, with each member selecting a different company. (In addition to the company's own Web site, a great source is the SEC's Electronic Data Gathering, Analysis, and Retrieval (EDGAR) service. This free source is available by going to the "Filings & Forms" section of www.sec.gov and clicking on "Search for Company Filings" and then "Company or fund name." Another resource being developed at the time of writing this book is the IDEA system (idea.sec.gov), which will provide greater access to companies' financial data.

Required:

1. On an individual basis, each team member should write a short report that lists the following information:
   a. What type of business organization is it?
   b. What types of products or services does it sell?
   c. On what day of the year does its fiscal year end?
   d. For how many years does it present complete balance sheets? Income statements? Cash flow statements?
   e. Are its financial statements audited by independent CPAs? If so, by whom?
   f. Did its total assets increase or decrease over the last year?
   g. Did its net income increase or decrease over the last year?

2. Then, as a team, write a short report comparing and contrasting your companies using these attributes. Discuss any patterns across the companies that you as a team observe. Provide potential explanations for any differences discovered.

S1-4 Ethical Decision Making: A Real-Life Example

LO2, 3, 4

Adelphia Communications

In June 2005, John Rigas, the 80-year-old founder and former chief executive officer (CEO) of Adelphia Communications was sentenced to 15 years in jail for defrauding investors and lenders of over a billion dollars. His son, the former chief financial officer (CFO), was sentenced to

20 years in jail. To understand the charges, you need to first understand a bit about Adelphia's history. Adelphia started as a one-town cable company in 1952 and, at the time the fraud accusations were made public, had grown into the sixth-largest cable television provider in the country. With the company starting as a family-owned business, Adelphia's operations were always a central part of the personal lives of the Rigas family members. However, the extent to which their personal lives were mixed in with the business activities was never clear to stockholders—at least, not nearly as clear as when they were reported in an article in the August 12, 2002, issue of *Fortune*. Below the following questions we present a table from that article, which summarizes how the Rigas family allegedly used over $1.2 billion of Adelphia's money—money that ultimately belonged to Adelphia's stockholders.

1. What is the accounting concept that the Rigas family is accused of violating?
2. Based on the information provided in the following table, can you determine which of the family's dealings are clearly inappropriate and which are clearly appropriate?
3. As a stockholder, how might you attempt to ensure that this kind of behavior does not occur or, at least, does not occur without you knowing about it?
4. Aside from Adelphia's stockholders, who else might be harmed by these actions committed by the Rigas family?

Family Assets, Sort Of		
Some of the notable ways the Rigas family used Adelphia shareholder dollars.		
On the Receiving End	Who's behind the Entity	How Much?
Dobaire Designs	Adelphia paid this company, owned by Doris Rigas (John's wife), for design services.	$371,000
Wending Creek Farms	Adelphia paid John Rigas's farm for lawn care and snowplowing.	$2 million
SongCatcher Films	Adelphia financed the production of a movie by Ellen Rigas (John's daughter).	$3 million
Eleni Interiors	The company made payments to a furniture store run by Doris Rigas and owned by John.	$12 million
The Golf Club at Wending Creek Farms	Adelphia began developing a ritzy golf club.	$13 million
Wending Creek 3656	The company bought timber rights that would eventually revert to a Rigas family partnership.	$26 million
Praxis Capital Ventures	Adelphia funded a venture capital firm run by Ellen Rigas's husband.	$65 million
Niagara Frontier Hockey LP	Adelphia underwrote the Rigas's purchase of the Buffalo Sabres hockey team.	$150 million
Highland 2000	Adelphia guaranteed loans to a Rigas family partnership, which used the funds to buy stock.	$1 billion
Total		$1,271,371,000

LO4 **S1-5 Ethical Decision Making: A Mini-Case**

You are one of three partners who own and operate Mary's Maid Service. The company has been operating for seven years. One of the other partners has always prepared the company's annual financial statements. Recently, you proposed that the statements be audited each year because it would benefit the partners and prevent possible disagreements about the division of profits. The partner who prepares the statements proposed that his uncle, who has a lot of financial experience, can do the job at little cost. Your other partner remained silent.

Required:

1. What position would you take on the proposal? Justify your response in writing.
2. What would you strongly recommend? Give the basis for your recommendation.

LO2, 3, 4 **S1-6 Critical Thinking: Developing a Balance Sheet and Income Statement**

On September 30, Ashley and Jason started arguing about who is better off. Jason said he was better off because he owned a PlayStation console that he bought last year for $350. He figures that, if needed, he could sell it to a friend for $280. Ashley argued that she was better off because she had $1,000 cash in her bank account and a vintage car that she bought two years ago for $800 but could now sell for $1,400. Jason countered that Ashley still owed $250 on her car loan and that Jason's dad promised to buy him a Porsche if he does really well in his accounting class. Jason said he had $6,000 cash in his bank account right now because he just received a $4,800 student loan. Ashley knows that Jason also owes a tuition installment of $800 for this term.

Ashley and Jason met again in early November. They asked how each other was doing. Ashley claimed that she'd become much more successful than Jason. She had a part-time job, where she earned $1,500 per month. Jason laughed at Ashley because he had won $1,950 on a lottery ticket he bought in October, and that was merely for the "work" of standing in line for a minute. It was just what he needed because his apartment costs $800 each month. Ashley, on the other hand, pays $470 for her share of the rent. Both Ashley and Jason have other normal living costs that total $950 each month.

1. Prepare a financial report that compares what Ashley and Jason each own and owe on September 30. Make a list of any decisions you had to make when preparing your report.
2. In a written report, identify and justify which of the two characters is better off. If you were a creditor, to whom would you rather lend money?
3. Prepare a report that compares what Ashley and Jason each earned during October. Make a list of any decisions you had to make when preparing your report.
4. In a written report, identify and justify which of the two characters is more successful. If you were a creditor considering a three-year loan to one of these characters, to whom would you rather lend money?

S1-7 Preparing an Income Statement and Balance Sheet

LO2

Electronic Arts is the world's leading developer and publisher of interactive entertainment software for personal computers and advanced entertainment systems made by Sony, Nintendo, and Microsoft. Assume that the company is revising its methods for displaying its financial statements, and the controller in the accounting department has asked you to create electronic worksheets that they can use as their standard format for financial statement reporting. The controller has provided you with an alphabetical list of statement categories and account names (below), with corresponding balances (in millions) as of September 30. She has asked you to use a spreadsheet program to create two worksheets that organize the accounts into a properly formatted balance sheet and income statement, and that use formulas to compute amounts marked by a ? below.

Electronic Arts Inc.

www.mhhe.com/phillips3e

Accounts Payable	$ 171	Liabilities		Revenue		
Accounts Receivable	328	Net Income	?	Sales Revenue	$675	
Assets		Notes Payable	$ 12	Selling Expense	223	
Cash	2,412	Other Assets	283	Stockholders' Equity		
Contributed Capital	986	Other Expenses	1	Total Assets	?	
Cost of Goods Sold Expense	284	Other Liabilities	587	Total Expenses	?	
Expenses		Promotion Expense	107	Total Liabilities	?	
Income Tax Expense	9	Property and Equipment	364	Total Liabilities and		
Inventories	367	Retained Earnings	1,998	Stockholders' Equity	?	
				Total Stockholders' Equity	?	

Not knowing where to start, you e-mailed your friend Owen for advice on using a spreadsheet. Owen's detailed reply follows.

Required:

Follow Owen's advice to create a balance sheet and income statement, with each statement saved on a separate worksheet in a file called *me*EA.xls where the *me* part of the filename uniquely identifies you.

From:	Owentheaccountant@yahoo.com
To:	Helpme@hotmail.com
Cc:	
Subject:	Excel Help

Hey pal. Long time, no chat. Here's the scoop on creating those worksheets, with a screenshot too. If you need more help, let me know and I'll submit an application for your position there. ☺

1. Start-up Excel to open a new spreadsheet file. You'll need only two worksheets for this assignment, so delete the third worksheet by right-clicking on the *Sheet3* tab at the bottom of the worksheet and selecting Delete. While you're at it, rename *Sheet1* and *Sheet2* to *Balance Sheet* and *Income Statement* by double-clicking on the worksheet tabs and typing in the new names.

2. Plan the layout for your reports. Use the first column as a blank margin, the second column for account names and their headings, and the third column for the numbers corresponding to each account name or total. If you want to apply the same format to all worksheets, begin by right-clicking on the tab at the bottom of a worksheet and choosing Select All Sheets. Next, resize the first column by clicking on the A at the top of that column, then from the Home tab, in the Cells group, click on Format then Column Width . . . , and enter a width of 2. Using this same procedure, resize columns B and C to 50 and 15, respectively.

3. Starting with cell B1, enter the company's name. Enter the report name and date in cells B2 and B3. To merge cells so these headings span more than one column, select the cells to be merged and then click on Format in the Cells group, select Format Cells . . . and click the Merge Cells box in the Text Control section of the Alignment tab. Continue with the body of the report in cell B5, entering any necessary amounts in column C.

4. To use formulas to compute subtotals and totals, the equals sign = is entered first into the cell and is followed immediately by the formula. So, to add a series of amounts, say C7 through C11, use a formula like =SUM(C7:C11), as shown in the screenshot below.

5. After you enter all the data and calculate totals, be sure to save the file. To do this, just click on the Office button in the top left and choose Save As. . . .

6. If you need to print the worksheets, it might be best to highlight what you want printed, then click on the Office button, choose Print. . . , and choose Selection in the Print What box.

7. Go to it, you accounting guru!

S1-7.xlsx - Microsoft Excel

C12 fx =SUM(C7:C11)

	A	B	C	D
1		Electronic Arts		
2		Balance Sheet		
3		As of September 30		
4		(in millions)		
5				
6		ASSETS		
7		Cash	$ 2,412	
8		Accounts Receivable	328	
9		Inventories	367	
10		Property and Equipment	364	
11		Other Assets	283	
12		Total Assets	$ 3,754	
13				
14		LIABILITIES		
15		Accounts Payable	$ 171	
16		Notes Payable	12	
17		Other Liabilities	587	
18		Total Liabilities	770	
19		STOCKHOLDERS' EQUITY		
20		Contributed Capital	986	
21		Retained Earnings	1,998	
22		Total Stockholders' Equity	2,984	
23		Total Liabilities and Stockholders' Equity	$ 3,754	
24				

Balance Sheet / Income Statement

Ready   100%

CONTINUING CASE

CC1 Financial Statements for a Business Plan   LO2, 3

Nicole Mackisey is thinking of forming her own spa business, Nicole's Getaway Spa (NGS). Nicole expects that she and two family members will each contribute $10,000 to the business and receive 1,000 shares each. Nicole forecasts the following amounts for the first year of operations, ending December 31, 2010: Cash on hand and in the bank, $2,150; amounts due from customers from spa treatments, $1,780; building and equipment, $70,000; amounts owed to beauty supply outlets for spa equipment, $4,660; notes payable to a local bank for $38,870. Cash dividends of $2,000 will be paid to the stockholders during the year. Nicole also forecasts that first year sales revenues will be $40,000; wages will be $24,000; the cost of supplies used up will be $7,000; selling and administrative expenses will be $5,000; and income taxes will be $1,600.

Required:

1. Based on Nicole's estimates, prepare a (forecasted) income statement for Nicole's Getaway Spa for the year ended December 31, 2010.
2. Prepare a (forecasted) statement of retained earnings for Nicole's Getaway Spa for the year ended December 31, 2010.
3. Prepare a (forecasted) balance sheet for Nicole's Getaway Spa at December 31, 2010.
4. As of December 31, 2010, would most of the financing for assets come from creditors or stockholders?

CHAPTER 2

Reporting Investing and Financing Results on the Balance Sheet

YOUR LEARNING OBJECTIVES

Understand the business

- LO1   Identify financial effects of common financing and investing activities.

Study the accounting methods

- LO2   Apply transaction analysis to financing and investing transactions.
- LO3   Use journal entries and T-accounts to show how transactions affect the balance sheet.
- LO4   Prepare a classified balance sheet.

Evaluate the results

- LO5   Interpret the balance sheet using the current ratio and an understanding of related concepts.

Review the chapter

THAT WAS
THEN

In the previous chapter, you were introduced to the four main financial statements: the balance sheet, income statement, statement of retained earnings, and statement of cash flows.

Lecture Presentation-LP2
www.mhhe.com/phillips3e

FOCUS COMPANY: Pizza Aroma, Ithaca, NY

PIZZA AROMA

I n Chapter 1 you heard about Mauricio Rosa's plans for starting a pizza company in New York. Mauricio's local CPA, Laurie, advised him that all businesses, big and small, need systems for gathering and organizing financial information. Just as FedEx must have a way to monitor and evaluate its use of $12.6 billion in delivery equipment,[1] smaller companies like Pizza Aroma, Inc., must track the financial results of their activities. With Laurie's help, Mauricio will implement an accounting system to do this for Pizza Aroma. This system will provide the financial information that he needs to manage the company and to report its results to others interested in his business.

The focus in this chapter is on the financing and investing activities that occurred during August when Mauricio was establishing Pizza Aroma, long before it could open its doors to customers. You will learn how these activities are captured in an accounting system, leading to the assets, liabilities, and stockholders' equity that are reported in a balance sheet. Later, in Chapter 3, you will learn about the operating activities that occur after a business opens its doors to customers and begins generating the revenues and expenses that are reported in an income statement. Your introduction to the accounting system will conclude in Chapter 4, where you will learn about the steps needed to adjust the accounting records before finalizing and evaluating a company's financial results.

THIS IS NOW

This chapter focuses on just the balance sheet and the accounting system used to produce it.

[1]http://www.fedex.com/us/investorrelations/financialinfo/2007annualreport/.

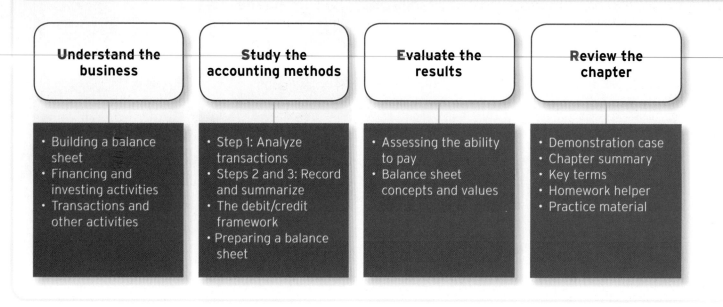

Understand the business	Study the accounting methods	Evaluate the results	Review the chapter
• Building a balance sheet • Financing and investing activities • Transactions and other activities	• Step 1: Analyze transactions • Steps 2 and 3: Record and summarize • The debit/credit framework • Preparing a balance sheet	• Assessing the ability to pay • Balance sheet concepts and values	• Demonstration case • Chapter summary • Key terms • Homework helper • Practice material

Understand the Business

BUILDING A BALANCE SHEET

Learning Objective 1
Identify financial effects of common financing and investing activities.

YOU SHOULD KNOW

Assets: Resources presently owned by a business that generate future economic benefits. **Liabilities:** Amounts presently owed by a business. **Stockholders' equity:** The amount invested and reinvested in a company by its stockholders.

After meeting with Laurie, Mauricio understood that before he could open his restaurant, he would first have to establish the business. This would involve acquiring **assets** that Pizza Aroma would use for many months or years to come. The assets would be owned by Pizza Aroma, but creditors would have a claim to those assets equal to the amount of **liabilities** that the company owes. As owners of Pizza Aroma, Mauricio and his wife also would have a claim on the company's assets (**stockholders' equity**), but their claim would be secondary to creditors' claims. Mauricio remembered that the balance sheet was structured like the basic accounting equation (A = L + SE), but it was only by accounting for Pizza Aroma's actual activities that he truly learned how a balance sheet was built.

FINANCING AND INVESTING ACTIVITIES

A key activity for any start-up company, such as Pizza Aroma, is to obtain financing. Two sources of financing are available to businesses: equity and debt. Equity refers to financing a business obtains through owners' contributions and reinvestments of profit. Debt refers to financing the business obtains through loans. A business is obligated to repay debt financing, but it is not obligated to repay its equity financing.

Like most small business owners, Mauricio and his wife used their personal savings to make an initial cash contribution to the company. They decided to contribute $50,000, which is more than they had originally planned, but by relying more on equity financing, the company wouldn't require quite as much debt financing. When a business receives cash contributions from its owners like this, it gives documents called stock certificates to the owners as evidence of their ownership.

Mauricio had determined that Pizza Aroma would need additional money to become established so, on behalf of the company, he applied for a loan from a bank. Soon after the loan was approved, Pizza Aroma received $20,000 cash in exchange for its promise to repay the loan in two years. The terms for repaying the loan were described in detail on a legal document called a promissory note. Pizza Aroma's initial financing activities are pictured in Exhibit 2.1.

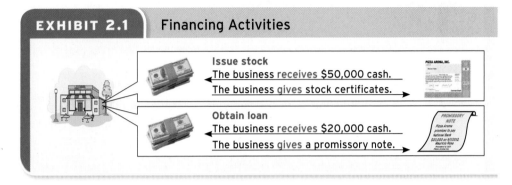

EXHIBIT 2.1 | **Financing Activities**

Issue stock
The business receives $50,000 cash.
The business gives stock certificates.

Obtain loan
The business receives $20,000 cash.
The business gives a promissory note.

After obtaining initial financing, a company will start **investing** in assets that will be used later when the business opens. In the case of Pizza Aroma, Mauricio first spent $42,000 cash by writing company checks to buy and install restaurant booths, cash registers, and other equipment. The company also needed to buy cookware and related items like pizza pans, pizza cutters, serving plates, cutlery, drink glasses, napkin holders, and cheese and spice shakers. These items could be purchased with cash, but that would be inconvenient and inefficient. Instead, businesses typically buy goods or services from others on credit, by promising to pay within 30 days of the purchase. Pizza Aroma bought $630 of these items on credit, as indicated by the supplier's bill (or "invoice"). These examples, pictured in Exhibit 2.2, are just a few of Pizza Aroma's investing activities.

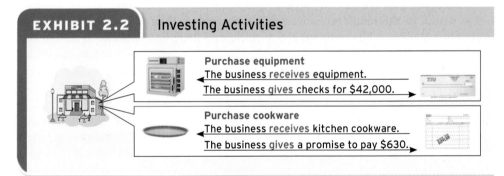

EXHIBIT 2.2 | **Investing Activities**

Purchase equipment
The business receives equipment.
The business gives checks for $42,000.

Purchase cookware
The business receives kitchen cookware.
The business gives a promise to pay $630.

By carefully reading Exhibits 2.1 and 2.2, you will see three features that will be important for understanding how accounting works.

1. The company always **documents** its activities. Stock certificates, promissory notes, checks, and invoices indicate the nature of the underlying business activity.

2. The company always **receives** something and **gives** something. This is a basic feature of all business activities. A business enters into an exchange either to earn a profit immediately or to obtain resources that will allow it to earn a profit later. This is the fundamental idea of business: to create value through exchange. Any exchange that affects the company's assets, liabilities, or stockholders' equity must be captured in and reported by the accounting system. Because the accounting system captures both what is received and what is given, it is often referred to as a "double-entry" system.

3. Each exchange is analyzed to determine a dollar amount that represents the value of items given and received. This value is called the **cost** and is used to measure the financial effects of the exchange, as required by the **cost principle**.

> **YOU SHOULD KNOW**
>
> **Cost principle:** Assets and liabilities should be initially recorded at their original cost to the company.

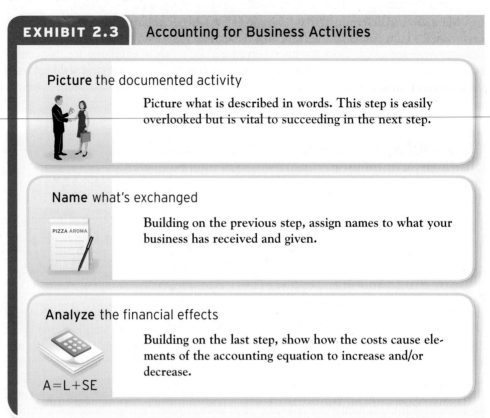

EXHIBIT 2.3   Accounting for Business Activities

Picture the documented activity

Picture what is described in words. This step is easily overlooked but is vital to succeeding in the next step.

Name what's exchanged

PIZZA AROMA

Building on the previous step, assign names to what your business has received and given.

Analyze the financial effects

A = L + SE

Building on the last step, show how the costs cause elements of the accounting equation to increase and/or decrease.

As illustrated in Exhibit 2.3, these three features are key inputs into the process used when accounting for business activities. After each activity is documented, accountants assign names to the items exchanged and then analyze their financial effects on the accounting equation. The ultimate goal is to capture these financial effects so that they can be reported in the financial statements for use by decision makers inside and outside the company. Take a moment right now to read Exhibit 2.3.

TRANSACTIONS AND OTHER ACTIVITIES

Business activities that affect the basic accounting equation ($A = L + SE$) are called **transactions.** Transactions are of special importance because they are the only activities that enter the financial accounting system. Transactions include two types of events:

YOU SHOULD KNOW

Transaction: An event or activity that has a direct and measurable financial effect on the assets, liabilities, or stockholders' equity of a business.

1. **External exchanges:** These are exchanges involving assets, liabilities, and/or stockholders' equity that you can see between the company and someone else. When Starbucks sells you a Frappucino®, it is exchanging an icy taste of heaven for your cash, so Starbucks would record this in its accounting system.

2. **Internal events:** These events do not involve exchanges with others outside the business, but rather occur within the company itself. For example, when the company Red Bull combines sugar, water, taurine, and caffeine, something magical happens: these ingredients turn into Red Bull Energy Drink. This internal event is a transaction because it has a direct financial effect whereby some assets (supplies of sugar, etc.) are used up to create a different asset (an inventory of Red Bull drinks).

During the first month of business, some important activities that occur will not be captured by the accounting system because they are not transactions. For example, Mauricio signed a contract on behalf of Pizza Aroma to rent restaurant space in a building. This activity was not a transaction because no assets or services were exchanged at that time. The landlord exchanged a promise to rent the building for Pizza Aroma's promise to pay rent, but an exchange of only promises is not an accounting transaction.

For this same reason, Pizza Aroma's accounting system did not capture other activities such as placing orders with suppliers or promising to hire employees. Documents were created to indicate that these activities occurred, but they were appropriately excluded from the accounting records because these were not transactions. Later, when these promises result in actually receiving or giving an asset or service, they will become transactions to be captured by the accounting system.

Study the Accounting Methods

A systematic accounting process is used to capture and report the financial effects of a company's activities. This process includes three basic steps:

① Analyze ⟶ ② Record ⟶ ③ Summarize

> **Learning Objective 2**
> Apply transaction analysis to financing and investing transactions.

STEP 1: ANALYZE TRANSACTIONS

The process in Exhibit 2.3 is commonly referred to as transaction analysis, which involves determining whether a transaction exists and, if it does, analyzing its impact on the accounting equation. Two simple ideas are used when analyzing transactions:

Video 2.1
www.mhhe.com/phillips3e

1. **Duality of effects.** It's a fancy name, but the idea is simple. Every transaction has at least two effects on the basic accounting equation. To remember this, just think of expressions like "give and receive" or "push and pull" or, if you're a closet scientist, Newton's Third Law of Motion.

2. **A = L + SE.** You know this already, right? Well, just remember that the dollar amount for assets must always equal the total of liabilities plus stockholders' equity for every accounting transaction. If it doesn't, then you are missing something and you should go back to the first (duality of effects) idea.

As part of transaction analysis, a name is given to each item exchanged. Accountants refer to these names as account titles. To ensure account titles are used consistently, every company establishes a **chart of accounts**—a list that designates a name and reference number that the company will use when accounting for each item it exchanges. A partial chart of accounts for Pizza Aroma is shown in Exhibit 2.4. (The chart of accounts shown in Chapter 2 includes only balance sheet accounts. Chapter 3 will expand this to include additional assets and liabilities as well as revenue and expense accounts.) A more comprehensive chart of accounts to use when completing homework assignments is presented in the Homework Helper on page 71.

> **YOU SHOULD KNOW**
> **Chart of accounts:** A summary of all account names (and corresponding account numbers) used to record financial results in the accounting system.

EXHIBIT 2.4	Pizza Aroma's (Partial) Chart of Accounts

Account Number	Account Name	Description
101	Cash	— Dollar amount of coins, paper money, funds in bank
113	Cookware	— Cost of cutlery, pizza pans, dishes, etc.
135	Equipment	— Cost of pizza ovens, restaurant booths, dishwashers, etc.
201	Accounts Payable	— Owed to suppliers for goods or services bought on credit
222	Note Payable	— Owed to lenders, as per terms of promissory note
301	Contributed Capital	— Stock issued for contributions made to the company
310	Retained Earnings	— Accumulated earnings (not yet distributed as dividends)

The chart of accounts is tailored to each company's business, so although some account titles are common across all companies (Cash, Accounts Payable), others may be used only by that particular company (Cookware). Depending on the company, you may see a liability for a bank loan called a Note Payable or a Loan Payable.[2]

The best way to learn how to account for business activities is to work through examples. So skim the names and descriptions in Exhibit 2.4 one more time and then let's look more closely at Pizza Aroma's financing and investing activities.

(a) Issue Stock to Owners   Mauricio Rosa incorporates Pizza Aroma, Inc., on August 1. The company issues stock to Mauricio and his wife as evidence of their contribution of $50,000 cash, which is deposited in the company's bank account.

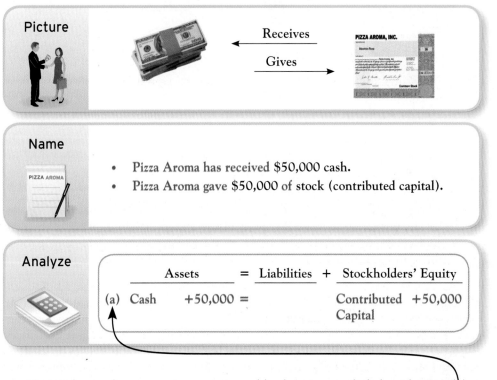

Analyze transactions from the standpoint of the business, not its owners.

Notice that in the accounting equation table above, we included a reference (a) so that we can refer back to the original transaction description if needed. You too should use transaction letters (or numbers or dates) as references in your homework problems. The goal of transaction analysis is to identify the specific accounts affected, the dollar amount of the change in the accounts, and the direction of this change (+ or −) on the accounting equation category. In example (a), an asset (Cash) increases by $50,000, which equals the increase in the stockholders' equity account (Contributed Capital).

(b) Invest in Equipment   Pizza Aroma pays $42,000 cash to buy restaurant booths and other equipment.

---

[2]The account names you see in the financial statements of most large businesses are actually aggregations (or combinations) of several specific accounts. For example, Papa John's International—a competitor of Pizza Aroma—keeps separate accounts for land, buildings, and equipment but combines them into one title on its balance sheet called Property and Equipment.

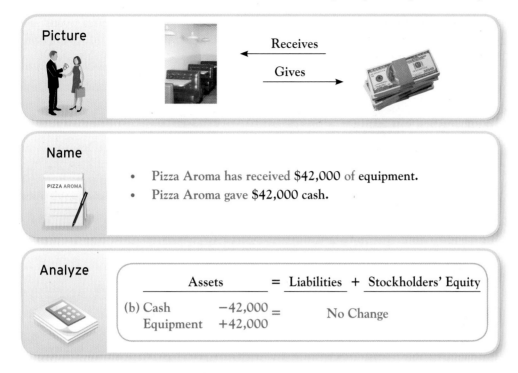

Picture

Receives ←

Gives →

Name

PIZZA AROMA

- Pizza Aroma has received $42,000 of equipment.
- Pizza Aroma gave $42,000 cash.

Analyze

	Assets	= Liabilities	+ Stockholders' Equity
(b) Cash	−42,000	=	No Change
Equipment	+42,000		

Notice that even though transaction (b) did not affect liabilities or stockholders' equity, the accounting equation remained in balance because the decrease in one asset (Cash) was offset by the increase in another asset (Equipment). **The accounting equation must always "balance" (be equal) for each transaction.**

(c) Obtain Loan from Bank Pizza Aroma **borrows $20,000 from a bank, depositing those funds in its bank account and signing a formal agreement to repay the loan in two years.**

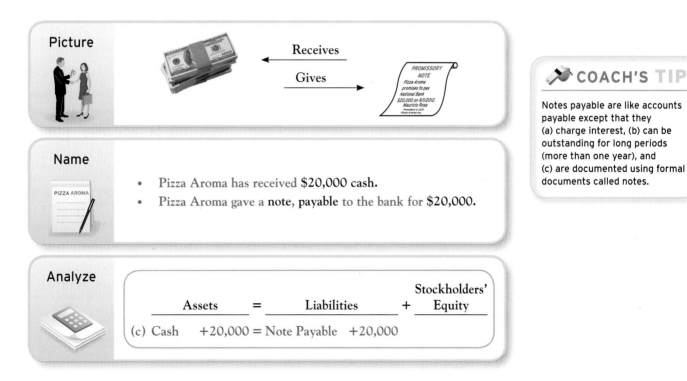

Picture

Receives ←

Gives →

PROMISSORY NOTE
Pizza Aroma promises to pay National Bank $20,000 on 9/1/2012.
Mauricio Rosa
President & CEO
Pizza Aroma Inc.

Name

PIZZA AROMA

- Pizza Aroma has received $20,000 cash.
- Pizza Aroma gave a **note, payable** to the bank for **$20,000.**

Analyze

	Assets	=	Liabilities	+	Stockholders' Equity
(c) Cash	+20,000	=	Note Payable	+20,000	

COACH'S TIP

Notes payable are like accounts payable except that they (a) charge interest, (b) can be outstanding for long periods (more than one year), and (c) are documented using formal documents called notes.

(d) Invest in Equipment   Pizza Aroma purchases $18,000 in pizza ovens and other restaurant equipment, paying $16,000 in cash and giving an informal promise to pay $2,000 at the end of the month.

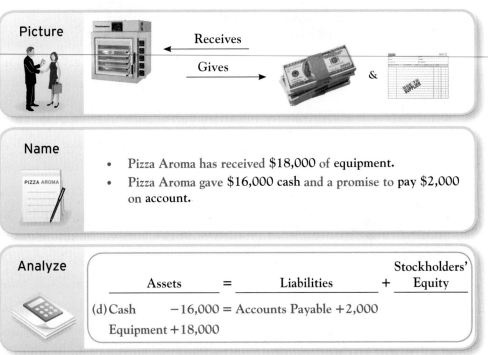

🐾 **COACH'S TIP**

Although we use the same format for all of our examples, the content in each differs. Don't skip this section with the plan of coming back to it later, because the next part of this chapter builds on this part. Most students say that, of all the topics in this course, transaction analysis is the one they wished they had spent more time on when first learning it.

Picture

Receives

Gives

Name

PIZZA AROMA

- Pizza Aroma has received $18,000 of equipment.
- Pizza Aroma gave $16,000 cash and a promise to pay $2,000 on account.

Analyze

	Assets	=	Liabilities	+	Stockholders' Equity
(d) Cash	−16,000	=	Accounts Payable +2,000		
Equipment	+18,000				

If you ever run into a transaction that you have no idea how to analyze, try to break it down. Rather than trying to solve it all at once, begin by looking just for what is received. Another strategy is to look for any cash exchanged because by getting a handle on that part of the transaction, the other parts often become easier to see. Always be sure to summarize the effects in terms of the accounting equation, because it must balance if you've detected all the accounts affected by the transaction.

(e) Order Cookware   Pizza Aroma orders $630 of pans, dishes, and other cookware. None have been received yet.

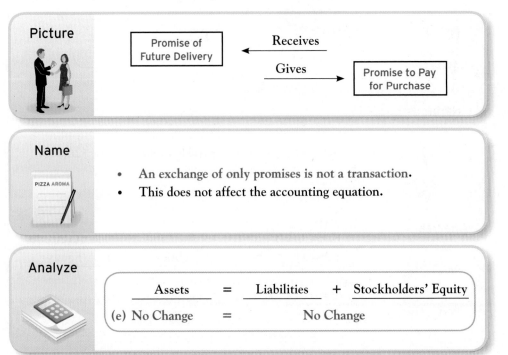

🐾 **COACH'S TIP**

Not all business activities are considered accounting transactions.

Picture

Promise of Future Delivery

Receives

Gives

Promise to Pay for Purchase

Name

PIZZA AROMA

- An exchange of only promises is not a transaction.
- This does not affect the accounting equation.

Analyze

	Assets	=	Liabilities	+	Stockholders' Equity
(e)	No Change	=	No Change		

Not all documented business activities are considered accounting transactions. As shown in (e), Pizza Aroma and the supplier have documented the order, but it involves an exchange of only promises, so it is not an accounting transaction.

(f) Pay Supplier   Pizza Aroma pays $2,000 to the equipment supplier in (d).

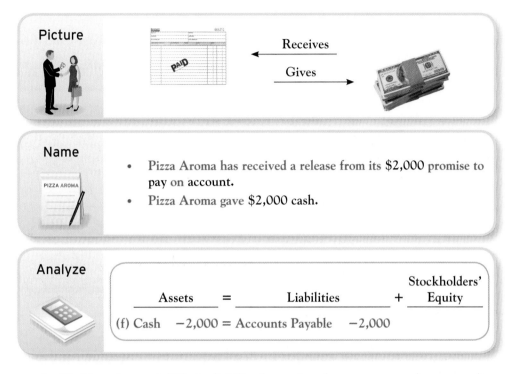

	Assets	**=**	**Liabilities**	**+**	**Stockholders' Equity**
(f) Cash	−2,000	=	Accounts Payable	−2,000	

In (f), Pizza Aroma fulfills its liability by paying the amount owed to a supplier. Thus, the Accounts Payable is decreased because, in exchange for its payment to the supplier, Pizza Aroma receives a release from its original promise to pay the supplier.

(g) Receive Cookware   Pizza Aroma receives $630 of the cookware ordered in (e) and promises to pay for it next month.

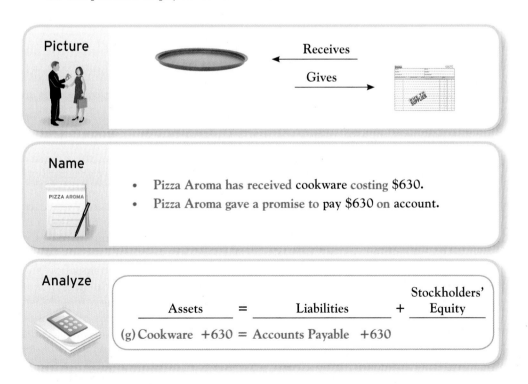

	Assets	**=**	**Liabilities**	**+**	**Stockholders' Equity**
(g) Cookware	+630	=	Accounts Payable	+630	

As we said, the best way to learn accounting is to do examples, so try the following practice question. (Cover the answers in the margin with your thumb until you're done.)

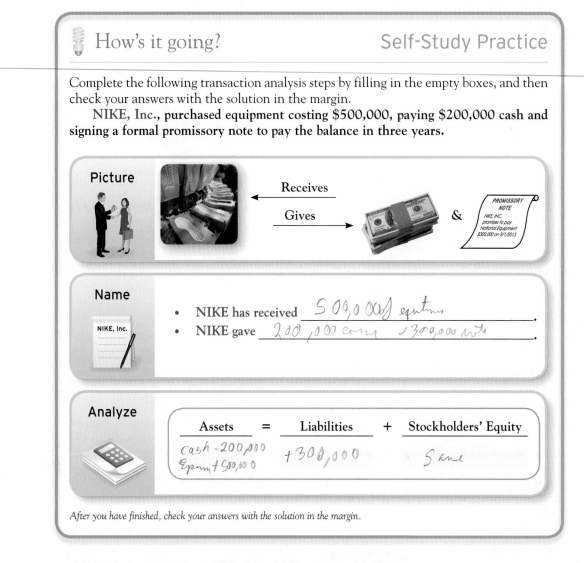

How's it going?   Self-Study Practice

Complete the following transaction analysis steps by filling in the empty boxes, and then check your answers with the solution in the margin.

NIKE, Inc., purchased equipment costing $500,000, paying $200,000 cash and signing a formal promissory note to pay the balance in three years.

Picture

Receives

Gives

PROMISSORY NOTE
NIKE, INC. promises to pay National Equipment $300,000 on 9/1/2013.

Name

NIKE, Inc.

- NIKE has received ___500,000 equipment___
- NIKE gave ___200,000 cash & 300,000 note___

Analyze

Assets	=	Liabilities	+	Stockholders' Equity
Cash -200,000		+300,000		Same
Equip +500,000				

After you have finished, check your answers with the solution in the margin.

Solution to Self-Study Practice

NIKE has received equipment costing $500,000.
NIKE gave $200,000 cash and a $300,000 note.

Assets	=	Liabilities	+	Stockholders' Equity
Cash	−200,000	= Note		
Equipment	+500,000	Payable +300,000		

STEPS 2 AND 3: RECORD AND SUMMARIZE

In the previous section, you learned how to analyze transactions, which ended with an understanding of the financial effects of each transaction on a company's asset, liability, and stockholders' equity accounts. In an academic setting, we have encouraged you to write down these accounting equation effects. In the workplace, an accountant would not actually capture the effects in this way. Instead, after determining the financial effects of a transaction, an accountant would capture the effects through two additional steps: recording and summarizing.

One way to record and summarize the financial effects of transactions would be to enter your understanding of their effects into a spreadsheet like the one shown in Exhibit 2.5. By summing each spreadsheet column, you could compute new balances at the end of each month and report them on a balance sheet.

A spreadsheet makes it easy to see the individual impact of each transaction and how transactions combine with beginning balances to yield ending balances, but it is impractical for most large organizations to use. Just imagine how big a spreadsheet would have to be to handle millions of transactions affecting hundreds of accounts. Rather than create a spreadsheet the size of three football fields, a more manageable system is used.

EXHIBIT 2.5	Using a Spreadsheet to Record and Summarize Transactions

Exhibit 2.5.xlsx - Microsoft Excel

Home   Insert   Page Layout   Formulas   Data   Review   View

		Assets			=	Liabilities		+	Stockholders' Equity
		Cash	Cookware	Equipment		Accounts Payable	Notes Payable		Contributed Capital
Beginning		0	0	0	=	0	0		0
(a)		+50,000			=				+50,000
(b)		-42,000		+42,000	=				
(c)		+20,000			=		+20,000		
(d)		-16,000		+18,000	=	+2,000			
(e)		no change			=	no change			
(f)		-2,000			=	-2,000			
(g)			+630		=	+630			
Ending		10,000	630	60,000	=	630	20,000	+	50,000

Exhibit 2.5

Ready   100%

Most companies record and summarize the financial effects of transactions with computerized accounting systems, which can handle a large number of transactions. These systems follow a cycle, called **the accounting cycle,** which **is repeated day-after-day, month-after-month, and year-after-year.** As shown in Exhibit 2.6, a three-step analyze-record-summarize process is applied to **daily transactions** and is then followed by **adjustments and closing processes at the end of the accounting period.** Our focus in Chapter 2 is on applying the three-step process during the period to activities that affect only balance sheet accounts. After you've become comfortable with this process, you will learn (in Chapter 3) to apply this process to operating activities that affect both balance sheet and income statement accounts. In Chapter 4, you will learn how the process is applied at the end of the accounting period, when the accounting records are adjusted and closed.

The three-step process of analyzing, recording, and summarizing is a lot like what you do as a student when attending class, taking notes, and preparing for exams. Day

EXHIBIT 2.6	Elements of the Accounting Process

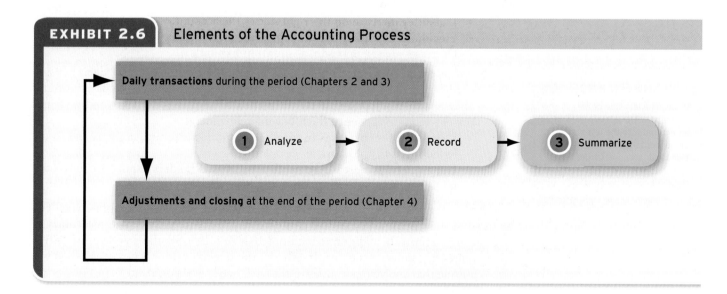

Daily transactions during the period (Chapters 2 and 3)

1 Analyze → 2 Record → 3 Summarize

Adjustments and closing at the end of the period (Chapter 4)

YOU SHOULD KNOW

Journals: Used to record the effects of each day's transactions; organized by date. **Ledger:** Used to summarize the effects of journal entries on each account; organized by account.

after day, you analyze what is said in class and you record important points in a notebook, which is kind of like an academic diary or journal. Later, when preparing for exams, you copy your notes to summary sheets to study from. The same ideas are used in the accounting cycle. Transactions are analyzed, and their financial effects are entered into **journals** each day they occur. Later, these journal entries are summarized in **ledger** accounts that keep track of the financial effects on each account. To make this process as efficient as possible, journals and ledger accounts share the same underlying framework discussed in the following section.

THE DEBIT/CREDIT FRAMEWORK

Learning Objective 3
Use journal entries and T-accounts to show how transactions affect the balance sheet.

The framework used for journals and ledger accounts was created more than 500 years ago, yet it continues to exist in accounting systems today. Although computers now perform many routine accounting tasks involving journals and ledger accounts, most computerized systems still require you to know how these accounting records work. To understand this framework, think of the accounting equation ($A = L + SE$) as an old-fashioned weight scale that tips at the equals sign. Assets—like Cash and Equipment—are put on the left side of the scale and liabilities and stockholders' equity accounts are put on the right. Likewise, each individual account has two sides, with one side used for increases and the other for decreases, similar to what is shown in Exhibit 2.7.

EXHIBIT 2.7 The Debit/Credit Framework

Take special note of two important rules illustrated in Exhibit 2.7:

1. **Accounts increase on the same side as they appear in $A = L + SE$.** Accounts on the left side of the accounting equation increase on the left side of the account and accounts on the right side of the equation increase on the right. So
   - Assets increase on the **left** side of the account.
   - Liabilities increase on the **right** side of the account.
   - Stockholders' equity accounts increase on the **right** side of the account.
   - Decreases are the opposite, as shown in Exhibit 2.7.

YOU SHOULD KNOW

Debit: The left side of an account, or the act of entering an amount into the left side of an account. **Credit:** The right side of an account, or the act of entering an amount into the right side of an account.

2. **Left is debit (*dr*), right is credit (*cr*).** The terms (and abbreviations) **debit** (*dr*) and **credit** (*cr*) come from Latin words that had meaning back in the day, but today they just mean *left* and *right*. When combined with how increases and decreases are entered into accounts, the following rules emerge:
   - Use debits for increases in assets (and for decreases in liabilities and stockholders' equity accounts).
   - Use credits for increases in liabilities and stockholders' equity accounts (and for decreases in assets).

Accountants didn't dream up this debit/credit framework just to confuse you. The purpose of this double-entry system is to introduce another check on the accuracy of accounting numbers. In addition to requiring that $A = L + SE$, the double-entry system also requires that **debits = credits**. If either of these relationships is not equal, then you know for sure that you've made an error that will need to be corrected.

Step 1: Analyzing Transactions

The debit/credit framework does not change this first step of the accounting process. Continue to use the approach shown in Exhibit 2.3 to determine the financial effects of transactions, which you will learn to enter into the accounting system in step 2.

Step 2: Recording Journal Entries

The financial effects of transactions are entered into a journal using a debits-equal-credits format, as shown in Exhibit 2.8. When looking at these **journal entries,** as they are called, notice the following:

- A date is included for each transaction.
- Debits appear first (on top). Credits are written below the debits and are indented to the right (both the words and the amounts). The order of the debited accounts or credited accounts doesn't matter, as long as for each journal entry debits are on top and credits are on the bottom and indented.
- Total debits equal total credits for each transaction (for example, see the entry on August 5 where $18,000 = $16,000 + $2,000).
- Dollar signs are not used because the journal is understood to be a record of financial effects.
- The reference column (Ref.) will be used later (in step 3) to indicate when the journal entry has been summarized in the ledger accounts.
- A brief explanation of the transaction is written below the debits and credits.
- The line after the explanation is left blank before writing the next journal entry.

> **YOU SHOULD KNOW**
>
> **Journal entries:** Indicate the effects of each day's transactions in a debits-equal-credits format.

Video 2.2
www.mhhe.com/phillips3e

EXHIBIT 2.8 Formal Journal Page

Date	Account Titles and Explanation	Ref.	Debit	Credit
General Journal				Page G1
2010				
Aug. 1	Cash		50,000	
	Contributed Capital			50,000
	(Financing from stockholders.)			
Aug. 2	Equipment		42,000	
	Cash			42,000
	(Bought equipment using cash.)			
Aug. 5	Equipment		18,000	
	Cash			16,000
	Accounts Payable			2,000
	(Bought equipment using cash and			
	credit.)			

When writing journal entries in this course, we'll make a few minor changes to the formal entries, which should make it easier for you to learn the most important aspects of recording journal entries. The way we would show the journal entry for August 5 is:

(d)   *dr* Equipment (+A).. 18,000
        cr Cash (−A) 16,000
        cr Accounts Payable (+L) 2,000

The main differences between our simplified format and a formal journal entry are:

- When a date is not given, use some form of reference for each transaction, such as (d), to identify the event.
- Omit the reference column and transaction explanation to simplify the entry.
- Indicate whether you are debiting (dr) or crediting (cr) each account. This will help to reinforce the debit/credit framework from Exhibit 2.7. Plus, it will make it easier to interpret journal entries when indents aren't clear (sometimes an issue in handwritten homework).
- Include the appropriate account type (A, L, or SE) along with the direction of the effect (+ or −) next to each account title to clarify the effects of the transaction on each account. Again, this will reinforce the debit/credit framework and help you to determine whether the accounting equation has remained in balance.

Step 3: Summarizing in Ledger Accounts

By themselves, journal entries show the effects of transactions, but they do not provide account balances. That's why ledger accounts are needed. After journal entries have been recorded (in step 2), their dollar amounts are copied ("posted") to each ledger account affected by the transaction so that account balances can be computed. In most computerized accounting systems, this happens automatically. In homework assignments, you'll have to do it yourself, so Exhibit 2.9 shows you how this is done using the journal entry for August 5. If account numbers are provided, keep track of the posting of journal entries to general ledger accounts by writing the account number in the Ref. column of the journal and the journal page number in the Ref. column of the ledger.

As we did earlier for journal entries, we will use a simplified format for ledger accounts to make it easier to focus on their main features. The simplified version of a ledger account is called a **T-account.** Each T-account represents the debit and credit

YOU SHOULD KNOW

T-account: A simplified version of a ledger account used for summarizing the effects of journal entries.

EXHIBIT 2.9   Posting from the Journal to the Ledger

columns of a ledger account. Exhibit 2.10 shows the T-accounts for Pizza Aroma's Equipment, Cash, and Accounts Payable based on transactions (a) through (d) on pages 50–52. It also shows how an individual journal entry's effects would be summarized in these T-accounts. The debit to Equipment in the journal entry is copied into the debit (left) side of its T-account. The credits to Cash and Accounts Payable are copied into the credit (right) side of those T-accounts. (If you've forgotten why the transaction is recorded this way, take a quick look back at Exhibit 2.7 on page 56 or the graphic to the right.)

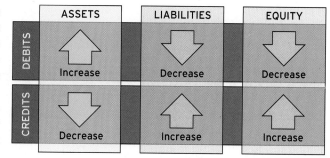

	ASSETS	LIABILITIES	EQUITY
DEBITS	Increase ⬆	Decrease ⬇	Decrease ⬇
CREDITS	Decrease ⬇	Increase ⬆	Increase ⬆

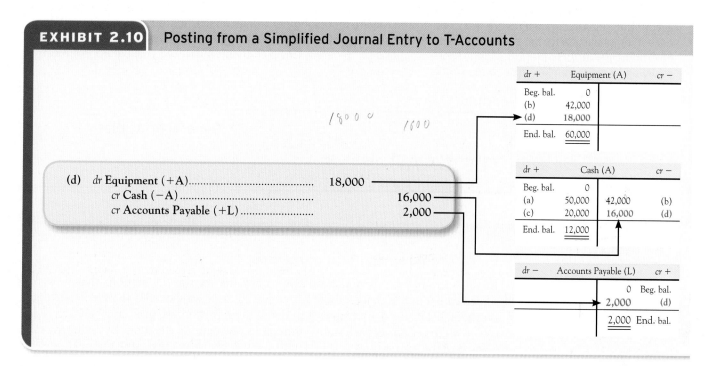

EXHIBIT 2.10   Posting from a Simplified Journal Entry to T-Accounts

dr +	Equipment (A)		cr −
Beg. bal.	0		
(b)	42,000		
(d)	18,000		
End. bal.	60,000		

dr +	Cash (A)		cr −
Beg. bal.	0		
(a)	50,000	42,000	(b)
(c)	20,000	16,000	(d)
End. bal.	12,000		

dr −	Accounts Payable (L)		cr +
		0	Beg. bal.
		2,000	(d)
		2,000	End. bal.

(d) dr Equipment (+A) 18,000
      cr Cash (−A) 16,000
      cr Accounts Payable (+L) 2,000

In Exhibit 2.10, notice the following:

• Every account starts with a beginning balance, usually on the side where increases are summarized. For balance sheet accounts, the ending balance from the prior period is the beginning balance for the current period. Because Pizza Aroma is in its first month of business, the beginning balance in each account is zero in this example.

• Dollar signs are not needed.

• Each amount is accompanied by a reference to the related journal entry, which makes it easy to trace back to the original transaction should errors occur.

• To find ending account balances, express the T-accounts as equations:

	Equipment	Cash	Accounts Payable
Beginning balance	0	0	0
Add: "+" side	42,000	+50,000	+2,000
	18,000	+20,000	
Subtract: "−" side		−42,000	
		−16,000	
Ending balance	60,000	12,000	2,000

COACH'S TIP

Assets normally end with a debit balance (because debits to assets normally exceed credits) and liabilities and stockholders' equity accounts normally end with credit balances (credits exceed debits).

Knowing how to use T-accounts in this way will help you answer homework questions that involve solving for missing values in accounts.

- The ending balance is double underlined to distinguish it from transactions and symbolize the final result of a computation. The ending balance is shown on the side that has the greater total dollar amount.

Spotlight On THE WORLD

Transaction Analysis Skills in Great Demand

The 3-step transaction analysis process in this chapter may become even more important in the future, as International Financial Reporting Standards (IFRS) are adopted around the world. In contrast to GAAP, which explain accounting rules in detail, IFRS are less detailed and require more judgment when analyzing transactions. This difference in emphasis exists because IFRS are used across many different countries, where business practices and legal environments vary. By placing slightly more emphasis on general principles than on detailed rules, IFRS are more easily and broadly applied around the world.

Detailed rules   **GAAP**   **IFRS**   General principles

Pizza Aroma's Accounting Records

In this section, we will work with you to account for the transactions that were presented earlier in this chapter for Pizza Aroma. Because we show the analyze step in detail on pages 49–54, we do not show it in detail here. Instead, we pick up where step 1 left off—with the effects of each transaction on the accounting equation. By reviewing steps 2 and 3 of the accounting cycle in detail, you will get to practice using the new concepts of debits, credits, journal entries, and T-accounts. **Study the following examples carefully.** The biggest mistake people make when first learning accounting is they think they understand how it all works without actually going through enough examples. To understand accounting, you have to practice, practice, practice, as if you're learning to play a new sport or a musical instrument.

(a) Issue Stock to Owners   Mauricio Rosa incorporates Pizza Aroma, Inc., on August 1. The company issues stock to Mauricio and his wife as evidence of their contribution of $50,000 cash, which is deposited in the company's bank account.

1 Analyze

	Assets		=	Liabilities	+	Stockholders' Equity	
(a) Cash	+50,000		=			Contributed Capital	+50,000

2 Record

(a)	*dr* **Cash** (+A)..	50,000	
	cr **Contributed Capital** (+SE)		50,000

3 Summarize

dr +	Cash (A)	*cr* −		*dr* −	Contributed Capital (SE)	*cr* +
Beg. bal.	0				0	Beg. bal.
(a)	50,000				50,000	(a)

(b) Invest in Equipment   Pizza Aroma pays $42,000 cash to buy restaurant booths and other equipment.

1 Analyze

	Assets	=	Liabilities	+	Stockholders' Equity
(b) Cash	−42,000				
Equipment	+42,000				

2 Record

(b)   *dr* **Equipment** (+A)... 42,000
         cr **Cash** (−A)... 42,000

3 Summarize

dr +	Cash (A)	*cr* −		*dr* +	Equipment (A)	*cr* −
Beg. bal.	0			Beg. bal.	0	
(a)	50,000 | 42,000	(b)		(b)	42,000	

(c) Obtain Loan from Bank   Pizza Aroma borrows $20,000 from a bank, depositing those funds in its bank account and signing a formal agreement to repay the loan in two years.

1 Analyze

	Assets	=	Liabilities		+	Stockholders' Equity
(c) Cash	+20,000	=	Note Payable	+20,000		

2 Record

(c)   *dr* **Cash** (+A)... 20,000
         cr **Note Payable** (+L)... 20,000

3 Summarize

dr +	Cash (A)	*cr* −		*dr* −	Note Payable (L)	*cr* +
Beg. bal.	0				0	Beg. bal.
(a)	50,000 | 42,000	(b)			20,000	(c)
(c)	20,000					

(d) Invest in Equipment   Pizza Aroma purchases $18,000 in pizza ovens and other restaurant equipment, paying $16,000 in cash and giving an informal promise to pay $2,000 at the end of the month.

1 Analyze

	Assets	=	Liabilities		+	Stockholders' Equity
(d) Cash	−16,000	=	Accounts Payable	+2,000		
Equipment	+18,000					

2 Record

(d)   *dr* **Equipment** (+A)... 18,000
         cr **Cash** (−A)... 16,000
         cr **Accounts Payable** (+L)... 2,000

3 Summarize

dr +	Cash (A)		cr −	dr +	Equipment (A)	cr −	dr −	Accounts Payable (L)	cr +
Beg. bal.	0			Beg. bal.	0			0	Beg. bal.
(a)	50,000	42,000	(b)	(b)	42,000			2,000	(d)
(c)	20,000	16,000	(d)	(d)	18,000				

(e) Order Cookware Pizza Aroma orders $630 of pans, dishes and other cookware. None have been received yet. Because this event involves the exchange of only promises, it is not considered a transaction. No journal entry is needed.

(f) Pay Supplier Pizza Aroma pays $2,000 to the equipment supplier in (d).

1 Analyze

Assets	=	Liabilities	+	Stockholders' Equity
(f) Cash −2,000	=	Accounts Payable −2,000		

2 Record

(f)	dr Accounts Payable (−L)	2,000	
	cr Cash (−A)...		2,000

3 Summarize

dr +	Cash (A)		cr −	dr −	Accounts Payable (L)		cr +
Beg. bal.	0					0	Beg. bal.
(a)	50,000	42,000	(b)	(f)	2,000	2,000	(d)
(c)	20,000	16,000	(d)				
		2,000	(f)				

(g) Receive Cookware Pizza Aroma receives $630 of the cookware ordered in (e) and promises to pay for it next month.

1 Analyze

Assets	=	Liabilities	+	Stockholders' Equity
(g) Cookware +630	=	Accounts Payable +630		

2 Record

(g)	dr Cookware (+A)...	630	
	cr Accounts Payable (+L)		630

3 Summarize

dr +	Cookware (A)	cr −	dr −	Accounts Payable (L)		cr +
Beg. bal.	0				0	Beg. bal.
(g)	630		(f)	2,000	2,000	(d)
					630	(g)

Exhibit 2.11 summarizes the journal entries and T-accounts affected by events (a) through (g) for Pizza Aroma. It also reports the ending balances for each account.

EXHIBIT 2.11	Journal Entries and T-Accounts for Pizza Aroma

Assets	=	Liabilities	+	Stockholders' Equity

Journal Entries

(a) *dr* Cash (+A)...................................... 50,000
        cr Contributed Capital (+SE).... 50,000

(b) *dr* Equipment (+A).......................... 42,000
        cr Cash (−A)............................... 42,000

(c) *dr* Cash (+A)..................................... 20,000
        cr Note Payable (+L) 20,000

(d) *dr* Equipment (+A).......................... 18,000
        cr Cash (−A)............................... 16,000
        cr Accounts Payable (+L).......... 2,000

(e) Not a transaction.

(f) *dr* Accounts Payable (−L)................ 2,000
        cr Cash (−A)............................... 2,000

(g) *dr* Cookware (+A)............................ 630
        cr Accounts Payable (+L).......... 630

Cash (A)

Beg. bal.	0		
(a)	50,000	42,000	(b)
(c)	20,000	16,000	(d)
		2,000	(f)
End. bal.	10,000		

Cookware (A)

Beg. bal.	0		
(g)	630		
End. bal.	630		

Equipment (A)

Beg. bal.	0		
(b)	42,000		
(d)	18,000		
End. bal.	60,000		

Accounts Payable (L)

		0	Beg. bal.
(f)	2,000	2,000	(d)
		630	(g)
		630	End. bal.

Note Payable (L)

	0	Beg. bal.
	20,000	(c)
	20,000	End. bal.

Contributed Capital (SE)

	0	Beg. bal.
	50,000	(a)
	50,000	End. bal.

PREPARING A BALANCE SHEET

Using the ending amount from each T-account, you could now prepare a balance sheet. Before you do this, however, it's a good idea to check that the accounting records are in balance by determining whether debits = credits. If total debits don't equal total credits, the balance sheet will not balance. The equality of debits and credits can be checked by preparing an internal accounting report called the trial balance, shown in Exhibit 2.12. Fortunately the column totals are equal, so the Pizza Aroma balance sheet can be prepared and shown to Mauricio.

> **Learning Objective 4**
> Prepare a classified balance sheet.

EXHIBIT 2.12	Trial Balance for Pizza Aroma

PIZZA AROMA, INC.
Trial Balance
At August 31, 2010

	Debit	Credit
Cash	10,000	
Cookware	630	
Equipment	60,000	
Accounts Payable		630
Note Payable		20,000
Contributed Capital		50,000
Totals	70,630	70,630

Trial balance provides a check on debits = credits equality

Ending balances in T-accounts in Exhibit 2.11

Exhibit 2.13 shows Pizza Aroma's balance sheet based on the transactions in this chapter. The balance sheet is prepared by taking the ending balances for each account and grouping them as assets, liabilities, and stockholders' equity in balance sheet format. We've used a balance sheet format in Exhibit 2.13 called the **classified balance sheet.**

> **YOU SHOULD KNOW**
>
> **Classified balance sheet:**
> A balance sheet that shows a subtotal for current assets and current liabilities.

EXHIBIT 2.13   Classified Balance Sheet

PIZZA AROMA

PIZZA AROMA, INC. Balance Sheet At August 31, 2010		Explanation of Classification
Assets		
Current Assets		Current assets will be used up or turned into cash within 12 months.
Cash	$10,000	Cash in the company's bank account will be used up before August 31, 2011.
Cookware	630	Pizza pans and dishes will likely be used up or replaced before August 31, 2011.
Total Current Assets	10,630	
Equipment	60,000	Ovens and restaurant booths will be used for many years.
Total Assets	$70,630	
Liabilities and Stockholders' Equity		
Current Liabilities		Current liabilities will be paid or fulfilled within 12 months.
Accounts Payable	$ 630	Amounts owed to suppliers are usually paid within one or two months.
Total Current Liabilities	630	
Note Payable	20,000	The promissory note is not required to be repaid until September 1, 2012.
Total Liabilities	20,630	
Stockholders' Equity		
Contributed Capital	50,000	
Retained Earnings	0	Stockholders' equity accounts are not classified as current or noncurrent.
Total Stockholders' Equity	50,000	
Total Liabilities and Stockholders' Equity	$70,630	

YOU SHOULD KNOW

Current assets: To be used up or converted into cash within 12 months of the balance sheet date. **Current liabilities:** Debts and obligations that will be paid, settled, or fulfilled within 12 months of the balance sheet date. **Noncurrent** (or long-term): Assets and liabilities that do not meet the definition of current.

A classified balance sheet contains subcategories for assets and liabilities labeled *current.* **Current assets** are assets the business will use up or turn into cash within 12 months of the balance sheet date. **Current liabilities** are debts and other obligations that will be paid or fulfilled within 12 months of the balance sheet date. In our example, Accounts Payable is the only current liability. The other liability—Note Payable—is expected to be paid in two years, so it is considered **noncurrent.** Most companies list assets in order of liquidity (how soon they will be used up or turned into cash) and liabilities in order of maturity (how soon they will be paid in cash or fulfilled by providing a service).

Like Pizza Aroma's Equipment and Note Payable accounts, its stockholders' equity accounts are understood to be long-term in nature, although they are not labeled as such. Exhibit 2.13 includes the Retained Earnings account in stockholders' equity despite its zero balance because we don't want you to forget about this account. It will become a key link to the income statement, when introduced in Chapter 3.

Evaluate the Results

Learning Objective 5
Interpret the balance sheet using the current ratio and an understanding of related concepts.

ASSESSING THE ABILITY TO PAY

The classified balance sheet format makes it easy to see whether current assets are sufficient to pay current liabilities. In Pizza Aroma's case, $10,630 of current assets is greater than the $630 of current liabilities, making it obvious that the company's current assets are sufficient to cover its current liabilities.

The only problem with looking at total dollar amounts is the difficulty in comparing across companies. It's far easier to express the relationship as a ratio, by dividing current assets by current liabilities. This calculation is known as the current ratio. It is used to evaluate liquidity, which is the ability to pay liabilities as they come due in the short run. Generally speaking, a high current ratio suggests good liquidity. Pizza Aroma's current ratio ($10,630 ÷ $630 = 16.9) is unusually high. Current ratios typically vary from 1.0 to 2.0. Recently, Papa John's current ratio was 0.87, as shown below.

Accounting Decision Tools		
Name of Measure	**Formula**	**What It Tells You**
Current ratio	$\dfrac{\text{Current Assets}}{\text{Current Liabilities}}$	• Whether current assets are sufficient to pay current liabilities • A higher ratio means better ability to pay

Spotlight On FINANCIAL REPORTING

Papa John's is significantly larger than Pizza Aroma, but the structure of the balance sheet and its account titles are quite similar. Its current ratio is typical of many large companies.

PAPA JOHN'S INTERNATIONAL, INC.
Balance Sheet
At September 28, 2008
(In thousands)

This implies nearly $13 million of cash.

Assets	
Current Assets	
Cash	$ 12,678
Accounts Receivable	22,808
Inventories	16,910
Other Current Assets	33,604
Total Current Assets	**86,000**
Property and Equipment	190,666
Other Assets	121,099
Total Assets	**$397,765**
Liabilities and Stockholders' Equity	
Current Liabilities	
Accounts Payable	$ 29,414
Income and Other Taxes Payable	7,509
Other Current Liabilities	61,905
Total Current Liabilities	**98,828**
Long-term Debt	145,085
Other Long-term Liabilities	32,600
Total Liabilities	**276,513**
Stockholders' Equity	
Contributed Capital	509
Retained Earnings	120,743
Total Stockholders' Equity	**121,252**
Total Liabilities and Stockholders' Equity	**$397,765**

Current assets

Noncurrent assets

Current liabilities

Noncurrent liabilities

Current ratio = $\dfrac{\$86,000}{\$98,828} = 0.87$

Spotlight On FINANCIAL REPORTING

What Is a Strong Balance Sheet?

During the fall of 2008, companies experienced a crisis unlike anything since the Great Depression of the 1930s. Financial institutions, such as Lehman Brothers, had collapsed or were on the verge of collapse. Consequently, banks became ultra-conservative and stopped lending to one another, which severely limited the amount of cash available to lend to businesses. The best way for a company to survive this credit crisis was to have a strong balance sheet, which meant having lots of cash and other current assets relative to the amount of liabilities owed.

BALANCE SHEET CONCEPTS AND VALUES

The purpose of a balance sheet is to report what a company owns and owes, but not necessarily what the company is worth. Some people mistakenly believe that the balance sheet reports a company's current value. To them, this isn't a crazy idea because the balance sheet lists a company's assets and liabilities, so the net difference between the two must be the company's worth. In fact, *net worth* is a term that many accountants and analysts use when referring to stockholders' equity. So why is it wrong to think that the balance sheet reports a company's current value?

The answer comes from knowing that accounting is based on recording and reporting transactions, as you have seen over and over in this chapter. This focus on transactions does two things to the balance sheet: (1) it affects what is (and is not) recorded, and (2) it affects the amounts assigned to recorded items.

1. **What is (and is not) recorded?**
   - Measurable exchanges, such as a purchase of ovens, are recorded. Pizza Aroma's gourmet pizza recipes, on the other hand, were not acquired in an exchange, so they are not listed on the balance sheet.

2. **What amounts are assigned to recorded items?**
   - Following the cost principle, assets and liabilities are first recorded at the amounts that were measurable at the time transactions occurred. Later, if an asset's value increases, the increase is generally not recorded under GAAP. However, if an asset's value falls, it is generally reported at that lower value. This **conservatism** is followed when doubt exists about the amount at which to report assets and liabilities (and revenues and expenses).

YOU SHOULD KNOW

Conservatism: Using the least optimistic measures when uncertainty exists about the value of an asset or liability.

Spotlight On FINANCIAL REPORTING

The Motivation to Be Conservative

Why are accountants conservative? It's primarily because they know that the financial statements are going to be used by outsiders such as bankers and investors to make decisions, and accountants don't want to mislead them. This is a very important issue for accountants. If they paint too rosy a picture and lead someone to buy stock in a questionable company, investors may lose their money when things go wrong. So, when faced with uncertainty about the numbers, accountants tend to take a conservative approach. Those who do not are said to be aggressive.

Summary of the Accounting Cycle

To show that the accounting process explained in this chapter can apply to any business, Exhibit 2.14 illustrates it for a fictitious construction company.

EXHIBIT 2.14	Summary of the Accounting Cycle

During the Accounting Period:

Transaction takes place	(e) Doe Construction purchases a loader, writing a check for $50,000.
Picture the documented activity.	Receives ← / Gives →
Name what's exchanged.	• Received a $50,000 loader. • Gave $50,000 cash.
Analyze the financial effects.	**Assets** = **Liabilities + Stockholders' Equity** (e) Cash −50,000 Equipment +50,000
Record a journal entry.	(e) *dr* Equipment (+A) .... 50,000 *cr* Cash (−A) 50,000
Summarize in T-accounts.	*dr+* **Equipment (A)** *cr−* *dr+* **Cash (A)** *cr−* Beg. bal. 160,000 Beg. bal. 62,000 (e) 50,000 ← 50,000 (e) End. bal. 210,000 End. bal. 12,000

At the End of the Accounting Period:

Prepare a trial balance.		Debit	Credit
	Cash	12,000	
	Supplies	2,000	
	Equipment	210,000	
	Accounts Payable		10,000
	Contributed Capital		214,000
	Retained Earnings		0
	Totals	224,000	224,000

Adjust the accounts.	Covered in Chapter 4

Prepare financial statements from the trial balance and distribute to users.
 	
(Because the company does not report any operations here, it prepares only the balance sheet.)
	DOE CONSTRUCTION
	Balance Sheet
	At December 31, 2010
	
	Assets
	Current Assets:
	 Cash $ 12,000
	 Supplies 2,000
	  Total Current Assets 14,000
	Equipment 210,000
	
	Total Assets $224,000
	
	Liabilities and Stockholders' Equity
	Current Liabilities:
	 Accounts Payable $ 10,000
	  Total Current Liabilities 10,000
	
	Stockholders' Equity:
	 Contributed Capital 214,000
	 Retained Earnings 0
	  Total Stockholders' Equity 214,000
	Total Liabilities and Stockholders' Equity $224,000

Close the books.	Covered in Chapter 4

REVIEW THE CHAPTER

This section provides a chance to solidify your understanding of key points. It's worth your time to work through the following demonstration case, scan the chapter summary, test your understand-ing of key terms, and then practice, practice, practice.

DEMONSTRATION CASE

COACH'S TIP

For possible account names, see the Homework Helper on page 71.

www.mhhe.com/phillips3e

On April 1, 2010, three college students started Goodbye Grass Corporation (GGC). A summary of GGC's transactions completed through April 30, 2010, follows:

a. Issued shares of stock to the three investors in exchange for cash contributions totaling $9,000.
b. Acquired rakes and other hand tools (equipment) for $600, paying the hardware store $200 cash and agreeing informally to pay the balance in three months.
c. Ordered lawn mowers and edgers costing $4,000 from XYZ Lawn Supply, Inc.
d. Purchased four acres of land for the future site of a storage garage. Paid cash, $5,000.
e. Received the mowers and edgers that had been ordered and signed a promissory note to pay XYZ Lawn Supply in full in 60 days.
f. Sold for $1,250 one acre of land to the city for a park and accepted a note from the city indi-cating payment will be received by GGC in six months.
g. One of the owners borrowed $3,000 from a local bank for personal use.

Required:

1. Analyze each event to determine its effects on the accounting equation.
2. Prepare journal entries to record transactions listed above (omit explanations).
3. Set up T-accounts for Cash, Note Receivable (from the city), Equipment (hand tools and mowing equipment), Land, Accounts Payable (to hardware store), Note Payable (to equip-ment supply company), and Contributed Capital. Indicate the beginning balances of $0 in each T-account, and then summarize the effects of each journal entry in the appropriate T-accounts. Determine the ending balance in each account.
4. Use the amounts in the T-accounts, developed in requirement 3, to prepare a classified bal-ance sheet for Goodbye Grass Corporation at April 30, 2010. Show the balances for all assets, liabilities, and stockholders' equity accounts.
5. As of April 30, 2010, has financing for GGC's assets come primarily from liabilities or stock-holders' equity?

Suggested Solution

1. Analyze transactions:

	Assets				=	Liabilities		+	Stockholders' Equity
	Cash	Note Receivable	Equipment	Land	=	Accounts Payable	Note Payable		Contributed Capital
(a)	+9,000				=				+9,000
(b)	−200		+600		=	+400			
(c)		No change*			=				No change
(d)	−5,000			+5,000	=				No change
(e)			+4,000		=		+4,000		
(f)		+1,250		−1,250	=				No change
(g)		No change*			=				No change

*Event (c) is not considered a transaction because it involves only the exchange of promises. Event (g) is not considered a transaction of the company because the separate entity assumption (from Chapter 1) states that transactions of the owners are separate from transactions of the business.

2. Record journal entries:
   a. *dr* Cash (+A) 9,000
         cr Contributed Capital (+SE) 9,000

   b. *dr* Equipment (+A) 600
         cr Cash (−A) 200
         cr Accounts Payable (+L) 400

   c. This is not an accounting transaction, so a journal entry is not needed.

   d. *dr* Land (+A) 5,000
         cr Cash (−A) 5,000

   e. *dr* Equipment (+A) 4,000
         cr Note Payable (+L) 4,000

   f. *dr* Note Receivable (+A) 1,250
         cr Land (−A) 1,250

   g. This is not a transaction of the business, so a journal entry is not needed.

3. Summarize journal entries in T-accounts:

Assets		=	Liabilities	+	Stockholders' Equity

Cash (A)

Beg. bal.	0	200	(b)
(a)	9,000	5,000	(d)
End. bal.	3,800		

Equipment (A)

Beg. bal.	0		
(b)	600		
(e)	4,000		
End. bal.	4,600		

Accounts Payable (L)

	0	Beg. bal.
	400	(b)
	400	End. bal.

Contributed Capital (SE)

	0	Beg. bal.
	9,000	(a)
	9,000	End. bal.

Note Receivable (A)

Beg. bal.	0		
(f)	1,250		
End. bal.	1,250		

Land (A)

Beg. bal.	0		
(d)	5,000	1,250	(f)
End. bal.	3,750		

Note Payable (L)

	0	Beg. bal.
	4,000	(e)
	4,000	End. bal.

4. Prepare a classified balance sheet from the T-accounts:

GOODBYE GRASS CORPORATION
Balance Sheet
At April 30, 2010

Assets		Liabilities	
Current Assets		Current Liabilities	
Cash	$ 3,800	Accounts Payable	$ 400
Note Receivable	1,250	Note Payable	4,000
Total Current Assets	5,050	Total Current Liabilities	4,400
Equipment	4,600		
Land	3,750	**Stockholders' Equity**	
		Contributed Capital	9,000
		Retained Earnings	0
		Total Stockholders' Equity	9,000
Total Assets	$13,400	Total Liabilities and Stockholders' Equity	$13,400

---

5. The primary source of financing for GGC's assets (totaling $13,400) has come from stockholders' equity ($9,000) rather than liabilities ($4,400).

CHAPTER SUMMARY

LO1   Identify financial effects of common financing and investing activities. p. 46

- Financing activities involve debt transactions with lenders (e.g., Notes Payable) or equity transactions with investors (e.g., Contributed Capital).
- Investing activities involve buying and selling long-term assets (e.g., Buildings, Equipment).

LO2   Apply transaction analysis to financing and investing transactions. p. 49

- Transactions include external exchanges and internal events.
- Transaction analysis is based on the duality of effects and the basic accounting equation. *Duality of effects* means that every transaction affects at least two accounts.
- Transaction analysis follows a systematic approach of picturing the documented business activity; naming the assets, liabilities, or stockholders' equity that are exchanged; and analyzing the financial effects on the basic accounting equation.

LO3   Use journal entries and T-accounts to show how transactions affect the balance sheet. p. 56

- Debit means left and credit means right.
- Debits increase assets and decrease liabilities and stockholders' equity.
- Credits decrease assets and increase liabilities and stockholders' equity.
- Journal entries express, in debits-equal-credits form, the effects of a transaction on various asset, liability, and stockholders' equity accounts. Journal entries are used to record financial information in the accounting system, which is later summarized by accounts in the ledger (T-accounts).
- T-accounts are a simplified version of the ledger, which summarizes transaction effects for each account. T-accounts show increases on the left (debit) side for assets, which are on the left side of the accounting equation. T-accounts show increases on the right (credit) side for liabilities and stockholders' equity, which are on the right side of the accounting equation.

LO4   Prepare a classified balance sheet. p. 63

- A *classified balance sheet* separately classifies assets as current if they will be used up or turned into cash within one year. Liabilities are classified as current if they will be paid, settled, or fulfilled within one year.

LO5   Interpret the balance sheet using the current ratio and an understanding of related concepts. p. 64

- The current ratio divides current assets by current liabilities to determine the extent to which current assets are likely to be sufficient for paying current liabilities.
- Because accounting is transaction-based, the balance sheet does not necessarily represent the current value of a business.
- Some assets are not recorded because they do not arise from transactions.
- The amounts recorded for assets and liabilities may not represent current values because under the cost principle they generally are recorded at cost, using the exchange amounts established at the time of the initial transaction.
- The concept of conservatism states that when uncertainty exists about the value of an asset or liability, care should be taken to not overstate the reported value of assets or understate the reported value of liabilities.

Accounting Decision Tools

Name of Measure	Formula	What It Tells You
Current ratio	$\dfrac{\text{Current Assets}}{\text{Current Liabilities}}$	• Whether current assets are sufficient to pay current liabilities • A higher ratio means better ability to pay

KEY TERMS

Assets p. 46

Chart of Accounts p. 49

Classified Balance Sheet p. 63

Conservatism p. 66

Cost Principle p. 47

Current Assets p. 64

Current Liabilities p. 64

Debits and Credits p. 56

Journal p. 56

Journal Entry p. 57

Ledger p. 56

Liabilities p. 46

Noncurrent p. 64

Stockholders' Equity p. 46

T-account p. 58

Transaction p. 48

See complete definitions in the glossary in the back of this text.

HOMEWORK HELPER

Account Name	Description
Assets	
Cash	Includes cash in the bank and in the cash register
Accounts Receivable	The right to collect from customers for prior sales on credit
Interest Receivable	The right to collect interest from others
Inventories	Goods on hand that are being held for resale
Supplies	Items on hand that will be used to make goods or provide services
Prepaid Insurance	Amount paid to obtain insurance covering future periods
Prepaid Rent	Amount paid for rent relating to future periods
Notes Receivable	Amounts loaned to others under a formal agreement ("note")
Land	Cost of land to be used by the business
Buildings	Cost of buildings the business will use for operations
Equipment	Cost of equipment used to produce goods or provide services
Intangible Assets	Trademarks, brand names, goodwill, and other assets that lack a physical presence
Liabilities	
Accounts Payable	Amounts owed to suppliers for goods or services bought on credit
Wages Payable	Amounts owed to employees for salaries, wages, and bonuses
Accrued Liabilities	Amounts owed to others for advertising, utilities, interest, etc.
Unearned Revenues	Amounts (customer deposits) received in advance of providing goods or services to customers
Notes Payable	Amounts borrowed from lenders; involves signing a promissory note
Interest Payable	Amount due on loans as the cost of borrowing
Bonds Payable	Amounts borrowed from lenders; involves issuance of bonds
Other Liabilities	A variety of liabilities with smaller balances
Stockholders' Equity	
Contributed Capital	Amount of cash (or other property) contributed in exchange for the company's stock
Retained Earnings	Amount of accumulated earnings not distributed as dividends

> **COACH'S TIP**
>
> Read this chart of accounts but don't memorize it. Also, don't try to force this chart of accounts on all problems. Account names vary from company to company.

Alternative terms

- Stockholders' equity also can be called shareholders' equity.

Helpful reminders

- It's easier to account for a transaction if you can accurately determine how it might affect Cash before determining its impact on other account(s).
- The word *pay* and the expression *purchase with cash* both imply a reduction in Cash.

Frequent mistakes

- When accounting for transactions, avoid thinking of yourself as the customer, investor, or creditor. Instead, put yourself in the position of the company you're accounting for.
- Stockholders' is plural; stockholder's is singular.

PRACTICE MATERIAL

QUESTIONS (⊖ Symbol indicates questions that require analysis from more than one perspective.)

1. Define the following:

   a. Asset
   b. Current asset
   c. Liability
   d. Current liability
   e. Contributed capital
   f. Retained earnings

2. Define a transaction and give an example of each of the two types of events that are considered transactions.

3. For accounting purposes, what is an account? Explain why accounts are used in an accounting system.

4. What is the basic accounting equation?

5. Explain what *debit* and *credit* mean.

6. Briefly explain what is meant by *transaction analysis*. What are the two principles underlying transaction analysis?

7. What two different accounting equalities must be maintained in transaction analysis?

8. What is a journal entry? What is the typical format of a journal entry?

9. What is a T-account? What is its purpose?

10. Explain what the following accounting terms mean:

    a. *Cost principle*
    b. *Conservatism*

11. To obtain financing for her hair salon, Valeri asked you to prepare a balance sheet for her business. When she sees it, she is disappointed that the assets exclude a value for her list of loyal customers. What can you tell her to explain why this "asset" has been excluded? Knowing this, what should she tell her banker when they meet next week? ⊖

12. Is transaction analysis expected to be as important under IFRS as it is under GAAP? Why or why not?

MULTIPLE CHOICE

1. Which of the following is not an asset?

   a. Cash
   b. Land
   c. Equipment
   d. Contributed capital

   Quiz 2
   www.mhhe.com/phillips3e

2. Which of the following statements describe transactions that would be recorded in the accounting system?

   a. An exchange of an asset for a promise to pay.
   b. An exchange of a promise for another promise.
   c. Both of the above.
   d. None of the above.

3. Total assets on a balance sheet prepared on any date must agree with which of the following?

   a. The sum of total liabilities and net income as shown on the income statement.
   b. The sum of total liabilities and contributed capital.
   c. The sum of total liabilities and retained earnings.
   d. The sum of total liabilities and contributed capital and retained earnings.

4. The *duality of effects* can best be described as follows:

   a. When a transaction is recorded in the accounting system, at least two effects on the basic accounting equation will result.
   b. When an exchange takes place between two parties, both parties must record the transaction.
   c. When a transaction is recorded, both the balance sheet and the income statement must be impacted.
   d. When a transaction is recorded, one account will always increase and one account will always decrease.

5. The T-account is used to summarize which of the following?

   a. Increases and decreases to a single account in the accounting system.
   b. Debits and credits to a single account in the accounting system.
   c. Changes in specific account balances over a time period.
   d. All of the above describe how T-accounts are used by accountants.

6. Which of the following describes how assets are listed on the balance sheet?

   a. In alphabetical order.
   b. In order of magnitude, lowest value to highest value.
   c. In the order they will be used up or turned into cash.
   d. From least current to most current.

7. A company was recently formed with $50,000 cash contributed to the company by stockholders. The company then borrowed $20,000 from a bank and bought $10,000 of supplies on account. The company also purchased $50,000 of equipment by paying $20,000 in cash and issuing a note for the remainder. What is the amount of total assets to be reported on the balance sheet?

   a. $110,000
   b. $100,000
   c. $90,000
   d. None of the above

8. Which of the following statements are true regarding debits and credits?

   a. In any given transaction, the total dollar amount of the debits and the total dollar amount of the credits must be equal.
   b. Debits decrease certain accounts and credits decrease certain accounts.
   c. Liabilities and stockholders' equity accounts usually end in credit balances, while assets usually end in debit balances.
   d. All of the above.

9. Which of the following statements are true regarding the balance sheet?

   a. One cannot determine the true current value of a company by reviewing just its balance sheet.
   b. The balance sheet reports assets only if they have been acquired through identifiable transactions.
   c. A balance sheet shows only the ending balances, in a summarized format, of balance sheet accounts in the accounting system as of a particular date.
   d. All of the above.

10. If a publicly traded company is trying to maximize its perceived value to decision makers external to the corporation, the company is most likely to report too small a value for which of the following on its balance sheet?

    a. Assets
    b. Liabilities
    c. Retained earnings
    d. Contributed capital

> For answers to the Multiple-Choice Questions **see page Q1** located in the last section of the book.

MINI-EXERCISES

M2-1 Identifying Increase and Decrease Effects on Balance Sheet Accounts   LO3

Complete the following table by entering either the word *increases* or *decreases* in each column.

	Debit	Credit
Assets		
Liabilities		
Stockholders' Equity		

M2-2 Identifying Debit and Credit Effects on Balance Sheet Accounts   LO3

Complete the following table by entering either the word *debit* or *credit* in each column.

	Increase	Decrease
Assets		
Liabilities		
Stockholders' Equity		

M2-3 Matching Terms with Definitions   LO2, 3, 5

Match each term with its related definition by entering the appropriate letter in the space provided. There should be only one definition per term. (That is, there are more definitions than terms.)

Term	Definition
____ 1. Journal entry	A. An exchange or event that has a direct and measurable financial effect.
____ 2. A = L + SE; Debits = Credits	B. Four periodic financial statements.
____ 3. Transaction	C. The two equalities in accounting that aid in providing accuracy.
____ 4. Liabilities	D. The results of transaction analysis in debits-equal-credits format.
____ 5. Assets	E. The account that is debited when money is borrowed from a bank.
____ 6. Income statement, balance sheet, statement of retained earnings, and statement of cash flows	F. A resource owned by a business, with measurable value and expected future benefits.
	G. Cumulative earnings of a company that are not distributed to the owners.
	H. Every transaction has a least two effects.
	I. Amounts presently owed by a business.
	J. Assigning dollar amounts to transactions.

LO1, 4   **M2-4 Classifying Accounts on a Balance Sheet**

The following are a few of the accounts of Aim Delivery Corporation:

____	1. Wages Payable	____	8. Income Taxes Payable
____	2. Accounts Payable	____	9. Equipment
____	3. Accounts Receivable	____	10. Notes Payable (due in six months)
____	4. Buildings	____	11. Retained Earnings
____	5. Cash	____	12. Supplies
____	6. Contributed Capital	____	13. Utilities Payable
____	7. Land		

In the space provided, classify each as it would be reported on a balance sheet. Use the following code:

    CA = Current Asset   CL = Current Liability   SE = Stockholders' Equity
    NCA = Noncurrent Asset   NCL = Noncurrent Liability

LO1, 3, 4   **M2-5 Identifying Accounts on a Classified Balance Sheet and Their Normal Debit or Credit Balances**

According to a recent report of Hasbro, Inc., the company is "a worldwide leader in children's and family games and toys." Hasbro produces products under several brands including Tonka, Milton Bradley, Playskool, and Parker Brothers. The following are several of the accounts from a recent balance sheet:

1. Accounts Receivable
2. Short-term Bank Loan
3. Contributed Capital
4. Long-term Debt
5. Income Taxes Payable
6. Property, Plant, and Equipment
7. Retained Earnings
8. Accounts Payable
9. Cash

Required:

1. Indicate how each account normally should be categorized on a classified balance sheet. Use CA for current asset, NCA for noncurrent asset, CL for current liability, NCL for noncurrent liability, and SE for stockholders' equity.
2. Indicate whether the account normally has a debit or credit balance.

LO1, 3, 4   **M2-6 Identifying Accounts on a Classified Balance Sheet and Their Normal Debit or Credit Balances**

Blockbuster, Inc.

Blockbuster, Inc., is the world's leading provider of rentable DVDs and videogames. Blockbuster estimates that 64 percent of the U.S. population lives within a 10-minute drive of a Blockbuster store. The following are several of the accounts included in a recent balance sheet:

1. Income Taxes Payable
2. Accounts Receivable
3. Cash
4. Contributed Capital
5. Long-term Debt
6. Property and Equipment
7. Retained Earnings
8. Accounts Payable

Required:

1. Indicate how each account normally should be categorized on a classified balance sheet. Use CA for current asset, NCA for noncurrent asset, CL for current liability, NCL for noncurrent liability, and SE for stockholders' equity.
2. Indicate whether the account normally has a debit or credit balance.

LO2   **M2-7 Identifying Events as Accounting Transactions**

TORO

Do the following events result in a recordable transaction for The Toro Company? Answer yes or no for each.

____ 1. Toro purchased robotic manufacturing equipment that it paid for by signing a note payable.

____ 2. Toro's president purchased stock in another company for his own portfolio.

____ 3. The company lent $550 to an employee.

____ 4. Toro ordered supplies from Office Max to be delivered next week.

____ 5. Six investors in Toro sold their stock to another investor.

____ 6. The company borrowed $2,500,000 from a local bank.

M2-8 Identifying Events as Accounting Transactions   LO2

With 80 locations in 15 states, Half Price Books is the country's favorite new and used bookstore chain. Do the following events result in a recordable transaction for Half Price Books? Answer yes or no for each.

____ 1. Half Price Books bought an old laundromat in Dallas.

____ 2. The privately held company issued stock to new investors.

____ 3. The company signed an agreement to rent store space in Columbia Plaza near Cleveland.

____ 4. The company paid for renovations to prepare its Seattle store for operations.

____ 5. The vice president of the company spoke at a literacy luncheon in Indiana, which contributed to building the company's reputation as a responsible company.

M2-9 Determining Financial Statement Effects of Several Transactions   LO2

For each of the following transactions of Spotlighter Inc. for the month of January 2010, indicate the accounts, amounts, and direction of the effects on the accounting equation. A sample is provided.

a. (Sample) Borrowed $3,940 from a local bank on a note due in six months.
b. Received $4,630 cash from investors and issued stock to them.
c. Purchased $920 in equipment, paying $190 cash and promising the rest on a note due in one year.
d. Paid $372 cash for supplies.
e. Bought $700 of supplies on account.

	Assets	=	Liabilities	+	Stockholders' Equity
a. Sample:	Cash +3,940		Notes Payable +3,940		

M2-10 Preparing Journal Entries   LO3

For each of the transactions in M2-9 (including the sample), write the journal entry using the format shown in this chapter (omit explanations).

M2-11 Posting to T-Accounts   LO3

For each of the transactions in M2-9 (including the sample), post the effects to the appropriate T-accounts and determine ending account balances.

+ Cash (A) −	+ Supplies (A) −	+ Equipment (A) −

− Accounts Payable (L) +	− Notes Payable (L) +	− Contributed Capital (SE) +

LO4   **M2-12   Reporting a Classified Balance Sheet**

Given the transactions in M2-9 (including the sample), prepare a classified balance sheet for Spotlighter Inc. as of January 31, 2010.

LO3   **M2-13   Identifying Transactions and Preparing Journal Entries**

J.K. Builders was incorporated on July 1, 2010. Prepare journal entries for the following events from the first month of business. If the event is not a transaction, write "no transaction."

a.   Received $55,000 cash invested by owners and issued stock.
b.   Bought an unused field from a local farmer by paying $45,000 cash. As a construction site for smaller projects, it is estimated to be worth $50,000 to J.K. Builders.
c.   A lumber supplier delivered lumber to J.K. Builders for future use. The lumber would have normally sold for $10,000, but the supplier gave J.K. Builders a 10 percent discount. J.K. Builders has not yet received a bill from the supplier.
d.   Borrowed $25,000 from the bank with a plan to use the funds to build a small workshop in August. The loan must be repaid in two years.
e.   One of the owners sold $10,000 worth of his stock to another shareholder for $11,000.

LO3   **M2-14   Identifying Transactions and Preparing Journal Entries**

Joel Henry founded bookmart.com at the beginning of August, which sells new and used books online. He is passionate about books but does not have a lot of accounting experience. Help Joel by preparing journal entries for the following events. If the event is not a transaction, write "no transaction."

a.   The company purchased bookshelves for $2,000 cash. The bookshelves are expected to be used for 10 or more years.
b.   Joel's business bought $8,000 worth of books from a publisher. The company will pay the publisher within 45–60 days.
c.   Joel's friend Sam lent $4,000 to the business. Sam had Joel write a note promising that bookmart.com would repay the $4,000 in four months. Because they are good friends, Sam is not going to charge Joel interest.
d.   The company paid $1,500 cash for books purchased on account earlier in the month.
e.   Bookmart.com repaid the $4,000 loan established in (c).

LO3   **M2-15   Identifying Transactions and Preparing Journal Entries**

Katy Williams is the manager of Blue Light Arcade. The company provides entertainment for parties and special events. Prepare journal entries for the following events relating to the year ended December 31. If the event is not a transaction, write "no transaction."

a.   Blue Light Arcade received $50 cash on account for a birthday party held two months ago.
b.   Agreed to hire a new employee at a monthly salary of $3,000. The employee starts work next month.
c.   Paid $2,000 for a table top hockey game purchased last month on account.
d.   Repaid a $5,000 bank loan. (Ignore interest.)
e.   The company purchased an air hockey table for $2,200, paying $1,000 cash and signing a short-term note for $1,200.

LO3   **M2-16   Identifying Transactions and Preparing Journal Entries**

Sweet Shop Co. is a chain of candy stores that has been in operation for the past ten years. Prepare journal entries for the following events, which occurred at the end of the most recent year. If the event is not a transaction, write "no transaction."

a.   Ordered and received $12,000 worth of cotton candy machines from Candy Makers Inc., which Sweet Shop Co. will pay for in 45 days.
b.   Sent a check for $6,000 to Candy Makers Inc. for the cotton candy machines from (a).
c.   Received $400 from customers who bought candy on account in previous months.
d.   To help raise funds for store upgrades estimated to cost $20,000, Sweet Shop Co. issued 1,000 shares for $15 each to existing stockholders.
e.   Sweet Shop Co. bought ice cream trucks for $50,000 total, paying $10,000 cash and signing a long-term note for $40,000.

M2-17 Ordering Current Assets and Current Liabilities within a Classified Balance Sheet

LO4

Charlie's Crispy Chicken (CCC) operates a fast-food restaurant. When accounting for its first year of business, CCC created several accounts. Using the following descriptions, prepare a classified balance sheet at September 30, 2010.

Account Name	Balance	Description
Accounts Payable	$ 2,000	Payment is due in 30 days
Bank Loan Payable	10,000	Payment is due in 2014
Cash	1,800	Includes cash in register and in bank account
Contributed Capital	20,000	Stock issued in exchange for owners' contributions
Food Ingredients	400	Includes frozen chicken, french fries, beverages, etc.
Kitchen Equipment	13,000	Includes deep fryers, microwaves, dishwasher, etc.
Kitchen Supplies	1,400	Includes serving trays, condiment dispensers, etc.
Land	8,900	Held for future site of new restaurant
Note Payable	15,000	Payment is due in 2016
Restaurant Booths	25,000	Likely to be used through 2020
Retained Earnings	3,000	Total earnings through September 30, 2010
Utilities Payable	300	Payment is due in 30–45 days
Wages Payable	200	Payment is due in 7 days

M2-18 Preparing a Classified Balance Sheet

LO4

The following accounts are taken from the financial statements of Trump Entertainments Resorts, Inc., at its September 30, 2008, year-end. (Amounts are in thousands.)

TRUMP
ENTERTAINMENT RESORTS
MARINA   PLAZA   TAJ MAHAL

General Expenses	$ 48,735
Salaries Payable	22,082
Interest Expense	32,066
Accounts Payable	58,462
Other Current Liabilities	115,663
Food and Beverage Revenue	12,065
Cash	88,761
Accounts Receivable	56,777
Other Current Assets	283,692
Property and Equipment	1,647,050
Long-term Note Payable	1,835,192
Contributed Capital	32
Retained Earnings	44,849

Required:

1. Prepare a classified balance sheet at September 30, 2008.

   TIP: This exercise requires you to remember material from Chapter 1. (Some of the above accounts are not reported on the balance sheet.)

2. Using the balance sheet, indicate whether the total assets of Trump Entertainments Resorts, Inc., at the end of the year were financed primarily by liabilities or stockholders' equity.

M2-19 Calculating and Interpreting the Current Ratio

LO5

The balance sheet of Mister Ribs Restaurant reports current assets of $30,000 and current liabilities of $15,000. Calculate and interpret the current ratio. Does it appear likely that Mister Ribs will be able to pay its current liabilities as they come due in the next year?

M2-20 Evaluating the Impact of Transactions on the Current Ratio

LO5

Refer to M2-19. Evaluate whether the current ratio of Mister Ribs Restaurant will increase or decrease as a result of the following transactions.

a. Paid $2,000 cash for a new oven.
b. Borrowed $5,000 cash from a bank, issuing a note that must be repaid in three years.
c. Received a $2,000 cash contribution from the company's main stockholder.
d. Purchased $500 of napkins, paper cups, and other disposable supplies on account.

LO5   **M2-21 Analyzing the Impact of Transactions on the Current Ratio**

BSO, Inc., has current assets of $1,000,000 and current liabilities of $500,000, resulting in a current ratio of 2.0. For each of the following transactions, determine whether the current ratio will increase, decrease, or remain the same.

a.   Purchased $20,000 of supplies on credit.
b.   Paid Accounts Payable in the amount of $50,000.
c.   Recorded $100,000 of cash contributed by a stockholder.
d.   Borrowed $250,000 from a local bank, to be repaid in 90 days.

EXERCISES

LO1, 2, 3, 5   **E2-1 Matching Terms with Definitions**

Match each term with its related definition by entering the appropriate letter in the space provided. There should be only one definition per term (that is, there are more definitions than terms).

Term	Definition
____ 1. Transaction	A. Economic resources to be used or turned into cash within one year.
____ 2. Separate Entity Assumption	B. Reports assets, liabilities, and stockholders' equity.
____ 3. Balance Sheet	
____ 4. Liabilities	C. Decrease assets; increase liabilities and stockholders' equity.
____ 5. Assets = Liabilities + Stockholders' Equity	D. Increase assets; decrease liabilities and stockholders' equity.
____ 6. Current Assets	E. An exchange or event that has a direct and measurable financial effect.
____ 7. Notes Payable	F. Accounts for a business separate from its owners.
____ 8. Duality of Effects	G. The principle that assets should be recorded at their original cost to the company.
____ 9. Retained Earnings	H. A standardized format used to accumulate data about each item reported on financial statements.
____ 10. Debit	I. The basic accounting equation.
	J. The two equalities in accounting that aid in providing accuracy.
	K. The account credited when money is borrowed from a bank using a promissory note.
	L. Cumulative earnings of a company that are not distributed to the owners.
	M. Every transaction has at least two effects.
	N. Amounts presently owed by the business.

LO1, 2, 5   **E2-2 Identifying Account Titles**

The following are independent situations.

a.   A company orders and receives 10 personal computers for office use for which it signs a note promising to pay $25,000 within three months.
b.   A company purchases for $21,000 cash a new delivery truck that has a list ("sticker") price of $24,000.
c.   A women's clothing retailer orders 30 new display stands for $300 each for future delivery.
d.   A new company is formed and issues 100 shares of stock for $12 per share to investors.

e. A company purchases a piece of land for $50,000 cash. An appraiser for the buyer valued the land at $52,500.
f. The owner of a local company buys a $10,000 car for personal use. Answer from the company's point of view.
g. A company borrows $1,000 from a local bank and signs a six-month note for the loan.
h. A company pays $1,500 owed on its note payable (ignore interest).

Required:

1. Indicate titles of the appropriate accounts, if any, affected in each of the preceding events. Consider what the company gives and receives.

2. At what amount would you record the delivery truck in *b*? The piece of land in *e*? What measurement principle are you applying?

3. What reasoning did you apply in *c*? For *f*, what accounting concept did you apply?

E2-3 **Classifying Accounts and Their Usual Balances**

As described in a recent annual report, Digital Diversions, Inc. (DDI) designs, develops, and distributes videogames for computers and advanced game systems such as Playnation, Y-Box, and Yeee. DDI has been operating for only one full year.

LO1, 3, 4

Required:

For each of the following accounts from DDI's recent balance sheet, complete the following table. Indicate whether the account is classified as a current asset (CA), noncurrent asset (NCA), current liability (CL), noncurrent liability (NCL), or stockholders' equity (SE), and whether the account usually has a debit (*dr*) or credit (*cr*) balance.

Account	Balance Sheet Classification	Debit or Credit Balance
1. Land		
2. Retained Earnings		
3. Notes Payable (due in three years)		
4. Accounts Receivable		
5. Supplies		
6. Contributed Capital		
7. Equipment		
8. Accounts Payable		
9. Cash		
10. Taxes Payable		

E2-4 **Determining Financial Statement Effects of Several Transactions**

LO1, 2

The following events occurred for Favata Company:

a. Received $10,000 cash from owners and issued stock to them.
b. Borrowed $7,000 cash from a bank and signed a note.
c. Purchased land for $12,000; paid $1,000 in cash and signed a note for the balance.
d. Bought $800 of equipment on account.
e. Purchased $3,000 of equipment, paying $1,000 in cash and signing a note for the rest.

Required:

For each of the events (*a*) through (*e*), perform transaction analysis and indicate the account, amount, and direction of the effect (+ for increase and − for decrease) on the accounting equation. Check that the accounting equation remains in balance after each transaction. Use the following headings:

Event	Assets	=	Liabilities	+	Stockholders' Equity

LO1, 2, 5

NIKE, Inc.

E2-5 Determining Financial Statement Effects of Several Transactions

NIKE, Inc., with headquarters in Beaverton, Oregon, is one of the world's leading manufacturers of athletic shoes and sports apparel. The following activities occurred during a recent year. The amounts are presented in millions of dollars.

a.   Purchased $216.3 in equipment; paid by signing a $5 long-term note and fulfilling the rest with cash.

b.   Issued $21.1 in additional stock for cash contributions made by stockholders.

c.   Several NIKE investors sold their own stock to other investors on the stock exchange for $21 per share of stock.

Required:

1.   For each of these events, perform transaction analysis and indicate the account, amount (in millions), and direction of the effect on the accounting equation. Check that the accounting equation remains in balance after each transaction. Use the following headings:

Event	Assets	=	Liabilities	+	Stockholders' Equity

2.   Explain your response to transaction (c).

LO3

E2-6 Recording Investing and Financing Activities

Refer to E2-4.

Required:

For each of the events in E2-4, prepare journal entries, checking that debits equal credits.

LO3, 5

E2-7 Recording Investing and Financing Activities

Refer to E2-5.

Required:

1.   For each of the events in E2-5, prepare journal entries, checking that debits equal credits.

2.   Explain your response to event (c).

LO2, 3, 5

E2-8 Analyzing the Effects of Transactions in T-Accounts

Mulkeen Service Company, Inc., was incorporated by Conor Mulkeen and five other managers. The following activities occurred during the year:

a.   Received $60,000 cash from the managers; each was issued 1,000 shares of stock.

b.   Purchased equipment for use in the business at a cost of $12,000; one-fourth was paid in cash and the company signed a note for the balance (due in six months).

c.   Signed an agreement with a cleaning service to pay it $120 per week for cleaning the corporate offices, beginning next week.

d.   Conor Mulkeen borrowed $10,000 for personal use from a local bank, signing a one-year note.

Required:

1.   Create T-accounts for the following accounts: Cash, Equipment, Note Payable, and Contributed Capital. Beginning balances are zero. For each of the above transactions, record its effects in the appropriate T-accounts. Include referencing and totals for each T-account.

2.   Using the balances in the T-accounts, fill in the following amounts for the accounting equation:

Assets $_____ = Liabilities $_____ + Stockholders' Equity $_____

3.   Explain your response to events (c) and (d).

LO1, 2, 4

E2-9 Inferring Investing and Financing Transactions and Preparing a Balance Sheet

During its first week of operations, January 1–7, 2010, Home Comfort Furniture Company completed six transactions with the dollar effects indicated in the following schedule:

	Assets			=	Liabilities	+ Stockholders' Equity
	Cash	Equipment	Land		Notes Payable	Contributed Capital
Beginning	$ 0	$ 0	$ 0	=	$ 0	$ 0
(1)	+12,000			=		+12,000
(2)	+50,000			=	+50,000	
(3)	−4,000		+12,000	=	+8,000	
(4)	+4,000			=	+4,000	
(5)	−7,000	+7,000		=		
(6)			+3,000	=	+3,000	
Ending	$	$	$	=	$	$

Required:

1. Write a brief explanation of transactions 1 through 6. Explain any assumptions that you made.
2. Compute the ending balance in each account and prepare a classified balance sheet for Home Comfort Furniture Company on January 7, 2010.
3. As of January 7, 2010, has most of the financing for Home Comfort's investments in assets come from liabilities or stockholders' equity?

E2-10 Inferring Investing and Financing Transactions and Preparing a Balance Sheet   LO1, 2, 4

During its first month of operations, March 2010, Faye's Fashions, Inc., completed four transactions with the dollar effects indicated in the following schedule:

	DOLLAR EFFECT OF EACH OF THE FOUR TRANSACTIONS				
Accounts	1	2	3	4	Ending Balance
Cash	$50,000	$(4,000)	$5,000	$(4,000)	
Computer Equipment				4,000	
Delivery Truck		25,000			
Short-term Bank Loan			5,000		
Long-term Notes Payable		21,000			
Contributed Capital	50,000				

Required:

1. Write a brief explanation of transactions 1 through 4. Explain any assumptions that you made.
2. Compute the ending balance in each account and prepare a classified balance sheet for Faye's Fashions, Inc., at the end of March 2010.
3. As of March 31, 2010, has most of the financing for Faye's investment in assets come from liabilities or stockholders' equity?

E2-11 Recording Journal Entries   LO1, 3, 5

Assume Down.com was organized on May 1, 2010 to compete with Despair.com—a company that sells de-motivational posters and office products. The following events occurred during the first month of Down.com's operations.

a. Received $60,000 cash from the investors who organized Down.com Corporation.
b. Borrowed $20,000 cash and signed a note due in two years.
c. Ordered computer equipment costing $16,000.
d. Purchased $10,000 in equipment, paying $1,000 in cash and signing a six-month note for the balance.
e. Received and paid for the computer equipment ordered in (c).

Required:

Prepare journal entries for each transaction. (Remember that debits go on top and credits go on the bottom, indented.) Be sure to use referencing and categorize each account as an asset (A), liability (L), or stockholders' equity (SE). If a transaction does not require a journal entry, explain the reason.

LO2, 3, 4   **E2-12 Analyzing the Effects of Transactions Using T-Accounts; Preparing and Interpreting a Balance Sheet**

Lee Delivery Company, Inc. (LDC), was incorporated in 2010. The following transactions occurred during the year:

a. Received $40,000 cash from organizers in exchange for stock in the new company.
b. Purchased land for $12,000, signing a two-year note (ignore interest).
c. Bought two used delivery trucks at the start of the year at a cost of $10,000 each; paid $2,000 cash and signed a note due in three years for the rest (ignore interest).
d. Paid $2,000 cash to a truck repair shop for a new motor, which increased the cost of one of the trucks.
e. Stockholder Jonah Lee paid $122,000 cash for a house for his personal use.

Required:

1. Analyze each item for its effects on the accounting equation of LDC, for the year ended December 31, 2010.

    TIP: Transaction (a) is presented below as an example.

Assets	=	Liabilities	+	Stockholders' Equity
(a) Cash +40,000 =				Contributed Capital +40,000

    TIP: The new motor in transaction (d) is treated as an increase to the cost of the truck.
2. Record the effects of each item using a journal entry.

    TIP: Use the simplified journal entry format shown in the demonstration case on page 69.
3. Summarize the effects of the journal entries by account, using the T-account format shown in the chapter.
4. Prepare a classified balance sheet for LDC at the end of 2010.
5. Using the balance sheet, indicate whether LDC's assets at the end of the year were financed primarily by liabilities or stockholders' equity.

LO1, 2, 3   **E2-13 Explaining the Effects of Transactions on Balance Sheet Accounts Using T-Accounts**

Heavey and Lovas Furniture Repair Service, a company with two stockholders, began operations on June 1, 2010. The following T-accounts indicate the activities for the month of June.

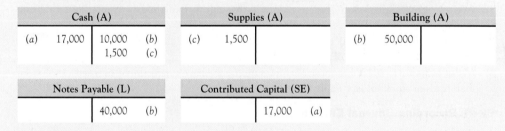

Cash (A)				Supplies (A)			Building (A)	
(a) 17,000	10,000 (b)		(c) 1,500			(b) 50,000	
	1,500 (c)						

Notes Payable (L)			Contributed Capital (SE)	
	40,000 (b)			17,000 (a)

Required:

Explain events (a) through (c) that resulted in the entries in the T-accounts. That is, for each account what transactions made it increase and/or decrease?

LO1, 5   **E2-14 Calculating and Evaluating the Current Ratio**

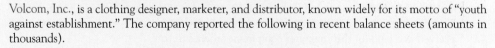

Volcom, Inc., is a clothing designer, marketer, and distributor, known widely for its motto of "youth against establishment." The company reported the following in recent balance sheets (amounts in thousands).

	September 30, 2008	December 31, 2007
Assets		
Current Assets:		
Cash	$ 73,324	$ 92,962
Accounts Receivable	81,336	58,270
Inventories	25,816	20,440
Other Current Assets	5,512	5,002
Total Current Assets	185,988	176,674
Property, Equipment, and Other Long-term Assets	54,128	25,820
Total Assets	$240,116	$202,494
Liabilities and Stockholders' Equity		
Current Liabilities:		
Accounts Payable	$ 19,207	$ 18,694
Other Current Liabilities	12,880	10,633
Income Taxes Payable	3,512	—
Total Current Liabilities	35,599	29,327
Long-term Liabilities	1,709	312
Stockholders' Equity	202,808	172,855
Total Liabilities and Stockholders' Equity	$240,116	$202,494

Required:

1. Calculate the current ratio at September 30, 2008, and December 31, 2007.

2. Did the company's current ratio increase or decrease? What does this imply about the company's ability to pay its current liabilities as they come due?

3. What would Volcom's current ratio have been if, on September 30, 2008, the company were to have paid down $10,000 of its Accounts Payable?

4. Are the company's total assets financed primarily by liabilities or stockholders' equity at September 30, 2008?

COACHED PROBLEMS

CP2-1 **Determining Financial Statement Effects of Various Transactions**

LO2, 5

www.mhhe.com/phillips3e

Lester's Home Healthcare Services (LHHS) was organized on January 1, 2010, by four friends. Each organizer invested $10,000 in the company and, in turn, was issued 8,000 shares of common stock. To date, they are the only stockholders. During the first month (January 2010), the company had the following five events:

a. Collected a total of $40,000 from the organizers and, in turn, issued the shares of stock.
b. Purchased a building for $65,000, equipment for $16,000, and three acres of land for $12,000; paid $13,000 in cash and signed a note for the balance, which is due to be paid in 15 years.
c. One stockholder reported to the company that 500 shares of his LHHS stock had been sold and transferred to another stockholder for $5,000 cash.
d. Purchased supplies for $3,000 cash.
e. Sold one acre of land for $4,000 cash to another company.

Required:

1. Was Lester's Home Healthcare Services organized as a partnership or corporation? Explain the basis for your answer.

2. During the first month, the records of the company were inadequate. You were asked to prepare a summary of the preceding transactions. To develop a quick assessment of their economic effects on Lester's Home Healthcare Services, you have decided to complete the spreadsheet that follows and to use plus (+) for increases and minus (−) for decreases for each account.

TIP: Transaction (*a*) is presented below as an example.

	Assets					=	Liabilities	+	Stockholders' Equity	
	Cash	Supplies	Land	Building	Equipment	=	Notes Payable		Contributed Capital	Retained Earnings
(*a*)	+40,000								+40,000	

3. Did you include the transaction between the two stockholders—event (*c*)—in the spreadsheet? Why?
   TIP: Think about whether this event caused LHHS to receive or give up anything.

4. Based only on the completed spreadsheet, provide the following amounts (show computations):
   a. Total assets at the end of the month.
   b. Total liabilities at the end of the month.
   c. Total stockholders' equity at the end of the month.
   d. Cash balance at the end of the month.
   e. Total current assets at the end of the month.

5. As of January 31, 2010, has the financing for LHHS's investment in assets primarily come from liabilities or stockholders' equity?

LO2, 3, 4, 5   **CP2-2 Recording Transactions (in a Journal and T-Accounts); Preparing and Interpreting the Balance Sheet**

Athletic Performance Company (APC) was incorporated as a private company on June 1, 2010. The company's accounts included the following at July 1, 2010:

Accounts Payable	$ 4,000	Land	$100,000
Building	200,000	Notes Payable	17,000
Cash	16,000	Retained Earnings	0
Contributed Capital	318,000	Supplies	5,000
Equipment	18,000		

During the month of July, the company had the following activities:

a. Issued 2,000 shares of stock for $200,000 cash.
b. Borrowed $30,000 cash from a local bank, payable June 30, 2012.
c. Bought a building for $141,000; paid $41,000 in cash and signed a three-year note for the balance.
d. Paid cash for equipment that cost $100,000.
e. Purchased supplies for $10,000 on account.

Required:

1. Analyze transactions (*a*)–(*e*) to determine their effects on the accounting equation. Use a spreadsheet format with a column for each account, enter the July 1, 2010, amounts in the first line under the account headings, and calculate ending balances.
   TIP: You won't need new accounts to record the transactions described above, so have a quick look at the ones listed before you begin.
   TIP: In transaction (*c*), three different accounts are affected.

2. Record the transaction effects determined in requirement 1 using journal entries.

3. Summarize the journal entry effects from requirement 2 using T-accounts.
   TIP: Create a T-account for each account listed above. Enter the July 1, 2010, balances as the month's beginning balances.

4. Prepare a classified balance sheet at July 31, 2010.

5. As of July 31, 2010, has the financing for APC's investment in assets primarily come from liabilities or stockholders' equity?

LO2, 3, 4, 5   **CP2-3 Recording Transactions (in a Journal and T-Accounts); Preparing and Interpreting the Balance Sheet**

Performance Plastics Company (PPC) has been operating for three years. The December 31, 2010, account balances are:

Cash	$ 35,000	Land	$ 30,000
Accounts Receivable	5,000	Supplies	5,000
Inventory	40,000	Accounts Payable	37,000
Notes Receivable (due 2013)	2,000	Notes Payable (due 2013)	80,000
Equipment	80,000	Contributed Capital	150,000
Factory Building	120,000	Retained Earnings	50,000

During the year 2011, the company had the following summarized activities:

a.   Purchased equipment that cost $21,000; paid $5,000 cash and signed a two-year note for the balance.

b.   Issued an additional 2,000 shares of stock for $20,000 cash.

c.   Borrowed $30,000 cash from a local bank, payable June 30, 2013.

d.   Purchased supplies for $4,000 cash.

e.   Built an addition to the factory for $41,000; paid $12,000 in cash and signed a three-year note for the balance.

f.   Hired a new president to start January 1, 2012. The contract was for $95,000 for each full year worked.

Required:

1.   Analyze transactions (a)–(f) to determine their effects on the accounting equation.

   TIP: You won't need new accounts to record the transactions described above, so have a quick look at the ones listed in the beginning of this question before you begin.

   TIP: In transaction (e), three different accounts are affected.

   TIP: In transaction (f), consider whether PPC owes anything to its new president for the year ended December 31, 2011.

2.   Record the transaction effects determined in requirement 1 using journal entries.

3.   Summarize the journal entry effects from requirement 2 using T-accounts.

   TIP: Create a T-account for each account listed above. Enter the December 31, 2010, balances as the 2011 beginning balances.

4.   Explain your response to event (f).

5.   Prepare a classified balance sheet at December 31, 2011.

6.   As of December 31, 2011, has the financing for PPC's investment in assets primarily come from liabilities or stockholders' equity?

GROUP A PROBLEMS

PA2-1 Determining Financial Statement Effects of Various Transactions

LO2, 5

eXcel

www.mhhe.com/phillips3e

Mallard Incorporated (MI) is a small manufacturing company that makes model trains to sell to toy stores. It has a small service department that repairs customers' trains for a fee. The company has been in business for five years. At the end of the most recent year, 2009, the accounting records reflected total assets of $500,000 and total liabilities of $200,000. During the current year, 2010, the following summarized events occurred:

a.   Issued additional shares of stock for $100,000 cash.

b.   Borrowed $120,000 cash from the bank and signed a 10-year note.

c.   Built an addition on the factory for $200,000 and paid cash to the contractor.

d.   Purchased equipment for the new addition for $30,000, paying $3,000 in cash and signing a note due in six months for the balance.

e.   Returned a $3,000 piece of equipment, from (d), because it proved to be defective; received a reduction of the note payable.

f.   Purchased a delivery truck (equipment) for $10,000; paid $5,000 cash and signed a nine-month note for the remainder.

g.   A stockholder sold $5,000 of his stock in Mallard Incorporated to his neighbor.

Required:

1.   Complete the spreadsheet that follows, using plus (+) for increases and minus (−) for decreases for each account. The first transaction is used as an example.

	Assets			=	Liabilities	+	Stockholders' Equity	
	Cash	Equipment	Building	=	Notes Payable		Contributed Capital	Retained Earnings
(a)	+100,000						+100,000	

2. Did you include event (g) in the spreadsheet? Why or why not?

3. Based on beginning balances plus the completed spreadsheet, provide the following amounts (show computations):

   a. Total assets at the end of the year.
   b. Total liabilities at the end of the year.
   c. Total stockholders' equity at the end of the year.

4. As of December 31, 2010, has the financing for MI's investment in assets primarily come from liabilities or stockholders' equity?

LO2, 3, 4, 5   **PA2-2 Recording Transactions (in a Journal and T-Accounts); Preparing and Interpreting the Balance Sheet**

Deliberate Speed Corporation (DSC) was incorporated as a private company on June 1, 2010. The company's accounts included the following at June 30, 2010:

Accounts Payable	$ 10,000	Land	$200,000
Factory Building	100,000	Notes Payable	2,000
Cash	26,000	Retained Earnings	259,000
Contributed Capital	180,000	Supplies	7,000
Equipment	118,000		

During the month of July, the company had the following activities:

a. Issued 4,000 shares of stock for $400,000 cash.
b. Borrowed $90,000 cash from a local bank, payable June 30, 2012.
c. Bought a factory building for $182,000; paid $82,000 in cash and signed a three-year note for the balance.
d. Paid cash for equipment that cost $200,000.
e. Purchased supplies for $30,000 on account.

Required:

1. Analyze transactions (a)–(e) to determine their effects on the accounting equation.
2. Record the transaction effects determined in requirement 1 using a journal entry format.
3. Summarize the journal entry effects from requirement 2 using T-accounts.
4. Prepare a classified balance sheet at July 31, 2010.
5. As of July 31, 2010, has the financing for DSC's investment in assets primarily come from liabilities or stockholders' equity?

LO2, 3, 4, 5   **PA2-3 Recording Transactions (in a Journal and T-Accounts); Preparing and Interpreting the Balance Sheet**

ETHAN ALLEN®

Ethan Allen Interiors, Inc., is a leading manufacturer and retailer of home furnishings in 291 retail stores in the United States and abroad. The following is adapted from Ethan Allen's balance sheet as of September 30, 2008. Dollars are in millions.

Cash	$ 80	Accounts Payable	$ 26
Accounts Receivable	12	Wages and Other Expenses Payable	111
Inventories	188	Long-term Debt	203
Other Current Assets	26	Other Long-term Liabilities	44
Property, Plant, and Equipment	355	Contributed Capital	356
Other Assets	99	Retained Earnings	20

Assume that the following events occurred in the quarter ended December 31. Dollars are in millions.

a. Paid $2 cash for an additional "other asset."
b. Issued additional shares of stock for $2 in cash.
c. Purchased property, plant, and equipment; paid $2 in cash and signed a note to pay the remaining $9 in two years.
d. Sold, at cost, other assets for $1 cash.
e. Conducted negotiations to purchase a sawmill, which is expected to cost $36.

Required:

1. Analyze transactions (a)–(e) to determine their effects on the accounting equation. Use the format shown in the demonstration case on page 68.
2. Record the transaction effects determined in requirement 1 using journal entries.
3. Summarize the journal entry effects from requirement 2 using T-accounts. Use the September 2008 ending balances as the beginning balances for the October–December 2008 quarter.
4. Explain your response to event (e).
5. Prepare a classified balance sheet at December 31, 2008.
6. As of December 31, 2008, has the financing for Ethan Allen's investment in assets primarily come from liabilities or stockholders' equity?

GROUP B PROBLEMS

PB2-1 Determining Financial Statement Effects of Various Transactions

LO2, 5

Swish Watch Corporation manufactures, sells, and services expensive, ugly watches. The company has been in business for three years. At the end of the most recent year, 2009, the accounting records reported total assets of $2,255,000 and total liabilities of $1,780,000. During the current year, 2010, the following summarized events occurred:

a. Issued additional shares of stock for $109,000 cash.
b. Borrowed $186,000 cash from the bank and signed a 10-year note.
c. A stockholder sold $5,000 of his stock in Swish Watch Corporation to another investor.
d. Built an addition on the factory for $200,000 and paid cash to the construction company.
e. Purchased equipment for the new addition for $44,000, paying $12,000 in cash and signing a six-month note for the balance.
f. Returned a $4,000 piece of equipment, from (e), because it proved to be defective; received a cash refund.

Required:

1. Complete the spreadsheet that follows, using plus (+) for increases and minus (−) for decreases for each account. The first transaction is used as an example.

	Assets			=	Liabilities	+	Stockholders' Equity	
	Cash	Equipment	Building	=	Notes Payable		Contributed Capital	Retained Earnings
(a)	+109,000						+109,000	

2. Did you include event (c) in the spreadsheet? Why?
3. Based on beginning balances plus the completed spreadsheet, provide the following amounts (show computations):
   a. Total assets at the end of the year.
   b. Total liabilities at the end of the year.
   c. Total stockholders' equity at the end of the year.
4. As of December 31, 2010, has the financing for Swish Watch Corporation's investment in assets primarily come from liabilities or stockholders' equity?

LO2, 3, 4, 5   **PB2-2 Recording Transactions (in a Journal and T-Accounts); Preparing and Interpreting the Balance Sheet**

Bearings & Brakes Corporation (B&B) was incorporated as a private company on June 1, 2010. The company's accounts included the following at June 30, 2010:

Accounts Payable	$ 50,000	Land	$444,000
Factory Building	500,000	Notes Payable	5,000
Cash	90,000	Retained Earnings	966,000
Contributed Capital	170,000	Supplies	9,000
Equipment	148,000		

During the month of July, the company had the following activities:

a. Issued 6,000 shares of stock for $600,000 cash.
b. Borrowed $60,000 cash from a local bank, payable June 30, 2012.
c. Bought a factory building for $166,000; paid $66,000 in cash and signed a three-year note for the balance.
d. Paid cash for equipment that cost $90,000.
e. Purchased supplies for $90,000 on account.

Required:

1. Analyze transactions (a)–(e) to determine their effects on the accounting equation. Use the format shown in the demonstration case on page 68.
2. Record the transaction effects determined in requirement 1 using a journal entry format.
3. Summarize the journal entry effects from requirement 2 using T-accounts.
4. Prepare a classified balance sheet at July 31, 2010.
5. As of July 31, 2010, has the financing for B&B's investment in assets primarily come from liabilities or stockholders' equity?

LO2, 3, 4, 5   **PB2-3 Recording Transactions (in a Journal and T-Accounts); Preparing and Interpreting the Balance Sheet**

Starbucks

Starbucks is a coffee company—a big coffee company. During a 10-year period, the number of Starbucks locations grew from 165 to over 5,800 stores in 30 countries. The following is adapted from Starbucks's annual report for the year ended September 30, 2008, and dollars are reported in thousands.

Cash	$ 269,800	Accounts Payable	$ 324,900
Accounts Receivable	329,500	Short-term Bank Loans	1,864,800
Inventories	692,800	Long-term Debt	549,600
Other Current Assets	455,900	Other Long-term Liabilities	442,400
Property, Plant, and Equipment	2,956,400	Contributed Capital	40,100
Other Long-term Assets	968,200	Retained Earnings	2,450,800

Assume that the following events occurred in the following quarter, which ended December 31, 2008. Dollars are in thousands.

a. Paid $10,000 cash for additional other long-term assets.
b. Issued additional shares of stock for $5,100 in cash.
c. Purchased property, plant, and equipment; paid $11,200 in cash and signed additional long-term loans for $9,500.
d. Sold, at cost, other long-term assets for $6,000 cash.
e. Conducted negotiations to purchase a coffee farm, which is expected to cost $8,400.

Required:

1. Analyze transactions (a)–(e) to determine their effects on the accounting equation. Use the format shown in the demonstration case on page 68.
2. Record the transaction effects determined in requirement 1 using journal entries.

3. Summarize the journal entry effects from requirement 2 using T-accounts. Use the September 2008 ending balances (reported above) as the beginning balances for the October–December 2008 quarter.

4. Explain your response to event (*e*).

5. Prepare a classified balance sheet at December 31, 2008.

6. As of December 31, 2008, has the financing for the investment in assets made by Starbucks primarily come from liabilities or stockholders' equity?

SKILLS DEVELOPMENT CASES

S2-1 Finding and Analyzing Financial Information   LO1, 4, 5

Refer to the financial statements of The Home Depot in Appendix A at the end of this book, or download the annual report from the *Cases* section of the text's Web site at www.mhhe.com/phillips3e.

Required:

1. What is the company's fiscal year-end? Where did you find the exact date?

2. Use the company's balance sheet to determine the amounts in the accounting equation (A = L + SE).

3. What is the amount of the company's current liabilities on February 1, 2009? Are current assets sufficient to cover current liabilities?

4. Has financing for the company's investment in assets primarily come from liabilities or stockholders' equity?

S2-2 Finding and Analyzing Financial Information   LO1, 4, 5

Lowe's

Refer to the financial statements of The Home Depot in Appendix A and Lowe's in Appendix B at the end of this book, or download the annual reports from the *Cases* section of the text's Web site at www.mhhe.com/phillips3e.

Required:

1. Use the company's balance sheet to determine the amounts in the accounting equation (A = L + SE). Is Lowe's or The Home Depot larger in terms of total assets?

2. Does Lowe's have more or less current liabilities than The Home Depot at the end of January 2009? Which company has a larger current ratio?

3. On the balance sheet, Lowe's reports inventories of $8,209,000,000. Does this amount represent the expected selling price? Why or why not?

4. Has financing for Lowe's investment in assets primarily come from liabilities or stockholders' equity at January 30, 2009? Thinking back to Chapter 1, what does this imply about the risk assumed by Lowe's investors, relative to those investing in The Home Depot?

S2-3 Team Research, Financial Analysis, Technology, and Communication: LO1, 4, 5
Examining the Balance Sheet

As a team, select an industry to analyze. Using your Web browser, each team member should access the annual report or 10-K for one publicly traded company in the industry, with each member selecting a different company. (See S1-3 in Chapter 1 for a description of possible resources for these tasks.)

Required:

1. On an individual basis, each team member should write a short report that lists the following information.
   a. The date of the balance sheet.
   b. The major noncurrent asset accounts and any significant changes in them.
   c. The major noncurrent liability accounts and any significant changes in them.
   d. Any significant changes in total stockholders' equity.
   e. Whether financing for the investment in assets primarily comes from liabilities or stockholders' equity.

2. Then, as a team, write a short report comparing and contrasting your companies using the above dimensions. Discuss any similarities across the companies that you as a team observe, and provide potential explanations for any differences discovered.

LO1, 2, 5   **S2-4** **Ethical Reasoning, Critical Thinking, and Communication: A Real-Life Fraud**

In the world of financial fraud, a "Ponzi scheme" is famous. Here is the story behind how the scam got its name. Charles Ponzi started the Security Exchange Company on December 26, 1919. He thought he had discovered a way to purchase American stamps in a foreign country at significantly lower amounts than they were worth in the United States. He claimed his idea was so successful that anyone who gave money to his company would be repaid their original loan plus 50 percent interest within 90 days. Friends and family quickly offered their money to Ponzi and they were handsomely rewarded, being repaid their original loan and the 50 percent interest within just 45 days. Thanks to an article in *The New York Times*, word spread quickly about Ponzi's business, attracting thousands of people seeking a similar payback. He might have had a successful business had his idea actually worked. The problem, however, was that it didn't. The 50 percent interest paid to early investors did not come from the profits of a successful underlying business idea (which didn't even exist) but instead was obtained fraudulently from funds contributed by later lenders. Eventually, the Ponzi scheme collapsed on August 10, 1920, after an auditor examined his accounting records.

Required:

1. Assume that on December 27, 1919, Ponzi's first three lenders provided his company with $5,000 each. Use the basic accounting equation to show the effects of these transactions on December 27, 1919.
2. If the first two lenders are repaid their original loan amounts plus the 50 percent interest promised to them, how much cash is left in Ponzi's business to repay the third lender? Given what you discovered, how was it possible for Ponzi's company to remain in "business" for over eight months?
3. Who was harmed by Ponzi's scheme?

Epilogue: After taking in nearly $15 million from 40,000 people, Ponzi's company failed with just $1.5 million in total assets. Ponzi spent four years in prison before jumping bail, to become involved in fraudulently selling swampland in Florida. We're not kidding. In December 2008, Bernard Madoff was arrested for using a modern-day Ponzi scheme to defraud investors of $65,000,000,000. On June 29, 2009, he was sentenced to 150 years in prison.

LO1, 5   **S2-5** **Ethical Reasoning, Critical Thinking, and Communication: A Mini-Case**

You work as an accountant for a small land development company that desperately needs additional financing to continue in business. The president of your company is meeting with the manager of a local bank at the end of the month to try to obtain this financing. The president has approached you with two ideas to improve the company's reported financial position. First, he claims that because a big part of the company's value comes from its knowledgeable and dedicated employees, you should report their "Intellectual Abilities" as an asset on the balance sheet. Second, he claims that although the local economy is doing poorly and almost no one is buying land or new houses, he is optimistic that eventually things will turn around. For this reason, he asks you to continue reporting the company's land on the balance sheet at its cost, rather than the much lower amount that real estate appraisers say it's really worth.

Required:

1. Thinking back to Chapter 1, why do you think the president is so concerned with the amount of assets reported on the balance sheet?
2. What accounting concept introduced in Chapter 2 relates to the president's first suggestion to report "Intellectual Abilities" as an asset?
3. What accounting concept introduced in Chapter 2 relates to the president's second suggestion to continue reporting land at its cost?
4. Who might be hurt by the president's suggestions, if you were to do as he asks? What should you do?

S2-6 **Financial Analysis and Critical Thinking: Evaluating the Reliability of a Balance Sheet**   LO1, 4, 5

Betsey Jordan asked a local bank for a $50,000 loan to expand her small company. The bank asked Betsey to submit a financial statement of the business to supplement the loan application. Betsey prepared the following balance sheet.

Balance Sheet
June 30, 2010

Assets	
Cash	$ 9,000
Inventory	30,000
Equipment	46,000
Personal Residence (monthly payments, $2,800)	300,000
Remaining Assets	20,000
Total Assets	$405,000
Liabilities	
Short-term Debt to Suppliers	$ 62,000
Long-term Debt on Equipment	38,000
Total Debt	100,000
Stockholders' Equity	305,000
Total Liabilities and Stockholders' Equity	$405,000

Required:

The balance sheet has several flaws. However, there is at least one major deficiency. Identify it and explain its significance.

S2-7 **Using Technology to Analyze Transactions and Prepare a Balance Sheet**   LO2

Elizabeth Arden, Inc.

Assume you recently obtained a part-time accounting position at the corporate headquarters of Elizabeth Arden, Inc., in Miami Lakes, Florida. Elizabeth Arden is a leading marketer and manufacturer of prestige beauty products, prominently led by the Red Door line of fragrances. The following table summarizes accounts and their balances (in thousands) reported by Elizabeth Arden, Inc., in a recent September 30 balance sheet.

www.mhhe.com/phillips3e

Cash	$ 14,300	Short-term Notes Payable	$ 125,000
Accounts Receivable	285,400	Accounts Payable	111,800
Inventories	199,700	Other Current Liabilities	75,700
Other Current Assets	31,600	Long-term Debt	323,600
Property and Equipment	35,800	Other Long-term Liabilities	10,100
Other Noncurrent Assets	224,100	Contributed Capital	101,800
		Retained Earnings	42,900

Assume the company entered into the following transactions during October (amounts in thousands):

(a) Purchased an additional manufacturing facility at a cost of $15,000 by issuing a promissory note that becomes payable in three years.
(b) Used $7,000 cash to repay one of the short-term loans.
(c) Issued additional stock for $20,000 cash contributed by stockholders.
(d) Used cash to buy land for $8,000.

Required:

The controller at Elizabeth Arden has asked you to create a spreadsheet in which to display:

a.   The account balances at September 30.
b.   The effects of the four October transactions.
c.   Totals that combine the September 30 balances with the October transactions. You feel like you might be ready to tackle this assignment, but just to be sure, you e-mail your friend Owen for advice. Here's his reply.

From: Owentheaccountant@yahoo.com
To: Helpme@hotmail.com
Cc:
Subject: Excel Help

Wow, I can't believe you gave up that great job at EA. Good thing you landed another one so quickly!

1. My thinking is that you'll really impress your boss if you set up the spreadsheet to look like a bunch of T-accounts, one beside another. Use two columns for each balance sheet account (with the account name spanning the two columns) to make it look just like a T-account. You do remember how to use the cell merge command to make a header span two columns, right? If not, check the last e-mail I sent you. Here's a screenshot of how your worksheet might look just before you enter the October transactions.

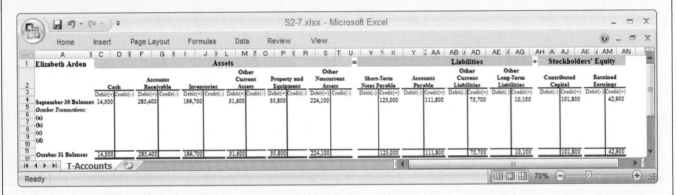

2. See S1-7 for my cell merge advice. For extra spreadsheet skills, you might also try creating a balance sheet with cells that are linked to the corresponding cells in the T-accounts. To do this, open a worksheet in the same file as the T-accounts. Then click on a cell in the balance sheet worksheet where you want to import a number from the T-accounts, then type =, then click on the tab for the T-account worksheet, click on the cell with the total to be transferred, and then press enter. This links the cells so that any changes to the T-accounts automatically update the balance sheet. Also, Excel will let you hide row and column gridlines if you want. Just search Excel's help index for "hide gridlines."

3. I guess the only thing that's left is to remind you that to compute the ending balances in each T-account you have to add the increases to the beginning balance and subtract the decreases. So, to compute the totals for a particular account, your formula might look like =(SUM(C4:C9)-SUM(D5:D9)).

4. Oh yeah, when you're all done, don't forget to save the file using a name that uniquely identifies you.

CONTINUING CASE

LO1, 2, 3, 4, 5   **CC2 Accounting for the Establishment of a Business**

Nicole has decided that she is going to start her business Nicole's Getaway Spa (NGS). A lot has to be done when starting a new business. Here are some transactions that have occurred prior to April 30, 2010.

a.   Received $80,000 cash when issuing 8,000 new shares.
b.   Purchased some land by paying $2,000 cash and signing a note payable for $7,000 due in 2013.
c.   Hired a new esthetician for a salary of $1,000 a month, starting next month.

d. Bought $1,000 in soaps and aromatherapy supplies for the spa on credit.
e. NGS purchased a company car for $18,000 cash (list price of $21,000) to assist in running errands for the business.
f. Nicole sold 100 of her own personal shares to Raea Gooding for $300.
g. Paid $350 of the amount owed in (d).

Required:

1. For each of the events, prepare journal entries if a transaction exists, checking that debits equal credits. If a transaction does not exist explain why there is no transaction.
2. Assuming that the beginning balances in each of the accounts are zero, complete T-accounts to summarize the transactions (a)–(g).
3. Prepare a classified balance sheet at April 30, 2010, using the information given in the transactions.
4. Calculate the current ratio at April 30, 2010. What does this ratio indicate about the ability of NGS to pay its current liabilities?

CHAPTER 3

Reporting Operating Results on the Income Statement

YOUR LEARNING OBJECTIVES

Understand the business

LO1   Describe common operating transactions and select appropriate income statement account titles.

Study the accounting methods

LO2   Explain and apply the revenue and matching principles.

LO3   Analyze, record, and summarize the effects of operating transactions, using the accounting equation, journal entries, and T-accounts.

LO4   Prepare an unadjusted trial balance.

Evaluate the results

LO5   Describe limitations of the income statement.

Review the chapter

THAT WAS
THEN

In the previous chapter, you learned how to analyze, record, and summarize the effects of transactions on balance sheet accounts.

Lecture Presentation-LP3
www.mhhe.com/phillips3e

FOCUS COMPANY: PIZZA AROMA, Ithaca, NY

I n Chapter 2, Mauricio Rosa, owner-manager of Pizza Aroma, established his new gourmet pizza business. Using money he had contributed plus a loan from the bank, he purchased the ovens, restaurant booths, and other equipment he needed to run the business. His next step is to draw customers into the restaurant and provide them with the service that will keep them coming back. These day-to-day operating activities will determine whether Pizza Aroma makes a profit.

The first goal of this chapter is to help you understand common operating activities and see how an income statement indicates whether a business generated a profit (or loss). Then, we'll show how the transaction analysis approach from Chapter 2 can be used to analyze and record transactions affecting the income statement. Finally, at the end of the chapter, we will highlight some limitations of the income statement.

THIS IS
NOW

This chapter focuses on analyzing, recording, and summarizing the effects of operating transactions on balance sheet and income statement accounts.

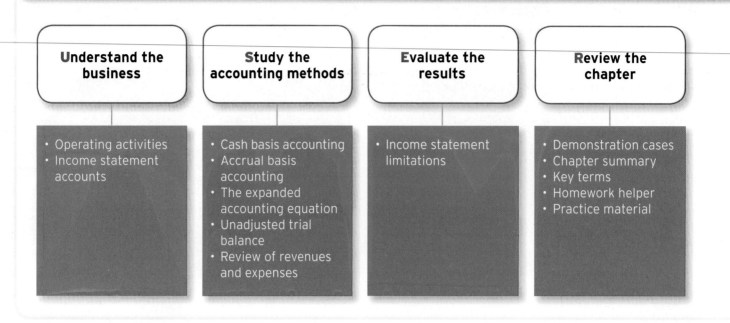

Understand the business	Study the accounting methods	Evaluate the results	Review the chapter
• Operating activities • Income statement accounts	• Cash basis accounting • Accrual basis accounting • The expanded accounting equation • Unadjusted trial balance • Review of revenues and expenses	• Income statement limitations	• Demonstration cases • Chapter summary • Key terms • Homework helper • Practice material

Understand the Business

OPERATING ACTIVITIES

Learning Objective 1
Describe common operating transactions and select appropriate income statement account titles.

Operating activities are the day-to-day functions involved in running a business. Unlike the investing and financing activities in Chapter 2 that occur infrequently and typically produce long-lasting effects, operating activities occur regularly and often have a shorter duration of effect. Operating activities include buying goods and services from suppliers and employees and selling goods and services to customers and then collecting cash from them. The period from buying goods and services through to collecting cash from customers is known as the operating cycle. Exhibit 3.1 illustrates the operating cycle for Pizza Aroma.

EXHIBIT 3.1 | **Typical Operating Cycle Activities**

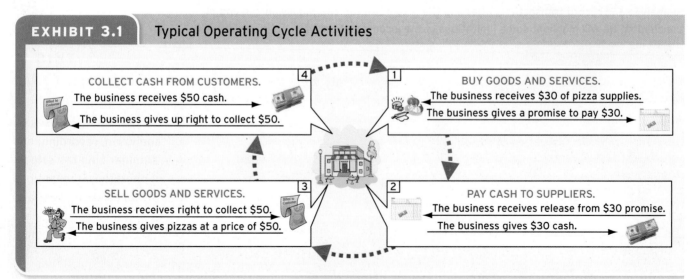

Although most businesses have the same steps in their operating cycles, the length of time for each step varies from company to company. For example, Pizza Aroma usually collects cash from restaurant customers within minutes of making a sale, whereas the breakfast cereal company Kellogg's might wait several weeks to collect on sales it makes to grocery stores.

To be successful, Mauricio must closely monitor Pizza Aroma's operating activities. **Operating activities are the primary source of revenues and expenses** and, thus, can determine whether a company earns a profit (or incurs a loss). Although Mauricio may intuitively sense how his business is doing, a more reliable management approach is to evaluate the revenues and expenses reported on the income statement. Mauricio takes a quick look at the income statement Laurie had prepared (Exhibit 3.2) based on the operating activities that were expected for Pizza Aroma (in Chapter 1). This projected income statement will provide a benchmark for him to evaluate actual results.

EXHIBIT 3.2	Income Statement		
			Explanation
PIZZA AROMA, INC. **Income Statement** **For the Month Ended September 30, 2010**			Who: Name of the business What: Title of the statement When: Accounting period
Revenues			
Pizza Revenue	$11,000		Revenue earned from the sale of pizza to customers in September
Total Revenues	11,000		**Total amount earned during September**
Expenses			
Supplies Expense	4,000		Cost of pizza ingredients used-up in September
Wages Expense	2,000		Cost of employee wages for work done in September
Rent Expense	1,500		Cost of rent for the month of September
Utilities Expense	600		Cost of utilities used in September
Insurance Expense	300		Cost of insurance coverage for September
Advertising Expense	100		Cost of advertising done in September
Income Tax Expense	500		Cost of taxes on September's income
Total Expenses	9,000		**Total expenses incurred in September to generate revenues**
Net Income	$ 2,000		**Difference between total revenues and total expenses**

INCOME STATEMENT ACCOUNTS

The income statement summarizes the financial impact of operating activities undertaken by the company during the accounting period. It includes three main sections: revenues, expenses, and net income.

Revenues

Revenues are the amounts a business charges its customers when it provides goods or services. If Pizza Aroma sells 1,100 pizzas in September and charges $10 per pizza, Pizza Revenue would total $11,000. The amount of revenues earned during the period is the first thing reported in the body of the income statement.

Expenses

Expenses are costs of operating the business, incurred to generate revenues in the period covered by the income statement. When a business uses up its resources to generate revenues during the period, it reports an expense, regardless of when the

> **YOU SHOULD KNOW**
>
> **Revenues:** Amounts earned by selling goods or services to customers. **Expenses:** Costs of business necessary to earn revenues.

resources were or will be paid for. Expenses are reported in the body of the income statement after revenues. Some of Pizza Aroma's typical expenses are listed in the income statement shown in Exhibit 3.2.

Net Income

YOU SHOULD KNOW

Net income: The excess of revenues over expenses.

COACH'S TIP

A more complete list of revenue and expense account titles appears in the Homework Helper section on page 120.

YOU SHOULD KNOW

Time period assumption: The long life of a company is divided into shorter periods, such as months, quarters, and years.

Net income is a total that is calculated by subtracting expenses from revenues; it is not an account like Pizza Revenue or Wages Expense. Because it is a total, net income summarizes the overall impact of revenues and expenses in a single number. It is called a net loss if expenses are greater than revenues, and net income if revenues are greater than expenses. **Net income indicates the amount by which stockholders' equity increases as a result of a company's profitable operations.** For this reason, net income (or loss) is a closely watched measure of a company's success.

Exhibit 3.2 shows how revenues, expenses, and net income would be reported in Pizza Aroma's income statement. Each account title describes the specific type of revenue or expense arising from the business's particular operations. This is true for all companies. Pizza Aroma reports "Pizza Revenues," but Blockbuster reports "Movie Rental Revenues." Google reports "Traffic Acquisition Expenses" and Southwest Airlines reports "Landing Fee Expenses." You'll become more comfortable with various account titles as this course progresses but to keep things simple right now we'll stick to common types of revenues and expenses.

The income statement in Exhibit 3.2 is for the month ended September 30, 2010. As it turns out, September 30, 2010, is a Thursday. You might wonder what's so special about this date. The answer is that there is nothing particularly special about this date—it's just the last day of the month. By dividing the company's long life into meaningful and shorter chunks of time, Mauricio can measure and evaluate Pizza Aroma's financial performance on a timely basis. This is known in accounting as the **time period assumption**. If net income is low in the current month, Mauricio will find out about it quickly and be able to take steps to become more profitable in the following month.

Notice that the income statement reports the financial effects of business activities that occurred during just the current period. They relate only to the current period. They do not have a lingering financial impact beyond the end of the current period. This is a key distinction between the income statement and the balance sheet. **The revenues and expenses on an income statement report the financial impact of activities in just the current period whereas items on a balance sheet will continue to have a financial impact beyond the end of the current period. Balance sheet accounts are considered permanent whereas income statement accounts are considered temporary.** Another way people describe this difference is that **the balance sheet takes stock of what exists at a point in time whereas the income statement depicts a flow of what happened over a period of time.**

Solution to Self-Study Practice

	Yes/No	Account Title
1.	Yes	Service Fee Revenue
2.	No	(a building is an asset not an expense)
3.	Yes	Delivery Expense
4.	No	(supplies are assets until used up)
5.	Yes	Salaries and Wages Expense

How's it going?   Self-Study Practice

For each item listed below, indicate whether the company should report it on the income statement this period (yes/no). If yes, indicate an appropriate account title for the item described.

	Description	Yes/No	Account Title
1.	Bank of America charges customers a monthly service fee.	Yes	
2.	Target buys a new building to use as a retail store.		
3.	Dell pays to deliver computers to customers.		
4.	Pizza Hut buys supplies to be used next month.		
5.	Abercrombie pays this week's wages to employees.		

After you have finished, check your answers with the solution in the margin.

Spotlight On ETHICS

www.mhhe.com/phillips3e

35 Days Hath September?

It seems some managers—specifically those at Computer Associates (CA)—haven't learned the **time period assumption.** CA was charged with financial statement fraud for improperly recording 35 days of sales in September–a month that has only 30 days. To make it look like managers had met their September sales targets, CA included the first five days of sales from October in its September income statement. This accounting fraud led managers to be paid bonuses they hadn't earned and tricked investors into thinking CA was a successful company. When the truth was revealed later, CA's stockholders quickly abandoned the company, causing its stock price to fall 43 percent in a single day. CA ultimately paid stockholders $225 million to make up for its bad accounting and agreed to ensure all inappropriate management bonuses were paid back to the company. In addition, several marketing and accounting personnel were sent to jail. Proper revenue reporting is obviously a very serious matter.

Study the Accounting Methods

CASH BASIS ACCOUNTING

What's a good way to determine whether you're doing well financially? Many people simply look at the balance in their bank accounts to gauge their financial performance. If the overall balance increased this month, they take that as a sign that they've done a good job of managing their finances. If it has gone down, that's a clue they need to tame their spending next month. The reason that the change in your bank balance tends to give a decent measure of financial performance is that your cash flows (in and out) occur close in time to the activities that cause those cash flows. Reporting your income on this basis, called **cash basis accounting**, is fine for managing personal finances, but not running a business.

Cash basis accounting doesn't measure financial performance very well when transactions are conducted using credit rather than cash. Credit often introduces a significant delay between the time an activity occurs and the time it impacts a bank account balance. If you are paid for work once a month, for example, the results of your hard work don't show up until the end of the month. Similarly, if you go crazy with your credit card at the mall, these transactions won't affect your bank balance until you pay the bill the following month.

Because most companies use credit for their transactions, cash basis accounting is not likely to correspond to the business activities that actually occur during a given period. UPS, for example, often pays its employees to deliver packages in one month but doesn't get paid by its customers until the following month. Under cash basis accounting, UPS would report expenses in Month 1 but wouldn't report revenues until it received payments from its customers in Month 2. This leads to a rather distorted view of the company's financial performance, as shown in Exhibit 3.3.

Video 3.1
www.mhhe.com/phillips3e

YOU SHOULD KNOW

Cash basis accounting: Reports revenues when cash is received and expenses when cash is paid; not allowed under GAAP.

EXHIBIT 3.3	Cash Basis Can Distort Reported Profits

	MONTH 1 (Delivery occurs, and **cash is paid**)		MONTH 2 (No delivery, but **cash is received**)	
Revenues	$	0	Revenues	$15,000
Expenses		10,000	Expenses	0
Net Income (Loss)	$(10,000)		Net Income	$15,000

Under cash basis accounting, the company would report a net loss in Month 1 and a huge net income in Month 2, when the truth is the business activities generate revenue of $15,000, expenses of $10,000, and net income of $5,000, all of which relate to the activities that occurred in Month 1 when the packages were delivered. A better method of accounting is needed—one that reports the revenues and related expenses during the same period.

ACCRUAL BASIS ACCOUNTING

Learning Objective 2
Explain and apply the revenue and matching principles.

YOU SHOULD KNOW

Accrual basis accounting:
Reports revenues when they are earned and expenses when they are incurred, regardless of the timing of cash receipts or payments; required under GAAP.

An alternative method of accounting would be for UPS to report revenues and expenses when packages are delivered, regardless of when cash is received or paid. This approach, called **accrual basis accounting**, produces a better measure of the profits arising from the company's activities. As shown in Exhibit 3.4, accrual accounting would require that UPS report all its revenues, expenses, and net income in the period the delivery occurs (Month 1). In the following month, UPS does not deliver packages, so it does not report revenues and expenses. According to GAAP and IFRS, the accrual basis is the only acceptable method for external reporting of income. The cash basis can be used internally by some small companies, but GAAP and IFRS do not allow it for external reporting. The "rule of accrual" is that the financial effects of business activities are measured and reported when the activities actually occur, not when the cash related to them is received or paid. That is, revenues are recognized when they are earned and expenses when they are incurred. The two basic accounting principles that determine when revenues and expenses are recognized under accrual basis accounting are called the *revenue principle* and the *matching principle*.

EXHIBIT 3.4	Accrual Basis Relates Profit to Underlying Activities

	MONTH 1 (Delivery occurs, and cash is paid)		MONTH 2 (No delivery, but cash is received)	
Revenues		$15,000	Revenues	$ 0
Expenses		10,000	Expenses	0
Net Income		$ 5,000	Net Income	$ 0

Revenue Principle—Revenue Recognition

YOU SHOULD KNOW

Revenue principle: The requirement under accrual basis accounting to record revenues when they are earned, not necessarily when cash is received for them.

According to the **revenue principle**, revenues should be recognized when they are earned. The word *recognized* means revenues are measured and recorded in the accounting system. The word *earned* means the company has performed the acts promised to the customer. For most businesses, these conditions are met at the point of delivery of goods or services.

All companies expect to receive cash in exchange for providing goods and services, but the timing of cash receipts does not dictate when revenues are recognized. Instead, the key factor in determining when to recognize revenue is whether the company has provided goods or services to customers during the accounting period. Regardless of the length of the period (month, quarter, or year), cash can be received (1) in the same period as the goods or services are provided, (2) in a period before they are provided, or (3) in a period after they are provided, as shown on the timeline in Exhibit 3.5. Let's see how to handle each of these cases.

1 ▷ Cash is received in the **same** period as the goods or services are provided. This is a common occurrence for Pizza Aroma. Pizza Aroma earns revenue by delivering pizza to the customer as ordered. Within minutes, Pizza Aroma receives cash from the customer.

| EXHIBIT 3.5 | Timing of Reporting Revenue versus Cash Receipts |

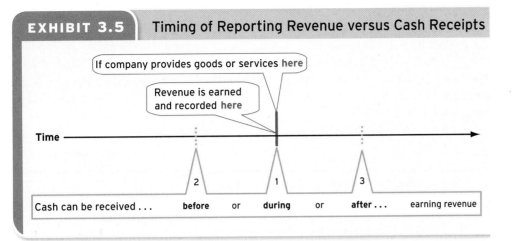

> **2** Cash is received in a period **before** goods or services are provided. This situation can occur when Pizza Aroma receives cash for gift cards that customers can use to pay for pizza in the future. Pizza Aroma will record the cash received, but since it hasn't delivered pizza for these customers, no revenue is recorded yet. Instead, Pizza Aroma has an obligation to accept the gift card as payment for pizza in the future. This obligation is a liability called **Unearned Revenue**, and it is recorded on the balance sheet equal in amount to the cash received for the gift card. Businesses that routinely receive cash before delivering goods or services include airlines, magazine publishers, and insurance companies.

> **3** Cash is to be received in a period **after** goods or services are provided. This situation typically arises when a company sells to a customer on account. Selling on account means that the company provides goods or services to a customer not for cash, but instead for the right to collect cash in the future. This right is an asset called Accounts Receivable. Thus, if Pizza Aroma delivers pizza sold on account to a college organization in September, it will report Pizza Revenue on the September income statement. Accounts Receivable will be reported on the balance sheet until Pizza Aroma receives the customer's payment, at which time Pizza Aroma will increase its Cash account and decrease its Accounts Receivable. No additional revenue is reported when the customer's payment is received because the revenue was already recorded when the pizza was delivered.

> **YOU SHOULD KNOW**
>
> **Unearned Revenue:** A liability representing a company's obligation to provide goods or services to customers in the future.

Spotlight On FINANCIAL REPORTING

Revenue Recognition Policy

Every company reports its revenue recognition policy in its notes to the financial statements. Pizza Aroma follows the same revenue recognition policy as Papa John's, which explains its policy as follows.

Papa John's International Inc.

Restaurant sales are recognized as revenues when the products are delivered to or carried out by customers.

It's worthwhile making sure you understand what sparks the recording of revenues because, in the next section, you'll see that this also triggers the recording of expenses. To ensure that you have a handle on this, spend a minute on the following Self-Study Practice.

Solution to Self-Study Practice

1. $32,000.

2. $5,200 in June (the remaining $3,000 will be recognized as revenue in July; until then, it is reported as a liability called Unearned Revenue).

3. No revenue in June for this activity; revenue was earned and recognized in May (along with Accounts Receivable). The cash received in June reduces Accounts Receivable.

How's it going?   Self-Study Practice

The following transactions are typical operating activities for Florida Flippers, a scuba diving and instruction company. Indicate the amount of revenue, if any, that should be recognized in June for each activity.

Operating Activity	Amount of Revenue Earned in June
1. In June, Florida Flippers provided $32,000 in diving instruction to customers for cash.	32,000
2. In June, new customers paid $8,200 cash for diving trips to be provided by Florida Flippers; $5,200 in trips were made in June and the rest will be provided in July.	5,200
3. In June, customers paid $3,900 cash for instruction they received in May.	0

After you have finished, check your answers with the solution in the margin.

Matching Principle—Expense Recognition

YOU SHOULD KNOW

Matching principle: The requirement under accrual basis accounting to record expenses in the same period as the revenues they generate, not necessarily the period in which cash is paid for them.

The business activities that generate revenues also create expenses. **Under accrual basis accounting, expenses are recognized in the same period as the revenues to which they relate,** not necessarily the period in which cash is paid for them. For example, for Pizza Aroma to deliver pizza in September, it must rent space in a building and have its employees work that month. Under accrual basis accounting, Pizza Aroma would report rent expense and wages expense in September, even if the rent were paid in August and the wages were paid in October. This is what accountants call the **matching principle:** record expenses in the same period as the revenues with which they can be reasonably associated. If an expense cannot be directly associated with revenues, it is recorded in the period that the underlying business activity occurs. For example, because it's not clear how or when advertising affects revenue, advertising expense is simply reported in the period that ads are run. Notice that it is the timing of the underlying business activities, not the cash payments, that dictates when expenses are recognized. Cash payments may occur (1) at the same time as, (2) before, or (3) after the related expenses are incurred to generate revenue, as shown in Exhibit 3.6.

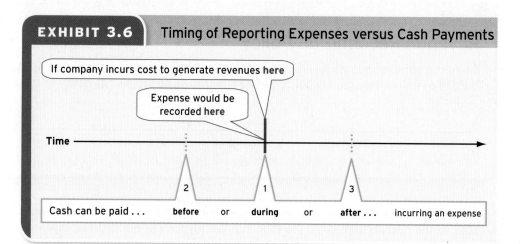

EXHIBIT 3.6   Timing of Reporting Expenses versus Cash Payments

1 ▷ **Cash is paid at the same time as the cost is incurred to generate revenue.** Although this isn't as common in business as in your personal life, expenses are sometimes paid for in the period that they arise. For example, Pizza Aroma could spend $50 cash for balloons to celebrate its grand opening this month. It would report this cost on this month's income statement because the balloons were used for an activity occurring this month. In other words, the benefits of incurring the cost are entirely used up in the current accounting period.

2 ▷ **Cash is paid before the expense is incurred to generate revenue.** It is common for businesses to pay for something that provides benefits only in future periods. For example, Pizza Aroma might buy paper napkins now but does not use them until next month. Given the matching principle, the expense from using these supplies is reported next month when the supplies are used to earn revenue, not in the current month when purchased. This month, the supplies represent an asset because they will benefit a future period. When they are used later, Supplies Expense will be reported on next month's income statement and the asset Supplies will decrease. Similar situations arise when a company prepays rent or insurance.

3 ▷ **Cash is paid after the cost is incurred to generate revenue.** Although rent is paid and supplies are purchased before they are used, many costs are paid after receiving and using goods or services. For example, Pizza Aroma uses electricity to heat the ovens and light the restaurant this month but does not pay for its electricity usage until next month. Because the cost of the electricity relates to revenues earned now, it represents an expense that will be reported on this month's income statement. Because the cost has not yet been paid at the end of the month, the balance sheet reports a corresponding liability called Accounts Payable. Similar situations arise when employees work in the current period but are not paid their wages until the following period. This period's wages are reported as Wages Expense on the income statement and any unpaid wages are reported as Wages Payable on the balance sheet.

> **COACH'S TIP**
>
> Promises exchanged for promises are not considered transactions, as you learned in Chapter 2. Here, a service has been received in exchange for a promise (of future payment), so it is considered a transaction.

It's time for you to practice determining which costs should be reported as expenses on an income statement prepared using accrual basis accounting. As you work through the next Self-Study Practice, feel free to glance at Exhibit 3.6 for help.

💡 How's it going?   Self-Study Practice

The following transactions are typical operating activities for Florida Flippers, a scuba diving and instruction company. Indicate the amount of expense, if any, that should be recognized in June for each activity.

Operating Activity	Amount of Expense Incurred in June
1. In June, Florida Flippers paid $6,000 cash for insurance for July–December.	*0*
2. In June, Florida Flippers paid $4,000 in wages to employees who worked in June.	*4,000*
3. In June, Florida Flippers used $2,400 of electricity, to be paid in July.	*2400*

⌐ *After you have finished, check your answers with the solution in the margin.*

Solution to Self-Study Practice
1. No expense in June for the $6,000 payment; the $6,000 will be reported as an asset called Prepaid Insurance until used up in July–December.
2. $4,000.
3. $2,400; this cost relates to business activities in June, so the $2,400 is reported as an expense in June (a corresponding liability is reported on the balance sheet).

Learning Objective 3
Analyze, record, and summarize the effects of operating transactions, using the accounting equation, journal entries, and T-accounts.

Video 3.2
www.mhhe.com/phillips3e

THE EXPANDED ACCOUNTING EQUATION

When we introduced the basic accounting equation in Chapter 2, we didn't mention how to account for the income statement effects of operating activities. You already had enough to learn, relating to the effects of investing and financing activities on assets, liabilities, and contributed capital. The time has now come for you to learn how to analyze, record, and summarize the effects of operating activities. To do this, you first need to know how the debit/credit framework works with revenues and expenses.

Let's start with the basic accounting equation from Chapter 2. That is, assets equal liabilities plus stockholders' equity, or A = L + SE. For now, we're going to focus on the stockholders' equity category. As you already know from Chapters 1 and 2, stockholders' equity represents stockholders' claims on the company, which come from either (1) Contributed Capital, given to the company by stockholders in exchange for stock, or (2) Retained Earnings, generated by the company itself through profitable operations. Retained earnings is the part that expands to include revenues and expenses, as shown in Exhibit 3.7.

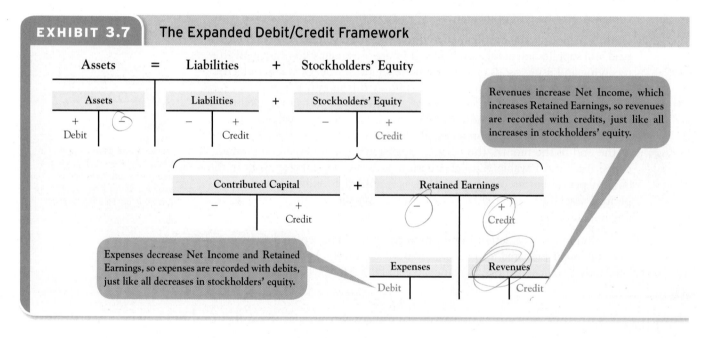

EXHIBIT 3.7 **The Expanded Debit/Credit Framework**

Take a moment to look at how Exhibit 3.7 encourages you to think of revenues and expenses as subcategories within retained earnings. They are shown this way because revenues and expenses eventually flow into Retained Earnings, but they aren't initially recorded there. Instead, each revenue and expense is accumulated in a separate account, making it easier to identify the amount to report for each item on the income statement. At the end of each accounting year, these separate revenue and expense accounts are transferred to (or "closed") into Retained Earnings through a process we'll demonstrate in Chapter 4. For now, just focus on learning how revenues and expenses are recorded to indicate increases and decreases in the company's earnings, with corresponding effects recorded in the company's asset and/or liability accounts.

Because revenue and expense accounts are subcategories of Retained Earnings, they are affected by debits and credits in the same way as all stockholders' equity accounts. You already know that increases in stockholders' equity are recorded on the right side. You also know that revenues increase net income, which increases the stockholders' equity account Retained Earnings. So putting these ideas together should lead to the conclusion that revenues are recorded on the right (credit). Here's the logic again: Increases in stockholders' equity are on the right, revenues increase stockholders' equity, so revenues are recorded on the right (credit). Decreases in stockholders' equity are recorded on the left side, so to show that expenses decrease net income and retained earnings, expenses are recorded on the left (debit). Exhibit 3.7 summarizes these effects.

Transaction Analysis, Recording, and Summarizing

To learn how to use your new knowledge of the revenue and matching principles, the expanded accounting equation, and the debit/credit framework, you'll need lots of practice. The best place to start is by reading our analysis of the following examples, which involve Pizza Aroma's operating activities during September.

(a) Provide Services for Cash In September, Pizza Aroma delivered pizza to customers for $15,000 cash. These activities qualify as accounting transactions because Pizza Aroma received cash and delivered pizza, which generates revenues. The increase in Cash (an asset) must be recorded (with a debit) along with the revenue (which, as a subcategory of stockholders' equity, is recorded with a credit). To indicate that the pizza deliveries increase revenue, which ultimately increases stockholders' equity, we use the notation (+R, +SE) in the journal entry. The increase in Cash is summarized in the Cash T-account, which carried a debit balance of $10,000 forward from the end of August (Chapter 2). The revenues earned are recorded in a new account called Pizza Revenue, which has a beginning balance of zero because the company began operating only this month.

1 Analyze

	Assets	=	Liabilities	+	Stockholders' Equity	
(a) Cash	+15,000	=			Pizza Revenue (+R)	+15,000

2 Record

(a)	dr Cash (+A)	15,000	
	cr Pizza Revenue (+R, +SE)		15,000

3 Summarize

dr +	Cash (A)	cr −	dr −	Pizza Revenue (R, SE)	cr +
Beg. bal.	10,000				0 Beg. bal.
(a)	15,000				15,000 (a)

(b) Receive Cash for Future Services Pizza Aroma sold three $100 gift cards at the beginning of September. Pizza Aroma receives cash but gives only gift cards, which creates an obligation to accept the gift cards as payment for pizzas in the future. This obligation is recorded as a liability called Unearned Revenue.

> **COACH'S TIP**
>
> The word *unearned* in the Unearned Revenue account means the company hasn't done everything it was paid to do. It has a liability to do the work or return the cash.

1 Analyze

	Assets	=	Liabilities	+	Stockholders' Equity
(b) Cash	+300	=	Unearned Revenue	+300	

2 Record

(b)	dr Cash (+A)	300	
	cr Unearned Revenue (+L)		300

3 Summarize

dr +	Cash (A)	cr −	dr −	Unearned Revenue (L)	cr +
Beg. bal.	10,000				0 Beg. bal.
(a)	15,000				300 (b)
(b)	300				

(c) Provide Services on Credit   Pizza Aroma **delivers $500 of pizza to a college organization, billing this customer on account.** Once again, this is another instance where revenues are recorded based on whether the work has been done, not whether cash has been received. Because the pizza has been delivered, Pizza Aroma has earned revenue and now has the right to collect $500 from the college organization. The right to collect money is an asset called Accounts Receivable.

1 Analyze

Assets	=	Liabilities	+	Stockholders' Equity
(c) Accounts Receivable +500 =				Pizza Revenue (+R) +500

2 Record

(c)	*dr* Accounts Receivable (+A)	500	
	cr Pizza Revenue (+R, +SE)		500

3 Summarize

dr +	Accounts Receivable (A)	*cr* −		*dr* −	Pizza Revenue (R, SE)	*cr* +
Beg. bal.	0				0	Beg. bal.
(c)	500				15,000	(a)
					500	(c)

(d) Receive Payment on Account   Pizza Aroma **received a $300 check from the college organization, as partial payment of its account balance.** This transaction does not involve additional pizza deliveries, so no additional revenue is generated. Instead, the receipt of cash reduces the amount that Pizza Aroma can collect from this customer in the future, so it causes a decrease in Accounts Receivable.

1 Analyze

Assets		=	Liabilities	+	Stockholders' Equity
(d) Cash	+300				
Accounts Receivable	−300				

2 Record

(d)	*dr* Cash (+A)	300	
	cr Accounts Receivable (−A)		300

3 Summarize

dr +	Cash (A)	*cr* −		*dr* +	Accounts Receivable (A)	*cr* −
Beg. bal.	10,000			Beg. bal.	0	
(a)	15,000			(c)	500	300	(d)
(b)	300					
(d)	300					

How's it going?   Self-Study Practice

Analyze, record, and summarize the following June transaction: Florida Flippers provided $3,000 of diving instruction in June to customers who will pay cash in July.

① Analyze

Assets	=	Liabilities	+	Stockholders' Equity
A/R +500				dividend, +R (500)

② Record

dr A/R   (+A) 3,000

   cr Diving revenue (+SE+R)   3,000

③ Summarize

dr Account/R (+A) cr	dr Diving Reve (+E,+R) cr
3,000	3,000

After you have finished, check your answers with the solution in the margin.

Solution to Self-Study Practice

1.

Assets	=	Liabilities	+	Stockholders' Equity
Accts. Receivable +3,000	=			Diving Revenue (+R) +3,000

2. dr Accounts Receivable (+A) 3,000
   cr Diving Revenue (+R, +SE)   3,000

3.

dr + Accts. Rec. (A) cr −	dr − Diving Revenue (R, SE) cr +
(June) 3,000	3,000 (June)

(e) Pay Cash to Employees

Pizza Aroma wrote checks to employees, totaling $8,100 for wages related to hours worked in September. The matching principle requires that all expenses that relate to revenues earned in the current period be recorded in the current period. Thus, this transaction involves an expense. We show (+E, −SE) because as expenses increase, net income decreases, which causes stockholders' equity to decrease.

> **COACH'S TIP**
>
> To review why expenses are recorded using a debit, see Exhibit 3.7 (page 104).

① Analyze

Assets	=	Liabilities	+	Stockholders' Equity
(e) Cash −8,100	=			Wages Expense (+E) −8,100

② Record

(e)   dr Wages Expense (+E, −SE) 8,100

      cr Cash (−A)   8,100

③ Summarize

dr +	Cash (A)		cr −		dr +	Wages Expense (E, SE)		cr −
Beg. bal.	10,000				Beg. bal.	0		
(a)	15,000	8,100	(e)		(e)	8,100		
(b)	300							
(d)	300							

(f) Pay Cash in Advance On September 1, Pizza Aroma **paid $7,200 in advance for September, October, and November rent.** This transaction involves paying for the right to use the rented building for three months following the payment. This payment provides an economic resource to Pizza Aroma (building space for three months), so it will be initially reported as an asset called Prepaid Rent. Each month, when the rented space has been used, Pizza Aroma will reduce Prepaid Rent and show the amount used up as Rent Expense. The adjustment needed to report September's share of the total rent expense (1/3 × $7,200 = $2,400) will be covered in Chapter 4. For now, we will record just the $7,200 rent prepayment.

Pay rent now

Rent benefits consumed later

Rent Expense recorded later

Record asset now
(Prepaid Rent)

1 Analyze

	Assets		=	Liabilities	+	Stockholders' Equity
(f) Cash		−7,200				
Prepaid Rent		+7,200				

2 Record

(f)	*dr* **Prepaid Rent** (+A)	7,200	
	cr **Cash** (−A)		7,200

3 Summarize

dr +	Cash (A)		*cr* −		*dr* +	Prepaid Rent (A)		*cr* −
Beg. bal.	10,000				Beg. bal.	0		
(a)	15,000	8,100	(e)		(f)	7,200		
(b)	300	7,200	(f)					
(d)	300							

Prepayments for insurance and other time-based services would be analyzed and recorded in a similar manner.

(g) Pay Cash in Advance On September 2, Pizza Aroma **wrote a check for $1,600 for pizza sauce, dough, cheese, and paper products.** This transaction provides another example of a prepayment that is initially recorded as an asset. The supplies are an asset because they can be used to make and sell pizza in the future. Later, when that happens and the supplies have been used up, Pizza Aroma will reduce the Supplies account balance and report the amount used up as Supplies Expense. The adjustment to be made at the end of September will be covered in Chapter 4.

1 Analyze

	Assets		=	Liabilities	+	Stockholders' Equity
(g) Cash		−1,600				
Supplies		+1,600				

2 Record

(g)	*dr* **Supplies** (+A)	1,600	
	cr **Cash** (−A)		1,600

3 Summarize

dr +	Cash (A)		*cr* −		*dr* +	Supplies (A)		*cr* −
Beg. bal.	10,000				Beg. bal.	0		
(a)	15,000	8,100	(e)		(g)	1,600		
(b)	300	7,200	(f)					
(d)	300	1,600	(g)					

(h) Incur Cost to Be Paid Later Pizza Aroma received a bill for $400 for running a newspaper ad in September. The bill will be paid in October. This cost was incurred for September advertising services, so according to the matching principle it should be recorded as an expense in September. Rather than pay cash for this expense, Pizza Aroma gave a promise to pay, which increases the liability called Accounts Payable.

> **COACH'S TIP**
>
> The beginning balance in Accounts Payable is carried forward from the previous month's activities discussed in Chapter 2.

1 Analyze

	Assets	=	Liabilities	+	Stockholders' Equity
(h)			Accounts Payable +400		Advertising Expense (+E) −400

2 Record

(h) dr Advertising Expense (+E, −SE) 400
       cr Accounts Payable (+L).. 400

3 Summarize

dr −	Accounts Payable (L)	cr +		dr +	Advertising Exp. (E, SE)	cr −
	630	Beg. bal.		Beg. bal.	0	
	400	(h)		(h)	400	

(i) Pay Cash for Expenses Pizza Aroma received and paid bills totaling $600 for September utilities services. Just like transaction (e), the cash payment and expense occurred during the same period.

1 Analyze

	Assets	=	Liabilities	+	Stockholders' Equity
(i) Cash	−600 =				Utilities Expense (+E) −600

2 Record

(i) dr Utilities Expense (+E, −SE) 600
       cr Cash (−A) 600

3 Summarize

dr +	Cash (A)		cr −		dr +	Utilities Expense (E, SE)	cr −
Beg. bal.	10,000				Beg. bal.	0	
(a)	15,000	8,100	(e)		(i)	600	
(b)	300	7,200	(f)				
(d)	300	1,600	(g)				
		600	(i)				

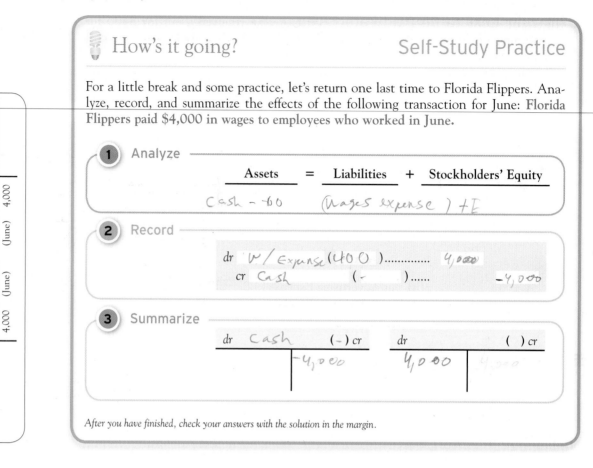

How's it going?   Self-Study Practice

For a little break and some practice, let's return one last time to Florida Flippers. Analyze, record, and summarize the effects of the following transaction for June: Florida Flippers paid $4,000 in wages to employees who worked in June.

1 Analyze

Assets	=	Liabilities	+	Stockholders' Equity
Cash − 4,000		(Wages expense) +E		

2 Record

dr W/ Expense (400)............. 4,000
  cr Cash   (−   )...... −4,000

3 Summarize

dr Cash (−) cr	dr ( ) cr
−4,000	4,000 4,000

After you have finished, check your answers with the solution in the margin.

Solution to Self-Study Practice

1.

Assets	=	Liabilities	+	Stockholders' Equity
Cash −4,000 =				Wages Expense (+E) −4,000

2. dr Wages Expense (+E, −SE) 4,000
   cr Cash (−A)   4,000

3.

dr +	Cash (A)	cr −	dr +	Wages Expense (E, SE)	cr −
	(June) 4,000	(June) 4,000			

Calculating Account Balances Having entered ("posted") the effects of each journal entry into the T-accounts, we can now calculate the ending balances. In Exhibit 3.8, we have included all the T-accounts for Pizza Aroma (from this chapter as well as Chapter 2). You've heard it before, but we'll just remind you that the ending balance in each account is the amount by which the total of the increase (+) side exceeds the total of the decrease (−) side.

UNADJUSTED TRIAL BALANCE

Learning Objective 4
Prepare an unadjusted trial balance.

After summarizing journal entries in the various accounts and then calculating ending balances for each account, you should check that the total recorded debits equal the total recorded credits. It's easy to make mistakes when you're doing the recording and summarizing steps by hand. Typical mistakes involve (a) forgetting to post both sides of a journal entry, (b) posting a debit in the credit column (or vice versa), (c) recording the wrong amount, or (d) miscalculating the ending account balance. The best way to ensure your accounts are "in balance" is to prepare a **trial balance**, like the one in Exhibit 3.9. A trial balance is an internal report used to determine whether total debits equal total credits. Also, as you will see in Chapter 4, it's a great tool to use when preparing the financial statements. Typically, a trial balance lists every account name in one column (usually in the order of assets, liabilities, stockholders' equity, revenues, and expenses). The ending balances obtained from the ledgers (T-accounts) are listed in the appropriate debit or credit column.

YOU SHOULD KNOW

Trial balance: An internal report that lists all accounts and their balances to check on the equality of total recorded debits and total recorded credits.

If your trial balance indicates that total debits don't equal total credits, you will experience a sickening feeling in your stomach because this means you've made an error somewhere in preparing or posting the journal entries to the T-accounts. Don't panic or start randomly changing numbers. The first thing to do when you find yourself in a hole is stop digging. Calmly look at the difference between total debits and credits and

EXHIBIT 3.8	T-Accounts for Pizza Aroma

Assets = Liabilities + Stockholders' Equity

dr + Cash (A) cr −

Beg. bal.	10,000			
(a)	15,000	8,100	(e)	
(b)	300	7,200	(f)	
(d)	300	1,600	(g)	
		600	(i)	
End. bal.	8,100			

dr + Accounts Receivable (A) cr −

Beg. bal.	0		
(c)	500	300	(d)
End. bal.	200		

dr + Supplies (A) cr −

Beg. bal.	0	
(g)	1,600	
End. bal.	1,600	

dr + Prepaid Rent (A) cr −

Beg. bal.	0	
(f)	7,200	
End. bal.	7,200	

dr + Cookware (A) cr −

Beg. bal.	630

dr + Equipment (A) cr −

Beg. bal.	60,000

dr − Accounts Payable (L) cr +

		630	Beg. bal.
		400	(h)
		1,030	End. bal.

dr − Unearned Revenue (L) cr +

		0	Beg. bal.
		300	(b)
		300	End. bal.

dr − Note Payable (L) cr +

	20,000	Beg. bal.

Beginning balances in this exhibit (September 1) are the ending balances in Exhibit 2.12 (August 31).

dr − Contributed Capital (SE) cr +

	50,000	Beg. bal.

dr − Retained Earnings cr +

	0	Beg. bal.

Pizza
dr − Revenue (R, SE) cr +

	0	Beg. bal.
	15,000	(a)
	500	(c)
	15,500	End. bal.

dr + Wages Expense (E, SE) cr −

Beg. bal.	0	
(e)	8,100	
End. bal.	8,100	

dr + Utilities Expense (E, SE) cr −

Beg. bal.	0	
(i)	600	
End. bal.	600	

dr + Advertising Exp. (E, SE) cr −

Beg. bal.	0	
(h)	400	
End. bal.	400	

consult the Homework Helper section on page 120 for tips on how to find the error causing that difference.

We don't want to depress you, but even if total debits equal total credits, it's still possible that you've made an error. For example, if you accidentally debit an asset rather than an expense or credit Accounts Payable instead of Unearned Revenue, total debits would still equal total credits. So if the trial balance doesn't balance, you know you've made an error for sure. If the trial balance does balance, it's still possible that you've made a mistake.

If you haven't already scanned the trial balance in Exhibit 3.9, take a moment to do it now. Notice that the title says **unadjusted** trial balance. It is called this because several adjustments will have to be made at the end of the accounting period to update the accounts. For example, some of the benefits of Prepaid Rent were used up in September, but this wasn't recorded yet. If you're really sharp, you'll also have noticed that income taxes haven't been calculated and recorded yet. Although it's possible to prepare preliminary financial statements using the numbers on the unadjusted

EXHIBIT 3.9	Sample Unadjusted Trial Balance

PIZZA AROMA, INC.
Unadjusted Trial Balance
At September 30, 2010

Account Name	Debits	Credits	
Cash	$ 8,100		
Accounts Receivable	200		
Supplies	1,600		
Prepaid Rent	7,200		Balance
Cookware	630		sheet
Equipment	60,000		accounts
Accounts Payable		$ 1,030	
Unearned Revenue		300	
Note Payable		20,000	
Contributed Capital		50,000	
Retained Earnings		0	
Pizza Revenue		15,500	
Wages Expense	8,100		Income
Utilities Expense	600		statement
Advertising Expense	400		accounts
Totals	$86,830	$86,830	

COACH'S TIP

A trial balance is prepared by simply listing and summing the T-account balances.

trial balance, most companies don't. They wait until after the final adjustments are made. These adjustments will ensure the revenues and expenses are up to date and complete so that the (adjusted) net income number will provide a good indication about whether the company was profitable during the period. Don't worry about how to make the end-of-period adjustments yet. We'll spend most of Chapter 4 on that. For now, just realize that the accounts still have to be adjusted before we can prepare financial statements that follow generally accepted accounting principles.

REVIEW OF REVENUES AND EXPENSES

Up to this point of the chapter, you've analyzed some transactions—nine actually—that involve operating activities. While this is a good introduction, it doesn't quite prepare you for the variety of operating activities that most companies engage in. What you really need is a general summary of everything you've learned about revenues, expenses, and journal entries, and then lots of practice applying it to a broad range of activities. Let's start with revenues.

Remember that revenues are recorded when the business fulfills its promise to provide goods or services to customers, which is not necessarily the same time that cash is received. Because of this, we look at three cases, where cash is received (1) before the revenue is earned by delivering goods or services, (2) in the same period the revenue is earned, and (3) after the revenue is earned. The journal entries for these situations are shown in the following panels.

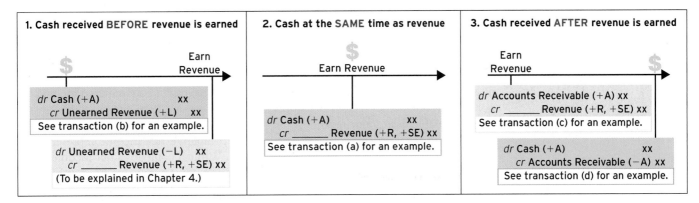

Although these three panels correspond to the revenue transactions for Pizza Aroma analyzed earlier in this chapter, they can be applied to any business. We use a generic label "_____ Revenue" with the expectation that you will fill in the blank with whatever type of revenue you are recording. That is, when accounting for revenue from delivering pizza, you should use an account name like Pizza Revenue. A more complete list of account names is provided in the Homework Helper section on page 120.

Let's look at a similar summary for expenses now. Under accrual accounting, expenses are recorded when incurred (by using up the economic benefits of acquired items). Expenses are not necessarily incurred at the same time that cash is paid. Because of this, we look at three cases, where cash is paid (1) before the expense is incurred, (2) in the same period the expense is incurred, and (3) after the expense is incurred. The corresponding journal entries are summarized in the following panels.

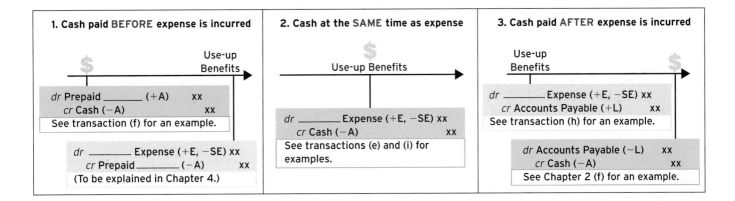

Again, we use generic labels like "Prepaid _____" and "_____ Expense" with the expectation that you will fill in the blank with whatever type of item you are recording (e.g., Prepaid Rent, Rent Expense).

Evaluate the Results

The income statement provides the main measure of a company's operating performance. The key thing to look for is whether net income is positive (revenues exceed expenses). Beyond that, it's useful to consider whether revenues are growing faster than expenses. If so, the company's net income will be increasing. To be successful, a company's net income should be stable or growing from period to period.

Learning Objective 5
Describe limitations of the income statement.

INCOME STATEMENT LIMITATIONS

Although an income statement is useful for assessing a company's performance, it does have some limitations that lead to common misconceptions. One of the most common is that some people think net income equals the amount of cash generated by the business during the period. While this is the way many of us think about our own income, it's not the way companies recognize revenues and expenses on the income statement when using accrual basis accounting.

A second, related misconception is that a company's net income represents the change in the company's value during the period. While a company's net income is one source of value to the company, many other determinants of its value are not included in the income statement. A good example is the increase in the value of Pizza Aroma's name as it grows its reputation for making great pizza.

A third common misconception is that the measurement of income involves only counting. Proper counting is critical to income measurement, but estimation also plays a role. For example, Pizza Aroma's equipment will not last forever. Instead, it will be "used up" over time to generate the company's revenue. It should therefore be expensed over the period in which it is used. Doing so requires an estimate of the period over which each category of equipment will be used. We will discuss this particular example in Chapter 4; many other examples of the role of estimates in income measurement will arise in later chapters.

Spotlight On ETHICS

Why All the Scandals?

You may have heard about accounting scandals, such as those at Enron and WorldCom (now owned by Verizon), in which managers have been accused of "cooking the books." Why did they do it? The simple answer is greed. Companies whose earnings have fallen often experience a decline in their stock prices, which usually leads to pay reductions or even job losses for senior executives. When a company is actually performing poorly, greed may lead some managers to falsify revenues and hide expenses to make it look like the company is still doing well.

While this sometimes fools people for a short time, it rarely works in the long run and often leads to very bad consequences. A few cases involving faulty revenue and expense accounting follow. As you look at these, imagine what it must have been like to be Bernie Ebbers—the person who received a 25-year prison sentence at age 65. It is probably just as bad as being Barry Minkow, who was sentenced to 25 years in jail when he was 21.

The CEO	The Fraud	Conviction/Plea	The Outcome
Bernie Ebbers, 65 WorldCom	Recorded operating expenses as if they were assets; resulted in the largest fraud in U.S. history	Convicted July 2005	Sentenced to 25 years
Sanjay Kumar, 44 Computer Associates	Recorded sales in the wrong accounting period	Pleaded guilty April 2006	Sentenced to 12 years
Martin Grass, 49 Rite Aid Corporation	Recorded rebates from drug companies before they were earned	Pleaded guilty June 2003	Sentenced to 8 years
Barry Minkow, 21 ZZZZ Best	Made up customers and sales to show profits when, in reality, the company was a sham	Convicted December 1988	Sentenced to 25 years

In this chapter, you learned how to measure and report revenues and expenses for the accounting period as a starting point for determining net income. The next step is to adjust the financial statements so that they will be complete and up to date at the end of the accounting period. Currently, Pizza Aroma's accounting records report revenues of $15,500 and expenses of $8,100, $600, and $400, suggesting a net income of $6,400. But Laurie cautions Mauricio that this measure of net income is preliminary and will change when the accounting records are adjusted at the end of September. The adjustment process is the main topic of Chapter 4.

REVIEW THE CHAPTER

DEMONSTRATION CASE A

Carnival Corporation

1. From the following list of balance sheet and income statement account balances for Carnival Corporation, prepare an income statement for the year ended November 30, 2008. (Amounts are reported in millions of U.S. dollars.)

2. Explain what the results suggest about the cruise ship company's operating performance. Net income for the same period last year was $2,408 (in millions of U.S. dollars).

Transportation Expenses	$ 2,232	Wage Expenses	$1,470	Selling Expenses	$1,629
Passenger Ticket Revenue	11,210	Fuel Expenses	1,774	Prepaid Expenses	267
Onboard Revenue	3,436	Accounts Payable	512	Ship Expenses	4,308
Food Expenses	856	Income Tax Expense	47	Unearned Revenue	2,519

Suggested Solution

1. Income Statement

CARNIVAL CORPORATION
Income Statement
For the Year Ended November 30, 2008
(amounts in millions of U.S. dollars)

Revenues	
Passenger Ticket Revenue	$11,210
Onboard Revenue	3,436
Total Revenues	14,646
Expenses	
Ship Expenses	4,308
Transportation Expenses	2,232
Selling Expenses	1,629
Fuel Expenses	1,774
Wage Expenses	1,470
Food Expenses	856
Income Tax Expense	47
Total Expenses	12,316
Net Income	$ 2,330

> **COACH'S TIP**
>
> Prepaid Expenses of $267 is excluded from the income statement because it is an asset on the balance sheet. Accounts Payable of $512 and Unearned Revenue of $2,519 are excluded from the income statement because they are liabilities on the balance sheet.

2. The net income of $2,330 (million) indicates that Carnival Corporation was profitable, meaning that the revenues it earned were greater than the expenses it incurred. Generally, this is a positive sign. However, the decline from the net income of $2,408 (million) reported in the prior year suggests the company is not doing as well as it once did.

DEMONSTRATION CASE B

This case is a continuation of the Goodbye Grass Corporation case introduced in Chapter 2. The company was established and property and equipment were purchased. The balance sheet at April 30, 2010, based on only the investing and financing activities (from Chapter 2) is as follows:

GOODBYE GRASS CORPORATION
Balance Sheet
At April 30, 2010

Assets		Liabilities	
Current Assets		Current Liabilities	
Cash	$ 3,800	Accounts Payable	$ 400
Note Receivable	1,250	Note Payable	4,000
Total Current Assets	5,050	Total Current Liabilities	4,400
Equipment	4,600	**Stockholders' Equity**	
Land	3,750	Contributed Capital	9,000
		Retained Earnings	0
		Total Stockholders' Equity	9,000
Total Assets	$13,400	Total Liabilities and Stockholders' Equity	$13,400

The following activities also occurred during April 2010:

a. Purchased and used gasoline for mowers and edgers, paying $90 in cash at a local gas station.
b. In early April, received $1,600 cash from the city in advance for lawn maintenance service for April through July ($400 each month). The entire amount is to be recorded as Unearned Revenue.
c. In early April, purchased $300 of insurance covering six months, April through September. The entire payment is to be recorded as Prepaid Insurance.
d. Mowed lawns for residential customers who are billed every two weeks. A total of $5,200 of service was billed and is to be recorded in April.
e. Residential customers paid $3,500 on their accounts.
f. Paid wages every two weeks. Total cash paid in April was $3,900.
g. Received a bill for $320 from the local gas station for additional gasoline purchased on account and used in April.
h. Paid $100 on accounts payable.

Required:

1. Analyze activities (a)–(h) with the goal of indicating their effects on the basic accounting equation (Assets = Liabilities + Stockholders' Equity), using the format shown in the chapter.
2. Prepare journal entries to record the transactions identified among activities (a)–(h).
    TIP: Treat insurance (in c) in the same manner as Pizza Aroma's rent in transaction (f) on page 108.
3. Summarize the effects of each transaction in the appropriate T-accounts. Before entering these effects, set up T-accounts for Cash, Accounts Receivable, Note Receivable, Prepaid Insurance, Equipment, Land, Accounts Payable, Unearned Revenue, Note Payable, Contributed Capital, Retained Earnings, Mowing Revenue, Wages Expense, and Fuel Expense. The beginning balance in each T-account should be the amount shown on the balance sheet above or $0 if the account does not appear on the above balance sheet. After posting the journal entries to the T-accounts, compute ending balances for each of the T-accounts.
4. Use the amounts in the T-accounts to prepare an unadjusted trial balance for Goodbye Grass Corporation at April 30, 2010.

    After completing the above requirements, check your answers with the following solution.

Suggested Solution

1. Transaction analysis:

	Assets		=	Liabilities		+	Stockholders' Equity	
a.	Cash	−90	=				Fuel Expense (+E)	−90
b.	Cash	+1,600	=	Unearned Revenue	+1,600			
c.	Cash	−300	=			No change		
	Prepaid Insurance	+300						
d.	Accounts Receivable	+5,200	=				Mowing Revenue (+R)	+5,200
e.	Cash	+3,500	=			No change		
	Accounts Receivable	−3,500						
f.	Cash	−3,900	=				Wages Expense (+E)	−3,900
g.	No change		=	Accounts Payable	+320		Fuel Expense (+E)	−320
h.	Cash	−100	=	Accounts Payable	−100			

2. Journal entries:

a.	dr Fuel Expense (+E, −SE)	90	
	cr Cash (−A)		90
b.	dr Cash (+A)	1,600	
	cr Unearned Revenue (+L)		1,600
c.	dr Prepaid Insurance (+A)	300	
	cr Cash (−A)		300
d.	dr Accounts Receivable (+A)	5,200	
	cr Mowing Revenue (+R, +SE)		5,200
e.	dr Cash (+A)	3,500	
	cr Accounts Receivable (−A)		3,500
f.	dr Wages Expense (+E, −SE)	3,900	
	cr Cash (−A)		3,900
g.	dr Fuel Expense (+E, −SE)	320	
	cr Accounts Payable (+L)		320
h.	dr Accounts Payable (−L)	100	
	cr Cash (−A)		100

3. T-Accounts:

Assets	=	Liabilities	+	Stockholders' Equity

dr +   Cash (A)   cr −

Beg. bal. 3,800			
(b) 1,600	90	(a)	
(e) 3,500	300	(c)	
	3,900	(f)	
	100	(h)	
End. bal. 4,510			

dr + Accounts Receivable (A) cr −

Beg. bal. 0			
(d) 5,200	3,500	(e)	
End. bal. 1,700			

dr + Note Receivable (A) cr −

Beg. bal. 1,250	
End. bal. 1,250	

dr + Prepaid Insurance (A) cr −

Beg. bal. 0	
(c) 300	
End. Bal. 300	

dr +   Equipment (A)   cr −

Beg. bal. 4,600	
End. bal. 4,600	

dr +   Land (A)   cr −

Beg. bal. 3,750	
End. bal. 3,750	

dr − Accounts Payable (L) cr +

		400	Beg. bal.
(h)	100	320	(g)
		620	End. bal.

dr − Unearned Revenue (L) cr +

0	Beg. bal.
1,600	(b)
1,600	End. bal.

dr −   Note Payable (L)   cr +

4,000	Beg. bal.
4,000	End. bal.

dr +   Wages Expense (E)   cr −

Beg. bal. 0	
(f) 3,900	
End. bal. 3,900	

dr +   Fuel Expense (E)   cr −

Beg. bal. 0	
(a) 90	
(g) 320	
End. bal. 410	

dr − Contributed Capital (SE) cr +

9,000	Beg. bal.
9,000	End. bal.

dr − Retained Earnings (SE) cr +

0	Beg. bal.
0	End. bal.

dr − Mowing Revenue (R) cr +

0	Beg. bal.
5,200	(d)
5,200	End. bal.

4. Unadjusted trial balance:

GOODBYE GRASS CORPORATION
Unadjusted Trial Balance
At April 30, 2010

Account Name	Debits	Credits
Cash	$ 4,510	
Accounts Receivable	1,700	
Note Receivable	1,250	
Prepaid Insurance	300	
Equipment	4,600	
Land	3,750	
Accounts Payable		$ 620
Unearned Revenue		1,600
Note Payable		4,000
Contributed Capital		9,000
Retained Earnings		0
Mowing Revenue		5,200
Wages Expense	3,900	
Fuel Expense	410	
Totals	$20,420	$20,420

CHAPTER SUMMARY

Describe common operating transactions and select appropriate income statement account titles. p. 96   **LO1**

- The income statement reports the results of transactions that affect net income, which includes

    Revenues—amounts charged to customers for sales of goods or services provided.

    Expenses—costs of business activities undertaken to earn revenues.

- See Exhibit 3.2 on page 97 for basic income statement format.

Explain and apply the revenue and matching principles. p. 100   **LO2**

- The two key concepts underlying accrual basis accounting and the income statement are

    Revenue principle—recognize revenues when they are earned by providing goods or services.

    Matching principle—recognize expenses when they are incurred in generating revenue.

Analyze, record, and summarize the effects of operating transactions, using the accounting equation, journal entries, and T-accounts. p. 104   **LO3**

- The expanded transaction analysis model includes revenues and expenses as subcategories of Retained Earnings. Increases, decreases, and normal account balances (*dr* or *cr*) are shown below.

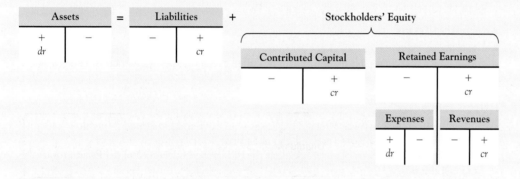

Prepare an unadjusted trial balance. p. 110   **LO4**

- The unadjusted trial balance is a list of all accounts and their unadjusted balances, and is used to check on the equality of recorded debits and credits.

Describe limitations of the income statement. p. 114   **LO5**

- The income statement indicates whether the company is profitable, but this might not explain whether cash increased or decreased.

- The income statement does not directly measure the change in value of a company during the period.

- Estimation plays a key role when measuring income.

KEY TERMS

Accrual Basis Accounting p. 100	**Net Income** p. 98	**Trial Balance** p. 110
Cash Basis Accounting p. 99	**Revenue Principle** p. 100	**Unearned Revenue** p. 101
Expenses p. 97	**Revenues** p. 97	
Matching Principle p. 102	**Time Period Assumption** p. 98	

See complete definitions in the glossary in the back of this text.

HOMEWORK HELPER

Account Name	Description
Revenues	
Sales	Arise from delivering products in the ordinary course of business
Service Revenues	Arise from providing services in the ordinary course of business
Rental Revenues	Amounts earned by renting out company property
Interest Revenues	Amounts earned on savings and loans to others
Dividend Revenues	Dividends earned from investing in other companies
Fees Earned	Fees that the company charges its customers
Expenses	
Cost of Goods Sold	Cost of products sold in the ordinary course of business
Repairs & Maintenance Expense	Cost of routine maintenance and upkeep of buildings/equipment
Advertising Expense	Cost of advertising services obtained during the period
Depreciation Expense	Cost of plant and equipment used up during the period
Insurance Expense	Cost of insurance coverage for the current period
Salaries and Wages Expense	Cost of employees' salaries and wages for the period
Rent Expense	Cost of rent for the period
Supplies Expense	Cost of supplies used up during the period
Delivery Expense	Cost of freight to deliver goods to customers
Utilities Expense	Cost of power, light, heat, Internet, and telephone for the period
Amortization Expense	Cost of intangible assets used up or expired during the period
Interest Expense	Interest charged on outstanding debts owed during the period
Income Tax Expense	Taxes charged on net income reported for the period

Alternative terms

- Net income also can be called net earnings.
- Prepaid Rent and Prepaid Insurance can be called Prepaid Expenses, which is reported as a current asset on the balance sheet.

Helpful reminders

- To properly understand why Prepaid Expenses is an asset and Unearned Revenue is a liability, emphasize the first word (prepaid and unearned).
- If the trial balance doesn't balance, look at the difference between total debits and total credits. If it is . . .
  - The same as one of your T-account balances, you probably forgot to include the account in your trial balance.
  - Twice the amount of an account balance, you may have included it in the wrong column of the trial balance.
  - Twice the amount of a transaction, you may have posted a debit as a credit or a credit as a debit in your T-accounts.
  - Evenly divisible by 9, you may have reversed the order of two digits in a number (a transposition error) or left a zero off the end of a number.
  - Evenly divisible by 3, you may have hit the key above or below the one you intended to hit (like a 9 instead of a 6) on your numeric keypad.

Frequent mistakes

- Accrual is <u>not</u> spelled accural.

PRACTICE MATERIAL

QUESTIONS (⊕ Symbol indicates questions that require analysis from more than one perspective.)

1. Show the income statement equation and define each element.

2. When accounting was developed in the 14th and 15th centuries, some businesses had very short lives. For instance, a business might have been created for a ship to sail from

Europe to North America and return with furs and other goods. After the goods were delivered and profits were distributed among those who financed the shipment, the business ceased to exist. In more recent centuries, businesses began to experience longer lives. Identify the accounting concept that is needed when accounting for businesses with long lives. Explain what this concept means and why it is necessary for modern-day accounting.

3. Define *accrual basis accounting* and contrast it with *cash basis accounting*.

4. Why is it appropriate to use cash basis accounting in your personal life but not in the business world?

5. What does it mean to *recognize* an accounting transaction?

6. When is revenue typically recognized under accrual basis accounting?

7. Explain the matching principle.

8. Explain why stockholders' equity is increased by revenues and decreased by expenses.

9. Explain why revenues are recorded as credits and expenses as debits.

10. Complete the following table by entering either *debit* or *credit* in each cell:

Item	Increase	Decrease
Revenues		
Expenses		

11. Complete the following table by entering either *increase* or *decrease* in each cell:

Item	Debit	Credit
Revenues		
Expenses		

12. What basic characteristic distinguishes items reported on the income statement from items reported on the balance sheet?

13. Which of the four basic accounting reports indicates that it is appropriate to consider revenues and expenses as subcategories of retained earnings? Explain.

14. What is the difference between Accounts Receivable and Revenue?

15. What is the difference between Accounts Payable for advertising and Advertising Expense?

16. For each of the following situations, indicate whether it represents an accounting error and explain why it is or is not an error. Also state whether a trial balance would indicate that an error exists for each situation.

   a. Cash received from a customer was debited to Accounts Receivable and credited to Cash.
   b. Revenue was recognized when a customer purchased a gift card for future use.
   c. An expense was recorded as an asset.
   d. The debit side of a journal entry was recorded in the accounts, but the credit side was not.
   e. A company shareholder purchased a new car, but this was not recorded by the company.

17. What are three limitations of the income statement that often lead to misconceptions?

MULTIPLE CHOICE

Quiz 3
www.mhhe.com/phillips3e

1. Which of the following items is not a specific account in a company's accounting records?
   a. Accounts Receivable   c. Sales Revenue
   b. Net Income   d. Unearned Revenue

2. Which of the following accounts normally has a debit balance?
   a. Unearned Revenue   c. Retained Earnings
   b. Rent Expense   d. Sales Revenue

3. The matching principle controls
   a. Where on the income statement expenses should be presented.
   b. When revenues are recognized on the income statement.
   c. The ordering of current assets and current liabilities on the balance sheet.
   d. When costs are recognized as expenses on the income statement.

4. When should companies that sell gift cards to customers report revenue?
   a. When the gift card is sold and cash is received.
   b. When the gift card is used by the customer.
   c. At the end of the year in which the gift card is sold.
   d. None of the above.

5. If a company incorrectly records a payment as an asset, rather than as an expense, how will this error affect net income in the current period?
   a. Net income will be too high.
   b. Net income will be too low.
   c. Net income will not be affected by this error.
   d. It's a mystery; nobody really knows.

6. When should a company report the cost of an insurance policy as an expense?
   a. When the company first signs the policy.
   b. When the company pays for the policy.
   c. When the company receives the benefits from the policy over its period of coverage.
   d. When the company receives payments from the insurance company for its insurance claims.

7. When expenses exceed revenues in a given period (and there are no gains or losses),
   a. Stockholders' equity will not be impacted.
   b. Stockholders' equity will be increased.
   c. Stockholders' equity will be decreased.
   d. One cannot determine the impact on stockholders' equity without information about the specific revenues and expenses.

8. Which account is *least* likely to be debited when revenue is recorded?

   a. Accounts Payable   c. Cash
   b. Accounts Receivable   d. Unearned Revenue

9. Webby Corporation reported the following amounts on its income statement: service revenues, $32,500; utilities expense, $300; net income, $1,600; and income tax expense, $900. If the only other amount reported on the income statement was for selling expenses, what amount would it be?

   a. $2,200   c. $30,000
   b. $29,700   d. $30,900

10. Which of the following is the entry to be recorded by a law firm when it receives a payment from a new client that will be earned when services are provided in the future?

   a. *Debit* Accounts Receivable; *credit* Legal Services Revenue.
   b. *Debit* Unearned Revenue; *credit* Legal Services Revenue.
   c. *Debit* Cash; *credit* Unearned Revenue.
   d. *Debit* Unearned Revenue; *credit* Cash.

> For answers to the Multiple-Choice Questions **see page Q1** located in the last section of the book.

MINI-EXERCISES

LO2   **M3-1 Reporting Cash Basis versus Accrual Basis Income**

Mostert Music Company had the following transactions in March:

a. Sold music lessons to customers for $10,000; received $6,000 in cash and the rest on account.
b. Paid $600 in wages for the month.
c. Received a $200 bill for utilities that will be paid in April.
d. Received $1,000 from customers as deposits on music lessons to be given in April.

Complete the following statements for March:

Cash Basis Income Statement			Accrual Basis Income Statement		
Revenues			Revenues		
Cash Sales		$	Sales to Customers		$
Customer Deposits					
Expenses			Expenses		
Wages Paid			Wages Expense		
			Utilities Expense		
Cash Income		$	Net Income		$

LO2   **M3-2 Identifying Accrual Basis Revenues**

The following transactions are July 2010 activities of Bill's Extreme Bowling, Inc., which operates several bowling centers. If revenue is to be recognized in July, indicate the amount. If revenue is not to be recognized in July, explain why.

Activity	Amount or Explanation
a. Bill's collected $12,000 from customers for games played in July.	
b. Bill's billed a customer for $250 for a party held at the center on the last day of July. The bill is to be paid in August.	
c. Bill's received $1,000 from credit sales made to customers last month (in June).	
d. The men's and women's bowling leagues gave Bill's advance payments totaling $1,500 for the fall season that starts in September.	

M3-3 Identifying Accrual Basis Expenses

LO2

The following transactions are July 2010 activities of Bill's Extreme Bowling, Inc., which operates several bowling centers. If an expense is to be recognized in July, indicate the amount. If an expense is not to be recognized in July, explain why.

Activity	Amount or Explanation
e. Bill's paid $1,500 to plumbers for repairing a broken pipe in the restrooms.	
f. Bill's paid $2,000 for the June electricity bill and received the July bill for $2,500, which will be paid in August.	
g. Bill's paid $5,475 to employees for work in July.	

M3-4 Recording Accrual Basis Revenues

LO3

For each of the transactions in M3-2, write the journal entry using the format shown in the chapter.

M3-5 Recording Accrual Basis Expenses

LO3

For each of the transactions in M3-3, write the journal entry using the format shown in the chapter.

M3-6 Determining the Accounting Equation Effects of Operating Activities Involving Revenues

LO2, 3

The following transactions are July 2010 activities of Bill's Extreme Bowling, Inc., which operates several bowling centers. For each of the following transactions, complete the spreadsheet, indicating the amount and effect (+ for increase and − for decrease) of each transaction under the accrual basis. Write NE if there is no effect. Include revenues as a subcategory of stockholders' equity, as shown for the first transaction, which is provided as an example.

Transaction	Assets	Liabilities	Stockholders' Equity
a. Bill's collected $12,000 from customers for games played in July.	+12,000	NE	Games Fee Revenue (+R) + 12,000
b. Bill's billed a customer for $250 for a party held at the center on the last day of July. The bill is to be paid in August.	+250	NE	~~Games Revenue~~ (+SE) 250
c. Bill's received $1,000 from credit sales made to customers last month (in June).			
d. The men's and women's bowling leagues gave Bill's advance payments totaling $1,500 for the fall season that starts in September.			

M3-7 Determining the Accounting Equation Effects of Operating Activities Involving Expenses

LO2, 3

The following transactions are July 2010 activities of Bill's Extreme Bowling, Inc., which operates several bowling centers. For each of the following transactions, complete the spreadsheet, indicating the amount and effect (+ for increase and − for decrease) of each transaction under the accrual basis. Write NE if there is no effect. Include expenses as a subcategory of stockholders' equity, as shown for the first transaction, which is provided as an example.

Transaction	Assets	Liabilities	Stockholders' Equity
e. Bill's paid $1,500 to plumbers for repairing a broken pipe in the restrooms.	−1,500	NE	Repairs Expense (+E) −1,500
f. Bill's paid $2,000 for the June electricity bill and received the July bill for $2,500, which will be paid in August.			
g. Bill's paid $5,475 to employees for work in July.			

LO1   **M3-8 Preparing an Income Statement**

Given the transactions in M3-6 and M3-7 (including the examples), prepare an income statement for Bill's Extreme Bowling, Inc., for the month ended July 31, 2010. (This income statement would be considered "preliminary" because it uses unadjusted balances.)

LO2   **M3-9 Identifying Accrual Basis Revenues**

The following transactions are February 2010 activities of Swing Hard Incorporated, which offers indoor golfing lessons in the northeastern United States. If revenue is to be recognized in February, indicate the amount. If revenue is not to be recognized in February, explain why.

Activity	Amount or Explanation
a. Swing Hard collected $15,000 from customers for lessons given in February.	
b. Swing Hard sold a gift card for golf lessons for $150 cash in February.	
c. Swing Hard received $4,000 from credit sales made to customers in January.	
d. Swing Hard collects $2,250 in advance payments for golf lessons to start in June.	
e. Swing Hard bills a customer $125 for golf lessons given between February 25 and February 28. The bill is to be paid in March.	

LO2   **M3-10 Identifying Accrual Basis Expenses**

The following transactions are February 2010 activities of Swing Hard Incorporated, which offers indoor golfing lessons in the northeastern United States. If an expense is to be recognized in February, indicate the amount. If an expense is not to be recognized in February, explain why.

Activity	Amount or Explanation
f. Swing Hard paid $4,750 to its golf instructors for the month of February.	
g. Swing Hard paid $1,750 for electricity used in the month of January.	
h. Swing Hard received an electricity bill for $800 for the month of February, to be paid in March.	

LO3   **M3-11 Recording Accrual Basis Revenues**

For each of the transactions in M3-9, write the journal entry using the format shown in the chapter.

LO3   **M3-12 Recording Accrual Basis Expenses**

For each of the transactions in M3-10, write the journal entry using the format shown in the chapter.

LO3   **M3-13 Preparing Accrual Basis Journal Entries for Business Activities**

Quick Cleaners, Inc. (QCI) has been in business for several years. It specializes in cleaning houses but has some small business clients as well. Prepare journal entries for the following transactions, which occurred during a recent month:

a. Incurred $600 of heating and electrical costs this month and will pay them next month.
b. Issued $25,000 of QCI stock for cash.
c. Paid wages for the current month, totalling $2,000.
d. Performed cleaning services on account worth $2,800.
e. Some of Quick Cleaners's equipment was repaired at a total cost of $150. The company paid the full amount immediately.

M3-14 Preparing Accrual Basis Journal Entries for Business Activities
LO3

Junktrader is an online company that specializes in matching buyers and sellers of used items. Buyers and sellers can purchase a membership with Junktrader, which provides them advance notice of potentially attractive offers. Prepare journal entries for the following transactions, which occurred during a recent month.

a. Junktrader provided online advertising services for another company for $200 on account.
b. On the last day of the month, Junktrader paid $50 cash to run an ad promoting the company's services. The ad ran that day in the local newspaper.
c. Received $200 cash in membership fees for the month from new members.
d. Received an electricity bill for $85, for usage this month. The bill will be paid next month.
e. Billed a customer $180 for helping sell some junk. Junktrader expects to receive the customer's payment by the end of next month.

M3-15 Preparing Accrual Basis Journal Entries for Business Activities
LO3

An international children's charity collects donations, which are used to buy clothing and toys for children in need. The charity records donations of cash and other items as Donations Revenue when received. Prepare journal entries for the following transactions, which occurred during a recent month.

a. Received $4,000 in cash and checks from a door-to-door campaign.
b. Paid $2,000 cash for employee wages this month.
c. Paid $1,000 cash on a loan from the bank (ignore interest).
d. Bought $3,000 worth of new toy supplies from a large toy manufacturer, paying $1,000 cash and signing a short-term note for $2,000.
e. The manufacturer generously donated an additional $2,500 of toy supplies.

M3-16 Preparing Accrual Basis Journal Entries for Business Activities
LO3

An auto-body repair shop has been in business for 23 years. Prepare journal entries for the following transactions, which occurred during a recent month.

a. Signed a long-term note and received a $150,000 loan from a local bank.
b. Billed a customer $2,000 for repair work just completed. Payment is expected in 45 days.
c. Wrote a check for $600 of rent.
d. Received $450 cash from a customer for work done the same day.
e. The company incurred $400 in advertising costs for the current month and is planning to pay these costs next month.

M3-17 Determining the Accounting Equation Effects of Operating Activities Involving Revenues
LO2, 3

The following transactions are February 2010 activities of Swing Hard Incorporated, which offers golfing lessons in the northeastern United States. For each of the following transactions, complete the spreadsheet, indicating the amount and effect (+ for increase and − for decrease) of each transaction under the accrual basis. Write NE if there is no effect. Include revenues as a subcategory of stockholders' equity, as shown for the first transaction, which is provided as an example.

Transaction	Assets	Liabilities	Stockholders' Equity
a. Swing Hard collected $15,000 from customers for lessons given in February.	+15,000	NE	Lesson Revenue (+R) +15,000
b. Swing Hard sold a gift card for golf lessons for $150 cash in February.			
c. Swing Hard received $4,000 from credit sales made to customers in January.			
d. Swing Hard collects $2,250 in advance payments for golf lessons to start in June.			
e. Swing Hard bills a customer $125 for golf lessons given between February 25 thru February 28. The bill is to be paid in March.			

LO2, 3   M3-18 Determining the Accounting Equation Effects of Operating Activities Involving Expenses

The following transactions are February 2010 activities of Swing Hard Incorporated, which offers golfing lessons in the northeastern United States. For each of the following transactions, complete the spreadsheet, indicating the amount and effect (+ for increase and − for decrease) of each transaction under the accrual basis. Write NE if there is no effect. Include expenses as a subcategory of stockholders' equity, as shown for the first transaction, which is provided as an example.

Transaction	Assets	Liabilities	Stockholders' Equity
f. Swing Hard paid $4,750 for wages to its golf instructors for the month of February.	−4,750 Cash	NE	Wages Expense (+E) −4,750
g. Swing Hard paid $1,750 for electricity used in the month of January.	−175 Cash	A/P 750	195 E
h. Swing Hard received an electricity bill for $800 for the month of February, to be paid in March.		A/P +800	+800 E

LO1   M3-19 Preparing an Income Statement

Given the transactions in M3-17 and M3-18 (including the examples), prepare an income statement for Swing Hard Incorporated for the month ended February 28, 2010. (This income statement would be considered "preliminary" because it uses unadjusted balances.)

LO1, 4   M3-20 Preparing Financial Statements from a Trial Balance (Dividends Included)

The following accounts are taken from Buck Up!, Inc., a company that specializes in horse-breaking services and rodeo lessons, as of December 31, 2010.

BUCK UP!, INC.
Unadjusted Trial Balance
At December 31, 2010

Account Name	Debits	Credits
Cash	$ 59,750	
Accounts Receivable	3,300	
Prepaid Insurance	1,200	
Equipment	64,600	
Land	23,000	
Accounts Payable		$ 29,230
Unearned Revenue		1,500
Long-term Notes Payable		74,000
Contributed Capital		5,000
Retained Earnings		14,500
Dividends	3,500	
Horse-breaking Revenue		25,200
Rodeo Lesson Revenue		10,500
Wages Expense	3,900	
Maintenance Expense	410	
Other Expenses	270	
Totals	$159,930	$159,930

Required:

Using the unadjusted trial balance provided, create a classified Balance Sheet, Statement of Retained Earnings, and Income Statement for Buck Up!, Inc., for the year ended December 31, 2010. (These financial statements would be considered "preliminary" because they use unadjusted balances.)

TIP: Create the Income Statement first, followed by the Statement of Retained Earnings, and finally the classified Balance Sheet. Follow the formats presented in Exhibits 1.2, 1.3, and 2.13.

M3-21 Preparing an Income Statement

The following accounts are taken from the December 31, 2007, financial statements of Time Warner, Inc. (Amounts are in millions.)

LO1, 4

Time Warner, Inc.

Subscription Revenue	$24,904
Other Revenues	12,779
Salaries Expense	9,653
Cash	1,516
Accounts Receivable	7,296
Interest Expense	2,299
Accounts Payable	1,470
Advertising Revenue	8,799
Long-term Debt	37,004
Other Expenses	381
Unearned Revenue	1,178
Equipment	18,048
Income Tax Expense	2,336
Operating Expense	27,426

Required:

Prepare an Income Statement for the year ended December 31, 2007.

TIP: Some of the above accounts are not reported on the income statement.

EXERCISES

E3-1 Matching Definitions with Terms

LO1

Match each definition with its related term by entering the appropriate letter in the space provided.

Term	Definition
____ 1. Expenses	A. Record expenses when incurred in earning revenue.
____ 2. Matching principle	B. A liability account used to record the obligation to provide future services or return cash that has been received before revenues have been earned.
____ 3. Revenue principle	
____ 4. Cash basis accounting	C. Costs that result when a company sacrifices resources to generate revenues.
____ 5. Unearned Revenue	
____ 6. Accrual basis accounting	D. Record revenues when earned, not necessarily when cash is received.
____ 7. Prepaid Expenses	E. Record revenues when received and expenses when paid.
	F. A type of asset account used to record the benefits obtained when cash is paid before expenses are incurred.
	G. Record revenues when earned and expenses when incurred.

LO1, 2

Apple

AT&T

American Airlines

E3-2 Identifying Accrual Basis Revenues

According to the revenue principle, revenues should be recognized when they are earned, which happens when the company performs acts promised to the customer. For most businesses, this condition is met at the point of delivery of goods or services. The following transactions occurred in September 2010:

a. A customer pays $10 cash for 10 song files from Apple's iTunes store. Answer from Apple's standpoint.

b. Home Depot provides a carpet installation for $2,000 cash. A comparable installation from other companies costs $3,000.

c. AT&T is scheduled to install digital cable at 1,000 Austin area homes next week. The installation charge is $100 per home. The terms require payment within 30 days of installation. Answer from AT&T's standpoint.

d. AT&T completes the installations described in (c). Answer from AT&T's standpoint.

e. AT&T receives payment from customers for the installations described in (c). Answer from AT&T's standpoint.

f. A customer purchases a ticket from American Airlines in September for $500 cash to travel in December. Answer from American Airlines's standpoint.

Required:

For each of the transactions, if revenue is to be recognized in September, indicate the amount. If revenue is not to be recognized in September, explain why.

LO1, 2

T-Mobile

E3-3 Identifying Accrual Basis Revenues

According to the revenue principle, revenues should be recognized when they are earned, which happens when the company performs acts promised to the customer. For most businesses, this condition is met at the point of delivery of goods or services. The following transactions occurred in September 2010:

a. Gillespie Enterprises Inc. issues $26 million in new common stock.

b. Cal State University receives $20,000,000 cash for 80,000 five-game season football tickets. None of the games have been played.

c. Cal State plays the first football game referred to in (b).

d. Hall Construction Company signs a contract with a customer for the construction of a new $500,000 warehouse. At the signing, Hall receives a check for $50,000 as a deposit to be applied against amounts earned during the first phase of construction. Answer from Hall's standpoint.

e. A popular snowboarding magazine company receives a total of $1,800 today from subscribers. The subscriptions begin in the next fiscal year. Answer from the magazine company's standpoint.

f. T-Mobile sells a $100 cell phone plan for service in September to a customer who charges the sale on his credit card. Answer from the standpoint of T-Mobile.

Required:

For each of the transactions, if revenue is to be recognized in September, indicate the amount. If revenue is not to be recognized in September, explain why.

LO1, 2

Gateway

E3-4 Identifying Accrual Basis Expenses

Under accrual basis accounting, expenses are recognized when incurred, which means the activity giving rise to the expense has occurred. Assume the following transactions occurred in January 2010:

a. Gateway pays its computer service technicians $90,000 in salary for work done in January 2010. Answer from Gateway's standpoint.

b. At the beginning of January, Turner Construction Company pays $4,500 in rent for February–April 2010.

c. The McGraw-Hill Companies—publisher of this textbook and *BusinessWeek*—uses $1,000 worth of electricity and natural gas in January for which it has not yet been billed.

d. Pooler Company receives and pays in January a $1,500 invoice from a consulting firm for services received in January.

e. The campus bookstore receives consulting services at a cost of $5,000. The terms indicate that payment is due within 30 days of the consultation.

f. Schergevitch Incorporated has its delivery van repaired in January for $280 and charges the amount on account.

Required:

For each of the transactions, if an expense is to be recognized in January, indicate the amount. If an expense is not to be recognized in January, indicate why.

E3-5 Identifying Accrual Basis Expenses

LO1, 2

Under accrual basis accounting, expenses are recognized when incurred. The following transactions occurred in January 2010:

American Express
Waste Management, Inc.

a. American Express pays its salespersons $3,500 in commissions related to December financial advisory services sales. Answer from American Express's standpoint.

b. On January 31, American Express determines that it will pay its salespersons $4,200 in commissions related to January sales. The payment will be made in early February. Answer from American Express's standpoint.

c. The city of Omaha hires Waste Management, Inc., to provide trash collection services beginning in January. The city pays $7.2 million for the entire year. Answer from the city's standpoint.

d. The University of Florida pays $10,000 in advance for refundable airline tickets to fly the baseball team to a tournament in California. The first game will be played in March. Answer from the university's standpoint.

e. A Houston Community College employee works eight hours, at $15 per hour, on January 31; payday is not until February 3. Answer from the college's point of view.

f. Wang Company paid $3,600 for a fire insurance policy on January 1. The policy covers 12 months beginning on January 1. Answer from Wang's point of view.

g. Ziegler Company, a farm equipment company, receives a phone bill for $230 of January calls. The bill has not been paid to date.

Required:

For each of the transactions, if an expense is to be recognized in January, indicate the amount. If an expense is not to be recognized in January, indicate why.

E3-6 Determining Accounting Equation Effects of Various Transactions

LO2, 3

The following transactions occurred during a recent year:

a. Paid wages of $1,000 for the current period (example).
b. Borrowed $5,000 cash from local bank.
c. Purchased $2,000 of equipment on credit.
d. Earned $400 of sales revenue, collected cash.
e. Received $800 of utilities services, on credit.
f. Earned $700 of service revenue, on credit.
g. Paid $300 cash on account to a supplier.
h. Incurred $70 of delivery expenses, paid cash.
i. Earned $400 of service revenue, collected half in cash, balance on credit.
j. Collected $100 cash from customers on account.
k. Incurred $300 of advertising costs, paid half in cash, balance on credit.

Required:

For each of the transactions, complete the table below, indicating the account, amount, and direction of the effect (+ for increase and − for decrease) of each transaction under the accrual basis. Write NE if there is no effect. Include revenues and expenses as subcategories of stockholders' equity, as shown for the first transaction, which is provided as an example.

Transaction	Assets	=	Liabilities	+	Stockholders' Equity
(a) (example)	Cash −1,000		NE		Wages Expense (+E) −1,000

LO2, 3

E3-7 Determining Accounting Equation Effects of Various Transactions

Wolverine World Wide, Inc., manufactures military, work, sport, and casual footwear and leather accessories under a variety of brand names, such as Caterpillar, Hush Puppies, Wolverine, and Steve Madden. The following transactions occurred during a recent year. Dollars are in thousands.

- a. Made cash sales of $49,000 (example).
- b. Purchased $3,000 of additional supplies on account.
- c. Borrowed $58,000 on long-term notes.
- d. Purchased $18,600 in additional equipment, paying in cash.
- e. Incurred $87,000 in selling expenses, paying two-thirds in cash and owing the rest on account.
- f. Paid $4,700 in rent for this period.

Required:

For each of the transactions, complete the table below, indicating the account, amount, and direction of the effect (+ for increase and − for decrease) and amount of each transaction under the accrual basis. Write NE if there is no effect. Include revenues and expenses as subcategories of stockholders' equity, as shown for the first transaction, which is provided as an example.

Transaction	Assets	Liabilities	Stockholders' Equity
(a) (example)	Cash +49,000	NE	Sales Revenue (+R) +49,000

LO2, 3

Sysco

E3-8 Recording Accrual Basis Journal Entries

Sysco, formed in 1969, is America's largest marketer and distributor of food service products, serving nearly 250,000 restaurants, hotels, schools, hospitals, and other institutions. The following transactions are typical of those that occurred in a recent year. (All amounts are rounded to the nearest thousand.)

- a. Borrowed $80,000 from a bank, signing a short-term note payable.
- b. Provided $10,000 in service to customers, with $9,500 on account and the rest received in cash.
- c. Purchased plant and equipment for $130,000 in cash.
- d. Paid employee wages of $1,000.
- e. Received $410 on account from a customer.
- f. Purchased and used fuel of $400 in delivery vehicles during the year (paid for in cash).
- g. Paid $8,200 cash on accounts payable.
- h. Incurred $20,000 in utility expenses during the year, of which $15,000 was paid in cash and the rest owed on account.

Required:

For each of the transactions, prepare journal entries. Determine whether the accounting equation remains in balance and debits equal credits after each entry.

LO2, 3

Greek Peak

E3-9 Recording Accrual Basis Journal Entries

Greek Peak is a ski resort in upstate New York. The company sells lift tickets, ski lessons, and ski equipment. It operates several restaurants and rents townhouses to vacationing skiers. The following hypothetical December 2010 transactions are typical of those that occur at the resort.

- a. Borrowed $500,000 from the bank on December 1, signing a note payable, due in six months.
- b. Purchased a new snowplow for $20,000 cash on December 31.
- c. Purchased ski supplies for $10,000 on account.
- d. Incurred $22,000 in routine maintenance expenses for the chairlifts; paid cash.
- e. Received $72,000 for season passes (beginning in the new year).
- f. Daily lift passes were sold this month for a total of $76,000 cash.
- g. Received a $320 deposit on a townhouse to be rented for five days in January 2011.
- h. Paid half the charges incurred on account in (c).
- i. Paid $18,000 in wages to employees for the month of December.

Required:

Prepare journal entries for each transaction. Be sure to categorize each account as an Asset (A), Liability (L), Stockholders' Equity (SE), Revenue (R), or Expense (E), and check that debits equal credits for each journal entry.

E3-10 Recording Accrual Basis Journal Entries

LO2, 3

Rowland & Sons Air Transport Service, Inc., has been in operation for three years. The following transactions occurred in February 2010:

Feb. 1	Paid $200 for rent of hangar space in February.
Feb. 2	Purchased fuel costing $450 on account for the next flight to Dallas.
Feb. 4	Received customer payment of $800 to ship several items to Philadelphia next month.
Feb. 7	Flew cargo from Denver to Dallas; the customer paid in full ($900 cash).
Feb. 10	Paid pilot $1,200 in wages for flying in February.
Feb. 14	Paid $60 for an advertisement run in the local paper on February 14.
Feb. 18	Flew cargo for two customers from Dallas to Albuquerque for $1,700; one customer paid $500 cash and the other asked to be billed $1,200.
Feb. 25	Purchased on account $1,350 in spare parts for the planes.

Required:

Prepare journal entries for each transaction. Be sure to categorize each account as an Asset (A), Liability (L), Stockholders' Equity (SE), Revenue (R), or Expense (E).

E3-11 Recording and Posting Accrual Basis Journal Entries

LO2, 3

Ricky's Piano Rebuilding Company has been operating for one year (2009). At the start of 2010, its income statement accounts had zero balances and its balance sheet account balances were as follows:

Cash	$ 6,000	Accounts Payable	$ 8,000
Accounts Receivable	25,000	Unearned Revenue (deposits)	3,200
Supplies	1,200	Notes Payable	40,000
Equipment	8,000	Contributed Capital	8,000
Land	6,000	Retained Earnings	9,000
Building	22,000		

Required:

1. Create T-accounts for the balance sheet accounts and for these additional accounts: Piano Rebuilding Revenue, Rent Revenue, Wages Expense, and Utilities Expense. Enter the beginning balances.
2. Prepare journal entries for the following January 2010 transactions, using the letter of each transaction as a reference:
   a. Received a $500 deposit from a customer who wanted her piano rebuilt in February.
   b. Rented a part of the building to a bicycle repair shop; $300 rent received for January.
   c. Delivered five rebuilt pianos to customers who paid $14,500 in cash.
   d. Delivered two rebuilt pianos to customers for $7,000 charged on account.
   e. Received $6,000 from customers as payment on their accounts.
   f. Received an electric and gas utility bill for $350 for January services to be paid in February.
   g. Ordered $800 in supplies.
   h. Paid $1,700 on account in January.
   i. Paid $10,000 in wages to employees in January for work done this month.
   j. Received and paid cash for the supplies in (g).
3. Post the journal entries to the T-accounts. Show the unadjusted ending balances in the T-accounts.

LO4   **E3-12 Preparing an Unadjusted Trial Balance**

Refer to E3-11.

Required:

Use the balances in the completed T-accounts in E3-11 to prepare an unadjusted trial balance at the end of January 2010.

LO2, 3, 4   **E3-13 Inferring Operating Transactions and Preparing an Unadjusted Trial Balance**

Virtual Golf Corporation operates indoor golf simulators that allow individual customers and golf club members to experience courses like Pebble Beach and Augusta without leaving their own neighborhood. Its stores are located in rented space in malls and shopping centers. During its first month of business ended April 30, 2010, Virtual Golf Corporation completed seven transactions with the dollar effects indicated in the following schedule:

	Assets				=	Liabilities	+	Stockholders' Equity	
Accounts	Cash	Accounts Receivable	Supplies	Equipment		Accounts Payable	Unearned Revenue	Contributed Capital	Retained Earnings
Beginning balance	$ 0	$ 0	$ 0	$ 0		$ 0	$ 0	$ 0	$ 0
a	+100,000							+100,000	
b	−30,000			+30,000					
c	−200		+1,000			+800			
d	+9,000	+1,000							Sales Revenue +10,000
e	−1,000								Wages Expense −1,000
f						+1,200			Utilities Expense −1,200
g	+2,000						+2,000		
Ending balance	$ 79,800	$ 1,000	$ 1,000	$ 30,000		$ 2,000	$ 2,000	$ 100,000	

Required:

1. Write a brief explanation of transactions (a) through (g). Include any assumptions that you made.
2. Using the ending balance in each account, prepare an unadjusted trial balance for Virtual Golf Corporation on April 30, 2010.

LO1, 2, 3

Dow Jones & Company

E3-14 Inferring Transactions and Computing Effects Using T-Accounts

A recent annual report of Dow Jones & Company, the world leader in business and financial news and information (and publisher of *The Wall Street Journal*), included the following accounts. Dollars are in millions.

dr + Accounts Receivable (A) cr −		dr + Prepaid Expenses (A) cr −		dr − Unearned Revenue (L) cr +	
1/1 313		1/1 25			240 1/1
2,573 [a]		43 [b]		[c]	328
12/31 295		12/31 26			253 12/31

Required:

1. For each T-account, describe the typical transactions that cause it to increase and decrease.
2. Express each T-account in equation format (Beginning + Increase Side − Decrease Side = Ending) and then solve for the missing amounts (in millions). For example, the Accounts Receivable T-account can be expressed as: 313 + 2,573 − a = 295. By rearranging the equation, you can solve for 313 + 2,573 − 295 = a.

E3-15 Determining Accounting Equation Effects of Several Transactions LO2, 3

In January 2010, Tongo, Inc., a branding consultant, had the following transactions. Indicate the accounts, amounts, and direction of the effects on the accounting equation under the accrual basis. A sample is provided.

a. *(Sample)* Received $9,500 cash for consulting services rendered in January.
b. Issued stock to investors for $10,000 cash.
c. Purchased $12,000 of equipment, paying 25% in cash and owing the rest on a note due in 2 years.
d. Received $7,500 cash for consulting services to be performed in February.
e. Bought $1,000 of supplies on account.
f. Received utility bill for January for $1,250, due February 15.
g. Consulted for customers in January for fees totaling $15,900, due in February.
h. Received $12,000 cash for consulting services rendered in December.
i. Paid $500 toward supplies purchased in (e).

a.	Assets	=	Liabilities	+	Stockholders' Equity
	Cash +9,500 =				Service Revenue (+R) +9,500

E3-16 Preparing Journal Entries LO3

For each of the transactions in E3-15 (including the sample), write the journal entry using the format shown in this chapter.

E3-17 Posting to T-Accounts LO3

For each of the transactions in E3-15 (including the sample), post the effects to the appropriate T-accounts and determine ending account balances. Beginning account balances have been given. The sample transaction has been posted as an example.

dr +	Cash (A)	cr −		dr − Accounts Payable (L) cr +		dr − Contributed Capital (SE) cr +
1/1/10	10,000			5,000 1/1/10		12,000 1/1/10
a.	9,500					

dr + Accounts Receivable (A) cr −		dr − Unearned Revenue (L) cr +		dr − Retained Earnings (SE) cr +
1/1/10 12,500		2,500 1/1/10		8,800 1/1/10

dr +	Supplies (A)	cr −		dr − Note Payable (L) cr +		dr − Service Revenues (R) cr +
1/1/10	800			0 1/1/10		0 1/1/10
						9,500 a.

dr +	Equipment (A)	cr −			dr + Utilities Expense (E) cr −
1/1/10	5,000				1/1/10 0

E3-18 Creating an Unadjusted Trial Balance LO4

Based on the transactions posted to T-accounts in E3-17, create an unadjusted trial balance for Tongo, Inc., for the month ended January 31, 2010. Distinguish the balance sheet and income statement accounts as shown in Exhibit 3.9.

E3-19 Inferring Transactions and Creating Financial Statements LO3

An analysis of transactions made during July 2010 by NepCo, an Internet service provider, during its first month of operations is shown below. Increases and decreases affecting revenues and expenses are explained.

	Assets				=	Liabilities	+	Stockholders' Equity	
	Cash	Accounts Receivable	Supplies	Equipment		Accounts Payable		Contributed Capital	Retained Earnings
(a)	+11,000							+11,000	
(b)						+710			−710 Utilities expense
(c)		+5,000							+5,000 Service revenue
(d)	−6,000			+10,000		+4,000			
(e)	+1,000								+1,000 Service revenue
(f)			+550			+550			
(g)	−3,000					−3,000			
(h)	−2,000								−2,000 Wage expense
(i)	−750								−750 Rent expense
(j)	+1,500	−1,500							
	1,750	3,500	550	10,000		2,260		11,000	2,540

Required:

1. Describe the business activities that led to the accounting equation effects for each transaction shown above.

2. Prepare an income statement and a statement of retained earnings for July, and a classified balance sheet as of July 31, 2010. (These financial statements would be considered "preliminary" because they use unadjusted balances.)

LO3   **E3-20 Determining the Effects of Various Transactions**

EZ Reader was founded by John "Bum" Andrews in January 2010 to provide text reading and recording services. Selected transactions for EZ Reader's first month of business are as follows:

a. Issued stock to investors for $50,000 cash.
b. Billed customers $10,500 for services performed in January.
c. Purchased car for $24,500 for use in the business. Paid in cash.
d. Purchased $2,400 of supplies on account.
e. Received $7,500 cash from customers billed in transaction (b).
f. Used $1,500 in utilities, which will be paid in February.
g. Paid employees $3,500 cash for work done in January.
h. Paid $1,200 cash toward supplies purchased in transaction (d).

Required:

For each transaction, give (a) the name of the account being debited or credited, (b) the basic account type (A, L, SE, R, E), (c) whether the account is increased (+) or decreased (−) due to the transaction, and (d) whether the account normally holds a debit or credit balance. Transaction (a) has been given as an example.

	Debit Side of Journal Entry					Credit Side of Journal Entry			
	Account Name	Account Type	Direction of Change	Normal Balance		Account Name	Account Type	Direction of Change	Normal Balance
(a)	Cash	A	+	Debit		Contributed Capital	SE	+	Credit

LO2, 3, 4, 5   **E3-21 Comprehensive Exercise**

Vanishing Games Corporation (VGC) operates a massively multiplayer online game, charging players a monthly subscription of $15. At the start of 2010, VGC's income statement accounts had zero balances and its balance sheet account balances were as follows:

Cash	$1,500,000	Accounts Payable	$ 108,000
Accounts Receivable	150,000	Unearned Revenue	73,500
Supplies	14,700	Notes Payable (due 2013)	60,000
Equipment	874,500	Contributed Capital	2,500,000
Land	1,200,000	Retained Earnings	1,419,700
Building	422,000		

In addition to the above accounts, VGC's chart of accounts includes the following: Subscription Revenue, Licensing Revenue, Wages Expense, Advertising Expense, and Utilities Expense.

Required:

1. Analyze the effect of the January 2010 transactions (shown below) on the accounting equation, using the format shown in this chapter's Demonstration Case B.
   a. Received $50,000 cash from customers for subscriptions that had already been earned in 2009.
   b. Received $25,000 cash from Electronic Arts, Inc., for licensing revenue earned in the month of January 2010.
   c. Purchased 10 new computer servers for $33,500; paid $10,000 cash and signed a three-year note for the remainder owed.
   d. Paid $10,000 for an Internet advertisement run on Yahoo! in January 2010.
   e. Sold 15,000 monthly subscriptions at $15 each for services provided during the month of January 2010. Half was collected in cash and half was sold on account.
   f. Received an electric and gas utility bill for $5,350 for January 2010 utility services. The bill will be paid in February.
   g. Paid $378,000 in wages to employees for work done in January 2010.
   h. Purchased $3,000 of supplies on account.
   i. Paid $3,000 cash to the supplier in (h).

2. Prepare journal entries for the January 2010 transactions listed in requirement 1, using the letter of each transaction as a reference.
3. Create T-accounts, enter the beginning balances shown above, post the journal entries to the T-accounts, and show the unadjusted ending balances in the T-accounts.
4. Prepare an unadjusted trial balance as of January 31, 2010.
5. Prepare an Income Statement for the month ended January 31, 2010, using unadjusted balances from requirement 4.
6. Prepare a Statement of Retained Earnings for the month ended January 31, 2010, using the beginning balance given above and the net income from requirement 5. Assume VGC has no dividends.
7. Prepare a classified Balance Sheet at January 31, 2010, using your response to requirement 6.
8. Why does the income statement total not equal the change in cash?

COACHED PROBLEMS

CP3-1 Recording Nonquantitative Journal Entries

LO1, 2, 3

The following list includes a series of accounts for B-ball Corporation, which has been operating for three years. These accounts are listed alphabetically and numbered for identification. Following the accounts is a series of transactions. For each transaction, indicate the account(s) that should be debited and credited by entering the appropriate account number(s) to the right of each transaction. If no journal entry is needed, write *none* after the transaction. The first transaction is used as an example.

TIP: In transaction (h), remember what the matching principle says.
TIP: Think of transaction (j) as two transactions: (1) incur expenses and liability and (2) pay part of the liability.

Account No.	Account Title	Account No.	Account Title
1	Accounts Payable	8	Note Payable
2	Accounts Receivable	9	Prepaid Insurance
3	Cash	10	Rent Expense
4	Contributed Capital	11	Service Revenue
5	Equipment	12	Supplies Expense
6	Income Tax Expense	13	Supplies
7	Income Tax Payable		

Transactions	Debit	Credit
a. Example: Purchased equipment for use in the business; paid one-third cash and signed a note payable for the balance.	5	3, 8
b. Issued stock to new investors.	——	——
c. Paid cash for rent this period.	——	——
d. Collected cash for services performed this period.	——	——
e. Collected cash on accounts receivable for services performed last period.	——	——
f. Performed services this period on credit.	——	——
g. Paid cash on accounts payable for expenses incurred last period.	——	——
h. Purchased supplies to be used later; paid cash.	——	——
i. Used some of the supplies for operations.	——	——
j. Paid three-fourths of the income tax expense for the year; the balance will be paid next year.	——	——
k. On the last day of the current period, paid cash for an insurance policy covering the next two years.	——	——

LO2, 3

CP3-2 Recording Journal Entries

Ryan Olson organized a new company, MeToo, Inc. The company provides networking management services on social network sites. You have been hired to record the transactions occurring in the first two weeks of operations, beginning May 1, 2010.

a. May 1: Issued 1,000 shares of stock to investors for $30 per share.
b. May 1: Borrowed $50,000 from the bank to provide additional funding to begin operations; the note is due in two years.
c. May 1: Paid $2,400 for a one-year fire insurance policy.
  TIP: For convenience, simply record the full amount of the payment as an asset (Prepaid Insurance). At the end of the month, this account will be adjusted to its proper balance. We will study this adjustment process in Chapter 4, so just leave it as Prepaid Insurance for now.
d. May 3: Purchased furniture and fixtures for the store for $15,000 on account. The amount is due within 30 days.
e. May 5: Placed advertisements in local college newspapers for a total of $250 cash.
f. May 9: Sold services for $400 cash.
g. May 14: Made full payment for the furniture and fixtures purchased on account on May 3.

Required:

For each of the transactions, prepare journal entries. Be sure to categorize each account as an asset (A), liability (L), stockholders' equity (SE), revenue (R), or expense (E).

LO1, 2, 3, 4

www.mhhe.com/phillips3e

CP3-3 Analyzing the Effects of Transactions Using T-Accounts and Preparing an Unadjusted Trial Balance

Barbara Jones opened Barb's Book Business on February 1, 2010. The company specializes in editing accounting textbooks. You have been hired as manager. Your duties include maintaining the company's financial records. The following transactions occurred in February 2010, the first month of operations.

a. Received shareholders' cash contributions totaling $16,000 to form the corporation; issued stock.
b. Paid $2,400 cash for three months' rent for office space.

TIP: For convenience, simply record the full amount of the payment as an asset (Prepaid Rent). At the end of the month, this account will be adjusted to its proper balance. We will study this adjustment process in Chapter 4, so just leave it as Prepaid Rent for now.

c. Purchased supplies for $300 cash.
d. Signed a promissory note, payable in two years; deposited $10,000 in the company's bank account.
e. Used the money from (d) to purchase equipment for $2,500 and furniture and fixtures for $7,500.
f. Placed an advertisement in the local paper for $425 cash.
g. Made sales totaling $1,800; $1,525 was in cash and the rest on accounts receivable.
h. Incurred and paid employee wages of $420.
i. Collected accounts receivable of $50 from customers.
j. Repaired one of the computers for $120 cash.

TIP: Most repairs involve costs that do *not* provide additional future economic benefits.

Required:

1. Set up appropriate T-accounts for Cash, Accounts Receivable, Supplies, Prepaid Rent, Equipment, Furniture and Fixtures, Notes Payable, Contributed Capital, Service Revenue, Advertising Expense, Wages Expense, and Repair Expense. All accounts begin with zero balances.

   TIP: When preparing the T-accounts, you might find it useful to group them by type: assets, liabilities, stockholders' equity, revenues, and expenses.

2. Record in the T-accounts the effects of each transaction for Barb's Book Business in February, referencing each transaction in the accounts with the transaction letter. Show the unadjusted ending balances in the T-accounts.

3. Prepare an unadjusted trial balance at the end of February.

4. Refer to the revenues and expenses shown on the unadjusted trial balance. Based on this information, write a short memo to Barbara offering your opinion on the results of operations during the first month of business.

GROUP A PROBLEMS

PA3-1 Recording Nonquantitative Journal Entries |ACCOUNTING LO1, 2, 3

The following is a series of accounts for Dewan & Allard, Incorporated, which has been operating for two years. The accounts are listed alphabetically and numbered for identification. Following the accounts is a series of transactions. For each transaction, indicate the account(s) that should be debited and credited by entering the appropriate account number(s) to the right of each transaction. If no journal entry is needed, write *none* after the transaction. The first transaction is given as an example.

Account No.	Account Title	Account No.	Account Title
1	Accounts Payable	9	Land
2	Accounts Receivable	10	Note Payable
3	Advertising Expense	11	Prepaid Insurance
4	Buildings	12	Service Revenue
5	Cash	13	Supplies Expense
6	Contributed Capital	14	Supplies
7	Income Tax Expense	15	Wages Expense
8	Income Tax Payable		

Transactions	Debit	Credit
a. Example: Issued stock to new investors.	5	6
b. Performed services for customers this period on credit.	2	12
c. Purchased on credit but did not use supplies this period.	14	1
d. Prepaid a fire insurance policy this period to cover the next 12 months.	11	5
e. Purchased a building this period by making a 20 percent cash downpayment and signing a note payable for the balance.	4	5,10
f. Collected cash for services that had been provided and recorded in the prior year.	5	2
g. Paid cash for wages that had been incurred this period.	15	5
h. Paid cash for supplies that had been purchased on accounts payable in the prior period.	1	5
i. Paid cash for advertising expense incurred in the current period.	3	5
j. Incurred advertising expenses this period to be paid next period.	3	7
k. Collected cash for services rendered this period.	5	12
l. Used supplies on hand to clean the offices.	13	14
m. Recorded income taxes for this period to be paid at the beginning of the next period.	7	8
n. This period a shareholder sold some shares of her stock to another person for an amount above the original issuance price.		

LO2, 3   **PA3-2 Recording Journal Entries**

Diana Mark is the president of ServicePro, Inc., a company that provides temporary employees for not-for-profit companies. ServicePro has been operating for five years; its revenues are increasing with each passing year. You have been hired to help Diana in analyzing the following transactions for the first two weeks of April 2010:

April 2	Purchased office supplies for $500 on account.
April 5	Billed the local United Way office $1,950 for temporary services provided.
April 8	Paid $250 for supplies purchased and recorded on account last period.
April 8	Placed an advertisement in the local paper for $400 cash.
April 9	Purchased new equipment for the office costing $2,300 cash.
April 10	Paid employee wages of $1,200, which were incurred in April.
April 11	Received $1,000 on account from the local United Way office billed on April 5.
April 12	Purchased land as the site of a future office for $10,000. Paid $2,000 down and signed a note payable for the balance.
April 13	Issued 2,000 additional shares of stock for $40 per share in anticipation of building a new office.
April 14	Billed Family & Children's Services $2,000 for services rendered this month.
April 15	Received the April telephone bill for $245 to be paid next month.

Required:

For each of the transactions, prepare journal entries. Be sure to categorize each account as an asset (A), liability (L), stockholders' equity (SE), revenue (R), or expense (E).

LO1, 2, 3, 4   **PA3-3 Analyzing the Effects of Transactions Using T-Accounts and Preparing an Unadjusted Trial Balance**

Spicewood Stables, Inc., was established in Dripping Springs, Texas, on April 1, 2010. The company provides stables, care for animals, and grounds for riding and showing horses. You have been

www.mhhe.com/phillips3e

hired as the new Assistant Controller. The following transactions for April 2010 are provided for your review.

a. Received contributions from five investors of $200,000 in cash ($40,000 each).
b. Built a barn for $142,000. The company paid half the amount in cash on April 1 and signed a three-year note payable for the balance.
c. Provided $15,260 in animal care services for customers, all on credit.
d. Rented stables to customers who cared for their own animals; received cash of $13,200.
e. Received from a customer $1,500 to board her horse in May, June, and July (record as Unearned Revenue).
f. Purchased hay and feed supplies on account for $3,210.
g. Paid $840 in cash for water utilities incurred in the month.
h. Paid $1,700 on accounts payable for previous purchases.
i. Received $1,000 from customers on accounts receivable.
j. Paid $4,000 in wages to employees who worked during the month.
k. At the end of the month, prepaid a two-year insurance policy for $3,600.
l. Received an electric utility bill for $1,200 for usage in April; the bill will be paid next month.

Required:

1. Set up appropriate T-accounts. All accounts begin with zero balances.
2. Record in the T-accounts the effects of each transaction for Spicewood Stables in April, referencing each transaction in the accounts with the transaction letter. Show the unadjusted ending balances in the T-accounts.
3. Prepare an unadjusted trial balance as of April 30, 2010.
4. Refer to the revenues and expenses shown on the unadjusted trial balance. Based on this information, write a short memo to the five owners offering your opinion on the results of operations during the first month of business.

GROUP B PROBLEMS

PB3-1 Recording Nonquantitative Journal Entries

LO1, 2, 3

Abercrombie & Fitch
The Limited

Abercrombie & Fitch Co. is a specialty retailer of casual apparel. The company's brand was established in 1892. It was first publicly traded in 1996 and was spun off from The Limited in 1998. The following is a series of accounts for Abercrombie. The accounts are listed alphabetically and numbered for identification. Following the accounts is a series of transactions. For each transaction, indicate the account(s) that should be debited and credited by entering the appropriate account number(s) to the right of each transaction. If no journal entry is needed, write *none* after the transaction. The first transaction is given as an example.

Account No.	Account Title	Account No.	Account Title
1	Accounts Payable	7	Prepaid Rent
2	Accounts Receivable	8	Rent Expense
3	Cash	9	Supplies Expense
4	Contributed Capital	10	Supplies
5	Equipment	11	Unearned Revenue
6	Interest Revenue	12	Wages Expense

Transactions	Debit	Credit
a. Example: Incurred wages expense; paid cash.	12	3
b. Collected cash on account.	___	___
c. Used up supplies (cash register tapes, etc.) this period.	___	___
d. Sold gift certificates to customers; none redeemed this period.	___	___
e. Purchased equipment, paying part in cash and charging the balance on account.	___	___
f. Paid cash to suppliers on account.	___	___
g. Issued additional stock for cash.	___	___
h. Paid rent to landlords for next month's use of mall space.	___	___
i. Earned and received cash for interest on investments.	___	___

LO2, 3   **PB3-2 Recording Journal Entries**

Robin Harrington established Time Definite Delivery on January 1, 2010. The following transactions occurred during the company's most recent quarter.

a.   Issued stock for $80,000.
b.   Provided delivery service to customers, receiving $72,000 in accounts receivable and $16,000 in cash.
c.   Purchased equipment costing $82,000 and signed a long-term note for the full amount.
d.   Incurred repair costs of $3,000 on account.
e.   Collected $65,000 from customers on account.
f.   Borrowed $90,000 by signing a long-term note.
g.   Prepaid $74,400 cash to rent equipment and aircraft next quarter.
h.   Paid employees $38,000 for work done during the quarter.
i.   Purchased (with cash) and used $49,000 in fuel for delivery equipment.
j.   Paid $2,000 on accounts payable.
k.   Ordered, but haven't yet received, $700 in supplies.

Required:

For each of the transactions, prepare journal entries. Be sure to categorize each account as an asset (A), liability (L), stockholders' equity (SE), revenue (R), or expense (E).

LO1, 2, 3, 4   **PB3-3 Analyzing the Effects of Transactions Using T-Accounts and Preparing an Unadjusted Trial Balance**

Jessica Pothier opened FunFlatables on June 1, 2010. The company rents out moon walks and inflatable slides for parties and corporate events. The company also has obtained the use of an abandoned ice rink located in a local shopping mall, where its rental products are displayed and available for casual hourly rental by mall patrons. The following transactions occurred during the first month of operations.

a.   Jessica contributed $50,000 cash to the company in exchange for its stock.
b.   Purchased inflatable rides and inflation equipment, paying $20,000 cash.
c.   Received $5,000 cash from casual hourly rentals at the mall.
d.   Rented rides and equipment to customers for $10,000. Received cash of $2,000 and the rest is due from customers.
e.   Received $2,500 from a large corporate customer as a deposit on a party booking for July 4.
f.   Began to prepare for the July 4 party by purchasing various party supplies on account for $600.
g.   Paid $6,000 in cash for renting the mall space this month.
h.   Prepaid next month's mall space rental charge of $6,000.
i.   Received $1,000 from customers on accounts receivable.
j.   Paid $4,000 in wages to employees for work done during the month.
k.   Paid $1,000 for running a television ad this month.

Required:

1.   Set up appropriate T-accounts. All accounts begin with zero balances.
2.   Record in the T-accounts the effects of each transaction for FunFlatables in June, referencing each transaction in the accounts with the transaction letter. Show the unadjusted ending balances in the T-accounts.
3.   Prepare an unadjusted trial balance for the end of June 2010.
4.   Refer to the revenues and expenses shown on the unadjusted trial balance and write a short memo to Jessica offering your opinion on the results of operations during the first month of business.

SKILLS DEVELOPMENT CASES

LO1   **S3-1 Finding Financial Information**

Refer to the financial statements of The Home Depot in Appendix A at the end of this book, or download the annual report from the *Cases* section of the text's Web site at www.mhhe.com/phillips3e.

Required:

1. Did The Home Depot's sales revenues increase or decrease in the year ended February 1, 2009? By how much? Calculate this change as a percentage of the previous year's sales revenues by dividing the amount of the change by the previous year's sales revenues and multiplying by 100.

2. State the amount of the largest expense on the most recent income statement and describe the transaction represented by the expense. Did this expense increase or decrease from the previous year and by what percentage?

S3-2 Comparing Financial Information

LO1

Refer to the financial statements of The Home Depot in Appendix A and Lowe's in Appendix B at the end of this book, or download the annual reports from the *Cases* section of the text's Web site at www.mhhe.com/phillips3e.

Lowe's

Required:

1. Did Lowe's sales revenues increase or decrease in the year ended January 30, 2009, as compared to the preview year? By how much? Calculate this change as a percentage of the previous year's sales revenues. Is the trend in Lowe's sales revenues more or less favorable than The Home Depot's?

2. State the amount of the largest expense on the income statement of Lowe's for the year ended January 30, 2009, and describe the transaction represented by the expense. Did this expense increase or decrease and by what percentage, as compared to the previous year? Is the trend in Lowe's largest expense more or less favorable than the trend for The Home Depot's largest expense?

S3-3 Internet-Based Team Research: Examining the Income Statement

LO1, 5

As a team, select an industry to analyze. Using your Web browser, each team member should access the annual report or 10-K for one publicly traded company in the industry, with each member selecting a different company. (See S1-3 in Chapter 1 for a description of possible resources for these tasks.)

Required:

1. On an individual basis, each team member should write a short report that lists the following information:
    a. The major revenue and expense accounts on the most recent income statement.
    b. Description of how the company has followed the conditions of the revenue principle.
    c. The percentage of revenues that go to covering expenses, and that are in excess of expenses (in other words, the percentage that remains as net income).

2. Then, as a team, write a short report comparing and contrasting your companies using these attributes. Discuss any patterns across the companies that you as a team observe. Provide potential explanations for any differences discovered.

S3-4 Ethical Decision Making: A Real-Life Example

LO1, 2, 3, 5

Read the following excerpt from a September 2, 2002, article in *Fortune* magazine and answer the questions that appear below.

> Forget about fraud. Companies don't need to lie, cheat, and steal to fool investors. Clever managers have always had, and continue to have, access to perfectly legal tricks to help make their balance sheets and income statements look better than they really are—tricks that *even today* won't jeopardize their ability to swear to the SEC that their books are on the up and up . . . One of the most controversial of all number games—the one that got WorldCom in trouble—is to capitalize expenses. That can have a tremendous impact on the bottom line.

1. When a company incurs a cost, its accountants have to decide whether to record the cost as an asset or expense. When costs are recorded as an asset, they are said to be *capitalized*. This builds on ideas first presented in Chapter 2, where you learned that it was appropriate

to record costs as assets, provided that they possess certain characteristics. What are those characteristics?

2. The author of the article argues that even with clear rules like those referenced in question 1 above, accounting still allows managers to use "tricks" like *capitalizing expenses*. What do you suppose the author means by the expression *capitalizing expenses?*

3. Suppose that, in the current year, a company inappropriately records a cost as an asset when it should be recorded as an expense. What is the effect of this accounting decision on the current year's net income? What is the effect of this accounting decision on the following year's net income?

4. Later in the article (not shown) the author says that the videogame industry is one where companies frequently capitalize software development costs as assets. These costs include wages paid to programmers, fees paid to graphic designers, and amounts paid to game testers. Evaluate whether software development costs are likely to possess the main characteristics possessed by all assets. Can you think of a situation where software development costs might not possess these main characteristics?

5. Do you think it is always easy and straightforward to determine whether costs should be capitalized or expensed? Do you think it is always easy and straightforward to determine whether a manager is acting ethically or unethically? Give examples to illustrate your views.

LO1, 2, 5   **S3-5 Ethical Decision Making: A Mini-Case**

Mike Lynch is the manager of an upstate New York regional office for an insurance company. As the regional manager, his pay package includes a base salary, commissions, and a bonus when the region sells new policies in excess of its quota. Mike has been under enormous pressure lately, stemming largely from two factors. First, he is experiencing mounting personal debt due to a family member's illness. Second, compounding his worries, the region's sales of new insurance policies have dipped below the normal quota for the first time in years.

You have been working for Mike for two years, and like everyone else in the office, you consider yourself lucky to work for such a supportive boss. You also feel great sympathy for his personal problems over the last few months. In your position as accountant for the regional office, you are only too aware of the drop in new policy sales and the impact this will have on the manager's bonus. While you are working on the year-end financial statements, Mike stops by your office.

Mike asks you to change the manner in which you have accounted for a new property insurance policy for a large local business. A check for the premium, substantial in amount, came in the mail on December 31, the last day of the reporting year. The premium covers a period beginning on January 5. You deposited the check and correctly debited Cash and credited Unearned Revenue. Mike says, "Hey, we have the money this year, so why not count the revenue this year? I never did understand why you accountants are so picky about these things anyway. I'd like you to change the way you've recorded the transaction. I want you to credit a revenue account. And anyway, I've done favors for you in the past, and I am asking for such a small thing in return." With that, he leaves your office.

Required:

How should you handle this situation? What are the ethical implications of Mike's request? Who are the parties who would be helped or harmed if you went along with the request? If you fail to comply with his request, how will you explain your position to him? Justify your answers in writing.

LO1, 2, 4   **S3-6 Critical Thinking: Analyzing Changes in Accounts and Preparing a Trial Balance**

Hordichuk Painting Service Company was organized on January 20, 2010, by three individuals, each receiving 5,000 shares of stock from the new company. The following is a schedule of the cumulative account balances immediately after each of the first 9 transactions ending on January 31, 2010.

Accounts	Cumulative Balances								
	a	b	c	d	e	f	g	h	i
Cash	$75,000	$70,000	$85,000	$71,000	$61,000	$61,000	$46,000	$44,000	$60,000
Accounts Receivable			12,000	12,000	12,000	26,000	26,000	26,000	10,000
Supplies					5,000	5,000	4,000	4,000	4,000
Equipment		20,000	20,000	20,000	20,000	20,000	20,000	20,000	20,000
Land				18,000	18,000	18,000	18,000	18,000	18,000
Accounts Payable					3,000	3,000	3,000	1,000	1,000
Notes Payable		15,000	15,000	19,000	19,000	19,000	19,000	19,000	19,000
Contributed Capital	75,000	75,000	75,000	75,000	75,000	75,000	75,000	75,000	75,000
Paint Revenue			27,000	27,000	27,000	41,000	41,000	41,000	41,000
Supplies Expense							1,000	1,000	1,000
Wages Expense					8,000	8,000	23,000	23,000	23,000

Required:

1. Analyze the changes in this schedule for each transaction; then explain the transaction. Transactions (*a*) and (*b*) are examples:
   a. Cash increased $75,000, and Contributed Capital (stockholders' equity) increased $75,000. Therefore, transaction (*a*) was an issuance of the capital stock of the corporation for $75,000 cash.
   b. Cash decreased $5,000, Equipment (an asset) increased $20,000, and Notes Payable (a liability) increased $15,000. Therefore, transaction (*b*) was a purchase of equipment for $20,000. Payment was made as follows: cash, $5,000; notes payable, $15,000.
2. Based only on the preceding schedule, prepare an unadjusted trial balance.

S3-7 Analyzing Transactions and Preparing an Unadjusted Trial Balance

LO2, 3, 4

e**X**cel

www.mhhe.com/phillips3e

Assume you recently started up a new company that rents machines for making frozen drinks like smoothies, frozen juices, tea slush, and iced cappuccinos. For $100, your business will deliver a machine, provide supplies (straws, paper cups), set up the machine, and pick up the machine the next morning. Drink mix and other supplies are sold by other businesses in your city. Being a one-person operation, you are responsible for everything from purchasing to marketing to operations to accounting.

You've decided that you'll just write notes about what happens during the month and then do the accounting at the end of the month. You figure this will be more efficient. Plus, by waiting until the end of the month to do the accounting, you'll be less likely to make a mistake because by that time you'll better understand the accounting cycle. Your notes said the following about your first month of operations:

Oct. 2	Incorporated Slusher Gusher Inc. and contributed $10,000 for stock in the company.
Oct. 12	Paid cash to buy three frozen drink machines on eBay at a total cost of $1,500. What a deal!
Oct. 13	Paid cash to buy $70 of supplies. Wal-Mart was packed.
Oct. 16	Received $500 cash for this past week's rentals. I'm rich!
Oct. 17	Determined that $45 of supplies had been used up. Hmm, looks like I'll need some more.
Oct. 20	Bought $100 of supplies on account. I can't believe the party store gave me credit like that.
Oct. 23	Feeling tired after a busy week (6 rentals this time). Received $400 cash and expect to receive $200 more sometime this week.
Oct. 25	Received $100 cash from one of the customers who hadn't paid up yet. Called the other customer to remind him I'm waiting.

Oct. 26   Ran an ad in the local paper today. Paid $25 cash.

Oct. 27   Received $150 cash for a two-machine All Saints Day party to be held on November 1. It's a good thing I got this money because no other bookings are in sight for the rest of the month.

Required:

Create a spreadsheet in which to record the effects of the October transactions and calculate end-of-month totals. Using the spreadsheet, prepare a trial balance that checks whether debits = credits. Because you're dealing with your own business this time, you want to be sure that you do this just right, so you e-mail your friend Owen for advice. Here's his reply:

From:	Owentheaccountant@yahoo.com
To:	Helpme@hotmail.com
Cc:	
Subject:	Excel Help

Wow, you're a CEO already? I always thought you were a mover and a shaker! So you want my advice on how to set up your spreadsheet? My advice is *read the last email I sent.* The main thing that's new here is you'll need to include some columns for revenue and expenses under the stockholders' equity heading. Here's a screenshot of how your worksheet might look just before you enter the October transactions. Notice that because stockholders' equity is decreased by expenses, the debit side is used to record expenses.

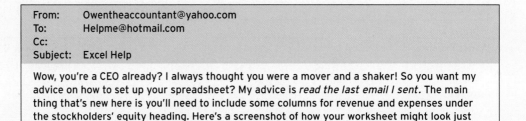

To prepare the trial balance, create three columns. In the first, enter the account names (one per row). In the second column, link in each debit balance by entering = in a cell and then clicking on the debit total from the T-account. Repeat this with all the accounts. Then do the same with the credit balances. At the bottom of the trial balance, use the SUM function to compute total debits and credits.

Don't forget to save the file using a name that uniquely identifies you (as my true hero).

CONTINUING CASE

L02, 3   **CC3 Accounting for Business Operations**

Starting in May 2010, Nicole has decided that she has everything that she needs to open her doors to customers. To keep up with competition, Nicole has added items such as gift certificates and has started to advertise her company more and put things into place to keep her business going in the long term. Here is a sample of some transactions that occurred in the month of May at Nicole's Getaway Spa.

May 1   Paid $3,000 cash for an insurance policy that covers the period from June 1 until May 31 next year.

May 4   Ordered five new massage tables from Spa Supplies Unlimited for $250 each for future delivery.

May 7	Provided $860 of spa services to customers on account.
May 10	Purchased spa supplies for $800 on account to use at Nicole's Getaway Spa.
May 13	Received a bill for $45 for running an advertisement in the newspaper in May. The bill was paid in cash.
May 16	Paid one-quarter of the amount owed from May 10.
May 19	Sold $1,900 of gift certificates to customers for cash.
May 20	Obtained financing from the bank by signing a $5,000 note payable.
May 22	Received two of the massage tables ordered on May 4 and paid the full amount in cash.
May 25	Paid $500 cash for utility bills for services received and billed in May.

Required:

For each of the transactions prepare journal entries, using the date of the transaction as the reference.

CHAPTER 4

Adjustments, Financial Statements, and Financial Results

YOUR LEARNING OBJECTIVES

Understand the business

LO1   Explain why adjustments are needed.

Study the accounting methods

LO2   Prepare adjustments needed at the end of the period.

LO3   Prepare an adjusted trial balance.

LO4   Prepare financial statements.

LO5   Explain the closing process.

Evaluate the results

LO6   Explain how adjustments affect financial results.

Review the chapter

THAT WAS
THEN

In the previous chapter, you learned how to analyze, record, and summarize the effects of operating transactions on balance sheet and income statement accounts.

Lecture Presentation-LP4
www.mhhe.com/phillips3e

FOCUS COMPANY: PIZZA AROMA, Ithaca, NY

I n Chapter 3, you saw that Pizza Aroma sold a lot of pizza during its first month of operations—more than owner-manager Mauricio Rosa had expected. Mauricio was very curious to know how the business performed, so he computed net income based on the company's unadjusted balances. When he saw that $15,500 of revenues had led to net income of $6,400, Mauricio was very excited.

Maurico's CPA, Laurie, cautioned him that because he had been using unadjusted amounts in his computations, his results were not meaningful. She emphasized that at the end of an accounting period, adjustments need to be made to (1) update amounts already recorded in the accounting records and (2) include events that had occurred but had not yet been recorded. These adjustments ensure that the recognition of revenues and expenses occurs in the proper period, and that assets and liabilities are reported at appropriate amounts.

In the first section of this chapter, we'll help you to understand why adjustments are a necessary part of accrual basis accounting. In the second part of the chapter, we'll show you how to determine what adjustments are needed and how they are recorded and summarized in the accounting system. This second section concludes with the final steps involved in the accounting cycle. In the third part of this chapter, you will learn the importance of adjustments for external financial statement users and, as always, the final section provides lots of opportunities for you to review and work with the material presented in this chapter.

THIS IS
NOW

This chapter concludes the accounting cycle by focusing on adjustments, financial statement preparation, and the closing process.

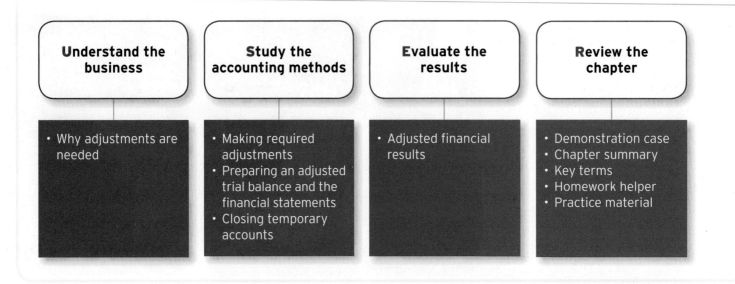

Understand the business	Study the accounting methods	Evaluate the results	Review the chapter
• Why adjustments are needed	• Making required adjustments • Preparing an adjusted trial balance and the financial statements • Closing temporary accounts	• Adjusted financial results	• Demonstration case • Chapter summary • Key terms • Homework helper • Practice material

Understand the Business

WHY ADJUSTMENTS ARE NEEDED

Learning Objective 1
Explain why adjustments are needed.

YOU SHOULD KNOW

Adjustments: Entries made at the end of every accounting period to report revenues and expenses in the proper period and assets and liabilities at appropriate amounts.

Video 4.1
www.mhhe.com/phillips3e

Accounting systems are designed to record most recurring daily transactions, particularly any involving cash. As cash is received or paid, it is recorded in the accounting system. This focus on cash works well, especially when cash receipts and payments occur in the same period as the activities that lead to revenues and expenses. However, as you learned in Chapter 3, cash is not always received in the period in which the company earns the related revenue; likewise, cash is not always paid in the period in which the company incurs the related expense. In these situations, **adjustments** are made to the accounting records at the end of the period to ensure assets and liabilities are reported at appropriate amounts. These adjustments also ensure the related revenues and expenses are reported in the proper period, as required by the revenue and matching principles.

Adjustments involve both income statement and balance sheet accounts. They are needed to ensure

- **Revenues** are recorded when earned (the revenue principle).
- **Expenses** are recorded in the same period as the revenues to which they relate (the matching principle).
- **Assets** are reported at amounts representing the economic benefits that remain at the end of the current period.
- **Liabilities** are reported at amounts owed at the end of the current period that will require a future sacrifice of resources.

Companies wait until the **end of the accounting period** to adjust their accounts because adjusting the records daily would be costly and time consuming. In practice, almost every financial statement account could require adjustment. Rather than try to memorize an endless list of examples, you should instead focus on learning what types of adjustments are needed in general. Later, we'll apply these general concepts to specific examples and give you lots of material to practice working with. In general, adjustments can be grouped into two categories: (1) deferrals, and (2) accruals.

1. Deferral Adjustments

The word *defer* means to postpone until later. In accounting, we say an expense or revenue has been deferred if we have postponed reporting it on the income statement until a later period. As you saw in Chapter 3, when Pizza Aroma pays its rent in advance, the expense is initially deferred as an asset on the balance sheet (in an account called Prepaid Rent). The adjustment part comes later, at the end of the month, when one month of the prepaid rent benefits have been used up. The deferral adjustment involves reducing Prepaid Rent and increasing Rent Expense on the income statement.

Deferral adjustments also can involve revenues. For example, when GQ receives cash for subscriptions before it has delivered magazines to subscribers, this revenue is initially deferred as a liability on the balance sheet (in an account called Unearned Subscriptions Revenue). The liability indicates the company's obligation to deliver magazines in the future. Later, when the company delivers the magazines, thereby meeting its obligation and earning the revenue, a deferral adjustment is made to reduce Unearned Subscriptions Revenue on the balance sheet and increase Subscriptions Revenue on the income statement.

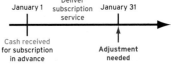

You should note two key ideas here.

1. **Deferral adjustments are used to decrease balance sheet accounts and increase corresponding income statement accounts.** Previously deferred amounts exist on the balance sheet because the company paid cash before incurring the expense or received cash before earning revenue. When revenues are earned (as defined by the revenue principle) or expenses incurred (as defined by the matching principle), the previously deferred amounts are adjusted and amounts are transferred to the income statement using a deferral adjustment.

2. **Each deferral adjustment involves one asset and one expense account, or one liability and one revenue account.** The left side of Exhibit 4.1 shows a partial list of accounts that require deferral adjustments.

EXHIBIT 4.1	Examples of Accounts Affected by Adjustments

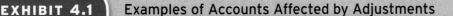

	Deferral Adjustments				Accrual Adjustments		
	Balance Sheet	Income Statement			Balance Sheet	Income Statement	
Assets	Supplies	Supplies Expense	**Expenses**	**Assets**	Interest Receivable	Interest Revenue	**Revenues**
	Prepaid Rent	Rent Expense			Rent Receivable	Rent Revenue	
	Prepaid Insurance	Insurance Expense					
Liabilities	Unearned Ticket Revenue	Ticket Sales Revenue	**Revenues**	**Liabilities**	Income Tax Payable	Income Tax Expense	**Expenses**
	Unearned Subscriptions Revenue	Subscriptions Revenue			Wages Payable	Wages Expense	
					Interest Payable	Interest Expense	

2. Accrual Adjustments

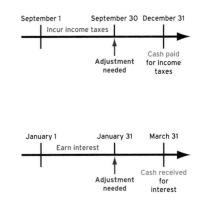

Accrual adjustments are needed when a company has earned revenue or incurred an expense in the current period but has not yet recorded it because the related cash will not be received or paid until a later period. For example, Pizza Aroma will eventually pay taxes on the income it earns this period, so an accrual adjustment will be needed at the end of the month to record increases in its Income Tax Expense and Income Tax Payable accounts. This adjustment matches Income Tax Expense to the period in which the company earned the income that caused the income taxes. Likewise, if interest revenue is earned on investments this month but not received in cash until a later month, an accrual adjustment is needed at the end of the current month to record increases in the company's Interest Revenue and Interest Receivable accounts.

You should note two key ideas here.

1. **Accrual adjustments are used to record revenue or expenses when they occur prior to receiving or paying cash, and to adjust corresponding balance sheet accounts.**

2. **Each accrual adjustment involves one asset and one revenue account, or one liability and one expense account.** Notice that this differs from deferral adjustments, which pair assets with expenses and liabilities with revenues. The right side of Exhibit 4.1 shows a partial list of accounts that require accrual adjustments.

How's it going?   Self-Study Practice

For each of the following, indicate whether a deferral (D) or accrual (A) adjustment is required on October 31, and what two accounts will be affected by it.

			ACCOUNTS AFFECTED	
		Type of Adjustment	Balance Sheet	Income Statement
1.	In October, American Airlines provided flight services to customers who had paid for their tickets in August.	D	unearned rev	Flt rev
2.	The Trump Organization earned office rent from tenants in October, but is not expecting payment until November.	A	rent receivable	rent rev
3.	In October, Fortune Magazine incurred interest on a bank loan that must be paid at the end of the year.	A	interest payable	interest exp
4.	In October, Apple Computer, Inc., used up one month of insurance coverage that it had prepaid in July.	D		

After you have finished, check your answers with the solution in the margin.

Solution to Self-Study Practice

Type / Balance Sheet & Income Statement Accounts

1. D / Unearned Revenue & Flight Service Revenue
2. A / Rent Receivable & Rent Revenue
3. A / Interest Payable & Interest Expense
4. D / Prepaid Insurance & Insurance Expense

Study the Accounting Methods

MAKING REQUIRED ADJUSTMENTS

Learning Objective 2
Prepare adjustments needed at the end of the period.

The process of making adjustments is similar to the process you learned in Chapters 2 and 3 when accounting for daily transactions. As shown in Exhibit 4.2, the main difference is that adjustments are made at the end of each accounting period immediately prior to preparing financial statements. Adjustments are not made on a daily basis because it's more efficient to do them all at once at the end of each period. After determining the necessary adjustments (in Step 1), they are recorded using **adjusting journal entries** (in Step 2) and then summarized in the accounts (in Step 3). An adjusted trial balance is prepared to ensure total debits still equal total credits after having posted the adjusting journal entries to the accounts. If the trial balance is in balance, the financial statements can be prepared and then distributed to interested users.

YOU SHOULD KNOW

Adjusting journal entries (AJEs): Record the effects of each period's adjustments in a debits-equal-credits format.

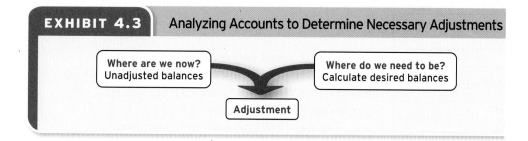

EXHIBIT 4.2 | Month-end Adjustments as Part of the Accounting Cycle

Timing	① Analyze	→	② Record	→	③ Summarize
Daily	Transactions		Journal entries (JEs)		• Ledgers (T-accounts) • Unadjusted trial balance
Month-end	Adjustments		Adjusting journal entries (AJEs)		• Ledgers (T-accounts) • Adjusted trial balance • Financial statements

Adjustment Analysis, Recording, and Summarizing

The first step, Analyze, involves determining the necessary adjustments to make to the accounting records. To complete this step, you need to know the balance currently reported in each account, then determine what should be reported as the balance, and finally figure out the adjustment that will take you from the current (unadjusted) balance to the desired (adjusted) balance. Exhibit 4.3 illustrates this thinking process.

EXHIBIT 4.3 | Analyzing Accounts to Determine Necessary Adjustments

Where are we now?
Unadjusted balances

Where do we need to be?
Calculate desired balances

Adjustment

The unadjusted trial balance is a key starting point for the adjustment process because it presents the unadjusted balances for every account, which will help you identify accounts that require adjustment. Exhibit 4.4 on page 152 shows Pizza Aroma's unadjusted trial balance at the end of September. This trial balance is identical to Exhibit 3.9 on page 112, except we've included balances for all accounts in Pizza Aroma's chart of accounts, including those that currently have zero balances. Alongside the unadjusted trial balance, we've identified accounts requiring adjustment at the end of September.

In the remainder of this section, we show how to analyze, record, and summarize the required adjustments. Read these pages carefully. They contain the topics that people typically find the most challenging in this chapter.

Deferral Adjustments   Let's begin by looking at deferral adjustments, which are used to update amounts that have been previously deferred on the balance sheet.

(a) Supplies Used during the Period   Of the $1,600 in supplies received in early September, $400 remain on hand at September 30.

The supplies were initially recorded as an asset on September 2 (in Chapter 3), but some of them have now been used up as of September 30. The **matching principle** requires an adjustment be made to report the cost of supplies used up this month as an expense (to match against revenues). To determine the cost of supplies used up, you have to do a

EXHIBIT 4.4	Unadjusted Trial Balance

PIZZA AROMA, INC.
Unadjusted Trial Balance
At September 30, 2010

Explanation of Adjustments Needed

Account Name	Debit	Credit	
Cash	$ 8,100		
Accounts Receivable	200		Increase for right to collect cash from Mauricio's friend for pizza delivery.
Supplies	1,600		Decrease for supplies used up during September.
Prepaid Rent	7,200		Decrease for prepaid September rent benefits now used up.
Cookware	630		
Equipment	60,000		} Adjust for equipment benefits used up in September.
Accumulated Depreciation		$ 0	
Accounts Payable		1,030	
Unearned Revenue		300	Decrease for gift card obligations met in September.
Wages Payable		0	Increase for September wages incurred but not yet paid.
Income Tax Payable		0	Increase for tax owed on income generated in September.
Interest Payable		0	Increase for interest owed on unpaid note in September.
Note Payable		20,000	
Contributed Capital		50,000	
Retained Earnings		0	
Dividends Declared	0		
Pizza Revenue		15,500	Increase for revenues earned by delivering pizza to Mauricio's friend.
Wages Expense	8,100		Increase for wages incurred, but not yet recorded, for employees' work in September.
Rent Expense	0		Increase for expense incurred for September rent.
Supplies Expense	0		Increase for supplies used up in September.
Depreciation Expense	0		Increase for expense incurred by using equipment in September.
Utilities Expense	600		
Advertising Expense	400		
Interest Expense	0		Increase for September interest incurred on unpaid note.
Income Tax Expense	0		Increase for taxes on income generated in September.
Totals	**$86,830**	**$86,830**	

little calculating. If you had $1,600 of supplies available for use and only $400 are left at the end of the month, then the $1,200 difference must be the cost of supplies used this month. In accounting terms, you should reduce the asset (Supplies) by $1,200 and show this amount as an expense (Supplies Expense).

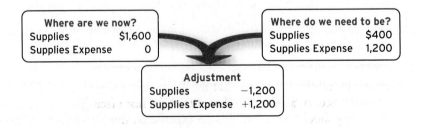

The effects of this adjustment on the accounting equation are shown on page 153, along with the required adjusting journal entry (AJE) and the accounts affected by it.

① Analyze

	Assets	=	Liabilities	+	Stockholders' Equity
(a) Supplies	−1,200	=			Supplies Expense (+E) −1,200

② Record

(a) *dr* Supplies Expense (+E, −SE) 1,200
       cr Supplies (−A)   1,200

③ Summarize

dr +	Supplies (A)	*cr* −		*dr* +	Supplies Expense (E, SE)	*cr* −
Unadj. bal. 1,600				Unadj. bal. 0		
	1,200 AJE (a)			AJE (a) 1,200		
Adj. bal. 400				Adj. bal. 1,200		

> **COACH'S TIP**
>
> The notation "Supplies Expense (+E, − SE) − 1,200" implies that the increase in an expense causes a decrease in stockholders' equity (through its negative impact on net income and retained earnings). To review this point see Exhibit 3.7 on page 104.

The financial statement effects of this adjustment are pictured in Exhibit 4.5.

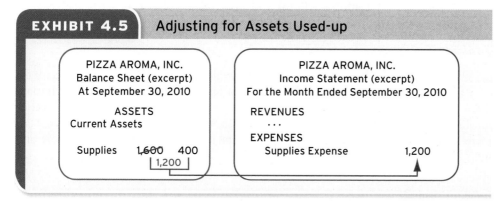

EXHIBIT 4.5 | **Adjusting for Assets Used-up**

PIZZA AROMA, INC.
Balance Sheet (excerpt)
At September 30, 2010

ASSETS
Current Assets

Supplies 1,600 400
         |1,200|

PIZZA AROMA, INC.
Income Statement (excerpt)
For the Month Ended September 30, 2010

REVENUES
...
EXPENSES
  Supplies Expense 1,200

(b) Rent Benefits Expired during the Period   Three months of rent were prepaid on September 1 for $7,200, but one month has now expired, leaving only two months prepaid at September 30.

To picture how costs relate to various time periods, it's useful to draw a timeline like the one shown in Exhibit 4.6.

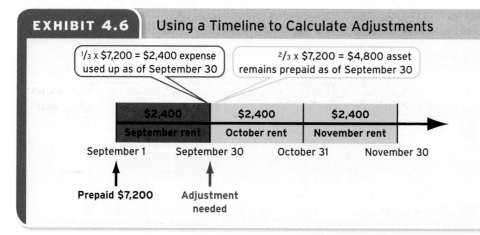

EXHIBIT 4.6 | **Using a Timeline to Calculate Adjustments**

$1/3$ × $7,200 = $2,400 expense used up as of September 30

$2/3$ × $7,200 = $4,800 asset remains prepaid as of September 30

$2,400	$2,400	$2,400
September rent	October rent	November rent

September 1   September 30   October 31   November 30

↑ Prepaid $7,200   ↑ Adjustment needed

The timeline in Exhibit 4.6 shows that the September prepayment of $7,200 represented three equal pieces of $2,400. The benefits of the first piece (pictured in red) have now expired, so they should be reported as an expense on the September income statement. Only two of the three months (2/3) remain prepaid on September 30. Thus, the $7,200 that was prepaid on September 1 needs to be adjusted on September 30 to $4,800 (2/3 × $7,200), which is the cost of the two remaining months of Prepaid Rent to be reported on the September 30 balance sheet (pictured in blue).

The preceding analysis has determined that an adjustment is needed to reduce Prepaid Rent by $2,400, from $7,200 to $4,800. Likewise, the adjustment needs to increase Rent Expense by $2,400. These effects are accounted for as follows:

1 Analyze

	Assets	=	Liabilities	+	Stockholders' Equity	
(b) Prepaid Rent	−2,400	=			Rent Expense (+E)	−2,400

2 Record

(b)	dr Rent Expense (+E, −SE)............................	2,400	
	cr Prepaid Rent (−A)................................		2,400

3 Summarize

dr +	Prepaid Rent (A)	cr −		dr +	Rent Expense (E, SE)	cr −
Unadj. bal. 7,200				Unadj. bal. 0		
		2,400 AJE (b)		AJE (b) 2,400		
Adj. bal. 4,800				Adj. bal. 2,400		

Similar adjustments are made for other prepayments such as Prepaid Insurance. If the company pays the cost of services in advance of receiving them, the company initially defers that cost as an asset on the balance sheet. At the end of each accounting period in which the services are used up, a deferral adjustment is made to decrease the asset and increase the related expense on the income statement. Practice doing this one more time in the following Self-Study Practice.

How's it going?   Self-Study Practice

On September 30, Apple, Inc., paid $24,000 for insurance for October, November, and December. On October 31, unadjusted balances for Prepaid Insurance and Insurance Expense were $24,000 and $0, respectively. Based on this information, (1) analyze the accounting equation effects of the adjustment required on October 31, (2) record the adjusting journal entry, and (3) summarize the effects of the adjusting journal entry in the T-accounts shown below.

1 Analyze

Assets	=	Liabilities	+	Stockholders' Equity
Prepaid insur −8000				Insuran expense −8000

2 Record

dr Insur expense	8000	
cr prepaid insur..............		8000

3 Summarize

dr +	Prepaid insur	cr −		dr +	Insurance expense	cr −
Unadj. bal.				Unadj. bal. 0		
24000	8000			AJE 8000		
Adj. bal. 16000				Adj. bal. 8000		

After you have finished, check your answers with the solution in the margin.

Solution to Self-Study Practice

1.

	Assets	=	Liabilities	+	Stockholders' Equity	
Prepaid Insurance	−8,000	=			Insurance Expense (+E)	−8,000

2.

dr Insurance Expense (+E, −SE)		8,000	
cr Prepaid Insurance (−A)			8,000

3.

dr +	Prepaid Insurance (A)	cr −		dr +	Insurance Expense (E, SE)	cr −
Unadj. bal. 24,000				Unadj. bal. 0		
		8,000 AJE		AJE 8,000		
Adj. bal. 16,000				Adj. bal. 8,000		

Notice that for events in (a), (b), and the Self-Study Practice, the deferral adjustments have two effects: (1) they reduce the **carrying value** of assets on the balance sheet, and (2) they transfer the amount of the reductions to related expense accounts on the income statement. This happens whether we're adjusting supplies, prepaid rent, or even long-term assets like buildings, vehicles, and equipment. When accounting for the use of long-term assets like buildings, vehicles, and equipment, there is one slight difference in how the carrying value is reduced, as we'll explain next.

(c) Depreciation Is Recorded for Use of Equipment   The restaurant equipment, which was estimated to last five years, has now been used for one month, representing an estimated expense of $1,000.

The **matching principle** indicates that when equipment is used to generate revenues in the current period, part of its cost should be transferred to an expense account in that period. This process is referred to as **depreciation,** so an account named Depreciation Expense reports the equipment cost that relates to the current period. Use of an expense account to report the part of an asset used up is not new to you. What is new, however, is that rather than take the amount of depreciation directly out of the Equipment account, a **contra-account** is created to keep track of all the depreciation recorded against the equipment. This contra-account, named Accumulated Depreciation, is like a negative asset account that is subtracted from the Equipment account in the assets section of the balance sheet, as shown in Exhibit 4.7.

> **YOU SHOULD KNOW**
>
> **Carrying value:** The amount an asset or liability is reported at ("carried at") in the financial statements. It is also known as "net book value" or simply "book value."

> **YOU SHOULD KNOW**
>
> **Depreciation:** The process of allocating the cost of buildings, vehicles, and equipment to the accounting periods in which they are used. **Contra-account:** An account that is an offset to, or reduction of, another account.

EXHIBIT 4.7	Reporting Accumulated Depreciation on the Balance Sheet

PIZZA AROMA, INC.
Balance Sheet (excerpt)
At September 30, 2010

Assets		
Equipment	$60,000	← Original cost of equipment
Less: Accumulated Depreciation	(1,000)	← Running total of depreciation recorded
Equipment, Net of Accumulated Depreciation	59,000	← Carrying value (or book value)

> **COACH'S TIP**
>
> Recording depreciation for the use of long-lived assets is a lot like recording the use of supplies. The only difference is that a contra-account is used so that the original costs of long-lived assets are maintained throughout their long lives.

In our analyses below, we use a small "x" to indicate a contra-account, so the notation for a contra-account for an asset is "xA." An increase in a contra-asset account (+xA) decreases the carrying value of the underlying asset (−A).

1 Analyze

Assets	= Liabilities +	Stockholders' Equity
(c) Accumulated Depreciation (+xA) −1,000 =		Depreciation Expense (+E) −1,000

2 Record

(c)   *dr* Depreciation Expense (+E, −SE).............................. 1,000
         cr Accumulated Depreciation (+xA, −A)................   1,000

3 Summarize

dr +	Equipment (A)	*cr* −
Unadj. bal.	60,000	
Adj. bal.	60,000	

dr −	Accumulated Depreciation (xA)	*cr* +
	0	Unadj. bal.
	1,000	AJE (c)
	1,000	Adj. bal.

dr +	Depreciation Expense (E, SE)	*cr* −
Unadj. bal.	0	
AJE (c)	1,000	
Adj. bal.	1,000	

There are four aspects of this example that you should note:

1. **Accumulated Depreciation is a balance sheet account and Depreciation Expense is an income statement account.** As a balance sheet account, Accumulated Depreciation will increase over time as it accumulates the depreciation of each period until the asset is no longer used. As an income statement account, Depreciation Expense will include only the depreciation of the current accounting year.

2. **By recording depreciation in Accumulated Depreciation separate from the Equipment account, you can report both the original cost of equipment and a running total of the amount that has been depreciated.** This gives financial statement users a rough idea of how much of the asset's original cost (representing its original usefulness) has been used up as of the balance sheet date. In our example, approximately 1/60 ($1,000/$60,000) of the equipment's total usefulness has been used up as of September 30, 2010.

3. **The normal balance in a contra-account is always the opposite of the account it offsets.** For example, the increase in Accumulated Depreciation is recorded with a credit because the account that it offsets, Equipment, is recorded with a debit.

4. **The amount of depreciation depends on the method used for determining it.** Depreciation methods (and their formulas) will be discussed in Chapter 9.

Just as deferral adjustments are used to record expenses incurred when assets are used up, they also are used to record the revenues earned when a company meets its obligation to provide goods or services to customers. For example, when American Airlines, Dow Jones, and T-Mobile receive cash in advance of providing flights, newspapers, and cell phone service, they initially increase (debit) Cash and increase (credit) a liability account called Unearned Revenue. Later, when they meet their obligations, a deferral adjustment is recorded, reducing the liability (with a debit) and reporting the revenue earned from these services (with a credit). Let's see how this idea applies to Pizza Aroma.

> **COACH'S TIP**
>
> The word "unearned" in the Unearned Revenue account means that the company hasn't done what it was paid to do. In other words, the company has an obligation (liability) to do the work or return the cash.

(d) Gift Cards Redeemed for Service   Pizza Aroma redeemed $160 of gift cards that customers used to pay for pizza.

The unadjusted trial balance reports $300 of Unearned Revenue, which represents Pizza Aroma's obligation to honor gift cards previously issued to customers. By accepting $160 of gift cards in exchange for pizza this month, Pizza Aroma has fulfilled a portion of its obligation and has earned additional revenue. Thus, a deferral adjustment is needed to reduce Unearned Revenue and increase Pizza Revenue.

1 Analyze

	Assets	=	Liabilities		+	Stockholders' Equity	
(d)			Unearned Revenue	−160		Pizza Revenue (+R)	+160

2 Record

(d) *dr* Unearned Revenue (−L) 160
     cr Pizza Revenue (+R, +SE).. 160

3 Summarize

dr −	Unearned Revenue (L)	*cr* +	*dr* −	Pizza Revenue (R, SE)	*cr* +
		300 Unadj. bal.			15,500 Unadj. bal.
AJE (d) 160					160 AJE (d)
		140 Adj. bal.			15,660 Adj. bal.

Accrual Adjustments   Let's now look at common examples of accrual adjustments, which are adjustments that make the accounting records complete by including transactions that occurred but have not been recorded.

(e) Revenues Earned but Not Yet Recorded   Pizza Aroma **provided $40 of Pizza to Mauricio's close friend on the last day of September, with payment to be received in October.**

Companies that regularly provide services on credit will design their accounting systems to record transactions like this on a daily basis. However, for a business like Pizza Aroma that does not typically extend credit to its customers, these kinds of events may require an accrual adjustment at month-end. Because these revenues and the right to collect them (Accounts Receivable) are earned in September, the **revenue principle** indicates they should be recorded in September. The accrual adjustment will increase Accounts Receivable on the balance sheet and increase Pizza Revenue on the income statement.

1 Analyze

	Assets	=	Liabilities	+	Stockholders' Equity	
(e)	Accounts Receivable +40	=			Pizza Revenue (+R)	+40

2 Record

(e)	dr Accounts Receivable (+A)....................................	40	
	cr Pizza Revenue (+R, +SE)....................................		40

3 Summarize

dr +	Accounts Receivable (A)	cr −		dr −	Pizza Revenue (R, SE)	cr +
Unadj. bal.	200				15,500	Unadj. bal.
AJE (e)	40				160	AJE (d)
Adj. bal.	240				40	AJE (e)
					15,700	Adj. bal.

Other situations require accrual adjustments for revenue earned but not yet recorded. For example, interest on investments is earned daily but typically is received in cash on a yearly basis, so each month an accrual adjustment is made to increase Interest Receivable and Interest Revenue for amounts earned but not yet recorded. Also, if a company provides professional accounting, advertising, or legal services over two or more accounting periods, it typically will not receive cash or bill its customer until the services have been provided in full. Consequently, an adjustment is needed to record the portion of the total revenue that has been earned as of the end of the month.

(f) Wage Expense Incurred but Not Yet Recorded   Pizza Aroma **owes $900 of wages to employees for work done in the last three days of September.**

Back in Chapter 3, Pizza Aroma paid employees $8,100 for work done through September 27 ($300 per day). As of September 30, three additional days of work have been completed at a cost of $900. Although this amount will not be paid until October, the expense relates to work done (and revenues generated) in September, so the **matching principle** requires an adjustment be made to accrue the $900 of additional wages incurred and owed by Pizza Aroma, as shown here.

September 2010						
S	M	T	W	T	F	S
		1	2	3	4	5	6
7	8	9	10	11	12	13
14	15	16	17	18	19	20
21	22	23	24	25	26	27
28	29	30	Owed			

Paid

1 ❯ Analyze

Assets	=	Liabilities		+	Stockholders' Equity	
(f)		Wages Payable	+900		Wages Expense (+E)	−900

2 ❯ Record

(f)	dr Wages Expense (+E, −SE)..	900	
	cr Wages Payable (+L)		900

3 ❯ Summarize

dr −	Wages Payable (L)	cr +		dr +	Wages Expense (E, SE)	cr −
	0	Unadj. bal.		Unadj. bal.	8,100	
	900	AJE (f)		AJE (f)	900	
	900	Adj. bal.		Adj. bal.	9,000	

When these $900 of wages are paid in cash the following month, Pizza Aroma will decrease Wages Payable (with a debit) and decrease Cash (with a credit).

(g) Interest Expense Incurred but Not Yet Recorded   Pizza Aroma has not paid or recorded the $100 interest that it owes for this month on its note payable to the bank.

As we saw in Exhibit 4.4, Pizza Aroma incurs interest on its unpaid note each month. An adjustment is needed to record the Interest Expense relating to September and, because this interest has not yet been paid, the adjustment also must record a liability called Interest Payable. Currently, the unadjusted trial balance shows $0 of Interest Payable and $0 of Interest Expense.

1 ❯ Analyze

Assets	=	Liabilities		+	Stockholders' Equity	
(g)		Interest Payable	+100		Interest Expense (+E)	−100

2 ❯ Record

(g)	dr Interest Expense (+E, −SE)	100	
	cr Interest Payable (+L)		100

3 ❯ Summarize

dr −	Interest Payable (L)	cr +		dr +	Interest Expense (E, SE)	cr −
	0	Unadj. bal.		Unadj. bal.	0	
	100	AJE (g)		AJE (g)	100	
	100	Adj. bal.		Adj. bal.	100	

Accrual adjustments also may be required for other expenses, like property taxes and utilities, if incurred and owed during the current period (but not yet recorded). The adjusting journal entry required for each of these items would be identical to the one shown in (g), except that the word *interest* would be replaced with the particular type of cost incurred and the applicable amounts would be used. For purposes of our Pizza Aroma example, we'll assume the only remaining expense to record is the accrual of income taxes that are incurred this month but won't be paid until a later period.

(h) Income Taxes Incurred but Not Yet Recorded   Pizza Aroma pays income tax at an average rate equal to 40 percent of the company's income before taxes.

Just like you, a corporation is responsible for income tax when it generates more revenue than expenses in the current period. Income tax is calculated by multiplying (1) the company's adjusted income (before income taxes) by (2) the company's tax rate. To calculate

adjusted income (before income tax), the following table starts with the unadjusted revenue and expense numbers from the unadjusted trial balance (Exhibit 4.4) and then includes
the effects of adjustments to revenues and expenses. Multiply the adjusted income before
income tax ($1,000) by the tax rate (40%) to get the amount of income tax ($400).

	Revenues	Expenses	
Unadjusted totals	$15,500	$ 9,100	← Calculated from Exhibit 4.4
			($9,100 = $8,100 + $600 + $400)
Adjustments: (a)		+1,200	
(b)		+2,400	
(c)		+1,000	
(d)	+ 160		
(e)	+ 40		
(f)		+ 900	
(g)		+ 100	
Adjusted totals	$ 15,700	− $14,700	= $1,000 ← Adjusted income before income tax expense

 **COACH'S TIP**

Always calculate income tax
expense **after** taking into
account all revenue and expense
adjustments.

The unadjusted trial balance shows that no income tax has been recorded (both
Income Tax Payable and Income Tax Expense are $0). Because income was reported
in September, the **matching principle** requires that we record the $400 tax expense in
September. Because the tax hasn't been paid yet, a liability also must be recorded.

1 Analyze

	Assets	=	Liabilities	+	Stockholders' Equity
(h)			Income Tax Payable +400		Income Tax Expense (+E) −400

2 Record

(h)	dr Income Tax Expense (+E, −SE)	400	
	cr Income Tax Payable (+L)		400

3 Summarize

dr − Income Tax Payable (L) cr +	dr + Income Tax Expense (E, SE) cr −
0 Unadj. bal.	Unadj. bal. 0
400 AJE (h)	AJE (h) 400
400 Adj. bal.	Adj. bal. 400

How's it going?   Self-Study Practice

Prior to accruing marketing expenses of $5 million, Pixar's adjusted income before
income taxes was $245 million. Assuming the company's average tax rate was 40%,
(1) analyze the effect of the required income tax adjustment on the accounting equation, and (2) prepare the adjusting journal entry, assuming that no amounts have been
recorded yet for income taxes.

1 Analyze

	Assets	=	Liabilities	+	Stockholders' Equity

2 Record

dr	....	
cr	....	

After you have finished, check your answers with the solution in the margin.

Solution to Self-Study Practice
1. Adjusted income before taxes = $245 − $5 = $240 (million).
    Income tax = $240 × 40% = $96 (million).

Assets	=	Liabilities	+	Stockholders' Equity
		Income Tax Payable +96		Income Tax Expense (+E) −96

2. dr Income Tax Expense (+E, −SE) 96
    cr Income Tax Payable (+L) 96

Additional Comments

There are three final points to learn before finishing this section. First, notice that none of the adjusting journal entries affected the Cash account. **Adjusting journal entries never involve cash.** Second, adjusting entries always include one balance sheet and one income statement account.

The third point doesn't relate to adjusting entries. Instead, it relates to dividends, which a corporation uses to distribute profits to stockholders as a return on their investment in the corporation. The decision to pay a dividend is made by the company's board of directors after profits have been generated, so **dividends are not expenses of the business.** Instead, they are a reduction of the retained earnings. Consequently, dividends are not reported on the income statement, but instead are subtracted on the Statement of Retained Earnings (as shown in Chapter 1). Dividends are recorded in their own special account called Dividends Declared. Because dividends reduce stockholders' equity, they are recorded with a debit just like all reductions in stockholders' equity. Now that we know Pizza Aroma has generated a profit for the month, we'll assume the company pays a dividend to stockholders. (Technically speaking, a dividend can occur any time during the year so it is typically recorded as a daily transaction when declared, rather than at the end of the period as an adjusting journal entry. But, we'll show it here for convenience.)

(i) Dividend Declared and Paid   Pizza Aroma declares and pays a $500 cash dividend.

The dividend is recorded as a reduction in stockholders' equity in a special account called Dividends Declared. Because it reduces stockholders' equity, it is recorded as a debit. The corresponding reduction in Cash is recorded as a credit.

1 Analyze

	Assets	=	Liabilities	+	Stockholders' Equity	
(i) Cash	−500 =				Dividends Declared (+D)	−500

2 Record

(i)	*dr* Dividends Declared (+D, −SE)	500	
	cr Cash (−A)		500

3 Summarize

dr +	Cash (A)	*cr* −		*dr* +	Dividends Declared (D, SE) *cr* −
Unadj. bal. 8,100				Unadj. bal. 0	
	500	(i)		(i) 500	
Adj. bal. 7,600				Adj. bal. 500	

Exhibit 4.8 summarizes the work we've done to this point. Starting with the unadjusted trial balance prepared at the end of Chapter 3 (see the left side of Exhibit 4.8), we determined the journal entries that needed to be recorded at the end of this month (see the right side of Exhibit 4.8). Next, we posted journal entries (a) through (i) to the T-accounts, as summarized in Exhibit 4.9. Next we need to check that the accounting records are still in balance by using the adjusted T-account balances to prepare an adjusted trial balance. Assuming the trial balance shows that debits equal credits, we will finally be able to prepare the financial statements.

PREPARING AN ADJUSTED TRIAL BALANCE AND THE FINANCIAL STATEMENTS

Learning Objective 3
Prepare an adjusted trial balance.

Adjusted Trial Balance

An **adjusted trial balance** is prepared to check that the accounting records are still in balance, after having posted all adjusting entries to the T-accounts. To prepare an adjusted

EXHIBIT 4.8	Summary of Unadjusted Balances and Adjusting Journal Entries

PIZZA AROMA, INC.
Unadjusted Trial Balance
At September 30, 2010

Account Name	Debit	Credit
Cash	$ 8,100	
Accounts Receivable	200	
Supplies	1,600	
Prepaid Rent	7,200	
Cookware	630	
Equipment	60,000	
Accumulated Depreciation		$ 0
Accounts Payable		1,030
Unearned Revenue		300
Wages Payable		0
Income Tax Payable		0
Interest Payable		0
Note Payable		20,000
Contributed Capital		50,000
Retained Earnings		0
Dividends Declared	0	
Pizza Revenue		15,500
Wages Expense	8,100	
Rent Expense	0	
Supplies Expense	0	
Depreciation Expense	0	
Utilities Expense	600	
Advertising Expense	400	
Interest Expense	0	
Income Tax Expense	0	
Totals	**$86,830**	**$86,830**

PIZZA AROMA, INC.
General Journal

(a)	dr Supplies Expense (+E, −SE)	1,200	
	cr Supplies (−A)		1,200
(b)	dr Rent Expense (+E, −SE)	2,400	
	cr Prepaid Rent (−A)		2,400
(c)	dr Depreciation Expense (+E, −SE)	1,000	
	cr Accumulated Depreciation (+xA, −A)		1,000
(d)	dr Unearned Revenue (−L)	160	
	cr Pizza Revenue (+R, +SE)		160
(e)	dr Accounts Receivable (+A)	40	
	cr Pizza Revenue (+R, +SE)		40
(f)	dr Wages Expense (+E, −SE)	900	
	cr Wages Payable (+L)		900
(g)	dr Interest Expense (+E, −SE)	100	
	cr Interest Payable (+L)		100
(h)	dr Income Tax Expense (+E, −SE)	400	
	cr Income Tax Payable (+L)		400
(i)	dr Dividends Declared (+D, −SE)	500	
	cr Cash (−A)		500

trial balance, just copy the adjusted T-account balances (Exhibit 4.9) into the debit or credit columns of the adjusted trial balance (left side of Exhibit 4.10).

List the accounts in the order they will appear in the balance sheet, statement of retained earnings, and income statement. As you can see in Exhibit 4.10 on page 163, the trial balance proves that Pizza Aroma's accounting records are in balance (total debits = $89,270 = total credits), so the financial statements can be prepared. The balance for each account in the trial balance is reported only once on either the income statement, statement of retained earnings, or balance sheet. Typically, the income statement is prepared first because the net income number from it flows into the statement of retained earnings, and then the retained earnings number from the statement of retained earnings flows into the balance sheet. As you will see in later chapters of this book, the statement of cash flows and notes to the financial statements are prepared last because they include information obtained from the income statement, statement of retained earnings, and balance sheet (plus other sources).

Income Statement and Statement of Retained Earnings

Prepare the income statement by creating the usual heading (who, what, when) and listing the names and amounts for each revenue and expense account from the adjusted

> **YOU SHOULD KNOW**
>
> **Adjusted trial balance:** A list of all accounts and their adjusted balances to check on the equality of recorded debits and credits.

> **Learning Objective 4**
> Prepare financial statements.

EXHIBIT 4.9   Pizza Aroma's Adjusted Accounts

dr +	Cash (A)	cr −
Unadj. bal.	8,100	
		500 (i)
Adj. bal.	7,600	

dr +	Accounts Receivable (A)	cr −
Unadj. bal.	200	
AJE (e)	40	
Adj. bal.	240	

dr +	Supplies (A)	cr −
Unadj. bal.	1,600	
		1,200 AJE (a)
Adj. bal.	400	

dr +	Prepaid Rent (A)	cr −
Unadj. bal.	7,200	
		2,400 AJE (b)
Adj. bal.	4,800	

dr +	Cookware (A)	cr −
Adj. bal.	630	

dr +	Equipment (A)	cr −
Adj. bal.	60,000	

dr −	Accumulated Depreciation (xA)	cr +
	0	Unadj. bal.
	1,000	AJE (c)
	1,000	Adj. bal.

dr −	Accounts Payable (L)	cr +
	1,030	Adj. bal.

dr −	Unearned Revenue (L)	cr +
		300 Unadj. bal.
AJE (d)	160	
		140 Adj. bal.

dr −	Wages Payable (L)	cr +
		0 Unadj. bal.
		900 AJE (f)
		900 Adj. bal.

dr −	Income Tax Payable (L)	cr +
		0 Unadj. bal.
		400 AJE (h)
		400 Adj. bal.

dr −	Interest Payable (L)	cr +
		0 Unadj. bal.
		100 AJE (g)
		100 Adj. bal.

dr −	Note Payable (L)	cr +
		20,000 Adj. bal.

dr −	Contributed Capital (SE)	cr +
		50,000 Adj. bal.

dr −	Retained Earnings (SE)	cr +
		0 Adj. bal.

dr +	Dividends Declared (D, SE)	cr −
Unadj. bal.	0	
(i)	500	
Adj. bal.	500	

dr −	Pizza Revenue (R, SE)	cr +
		15,500 Unadj. bal.
		160 AJE (d)
		40 AJE (e)
		15,700 Adj. bal.

dr +	Wages Expense (E, SE)	cr −
Unadj. bal.	8,100	
AJE (f)	900	
Adj. bal.	9,000	

dr +	Rent Expense (E, SE)	cr −
Unadj. bal.	0	
AJE (b)	2,400	
Adj. bal.	2,400	

dr +	Supplies Expense (E, SE)	cr −
Unadj. bal.	0	
AJE (a)	1,200	
Adj. bal.	1,200	

dr +	Depreciation Expense (E, SE)	cr −
Unadj. bal.	0	
AJE (c)	1,000	
Adj. bal.	1,000	

dr +	Utilities Expense (E, SE)	cr −
Adj. bal.	600	

dr +	Advertising Expense (E, SE)	cr −
Adj. bal.	400	

dr +	Interest Expense (E, SE)	cr −
Unadj. bal.	0	
AJE (g)	100	
Adj. bal.	100	

dr +	Income Tax Expense (E, SE)	cr −
Unadj. bal.	0	
AJE (h)	400	
Adj. bal.	400	

trial balance, as shown in Exhibit 4.10. Notice that each major category of items on the income statement is subtotaled prior to computing net income for the period.

Account balances from the adjusted trial balance are also used in the statement of retained earnings, as shown in Exhibit 4.10. Notice that **the amount coming from the adjusted trial balance is the beginning-of-year balance for Retained Earnings.** This account balance doesn't yet include revenues, expenses, and dividends for the current period because they've been recorded in their own separate accounts. Eventually we will transfer ("close") those accounts into Retained Earnings, but that's

| EXHIBIT 4.10 | Preparing the Income Statement and Statement of Retained Earnings |  |

PIZZA AROMA, INC.
Adjusted Trial Balance
At September 30, 2010

Account Name	Debits	Credits
Cash	$ 7,600	
Accounts Receivable	240	
Supplies	400	
Prepaid Rent	4,800	
Cookware	630	
Equipment	60,000	
Accumulated Depreciation		$ 1,000
Accounts Payable		1,030
Unearned Revenue		140
Wages Payable		900
Income Tax Payable		400
Interest Payable		100
Note Payable		20,000
Contributed Capital		50,000
Retained Earnings		0
Dividends Declared	500	
Pizza Revenue		15,700
Wages Expense	9,000	
Rent Expense	2,400	
Supplies Expense	1,200	
Depreciation Expense	1,000	
Utilities Expense	600	
Advertising Expense	400	
Interest Expense	100	
Income Tax Expense	400	
Totals	$89,270	$89,270

PIZZA AROMA, INC.
Income Statement
For the Month Ended September 30, 2010

Revenues	
Pizza Revenue	$15,700
Total Revenues	15,700
Expenses	
Wages Expense	9,000
Rent Expense	2,400
Supplies Expense	1,200
Depreciation Expense	1,000
Utilities Expense	600
Advertising Expense	400
Interest Expense	100
Income Tax Expense	400
Total Expenses	15,100
Net Income	$ 600

PIZZA AROMA, INC.
Statement of Retained Earnings
For the Month Ended September 30, 2010

Retained Earnings, September 1	$ 0
Add: Net Income	600
Subtract: Dividends Declared	(500)
Retained Earnings, September 30	$ 100

To the Balance Sheet on page 164.

only done at the end of the year. For now, the Retained Earnings account on the adjusted trial balance provides the opening amount on the statement of retained earnings. The amount for Net Income on the next line of the statement of retained earnings comes from the income statement, and the Dividends Declared number comes from the adjusted trial balance.

Balance Sheet

Like the other statements, the balance sheet is prepared from the adjusted trial balance, as shown in Exhibit 4.11. When preparing the balance sheet, watch out for three things. First, remember to classify assets and liabilities as current if they will be turned into cash or used up within 12 months. Liabilities should be classified as current if they will be ful-filled (paid) within 12 months. Second, note that Accumulated Depreciation is subtracted from Equipment in the assets section. Third, get the Retained Earnings balance from the

> **COACH'S TIP**
>
> Dividends Declared is reported only on the statement of retained earnings.

| EXHIBIT 4.11 | Preparing the Balance Sheet | PIZZA AROMA |

PIZZA AROMA, INC.
Adjusted Trial Balance
At September 30, 2010

Account Name	Debits	Credits
Cash	$ 7,600	
Accounts Receivable	240	
Supplies	400	
Prepaid Rent	4,800	
Cookware	630	
Equipment	60,000	
Accumulated Depreciation		$ 1,000
Accounts Payable		1,030
Unearned Revenue		140
Wages Payable		900
Income Tax Payable		400
Interest Payable		100
Note Payable		20,000
Contributed Capital		50,000
Retained Earnings		0
Dividends Declared	500	
Pizza Revenue		15,700
Wages Expense	9,000	
Rent Expense	2,400	
Supplies Expense	1,200	
Depreciation Expense	1,000	
Utilities Expense	600	
Advertising Expense	400	
Interest Expense	100	
Income Tax Expense	400	
Totals	$89,270	$89,270

PIZZA AROMA, INC.
Balance Sheet
At September 30, 2010

Assets

Current Assets		
Cash		$ 7,600
Accounts Receivable		240
Supplies		400
Prepaid Rent		4,800
Cookware		630
Total Current Assets		13,670
Equipment	$60,000	
Accumulated Depreciation	(1,000)	59,000
Total Assets		$72,670

Liabilities and Stockholders' Equity

Liabilities		
Current Liabilities		
Accounts Payable		$ 1,030
Unearned Revenue		140
Wages Payable		900
Income Tax Payable		400
Interest Payable		100
Total Current Liabilities		2,570
Note Payable		20,000
Total Liabilities		22,570
Stockholders' Equity		
Contributed Capital		50,000
Retained Earnings		100
Total Stockholders' Equity		50,100
Total Liabilities and Stockholders' Equity		$72,670

From the Statement of Retained Earnings on page 163.

statement of retained earnings, not from the adjusted trial balance. (The adjusted trial balance still only reports the period's opening Retained Earnings balance.)

Statement of Cash Flows and Notes

We don't want you to forget that the statement of cash flows (SCF) and notes to the financial statements must also be prepared as part of the financial statements. But you look a little tired, so we'll leave the SCF for Chapter 12 and we'll slide information about financial statement notes into each of the remaining chapters.

CLOSING TEMPORARY ACCOUNTS

Learning Objective 5
Explain the closing process.

The last step of the accounting cycle is referred to as the *closing process*. As shown in the first column in Exhibit 4.12, this step is performed only at the end of the year, after the financial statements have been prepared. The closing process cleans up the accounting

Timing	① Analyze ⟶	② Record ⟶	③ Summarize
Daily	Transactions	Journal entries (JEs)	• Ledgers (T-accounts) • Unadjusted trial balance
Month-end	Adjustments	Adjusting journal entries (AJEs)	• Ledgers (T-accounts) • Adjusted trial balance • Financial statements
Year-end	Closing	Closing journal entries (CJEs)	• Ledgers (T-accounts) • Post-closing trial balance

EXHIBIT 4.12 — Year-end Closing Concludes the Accounting Cycle

records to get them ready to begin tracking the results in the following year. It's kind of like hitting the trip odometer on your car or the reset button on your X-box.

Closing Income Statement and Dividend Accounts

In Chapter 3, you learned to think of revenue and expense accounts as subcategories of Retained Earnings, which are used to track earnings-related transactions of the current year. Earlier in this chapter, you saw that the Dividends Declared account is similarly used to track dividends declared during the current year. All revenue, expense, and dividends declared accounts are known as **temporary accounts** because they are used to track only the current year's results. At the end of each year, after all the year's transactions and adjustments are recorded, these temporary accounts are analyzed and closing journal entries are recorded to move the balances from the temporary accounts to where they belong—in Retained Earnings. The Retained Earnings account, like all other balance sheet accounts, is a **permanent account** because its ending balance from one year becomes its beginning balance for the following year.

The closing process serves two purposes:

1. **Transfer net income (or loss) and dividends to Retained Earnings.** After the closing journal entries are prepared and posted, the balance in the Retained Earnings account will agree with the statement of retained earnings and the balance sheet.

2. **Establish zero balances in all income statement and dividend accounts.** After the closing journal entries are prepared and posted, the balances in the temporary accounts are reset to zero to start accumulating next year's results.

Closing journal entries follow the usual debits-equal-credits format used for the transaction journal entries (in Chapters 2 and 3) and adjusting journal entries (shown earlier in this chapter). Because they're the last thing done during the year, they're posted immediately to the accounts. (Some computerized systems record and post closing journal entries automatically.) Two closing journal entries are needed:[1]

1. Debit each revenue account for the amount of its credit balance, credit each expense account for the amount of its debit balance, and record the difference in Retained Earnings. If you've done it right, **the amount credited to Retained Earnings should equal Net Income on the Income Statement.** (If the company has a net loss, Retained Earnings will be debited.)

2. Credit the Dividends Declared account for the amount of its debit balance and debit Retained Earnings for the same amount.

Exhibit 4.13 shows the closing process for Pizza Aroma (assuming, for sake of illustration, that it closes its books on the last day of September).

YOU SHOULD KNOW

Temporary accounts: Accounts that track financial results for a limited period of time by having their balances zeroed out at the end of each accounting year.
Permanent accounts: Accounts that track financial results from year to year by carrying their ending balances into the next year.

Video 4.2
www.mhhe.com/phillips3e

---

[1]Some companies use a four-step process, by closing (1) revenue and (2) expense accounts to a special summary account, called (3) Income Summary, which then is closed to (4) Retained Earnings, along with Dividends Declared.

EXHIBIT 4.13 | **Analyzing, Preparing, and Summarizing the Closing Journal Entries**

(1) Analyze

The analysis step for closing the temporary accounts only requires that you identify, from the adjusted trial balance, the temporary accounts with debit balances (to be credited below) and credit balances (to be debited below).

(2) Record

CJE 1. Close revenue and expense accounts:

dr Pizza Revenue (−R)	15,700	
cr Wages Expense (−E)		9,000
cr Rent Expense (−E)		2,400
cr Supplies Expense (−E)		1,200
cr Depreciation Expense (−E)		1,000
cr Utilities Expense (−E)		600
cr Advertising Expense (−E)		400
cr Interest Expense (−E)		100
cr Income Tax Expense (−E)		400
cr Retained Earnings (+SE)		600

CJE 2. Close the dividends declared account:

dr Retained Earnings (−SE)	500	
cr Dividends Declared (−D)		500

(3) Summarize

dr −	Pizza Revenue (R, SE)		cr +
		15,700	Adj. bal.
CJE (1)	15,700		
		0	Closed bal.

dr +	Advertising Expense (E, SE)		cr −
Adj. bal.	400		
		400	CJE (1)
Closed bal.	0		

dr +	Wages Expense (E, SE)		cr −
Adj. bal.	9,000		
		9,000	CJE (1)
Closed bal.	0		

dr +	Interest Expense (E, SE)		cr −
Adj. bal.	100		
		100	CJE (1)
Closed bal.	0		

dr +	Rent Expense (E, SE)		cr −
Adj. bal.	2,400		
		2,400	CJE (1)
Closed bal.	0		

dr +	Income Tax Expense (E, SE)		cr −
Adj. bal.	400		
		400	CJE (1)
Closed bal.	0		

dr +	Supplies Expense (E, SE)		cr −
Adj. bal.	1,200		
		1,200	CJE (1)
Closed bal.	0		

dr +	Dividends Declared (D, SE)		cr −
Adj. bal.	500		
		500	CJE (2)
Closed bal.	0		

dr +	Depreciation Expense (E, SE)		cr −
Adj. bal.	1,000		
		1,000	CJE (1)
Closed bal.	0		

dr −	Retained Earnings (SE)		cr +
		0	Adj. bal.
CJE (2)	500	600	CJE (1)
		100	Closed bal.

dr +	Utilities Expense (E, SE)		cr −
Adj. bal.	600		
		600	CJE (1)
Closed bal.	0		

Post-Closing Trial Balance

After the closing journal entries are posted, all temporary accounts should have zero balances. These accounts will be ready for summarizing transactions recorded next year. The ending balance in Retained Earnings is now up to date (it matches the year-end amount on the statement of retained earnings and balance sheet) and is carried forward as the beginning balance for the next year. As the last step of the accounting cycle, you should prepare a **post-closing trial balance** (as shown in Exhibit 4.14). In this context, *post* means "after," so a post-closing trial balance is an "after-closing" trial balance that is prepared as a final check that total debits still equal total credits and that all temporary accounts have been closed.

YOU SHOULD KNOW

Post-closing trial balance: An internal report prepared as the last step in the accounting cycle to check that debits equal credits and all temporary accounts have been closed.

EXHIBIT 4.14 Pizza Aroma's Post-Closing Trial Balance

PIZZA AROMA, INC.
Post-Closing Trial Balance
At September 30, 2010

Account Name	Debits	Credits
Cash	$ 7,600	
Accounts Receivable	240	
Supplies	400	
Prepaid Rent	4,800	
Cookware	630	
Equipment	60,000	
Accumulated Depreciation		$ 1,000
Accounts Payable		1,030
Unearned Revenue		140
Wages Payable		900
Income Tax Payable		400
Interest Payable		100
Note Payable		20,000
Contributed Capital		50,000
Retained Earnings		100
Dividends Declared	0	
Pizza Revenue		0
Wages Expense	0	
Rent Expense	0	
Supplies Expense	0	
Depreciation Expense	0	
Utilities Expense	0	
Advertising Expense	0	
Interest Expense	0	
Income Tax Expense	0	
Totals	$73,670	$73,670

COACH'S TIP

Total debits on the post-closing trial balance don't equal the total assets on the balance sheet because Accumulated Depreciation (a credit balance on the trial balance) is subtracted from assets on the Balance Sheet.

EXHIBIT 4.15	The Accounting Process

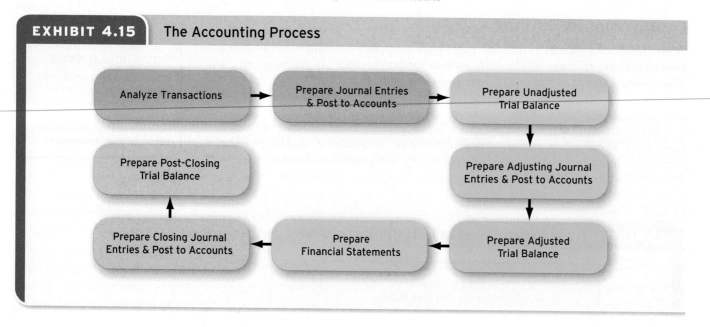

Now that we've completed the accounting cycle, it seems appropriate to summarize it one more time. Exhibit 4.12 (on page 165) showed one way to organize the various steps of the accounting cycle. Exhibit 4.15 presents the same ideas in a slightly different format. The steps in the coral, blue, and gold boxes are done daily, monthly, and yearly, respectively.

Evaluate the Results

ADJUSTED FINANCIAL RESULTS

Learning Objective 6
Explain how adjustments affect financial results.

Throughout this chapter, you learned various adjustments that must be made to the accounting records when finalizing and preparing the financial statements. These adjustments help to ensure that all revenues and expenses are reported in the period in which they are earned and incurred. As a result of these adjustments, the financial statements present the best picture of whether the company's business activities were profitable that period and what economic resources the company owns and owes at the end of that period. Without these adjustments, the financial statements present an incomplete and misleading picture of the company's financial performance.

Pizza Aroma provides a good example of the extent to which unadjusted balances may change during the adjustment process. In contrast to Mauricio's initial impression that Pizza Aroma had earned a sizable profit (net income of $6,400 from revenue of $15,500), the company's adjusted results indicated a much different picture (net income of $600 from revenue of $15,700). Consequently, Mauricio learned that he had much to improve upon in the upcoming months. He set a goal of attempting to increase the company's revenue by expanding his customer base, while at the same time trying to control expenses. He was well aware that even large companies go out of business if they fail to maintain revenues and control their expenses (as demonstrated in the following Spotlight on Financial Reporting).

Spotlight On FINANCIAL REPORTING

www.mhhe.com/phillips3e

Anatomy of a Business Failure

Until its bankruptcy in late 2008 and liquidation in early 2009, Circuit City was one of the largest electronics stores in the United States. However, Circuit City's inability to maintain sales and control expenses ultimately led to its demise. Notice how quickly the company's stock price fell as it reported deteriorating financial results.

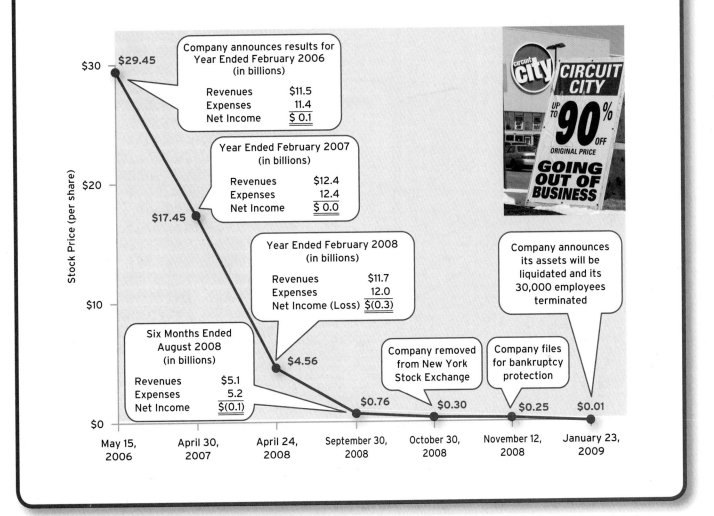

REVIEW THE CHAPTER

DEMONSTRATION CASE

We take our final look at the accounting activities of Goodbye Grass Corporation by illustrating the activities at the end of the accounting cycle: the adjustment process, financial statement preparation, and the closing process. No adjustments have been made to the

www.mhhe.com/phillips3e

accounts yet. Your starting point will be the following unadjusted trial balance dated April 30, 2010:

GOODBYE GRASS CORPORATION
Unadjusted Trial Balance
At April 30, 2010

Account Name	Debits	Credits
Cash	$ 4,510	
Accounts Receivable	1,700	
Note Receivable	1,250	
Interest Receivable	0	
Prepaid Insurance	300	
Equipment	4,600	
Accumulated Depreciation		$ 0
Land	3,750	
Accounts Payable		620
Unearned Revenue		1,600
Wages Payable		0
Interest Payable		0
Income Tax Payable		0
Note Payable		4,000
Contributed Capital		9,000
Retained Earnings		0
Mowing Revenue		5,200
Interest Revenue		0
Wages Expense	3,900	
Fuel Expense	410	
Insurance Expense	0	
Depreciation Expense	0	
Interest Expense	0	
Income Tax Expense	0	
Totals	$20,420	$20,420

By reviewing the unadjusted trial balance, you identify three deferral accounts (Prepaid Insurance, Equipment, and Unearned Revenue) that may need to be adjusted in addition to accruals that may be necessary relating to wages, income taxes, and interest on the Note Receivable and Note Payable. The following information is determined at the end of the accounting cycle:

Deferral Adjustments

a. One-fourth of the $1,600 cash received from the city at the beginning of April for future mowing service has been earned in April. The $1,600 in Unearned Revenue represents four months of service (April through July).

b. Insurance purchased at the beginning of April for $300 provides coverage for six months (April through September). The insurance coverage for April has now been used.
    TIP: Account for the expiry of prepaid insurance just like the expiry of prepaid rent.

c. Mowers, edgers, rakes, and hand tools (equipment) have been used in April to generate revenues. The company estimates $300 in depreciation each year.

Accrual Adjustments

d. Wages have been paid through April 28. Employees worked the last two days of April and will be paid in May. Wages amount to $200 per day.

e. Interest incurred and payable on the note payable is $45 for the month of April.

f. Interest earned and receivable on the note receivable is $10 for the month of April.

g. The estimated income tax rate for Goodbye Grass Corporation is 35 percent.

Required:

1. Analyze items (*a*)–(*g*) with the goal of identifying the effects of required adjustments on the basic accounting equation (Assets = Liabilities + Stockholders' Equity), using the format shown in the chapter.

2. Record the adjusting journal entries required at the end of April.

3. Summarize the effects of each adjusting journal entry in T-accounts for each account affected. Obtain beginning balances from the unadjusted trial balance, then post the adjusting journal entries from requirement 2, and calculate adjusted April 30 balances.

4. Prepare an adjusted trial balance to ensure debit and credit balances are equal, remembering to include all accounts in the trial balance (and not just the ones affected by the adjusting journal entries).

5. Prepare an income statement, statement of retained earnings, and classified balance sheet from the amounts in the adjusted trial balance.

6. Prepare the closing journal entries that would be required if Goodbye Grass Corporation's fiscal year ended April 30, 2010.

   After completing requirements 1–6, check your answers with the following solution.

Suggested Solution

1. Adjustment analysis:

   a. The unadjusted balances are $1,600 for Unearned Revenue and $5,200 for Mowing Revenue. One-fourth of the $1,600 has been earned in April ($400 = ¼ × $1,600), bringing total mowing revenues for the month to $5,600 ($5,200 + $400). Three-fourths of the $1,600 remain unearned at the end of April ($1,200 = ¾ × $1,600). To reach these desired balances, we need an adjustment that decreases Unearned Revenue by $400 and increases Mowing Revenue by $400.

Assets	=	Liabilities	+	Stockholders' Equity
		Unearned Revenue −400		Mowing Revenue (+R) +400

   b. The unadjusted balances are $300 for Prepaid Insurance and $0 for Insurance Expense. One-sixth of the $300 has expired in April resulting in an insurance expense for the month of $50 (= ⅙ × $300). Five of the six months of insurance coverage remain unused at the end of April ($250 = ⅚ × $300). To reach these desired balances, we need an adjustment that decreases Prepaid Insurance by $50 and increases Insurance Expense by $50.

Assets	=	Liabilities	+	Stockholders' Equity
Prepaid Insurance −50				Insurance Expense (+E) −50

   c. The unadjusted balances are $0 for Accumulated Depreciation and $0 for Depreciation Expense. Yearly depreciation of $300 equals $25 for just one month ($300 × 1/12). To go from the unadjusted balances of $0 to the desired adjusted balances of $25, we increase the expense and contra-account balances by $25.

Assets	=	Liabilities	+	Stockholders' Equity
Accumulated Depreciation (+xA) −25				Depreciation Expense (+E) −25

   d. The unadjusted balances are $0 for Wages Payable and $3,900 for Wages Expense. Because the final two days of work done in April are unpaid, we need to record a liability for $400 (2 × $200). Total wages expense for the month should include the $3,900 paid for work from April 1–28 plus the $400 not yet paid for work on April 29 and 30. To reach these desired balances, we need an adjustment increasing Wages Payable by $400 and increasing Wages Expense by $400.

Assets	=	Liabilities	+	Stockholders' Equity
		Wages Payable +400		Wages Expense (+E) −400

   e. The unadjusted balances are $0 for Interest Payable and $0 for Interest Expense. Interest of $45 was incurred in April, so the adjustment needs to increase both accounts by $45.

Assets	=	Liabilities	+	Stockholders' Equity
		Interest Payable +45		Interest Expense (+E) −45

f. The unadjusted balances are $0 for Interest Receivable and $0 for Interest Revenue. Interest of $10 was earned in April, so the adjustment needs to increase both accounts by $10.

Assets	=	Liabilities	+	Stockholders' Equity
Interest Receivable +10				Interest Revenue (+R) +10

g. The unadjusted balances are $0 for Income Tax Payable and $0 for Income Tax Expense. The amount of calculated income taxes will increase both of these accounts. Income taxes are calculated as 35 percent of adjusted income before tax for the month, as follows:

		Revenues	Expenses	
Unadjusted totals		$5,200	$4,310	← Calculated from unadjusted trial balance
Adjustments:	(a)	+400		($4,310 = $3,900 + $410)
	(b)		+ 50	
	(c)		+ 25	
	(d)		+ 400	
	(e)		+ 45	
	(f)	+ 10		
Adjusted totals		$5,610	− $4,830	= $780 Adjusted income before income tax
				× 35% Tax rate
				$273 **Income tax**

Assets	=	Liabilities	+	Stockholders' Equity
		Income Tax Payable +273		Income Tax Expense (+E) −273

2. Adjusting journal entries:

a.   dr Unearned Revenue (−L) 400
      cr Mowing Revenue (+R, +SE)   400

b.   dr Insurance Expense (+E, −SE) 50
      cr Prepaid Insurance (−A)   50

c.   dr Depreciation Expense (+E, −SE) 25
      cr Accumulated Depreciation (+xA, −A)   25

d.   dr Wages Expense (+E, −SE) 400
      cr Wages Payable (+L)   400

e.   dr Interest Expense (+E, −SE) 45
      cr Interest Payable (+L)   45

f.   dr Interest Receivable (+A) 10
      cr Interest Revenue (+R, +SE)   10

g.   dr Income Tax Expense (+E, −SE) 273
      cr Income Tax Payable (+L)   273

3. T-accounts affected by adjusting journal entries:*

dr +	Interest Receivable (A)		cr −
Beg. bal.	0		
(f)	10		
End. bal.	10		

dr −	Interest Payable (L)		cr +
		0	Beg. bal.
		45	(e)
		45	End. bal.

dr +	Insurance Expense (E)		cr −
Beg. bal.	0		
(b)	50		
End. bal.	50		

dr +	Prepaid Insurance (A)		cr −
Beg. bal.	300		
		50	(b)
End. bal.	250		

dr −	Income Tax Payable (L)		cr +
		0	Beg. bal.
		273	(g)
		273	End. bal.

dr +	Depreciation Expense (E)		cr −
Beg. bal.	0		
(c)	25		
End. bal.	25		

---

*See page 115 (Chapter 3) for balances of T-accounts not affected by adjusting journal entries.

dr −	Accumulated Depreciation (xA)	cr +		dr −	Mowing Revenue (R, SE)	cr +		dr +	Interest Expense (E, SE)	cr −
	0	Beg. bal.			5,200	Beg. bal.		Beg. bal.	0	
	25	(c)			400	(a)		(e)	45	
	25	End. bal.			5,600	End. bal.		End. bal.	45	

dr −	Unearned Revenue (L)	cr +		dr −	Interest Revenue (R, SE)	cr +		dr +	Income Tax Expense (E, SE)	cr −
	1,600	Beg. bal.			0	Beg. bal.		Beg. bal.	0	
(a) 400					10	(f)		(g)	273	
	1,200	End. bal.			10	End. bal.		End. bal.	273	

dr −	Wages Payable (L)	cr +		dr +	Wages Expense (E, SE)	cr −
	0	Beg. bal.		Beg. bal.	3,900	
	400	(d)		(d)	400	
	400	End. bal.		End. bal.	4,300	

4.   Adjusted trial balance:

GOODBYE GRASS CORPORATION
Adjusted Trial Balance
At April 30, 2010

Account Name	Debits	Credits	
Cash	$ 4,510		
Accounts Receivable	1,700		
Note Receivable	1,250		
Interest Receivable	10		
Prepaid Insurance	250		
Equipment	4,600		
Accumulated Depreciation		$ 25	
Land	3,750		To Balance Sheet
Accounts Payable		620	
Unearned Revenue		1,200	
Wages Payable		400	
Interest Payable		45	
Income Tax Payable		273	
Note Payable		4,000	
Contributed Capital		9,000	
Retained Earnings		0	To Statement of Retained Earnings
Mowing Revenue		5,600	
Interest Revenue		10	
Wages Expense	4,300		
Fuel Expense	410		To Income Statement
Insurance Expense	50		
Depreciation Expense	25		
Interest Expense	45		
Income Tax Expense	273		
Totals	$21,173	$21,173	

5. Income statement, statement of retained earnings, and balance sheet:

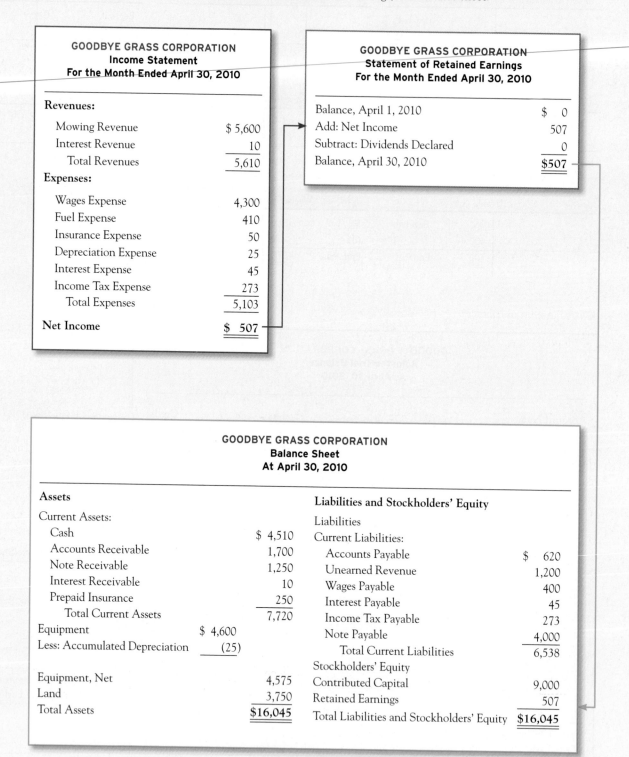

GOODBYE GRASS CORPORATION
Income Statement
For the Month Ended April 30, 2010

Revenues:

Mowing Revenue	$ 5,600
Interest Revenue	10
Total Revenues	5,610

Expenses:

Wages Expense	4,300
Fuel Expense	410
Insurance Expense	50
Depreciation Expense	25
Interest Expense	45
Income Tax Expense	273
Total Expenses	5,103
Net Income	**$ 507**

GOODBYE GRASS CORPORATION
Statement of Retained Earnings
For the Month Ended April 30, 2010

Balance, April 1, 2010	$ 0
Add: Net Income	507
Subtract: Dividends Declared	0
Balance, April 30, 2010	$507

GOODBYE GRASS CORPORATION
Balance Sheet
At April 30, 2010

Assets			Liabilities and Stockholders' Equity	
Current Assets:			Liabilities	
Cash		$ 4,510	Current Liabilities:	
Accounts Receivable		1,700	Accounts Payable	$ 620
Note Receivable		1,250	Unearned Revenue	1,200
Interest Receivable		10	Wages Payable	400
Prepaid Insurance		250	Interest Payable	45
Total Current Assets		7,720	Income Tax Payable	273
Equipment	$ 4,600		Note Payable	4,000
Less: Accumulated Depreciation	(25)		Total Current Liabilities	6,538
			Stockholders' Equity	
Equipment, Net		4,575	Contributed Capital	9,000
Land		3,750	Retained Earnings	507
Total Assets		$16,045	Total Liabilities and Stockholders' Equity	$16,045

6. Closing journal entry:

If Goodbye Grass Corporation had adopted an April 30 year-end, the company would require a journal entry to close its revenue and expense accounts into Retained Earnings. Because the company has not declared a dividend, a Dividends Declared account does not exist to be closed into Retained Earnings. The closing journal entry needed to close revenues and expenses into Retained Earnings is

dr Mowing Revenue (−R)	5,600	
dr Interest Revenue (−R)	10	
cr Wages Expense (−E)		4,300
cr Fuel Expense (−E)		410
cr Insurance Expense (−E)		50
cr Depreciation Expense (−E)		25
cr Interest Expense (−E)		45
cr Income Tax Expense (−E)		273
cr Retained Earnings (+SE)		507

CHAPTER SUMMARY

Explain why adjustments are needed. p. 148
LO1

Adjustments are needed to ensure:

- Revenues are recorded when earned (the revenue principle),
- Expenses are recorded when incurred to generate revenues (the matching principle),
- Assets are reported at amounts representing the economic benefits that remain at the end of the current period, and
- Liabilities are reported at amounts owed at the end of the current period that will require a future sacrifice of resources.

Prepare adjustments needed at the end of the period. p. 150
LO2

- The process for preparing adjustments includes
  1. Analyzing the unadjusted balances in balance sheet and income statement accounts, and calculating the amount of the adjustment needed, using a timeline where appropriate.
  2. Preparing an adjusting journal entry to make the adjustment.
  3. Summarizing the adjusting journal entry in the applicable ledger (T-accounts).
- Each adjusting journal entry affects one balance sheet and one income statement account.

Prepare an adjusted trial balance. p. 160
LO3

An adjusted trial balance is a list of all accounts with their adjusted debit or credit balances indicated in the appropriate column to provide a check on the equality of the debits and credits.

Prepare financial statements. p. 161
LO4

Adjusted account balances are used in preparing the following financial statements:

- Income Statement: Revenues − Expenses = Net Income.
- Statement of Retained Earnings: Beginning Retained Earnings + Net Income − Dividends Declared = Ending Retained Earnings.
- Balance Sheet: Assets = Liabilities + Stockholders' Equity.
- The statement of cash flows and notes to the financial statements are important components of adjusted financial statements, but they will be studied in later chapters.

Explain the closing process. p. 164
LO5

- Closing journal entries are required to (*a*) transfer net income (or loss) and dividends declared into retained earnings, and (*b*) prepare all temporary accounts (revenues, expenses, dividends declared) for the following year by establishing zero balances in these accounts.
- Two closing journal entries are needed:
  1. Debit each revenue account, credit each expense account, and record the difference (equal to net income) in Retained Earnings.
  2. Credit the Dividends Declared account for the amount of its balance and debit Retained Earnings for the same amount.

LO6   Explain how adjustments affect financial results. p. 168

Adjustments help ensure all revenues and expenses are reported in the period in which they are earned and incurred, as a result of a company's activities. Without these adjustments, the financial statements present an incomplete and potentially misleading picture of the company's financial performance.

KEY TERMS

Adjusted Trial Balance p. 161

Adjusting Journal
    Entries p. 150

Adjustments p. 148

Carrying Value (Net Book Value,
    Book Value) p. 155

Contra-Account p. 155

Depreciation p. 155

Permanent Accounts p. 165

Post-Closing Trial
    Balance p. 167

Temporary Accounts p. 165

See complete definitions in the glossary in the back of this text.

HOMEWORK HELPER

Alternative terms

- Accrued Liabilities is a generic account name that can include liabilities recorded using accrual adjustments for salaries, utilities, income taxes, and many other items.

Helpful reminders

- When determining each adjustment, draw timelines to picture where we are now, where we need to be, and the adjustment to get us there.
- Cash is never part of an accrual or deferral adjustment.
- The income statement is the temporary home for revenue and expense accounts, and Retained Earnings in the stockholders' equity section of the balance sheet is their permanent home.

Frequent mistakes

- Accumulated Depreciation and Depreciation Expense are not the same accounts. Accumulated Depreciation is a permanent, balance sheet account that accumulates each period of depreciation. Depreciation Expense is a temporary, income statement account that reports only the current period's depreciation.
- Dividends are not expenses, but rather are distributions to stockholders of the company's prior profits that have accumulated in Retained Earnings.
- The amount in Retained Earnings on an adjusted trial balance is not reported on the balance sheet; it is the beginning balance on the statement of retained earnings. The ending balance from the statement of retained earnings is reported on the balance sheet.

PRACTICE MATERIAL

QUESTIONS (⊕ Symbol indicates questions that require analysis from more than one perspective.)

1. Briefly explain the purposes of adjustments.

2. Explain the relationships between adjustments and the following Chapter 3 concepts: (*a*) the time period assumption, (*b*) the revenue principle, and (*c*) the matching principle.

3. List the two types of adjustments and give an example of an adjustment affecting revenues and expenses for each type.

4. Explain the effect of adjusting journal entries on cash.

5. What is a contra-asset? Give an example of one.

6. Explain the differences between depreciation expense and accumulated depreciation.

7. What is an adjusted trial balance? What is its purpose?

8. On December 31, a company makes a $9,000 payment for renting a warehouse in January, February, and March of the following year. Show the accounting equation effects of the transaction on December 31, as well as the adjustments required on January 31, February 28, and March 31.

9. Using the information in question 8, determine the amounts and accounts that will be reported on the January 31 balance sheet and the income statement for the month ended January 31.

10. Using the information in question 8, prepare the journal entry and adjusting journal entries to be made on December 31, January 31, February 28, and March 31.

11. What is the equation for each of the following statements: (*a*) income statement, (*b*) balance sheet, and (*c*) statement of retained earnings?

12. Explain how the financial statements in question 11 relate to each other.

13. What is the purpose of closing journal entries?

14. How do permanent accounts differ from temporary accounts?

15. Why are the income statement accounts closed but the balance sheet accounts are not?

16. Is Dividends Declared considered an asset, liability, or stockholders' equity account? Is it a permanent or temporary account? Does it normally have a debit or credit balance?

17. What is a post-closing trial balance? Is it a useful part of the accounting cycle? Explain.

18. The owner of a local business complains that the adjustments process consumes a lot of time and delays reporting month-end financial results. How would you convince her of the importance of this process?

MULTIPLE CHOICE

1. Which of the following accounts would not appear in a closing journal entry?
   a. Interest Revenue
   b. Accumulated Depreciation
   c. Retained Earnings
   d. Salary Expense

   Quiz 4
   www.mhhe.com/phillips3e

2. Which account is least likely to appear in an adjusting journal entry?
   a. Cash
   b. Interest Receivable
   c. Income Tax Expense
   d. Salaries Payable

3. When a concert promotions company collects cash for ticket sales two months in advance of the show date, which of the following accounts is recorded?
   a. Accrued Liability
   b. Accounts Receivable
   c. Prepaid Expense
   d. Unearned Revenue

4. On December 31, an adjustment is made to reduce unearned revenue and report (earned) revenue. How many accounts will be included in this adjusting journal entry?
   a. None
   b. One
   c. Two
   d. Three

5. An adjusting journal entry to recognize accrued salaries payable would cause which of the following?
   a. A decrease in assets and stockholders' equity.
   b. A decrease in assets and liabilities.
   c. An increase in expenses, liabilities, and stockholders' equity.
   d. An increase in expenses and liabilities and a decrease in stockholders' equity.

6. An adjusted trial balance
   a. Shows the ending balances in a debit and credit format before posting the adjusting journal entries.
   b. Is prepared after closing entries have been posted.
   c. Is a tool used by financial analysts to review the performance of publicly traded companies.
   d. Shows the ending balances resulting from the adjusting journal entries in a debit-and-credit format.

7. Company A has owned a building for several years. Which of the following statements regarding depreciation is false from an accounting perspective?
   a. Depreciation Expense for the year will equal Accumulated Depreciation.
   b. Depreciation is an estimated expense to be recorded each period during the building's life.
   c. As depreciation is recorded, stockholders' equity is reduced.
   d. As depreciation is recorded, total assets are reduced.

8. Which of the following trial balances is used as a source for preparing the income statement?
   a. Unadjusted trial balance
   b. Pre-adjusted trial balance
   c. Adjusted trial balance
   d. Post-closing trial balance

9. Assume the balance in Prepaid Insurance is $2,500 but it should be $1,500. The adjusting journal entry should include which of the following?
   a. Debit to Prepaid Insurance for $1,000.
   b. Credit to Insurance Expense for $1,000.
   c. Debit to Insurance Expense for $1,000.
   d. Debit to Insurance Expense for $1,500.

10. Assume a company receives a bill for $10,000 for advertising done during the current year. If this bill is not yet recorded at the end of the year, what will the adjusting journal entry include?
    a. Debit to Advertising Expense of $10,000.
    b. Credit to Advertising Expense of $10,000.
    c. Debit to Accrued Liabilities of $10,000.
    d. Need more information to determine.

For answers to the Multiple-Choice Questions **see page Q1** located in the last section of the book.

MINI-EXERCISES

LO1

Northwest Airlines
Abercrombie
GSD + M
Tiger Woods Foundation

M4-1 Understanding Concepts Related to Adjustments

Match each situation below to two applicable reasons that require an adjustment to be made.

____ 1. Northwest Airlines provided flights this month for customers who paid cash last month for tickets.	A. Revenue has been earned.
____ 2. Abercrombie received a telephone bill for services this month, which must be paid next month.	B. Expense has been incurred.
____ 3. GSD + M completed work on an advertising campaign that will be collected next month.	C. Liability has been incurred.
	D. Liability has been fulfilled.
____ 4. The Tiger Woods Foundation used up some of the benefits of its 35,000 square foot building (when teaching students about forensic science, aerospace, and video production).	E. Asset has been acquired.
	F. Asset has been used up.

LO1, 2

M4-2 Matching Transactions with Type of Adjustment

Match each transaction with the type of adjustment that will be required, by entering the appropriate letter in the space provided.

Transaction	Type of Adjustment
____ 1. An expense has not yet been incurred, but has been paid in advance.	A. Accrual adjustment
____ 2. Rent has not yet been collected, but is already earned.	B. Deferral adjustment
____ 3. Office supplies on hand will be used next accounting period.	
____ 4. An expense has been incurred, but not yet paid or recorded.	
____ 5. Revenue has been collected in advance and will be earned later.	

LO1, 2

M4-3 Matching Transactions with Type of Adjustment

Match each transaction with the type of adjustment that will be required, by entering the appropriate letter in the space provided.

Transaction	Type of Adjustment
____ 1. Supplies for office use were purchased during the year for $500, of which $100 remained on hand (unused) at year-end.	A. Accrual adjustment
____ 2. Interest of $250 on a note receivable was earned at year-end, although collection of the interest is not due until the following year.	B. Deferral adjustment
____ 3. At year-end, wages payable of $3,600 had not been recorded or paid.	
____ 4. At year-end, one-half of a $2,000 advertising project had been completed for a client, but nothing had been billed or collected.	

LO2

M4-4 Recording Adjusting Journal Entries

Using the information in M4-3, prepare the adjusting journal entries required.

M4-5 Determine Accounting Equation Effects of Adjustments

LO2

For each of the following transactions for the Sky Blue Corporation, give the accounting equation effects of the adjustments required at the end of the month on December 31, 2009:

a. Collected $1,200 rent for the period December 1, 2009, to February 28, 2010, which was credited to Unearned Rent Revenue on December 1, 2009.

b. Paid $2,400 for a two-year insurance premium on December 1, 2009; debited Prepaid Insurance for that amount.

c. Used a machine purchased on December 1, 2009, for $48,000. The company estimates *annual* depreciation of $4,800.

M4-6 Recording Adjusting Journal Entries

LO2

Using the information in M4-5, prepare the adjusting journal entries required on December 31, 2009.

M4-7 Determining Accounting Equation Effects of Adjustments

LO2

For each of the following transactions for the Sky Blue Corporation, give the accounting equation effects of the adjustments required at the end of the month on December 31, 2010:

a. Received a $600 utility bill for electricity usage in December to be paid in January 2011.

b. Owed wages to 10 employees who worked three days at $100 each per day at the end of December. The company will pay employees at the end of the first week of January 2011.

c. On December 1, 2010, loaned money to an employee who agreed to repay the loan in one year along with $1,200 for one full year of interest. No interest has been recorded yet.

M4-8 Recording Adjusting Journal Entries

LO2

Using the information in M4-7, prepare the adjusting journal entries required on December 31, 2010.

M4-9 Preparing Journal Entries for Deferral Transactions and Adjustments

LO2

For each of the following independent situations, prepare journal entries to record the initial transaction on September 30 and the adjustment required on October 31.

a. Hockey Helpers paid $2,000 cash on September 30, to rent an arena for the months of October and November.

b. Super Stage Shows received $6,000 on September 30, for season tickets that admit patrons to a theatre event that will be held twice (on October 31 and November 30).

c. Risky Ventures paid $3,000 on September 30, for insurance coverage for the months of October, November, and December.

M4-10 Preparing Journal Entries for Deferral Transactions and Adjustments

LO2

For each of the following independent situations, prepare journal entries to record the initial transaction on December 31 and the adjustment required on January 31.

a. Magnificent Magazines received $12,000 on December 31, 2010, for subscriptions to magazines that will be published and distributed in January through December 2011.

b. Walker Window Washing paid $1,200 cash for supplies on December 31, 2010. As of January 31, 2011, $200 of these supplies had been used up.

c. Indoor Raceway received $3,000 on December 31, 2010, from race participants for three races. One race is held January 31, 2011, and the other two will be held in March 2011.

M4-11 Preparing an Adjusted Trial Balance

LO3

Macro Company has the following adjusted accounts and balances at year-end (June 30, 2010):

Accounts Payable	$ 300	Cash	$1,020	Prepaid Expenses	$ 40
Accounts Receivable	550	Contributed Capital	300	Salaries Expense	660
Accrued Liabilities	150	Depreciation Expense	110	Sales Revenue	3,600
Accumulated		Income Tax Expense	110	Supplies	710
Depreciation	250	Income Tax Payable	30	Rent Expense	400
Administrative		Interest Expense	180	Retained Earnings	120
Expense	820	Interest Revenue	50	Unearned Revenue	100
Buildings and		Land	200		
Equipment	1,400	Long-term Debt	1,300		

Required:

Prepare an adjusted trial balance for Macro Company at June 30, 2010.

LO4   **M4-12 Reporting an Income Statement**

The Sky Blue Corporation has the following adjusted trial balance at December 31, 2009.

	Debit	Credit
Cash	$ 1,230	
Accounts Receivable	2,000	
Prepaid Insurance	2,300	
Notes Receivable	3,000	
Equipment	12,000	
Accumulated Depreciation		$ 2,600
Accounts Payable		1,600
Accrued Liabilities Payable		3,820
Wages Payable		1,000
Income Taxes Payable		2,900
Unearned Rent Revenue		600
Contributed Capital		2,400
Retained Earnings		1,000
Dividends Declared	300	
Sales Revenue		42,030
Rent Revenue		300
Wages Expense	21,600	
Depreciation Expense	1,300	
Utilities Expense	1,220	
Insurance Expense	1,400	
Rent Expense	9,000	
Income Tax Expense	2,900	
Total	$58,250	$58,250

Prepare an income statement for the year ended December 31, 2009. How much net income did the Sky Blue Corporation generate during 2009?

LO4   **M4-13 Reporting a Statement of Retained Earnings**

Refer to M4-12. Prepare a statement of retained earnings for 2009.

LO4   **M4-14 Reporting a Balance Sheet**

Refer to M4-12. Prepare a classified balance sheet at December 31, 2009. Are the Sky Blue Corporation's assets financed primarily by debt or equity?

LO5   **M4-15 Recording Closing Journal Entries**

Refer to the adjusted trial balance in M4-12. Prepare closing journal entries on December 31, 2009.

LO2   **M4-16 Preparing and Posting Adjusting Journal Entries**

At December 31, the unadjusted trial balance of H&R Tacks reports Supplies Inventory of $9,000 and Supplies Expense of $0. On December 31, supplies costing $1,300 are on hand. Prepare the adjusting journal entry on December 31. In separate T-accounts for each account, enter the unadjusted balances, post the adjusting journal entry, and report the adjusted balance.

LO2   **M4-17 Preparing and Posting Adjusting Journal Entries**

At December 31, the unadjusted trial balance of H&R Tacks reports Equipment of $30,000 and zero balances in Accumulated Depreciation and Depreciation Expense. Depreciation for the period is estimated to be $6,000. Prepare the adjusting journal entry on December 31. In separate T-accounts for each account, enter the unadjusted balances, post the adjusting journal entry, and report the adjusted balance.

LO2   **M4-18 Preparing and Posting Adjusting Journal Entries**

At December 31, the unadjusted trial balance of H&R Tacks reports Prepaid Insurance of $7,200 and Insurance Expense of $0. The insurance was purchased on July 1 and provides coverage for 12 months. Prepare the adjusting journal entry on December 31. In separate T-accounts for each account, enter the unadjusted balances, post the adjusting journal entry, and report the adjusted balance.

M4-19 Preparing and Posting Adjusting Journal Entries   LO2

At December 31, the unadjusted trial balance of H&R Tacks reports Unearned Revenue of $5,000
and Sales and Service Revenues of $33,800. One-half of the unearned revenues have been earned   *2500*
as of December 31. Prepare the adjusting journal entry on December 31. In separate T-accounts
for each account, enter the unadjusted balances, post the adjusting journal entry, and report the
adjusted balance.

M4-20 Preparing and Posting Adjusting Journal Entries   LO2

At December 31, the unadjusted trial balance of H&R Tacks reports Wages Payable of $0 and
Wages Expense of $20,000. Employees have been paid for work done up to December 27, but the
$1,200 they have earned for December 28–31 has not yet been paid or recorded. Prepare the
adjusting journal entry on December 31. In separate T-accounts for each account, enter the unadjusted balances, post the adjusting journal entry, and report the adjusted balance.

M4-21 Preparing and Posting Adjusting Journal Entries   LO2

At December 31, the unadjusted trial balance of H&R Tacks reports Interest Payable of $0 and
Interest Expense of $0. Interest incurred and owed in December totals $500. Prepare the adjusting
journal entry on December 31. In separate T-accounts for each account, enter the unadjusted balances, post the adjusting journal entry, and report the adjusted balance.

M4-22 Preparing and Posting Journal Entries for Dividends   LO2

At December 31, the unadjusted trial balance of H&R Tacks reports Dividends Declared of $0
and Dividends Payable of $0. A $200 dividend was declared on December 27, with payment in
cash to occur three weeks later. Prepare the required journal entry. In separate T-accounts for each
account, enter the unadjusted balances, post the journal entry, and report the adjusted balance.

M4-23 Preparing an Adjusted Trial Balance   LO3

The unadjusted trial balance for H&R Tacks reported the following account balances: Cash
$5,000; Accounts Receivable $500; Supplies $9,000; Prepaid Insurance $7,200; Equipment
$28,000; Accounts Payable $200; Unearned Revenue $5,000; Notes Payable $3,000; Contributed
Capital $22,000; Retained Earnings $5,700; Sales and Service Revenue $33,800; and Wages
Expense $20,000. Prepare an adjusted trial balance as of December 31 that includes the entries
required in M4-16 through M4-22.

M4-24 Progression of Prepaid Expenses over Several Periods   LO2, 4, 5

Midwest Manufacturing purchased a three-year insurance policy for $30,000 on January 2, 2009.
Prepare any journal entries, adjusting journal entries, and closing journal entries required on
January 2, 2009, December 31, 2009, and December 31, 2010. Summarize these entries in T-accounts
for Prepaid insurance, Insurance Expense, Cash, and Retained Earnings. Assume the January 2,
2009, balances in these accounts were $0, $0, $90,000, and $80,000, respectively. Given only the
entries for insurance, indicate what amounts would be reported for each of these accounts on the
balance sheet and income statement prepared on December 31, 2009, and December 31, 2010.

EXERCISES   McGraw Hill **connect**™
                                                           |ACCOUNTING

E4-1 Preparing an Adjusted Trial Balance from Adjusted   LO3
Account Balances

Gibson Consultants, Inc., provides marketing research for clients in the retail industry. The company had the following adjusted balances at December 31, 2009 (listed alphabetically):

Accounts Payable	Accumulated Depreciation	Consulting Fees Earned	General and Administrative Expense
86,830	18,100	2,564,200	320,050

Accounts Receivable	Building and Equipment	Contributed Capital	Income Taxes Payable
225,400	323,040	233,370	2,030

Accrued Liabilities	Cash	Dividends Declared	Interest Expense
25,650	173,000	5,000	17,200

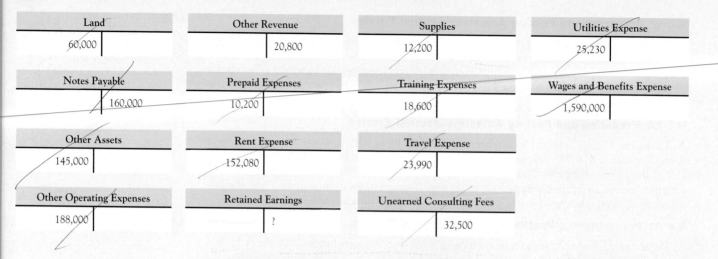

Land			Other Revenue			Supplies			Utilities Expense		
60,000				20,800		12,200			25,230		

Notes Payable			Prepaid Expenses			Training Expenses			Wages and Benefits Expense		
	160,000		10,200			18,600			1,590,000		

Other Assets			Rent Expense			Travel Expense		
145,000			152,080			23,990		

Other Operating Expenses			Retained Earnings			Unearned Consulting Fees		
188,000			?			32,500		

Required:

1. Prepare an adjusted trial balance listing the accounts in proper order at December 31, 2009. Solve for the "?" in Retained Earnings.
2. Does the Retained Earnings balance determined in requirement 1 represent the balance at December 31, 2009, or December 31, 2008? Explain.

L01   **E4-2 Identifying Adjustments by Scanning a Trial Balance**

Coach, Inc.—the maker of handbags and other women's and men's accessories—was previously owned by Sara Lee Corporation until April 2001, when Coach was spun off as a separate company. Assume the following were reported in Coach's adjusted trial balance and were used to prepare its June 28, 2008, year-end financial statements.

COACH INCORPORATED
Adjusted Trial Balance
At June 28, 2008
(millions of dollars)

	Debit	Credit
Cash	$ 698	
Accounts Receivable	107	
Inventories	345	
Prepaid Expenses	234	
Property and Equipment	755	
Accumulated Depreciation		$ 291
Other Assets	426	
Accounts Payable		134
Wages Payable		304
Income Taxes Payable		12
Other Current Liabilities		308
Contributed Capital		24
Retained Earnings		709
Sales Revenue		3,181
Cost of Sales	774	
Selling, General and Administrative Expenses	1,260	
Interest Revenue		48
Income Tax Expense	412	
	$5,011	$5,011

Required:

1. Based on the information in the trial balance, list two pairs of balance sheet and income statement accounts that likely required *deferral adjustments* as of June 30 (no computations are necessary).

2. Based on the information in the trial balance, list two pairs of balance sheet and income statement accounts that likely required *accrual adjustments* as of June 30 (no computations are necessary).

E4-3 Recording Initial Transactions and Subsequent Adjustments   LO1, 2

During the month of September, the Texas Go-Kart Company had the following business activities:

a. On September 1, paid rent on the track facility for six months at a total cost of $12,000.
b. On September 1, received $60,000 for season tickets for 12-month admission to the race track.
c. On September 1, booked the race track for a private organization that will use the track one day per month for $2,000 each time, to be paid in the following month. The organization uses the track on September 30.
d. On September 1, hired a new manager at a monthly salary of $3,000, to be paid the first Monday following the end of the month.

Required:

First prepare the journal entry, if any, required to record each of the initial business activities on September 1. Then, prepare the adjusting journal entries, if any, required on September 30.

E4-4 Recording Adjusting Journal Entries   LO1, 2

Mobo, a wireless phone carrier, completed its first year of operations on December 31, 2009. All of the 2009 entries have been recorded, except for the following:

a. At year-end, employees earned wages of $6,000, which will be paid on the next payroll date, January 6, 2010.
b. At year-end, the company had earned interest revenue of $3,000. It will be collected March 1, 2010.

Required:

1. What is the annual reporting period for this company?
2. Identify whether each required adjustment is a deferral or an accrual.
3. Show the accounting equation effects of each required adjustment, using the format shown in the demonstration case.
4. Why are these adjustments needed?

E4-5 Recording Adjusting Journal Entries   LO1, 2

Refer to E4-4.

Required:

Record the required adjusting journal entry for transactions (a) and (b).

E4-6 Determining Adjustments and Accounting Equation Effects   LO1, 2

Fes Company is making adjusting journal entries for the year ended December 31, 2010. In developing information for the adjusting journal entries, you learned the following:

a. A two-year insurance premium of $7,200 was paid on January 1, 2010, for coverage beginning on that date. As of December 31, 2010, the unadjusted balances were $7,200 for Prepaid Insurance and $0 for Insurance Expense.
b. At December 31, 2010, you obtained the following data relating to shipping supplies.

Unadjusted balance in Shipping Supplies on December 31, 2010	$15,000
Unadjusted balance in Shipping Supplies Expense on December 31, 2010	72,000
Shipping supplies on hand, counted on December 31, 2010	10,000

Required:

1. Of the $7,200 paid for insurance, what amount should be reported on the 2010 income statement as Insurance Expense? What amount should be reported on the December 31, 2010, balance sheet as Prepaid Insurance?

2. What amount should be reported on the 2010 income statement as Shipping Supplies Expense? What amount should be reported on the December 31, 2010, balance sheet as Shipping Supplies?

3. Using the format shown in the demonstration case, indicate the accounting equation effects of the adjustment required for (*a*) insurance and (*b*) shipping supplies.

LO1, 2   **E4-7   Recording Adjusting Journal Entries**

Refer to E4-6.

Required:

Prepare adjusting journal entries at December 31, 2010, for (*a*) insurance, and (*b*) shipping supplies.

LO1, 2, 6   **E4-8   Recording Typical Adjusting Journal Entries**

Jaworski's Ski Store is completing the accounting process for its first year ended December 31, 2010. The transactions during 2010 have been journalized and posted. The following data are available to determine adjusting journal entries:

a. The unadjusted balance in Office Supplies was $850 at December 31, 2010. The unadjusted balance in Supplies Expense was $0 at December 31, 2010. A year-end count showed $100 of supplies on hand.

b. Wages earned by employees during December 2010, unpaid and unrecorded at December 31, 2010, amounted to $3,700. The last paychecks were issued December 28; the next payments will be made on January 6, 2011. The unadjusted balance in Wages Expense was $40,000 at December 31, 2010.

c. A portion of the store's basement is now being rented for $1,100 per month to K. Frey. On November 1, 2010, the store collected six months' rent in advance from Frey in the amount of $6,600. It was credited in full to Unearned Rent Revenue when collected. The unadjusted balance in Rent Revenue was $0 at December 31, 2010.

d. The store purchased delivery equipment at the beginning of the year. The estimated depreciation for 2010 is $3,000, although none has been recorded yet.

e. On December 31, 2010, the unadjusted balance in Prepaid Insurance was $4,800. This was the amount paid in the middle of the year for a two-year insurance policy with coverage beginning on July 1, 2010. The unadjusted balance in Insurance Expense was $800, which was the cost of insurance from January 1 to June 30, 2010.

f. Jaworski's store did some ski repair work for Frey. At the end of December 31, 2010, Frey had not paid for work completed amounting to $750. This amount has not yet been recorded as Repair Shop Revenue. Collection is expected during January 2011.

Required:

Earlier in 2010, Jaworski's store had already provided, recorded, and collected cash for $5,000 of repair services for other customers.

1. For each of the items listed above, indicate the account names and adjusted balances that should be reported on Jaworski's year-end balance sheet and income statement.

2. For each situation, prepare the adjusting journal entry that should be recorded for Jaworski's at December 31, 2010.

LO2, 6   **E4-9   Determining Accounting Equation Effects of Typical Adjusting Journal Entries**

Refer to E4-8.

Required:

For each of the transactions in E4-8, indicate the amount and direction of effects of the adjusting journal entry on the elements of the accounting equation. Using the following format, indicate + for increase, − for decrease, and NE for no effect. Include account names using the format shown for the following sample.

Transaction	Assets	Liabilities	Stockholders' Equity
a	Office Supplies −750		Supplies Expense (+E) −750
etc.			

E4-10 Recording Transactions Including Adjusting and Closing Journal Entries

LO2, 5

The following accounts are used by Mouse Potato, Inc., a computer game maker.

Codes	Accounts	Codes	Accounts
A	Accounts Receivable	K	Note Payable
B	Accumulated Depreciation	L	Office Equipment
C	Cash	M	Office Supplies
D	Contributed Capital	N	Retained Earnings
E	Depreciation Expense	O	Service Revenue
F	Dividends Declared	P	Supplies Expense
G	Dividends Payable	Q	Unearned Service Revenue
H	Interest Expense	R	Wage Expense
I	Interest Payable	S	Wages Payable
J	Interest Revenue	T	None of the above

Required:

For each of the following independent situations, give the journal entry by entering the appropriate code(s) and amount(s). We've done the first one for you as an example.

		Debit		Credit	
	Independent Situations	Code	Amount	Code	Amount
a.	Accrued wages, unrecorded and unpaid at year-end, $400 (example).	R	400	S	400
b.	Service revenue collected in advance, $600.				
c.	Dividends declared and paid during year, $900.				
d.	Depreciation expense for year, $1,000.				
e.	Service revenue earned but not yet collected at year-end, $1,000.				
f.	Balance in Office Supplies account, $400; supplies on hand at year-end, $150.				
g.	At year-end, interest on note payable not yet recorded or paid, $220.				
h.	Adjusted balance at year-end in Service Revenue account, $75,000. Give the journal entry to close this one account at year-end.				
i.	Adjusted balance at year-end in Interest Expense account, $420. Give the journal entry to close this one account at year-end.				

E4-11 Inferring Transactions from Accrual and Deferral Accounts

LO1, 2

Deere & Company was incorporated in 1868 and today is the world's leading producer of agricultural equipment. The following information is taken from its annual report for the year ended October 31, 2008 (in millions of dollars):

Deere & Company

Income Tax Payable			Wages Payable			Interest Payable		
	135	Beg. bal.		1,060	Beg. bal.		140	Beg. bal.
712	?	(a)	(b) ?	19,575		1,127	?	(c)
	79	End. bal.		1,175	End. bal.		150	End. bal.

Required:

1. For each accrued liability account, describe the typical transactions that cause it to increase and decrease.

2. Express each T-account in equation format and then solve for the missing amounts for (a), (b), and (c) (in millions). For example, the Interest Payable T-account can be expressed as: Beg. bal. (140) + increases (?) − decreases (1,127) = End. bal. (150). By rearranging the equation, you can solve for ? = 150 + 1,127 − 140.

LO2, 6   **E4-12 Analyzing the Effects of Adjusting Journal Entries on the Income Statement and Balance Sheet**

On December 31, 2009, Alan and Company prepared an income statement and balance sheet but failed to take into account four adjusting journal entries. The income statement, prepared on this incorrect basis, reported income before income tax of $30,000. The balance sheet (before the effect of income taxes) reflected total assets, $90,000; total liabilities, $40,000; and stockholders' equity, $50,000. The data for the four adjusting journal entries follow:

a. Depreciation of $8,000 for the year on equipment was not recorded.
b. Wages amounting to $17,000 for the last three days of December 2009 were not paid and not recorded (the next payroll will be on January 10, 2010).
c. Rent revenue of $4,800 was collected on December 1, 2009, for office space for the three-month period December 1, 2009, to February 28, 2010. The $4,800 was credited in full to Unearned Rent Revenue when collected.
d. Income taxes were not recorded. The income tax rate for the company is 30 percent.

Required:

Complete the following table to show the effects of the four adjusting journal entries (indicate deductions with parentheses):

Items	Net Income	Total Assets	Total Liabilities	Stockholders' Equity
Amounts reported	$30,000	$90,000	$40,000	$50,000
Effect of depreciation				
Effect of wages				
Effect of rent revenue				
Adjusted balances	6,600	82,000	55,400	26,600
Effect of income tax				
Correct amounts				

LO2, 4, 6   **E4-13 Reporting an Adjusted Income Statement**

Dyer, Inc., completed its first year of operations on December 31, 2010. Because this is the end of the annual accounting period, the company bookkeeper prepared the following preliminary income statement:

Income Statement, 2010

Rental Revenue		$114,000
Expenses:		
Salaries and Wages Expense	$28,500	
Maintenance Expense	12,000	
Rent Expense	9,000	
Utilities Expense	4,000	
Gas and Oil Expense	3,000	
Other Expenses	1,000	
Total Expenses		57,500
Income		$ 56,500

You are an independent CPA hired by the company to audit the firm's accounting systems and financial statements. In your audit, you developed additional data as follows:

a. Wages for the last three days of December amounting to $310 were not recorded or paid.
b. The $400 telephone bill for December 2010 has not been recorded or paid.
c. Depreciation on rental autos, amounting to $23,000 for 2010, was not recorded.
d. Interest of $500 was not recorded on the note payable by Dyer, Inc.
e. The Rental Revenue account includes $4,000 of revenue to be earned in January 2011.
f. Maintenance supplies costing $600 were used during 2010, but this has not yet been recorded.
g. The income tax expense for 2010 is $7,000, but it won't actually be paid until 2011.

Required:

1. What adjusting journal entry for each item (*a*) through (*g*) should be recorded at December 31, 2010? If none is required, explain why.

2. Prepare, in proper form, an adjusted income statement for 2010.

3. Did the adjustments have a significant overall effect on the company's net income?

E4-14 Recording Adjusting Entries and Preparing an Adjusted Trial Balance   LO2, 3

Ninja Sockeye Star prepared the following unadjusted trial balance at the end of its second year of operations ending December 31, 2009.

Account Titles	Debit	Credit
Cash	$12,000	
Accounts Receivable	6,000	
Prepaid Rent	2,400	
Machinery	21,000	
Accumulated Depreciation		$ 1,000
Accounts Payable		1,000
Utilities Payable		0
Income Tax Payable		0
Contributed Capital		29,800
Retained Earnings		2,100
Sales Revenue		45,000
Wages Expense	25,000	
Utilities Expense	12,500	
Rent Expense	0	
Depreciation Expense	0	
Income Tax Expense	0	
Totals	$78,900	$78,900

Other data not yet recorded at December 31, 2009:

a. Rent expired during 2009, $1,200.
b. Depreciation expense for 2009, $1,000.
c. Utilities payable, $9,000.
d. Income tax expense, $800.

Required:

1. Using the format shown in the demonstration case, indicate the accounting equation effects of each required adjustment.

2. Prepare the adjusting journal entries required at December 31, 2009.

3. Summarize the adjusting journal entries in T-accounts. After entering the beginning balances and computing the adjusted ending balances, prepare an adjusted trial balance as of December 31, 2009.

LO2, 3   **E4-15 Recording Four Adjusting Journal Entries and Preparing an Adjusted Trial Balance**

Mint Cleaning Inc. prepared the following unadjusted trial balance at the end of its second year of operations ending December 31, 2010. To simplify this exercise, the amounts given are in thousands of dollars.

Account Titles	Debit	Credit
Cash	$ 38	
Accounts Receivable	9	
Prepaid Insurance	6	
Machinery	80	
Accumulated Depreciation		$ 0
Accounts Payable		9
Contributed Capital		76
Retained Earnings		4
Sales Revenue		80
Administrative Expenses	26	
Wages Expense	10	
Totals	$169	$169

Other data not yet recorded at December 31, 2010:

a.   Insurance expired during 2010, $5.
b.   Depreciation expense for 2010, $4.
c.   Wages payable, $7.
d.   Income tax expense, $9.

Required:

1.   Prepare the adjusting journal entries for 2010.
2.   Using T-accounts, determine the adjusted balances in each account and prepare an adjusted trial balance as of December 31, 2010.

LO4   **E4-16 Reporting an Income Statement, Statement of Retained Earnings, and Balance Sheet**

Refer to E4-15.

Required:

Using the adjusted balances in E4-15, prepare an income statement, statement of retained earnings, and balance sheet for 2010.

LO5   **E4-17 Recording Closing Entries**

Refer to E4-15.

Required:

Using the adjusted balances in E4-15, give the closing journal entry for 2010. What is the purpose of "closing the books" at the end of the accounting period?

LO1, 2, 6   **E4-18 Analyzing, Recording, and Summarizing Business Activities and Adjustments**

The following relates to a magazine company called My Style Mag (MSM). You will use your understanding of the relationships among: (1) business activities, (2) accounting equation effects, (3) journal entries, and (4) T-accounts, to complete a four-part table similar to the following. Prepare a separate table for each item (a)–(f) listed below.

(1)	(Description of the business activity.)

(2)	Assets	=	Liabilities	+	Stockholders' Equity

(3)	Account Names	Debit	Credit

(4)		

Required:

For each item (a)–(f) listed below, use the information provided to prepare and complete a four-part table similar to that shown above.

a.

(1)	On January 22, 2009, MSM received $24,000 cash from customers for one-year subscriptions to the magazine for February 2009–January 2010.

b.

(3)	Account Names	Debit	Credit
Jan. 31	Utilities Expense (+E, −SE)	3,000	
	Accounts Payable (+L)		3,000

c.

(2)	Assets	=	Liabilities	+	Stockholders' Equity
Feb. 28			Unearned Subscription Revenue −2,000		Subscription Revenue (+R) +2,000

d.

(1)	On March 31, 2009, MSM recorded an adjusting entry for the month's depreciation of $10,000.

e.

(4)	Cash	Prepaid Rent

	Cash		Prepaid Rent	
	5,000	Apr. 1	Apr. 1 5,000	

f.

(4)	Accounts Receivable	Advertising Revenue

	Accounts Receivable		Advertising Revenue	
Apr. 30	10,000		10,000 Apr. 30	

COACHED PROBLEMS

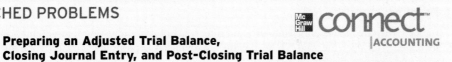

|ACCOUNTING   **L03, 5**

CP4-1 **Preparing an Adjusted Trial Balance, Closing Journal Entry, and Post-Closing Trial Balance**

Building on its brand's success in boardsports, Volcom, Inc., has become a premium designer, marketer, and distributor of clothing and accessories for young men and women. The following is a list of accounts and amounts reported for the fiscal year ended December 31, 2008. The accounts have normal debit or credit balances and the dollars are rounded to the nearest thousand.

Accounts Payable	$ 15,291	Long-term Debt	$ 531
Accounts Receivable	60,914	Other Assets	27,294
Accrued Liabilities	12,098	Other Revenue	1,288
Accumulated Depreciation	7,315	Product Cost Expense	171,208
Cash	79,613	Property and Equipment	34,031
Contributed Capital	91,768	Retained Earnings	80,226
Income Tax Expense	11,787	Sales Revenue	332,110
Inventories	27,086	Selling, General, and	
		Administrative Expenses	128,694

Required:

1. Prepare an adjusted trial balance at December 31, 2008. Is the Retained Earnings balance of $80,226 the amount that would be reported on the balance sheet as of December 31, 2008?
   TIP: Volcom, Inc., did not declare a dividend during 2008 but it did earn net income.
2. Prepare the closing entry required at December 31, 2008.
3. Prepare a post-closing trial balance at December 31, 2008.

LO1, 2

www.mhhe.com/phillips3e

CP4-2 Analyzing and Recording Adjusting Journal Entries

Jordan Company's annual accounting year ends on December 31. It is now December 31, 2009, and all of the 2009 entries have been made except for the following:

a. The company owes interest of $400 on a bank loan. The interest will be paid when the loan is repaid on September 30, 2010. No interest has been recorded.
b. On September 1, 2009, Jordan collected six months' rent of $4,800 on storage space. At that date, Jordan debited Cash and credited Unearned Rent Revenue for $4,800.
c. The company earned service revenue of $3,000 on a special job that was completed December 29, 2009. Collection will be made during January 2010. No entry has been recorded.
d. On November 1, 2009, Jordan paid a one-year premium for property insurance of $4,200, for coverage starting on that date. Cash was credited and Prepaid Insurance was debited for this amount.
e. At December 31, 2009, wages earned by employees but not yet paid totaled $1,100. The employees will be paid on the next payroll date, January 15, 2010.
f. Depreciation of $1,000 must be recognized on a service truck purchased this year.
g. On December 27, 2009, the company received a tax bill of $400 from the city for 2009 property taxes on land. The tax bill is payable during January 2010.
h. The income before any of the adjustments or income taxes was $27,400. The company's income tax rate is 30 percent. Compute adjusted income based on (a) through (g) to determine and record income tax expense.

Required:

1. Determine the accounting equation effects of each required adjustment.
   TIP: In transaction (b), Jordan Company has met its obligation for four of the six months, thereby earning 4/6 of the rent collected.
   TIP: In transaction (d), two months of insurance coverage has now expired.
   TIP: Adjusted income based on (a) through (g) should be $30,000.
2. Give the adjusting journal entry required for each transaction at December 31, 2009.

LO2, 6

CP4-3 Determining Accounting Equation Effects of Adjusting Journal Entries

Refer to CP4-2.

Required:

Indicate the effects (account, amount, and direction) of each adjusting journal entry. Use + for increase, − for decrease, and NE for no effect. Provide an appropriate account name for any revenue and expense effects.

TIP: The first transaction is done for you as an example.

Transaction	Assets	Liabilities		Stockholders' Equity	
a	NE	Interest Payable	+400	Interest Expense (+E)	−400
b					
etc.					

CP4-4 Identifying and Preparing Adjusting Journal Entries

LO1, 2, 3, 6

Golf Academy, Inc., provides private golf lessons. Its unadjusted trial balance at December 31, 2009, follows, along with information about selected accounts.

Account Names	Debit	Credit	Further Information
Cash	$ 31,900		As reported on December 31 bank statement.
Supplies	600		Based on count, only $200 of supplies still exist.
Unearned Revenue		$ 3,500	Of this amount, $3,000 was received for December lessons and $500 for January lessons.
Wages Payable		0	Employees were paid $1,000 for 10 days of work through December 28. They have not yet been paid for work on December 29 and 30.
Income Tax Payable		0	The company has paid last year's income tax but not this year's tax.
Interest Payable		0	The company has not paid the $100 of interest owed on its note payable for the current period.
Note Payable		12,000	This one-year note was taken out this year on December 1.
Contributed Capital		1,000	This amount was contributed to the company in prior years.
Retained Earnings		3,000	This is the balance reported at the end of last year.
Lesson Revenue		51,500	Most customers pay cash for lessons each time they are provided, but some customers pay in advance.
Wages Expense	36,100		Employees worked through December 30, but did not work on December 31.
Supplies Expense	2,400		This is the cost of supplies used through November 30.
Interest Expense	0		The company has not paid the $100 of interest owed on its note payable for the current period.
Income Tax Expense	0		The company has an average tax rate of 30 percent.
Totals	$71,000	$71,000	

Required:

1. Calculate the (preliminary) unadjusted net income for the year ended December 31, 2009.
2. Name the five pairs of balance sheet and income statement accounts that require adjustment.
3. Calculate the desired balances for each account listed in the unadjusted trial balance.
4. Prepare the adjusting journal entries that are required at December 31, 2009.
5. Calculate the adjusted net income that the company should report for the year ended December 31, 2009. By how much did the adjustments in requirement (4) cause net income to increase or decrease?

CP4-5 Comprehensive Review Problem: From Recording Transactions (Including Adjusting Journal Entries) to Preparing Financial Statements and Closing Journal Entries (Chapters 2, 3, and 4)

LO1, 2, 3, 4, 5, 6

Brothers Harry and Herman Hausyerday began operations of their machine shop (H & H Tool, Inc.) on January 1, 2007. The annual reporting period ends December 31. The trial balance on January 1, 2009, follows (the amounts are rounded to thousands of dollars to simplify):

Account Titles	Debit	Credit
Cash	$ 3	
Accounts Receivable	5	
Supplies	12	
Land	0	
Equipment	60	
Accumulated Depreciation (on Equipment)		$ 6
Other Assets	4	
Accounts Payable		5
Notes Payable		0
Wages Payable		0
Interest Payable		0
Income Tax Payable		0
Contributed Capital		65
Retained Earnings		8
Dividends Declared	0	
Service Revenue	0	
Depreciation Expense	0	
Income Tax Expense	0	
Interest Expense	0	
Supplies and Operating Expenses	0	
Totals	$84	$84

Transactions during 2009 (summarized in thousands of dollars) follow:

a. Borrowed $12 cash on a six-month note payable dated March 1, 2009.
b. Purchased land for future building site, paid cash, $9.
c. Earned revenues for 2009, $160, including $40 on credit and $120 collected in cash.
d. Issued additional shares of stock for $3.
e. Recognized operating expenses for 2006, $85, including $15 on credit and $70 paid in cash.
f. Collected accounts receivable, $24.
g. Purchased other assets, $10 cash.
h. Paid accounts payable, $13.
i. Purchased supplies on account for future use, $18.
j. Signed a $25 service contract to start February 1, 2010.
k. Declared and paid a cash dividend, $17.

Data for adjusting journal entries:

l. Supplies counted on December 31, 2009, $10.
m. Depreciation for the year on the equipment, $6.
n. Accrued interest on notes payable of $1.
o. Wages earned since the December 24 payroll not yet paid, $12.
p. Income tax for the year was $8. It will be paid in 2010.

Required:

1. Set up T-accounts for the accounts on the trial balance and enter beginning balances.
2. Record journal entries for transactions (a) through (k), and post them to the T-accounts.

   TIP: In transaction (e), when operating costs are incurred on credit, Accounts Payable typically is used rather than Accrued Liabilities. The account Accrued Liabilities typically is used only for accrual adjustments made at the end of the period.

3. Prepare an unadjusted trial balance.
4. Record and post the adjusting journal entries (*l*) through (*p*).

   TIP: To determine the adjustment in (*l*), consider the beginning account balance shown in the trial balance and the information in (*i*) and (*l*).

5. Prepare an adjusted trial balance.
6. Prepare an income statement, statement of retained earnings, and balance sheet.
7. Prepare and post the closing journal entries.
8. Prepare a post-closing trial balance.
9. How much net income did H & H Tool, Inc., generate during 2009? Is the company financed primarily by liabilities or stockholders' equity?

GROUP A PROBLEMS

_{Mc Graw Hill} **connect**™ |ACCOUNTING   **LO3, 5**

PA4-1 Preparing a Trial Balance, Closing Journal Entry, and Post-Closing Trial Balance

Starbooks Corporation provides an online bookstore for electronic books. The following is a simplified list of accounts and amounts reported in its accounting records. The accounts have normal debit or credit balances and the dollars are rounded to the nearest thousand. Assume the year ended on September 30, 2009.

Accounts Payable	$ 221	Other Current Assets	$ 71
Accounts Receivable	191	Other Long-lived Assets	461
Accrued Liabilities	354	Other Operating Expenses	197
Accumulated Depreciation	300	Prepaid Expenses	94
Cash	307	Property and Equipment	2,142
Contributed Capital	151	Retained Earnings	1,445
Depreciation Expense	340	Selling Expenses	2,605
General and		Service Revenues	6,369
Administrative Expenses	357	Short-term Bank Loan	476
Income Tax Expense	302	Store Operating Expenses	2,166
Interest Revenue	92	Supplies	546
Long-term Debt	196	Unearned Revenue	175

Required:

1. Prepare an adjusted trial balance at September 30, 2009. Is the Retained Earnings balance of $1,445 the amount that would be reported on the balance sheet as of September 30, 2009?
2. Prepare the closing entry required at September 30, 2009.
3. Prepare a post-closing trial balance at September 30, 2009.

PA4-2 Analyzing and Recording Adjusting Journal Entries   **LO1, 2**

Brokeback Towing Company is at the end of its accounting year, December 31, 2010. The following data that must be considered were developed from the company's records and related documents:

a. On July 1, 2010, a three-year insurance premium on equipment in the amount of $600 was paid and debited in full to Prepaid Insurance on that date. Coverage began on July 1.
b. At the end of 2010, the unadjusted balance in the Office Supplies account was $1,000. A physical count of supplies on December 31, 2010, indicated supplies costing $300 were still on hand.
c. On December 31, 2010, YY's Garage completed repairs on one of Brokeback's trucks at a cost of $800. The amount is not yet recorded. It will be paid during January 2011.
d. In December the 2010 property tax bill for $1,600 was received from the city. The taxes, which have not been recorded, will be paid on February 15, 2011.
e. On December 31, 2010, the company completed a contract for an out-of-state company for $7,900 payable by the customer within 30 days. No cash has been collected and no journal entry has been made for this transaction.

f. On July 1, 2010, the company purchased a new hauling van. Depreciation for July–December 2010, estimated to total $2,750, has not been recorded.

g. As of December 31, the company owes interest of $500 on a bank loan taken out on October 1, 2010. The interest will be paid when the loan is repaid on September 30, 2011. No interest has been recorded yet.

h. The income before any of the adjustments or income taxes was $30,000. The company's federal income tax rate is 30 percent. Compute adjusted income based on all of the preceding information, and then determine and record income tax expense.

Required:

1. Determine the accounting equation effects of each required adjustment.
2. Give the adjusting journal entry required for each transaction at December 31, 2010.

LO2, 4, 6

eXcel

www.mhhe.com/phillips3e

PA4-3 Determining Accounting Equation Effects of Adjusting Journal Entries

Refer to PA4-2.

Required:

Indicate the accounting equation effects (amount and direction) of each adjusting journal entry. Use + for increase, − for decrease, and NE for no effect. Provide an appropriate account name for any revenue and expense effects.

Transaction	Assets	Liabilities	Stockholders' Equity
a			
b			
etc.			

LO1, 2 3, 6

PA4-4 Identifying and Preparing Adjusting Journal Entries

Val's Hair Emporium operates a hair salon. Its unadjusted trial balance as of December 31, 2010, follows along with information about selected accounts.

Account Names	Debit	Credit	Further Information
Cash	$ 3,800		As reported on December 31 bank statement.
Supplies	4,300		Based on count, only $3,200 of supplies still exist.
Prepaid Rent	6,000		This amount was paid November 1 for rent through the end of January.
Accounts Payable		$ 1,500	This represents the total amount of bills received for supplies and utilities through December 15. Val estimates that the company has received $450 of utility services through December 31 for which it has not yet been billed.
Wages Payable		0	Stylists have not yet been paid $150 for their work on December 31.
Income Tax Payable		0	The company has paid last year's income taxes but not this year's taxes.
Contributed Capital		2,000	This amount was contributed to the company in prior years.
Retained Earnings		900	This is the balance reported at the end of last year.
Hair Styling Revenue		75,800	Customers pay cash when they receive services.
Wages Expense	29,100		This is the cost of stylist wages through December 30.
Utilities Expense	12,200		This is the cost of utilities through December 15.
Rent Expense	20,000		This year's rent was $2,000 per month.
Supplies Expense	4,800		This is the cost of supplies used through November 30.
Income Tax Expense	0		The company has an average tax rate of 30 percent.
Totals	$80,200	$80,200	

Required:

1. Calculate the (preliminary) unadjusted net income for the year ended December 31, 2010.
2. Name the five pairs of balance sheet and income statement accounts that require adjustment.

3. Calculate the desired balances for each account listed in the unadjusted trial balance.

4. Prepare the adjusting journal entries that are required at December 31, 2010.

5. Calculate the adjusted net income that the company should report for the year ended December 31, 2010. By how much did the adjustments in requirement (4) cause net income to increase or decrease?

PA4-5 Comprehensive Review Problem: From Recording Transactions (Including Adjusting Journal Entries) to Preparing Financial Statements and Closing Journal Entries (Chapters 2, 3, and 4)

LO1, 2, 3, 4, 5, 6

www.mhhe.com/phillips3e

Drs. Glenn Feltham and Gary Entwistle began operations of their physical therapy clinic called Northland Physical Therapy on January 1, 2008. The annual reporting period ends December 31. The trial balance on January 1, 2009, was as follows (the amounts are rounded to thousands of dollars to simplify):

Account Titles	Debit	Credit
Cash	$ 7	
Accounts Receivable	3	
Supplies	3	
Equipment	6	
Accumulated Depreciation (equipment)		$ 1
Other Assets	6	
Accounts Payable		5
Notes Payable		0
Wages Payable		0
Interest Payable		0
Income Taxes Payable		0
Unearned Revenue		0
Contributed Capital		15
Retained Earnings		4
Dividends Declared	0	
Service Revenue		0
Depreciation Expense	0	
Income Tax Expense	0	
Interest Expense	0	
Operating Expenses	0	
Totals	$25	$25

Transactions during 2009 (summarized in thousands of dollars) follow:

a. Borrowed $22 cash on July 1, 2009, signing a six-month note payable.
b. Purchased equipment for $25 cash on July 1, 2009.
c. Issued additional shares of stock for $5.
d. Earned revenues for 2009 of $55, including $8 on credit and $47 received in cash.
e. Recognized operating expenses for 2009 of $30, including $5 on credit and $25 in cash.
f. Purchased other assets, $3 cash.
g. Collected accounts receivable, $9.
h. Paid accounts payable, $10.
i. Purchased supplies on account for future use, $7.
j. Received a $3 deposit from a hospital for a contract to start January 5, 2010.
k. Declared and paid a cash dividend, $4.

Data for adjusting journal entries:

l. Supplies of $3 were counted on December 31, 2009.
m. Depreciation for 2009, $4.
n. Accrued interest on notes payable of $1.
o. Wages incurred since the December 27 payroll not yet paid, $3.
p. Income tax expense for 2009 was $4, and will be paid in 2010.

Required:

1. Set up T-accounts for the accounts on the trial balance and enter beginning balances.
2. Record journal entries for transactions (a) through (k), and post them to the T-accounts.
3. Prepare an unadjusted trial balance.
4. Record and post the adjusting journal entries (l) through (p).
5. Prepare an adjusted trial balance.
6. Prepare an income statement, statement of retained earnings, and balance sheet.
7. Prepare and post the closing journal entries.
8. Prepare a post-closing trial balance.
9. How much net income did the physical therapy clinic generate during 2009? Is the business financed primarily by liabilities or stockholders' equity?

GROUP B PROBLEMS

LO3, 5

Regis Corporation

PB4-1 Preparing a Trial Balance, Closing Journal Entry, and Post-Closing Trial Balance

Regis Corporation operates hair salons under various brand names including Supercuts, Mia & Maxx, and Style America. The following is a simplified list of accounts and amounts (in millions) reported in the company's accounts for the year ended June 30, 2008.

Accounts Payable	$ 70	Income Tax Expense	$ 54
Accounts Receivable	38	Interest Expense	36
Accrued Liabilities	208	Inventories	212
Accumulated Depreciation	586	Long-term Liabilities	982
Cash	128	Other Current Assets	67
Contributed Capital	247	Other Long-lived Assets	1,309
Cost of Operations	1,690	Property, Plant, and Equipment	1,068
Depreciation Expense	131	Retained Earnings	644
General and		Rent Expense	406
Administrative Expenses	337	Salon Revenue	2,739

Required:

1. Prepare an adjusted trial balance at June 30, 2008. Is the Retained Earnings balance of $644 the amount that would be reported on the balance sheet as of June 30, 2008?
2. Prepare the closing entry required at June 30, 2008.
3. Prepare a post-closing trial balance at June 30, 2008.

LO1, 2

PB4-2 Recording Adjusting Journal Entries

Cactus Company's annual accounting year ends on June 30. It is June 30, 2010, and all of the 2010 entries except the following adjusting journal entries have been made:

a. The company earned service revenue of $2,000 on a special job that was completed June 29, 2010. Collection will be made during July 2010; no entry has been recorded.

b. On March 31, 2010, Cactus paid a six-month premium for property insurance in the amount of $3,200 for coverage starting on that date. Cash was credited and Prepaid Insurance was debited for this amount.

c. At June 30, 2010, wages of $900 were earned by employees but not yet paid. The employees will be paid on the next payroll date, which is July 15, 2010.

d. On June 1, 2010, Cactus collected two months' maintenance revenue of $450. At that date, Cactus debited Cash and credited Unearned Maintenance Revenue for $450. One-half of it has now been earned but not yet recorded.

e. Depreciation of $1,500 must be recognized on a service truck purchased on July 1, 2009.

f. Cash of $4,200 was collected on May 1, 2010, for services to be rendered evenly over the next year beginning on May 1. Unearned Service Revenue was credited when the cash was received. Some of it has now been earned but not yet recorded.

g. The company owes interest of $600 on a bank loan taken out on February 1, 2010. The interest will be paid when the loan is repaid on January 31, 2011.

h. The income before any of the adjustments or income taxes was $31,675. The company's federal income tax rate is 30 percent. Compute adjusted income based on all of the preceding information, and then determine and record income tax expense.

Required:

1. Determine the accounting equation effects of each required adjustment.
2. Give the adjusting journal entry required for each transaction at June 30, 2010.

PB4-3 Determining Accounting Equation Effects of Adjusting Journal Entries   LO2, 6

Refer to PB4-2.

Required:

Indicate the accounting equation effects (amount and direction) of each adjusting journal entry. Use + for increase, − for decrease, and NE for no effect. Provide an appropriate account name for any revenue and expense effects.

Transaction	Assets	Liabilities	Stockholders' Equity
a			
b			
c			
etc.			

PB4-4 Identifying and Preparing Adjusting Journal Entries   LO1, 2, 3, 6

Learn to Play, Inc., is a one-person company that provides private piano lessons. Its unadjusted trial balance at December 31, 2010, follows along with information about selected accounts.

Account Names	Debit	Credit	Further Information
Cash	$ 23,800		As reported on December 31 bank statement.
Supplies	300		Based on count, only $200 of supplies still exist.
Unearned Revenue		$ 1,500	Of this amount, $500 was received for December lessons and $1,000 for January lessons.
Wages Payable		0	The employee was paid $500 for 10 days of work through December 28. She has not yet been paid for work on December 29 and 30.
Income Tax Payable		0	The company has paid last year's income taxes but not this year's taxes.
Interest Payable		0	The company has not paid the $100 of interest owed on its note payable for the current period.
Note Payable		12,000	This one-year note was taken out this year on December 1.
Contributed Capital		1,000	This amount was contributed to the company in prior years.
Retained Earnings		3,000	This is the balance reported at the end of last year.
Lesson Revenue		25,500	Most customers pay cash for lessons each time they are provided, but some customers paid in advance.
Wages Expense	18,100		The company's employee worked through December 30, but did not work on December 31.
Supplies Expense	800		This is the cost of supplies used through November 30.
Interest Expense	0		The company has not paid the $100 of interest owed on its note payable for the current period.
Income Tax Expense	0		The company has an average tax rate of 30 percent.
Totals	$43,000	$43,000	

Required:

1. Calculate the (preliminary) unadjusted net income for the year ended December 31, 2010.
2. Name the five pairs of balance sheet and income statement accounts that require adjustment.
3. Calculate the desired balances for each account listed in the unadjusted trial balance.
4. Prepare the adjusting journal entries that are required at December 31, 2010.
5. Calculate the adjusted net income that the company should report for the year ended December 31, 2010. By how much did the adjustments in requirement (4) cause net income to increase or decrease?

LO1, 2, 3, 4, 5, 6   **PB4-5 Comprehensive Review Problem: From Recording Transactions (Including Adjusting Journal Entries) to Preparing Financial Statements and Closing Journal Entries (Chapters 2, 3, and 4)**

Alison and Chuck Renny began operations of their furniture repair shop (Lazy Sofa Furniture, Inc.) on January 1, 2008. The annual reporting period ends December 31. The trial balance on January 1, 2009, was as follows (the amounts are rounded to thousands of dollars to simplify):

Account Titles	Debit	Credit
Cash	$ 5	
Accounts Receivable	4	
Supplies	2	
Small Tools	6	
Equipment	0	
Accumulated Depreciation		$ 0
Other Assets	9	
Accounts Payable		7
Notes Payable		0
Wages Payable		0
Interest Payable		0
Income Tax Payable		0
Unearned Revenue		0
Contributed Capital		15
Retained Earnings		4
Dividends Declared	0	
Service Revenue		0
Depreciation Expense	0	
Income Tax Expense	0	
Interest Expense	0	
Operating Expenses	0	
Totals	$26	$26

Transactions during 2009 (summarized in thousands of dollars) follow:

a. Borrowed $21 cash on July 1, 2009, signing a six-month note payable.
b. Purchased equipment for $18 cash on July 1, 2009.
c. Issued additional shares of stock for $5.
d. Earned revenues for 2009 in the amount of $65, including $9 on credit and $56 received in cash.
e. Recognized operating expenses for 2009, $35, including $7 on credit and $28 in cash.
f. Purchased additional small tools, $3 cash.

g.   Collected accounts receivable, $8.
h.   Paid accounts payable, $11.
i.   Purchased on account supplies for future use, $10.
j.   Received a $3 deposit on work to start January 15, 2010.
k.   Declared and paid a cash dividend, $10.

Data for adjusting journal entries:

l.   Supplies of $4 were counted on December 31, 2009.
m. Depreciation for 2009, $2.
n.   Accrued interest on notes payable of $1.
o.   Wages earned since the December 24 payroll not yet paid, $3.
p.   Income tax for 2009 was $4, and will be paid in 2010.

Required:

1.   Set up T-accounts for the accounts on the trial balance and enter beginning balances.
2.   Record journal entries for transactions (a) through (k), and post them to the T-accounts.
3.   Prepare an unadjusted trial balance.
4.   Record and post the adjusting journal entries (l) through (p).
5.   Prepare an adjusted trial balance.
6.   Prepare an income statement, statement of retained earnings, and balance sheet.
7.   Prepare and post the closing journal entries.
8.   Prepare a post-closing trial balance.
9.   How much net income did Lazy Sofa Furniture, Inc., generate during 2009? Is the company financed primarily by liabilities or stockholders' equity?

SKILLS DEVELOPMENT CASES

S4-1 Finding Financial Information

LO1, 6

Refer to the financial statements of The Home Depot in Appendix A at the end of this book, or download the annual report from the *Cases* section of the text's Web site at www.mhhe.com/phillips3e.

Required:

1.   The company's Prepaid Advertising Expenses are included in the February 1, 2009, balance sheet under Other Current Assets. Refer to the notes to the financial statements to determine the amount of the Prepaid Advertising Expenses as of February 1, 2009 (fiscal 2008).
2.   How much did The Home Depot owe for salaries and related expenses at February 1, 2009? Was this an increase or decrease from the previous year?
3.   Refer to the Revenues note in the Summary of Significant Accounting Policies that follows The Home Depot's statements of cash flows. How does the company account for customer payments received in advance of providing services? What adjusting journal entry must The Home Depot make when it provides these services?

S4-2 Comparing Financial Information

LO1, 6

Refer to the financial statements of The Home Depot in Appendix A and Lowe's in Appendix B at the end of this book, or download the annual reports from the *Cases* section of the text's Web site at www.mhhe.com/phillips3e.

Lowe's

Required:

1.   Refer to the notes to the financial statements to determine how much The Home Depot and Lowe's each spent on advertising expenses in the year ended January 30, 2009 (fiscal 2008).
2.   How much did The Home Depot and Lowe's each owe for salaries and wages at January 30, 2009? Provide one reason that would explain the difference between the two companies' accrued payroll liabilities.

LO1, 4   **S4-3 Internet-Based Team Research: Examining Deferrals and Accruals**

As a team, select an industry to analyze. Using your Web browser, each team member should access the annual report or 10-K for one publicly traded company in the industry, with each member selecting a different company. (See S1-3 in Chapter 1 for a description of possible resources for these tasks.)

Required:

1. On an individual basis, each team member should write a short report listing the following:
    a. The company's total assets and total liabilities at the end of each year.
    b. The company's prepaid expenses and accrued liabilities at the end of each year.
    c. The percentage of prepaid expenses to total assets and the percentage of accrued liabilities to total liabilities.
    d. Describe and explain the types of accrued liabilities reported in the notes to the financial statements.

2. Discuss any patterns that you as a team observe. Then, as a team, write a short report comparing and contrasting your companies according to the preceding attributes. Provide potential explanations for any differences discovered.

LO1, 2, 6

Safety-Kleen Corp.

S4-4 Ethical Decision Making: A Real-Life Example

On December 12, 2002, the SEC filed a lawsuit against four executives of Safety-Kleen Corp., one of the country's leading providers of industrial waste collection and disposal services. The primary issue was that the executives had directed others in the company to record improper adjustments in 1999 and 2000, which had the effect of overstating net income during those periods. The following table was included in the SEC's court documents to demonstrate the (combined) effect of proper and improper adjustments on net income. (All amounts are in millions.)

	Year (Quarter)				
	1999 (Q1)	1999 (Q2)	1999 (Q3)	1999 (Q4)	2000 (Q1)
Net income before adjustments	$ 90.9	$ 76.7	$ 47.9	$ 57.3	$ 47.0
Effect of adjustments	36.6	30.9	75.5	53.1	69.8
Net income after adjustments	$127.5	$107.6	$123.4	$110.4	$116.8

The following excerpts from the SEC's complaint describe two of the allegedly improper adjustments:

Improper Capitalization of Operating Expenses

26. As part of the fraudulent accounting scheme, [three top executives] improperly recorded several adjusting entries to capitalize certain operating expenses. These adjustments caused the company to materially overstate both its assets and its earnings. For example, at the end of the third quarter of fiscal 1999, they improperly capitalized approximately $4.6 million of payroll expenses relating to certain marketing and start-up activities.

Improper Treatment of Accruals

33. During the fourth quarter of fiscal 1999, Humphreys [the CFO] created additional fictitious income by directing [other accounting executives] to eliminate a $7.6 million accrual that had been established to provide for management bonuses that had been earned in fiscal 1999, but were to be paid the following quarter. Humphreys' action suggested that no bonuses were going to be paid for that year. In fact, the bonuses for 1999 were paid as scheduled.

Required:

1. Discuss whether large adjustments, such as those included by Safety-Kleen in 1999 and 2000, necessarily indicate improper accounting procedures.

2. What does the SEC's document mean in paragraph 26 when it says three top executives "improperly recorded several adjusting entries to *capitalize* certain operating expenses"? Drawing on concepts presented in Chapters 2 and 3, explain why it is improper to record payroll expenses for marketing personnel as assets.

3. Assume the $7.6 million in bonuses referred to in paragraph 33 were recorded in the third quarter of 1999. What journal entry would have been used to record this accrual? Assume this accrual was eliminated in the fourth quarter of 1999. What adjusting journal entry would have been recorded to eliminate (remove) the previous accrual? What journal entry would have been used to record the $7.6 million in bonuses paid in the first quarter of 2000 (assuming the accrual had been removed in the fourth quarter of 1999)? What accounting concept is violated by recording an expense for management bonuses when they are paid rather than when they are earned by managers?

Epilogue:
In April 2005, a federal judge found the company's former CEO and CFO liable for $200 million for their role in the fraud.

S4-5 Ethical Decision Making: A Mini-Case

LO1, 4, 6

Blockbuster Inc.

Assume you work as an assistant accountant in the head office of a national movie rental business, a la Blockbuster Inc. With the increasing popularity of online movie rental operations, your company has struggled to meet its earnings targets for the year. It is important for the company to meet its earnings targets this year because the company is renegotiating a bank loan next month, and the terms of that loan are likely to depend on the company's reported financial success. Also, the company plans to issue more stock to the public in the upcoming year, to obtain funds for establishing its own presence in the online movie rental business. The chief financial officer (CFO) has approached you with a solution to the earnings dilemma. She proposes that the depreciation period for the stock of reusable DVDs be extended from 3 months to 15 months. She explains that by lengthening the depreciation period, a smaller amount of depreciation expense will be recorded in the current year, resulting in a higher net income. She claims that generally accepted accounting principles require estimates like this, so it wouldn't involve doing anything wrong.

Required:

Discuss the CFO's proposed solution. In your discussion, consider the following questions. Will the change in depreciation affect net income in the current year in the way that the CFO described? How will it affect net income in the following year? Is the CFO correct when she claims that the change in estimated depreciation is allowed by GAAP? Who relies on the video company's financial statements when making decisions? Why might their decisions be affected by the CFO's proposed solution? Is it possible that their decisions would not be affected? What should you do?

S4-6 Critical Thinking: Adjusting an Income Statement and Balance Sheet for Deferrals and Accruals

LO1, 2, 4, 6

Pirate Pete Moving Corporation has been in operation since January 1, 2009. It is now December 31, 2009, the end of the annual accounting period. The company has not done well financially during the first year, although revenue has been fairly good. Three stockholders manage the company, but they have not given much attention to recordkeeping. In view of a serious cash shortage, they have applied to your bank for a $20,000 loan. As a loan officer, you requested a complete set of financial statements. The following 2009 annual financial statements were prepared by the company's office staff.

PIRATE PETE MOVING CORPORATION
Income Statement
For the Period Ended December 31, 2009

Transportation Revenue	$85,000
Expenses:	
Salaries Expense	17,000
Supplies Expense	12,000
Other Expenses	18,000
Total Expenses	47,000
Net Income	$38,000

PIRATE PETE MOVING CORPORATION
Balance Sheet
At December 31, 2009

Assets	
Cash	$ 2,000
Accounts Receivable	3,000
Supplies	6,000
Equipment	40,000
Prepaid Insurance	4,000
Remaining Assets	27,000
Total Assets	$82,000
Liabilities	
Accounts Payable	$ 9,000
Stockholders' Equity	
Contributed Capital	35,000
Retained Earnings	38,000
Total Liabilities and Stockholders' Equity	$82,000

After briefly reviewing the statements and "looking into the situation," you requested that the statements be redone (with some expert help) to "incorporate depreciation, accruals, supply counts, income taxes, and so on." As a result of a review of the records and supporting documents, the following additional information was developed:

a. Supplies of $6,000 shown on the balance sheet has not been adjusted for supplies used during 2009. A count of the supplies on hand on December 31, 2009, showed $1,800.

b. The insurance premium paid in 2009 was for years 2009 and 2010. The total insurance premium was debited in full to Prepaid Insurance when paid in 2009 and no adjustment has been made.

c. The equipment cost $40,000 when purchased January 1, 2009. It had an estimated annual depreciation of $8,000. No depreciation has been recorded for 2009.

d. Unpaid (and unrecorded) salaries at December 31, 2009, amounted to $2,200.

e. At December 31, 2009, transportation revenue collected in advance amounted to $7,000. This amount was credited in full to Transportation Revenue when the cash was collected earlier during 2009.

f. Income taxes for the year are calculated as 25 percent of income before tax.

Required:

1. Prepare the adjusting journal entries required on December 31, 2009, based on the preceding additional information. You may need to create new accounts not yet included in the income statement or balance sheet.

2. Redo the preceding statements after taking into account the adjusting journal entries. One way to organize your response follows:

		Changes		
Items	Amounts Reported	Plus	Minus	Corrected Amounts
(List here each item from the two statements)				

3. The effects of recording the adjusting journal entries were to
   a. *Increase* or *decrease* (select one) net income by $_____.
   b. *Increase* or *decrease* (select one) total assets by $_____.

4. Write a letter to the company explaining the results of the adjustments and your preliminary analysis.

S4-7 Aggregating Accounts on an Adjusted Trial Balance to Prepare an Income Statement, Statement of Retained Earnings, and Balance Sheet

LO3, 4, 6

Assume you recently were hired for a job in Evansville, Indiana, at the head office of Escalade, Inc.—the company that makes Goalrilla™ and Goaliath® basketball systems, and is the exclusive supplier of Ping Pong® and Stiga® equipment for table tennis. Your first assignment is to review the company's lengthy adjusted trial balance to determine the accounts that can be combined ("aggregated") into single line-items that will be reported on the financial statements. By querying the accounting system, you were able to obtain the following alphabetical list of accounts and their adjusted balances (in thousands) for the year ended December 31.

Escalade, Inc.

www.mhhe.com/phillips3e

Account	Balance	Account	Balance	Account	Balance
Accounts Payable	$ 2,792	Inventory of Finished Goods	$ 10,263	Prepaid Insurance	$ 108
Accounts Receivable	34,141	Inventory of Goods being Made	4,536	Prepaid Rent	434
Accrued Interest Payable	42	Inventory of Supplies and Materials	5,750	Rent Expense	7,350
Accrued Wages Payable	5,856	Long-term Bank Loan	14,000	Retained Earnings	27,571
Accrued Warranties Payable	1,324	Long-term Contract Payable	1,837	Salaries Expense	3,582
Accumulated Depreciation	26,198	Long-term Note Payable	2,700	Sales Commissions Expense	3,349
Cash	3,370	Manufacturing Equipment	12,962	Sales of Basketball Systems	98,998
Contributed Capital	7,165	Notes Payable (current)	11,390	Sales of Other Products	28,710
Cost of Goods Sold	111,164	Notes Receivable	400	Sales of Ping Pong Tables	27,747
Depreciation Expense	862	Office Building	2,301	Shipping Expenses	1,448
Factory Buildings	7,070	Office Equipment	2,363	Transport Equipment	7,560
Income Tax Expense	5,804	Office Supplies Expense	69	Unearned Revenue	8,144
Income Tax Payable	1,189	Other Accrued Liabilities	1,638	Utilities Expense	2,111
Insurance Expense	2,368	Other Long-term Assets	28,310	Wages Expense	3,024
Interest Expense	950	Packaging Expenses	1,010	Warranties Expense	1,226
Interest Receivable	415			Warehouse Buildings	3,001

Required:

With the above account names and balances, prepare an adjusted trial balance using a spreadsheet. Also prepare an income statement, statement of retained earnings, and balance sheet that import their numbers from the adjusted trial balance or from the other statements where appropriate. If similar accounts can be aggregated into a single line-item for each financial statement, use a formula to compute the aggregated amount. To be sure that you understand how to import numbers from other parts of a spreadsheet, you e-mail your friend Owen for advice. His reply is as follows.

From: Owentheaccountant@yahoo.com
To: Helpme@hotmail.com
Cc:
Subject: Excel Help

Hey pal. You're bouncing from job to job like one of those ping-pong balls that your company sells. Okay, to import a number from another spreadsheet, you first click on the cell where you want the number to appear. For example, if you want to enter the Cash balance in the balance sheet, click on the cell in the balance sheet where the cash number is supposed to appear. Enter the equals sign (=) and then click on the tab that takes you to the worksheet containing the adjusted trial balance. In that worksheet, click on the cell that contains the amount you want to import into the balance sheet and then press enter. This will create a link from the adjusted trial balance cell to the balance sheet cell. At the end of this message, I've pasted a screen shot showing the formula I would enter on the balance sheet to import the total of three related inventory accounts from the adjusted trial balance. Don't forget to save the file using a name that indicates who you are.

S4-7.xls - Microsoft Excel

Home | Insert | Page Layout | Formulas | Data | Review | View

C7   fx =SUM('Trial Balance'!C8:C10)

	A	B	C
1		Escalade, Inc.	
2		Balance Sheet	
3		As of December 31 (in thousands)	
4		ASSETS	
5		Cash	$ 3,370
6		Receivables	34,956
7		Inventories	20,549
8		Prepaids	542
9		Total Current Assets	59,417
10		Property, plant, and equipment	35,257
11		less accumulated depreciation	(26,198)
12		Other long-term assets	28,310
13		Total Assets	$ 96,786
14		LIABILITIES	
15		Accounts payable	$ 2,792
16		Notes payable	11,390
17		Income tax payable	1,189
18		Unearned revenue	8,144
19		Other liabilities	8,860
20		Total Current Liabilities	32,375
21		Long-term debt	18,537
22		Total Liabilities	50,912
23		STOCKHOLDERS' EQUITY	
24		Contributed capital	7,165
25		Retained earnings	38,709
26		Total Stockholders' Equity	45,874
27		Total Liabilities and Stockholders' Equity	$ 96,786
28			

Trial Balance / Income Statement / Statement of

Ready   100%

CONTINUING CASE

CC4 Adjusting the Accounting Records

|ACCOUNTING   LO1, 2

Assume it is now December 31, 2010, and Nicole has just completed her first year of operations at Nicole's Getaway Spa. After looking through her trial balance, she noticed that there are some items that have either not been recorded or are no longer up-to-date.

a. Nicole's Getaway Spa is renting its space at a cost of $600 per month. On September 1, 2010, Nicole paid eight months rent in advance using cash. This prepayment was recorded in the account Prepaid Rent back in September.

b. The building purchased at the beginning of the year for $47,000 cash has estimated depreciation of $2,000 for 2010, but none has been recorded yet.

c. Wages to the support staff at Nicole's Getaway Spa have been paid up to December 26, 2010. The support staff worked both December 27 and 28 and will be paid on January 5, 2011. Wages amount to $1,000 per day.

d. The insurance policy, purchased on June 1 for $3,000 cash, provides coverage for 12 months. The insurance coverage since June has now been used up.

e. The unadjusted amount in the Spa Supplies account was $2,000 at December 31, 2010, for supplies purchased on account. A year-end count showed $700 of supplies remain on hand.

f. On the last day of December, a customer obtained spa services by using a $90 gift certificate which was purchased earlier in the month. Use of the gift certificate to pay for these services had not yet been recorded.

Required:

1. For each of the items listed above, identify whether an accrual adjustment, a deferral adjustment, or no adjustment is required.

2. For each of the deferral adjustments, prepare the initial journal entry that would have been recorded.

3. Prepare the adjusting journal entries that should be recorded for Nicole's Getaway Spa at December 31, 2010, assuming that the items have not been adjusted prior to December 31, 2010.

CHAPTER 5

Financial Reporting and Analysis

YOUR LEARNING OBJECTIVES

Understand the business

LO1   Explain the needs of financial statement users.

LO2   Describe the environment for financial reporting, including the Sarbanes-Oxley Act.

Study the accounting methods

LO3   Prepare a comparative balance sheet, multiple-step income statement, and statement of stockholders' equity.

LO4   Describe other significant aspects of the financial reporting process, including external audits and the distribution of financial information.

LO5   Explain the reasons for, and financial statement presentation effects of, adopting IFRS.

Evaluate the results

LO6   Compare results to common benchmarks.

LO7   Calculate and interpret the debt-to-assets, asset turnover, and net profit margin ratios.

Review the chapter

THAT WAS
THEN

In the previous chapters, you learned about the accounting system that produces the basic financial statements.

Lecture Presentation-LP5
www.mhhe.com/phillips3e

FOCUS COMPANY: Activision

www.activision.com

ACTIVISION®

As you have seen in Chapters 1 through 4, accounting plays a vital role when establishing and operating a small business like Pizza Aroma. Chapter 5 will continue to broaden your understanding by looking at the role accounting plays in large public companies that carry out their business activities in many cities and countries throughout the world. As you will learn in this chapter, accounting is actually one of the most pressure-filled, fast-paced elements of business. In the past 10 years alone, the accounting world has tackled frauds and scandals, increasing regulation, globalization, and economic turmoil. The purposes of this chapter are to explain these four major topics and begin to equip you with tools that will help you use financial statement information.

In keeping with the theme that accounting can be useful and fun, we focus on an exciting company that is bringing smiles to people of all ages, whether they live in India, China, or Europe, or the home of its headquarters in Santa Monica, California. Activision started as a private company in 1979, went public in 1983, survived economic troubles in the late 1980s, and became known as Activision Blizzard in late 2008 when it merged with a European video game company (Vivendi Games) to create the world's largest video game company. Famous for its Guitar Hero® video games and World of Warcraft® online role-playing game, Activision Blizzard provides an ideal background for learning about the role of accounting in business and the ways in which U.S. accounting rules are changing to become more comparable with those used in Europe and other countries throughout the world.

THIS IS NOW

This chapter describes the environment in which financial statements are used, and introduces common ratio analyses.

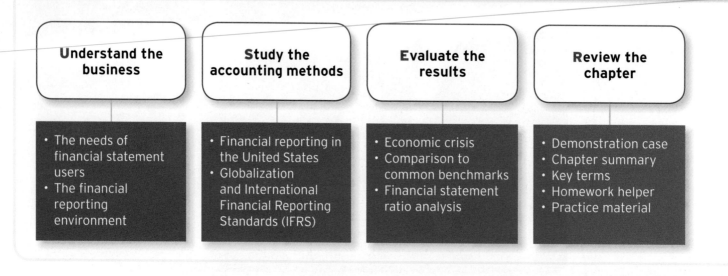

Understand the business	Study the accounting methods	Evaluate the results	Review the chapter
• The needs of financial statement users • The financial reporting environment	• Financial reporting in the United States • Globalization and International Financial Reporting Standards (IFRS)	• Economic crisis • Comparison to common benchmarks • Financial statement ratio analysis	• Demonstration case • Chapter summary • Key terms • Homework helper • Practice material

Understand the Business

THE NEEDS OF FINANCIAL STATEMENT USERS

Learning Objective 1
Explain the needs of financial statement users.

Chapter 1 provided an overview of the many people who use financial statements to make decisions. A more detailed look at the main user groups is presented in Exhibit 5.1 and explained below.

Managers

Managers at all levels within a company use accounting information to run the business. To make good decisions at Activision Blizzard, managers need to know detailed information such as sales by game (e.g., Guitar Hero, Tony Hawk) and game platform (PlayStation, X-box, Wii, PC), profits by genre (e.g., action, role-playing, etc.), and costs by game developer. When accounting information is used to manage the business, it is being used to fulfill a *management* function.

Directors

Directors is the short title used to describe members of the board of directors, who are elected by the company's stockholders to serve as their representatives. Directors oversee the managers of the company, with the primary goal of ensuring that management and financial decisions aim to benefit stockholders. Directors will use the financial

Directors
oversee
↓
Officers and
Top Managers

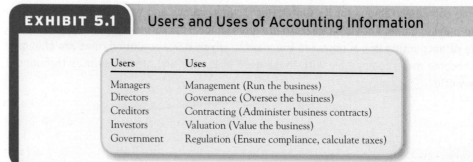

EXHIBIT 5.1	Users and Uses of Accounting Information

Users	Uses
Managers	Management (Run the business)
Directors	Governance (Oversee the business)
Creditors	Contracting (Administer business contracts)
Investors	Valuation (Value the business)
Government	Regulation (Ensure compliance, calculate taxes)

statements to evaluate whether the Chief Executive Officer (CEO), Chief Financial Officer (CFO), and other top managers have made wise decisions about the amount to invest in assets and have managed to generate sufficient sales and net income from those assets. When accounting information is used to oversee the business, it is being used in a *governance* role.

Creditors

All creditors use accounting information. Suppliers, for example, use it to decide whether to enter into contracts to supply other companies, based in part on whether those companies have sufficient assets to pay their liabilities. Bankers use financial statement information to evaluate (and sometimes limit) a company's activities by measuring the company's ability to satisfy certain financial targets such as maintaining specific levels of assets or stockholders' equity. These **loan covenants** help to ensure the company will be able to repay loans owed to the bank. When accounting information is used to administer contract terms such as these, it is being used in a *contracting* role.

Investors

Investors (and their advisers) look to accounting information to help assess the financial strength of a business and, ultimately, to estimate its value. Part of this analysis involves forecasting the company's future revenues, expenses, and net income. Ultimately, the goal is to determine whether to buy, hold, or sell shares of the company's stock. When this text was written, investment advisers had mixed opinions about Activision's stock. Many recommended buying it, but some said to "hold," which meant investors should hit the pause button—the price was not attractive enough to recommend buying the company's stock nor bad enough to recommend selling. When accounting information is used to assess stock prices, it is being used in a *valuation* role.

Government

Several government agencies look closely at the financial statements prepared by companies. The Securities and Exchange Commission (SEC), for example, is responsible for the functioning of stock markets, so it keeps a close watch on the information that public companies report in financial statements. The Internal Revenue Service (IRS) also is interested in financial statements because the income statement provides a starting point for determining the amount of taxes that should be paid by private and public corporations. Other government agencies rely on financial statements to fulfill their responsibilities, as explained in the following Spotlight.

> **YOU SHOULD KNOW**
>
> **Loan covenants:** Terms of a loan agreement which, if broken, entitle the lender to renegotiate loan terms or force repayment.

Spotlight On BUSINESS DECISIONS

Banks Feeling the Stress

When determining how to help struggling banks in 2009, the U.S. Treasury Department used a "stress test" to forecast whether the banks would survive a worse-than-expected decline in the economy. This test involved looking at the financial effects of deteriorating economic conditions, including the extent to which each banking company would have sufficient stockholders' equity on the balance sheet to absorb the losses that it would report on the income statement if home prices were to fall or unemployment rates were to rise.

As Exhibit 5.1 indicates, many different groups use accounting information to make decisions. These decisions can be wide-ranging, affecting employee bonuses, stock prices, and the interest paid on loans. All this attention to a company's financial results creates a high-pressure and potentially explosive environment, as discussed in the next section.

Learning Objective 2
Describe the environment for financial reporting, including the Sarbanes-Oxley Act.

THE FINANCIAL REPORTING ENVIRONMENT

The accounting world was rocked in the last decade with scandal and fraud, leading to significant changes in the financial reporting environment. In this section, we describe what appears to have fueled the fraud and how accounting regulators have responded with changes that are likely to affect your future career.

Accounting Fraud

Three things have to exist for accounting fraud to occur. First, there must be an incentive for someone to commit the fraud. Second, an opportunity must exist to commit the fraud. Third, the person committing the fraud must possess a personality that leads to rationalizing and concealing the fraud. Fraud investigators refer to these three elements as the *fraud triangle*, which is shown in Exhibit 5.2.

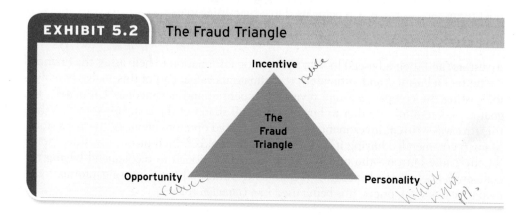

EXHIBIT 5.2   The Fraud Triangle

Incentive to Commit Fraud   Financial misreporting is both unethical and illegal, so there must be enormous incentives driving some accountants and business managers to commit fraud. As shown in Exhibit 5.3 below, incentives can be divided into two categories: (1) creating business opportunities and (2) satisfying personal greed.

1. **Creating business opportunities.** Management is under constant pressure to produce pleasing financial results for at least three business reasons:
   - *Satisfy loan covenants.* As you learned earlier in this chapter, lenders rely on financial statements to determine whether a company has violated its loan covenants by failing to meet specific financial targets. By overstating their company's financial condition, managers can avoid violating loan covenants which otherwise could require the company to pay a higher interest rate, repay its loan balance right away, or be forced to put up extra collateral to secure its loan.
   - *Increase equity financing.* The amount of money obtained from issuing stock depends, in part, on the price of the stock when it is issued. An issuance of 100,000 shares will yield double the money if the stock price is $20 per share

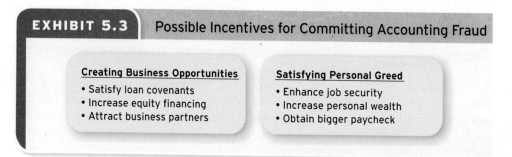

EXHIBIT 5.3   Possible Incentives for Committing Accounting Fraud

Creating Business Opportunities
- Satisfy loan covenants
- Increase equity financing
- Attract business partners

Satisfying Personal Greed
- Enhance job security
- Increase personal wealth
- Obtain bigger paycheck

rather than $10 per share. Managers can lead investors to pay more for the company's stock if they overstate the company's financial performance.

- *Attract business partners.* By making the business appear more stable than it actually is, management can mislead suppliers and other companies into wanting to pursue a business relationship with the company.

2. **Satisfying personal greed.** By producing pleasing financial results, members of top management can benefit personally in three ways:

- *Enhance job security.* The financial statements are a report card on both the company and the company's management. If top management reports strong financial results, they'll likely get to keep their high-paying jobs.
- *Increase personal wealth.* Members of top management often own shares of their company's stock, so their personal shareholdings will be worth more (and their personal wealth will increase) if their company reports financial results that increase its stock price.
- *Obtain a bigger paycheck.* Managers often receive cash bonuses based on the strength of their company's reported financial performance. The more net income they report, the bigger the bonuses they'll get. One of Activision's competitors (Take-Two Interactive) paid a $3 million bonus to its (former) CEO a few years ago, but was soon investigated by the SEC for overstating its profits.

Opportunity to Commit Fraud   As you saw in Chapters 2–4, financial statements are produced by an accounting system that involves analyzing, recording, and summarizing the results of business activities. Weaknesses in this system create an opportunity for fraudulent information to be entered into it, which increases the risk that the financial statements will be fraudulently misreported. To reduce this risk, certain procedures and policies can be put in place to help ensure that information entered into the accounting system and reported in the financial statements is accurate and complete. These internal controls, as they are called, can't completely eliminate the opportunity for fraud, but they can limit it if they operate effectively. You will learn about internal controls in detail in Chapter 6.

Personality to Rationalize and Conceal Fraud   For people to commit fraud and keep it secret, they have to feel "okay" with their actions. Most fraudsters achieve this through a sense of personal entitlement, which outweighs other moral principles, such as fairness, honesty, and concern for others. Many are said to be egotistical and possess an ability to lie or pressure others to look the other way.[1] It's not easy to counteract these undesirable traits, but recent changes in the financial reporting environment begin to do so, as we discuss in the next section.

The Sarbanes-Oxley Act

The **Sarbanes-Oxley (SOX) Act** is one of the most significant changes to the financial reporting environment in the United States since the Securities Acts were introduced in the 1930s. All companies that trade on U.S. stock exchanges must comply with the requirements of SOX. The impact of SOX has been felt by nearly everyone in the business world. Whether you're an accounting major or not, you will likely be affected by SOX.

SOX was created in response to the many financial frauds and scandals occurring in the late 1990s and early 2000s. Confidence in the stock markets had been shaken by frauds involving Enron (now bankrupt) and WorldCom (now owned by Verizon), so the U.S. Congress passed the act in an attempt to improve the financial reporting environment and restore investor confidence. SOX introduced many new requirements. Some of the key changes are summarized in Exhibit 5.4.

> **YOU SHOULD KNOW**
>
> **Sarbanes-Oxley (SOX) Act:** A set of regulations passed by Congress in 2002 in an attempt to improve financial reporting and restore investor confidence.

---

[1]David T. Wolfe and Dana R. Hermanson, "The Fraud Diamond: Considering the Four Elements of Fraud," *The CPA Journal,* December 2004, pp. 38–41.

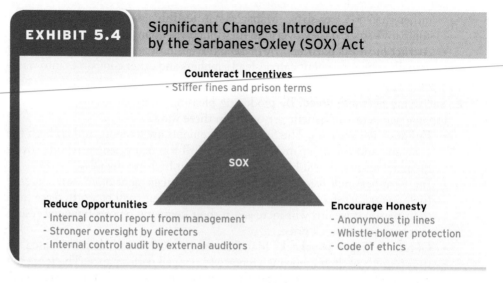

EXHIBIT 5.4 Significant Changes Introduced by the Sarbanes-Oxley (SOX) Act

Counteract Incentives for Committing Fraud Those who willfully misrepresent financial results face stiff penalties, including fines of up to $5 million. Also, maximum jail sentences are now 20 years, which can really add up because federal sentencing guidelines allow judges to declare consecutive jail terms for each violation.

Reduce Opportunities for Fraud Of the three parts of the fraud triangle, this is the area that business owners, managers, and accountants can do the most about. Not surprisingly, then, it's also the area affected most by SOX. The main thrust of SOX, as it applies to this area, is to improve internal control over companies' financial reporting. SOX aims to achieve this in three ways:

1. Managers must review how well their company's internal controls worked during the year and issue a report that indicates whether the controls over financial reporting operated effectively. This requirement means that most marketing managers, for example, now have some accounting responsibilities such as determining whether their staff submit accurate sales and expense reports.

2. The company's board of directors is required to establish an audit committee of independent directors to oversee financial matters of the company. One of the primary functions of this committee is to communicate with external auditors and ensure they are able to effectively perform the work described below in 3.

3. The company's external auditors must test the effectiveness of the company's internal controls and issue a report that gives an opinion about the company's internal controls over financial reporting. As was the case before SOX, the external auditors also must examine the company's financial statements and report whether they were presented fairly (no material misstatements) in accordance with GAAP.

Encourage Honesty in Employees Admittedly, it's difficult for any law to achieve this, but some provisions of SOX should help honest employees confront those with a questionable personality. For example, audit committees are now required to create tip lines that allow employees to secretly submit concerns about questionable accounting or auditing practices being committed by others. Further, SOX grants legal protection to these whistle-blowers so they aren't retaliated against by those charged with fraud. If you tattle on your boss for submitting a fraudulent expense claim, you can't be fired for it. Finally, to reinforce the importance of good character, companies are required to adopt a code of ethics for their senior financial officers. Google begins its code with "Don't be evil" and then explains what this means in plain English (see investor.google.com/conduct.html).

How's it going?   Self-Study Practice

Identify whether each of the following increases (+) or decreases (−) the risk of fraud, arising from incentives (I), opportunities (O), or personality (P).

	+/−	I/O/P
1. Enron was notorious for its "rank and yank" practice that involved ranking the financial performance of each business unit and then firing managers in the lowest 20%.		
2. Microsoft Corporation invites anonymous or confidential submission of questionable accounting or auditing matters to msft.buscond@alertline.com.		
3. The H. J. Heinz Company board of directors is one of the strongest boards in America, according to Institutional Shareholder Services.		

After you have finished, check your answers with the solution in the margin.

Solution to Self-Study Practice
1. + I (greater pressure to report stronger financial results)
2. − P (less likely that unethical behavior will go unreported)
3. − O (strong oversight by directors)

Spotlight On ETHICS

You Can't Count That!

Most of the big accounting frauds involve uncertain judgments or complex accounting decisions that later are found to be inappropriate. However, some frauds have involved blatantly unethical acts. In one famous case, managers at Bausch & Lomb shipped as much as two years' worth of contact lenses to opticians who hadn't even ordered them. These shipments were counted as sales revenue, which led to overstated financial results and unwarranted bonuses. An investigation later found: (1) an environment of extreme pressure created incentives, (2) weak internal controls provided opportunities, and (3) unscrupulous managers possessed the personalities to commit the fraud.

Study the Accounting Methods

In the previous section, we discussed some of the *regulatory* changes made to improve the quality of publicly reported financial statements. In this section, we describe some of the *financial reporting* changes that publicly traded companies make to improve the quality and usefulness of their financial statements. We also describe how increasing globalization has created a need for common accounting rules worldwide, which is leading companies in the United States to adopt International Financial Reporting Standards (IFRS)—a move that will further change financial statement reporting.

> **Learning Objective 3**
> Prepare a comparative balance sheet, multiple-step income statement, and statement of stockholders' equity.

FINANCIAL REPORTING IN THE UNITED STATES

The good news is that the accounting and financial statement preparation processes that you learned in Chapters 1–4 for small, private companies continue to apply for even the largest, publicly traded corporations. To further improve the usefulness of financial statements for their external users, though, all public companies and some private companies take three additional steps: (1) enhance the financial statement format, (2) obtain an independent external audit, and (3) release additional financial information. Exhibit 5.5 presents a timeline showing how this financial reporting process typically occurs for a company that ends its year on December 31, 2010.

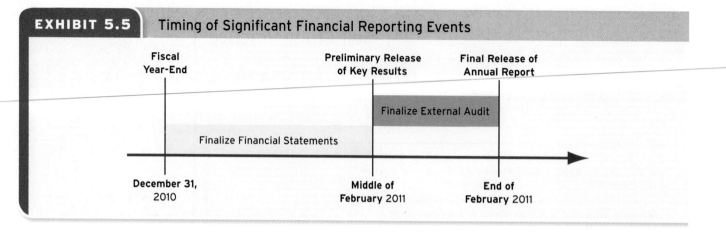

EXHIBIT 5.5 | Timing of Significant Financial Reporting Events

Financial Statement Formatting

The financial statements shown in previous chapters provided a good introduction to their basic structure and content. However, in comparison to what you'll see in the corporate world, they were somewhat simplified. In this section, we show three enhancements that are intended to provide additional information for financial statement users: comparative financial statements, multiple-step income statements, and the statement of stockholders' equity.

Comparative Financial Statements   To make it easy for financial statement users to compare account balances from one period to the next, most companies report **comparative financial statements.** Comparative financial statements contain two or more columns of numbers, with each column representing the financial results for different time periods. For example, Activision's comparative balance sheets in Exhibit 5.6 show one column with account balances at the end of the most recent year (March 31, 2008) and another column with balances at the end of the previous year (March 31, 2007). This allows you to quickly see that Short-Term Investments dropped dramatically (from $570 million to $53 million) while Cash increased by more than $1 billion. Note that the balance sheet is still classified, as introduced in Chapter 2. The only difference in a comparative balance sheet is that it uses separate columns to report different points in time.

Income statements also can be presented in a comparative format, often reporting three periods of results as shown in Exhibit 5.7. By including three columns, managers and accountants help reveal trends that persist over longer periods of time. For example, Exhibit 5.7 indicates that Activision has grown its revenues and net income each year since 2006, with a huge jump in 2008 when Activision had two of the best-selling video games in the world (Guitar Hero and Call of Duty).

Multiple-step Income Statements   If you look carefully at Exhibit 5.7, you'll notice the income statement format differs in another way from that used in earlier chapters. Earlier chapters used a format that contained a single grouping of revenues and a single grouping of expenses in what is typically called a **single-step income statement** format. Exhibit 5.7 presents a variation on the single-step income statement by displaying subtotals that indicate multiple steps before reaching Net Income at the bottom. **The purpose of these multiple steps is to display important measures of profit in addition to net income.** Exhibit 5.7 shows two new subtotals:

1. **Income from Operations**—As an investor or creditor interested in Activision's long-term success, you probably care most about the company's ability to generate income from its core business activities like developing, making, and selling video games. Peripheral activities, like earning revenue from investments, aren't as important in the long-run because they're not the key reason Activision is in business (and they're not as likely to recur in the future). To make it easy for you to distinguish core and peripheral results, the top portion of the income

YOU SHOULD KNOW

Comparative financial statements: Report numbers for two or more time periods.

YOU SHOULD KNOW

Single-step income statement: Reports net income by subtracting a single group of expenses from a single group of revenues.

| EXHIBIT 5.6 | Comparative Balance Sheet | ACTIVISION |

ACTIVISION, INC.
Balance Sheet
(in millions of U.S. dollars)

	March 31, 2008	March 31, 2007	
Assets			
Current Assets:			
Cash	$ 1,396	$ 384	A comparative format reveals changes over time, such as Activision's huge increase in Cash and decline in Short-term Investments.
Short-term Investments	53	570	
Accounts Receivable	203	149	
Inventories	147	91	
Other Current Assets	180	207	
Total Current Assets	1,979	1,401	
Property and Equipment, net	55	47	
Other Noncurrent Assets	217	151	
Goodwill	279	195	
Total Assets	$ 2,530	$ 1,794	
Liabilities and Stockholders' Equity			
Current Liabilities:			
Accounts Payable	$ 130	$ 136	
Accrued and Other Liabilities	426	205	
Total Current Liabilities	556	341	
Other Noncurrent Liabilities	26	41	
Total Liabilities	582	382	
Stockholders' Equity:			
Contributed Capital	1,175	984	Changes in stockholders' equity accounts are shown in the Statement of Stockholders' Equity, as shown in Exhibit 5.8.
Retained Earnings	773	428	
Total Stockholders' Equity	1,948	1,412	
Total Liabilities and Stockholders' Equity	$ 2,530	$ 1,794	

| EXHIBIT 5.7 | Income Statement with Multiple Steps | ACTIVISION |

ACTIVISION, INC.
Income Statement
(in millions of U.S. dollars)

	Year Ended March 31,			
	2008	2007	2006	
Sales and Service Revenues	$ 2,898	$ 1,513	$ 1,468	
Expenses:				**Core results**—include revenues and expenses from the company's main business activities. Expenses are reported by function (e.g., production, research, marketing, general operations).
Production	1,645	979	942	
Research and Development	270	133	132	
Marketing and Sales	308	196	283	
General and Administrative	195	132	96	
Total Operating Expenses	2,418	1,440	1,453	
Income from Operations	480	73	15	
Revenue from Investments	51	37	31	**Peripheral results**—include any revenues and expenses from activities other than the company's main business.
Income before Income Tax Expense	531	110	46	
Income Tax Expense	186	24	6	
Net Income	$ 345	$ 86	$ 40	

statement reports revenues and expenses relating only to core activities, as shown in Exhibit 5.7. Public companies in the United States group their expenses by the type of business function (e.g., production, research, marketing, general operations) rather than by the nature of each expense (e.g., salaries, rent, supplies, electricity). After the core revenues and expenses, a multiple-step income statement presents a subtotal called Income from Operations. This is a useful measure, because in Activision's case, it reveals that the company's core business became much more profitable in 2008. Revenue from Investments did contribute to net income so it is included in the income statement, but since it's not a core business activity for Activision it is shown after Income from Operations. Other companies, particularly financial institutions like Capital One and Bank of America, would consider Revenue from Investments a core business activity. But Activision is in business to generate profit from video game sales, not from interest on investments.

2. **Income before Income Tax Expense**—This other new subtotal in Exhibit 5.7 indicates how much profit the company would have reported had there been no income taxes. This subtotal is useful because not all companies pay the same rate of tax. So, if you're trying to decide whether to invest in Pfizer or FedEx, which had effective tax rates in 2008 ranging from 11 to 44 percent, you might be interested in comparing their pretax levels of income. Of course, you will also care about Net Income, which is obtained by subtracting Income Tax Expense from Income before Income Tax Expense. Net Income is the same whether a single-step or multiple-step income statement is presented.

Statement of Stockholders' Equity   Previous chapters indicated that companies report a statement of retained earnings to show how net income increased and dividends decreased the retained earnings balance during the period. While this information is useful, it doesn't tell the full story because Retained Earnings is only one of the stockholders' equity accounts. Contributed Capital is another important stockholders' equity account whose balance increases and decreases during the accounting period. To show all the changes, public companies report a more comprehensive version of the statement of retained earnings called the statement of stockholders' equity. The statement of stockholders' equity has a column for each stockholders' equity account and shows the factors that increased and decreased these account balances during the period. Exhibit 5.8 shows a modified version of Activision's statement. Notice how the beginning and

| EXHIBIT 5.8 | Statement of Stockholders' Equity | ACTIVISION. |

ACTIVISION, INC.
Statement of Stockholders' Equity
For the Year Ended March 31, 2008
(in millions of U.S. dollars)

	Contributed Capital	Retained Earnings
Balances at March 31, 2007	$ 984	$ 428
Net Income		345
Dividends Declared		(-0-)
Issued Shares of Stock	191	
Repurchased Shares of Stock	(-0-)	
Balances at March 31, 2008	$ 1,175	$ 773

How's it going?   Self-Study Practice

Complete the blanks in the following comparative income statements, statement of stockholders' equity, and balance sheets.

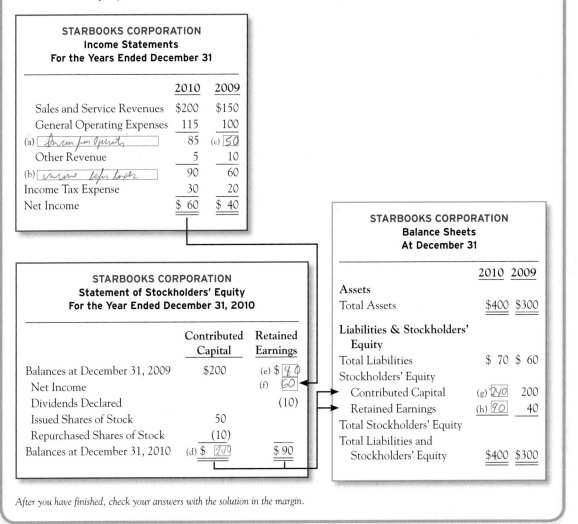

STARBOOKS CORPORATION
Income Statements
For the Years Ended December 31

	2010	2009
Sales and Service Revenues	$200	$150
General Operating Expenses	115	100
(a) _Income from Operations_	85	(c) 50
Other Revenue	5	10
(b) _Income before Income Taxes_	90	60
Income Tax Expense	30	20
Net Income	$ 60	$ 40

STARBOOKS CORPORATION
Statement of Stockholders' Equity
For the Year Ended December 31, 2010

	Contributed Capital	Retained Earnings
Balances at December 31, 2009	$200	(e) $ 40
Net Income		(f) 60
Dividends Declared		(10)
Issued Shares of Stock	50	
Repurchased Shares of Stock	(10)	
Balances at December 31, 2010	(d) $ 240	$ 90

STARBOOKS CORPORATION
Balance Sheets
At December 31

	2010	2009
Assets		
Total Assets	$400	$300
Liabilities & Stockholders' Equity		
Total Liabilities	$ 70	$ 60
Stockholders' Equity		
Contributed Capital	(g) 240	200
Retained Earnings	(h) 90	40
Total Stockholders' Equity		
Total Liabilities and Stockholders' Equity	$400	$300

After you have finished, check your answers with the solution in the margin.

Solution to Self-Study Practice
(a) Income from Operations (b) Income before Income Tax Expense (c) 50 (d) 240
(e) 40 (from the balance sheet on December 31, 2009) (f) 60 (g) 240 (h) 90

ending balances for each account correspond to the balance sheet (in Exhibit 5.6). From this statement, we can see that Activision issued additional shares of stock in 2008, but the biggest increase in stockholders' equity ($345 million) came from the company's own generation (and retention) of net income.

Independent External Audit

To ensure that the financial statements, shown in the previous section, are prepared properly, the SEC requires all publicly traded companies to have their internal controls and financial statements audited by external auditors. Many privately owned companies have their financial statements audited, too, often at the request of lenders or private investors. External audits are conducted by Certified Public Accountants (CPAs) who are independent of the company. These trained professionals examine the company's financial statements (and its accounting system) with the goal of detecting **material misstatements**. It is not practical for auditors to check every single business transaction

> **Learning Objective 4**
> Describe other significant aspects of the financial reporting process, including external audits and the distribution of financial information.

YOU SHOULD KNOW

Material misstatements:
Large enough to influence
the decisions of financial
statement users. **Unqualified
audit opinion:** Indicates that
the financial statements are
presented in accordance
with GAAP. **Qualified audit
opinion:** Indicates that either
the financial statements
do not follow GAAP or the
auditors were not able to
complete the tests needed to
determine whether the financial
statements follow GAAP.

to ensure it was accurately reported, so they can't be 100 percent sure they have caught *every* error. Instead, their audits provide *reasonable* assurance to financial statement users. After completing the audit, external auditors will attach a report to the financial statements that gives a pass/fail type of opinion. An **unqualified audit opinion** represents a passing grade. For an example of an unqualified audit report, see the one on page A.1 for The Home Depot. If the financial statements fail to follow GAAP or if the auditors were not able to complete the tests needed to determine whether GAAP was followed, the auditors will issue a **qualified audit opinion**.

Releasing Financial Information

Preliminary Releases   To provide timely information for all external users, public companies announce annual (and quarterly) results through a press release sent to news agencies. This press release is issued three to five weeks after the accounting period ends. The press release typically includes key figures, management's discussion of the results, and attachments containing a condensed income statement and balance sheet. Exhibit 5.9 shows an excerpt from a typical press release for Activision. Notice that five weeks elapsed between the end of the company's year (March 31) and the date of the press release (May 8). During this time, Activision's accountants were busy making adjusting journal entries and finalizing the financial statements, and its managers were preparing an analysis and discussion of the results.

Many companies, including Activision, follow up the press release with a conference call broadcast on the Internet that allows analysts to grill the company's senior executives with questions about the financial results. By listening to these calls, you can learn a lot about a company's business strategy, its expectations for the future, and the key factors that analysts consider when they evaluate a company. You can check out this useful source of information by visiting each company's own Web site or the archive of conference calls at biz.yahoo.com/cc.

Financial Statement Release   Several weeks after the preliminary press release, public companies release their complete financial statements as part of an annual (or quarterly) report. The annual report is organized into two main sections. The first part of the report usually begins with a friendly letter to investors from the company's CEO. This is followed by glossy pictures of the company's products and commentaries about the company's positioning in its industry. The annual report then presents the financial section. The typical elements of an annual report's financial section are listed and

COACH'S TIP

Companies require several
weeks after the preliminary
press release to gather
information reported in the
financial statement notes or in
other parts of the annual report.
External auditors also complete
their work during this time.

EXHIBIT 5.9	Preliminary Release of Key Results

ACTIVISION REPORTS RECORD Q4 AND FISCAL YEAR 2008 RESULTS

SANTA MONICA, CA—May 8, 2008—Activision, Inc. (Nasdaq: ATVI) today announced record fiscal year 2008 and fourth quarter results.

Net revenues for the fiscal year ended March 31, 2008, were $2.90 billion, as compared to $1.51 billion for the fiscal year ended March 31, 2007. Net income for the fiscal year was $344.9 million, or $1.10 in earnings per share, as compared to net income of $85.8 million for the last fiscal year.

Robert Kotick, chairman and CEO of Activision, Inc. commented, "Fiscal 2008 was the best year in our history and Q4 was the largest and most profitable nonholiday quarter, even though we did not release any new titles. During the fiscal year, we were the #1 U.S. console and handheld publisher in dollars for the first time ever."

Today at 4:30 p.m. EDT, Activision's management will host a conference call and Webcast to discuss its fiscal 2008 year-end results and outlook for fiscal 2009.

EXHIBIT 5.10	Typical Elements of an Annual Report's Financial Section

Name of Financial Section	Information Presented	Example in Appendix A or Online
1. Summarized financial data	• key figures covering a period of 5 or 10 years.	Online
2. Management's discussion and analysis (MD&A)	• an honest and detailed analysis of the company's financial condition and operating results; a must-read for any serious financial statement user.	Online
3. Management's report on internal control	• statements that describe management's responsibility for ensuring adequate internal control over financial reporting and that report on the effectiveness of these controls during the year.	Online
4. Auditor's report	• the auditor's conclusion about whether GAAP was followed (and, for public companies, whether internal controls were effective).	p. A.3
5. Comparative financial statements	• a multi-year presentation of the four basic statements.	p. A.5
6. Financial statement notes	• further information about the financial statements; crucial to understanding the financial statement data.	p. A.9
7. Recent stock price data	• brief summary of highs and lows during the year.	Online
8. Unaudited quarterly data	• condensed summary of each quarter's results.	Online
9. Directors and officers	• a list of who's overseeing and running the company.	Online

explained in Exhibit 5.10, along with references to pages in Appendix A (at the end of this book) or online (at www.mhhe.com/phillips3e) where you should look to see an example of each.

A company's **quarterly** report is like a supercondensed version of its annual report. Following a short letter to stockholders and abbreviated discussion of the financial results, a quarterly report presents a condensed income statement for the quarter, a condensed balance sheet dated at the end of the quarter, and a condensed statement of cash flows. These condensed financial statements typically show less detail than the annual statements, often omitting items 4, 7, 8, and 9 in Exhibit 5.10. Quarterly financial statements are not audited, so they are labeled as unaudited. Obviously, with all these limitations, the quarterly reports aren't quite as informative as the annual reports, but they have the benefit of being released on a timelier basis (every three months rather than every year).

Securities and Exchange Commission (SEC) Filings   To ensure sufficient, relevant information is available to investors, the SEC requires public companies to electronically file certain reports with the SEC, including an **annual report on Form 10-K**, **quarterly reports on Form 10-Q**, and **current event reports on Form 8-K**. (We wouldn't burden you with the details of the form numbers except that most people refer to them by number.) Several of these reports require release of additional information beyond that reported in quarterly or annual reports. In fact, many companies use these reports as substitutes for their glossy annual and quarterly reports. The additional information in the SEC filings can provide great insight about a company. For example, Activision's 2008 10-K describes 30 significant business risks that the company faces and outlines the business strategies for addressing those risks. The 8-K reports significant business events that occur between financial statement dates, such as the acquisition of another company (e.g., Activision's combination with Vivendi Games), a change in its year-end (from March 31 to December 31), or a change in auditor.

These filings are available to the public as soon as they are received by the SEC's Electronic Data Gathering and Retrieval service (EDGAR). As a result, most users can get all the details about a company's financial results in the SEC filings several weeks before the company's glossy reports reach them in the mail or are posted on the company's Web site. To find a company's SEC filings, click on "Search for Company Filings" at www.sec.gov or go to idea.sec.gov.

Spotlight On FINANCIAL REPORTING

Speaking a New Language–XBRL (eXtensible Business Reporting Language)

On December 18, 2008, the SEC voted to require public companies and mutual funds to use interactive data for financial information. This means that each fact in a financial report soon will be "tagged" to identify its source and meaning. This tagging system (called **XBRL**) will allow software applications to retrieve and compare financial data from a broad range of businesses, making comparisons far more efficient and reliable than in the past. Previously, you could never know whether investor information Web sites, like reuters.com/finance or Yahoo!Finance, had correctly entered financial information into their databases. Data error rates in some industries were as high as 34 percent but have fallen to near zero since XBRL was adopted.* For you, this means it just got a little easier to compare financial data (which should simplify some of the skills development cases at the end of this chapter). For further information, go to xbrl.org.

Yahoo! My Yahoo! Mail

YAHOO! FINANCE Sign In
New User? Sign Up

Welcome [Sign In]
Yahoo! Finance

Enter symbol(s): e.g. YHOO, ^DJI [   ] [Go] Symbol Lookup | Finance Search

*Leone, M. "10-Ks, 8-Ks a Thing of the Past?" *CFO.com*, September 25, 2006. Retrieved March 24, 2009, from www.cfo.com/article.cfm/7960677/1/c_2984312.

Learning Objective 5
Explain the reasons for, and financial statement presentation effects of, adopting IFRS.

YOU SHOULD KNOW

International Financial Reporting Standards (IFRS): Accounting rules established by the International Accounting Standards Board for use in over 100 countries around the world.

GLOBALIZATION AND INTERNATIONAL FINANCIAL REPORTING STANDARDS (IFRS)

It's become an old cliché but business really has gone global. Abercrombie is opening stores in Sweden, and Swedish companies like IKEA and H&M are opening stores throughout the United States. Similar trends are occurring in the investing world, where shares of foreign companies like Benetton and British Airways are traded on the New York Stock Exchange (NYSE). Until recently, investors struggled to compare the financial statements of companies like these because different countries used different accounting rules. All this is changing now with the increasing acceptance of **International Financial Reporting Standards** (abbreviated IFRS).

IFRS are developed by the International Accounting Standards Board (IASB), which is the international counterpart to the FASB in the United States. Over 100 different countries including Australia, China, the European Union, South Africa, and New Zealand currently require or permit the use of IFRS, or a local version of IFRS. This number is continuing to grow with IFRS becoming official in Brazil (2010), Canada (2011), India (2011), and other countries. Although the United States has not yet switched to IFRS, such a change is coming. In 2007, the Securities and Exchange Commission (SEC) began moving in this direction by allowing foreign companies like Benetton and British Airways to issue stock in the United States without having to convert their IFRS-based accounting numbers to U.S. generally accepted accounting principles (GAAP). In 2008, the SEC announced a plan to allow some U.S. companies to use IFRS in 2009 and could require mandatory use of IFRS starting in 2014. Many foreign-owned private companies in the United States, such as Mack Trucks and Dreyer's Grand Ice Cream, already use IFRS to make it easy to combine their financial statements with their foreign owners' financial statements.

Although IFRS differ from GAAP, they do not dramatically alter what you have learned to this point in this course. IFRS use the same system of analyzing, recording, and summarizing the results of business activities that you learned in Chapters 1–4.

The most significant differences between IFRS and GAAP relate to technical issues that are typically taught in intermediate and advanced accounting courses. For the topics discussed in this introductory course, differences between IFRS and GAAP are limited. One place where IFRS differ from GAAP is in the formatting of financial statements.

IFRS Formatting of Financial Statements

Although financial statements prepared using GAAP and IFRS include the same items (assets, liabilities, revenues, expenses, etc.), a single, consistent format has not been mandated. Consequently, various formats have evolved over time, with those in the United States differing from those typically used internationally. You can gain a good understanding of the most common differences by reading Exhibit 5.11.

[handwritten: know what IFRS is]

EXHIBIT 5.11	Financial Statement Presentation under GAAP and IFRS	

	GAAP	IFRS
Financial Statement Titles • The financial statements report similar items but under different titles.	Balance sheet Income statement Statement of stockholders' equity Statement of cash flows	Statement of financial position Statement of comprehensive income Statement of shareholders' equity Statement of cash flows
Presentation of Expenses • Similar expenses are reported, but may be grouped in different ways.	Public companies categorize expenses by business **function** (e.g., production, research, marketing, general operations).	Companies can categorize expenses by either function **or nature** (e.g., salaries, rent, supplies, electricity).

Balance Sheet Order
• Similar accounts are shown, but differ in order of liquidity (for assets) and order of maturity (for liabilities).
	Assets
	  Current
	  Noncurrent
	Liabilities
	  Current
	  Noncurrent
	Stockholders' Equity
		Assets
		  Noncurrent
		  Current
		Shareholders' Equity
		Liabilities
		  Noncurrent
		  Current

Of the differences listed in Exhibit 5.11, balance sheet order is the most striking. Most companies that follow GAAP begin with current items whereas those that follow IFRS tend to begin with noncurrent items. Consistent with this, **assets are listed in decreasing order of liquidity under GAAP, but internationally they are usually listed in increasing order of liquidity.** IFRS similarly emphasize longer-term financing sources by listing equity before liabilities and, within liabilities, by listing noncurrent liabilities before current liabilities (**decreasing time to maturity**).

Activision provides an ideal case for illustrating these differences because its balance sheet is prepared using GAAP, but its main stockholder (a European company named Vivendi) reports a statement of financial position based on IFRS. A side-by-side comparison is shown in Exhibit 5.12. As you can see, Vivendi is a larger company than Activision (one euro is equal to about $1.25 in U.S. dollars) and it reports its assets, liabilities, and stockholders' equity accounts in the typical IFRS order. But, despite these differences in appearance, the two companies are involved in the same sort of business activities, so the specific items on the financial statements are similar. It may take you a moment or two, but you should be able to find Cash, Short-term Investments, and so on, on both companies' financial statements. Locating this kind of information is the first step to evaluating the companies' financial results, as you will see in the next section.

EXHIBIT 5.12   Comparison of GAAP Balance Sheet to IFRS Statement of Financial Position

ACTIVISION, INC.
Balance Sheet
(in millions of U.S. dollars)

	March 31, 2008	March 31, 2007
Assets		
Current Assets:		
Cash	$ 1,396	$ 384
Short-term Investments	53	570
Accounts Receivable	203	149
Inventories	147	91
Other Current Assets	180	207
Total Current Assets	1,979	1,401
Property and Equipment, net	55	47
Other Noncurrent Assets	217	151
Goodwill	279	195
Total Assets	$ 2,530	$ 1,794
Liabilities and Stockholders' Equity		
Current Liabilities:		
Accounts Payable	$ 130	$ 136
Accrued and Other Liabilities	426	205
Total Current Liabilities	556	341
Other Noncurrent Liabilities	26	41
Total Liabilities	582	382
Stockholders' Equity:		
Contributed Capital	1,175	984
Retained Earnings	773	428
Total Stockholders' Equity	1,948	1,412
Total Liabilities and Stockholders' Equity	$ 2,530	$ 1,794

Differences
← Title →

Order
← of →
Liquidity
(Decreasing
vs.
Increasing)

Time
← to →
Maturity
(Increasing
vs.
Decreasing)

VIVENDI
Statement of Financial Position
(in millions of euros)

	December 31, 2008	December 31, 2007
Assets		
Goodwill	€22,612	€15,427
Other Noncurrent Assets	15,229	15,361
Property and Equipment, net	6,317	4,675
Total Noncurrent Assets	44,158	35,463
Current Assets:		
Inventories	763	429
Other Current Assets	1,529	1,743
Accounts Receivable	6,777	5,208
Short-term Investments	287	187
Cash	3,152	2,049
Total Current Assets	12,508	9,616
Total Assets	€56,666	€45,079
Equity and Liabilities		
Stockholders' Equity:		
Contributed Capital	€13,840	€13,736
Retained Earnings and Other	12,786	8,506
Total Stockholders' Equity	26,626	22,242
Long-term Borrowings	9,975	5,610
Other Noncurrent Liabilities	4,370	3,768
Total Noncurrent Liabilities	14,345	9,378
Current Liabilities:		
Accrued and Other Current Liabilities	822	909
Short-term Borrowings	1,655	1,766
Accounts Payable	13,218	10,784
Total Current Liabilities	15,695	13,459
Total Liabilities	30,040	22,837
Total Stockholders' Equity and Liabilities	€56,666	€45,079

Spotlight On THE WORLD

Financial Statement Reporting Continues to Evolve

The FASB and IASB continue to explore alternative financial statement formats that better show how information flows from one financial statement to another. The following chart summarizes a recent proposal for each financial statement to use the same section names and categories. **Don't worry about memorizing the following details, just be aware that financial reporting is always evolving**.

Statement of Financial Position	Statement of Comprehensive Income	Statement of Cash Flows
Business • Operating assets and liabilities • Investing assets and liabilities	**Business** • Operating income and expenses • Investing income and expenses	**Business** • Operating cash flows • Investing cash flows
Financing • Financing assets • Financing liabilities	**Financing** • Financing asset income • Financing liability expenses	**Financing** • Financing asset cash flows • Financing liability cash flows
Income Taxes	**Income Taxes**	**Income Taxes**
Discontinued Operations	**Discontinued Operations**	**Discontinued Operations**
	Other	
Equity		**Equity**

For further developments, check out our Web site at www.mhhe.com/phillips3e.

Evaluate the Results

ECONOMIC CRISIS

The end of 2008 and early 2009 was a difficult time for most businesses, whether they were based in the United States, or China, or India, or Europe. Companies were unable to find financing and they struggled to generate sales. In an effort to control expenses, they cut back on workers through massive layoffs (e.g., 1,000 at Electronic Arts, 6,700 at Starbucks, 52,000 at Citigroup, 66,000 at General Motors). Whether they will withstand this economic turmoil is still being determined, but by understanding how to read financial statements, you're in a better position to identify the companies that are likely to survive.

COMPARISON TO COMMON BENCHMARKS

If you're like most people, you probably find it hard to know whether Activision's $345 million in net income is a decent level of performance. It seems like a good number, but to interpret financial statement amounts, it's useful to have points of comparison, or benchmarks. Two commonly used benchmarks are

1. **Prior periods.** By comparing a company's current period results to its own results in prior periods, we can gain a sense of how the company's performance is changing over time. The trend is your friend. In Wall Street language, this comparison of the same company over a series of prior time periods is called **time-series analysis.**

2. **Competitors.** Although an analysis focused on one company is useful, it doesn't show what's happening in the industry. It's possible that the company is improving (good), but still hasn't caught up to others in the same industry (not so good).

> **Learning Objective 6**
> Compare results to common benchmarks.

> **YOU SHOULD KNOW**
>
> **Time-series analysis:** Compares a company's results for one period to its own results over a series of time periods.

YOU SHOULD KNOW

Cross-sectional analysis:
Compares the results of one
company with those of others
in the same section of the
industry.

Or it could be that the company's performance is declining (bad), but it has avoided the severe financial problems others experienced (not so bad). To get this industrywide perspective, most analysts will compare competitors within a particular industry. The name for comparing across companies that compete in the same section of an industry is **cross-sectional analysis.**

In Exhibit 5.13, we present a time-series chart that compares Activision to itself on several key totals from the balance sheet and income statement. From the chart, we can see that Activision grew significantly, in all dimensions, between 2007 and 2008. To gain an understanding of whether this growth enhances Activision's standing in the video game industry, analysts also would compare Activision to competitors, such as Electronic Arts (maker of Rock Band and Madden NFL).

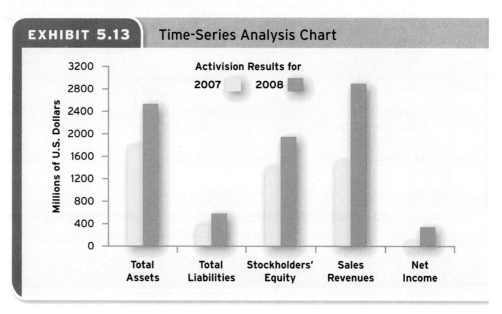

EXHIBIT 5.13   Time-Series Analysis Chart

In Exhibit 5.14, we present a cross-sectional chart that compares Activision to Electronic Arts (stock ticker symbol ERTS) based on financial statement data for the fiscal year ended March 31, 2008.

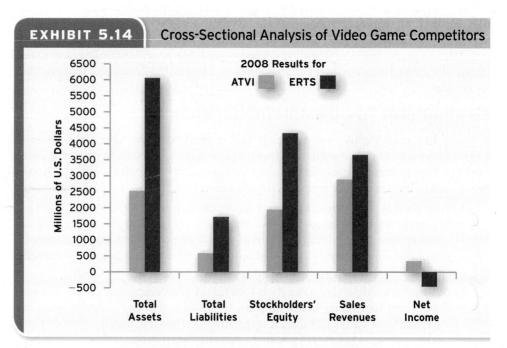

EXHIBIT 5.14   Cross-Sectional Analysis of Video Game Competitors

COACH'S TIP

Average measures for each
industry also can be used in
cross-sectional analysis. Obtain
these measures from the *Annual
Statement Studies* published
by the Risk Management
Association or by clicking on the
ratios link in the stock section of
reuters.com/finance.

The bar chart in Exhibit 5.14 shows that Electronic Arts towers over Activision in almost every category. Given these mammoth differences in size, do analysts simply conclude that Electronic Arts is the winner and give them a pocketful of investment tokens? In a word, no. This means only that Electronic Arts is a bigger company. It says nothing about whether it's best at using the resources provided to it. In fact, the differences in Net Income suggest that Activision may have been more successful. To fully understand the differences, analysts rely on financial statement ratio analysis.

FINANCIAL STATEMENT RATIO ANALYSIS

> **Learning Objective 7**
> Calculate and interpret the debt-to-assets, asset turnover, and net profit margin ratios.

The goal of ratio analysis is to get to the heart of how well a company performed given the resources it had available. By using ratios, you can take into account differences in company size and uncover results that aren't easily detected by looking at total dollar amounts. For example, as you will see below, ratios allow you to discover that although Activision's sales were lower than Electronic Arts's sales, Activision was more efficient in generating sales.

A Basic Business Model

Before evaluating Activision's financial performance, it is useful to first consider what's involved in running a business. Most businesses can be broken down into four elements:

① **Obtain financing** from lenders and investors, which is used to invest in assets.

② **Invest in assets**, which are used to generate revenues.

③ **Generate revenues**, which lead to producing net income.

④ **Produce net income**, which is needed to comfort lenders, satisfy investors, and provide resources for future expansion.

From this description, a business model can be created, as shown in Exhibit 5.15. This business model includes the key financial measures analyzed earlier, including total liabilities (debt), stockholders' equity, assets, revenues, and net income. What's really useful about this business model is that it links one business element to another, so you aren't limited to looking at just total dollar amounts, as we did before.

The business model in Exhibit 5.15 provides a framework for understanding the ratios that we introduce in the next section. Ratios provide measures of key business results, often examining relationships between one element of the business and the next. This is a useful way to think about ratios because it's the same way businesses operate—as a series of interconnected decisions. The last thing we want is for you to view ratios just as a list of individual formulas to memorize without understanding what they mean. Rather, we want you to think of ratios as ways to measure key relationships within a business. It's like using your speedometer to gauge how fast you're going in the car, and then using miles per gallon to understand how it's affecting your fuel efficiency.

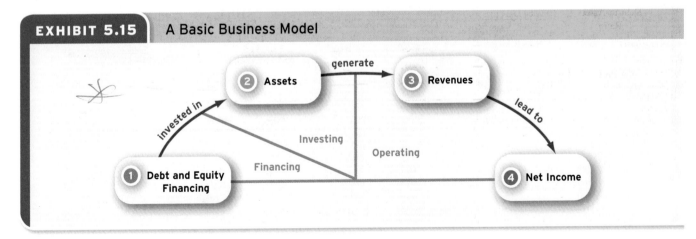

| EXHIBIT 5.15 | A Basic Business Model |

Financial Statement Ratios

The business model in Exhibit 5.15 contains three links: (1) debt and equity financing is invested in assets, (2) assets are used to generate revenues, and (3) revenues lead to net income. Using these links, three key financial ratios can be created, as shown below.

Accounting Decision Tools		
Name of Measure	**Formula**	**What It Tells You**
1. Debt-to-assets ratio	$\dfrac{\text{Total Liabilities}}{\text{Total Assets}}$	• The percentage of assets financed by debt • A higher ratio means greater financing risk
2. Asset turnover ratio	$\dfrac{\text{Sales Revenue}}{\text{Average Total Assets}}$	• How well assets are used to generate revenues • A higher ratio means greater efficiency
3. Net profit margin ratio	$\dfrac{\text{Net Income}}{\text{Sales Revenue}}$	• How well expenses are controlled • A higher ratio means better performance

These three ratios are calculated in the top panel of Exhibit 5.16, using relevant amounts (in the bottom panel) from the financial statements of Activision, Electronic Arts, and Ubisoft (a European company that makes Rayman and Petz games). In addition to making it possible to compare companies of different sizes, a benefit of ratio analysis is that it enables comparisons between companies reporting in different currencies (dollars vs. euros).[2]

Note that, to calculate average total assets in the bottom of the asset turnover ratio, you need amounts from two balance sheets. An average is needed in the asset turnover ratio so that the bottom part spans the entire year, just like the top part. In the following discussion, we explain the significance of each of the three ratios and provide examples of how you could conduct similar analyses with other companies.

---

[2]Any differences in accounting methods, which are discussed in later chapters, can limit the ability to draw conclusions from ratio analysis. One of the goals in moving to IFRS is to eliminate cross-country differences and thereby improve comparability.

EXHIBIT 5.16   **Analysis of Video Game Companies**

		Ubisoft		Activision Inc.		Electronic Arts Inc.	
Ratios							
Debt-to-Assets Ratio	$\dfrac{\text{Total Liabilities}}{\text{Total Assets}}$	$\dfrac{€416}{€1,050} = 0.396$		$\dfrac{\$582}{\$2,530} = 0.230$		$\dfrac{\$1,720}{\$6,059} = 0.284$	
Asset Turnover Ratio	$\dfrac{\text{Sales Revenue}}{\text{Average Total Assets}}$	$\dfrac{€928}{(€1,050 + €822)/2} = 0.99$		$\dfrac{\$2,898}{(\$2,530 + \$1,794)/2} = 1.34$		$\dfrac{\$3,665}{(\$6,059 + \$5,146)/2} = 0.65$	
Net Profit Margin Ratio	$\dfrac{\text{Net Income}}{\text{Sales Revenue}}$	$\dfrac{€110}{€928} = 0.119$		$\dfrac{\$345}{\$2,898} = 0.119$		$\dfrac{\$(454)}{\$3,665} = (0.124)$	
Financial Statement Information (millions)		**2008**	**2007**	**2008**	**2007**	**2008**	**2007**
Total assets		€1,050	€822	$2,530	$1,794	$6,059	$5,146
Total liabilities		416	300	582	382	1,720	1,114
Total stockholders' equity		634	522	1,948	1,412	4,339	4,032
Total sales revenue		928	680	2,898	1,513	3,665	3,091
Net income (loss)		110	41	345	86	(454)	76

1. Debt-to-Assets Ratio The **debt-to-assets ratio** compares total liabilities to total assets. It is usually calculated to three decimal places, and can be expressed as a percentage by multiplying by 100. This ratio indicates the proportion of total assets that are financed by debt. It's important to know how much debt is used to finance assets because debt has to be repaid whether or not a company is doing well financially. If assets are financed mainly by debt, rather than equity, then this ratio will be high, which would suggest the company has adopted a risky financing strategy. Ultimately, a company could be forced into bankruptcy if it took on more debt than it ever could repay. Exhibit 5.16 shows that, for all three companies, debt plays a fairly small role in financing the companies' assets. Activision is the lowest with a debt-to-assets ratio (0.230 or 23.0%) that is lower than either Electronic Arts (0.284 or 28.4%) or Ubisoft (0.396 or 39.6%). This means that the likelihood of Activision being able to repay its existing liabilities is very high, so the company has little financing risk.

YOU SHOULD KNOW

Debt-to-assets ratio: Indicates financing risk by computing the proportion of total assets financed by debt.

2. Asset Turnover Ratio The **asset turnover ratio** compares total sales revenue to average total assets. It is usually calculated to two decimal places and not expressed as a percentage. This ratio indicates the sales revenue per dollar invested in the assets of the business. The higher the ratio, the more efficiently the company is utilizing its assets. Inefficiently run businesses will have lower ratios because their assets will be more likely to sit around idle and not generate revenue. Exhibit 5.16 shows that Activision is the only company generating more than one dollar in sales revenue per dollar invested in assets (as indicated by the ratio of 1.34). In contrast, Electronic Arts appears sluggish, with an asset turnover ratio of 0.65. This indicates that Electronic Arts generated $0.65 dollars of sales revenue (65 cents) per dollar of assets, which is quite a bit less than Activision or Ubisoft. By reading the notes to the financial statements of Electronic Arts, we found that part of the reason for this lower ratio is that Electronic Arts bought the assets of another company late in the year and has not yet been able to use those assets to generate significant sales.

YOU SHOULD KNOW

Asset turnover ratio: Indicates how well assets are being used to generate revenues by dividing total assets into total revenue.

3. Net Profit Margin Ratio The **net profit margin ratio** measures the amount of net income (profit) generated from each dollar of sales revenue. It is usually calculated to three decimal places and can be expressed as a percentage by multiplying by 100. Net profit margin is a key ratio because it indicates how well a company has controlled its expenses. Although it's important for companies to generate lots of revenue, it's equally important to control expenses. A company generating tons of revenue will go bankrupt if its expenses are out of control. Exhibit 5.16 shows that Activision and Ubisoft were equally good at controlling their expenses because they were able to generate net profit margins of 0.119 (or 11.9%). In other words, each dollar (or euro) in sales revenue produced $0.12 (or €0.12) in profit. Once again, Electronic Arts stumbled, as indicated by its loss of over $0.12 on each dollar of sales. As world economies struggle, these kinds of financial results become more typical. **A small negative net profit margin (NPM) does not usually cause a company to go out of business; however, large or repeating negative NPMs are definitely cause for concern.** Look back at the Circuit City spotlight on page 169 for an example of a company that failed within a year of reporting its first *negative* NPM.

YOU SHOULD KNOW

Net profit margin ratio: Indicates how well expenses are controlled, by dividing net income by revenue.

Although it is useful to consider each of the ratios separately, it is even more informative to consider them together, to tell a "story" about the company's financial results. Based on the 2008 ratios in Exhibit 5.16, Activision appears to be the clear leader in its industry. Of the three companies, Activision relied the least on debt financing (debt-to-assets ratio of 0.230), it generated the most sales for each dollar invested in assets (asset turnover ratio of 1.34), and it was a top performer in converting these sales into profit (NPM ratio of 0.119). This explains why the company was so upbeat in the press release announcing its financial results (see Exhibit 5.9 again, on page 218).

Many other financial statement ratios exist to assess profitability (the ability to generate income in the current period), liquidity (the ability to use current assets to pay liabilities), and solvency (the ability to repay lenders when debt matures). Rather than load you up with them all at once, we will introduce them gradually in Chapters 6–12, and then we'll summarize and apply them in a comprehensive analysis in Chapter 13.

Solution to Self-Study Practice

(a) Debt-to-assets ratio = 30,040/56,666 = 0.530

This indicates higher financing risk than Activision's 0.230.

(b) Asset turnover ratio = $\dfrac{25,392}{(56,666 + 45,079)/2}$ = 0.50

This indicates lower asset efficiency than Activision's 1.34.

(c) Net profit margin ratio = 3,699/25,392 = 0.146

This indicates higher profitability than Activision's 0.119.

How's it going?   Self-Study Practice

Vivendi owns a significant part of Activision (now doing business under the name Activision Blizzard). In the year ended December 31, 2008, Vivendi reported (in millions of euros) total sales revenues of €25,392 and net income of €3,699. Using this information and Exhibit 5.12, calculate ratios to indicate whether, relative to Activision, Vivendi has higher or lower levels of (a) financing risk, (b) asset efficiency, and (c) profitability.

After you have finished, check your answers with the solution in the margin.

How Transactions Affect Ratios

To properly interpret financial statement ratios, you will find it useful to understand how they are affected by transactions. Apply the following three-step process to determine the impact of each transaction on a particular ratio:

1. **Analyze the transaction to determine its effects on the accounting equation,** just as you have learned to do in Chapters 2–4.
2. **Relate the effects in step 1 to the ratio's components,** to determine whether each component increases, decreases, or stays the same.
3. **Evaluate the combined impact of the effects in step 2 on the overall ratio.**

A ratio will increase if (a) its top number increases and the bottom number does not change, (b) its bottom number decreases and its top number does not change, or (c) the top number increases while the bottom number decreases. Changes in the opposite direction have the opposite effect. A ratio will decrease if (a) its top number decreases and the bottom number does not change, (b) its bottom number increases and its top number does not change, or (c) the top number decreases while the bottom number increases.

When a transaction causes both the top and bottom numbers to change in the same direction, the overall impact on a ratio depends on whether the ratio is greater or less than 1.0 before the transaction. A useful approach for determining the impact of a transaction on a ratio in these cases is to assume some simple numbers for the ratio's starting point and then recalculate the ratio after taking into account the effects of the transaction. Exhibit 5.17 illustrates this approach for two situations.

EXHIBIT 5.17	Changes in Ratios Given Changes in Its Components		
Situation	Before	Change	After
1. Ratio < 1	$\dfrac{5}{10}$	$\dfrac{+5}{+5}$	$\dfrac{10}{15}$
	= 0.50		= 0.67
2. Ratio > 1	$\dfrac{10}{5}$	$\dfrac{+5}{+5}$	$\dfrac{15}{10}$
	= 2.0		= 1.5

In the first situation, the $5 increases in the top and bottom of the ratio cause the overall ratio to increase from 0.50 to 0.67. In the second situation, the $5 increases cause the overall ratio to decrease from 2.0 to 1.5. These different outcomes occur because in situation (1), the increase has a greater proportionate effect on the top number than on the bottom, whereas in situation (2), the change has a greater proportionate effect on the bottom number than on the top.

For many situations, you will know whether a ratio is greater or less than one, as a result of understanding the relationship between the ratio's components. For example, the debt-to-assets ratio is likely to be less than 1.0 because the balance sheet equation $(A = L + SE)$ indicates that liabilities are less than assets. Similarly, the net profit margin ratio is less than 1.0 because the income statement equation (Revenues − Expenses = Net Income) implies that revenues are greater than net income. Only in a few cases (e.g., asset turnover ratio) will you need to know whether the ratio is greater or less than 1.0 to determine the impact of a transaction that causes both the top and bottom numbers of a ratio to change in the same direction.

REVIEW THE CHAPTER

DEMONSTRATION CASE

Some analysts claim the video game business is similar to the book business. In this demonstration case, we'll take a look at just how similar they are in terms of financial results. While we're tempted to analyze the financial statements of the company that published this textbook, it wouldn't provide a clean comparison because McGraw-Hill doesn't just publish books—it also runs Standard & Poor's (a financial services company). So, instead, we'll analyze the financial statements of one of our publisher's main competitors, John Wiley & Sons—a company that operates only in the book business. Shortened versions of that company's financial statements are shown below:

John Wiley & Sons

www.mhhe.com/phillips3e

JOHN WILEY & SONS, INC. Income Statement (modified) (U.S. dollars in millions) For the Years Ended April 30		
	2008	2007
Total Sales Revenue	$1,674	$1,235
Cost of Sales	537	394
Operating and Administrative Expenses	875	659
Other Expenses	39	21
Income from Operations	223	161
Interest Expense	61	21
Income before Income Tax Expense	162	140
Income Tax Expense	14	40
Net Income	$ 148	$ 100

JOHN WILEY & SONS, INC.
Balance Sheet (modified)
(U.S. dollars in millions)
April 30

	2008	2007
Assets		
Current Assets	$ 448	$ 421
Other Assets	2,141	2,132
Total Assets	$2,589	$2,553
Liabilities and Stockholders' Equity		
Current Liabilities	$ 691	$ 620
Other Liabilities	1,209	1,403
Total Liabilities	1,900	2,023
Stockholders' Equity	689	530
Total Liabilities and Stockholders' Equity	$2,589	$2,553

1026

Required:

1. Compute Wiley's debt-to-assets ratio at the end of the 2008 and 2007 fiscal years. How has Wiley changed its financing strategy from 2007 to 2008? Is this likely to be considered a riskier or safer strategy? How similar is the proportion of debt financing used by the book publisher to that used by the video game companies analyzed in Exhibit 5.16?

2. Compute Wiley's asset turnover ratio for 2008 and 2007. (In millions, Wiley's total assets at April 30, 2006, were $1,026.) Between 2007 and 2008, was there a change in Wiley's efficiency in using its assets to generate revenues? Does the book publisher generate more or less sales from each dollar invested in assets than the video game companies analyzed in Exhibit 5.16?

3. Compute Wiley's net profit margin ratio for the 2008 and 2007 fiscal years. How has this aspect of Wiley's financial performance changed? Does the book publisher make more or less profit from each dollar of sales than the video game companies analyzed in Exhibit 5.16?

4. In the aftermath of the 2001 Enron financial scandal, one of the biggest auditing firms in the world (Arthur Andersen) shut down. On April 15, 2002, John Wiley & Sons announced that KPMG would replace Arthur Andersen as the company's auditor. How would Wiley report this news to the SEC?

After completing requirements 1–4, check your answers with the following solution.

Suggested Solution

1. Debt-to-Assets Ratio = Total Liabilities ÷ Total Assets

	2008	2007
$\dfrac{\text{Total Liabilities}}{\text{Total Assets}}$	$\dfrac{\$1,900}{\$2,589} = 0.734$ or 73.4%	$\dfrac{\$2,023}{\$2,553} = 0.792$ or 79.2%

Wiley has moved toward a safer financing strategy in 2008, by relying less on debt (down from 79.2 percent in 2007 to 73.4 percent in 2008). Despite this change, Wiley still relies much more on debt than the video game companies in Exhibit 5.16, which financed less than 40 percent of their total assets using debt.

2. Asset Turnover Ratio = Sales Revenue ÷ Average Total Assets

	2008	2007
$\dfrac{\text{Total Sales Revenue}}{\text{Average Total Assets}}$	$\dfrac{\$1,674}{(\$2,589 + \$2,553)/2} = 0.65$	$\dfrac{\$1,235}{(\$2,553 + \$1,026)/2} = 0.69$

Wiley generated weaker sales per dollar invested in assets in 2008 (0.65) than in 2007 (0.69). In comparison to the video game companies in Exhibit 5.16, it appears Wiley's assets are generating sales with less efficiency.

3. Net Profit Margin Ratio = Net Income ÷ Sales Revenue

	2008		2007	
$\dfrac{\text{Net Income}}{\text{Total Sales Revenue}}$	$\dfrac{\$148}{\$1,674}$	$= 0.088$ or 8.8%	$\dfrac{\$100}{\$1,235}$	$= 0.081$ or 8.1%

Wiley has improved its net profit margin from 8.1 percent in 2007 to 8.8 percent in 2008. This means that, in 2008, Wiley made about 8.8 cents of profit for each dollar of sales. These ratios are lower than those for Activision and Ubisoft.

4. Form 8-K is used to report significant events such as this change in auditor.

CHAPTER SUMMARY

Explain the needs of financial statement users. p. 208 LO1

- The main financial statement users are:

    Managers, who use accounting information to run the business.

    Directors, who use accounting information to oversee the business.

    Creditors, who use accounting information to administer business contracts.

    Investors, who use accounting information to value the business.

    Government, which uses accounting information to ensure compliance with regulations.

Describe the environment for financial reporting, including the Sarbanes-Oxley Act. p. 210 LO2

- For someone to commit fraud, three things must exist: incentive, opportunity, and the personality to rationalize and conceal.

- Incentives that motivate managers to misreport financial results include creating business opportunities (by satisfying loan covenants, increasing equity financing, and attracting business partners) and satisfying personal greed (enhancing job security, increasing personal wealth, and obtaining a bigger paycheck).

- The Sarbanes-Oxley (SOX) Act reduced the incentive to commit fraud by introducing stiffer penalties. It also limited opportunities by improving internal controls through management reporting, audit committee functioning, and external audit reporting. Finally, it attempted to support honest employees confronting those with questionable personalities.

Prepare a comparative balance sheet, multiple-step income statement, and statement of stockholders' equity. p. 213 LO3

- Comparative financial statements include separate columns for each period's results. See Exhibit 5.6 (p. 215) for an example.

- A multiple-step income statement displays subtotals that indicate multiple steps before reaching Net Income at the bottom. See Exhibit 5.7 (p. 215) for an example.

- The statement of stockholders' equity, which replaces the statement of retained earnings, has columns for each stockholders' equity account and shows the factors that increased and decreased these account balances during the period. See Exhibit 5.8 (p. 216) for an example.

Describe other significant aspects of the financial reporting process, including external audits and the distribution of financial information. p. 217 LO4

- Financial information can be distributed through press releases, SEC filings, investor information Web sites, and quarterly and annual reports.

- Press releases typically include key figures (sales revenues, net income), management's discussion of the results, and attachments containing a condensed income statement and balance sheet.

- Form 10-K is the SEC's version of the annual report, which includes the annual financial statements, auditor's report, management's discussion and analysis, stock price data, and other financial schedules. Form 10-Q is the SEC's version of the quarterly report, which includes the quarterly financial statements and management's discussion and analysis. Form 8-K is the SEC's form that companies use to report significant current events, such as changes in auditors, press releases issued, and acquisitions of other companies.

LO5   **Explain the reasons for, and financial statement presentation effects of, adopting IFRS. p. 220**

- IFRS are intended to reduce or eliminate differences in accounting rules that have developed previously on a country-by-country basis.

- These improvements in comparability are needed as a result of increasing globalization in corporate operations and investing.

- IFRS introduce new financial statement titles, order of balance sheet accounts, and groupings of expenses, as summarized in Exhibit 5.11 (p. 221).

LO6   **Compare results to common benchmarks. p. 223**

- Common benchmarks include: prior periods (used in time-series analysis) and competitors (used in cross-sectional analysis).

LO7   **Calculate and interpret the debt-to-assets, asset turnover, and net profit margin ratios. p. 225**

- The debt-to-assets ratio is calculated by dividing total liabilities by total assets. It indicates the percentage of assets financed by debt, with a higher ratio indicating a riskier financing strategy.

- The asset turnover ratio is calculated by dividing total sales revenue for the period by average total assets held during the period. Average total assets usually is calculated by adding the beginning and ending total assets together and dividing by 2. The asset turnover ratio indicates how well assets are used to generate sales, with a higher ratio indicating greater efficiency.

- The net profit margin ratio is calculated by dividing net income by total sales revenue. It indicates the ability to control expenses, with a higher ratio indicating better performance.

Accounting Decision Tools

Name of Measure	Formula	What It Tells You
1. Debt-to-assets ratio	$\dfrac{\text{Total Liabilities}}{\text{Total Assets}}$	• The percentage of assets financed by debt • A higher ratio means greater financing risk
2. Asset turnover ratio	$\dfrac{\text{Sales Revenue}}{\text{Average Total Assets}}$	• How well assets are used to generate sales • A higher ratio means greater efficiency
3. Net profit margin ratio	$\dfrac{\text{Net Income}}{\text{Sales Revenue}}$	• How well expenses are controlled • A higher ratio means better performance

KEY TERMS

Asset Turnover Ratio p. 227

Comparative Financial Statements p. 214

Cross-Sectional Analysis p. 224

Debt-to-Assets Ratio p. 227

Loan Covenants p. 209

International Financial Reporting Standards (IFRS) p. 220

Material Misstatements p. 218

Net Profit Margin Ratio p. 227

Qualified Audit Opinion p. 218

Sarbanes-Oxley (SOX) Act p. 211

Single-Step Income Statement p. 214

Time-Series Analysis p. 223

Unqualified Audit Opinion p. 218

See complete definitions in the glossary in the back of this text.

HOMEWORK HELPER

Alternative terms

- Under IFRS, the balance sheet is called the statement of financial position, and the income statement is called the statement of comprehensive income.

Helpful reminders

- If you're not sure how a transaction affects a particular ratio, assume simple numbers for the ratio's starting point (before the transaction) and then recalculate the ratio after taking into account the effects of the transaction.

Frequent mistakes

- Some students assume that a ratio does not change when its numerator and denominator change by the same amount. A ratio is likely to change even if both its top and bottom parts increase (or decrease) by an equal dollar amount.

PRACTICE MATERIAL

QUESTIONS   (⊕ Symbol indicates questions that require analysis from more than one perspective.)

1. Describe one way that each of the main financial statement user groups uses financial statement information.

2. What are the three points of the fraud triangle? Is fraud more or less likely to occur if one of these elements is missing?

3. Why would managers misrepresent the financial results of their companies? What are the incentives for doing this?

4. What aspect(s) of the Sarbanes-Oxley Act might counteract the incentive to commit fraud?

5. What aspect(s) of the Sarbanes-Oxley Act might reduce opportunities for fraud?

6. What aspect(s) of the Sarbanes-Oxley Act might allow honest employees to prevail?

7. What roles do auditors play in the financial reporting process?

8. In what ways are fraudulent financial reporting and academic dishonesty (e.g., cheating on exams) similar? Consider the three points of the fraud triangle.

9. Companies will incur substantial costs to implement XBRL. What are some benefits of requiring companies to report interactive data in this format? ⊕

10. In what three ways might corporate financial statements in the United States differ from the examples shown in Chapters 1–4?

11. Switching to International Financial Reporting Standards (IFRS) will require companies to incur significant costs. What are the benefits of countries adopting IFRS? ⊕

12. In what three general ways might financial statements prepared using IFRS differ from those prepared using GAAP?

13. What two benchmarks are commonly used to interpret and evaluate amounts reported for specific financial statement items?

14. What is the goal of ratio analysis?

15. Explain the simple business model that starts with obtaining financing and then proceeds through other investing and operating decisions.

16. Why do some ratios use just the ending balance sheet amounts whereas others use averages of the beginning and ending balances?

17. What are the key business activities that the debt-to-assets, asset turnover, and net profit margin ratios assess?

MULTIPLE CHOICE

Quiz 5
www.mhhe.com/phillips3e

1. If total assets increase but total liabilities remain the same, what is the impact on the debt-to-assets ratio?
   a. Increases.
   b. Decreases.
   c. Remains the same.
   d. Cannot be determined without additional information.

2. Costco and Sam's Club are two companies that offer low prices for items packaged in bulk. This strategy increases total sales volume but generates less profit for each dollar of sales. Which of the following ratios is improved by this strategy?
   a. Net profit margin.
   b. Asset turnover.
   c. Debt-to-assets.
   d. All of the above.

3. Which of the following would increase the net profit margin ratio in the current year?

   a. Increase the amount of research and development in the last month of the year.

   b. Decrease the amount of sales in the last month of the year.

   c. Postpone routine maintenance work that was to be done this year.

   d. All of the above.

4. The asset turnover ratio is directly affected by which of the following categories of business decisions?

   a. Operating and investing decisions.

   b. Operating and financing decisions.

   c. Investing and financing decisions.

   d. Operating, investing, and financing decisions.

5. Which of the following reports is filed annually with the SEC?

   a. Form 10-Q

   b. Form 10-K

   c. Form 8-K

   d. Press release

6. Which of the following describes the order in which assets are reported under IFRS?

   a. Increasing order of liquidity.

   b. Increasing time to maturity.

   c. Decreasing order of liquidity.

   d. Decreasing time to maturity.

7. Which of the following describes a time-series analysis of your academic performance?

   a. Counting the number of A's on your transcript.

   b. Comparing the number of A's you received this year to the number you received last year.

   c. Comparing the number of A's you received this year to the number your friend received.

   d. Counting the total number of A's given out to your class as a whole.

8. Which of the following is always included in an annual report but never in a quarterly report?

   a. Balance sheet.

   b. Income statement.

   c. Management's discussion and analysis.

   d. Auditor's report.

9. Which of the following transactions will increase the debt-to-assets ratio?

   a. The company issues stock to investors.

   b. The company uses cash to buy land.

   c. The company issues a note payable to buy machinery.

   d. None of the above.

10. What type of audit report does a company hope to include with its annual report?

   a. Conservative report

   b. Qualified report

   c. Comparable report

   d. Unqualified report

For answers to the Multiple-Choice Questions **see page Q1** located in the last section of the book.

MINI-EXERCISES

LO1   **M5-1 Matching Players in the Financial Reporting Process with Their Definitions**

Match each player with the related definition by entering the appropriate letter in the space provided.

Players	Definitions
___ 1. Independent auditors	A. Investors and creditors (among others).
___ 2. External users	B. People who are elected by stockholders to oversee a company's management.
___ 3. Directors	C. CPAs who examine financial statements and attest to their fairness.

LO2   **M5-2 Matching Sarbanes-Oxley (SOX) Requirements to the Fraud Triangle**

Match each of the following SOX requirements to the corresponding element of the fraud triangle by entering the appropriate letter in the space provided.

___ 1. Establish a tip line for employees to report questionable acts.	A. Incentive
___ 2. Increase maximum fines to $5 million.	B. Opportunity
___ 3. Require management to report on effectiveness of internal controls.	C. Personality
___ 4. Legislate whistle-blower protections.	
___ 5. Require external auditors' report on internal control effectiveness.	

M5-3 Identifying the Sequence of Financial Reports and Disclosures

LO4

Indicate the order in which the following reports and disclosures are normally issued by public companies in any given year.

No.	Title
____	Form 10-K
____	Annual Report
____	Press release announcing annual earnings

M5-4 Preparing and Interpreting a Multiple-step Income Statement

LO3, 7

Nutboy Theater Company reported the following single-step income statement. Prepare a multiple-step income statement that distinguishes the financial results of the local theater company's core and peripheral activities. Also, calculate the net profit margin and compare it to the 8% earned in 2009. In which year did the company generate more profit from each dollar of sales?

NUTBOY THEATER COMPANY
Income Statement
For the year ended December 31, 2010

Revenues	
Ticket Sales	$50,000
Concession Sales	2,500
Interest Revenue	200
Other Revenue	50
Total revenues	52,750
Expenses	
Salaries and Wage Expense	30,000
Advertising Expense	8,000
Utilities Expense	7,000
Income Tax Expense	2,500
Total Expenses	47,500
Net Income	$ 5,250

M5-5 Preparing a Statement of Stockholders' Equity

LO3

On December 31, 2008, WER Productions reported $100,000 of contributed capital and $20,000 of retained earnings. During 2009, the company had the following transactions. Prepare a statement of stockholders' equity for the year ended December 31, 2009.

a. Issued stock for $50,000.
b. Declared and paid a cash dividend of $5,000.
c. Reported total revenue of $120,000 and total expenses of $87,000.

M5-6 Determining the Accounting Equation Effects of Transactions

LO3

Complete the following table, indicating the sign and amount of the effect (+ for increase, − for decrease, and NE for no effect) of each transaction. Provide an account name for any revenue or expense transactions included in stockholders' equity. Consider each item independently.

a. Recorded services provided to a customer on account for $500.
b. Recorded $50 of supplies purchased from a supplier on account.
c. Recorded advertising services of $1,000 received but not yet paid for.

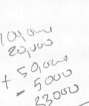

$A = L + E$

Transaction	Assets	Liabilities	Stockholders' Equity
a			
b			
c			

LO7   **M5-7 Determining the Effects of Transactions on Debt-to-Assets, Asset Turnover, and Net Profit Margin Ratios**

Using the transactions in M5-6, complete the following table by indicating the sign of the effect (+ for increase, − for decrease, NE for no effect, and CD for cannot determine) of each transaction. Consider each item independently.

Transaction	Debt-to-Assets	Asset Turnover	Net Profit Margin
a			
b			
c			

LO3   **M5-8 Determining the Accounting Equation Effects of Transactions**

Complete the following table, indicating the sign and amount of the effect (+ for increase, − for decrease, and NE for no effect) of each transaction. Provide an account name for any revenue or expense transactions included in stockholders' equity. Consider each item independently.

a.   Issued 10,000 shares of stock for $90,000 cash.
b.   Equipment costing $4,000 was purchased by issuing a note payable.
c.   Recorded depreciation of $1,000 on the equipment.

Transaction	Assets	Liabilities	Stockholders' Equity
a			
b			
c			

LO7   **M5-9 Determining the Effects of Transactions on Debt-to-Assets, Asset Turnover, and Net Profit Margin Ratios**

Using the transactions in M5-8, complete the following table by indicating the sign of the effect (+ for increase, − for decrease, NE for no effect, and CD for cannot determine) of each transaction. Consider each item independently.

Transaction	Debt-to-Assets	Asset Turnover	Net Profit Margin
a	NE	−	NE
b	+	−	NE
c	+	+	−

LO3   **M5-10 Preparing Comparative Financial Statements**

Complete the blanks in the following comparative income statements, statement of stockholders' equity, and balance sheets.

STARBOOKS CORPORATION
Income Statements
For the Years Ended December 31

	2010	2009
Sales and Service Revenues	$400	$300
General Operating Expenses	230	200
(a) ⌐Totl Oping Rovrne¬	170	(c) ⌐160⌐
Other Revenue	10	20
(b) ⌐Total Rev befre X At Enpsh¬	180	120
Income Tax Expense	60	40
Net Income	$120	$ 80

STARBOOKS CORPORATION
Statement of Stockholders' Equity
For the Year Ended December 31, 2010

	Contributed Capital	Retained Earnings
Balances at December 31, 2009	$400	(e) $☐
Net Income		(f) ☐
Dividends Declared		(20)
Issued Shares of Stock	100	
Repurchased Shares of Stock	(20)	
Balances at December 31, 2010	(d) $☐	$180

STARBOOKS CORPORATION
Balance Sheets
December 31

	2010	2009
Assets		
Total Assets	$800	$600
Liabilities & Stockholders' Equity		
Total Liabilities	$140	$120
Stockholders' Equity		
Contributed Capital	(g) ☐	400
Retained Earnings	(h) ☐	80
Total Stockholders' Equity		
Total Liabilities & Stockholders' Equity	$800	$600

M5-11 Preparing a Financial Statement under IFRS   LO5

Show how the balance sheet in M5-10 would be presented under International Financial Reporting Standards.

M5-12 Computing and Interpreting the Net Profit Margin Ratio   LO7

Happy's Golf Corporation recently reported the following December 31 amounts in its financial statements (in thousands):

	Prior Year	Current Year
Income from Operations	$ 1,700	$1,400
Net Income	850	700
Total Assets	10,000	9,000
Total Stockholders' Equity	8,000	7,500
Sales Revenue	9,000	7,000

Compute the net profit margin ratio for the current and prior years. What do these analyses indicate?

M5-13 Computing and Interpreting the Debt-to-Assets Ratio   LO7

Using the data in M5-12, compute the debt-to-assets ratio for the current and prior years. What do these analyses indicate?

LO7   **M5-14 Computing and Interpreting the Asset Turnover Ratio**

Using the data in M5-12, compute the asset turnover ratio for the current year. Assuming the asset turnover ratio in the prior year was 85.2 percent (0.852), what does your analysis indicate?

LO6, 7   **M5-15 Computing and Interpreting Financial Ratios**

Columbia Sportswear
Levi Strauss

Key financial data for Columbia Sportswear and Levi Strauss follow (amounts in millions). Using two ratios included in this chapter, compare their relative abilities to generate (a) sales from assets and (b) net income from sales. Which company appears more successful on each of the measures?

	Columbia Sportswear	Levi Strauss and Co.
Sales	$1,318	$4,303
Net Income	95	229
Total Assets, 2008	1,148	2,777
Total Assets, 2007	1,166	2,851

EXERCISES

LO1, 4   **E5-1 Matching Components of the Financial Reporting Process with Their Definitions**

Match each component with the related definition by entering the appropriate letter in the space provided.

Components	Definitions
___ 1. Investor information Web site	A. Individual who purchases stock in companies for personal ownership or for pension funds or mutual funds.
___ 2. External auditor	
___ 3. Investor	
___ 4. Creditor	B. Financial institution or supplier that lends money to the company.
___ 5. SEC	C. Independent CPA who examines financial statements and attests to their fairness.
	D. Securities and Exchange Commission, which regulates financial disclosure requirements.
	E. Gathers, combines, and transmits financial and related information from various sources.

LO4   **E5-2 Matching Definitions with Information Releases Made by Public Companies**

Following are the titles of various information releases. Match each definition with the related release by entering the appropriate letter in the space provided.

Information Release	Definitions
___ 1. Annual report	A. Comprehensive report containing the four basic financial statements and related notes, statements by management and auditors, and other descriptions of the company's activities.
___ 2. Form 8-K	
___ 3. Press release	
___ 4. Form 10-Q	B. Annual report filed by public companies with the SEC that contains detailed financial information.
___ 5. Quarterly report	C. Quarterly report filed by public companies with the SEC that contains unaudited financial information.
___ 6. Form 10-K	D. A company-prepared news announcement that is normally distributed to major news agencies.
	E. Brief unaudited report for the quarter, normally containing condensed income statement and balance sheet (unaudited).
	F. Report of special events (e.g., auditor changes, mergers and acquisitions) filed by public companies with the SEC.

E5-3 Finding Financial Information: Matching Information Items to Financial Reports

Following are information items included in various financial reports. Match each information item with the report(s) where it would most likely be found by entering the appropriate letter(s) in the space provided.

Information Item	Report
_____ 1. Initial announcement of hiring of new vice president for sales.	A. Annual report
_____ 2. Initial announcement of quarterly earnings.	B. Form 8-K
_____ 3. Initial announcement of a change in auditors.	C. Press release
_____ 4. Complete quarterly income statement, balance sheet, and cash flow statement.	D. Form 10-Q
_____ 5. The four basic financial statements for the year.	E. Quarterly report
_____ 6. Summarized income statement information for the quarter.	F. Form 10-K
_____ 7. Detailed discussion of the company's business risks and strategies.	G. None of the above
_____ 8. Detailed notes to financial statements.	
_____ 9. Summarized financial data for 5- or 10-year period.	

E5-4 Understanding the Financial Reporting Process

During the first half of 2007, Mad Catz Interactive, Inc., completed its fiscal year, filed reports with the SEC, and issued various reports to the public. Match each date in the table below with the related activity by entering the appropriate letter in the space provided.

Date Filed/Issued	Activity
_____ 1. March 31, 2007	A. Issued annual earnings press release
_____ 2. June 5, 2007	B. Filed Form 8-K announcing press release
_____ 3. June 5, 2007	C. Filed Form 10-K
_____ 4. June 29, 2007	D. Completed fiscal year

E5-5 Matching Events with Concepts

Following are accounting concepts covered in Chapters 1 through 5. Match each event (A–J) with its related concept (1–10) by entering the appropriate letter in the space provided. Use one letter for each blank.

Concepts	Events
_____ 1. Users of financial statements	A. Counted unused supplies at the end of the period and valued them in U.S. dollars.
_____ 2. Objective of financial statements	B. Valued an asset at the amount paid to acquire it, even though its market value has increased considerably.
_____ 3. Faithful representation	C. Analyzed the financial statements to assess the company's performance.
_____ 4. Comparability	D. Established an accounting policy that sales revenue shall be recognized only when services have been provided to the customer.
_____ 5. Separate entity	
_____ 6. Unit of measure	E. Prepared and distributed financial statements that provide useful financial information for creditors and investors.
_____ 7. Cost principle	F. Established a policy not to include in the financial statements the personal financial affairs of the owners of the business.
_____ 8. Revenue principle	G. Used the same accounting policies over several years to facilitate analysis.
_____ 9. Matching principle	H. Established policies to report the company's business activities in a way that depicts their economic substance.
_____ 10. Conservatism	I. Adjusted the rent accounts to show the cost of rent used up in the current period.
	J. Acquired a vehicle for use in the business, reporting it at the agreed-upon purchase price rather than its higher sticker price.

LO1, 4, 7

Atari Incorporated

E5-6 Understanding the Characteristics of Useful Financial Information and the Financial Reporting Process

Atari Incorporated began with $250 and an idea for a video game named Pong, eventually becoming a $28 million enterprise. Over the years, Atari has been owned by a variety of companies, including Time-Warner, Hasbro, and, most recently, Infogrames (a public company in France). Infogrames made the following announcement:

> On March 28, 2003, the Company announced that it has changed its fiscal year-end from June 30 to March 31. As a result of this change, the Company's fiscal year 2003 was a nine-month period. The Company believes that the March 31 year-end is consistent with more of its peers in the video game industry, allowing for more meaningful analysis and comparisons within the sector.

Required:

1. To which of the four factors that enhance the usefulness of information, introduced in Chapter 1, is the company referring?
   TIP: Rather than look for key words in the announcement, read it for meaning.
2. On what SEC form would the change in year-end be reported?
3. Since the 2003 fiscal period includes only nine months, will the debt-to-assets, asset turnover, and net profit margin ratios be meaningful in 2003? Explain your reasoning.

LO1, 4, 7

THQ, Inc.

E5-7 Understanding the Characteristics of Useful Financial Information and the Financial Reporting Process

THQ, Inc., is among the biggest video game makers in the world. THQ made the following announcement:

> On February 13, 2003, we announced a fiscal year-end change from December 31 of each year to March 31 of each year, effective March 31, 2003. We believe that the change in fiscal year will better reflect our natural business year and allow us to provide financial guidance after the holiday selling season.

Required:

1. Does the reason given for the change in year-end indicate that this change will make THQ's financial statements more useful to users? Can you think of a reason that the change in year-end ultimately will result in more useful information for users?
2. On what SEC form would the change in year-end be reported?
3. Since the March 31, 2003, fiscal period includes only three months, will the debt-to-assets, asset turnover, and net profit margin ratios be meaningful in this period? Explain your reasoning.

LO7

Cendant Corporation

E5-8 Computing and Interpreting the Net Profit Margin Ratio

Before spinning off its businesses in 2006, Cendant Corporation owned and operated Super 8 Motels, Ramada, Howard Johnson, Century 21, Orbitz.com, Avis, and Budget. Cendant also was notorious for committing a $3.3 billion accounting fraud in the late 1990s, which sent its former vice chairman to prison for 10 years. On February 13, 2006, the company issued a press release that reported the following amounts (in millions) for the year just ended on December 31, 2005:

	2005	2004
Total Fee Revenue	$18,236	$16,689
Income from Operations	869	1,365
Net Income	1,341	2,082

Required:

Compute the net profit margin ratio for the current and prior years. What do these analyses indicate?

E5-9 Understanding the Financial Reporting Process

1. The information in E5-8 indicated that the Cendant Corporation press release was issued on February 13, yet the company's year-end was six weeks earlier on December 31. Why did the company wait so long to issue the press release? Why weren't the financial results announced on January 1?
2. The 10-K was filed on March 1, 2006. Why would the company wait so long to file the 10-K? Why wouldn't it be filed at the same time the press release was issued?
3. Is the company's glossy annual report likely to be issued before or after the 10-K?

LO4

Cendant Corporation

E5-10 Analyzing and Interpreting Asset Turnover and Net Profit Margin Ratios

Papa John's is one of the fastest-growing pizza delivery and carry-out restaurant chains in the country. Presented here are selected income statement and balance sheet amounts (in millions).

LO1, 7

Better Ingredients.
Better Pizza.

	2008	2007
Total Revenues	$1,132	$1,064
Net Income	37	33
Total Assets, beginning of year	402	380
Total Assets, end of year	386	402

Required:

1. Compute the asset turnover and net profit margin ratios for 2008 and 2007.
2. Would analysts more likely increase or decrease their estimates of stock value on the basis of these changes? Explain by interpreting what the changes in these two ratios mean.

E5-11 Analyzing and Interpreting Asset Turnover and Net Profit Margin Ratios

RadioShack Corporation has populated the world with stores from Greece to Canada, and in the United States, an estimated 94 percent of all Americans live or work within five minutes of the electronics retailer—not bad for a company that originally started business as American Hide & Leather Company. The following amounts (in millions) were reported in RadioShack's income statement and balance sheet.

LO1, 7

(R) **RadioShack**®

	2008	2007	2006
Sales Revenue	$4,225	$4,252	$4,778
Net Income	192	237	73
Total Assets	2,284	1,990	2,070
Total Liabilities	1,466	1,220	1,416

(handwritten annotations:) o8   4225   (2284 + 1990)/2   o 7   4252   (1990 + 2070)/2

Required:

1. Compute the asset turnover and net profit margin ratios for 2008 and 2007.
2. Would analysts be more likely to increase or decrease their estimates of stock value on the basis of these changes? Explain what the changes in these two ratios mean.
3. Compute the debt-to-assets ratio for 2008 and 2007.
4. Would analysts be more likely to increase or decrease their estimates of RadioShack's ability to repay lenders on the basis of this change? Explain by interpreting what the change in this ratio means.

E5-12 Determining the Accounting Equation Effects of Transactions

La-Z-Boy Incorporated is a furniture manufacturer. Listed here are typical aggregate transactions from the first quarter of a recent year (in millions). Complete the following table, indicating the sign (+ for increase, − for decrease, and NE for no effect) and amount of the effect of each transaction. Provide an account name for any revenue or expense transactions included in stockholders' equity. Consider each item independently.

a. Repaid $10 on a note payable to a bank. (Interest was paid separately.)
b. Recorded collections of cash from customers who owed $32.

LO3

La-Z-Boy Incorporated

Transaction	Assets	Liabilities	Stockholders' Equity
a	−10	−10	NE
b	+/−32	NE	NE

LO7   **E5-13 Determining the Effects of Transactions on Debt-to-Assets, Asset Turnover, and Net Profit Margin Ratios**

Using the transactions in E5-12, complete the following table by indicating the sign of the effect (+ for increase, − for decrease, NE for no effect, and CD for cannot determine) of each transaction. Consider each item independently.

Transaction	Debt-to-Assets	Asset Turnover	Net Profit Margin
a	−	+	NE
b	NE	NE	NE

LO3, 6, 7   **E5-14 Preparing and Interpreting Financial Statements**

The December 31, 2010 and 2009 adjusted trial balances for Sportlife Gym Corporation are shown below.

	2010		2009	
	Debit	Credit	Debit	Credit
Cash	$ 31,500		$ 30,000	
Accounts Receivable	2,500		2,000	
Supplies	13,000		13,000	
Prepaid Rent	3,000		3,000	
Equipment	350,000		350,000	
Accumulated Depreciation		$ 20,000		$ 10,000
Other Long-term Assets	20,000		12,000	
Accounts Payable		5,000		6,000
Unearned Revenue		72,000		80,000
Income Taxes Payable		13,000		14,000
Long-term Debt		10,000		200,000
Contributed Capital		214,000		50,000
Retained Earnings		50,000		19,400
Dividends Declared	5,000		0	
Membership Revenue		399,000		398,000
Coaching Revenue		11,000		10,000
Coaching and Assistants' Wages	221,000		219,400	
Management Salaries	100,000		100,000	
Facilities Rent Expense	12,000		12,000	
Depreciation Expense	10,000		10,000	
General Operating Expenses	6,150		7,700	
Interest Revenue		750		700
Interest Expense	600		15,000	
Income Tax Expense	20,000		14,000	
	$794,750	$794,750	$788,100	$788,100

Required:

1. Prepare a comparative income statement for 2010 and 2009, a statement of stockholders' equity for 2010, and a comparative classified balance sheet for 2010 and 2009. The income statement should distinguish the gym's core and peripheral results, and group expenses by function (coaching, facilities, and general management). The change in Contributed Capital was caused by the issuance of new stock in 2010.

2. Identify two balance sheet and two income statement accounts that changed significantly in 2010. What might be the cause of these changes?

3. Calculate and interpret the debt-to-assets, asset turnover, and net profit margin ratios in 2010 and 2009. Total assets were $400,000 on December 31, 2008.

E5-15 Preparing Financial Statements using IFRS   LO5

Refer to E5-14.

Required:

1. Prepare a comparative classified statement of financial position, as typically presented using IFRS.
2. Prepare a comparative income statement, which IFRS calls a statement of comprehensive income.
   TIP: Use Exhibit 5.7 as a guide, except group expenses by nature (e.g., salaries and wages, rent, etc.) as outlined in Exhibit 5.11.

E5-16 Finding Financial Statement Information   LO3

Indicate whether each of the following would be reported on the balance sheet (B/S), income statement (I/S), or statement of stockholders' equity (SSE).

1. Insurance costs paid this year, to expire next year. *BS*
2. Insurance costs expired this year. *IS*
3. Insurance costs still owed. *BS*
4. Cost of equipment used up this accounting year. *BS*
5. Equipment book value (carrying value). *BS*
6. Amounts contributed by stockholders during the year. *SSI /BS*
7. Cost of supplies unused at the end of the year. *BS*
8. Cost of supplies used during the accounting year. *IS*
9. Amount of unpaid loans at end of year. *BS*
10. Dividends declared and paid during this year. *SEL*

[Handwritten margin notes:]
I = E & R
B = A & L
SE = CC & RE

COACHED PROBLEMS

CP5-1 Determining the Accounting Equation Effects   LO3
of Transactions

Yahoo! Inc. is a leading provider of Internet products and services. Listed here are selected aggregate transactions from 2008 (in millions). Complete the following table, indicating the sign (+ for increase, − for decrease, and NE for no effect) and amount of the effect of each transaction. Provide an account name for any revenue or expense transactions included in stockholders' equity. Consider each item independently.

www.mhhe.com/phillips3e

a.   Recorded marketing revenues on account of $7,208.
b.   Obtained $363 cash by issuing stock.
c.   Incurred product development expense of $1,222, which was paid in cash.

Transaction	Assets	Liabilities	Stockholders' Equity
a			
b			
c			

CP5-2 Determining the Effects of Transactions on Debt-to-Assets, Asset   LO7
Turnover, and Net Profit Margin Ratios

Using the transactions in CP5-1, complete the following table by indicating the sign of the effect (+ for increase, − for decrease, NE for no effect, and CD for cannot determine) of each transaction. Consider each item independently.

TIP: To determine the impact of a transaction on a ratio, try an example with numbers. For example, assume asset turnover ratios of 9/10 or 10/9 and see how an increase of 1 in the top and bottom numbers affects the ratios.

TIP: A = L + SE implies that total assets are almost always greater than total liabilities. This means that if assets and liabilities change by the same dollar amount, the impact on liabilities will be proportionally bigger than the impact on assets.

Transaction	Debt-to-Assets	Asset Turnover	Net Profit Margin
a			
b			
c			

L07   CP5-3 Interpreting Debt-to-Assets, Asset Turnover, and Net Profit Margin Ratios

Best Buy Co. Inc.
GameStop Corp.

The following ratios for Best Buy Co. Inc. and its competitor GameStop Corp. were obtained from reuters.com/finance. Compare the two companies based on the following ratios:

Ratio	Best Buy	GameStop Corp.
Debt-to-assets	0.42	0.21
Asset turnover ratio	2.42	2.10
Net profit margin	2.69%	4.35%

Required:

1. Which company appears to rely more on debt financing? Describe the ratio that you used to reach this decision, and explain what the ratio means.

2. Which company appears to use its assets more efficiently? Describe the ratio that you used to reach this decision, and explain what the ratio means.

3. Which company appears to better control its expenses? Describe the ratio that you used to reach this decision, and explain what the ratio means.

LO5, 6, 7   CP5-4 Preparing and Interpreting IFRS Financial Statements

H&M

H&M is a retail clothing company headquartered in Sweden with operations in 33 countries, including 169 stores in the United States. The company began its 2008 fiscal year with assets totaling 41,734 (in millions of Swedish krona) but ended the year (on November 30, 2008) with 51,243 in total assets. Account balances on November 30, 2008, are listed below (in millions of Swedish krona).

Accounts Payable	3,658	Long-term Liabilities	2,414
Accounts Receivable	3,197	Other Current Liabilities	4,534
Accrued Liabilities	3,687	Other Non-current Assets	1,775
Accumulated Depreciation	9,243	Prepaid Expenses	948
Buildings and Equipment	21,616	Profit for the Year (Net Income)	15,294
Contributed Capital	1,617	Retained Earnings, Dec. 1, 2007	20,039
Goodwill and Intangible Assets	1,656	Sales Revenues	192,573
Land	68	Stock-in-Trade (Inventory)	8,500
Liquid Funds (Cash)	22,726		

Required:

1. Prepare a statement of financial position at November 30, 2008, using Exhibit 5.12 as a guide.
   TIP: Not all of the accounts listed are reported on the Statement of Financial Position.

2. Use an appropriate ratio to compute H&M's financing risk. Compare H&M's ratio to the 0.126 reported for Volcom (a clothing company headquartered in California) on December 31, 2008. Which company appears more likely to pay its liabilities?

3. Use an appropriate ratio to compute the amount of profit H&M earns from each dollar of sales. Compare H&M's ratio to that of Volcom, which earned 6.5 cents of profit for each dollar of sales in the year ended December 31, 2008.

4. Use an appropriate ratio to compute H&M's efficiency at using assets to generate sales. Compare H&M's ratio to the 1.58 reported for Volcom for the year ended December 31, 2008.

GROUP A PROBLEMS

www.mhhe.com/phillips3e

PA5-1 Determining the Accounting Equation Effects of Transactions

LO3

Papa John's International began in the back of a tavern in Jeffersonville, Indiana, and has since become the third-largest pizza company in America. Listed here are transactions that typically occur each year (in millions). Complete the following table, indicating the sign (+ for increase, − for decrease, and NE for no effect) and amount of the effect of each transaction. Provide an account name for any revenue or expense transactions included in stockholders' equity. Consider each item independently.

a. Repaid bank loan payable of $7. (Interest was paid separately.)
b. Paid cash to purchase property and equipment costing $6.
c. Purchased additional property and equipment costing $2 by issuing a note payable.
d. Recorded franchise royalty revenues on account of $20.

Transaction	Assets	Liabilities	Stockholders' Equity
a			
etc.			

PA5-2 Determining the Effects of Transactions on Debt-to-Assets, Asset Turnover, and Net Profit Margin Ratios

LO7

Using the transactions in PA5-1, complete the following table by indicating the sign of the effect (+ for increase, − for decrease, NE for no effect, and CD for cannot determine) of each transaction. Consider each item independently.

www.mhhe.com/phillips3e

Transaction	Debt-to-Assets	Asset Turnover	Net Profit Margin
a			
etc.			

PA5-3 Interpreting Debt-to-Assets, Asset Turnover, and Net Profit Margin Ratios

LO7

Kohl's Corporation
Dillard's, Inc.

The following ratios for Kohl's Corporation and its competitor Dillard's, Inc., were obtained from reuters.com/finance. Compare the two companies based on the following ratios:

Ratio	Kohl's	Dillard's
Debt-to-assets	0.24	0.35
Asset turnover ratio	1.50	1.39
Net profit margin	5.4%	−3.4%

Required:

1. Which company appears to rely more on debt for financing? Describe the ratio that you used to reach this decision, and explain what the ratio means.
2. Which company appears to use its assets more efficiently? Describe the ratio that you used to reach this decision, and explain what the ratio means.
3. Which company appears to better control its expenses? Describe the ratio that you used to reach this decision, and explain what the ratio means.

PA5-4 Preparing and Interpreting IFRS Financial Statements

LO5, 6, 7

Glücklich Golfspieler (GG) is a golf club company headquartered in Germany. The company began its 2009 fiscal year with assets totaling 10 million euro but ended the year (on December 31, 2010) with 13 million euro of total assets. Account balances on December 31, 2010, appear below (in thousands of euro).

Accounts Payable	1,000	Contributed Capital	400	Other Non-current Assets	400
Accounts Receivable	500	Goodwill and Intangible Assets	450	Prepaid Expenses	250
Accrued Liabilities	900	Inventory	2,500	Profit for the Year (Net Income)	4,000
Accumulated Depreciation	2,500	Land	100	Retained Earnings, Jan. 1, 2010	5,000
Buildings and Equipment	5,500	Notes Payable, due 2012	600	Sales Revenues	44,000
Cash	5,800	Other Long-term Liabilities	1,100		

Required:

1. Prepare a statement of financial position at December 31, 2010, using Exhibit 5.12 as a guide.
2. Use an appropriate ratio to compute GG's financing risk. Compare GG's ratio to the 0.20 reported for one of its close competitors. Which company appears more likely to pay its liabilities?
3. Use an appropriate ratio to compute the amount of profit GG earns from each euro of sales. Compare GG's ratio to its competitor, which had a ratio of 0.05. Which company is better able to control its expenses?
4. Use an appropriate ratio to compute GG's efficiency at using assets to generate sales. Compare GG's ratio to the 2.60 reported for its competitor. Which company is more efficient at using its assets to generate sales?

GROUP B PROBLEMS

LO3

Regal Entertainment Group

PB5-1 Determining the Accounting Equation Effects of Transactions

Regal Entertainment Group is the largest movie company in the world, taking in over 20 percent of the box office receipts in the United States. Listed here are transactions that typically occur each quarter (in millions). Complete the following table, indicating the sign (+ for increase, − for decrease, and NE for no effect) and amount of the effect of each transaction. Provide an account name for any revenue or expense transactions included in stockholders' equity. Consider each item independently.

a. Paid cash to purchase property and equipment costing $30.
b. Declared and paid a cash dividend totaling $40.
c. Recorded depreciation on property and equipment totaling $78.
d. Recorded cash admissions revenues of $450.

Transaction	Assets	Liabilities	Stockholders' Equity
a			
etc.			

LO7

PB5-2 Determining the Effects of Transactions on Debt-to-Assets, Asset Turnover, and Net Profit Margin Ratios

Using the transactions in PB5-1, complete the following table by indicating the sign of the effect (+ for increase, − for decrease, NE for no effect, and CD for cannot determine) of each transaction. Consider each item independently.

Transaction	Debt-to-Assets	Asset Turnover	Net Profit Margin
a			
etc.			

PB5-3 Interpreting Debt-to-Assets, Asset Turnover, and Net Profit Margin Ratios

LO7

i'm lovin' it

YUM Brands, Inc.

The following ratios for McDonald's Corporation and its competitor YUM Brands, Inc., (the owner of KFC, Pizza Hut, and Taco Bell) were obtained from reuters.com/finance. Compare the two companies based on the following ratios:

Ratio	McDonald's	YUM
Debt-to-Assets	0.43	0.99
Asset Turnover Ratio	0.81	1.64
Net Profit Margin	18.34%	8.6%

Required:

1. Which company appears to rely more on debt than stockholders' equity for financing? Describe the ratio that you used to reach this decision, and explain what the ratio means.

2. Which company appears to use its assets more efficiently? Describe the ratio that you used to reach this decision, and explain what the ratio means.

3. Which company appears to better control its expenses? Describe the ratio that you used to reach this decision, and explain what the ratio means.

PB5-4 Preparing and Interpreting IFRS Financial Statements

LO5, 6, 7

Latteria Limited (LL) is a dairy company headquartered in Italy. The company began its 2009 fiscal year with assets totaling 9 million euro but ended the year (on December 31, 2010) with 13 million euro of total assets. Account balances on December 31, 2010, appear below (in thousands of euro).

Accounts Payable	1,300	Cash	1,200	Prepaid Expenses	250
Accounts Receivable	500	Contributed Capital	400	Profit for the Year (Net Income)	2,200
Accrued Liabilities	600	Inventory	2,500	Retained Earnings, Jan. 1, 2010	6,800
Accumulated Depreciation	3,600	Land	5,550	Sales Revenues	22,000
Buildings and Equipment	6,600	Notes Payable, due 2012	1,700		

Required:

1. Prepare a statement of financial position at December 31, 2010, using Exhibit 5.12 as a guide.

2. Use an appropriate ratio to compute LL's financing risk. Compare LL's ratio to the 0.40 reported in a recent year for Saputo, Inc. (a dairy company based in Montreal, Canada). Which company appears more likely to pay its liabilities?

3. Use an appropriate ratio to compute the amount of profit LL earns from each euro of sales. Compare LL's ratio to Saputo, which had a ratio of 0.06. Which company is better able to control its expenses?

4. Use an appropriate ratio to compute LL's efficiency at using assets to generate sales. Compare LL's ratio to the 1.94 reported for Saputo. Which company is more efficient at using its assets to generate sales?

SKILLS DEVELOPMENT CASES

S5-1 Finding Financial Information

LO7

Refer to the financial statements of The Home Depot in Appendix A at the end of this book, or download the annual report from the *Cases* section of the text's Web site at www.mhhe.com/phillips3e.

Required:

1. Calculate the debt-to-assets ratio at February 1, 2009, and February 3, 2008. Based on these calculations, has The Home Depot's financing become more or less risky over these two years?

2. Calculate the asset turnover ratio for the February 2009 and 2008 year-ends. The Home Depot's total assets at the end of fiscal 2007 were $52,263 million. Based on these calculations, has The Home Depot used its assets more or less efficiently in 2008–2009 than in 2007–2008?

3. Calculate the net profit margin ratio for 2008–2009 and 2007–2008. Based on these calculations, has The Home Depot generated more or less profit per dollar of sales in 2008–2009 than in 2007–2008?

LO6, 7

Lowe's

S5-2 Comparing Financial Information

Refer to the financial statements of The Home Depot in Appendix A and Lowe's in Appendix B at the end of this book, or download the annual reports from the *Cases* section of the text's Web site at www.mhhe.com/phillips3e.

Required:

1. Calculate the debt-to-assets ratio for Lowe's at January 30, 2009. Based on this calculation, was Lowe's financing more or less risky than The Home Depot's at the end of January 2009?

2. Calculate the asset turnover ratio for Lowe's for the year ended January 30, 2009. Lowe's total assets at the end of fiscal 2007 were $30,869 million. Based on this calculation, did Lowe's use its assets more or less efficiently than The Home Depot in 2008–2009?

3. Calculate the net profit margin ratio for Lowe's for the year ended January 30, 2009. Based on this calculation, did Lowe's generate more or less profit per dollar of sales than The Home Depot in 2008–2009?

LO6, 7

S5-3 Internet-Based Team Research: Examining an Annual Report

As a team, select an industry to analyze. Using your Web browser, each team member should access the annual report or 10-K for one publicly traded company in the industry, with each member selecting a different company (see S1-3 in Chapter 1 for a description of possible resources for these tasks).

Required:

1. On an individual basis, each team member should write a short report that incorporates the following:
   a. Calculate the debt-to-assets ratio at the end of the current and prior years, and explain any change between the two years.
   b. Calculate the asset turnover ratio at the end of the current and prior years and explain any change between the two years. (To calculate average assets for the prior year, you will need the total assets number for the beginning of the prior year. If this isn't reported in the summarized financial data section in the current annual report, you will need to get it from the prior year's annual report or 10-K.)
   c. Calculate the net profit margin ratio at the end of the current and prior years and explain any change between the two years.

2. Then, as a team, write a short report comparing and contrasting your companies using these attributes. Discuss any patterns across the companies that you observe as a team. Provide potential explanations for any differences discovered.

LO1, 2, 7

Aurora Foods Inc.

S5-4 Ethical Decision Making: A Real-Life Example

On February 18, 2000, the board of directors of Aurora Foods Inc.—the maker of Duncan Hines® and Mrs. Butterworth's® products—issued a press release announcing that a special committee had been formed to conduct an investigation into the company's accounting practices. During the financial statement audit for the year ended December 31, 1999, Aurora's auditors had discovered documents that raised questions about how the company accounted for marketing costs incurred to entice grocery stores to promote Aurora's products. The company's stock price fell by 50 percent in the week following this announcement.

After nearly a year of investigation, Aurora filed revised quarterly reports with the SEC, showing that the company had not accrued adequately for liabilities and expenses that had been incurred during the third and fourth quarters of 1998 and during the first three quarters of 1999. Key financial figures for these quarters as initially reported and as later restated are shown below.

(in millions of U.S. dollars)	1998 Q3 (September 30)		1998 Q4 (December 31)		1999 Q1 (March 31)		1999 Q2 (June 30)		1999 Q3 (September 30)	
	Initial Report	Restated Report	Initial Report	Restated Report	Initial Report	Restated Report	Initial Report	Restated Report	Initial Report	Restated Report
Assets	$1,457	$1,455	$1,434	$1,448	$1,474	$1,463	$1,558	$1,521	$1,614	$1,553
Liabilities	869	879	830	868	862	882	937	944	983	972
Revenues	220	219	280	277	261	254	222	214	238	231
Net income (loss)	1	(12)	16	5	8	0	8	(4)	11	4

The SEC also investigated and filed a legal claim alleging that Aurora's 36-year-old chief financial officer (CFO) had violated federal securities laws by instructing accounting staff to make false journal entries and prepare two sets of records—one for the company's internal use and another to be provided to the auditors. The SEC alleged that her actions allowed Aurora to meet the net income targets set by Wall Street analysts and the expectations of Aurora investors and to obtain loans from Chase Manhattan Bank and other lenders. The CFO pled guilty to the charges, was sentenced to 57 months in prison, was barred for life from ever serving as an executive of a public company, and had to return to the company the stock and bonuses that had been awarded to her on the basis of Aurora's false and substantially inflated financial results.

Epilogue: On December 8, 2003, Aurora Foods filed for bankruptcy protection after violating several of its lenders' loan covenants. On March 19, 2004, Aurora emerged from bankruptcy and has since merged with Pinnacle Foods, the maker of Vlasic pickles and Swanson TV dinners.

Required:

1. Using the initially reported numbers, calculate the debt-to-assets, asset turnover, and net profit margin ratios at the end of each quarter. (Note that the asset turnover ratio will be substantially less than the examples shown earlier in this chapter because they use only three months of revenues. Do not attempt to convert them to annual amounts.)

2. Using the restated numbers, calculate the debt-to-assets, asset turnover, and net profit margin ratios at the end of each quarter.

3. On an overall basis, did the initially reported numbers suggest more or less financing risk than the restated numbers? Of the financial statement users mentioned earlier in this chapter in Exhibit 5.1, which would be most influenced by this impact on the debt-to-assets ratio?

4. On an overall basis, did the initially reported numbers or the restated numbers present Aurora's efficiency in using assets to generate sales in a better light? Of the financial statement users mentioned earlier in this chapter in Exhibit 5.1, which would be most influenced by this impact on the asset turnover ratio?

5. On an overall basis, did the initially reported numbers or the restated numbers present Aurora's profitability in a better light? Of the financial statement users mentioned earlier in this chapter in Exhibit 5.1, which would be most influenced by this impact on the net profit margin ratio?

6. What important role(s) did Aurora's auditors play in this case?

7. Based on specific information in the case, identify the incentives or goals that might have led the CFO to misreport Aurora's financial results. Looking back at the consequences of her dishonest actions, did she fulfill those goals in the short run and long run? Speculate about how the requirements of the Sarbanes-Oxley Act might have affected the CFO, had this legislation existed prior to 1998.

S5-5 Ethical Decision Making: A Mini-Case   LO1, 2, 7

Assume you've been hired to replace an accounting clerk for a small public company. After your second month on the job, the chief financial officer (CFO) approached you directly with a "special project." The company had just finished installing a new production line earlier in the year, and the CFO wanted you to go through all of the company's expense accounts with the goal of finding any costs that might be related to the machinery's installation or to "tinkering with it" to get the line working just right. He said that the previous accounting clerk, whom you had replaced, didn't understand that these costs should have been recorded as part of the production line (an asset) rather than as expenses of the period. The CFO indicated that there was some urgency, as the company had to finalize its quarterly financial statements so that they could be filed with the SEC. Also, the company was close to violating its loan covenants and it needed a few extra dollars of profit this quarter to ensure the bank didn't demand immediate repayment of the loan. As you thought about this situation, you tried to remember what Chapter 2 in your accounting textbook said regarding the key characteristics of assets.

Required:

1. Which of the three ratios discussed in this chapter (debt-to-assets, asset turnover, and net profit margin) are affected by the decision to record costs as an asset rather than an expense? Indicate whether each ratio will be higher or lower if costs are recorded as an asset rather than an expense.
2. Is there anything in the case that makes you uncomfortable with the work that you've been asked to do?
3. What should you do?

LO2, 7

S5-6 Critical Thinking: Analyzing Income Statement–Based Executive Bonuses

Callaway Golf believes in tying executives' compensation to the company's performance as measured by accounting numbers. Suppose, in a recent year, Callaway had agreed to pay its executive officers bonuses if (a) asset turnover meets or exceeds 0.8, and (b) net profit margin meets or exceeds 5.0 percent. Their bonuses will be even larger if asset turnover meets (or exceeds) 1.6 and net profit margin meets (or exceeds) 7.0 percent. Total assets were $855 (million) and $838 (million) at December 31, 2008 and 2007, respectively. For the year ended December 31, 2008, total sales revenue was $1,117 (million) and net income was $66 (million).

Required:

1. Use the preceding information to determine whether Callaway executives met the two bonus targets in 2008.
2. Explain why the bonus arrangement might be based on both asset turnover and net profit margin ratios, rather than just one of these two ratios.

LO6, 7

www.mhhe.com/phillips3e

Hershey Foods Corporation

S5-7 Computing, Charting, and Interpreting Time-Series and Cross-Sectional Analyses

Assume that *Candy Industry Magazine* has contracted you to write an article discussing the financial status of Hershey Foods Corporation over the last few years. The editor suggests that your article should also compare Hershey's recent financial performance to competitors like Tootsie Roll Industries and Rocky Mountain Chocolate Factory. You gather the following information from the 2008 10-Ks of the three companies.

(in millions of U.S. dollars)	Hershey Foods Corporation			Tootsie Roll Industries	Rocky Mountain Chocolate Factory
	2006	2007	2008	2008	2008
Total Liabilities	$3,474	$3,626	$3,285	$177	$ 4
Total Assets	4,157	4,247	3,634	812	16
Sales Revenues	4,944	4,947	5,133	496	32
Net Income	559	214	311	39	5

Required:

Enter the above information into a spreadsheet and perform the following analyses:

1. *Time-series analysis:* Demonstrate the changes in Hershey's size over the three years by charting its total liabilities, total assets, sales revenues, and net income.

2. *Cross-sectional analysis:* Demonstrate the size of Hershey relative to Tootsie Roll and Rocky Mountain Chocolate Factory by charting the three companies' total liabilities, total assets, sales revenues, and net income for 2008.

3. *Ratio analysis:* Compare the performance of Hershey relative to Tootsie Roll and Rocky Mountain Chocolate Factory by computing the debt-to-assets and net profit margin ratios for 2008.

CONTINUING CASE

Mc Graw Hill **connect**™

|ACCOUNTING   LO7

CC5 Evaluating the Impact of Typical Transactions

After finishing her first year of operations, Nicole used the debt-to-assets, asset turnover, and net profit margin ratios to determine how effective she was in running the business. Listed here are a few company transactions from the past quarter that may have influenced these ratios.

a. Acquired, but haven't yet paid for, equipment costing $320.
b. Recorded spa treatment revenues of $1,500 on account.
c. Incurred advertising expense of $40, paid in cash.
d. Accrued $750 for utility bills.
e. Received $50,000 cash from an investor in exchange for company shares.
f. Received $2,500 cash by signing a note payable.
g. Recorded $1,800 in depreciation expense.
h. Customers used $200 of gift certificates to pay for spa services.

Required:

1. Complete the following table, indicating the effects (account, amount, and direction) of each transaction. Use + for increase, − for decrease, and NE for no effect.

Transaction	Assets	Liabilities	Stockholders' Equity
a			
etc.			

2. Complete the following table, indicating the sign (+ for increase, − for decrease, and NE for no effect) for each transaction. Assume that, prior to recording items (a)–(h), Nicole's Getaway Spa had more assets than liabilities, more revenues than net income, and more revenues than average assets.

Transaction	Debt-to-Assets	Asset Turnover	Net Profit Margin
a			
etc.			

CHAPTER 6

Internal Control and Financial Reporting for Cash and Merchandise Sales

YOUR LEARNING OBJECTIVES

Understand the business

LO1   Distinguish among service, merchandising, and manufacturing operations.

LO2   Explain common principles and limitations of internal control.

Study the accounting methods

LO3   Apply internal control principles to cash receipts and payments.

LO4   Perform the key control of reconciling cash to bank statements.

LO5   Explain the use of a perpetual inventory system as a control.

LO6   Analyze sales transactions under a perpetual inventory system.

Evaluate the results

LO7   Analyze a merchandiser's multistep income statement.

Review the chapter

THAT WAS
THEN

Earlier chapters have focused on companies whose operating activities relate to providing services to customers, rather than selling goods.

Lecture Presentation-LP6
www.mhhe.com/phillips3e

FOCUS COMPANY: Wal-Mart

www.walmart.com

Seventeen years after the company was founded, Wal-Mart rang up yearly sales of $1 billion. Fourteen years later, it sold that much in a week. Thanks to you and the 200 million other Americans who shop at Wal-Mart, its sales now average over $1 billion a day. And that's not all. Wal-Mart has been able to earn sizable profits, even during difficult economic times. One secret to its success is the state-of-the-art accounting system that controls Wal-Mart's merchandise sales and cash collections. In this chapter, you will learn about this kind of system and the other aspects of merchandising companies that make them unique and interesting. You'll also learn how to analyze a merchandiser's financial statements to figure out the amount of mark-up that it includes in the prices you pay. You might be surprised by how much you're contributing to Wal-Mart's profits.

THIS IS
NOW

This chapter focuses on companies that sell merchandise to customers, and the way they control and report their operating results.

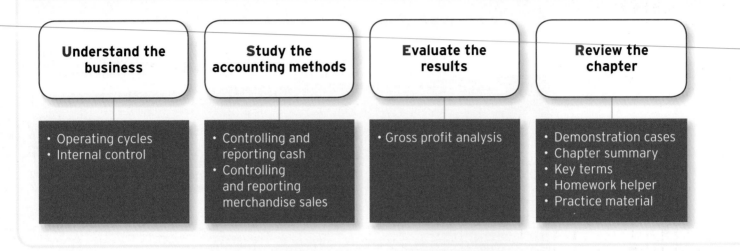

Understand the business	Study the accounting methods	Evaluate the results	Review the chapter
• Operating cycles • Internal control	• Controlling and reporting cash • Controlling and reporting merchandise sales	• Gross profit analysis	• Demonstration cases • Chapter summary • Key terms • Homework helper • Practice material

Understand the Business

OPERATING CYCLES

Learning Objective 1
Distinguish among service, merchandising, and manufacturing operations.

For any company to be successful, it must be able to efficiently circle through its operating cycle. **The operating cycle is a series of activities that a company undertakes to generate sales and, ultimately, cash.** Exhibit 6.1 contrasts the operating cycles of three types of businesses: (1) service companies, (2) merchandising companies, and (3) manufacturing companies.

Service companies such as WorldGym follow a simple operating cycle: sell services to customers, collect cash from them, and use that money to pay for operating expenses. **Merchandising companies** differ in that their cycle begins with buying products. These products, which are called Inventory, are sold to customers, which leads to collecting cash that can be used to pay for operating expenses and buy more inventory. Merchandising companies such as Wal-Mart and Costco are called **retailers** when they sell directly to individual consumers and **wholesalers** when they sell their inventory to retail businesses for resale to consumers. This chapter applies equally to both retail and wholesale merchandisers. This chapter does not include **manufacturing companies** such as Mattel and Goodyear because they make their own products from raw materials rather than acquire them in a ready-to-sell format. The manufacturing process involves complexities that require much more discussion than is possible in this introductory course. Consequently, accounting for manufacturing companies is discussed in detail in managerial and cost accounting courses.

YOU SHOULD KNOW

Service company: Sells services rather than physical goods.
Merchandising company: Sells goods that have been obtained from a supplier. **Manufacturing company:** Sells goods that it has made itself.

A goal of most merchandising companies is to generate more and more cash by reducing the time they take to circle through their operating cycles. To promote this efficiency, companies establish and follow specific procedures and policies that describe how the business is to be run. These procedures and policies are called **internal controls.** In your personal life, internal controls include basic precautions such as locking your car door and checking the accuracy of your bank statement. As you will learn in the following section, similar controls apply to all government, not-for-profit, and business organizations, both large and small. When internal controls operate effectively, they contribute not only to improving operating efficiency, but also to reducing waste, minimizing unintentional

YOU SHOULD KNOW

Internal controls: Methods to protect against theft of assets, enhance the reliability of accounting information, promote efficient and effective operations, and ensure compliance with applicable laws and regulations.

EXHIBIT 6.1	Operating Cycles for Service, Merchandising, and Manufacturing Companies

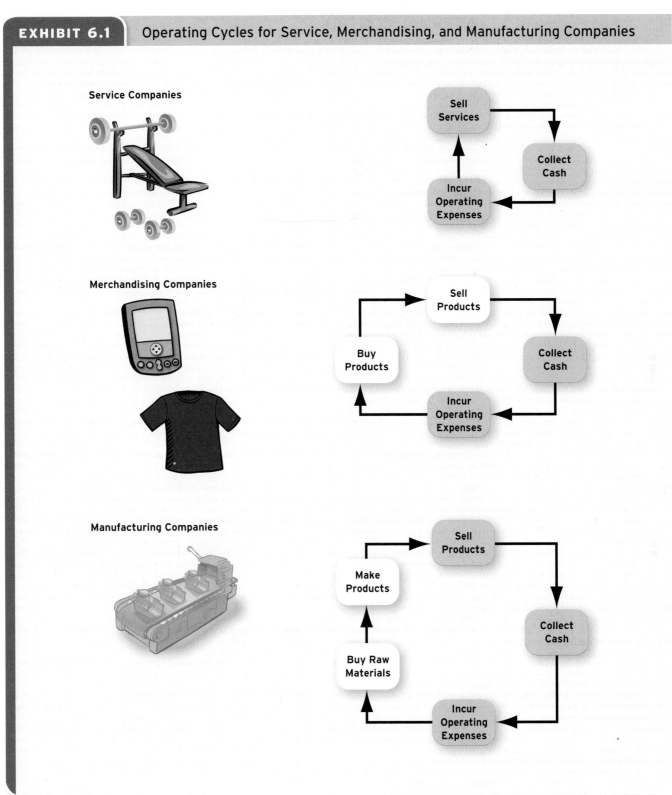

errors, and deterring fraud. It's little wonder, then, that Wal-Mart has established strong internal controls at each of its 7,200 store locations, to ensure the company's transactions are processed with efficiency, consistency, accuracy, and honesty.

Learning Objective 2
Explain common principles
and limitations of internal
control.

INTERNAL CONTROL

Internal control has always been important to all types and sizes of organizations. However, with the business failures and accounting scandals involving Enron and other companies in the early 2000s, internal control has gained a lot more attention. As you may recall from Chapter 5, the Sarbanes-Oxley (SOX) Act requires public companies to report on and have an independent auditor assess the effectiveness of internal controls over financial reporting. These rules have led companies to strengthen their internal controls and better inform financial statement users about how effective their accounting systems are in producing accurate financial statements. **Effective internal controls play an essential role in creating an ethical business environment** and in improving financial performance.[1]

Common Control Principles

From the perspective of a company's chief executive officer (CEO), chief financial officer (CFO), and board of directors, internal control is a broad concept that includes more than accounting. It includes setting strategic objectives, identifying risks the company faces, hiring good employees, instilling ethical principles in them, motivating them to achieve the company's objectives, and providing the resources and information they need to fulfill those objectives. Rather than overwhelm you with the list of 20 control principles that senior executives must think about,[2] we focus on just five basic principles that you are likely to see in your own work. We want you to understand why certain types of control exist so that when you encounter them during your career, you will appreciate them and ensure that others respect them.

Video 6.1
www.mhhe.com/phillips3e

All good systems of internal control are based on these five common principles, which are summarized in Exhibit 6.2. These principles are typically applied to all aspects of a company's business activities, including human resource management, finance, marketing, and general business operations. Our focus here, however, is on their relationship to accounting.

1 Establish responsibility. Whenever possible, assign each task to only one employee. Doing so will allow you to determine who caused any errors or thefts that occur. That's the reason Wal-Mart assigns a separate cash register drawer to each employee at the beginning of a shift. If two cashiers were to use the same drawer, it would be impossible to know which cashier caused the drawer to be short on cash. With only one person responsible for adding and removing money from the drawer, there's no doubt about who is responsible for a cash shortage.

YOU SHOULD KNOW

Segregation of duties: An
internal control designed
into the accounting system
to prevent an employee from
making a mistake or commiting
a dishonest act as part of one
assigned duty, and then also
covering it up through another
assigned duty.

2 Segregate duties. **Segregation of duties** involves assigning responsibilities so that one employee can't make a mistake or commit a dishonest act without someone else knowing it. That's why cashiers at Wal-Mart need a manager to approve price changes at the checkout. Without this control, cashiers could lower the sales price for a friend. Segregation of duties is most effective when a company assigns responsibilities for related activities to two or more people and assigns responsibilities for recordkeeping to people who do not handle the assets that they are accounting for. One employee should not initiate, approve, record, and have access to the items involved in the same transaction.

---

[1]One study found that companies emphasizing strong internal control and an ethical culture grew their revenues four times faster and increased their stock prices 12 times as much as companies without these practices. "Corporate Culture and Performance," by J.P. Kotter and J.L. Heskett, New York: Maxwell MacMillan International.

[2]These 20 principles are outlined in "Internal Control for Financial Reporting—Guidance for Smaller Public Companies," published June 2006 at www.coso.org by The Committee of Sponsoring Organizations (COSO).

EXHIBIT 6.2	Five Common Principles of Internal Control

Principle	Explanation	Examples	
① Establish responsibility	Assign each task to only one employee.	Each Wal-Mart cashier uses a different cash drawer.	
② Segregate duties	Do not make one employee responsible for all parts of a process.	Wal-Mart cashiers, who ring up sales, do not also approve price changes.	
③ Restrict access	Do not provide access to assets or information unless it is needed to fulfill assigned responsibilities.	Wal-Mart secures valuable assets such as cash and restricts access to its computer systems (via passwords, firewalls).	
④ Document procedures	Prepare documents to show activities that have occurred.	Wal-Mart pays suppliers using prenumbered checks.	
⑤ Independently verify	Check others' work.	Wal-Mart compares the cash balances in its accounting records to the cash balances reported by its bank, and accounts for any differences.	

③ **Restrict access.** Some controls involve rather obvious steps such as physically locking up valuable assets and electronically securing access to other assets and information. Wal-Mart restricts access to check-signing equipment, requires a password to open cash registers, and protects computer systems with firewalls. The company provides access to important assets and valuable information on an as-needed basis. If employees do not need assets or information to fulfill their assigned responsibilities, they are denied access.

④ **Document procedures.** Digital and paper documents are such common features of business that you may not realize they represent an internal control. By documenting each business activity, a company creates a record of whether goods were shipped, customers were billed, cash was received, and so on. Without these documents, a company wouldn't know what transactions have been or need to be entered into the accounting system. To enhance this control, most companies assign sequential numbers to their documents and then check at the end of every accounting period that each document number corresponds to one and only one accounting entry. Wal-Mart's computer system automatically assigns sequential numbers to cash sales so that the accounting staff can ensure that every sale has been recorded.

⑤ **Independently verify.** A business can perform independent verification in various ways. The most obvious is to hire someone (an auditor) to check that the work done by others within the company is appropriate and supported by documentation. Independent verification also can be made part of a person's job. For example, before Wal-Mart issues a check to pay the bill for a truckload of merchandise, a clerk first verifies that the bill relates to goods actually received and is calculated correctly. A third form of independent verification involves comparing the company's accounting information to information kept by an independent third party. For example, the company may compare internal cash records to a statement of account issued by the bank. The next section of this chapter demonstrates this procedure, called a bank reconciliation.

Control Limitations

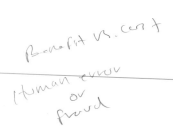

Internal controls can never completely prevent and detect errors and fraud for two reasons. First, an organization will implement internal controls only to the extent that their benefits exceed their costs. Wal-Mart could nearly eliminate shoplifting by body searching every customer who leaves the store, but such an irritating policy would soon drive customers away. The cost of the lost sales would far exceed the benefits of reduced shoplifting. For smaller companies, the cost of hiring additional employees to fully segregate duties exceeds the benefits. In these cases, other controls such as independent verification by top management must compensate for the lack of segregation of duties. A second limitation is that internal controls can fail as a result of human error or fraud. People do make simple mistakes in performing control procedures, especially if they are tired, careless, or confused. Criminally minded employees have been known to **override** (disarm) internal controls or **collude** (work together) to get around them.

Spotlight On CONTROLS

Is That a Control, Too?

The five principles covered in this section do not represent all possible forms of internal control. Many other policies and procedures exist, some of which contribute in subtle ways to internal control. For example, most businesses establish a **mandatory vacation** policy for employees who handle cash because it is difficult for them to cover prior thefts while they are away from the business. Another simple control is an **anonymous hotline** that allows anyone to tip off independent auditors about suspected fraud. The Association of Certified Fraud Examiners claims that more than 46 percent of workplace fraud cases are identified in this way. A final example of a control that can limit losses from theft is **bonding** employees, which involves obtaining an insurance policy that partially reimburses the organization for losses caused by employee fraud.

Study the Accounting Methods

CONTROLLING AND REPORTING CASH

Learning Objective 3
Apply internal control principles to cash receipts and payments.

Internal control of cash is important to any organization for two main reasons. First, because the volume of transactions affecting cash is enormous, any errors that are made in handling cash can quickly add up. By our estimates, Wal-Mart received about $405 billion from customers in 2009 and paid $380 billion for inventory, wages, and other operating expenses. Second, because cash is valuable, portable, and "owned" by the person who possesses it, thieves often target it. The Association of Certified Fraud Examiners reports that 86 percent of all known asset thefts involve cash. The following discussion describes common applications of internal control principles to cash receipts and cash payments.

Cash Receipts

Businesses can receive cash in two different ways. They can receive it in person at the time of a sale, or they can receive it from a remote source as payment on an account. Most businesses, including Wal-Mart, receive cash either physically, in the form of dollars, coins, and checks payable to the business, or through electronic transactions involving credit cards, debit cards, and electronic funds transfers. Generally speaking, Wal-Mart applies similar controls to cash received in both these forms, so in the following discussion, we do not distinguish between them. Regardless of the way or form in which a business receives cash, **the primary internal control goal for cash receipts is to ensure that the business receives the appropriate amount of cash and safely deposits it in the bank.**

Cash Received in Person To properly segregate duties involving cash receipts, specific responsibilities are established and usually assigned to three different employee groups, as shown in the left side of Exhibit 6.3. First, cashiers are responsible for collecting cash and issuing a receipt at the point of sale. Second, a supervisor is responsible for taking custody of the cash at the end of each cashier's shift and depositing it in the bank. Third, members of the accounting staff are responsible for ensuring that the receipts from cash sales are properly recorded in the accounting system. If this segregation of duties did not exist, employees could steal the cash and cover up the theft by changing the accounting records. Segregating the duties ensures that those who handle the cash (the cashiers and supervisor) do not have access to those who record it (the accounting staff).

The cash register, shown in Exhibit 6.3, performs three important functions: (1) it restricts access to cash, (2) it documents the amount charged for each item sold, and (3) it summarizes the total cash sales. By restricting access, the cash register reduces the risk of cash being lost or stolen. In documenting each item sold (both on screen and on a paper receipt), the cash register reduces errors by allowing customers to dispute overcharges should they occur. By summarizing the total cash sales, the cash register provides an independent record of the amount of cash the cashier should have collected and passed on for deposit at the bank. This record is securely forwarded to the accounting department (see the **black arrow** in Exhibit 6.3). The cashier also uses it to complete a cash count sheet at the end of each shift (see the red arrow in Exhibit 6.3).

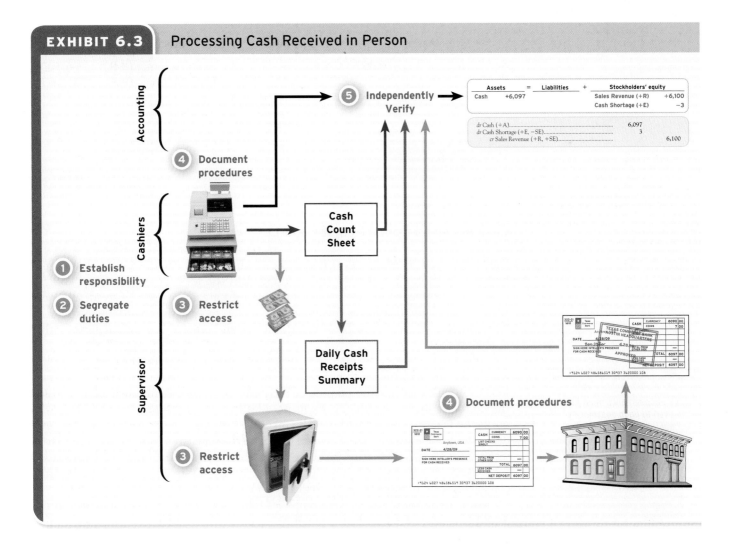

EXHIBIT 6.3 | **Processing Cash Received in Person**

The **cash count sheet** is used to determine the amount of cash available for deposit at the bank. The cash count sheet documents the amount of cash the cashier received and determines any cash short or over that occurred during the shift. The supervisor independently verifies each cashier's count sheet and prepares a daily cash receipts summary that summarizes all cashiers' count sheets and sends one copy to the accounting department (see the blue arrow in Exhibit 6.3). The supervisor is also responsible for placing the cash in a locked safe until the end of the day, at which time it is taken to the bank for deposit. At that time, a deposit slip listing the amounts included in the deposit is prepared and presented to the bank for a teller to verify. After verifying and receiving the funds, the bank teller stamps the deposit slip, which is then forwarded to the company's accounting department. The green arrows in Exhibit 6.3 indicate this process.

The accounting department compares the record of cash sales maintained by the cash register with the count sheet prepared by the cashier, the daily cash receipts summary prepared by the supervisor, and the stamped bank deposit slip returned by the bank (see Exhibit 6.3). This comparison provides independent verification that the amount of cash rung up at the time of sale was deposited into the bank account. Based on this information, a journal entry is prepared to record Sales Revenue at the amount rung up by the cash register and Cash at the amount deposited in the bank. Any difference between the two amounts is recorded in a Cash Shortage (or Overage) account, which is reported on the income statement as a miscellaneous expense (or revenue). For example, if cashiers rung up sales totalling $6,100, but had only $6,097 to deposit, the following financial statement effects would be recorded with the journal entry that follows.

1 Analyze

	Assets		=	Liabilities	+	Stockholders' Equity	
Cash	+ 6,097					Sales Revenue (+R)	+6,100
						Cash Shortage (+E)	−3

2 Record

dr Cash (+A)..	6,097	
dr Cash Shortage (+E, −SE)	3	
cr Sales Revenue (+R, +SE)		6,100

Cash Received from a Remote Source

Cash Received by Mail   Businesses receive checks in the mail when customers pay on account. Because this cash is not received in the form of currency and coins, a cashier is not needed to enter these amounts into a cash register. Instead, the clerk who opens the mail performs this function. In fact, to visualize the following description, you need only glance back at Exhibit 6.3 and replace the cash register with a mail clerk.

Like a cash register, the mail clerk lists all amounts received on the cash receipt list, which also includes the customers' names and the purpose of each payment. The customer typically explains the purpose of the payment using a **remittance advice**, which the customer includes with the payment. Ideally, someone supervises the clerk who opens the mail to ensure that he or she takes no cash receipts for personal use. As evidence of this supervision, both the mail clerk and the supervisor sign the completed cash receipts list. To ensure that no one diverts the checks for personal use, the clerk stamps each check "For Deposit Only," which instructs the bank to deposit the check in the company's account rather than exchange it for cash.

After these steps have been completed, the cash received is separated from the record of cash received, and each follows a separate route similar to the routes shown in

COACH'S TIP

Because payments must be credited to each customer's account, it is important that the cash receipt list include the customer's name and payment purpose.

Exhibit 6.3 (page 259). Checks and money orders are given to the person who prepares the bank deposit whereas the cash receipts list and remittance advices are sent to the accounting department. The accounting department then independently verifies that all cash received by mail was deposited in the bank by ensuring that the total on the cash receipts list equals the stamped deposit slip received from the bank. The accounting department then uses the cash receipts list to record the journal entries that debit Cash and credit Accounts Receivable from each customer.

Cash Received Electronically   Businesses also receive payments from customers via **electronic funds transfer (EFT).** An EFT occurs when a customer electronically transfers funds from its bank account to the company's bank account. Most businesses encourage customers to use EFTs because they speed up collections. A company may not receive mailed payments for five to seven days, but it receives EFTs immediately. And because these payments are deposited directly into the company's bank account, EFTs eliminate the need for some internal controls. To process an EFT, the accounting department merely records journal entries to debit Cash and credit each customer's account receivable.

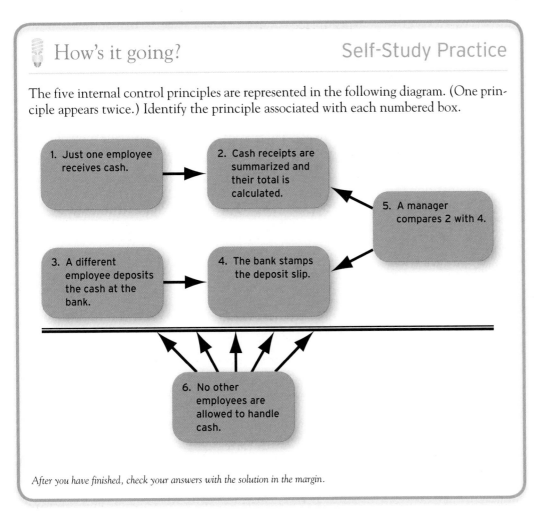

How's it going?   Self-Study Practice

The five internal control principles are represented in the following diagram. (One principle appears twice.) Identify the principle associated with each numbered box.

1. Just one employee receives cash.

2. Cash receipts are summarized and their total is calculated.

3. A different employee deposits the cash at the bank.

4. The bank stamps the deposit slip.

5. A manager compares 2 with 4.

6. No other employees are allowed to handle cash.

After you have finished, check your answers with the solution in the margin.

Solution to Self-Study Practice
1. Establish responsibility
2. Document procedures
3. Segregate duties
4. Document procedures
5. Independently verify
6. Restrict access

Cash Payments

Companies rarely use dollar bills and coins to pay for purchases. Instead, most cash payments involve (1) writing a check to a supplier, or (2) paying employees via EFT. **The primary goal of internal controls for cash payments is to ensure that the business pays only for properly authorized transactions.**

Cash Paid by Check for Purchases on Account   Most businesses purchase goods and services on account and pay for them later by check. Purchases and payments cause increases and decreases in Accounts Payable, so they are closely controlled for financial reporting reasons. Control over purchases and payments is also important to avoid inefficiency and fraud. Because companies incur substantial internal costs to process each transaction with a supplier, controls that promote efficiency can significantly improve a company's profits. Companies can also avoid or reduce losses due to fraud by having strong internal controls. A 2008 report by the Association of Certified Fraud Examiners estimated that most fraud losses involved falsified purchases (24 percent of cases) or illegitimate payments (15 percent of cases).

Most companies rely on a voucher system to control these transactions. A **voucher system** is a process for approving and documenting all purchases and payments made on account. The voucher includes the documents prepared at each step in the system. See Exhibit 6.4 for the typical steps involved in obtaining goods or services from a supplier and the documentation prepared at each step. Exhibit 6.4 also gives some examples of the related cash controls and applicable control principles. **Study this exhibit in detail,** noticing how at each step employee responsibilities are limited to specific tasks that occur only after obtaining and documenting proper authorization in the prior step. The purchasing, receiving, and bill payment duties are segregated to ensure that the company obtains and pays only for the goods or services that have been properly authorized.

Cash Paid to Employees via Electronic Funds Transfer   Most companies pay cash to their employees through EFTs, which are known by employees as **direct deposits.** The company initiates the EFT when it instructs its bank to transfer the net pay due each employee directly from the company's bank account to each employee's checking account. This system is convenient and efficient for the employer because it eliminates

YOU SHOULD KNOW

Voucher system: A process for approving and documenting all purchases and payments on account.

EXHIBIT 6.4 | **Steps, Documentation, and Controls in a Voucher System**

Steps	Documentation	Sample Control(s)		Control Principle
1. Request that goods or services be ordered.	Purchase requisition	Ensure that the request is made by someone who is approved to order goods or services of the type and amount requested.	1	Establish responsibility.
2. Order goods or services.	Purchase order	Place the order only with approved suppliers at approved prices.	3	Restrict access.
3. Receive goods or services.	Receiving report	Record goods received.	4	Document procedures.
		Notify the accounting department so that the purchase and liability can be recorded.	2	Segregate duties.
4. Obtain bill for goods or services.	Supplier invoice	Ensure that the supplier charges only for items received at approved prices.	5	Independently verify.
5. Write check to pay the bill.	Company check	Use prenumbered checks and account for their sequence. Missing checks may signal theft.	4	Document procedures.
		Make payments only when a purchase is supported by complete voucher documentation.	5	Independently verify.
		Mark the voucher "paid" after each check is written to avoid duplicating the payment.	4	Document procedures.
		Notify the accounting department of the payment so that it can be recorded.	2	Segregate duties.

the tasks of physically writing and distributing the checks and for the employee who has access to the funds without having to deposit a check. One risk, however, is that the bank might accidentally overpay or underpay an employee by transfering the wrong amount of money out of the company's bank account.

To avoid this risk, many companies use an imprest system for paying employees. An **imprest system** restricts the total amount paid to others by limiting the amount of money available to be transferred. Using an imprest payroll system, the company instructs the bank to transfer the total net pay of all employees for the pay period out of the company's general bank account and into a special payroll account established for that purpose. Then the bank transfers the individual amounts from the payroll account to the employees' checking accounts. If the transfers occur without error, the special payroll account equals zero after all employees have been paid. If the account is overdrawn or a balance remains, the company knows that an error has occurred.

An imprest payroll system is one example of how banking procedures can help a company control its cash. Other basic banking procedures contribute to a company's internal control, as discussed in the next section.

YOU SHOULD KNOW

Imprest system: A process that controls the amount paid to others by limiting the total amount of money available for making payments to others.

Bank Procedures and Reconciliation

Banks provide important services to individuals and businesses. They accept deposits, process payments to others, and provide statements that account for these and other transactions. Their services help businesses to control cash in several ways:

Learning Objective 4
Perform the key control of reconciling cash to bank statements.

1. **Restricting access.** Because banks provide a secure place to deposit cash, businesses need to keep only a limited amount of cash on hand, which reduces the risk that it will be stolen or misplaced.

2. **Documenting procedures.** By processing payments made by check or EFT, banks facilitate and document business transactions.

3. **Independently verifying.** Company accountants can use the statement of account prepared by the bank to double-check the accuracy of the cash records. By comparing these two sets of records and investigating any differences, they can verify that the company's records are accurate or identify necessary adjustments.

The process of comparing two sets of records is called reconciling. Thus, the internal accounting report that compares the company's cash records with the bank's is a **bank reconciliation**. A bank reconciliation is a key internal control because it provides independent verification of all cash transactions that the bank has processed for the company. This procedure is done monthly, ideally by a company employee whose duties are segregated from recording and handling cash. You should prepare a bank reconciliation in your own life too, every month. To prepare a bank reconciliation, you must first understand the items on a bank statement.

YOU SHOULD KNOW

Bank reconciliation: An internal report prepared to verify the accuracy of both the bank statement and the cash accounts of a business or individual.

Bank Statement   Large businesses such as Wal-Mart can have many bank accounts. For each account a business opens, the bank generates a monthly statement that it either mails to the business or makes available online. The format varies from bank to bank, but the statement in Exhibit 6.5 is typical. This statement, prepared by Texas Commerce Bank for one of the accounts opened by Wonderful Merchandise and Things (WMT), provides an overall summary of the activity in the account (labeled ① in Exhibit 6.5). The summary is followed by a list of specific transactions posted to the account (labeled ② through ④) and a running balance in the account (labeled ⑤). In the following section, we explain the transactions that caused changes in the account's balance.

Checks Cleared   After a check is written, the payee (to whom the check is written) usually presents the check to a financial institution for deposit or cash. That financial institution contacts the check writer's bank, which in turn withdraws the amount of the check from the check writer's account and reports it as a deduction on the bank statement. The check is then said to have **cleared the bank.**

EXHIBIT 6.5 | Sample Bank Statement

TEXAS COMMERCE BANKING ONLINE

★ TEXAS COMMERCE BANK

| Transfer | Account | Payment | Options | Services | Help | | Log Out |

Details   Print Statement   Daily Activity Report

STATEMENT

★ Texas Commerce Bank

Austin
NATIONAL ASSOCIATION

7TH & LAVACA
AUSTIN, TEXAS 78789
PHONE: 512/555-6611

ACCOUNT NUMBER	STATEMENT DATE
877-95861	6-30-2010

Wonderful Merchandise and Things (WMT)
1000 Blank Road
Austin, Texas 78703

STATEMENT OF ACCOUNT
Please examine statement and checks
promptly. If no error is reported within ten
days, the account will be considered correct.
Please report change of address.
For questions or problems
call TCB-Austin's Hotline—555-6100

BALANCE LAST STATEMENT	CHECKS CLEARED		DEPOSITS MADE		OTHER		BALANCE THIS STATEMENT
	No.	Total Amount	No.	Total Amount	No.	Net Amount	
7,762.40	4	$720.00	2	$3,500.00	4	$96.00	$10,638.40

Date	Checks Cleared		Deposits Made	Other Transactions		Daily Balance
06-01						7,762.40
06-06	#100	500.00	3,000.00			10,262.40
06-19	#101	55.00				10,207.40
06-23	#102	100.00	500.00			10,607.40
06-24				Interest earned	20.00	10,627.40
06-25				NSF check	18.00	10,609.40
06-26				EFT deposit	100.00	10,709.40
06-30	#104	65.00		Service charge	6.00	$10,638.40

MEMBER F.D.I.C.

Checks are listed on the bank statement in the order in which they clear the bank. Look closely at column ② in Exhibit 6.5 and you will see that four checks cleared the bank in June. Because WMT's checks are used in their prenumbered order, the bank statement provides a hint that check 103 did not clear the bank this month. (This fact will be important later when we prepare the bank reconciliation.)

Deposits Made   Deposits are listed on the bank statement in the order in which the bank processes them. If you make a deposit after the bank closes (using an ATM or a night deposit chute), it will not appear on the bank statement until the bank processes it the following business day. Knowing this detail will help you to prepare the bank reconciliation.

Other Transactions   The balance in a bank account can change for a variety of reasons other than checks and deposits. For example, the account balance increases when the account earns interest and when funds are transferred into the account electronically. The account balance decreases when the bank charges a service fee or transfers funds out of the account electronically.

To understand how these items are reported on a bank statement, it is important to realize that the bank statement is presented from the bank's point of view. The amounts in a company's bank account are liabilities to the bank because they will eventually be used by or returned to the company. As with all liabilities, increases are reported as credits on the bank statement. Amounts that are removed from a bank account reduce the bank's liability, so they are reported as debits on the bank statement. Banks typically explain the reasons for these increases (credits) and decreases (debits) with symbols or in a short memo, appropriately called a credit memo or debit memo.

🏈 **COACH'S TIP**

Bank statements often refer to checks as debits and deposits as credits. This apparent reversal of debit and credit rules occurs because the bank reports from its perspective, not yours. To the bank, your account is a liability that decreases when you take money out (debit the liability) and increases when you deposit money (credit the liability).

Need for Reconciliation   A bank reconciliation involves comparing the company's records to the bank's statement of account to determine whether they agree. The company's records can differ from the bank's records for two basic reasons: (1) the company has recorded some items that the bank doesn't know about at the time it prepares the statement of account or (2) the bank has recorded some items that the company doesn't know about until the bank statement arrives. Exhibit 6.6 lists specific causes of these differences, which we discuss below.

1. **Bank errors.** Bank errors happen in real life, just as they do in Monopoly. If you discover a bank error, you should ask the bank to correct its records, but you should not change yours.

2. **Time lags.** Time lags are common. A time lag occurs, for example, when you make a deposit after the bank's normal business hours. *You* know you made the deposit, but your bank does not know until it processes the deposit the next day. Time lags involving deposits are called deposits in transit. Another common time lag is an outstanding check. This lag occurs when you write and mail a check to a company, but your bank doesn't find out about it until that company deposits the check in its own bank, which then notifies your bank. As you will see later, although deposits in transit and outstanding checks may be a significant part of a bank reconciliation, they do not require any further action on your part because you have already recorded them.

3. **Interest deposited.** You may know that your bank pays interest, but you probably do not know exactly how much interest you'll get because it varies depending on the average balance in your account. When you read your bank statement, you'll learn how much interest to add to your records.

4. **Electronic funds transfer (EFT).** It doesn't happen every day, but occasionally funds may be transferred into or out of your account without your knowing about it. If you discover these electronic transfers on your bank statement, you will need to adjust your records.

5. **Service charges.** These are the amounts the bank charges for processing your transactions. Rather than send you a bill and wait for you to pay it, the bank just takes the amount directly out of your account. You will need to reduce the Cash balance in your accounting records for these charges.

6. **NSF checks.** Checks that were deposited in the bank but were later rejected ("bounced") because of insufficient funds in the check writer's account are referred to as **NSF (not sufficient funds) checks.** Because the bank increased your account when the check was deposited, the bank decreases your account when it discovers that the deposit was not valid. You will need to reduce your Cash balance by the amount of these bounced checks (and any additional bank charges), and you will have to try to collect these amounts from the check writer.

7. **Your errors.** You may have made mistakes or forgotten to record some amounts in your checkbook. If so, you will need to adjust your records for these items.

> **YOU SHOULD KNOW**
>
> **Checks:** Another name for bounced checks. **NSF (not sufficient funds):** They arise when the check writer (your customer) does not have sufficient funds to cover the amount of the check.

EXHIBIT 6.6	Reconciling Differences

Your Bank May Not Know About	You May Not Know About
1. Errors made by the bank	3. Interest the bank has put into your account
2. Time lags	4. Electronic funds transfers (EFTs)
a. Deposits that you made recently	5. Service charges taken out of your account
b. Checks that you wrote recently	6. Customer checks you deposited but that bounced
	7. Errors made by you

> **COACH'S TIP**
>
> You'll need to adjust your cash records only for items that appear on the right-hand side of this table.

Bank Reconciliation   The ending cash balance as shown on the bank statement does not usually agree with the ending cash balance shown by the related Cash account on the books of the company. For example, the Cash account of WMT at the end of June might contain the information shown in the following T-account.

dr +		Cash (A)			cr −
June 1 balance	7,762.40				
June 6 deposit	3,000.00		500.00	Check # 100 written June 4	
June 23 deposit	500.00		55.00	Check # 101 written June 17	
June 30 deposit	1,800.00		100.00	Check # 102 written June 20	
			145.00	Check # 103 written June 24	
			56.00	Check # 104 written June 30	
			815.00	Check # 105 written June 30	
Ending balance	11,391.40				

Notice that WMT's ending cash balance of $11,391.40 differs from the $10,638.40 ending cash balance shown on the bank statement in Exhibit 6.5 (page 264). To determine the appropriate cash balance, these balances need to be reconciled.

Exhibit 6.7 shows the bank reconciliation prepared by WMT for the month of June. The completed reconciliation finds that the up-to-date cash balance is $11,478.40, an amount that differs from both the bank's statement and WMT's accounting records. This balance is the amount that WMT will report as Cash on its balance sheet after adjusting its records with the journal entries that we present later.

To prepare the bank reconciliation in Exhibit 6.7, WMT compared the entries in its Cash account to the bank statement (Exhibit 6.5) with the following goals:

1. **Identify the deposits in transit.** A comparison of WMT's recorded deposits with those listed on the bank statement revealed that WMT made a deposit of $1,800 on June 30 that was not listed on the bank statement. More than likely, the bank will process this deposit the next business day (July 1). WMT doesn't have to change its records for this item because it already was in WMT's books on June 30. It is simply a timing difference so WMT entered the amount on the bank reconciliation as an addition to update the bank's records.

2. **Identify the outstanding checks.** A comparison of the checks listed on the bank statement with the company's record of written checks showed checks numbered 103 and 105 were still outstanding at the end of June (that is, they had not cleared

---

EXHIBIT 6.7   Sample Bank Reconciliation

WMT BANK RECONCILIATION
At June 30, 2010

UPDATES TO BANK STATEMENT			UPDATES TO COMPANY'S BOOKS	
Ending cash balance per bank statement		$10,638.40	Ending cash balance per books	$11,391.40
Additions			Additions	
(1) Deposit in transit		1,800.00	(3a) Interest received from the bank	20.00
		12,438.40	(3b) EFT received from customer	100.00
				11,511.40
Deductions				
(2) Outstanding checks:			Deductions	
# 103	145.00		(3c) NSF check of R. Smith	18.00
# 105	815.00	960.00	(3d) Bank service charges	6.00
Up-to-date ending cash balance		$11,478.40	(4) Error in recording check no. 104	9.00
			Up-to-date ending cash balance	$11,478.40

the bank). They were entered on the reconciliation (in Exhibit 6.7) as a deduction from the bank account because the bank will eventually reduce the account balance when these checks clear the bank. (WMT had already deducted Checks 103 and 105 from its cash records.)

3. **Record other transactions on the bank statement.**
   a. **Interest received** from the bank, $20—entered on the bank reconciliation in Exhibit 6.7 as an addition to the book balance because it's included in the bank balance but not yet in the company's books.
   b. **Electronic funds transfer** received from customer, $100—entered on the bank reconciliation as an addition to the book balance because it's included in the bank balance but not yet in the company's books.
   c. **NSF check** rejected, $18—entered on the bank reconciliation as a deduction from the book balance because it was deducted from the bank statement balance but has not yet been deducted from the company's cash records.
   d. **Service charges,** $6—entered on the bank reconciliation as a deduction from the book balance because it has been deducted from the bank balance but not yet removed from the Cash account in the company's books.

4. **Determine the impact of errors.** After performing the three steps listed above, WMT found that the reconciliation was out of balance by $9. Upon checking the journal entries made during the month, WMT found that Check 104 was recorded in the company's accounts as $56 when, in fact, the check had been filled out for $65 (in payment of Accounts Payable). As Exhibit 6.5 shows on page 264, the bank correctly processed the check (on June 30) as $65. To correct its own error, WMT must deduct $9 ($65 − $56) from the Company's Books side of the bank reconciliation.

Now that we know the up-to-date cash balance is $11,478.40, we need to prepare and record journal entries that will bring the Cash account to that balance. Remember that the entries on the Bank Statement side of the bank reconciliation do not need to be adjusted by WMT because they will work out automatically when the bank processes them next month. Only the items on the Company's Books side of the bank reconciliation need to be recorded in the company's records, using the following journal entries:

COACH'S TIP

This example involves the company's error in recording the amount of the check. In other cases, the bank errs if it processes the check at the wrong amount. In all instances, the amount written on the check is the correct amount at which the transaction should be recorded.

Interest Received:
(a) dr Cash (+A) 20
    cr Interest Revenue (+R, +SE) 20
    To record interest received from the bank.

EFT Received from Customer:
(b) dr Cash (+A) 100
    cr Accounts Receivable (−A) 100
    To record electronic funds transfer received from customer.

Customer's Check Rejected as NSF:
(c) dr Accounts Receivable (+A) 18
    cr Cash (−A) 18
    To record amount rejected by bank and still owed by customer.

Service Charges:
(d) dr Office Expenses (+E, −SE) 6
    cr Cash (−A) 6
    To record service charge deducted by bank.

Company Error (Understated Payment to Supplier):
(e) dr Accounts Payable (−L) 9
    cr Cash (−A) 9
    To correct error made in recording a check paid to a creditor.

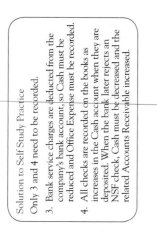

Solution to Self Study Practice

Only 3 and 4 need to be recorded.

3. Bank service charges are deducted from the company's bank account, so Cash must be reduced and Office Expense must be recorded.

4. All checks are recorded on the books as increases in the Cash account when they are deposited. When the bank later rejects an NSF check, Cash must be decreased and the related Accounts Receivable increased.

How's it going?   Self-Study Practice

Indicate which of the following items discovered when preparing a bank reconciliation for Target will need to be recorded in the Cash account on the company's books.

1. Outstanding checks.

2. Deposits in transit.

3. Bank service charges.

4. NSF checks that were deposited.

After you have finished, check your answers with the solution in the margin.

YOU SHOULD KNOW

Cash: Money or any instrument that banks will accept for deposit and immediate credit to a company's account. **Cash equivalents:** Short-term, highly liquid investments purchased within three months of maturity.

Reporting Cash and Cash Equivalents   The account called Cash on the balance sheet includes **cash** deposited with banks as well as cash on hand (also called petty cash) and cash equivalents. **Cash equivalents** are short-term, highly liquid investments purchased within three months of maturity. They are considered equivalent to cash because they are both readily convertible to known amounts of cash and so near to maturity that there is little risk their value will change. In your personal life, cash equivalents could include certificates of deposit (CDs) you've purchased within three months of maturity.

Spotlight On CONTROLS   www.mhhe.com/phillips3e

Granny Does Time

Grandmothers seem so trustworthy. But in one well-known case, a granny stole nearly half a million dollars from the small company where she worked as a bookkeeper. How did she do it? It was easy because the owner knew little accounting, so he gave her responsibility for all of the company's accounting work but never independently verified her work. Granny realized this lack of internal control gave her unlimited opportunity, so she wrote checks to herself and recorded them as inventory purchases. Then, when she did the bank reconciliation, she destroyed the checks to cover her tracks. Granny kept this fraud going for eight years, but then confessed after becoming overwhelmed with guilt. If you're wondering why no one ever became suspicious about the recorded inventory purchases that didn't actually occur, keep reading. The next section will tell you why.

Learning Objective 5
Explain the use of a perpetual inventory system as a control.

Video 6.2
www.mhhe.com/phillips3e

CONTROLLING AND REPORTING MERCHANDISE SALES

The success of all merchandisers depends on their ability to sell large quantities of merchandise at prices that exceed their cost. Knowing this, merchandisers spend a great deal of time and money tracking their inventory transactions. A strong accounting system plays three roles in this process:

1. It provides information on inventory quantities so that managers can control inventory levels.

2. It provides information on inventory costs so that managers can set appropriate selling prices.

3. It provides information for preparing financial statements, which can be used to evaluate the amount of profit generated from merchandise sales in the current period. Until inventory is sold, it is an asset reported at its cost on the balance sheet. After inventory is sold, its cost is removed from the balance sheet and reported on the income statement as an expense, called Cost of Goods Sold. The difference between the selling price (reported as Sales Revenue) and the Cost of Goods Sold is the gross profit earned by the merchandiser.

To perform these functions, companies can use either of two types of inventory accounting system: perpetual or periodic.

Perpetual Inventory System

A **perpetual inventory system** updates inventory records every time an item is bought, sold, or returned. You may not realize it, but the bar-code readers at Wal-Mart's checkouts serve two purposes: (1) they calculate and record the sales revenue for each product you're buying, and (2) they remove the product and its cost from Wal-Mart's inventory records. Similar scanners are used back in the "employees only" part of the store, where products are unloaded from the trucks or returned to suppliers. As a result of this continuous, or "perpetual," updating, the balances in Wal-Mart's Inventory and Cost of Goods Sold accounts are always up to date.

YOU SHOULD KNOW

Perpetual inventory system: Inventory records are updated "perpetually," every time inventory is bought, sold, or returned.

Periodic Inventory System

Unlike a perpetual system, which updates the inventory records immediately after each purchase, sale, and return of merchandise, a **periodic inventory system** updates the inventory records only at the end of the accounting period. Although simple to maintain, a major drawback of a periodic system is that accurate records of the inventory on hand and the inventory that has been sold are unavailable. To determine these amounts, employees must physically count the inventory, which they do at the end of the period, when the store is "closed for inventory." This inventory count is then used to adjust the balances for Inventory and Cost of Goods Sold.

YOU SHOULD KNOW

Periodic inventory system: Inventory records are updated "periodically," at the end of the accounting period. To determine how much merchandise has been sold, periodic systems require that inventory be physically counted at the end of the period.

Inventory Control

A perpetual inventory system provides the best inventory control because its continuous tracking of transactions allows companies to instantly determine the quantity of products on the shelves and to evaluate the amount of time they have spent there. Using this information, companies can better manage their inventory and save a great deal of money in financing and storage charges. This also benefits consumers, who pay less for the products they buy. When companies use less money or labor to produce a product or service, the productivity of our entire economy goes up.

Another benefit of a perpetual inventory system is that it allows managers to estimate **shrinkage,** the term for loss of inventory from theft, fraud, and error. You might wonder how companies can estimate how much of their inventory is missing; because isn't it, by definition, *missing?* They use the information in the perpetual inventory system and their understanding of the following inventory equation. Assume Wal-Mart reports the following for one of its lines of cell phones.

Equation	Quantity		Cost per Unit		Total Cost		Physical inventory count
Beginning Inventory	3	×	$100	=	$300		
+ **Purchases**	3	×	$100	=	300		
− **Goods Sold**	(2)	×	$100	=	(200)	vs.	
= **Ending Inventory**	4	×	$100	=	$400		

Information in the company's perpetual records

Because a perpetual inventory system records all goods purchased and sold, the ending inventory in the company's perpetual records indicates how many units should be on hand. In our example, four units should be on hand at a unit cost of $100, for a total cost of $400. By physically counting the inventory that is actually on hand, the company can determine whether items have been physically removed without being recorded as an approved transaction. In our example, just three units were on hand, so the shrinkage was one unit, with a cost of $100.

Notice that you can't do this kind of detective work with a periodic inventory system because it doesn't provide an up-to-date record of the inventory that should be on hand when you count it. Also note that, even if you're using a perpetual inventory system, you still need to count the inventory occasionally (at least yearly) to ensure the accounting records are accurate and that any shrinkage is detected. If you don't do this physical count, you could end up like the company in the Spotlight on Controls on page 268. The grandmother was able to falsely record payments to herself as if they were inventory purchases because no one checked to see whether the recorded inventory actually existed.

Until recently, perpetual inventory systems were too costly for most merchandisers to implement. Today, however, computerized inventory systems have become so cheap that most merchandisers use a perpetual system. Accordingly, this chapter focuses on the accounting process that perpetual systems use. Because you may still encounter a periodic system, particularly in small companies or large ones that have been slow to switch, we discuss the accounting process for periodic systems in Chapter 7.

Spotlight On ETHICS

Sources of Inventory Shrinkage

Independent verification of inventory quantities is important. A recent study suggests that more than $37 billion of inventory goes missing from U.S. retailers each year.* Although shoplifting is a major cause of shrinkage (accounting for 33 percent of lost units), an even larger portion (47 percent) results from employee theft. To avoid hiring dishonest employees, companies screen job applicants using employment and criminal background checks. To deter and detect employee theft, they use security tags, closed-circuit TV, and complex computer programs that monitor cash registers.

*Richard Hollinger, "2005 National Retail Security Survey," University of Florida, 2006.

Sales Transactions

Learning Objective 6
Analyze sales transactions under a perpetual inventory system.

As required by the revenue principle, merchandisers record revenue when it is earned. Merchandisers earn revenues by making a "sale," which means transferring ownership of merchandise to a customer, either for cash or on credit. For a retail merchandiser like Wal-Mart, this transfer of ownership occurs when a customer buys and takes possession of the goods at checkout. For a wholesale merchandiser who is shipping goods to a customer, the transfer of ownership occurs at a time stated in the written sales agreement. The sales agreement will specify one of two possible times:

YOU SHOULD KNOW

FOB shipping point: A term of sale indicating that goods are owned by the customer the moment they leave the seller's premises. **FOB destination:** A term of sale indicating that goods are owned by the seller until they are delivered to the customer.

1. **FOB shipping point**—the sale is recorded when the goods leave the seller's shipping department.
2. **FOB destination**—the sale is recorded when the goods reach their destination (the customer).

Unless otherwise indicated, the examples in this book assume that ownership transfers when goods are shipped (FOB shipping point), which usually means the buyer pays for all transportation costs.[3]

---

[3] Any transportation costs paid by the seller (called freight-out) are reported as Delivery Expenses on the seller's income statement. Chapter 7 discusses buyers' accounting for transportation costs.

Every merchandise sale has two components, each of which requires an entry in a perpetual inventory system:

1. **Selling price.** Wal-Mart's *sales price* is recorded as an increase in Sales Revenue and a corresponding increase in either Cash (for a cash sale) or Accounts Receivable (for a credit sale).

2. **Cost.** The *cost* that Wal-Mart incurred to initially buy the merchandise is removed from Inventory and reported as an expense called Cost of Goods Sold (CGS).

For example, assume Wal-Mart sells two Schwinn mountain bikes at a selling price of $200 per bike, for a total of $400 cash. The bikes had previously been recorded in Wal-Mart's Inventory at a total cost of $350. This transaction is illustrated, analyzed, and recorded in Exhibit 6.8.

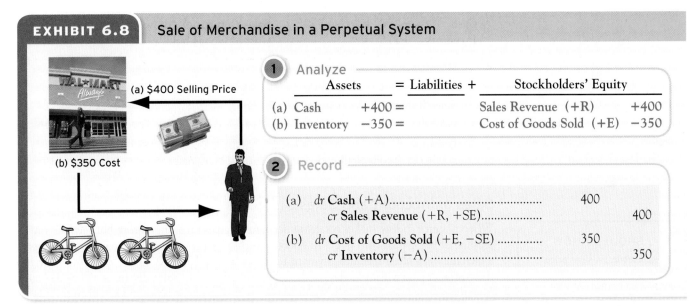

EXHIBIT 6.8 | **Sale of Merchandise in a Perpetual System**

(a) $400 Selling Price

(b) $350 Cost

1 Analyze

	Assets	= Liabilities +	Stockholders' Equity	
(a) Cash	+400 =		Sales Revenue (+R)	+400
(b) Inventory	−350 =		Cost of Goods Sold (+E)	−350

2 Record

(a)	*dr* **Cash** (+A)...	400	
	cr **Sales Revenue** (+R, +SE)..................		400
(b)	*dr* **Cost of Goods Sold** (+E, −SE)	350	
	cr **Inventory** (−A)		350

Notice in Exhibit 6.8 that the first part of Wal-Mart's journal entry involving Cash and Sales Revenue is recorded at the total selling price ($400). The second part involving Cost of Goods Sold and Inventory uses Wal-Mart's total cost ($350). The $50 difference between selling price and cost ($400 − $350) is called the *gross profit*. **Gross profit is not directly recorded in an account by itself,** but instead is a subtotal produced by subtracting Cost of Goods Sold from Sales Revenue on the income statement.

To keep things simple, we use only one Sales Revenue account and one Cost of Goods Sold account for our examples. In the workplace, however, merchandising companies use different Sales and Cost of Goods Sold accounts for different product lines. This allows managers at Wal-Mart to separately evaluate sales of different products. When reporting to external financial statement users, Wal-Mart combines these individual accounts into a single number for Sales and a single number for Cost of Goods Sold, which avoids cluttering its income statement with numerous accounts and also prevents its competitors from discovering details about its sales of specific products.

Sales Returns and Allowances

When goods sold to a customer arrive in damaged condition or are otherwise unsatisfactory, the customer can (1) return them for a full refund or (2) keep them and ask for a reduction in the selling price, called an *allowance*. These **sales returns and allowances** require Wal-Mart to revise the previously recorded sale and, in the case of returns, to revise the previously recorded inventory reduction and cost of goods sold. To illustrate this, suppose that after Wal-Mart sold the two Schwinn mountain bikes, the customer returned one to Wal-Mart. Assuming that the bike is still like new, Wal-Mart would refund the $200 selling price to the customer and take the bike back into inventory.

YOU SHOULD KNOW

Sales returns and allowances: Refunds and price reductions given to customers after goods have been sold and found unsatisfactory.

To account for this transaction, Wal-Mart would make two entries to basically reverse the entries recorded when the bike was sold. We say "basically" because there is one catch: Wal-Mart does not directly reduce its Sales Revenue account. Instead, Wal-Mart tracks sales returns and allowances in a contra-revenue account that is deducted from total sales revenue.

Just as a contra-asset account such as Accumulated Depreciation reduces the total in an asset account such as Equipment, a contra-revenue account such as Sales Returns and Allowances reduces the total in a revenue account such as Sales Revenues. Using a contra-revenue account instead of directly reducing the Sales account allows Wal-Mart to track the value of goods returned, providing clues about whether customers are happy with the quality and price of Wal-Mart's products.[4] Sales returns are recorded as follows:

COACH'S TIP

To indicate that an increase in a contra-revenue account reduces revenues, which reduces stockholders' equity, use (+xR, −SE).

1 Analyze

Assets		=	Liabilities	+	Stockholders' Equity	
Cash	−200	=			Sales Returns & Allowances (+xR)	−200
Inventory	+175	=			Cost of Goods Sold (−E)	+175

2 Record

dr Sales Returns & Allowances (+xR, −SE) 200	
cr Cash (−A)	200
dr Inventory (+A) 175	
cr Cost of Goods Sold (−E, +SE).........................	175

Sales on Account and Sales Discounts

When a merchandiser makes a sale on account, it gives up its inventory but receives only a promise of being paid cash later. To encourage customers to make these payments promptly, a merchandiser often specifies payment terms such as "2/10, n/30." The "2/10" means that if the customer pays within 10 days of the sale date, a 2 percent **sales discount** will be deducted from the selling price. The "n/30" part implies that if payment is not made within the 10-day discount period, the full amount will be due 30 days after the date of sale. See Exhibit 6.9 for an illustration of a 2/10, n/30 sale that occurred on November 1.

When a sales discount is offered to and later taken by the customer, the seller accounts for two transactions: (1) the initial sale, and (2) the sales discount taken by

YOU SHOULD KNOW

Sales discount: A sales price reduction given to customers for prompt payment of their account balance.

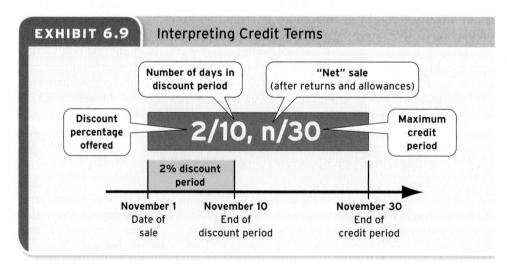

EXHIBIT 6.9 Interpreting Credit Terms

---

[4]We have assumed that the return occurs in the same period as the sale. When significant returns are likely to occur after the period of sale, the seller records an estimate of those expected returns, using methods described in Chapter 8. We also have assumed the returned bike was as good as new. Chapter 7 describes how to account for damaged inventory.

the customer. Suppose Wal-Mart's warehouse store (Sam's Club) sells printer paper on account to a local business for $1,000 with payment terms of 2/10, n/30. The paper cost Sam's Club $700. Wal-Mart accounts for this initial sale as follows:

1 Analyze

Assets		=	Liabilities	+	Stockholders' Equity	
Accounts Receivable	+1,000				Sales Revenue (+R)	+1,000
Inventory	−700				Cost of Goods Sold (+E)	−700

2 Record

dr Accounts Receivable (+A)...	1,000	
cr Sales Revenue (+R, +SE)		1,000
dr Cost of Goods Sold (+E, −SE)..	700	
cr Inventory (−A)..		700

To take advantage of this 2 percent discount, the customer must pay Wal-Mart within 10 days. If the customer does so, it will deduct the $20 discount (2% × $1,000) from the total owed ($1,000), and then pay $980 to Wal-Mart. Wal-Mart accounts for the $20 sales discount using a contra-revenue account, as follows:

1 Analyze

Assets		=	Liabilities	+	Stockholders' Equity	
Cash	+ 980				Sales Discounts (+xR)	−20
Accounts Receivable	−1,000					

2 Record

dr Cash (+A)..	980	
dr Sales Discounts (+xR, −SE)	20	
cr Accounts Receivable (−A)...		1,000

If the customer doesn't pay by the end of the discount period, Wal-Mart would not allow the customer to take a discount for early payment. Instead, the customer would have to pay the full $1,000, which Wal-Mart would record as an increase in Cash (debit) and a decrease in Accounts Receivable (credit). What if a customer doesn't pay at all? We discuss that important issue in detail in Chapter 8.

Before leaving the topic of sales discounts, we should clear up a common misconception. Sales discounts differ from the discount that you get as a consumer buying clearance items at a reduced selling price. Reductions in the selling price of merchandise that occur before a sale is made—what Wal-Mart calls "rolling back" prices—are not captured in the accounting system because they are not transactions. To be considered a transaction, a sales discount must occur after the initial sale has been made. These types of sales discounts are given in business-to-business (B2B) transactions for prompt payment on account. We're sorry to say that, as a consumer, you're not likely to be offered this kind of discount.

Summary of Sales-Related Transactions

The sales returns and allowances and sales discounts introduced in this section were recorded using contra-revenue accounts. Exhibit 6.10 summarizes their effects on sales reporting. See the Homework Helper on page 280 for further illustration.

> **COACH'S TIP**
>
> Sales discounts are calculated after taking into account any sales returns and allowances. Customers that pay a portion of what they owe are entitled to a discount on that portion if they pay within the discount period.

EXHIBIT 6.10	Effects of Sales-Related Transactions on Net Sales

Sales Revenue	$1,400*
Less: Sales Returns and Allowances	(200)
Sales Discounts	(20)
Net Sales	$1,180

* $1,400 = $400 (bikes) + $1,000 (printer paper)

Spotlight On FINANCIAL REPORTING

The Makeup of Net Sales

As you have seen, the documentation procedure involving contra-revenue accounts allows managers to monitor and control how sales discounts, returns, and allowances affect the company's revenues. For example, frequent returns of defective products would show up as an increase in the Sales Returns and Allowances account. In response to such an increase, Wal-Mart's managers might decide to discontinue the product or find a new supplier.

Detailed information relating to sales discounts and returns is a key part of a merchandiser's business operations. To avoid revealing these secrets to competitors, most companies report these contra-accounts only on their internal financial statements as in Exhibit 6.10. Externally reported income statements almost never include contra-revenue accounts. Instead, externally reported income statements begin with **Net Sales.** Despite this secrecy, external financial statement users can still conduct useful financial statement analyses, as we'll see in the next section.

Evaluate the Results

GROSS PROFIT ANALYSIS

Learning Objective 7
Analyze a merchandiser's multistep income statement.

One of the basic facts of merchandising is that to survive, a merchandiser must sell goods for more than their cost. Sure, cash has to be controlled, but the fact remains that there won't be much cash to control unless goods are sold at a profit. That's the only way companies like Wal-Mart can generate enough money to cover their operating expenses. To make it easy for financial statement users to see how much is earned from product sales, without being clouded by other operating costs, merchandise companies often present their income statement using a multistep format.

A **multistep income statement** is similar to what you saw in the first few chapters, with expenses being subtracted from revenues to arrive at net income. The difference is that a multistep format separates the revenues and expenses that relate to core operations from all the other (peripheral) items that affect net income. For merchandisers, a key measure is the amount of profit earned over the cost of goods sold, so their multistep income statements separate Cost of Goods Sold from other expenses. As shown in Exhibit 6.11, this extra step produces a subtotal called **gross profit**, which is the amount the company earned from selling goods, over and above the cost of the goods. If you buy something for $70 and sell it for $100, you'll have a gross profit of $30.

Notice in Exhibit 6.11 that after the gross profit line, the multistep income statement presents other items in a format similar to what you saw for a service company in Chapter 3 (Exhibit 3.2). The category called *Selling, General, and Administrative Expenses* includes a variety of operating expenses including wages, utilities, advertising, rent, and the costs of delivering merchandise to customers. These expenses are subtracted from gross profit to yield Income from Operations, which is a measure of the company's income from regular operating activities, before considering the effects of interest, income taxes, and any nonrecurring items.

YOU SHOULD KNOW

Multistep income statement: Presents important subtotals, such as gross profit, to help distinguish core operating results from other, less significant items that affect net income. **Gross profit** (also called *gross margin* or simply *margin*): Net sales minus cost of goods sold. It is a subtotal, not an account.

| EXHIBIT 6.11 | Sample Multistep Income Statement | Walmart |

On Test

Gross Profit / Net sales

Coming from Trial Balance

WAL-MART STORES, INC.
Income Statements
For the Years Ended January 31
(amounts in millions)

	2009	2008	2007
Net Sales	$405,607	$378,476	$348,368
Cost of Goods Sold	306,158	286,350	263,979
Gross Profit	99,449	92,126	84,389
Selling, General, and Administrative Expenses	76,651	70,174	63,892
Income from Operations	22,798	21,952	20,497
Other Expenses	2,253	2,332	2,859
Income before Income Taxes	20,545	19,620	17,638
Income Tax Expense	7,145	6,889	6,354
Net Income	$ 13,400	$ 12,731	$ 11,284

Gross Profit Percentage

Gross profit % = Gross profit / Net Sales

Let's focus again on the gross profit line on the income statement in Exhibit 6.11. Although the dollar amount of gross profit can be impressive—yes, Wal-Mart really did generate over $99 billion of gross profit in 2009—this number is difficult to interpret by itself. In Exhibit 6.11, we see that Wal-Mart's gross profit increased from 2007 to 2008 to 2009. The difficulty in interpreting this is that Wal-Mart also increased its sales over these three years, so we don't know whether the increase in gross profit dollars arises because Wal-Mart increased its sales volume or whether it is generating more profit per sale. To determine the amount of gross profit included in each dollar of sales, analysts typically evaluate the gross profit percentage.

Accounting Decision Tools		
Name of Measure	**Formula**	**What It Tells You**
Gross profit percentage	$\dfrac{\text{Net Sales} - \text{CGS}}{\text{Net Sales}} \times 100$	• The percentage of profit earned on each dollar of sales, after considering the cost of products sold • A higher ratio means that greater profit is available to cover operating and other expenses

The **gross profit percentage** measures the percentage of profit earned on each dollar of sales. As discussed below, this ratio is used (1) to analyze changes in the company's operations over time, (2) to compare one company to another, and (3) to determine whether a company is earning enough on each sale to cover its operating expenses. A higher gross profit percentage means that the company is selling products for a greater markup over its cost.

As we can see in the graphic in the margin on page 276, Wal-Mart's gross profit percentage increased slightly from 2007 through 2009. Each dollar of sales in 2009

> **YOU SHOULD KNOW**
>
> **Gross profit percentage:** A ratio indicating the percentage of profit earned on each dollar of sales, after considering the cost of products sold.

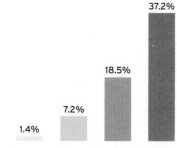

WAL-MART'S GROSS PROFIT PERCENTAGE			
	2009	2008	2007
$\frac{\text{Gross Profit}}{\text{Net Sales}}$	$\frac{\$\ 99,449}{\$405,607}$	$\frac{\$\ 92,126}{\$378,476}$	$\frac{\$\ 84,389}{\$348,368}$
=	0.245	0.243	0.242
	× 100	× 100	× 100
=	24.5%	24.3%	24.2%

included 24.5 cents of gross profit whereas in the prior two years, an average dollar of sales included 24.3 or 24.2 cents of gross profit. So not only did Wal-Mart sell more in 2009 than in the prior years, it also generated more profit per sale. How was this possible? To find out, you could read the Management's Discussion and Analysis section of Wal-Mart's annual report. You'd find out that Wal-Mart has reduced inventory shrinkage and markdowns, which means more profit from each dollar of sales. You might wonder whether it's even worth talking about a gross profit percentage increase of less than half a percent. Just remember that a small change in the gross profit percentage can lead to a big change in net income. In Wal-Mart's case, because the company has such a huge sales volume ($405 billion), even just one-tenth of a percentage point increase in gross profit translates into almost half a billion dollars. Yes, that's billion with a **b** ($405 billion × 0.001 = $0.4 billion).

Comparing Operating Results across Companies and Industries   Be aware that gross profit percentages can vary greatly between companies. Wal-Mart's gross profit percentage of 24.5 percent is characteristic of its slogan of "Saving people money so they can live better." Wal-Mart's strategy is to earn a relatively small amount of profit on each dollar of sales, but to compensate by generating a huge volume of sales. In contrast, high-end department stores carry fashions with high-end prices, resulting in fewer sales, but more profit on each sale. In 2009, Sak's reported a 31.9 percent gross profit percentage.

Gross profit percentages can vary across industries too. Oil and gas companies recently reported an average gross profit percentage of 37.2 percent, which they need to cover their research and exploration expenses.[5]

Gross Profit Percentage by Industry

- 1.4% Consumer Electronics
- 7.2% Drug Stores
- 18.5% Non-alcoholic Beverages
- 37.2% Oil and Gas

REVIEW THE CHAPTER

eXcel

www.mhhe.com/phillips3e

DEMONSTRATION CASE A: BANK RECONCILIATION

Kat Bardash, a student at a small state college, has just received her first checking account statement for the month ended September 30. This was her first chance to attempt a bank reconciliation. The bank's statement of account showed the following:

Bank balance, September 1	$1,150
Deposits during September	650
Checks cleared during September	900
Bank service charge	25
Interest earned	5
Bank balance, September 30	880

Kat was surprised that her bank had not yet reported the deposit of $50 she made on September 29 and was pleased that a check she wrote for $200 had not cleared her account. Her September 30 checkbook balance was $750.

Required:

1. Complete Kat's bank reconciliation. What adjustments, if any, does she need to make in her checkbook?

2. Why is it important for individuals and businesses to do a bank reconciliation each month?

---

[5]Industry statistics were retrieved on April 13, 2009, from www.reuters.com/finance/industries.

Suggested Solution

1. Kat's bank reconciliation:

Updates to Bank Statement		Updates to Kat's Books	
September 30 cash balance	$ 880	September 30 cash balance	$750
Additions		Additions	
Deposit in transit	50	Interest earned	5
Deductions		Deductions	
Outstanding check	(200)	Bank service charge	(25)
Up-to-date cash balance	$ 730	Up-to-date cash balance	$730

Kat should increase her checkbook balance by $5 for the cash given by the bank for interest and reduce her checkbook balance by $25 for the cash given to the bank for service charges. In journal entry format, this would involve:

dr Cash (+A)	5	
cr Interest Revenue (+R, +SE)		5
dr Office Expenses (+E, −SE)..	25	
cr Cash (−A)		25

2. Bank statements, whether personal or business, should be reconciled each month to help ensure that a correct balance is reflected in the depositor's books. Failure to reconcile a bank statement increases the chance that an error will not be discovered and may result in NSF checks being written. Businesses reconcile their bank statements for an additional reason: The up-to-date balance that is calculated during reconciliation is reported on the balance sheet.

DEMONSTRATION CASE B: MERCHANDISE SALES

Sunglass Hut

Assume Oakley, Inc.—the maker of sunglasses, goggles, and other products—made merchandise costing $137,200 and sold it on credit to Sunglass Hut for $405,000 with terms 2/10, n/30. Some of the merchandise differed from what Sunglass Hut had ordered, so Oakley agreed to give an allowance of $5,000. Sunglass Hut satisfied the remaining balance (of $400,000) by paying within the discount period.

Required:

1. Assuming that Oakley uses a perpetual inventory system, analyze the accounting equation effects and record the journal entries that Oakley would use for the following transactions:
    a. Sale from Oakley to Sunglass Hut.
    b. Allowance granted by Oakley.
    c. Payment made by Sunglass Hut to Oakley.
2. Compute Oakley's net sales, assuming that sales returns and allowances and sales discounts are treated as contra-revenues.
3. Compute Oakley's gross profit and gross profit percentage on the sale. Compare this ratio to the 66.5 percent gross profit percentage earned in 2008 by the Luxottica Group—the Italian company that makes Killer Loop® and Ray-Ban® sunglasses, which are sold through its Sunglass Hut stores. What does it imply about the two companies?

Suggested Solution

1. **a.** Sale from Oakley to Sunglass Hut

① Analyze

Assets	= Liabilities +	Stockholders' Equity
Accounts Receivable +405,000		Sales Revenue (+R) +405,000
Inventory −137,200		Cost of Goods Sold (+E) −137,200

② Record

dr Accounts Receivable (+A)...	405,000	
cr Sales Revenue (+R, +SE)		405,000
dr Cost of Goods Sold (+E, −SE)...	137,200	
cr Inventory (−A)		137,200

b. Allowance granted by Oakley

① Analyze

Assets	= Liabilities +	Stockholders' Equity
Accounts Receivable −5,000		Sales Returns and Allowances (+xR) −5,000

② Record

dr Sales Returns and Allowances (+xR, −SE)........................	5,000	
cr Accounts Receivable (−A).....................................		5,000

c. Payment made by Sunglass Hut to Oakley

① Analyze

Assets	= Liabilities +	Stockholders' Equity
Cash +392,000		Sales Discounts (+xR) −8,000
Accounts Receivable −400,000		

② Record

dr Cash (+A)...	392,000	
dr Sales Discounts (+xR, −SE)	8,000	
cr Accounts Receivable (−A).....................................		400,000

2. Sales returns and allowances and sales discounts should be subtracted from sales revenue to compute net sales:

COACH'S TIP

Transaction b depicts an allowance but no return of goods. Had goods been returned, Oakley also would increase its Inventory and decrease its Cost of Goods Sold.

Sales Revenue		$405,000
Less: Sales Returns and Allowances		5,000
Sales Discounts		8,000*
Net Sales		392,000
*$8,000 = 2% × ($405,000 − $5,000)		

3. Gross profit and gross profit percentage are calculated as follows:

	In Dollars	Percent of Net Sales
Net Sales (calculated in 2.)	$392,000	100.0%
Less: Cost of Goods Sold	137,200	35.0
Gross Profit	$254,800	65.0%

The 65% gross profit percentage indicates that Oakley generates 65 cents of gross profit on each dollar of sales. This is 1.5 cents less gross profit on each dollar of sales than Luxottica ($1.5 = 66.5 - 65.0$). This difference implies that Luxottica is including a higher markup in its selling prices than Oakley.

CHAPTER SUMMARY

Distinguish among service, merchandising, and manufacturing operations. p. 254   LO1

- Service companies sell services rather than physical goods; consequently, their income statements show costs of services rather than cost of goods sold.

- Merchandise companies sell goods that have been obtained from a supplier. Retail merchandise companies sell directly to consumers whereas wholesale merchandise companies sell to retail companies.

- Manufacturing companies sell goods that they have made themselves.

Explain common principles and limitations of internal control. p. 256   LO2

- The concept of internal control is broad. Most employees working within a company will encounter five basic principles: (1) establish responsibility for each task; (2) segregate duties so that one employee cannot initiate, record, approve, and handle a single transaction; (3) restrict access to those employees who have been assigned responsibility; (4) document procedures performed; and (5) independently verify work done by others inside and outside the business.

- Internal controls may be limited by cost, human error, and fraud.

Apply internal control principles to cash receipts and payments. p. 258   LO3

- When applied to cash receipts, internal control principles require that (1) cashiers be held individually responsible for the cash they receive, (2) different individuals be assigned to receive, maintain custody of, and record cash, (3) cash be stored in a locked safe until it has been securely deposited in a bank, (4) cash register receipts, cash count sheets, daily cash summary reports, and bank deposit slips be prepared to document the cash received and deposited, and (5) cash register receipts be matched to cash counts and deposit slips, to independently verify that all cash was received and deposited.

- When applied to cash payments, internal control principles require that (1) only certain individuals or departments initiate purchase requests, (2) different individuals be assigned to order, receive, and pay for purchases, (3) access to checks and valuable property be restricted, (4) purchase requisitions, purchase orders, receiving reports, and prenumbered checks be used to document the work done, and (5) each step in the payment process occurs only after the preceding step has been independently verified using the documents listed in (4).

Perform the key control of reconciling cash to bank statements. p. 263   LO4

- The bank reconciliation requires determining two categories of items: (1) those that have been recorded in the company's books but not in the bank's statement of account, and (2) those that have been reported in the bank's statement of account but not in the company's books. The second category of items provides the data needed to adjust the Cash account to the balance that will be reported on the balance sheet.

Explain the use of a perpetual inventory system as a control. p. 268   LO5

- Perpetual inventory systems protect against undetected theft because they provide an up-to-date record of inventory that should be on hand at any given time, which can be compared to a count of the physical quantity that actually is on hand.

- Perpetual inventory systems serve to promote efficient and effective operations because they are updated every time inventory is purchased, sold, or returned.

LO6   Analyze sales transactions under a perpetual inventory system. p. 270

- In a perpetual inventory system, two entries are made every time inventory is sold: one entry records the sale (and corresponding debit to Cash or Accounts Receivable) and the other entry records the Cost of Goods Sold (and corresponding credit to Inventory).

- Sales discounts and sales returns and allowances are reported as contra-revenues, reducing net sales.

LO7   Analyze a merchandiser's multistep income statement. p. 274

- One of the key items in a merchandiser's multistep income statement is gross profit, which is a subtotal calculated by subtracting cost of goods sold from net sales. The gross profit percentage is calculated and interpreted as follows.

Accounting Decision Tools

Name of Measure	Formula	What It Tells You
Gross profit percentage	$\dfrac{\text{Net Sales} - \text{CGS}}{\text{Net Sales}} \times 100$	• The percentage of profit earned on each dollar of sales, after considering the cost of products sold • A higher ratio means that greater profit is available to cover operating and other expenses

KEY TERMS

Bank Reconciliation p. 263

Cash p. 268

Cash Equivalents p. 268

FOB Destination p. 270

FOB Shipping Point p. 270

Gross Profit (or Gross Margin) p. 274

Gross Profit Percentage p. 275

Imprest System p. 263

Internal Controls p. 254

Manufacturing Company p. 254

Merchandising Company p. 254

Multistep Income Statement p. 274

NSF (Not Sufficient Funds) Check p. 265

Periodic Inventory System p. 269

Perpetual Inventory System p. 269

Sales Discount p. 272

Sales Returns and Allowances p. 271

Segregation of Duties p. 256

Service Company p. 254

Voucher System p. 262

See complete definitions in the glossary in the back of this text.

HOMEWORK HELPER

Multistep Income Statement Format

Sales Revenue	$100,000	
Less: Sales Returns and Allowances	(2,500)	
Sales Discounts	(1,500)	
Net Sales	96,000	
Cost of Goods Sold	55,000	
Gross Profit	41,000	
Selling, General, and Administrative Expenses	21,000	
Income from Operations	20,000	
Other Revenue (Expenses)	5,000	
Income before Income Tax Expense	25,000	
Income Tax Expense	10,000	
Net Income	$ 15,000	

Reported Internally

Reported Externally

Alternative terms

- Gross profit is also called gross margin or margin.

Helpful reminders

- When preparing a bank reconciliation, your goals are to determine which transactions the bank has not yet processed and which transactions your company has not yet processed. You will record transactions correctly processed by the bank but not yet processed by your company.
- Sales Returns have two components: (1) an adjustment to the selling price (record a contra-revenue and a decrease in Cash or Accounts Receivable) and (2) return of goods previously recorded as sold (record an increase in Inventory and a decrease in Cost of Goods Sold). Sales Allowances involve only the first component, because no goods are returned to the seller.

Frequent mistakes

- Discounts (or "markdowns") in the selling price of merchandise occur prior to making a sale, so they are not recorded. Sales Discounts, given to customers after making a sale, are recorded in a contra-revenue account, to offset the Sales Revenue recorded on the initial sales transaction.
- Gross profit percentage is calculated as a percentage of Net Sales, not Cost of Goods Sold.

PRACTICE MATERIAL

QUESTIONS (⊖ Symbol indicates questions that require analysis from more than one perspective.)

1. What is the distinction between service and merchandising companies? What is the distinction between merchandising and manufacturing companies? What is the distinction between retail and wholesale merchandising companies?

2. From the perspective of a CEO or CFO, what does internal control mean?

3. What are five common internal control principles?

4. Why is it a good idea to assign each task to only one employee?

5. Why should responsibilities for certain duties, like cash handling and cash recording, be separated? What types of responsibilities should be separated?

6. What are some of the methods for restricting access?

7. In what ways does documentation act as a control?

8. In what ways can independent verification occur?

9. In what way does a mandatory vacation policy act as a control?

10. What are two limitations of internal control?

11. What is the primary internal control goal for cash receipts?

12. What internal control functions are performed by a cash register? How are these functions performed when cash is received by mail? ⊖

13. How is cash received in person independently verified?

14. What is the primary internal control goal for cash payments?

15. What are the purposes of a bank reconciliation? What balances are reconciled?

16. Define Cash and Cash Equivalents, and indicate the types of items that should be reported as cash and cash equivalents.

17. What is the main distinction between perpetual and periodic inventory systems? Which type of system provides better internal control over inventory? Explain why.

18. Why is a physical count of inventory necessary in a periodic inventory system? Why is it still necessary in a perpetual inventory system?

19. What is the difference between FOB shipping point and FOB destination? How do these terms relate to the revenue principle?

20. Describe in words the journal entries that are made in a perpetual inventory system when inventory is sold on credit.

21. What is the distinction between Sales Returns and Sales Allowances?

22. What is a Sales Discount? Use 1/10, n/30 in your explanation.

23. In response to the weak economy, your company's sales force is urging you, the sales manager, to change sales terms from 1/10, n/30 to 2/10, n/45. Explain what these terms mean and how this switch could increase or decrease your company's profits. ⊖

24. Explain the difference between Sales Revenue and Net Sales.

25. Why are contra-revenue accounts used rather than directly deducting from the Sales Revenue account?

26. What is gross profit? How is the gross profit percentage computed? Illustrate its calculation and interpretation assuming Net Sales is $100,000 and Cost of Goods Sold is $60,000.

MULTIPLE CHOICE

1. Mountain Gear, Inc., buys bikes, tents, and climbing supplies from Rugged Rock Corporation for sale to consumers. What type of company is Mountain Gear, Inc.?
   Quiz 6
   www.mhhe.com/phillips3e

   a. Service
   b. Retail merchandiser
   c. Wholesale merchandiser
   d. Manufacturer

2. Which of the following does not enhance internal control?

   a. Assigning different duties to different employees.
   b. Ensuring adequate documentation is maintained.
   c. Allowing access only when required to complete assigned duties.
   d. None of the above—all enhance internal control.

3. Which of the following internal control principles underlies the requirement that all customers be given a sales receipt?

   a. Segregate duties
   b. Establish responsibility
   c. Restrict access
   d. Document procedures

4. Upon review of your company's bank statement, you discover that you recently deposited a check from a customer that was rejected by your bank as NSF. Which of the following describes the actions to be taken when preparing your company's bank reconciliation?

	Balance per Bank	Balance per Book
a.	Decrease	No change
b.	Increase	Decrease
c.	No change	Decrease
d.	Decrease	Increase

5. Upon review of the most recent bank statement, you discover that a check was made out to your supplier for $76 but was recorded in your Cash and Accounts Payable accounts as $67. Which of the following describes the actions to be taken when preparing your bank reconciliation?

	Balance per Bank	Balance per Book
a.	Decrease	No change
b.	Increase	Decrease
c.	No change	Decrease
d.	Decrease	Increase

6. Which of the following is false regarding a perpetual inventory system?

   a. Physical counts are never needed because records are maintained on a transaction-by-transaction basis.
   b. The Inventory records are updated with each inventory purchase, sale, or return transaction.
   c. Cost of Goods Sold is increased as sales are recorded.
   d. A perpetual inventory system can be used to detect shrinkage.

7. Sales discounts with terms 2/10, n/30 mean

   a. 10 percent discount for payment received within 30 days of the date of sale.
   b. 2 percent discount for payment received within 10 days or the full amount (less returns) is due within 30 days.
   c. Two-tenths of a percent discount for payment received within 30 days.
   d. None of the above.

8. Which of the following is not a component of Net Sales?

   a. Sales Returns and Allowances
   b. Sales Discounts
   c. Cost of Goods Sold
   d. Sales Revenue

9. A $1,000 sale is made on May 1 with terms 2/10, n/30. Items with a $100 selling price are returned on May 3. What amount, if received on May 9, will be considered payment in full?

   a. $700
   b. $800
   c. $882
   d. $900

10. This year your company has purchased less expensive merchandise inventory but has not changed its selling prices. What effect will this change have on the company's gross profit percentage this year, in comparison to last year?

   a. The ratio will not change.
   b. The ratio will increase.
   c. The ratio will decrease.
   d. Cannot determine.

> For answers to the Multiple-Choice Questions **see page Q1** located in the last section of the book.

MINI-EXERCISES

LO1   M6-1 Distinguishing among Operating Cycles

Identify the type of business as service (S), retail merchandiser (RM), wholesale merchandiser (WM), or manufacturer (M) for each of the following.

_____ 1. The company reports no inventory on its balance sheet.

_____ 2. The company is a true "middleman," buying from a manufacturer and selling to other companies.

_____ 3. The company's inventory includes raw materials that will be processed into ready-to-use goods.

_____ 4. The company sells goods to consumers.

M6-2 Identifying Internal Controls over Financial Reporting   LO2, 3

Fox Erasing has a system of internal control with the following procedures. Match the procedure to the corresponding internal control principle.

Procedure	Internal Control Principle
_____ 1. The treasurer signs checks.	A. Establish responsibility
_____ 2. The treasurer is not allowed to make bank deposits.	B. Segregate duties
	C. Restrict access
_____ 3. The company's checks are prenumbered.	D. Document procedures
_____ 4. Unused checks are stored in the vault.	E. Independently verify
_____ 5. A bank reconciliation is prepared each month.	

M6-3 Identifying Internal Control Principles Applied by a Merchandiser   LO2

Identify the internal control principle represented by each point in the following diagram.

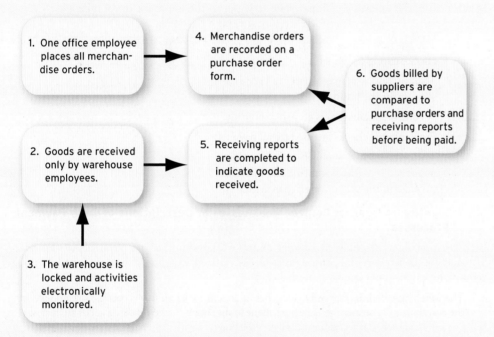

1. One office employee places all merchandise orders.

4. Merchandise orders are recorded on a purchase order form.

6. Goods billed by suppliers are compared to purchase orders and receiving reports before being paid.

2. Goods are received only by warehouse employees.

5. Receiving reports are completed to indicate goods received.

3. The warehouse is locked and activities electronically monitored.

M6-4 Matching Cash Receipt Processes to Internal Control Principles   LO3

Match each of the following cash receipt activities to the internal control principle to which they best relate. Enter the appropriate letter in the space provided.

_D_ 1. A list of checks received in the mail is prepared.	A. Establish responsibility
_E_ 2. Total cash receipts are compared to the amount on the bank deposit slip.	B. Segregate duties
_C_ 3. A password is required to open the cash register.	C. Restrict access
_B_ 4. Price changes at the checkout require a manager's approval.	D. Document procedures
_A_ 5. Cashiers are required to count the cash in their register at the beginning and end of each shift.	E. Independently verify

LO3   **M6-5 Identifying Internal Control Weaknesses in Descriptions of Cash Receipts Process**

Each situation below describes an internal control weakness in the cash receipts process. Identify which of the five internal control principles is violated, explain the weakness, and then suggest a change that would improve internal control.

a. Cashiers prepare a cash count summary, attach tapes from the cash register showing total receipts, and then prepare a bank deposit slip, which they take to the bank for deposit. After the deposit is made, all documents are forwarded to the accounting department for review and recording.

b. The receptionist opens the mail each morning, sorts it into piles, and then gives checks received from customers to the mail clerk for delivery to the accounting department, where a cash receipts list is prepared.

c. The accounting department receives cash register totals each day and promptly files them by cash register number. The accounting department also receives cash count sheets from cashiers each day and files them by employee number. The accounting department receives stamped bank deposit slips the morning after the bank deposit is made, prepares the journal entry, and files the deposit slips by date.

d. To avoid boredom, the employee who works the cash register at the movie theater trades off with either the employee who collects the tickets or an employee who works at the concessions stand.

e. To enhance efficiency, cashiers are assigned the responsibility of authorizing price changes at the cash register.

LO3   **M6-6 Matching Cash Payment Processes to Internal Control Principles**

Match each of the following cash payment activities to the internal control principle to which they best relate. Enter the appropriate letter in the space provided.

_____ 1. The business manager has the only key to the check-signing equipment.

_____ 2. The purchasing manager orders all goods and services for the business.

_____ 3. A bank reconciliation is prepared monthly.

_____ 4. Prenumbered checks are used for all payments.

_____ 5. The company asks suppliers to deliver their merchandise to the warehouse but mail their invoices to the accounting department.

A. Establish responsibility
B. Segregate duties
C. Restrict access
D. Document procedures
E. Independently verify

LO3   **M6-7 Identifying Internal Control Weaknesses in Descriptions of Cash Payment Processes**

Each situation below describes an internal control weakness in the cash payments process. Identify which of the five internal control principles is violated, explain the weakness, and then suggest a change that would improve internal control.

a. The warehouse clerk is responsible for ordering inventory when levels become low and advising the accounting department to issue a payment to the supplier when ordered goods are received.

b. For each purchase, the accountant compares the purchase order (prepared by the purchasing manager) to the receiving report (prepared by warehouse employees), and then attaches these documents to the corresponding supplier invoice and files them by supplier name. The accountant then prepares a check, which the owner merrily signs and sends to the mail clerk for mailing.

c. The check-signing machine is stored with a supply of blank checks in the lunch room closet.

d. Purchase orders can be approved by the purchasing manager, accountant, or warehouse supervisor, depending on who is least busy.

LO4   **M6-8 Organizing Items on the Bank Reconciliation**

Indicate whether the following items would be added (+) or subtracted (−) from the company's books or the bank statement side of a bank reconciliation.

Reconciling Item	Bank Statement	Company's Books
a. Outstanding checks of $12,000		
b. Bank service charge of $15		
c. Deposit in transit of $2,300		
d. Interest earned of $5		

M6-9 Preparing Journal Entries after a Bank Reconciliation

LO4

Using the information in M6-8, prepare any journal entries needed to adjust the company's books.

M6-10 Choosing between a Perpetual and Periodic Inventory System

LO5

Nordstrom, Inc., started in business in 1901. It only took 100 years, but eventually the company changed from a periodic inventory system to a perpetual inventory system (in 2002). Write a brief report describing how this change would improve the company's inventory control.

Nordstrom, Inc.

M6-11 Calculating Shrinkage in a Perpetual Inventory System

LO5

Corey's Campus Store has $50,000 of inventory on hand at the beginning of the month. During the month, the company buys $8,000 of merchandise and sells merchandise that had cost $30,000. At the end of the month, $25,000 of inventory is on hand. How much shrinkage occurred during the month?

M6-12 Choosing between FOB Shipping Point and FOB Destination

LO6

In its 2009 annual report, American Eagle Outfitters states that its "e-commerce operation records revenue upon the estimated customer receipt date of the merchandise." Is this FOB shipping point or FOB destination? If American Eagle were to change to the other terms of shipment, would it report its Sales Revenues earlier, or later?

AMERICAN EAGLE
OUTFITTERS
ae.com

M6-13 Reporting Net Sales and Gross Profit with Sales Discounts

LO6

Merchandise costing $1,500 is sold for $2,000 on terms 2/10, n/30. If the buyer pays within the discount period, what amount will be reported on the income statement as net sales and as gross profit?

M6-14 Recording Journal Entries for Sales and Sales Discounts

LO6

Using the information in M6-13, prepare the journal entries needed at the time of sale and collection, assuming the company uses a perpetual inventory system.

M6-15 Journal Entries to Record Sales Discounts

LO6

Inventory that cost $500 is sold for $700, with terms of 2/10, n/30. Give the journal entries to record (a) the sale of merchandise and (b) collection of the accounts receivable assuming that it occurs during the discount period.

M6-16 Preparing a Multistep Income Statement

LO7

Sellall Department Stores reported the following amounts in its adjusted trial balance prepared as of its December 31, 2010, year-end: Administrative Expenses, $2,400; Cost of Goods Sold, $22,728; Income Tax Expense, $3,000; Interest Expense, $1,600; Interest Revenue, $200; General Expenses, $2,600; Sales Revenue, $42,000; Sales Discounts, $2,200; Sales Returns and Allowances, $1,920; and Delivery (freight-out) Expense, $300. Prepare a multistep income statement for distribution to external financial statement users, using a format similar to Exhibit 6.11.

M6-17 Computing and Interpreting the Gross Profit Percentage

LO7

Using the information in M6-16, calculate the gross profit percentage for 2010. How has Sellall performed, relative to the gross profit percentages reported for Wal-Mart in the chapter?

M6-18 Computing and Interpreting the Gross Profit Percentage

LO7

Ziehart Pharmaceuticals reported Net Sales of $178,000 and Cost of Goods Sold of $58,000. Candy Electronics Corp. reported Net Sales of $36,000 and Cost of Goods Sold of $26,200. Calculate the gross profit percentage for both companies. From these calculations, can you determine which company is more successful? Explain.

M6-19 Calculating the Impact of Changes in Gross Profit Percentage on Operating Income

LO7

Luxottica Group, the Italian company that sells Ray Ban and Killer Loop sunglasses, reported a gross profit percentage of 68.3 percent in 2007 and 66.5 percent in 2008. In each of these two years, the company's net sales was fairly steady at approximately 5 million euro. Assuming that Luxottica's operating expenses were 2.6 million euro in each year, how much more (or less) income from operations did Luxottica report in 2008 than in 2007?

Luxottica Group

LO7   **M6-20 Determining the Cause of Decreasing Gross Profit**

Fortune Brands, Inc., sells a variety of products including Titleist and Pinnacle golf balls, Footjoy golf shoes, and Master Lock padlocks. Like many other companies, Fortune Brands reported a drop in net sales from $8.6 million in 2007 to $7.6 million in 2008, and a drop in gross profit from $4.0 million in 2008 to $3.6 million in 2007. Based on these numbers, determine whether the drop in gross profit was caused by a decline in gross profit per sale, a decline in sales volume, or a combination of the two.

EXERCISES

LO2   **E6-1 Identifying Internal Control Principle and Financial Reporting Control Objective**

At most movie theaters, one employee sells tickets and another employee collects them. One night, when you're at the movies, your friend comments that this is a waste of the theater's money.

Required:

1. Identify the name of the control principle to which this situation relates.
2. Explain to your friend what could happen if the same person did both jobs.

LO2   **E6-2 Identifying Financial Reporting Control Objectives**

Your student club recently volunteered to go door-to-door collecting cash donations on behalf of a local charity. The charity's accountant went berserk when you said you wrote receipts only for donors who asked for one.

Required:

Identify the control principle that you violated, and explain why the accountant reacted so strongly. What controls might be appropriate to use in the future?

LO3   **E6-3 Identifying Internal Control Principles in Cash Receipt Processes**

Locker Rentals Corp. (LRC) operates locker rental services at several locations throughout the city including the airport, bus depot, shopping malls, and athletics facilities. Unlike some of the old mechanical lockers that charge a fixed amount per use, LRC's lockers operate electronically and are able to charge based on hours of use. The locker system transmits a daily message to LRC's office indicating the number of hours that lockers have been used, which the office manager uses to determine when cash should be picked up at each location. LRC's cash receipts system is described below.

   a. Two employees ("cash collection clerks") are responsible for collecting cash from the lockers. Based on instructions from the office manager, one clerk collects cash from specific locations on the west side of the city and the other collects from specific locations on the east side.

   b. When each cash collection clerk returns the cash, a supervisor counts the cash and prepares a cash count sheet.

   c. The supervisor summarizes the cash count sheets in a prenumbered daily cash summary, and files the prenumbered cash count sheets by date.

   d. The supervisor places the cash in a locked cashbox until it is taken to the bank for deposit.

   e. The supervisor, not the cash collection clerks, takes the cash to the bank for deposit.

   f. The supervisor prepares a duplicate deposit slip, which the bank stamps after the deposit is made, to indicate the date and amount of the deposit.

   g. The supervisor sends the stamped bank deposit slip and daily cash summary to the accountant, who compares them before preparing a journal entry debiting Cash and crediting Locker Rental Revenue.

Required:

1. For each statement (*a*)–(*g*), identify the internal control principle being applied.
2. Prepare a diagram similar to Exhibit 6.3 showing the flow of information and materials. In what ways does LRC's system differ from Exhibit 6.3?
3. After several months, LRC's supervisor is arrested for stealing nearly $10,000 from the company. Identify the internal control weakness that allowed this theft to occur.

E6-4 Identifying Internal Control Principles in Cash Payment Processes   LO3

Home Repair Corp. (HRC) operates a building maintenance and repair business. The business has three office employees—a sales manager, a materials/crew manager, and an accountant. HRC's cash payments system is described below.

a. After a contract is signed with a customer, the sales manager prepares a prenumbered purchase requisition form that indicates the materials needed for the work at the repair site.

b. Based on the purchase requisition form, the materials/crew manager prepares and sends a prenumbered purchase order to suppliers of materials, advising them of the specific materials needed and the repair site to which they should be delivered.

c. The materials/crew manager is the only employee authorized to order goods.

d. Upon receiving a supplier's invoice, the accountant compares it to terms indicated on the purchase order, noting in particular the prices charged and quantity ordered.

e. If these documents are in agreement, the accountant prepares a prenumbered check, stamps the invoice "paid," and prepares a journal entry to record the payment. The journal entry explanation references the sequential number on the purchase order.

f. HRC's owner prepares a monthly bank reconciliation, and review checks returned with the bank statement to ensure they have been issued to valid suppliers.

Required:

1. For each statement (a)–(f), identify the internal control principle being applied.

2. Using the above description, prepare a list of steps and documentation similar to Exhibit 6.4. Which document in Exhibit 6.4 is excluded from the above description?

3. After several months, HRC's materials/crew manager is arrested for having $20,000 of materials delivered to his home, but charged to the company. Identify the internal control weakness that allowed this theft to occur.

E6-5 Preparing a Bank Reconciliation and Journal Entries, and Reporting Cash   LO4

Hills Company's June 30, 2010, bank statement and the June ledger account for cash are summarized here:

BANK STATEMENT				
	Checks	Deposits	Other	Balance
Balance, June 1, 2010				$ 7,200
Deposits during June		$18,000		25,200
Checks cleared during June	$19,100			6,100
Bank service charges			$30	6,070
Balance, June 30, 2010				6,070

		+	Cash (A)	−		
June 1	Balance	6,800				
June	Deposits	19,000		19,400	Checks written	June
June 30	Balance	6,400				

Required:

1. Prepare a bank reconciliation. A comparison of the checks written with the checks that have cleared the bank shows outstanding checks of $700. Some of the checks that cleared in June were written prior to June. No deposits in transit were noted in May, but a deposit is in transit at the end of June.

2. Give any journal entries that should be made as a result of the bank reconciliation.

3. What is the balance in the Cash account after the reconciliation entries?

4. In addition to the balance in its bank account, Hills Company also has $300 cash on hand. This amount is recorded in a separate T-account called Cash on Hand. What is the total amount of cash that should be reported on the balance sheet at June 30?

LO4   **E6-6 Preparing a Bank Reconciliation and Journal Entries, and Reporting Cash**

The September 30, 2011, bank statement for Cadieux Company and the September ledger account for cash are summarized here:

BANK STATEMENT	Checks	Deposits	Other	Balance
Balance, September 1, 2011				$ 2,000
September 7			NSF check $100	1,900
September 11		$3,000 √		4,900
September 12	#101 $ 800 √			4,100
September 17	#102 1,700 √			2,400
September 26	#103 2,300 √			100
September 29			√EFT deposit 150	250
September 30			Service charge 20	230

		+	Cash (A)	−		
Sept 1	Balance	√2,000				
Sept 10		√3,000	800 √	Sept 10	#101	
Sept 30		√2,500	1,700 √	Sept 15	#102	
			2,300	Sept 22	#103	
			√50	Sept 28	#104	
Sept 30	Balance	2,650				

No outstanding checks and no deposits in transit were noted in August. However, there are deposits in transit and checks outstanding at the end of September. The NSF check and electronic funds transfer (EFT) involved transactions with Cadieux Company's customers.

Required:

1. Prepare a bank reconciliation.
2. Give any journal entries that should be made as the result of the bank reconciliation.
3. What should the balance in the Cash account be after recording the journal entries in requirement 2?
4. If the company also has $400 of cash on hand (recorded in a separate account), what total amount of cash should the company report on the September 30 balance sheet?

LO5   **E6-7 Identifying Shrinkage and Other Missing Inventory Information**

Calculate the missing information for each of the following independent cases:

Cases	Beginning Inventory	Purchases	Cost of Goods Sold	Ending Inventory (perpetual system)	Ending Inventory (as counted)	Shrinkage
A	$100	$700	$300	?	$420	$?
B	200	800	?	150	150	?
C	150	500	200	450	?	10
D	260	?	650	210	200	?

LO5   **E6-8 Inferring Shrinkage Using a Perpetual Inventory System**

JCPenney Company, Inc.

JCPenney Company, Inc., is a major retailer with department stores in all 50 states. The main part of the company's business consists of providing merchandise and services to consumers through department stores. In 2008, JCPenney reported cost of goods sold of $11,571 million, ending inventory for the current year of $3,259 million, and ending inventory for the previous year (2007) of $3,641 million.

Required:

If you knew that the cost of inventory purchases was $11,289 million, could you estimate the cost of shrinkage during the year? If so, prepare the estimate and, if not, explain why.

E6-9 Reporting Net Sales with Credit Sales and Sales Discounts

LO6

During the months of January and February, Solitare Corporation sold goods to three customers. The sequence of events was as follows:

Jan. 6	Sold goods for $100 to Wizard Inc. with terms 2/10, n/30. The goods cost Solitare $70.	
6	Sold goods to SpyderCorp. for $80 with terms 2/10, n/30. The goods cost Solitare $60.	*98* *80* *50*
14	Collected cash due from Wizard Inc.	
Feb. 2	Collected cash due from SpyderCorp.	*228*
28	Sold goods for $50 to Bridges with terms 2/10, n/45. The goods cost Solitare $30.	

Required:

Assuming that Sales Discounts are reported as contra-revenue, compute Net Sales for the two months ended February 28.

E6-10 Recording Journal Entries for Net Sales with Credit Sales and Sales Discounts

LO6

Using the information in E6-9, prepare journal entries to record the transactions, assuming Solitare uses a perpetual inventory system.

E6-11 Reporting Net Sales with Credit Sales and Sales Discounts

LO6

The following transactions were selected from the records of Evergreen Company:

July 12	Sold merchandise to Wally Butler, who paid the $1,000 purchase with cash. The goods cost Evergreen Company $600.	*1000*
15	Sold merchandise to Claudio's Chair Company at a selling price of $5,000 on terms 3/10, n/30. The goods cost Evergreen Company $3,500.	*4 850*
20	Sold merchandise to Otto's Ottomans at a selling price of $3,000 on terms 3/10, n/30. The goods cost Evergreen Company $1,900.	
23	Collected payment from Claudio's Chair Company from the July 15 sale.	
Aug. 25	Collected payment from Otto's Ottomans from the July 20 sale.	*5000*

Required:

210 = 260 + x - 650

Assuming that Sales Discounts are reported as contra-revenue, compute Net Sales for the two months ended August 31.

E6-12 Recording Journal Entries for Net Sales with Credit Sales and Sales Discounts

LO6

Using the information in E6-11, prepare journal entries to record the transactions, assuming Evergreen Company uses a perpetual inventory system.

E6-13 Reporting Net Sales with Credit Sales, Sales Discounts, and Sales Returns

LO6

The following transactions were selected from among those completed by Bear's Retail Store in 2010:

Nov. 20	Sold two items of merchandise to Cheryl Jahn, who paid the $400 sales price in cash. The goods cost Bear's $300.	
25	Sold 20 items of merchandise to Vasko Athletics at a selling price of $4,000 (total); terms 3/10, n/30. The goods cost Bear's $2,500.	
28	Sold 10 identical items of merchandise to Nancy's Gym at a selling price of $6,000 (total); terms 3/10, n/30. The goods cost Bear's $4,000.	
29	Nancy's Gym returned one of the items purchased on the 28th. The item was in perfect condition, and credit was given to the customer.	
Dec. 6	Nancy's Gym paid the account balance in full.	
30	Vasko Athletics paid in full for the invoice of November 25, 2010.	

Required:

Assuming that Sales Returns and Sales Discounts are reported as contra-revenues, compute Net Sales for the two months ended December 31, 2010.

LO6 **E6-14 Recording Journal Entries for Net Sales with Credit Sales, Sales Discounts, and Sales Returns**

Using the information in E6-13, prepare journal entries to record the transactions, assuming Bear's Retail Store uses a perpetual inventory system.

LO6, 7 **E6-15 Determining the Effects of Credit Sales, Sales Discounts, and Sales Returns and Allowances on Income Statement Categories**

Rockland Shoe Company records Sales Returns and Allowances and Sales Discounts as contra-revenues. Complete the following table, indicating the amount and direction of effect (+ for increase, − for decrease, and NE for no effect) of each transaction on each item reported in Rockland's income statement prepared for internal use. Be sure to total the effects.

July 12	Rockland sold merchandise to Kristina Zee at its factory store. Kristina paid for the $300 purchase in cash. The goods cost Rockland $160.
15	Sold merchandise to Shoe Express at a selling price of $5,000, with terms 3/10, n/30. Rockland's cost was $3,000.
20	Collected cash due from Shoe Express.
21	Sold merchandise to Fleet Foot Co. at a selling price of $2,000, with terms 2/10, n/30. Rockland's cost was $1,200.
23	Fleet Foot Co. returned $1,000 of shoes and promised to pay for the remaining goods in August. The returned shoes were in perfect condition and had cost Rockland $600.

Transaction Date:	July 12	July 15	July 20	July 21	July 23	Totals
Sales Revenues						
Sales Returns and Allowances						
Sales Discounts						
Net Sales						
Cost of Goods Sold						
Gross Profit						

LO6, 7 **E6-16 Analyzing and Recording Sales and Gross Profit with and without Sales Discounts**

Cycle Wholesaling sells merchandise on credit terms of 2/10, n/30. A sale for $800 (cost of goods sold of $500) was made to Sarah's Cycles on February 1, 2010. Assume Cycle Wholesaling uses a perpetual inventory system.

Required:

1. Give the journal entry Cycle Wholesaling would make to record the sale to Sarah's Cycles.
2. Give the journal entry to record the collection of the account, assuming it was collected in full on February 9, 2010.
3. Give the journal entry, assuming, instead, that the account was collected in full on March 2, 2010.
4. Calculate the gross profit percentage for the sale to Sarah's Cycles, assuming the account was collected in full on February 9, 2010.

LO7 **E6-17 Inferring Missing Amounts Based on Income Statement Relationships**

Supply the missing dollar amounts for the income statement of Williamson Company for each of the following independent cases:

	Case A	Case B	Case C
Sales Revenues	$8,000	$6,000	$?
Sales Returns and Allowances	150	?	275
Net Sales	?	?	5,920
Cost of Goods Sold	5,750	4,050	5,400
Gross Profit	?	1,450	?

E6-18 Analyzing Gross Profit Percentage on the Basis of a Multistep Income Statement   LO7

The following summarized data were provided by the records of Mystery Incorporated for the year ended December 31, 2010:

Administrative Expense	$ 19,000
Cost of Goods Sold	165,000
Income Tax Expense	17,600
Sales Returns and Allowances	7,000
Selling Expense	40,200
Sales of merchandise on cash	240,000
Sales of merchandise for credit	42,000

Required:

1. Based on these data, prepare a multistep income statement for internal reporting purposes (showing all appropriate subtotals and totals).
2. What was the amount of gross profit? What was the gross profit percentage (calculated using the formula shown in this chapter)? Explain what these two amounts mean.
3. Evaluate the 2010 results in light of the company's 38% gross profit percentage in 2009.

E6-19 Analyzing Gross Profit Percentage on the Basis of an Income Statement   LO7

Wolverine World Wide Inc. prides itself as being the "world's leading marketer of U.S. branded non-athletic footwear." The following data (in millions) were taken from its annual report for the fiscal year ended January 3, 2009:

Wolverine World Wide Inc.

Sales of Merchandise	$1,220
Income Tax Expense	45
Cash Dividends Paid	21
Selling and Administrative Expense	345
Cost of Products Sold	735
Interest Expense	3
Other Revenues	3

Required:

1. Based on these data, prepare a multistep income statement.
2. How much was the gross profit? What was the gross profit percentage? (Round to the nearest tenth of a percent.) Explain what these two amounts mean.
3. Evaluate the results in light of the company's 39.2% gross profit percentage in the prior year.
4. Compare Wolverine's gross profit percentage to Wal-Mart's average gross profit percentage of 24.5%. From this information, can you determine which company is more successful? Why or why not?

E6-20 Evaluating the Effect of Discounts and Returns on Gross Profit   LO7

One of the few companies to ever report the extent of sales discounts and returns was sunglass maker Oakley, Inc. In the Management Discussion and Analysis section of its 2005 annual report, Oakley reported the following information about its Sales Discounts and Returns.

	Year Ended December 31,	
(in thousands)	2005	2004
Gross Sales	$693,342	$621,652
Sales Discounts and Returns	(45,211)	(36,184)
Net Sales	648,131	585,468
Cost of Goods Sold	277,230	262,483
Gross Profit	370,901	322,985

Required:

1. For each year, calculate the percentage of sales discounts and returns by dividing Sales Discounts and Returns by Gross Sales and multiplying by 100. Based on these percentages, explain whether Sales Discounts and Returns have a greater impact in 2005 or 2004.

2. For each year, calculate the gross profit percentage using the formula shown in this chapter (i.e., using net sales). Did Oakley's gross profit improve or worsen in 2005, as compared to 2004?

COACHED PROBLEMS

LO3   **CP6-1 Evaluating Internal Control Strengths and Weaknesses in Cash Receipts and Disbursements**

The following procedures are used by Richardson Light Works.

a. When customers pay cash for lighting products, the cash is placed in a cash register and a receipt is issued to the customer.
b. At the end of each day, the cash is counted by the cashier and a cash count sheet is prepared.
c. The manager checks the accuracy of the cash count sheet before taking the cash to the bank for deposit.
d. The journal entry to record cash sales is prepared using the cash count sheets.
e. Checks are written to suppliers immediately after supplier invoices are received.
f. Receiving reports are prepared to indicate the quantity and condition of goods received from suppliers, based on inspections made by warehouse personnel.

Required:

1. Indicate whether each procedure represents a strength or weakness. Explain your reasons.
2. For each weakness, describe a change in procedures that would address the weakness.

LO4   **CP6-2 Preparing a Bank Reconciliation and Journal Entries, and Reporting Cash**

eXcel

www.mhhe.com/phillips3e

The April 30, 2010, bank statement for KMaxx Company and the April ledger account for cash are summarized here:

BANK STATEMENT				
	Checks	Deposits	Other	Balance
Balance, April 1, 2010				$6,000
April 5	#101 $700			5,300
April 9		$2,500		7,800
April 12	#102 200			7,600
April 19	#103 500			7,100
April 22	#104 1,000			6,100
April 27			EFT payment $200	5,900
April 29			NSF check 100	5,800
April 30			Service charge 25	5,775

	+	Cash (A)	−	
April 1 Balance	6,000			
April 8	2,500	700	April 2 #101	
April 28	500	200	April 10 #102	
		500	April 15 #103	
		1,100	April 20 #104	
		300	April 29 #105	
April 30 Balance	6,200			

No outstanding checks and no deposits in transit were noted in March. However, there are deposits in transit and checks outstanding at the end of April. The electronic funds transfer (EFT) involved an automatic monthly payment to one of KMaxx's creditors. Check #104 was written for $1,100. The NSF check had been received from a customer.

Required:

1. Prepare a bank reconciliation for April.
   TIP: Put a check mark beside each item that appears on both the bank statement and what's already been recorded in the accounting records (shown in the T-account). Items left unchecked will be used in the bank reconciliation.
2. Give any journal entries that should be made as a result of the bank reconciliation.
   TIP: Remember to make entries only for items that affect the company's books, not the bank.
3. What should the balance in the Cash account be after recording the journal entries in requirement 2?
4. If the company also has $1,000 of cash on hand (recorded in a separate account), what total amount should the company report as Cash and Cash Equivalents on the April 30 balance sheet?

CP6-3 Identifying Outstanding Checks and Deposits in Transit and Preparing a Bank Reconciliation and Journal Entries   LO4

The August 2010 bank statement and cash T-account for Martha Company follow:

BANK STATEMENT

Date	Checks	Deposits	Other	Balance
Aug. 1				$17,470
2	$300			17,170
3		$12,000		29,170
4	400			28,770
5	250			28,520
9	890			27,630
10	310			27,320
15		4,000		31,320
21	400			30,920
24	21,000			9,920
25		7,000		16,920
30	800			16,120
30			Interest earned $20	16,140
31			Service charge 10	16,130

	+	Cash (A)	−	
Aug. 1 Balance		17,470	Checks written	
Deposits				
Aug. 2		12,000	300	Aug. 1
12		4,000	400	2
24		7,000	250	3
31		5,000	310	4
			890	5
			290	15
			550	17
			800	18
			400	19
			21,000	23
Aug. 31 Balance		20,280		

No deposits were in transit and no checks were outstanding at the end of July.

Required:

1. Identify and list the deposits in transit at the end of August.

    TIP: Put a check mark beside each item that appears on both the bank statement and what's already been recorded in the accounting records (shown in the T-account).

2. Identify and list the outstanding checks at the end of August.

3. Prepare a bank reconciliation for August.

    TIP: Any item in the accounting records without check marks should appear on the bank statement side of the bank reconciliation. Any items in the bank statement without check marks should appear on the company's books side of the bank reconciliation.

4. Give any journal entries that the company should make as a result of the bank reconciliation. Why are they necessary?

5. After the reconciliation journal entries are posted, what balance will be reflected in the Cash account in the ledger?

6. If the company also has $100 on hand, which is recorded in a different account called Cash on Hand, what total amount of Cash and Cash Equivalents should be reported on the August 31, 2010, balance sheet?

LO7   **CP6-4 Preparing a Multistep Income Statement with Sales Discounts and Sales Returns and Allowances and Computing the Gross Profit Percentage**

Psymon Company, Inc., sells construction equipment. The annual fiscal period ends on December 31. The following adjusted trial balance was created from the general ledger accounts on December 31, 2010:

Account Titles	Debits	Credits
Cash	$ 42,000	
Accounts Receivable	18,000	
Inventory	65,000	
Property and Equipment	50,000	
Accumulated Depreciation		$ 21,000
Liabilities		30,000
Contributed Capital		90,000
Retained Earnings, January 1, 2010		11,600
Sales Revenue		182,000
Sales Returns and Allowances	7,000	
Sales Discounts	8,000	
Cost of Goods Sold	98,000	
Selling Expense	17,000	
Administrative Expense	18,000	
General Expenses	2,000	
Income Tax Expense	9,600	
Totals	$334,600	$334,600

Required:

1. Prepare a multistep income statement that would be used for internal reporting purposes. Treat Sales Discounts and Sales Returns and Allowances as contra-revenue accounts.

    TIP: Some of the accounts listed will appear on the balance sheet rather than the income statement.

2. Prepare a multistep income statement that would be used for external reporting purposes, beginning with the amount for Net Sales.

3. Compute and interpret the gross profit percentage (using the formula shown in this chapter).

LO6, 7   **CP6-5 Recording Cash Sales, Credit Sales, Sales Discounts, Sales Returns, and Sales Allowances and Analyzing Gross Profit Percentage**

Campus Stop, Incorporated, is a student co-op. Campus Stop uses a perpetual inventory system. The following transactions (summarized) have been selected from 2010:

a.	Sold merchandise for cash (cost of merchandise $152,070).	$275,000
b.	Received merchandise returned by customers as unsatisfactory (but in perfect condition), for cash refund (original cost of merchandise $800).	1,600
c.	Sold merchandise (costing $9,000) to a customer, on account with terms 2/10, n/30.	20,000
d.	Collected half of the balance owed by the customer in (c) within the discount period.	9,800
e.	Granted an allowance to the customer in (c).	1,800

Required:

1. Compute Sales Revenue, Net Sales, and Gross Profit for Campus Stop.
2. Compute the gross profit percentage (using the formula shown in this chapter).
3. Prepare journal entries to record transactions (a)–(e).
4. Campus Stop is considering a contract to sell merchandise to a campus organization for $15,000. This merchandise will cost Campus Stop $12,000. Would this contract increase (or decrease) Campus Stop's gross profit and gross profit percentage? How should Campus Stop decide whether to accept the contract?

   TIP: The impact on gross profit (a dollar amount) may differ from the impact on gross profit percentage.

**CP6-6 Sales Transactions between Wholesale and Retail Merchandisers, with   LO6, 7
Sales Allowances and Sales Discounts Using a Perpetual Inventory
System**

The transactions listed below are typical of those involving Amalgamated Textiles and American Fashions. Amalgamated is a wholesale merchandiser and American Fashions is a retail merchandiser. Assume all sales of merchandise from Amalgamated to American Fashions are made with terms 2/10, n/30, and that the two companies use perpetual inventory systems. Assume the following transactions between the two companies occurred in the order listed during the year ended December 31, 2010.

a. Amalgamated sold merchandise to American Fashions at a selling price of $230,000. The merchandise had cost Amalgamated $175,000.
b. Two days later, American Fashions complained to Amalgamated that some of the merchandise differed from what American Fashions had ordered. Amalgamated agreed to give an allowance of $5,000 to American Fashions.
c. Just three days later, American Fashions paid Amalgamated, which settled all amounts owed.

Required:

1. For each of the events (a) through (c), indicate the amount and direction of the effect (+ for increase, − for decrease, and NE for no effect) on Amalgamated Textiles in terms of the following items.

Sales Revenues	Sales Returns and Allowances	Sales Discounts	Net Sales	Cost of Goods Sold	Gross Profit

2. Which of the above items are likely to be reported on Amalgamated's external financial statements, and which items will be combined "behind the scenes"?
3. Prepare the journal entries that Amalgamated Textiles would record, and show any computations.

   TIP: When using a perpetual inventory system, the seller always makes two journal entries when goods are sold.

GROUP A PROBLEMS

**PA6-1 Evaluating Internal Control Strengths |ACCOUNTING   LO3
and Weaknesses in Cash Receipts and Disbursements**

The following procedures are used by The Taco Shop.

a. Customers pay cash for all food orders. Cash is placed in a cash register and a receipt is issued upon request by the customer.
b. At the end of each day, the cashier counts the cash, prepares a cash count sheet, and has the manager review and sign the cash count sheet.
c. At three times during the day, excess cash is removed from the cash registers and placed in a vault until it is taken for night deposit at the local bank.

d. Orders for drink cups, straws, condiments, and other supplies are written on prenumbered purchase order forms and are approved by the manager before being sent to an authorized supplier.

e. When supplies are received, they are stacked just inside the back door to the kitchen, which is left unlocked because part-time employees frequently arrive and leave at various times during the day.

Required:

1. Indicate whether each procedure represents a strength or weakness. Explain your reasons.

2. For each weakness, describe a change in procedures that would address the weakness.

LO4

eXcel
www.mhhe.com/phillips3e

PA6-2 Preparing a Bank Reconciliation and Journal Entries, and Reporting Cash

The bookkeeper at Martin Company has asked you to prepare a bank reconciliation as of May 31, 2010. The May 31, 2010, bank statement and the May T-account for cash showed the following (summarized):

Martin Company's bank reconciliation at the end of April 2010 showed a cash balance of $18,800. No deposits were in transit at the end of April, but a deposit was in transit at the end of May.

BANK STATEMENT						
		Checks	Deposits	Other		Balance
Balance, May 1, 2010						$18,800
May 2			$ 8,000			26,800
May 5	#301	$11,000				15,800
May 7	#302	6,000				9,800
May 8			10,000			19,800
May 14	#303	500				19,300
May 17				Interest	$120	19,420
May 22				NSF check	280	19,140
May 27	#304	4,600				14,540
May 31				Service charge	60	14,480
Balance, May 31, 2010						14,480

		+	Cash (A)	−	
May 1	Balance	18,800			
May 1		8,000	11,000	#301	May 2
May 7		10,000	6,000	#302	May 4
May 29		4,000	500	#303	May 11
			4,600	#304	May 23
			1,300	#305	May 29
May 31	Balance	17,400			

Required:

1. Prepare a bank reconciliation for May.

2. Prepare any journal entries required as a result of the bank reconciliation. Why are they necessary?

3. After the reconciliation journal entries are posted, what balance will be reflected in the Cash account in the ledger?

4. If the company also has $50 on hand, which is recorded in a different account called Cash on Hand, what total amount of Cash and Cash Equivalents should be reported on the balance sheet at the end of May?

PA6-3 Identifying Outstanding Checks and Deposits in Transit and Preparing a Bank Reconciliation and Journal Entries

The December 2010 bank statement and cash T-account for Stewart Company follow:

BANK STATEMENT					
Date	Checks	Deposits	Other		Balance
Dec. 1					$48,000
2	$ 500				47,500
4	7,000				40,500
6	120				40,380
11	550	$28,000			67,830
13	1,900				65,930
17	12,000				53,930
23	60	36,000			89,870
26	900				88,970
28	2,200				86,770
30	17,000	19,000	NSF*	$300	88,470
31	1,650		Interest earned	50	86,870
31			Service charge	150	86,720

*NSF check from J. Left, a customer.

+	Cash (A)	−		
Dec. 1 Balance	48,000	Checks written during December:		
Deposits				
Dec. 11	28,000	500		60
23	36,000	7,000		900
30	19,000	120		150
31	13,000	550		17,000
		1,900		3,500
		12,000		1,650
		2,200		
Dec. 31 Balance	96,470			

There were no deposits in transit or outstanding checks at November 30.

Required:

1. Identify and list the deposits in transit at the end of December.
2. Identify and list the outstanding checks at the end of December.
3. Prepare a bank reconciliation for December.
4. Give any journal entries that the company should make as a result of the bank reconciliation. Why are they necessary?
5. After the reconciliation journal entries are posted, what balance will be reflected in the Cash account in the ledger?
6. If the company also has $300 on hand, which is recorded in a different account called Cash on Hand, what total amount of Cash and Cash Equivalents should be reported on the December 31, 2010, balance sheet?

LO7   **PA6-4 Preparing a Multistep Income Statement with Sales Discounts and Sales Returns and Allowances and Computing the Gross Profit Percentage**

Big Tommy Corporation is a local grocery store organized seven years ago as a corporation. The store is in an excellent location, and sales have increased each year. At the end of 2010, the bookkeeper prepared the following statement (assume that all amounts are correct, but note the incorrect terminology and format):

	Debit	Credit
BIG TOMMY CORPORATION		
Profit and Loss		
December 31, 2010		
Sales		$420,000
Cost of Goods Sold	$279,000	
Sales Returns and Allowances	10,000	
Sales Discounts	6,000	
Selling Expense	58,000	
Administrative Expense	16,000	
General Expenses	1,000	
Income Tax Expense	15,000	
Net Profit	35,000	
Totals	$420,000	$420,000

Required:

1. Prepare a multistep income statement that would be used for internal reporting purposes. Treat Sales Returns and Allowances and Sales Discounts as contra-revenue accounts.

2. Prepare a multistep income statement that would be used for external reporting purposes, beginning with the amount for Net Sales.

3. Compute and interpret the gross profit percentage (using the formula shown in this chapter).

LO6, 7   **PA6-5 Recording Sales with Discounts and Returns and Analyzing Gross Profit Percentage**

Hair World Inc. is a wholesaler of hair supplies. Hair World uses a perpetual inventory system. The following transactions (summarized) have been selected from 2010:

a. Sold merchandise for cash (cost of merchandise $28,797). $51,200
b. Received merchandise returned by customers as unsatisfactory
    (but in perfect condition), for cash refund (original cost of merchandise $360).   600
c. Sold merchandise (costing $4,750) to a customer, on account with terms 2/10, n/30.   10,000
d. Collected half of the balance owed by the customer in (c) within the discount period.   4,900
e. Granted an allowance to the customer in (c).   160

Required:

1. Compute Sales Revenue, Net Sales, and Gross Profit for Hair World.
2. Compute the gross profit percentage (using the formula shown in this chapter).
3. Prepare journal entries to record transactions (a)–(e).
4. Hair World is considering a contract to sell merchandise to a hair salon chain for $15,000. This merchandise will cost Hair World $10,000. Would this contract increase (or decrease) Hair World's gross profit and gross profit percentage? How should Hair World decide whether to accept the contract?

PA6-6 Reporting Sales Transactions between Wholesale and Retail Merchandisers, with Sales Allowances and Sales Discounts Using a Perpetual Inventory System

LO6, 7

www.mhhe.com/phillips3e

The transactions listed below are typical of those involving New Books Inc. and Readers' Corner. New Books is a wholesale merchandiser and Readers' Corner is a retail merchandiser. Assume all sales of merchandise from New Books to Readers' Corner are made with terms 2/10, n/30, and that the two companies use perpetual inventory systems. Assume the following transactions between the two companies occurred in the order listed during the year ended August 31, 2010.

a. New Books sold merchandise to Readers' Corner at a selling price of $550,000. The merchandise had cost New Books $415,000.

b. Two days later, Readers' Corner complained to New Books that some of the merchandise differed from what Readers' Corner had ordered. New Books agreed to give an allowance of $10,000 to Readers' Corner.

c. Just three days later, Readers' Corner paid New Books, which settled all amounts owed.

Required:

1. For each of the events (a) through (c), indicate the amount and direction of the effect (+ for increase, − for decrease, and NE for no effect) on New Books in terms of the following items.

Sales Revenues	Sales Returns and Allowances	Sales Discounts	Net Sales	Cost of Goods Sold	Gross Profit

2. Which of the above items are likely to be reported on New Books's external financial statements, and which items will be combined "behind the scenes"?

3. Prepare the journal entries that New Books would record, and show any computations.

GROUP B PROBLEMS

PB6-1 Evaluating Internal Control Strengths and Weaknesses in Cash Receipts and Disbursements

LO3

The following procedures are used by Complete Wholesale Incorporated.

a. All sales are made on account, with each sale being indicated on a sequentially numbered sales invoice.

b. Customer payments are received in the mail by the office receptionist, who sends the checks to a cashier for deposit and the remittance advices to the accounting department for recording against the customer's account balance.

c. The office receptionist is assigned the job of handling all customer complaints.

d. When a customer has a legitimate complaint about goods sold to the customer on account, the receptionist will phone the accounting department to request that the customer's account be credited for the sales allowance.

e. The company's inventory is stored in a locked warehouse that is monitored by surveillance cameras.

f. Payments to the company's suppliers are made only after the supplier's invoice is received and compared to the receiving report.

Required:

1. Indicate whether each procedure represents a strength or weakness. Explain your reasons.

2. For each weakness, describe a change in procedures that would address the weakness.

LO4   PB6-2 Preparing a Bank Reconciliation and Journal Entries and Reporting Cash

The bookkeeper at Tony Company has asked you to prepare a bank reconciliation as of February 28, 2010. The February 28, 2010, bank statement and the February T-account for cash showed the following (summarized):

BANK STATEMENT						
		Checks	Deposits	Other		Balance
Balance, February 1, 2010						$49,400
February 2	#101	$15,000				34,400
February 4			$ 7,000			41,400
February 5				NSF	$320	41,080
February 9	#102	11,000				30,080
February 12	#103	7,500				22,580
February 14			9,500			32,080
February 19	#104	9,000				23,080
February 23			14,150			37,230
February 26	#105	6,700				30,530
February 27				Interest earned	150	30,680
February 28				Service charge	40	30,640

		+	Cash (A)	−	
Feb 1	Balance	49,400			
Feb 2		7,000	15,000	Feb 1 #101	
Feb 13		9,500	11,000	Feb 7 #102	
Feb 21		14,150	7,500	Feb 11 #103	
Feb 28		7,800	9,000	Feb 17 #104	
			6,700	Feb 25 #105	
			1,200	Feb 29 #106	
Feb 28	Balance	37,450			

Tony Company's bank reconciliation at the end of January 2010 showed no outstanding checks. No deposits were in transit at the end of January, but a deposit was in transit at the end of February.

Required:

1. Prepare a bank reconciliation for February.
2. Prepare any journal entries required as a result of the bank reconciliation. Why are they necessary?
3. After the reconciliation journal entries are posted, what balance will be reflected in the Cash account in the ledger?
4. If the company also has $50 on hand, which is recorded in a different account called Cash on Hand, what total amount of Cash and Cash Equivalents should be reported on the balance sheet at the end of February?

PB6-3 Identifying Outstanding Checks and Deposits in Transit and Preparing   **LO4**
     a Bank Reconciliation and Journal Entries

The September 2011 bank statement and cash T-account for Terrick Company follow:

		BANK STATEMENT		
Date	Checks	Deposits	Other	Balance
Sept. 1				$ 75,900
2	$620			75,280
4	2,000			73,280
6	1,500			71,780
11	300	14,000		85,480
13	650			84,830
17	10,000			74,830
23	90	27,000		101,740
26	700			101,040
28	8,000			93,040
29	730	17,000	NSF* $500	108,810
30	400		Interest earned 60	108,470
30			Service charge 40	108,430

*NSF check from B. Frank, a customer.

		+	Cash (A)	−	
Sept. 1	Balance	75,900	Checks written during September:		
Deposits			620	8,000	
Sept. 11		14,000	2,000	730	
23		27,000	1,500	400	
29		17,000	300	500	
30		21,000	650	6,000	
			10,000	90	
			700		
Sept. 30	Balance	123,410			

There were no deposits in transit or outstanding checks at August 31.

Required:

1. Identify and list the deposits in transit at the end of September.
2. Identify and list the outstanding checks at the end of September.
3. Prepare a bank reconciliation for September.
4. Give any journal entries that the company should make as a result of the bank reconciliation. Why are they necessary?
5. After the reconciliation journal entries are posted, what balance will be reflected in the Cash account in the ledger?
6. If the company also has $200 on hand, which is recorded in a different account called Cash on Hand, what total amount of Cash and Cash Equivalents should be reported on the September 30, 2011, balance sheet?

PB6-4 Preparing a Multistep Income Statement with Sales Discounts and Sales   **LO7**
     Returns and Allowances and Computing the Gross Profit Percentage

Emily's Greenhouse Corporation is a local greenhouse organized 10 years ago as a corporation. The greenhouse is in an excellent location, and sales have increased each year. At the end of

2011, the bookkeeper prepared the following statement (assume that all amounts are correct, but note the incorrect terminology and format):

EMILY'S GREENHOUSE CORPORATION
Profit and Loss
December 31, 2011

	Debit	Credit
Sales		$504,000
Cost of Goods Sold	$311,000	
Sales Returns and Allowances	11,000	
Sales Discounts	8,000	
Selling Expense	61,000	
Administrative Expense	13,000	
General Expenses	3,000	
Income Tax Expense	18,000	
Net Profit	79,000	
Totals	$504,000	$504,000

Required:

1. Prepare a multistep income statement that would be used for internal reporting purposes. Treat Sales Returns and Allowances and Sales Discounts as contra-revenue accounts.

2. Prepare a multistep income statement that would be used for external reporting purposes, beginning with the amount for Net Sales.

3. Compute and interpret the gross profit percentage (using the formula shown in this chapter).

LO6, 7   PB6-5 Recording Sales and Purchases with Discounts and Returns and Analyzing Gross Profit Percentage

Larry's Building Supplies (LBS) is a locally owned and operated hardware store. LBS uses a perpetual inventory system.

The following transactions (summarized) have been selected from 2010:

a.	Sold merchandise for cash (cost of merchandise $224,350).	$500,000
b.	Received merchandise returned by customers as unsatisfactory (but in perfect condition), for cash refund (original cost of merchandise $1,900).	3,000
c.	Sold merchandise (costing $3,000) to a customer, on account with terms 2/10, n/30.	5,000
d.	Collected half of the balance owed by the customer in (c) within the discount period.	2,450
e.	Granted an allowance to the customer in (c).	950

Required:

1. Compute Sales Revenue, Net Sales, and Gross Profit for LBS.

2. Compute the gross profit percentage (using the formula shown in this chapter).

3. Prepare journal entries to record transactions (a)–(e).

4. LBS is considering a contract to sell building supplies to a local home builder for $20,000. These materials will cost LBS $16,000. Would this contract increase (or decrease) LBS's gross profit and gross profit percentage? How should LBS decide whether to accept the contract?

LO5, 6, 7   PB6-6 Reporting Sales Transactions between Wholesale and Retail Merchandisers, with Sales Allowances and Sales Discounts Using a Perpetual Inventory System

The transactions listed below are typical of those involving Southern Sporting Goods and Sports R Us. Southern Sporting Goods is a wholesale merchandiser and Sports R Us is a retail merchandiser. Assume all sales of merchandise from Southern Sporting Goods to Sports R Us are made with terms 2/10, n/30, and that the two companies use perpetual inventory systems. Assume the following transactions between the two companies occurred in the order listed during the year ended December 31, 2011.

a. Southern Sporting Goods sold merchandise to Sports R Us at a selling price of $125,000. The merchandise had cost Southern Sporting Goods $94,000.

b. Two days later, Sports R Us complained to Southern Sporting Goods that some of the merchandise differed from what Sports R Us had ordered. Southern Sporting Goods agreed to give an allowance of $3,000 to Sports R Us.

c. Just three days later Sports R Us paid Southern Sporting Goods, which settled all amounts owed.

Required:

1. For each of the events (*a*) through (*c*), indicate the amount and direction of the effect (+ for increase, − for decrease, and NE for no effect) on Southern Sporting Goods in terms of the following items.

Sales Revenues	Sales Returns and Allowances	Sales Discounts	Net Sales	Cost of Goods Sold	Gross Profit

2. Which of the above items are likely to be reported on Southern Sporting Goods's external financial statements, and which items will be combined "behind the scenes"?

3. Prepare the journal entries that Southern Sporting Goods would record and show any computations.

SKILLS DEVELOPMENT CASES

Mc Graw Hill **connect™** |ACCOUNTING

L02, 7

S6-1 Finding Financial Information

Refer to the financial statements of The Home Depot in Appendix A at the end of this book, or download the annual report from the *Cases* section of the text's Web site at www.mhhe.com/phillips3e.

Required:

1. What amount of Net Sales does the company report during the year ended February 1, 2009?

2. Assuming that Cost of Sales is the same thing as Cost of Goods Sold, compute the company's gross profit percentage for the most recent two years. Has it risen or fallen? Explain the meaning of the change.

3. Assume that The Home Depot experienced no shrinkage in the most current year. Using the balance sheet and income statement, estimate the amount of purchases in the year ended February 1, 2009.

4. Refer to the "Report of Independent Registered Public Accounting Firm" in the annual report. To what "inherent limitations" of internal control is KPMG referring?

S6-2 Comparing Financial Information

L02, 7

Refer to the financial statements of The Home Depot in Appendix A and Lowe's in Appendix B at the end of this book, or download the annual reports from the *Cases* section of the text's Web site at www.mhhe.com/phillips3e.

Lowe's

1. Does Lowe's report higher or lower Net Sales than The Home Depot during the year ending near January 31, 2009?

2. Assuming that Cost of Sales is the same thing as Cost of Goods Sold, compute Lowe's gross profit percentage for the most recent two years. Is it greater or less than The Home Depot's? Based on this, where are consumers likely to find lower mark-ups?

3. Assume that Lowe's and The Home Depot experienced no shrinkage in the most recent year. Using the balance sheet and income statement, estimate the amount of purchases in the 2008–2009 year. How much greater (or less) were Lowe's purchases than The Home Depot's in that year?

4. Refer to the "Report of Independent Registered Public Accounting Firm" in The Home Depot's annual report and Lowe's annual report. Were the two companies' internal controls operating effectively?

S6-3 Internet-Based Team Research: Examining an Annual Report

L01, 7

As a team, select an industry to analyze. Using your Web browser, each team member should access the annual report or 10-K for one publicly traded company in the industry, with each member selecting a different company. (See S1-3 in Chapter 1 for a description of possible resources for these tasks.)

Required:

1. On an individual basis, each team member should write a short report that incorporates the following:

   a. Describe the company's business in sufficient detail to be able to classify it as a service, merchandising, or manufacturing company. What products or services does the company provide?

   b. Calculate the gross profit percentage at the end of the current and prior year, and explain any change between the two years.

2. Then, as a team, write a short report comparing and contrasting your companies using these attributes. Discuss any patterns across the companies that you as a team observe. Provide potential explanations for any differences discovered.

LO2, 5 **S6-4 Ethical Decision Making: A Real-Life Example**

When some people think about inventory theft, they imagine a shoplifter running out of a store with goods stuffed inside a jacket or bag. But that's not what the managers thought at the Famous Footwear store on Chicago's Madison Street. No, they suspected their own employees were the main cause of their unusually high shrinkage. One scam involved dishonest cashiers who would let their friends take a pair of Skechers without paying for them. To make it look like the shoes had been bought, cashiers would ring up a sale, but instead of charging $50 for shoes, they would charge only $2 for a bottle of shoe polish. That's when the company's managers decided to put its accounting system to work. In just two years, the company cut its Madison Street inventory losses in half. Here's how a newspaper described the store's improvements:

> ### Retailers Crack Down on Employee Theft
> *SouthCoast Today,* September 10, 2000, Chicago
> By Calmetta Coleman, *Wall Street Journal* Staff Writer
>
> . . . Famous Footwear installed a chainwide register-monitoring system to sniff out suspicious transactions, such as unusually large numbers of refunds or voids, or repeated sales of cheap goods.
>
> . . . [B]efore an employee can issue a cash refund, a second worker must be present to see the customer and inspect the merchandise.
>
> . . . [T]he chain has set up a toll-free hotline for employees to use to report suspicions about co-workers.

These improvements in inventory control came as welcome news for investors and creditors of Brown Shoe Company, the company that owns Famous Footwear. Despite these improvements at the Chicago store, Brown Shoe has been forced to shut down operations in other cities.

Required:

1. Explain how the register-monitoring system would allow Famous Footwear to cut down on employee theft.
2. What is the name of the control principle that is addressed by Famous Footwear's new cash refund procedure?
3. If Famous Footwear used a periodic inventory system, rather than a perpetual inventory system, how would the company detect shrinkage?
4. Think of and describe at least four different parties that are harmed by the type of inventory theft described in this case.

LO6, 7 **S6-5 Ethical Decision Making: A Mini-Case**

Assume you work as an accountant in the merchandising division of a large public company that makes and sells athletic clothing. To encourage the merchandising division to earn as much profit on each individual sale as possible, the division manager's pay is based, in part, on the division's gross profit percentage. To encourage control over the division's operating expenses, the manager's pay also is based on the division's net income.

You are currently preparing the division's financial statements. The division had a good year, with sales of $100,000, cost of goods sold of $50,000, sales returns and allowances of $6,000, sales discounts of $4,000, and other selling expenses of $30,000. (Assume the division does not report income taxes.) The division manager stresses that "*it would be in your personal interest*" to classify sales returns and allowances and sales discounts as selling expenses rather than as contra-revenues on the division's income statement. He justifies this "friendly advice" by saying that he's not asking you to fake the numbers—he just believes that those items are more accurately reported as expenses. Plus, he claims, being a division of a larger company, you don't have to follow GAAP.

Required:

1. Prepare an income statement for the division using the classifications shown in this chapter. Using this income statement, calculate the division's gross profit percentage.
2. Prepare an income statement for the division using the classifications advised by the manager. Using this income statement, calculate the division's gross profit percentage.

3. What reason (other than reporting "more accurately") do you think is motivating the manager's advice to you?
4. Do you agree with the manager's statement that "he's not asking you to fake the numbers"?
5. Do you agree with the manager's statement about not having to follow GAAP?
6. How should you respond to the division manager's "friendly advice"?

S6-6 Critical Thinking: Analyzing Internal Control Weaknesses

LO2

Snake Creek Company has a trusted employee who, as the owner said, "handles all of the book-keeping and paperwork for the company." This employee is responsible for counting, verifying, and recording cash receipts and payments, making the weekly bank deposit, preparing checks for major expenditures (signed by the owner), making small expenditures from the cash register for daily expenses, and collecting accounts receivable. The owner asked the local bank for a $20,000 loan. The bank asked that an audit be performed covering the year just ended. The independent auditor (a local CPA), in a private conference with the owner, presented some evidence of the following activities of the trusted employee during the past year:

a. Cash sales sometimes were not entered in the cash register, and the trusted employee pocketed approximately $50 per month.
b. Cash taken from the cash register (and pocketed by the trusted employee) was replaced with expense memos with fictitious signatures (approximately $12 per day).
c. $300 collected on an account receivable from a valued out-of-town customer was pocketed by the trusted employee and was covered by making a $300 entry as a debit to Sales Returns and a credit to Accounts Receivable.
d. $800 collected on an account receivable from a local customer was pocketed by the trusted employee and was covered by making an $800 entry as a debit to Sales Discounts and a credit to Accounts Receivable.

Required:

1. What was the approximate amount stolen during the past year?
   TIP: Assume employees work 5 days a week, 52 weeks a year.
2. What would be your recommendations to the owner?

S6-7 Preparing Multistep Income Statements and Calculating Gross Profit Percentage

LO6, 7

www.mhhe.com/phillips3e

Assume that you have been hired by Big Sky Corporation as a summer intern. The company is in the process of preparing its annual financial statements. To help in the process, you are asked to prepare an income statement for internal reporting purposes and an income statement for external reporting purposes. Your boss has also requested that you determine the company's gross profit percentage based on the statements that you are to prepare. The following adjusted trial balance was created from the general ledger accounts on May 31, 2010.

Account Titles	Debits	Credits
Cash	$ 57,000	
Accounts Receivable	67,000	
Inventory	103,000	
Property and Equipment	252,000	
Accumulated Depreciation		$103,000
Liabilities		75,000
Contributed Capital		120,000
Retained Earnings, June 1, 2009		145,900
Sales Revenue		369,000
Sales Returns and Allowances	9,500	
Sales Discounts	14,000	
Cost of Goods Sold	248,000	
Selling Expense	19,000	
Administrative Expense	23,000	
General Expenses	5,000	
Income Tax Expense	15,400	
Totals	$812,900	$812,900

Your boss wants you to create the spreadsheet in a way that automatically recalculates net sales and any other related amounts whenever changes are made to the contra-revenue accounts. To do this, you know that you'll have to use formulas throughout the worksheets and even import or link cells from one worksheet to another. Once again, your friend Owen is willing to help.

From: Owentheaccountant@yahoo.com
To: Helpme@hotmail.com
Cc:
Subject: Excel Help

Sounds like you are going to get some great experience this summer. Okay, to import a number from another spreadsheet, you first click on the cell where you want the number to appear. For example, if you want to enter the Net Sales balance in the external income statement, click on the cell in the external income statement where the Net Sales number is supposed to appear. Enter the equals sign (=) and then click on the tab that takes you to the worksheet containing the internal income statement. In that worksheet, click on the cell that contains the amount you want to import into the external income statement and then press enter. This will create a link from the internal income statement cell to the external income statement cell. Here's a screen shot showing the formula that will appear after you import the number.

	S6-7 - Microsoft Excel	

Home	Insert	Page Layout	Formulas	Data	Review	View

G5 f_x ='Internal Income Statement'!G8

	A	B	C	D	E	F	G	H
1				Big Sky Corporation				
2				Income Statement				
3				For the Year Ended May 31, 2010				
4								
5	Net sales						345,500	
6	Cost of goods sold						248,000	
7	Gross profit							
8								

Internal Income Statement   **External Income Statement**

Ready   100%

Don't forget to save the file using a name that indicates who you are.

Required:

Enter the trial balance information into a spreadsheet and complete the following:
1. Prepare a multistep income statement that would be used for internal reporting purposes. Classify sales returns and allowances and sales discounts as contra-revenue accounts.
2. Prepare a multistep income statement that would be used for external reporting purposes, beginning with the amount for Net Sales.
3. Compute the gross profit percentage.

CONTINUING CASE

LO6, 7   **CC6 Accounting for Merchandising Operations**

Nicole's Getaway Spa (NGS) has been so successful that Nicole has decided to expand her spa by selling merchandise. She sells things such as nail polish, at-home spa kits, cosmetics, and aromatherapy items. Nicole uses a perpetual inventory system and is starting to realize all of the work that is created when inventory is involved in a business. The following transactions were selected from among those completed by NGS in August.

Aug. 2   Sold 10 items of merchandise to Salon World on account at a selling price of $1,000 (total); terms 2/10, n/30. The goods cost NGS $650.

Aug. 3   Sold 5 identical items of merchandise to Cosmetics R Us on account at a selling price of $825 (total); terms 2/10, n/30. The goods cost NGS $400.

Aug. 6   Cosmetics R Us returned one of the items purchased on August 3. The item could still be sold by NGS in the future, and credit was given to the customer.

Aug. 10   Collected payment from Salon World, fully paying off the account balance.

Aug. 20   Sold two at-home spa kits to Meghan Witzel for $300 cash. The goods cost NGS $96.

Aug. 22   Cosmetics R Us paid its remaining account balance in full.

Required:

1. Prepare journal entries for each transaction.
2. Calculate the amount of Net Sales and Cost of Goods Sold for the transactions listed above. What is Nicole's Getaway Spa's gross profit percentage? Explain to Nicole what this gross profit percentage means.
3. At the end of August, Nicole noticed that the bank account balance did not equal the company's Cash account balance. Explain to her why these balances do not equal and what related internal control she needs to establish.

CHAPTER 7

Reporting and Interpreting Inventories and Cost of Goods Sold

YOUR LEARNING OBJECTIVES

Understand the business

LO1   Describe the issues in managing different types of inventory.

Study the accounting methods

LO2   Explain how to report inventory and cost of goods sold.

LO3   Compute costs using four inventory costing methods.

LO4   Report inventory at the lower of cost or market.

LO5   Analyze and record inventory purchases, transportation, returns and allowances, and discounts.

Evaluate the results

LO6   Evaluate inventory management by computing and interpreting the inventory turnover ratio.

Review the chapter

THAT WAS

THEN

In the previous chapter, we focused on selling goods that were purchased at the same cost per unit.

Lecture Presentation-LP7
www.mhhe.com/phillips3e

FOCUS COMPANY: American Eagle Outfitters

www.ae.com

AMERICAN EAGLE
OUTFITTERS
ae.com

Whether you are shopping for gasoline, groceries, or a new flat-screen TV, prices always seem to be changing. The political situation in oil-producing nations can cause a stunning increase in prices at the pump. A late freeze in Florida can hike the price of orange juice. Increasing competition can dramatically lower the cost of that new TV.

Like you, companies face similar price changes when they purchase or produce goods. Increases in demand can cause the cost of inventory to increase over time; technological innovation can cause it to decrease. Either way, inventory is likely to include some items that were acquired at a lower unit cost and others that were acquired at a higher unit cost.

Suppose clothing retailer American Eagle Outfitters buys three batches of its AE Fleece Jackets at a cost of $20 per jacket for the first batch, $30 per jacket for the second batch, and $40 per jacket for the third. When American Eagle sells a jacket, what cost should it use to compute the Cost of Goods Sold? And, what happens at the end of the season when the value of its jackets falls below cost? As you will learn in this chapter, accounting rules allow different methods to be used when accounting for inventory, each of which leads to reporting different dollar amounts for Cost of Goods Sold (and the items remaining in inventory). This flexibility allows managers to choose the method that best fits their business environment. But it also means that you must know which method managers are using and how it works. That's what we'll look at in this chapter.

THIS IS
NOW

This chapter demonstrates how to account for goods purchased at different unit costs.

ORGANIZATION OF THE CHAPTER

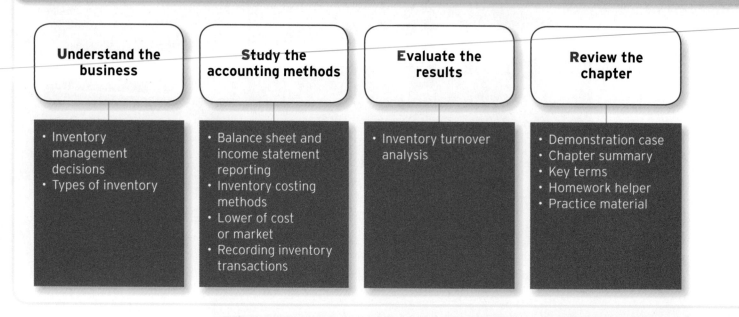

Understand the business	**Study the accounting methods**	**Evaluate the results**	**Review the chapter**
• Inventory management decisions • Types of inventory	• Balance sheet and income statement reporting • Inventory costing methods • Lower of cost or market • Recording inventory transactions	• Inventory turnover analysis	• Demonstration case • Chapter summary • Key terms • Homework helper • Practice material

Understand the Business

Learning Objective 1
Describe the issues in managing different types of inventory.

INVENTORY MANAGEMENT DECISIONS

You may not make or sell inventory, but you buy it all the time. The things that concern you as a consumer also concern managers who make inventory decisions. The primary goals of inventory managers are to (1) maintain a sufficient **quantity** of inventory to meet customers' needs and (2) ensure inventory **quality** meets customers' expectations and company standards. At the same time, they try to (3) minimize the **cost** of acquiring and carrying inventory (including costs related to purchasing, production, storage, spoilage, theft, obsolescence, and financing). These factors are tricky to manage because as one of them changes (e.g., quality) so, too, do the others (e.g., cost). Ultimately, inventory management often comes down to purchasing goods that can be sold soon after they are acquired.

TYPES OF INVENTORY

The generic term *inventory* means goods that are held for sale in the normal course of business or are used to produce other goods for sale. Merchandisers hold **merchandise inventory,** which consists of products acquired in a finished condition, ready for sale without further processing. Manufacturers often hold three types of inventory, with each representing a different stage in the manufacturing process. They start with **raw materials inventory** such as plastic, steel, or fabrics. When these raw materials enter the production process, they become part of **work in process inventory,** which includes goods that are in the process of being manufactured. When completed, work in process inventory becomes **finished goods inventory,** which is ready for sale just like merchandise inventory. For purposes of this chapter, we'll focus on merchandise inventory, but be aware that the concepts we cover apply equally to manufacturers' inventory.

Two other accounting terms may be used to describe inventory. **Consignment inventory** refers to goods a company is holding on behalf of the goods' owner. Typically, this arises when a company is willing to sell the goods for the owner (for a fee) but does not want to take ownership of the goods in the event the goods are difficult to sell. Consignment inventory is reported on the balance sheet of the owner, not the company holding the inventory. **Goods in transit** are inventory items being transported. This type of inventory is reported on the balance sheet of the owner, not the company transporting it. As you may remember

310

from Chapter 6, ownership of inventory is determined by the terms of the inventory sales agreement. If a sale is made FOB destination, the goods belong to the seller until they reach their destination (the customer). If a sale is made FOB shipping point, inventory belongs to the customer at the point of shipping (from the seller's premises).

Study the Accounting Methods

BALANCE SHEET AND INCOME STATEMENT REPORTING

Because inventory will be used or converted into cash within one year, it is reported on the balance sheet as a current asset. Goods placed in inventory are initially recorded at cost, which is the amount paid to acquire the asset and prepare it for sale. See Exhibit 7.1 for the way American Eagle reports inventory.

> **Learning Objective 2**
> Explain how to report inventory and cost of goods sold.

EXHIBIT 7.1	Reporting Inventory on the Balance Sheet (Partial)

AMERICAN EAGLE
OUTFITTERS
ae.com

AMERICAN EAGLE OUTFITTERS, INC.
Balance Sheets (Partial)
At January 31, 2009 and 2008

(in millions)	2009	2008
Assets		
Current Assets		
Cash and Cash Equivalents	$473	$116
Short-term Investments	11	504
Inventory	295	286
Accounts and Note Receivable	41	32
Prepaid Expenses and Other	105	82

When a company sells goods, it removes their cost from the Inventory account and reports the cost on the income statement as the expense Cost of Goods Sold. See Exhibit 7.2 for how American Eagle reports the Cost of Goods Sold (CGS) on its partial income statement. Notice that it follows directly after Net Sales. The difference between these two line items is a subtotal called Gross Profit.

EXHIBIT 7.2	Reporting Cost of Goods Sold on the Income Statement (Partial)

AMERICAN EAGLE
OUTFITTERS
ae.com

AMERICAN EAGLE OUTFITTERS, INC.
Income Statements (Partial)
For the Years Ended January 31, 2009, 2008, and 2007

(in millions)	2009	2008	2007
Net Sales	$2,989	$3,055	$2,794
Cost of Goods Sold	1,815	1,632	1,454
Gross Profit	1,174	1,423	1,340

Cost of Goods Sold Equation

Although the cost of inventory and the cost of goods sold are reported on different financial statements, they are related. A company starts each accounting period with a stock of inventory called **beginning inventory (BI).** During the accounting period, new **purchases (P)** are added to the beginning inventory. As in Exhibit 7.3, the sum of these two amounts (BI + P) becomes the cost of **goods available for sale** during the period.

YOU SHOULD KNOW

Goods available for sale: The sum of beginning inventory and purchases for the period.

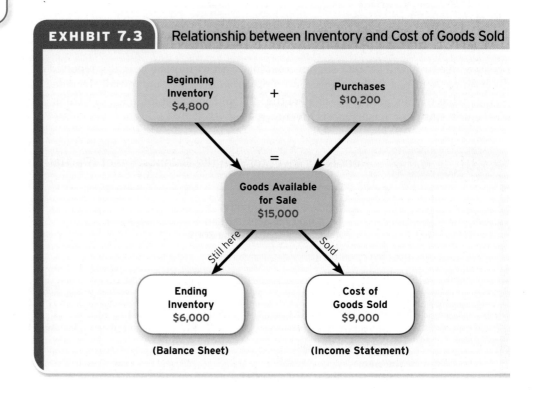

EXHIBIT 7.3 | Relationship between Inventory and Cost of Goods Sold

Goods available for sale either will be sold during the period (reported as the cost of goods sold on the income statement) or not (reported as **ending inventory (EI)** on the balance sheet). The ending inventory for one accounting period then becomes the beginning inventory for the next period. The **cost of goods sold (CGS) equation** summarizes the relationships between these inventory amounts:

YOU SHOULD KNOW

Cost of goods sold (CGS) equation: BI + P − EI = CGS.

$$BI + P - CGS = EI$$

To illustrate the CGS equation, assume that, as in Exhibit 7.3, American Eagle Outfitters began the period with $4,800 of Vintage Jeans in beginning inventory. During the period, the company purchased more of these jeans for $10,200. This meant that American Eagle had goods costing $15,000 that were available for sale. If the cost of goods sold for the period was $9,000, $6,000 of jeans was left in inventory at the end of the period. These amounts can be represented in the following cost of goods sold equation or Inventory T-account:

Cost of Goods Sold Calculation

Beginning Inventory	$ 4,800
+ Purchases	+10,200
Goods Available for Sale	15,000
− Cost of Goods Sold	− 9,000
Ending Inventory	$ 6,000

+	Inventory (A)		−
Beginning Inventory	4,800		
Purchases of Inventory	10,200	9,000	Cost of Goods Sold
Ending Inventory	6,000		

If one of these values is unknown, you can use either the cost of goods sold equation or the inventory T-account to solve for the missing value. See for yourself in the following Self-Study Practice.

How's it going?   Self-Study Practice

Use the cost of goods sold equation to solve for the missing information for cases 1 and 2. Then enter the information for either case 1 or case 2 into the T-account on the right.

		Case 1	Case 2
Beginning Inventory	5 units × $10	$ 50	$ 50
+ Purchases	20 units × $10	200	200
Goods Available for Sale			250
− Ending Inventory		100	
Cost of Goods Sold			$150

dr +	Inventory		cr −
Beginning	50		
Purchases	200		
Goods Available			
			Goods Sold
Ending Inventory			

After you have finished, check your answers with the solution in the margin.

Solution to Self-Study Practice
Case 1: Goods available = $250, CGS = $150
Case 2: Ending inventory = $100

dr +	Inventory		cr −
Beginning Inventory	50		
Purchases	200		
Goods Available	250	150	Goods Sold
Ending Inventory	100		

INVENTORY COSTING METHODS

In the example presented in the Self-Study Practice, the cost of all units of the item was the same—$10. If inventory costs normally remained constant, we'd be done right now. But just as you notice every time you fill up your car with gas, the cost of goods does not always stay the same. In recent years, the costs of many items have risen moderately. In other cases, such as LCD TVs, costs have dropped dramatically.

When the costs of inventory change over time, it is not obvious how to determine the cost of goods sold (and the cost of ending inventory). To see why, think about the following simple example:

May 3	Purchased 1 unit for **$70.**
May 5	Purchased 1 more unit for **$75.**
May 6	Purchased 1 more unit for **$95.**
May 8	Sold 2 units for $125 each.

The sale on May 8 of two units, at a selling price of $125 each, would generate sales revenue of $250 ($125 × 2), but what amount would be considered the cost of goods sold? The answer depends on which goods are assumed to have been sold.

Four generally accepted inventory costing methods are available for determining the cost of goods sold and the cost of goods remaining in ending inventory. The method chosen does not have to correspond to the physical flow of goods, so any one of these four methods is acceptable under GAAP in the United States.

The **specific identification** method individually identifies and records the cost of each item sold as Cost of Goods Sold. This method requires accountants to keep track of the purchase cost of each item. In the example just given, if the items sold were identified as the ones received on May 3 and May 6, which cost $70 and $95, the total cost of those items ($70 + $95 = $165) would be reported as Cost of Goods Sold. The cost of the remaining item ($75) would be reported as Inventory on the balance sheet at the end of the period. Companies tend to use the specific identification method when accounting for individually expensive and unique items. Toll Brothers, the country's leading builder of luxury homes, reports the costs of home construction using the specific identification method. Car Max, a national auto dealership, uses specific identification too.

The units within each American Eagle product line are identical, so the company does not use the specific identification method. Like most companies, American Eagle uses

Learning Objective 3
Compute costs using four inventory costing methods.

Video 7.1
www.mhhe.com/phillips3e

YOU SHOULD KNOW

Specific identification: The inventory costing method that identifies the cost of the specific item that was sold.

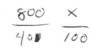

YOU SHOULD KNOW

First-in, first-out (FIFO):
Assumes that the costs of the
first goods purchased (first in)
are the costs of the first goods
sold (first out).

YOU SHOULD KNOW

Last-in, first-out (LIFO):
Assumes that the costs of the
last goods purchased (last in)
are the costs of the first goods
sold (first out).

YOU SHOULD KNOW

Weighted average cost: An
inventory costing assumption
that uses the weighted average
unit cost of the goods available
for sale for both cost of goods
sold and ending inventory.

one of the three other cost flow methods to account for inventory items. These three other inventory costing methods are **not based on the physical flow** of goods on and off the shelves. Instead, these methods are based on **assumptions** that accountants make about the flow of inventory costs. These three cost flow assumptions are applied to our simple three-unit example in Exhibit 7.4.

1. **First-in, first-out (FIFO)** assumes that the inventory costs flow out in the order the goods are received. As in Exhibit 7.4, the earliest items received, the $70 and $75 units received on May 3 and 5, become the $145 Cost of Goods Sold on the income statement and the remaining $95 unit received on May 6 becomes ending Inventory on the balance sheet.

2. **Last-in, first-out (LIFO)** assumes that the inventory costs flow out in the opposite of the order the goods are received. As in Exhibit 7.4, the latest items received, the $95 and $75 units received on May 6 and 5, become the $170 Cost of Goods Sold on the income statement, and the remaining $70 unit received on May 3 becomes ending Inventory on the balance sheet.

3. **Weighted average cost** uses the weighted average of the costs of goods available for sale for both the cost of each item sold and those remaining in inventory. As in Exhibit 7.4, the average of the costs [($70 + $75 + $95) ÷ 3 = $80] is assigned to the two items sold, resulting in $160 as Cost of Goods Sold on the income statement. The same $80 average cost is assigned to the one item in ending Inventory reported on the balance sheet.

As Exhibit 7.4 illustrates, the choice of cost flow assumption can have a major effect on Gross Profit on the income statement and Inventory on the balance sheet. Exxon Mobil, for example, could increase its Gross Profit by nearly $10 billion if it were to switch from LIFO to FIFO. But doing so would also increase the company's income taxes, so it hasn't made the switch.

Notice that although they're called "inventory" costing methods, their names actually describe how to calculate the cost of goods sold. That is, the "first-out" part of FIFO and LIFO refers to the goods that are sold (i.e., first out) not the goods that are still in ending inventory. Also notice that the cost flows assumed for LIFO are the exact opposite of FIFO, and weighted average is a middle-of-the-road method. Here's

EXHIBIT 7.4   **Cost Flow Assumptions and Financial Statement Effects**

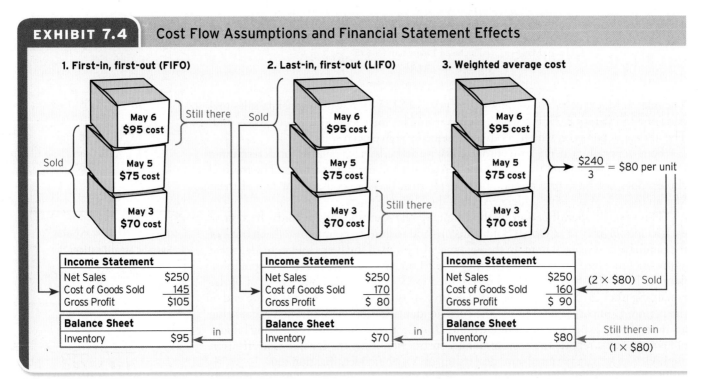

1. First-in, first-out (FIFO)

Sold

May 6 $95 cost	Still there
May 5 $75 cost	
May 3 $70 cost	

Income Statement

Net Sales	$250
Cost of Goods Sold	145
Gross Profit	$105

Balance Sheet

| Inventory | $95 |

in

2. Last-in, first-out (LIFO)

Sold

May 6 $95 cost	
May 5 $75 cost	
May 3 $70 cost	Still there

Income Statement

Net Sales	$250
Cost of Goods Sold	170
Gross Profit	$ 80

Balance Sheet

| Inventory | $70 |

in

3. Weighted average cost

May 6 $95 cost	
May 5 $75 cost	$\frac{\$240}{3} = \$80$ per unit
May 3 $70 cost	

Income Statement

Net Sales	$250	
Cost of Goods Sold	160	(2 × $80) Sold
Gross Profit	$ 90	

Balance Sheet

| Inventory | $80 | Still there in (1 × $80) |

a summary of whether the oldest, newest, or average unit costs are used to calculate amounts on the balance sheet or income statement.

	FIFO	LIFO	Weighted Average
Cost of Goods Sold (Income Statement)	Oldest cost	Newest cost	Average cost
Inventory (Balance Sheet)	Newest cost	Oldest cost	Average cost

Inventory Cost Flow Computations

Now that you've seen how these cost flow assumptions work and that they actually make a difference in a company's balance sheet and income statement, you're ready for a more realistic example. So, let's assume that during the first week of October American Eagle entered into the following transactions for its Henley T-shirt product line. All sales were made at a selling price of $15 per unit. These sales occurred after American Eagle made two batches of T-shirt purchases, which were added to inventory purchased the previous month.

Date	Description	# of Units	Cost per Unit	Total Cost
Oct. 1	Beginning Inventory	10	$ 7	$ 70
Oct. 3	Purchase	30	8	240
Oct. 5	Purchase	10	10	100
Oct. 6	Sales	(35)	To calculate	To calculate
	Ending Inventory	15	To calculate	To calculate

FIFO (First-in, first-out)   The first-in, first-out (FIFO) method assumes that the oldest goods (the first in to inventory) are the first ones sold (the first out of inventory). So **to calculate the cost of the 35 units sold, use the costs of the first-in (oldest) goods** (10 units at $7 plus 25 of the 30 units at $8 = a total of $270). The **costs of the newer goods are included in the cost of the ending inventory** (10 units at $10 plus 5 units remaining from the 30 units at $8 = a total of $140). These calculations are summarized in the table below.

FIFO		
Beginning Inventory	10 units × $7	$ 70
+ Purchases	30 units × $8	240
	10 units × $10	100
Goods Available for Sale		410
− Ending Inventory (10 × $10) + (5 × $8)		**140**
Cost of Goods Sold (10 × $7) + (25 × $8)		$270

> **COACH'S TIP**
>
> Notice that the name of the method (first-in, first-out) describes how to calculate the cost of goods sold. The cost of ending inventory using FIFO is based on costs last-in.

Notice in the table that the Cost of Goods Sold can be calculated directly (10 times $7 plus 25 times $8 = a total of $270) or it can be "backed into" by subtracting the cost of ending inventory from the cost of goods available for sale ($410 − $140 = $270). This latter approach is helpful if the number of units sold is not known, which can occur when a company uses a periodic inventory system.[1]

---

[1]By showing all purchases taking place before any Sales and Cost of Goods Sold are computed, we are demonstrating a periodic inventory system. You might think it's odd that we use a periodic system when we said in Chapter 6 that most modern companies use perpetual inventory systems. We actually have several good reasons for doing this, which we explain in Supplement 7A at the end of this chapter. To learn how cost flow assumptions are applied in more complex situations involving perpetual inventory systems, see Supplement 7A. For purposes of examples shown in the chapter and for problem materials at the end of this chapter, we assume no shrinkage (a topic discussed in Chapter 6).

LIFO (Last-in, first-out) The last-in, first-out (LIFO) method assumes that the newest goods (the last in to inventory) are the first ones sold (the first out of inventory). So to calculate the cost of the 35 units sold, use the costs of the last-in (newest) goods (10 units at $10 plus 25 of the 30 units at $8 = total of $300). The costs of the older goods are included in the cost of the ending inventory (10 units at $7 plus 5 units remaining from the 30 units at $8 = a total of $110). These calculations are summarized in the table below.

COACH'S TIP

The name of the method (last-in, first-out) describes how to calculate the cost of goods sold. The cost of ending inventory using LIFO is based on costs first-in. (Think of this as "first-in, still there" or FIST.)

LIFO

Beginning Inventory	10 units × $7	$ 70
+ Purchases	30 units × $8	240
	10 units × $10	100
Goods Available for Sale		410
− Ending Inventory (10 × $7) + (5 × $8)		110
Cost of Goods Sold (10 × $10) + (25 × $8)		$300

As in the table, Cost of Goods Sold can be calculated directly (10 times $10 plus 25 times $8 = a total of $300) or it can be "backed into" by subtracting the cost of ending inventory from the cost of goods available for sale ($410 − $110 = $300). We actually recommend that you do both, as a way to double-check your calculations.

Weighted Average Cost The weighted average cost method is calculated in two steps. The first step is to calculate the total cost of the goods available for sale. You multiply the number of units at each cost by the cost per unit and then add to get the total cost:

Beginning Inventory	10 units × $7	$ 70
+ Purchases	30 units × $8	240
	10 units × $10	100
Goods Available for Sale	50 units	$410

Then you calculate the weighted average cost per unit using the following formula:

$$\text{Weighted Average Cost} = \frac{\text{Cost of Goods Available for Sale}}{\text{Number of Units Available for Sale}} = \frac{\$410}{50 \text{ units}} = \$8.20 \text{ per unit}$$

Cost of goods sold and ending inventory are both calculated using the same weighted average cost per unit, as in the following table.

COACH'S TIP

To calculate weighted average cost, be sure to weight the costs by the number of units at each unit cost. Don't simply average the unit costs [($7 + $8 + $10) ÷ 3 = $8.33]. That is a simple average—not a weighted average.

Weighted Average

Beginning Inventory	10 units × $7	$ 70
+ Purchases	30 units × $8	240
	10 units × $10	100
Goods Available for Sale	50 units	410
− Ending Inventory (15 × $8.20)		123
Cost of Goods Sold (35 × $8.20)		$287

Financial Statement Effects Exhibit 7.5 summarizes the financial statement effects of the FIFO, LIFO, and weighted average cost methods. Remember that these methods differ only in the way they split the cost of goods available for sale between ending inventory and cost of goods sold. If a cost goes into Inventory, it doesn't go into

EXHIBIT 7.5	Financial Statement Effects of Inventory Costing Methods

Effects on the Income Statement	FIFO	LIFO	Weighted Average
Sales	$525	$525	$525
Cost of Goods Sold	270	300	287
Gross Profit	255	225	238
Operating Expenses	125	125	125
Income from Operations	130	100	113
Other Revenue (Expenses)	20	20	20
Income before Income Tax Expense	150	120	133
Income Tax Expense (assume 30%)	45	36	40
Net Income	$105	$ 84	$ 93
Effects on the Balance Sheet			
Inventory	$140	$110	$123

Cost of Goods Sold. Thus, the method that assigns the highest cost to ending inventory will assign the lowest cost to cost of goods sold (and vice versa). As you can see in Exhibit 7.5, the effect on Cost of Goods Sold affects many other items on the income statement including Gross Profit, Income from Operations, Income before Income Tax Expense, Income Tax Expense, and Net Income.

Depending on whether costs are rising or falling, different methods have different effects on the financial statements. **When costs are rising,** as they are in our example, FIFO produces a higher inventory value (making the balance sheet **appear** to be stronger) and a lower cost of goods sold (resulting in a higher gross profit, which makes the company **look** more profitable). **When costs are falling,** these effects are reversed; FIFO produces a lower ending inventory value and a higher cost of goods sold—a double whammy. These are not "real" economic effects, however, because the same number of units is sold or held in ending inventory under either method. The following table summarizes the effects:

Effects of Increasing Costs on the Financial Statements		
	FIFO	**LIFO**
Inventory (Balance Sheet)	Higher	Lower
Cost of Goods Sold (Income Statement)	Lower	Higher
Effects of Decreasing Costs on the Financial Statements		
	FIFO	**LIFO**
Inventory (Balance Sheet)	Lower	Higher
Cost of Goods Sold (Income Statement)	Higher	Lower

Tax Implications and Cash Flow Effects Given the financial statement effects, you might wonder why a company would ever use a method that produces a lower inventory amount and a higher cost of goods sold. The answer is suggested in Exhibit 7.5, in the line called Income Tax Expense. **When faced with increasing costs per unit,** as in our example, **a company that uses FIFO will have a higher income tax expense.** This income tax effect is a real cost, in the sense that the company will actually have to pay more income taxes in the current year, thereby reducing the company's cash.

Solution to Self-Study Practice

	(a) FIFO	(b) Weighted Average	(c) LIFO
Sales Revenue (3 × $1,000)	$3,000	$3,000	$3,000
Cost of Goods Sold*	1,000	1,050	1,200
Gross Profit	2,000	1,950	1,800
Ending Inventory	$ 400	$ 350	$ 200

*(a) $1,000 = (1 × $200) + (2 × $400); (b) $1,050 = 3 × [(1 × $200) + (3 × $400)]/4; (c) $1,200 = 3 × $400

LIFO minimizes Ultimo's gross profit and, therefore, minimizes its income taxes.

How's it going?   Self-Study Practice

Ultimo Euromoda, Inc., purchased one designer suit at a cost of $200 and then purchased three more for $400 each. Three of the suits are then sold at a price of $1,000 each. Compute the Sales Revenue, Cost of Goods Sold, Gross Profit, and the cost of ending Inventory using (a) FIFO, (b) weighted average, and (c) LIFO. Which inventory costing method will minimize Ultimo's income taxes?

After you have finished, check your answers with the solution in the margin.

Consistency in Reporting   A common question people ask is whether managers are free to choose LIFO one period, FIFO the next, and then back to LIFO, depending on whether unit costs are rising or declining during the period. Because this constant switching would make it difficult to compare financial results across periods, accounting rules discourage it. A change in method is allowed only if it will improve the accuracy with which the company's financial results and financial position are measured. A company can, however, use different methods for inventories that differ in nature or use, provided that the methods are used consistently over time. Tax rules also limit the methods that can be used. In the United States, the LIFO Conformity Rule requires that if LIFO is used on the income tax return, it also must be used in financial statement reporting.

Spotlight On THE WORLD

No LIFO

Approximately 36 percent of companies in the United States currently use LIFO,* but **International Financial Reporting Standards (IFRS) do not allow LIFO** so a switch to IFRS will require many U.S. companies to stop using LIFO in their financial statements. And if these companies stop using LIFO in their financial statements, the LIFO Conformity Rule will require that they stop using LIFO in their tax returns. Without LIFO, these companies will have higher tax bills (as illustrated in Exhibit 7.5), the total cost of which is estimated to be more than $100 billion.‡

*American Institute of Certified Public Accountants, *Accounting Trends and Techniques*, 62nd ed. 2008, p. 159.

‡House Ways and Means Committee, "H.R. 3970, Tax Reduction and Reform Act of 2007 (October 29, 2007)."

Learning Objective 4
Report inventory at the lower of cost or market.

LOWER OF COST OR MARKET

The value of inventory can fall below its recorded cost for two reasons: (1) it's easily replaced by identical goods at a lower cost, or (2) it's become outdated or damaged. The first case typically involves high-tech goods such as cell phones. As companies become more efficient at making these cutting-edge products, they become cheaper to make. The second case commonly occurs with fad items or seasonal goods such as American Eagle's winter coats, which tend to drop in value at the end of the season.

In either instance, when the value of inventory falls below its recorded cost, GAAP require that the amount that was originally recorded for inventory be written down to its lower market value. This rule is known as reporting inventories at the **lower of cost or market (LCM).** It results in reporting inventory conservatively, at an amount that does not exceed its actual value. Also, by recording the write-down in the period in which a loss in value occurs, companies better match their revenues and expenses of that period.

YOU SHOULD KNOW

Lower of cost or market (LCM): A valuation rule that requires Inventory to be written down when its market value falls below its cost.

Let's look at how the inventory write-down is determined and recorded. Assume that American Eagle's ending inventory includes two items whose replacement costs have recently changed: leather coats and vintage jeans.[2] The replacement costs of these items can be used as estimates of market value and compared to the original recorded cost per unit. You then take the lower of those two amounts (the lower of cost or market) and multiply it by the number of units on hand. The result is the amount at which the inventory should be reported after all adjustments have been made:

Item	Cost per Item	Market Value per Item	LCM per Item	Quantity	Total Lower of Cost or Market	Total Cost	Write-down
Leather coats	$165	$150	$150	1,000	1,000 × $150 = $150,000	$165,000	$15,000
Vintage jeans	20	25	20	400	400 × $ 20 = 8,000	8,000	0

Because the market value of the 1,000 leather coats ($150) is **lower** than the recorded cost ($165), the recorded amount for ending inventory should be written down by $15 per unit ($165 − $150). If American Eagle has 1,000 units in inventory, the total write-down should be $15,000 ($15 × 1,000). The effect of this write-down on the accounting equation and the journal entry to record it would be:

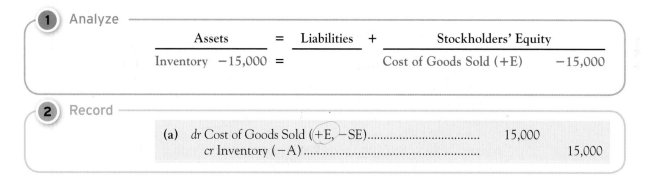

1 Analyze

Assets	=	Liabilities	+	Stockholders' Equity	
Inventory −15,000	=			Cost of Goods Sold (+E)	−15,000

2 Record

(a) *dr* Cost of Goods Sold (+E, −SE).................................	15,000	
cr Inventory (−A)...		15,000

Because the market value of the vintage jeans ($25) is higher than the original cost ($20), no write-down is necessary. The vintage jeans remain on the books at their cost of $20 per unit ($8,000 in total). Their value should not be increased based on the higher replacement cost because GAAP require that they be reported at the **lower** of cost or market.

Most companies report their inventory write-down expense as Cost of Goods Sold, even though the written-down goods may not have been sold. This reporting is appropriate because writing down goods that haven't yet sold is a necessary cost of carrying the goods that did sell. By recording the write-down in the period in which a loss in value occurs, companies better match their revenues and expenses of that period.

COACH'S TIP

Companies generally report their accounting policy for inventory in the first note to the financial statements.

Spotlight On THE WORLD

Recovery in Inventory Value

Like GAAP, IFRS require that inventory be reported at the lower of cost or market (LCM). However, inventory LCM rules under IFRS differ from GAAP in an important way. With IFRS, if a decline in market value reverses, for example because of an economic recovery, the value of inventory is written back up to its original cost and the recovery is credited to Cost of Goods Sold. With GAAP, reversals of inventory write-downs are not allowed.

[2]We apply lower of cost or market on an item basis. It also may be applied on a product line basis.

Most analysts view an inventory write-down to LCM as a sign of inventory management problems. Knowing this, some executives have gone out of their way to avoid inventory write-downs, as the following Spotlight on Ethics explains. The failure to follow inventory LCM rules is one of the most common types of financial statement misstatements. To learn more about how this misstatement and other inventory errors can affect the financial statements, see Supplement 7B at the end of this chapter.

Spotlight On ETHICS

www.mhhe.com/phillips3e

Dodging Bullets

David H. Brooks, the founder and former chief executive officer of DHB Industries, Inc., was charged in October 2007 for his involvement in fraudulently misstating DHB's financial statements. His company produced 50,000 bulletproof vests using a material (Zylon) that allegedly was known to degrade rapidly. The fraud charge claims that DHB knew that these quality problems led to a decline in the inventory's market value but failed to write down the inventory to LCM on a timely basis. The company eventually did record inventory write-downs totaling $18 million, causing a reduction in assets and net income. But this information came too late for some DHB stockholders who had unsuspectingly invested in a failing company. To learn more about this fraud, see E7-12 at the end of this chapter.

Learning Objective 5
Analyze and record inventory purchases, transportation, returns and allowances, and discounts.

RECORDING INVENTORY TRANSACTIONS

To this point in the chapter, we have described the requirement that inventory be reported at the lower of cost or market, and we have shown how those values are determined. But we haven't discussed the details about how to record inventory transactions. Until now, we have considered only inventory purchases but not other related transactions including transportation, purchase returns and allowances, and purchase discounts. In this section, we demonstrate the accounting for these other transactions. For purposes of this demonstration, we record all inventory-related transactions in the Inventory account. This approach is generally associated with a **perpetual inventory system** because it maintains an up-to-date balance in the Inventory account at all times. An alternative approach, which maintains separate accounts for purchases, transportation, and so on, is generally used in a **periodic inventory system** and is demonstrated in Supplement 7C at the end of this chapter.

Inventory Purchases

To enhance efficiency and internal control, most companies buy inventory on credit rather than with cash. If American Eagle Outfitters purchases $10,500 of vintage jeans on credit, the transaction would affect the accounting equation and would be recorded as follows.

① Analyze

Assets	=	Liabilities	+	Stockholders' Equity
Inventory +10,500		Accounts Payable +10,500		

② Record

dr Inventory (+A)...	10,500	
cr Accounts Payable (+L)...................................		10,500

The $10,500 owed to the supplier remains in Accounts Payable until it is paid, at which time Accounts Payable is decreased (with a debit) and Cash is decreased (with a credit). The Inventory account remains at $10,500, unless the inventory is sold or any of the following transactions occur.

Transportation Cost

The inventory that American Eagle purchases does not magically appear in its stores. It must be shipped from the supplier to American Eagle. If the terms are **FOB shipping**

point, the purchaser pays for the shipping. If the terms are **FOB destination**, the seller pays for the shipping. When the purchaser pays for the shipping, the additional cost of transporting the goods (called freight-in) is added to the Inventory account.

Assume that American Eagle pays $400 cash to a trucker who delivers the $10,500 of vintage jeans to one of its stores. American Eagle would account for this transportation cost as follows:

1 Analyze

	Assets	=	Liabilities	+	Stockholders' Equity
Cash	−400				
Inventory	+400				

2 Record

dr Inventory (+A)...	400	
cr Cash (−A)...		400

In general, a purchaser should include in the Inventory account any costs needed to get the inventory into a condition and location ready for sale. Costs that are incurred after the inventory has been made ready for sale, such as freight-out to deliver goods to customers, should be treated as selling expenses.

Purchase Returns and Allowances

When goods purchased from a supplier arrive in damaged condition or fail to meet specifications, the buyer can (1) return them for a full refund or (2) keep them and ask for a cost reduction, called an allowance. Either way, these **purchase returns and allowances** are accounted for by reducing the cost of the inventory and either recording a cash refund or by reducing the liability owed to the supplier.

Assume, for example, that American Eagle returned some of the vintage jeans to the supplier and received a $500 reduction in the balance owed. This purchase return would be analyzed and recorded as follows:

YOU SHOULD KNOW

Purchase returns and allowances: A reduction in the cost of inventory purchases associated with unsatisfactory goods.

1 Analyze

	Assets	=	Liabilities		+	Stockholders' Equity
Inventory	−500		Accounts Payable	−500		

2 Record

dr Accounts Payable (−L).....................................	500	
cr Inventory (−A)...		500

Purchase Discounts

When inventory is bought on credit, terms such as "2/10, n/30" may be specified. Chapter 6 provided a lengthy description of how to interpret these terms from the seller's perspective. From the purchaser's perspective, these terms mean that the purchaser is allowed to deduct a 2 percent **purchase discount** if payment is made within 10 days of the date of purchase, otherwise the purchase cost (net of any returns or allowances) is due within 30 days of the purchase date.

When offered a purchase discount at the time of purchase, the purchaser accounts for it in two stages. Initially, the purchase is accounted for at full cost because it is not clear whether the company will take advantage of the discount. Later, if payment is made within the discount period, the purchaser reduces the Inventory account by the amount of the discount because it effectively reduces the cost of the inventory. The purchase discount is calculated using the net amount owing to the supplier, after considering purchase returns and allowances.

YOU SHOULD KNOW

Purchase discount: A cash discount received for prompt payment of a purchase on account.

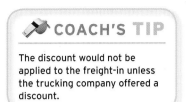

COACH'S TIP

The discount would not be applied to the freight-in unless the trucking company offered a discount.

Assume, for example, that American Eagle's purchase of vintage jeans for $10,500 occurred with terms 2/10, n/30. The initial purchase would be accounted for as shown earlier, by recording a $10,500 increase in Inventory (with a debit) and a $10,500 increase in Accounts Payable (with a credit). In our example, American Eagle returned inventory costing $500 and received a $500 reduction in its Accounts Payable. Consequently, American Eagle owed the supplier $10,000 for the purchase. Multiplying this balance by the 2 percent discount, we find that American Eagle's purchase discount is $200 (2% × $10,000 = $200). This discount means that American Eagle has to pay only $9,800 ($10,000 − $200 = $9,800) to fully satisfy its $10,000 of Accounts Payable. The $200 discount also reduces the cost of inventory as follows:

1 Analyze

Assets		=	Liabilities		+ Stockholders' Equity
Cash	−9,800		Accounts Payable	−10,000	
Inventory	−200				

2 Record

dr Accounts Payable (−L)...	10,000	
cr Cash (−A)...		9,800
cr Inventory (−A)..		200

COACH'S TIP

To review how to account for sales of inventory, see page 270 in Chapter 6.

Summary of Inventory Transactions

You have now seen how several types of inventory transactions affect the Inventory account on the balance sheet. Exhibit 7.6 summarizes, in table and T-account forms, how these transactions affect inventory, assuming beginning inventory was $4,800. Take a moment to flip back to Exhibit 7.3 on page 312 so that you can see that these are the values that will either become assigned to Cost of Goods Sold (when the goods are sold) or remain in Inventory.

EXHIBIT 7.6 **Effects of Inventory Transactions Related to Purchases**

Beginning Inventory		$ 4,800	
+ Purchases	$10,500		
+ Freight-in	400		
− Purchase Returns and Allowances	(500)		
− Purchase Discounts	(200)		
Net Purchases		10,200	
Cost of Goods Available for Sale		$15,000	

dr +	Inventory		cr −
Beginning	4,800		
Purchases	10,500	500	Purchase Returns
Freight-in	400	200	Purchase Discounts
Goods Available	15,000		

Evaluate the Results

INVENTORY TURNOVER ANALYSIS

Learning Objective 6
Evaluate inventory management by computing and interpreting the inventory turnover ratio.

If a company's inventory balance increases from $100,000 in one period to $130,000 in the next, is that good news or bad news? If the increase occurs because management is building up stock in anticipation of higher sales, it could be good news. But if it results from an accumulation of old inventory items that nobody wants, it is probably bad news. Those who work inside the company can easily determine whether the change is good or bad news by talking with the sales managers. But if you are looking at the company's financial statements from the outside, how can you tell?

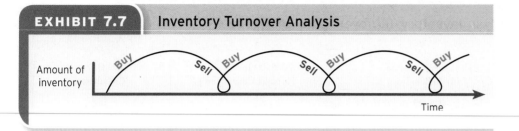

EXHIBIT 7.7 | Inventory Turnover Analysis

Amount of inventory

Buy Sell Buy Sell Buy Sell Buy

Time

The method most analysts use to evaluate such changes is called inventory turnover analysis. Exhibit 7.7 illustrates the idea behind inventory turnover analysis. As a company buys goods, its inventory balance goes up; as it sells goods, its inventory balance goes down. This process of buying and selling, which is called **inventory turnover,** is repeated over and over during each accounting period for each line of products.

Analysts can assess how many times, on average, inventory has been bought and sold during the period by calculating the inventory turnover ratio. A higher ratio indicates that inventory moves more quickly from purchase to sale, reducing storage and obsolescence costs. Because less money is tied up in inventory, the excess can be invested to earn interest or reduce borrowing, which reduces interest expense. More efficient purchasing and production techniques as well as high product demand will boost this ratio. A sudden decline in the inventory turnover ratio may signal an unexpected drop in demand for the company's products or sloppy inventory management.

Rather than evaluate the **number of times** inventory turns over during the year, some analysts prefer to think in terms of the **length of time** (in days) required to sell inventory. Converting the inventory turnover ratio to the number of days needed to sell the inventory is easy. You simply divide 365 days by the year's inventory turnover ratio to get the **days to sell.** This measure provides the same basic information, but it is a little easier to interpret than the inventory turnover ratio. In terms of Exhibit 7.7, the inventory turnover ratio indicates the number of loops in a given period; days to sell indicates the average number of days between loops.

YOU SHOULD KNOW

Inventory turnover: The process of buying and selling inventory.

YOU SHOULD KNOW

Days to sell: A measure of the average number of days from the time inventory is bought to the time it is sold.

Accounting Decision Tools		
Name of Measure	Formula	What It Tells You
Inventory turnover ratio	$\dfrac{\text{Cost of Goods Sold}}{\text{Average Inventory}}$	• The number of times inventory turns over during the period • A higher ratio means faster turnover
Days to sell	$\dfrac{365}{\text{Inventory Turnover Ratio}}$	• Average number of days from purchase to sale • A higher number means a longer time to sell

Comparison to Benchmarks

Inventory turnover ratios and the number of days to sell can be helpful in comparing different companies' inventory management practices. But use them cautiously because these measures can vary significantly between industries. For merchandisers, inventory turnover refers to buying and selling goods, whereas for manufacturers, it refers to producing inventory and delivering it to customers. These differences are reflected in Exhibit 7.8, which shows that McDonald's has a turnover ratio of 47.1, which means it takes about 7–8 days to sell its entire food inventory (including the stuff in its freezers). The motorcycles at Harley-Davidson hog more time, as indicated by its inventory turnover ratio of 9.8, which equates to about 37 days to produce and sell. American Eagle's inventory turned over only 6.2 times during the year, which is just once every 58.9 days.

EXHIBIT 7.8	Summary of Inventory Turnover Ratio Analyses

Company	Relevant Information (in millions)			2008–09 Inventory Turnover Calculation	2008–09 Days to Sell Calculation
HARLEY-DAVIDSON MOTORCYCLES		2008–09	2007–08	$\dfrac{\$3,663}{(\$401 + \$350)/2} = 9.8 \text{ times}$	$\dfrac{365 \text{ days}}{9.8 \text{ times}} = 37.2 \text{ days}$
	CGS	$3,663	$3,613		
	Inventory	$401	$350		
i'm lovin' it		2008–09	2007–08	$\dfrac{5,586}{(\$112 + \$125)/2} = 47.1 \text{ times}$	$\dfrac{365 \text{ days}}{47.1 \text{ times}} = 7.7 \text{ days}$
	CGS	$5,586	$5,487		
	Inventory	$112	$125		
AMERICAN EAGLE OUTFITTERS ae.com		2008–09	2007–08	$\dfrac{\$1,815}{(\$295 + \$286)/2} = 6.2 \text{ times}$	$\dfrac{365 \text{ days}}{6.2 \text{ times}} = 58.9 \text{ days}$
	CGS	$1,815	$1,632		
	Inventory	$295	$286		

Inventory turnover also can vary significantly between companies within the same industry, particularly if they take different approaches to pricing their inventories. In Chapter 6, we saw that Wal-Mart follows a low-cost pricing policy, which means setting its sales prices only slightly above cost. This policy led Wal-Mart to earn about 24.5 cents of gross profit on each dollar of sales whereas Saks earned 31.9 cents of gross profit. But when you consider the inventory turnover measures, you can see the full implications of this pricing policy. Wal-Mart turns its inventory over about 8.8 times a year (41 days), whereas Saks turns inventory over 2.6 times a year (140 days). **Often, the company with a lower gross profit percentage has a faster inventory turnover.**

With inventory turnover ratios varying between industries and companies, it's most useful to compare a company's turnover with its own results from prior periods. For practice at computing and comparing to prior periods, try the following Self-Study Practice.

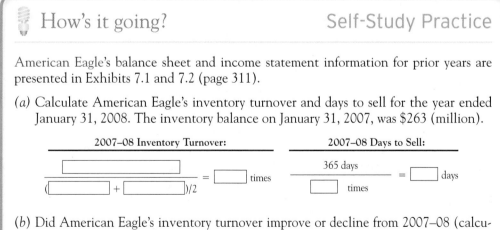

How's it going?   Self-Study Practice

American Eagle's balance sheet and income statement information for prior years are presented in Exhibits 7.1 and 7.2 (page 311).

(*a*) Calculate American Eagle's inventory turnover and days to sell for the year ended January 31, 2008. The inventory balance on January 31, 2007, was $263 (million).

2007–08 Inventory Turnover:	2007–08 Days to Sell:
$\dfrac{\boxed{}}{(\boxed{} + \boxed{})/2} = \boxed{} \text{ times}$	$\dfrac{365 \text{ days}}{\boxed{} \text{ times}} = \boxed{} \text{ days}$

(*b*) Did American Eagle's inventory turnover improve or decline from 2007–08 (calculated in *a*) to 2008–09 (shown in Exhibit 7.8)?

After you have finished, check your answers with the solution in the margin.

Solution to Self-Study Practice

a. $\dfrac{\$1,632}{(\$286 + \$263)/2} = 5.9 \text{ times}$

   $365 \div 5.9 = 61.9 \text{ days}$

b. American Eagle's inventory turnover improved in 2008–09 (3 fewer days to sell).

Spotlight On FINANCIAL REPORTING

Impact of Inventory Cost Flow Assumptions

As you saw in Exhibit 7.4, different cost flow assumptions often yield different amounts for Inventory and Cost of Goods Sold. GAAP require that any company that chooses to use LIFO must report in the notes to the financial statements what the inventory balance would have been had it used FIFO instead. This isn't a big burden on accountants because most LIFO companies actually keep track of the costs of inventory and goods sold during the year using FIFO and then adjust the accounts to LIFO at the end of the year, using what is called a **LIFO Reserve.** Deere & Company, the manufacturer of John Deere farm and lawn equipment, disclosed this information as follows.

DEERE & COMPANY
Notes to the Consolidated Financial Statements

Note 15—Inventories

Most inventories owned by Deere & Company and its United States equipment subsidiaries are valued at cost, on the "last-in, first-out" (LIFO) basis. If all inventories had been valued on a FIFO basis, estimated inventories at October 31 in millions of dollars would have been as follows:

	2008	2007
Total FIFO value	$4,366	$3,570
Adjustment to LIFO basis	1,324	1,233
Inventories (LIFO value)	$3,042	$2,337

Notice how huge the difference between FIFO and LIFO can be for an old business like John Deere, which was incorporated in 1868. The cost of inventory under the FIFO assumption ($4,366 in 2008) was more than 1.4 times higher than the cost of inventory under the LIFO assumption ($3,042 in 2008). The lesson here is that in analyzing a company's inventory or cost of goods sold, you should compare that company's results only to its own results in prior periods or to those of another company that uses the same inventory cost flow assumption.

SUPPLEMENT 7A: FIFO, LIFO, and Weighted Average in a Perpetual Inventory System

There were several good reasons for showing, in the previous sections of this chapter, how cost flow assumptions are applied in a periodic inventory system, even though most modern companies use perpetual inventory systems. First, only the LIFO and weighted average calculations differ between periodic and perpetual inventory systems. As we show in the following example, FIFO calculations don't differ between periodic and perpetual systems. Nearly half of all U.S. companies use FIFO, so even if they calculate costs under a perpetual system, it is identical to calculating costs under a periodic system. Second, most LIFO companies actually use FIFO during the period and then adjust to LIFO at the end of the period. By waiting to the end of the period to calculate this LIFO adjustment, it's *as if* all purchases during the period were recorded before the Cost of Goods Sold is calculated and recorded. In other words, it's as if these companies use a periodic inventory system to determine their LIFO inventory numbers, even though they actually track the number of units bought and sold on a perpetual basis. Third, companies typically adjust their records at year-end to match a physical count of the

inventory on hand, so as a practical matter, these companies are in substance on a periodic costing system. Fourth, the periodic inventory system is easier to visualize, so it's easier for you to learn.

Despite these reasons, it can be useful to know how to apply cost flow assumptions in a perpetual inventory system. In this supplement, we show how to calculate the Cost of Goods Sold and cost of ending Inventory on a perpetual basis using the same basic cost flow information used in the body of the chapter (on pages 315–317). The only difference in the following table is that we have assumed the sales occurred on October 4, prior to the final inventory purchase.

Date	Description	# of Units	Cost per Unit	Total Cost
Oct. 1	Beginning Inventory	10	$ 7	$ 70
Oct. 3	Purchase	30	$ 8	240
Oct. 4	Sales	(35)	To calculate	To calculate
Oct. 5	Purchase	10	$10	100
	Ending Inventory	15	To calculate	To calculate

FIFO (First-in, First-out)

The first-in, first-out (FIFO) method assumes that the oldest goods (the first in to inventory) are the first ones sold (the first out of inventory). So to calculate the cost of the 35 units sold, use the costs of the first-in (oldest) goods (10 units at $7 plus 25 of the 30 units at $8 = a total of $270). The costs of the newer goods are included in the cost of the ending inventory (5 units remaining from the 30 units at $8 plus 10 units at $10 = a total of $140). These calculations are summarized in the left-hand side of the following table (the right-hand side summarizes periodic calculations, which were explained in the body of the chapter). As you can see, FIFO yields identical amounts under perpetual and periodic. The only difference is that perpetual does not allow you to "back into" the Cost of Goods Sold; you must calculate it directly.

FIFO – Perpetual

Beginning Inventory	10 units × $7	$ 70
+ Purchases	30 units × $8	240
	10 units × $10	100
Goods Available for Sale		410
− Cost of Goods Sold (10 × $7) + (25 × $8)		270
Ending Inventory (10 × $10) + (5 × $8)		$140

FIFO – Periodic

Beginning Inventory	10 units × $7	$ 70
+ Purchases	30 units × $8	240
	10 units × $10	100
Goods Available for Sale		410
− Ending Inventory (10 × $10) + (5 × $8)		140
Cost of Goods Sold (10 × $7) + (25 × $8)		$270

LIFO (Last-in, First-out)

The last-in, first-out (LIFO) method assumes that the newest goods (the last in to inventory) as of the date of the sale are the first ones sold (the first out of inventory). So to calculate the cost of the 35 units sold, use the costs of the last-in (newest) goods as of the date of the sale (30 units at $8 plus 5 of the 10 units at $7 = a total of $275). The costs of the older goods (5 units remaining from the 10 units at $7 = $35) plus any later purchases (10 units at $10 = $100) are included in the cost of the ending inventory ($35 + $100 = $135). These calculations appear in the following table on the left.

LIFO – Perpetual

Beginning Inventory	10 units × $7	$ 70
+ Purchase	30 units × $8	240
Goods Available for Sale		310
− Cost of Goods Sold (30 × $8) + (5 × $7)		275
Goods Available for Sale	5 units × $7	35
+ Purchase	10 units × $10	100
Ending Inventory (5 × $7) + (10 × $10)		$135

LIFO – Periodic

Beginning Inventory	10 units × $7	$ 70
+ Purchases	30 units × $8	240
	10 units × $10	100
Goods Available for Sale		410
− Ending Inventory (10 × $7) + (5 × $8)		110
Cost of Goods Sold (10 × $10) + (25 × $8)		$300

Notice that LIFO–Perpetual calculates Cost of Goods Sold using the cost of goods last-in at the time of the sale, whereas LIFO–Periodic uses the cost of goods last-in at the end of the period.

Weighted Average Cost

In a perpetual inventory system, the weighted average cost must be calculated each time a sale is recorded. Use the same two steps shown in the body of the chapter: (1) calculate the total cost of the goods available for sale, and (2) divide by the number of units available for sale. For example, in the following table on the left, the weighted average cost at the time of sale is calculated by dividing $310 by the 40 units available for sale ($310 ÷ 40 = $7.75 per unit). This cost is then multiplied by the number of units sold to calculate Cost of Goods Sold (35 × $7.75 = $271.25). The remaining 5 units are also valued at the same weighted average cost (5 × $7.75 = $38.75). Additional inventory purchases ($100) are added to these inventory costs to calculate the cost of ending inventory ($38.75 + $100 = $138.75).[3]

WA – Perpetual

Beginning Inventory	10 units × $7	$ 70.00
+ Purchase	30 units × $8	240.00
Goods Available for Sale	40 units	310.00
− Cost of Goods Sold (35 × $7.75)		271.25
Goods Available for Sale	5 units	38.75
+ Purchase	10 units × $10	100.00
Ending Inventory	15 units	$138.75

WA – Periodic

Beginning Inventory	10 units × $7	$ 70
+ Purchases	30 units × $8	240
	10 units × $10	100
Goods Available for Sale	50 units	410
− Ending Inventory (15 × $8.20)		123
Cost of Goods Sold (35 × $8.20)		$287

Financial Statement Effects

Exhibit 7A.1 summarizes the financial statement effects of using a perpetual inventory system with FIFO, LIFO, or weighted average cost methods. These methods differ only

EXHIBIT 7A.1	**Financial Statement Effects of Inventory Costing Methods (Perpetual)**

Effects on the Income Statement	FIFO	LIFO	Weighted Average
Sales	$525	$525	$ 525.00
Cost of Goods Sold	270	275	271.25
Gross Profit	255	250	253.75
Effects on the Balance Sheet			
Inventory	$140	$135	$138.75

---

[3]If inventory is sold immediately after the $100 purchase, the weighted average cost will need to be calculated again ($138.75 ÷ 15 = $9.25 per unit). Notice the change in weighted average cost from $7.75 to $9.25 per unit. Because the weighted average unit cost changes, weighted average perpetual is also called the moving average method.

in the way they split the cost of goods available for sale between ending inventory and cost of goods sold. If a cost goes into Cost of Goods Sold, it must be taken out of Inventory. Thus, the method that assigns the highest cost to cost of goods sold assigns the lowest cost to ending inventory (and vice versa).

SUPPLEMENT 7B: The Effects of Errors in Ending Inventory

As mentioned earlier in the chapter, the failure to correctly apply the LCM rule to ending inventory is considered an error. Other errors can occur when inappropriate quantities or unit costs are used in calculating inventory cost. Regardless of the reason, errors in inventory can significantly affect both the balance sheet and the income statement. As the cost of goods sold equation indicates, a direct relationship exists between ending inventory and cost of goods sold because items not in the ending inventory are assumed to have been sold. Thus, any errors in ending inventory will affect the balance sheet (current assets) and the income statement (Cost of Goods Sold, Gross Profit, and Net Income). The effects of inventory errors are felt in more than one year because the ending inventory for one year becomes the beginning inventory for the next year.

To determine the effects of inventory errors on the financial statements in both the current year and the following year, use the cost of goods sold equation. For example, let's assume that ending inventory was overstated in 2009 by $10,000 due to an error that was not discovered until 2010. This would have the following effects in 2009:

2009	
Beginning Inventory	Accurate
+ Purchases	Accurate
− Ending Inventory	Overstated $10,000
= Cost of Goods Sold	Understated $10,000

Because Cost of Goods Sold was understated, Gross Profit and Income before Income Tax Expense would be overstated by $10,000 in 2009, as shown in Exhibit 7B.1. (Net Income would be overstated as well, although the effects would be offset somewhat by overstated Income Tax Expense.)

The 2009 ending inventory becomes the 2010 beginning inventory, so even if 2010 ending inventory is calculated correctly, the error in 2009 creates an error in 2010, as shown in the following table:

2010	
Beginning Inventory	Overstated $10,000
+ Purchases	Accurate
− Ending Inventory	Accurate
= Cost of Goods Sold	Overstated $10,000

Because Cost of Goods Sold is overstated in 2010, that year's Gross Profit and Income before Income Tax Expense would be understated by the same amount in 2010. (Net

EXHIBIT 7B.1	Two-Year Income Effects of Inventory Error

	2009				2010			
	With an Error		Without an Error		With an Error		Without an Error	
Sales		$120,000		$120,000		$110,000		$110,000
Beginning Inventory	$ 50,000		$ 50,000		$45,000		$35,000	
Purchases	75,000		75,000		70,000		70,000	
Cost of Goods Available for Sale	125,000		125,000		115,000		105,000	
Ending Inventory	45,000		35,000		20,000		20,000	
Cost of Goods Sold		80,000		90,000		95,000		85,000
Gross Profit		40,000		30,000		15,000		25,000
Operating Expenses		10,000		10,000		10,000		10,000
Net Income (before income tax)		$ 30,000		$ 20,000		$ 5,000		$ 15,000

Net Income overstated by $10,000 ⟶ Cancels out ⟵ Net Income understated by $10,000

Income would be understated as well, although the effects would be offset somewhat by understated Income Tax Expense.)

Ignoring income taxes, the effects of these errors on Net Income in each of the two years is shown in Exhibit 7B.1. Notice that the Cost of Goods Sold is understated in the first year and overstated in the second year. Over the two years, these errors offset one another. Inventory errors will "self-correct" like this only if ending inventory is accurately calculated at the end of the following year and adjusted to that correct balance. (The fact that these errors are self-correcting does not make them "okay.")

SUPPLEMENT 7C: Recording Inventory Transactions in a Periodic System

As you have learned, businesses using a periodic inventory system update inventory records only at the end of the accounting period. Unlike a perpetual inventory system, a periodic system does not track the cost of goods sold during the accounting period.

This supplement illustrates typical journal entries made when using a periodic inventory system. The table that follows contrasts those entries with the entries that would be recorded using a perpetual inventory system. A summary of the effects of the journal entries on the accounting equation follows them. Note that the total effects and the resulting financial statements are identical. Only the timing and nature of the entries differ.

Assume for the purposes of this illustration that a local cell phone dealer stocks and sells just one item, the MOTORAZR phone, and that only the following events occurred in 2010:

Jan. 1   Beginning inventory: 80 units at a unit cost of $60.

Apr. 14   Purchased 170 additional units on account at a unit cost of $60.

Nov. 30   Sold 150 units on account at a unit sales price of $80.

Dec. 31   Counted 100 units at a unit cost of $60.

A. Record purchases:

April 14, 2010:

Purchases (+A) (170 units at $60)	10,200	
Accounts Payable (+L)		10,200

B. Record sales (but not cost of goods sold):

November 30, 2010:

Accounts Receivable (+A)	12,000	
Sales Revenue (+R, +SE) (150 units at $80)		12,000

No cost of goods sold entry

C. Record end-of-period adjustments:

    a. Count the number of units on hand.
    b. Compute the dollar valuation of the ending inventory.
    c. Compute and record the cost of goods sold.

Beginning Inventory (last period's ending) (80 units at $60)	$ 4,800
Add: Net Purchases	10,200
Cost of Goods Available for Sale	15,000
Deduct: Ending Inventory (physical count—100 units at $60)	6,000
Cost of Goods Sold	$ 9,000

December 31, 2010:

Transfer beginning inventory and net purchases to cost of goods sold (act as if all goods were sold):

Cost of Goods Sold (+E, −SE)	15,000	
Inventory (−A) (beginning)		4,800
Purchases (−A)		10,200

Adjust the cost of goods sold by subtracting the amount of ending inventory still on hand (recognize that not all goods were sold):

Inventory (+A) (ending)	6,000	
Cost of Goods Sold (−E, +SE)		6,000

A. Record purchases:

April 14, 2010:

Inventory (+A) (170 units at $60)	10,200	
Accounts Payable (+L)		10,200

B. Record sales and cost of goods sold:

November 30, 2010:

Accounts Receivable (+A)	12,000	
Sales Revenue (+R, +SE) (150 units at $80)		12,000

Cost of Goods Sold (+E, −SE)	9,000	
Inventory (−A) (150 units at $60)		9,000

C. Record end-of-period adjustments:

At the end of the accounting period, the balance in the Cost of Goods Sold account is reported on the income statement. Computing the cost of goods sold is not necessary because the **Cost of Goods Sold** account is up to date. Also, the **Inventory** account shows the ending inventory amount reported on the balance sheet. A physical inventory count is still necessary to assess the accuracy of the perpetual records and identify theft and other forms of shrinkage. Any shrinkage would be recorded by reducing the **Inventory** account and increasing an expense account (such as **Inventory Shrinkage** or **Cost of Goods Sold**). This illustration assumes that no shrinkage has been detected.

No entries

PERIODIC

Assets	=	Liabilities	+	Stockholders' Equity	
Purchases +10,200		Accounts Payable +10,200			
Accts. Rec. +12,000				Sales Revenue (+R)	+12,000
Inventory −4,800				Cost of Goods Sold (+E)	−15,000
Purchases −10,200					
Inventory +6,000				Cost of Goods Sold (−E)	+6,000
Totals +13,200	=	+10,200			+3,000

PERPETUAL

Assets	=	Liabilities	+	Stockholders' Equity	
Inventory +10,200		Accounts Payable +10,200			
Accts. Rec. +12,000				Sales Revenue (+R)	+12,000
Inventory −9,000				Cost of Goods Sold (+E)	−9,000
Totals +13,200	=	+10,200			+3,000

REVIEW THE CHAPTER

DEMONSTRATION CASE

Ebert Electronics sells one type of consumer electronics product. Assume that the following sum-marized transactions were completed during the month ended January 31, 2010, in the order given.

www.mhhe.com/phillips3e

	Units	Unit Cost
Beginning inventory (January 1)	11	$200
New inventory purchases (January 3)	5	209
New inventory purchases (January 4)	9	220
Sale (January 5 at a price of $420 per item)	(12)	
	13	

Required:

1. Using the formats shown in the chapter, compute the Cost of Goods Available for Sale, Ending Inventory, and Cost of Goods Sold under (*a*) FIFO, (*b*) LIFO, and (*c*) weighted average.
2. Which method would minimize income taxes? Explain your answer.
3. Assuming that operating expenses were $500 and the income tax rate is 25 percent, prepare the income statement for the month using the method selected in requirement 2.
4. If the replacement cost fell to $205 in February, compute the adjustment that would be made to the Inventory account assuming the company uses (*a*) FIFO, (*b*) LIFO, and (*c*) weighted average.
5. Describe the impact of an adjustment in requirement 4 on the inventory turnover ratio. Computations are not required.

Suggested Solution

1.

(a) FIFO

Beginning Inventory	11 units × $200	$ 2,200
+ Purchases	5 units × $209	1,045
	9 units × $220	1,980
Goods Available for Sale		5,225
− Ending Inventory (9 × $220) + (4 × $209)		2,816
Cost of Goods Sold (11 × $200) + (1 × $209)		$2,409

(b) LIFO

Beginning Inventory	11 units × $200	$ 2,200
+ Purchases	5 units × $209	1,045
	9 units × $220	1,980
Goods Available for Sale		5,225
− Ending Inventory (11 × $200) + (2 × $209)		2,618
Cost of Goods Sold (9 × $220) + (3 × $209)		$2,607

(c) Weighted Average

Beginning Inventory	11 units × $200	$ 2,200
+ Purchases	5 units × $209	1,045
	9 units × $220	1,980
Goods Available for Sale	25 units	5,225

$$\text{Weighted Average Cost} = \frac{\text{Cost of Goods Available for Sale}}{\text{Number of Units Available for Sale}} = \frac{\$5,225}{25 \text{ units}} = \frac{\$209}{\text{per unit}}$$

(c) Weighted Average

Beginning Inventory	11 units × $200	$ 2,200
+ Purchases	5 units × $209	1,045
	9 units × $220	1,980
Goods Available for Sale		5,225
− Ending Inventory (13 × $209)		2,717
Cost of Goods Sold (12 × $209)		$2,508

2. LIFO would minimize income taxes. Because costs are rising, LIFO produces higher Cost of Goods Sold, lower Income before Income Tax Expense, and lower Income Tax Expense.

3.

EBERT ELECTRONICS
Income Statement
For the Month Ended January 31, 2010

Sales (12 × $420)	$5,040
Cost of Goods Sold	2,607
Gross Profit	2,433
Operating Expenses	500
Income before Income Tax Expense	1,933
Income Tax Expense (25%)	483
Net Income	$1,450

4. The total market value of the 13 units in ending inventory, with a per unit replacement cost of $205, is $2,665 (13 × $205 = $2,665). The LCM analysis follows:

	Cost	Market	LCM	Adjustment Needed
(a) FIFO	$2,816	$2,665	$2,665	$(151) = $2,816 − $2,665
(b) LIFO	$2,618	$2,665	$2,618	0
(c) Weighted Average	$2,717	$2,665	$2,665	(52) = $2,717 − $2,665

5. An adjustment for LCM decreases the Inventory balance and increases the Cost of Goods Sold. Both of these changes (individually or together) increase the inventory turnover ratio.

CHAPTER SUMMARY

LO1   Describe the issues in managing different types of inventory. p. 310

- Make or buy a sufficient *quantity* of *quality* products, at the lowest possible *cost*, so that they can be sold as quickly as possible to earn the desired amount of gross profit.

- *Merchandise inventory* is bought by merchandisers in a ready to sell format. When *raw materials* enter a manufacturer's production process, they become *work in process* inventory, which is further transformed into *finished goods* that are ultimately sold to customers.

LO2   Explain how to report inventory and cost of goods sold. p. 311

- The costs of goods purchased are added to Inventory (on the balance sheet).

- The costs of goods sold are removed from Inventory and reported as an expense called Cost of Goods Sold (on the income statement).

- The costs remaining in Inventory at the end of a period become the cost of Inventory at the beginning of the next period.

- The relationships among beginning inventory (BI), purchases (P), ending inventory (EI), and cost of goods sold (CGS) are: BI + P − EI = CGS or BI + P − CGS = EI.

Compute costs using four inventory costing methods. p. 313 LO3

- Under GAAP, any of four generally accepted methods can be used to allocate the cost of inventory available for sale between goods that are sold and goods that remain on hand at the end of the accounting period.
- Specific identification assigns costs to ending inventory and cost of goods sold by tracking and identifying each specific item of inventory.
- Under FIFO, the costs first in are assigned to cost of goods sold, and the costs last in (most recent) are assigned to the inventory that is still on hand in ending inventory.
- Under LIFO, the costs last in are assigned to cost of goods sold, and the costs first in (oldest) are assigned to the inventory that is still on hand in ending inventory.
- Under weighted average cost, the weighted average cost per unit of inventory is assigned equally to goods sold and those still on hand in ending inventory.

Report inventory at the lower of cost or market. p. 318 LO4

- The LCM rule ensures inventory assets are not reported at more than they are worth.

Analyze and record inventory purchases, transportation, returns and allowances, and discounts. p. 320 LO5

- The Inventory account should include costs incurred to get inventory into a condition and location ready for sale.
- The cost of inventory includes its purchase price and transportation (freight-in) minus cost reductions for purchase returns and allowances and purchase discounts. Costs to deliver inventory to customers (freight-out) are a selling expense and are not included in inventory.

Evaluate inventory management by computing and interpreting the inventory turnover ratio. p. 322 LO6

- The inventory turnover ratio measures the efficiency of inventory management. It reflects how many times average inventory was acquired and sold during the period. The inventory turnover ratio is calculated by dividing Cost of Goods Sold by Average Inventory.
- To help financial statement users compare the inventory levels and ratios of companies that use different inventory cost flow assumptions, LIFO companies report FIFO numbers in their financial statement notes. Most companies use a LIFO Reserve to show how FIFO numbers are converted into LIFO numbers.

Accounting Decision Tools

Name of Measure	Formula	What It Tells You
Inventory turnover ratio	$\dfrac{\text{Cost of Goods Sold}}{\text{Average Inventory}}$	• The number of times inventory turns over during the period • A higher ratio means faster turnover
Days to sell	$\dfrac{365}{\text{Inventory Turnover Ratio}}$	• Average number of days from purchase to sale • A higher number means a longer time to sell

KEY TERMS

See complete definitions in the glossary in the back of this text.

HOMEWORK HELPER

Alternative terms

- Cost of Goods Sold is also called Cost of Sales.
- Days to Sell is also called "days in inventory" and "days' sales in inventory."

Helpful reminders

- The "first-out" part of FIFO and LIFO describes the costs going out of inventory into Cost of Goods Sold. To calculate ending inventory cost using LIFO, think FIST (first-in, still there). For FIFO inventory, think LIST (last-in, still there).
- Purchase discounts are calculated after taking into account any purchase returns and allowances. A partial payment within the discount period (such as one-half of the total cost) usually entitles the purchaser to a partial discount (apply the discount to one-half of the total cost).

Frequent mistakes

- Do not calculate purchase discounts on transportation costs unless the shipping company offers a purchase discount for early payment. Do not apply purchase discounts to returned merchandise.
- Do not simply average the costs per unit when calculating weighted average cost. Instead, divide the total cost of goods available for sale by the number of goods available for sale.
- Do not use Sales Revenue when calculating inventory turnover (use Cost of Goods Sold). Also, use the average inventory, not the ending Inventory balance.

PRACTICE MATERIAL

QUESTIONS (⊖ Symbol indicates questions that require analysis from more than one perspective.)

1. What are three goals of inventory management?

2. Describe the specific types of inventory reported by merchandisers and manufacturers.

3. If a Chicago-based company ships goods on September 30 to a customer in Hawaii with sales terms FOB destination, does the Chicago-based company include the inventory or the sale in its September financial statements?

4. Define *goods available for sale*. How does it differ from cost of goods sold?

5. Define *beginning inventory* and *ending inventory*.

6. The chapter discussed four inventory costing methods. List the four methods and briefly explain each.

7. Which inventory cost flow method is most similar to the flow of products involving (*a*) a gumball machine, (*b*) bricks off a stack, and (*c*) gasoline out of a tank?

8. "Where possible, the inventory costing method should mimic actual product flows." Do you agree? Explain.

9. Contrast the effects of LIFO versus FIFO on ending inventory when (*a*) costs are rising and (*b*) costs are falling.

10. Contrast the income statement effect of LIFO versus FIFO (on Cost of Goods Sold and Gross Profit) when (*a*) costs are rising and (*b*) costs are falling.

11. Several managers in your company are experiencing personal financial problems and have asked that your company switch from LIFO to FIFO so that they can receive bigger bonuses, which are tied to the company's net income. How would you respond to this request if you were the company's chief financial officer (CFO)? Would such a switch help the managers? Who could it hurt? ⊖

12. Explain briefly the application of the LCM rule to ending inventory. Describe its effect on the balance sheet and income statement when market is lower than cost.

13. Describe how transportation costs to obtain inventory (freight-in) are accounted for by a merchandising company using a perpetual inventory system. Explain the reasoning behind this accounting treatment.

14. As a sales representative for a publicly traded pharmaceutical company, you become aware of new evidence that one of your company's main drugs has significant life-threatening side effects that were not previously reported. Your company has a significant inventory of this drug. What income statement accounts other than Net Sales will be affected by the news? A friend asks you whether he should invest in your company. What should you say? ⊖

15. You work for a made-to-order clothing company, whose reputation is based on its fast turnaround from order to delivery. The owner of your company is considering outsourcing much of the clothing production because she thinks this will improve inventory turnover and customer satisfaction. In what way is she correct? In what way might she be wrong? ⊖

16. (Supplement A) Distinguish perpetual inventory systems from periodic inventory systems by describing when and how cost of goods sold is calculated when using LIFO.

17. (Supplement B) Explain why an error in ending inventory in one period affects the following period.

18. (Supplement C) The summary in Supplement C shows two entries recorded in a periodic system that are not recorded in a perpetual system and only one entry in the perpetual system that is not recorded in a periodic system. Why then is a periodic system considered less onerous than a perpetual system?

MULTIPLE CHOICE

1. Which of the following statements are true regarding Cost of Goods Sold?

   (i) Cost of Goods Sold represents the costs that a company incurred to purchase or produce inventory in the current period.

   (ii) Cost of Goods Sold is an expense on the income statement.

   (iii) Cost of Goods Sold is affected by the inventory method selected by a company (FIFO, LIFO, etc.).

   a. (i) only
   b. (ii) only
   c. (ii) and (iii)
   d. All of the above.

2. The inventory costing method selected by a company can affect

   a. The balance sheet.
   b. The income statement.
   c. The statement of retained earnings.
   d. All of the above.

3. Which of the following is not a name for a specific type of inventory?

   a. Finished goods.
   b. Merchandise inventory.
   c. Raw materials.
   d. Goods available for sale.

4. Each period, the Cost of Goods Available for Sale is allocated between

   a. Assets and Liabilities.
   b. Assets and Expenses.
   c. Assets and Revenues.
   d. Expenses and Liabilities.

5. A New York bridal dress designer that makes high-end custom wedding dresses and needs to know the exact cost of each dress most likely uses which inventory costing method?

   a. FIFO
   b. LIFO
   c. Weighted Average
   d. Specific Identification

6. If costs are rising, which of the following will be true?

   a. The cost of goods sold will be greater if LIFO is used rather than weighted average.
   b. The cost of ending inventory will be greater if FIFO is used rather than LIFO.
   c. The gross profit will be greater if FIFO is used rather than LIFO.
   d. All of the above are true.

 Quiz 7
www.mhhe.com/phillips3e

7. Which inventory method provides a better matching of current costs with sales revenue on the income statement but also results in older values being reported for inventory on the balance sheet?

   a. FIFO
   b. Weighted Average
   c. LIFO
   d. Specific Identification

8. Which of the following regarding the *lower of cost or market* rule for inventory are true?

   (i) The lower of cost or market rule is an example of the historical cost principle.

   (ii) When the replacement cost of inventory drops below the original cost of inventory shown in the financial records, net income is reduced.

   (iii) When the replacement cost of inventory drops below the original cost of inventory shown in the financial records, total assets are reduced.

   a. (i) only
   b. (ii) only
   c. (ii) and (iii)
   d. All of the above.

9. An increasing inventory turnover ratio

   a. Indicates a longer time span between the ordering and receiving of inventory.
   b. Indicates a shorter time span between the ordering and receiving of inventory.
   c. Indicates a shorter time span between the purchase and sale of inventory.
   d. Indicates a longer time span between the purchase and sale of inventory.

10. A company that purchases inventory costing $10,000 on terms 2/10, n/30, but first returns one-half of those goods, will receive a discount of what amount if it pays on the last day of the discount period?

    a. $0
    b. $100
    c. $200
    d. $5,000

> For answers to the Multiple-Choice Questions **see page Q1** located in the last section of the book.

MINI-EXERCISES

M7-1 **Items Included in Inventory**

L01

The Knot, Inc.

Explain whether the following items should be included in the inventory of The Knot, Inc., a company that arranges and supplies wedding services for couples and other wedding consultants.

a. Goods are being held by The Knot on consignment from Emerald Bridal.
b. Goods in transit to Winston Wedding Consultants, sold by The Knot FOB shipping point.
c. Goods in transit to The Knot, purchased by The Knot FOB shipping point.

LO1 **M7-2 Matching Inventory Items to Type of Business**

Match the type of inventory with the type of business by placing checkmarks in the applicable columns:

	Type of Business	
Type of Inventory	Merchandising	Manufacturing
Merchandise		
Finished goods		
Work in process		
Raw materials		

LO2 **M7-3 Inferring Purchases Using the Cost of Goods Sold Equation**

Dillard's, Inc.

Dillard's, Inc., operates 315 department stores located in 29 states primarily in the Southwest, Southeast, and Midwest. In its annual report for the year ended January 31, 2009, the company reported Cost of Goods Sold of $4,827 million, ending inventory for the current year of $1,374 million, and ending inventory for the previous year of $1,779 million. Is it possible to develop a reasonable estimate of the merchandise purchases for the year? If so, prepare the estimate. If not, explain why.

LO3 **M7-4 Matching Financial Statement Effects to Inventory Costing Methods**

Complete the following table by indicating which inventory costing method (FIFO or LIFO) would lead to the effects noted in the rows, for each of the circumstances described in the columns.

	1. Rising Costs	2. Declining Costs
a. Lowest net income		
b. Lowest ending inventory		

LO3 **M7-5 Matching Inventory Costing Method Choices to Company Circumstances**

Indicate whether a company interested in minimizing its income taxes should choose the FIFO or LIFO inventory costing method under each of the following circumstances.

a. Declining costs _____
b. Rising costs _____

LO3 **M7-6 Calculating Cost of Goods Available for Sale, Ending Inventory, Sales, Cost of Goods Sold, and Gross Profit under Periodic FIFO, LIFO, and Weighted Average Cost**

Given the following information, calculate cost of goods available for sale and ending inventory, then sales, cost of goods sold, and gross profit, under (a) FIFO, (b) LIFO, and (c) weighted average. Assume a periodic inventory system is used.

		Units	Unit Cost	Unit Selling Price
July 1	Beginning Inventory	100	$10	
July 13	Purchase	500	13	
July 25	Sold	(200)		$15
July 31	Ending Inventory	400		

LO3 **M7-7 Calculating Cost of Goods Available for Sale, Cost of Goods Sold, and Ending Inventory under FIFO, LIFO, and Weighted Average Cost (Periodic Inventory)**

Aircard Corporation tracks the number of units purchased and sold throughout each accounting period, but applies its inventory costing method at the end of each period as if it uses a periodic inventory system. Given the following information, calculate the cost of goods available for sale, ending inventory, and cost of goods sold, if Aircard uses (a) FIFO, (b) LIFO, or (c) weighted average cost.

		Units	Unit Cost
July 1	Beginning Inventory	2,000	$20
July 5	Sold	1,000	
July 13	Purchased	6,000	22
July 17	Sold	3,000	
July 25	Purchased	8,000	25
July 27	Sold	5,000	

M7-8 Calculating Cost of Goods Available for Sale, Cost of Goods Sold, and Ending Inventory under Periodic FIFO, LIFO, and Weighted Average Cost

LO3

In its first month of operations, Literacy for the Illiterate opened a new bookstore and bought merchandise in the following order: (1) 300 units at $7 on January 1, (2) 450 units at $8 on January 8, and (3) 750 units at $9 on January 29. Assuming 900 units are on hand at the end of the month, calculate the cost of goods available for sale, ending inventory, and cost of goods sold under the (a) FIFO, (b) LIFO, and (c) weighted average cost flow assumptions. Assume a periodic inventory system is used.

M7-9 Reporting Inventory under Lower of Cost or Market

LO4

The Jewel Fool had the following inventory items on hand at the end of the year.

	Quantity	Cost per Item	Replacement Cost per Item
Necklaces	50	$75	$70
Bracelets	25	60	50

Determine the lower of cost or market per unit and the total amount that should be reported on the balance sheet for each item of inventory.

M7-10 Preparing the Journal Entry to Record Lower of Cost or Market (LCM) Adjustments

LO4

In its annual report filed with the SEC for the year ended December 31, 2008, General Motors reported that it wrote down inventory by $336 million because its cost exceeded its market value. Show the effects of this adjustment on the accounting equation as well as the journal entry that the company would have made to record it.

General Motors

M7-11 Evaluating Inventory Cost Components

LO5

Assume Anderson's General Store bought, on credit, a truckload of merchandise from American Wholesaling costing $23,000. If the company was charged $650 in transportation cost by National Trucking, immediately returned goods to American Wholesaling costing $1,200, and then took advantage of AmericanWholesaling's 2/10, n/30 purchase discount, how much did this inventory cost Anderson's?

M7-12 Preparing Journal Entries for Purchases, Purchase Discounts, and Purchase Returns Using a Perpetual System

LO5

Using the information in M7-11, prepare journal entries to record the inventory transactions, assuming Anderson's uses a perpetual inventory system.

M7-13 Recording Journal Entries for Purchases and Sales Using a Perpetual Inventory System

LO2, LO5

Inventory at the beginning of the year cost $13,400. During the year, the company purchased (on account) inventory costing $54,000. Inventory that had cost $60,000 was sold on account for $75,000. At the end of the year, inventory was counted and its cost was determined to be $7,400. (a) Show the cost of goods sold equation using these numbers. (b) What was the Gross Profit? (c) Prepare journal entries to record these transactions, assuming a perpetual inventory system is used.

LO6

M7-14 Determining the Effects of Inventory Management Changes on the Inventory Turnover Ratio

Indicate the most likely effect of the following changes in inventory management on the inventory turnover ratio (+ for increase, − for decrease, and NE for no effect).

_____ a. Inventory delivered by suppliers daily (small amounts) instead of weekly (larger amounts).
_____ b. Shorten production process from 10 days to 8 days.
_____ c. Extend payments for inventory purchases from 15 days to 30 days.

LO6

Dillard's

★macy's

M7-15 Calculating the Inventory Turnover Ratio and Days to Sell

Using the data in M7-3, calculate to one decimal place the inventory turnover ratio and days to sell for Dillard's. In a recent year, Macy's reported an inventory turnover ratio of 3.1. Which company's inventory turnover is faster?

LO6

Koss Corporation

M7-16 Reporting FIFO Ending Inventory in the Financial Statement Notes

Koss Corporation is a public company with 76 employees involved exclusively in making and selling stereo headphones. Koss reported ending inventory at June 30, 2008, of $9,374,344 under the LIFO costing method. In Note 1 to its financial statements, Koss reported that its FIFO inventory cost was $1,218,866 higher than LIFO at June 30, 2008. Show how Koss would report this in its financial statement notes.

M7-17 (Supplement 7A) Calculating Cost of Goods Sold and Ending Inventory under FIFO and LIFO (Perpetual Inventory)

Refer to M7-7. Calculate the cost of ending inventory and cost of goods sold assuming a perpetual inventory system is used in combination with (a) FIFO and (b) LIFO.

M7-18 (Supplement 7A) Calculating Cost of Goods Sold and Ending Inventory under Perpetual FIFO, LIFO, and Weighted Average Cost

Repeat M7-8, except assume Literacy for the Illiterate uses a perpetual inventory system and it sold 600 units between January 9 and January 28.

M7-19 (Supplement 7B) Determining the Financial Statement Effects of Inventory Errors

Assume the 2009 ending inventory of Shea's Shrimp Shack was understated by $10,000. Explain how this error would affect the amounts reported for cost of goods sold and gross profit for 2009 and 2010.

M7-20 (Supplement 7B) Determining the Financial Statement Effects of Inventory Errors

Repeat M7-19, except assume the 2009 ending inventory was *overstated* by $100,000.

EXERCISES

LO1, 2

PC Mall, Inc.

E7-1 Items Incuded in Inventory

PC Mall, Inc., is a direct marketer of computer hardware, software, peripherals, and electronics. In its 2008 annual report, the company reported that its revenue is "recognized upon receipt of the product by the customer" and that its "inventories include goods-in-transit to customers at December 31, 2008."

Required:

1. Indicate whether PC Mall's sales terms are FOB shipping point or FOB destination.
2. Assume PC Mall sold inventory on account to eCOST.com on December 28, 2008, which was to be delivered January 3, 2009. The inventory cost PC Mall $25,000 and the selling price was $30,000. What amounts, if any, related to this transaction would be reported on PC Mall's balance sheet and income statement in 2008? In 2009?
3. PC Mall placed inventory on consignment with one of its customers. Would this inventory have been reported on the balance sheet of PC Mall or its customer?
4. Assume PC Mall purchased electronics on December 29, 2008, which were received on January 2, 2009. Would these goods be included in PC Mall's inventory on December 31, 2008, under FOB destination or FOB shipping point?

E7-2 Inferring Missing Amounts Based on Income Statement Relationships

Supply the missing dollar amounts for the income statement of Lewis Retailers for each of the following independent cases:

LO2

Cases	Sales Revenue	Beginning Inventory	Purchases	Cost of Goods Available for Sale	Cost of Goods Sold	Cost of Ending Inventory	Gross Profit
A	$ 650	$100	$700	?	$300	$?	$?
B	900	200	800	?	?	150	?
C	?	150	?	?	200	300	400
D	800	?	600	?	650	250	?
E	1,000	50	900	?	?	?	500

E7-3 Inferring Missing Amounts Based on Income Statement Relationships

Supply the missing dollar amounts for the income statement of Lewis Retailers for each of the following independent cases:

LO2

(handwritten: COGS = BI + P – EI)
(handwritten: 100 700 – 80)

Cases	Sales Revenue	Beginning Inventory	Purchases	Total Available	Ending Inventory	Cost of Goods Sold	Gross Profit	Selling and General Expenses	Income from Operations
A	$800	$100	$700	$? *(800)*	$500	$? *(300)*	$? *(500)*	$200	$? *(300)*
B	900	200	700	? *(700)*	? *(-50)*	? *(750)*	? *(150)*	150	*(0)*
C	? *(600)*	150	? *(200)*	? *(450)*	250	200	400	100	? *(300)*
D	800	? *(100)*	600	? *(700)*	250	? *(450)*	? *(350)*	250	100

E7-4 Inferring Merchandise Purchases

The Gap, Inc., is a specialty retailer that operates stores selling clothes under the trade names Gap, Banana Republic, and Old Navy. Assume that you are employed as a stock analyst and your boss has just completed a review of The Gap annual report for the year ended January 31, 2009. She provided you with her notes, but they are missing some information that you need. Her notes show that the ending inventory for Gap in the current year was $1,506 million and in the previous year it was $1,575 million. Net Sales for the current year were $14,526 million. Gross Profit was $5,447 million and Net Income was $967 million. For your analysis, you determine that you need to know the amount of Cost of Goods Sold and Purchases for the year.

LO2

The Gap, Inc.

(handwritten: 450 = X + 600 + Y)

Required:

Do you need to ask your boss for her copy of the annual report, or can you develop the information from her notes? Explain and show calculations.

E7-5 Calculating Cost of Ending Inventory and Cost of Goods Sold under Periodic FIFO, LIFO, and Weighted Average Cost

LO3

Oahu Kiki tracks the number of units purchased and sold throughout each accounting period but applies its inventory costing method at the end of each month, as if it uses a periodic inventory system. Assume Oahu Kiki's records show the following for the month of January. Sales totaled 240 units.

	Date	Units	Unit Cost	Total Cost
Beginning Inventory	January 1	120	$ 8	$ 960
Purchase	January 15	380	9	3,420
Purchase	January 24	200	11	2,200

Required:

1. Calculate the number and cost of goods available for sale.
2. Calculate the number of units in ending inventory.
3. Calculate the cost of ending inventory and cost of goods sold using the (a) FIFO, (b) LIFO, and (c) weighted average cost methods.

LO3   **E7-6 Analyzing and Interpreting the Financial Statement Effects of Periodic FIFO, LIFO, and Weighted Average Cost**

Orion Iron Corp. tracks the number of units purchased and sold throughout each year but applies its inventory costing method at the end of the year, as if it uses a periodic inventory system. Assume its accounting records provided the following information at the end of the annual accounting period, December 31, 2009.

Transactions	Units	Unit Cost
a. Inventory, December 31, 2008	3,000	$12
For the year 2009:		
b. Purchase, April 11	9,000	10
c. Purchase, June 1	8,000	13
d. Sale, May 1 (sold for $40 per unit)	3,000	
e. Sale, July 3 (sold for $40 per unit)	6,000	
f. Operating expenses (excluding income tax expense), $195,000		

Required:

1. Calculate the number and cost of goods available for sale.
2. Calculate the number of units in ending inventory.
3. Compute the cost of ending inventory and cost of goods sold under (a) FIFO, (b) LIFO, and (c) weighted average cost.
4. Prepare an Income Statement that shows 2009 amounts for the FIFO method in one column, the LIFO method in another column, and the weighted average method in a final column. Include the following line items in the income statement: Sales, Cost of Goods Sold, Gross Profit, Operating Expenses, and Income from Operations.
5. Compare the Income from Operations and the ending inventory amounts that would be reported under the three methods. Explain the similarities and differences.
6. Which inventory costing method may be preferred by Orion Iron Corp. for income tax purposes? Explain.

LO3   **E7-7 Analyzing and Interpreting the Financial Statement Effects of FIFO, LIFO, and Weighted Average Cost**

Scoresby Inc. tracks the number of units purchased and sold throughout each year but applies its inventory costing method at the end of the year, as if it uses a periodic inventory system. Assume its accounting records provided the following information at the end of the annual accounting period, December 31, 2010.

Transactions	Units	Unit Cost
a. Inventory, December 31, 2009	3,000	$ 8
For the year 2010:		
b. Purchase, March 5	9,500	9
c. Purchase, September 19	5,000	11
d. Sale, April 15 (sold for $29 per unit)	4,000	
e. Sale, October 31 (sold for $31 per unit)	8,000	
f. Operating expenses (excluding income tax expense), $250,000		

Required:

1. Calculate the number and cost of goods available for sale.
2. Calculate the number of units in ending inventory.
3. Compute the cost of ending inventory and cost of goods sold under (a) FIFO, (b) LIFO, and (c) weighted average cost.
4. Prepare an income statement that shows 2010 amounts for the FIFO method in one column, the LIFO method in another column, and the weighted average method in a final column. Include the following line items in the income statement: Sales, Cost of Goods Sold, Gross Profit, Operating Expenses, and Income from Operations.
5. Compare the Income from Operations and the ending inventory amounts that would be reported under the three methods. Explain the similarities and differences.
6. Which inventory costing method may be preferred by Scoresby for income tax purposes? Explain.

E7-8 Evaluating the Effects of Inventory Methods on Income from Operations, Income Taxes, and Net Income (Periodic)   LO3

Courtney Company uses a periodic inventory system. Data for 2009: beginning merchandise inventory (December 31, 2008), 1,000 units at $35; purchases, 4,000 units at $38; operating expenses (excluding income taxes), $91,500; ending inventory per physical count at December 31, 2009, 900 units; sales price per unit, $75; and average income tax rate, 30 percent.

Required:

1. Prepare income statements under the FIFO, LIFO, and weighted average costing methods. Use a format similar to the following:

Income Statement	Units	FIFO	LIFO	Weighted Average
		Inventory Costing Method		
Sales Revenue	___	$ ___	$ ___	$ ___
Cost of Goods Sold*	___	___	___	___
Gross Profit		___	___	___
Operating Expenses		___	___	___
Income from Operations		___	___	___
Income Tax Expense		___	___	___
Net Income		___	___	___

*Cost of goods sold equation:

		FIFO	LIFO	Weighted Average
Beginning Inventory	___	$ ___	$ ___	$ ___
Purchases	___	___	___	___
Goods Available for Sale	___	___	___	___
Ending Inventory	___	___	___	___
Cost of Goods Sold	___	___	___	___

2. Between FIFO and LIFO, which method is preferable in terms of (a) maximizing income from operations or (b) minimizing income taxes? Explain.
3. What would be your answer to requirement 2 if costs were falling? Explain.

E7-9 Choosing LIFO versus FIFO When Costs Are Rising and Falling   LO3

Use the following information to complete this exercise: sales, 550 units for $12,500; beginning inventory, 300 units; purchases, 400 units; ending inventory, 150 units; and operating expenses, $4,000. Begin by setting up the following table and then complete the requirements that follow.

	Situation A FIFO	Situation B LIFO	Situation C FIFO	Situation D LIFO
	Costs Rising		Costs Falling	
Sales Revenue	$12,500	$12,500	$12,500	$12,500
Beginning Inventory	$3,600			
Purchases	5,200	___	___	___
Goods Available for Sale	8,800			
Ending Inventory	1,950	___	___	___
Cost of Goods Sold	6,850	___	___	___
Gross Profit	5,650			
Operating Expenses	4,000	4,000	4,000	4,000
Income from Operations	1,650			
Income Tax Expense (30%)	495	___	___	___
Net Income	$ 1,155	___	___	___

Required:

1. Complete the table for each situation. In Situations A and B (costs rising), assume the following: beginning inventory, 300 units at $12 = $3,600; purchases, 400 units at $13 = $5,200. In Situations C and D (costs falling), assume the opposite; that is, beginning inventory, 300 units at $13 = $3,900; purchases, 400 units at $12 = $4,800. Use periodic inventory procedures.

2. Describe the relative effects on Income from Operations as demonstrated by requirement 1 when costs are rising and when costs are falling.

3. Describe the relative effects on Income Tax Expense for each situation.

LO4   **E7-10 Reporting Inventory at Lower of Cost or Market**

Peterson Furniture Designs is preparing the annual financial statements dated December 31, 2009. Ending inventory information about the five major items stocked for regular sale follows:

| | Ending Inventory, 2009 | | | | |
Item	Quantity on Hand	Unit Cost When Acquired (FIFO)	Market Value at Year-End	LCM per Item	Total LCM
Alligator Armoires	50	$15	$12		
Bear Bureaus	75	40	40		
Cougar Beds	10	50	52		
Dingo Cribs	30	30	30		
Elephant Dressers	400	10	6		

Required:

1. Complete the final two columns of the table and then compute the amount that should be reported for the 2009 ending inventory using the LCM rule applied to each item.

2. Prepare the journal entry that Peterson Furniture Designs would record on December 31, 2009.

3. If the market values recovered by June 30, 2010, to greater than original cost, would the journal entry in requirement 2 be reversed under GAAP? Under IFRS?

LO4   **E7-11 Reporting Inventory at Lower of Cost or Market**

Sandals Company was formed on January 1, 2010, and is preparing the annual financial statements dated December 31, 2010. Ending inventory information about the four major items stocked for regular sale follows:

| | Ending Inventory, 2010 | | |
Product Line	Quantity on Hand	Unit Cost When Acquired (FIFO)	Market Value at Year-End
Air Flow	20	$12	$14
Blister Buster	75	40	38
Coolonite	35	55	50
Dudesly	10	30	35

Required:

1. Compute the amount that should be reported for the 2010 ending inventory using the LCM rule applied to each item.

2. How will the write-down of inventory to lower of cost or market affect the company's expenses reported for the year ended December 31, 2010?

3. How would the methods used by Sandals Company to account for its inventory be affected by a switch from GAAP to IFRS?

E7-12 Failing to Report Inventory at the Lower of Cost or Market

David H. Brooks, a university graduate with an accounting degree and the former CEO of DHB Industries, Inc., was charged in October 2007 with accounting and securities fraud for failing to report the company's inventory at the lower of cost or market. From 2001 to 2005, DHB purchased large quantities of a material called Zylon and used it in making bulletproof vests that were sold to the U.S. military and local law enforcement agencies. During this same period, DHB learned that Zylon deteriorated rapidly when exposed to light, heat, and body perspiration. DHB knew that one of its competitors, Second Chance Body Armor, had stopped using Zylon in its vests and, eventually, discontinued its business because customer demand for its Zylon-based vests had evaporated. DHB did not write down its own inventory of Zylon and Zylon-based vests because it had a large contract to supply the U.S. military with bulletproof vests. In its financial statements for the year ended December 31, 2004, DHB reported inventories of $86 million, sales of $90 million, net income of $8.3 million, but no inventory write-down. Yet, only eight months later, DHB admitted it should have written down its inventory by $18 million.

Required:

1. Show the impact of the inventory write-down on the accounting equation, and also show the journal entry that should have been recorded on December 31, 2004.

2. Calculate (*a*) the Inventory balance that should have been reported on December 31, 2004, and (*b*) the amount of Net Income that should have been reported for the year ended December 31, 2004. (Assume the inventory write-down does not affect income tax.)

3. DHB's share price reached an all-time high ($20–$22 per share) in November and December 2004, but then the company's CEO, CFO, and other executives began selling their shares in the company. Within a few weeks, they had cashed in over $200 million of stock. In August 2005, after DHB announced its inventory would have to be written down, the stock price fell to less than $5 per share. If you were an attorney representing DHB's investors, what evidence would you present to assert that a fraud had occurred? If you were an attorney defending DHB, what counterarguments would you make?

E7-13 Reporting Purchases and Purchase Discounts Using a Perpetual Inventory System

During the months of January and February, Axe Corporation purchased goods from three suppliers. The sequence of events was as follows:

Jan. 6	Purchased goods for $1,200 from Green with terms 2/10, n/30.
6	Purchased goods from Munoz for $900 with terms 2/10, n/30.
14	Paid Green in full.
Feb. 2	Paid Munoz in full.
28	Purchased goods for $350 from Reynolds with terms 2/10, n/45.

Required:

Assume that Axe uses a perpetual inventory system, the company had no inventory on hand at the beginning of January, and no sales were made during January and February. Calculate the cost of inventory as of February 28.

E7-14 Recording Journal Entries for Purchases and Purchase Discounts Using a Perpetual Inventory System

Using the information in E7-13, prepare journal entries to record the transactions, assuming Axe uses a perpetual inventory system.

E7-15 Reporting Purchases, Purchase Discounts, and Purchase Returns Using a Perpetual Inventory System

During the month of June, Ace Incorporated purchased goods from two suppliers. The sequence of events was as follows:

June 3	Purchased goods for $3,200 from Diamond Inc. with terms 2/10, n/30.
5	Returned goods costing $1,100 to Diamond Inc. for full credit.
6	Purchased goods from Club Corp. for $1,000 with terms 2/10, n/30.
11	Paid the balance owed to Diamond Inc.
22	Paid Club Corp. in full.

Required:

Assume that Ace uses a perpetual inventory system and that the company had no inventory on hand at the beginning of the month. Calculate the cost of inventory as of June 30.

LO5

E7-16 Recording Journal Entries for Purchases, Purchase Discounts, and Purchase Returns Using a Perpetual Inventory System

Using the information in E7-15, prepare journal entries to record the transactions, assuming Ace uses a perpetual inventory system.

LO6

Polaris Industries Inc.
Arctic Cat

E7-17 Analyzing and Interpreting the Inventory Turnover Ratio

Polaris Industries Inc. is the biggest snowmobile manufacturer in the world. It reported the following amounts in its financial statements (in millions):

	2008	2007	2006	2005
Net Sales Revenue	$1,948	$1,780	$1,657	$1,870
Cost of Goods Sold	1,502	1,387	1,297	1,452
Average Inventory	220	224	216	188

Required:

1. Calculate to one decimal place the inventory turnover ratio and average days to sell inventory for 2008, 2007, and 2006.
2. Comment on any trends, and compare the effectiveness of inventory managers at Polaris to inventory managers at its main competitor, Arctic Cat, where inventory turns over 4.5 times per year (81.1 days to sell). Both companies use the same inventory costing method (FIFO).

LO2, 3, 6

E7-18 Analyzing and Interpreting the Effects of the LIFO/FIFO Choice on Inventory Turnover Ratio

Simple Plan Enterprises uses a periodic inventory system. Its records showed the following:

Inventory, December 31, 2009, using FIFO → 38 Units @ $14 = $532
Inventory, December 31, 2009, using LIFO → 38 Units @ $10 = $380

Transactions	Units	Unit Cost	Total Cost
Purchase, January 9, 2010	50	15	$ 750
Purchase, January 20, 2010	100	16	1,600
Sale, January 11, 2010 (at $38 per unit)	80		
Sale, January 27, 2010 (at $39 per unit)	56		

Required:

1. Compute the number and cost of goods available for sale, the cost of ending inventory, and the cost of goods sold under FIFO and LIFO.
2. Compute the inventory turnover ratio under the FIFO and LIFO inventory costing methods (show computations).
3. Based on your answer to 2, explain whether analysts should consider the inventory costing method when comparing companies' inventory turnover ratios.

LO6

Ford Motor Company

E7-19 Analyzing Notes to Adjust Inventory from LIFO to FIFO and Calculating the Effects on the Inventory Turnover Ratio and Days to Sell

The Ford Motor Company uses the LIFO method to determine the cost of most of its inventories, which were reported at December 31, 2008, as follows:

	Inventory (in millions)	
	2008	2007
Finished products	$6,493	$ 6,861
Raw material and work in process, supplies	3,016	4,360
Total inventories at FIFO	9,509	11,221
Less: LIFO adjustment	(891)	(1,100)
Total inventories	$8,618	$10,121

Required:

1. Given the amount of Ford's LIFO Reserve at the end of 2008, are costs rising or falling in this industry?

2. The Cost of Goods Sold reported by Ford for 2008 was $127,103 million. Using the CGS equation and the LIFO balances reported above, determine the cost of inventory acquired (purchases) during 2008.

3. If Ford had used FIFO, its Cost of Goods Sold would have been $127,312 for 2008 (under LIFO it was $127,103 million). Calculate the inventory turnover ratio and days to sell under LIFO and FIFO, and comment on the significance of the inventory costing methods to these analyses of Ford's inventory.

E7-20 (Supplement 7A) Calculating Cost of Ending Inventory and Cost of Goods Sold under Perpetual FIFO and LIFO

Refer to the information in E7-5. Assume Oahu Kiki applies its inventory costing method perpetually at the time of each sale. The company sold 240 units between January 16 and 23. Calculate the cost of ending inventory and the cost of goods sold using the FIFO and LIFO methods.

E7-21 (Supplement 7A) Calculating Cost of Ending Inventory and Cost of Goods Sold under Perpetual FIFO and LIFO

Refer to the information in E7-6. Assume Orion Iron applies its inventory costing method perpetually at the time of each sale. Calculate the cost of ending inventory and the cost of goods sold using the FIFO and LIFO methods.

E7-22 (Supplement 7B) Analyzing and Interpreting the Impact of an Inventory Error

Dallas Corporation prepared the following two income statements:

	First Quarter 2009		Second Quarter 2009	
Sales Revenue		$15,000		$18,000
Cost of Goods Sold				
Beginning Inventory	$ 3,000		$ 4,000	
Purchases	7,000		12,000	
Goods Available for Sale	10,000		16,000	
Ending Inventory	4,000		9,000	
Cost of Goods Sold		6,000		7,000
Gross Profit		9,000		11,000
Operating Expenses		5,000		6,000
Income from Operations		$ 4,000		$ 5,000

During the third quarter, the company's internal auditors discovered that the ending inventory for the first quarter should have been $4,400. The ending inventory for the second quarter was correct.

Required:

1. What effect would the error have on total Income from Operations for the two quarters combined? Explain.

2. What effect would the error have on Income from Operations for each of the two quarters? Explain.

3. Prepare corrected income statements for each quarter. Ignore income taxes.

E7-23 (Supplement 7C) Recording Purchases and Sales Using Perpetual and Periodic Inventory Systems

Kangaroo Jim Company reported beginning inventory of 100 units at a per unit cost of $25. It had the following purchase and sales transactions during 2009:

Jan. 14	Sold 25 units at unit sales price of $45 on account.
Apr. 9	Purchased 15 additional units at a per unit cost of $25 on account.
Sep. 2	Sold 50 units at a sales price of $50 on account.
Dec. 31	Counted inventory and determined 40 units were still on hand.

Required:

Record each transaction, assuming that Kangaroo Jim Company uses *(a)* a perpetual inventory system and *(b)* a periodic inventory system.

COACHED PROBLEMS

CP7-1 Analyzing the Effects of Four Alternative Inventory Costing Methods

LO3

Scrappers Supplies tracks the number of units purchased and sold throughout each accounting period but applies its inventory costing method at the end of each period, as if it uses a periodic inventory system. Assume its accounting records provided the following information at the end of the annual accounting period, December 31, 2010.

Transactions	Units	Unit Cost
Beginning inventory, January 1, 2010	200	$30
Transactions during 2010:		
a. Purchase on account, March 2	300	32
b. Cash sale, April 1 ($46 each)	(350)	
c. Purchase on account, June 30	250	36
d. Cash sale, August 1 ($46 each)	(50)	

TIP: Although the purchases and sales are listed in chronological order, Scrappers determines the cost of goods sold *after* all of the purchases have occurred.

Required:

1. Compute the cost of goods available for sale, cost of ending inventory, and cost of goods sold at December 31, 2010, under each of the following inventory costing methods:
   a. Last-in, first-out.
   b. Weighted average cost.
   c. First-in, first-out.
   d. Specific identification, assuming that the April 1, 2010, sale was selected one-fifth from the beginning inventory and four-fifths from the purchase of March 2, 2010. Assume that the sale of August 1, 2010, was selected from the purchase of June 30, 2010.

2. Of the four methods, which will result in the highest gross profit? Which will result in the lowest income taxes?

LO4

CP7-2 Evaluating the Income Statement and Income Tax Effects of Lower of Cost or Market

Smart Company prepared its annual financial statements dated December 31, 2010. The company used the FIFO inventory costing method, but it failed to apply LCM to the ending inventory. The preliminary 2010 income statement follows:

Sales Revenue		$280,000
Cost of Goods Sold		
Beginning Inventory	$ 30,000	
Purchases	182,000	
Goods Available for Sale	212,000	
Ending Inventory (FIFO cost)	44,000	
Cost of Goods Sold		168,000
Gross Profit		112,000
Operating Expenses		61,000
Income from Operations		51,000
Income Tax Expense (30%)		15,300
Net Income		$ 35,700

TIP: Inventory write-downs do not affect the cost of goods available for sale. Instead, the effect of the write-down is to reduce ending inventory, which increases Cost of Goods Sold and then affects other amounts reported lower in the income statement.

Assume that you have been asked to restate the 2010 financial statements to incorporate LCM. You have developed the following data relating to the 2010 ending inventory:

Item	Quantity	Purchase Cost Per Unit	Purchase Cost Total	Current Replacement Cost per Unit (Market)
A	3,000	$3	$ 9,000	$4
B	1,500	4	6,000	2
C	7,000	2	14,000	4
D	3,000	5	15,000	2
			$44,000	

Required:

1. Restate the income statement to reflect LCM valuation of the 2010 ending inventory. Apply LCM on an item-by-item basis and show computations.
2. Compare and explain the LCM effect on each amount that was changed in requirement 1.
3. What is the conceptual basis for applying LCM to merchandise inventories?

CP7-3 Accounting for Inventory Purchase Transactions including Allowances and Discounts Using a Perpetual Inventory System   LO5

Use the information in CP6-6 (page 295 in Chapter 6) to complete the following requirements.

Required:

1. Indicate the effect (direction and amount) of each transaction on the Inventory balance of American Fashions.
2. Prepare the journal entries that American Fashions would record and show any computations.
    TIP: The selling price charged by the seller is the purchaser's cost.

CP7-4 Calculating and Interpreting the Inventory Turnover Ratio and Days to Sell   LO6

Best Buy is a leading national retailer of brand-name consumer electronics, personal computers, and entertainment software. The company reported the following amounts in its financial statements (in millions).

Best Buy
GameStop

	2009	2008
Net Sales Revenue	$45,015	40,023
Cost of Goods Sold	34,017	30,477
Beginning Inventory	4,708	4,028
Ending Inventory	4,753	4,708

Required:

1. Determine the inventory turnover ratio and average days to sell inventory for 2009 and 2008. Round your answers to one decimal place.
    TIP: Remember to use costs in both the numerator (CGS) and denominator (average inventory).
2. Comment on any changes in these measures, and compare the effectiveness of inventory managers at Best Buy with GameStop, where inventory turns over 7.0 times per year (52 days to sell).

CP7-5 (Supplement 7A) Analyzing the Effects of the LIFO Inventory Method in a Perpetual Inventory System

Using the information in CP7-1, calculate the Cost of Goods Sold and Ending Inventory for Scrappers Supplies assuming it applies the LIFO cost method perpetually at the time of each sale. Compare these amounts to the periodic LIFO calculations in requirement 1a of CP7-1. Does the use of a perpetual inventory system result in a higher or lower Cost of Goods Sold when costs are rising?

TIP: In CP7-5, the sale of 350 units on April 1 is assumed, under LIFO, to consist of the 300 units purchased March 2 and 50 units from beginning inventory.

CP7-6 (Supplement 7B) Analyzing and Interpreting the Effects of Inventory Errors

Partial income statements for Murphy & Murphy (M & M) reported the following summarized amounts:

	2007	2008	2009	2010
Net Sales	$50,000	$49,000	$71,000	$58,000
Cost of Goods Sold	32,500	35,000	43,000	37,000
Gross Profit	17,500	14,000	28,000	21,000

After these amounts were reported, M & M's accountant determined that the inventory on December 31, 2008, was understated by $3,000. The inventory balance on December 31, 2009, was accurately stated.

Required:

1. Restate the partial income statements to reflect the correct amounts, after fixing the inventory error.

2. Compute the gross profit percentage for all four years both (*a*) before the correction and (*b*) after the correction. Does the pattern of gross profit percentages lend confidence to your corrected amounts? Explain. Round your answer to the nearest percentage.
    TIP: Gross profit percentage is calculated as (Gross Profit ÷ Net Sales) × 100.

CP7-7 (Supplement 7C) Journalizing Inventory Transactions Using a Periodic Inventory System

Prepare journal entries to record the transactions in CP7-1 assuming that a periodic inventory system is used, with inventory costs being determined on a FIFO basis.

GROUP A PROBLEMS

LO3

PA7-1 Analyzing the Effects of Four Alternative Inventory Methods in a Periodic Inventory System

www.mhhe.com/phillips3e

Gladstone Company tracks the number of units purchased and sold throughout each accounting period but applies its inventory costing method at the end of each period, as if it uses a periodic inventory system. Assume its accounting records provided the following information at the end of the annual accounting period, December 31, 2009.

Transactions	Units	Unit Cost
Beginning inventory, January 1, 2009	1,800	$5.00
Transactions during 2009:		
a. Purchase, January 30	2,500	6.20
b. Sale, March 14 ($10 each)	(1,450)	
c. Purchase, May 1	1,200	8.00
d. Sale, August 31 ($10 each)	(1,900)	

Required:

1. Compute the amount of goods available for sale, ending inventory, and cost of goods sold at December 31, 2009, under each of the following inventory costing methods:
    a. Last-in, first-out.
    b. Weighted average cost.
    c. First-in, first-out.
    d. Specific identification, assuming that the March 14, 2009, sale was selected two-fifths from the beginning inventory and three-fifths from the purchase of January 30, 2009. Assume that the sale of August 31, 2009, was selected from the remainder of the beginning inventory, with the balance from the purchase of May 1, 2009.

2. Of the four methods, which will result in the highest gross profit? Which will result in the lowest income taxes?

PA7-2 Evaluating the Income Statement and Income Tax Effects of Lower of Cost or Market

LO4

www.mhhe.com/phillips3e

Springer Anderson Gymnastics prepared its annual financial statements dated December 31, 2009. The company used the FIFO inventory costing method, but it failed to apply LCM to the ending inventory. The preliminary 2009 income statement follows:

Sales Revenue		$140,000
Cost of Goods Sold		
Beginning Inventory	$ 15,000	
Purchases	91,000	
Goods Available for Sale	106,000	
Ending Inventory (FIFO cost)	22,000	
Cost of Goods Sold		84,000
Gross Profit		56,000
Operating Expenses		31,000
Income from Operations		25,000
Income Tax Expense (30%)		7,500
Net Income		$ 17,500

Assume that you have been asked to restate the 2009 financial statements to incorporate LCM. You have developed the following data relating to the 2009 ending inventory:

		Purchase Cost		Current Replacement Cost per Unit (Market)
Item	Quantity	Per Unit	Total	
A	1,500	$3	$ 4,500	$4
B	750	4	3,000	2
C	3,500	2	7,000	1
D	1,500	5	7,500	3
			$22,000	

Required:

1. Restate the income statement to reflect LCM valuation of the 2009 ending inventory. Apply LCM on an item-by-item basis and show computations.
2. Compare and explain the LCM effect on each amount that was changed in requirement 1.
3. What is the conceptual basis for applying LCM to merchandise inventories?

PA7-3 Accounting for Inventory Purchase Transactions Including Allowances and Discounts Using a Perpetual Inventory System

LO5

Use the information in PA6-6 (page 299 in Chapter 6) to complete the following requirements.

Required:

1. Indicate the effect (direction and amount) of each transaction on the Inventory balance of Readers' Corner.
2. Prepare the journal entries that Readers' Corner would record and show any computations.

PA7-4 Calculating and Interpreting the Inventory Turnover Ratio and Days to Sell

LO6

Harman International Industries is a world leading producer of loudspeakers and other electronics products, which are sold under brand names like JBL, Infinity, and Harman/Kardon. The company reported the following amounts in its financial statements (in millions):

Harman International Industries
Pioneer Corporation

www.mhhe.com/phillips3e

	2008	2007
Net Sales	$4,113	$3,551
Cost of Goods Sold	3,003	2,340
Beginning Inventory	453	345
Ending Inventory	391	453

Required:

1. Determine the inventory turnover ratio and average days to sell inventory for 2008 and 2007. Round to one decimal place.

2. Comment on any changes in these measures, and compare the effectiveness of inventory managers at Harman to inventory managers at Pioneer Corporation, where inventory turns over 5.7 times per year (64 days to sell). Both companies use the same inventory costing method (FIFO).

PA7-5 (Supplement 7A) Analyzing the Effects of the LIFO Inventory Method in a Perpetual Inventory System

Using the information in PA7-1, calculate the cost of goods sold and ending inventory for Gladstone Company assuming it applies the LIFO cost method perpetually at the time of each sale. Compare these amounts to the periodic LIFO calculations in requirement 1a of PA7-1. Does the use of a perpetual inventory system result in a higher or lower cost of goods sold when costs are rising?

PA7-6 (Supplement 7B) Analyzing and Interpreting the Effects of Inventory Errors

www.mhhe.com/phillips3e

Partial income statements for Sherwood Company summarized for a four-year period show the following:

	2007	2008	2009	2010
Net Sales	$2,000,000	$2,400,000	$2,500,000	$3,000,000
Cost of Goods Sold	1,400,000	1,660,000	1,770,000	2,100,000
Gross Profit	600,000	740,000	730,000	900,000

An audit revealed that in determining these amounts, the ending inventory for 2008 was overstated by $20,000. The inventory balance on December 31, 2009, was accurately stated. The company uses a periodic inventory system.

Required:

1. Restate the partial income statements to reflect the correct amounts, after fixing the inventory error.

2. Compute the gross profit percentage for each year (a) before the correction and (b) after the correction, rounding to the nearest percentage. Do the results lend confidence to your corrected amounts? Explain.

PA7-7 (Supplement 7C) Journalizing Inventory Transactions Using a Periodic Inventory System

Prepare journal entries to record the transactions in PA7-1 assuming that a periodic inventory system is used, with inventory costs being determined on a FIFO basis.

GROUP B PROBLEMS

LO3

PB7-1 Analyzing the Effects of Four Alternative Inventory Methods in a Periodic Inventory System

Mojo Industries tracks the number of units purchased and sold throughout each accounting period but applies its inventory costing method at the end of each period, as if it uses a periodic inventory system. Assume its accounting records provided the following information at the end of the accounting period, January 31, 2009. The inventory's selling price is $9 per unit.

Transactions	Unit Cost	Units	Total Cost
Inventory, January 1, 2009	$2.50	250	$625
Sale, January 10		(200)	
Purchase, January 12	3.00	300	900
Sale, January 17		(150)	
Purchase, January 26	4.00	80	320

Required:

1. Compute the amount of goods available for sale, ending inventory, and cost of goods sold at January 31, 2009, under each of the following inventory costing methods:

    a. Weighted average cost.
    b. First-in, first-out.
    c. Last-in, first-out.
    d. Specific identification, assuming that the January 10 sale was from the beginning inventory and the January 17 sale was from the January 12 purchase.

2. Of the four methods, which will result in the highest gross profit? Which will result in the lowest income taxes?

PB7-2 Evaluating the Income Statement and Income Tax Effects of Lower of Cost or Market   LO4

Mondetta Clothing prepared its annual financial statements dated December 31, 2010. The company used the FIFO inventory costing method, but it failed to apply LCM to the ending inventory. The preliminary 2010 income statement follows:

Net Sales		$420,000
Cost of Goods Sold		
Beginning Inventory	$ 45,000	
Purchases	273,000	
Goods Available for Sale	318,000	
Ending Inventory (FIFO cost)	66,000	
Cost of Goods Sold		252,000
Gross Profit		168,000
Operating Expenses		93,000
Income from Operations		75,000
Income Tax Expense (30%)		22,500
Net Income		$ 52,500

Assume that you have been asked to restate the 2010 financial statements to incorporate LCM. You have developed the following data relating to the 2010 ending inventory:

Item	Quantity	Acquisition Cost Per Unit	Acquisition Cost Total	Current Replacement Cost per Unit (Market)
A	3,000	$4.50	$13,500	$6.00
B	1,500	6.00	9,000	3.00
C	7,000	3.00	21,000	6.00
D	3,000	7.50	22,500	4.50
			$66,000	

Required

1. Restate the income statement to reflect LCM valuation of the 2010 ending inventory. Apply LCM on an item-by-item basis and show computations.
2. Compare and explain the LCM effect on each amount that was changed in requirement 1.
3. What is the conceptual basis for applying LCM to merchandise inventories?

PB7-3 Accounting for Inventory Purchase Transactions Including Allowances and Discounts Using a Perpetual Inventory System   LO5

Use the information in PB6-6 (page 302 in Chapter 6) to complete the following requirements.

Required:

1. Indicate the effect (direction and amount) of each transaction on the Inventory balance of Sports R Us.
2. Prepare the journal entries that Sports R Us would record and show any computations.

L06   **PB7-4 Calculating and Interpreting the Inventory Turnover Ratio and Days to Sell**

Amazon.com
Borders

Amazon.com reported the following amounts in its financial statements (in millions):

	2008	2007
Net Sales	$19,166	$14,835
Cost of Goods Sold	14,896	11,482
Beginning Inventory	1,200	877
Ending Inventory	1,399	1,200

Required:

1. Determine the inventory turnover ratio and average days to sell inventory for 2008 and 2007. Round to one decimal place.

2. Comment on any changes in these measures and compare the inventory turnover at Amazon.com to inventory turnover at Borders, where inventory turned over 2.3 times during 2008 (158.7 days to sell). Based on your own experience, what's the key difference between Amazon.com and Borders that leads one company's results to be the picture of über-efficiency and the other to seem like a library?

PB7-5 (Supplement 7A) Analyzing the Effects of the LIFO Inventory Method in a Perpetual Inventory System

Using the information in PB7-1, calculate the cost of goods sold and ending inventory for Mojo Industries assuming it applies the LIFO cost method perpetually at the time of each sale. Compare these amounts to the periodic LIFO calculations in requirement 1(*c*) of PB7-1. Does the use of a perpetual inventory system result in a higher or lower cost of goods sold when costs are rising?

PB7-6 (Supplement 7B) Analyzing and Interpreting the Effects of Inventory Errors

Spears & Cantrell announced inventory had been overstated by $30 (million) at the end of its 2009 second quarter. The error wasn't discovered and corrected in the company's periodic inventory system until after the end of the third quarter. The following table shows the amounts (in millions) that were originally reported by the company.

	Q1	Q2	Q3
Net Sales	$3,000	$3,600	$3,750
Cost of Goods Sold	2,100	2,490	2,655
Gross Profit	900	1,110	1,095

Required:

1. Restate the income statements to reflect the correct amounts, after fixing the inventory error.

2. Compute the gross profit percentage for each quarter (*a*) before the correction and (*b*) after the correction, rounding to the nearest percentage. Do the results lend confidence to your corrected amounts? Explain.

PB7-7 (Supplement 7C) Journalizing Inventory Transactions Using a Periodic Inventory System

Prepare journal entries to record the transactions in PB7-1 assuming that a periodic inventory system is used, with inventory costs being determined on a FIFO basis.

COMPREHENSIVE PROBLEM

L03, 5, 6   **C7-1 Comprehensive Problem (Chapters 4, 6, and 7)**

College Coasters is a San Antonio–based merchandiser specializing in logo-adorned drink coasters. The company reported the following balances in its unadjusted trial balance at December 1, 2009.

Cash	$10,005	Accounts Payable	$ 1,500	Cost of Goods Sold	$8,900
Accounts Receivable	2,000	Wages Payable	300	Rent Expense	1,100
Inventory	500	Taxes Payable	0	Wages Expense	2,000
Prepaid Rent	600	Contributed Capital	6,500	Depreciation Expense	110
Equipment	810	Retained Earnings	3,030	Income Tax Expense	0
Accumulated Depreciation	110	Sales Revenue	15,985	Selling Expenses	1,400

The company buys coasters from one supplier. All amounts in Accounts Payable on December 1 are owed to that supplier. The inventory on December 1, 2009, consisted of 1,000 coasters, all of which were purchased in a batch on July 10 at a unit cost of $0.50. College Coasters uses the FIFO cost flow method.

During December 2009, the company entered into the following transactions. Some of these transactions are explained in greater detail below.

Dec. 1	Purchased 500 coasters on account from the regular supplier at a unit cost of $0.52, with terms of 2/10, n/30.
Dec. 2	Purchased 1,000 coasters on account from the regular supplier at a unit cost of $0.55, with terms of 2/10, n/30.
Dec. 15	Paid the supplier $1,600 cash on account.
Dec. 17	Sold 2,000 coasters on account at a unit price of $0.90.
Dec. 23	Paid employees $500, $300 of which related to work done in November and $200 for wages up to December 22.
Dec. 24	Collected $1,000 from customers on account.
Dec. 31	Loaded 1,000 coasters on a cargo ship to be delivered to a customer in Hawaii. The sale was made FOB destination with terms of 2/10, n/30.

Other relevant information includes the following:

a. College Coasters has not yet recorded $200 of selling expenses incurred in December on account.
b. The company estimates that the equipment depreciates at a rate of $10 per month. One month of depreciation needs to be recorded.
c. Wages for the period from December 23–31 are $100 and will be paid on January 15, 2010.
d. The $600 of Prepaid Rent relates to a six-month period ending on May 31, 2010.
e. No shrinkage or damage was discovered when the inventory was counted on December 31, 2009.
f. The company did not declare dividends and there were no transactions involving contributed capital.
g. The company has a 30 percent tax rate and has made no tax payments this year.

Required:

1. Analyze the accounting equation effects of each transaction and any adjustments required at month-end.
2. Prepare journal entries to record each transaction and any adjustments required at month-end.
3. Summarize the journal entries in T-accounts. Be sure to include the balances on December 1, 2009, as beginning account balances.
4. Prepare an Income Statement, Statement of Stockholders' Equity, and classified Balance Sheet, using the formats presented in Exhibits 6.11, 5.8, and 5.6.
5. Calculate to one decimal place the inventory turnover ratio and days to sell in 2009, assuming that inventory was $500 on January 1, 2009. Evaluate these measures in comparison to an inventory turnover ratio of 12.0 during the year ended December 31, 2008.

SKILLS DEVELOPMENT CASES

S7-1 Finding Financial Information

LO2, 4, 6

Refer to the financial statements of The Home Depot in Appendix A at the end of this book, or download the annual report from the *Cases* section of the text's Web site at www.mhhe.com/phillips3e.

1. How much inventory does the company hold on February 1, 2009? Does this represent an increase or decrease in comparison to the prior year?
2. Does the company follow the lower of cost or market rule? What method(s) does the company use to determine the cost of its inventory? Describe where you found this information.
3. Compute to one decimal place the company's inventory turnover ratio and days to sell for the most recent year.
4. Does the company believe FIFO, or weighted average cost, is a better method?
    TIP: See financial statement Note 3.

Lowe's

LO2, 4, 6

S7-2 Comparing Financial Information

Refer to the financial statements of The Home Depot in Appendix A and Lowe's in Appendix B at the end of this book, or download the annual reports from the *Cases* section of the text's Web site at www.mhhe.com/phillips3e.

1. Does Lowe's hold more or less inventory than The Home Depot at the end of January 2009?
2. Does Lowe's follow the lower of cost or market rule? What method does Lowe's use to determine the cost of its inventory? Comment on how this affects comparisons you might make between Lowe's and The Home Depot's inventory turnover ratios.
3. Compute to one decimal place Lowe's inventory turnover ratio and days to sell for the 2008–09 fiscal year and compare to The Home Depot's. What does this analysis suggest to you?

LO1, 2, 3, 4, 6

S7-3 Internet-Based Team Research: Examining an Annual Report

As a team, select an industry to analyze. Using your Web browser, each team member should access the annual report or 10-K for one publicly traded company in the industry, with each member selecting a different company. (See S1-3 in Chapter 1 for a description of possible resources for these tasks.)

Required:

1. On an individual basis, each team member should write a short report that incorporates the following:
   a. Describe the types of inventory held by the company. Does the company indicate its inventory management goals anywhere in its annual report?
   b. Describe the inventory costing method that is used. Why do you think the company chose this method rather than the other acceptable methods? Do you think its inventory costs are rising or falling?
   c. Calculate the inventory turnover ratio for the current and prior year, and explain any change between the two years. (To obtain the beginning inventory number for the prior year, you will need the prior year's annual report.)
   d. Search the 10-K for information about the company's approach for applying the LCM rule to inventory. Did the company report the amount of inventory written down during the year?
2. Then, as a team, write a short report comparing and contrasting your companies using these attributes. Discuss any patterns across the companies that you as a team observe. Provide potential explanations for any differences discovered.

LO2, 4

S7-4 Ethical Decision Making: A Real-Life Example

Assume you are on a jury hearing a trial involving a large national drugstore company. Your immediate task is to identify suspicious events in the following evidence that suggest financial fraud may have occurred.

In just seven years, the company grew from 15 to 310 stores, reporting sales of more than $3 billion. Some retail experts believed the company was going to be the next Wal-Mart. The apparent secret to the company's success was its ability to attract customers to its stores by selling items below cost. Then the company would make it easy for customers to buy other items, particularly pharmaceuticals, which earned a high gross profit. This strategy appeared to be working, so the company's top executives built up massive pharmaceutical inventories at its stores, causing total inventory to increase from $11 million to $36 million to $153 million in the last three years. The company hadn't installed a perpetual inventory system, so inventory had to be physically counted at each store to determine the cost of goods sold. To help its auditors verify the accuracy of these inventory counts, top management agreed to close selected stores on the day inventory was counted. All they asked was that they be given advance notice of which stores' inventory counts the auditors were planning to attend, so that the temporary closures could be conveyed to employees and customers at those stores. The external auditors selected four stores to test each year and informed the company several weeks in advance. To further assist the auditors with counting the inventory, top management reduced the inventory levels at the selected stores by shipping some of their goods to other stores that the auditors weren't attending.

After the inventory was counted and its cost was calculated, the company applied the LCM test. On a store-by-store basis, top management compared the unit cost and market value of inventory items and then prepared journal entries to write down the inventory. Some of the journal entries were large in amount and involved debiting an account called "Cookies" and crediting the inventory account. Management reported that the Cookies account was used to accumulate the required write-downs for all the company's stores. Just before the financial statements were finalized, the Cookies account was emptied by allocating it back to each of the stores. In one instance, $9,999,999.99 was allocated from Cookies to a store's account called "Accrued Inventory."

Required:

Prepare a list that summarizes the pieces of evidence that indicate that fraud might have occurred and, for each item on the list, explain why it contributes to your suspicion.

Epilogue:
This case is based on a fraud involving Phar Mor, as described by David Cottrell and Steven Glover in the July 1997 issue of the *CPA Journal*. Phar Mor's management was collectively fined over $1 million and two top managers received prison sentences ranging from 33 months to five years. The company's auditors paid over $300 million in civil judgments for failing to uncover the fraud.

Phar Mor

S7-5 Ethical Decision Making: A Mini-Case

LO3

David Exler is the CEO of AquaGear Enterprises, a seven-year-old manufacturer of boats. After many long months of debate with the company's board of directors, David obtained the board's approval to expand into water ski sales. David firmly believed that AquaGear could generate significant profits in this market, despite recent increases in the cost of skis. A board meeting will be held later this month for David to present the financial results for the first quarter of ski sales. As AquaGear's corporate controller, you reported to David that the results weren't great. Although sales were better than expected at $165,000 (3,000 units at $55 per unit), the cost of goods sold was $147,500. This left a gross profit of $17,500. David knew this amount wouldn't please the board. Desperate to save the ski division, David asks you to "take another look at the cost calculations to see if there's any way to reduce the cost of goods sold. I know you accountants have different methods for figuring things out, so maybe you can do your magic now when I need it most." You dig out your summary of inventory purchases for the quarter to recheck your calculations, using the LIFO method that has always been used for the company's inventory of boats.

	Date	Units	Unit Cost	Total Cost
Beginning inventory of water skis	January 1	0	—	—
Purchases	January 15	1,500	$30	$45,000
Purchases	February 18	2,000	45	90,000
Purchases	March 29	2,500	50	125,000

Required:

1. Calculate Cost of Goods Sold using the LIFO method. Does this confirm the statement you made to David about the Gross Profit earned on water ski sales in the first quarter?
2. Without doing any calculations, is it likely that any alternative inventory costing method will produce a lower Cost of Goods Sold? Explain.
3. Calculate Cost of Goods Sold using the FIFO method. Would use of this method solve David's current dilemma?
4. Is it acceptable within GAAP to report the water skis using one inventory costing method and the boats using a different method?
5. Do you see any problems with using the FIFO numbers for purposes of David's meeting with the board?

LO3   **S7-6 Critical Thinking: Income Manipulation under the LIFO Inventory Method**

Mandalay Industries is a private company that sells electronic test equipment. During the year 2010, the inventory records reflected the following:

	Units	Unit Cost	Total Cost
Beginning Inventory	15	$12,000	$180,000
Purchases	40	10,000	400,000
Sales (45 units at $25,000 each)			

To minimize income taxes, inventory is valued at cost using the LIFO inventory method. On December 28, 2010, Mandalay's supplier increased the unit cost of new test equipment to $15,000.

Required:

1. Determine the company's Income from Operations and the cost of ending inventory. The company's operating expenses (excluding Cost of Goods Sold) were $300,000 and the company applies LIFO with a periodic inventory system.

2. Mandalay's management is considering buying 20 additional units on December 31, 2010, at $15,000 each. Redo the income statement and ending inventory calculations, assuming that this purchase is made on December 31, 2010.

3. How much did Income from Operations change because of the decision to purchase additional units on December 31, 2010? Is there any evidence of deliberate income manipulation? Is this tax fraud? Explain.

LO4   **S7-7 Calculating and Recording the Effects of Lower of Cost or Market (LCM) on Ending Inventory**

Perfumania

www.mhhe.com/phillips3e

Assume you recently obtained a job in the Miami head office of Perfumania, the largest specialty retailer of discounted fragrances in the United States. Your job is to estimate the amount of write-down required to value inventory at the lower of cost or market. The cost of inventory is calculated using the weighted average cost method and, at $368 million, it represents the company's biggest and most important asset. Assume the corporate controller asked you to prepare a spreadsheet that can be used to determine the amount of LCM write-down for the current year. The controller provides the following hypothetical numbers for you to use in the spreadsheet.

Product Line	Weighted Average Unit Cost	Replacement Cost (Market) at Year-End	Quantity on Hand
Alfred Sung Shi	$22	$20	80
Animale	15	16	75
Azzaro	10	10	50
Mambo	16	17	30
OP Juice	8	7	400

You realize that you'll need to multiply the quantity of each item by the lower of cost or market per unit. You e-mailed your friend Owen for Excel help.

From:	Owentheaccountant@yahoo.com
To:	Helpme@hotmail.com
Cc:	
Subject:	Excel Help

So you don't have a sniff about how to pick the lower of cost or market? You can do this several different ways, but the easiest is to use the MIN command. Set up your spreadsheet similar to the table you sent me, and then add two new columns. In the first new column, enter the command "= MIN(costcell, marketcell)" where costcell is the cell containing the cost per unit and marketcell is the cell containing the market value per unit. Next, in the second new column, multiply the quantity by the LCM per unit, and then SUM the column.

Required:

1. Prepare a spreadsheet that calculates total LCM for inventory, applied on an item-by-item basis.
2. Prepare a journal entry to record the inventory LCM write-down.

CONTINUING CASE

CC7 **Accounting for Changing Inventory Costs**

|ACCOUNTING   LO3, 5, 6

In October 2010, Nicole eliminated all existing inventory of cosmetic items. The trouble of ordering and tracking each product line had exceeded the profits earned. In December, a supplier asked her to sell a prepackaged spa kit. Feeling she could manage a single product line, Nicole agreed. Nicole's Getaway Spa would make monthly purchases from the supplier at a cost that included production costs and a transportation charge. Nicole's Getaway Spa would keep track of its new inventory using a perpetual inventory system.

On December 30, 2010, Nicole's Getaway Spa purchased 10 units at a total cost of $6 per unit. Nicole purchased 30 more units at $8 in February 2011, but returned 5 defective units to her supplier. In March, Nicole purchased 15 units at $10 per unit. In May, 50 units were purchased at $10 per unit; however, Nicole took advantage of a 2/10, n/30 discount from her supplier. In June, NGS sold 50 units at a selling price of $12 per unit and 35 units at $10 per unit.

Required:

1. Explain whether the transportation cost included in each purchase should be recorded as a cost of the inventory or immediately expensed.
2. Compute the Cost of Goods Available for Sale, Cost of Goods Sold, and Cost of Ending Inventory using the first-in, first-out (FIFO) method.
3. Calculate the inventory turnover ratio (round to one decimal place), using the inventory on hand at December 31, 2010, as the beginning inventory. The supplier reported that the typical inventory turnover ratio was 7.9. How does NGS's ratio compare?
4. Would a different inventory cost flow assumption allow Nicole's Getaway Spa to better minimize its income tax?

CHAPTER 8

Reporting and Interpreting Receivables, Bad Debt Expense, and Interest Revenue

YOUR LEARNING OBJECTIVES

Understand the business

LO1   Describe the trade-offs of extending credit.

Study the accounting methods

LO2   Estimate and report the effects of uncollectible accounts.

LO3   Compute and report interest on notes receivable.

Evaluate the results

LO4   Compute and interpret the receivables turnover ratio.

Review the chapter

Lecture Presentation-LP8
www.mhhe.com/phillips3e

THAT WAS
THEN

In previous chapters, we quietly assumed that all sales on account ultimately are collected as cash.

FOCUS COMPANY: Skechers Shoes

www.skechers.com

One of the most challenging parts of your academic and professional career will be managing events that you can't completely control. Think, for example, about a group project that you must complete this term. You may believe that, in theory, the work should take only six days from start to finish. You know from experience, however, that someone in your group is likely to be late with the assigned work or may fail to complete it at all. The problem is you don't know who it will be or how long the delay will be—these matters are largely beyond your control. To allow for the possibility that someone may be late, you might set a shorter time period (say, four days) to complete the work. Establishing a two-day allowance will give you a realistic basis for planning and successfully completing the project.

This situation is similar to a problem faced by many companies, including Skechers, a shoe company that sells on credit to retailers such as Foot Locker. Skechers's managers know from experience that some customers won't pay their bills, especially in difficult economic times. The problem is that at the time sales are made, Skechers can't identify which particular customers will be "bad customers." In this chapter, you'll learn about a method of accounting for such uncertainties—one that is similar to the allowance approach you took with your group project. This method allows Skechers's managers to report in a timely manner how much money the company is likely to collect from customers. Also in this chapter, you will learn about notes receivable, which arise from selling or lending to others under contract.

THIS IS
NOW

In this chapter, you'll learn how companies handle the situation where customers don't pay all that they owe.

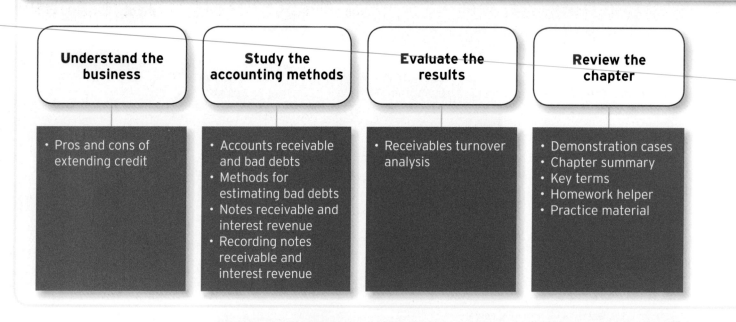

Understand the business	Study the accounting methods	Evaluate the results	Review the chapter
• Pros and cons of extending credit	• Accounts receivable and bad debts • Methods for estimating bad debts • Notes receivable and interest revenue • Recording notes receivable and interest revenue	• Receivables turnover analysis	• Demonstration cases • Chapter summary • Key terms • Homework helper • Practice material

Understand the Business

At December 31, 2008, accounts receivable and notes receivable accounted for over 20 percent of Skechers's total assets. If the company is to be successful, these assets have to be effectively managed. But what factors do managers consider when extending credit on account (accounts receivable) or under contract (notes receivable)?

PROS AND CONS OF EXTENDING CREDIT

Learning Objective 1
Describe the trade-offs of extending credit.

Skechers allows business customers (like DSW and Foot Locker) to open an account and buy shoes on credit, yet its retail outlets do not extend this option to you—the individual consumer. The reason Skechers is willing to create an account receivable from business customers but not individual consumers is that they carry different advantages and disadvantages. The advantage of extending credit is that it helps customers buy products and services, thereby increasing the seller's revenues. The disadvantages of extending credit are the following additional costs introduced:

1. **Increased wage costs.** If credit is extended, Skechers will have to hire people to (*a*) evaluate whether each customer is creditworthy, (*b*) track how much each customer owes, and (*c*) follow up to collect the receivable from each customer.

2. **Bad debt costs.** Inevitably, some customers dispute what they owe, or they run into financial difficulties and pay only a fraction of their account balances. These "bad debts," as they are called, can be a significant additional cost of extending credit. At December 31, 2008, Skechers estimated that nearly 8 percent of its receivables would not be collected.

3. **Delayed receipt of cash.** Even if Skechers were to collect in full from customers, it would likely have to wait 30–60 days before receiving the cash. During this period, Skechers may have to take out a short-term bank loan to pay for other business activities. The interest on such a loan would be another cost of extending credit to customers.

Most managers find that the additional revenue (or, more accurately, the gross profit) to be gained from selling on account to business customers is greater than the additional costs mentioned above. However, when it comes to individual consumers, the additional gross profit doesn't cover all the additional costs that Skechers would incur.

Spotlight On BUSINESS DECISIONS

Deciding Whether to Grant Credit

Many companies, including Skechers, do not grant credit to individual consumers because the expected costs outweigh the benefits. However, some companies such as Target Corporation are able to profit by extending credit to individuals. Through its Target credit card program, Target allows consumers to purchase merchandise on credit. For Target, extending credit has allowed the company to generate more profit,* even in 2008, when the economy struggled and its bad debts nearly tripled (in millions of dollars):

	2008		2007	
Additional revenues		$2,064		$1,896
Additional expenses				
Wages and administration	$ 491		$485	
Bad debts	**1,251**		**481**	
Interest	167	1,909	133	1,099
Additional profit		$ 155		$ 797

*Target Corporation 2008 Form 10-K, Item 7, Management's Discussion and Analysis.

Similar advantages and disadvantages are considered when deciding whether to create notes receivable. A **note receivable** is created when a formal written contract ("note") is established outlining the terms by which a company will receive amounts it is owed. Notes receivable differ from accounts receivable in that notes generally charge interest from the day they are signed to the day they are collected. Notes receivable are viewed as a stronger legal claim than accounts receivable, but a new note needs to be created for every transaction, so they are used less frequently—typically when a company sells large dollar-value items (e.g., cars), offers extended payment periods, or lends money to individuals or businesses.

YOU SHOULD KNOW

Note receivable: A promise that requires another party to pay the business according to a written agreement.

Study the Accounting Methods

ACCOUNTS RECEIVABLE AND BAD DEBTS

You already know from earlier chapters that **accounts receivable** arise from the sale of goods or services on credit. What you may not know is that some accounts receivable are never collected. Like that "friend" of yours who *says* he'll pay you later but for one reason or another never gets around to it, some customers just do not pay their bills.

Two objectives when accounting for accounts receivable and bad debts are: (1) report Accounts Receivable at the amount the company expects to collect ("net realizable value"), and (2) match the cost of bad debts to the accounting period in which the related credit sales are made. These two objectives point to the same solution: reduce both Accounts Receivable and Net Income by the amount of credit sales that are unlikely to be collected as cash.

The only problem with this solution is that, just as it takes you a while to find out which friends you can't trust, some time will pass before Skechers discovers which particular credit sales and customer balances aren't going to be collected. More than likely,

Learning Objective 2
Estimate and report the effects of uncollectible accounts.

YOU SHOULD KNOW

Accounts receivable: Amounts owed to a business by its customers.

Video 8.1
www.mhhe.com/phillips3e

EXHIBIT 8.1	Distortion Occurs If Bad Debts Are Not Matched to Sales

PERIOD 1 (Credit Sale Occurs)		PERIOD 2 (Bad Debt Discovered)	
Sales Revenues	$10,000	Sales Revenues	$ 0
Cost of Goods Sold	8,000	Cost of Goods Sold	0
Bad Debt Expense	0	Bad Debt Expense	1,000
Net Income	$ 2,000	Net Income (Loss)	$(1,000)

these bad debts will be discovered in an accounting period following the sale, rather than in the same period as the sale. As Exhibit 8.1 shows, if you record sales in one period when they occur and bad debts in a different period when they are discovered, you will violate the **matching principle.** This failure to match Bad Debt Expense with Sales Revenue in the same period will lead to distorted views of Net Income in the period of the sale as well as in the period the bad debt is discovered. To see how this could be a problem, take a moment to read Exhibit 8.1 right now.

Clearly, we need to **record bad debts in the same period as the sale.** The only way to do this is to estimate the amount of bad debts when the sale is recorded. Later, the accounting records can be adjusted when uncollectible amounts become known with certainty. This approach is called the **allowance method** and it follows a two-step process, which we'll walk you through below:

YOU SHOULD KNOW

Allowance method: A method of accounting that reduces accounts receivable (as well as net income) for an estimate of uncollectible accounts (bad debts).

1. Make an end-of-period adjustment to **record the estimated bad debts in the period credit sales occur.**
2. Remove ("write off") specific customer balances when they are known to be uncollectible.

1. Adjust for Estimated Bad Debts

Credit sales, when first recorded, affect both the balance sheet (an increase in Accounts Receivable) and the income statement (an increase in Sales Revenue). On occasion, a company will fail to collect receivables that arise from credit sales. To account for these bad sales on account that have been recorded in Sales Revenue and Accounts Receivable, we record offsetting amounts in both the balance sheet and income statement. This adjustment is made at the end of each accounting period to reduce Accounts Receivable (using a contra-asset account called Allowance for Doubtful Accounts) and reduce Net Income (using an expense account called **Bad Debt Expense**). If Skechers were to estimate $900 of bad debts this period, the effects on the accounting equation and adjusting journal entry to record them would be:

YOU SHOULD KNOW

Bad Debt Expense: Reports the estimated amount of this period's credit sales that customers will fail to pay.

1 Analyze

Assets	=	Liabilities	+	Stockholders' Equity	
Allowance for Doubtful Accounts (+xA)	−900			Bad Debt Expense (+E)	−900

2 Record

dr Bad Debt Expense (+E, −SE) 900
  cr Allowance for Doubtful Accounts (+xA, −A) 900

EXHIBIT 8.2	Recording and Reporting Estimated Bad Debts

Jan. 1   Jan. 31

Record sales on account   Record estimate of bad sales/receivables

| *dr* Accounts Receivable (+A) | 120,000 | | *dr* Bad Debt Expense (+E, −SE) | 900 | |
| *cr* Sales Revenue (+R, +SE) | | 120,000 | *cr* Allowance for Doubtful Accounts (+xA, −A) | | 900 |

Balance Sheet (excerpt)		
Cash		$115,000
Accounts Receivable	$200,000	
Less: Allowance for Doubtful Accounts	(15,000)	
Accounts Receivable, Net of Allowance		185,000
Inventory		260,000
Other Current Assets		40,000
Total Current Assets		600,000

Income Statement (excerpt)	
Sales Revenue	$120,000
Cost of Goods Sold	70,000
Gross Profit	50,000
Salaries and Wages Expense	44,000
Bad Debt Expense	900
Other Expenses	600
Income from Operations	4,500

Exhibit 8.2 uses blue and red text to show how the accounts in the end-of-period adjusting entry partially offset the original sales on account. The exhibit also shows where the accounts appear in the balance sheet and income statement.

Like all contra-asset accounts, such as Accumulated Depreciation, the Allowance for Doubtful Accounts is a permanent account, so its balance carries forward from one accounting period to the next. Bad Debt Expense, which is a temporary account, will have its balance closed (zeroed out) at the end of each accounting period. Consequently, the balance in the Allowance for Doubtful Accounts will differ from the balance in Bad Debt Expense, except during the first year that the Allowance for Doubtful Accounts is used. This explains why the Allowance for Doubtful Accounts in the balance sheet in Exhibit 8.2 does not equal the Bad Debt Expense in the income statement.

For billing and collection purposes, Skechers internally keeps a separate accounts receivable account (called a **subsidiary account**) for each customer. The total of these accounts is reported as Accounts Receivable on the balance sheet. Given this, you might wonder why the estimated uncollectible accounts aren't taken directly out of these individual accounts. The reason is that, at the time the Allowance for Doubtful Accounts is estimated, no one knows which particular customers' accounts receivable are uncollectible. If Skechers were to remove the specific customer accounts believed to be uncollectible, it would lose track of which customers still owed money. If this were to happen, Skechers would no longer know which customers it should continue pursuing for payment.

2. Remove (Write Off) Specific Customer Balances

Throughout the year, when it becomes clear that a particular customer will never pay, Skechers removes the customer's account from the accounts receivable records. After removing the receivable, Skechers no longer needs to make an allowance for it, so the company removes the corresponding amount from the Allowance for Doubtful Accounts. Removing the uncollectible account and a corresponding amount from the allowance is called a **write-off**. The purpose of writing off some or all of a customer's account balance is to remove amounts that are known with near certainty to have no chance of collection.

To illustrate, assume Skechers decides to write off an $800 receivable from Fast Footwear. Skechers would record an $800 decrease in Accounts Receivable, which would be offset by an $800 decrease in the contra-account Allowance for Doubtful Accounts. These accounting equation effects and the journal entry to record them follow.

> **COACH'S TIP**
>
> Accounts Receivable, Net of Allowance (shown in Exhibit 8.2) is not a separate account. It is a subtotal that is computed by subtracting the contra-asset account *Allowance for Doubtful Accounts* from the asset account *Accounts Receivable*.

> **YOU SHOULD KNOW**
>
> **Write-off:** The act of removing an uncollectible account and its corresponding allowance from the accounting records.

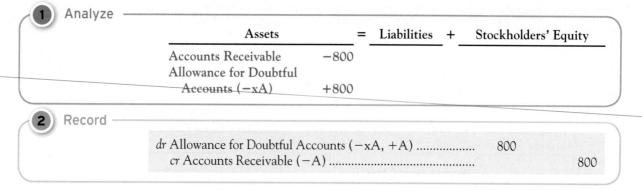

1 Analyze

Assets	= Liabilities +	Stockholders' Equity
Accounts Receivable	−800	
Allowance for Doubtful Accounts (−xA)	+800	

2 Record

dr Allowance for Doubtful Accounts (−xA, +A) 800
    cr Accounts Receivable (−A) 800

Notice that **a write-off does not affect income statement accounts.** The estimated Bad Debt Expense relating to these uncollectible accounts was already recorded with an adjusting entry in the period the sale was recorded. Therefore, no additional expense is incurred when the account is finally written off.

The effects of these two steps on Skechers's accounting records can be summarized in terms of the following changes in the related T-accounts:

dr + Accounts Receivable (A) cr −			dr − Allow. for Doubtful Accts (xA) cr +			dr + Bad Debt Expense (E, SE) cr −		
Beg. bal.	200,800				14,900	Beg. bal.	Beg. bal.	0	
		800 (2) Write-offs	(2) Write-offs	800	900	(1) Estimate	(1) Estimate	900	
End. bal.	200,000				15,000	End. bal.	End. bal.	900	

Summary of the Allowance Method

A summary of the two main steps in the allowance method follows:

Step	Timing	Journal Entry	FINANCIAL STATEMENT EFFECTS

1. Adjust for estimated bad debts	End of each period	dr Bad Debt Expense (+E, −SE)
		  cr Allowance for Doubtful Accounts (+xA, −A)
			Balance Sheet
			Accounts Receivable — *no effect*
			Less: Allowance — *increase*
			Accounts Receivable, Net — *decrease*
			
			Income Statement
			Revenues — *no effect*
			Expenses
			  Bad Debt Expense — *increase*
			Net Income — *decrease*

2. Write off specific customer balances	When known to be uncollectible	dr Allowance for Doubtful Accounts (−xA, +A)
		  cr Accounts Receivable (−A)
			Balance Sheet
			Accounts Receivable — *decrease*
			Less: Allowance — *decrease*
			Accounts Receivable, Net — *no effect*
			
			Income Statement
			Revenues — *no effect*
			Expenses
			  Bad Debt Expense — *no effect*
			Net Income — *no effect*

How's it going?   Self-Study Practice

Indicate the effect (+ / − / No Effect) of each of the following on net income and total assets.

	Net Income	Total Assets
1. Polaris Industries recorded an increase in estimated bad debts on December 31, 2009.		
2. Kellogg's wrote off twelve customer account balances during 2009.		

After you have finished, check your answers with the solution in the margin.

Solution to Self-Study Practice

	Net Income	Total Assets
1.	−	−
2.	NE	NE*

*The decrease in Accounts Receivable is offset by the decrease in Allowance for Doubtful Accounts.

METHODS FOR ESTIMATING BAD DEBTS

In the examples given so far, we simply stated the estimated amount of uncollectibles to record. In the workplace, these bad debts must be estimated. Such estimates may be based on either (1) a **percentage of credit sales** for the period or (2) an **aging of accounts receivable**. Both methods are acceptable under GAAP and IFRS. The percentage of credit sales method is simpler to apply, but the aging method is generally more accurate. Some companies use the simpler method on a weekly or monthly basis and the more accurate method on a monthly or quarterly basis to check the accuracy of earlier estimates.

Percentage of Credit Sales Method

The percentage of credit sales method estimates bad debt expense by multiplying the historical percentage of bad debt losses by the current period's credit sales. Assume, for example, that Skechers has experienced bad debt losses of ¾ of 1 percent of credit sales in prior periods. If credit sales in January total $120,000, Skechers could estimate the month's bad debt expense as:

Credit sales this month	$120,000
× Bad debt loss rate (0.75%)	× 0.0075
Bad debt expense this month	$ 900

This estimate would be recorded using the journal entry previously shown on page 362.

Aging of Accounts Receivable Method

While the percentage of credit sales method focuses on estimating Bad Debt Expense for the period, the aging of accounts receivable method focuses on estimating the ending balance in the Allowance for Doubtful Accounts. The aging method gets its name because it is based on the "age" of each amount in Accounts Receivable. The older and more overdue an account receivable becomes, the less likely it is to be collectible. Based on this idea, credit managers and accountants use their experience to estimate what portion of receivables of a specific age will not be paid.

To illustrate the aging of accounts receivable method, we assume Skechers applies this method to its accounts receivable balances when its quarter ends on March 31. The method includes three steps as shown in Exhibit 8.3:

1 **Prepare an aged listing of accounts receivable** with totals for each age category. Most accounting software will produce this report automatically by counting back the number of days to when each receivable was first recorded.

YOU SHOULD KNOW

Percentage of credit sales method (also called the income statement approach): Estimates bad debts based on the historical percentage of sales that lead to bad debt losses.
Aging of accounts receivable method (also called the balance sheet approach): Estimates uncollectible accounts based on the age of each account receivable.

EXHIBIT 8.3	Estimating Uncollectible Amounts with an Aging of Accounts Receivable

Customer	Total	Number of Days Unpaid			
		0–30	31–60	61–90	Over 90
Adam's Sports	$ 700	$ 400	$ 200	$ 100	
Backyard Shoe	2,300				$ 2,300
Others (not shown to save space)	189,000	97,600	49,800	37,900	3,700
Zoom Athletics	6,000	4,000	2,000		
Total Accounts Receivable	**$198,000**	**$102,000**	**$52,000**	**$38,000**	**$6,000**
Estimated Uncollectible (%)		× 2%	× 10%	× 20%	× 40%
Estimated Uncollectible ($)	**$ 17,240**	**$ 2,040**	**$ 5,200**	**$ 7,600**	**$2,400**

← Step ① —Age

← Step ② —Estimate

← Step ③ —Compute

② **Estimate bad debt loss percentages for each category.** The percentage each company uses varies according to its circumstances and past experience. Generally, higher percentages are applied to increasingly older receivables.

③ **Compute the total estimate by multiplying the totals in Step 1 by the percentages in Step 2 and then summing across all categories.** The total across all aging categories ($2,040 + $5,200 + $7,600 + $2,400 = $17,240) equals the balance to which the Allowance for Doubtful Accounts will need to be adjusted at the end of the period.

Allowance for
dr — **Doubtful Accounts** *cr* +

	15,000 Unadj. bal.
	? AJE
	17,240 Desired bal.

The amount computed in Step 3 is the desired balance in the Allowance for Doubtful Accounts, not the amount of the adjustment. To compute the amount of the adjustment, you must determine how much to increase (credit) the Allowance for Doubtful Accounts to reach the desired adjusted balance computed in Step 3. Assume, for example, Skechers had an unadjusted credit balance in the Allowance for Doubtful Accounts of $15,000 on March 31 and computed a desired credit balance of $17,240 as shown in Exhibit 8.3. An adjustment of $2,240 ($17,240 − $15,000) needs to be recorded as a credit to the account. A corresponding amount is debited to Bad Debt Expense, as follows.

① Analyze

	Assets	= Liabilities +	Stockholders' Equity
Allowance for Doubtful Accounts (+xA)	−2,240		Bad Debt Expense (+E) −2,240

② Record

dr Bad Debt Expense (+E, −SE) 2,240
    cr Allowance for Doubtful Accounts (+xA, −A) 2,240

③ Summarize

dr —	**Allow. for Doubtful Accts. (xA)**	*cr* +
	15,000	Unadj. bal.
	2,240	AJE
	17,240	Adj. bal.

dr +	**Bad Debt Expense (E, SE)**	*cr* −
Beg. bal.	900	
AJE	2,240	
End. bal.	3,140	

Although the Allowance for Doubtful Accounts normally has a credit balance, it may have a **debit balance** before it is adjusted. This happens when a company has recorded write-offs that exceed previous estimates of uncollectible accounts. If this happens, you can still calculate the amount of the adjustment needed to reach the desired balance under the aging of accounts receivable method. The only difference is that to reach the desired balance, you need to record an amount equal to the desired balance **plus** the existing debit balance. After the adjustment is recorded, the Allowance for Doubtful Accounts will once again return to a credit balance.

Spotlight On BUSINESS DECISIONS

Focus Collection Efforts with the Aged Listing of Accounts Receivable

The aged listing of accounts receivable, shown in Exhibit 8.3, is useful when estimating uncollectible accounts. But it also is useful when credit managers identify customers at risk of failing to pay their accounts. Some sources report that this risk doubles every month that an account ages beyond 90 days. Knowing this, employees in Skechers's credit department would be especially concerned with the $2,300 shown in Exhibit 8.3 as receivable from Backyard Shoe. If a follow-up phone call does not prompt the customer to pay, Skechers could turn the account over to a collection agency.

How's it going?   Self-Study Practice

For the years ended March 31, 2008 and 2007, Mad Catz reported credit balances in the Allowance for Doubtful Accounts of $4,514 and $3,583, respectively. It also reported that write-offs during the year ended March 31, 2008, amounted to $7,273 (all numbers in thousands of dollars). Assuming no other changes in the account, what amount did Mad Catz record as Bad Debt Expense for the period? Use the following T-accounts to solve for the missing value.

dr –	Allow. for Doubtful Accts. (xA)	cr +		dr +	Bad Debt Expense (E, SE)	cr –
	3,583	March 31, 2007		Beg. bal.	0	
7,273		Estimate		Estimate		
	4,514	March 31, 2008		March 31, 2008		

After you have finished, check your answers with the solution in the margin.

Other Issues

Revising Estimates   Bad debt estimates always differ from the amounts that are later written off. If these differences are material, companies are required to revise their bad debt estimates for the current period. That is, they correct overestimates of prior periods by lowering estimates in the current period, or they raise estimates in the current period to correct underestimates of prior periods.

Account Recoveries   In the same way that someone you've written off as a friend might do something to win you back, a customer might pay an account balance that was previously written off. Collection of a previously written off account is called a **recovery** and it is accounted for in two parts. First, put the receivable back on the books by recording

Solution to Self-Study Practice

dr –	Allow. for Doubtful Accts.	cr +
	3,583	March 31, 2007
Write-offs 7,273	8,204	Estimate
	4,514	March 31, 2008

dr +	Bad Debt Expense	cr –
	Beg. bal.	0
	Estimate 8,204	
	Adj. bal. 8,204	

Beginning + Bad debt estimate – Write-offs = Ending
3,583 + X – 7,273 = 4,514; X = 8,204

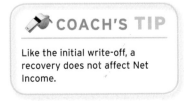

COACH'S TIP

Like the initial write-off, a recovery does not affect Net Income.

the opposite of the write-off. Second, record the collection of the account. To illustrate, let's assume that Skechers collects the $800 from Fast Footwear that was previously written off. This recovery would be recorded with the following journal entries:

Reverse the write-off
| (1) | dr Accounts Receivable (+A) .... | 800 | |
| | cr Allowance for Doubtful Accounts (+xA, −A) .... | | 800 |

Record the collection
| (2) | dr Cash (+A) .... | 800 | |
| | cr Accounts Receivable (−A) .... | | 800 |

Look closely at the journal entries for recording a recovery and you'll see that Accounts Receivable is debited and then credited for $800. It's tempting to cancel these two out, but don't do it because it would create an inaccurate credit history for the customer. After all is said and done, the customer's balance was removed because it was actually collected, not written off, so the accounting records should reflect that.

Alternative Methods   You should be aware that some small companies don't use the allowance method. Instead, they use an alternative approach called the **direct write-off method**, which we demonstrate in Supplement 8A at the end of this chapter. This alternative method records Bad Debt Expense only when a company writes off specific accounts. Although this alternative method is easier to use, it overstates the value of Accounts Receivable and it violates the matching principle as explained in Supplement 8A. Thus, it is not considered a generally accepted accounting method. However, the Internal Revenue Service (IRS), which discourages the use of accounting estimates, requires this method for tax purposes.

NOTES RECEIVABLE AND INTEREST REVENUE

Learning Objective 3
Compute and report interest on notes receivable.

A company reports Notes Receivable if it uses a promissory note to document its right to collect money from another party. This usually happens in the following three situations: (1) the company loans money to employees or businesses, (2) the company sells expensive items for which customers require an extended payment period, or (3) the company converts an existing account receivable to a note receivable to allow an extended payment period.

The accounting issues for notes receivable are similar to those for accounts receivable, with one exception. Unlike accounts receivable, which are interest-free until they become overdue, notes receivable charge interest from the day they are created to the day they are due (their **maturity date**). Although interest on a note receivable is earned each day, interest payments typically are received only once or twice a year. This means that a company with a note receivable needs to accrue Interest Revenue and Interest Receivable. Let's look at how to calculate interest.

YOU SHOULD KNOW

Interest formula: $I = P \times R \times T$ where I = interest calculated, P = principal, R = annual interest rate, and T = time period covered in the interest calculation (number of months out of 12).

Calculating Interest

To calculate interest, you need to consider three variables: (1) the **principal**, which is the amount of the note receivable, (2) the annual **interest rate** charged on the note, and (3) the **time** period covered in the interest calculation. Because **interest rates are always stated as an annual percentage even if the note is for less than a year**, the time period is the portion of a year for which interest is calculated. Ask yourself how many months out of 12 or how many days out of 365 the interest period covers. Then use the following **interest formula** to calculate the interest:

**COACH'S TIP**

The "time" variable refers to the portion of a year for which interest is calculated, not the portion of the note's entire life. A 2-month interest calculation on a 3-year note has a time variable of 2/12 not 2/36.

$$\text{Interest (I)} = \text{Principal (P)} \times \text{Interest Rate (R)} \times \text{Time (T)}$$

Many financial institutions use the number of days out of 365 to compute interest. In doing homework assignments, assume that the time is measured in terms of number of months out of 12. See Exhibit 8.4 for the computation of interest for three notes with

EXHIBIT 8.4	Sample Interest Computations

GIVEN INFORMATION		INTEREST CALCULATION				
Terms of note	Interest period	Principal	Rate		Time	Interest
$100,000, 6%, due in two years	November 1–October 31	$100,000 ×	6%	×	12/12 =	$6,000
$100,000, 6%, due in one year	January 1–October 31	100,000 ×	6	×	10/12 =	5,000
$100,000, 6%, due in 100 days	November 1–December 31	100,000 ×	6	×	2/12 =	1,000

different terms and different lengths of interest periods. Notice how the time variable depends on the interest period, not the due date for the note.

RECORDING NOTES RECEIVABLE AND INTEREST REVENUE

The four key events that occur with any note receivable are (1) establishing the note, (2) accruing interest earned but not received, (3) recording interest payments received, and (4) recording principal payments received. Assume that on November 1, 2009, Skechers lent $100,000 to a company by creating a note that required the company to pay Skechers 6 percent interest and the $100,000 principal on October 31, 2010. Skechers prepared year-end financial statements as of December 31, 2009, but made no other adjustments for interest during the year.

Establishing a Note Receivable

The $100,000 loan that created the note receivable has the following accounting equation effects, which Skechers would record using the following journal entry:

1 Analyze

	Assets	=	Liabilities	+	Stockholders' Equity
Note Receivable	+100,000				
Cash	−100,000				

2 Record

dr Note Receivable (+A)...	100,000	
cr Cash (−A)		100,000

Notice that no interest is recorded on the day the note is established. Interest is earned over time.

Accruing Interest Earned

Under accrual basis accounting, interest revenue is recorded when it is earned. Rather than record the interest earned as each day passes, Skechers waits until it either receives an interest payment or reaches the end of its accounting period.

The timeline in Exhibit 8.5 shows how Skechers should account for the interest revenue earned from the note over its one-year term. Note that between the date of the note's creation (November 1, 2009) and the year-end (December 31, 2009), Skechers earned two months of interest revenue (the red portion of the time line) because the note was outstanding for all of November and December 2009. As you learned in Chapter 4, when a company has earned interest in the current period but has not yet recorded the interest, the company must make an adjusting entry at the end of the current period to accrue the interest earned. The amount of interest to record for the two months of 2009 is computed as follows:

COACH'S TIP

Except for banks, interest is considered a peripheral source of revenue, so it is reported on the income statement immediately following the Income from Operations subtotal.

$$\text{Interest (I)} = \text{Principal (P)} \times \text{Interest Rate (R)} \times \text{Time (T)}$$
$$\$1{,}000 = \$100{,}000 \times 6\% \times 2/12$$

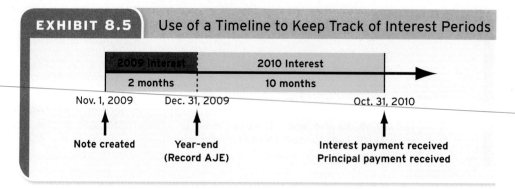

EXHIBIT 8.5   Use of a Timeline to Keep Track of Interest Periods

The effect of this adjustment, along with the adjusting journal entry to record the $1,000 of interest revenue that is receivable on December 31, 2009, is as follows.

1 Analyze

Assets	= Liabilities +	Stockholders' Equity
Interest Receivable +1,000		Interest Revenue (+R) +1,000

2 Record

dr Interest Receivable (+A)	1,000	
cr Interest Revenue (+R, +SE)		1,000

Recording Interest Received

On October 31, 2010, Skechers receives a cash interest payment of $6,000 (= $100,000 × 6% × 12/12). As shown on the following timeline, this $6,000 of interest includes the $1,000 that was accrued as Interest Receivable at December 31, 2009, plus $5,000 earned during the 10-month period from January 1 to October 31, 2010, which had yet to be recorded.

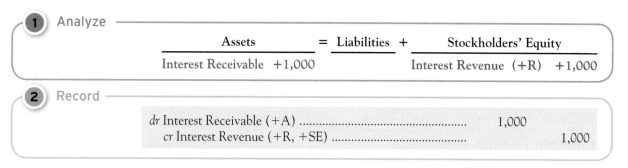

When Skechers receives the interest payment, it will record the $6,000 increase in cash, and it will reduce the $1,000 Interest Receivable that was previously recorded and record the remaining $5,000 as interest revenue in 2010. These effects and the journal entry to record them follow:

1 Analyze

Assets	= Liabilities +	Stockholders' Equity
Cash +6,000		
Interest Receivable −1,000		Interest Revenue (+R) +5,000

2 Record

dr Cash (+A)	6,000	
cr Interest Receivable (−A)		1,000
cr Interest Revenue (+R, +SE)		5,000

Recording Principal Received

The collection of a note receivable is accounted for just like the collection of an account receivable. Assuming that Skechers receives the $100,000 principal that is due, the accounting equation effects and journal entry for this transaction would be:

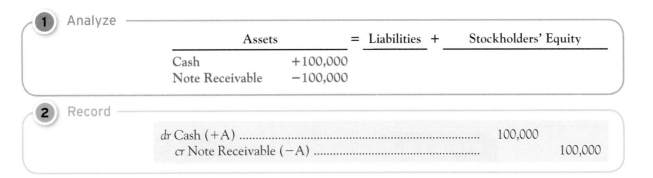

1 Analyze

	Assets	= Liabilities +	Stockholders' Equity
Cash	+100,000		
Note Receivable	−100,000		

2 Record

dr Cash (+A) 100,000
    cr Note Receivable (−A)   100,000

Accounting for Uncollectible Notes

Just as companies may not collect their accounts receivable in full, they also might not collect the full principal (and interest) that they are owed on a note receivable. When the collection of notes receivable is in doubt, a company should record an Allowance for Doubtful Accounts against the Notes Receivable, just as it records an Allowance for Doubtful Accounts against Accounts Receivable.

💡 How's it going?   Self-Study Practice

Assume that Mad Catz loaned $12,000 to an employee on October 1, 2009, by creating a note that required that the employee pay the principal and 8 percent interest on September 30, 2010. Assume that the company makes adjusting entries only at year-end on December 31.

1. Record the creation of the note.
2. Record any necessary end-of-period adjusting entry to be made at the end of 2009.
3. Record the receipt of interest and principal on September 30, 2010.

After you have finished, check your answers with the solution in the margin.

Solution to Self-Study Practice

1. dr Note Receivable (+A) 12,000
   cr Cash (−A) 12,000

2. dr Interest Receivable (+A) ($12,000 × 8% × 3/12) 240
   cr Interest Revenue (+R, +SE) 240

3. dr Cash (+A) ($12,000 × 8% × 12/12) 12,960
   cr Interest Receivable (−A) ($12,000 × 8% × 3/12) 240
   cr Interest Revenue (+R, +SE) ($12,000 × 8% × 9/12) 720
dr Cash (+A) 12,000
   cr Note Receivable (−A) 12,000

Spotlight On ETHICS

www.mhhe.com/phillips3e

Resetting the Clock

Earlier in this chapter, you saw that as customer balances get older, the Allowance for Doubtful Accounts should be increased. Because increases in the Allowance for Doubtful Accounts require increases in Bad Debt Expense, the result of older customer accounts should be a decrease in net income.

A credit manager at MCI knew about these accounting effects. To avoid reducing net income, he "reset the clock" on amounts owed by customers. He did so by making loans to customers, who then used the money to pay off their account balances. By replacing old accounts receivable with new notes receivable, he avoided recording approximately $70 million in bad debts. His scheme didn't last long, though. After the fraud was revealed, the credit manager spent several years in prison and he has been working to pay off over $10 million in fines. To learn more about this fraud, see S8-4 at the end of this chapter.

Evaluate the Results

RECEIVABLES TURNOVER ANALYSIS

YOU SHOULD KNOW

Receivables turnover: The process of selling and collecting on account. The receivables turnover ratio determines the average number of times this process occurs during the period.

Managers, directors, investors, and creditors can evaluate the effectiveness of a company's credit-granting and collection activities by conducting a receivables turnover analysis. The idea behind a receivables turnover analysis is shown in Exhibit 8.6. When a company sells goods or services on credit, its receivables balance goes up, and when it collects from customers, the receivables balance goes down. This process of selling and collecting is called **receivables turnover** and it is repeated over and over during each accounting period, for each customer.

$$\frac{31,944}{3,203.5} = 10$$

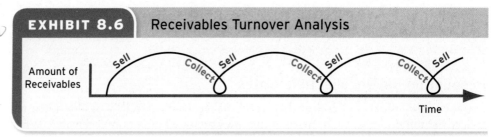

EXHIBIT 8.6 Receivables Turnover Analysis

COACH'S TIP

The bottom of the receivables turnover ratio uses the average beginning and ending Net Receivables, so that it spans the same period as the numerator. Ideally, the ratio would use only credit sales, but it is not reported separately, so use Net Sales instead.

The receivables turnover ratio indicates how many times, on average, this process of selling and collecting is repeated during the period. The higher the ratio, the faster the collection of receivables. And, the faster the collection of receivables, the shorter your company's operating cycle, which means more cash available for running the business. A low turnover ratio can be a warning sign, suggesting that the company is allowing too much time for customers to pay. As you learned earlier in this chapter (on page 365), the longer an account goes without being collected, the bigger the risk that it will never be collected. Analysts watch for changes in the receivables turnover ratio because a sudden decline may mean that a company is recording sales of merchandise that customers are likely to return later. It also may mean that the company is selling to less financially secure customers or is allowing customers more time to pay their accounts to entice them to buy as much as possible—a practice known as **channel stuffing**.

YOU SHOULD KNOW

Days to collect: A measure of the average number of days from the time a sale is made on account to the time it is collected.

Rather than evaluate the **number of times** accounts receivable turn over during a year, some people find it easier to think in terms of the **length of time** (in days) it takes to collect accounts receivable (called **days to collect**). Converting the year's receivables turnover ratio into the average days to collect is easy. Simply divide 365 by the year's receivables turnover ratio. This alternative measure provides the same basic information about the company's ability to collect receivables, but it's a little easier to interpret. In terms of Exhibit 8.6, the receivables turnover ratio counts the number of loops in a given period of time, whereas days to collect tells you the average number of days between loops.

Accounting Decision Tools		
Name of Measure	**Formula**	**What It Tells You**
Receivables turnover ratio	$\dfrac{\text{Net Sales Revenue}}{\text{Average Net Receivables}}$	• The number of times receivables turn over during the period • A higher ratio means faster (better) turnover
Days to collect	$\dfrac{365}{\text{Receivables Turnover Ratio}}$	• Average number of days from sale on account to collection • A higher number means a longer (worse) time to collect

Comparison to Benchmarks

Credit Terms   By calculating days to collect you can compare a company's collection performance to its stated collections policy. You might remember from Chapter 6 that when companies sell on account, they specify the length of credit period (as well as any discounts for prompt payment). By comparing the number of days to collect to the length of credit period, you can gain a sense of whether customers are complying with the stated policy. Managers inside a company watch this closely, and so do investors and creditors on the outside. Why? If customers appear to be disregarding the stated credit period, they may be dissatisfied with the product or service they bought.

Spotlight On FINANCIAL REPORTING

Comparing Days to Collect with Stated Credit Terms   *Kellogg's*

Kellogg Company—the cereal maker—is one of the rare companies that provides information about its normal credit policies in its annual report. In the notes to the financial statements, Kellogg indicates that its stated policy is to require payment from customers within 16 days of making a sale (**1/15, n/16**). The company's collection period of 19 days suggests that customers are generally willing to comply with this policy.

Other Companies   Receivables turnover ratios and the number of days to collect often vary across industries. To illustrate, we have calculated these measures in Exhibit 8.7 for Skechers, Crocs (another footwear company), and Boeing (an airplane manufacturer). As Exhibit 8.7 shows, Skechers turned over its receivables 8.4 times, which is once every 43.5 days. Boeing had a turnover ratio of 10.7 times, which means a jet-fast collection period of about 34 days. Crocs shuffled along behind, with a receivables turnover ratio of 7.7, which is about 47.4 days to collect. Because these measures typically vary between industries, you should compare a company's turnover only with other companies in the same industry or with its figures from prior

---

EXHIBIT 8.7	Summary of Receivables Turnover Ratio Analyses

Company	Relevant Information (in millions)		2008 Accounts Receivable Turnover Calculation	2008 Days to Collect Calculation
		2008 **2007**		
SKECHERS	Net Sales	$1,440 $1,394	$\dfrac{\$1,440}{(\$175 + \$167)/2} = 8.4$ times	$\dfrac{365\,\text{days}}{8.4\,\text{times}} = 43.5\,\text{days}$
	Net Accounts Receivable	175 167		
		2008 **2007**		
crocs	Net Sales	$722 $847	$\dfrac{\$722}{(\$35 + \$153)/2} = 7.7$ times	$\dfrac{365\,\text{days}}{7.7\,\text{times}} = 47.4\,\text{days}$
	Net Accounts Receivable	35 153		
		2008 **2007**		
BOEING	Net Sales	$60,909 $66,387	$\dfrac{\$60,909}{(\$5,602 + \$5,740)/2} = 10.7$ times	$\dfrac{365\,\text{days}}{10.7\,\text{times}} = 34.1\,\text{days}$
	Net Accounts Receivable	5,602 5,740		

periods. For practice at computing and comparing to prior periods, try the Self-Study Practice that follows.

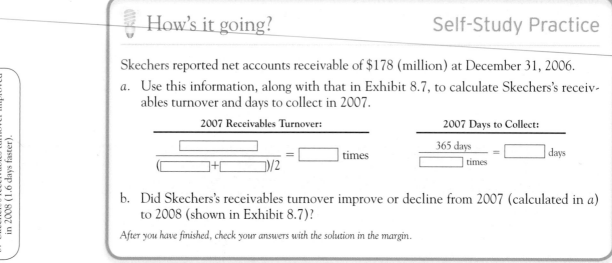

How's it going?   Self-Study Practice

Skechers reported net accounts receivable of $178 (million) at December 31, 2006.

a. Use this information, along with that in Exhibit 8.7, to calculate Skechers's receivables turnover and days to collect in 2007.

2007 Receivables Turnover:

$$\frac{\boxed{}}{(\boxed{}+\boxed{})/2} = \boxed{} \text{ times}$$

2007 Days to Collect:

$$\frac{365 \text{ days}}{\boxed{} \text{ times}} = \boxed{} \text{ days}$$

b. Did Skechers's receivables turnover improve or decline from 2007 (calculated in *a*) to 2008 (shown in Exhibit 8.7)?

After you have finished, check your answers with the solution in the margin.

Solution to Self-Study Practice

a. $\dfrac{\$1,394}{(\$167 + \$178)/2} = 8.1$ times

  $365 \div 8.1 = 45.1$ days

b. Skechers's receivables turnover improved in 2008 (1.6 days faster).

Speeding Up Collections

Factoring Receivables   To generate the cash needed to pay for a company's business activities, managers must ensure that receivables are collected on a timely basis. You might wonder what managers can do to speed up sluggish receivables collections. One obvious tactic is to start hounding customers for payment. This forceful approach has at least two drawbacks: (1) it is time-consuming and costly, and (2) it can annoy customers and cause them to take their business elsewhere. An alternative approach is to sell outstanding accounts receivable to another company (called a **factor**). The way this **factoring** arrangement works is that your company receives cash for the receivables it sells to the factor (minus a factoring fee) and the factor then has the right to collect the outstanding amounts owed by your customers. Factoring is a fast and easy way for your company to get cash for its receivables but with costs. First, factoring could send a potentially negative message because it might be seen as a last resort for collecting accounts. Second, the factoring fee can be as much as 3 percent of the receivables sold. If Skechers sold $100,000 of receivables to a factor under such an arrangement, Skechers would receive only $97,000 cash but would give up the potential to collect the full $100,000, resulting in an expense of $3,000. For a company that regularly sells its receivables, this cost of factoring is reported on the income statement as a selling expense. If a company factors infrequently, the fee is considered a peripheral "other" expense.

Credit Card Sales   Another way to avoid lengthy collection periods is to allow customers to pay for goods using national credit cards like Visa, MasterCard, American Express, and Discover Card. Unlike private credit card programs that require the seller to pursue collection from customers, national credit card companies pay the seller within one to three days of the sale. Some banks accept credit card receipts as overnight deposits into the company's bank account as if they're cash. This not only speeds up the seller's cash collection, but also reduces losses from customers writing bad checks. But, just like factoring, these benefits come at a cost. Credit card companies charge a fee for their services, often around 3 percent of the total sales price. If credit card sales amounted to $100,000, a credit card fee of $3,000 would be deducted, leaving the equivalent of $97,000 cash. These credit card fees are included with selling expenses on the income statement.

YOU SHOULD KNOW

Factoring: An arrangement where receivables are sold to another company (called a factor) for immediate cash (minus a factoring fee).

Spotlight On CONTROLS

Segregating Collections and Write-Offs

One way to control accounts receivable is to ensure that the same person does not both receive collections from customers and write off account balances. This segregation of duties helps to prevent errors and fraud. Without adequate segregation between these duties, a single dishonest employee could divert customer payments to his or her own bank account and then cover up the theft by writing off the customer's balance.

SUPPLEMENT 8A: Direct Write-Off Method

As described earlier in this chapter, an alternative method exists to account for uncollectible accounts. This alternative approach, called the **direct write-off method**, does not estimate bad debts and does not use an Allowance for Doubtful Accounts. Instead, it reports Sales when they occur and Bad Debt Expense when it is discovered. This is required for tax purposes but it is not acceptable under generally accepted accounting principles or IFRS. Consequently, it isn't used very often for external financial reporting.

The reason the direct write-off method isn't considered a GAAP method is that it reports Accounts Receivable at the total amount owed by customers (an overly optimistic point of view) rather than what is estimated to be collectible (a more realistic viewpoint). The direct write-off method also breaks the matching principle by recording Bad Debt Expense in the period that customer accounts are determined to be bad rather than matching the expense to the revenues reported in the period when the credit sales are actually made. As illustrated in Exhibit 8.1 on page 362, the failure to match Bad Debt Expense to Sales has a distorting effect on Net Income in the period of the sale as well as in later periods when bad debts are discovered. The only advantage of this method is that it doesn't require estimating uncollectible amounts.

Under the direct write-off method, no journal entries are made until a bad debt is discovered. The journal entry used by the direct write-off method to record $1,000 of Bad Debt Expense when a customer account is determined to be uncollectible is:

> **YOU SHOULD KNOW**
>
> **Direct write-off method:** A non-GAAP alternative to the allowance method of accounting for uncollectible accounts.

dr Bad Debt Expense (+E, −SE)	1,000	
cr Accounts Receivable (−A)		1,000

REVIEW THE CHAPTER

DEMONSTRATION CASE A: BAD DEBTS

Shooby Dooby Shoe (SDS) reported credit sales of $95,000 during January 2010. Later in 2010, SDS determined that it would not be able to collect a $500 account balance that was owed by a deceased customer (Captain Cutler). SDS uses the percentage of credit sales method for estimating monthly Bad Debt Expense, and the aging of accounts receivable method at its December 31 year-end.

www.mhhe.com/phillips3e

Required:

1. If SDS estimates that 1 percent of credit sales will result in bad debts, what will be the effects on the accounting equation of recording the January 2010 estimate? Prepare the journal entry to record these effects.

2. Show how the write-off of the account receivable from Captain Cutler would affect the accounting equation, and prepare the journal entry to record these effects.

3. Assume that SDS estimates that $11,000 of its year-end Accounts Receivable is uncollectible as shown below. As of December 31, 2010, the Allowance for Doubtful Accounts had an unadjusted credit balance of $3,000. Show the accounting equation effects of recording the bad debt estimate, and prepare a journal entry to record these effects.

		Number of Days Unpaid			
	Total	0–30	31–60	61–90	>90
Total Accounts Receivable	$171,000	$50,000	$80,000	$40,000	$1,000
Estimated uncollectible (%)		× 1%	× 5%	× 15%	× 50%
Estimated uncollectible ($)	$ 11,000	$ 500	$ 4,000	$ 6,000	$ 500

4. Assume that SDS reported total sales of $950,000 in 2010, Net Accounts Receivable of $160,000 at December 31, 2010, and $167,586 at December 31, 2009. Calculate the receivables turnover ratio for 2010.

5. If the receivables turnover ratio was 6.4 in 2009, what was the number of days to collect in 2009? Given your calculations in 4, conclude whether SDS collections are faster or slower in 2010 than in 2009.

Suggested Solution

1. The percentage of credit sales method multiplies historical bad debt losses (1%) by this period's credit sales ($95,000) to directly estimate the amount of Bad Debt Expense to record ($950 = 1% × $95,000).

Assets	= Liabilities +	Stockholders' Equity
Allowance for Doubtful Accounts (+xA) −950		Bad Debt Expense (+E) −950

dr Bad Debt Expense (+E, −SE)(0.01 × $95,000) 950
   cr Allowance for Doubtful Accounts (+xA, −A) 950

2.

Assets	= Liabilities + Stockholders' Equity
Accounts Receivable −500	
Allowance for Doubtful Accounts (−xA) +500	

dr Allowance for Doubtful Accounts (−xA, +A) 500
   cr Accounts Receivable (−A).. 500

3. Under the aging of accounts receivable method, we determine the estimated balance for the Allowance for Doubtful Accounts ($11,000) and then subtract its unadjusted balance ($3,000) to determine the amount of the adjustment ($8,000 = $11,000 − $3,000).

Assets	= Liabilities +	Stockholders' Equity
Allowance for Doubtful Accounts (+xA) −8,000		Bad Debt Expense (+E) −8,000

dr Bad Debt Expense (+E, −SE) 8,000
   cr Allowance for Doubtful Accounts (+xA, −A) 8,000

4. Receivables turnover ratio is calculated as Net Sales ÷ Average Accounts Receivable. The average accounts receivable in 2010 was $163,793 (= ($160,000 + $167,586)/2), so the receivables turnover ratio for 2010 was 5.8 (= $950,000 ÷ $163,793).

5. Days to collect is calculated as 365 ÷ receivables turnover ratio. The 6.4 turnover in 2009 equates to 57 days (and the 5.8 turnover in 2010 equates to 63 days). Collections are slower in 2010 than in 2009.

DEMONSTRATION CASE B: NOTES RECEIVABLE

As of February 28, 2008, Rocky Mountain Chocolate Factory, Inc. (RMCF), reported it had approximately $240,000 of Notes Receivable, with an annual interest rate of 8 percent. As a public company, RMCF prepares financial statements for external reporting every quarter, ending on May 31, August 31, November 30, and February 28. Assume that the notes were created on March 1, 2007, when money was loaned to another company, and that RMCF receives interest payments semi-annually, on July 31 and January 31.

Required:

1. Using the interest formula, calculate the amount of interest that RMCF earns each month on the notes.
2. Using the interest formula, calculate the amount of interest payment that RMCF received on July 31, 2008, and on January 31, 2009.
3. Prepare a timeline showing the amount of interest earned each quarter and received on each payment date.
4. Prepare journal entries to record the note's issuance, interest earned, and interest payments received for each quarter and on each payment date.

Suggested Solution

1. Interest earned = Principal × Interest Rate × Time
   $$= \$240{,}000 \times 8\% \times 1/12 = \$1{,}600 \text{ per month.}$$

2. The period from March 1 to July 31 is five months whereas the period from August 1 to January 31 is six months.

   Interest payment = Principal × Interest Rate × Time
   $$= \$240{,}000 \times 8\% \times 5/12 = \$8{,}000 \text{ on July 31.}$$

   Interest payment = Principal × Interest Rate × Time
   $$= \$240{,}000 \times 8\% \times 6/12 = \$9{,}600 \text{ on January 31.}$$

3. Timeline

March 1	May 31	July 31	Aug. 31	Nov. 30	Jan. 31	Feb. 28
$4,800	$3,200	$1,600	$4,800	$3,200	$1,600	
	$8,000			$9,600		

4. Journal Entries

   <u>March 1, 2007 (Notes Issued)</u>

dr Notes Receivable (+A)	240,000	
cr Cash (−A)		240,000

   <u>May 31, 2007 (Interest Accrued)</u>

dr Interest Receivable (+A)	4,800	
cr Interest Revenue (+R, +SE)		4,800

   <u>July 31, 2007 (Interest Payment Received)</u>

dr Cash (+A)	8,000	
cr Interest Receivable (−A)		4,800
cr Interest Revenue (+R, +SE)		3,200

   <u>August 31, 2007 (Interest Accrued)</u>

dr Interest Receivable (+A)	1,600	
cr Interest Revenue (+R, +SE)		1,600

   <u>November 30, 2007 (Interest Accrued)</u>

dr Interest Receivable (+A)	4,800	
cr Interest Revenue (+R, +SE)		4,800

January 31, 2008 (Interest Payment Received)

dr Cash (+A)	9,600	
cr Interest Receivable (−A)		6,400
cr Interest Revenue (+R, +SE)		3,200

February 28, 2008 (Interest Accrued)

dr Interest Receivable (+A)	1,600	
cr Interest Revenue (+R, +SE)		1,600

CHAPTER SUMMARY

LO1 **Describe the trade-offs of extending credit. p. 360**

- By extending credit to customers, a company is likely to attract a greater number of customers willing to buy from it.
- The additional costs of extending credit include increased wage costs, bad debt costs, and delayed receipt of cash.

LO2 **Estimate and report the effects of uncollectible accounts. p. 361**

- Under generally accepted accounting principles, companies must use the allowance method to account for uncollectibles. This method involves the following steps:
  1. Estimate and record uncollectibles with an end-of-period adjusting journal entry that increases Bad Debt Expense (debit) and increases the Allowance for Doubtful Accounts (credit).
  2. Identify and write off specific customer balances in the period that they are determined to be uncollectible.
- The adjusting entry (in 1) reduces Net Income as well as Net Accounts Receivable. The write-off (in 2) has offsetting effects on Accounts Receivable and the Allowance for Doubtful Accounts, ultimately yielding no net effect on Net Accounts Receivable or on Net Income.

LO3 **Compute and report interest on notes receivable. p. 368**

- Interest is calculated by multiplying the principal, interest rate, and time period (number of months out of 12). As time passes and interest is earned on the note, accountants must record an adjusting journal entry that accrues the interest revenue that is receivable on the note.

LO4 **Compute and interpret the receivables turnover ratio. p. 372**

- The receivables turnover ratio measures the effectiveness of credit-granting and collection activities. It reflects how many times average trade receivables were recorded and collected during the period.
- Analysts and creditors watch this ratio because a sudden decline may mean that a company is extending payment deadlines in an attempt to prop up lagging sales. Or it may mean that a company is recording sales of merchandise that customers are likely to return later.

Accounting Decision Tools		
Name of Measure	Formula	What It Tells You
Receivables turnover ratio	$\dfrac{\text{Net Sales Revenue}}{\text{Average Net Receivables}}$	• The number of times receivables turn over during the period • A higher ratio means faster (better) turnover
Days to collect	$\dfrac{365}{\text{Receivables Turnover Ratio}}$	• Average number of days from sale on account to collection • A higher number means a longer (worse) time to collect

KEY TERMS

Accounts Receivable p. 361

Aging of Accounts Receivable Method p. 365

Allowance Method p. 362

Bad Debt Expense p. 362

Days to Collect p. 372

Direct Write-Off Method p. 375

Factoring p. 374

Interest Formula p. 368

Notes Receivable p. 361

Percentage of Credit Sales Method p. 365

Receivables Turnover p. 372

Write-Off p. 363

See complete definitions in the glossary in the back of this text.

HOMEWORK HELPER

Alternative terms

- Days to Collect is also called "days' sales outstanding."

Helpful reminders

- The percentage of credit sales method calculates the amount to record as Bad Debt Expense. The aging of accounts receivable method calculates the desired balance in the Allowance for Doubtful Accounts. This desired balance is compared to the existing balance to determine the amount to record as Bad Debt Expense.
- Interest rates always are for a full year. To calculate interest for a shorter period, multiply the interest rate by the fraction of the year for which you are calculating interest.

Frequent mistakes

- Some students mistakenly think a write-off is an expense. It isn't. It is merely a way to clean up the accounts receivable records. Under the allowance method, no Bad Debt Expense is recorded when removing (writing off) specific customer accounts.

PRACTICE MATERIAL

QUESTIONS (⊖ Symbol indicates questions that require analysis from more than one perspective.)

1. What are the advantages and disadvantages of extending credit to customers?

2. In April 2006, Kohl's Corporation decided to discontinue its Kohl's credit card operations. What factors would this department store company have considered prior to making this decision? ⊖

3. Which basic accounting principles does the allowance method of accounting for bad debts satisfy?

4. Using the allowance method, is Bad Debt Expense recognized in the period in which (a) sales related to the uncollectible account were made or (b) the seller learns that the customer is unable to pay?

5. What is the effect of the write-off of uncollectible accounts (using the allowance method) on (a) net income and (b) net accounts receivable?

6. How does the use of calculated estimates differ between the aging of accounts receivable method and the percentage of credit sales method?

7. A local phone company had a customer who rang up $300 in charges during September 2009, but did not pay. Despite reminding the customer of this balance, the company was unable to collect in October, November, or December. In March 2010, the company finally gave up and wrote off the account balance. What amount of Sales, Bad Debt Expense, and Net Income would the phone company report from these events in 2009 and 2010 if it used the allowance method of accounting for uncollectible accounts? Assume the company estimates 5 percent of credit sales will go bad.

8. What is the primary difference between accounts receivable and notes receivable?

9. What are the three components of the interest formula? Explain how this formula adjusts for interest periods that are less than a full year.

10. As of February 1, 2009, Krispy Kreme Doughnuts had $100,000 of Notes Receivable due before January 31, 2010, $1,268,000 of Accounts Receivable, and $249,000 in its Allowance for Doubtful Accounts (all related to accounts receivable). How should these accounts be reported on a balance sheet prepared following GAAP? What if the balance sheet follows IFRS, as described in Chapter 5?

11. Does an increase in the receivables turnover ratio generally indicate faster or slower collection of receivables? Explain.

12. What two approaches can managers take to speed up sluggish collections of receivables? List one advantage and disadvantage for each approach.

13. When customers experience economic difficulties, companies consider extending longer credit periods. What are the possible consequences of longer credit periods on Sales, Accounts Receivable, Allowance for Doubtful Accounts, Net Income, and the receivables turnover ratio? ●

14. (Supplement 8A) Describe how (and when) the direct write-off method accounts for uncollectible accounts. What are the disadvantages of this method?

15. (Supplement 8A) Refer to question 7. What amounts would be reported if the direct write-off method were used? Which method (allowance or direct write-off) more accurately reports the financial results?

MULTIPLE CHOICE

Quiz 8
www.mhhe.com/phillips3e

1. When a company using the allowance method writes off a specific customer's account receivable from the accounting system, how many of the following are true?

   • Total stockholders' equity remains the same.
   • Total assets remain the same.
   • Total expenses remain the same.

   a. None
   b. One
   c. Two
   d. Three

2. When using the allowance method, as Bad Debt Expense is recorded,

   a. Total assets remain the same and stockholders' equity remains the same.
   b. Total assets decrease and stockholders' equity decreases. ₤
   c. Total assets increase and stockholders' equity decreases.
   d. Total liabilities increase and stockholders' equity decreases.

3. For many years, Carefree Company has estimated Bad Debt Expense using the aging of accounts receivable method. Assuming Carefree has no write-offs or recoveries, its estimate of uncollectible receivables resulting from the aging analysis equals

   a. Bad Debt Expense for the current period.
   b. The ending balance in the Allowance for Doubtful Accounts for the period.
   c. The change in the Allowance for Doubtful Accounts for the period.
   d. Both (a) and (c).

4. Which of the following best describes the proper presentation of accounts receivable in the financial statements?

   a. Accounts Receivable plus the Allowance for Doubtful Accounts in the asset section of the balance sheet.
   b. Accounts Receivable in the asset section of the balance sheet and the Allowance for Doubtful Accounts in the expense section of the income statement.
   c. Accounts Receivable less Bad Debt Expense in the asset section of the balance sheet.
   d. Accounts Receivable less the Allowance for Doubtful Accounts in the asset section of the balance sheet.

5. If the Allowance for Doubtful Accounts opened with a $10,000 credit balance, had write-offs of $5,000 (with no recoveries) during the period, and had a desired ending balance of $20,000 based on an aging analysis, what was the amount of Bad Debt Expense?

   a. $5,000
   b. $10,000
   c. $15,000
   d. $20,000

6. When an account receivable is "recovered"

   a. Total assets increase.
   b. Total assets decrease.
   c. Stockholders' equity increases.
   d. None of the above.

7. If a 10 percent note receivable for $10,000 is created on January 1, 2009, and it has a maturity date of December 31, 2013,

   a. No interest revenue will be recorded in 2009.
   b. The note receivable will be classified as a current asset.
   c. Interest Revenue of $1,000 will be recorded in 2009.
   d. None of the above.

8. If the receivables turnover ratio decreased during the year,

   a. The days to collect also decreased.
   b. Receivables collections slowed down.
   c. Sales Revenues increased at a faster rate than Accounts Receivable increased.
   d. None of the above.

9. In 2008, Coca-Cola Enterprises had a receivables turnover ratio of 8.5. Which of the following could Coca-Cola do to cause the ratio to increase?

   a. Pursue collections more aggressively.
   b. Increase the percentages used to estimate bad debts.
   c. Factor its receivables.
   d. All of the above.

10. All else equal, if Skechers incurs a 3 percent fee to factor $10,000 of its Accounts Receivable, its Net Income will

   a. Increase by $10,000.
   b. Increase by $9,700.
   c. Increase by $300.
   d. Decrease by $300.

> For answers to the Multiple-Choice Questions see page Q1 located in the last section of the book.

MINI-EXERCISES

|ACCOUNTING

LO1   M8-1   Evaluating the Decision to Extend Credit

Nutware Productions Inc. generated sales of $30,000 and gross profit of $10,000 last year. The company estimates that it would have generated sales of $60,000 had it extended credit, but there would be additional costs for associated wages and bad debts totaling $25,000. Should the company extend credit?

M8-2 Evaluating the Decision to Extend Credit

LO1

JCPenney currently allows customers to purchase merchandise using national credit cards like Visa and Mastercard, yet it had discontinued its own private credit card program in 1999. What pros and cons would lead JCPenney to continue with national credit cards but not its own private credit card program? In its annual report for the year ended January 31, 2009, JCPenney removed from Accounts Receivable $56 million of credit card transactions awaiting settlement and instead reported them as Cash and Cash Equivalents. What characteristic of national credit cards makes this reclassification appropriate?

JCPenney

M8-3 Reporting Accounts Receivable and Recording Write-Offs Using the Allowance Method

LO2

At the end of 2009, Extreme Fitness has adjusted balances of $800,000 in Accounts Receivable and $55,000 in Allowance for Doubtful Accounts. On January 2, 2010, the company learns that certain customer accounts are not collectible, so management authorizes a write-off of these accounts totaling $5,000.

a. Show how the company would have reported its receivable accounts on December 31, 2009. As of that date, what amount did Extreme Fitness expect to collect?
b. Prepare the journal entry to write off the accounts on January 2, 2010.
c. Assuming no other transactions occurred between December 31, 2009, and January 3, 2010, show how Extreme Fitness would have reported its receivable accounts on January 3, 2010. As of that date, what amount did Extreme Fitness expect to collect? Has this changed from December 31, 2009? Explain why or why not.

M8-4 Recording Recoveries Using the Allowance Method

LO2

Let's go a bit further with the example from M8-3. Assume that on February 2, 2010, Extreme Fitness received a payment of $500 from one of the customers whose balance had been written off. Prepare the journal entries to record this transaction.

M8-5 Recording Write-Offs and Bad Debt Expense Using the Allowance Method

LO2

Prepare journal entries for each transaction listed.

a. During the period, customer balances are written off in the amount of $17,000.
b. At the end of the period, bad debt expense is estimated to be $14,000.

M8-6 Determining Financial Statement Effects of Write-Offs and Bad Debt Expense Using the Allowance Method

LO2

Using the following categories, indicate the effects of the following transactions. Use + for increase and − for decrease and indicate the accounts affected and the amounts.

a. During the period, customer balances are written off in the amount of $8,000.
b. At the end of the period, bad debt expense is estimated to be $10,000.

Assets	=	Liabilities	+	Stockholders' Equity

M8-7 Estimating Bad Debts Using the Percentage of Credit Sales Method

LO2

Assume Simple Co. had credit sales of $250,000 and cost of goods sold of $150,000 for the period. Simple uses the percentage of credit sales method and estimates that ½ percent of credit sales would result in uncollectible accounts. Before the end-of-period adjustment is made, the Allowance for Doubtful Accounts has a credit balance of $250. What amount of Bad Debt Expense would the company record as an end-of-period adjustment?

M8-8 Estimating Bad Debts Using the Aging Method

LO2

Assume that Simple Co. had credit sales of $250,000 and cost of goods sold of $150,000 for the period. Simple uses the aging method and estimates that the appropriate ending balance in the Allowance for Doubtful Accounts is $1,600. Before the end-of-period adjustment is made, the Allowance for Doubtful Accounts has a credit balance of $250. What amount of Bad Debt Expense would the company record as an end-of-period adjustment?

M8-9 Recording Bad Debt Estimates Using the Two Estimation Methods

LO2

Using the information in M8-7 and M8-8, prepare the journal entry to record the end-of-period adjustment for bad debts under the (a) percentage of credit sales method, and (b) aging of accounts receivable method. Which of these methods is required by GAAP?

LO3   M8-10 Using the Interest Formula to Compute Interest

Complete the following table by computing the missing amounts (?) for the following independent cases.

	Principal Amount on Note Receivable	Annual Interest Rate	Time Period	Interest Earned
a.	$100,000	10%	6 months	?
b.	?	10%	12 months	$4,000
c.	$50,000	?	9 months	$3,000

LO3   M8-11 Recording Note Receivable Transactions

Scotia Corporation hired a new product manager and agreed to provide her a $20,000 relocation loan on a six-month, 7 percent note. Prepare journal entries to record the following transactions for Scotia Corporation. Rather than use letters to reference each transaction, use the date of the transaction.

a.   The company loans the money on January 1, 2010.
b.   The new employee pays Scotia the full principal and interest on its maturity date.

LO3   M8-12 Recording Note Receivable Transactions

RecRoom Equipment Company received an $8,000, six-month, 6 percent note to settle an $8,000 unpaid balance owed by a customer. Prepare journal entries to record the following transactions for RecRoom. Rather than use letters to reference each transaction, use the date of the transaction.

a.   The note is accepted by RecRoom on November 1, 2009, causing the company to increase its Notes Receivable and decrease its Accounts Receivable.
b.   RecRoom adjusts its records for interest earned to December 31, 2009.
c.   RecRoom receives the principal and interest on the note's maturity date.

LO2, 3   M8-13 Reporting Accounts and Notes Receivable in a Classified Balance Sheet

Caterpillar, Inc.

Caterpillar, Inc., reported the following accounts and amounts (in millions) in its December 31, 2008, year-end financial statements. Prepare the current assets section of a classified balance sheet. Assume that the Allowance for Doubtful Accounts relates to Accounts Receivable rather than Notes Receivable.

Accounts Payable	$ 4,827	Long-Term Debt	$22,834
Accounts Receivable	9,788	Long-Term Notes Receivable	15,743
Accumulated Depreciation	10,963	Notes Receivable—Current	8,731
Allowance for Doubtful Accounts	391	Other Current Assets	1,988
Cash and Cash Equivalents	2,736	Other Current Liabilities	14,033
Inventories	8,781	Other Noncurrent Assets	9,105
Loans Payable—Current	7,209	Property, Plant, and Equipment	23,487

LO4   M8-14 Determining the Effects of Credit Policy Changes on Receivables Turnover Ratio and Days to Collect

Indicate the most likely effect of the following changes in credit policy on the receivables turnover ratio and days to collect (+ for increase, − for decrease, and NE for no effect).

a.   Granted credit to less creditworthy customers.
b.   Granted credit with shorter payment deadlines.
c.   Increased effectiveness of collection methods.

LO4   M8-15 Evaluating the Effect of Factoring on the Receivables Turnover Ratio and Computing the Cost of Factoring

After noting that its receivables turnover ratio had declined, Imperative Company decided for the first time in the company's history to sell $500,000 of receivables to a factoring company. The factor charges a factoring fee of 3 percent of the receivables sold. How much cash does Imperative receive on the sale? Calculate the factoring fee and describe how it is reported by Imperative Company. All else equal, how will this affect Imperative's receivables turnover ratio in the future?

M8-16 (Supplement 8A) Recording Write-Offs and Reporting Accounts Receivable Using the Direct Write-Off Method

Complete all the requirements of M8-3, except assume that Extreme Fitness uses the direct write-off method. Note that this means Extreme does not have an Allowance for Doubtful Accounts balance.

EXERCISES

E8-1 Recording Bad Debt Expense Estimates and Write-Offs Using the Aging of Receivables Method

LO2

At the end of 2010, Blackhorse Productions, Inc., used the aging of accounts receivable method to estimate that its Allowance for Doubtful Accounts should be $19,750. The account had an unadjusted credit balance of $10,000 at December 31, 2010.

Required:

Prepare journal entries for each transaction.

a. The appropriate bad debt adjustment was recorded for the year 2010.
b. On January 31, 2011, an account receivable for $1,000 from March 2010 was determined to be uncollectible and was written off.

E8-2 Determining Financial Statement Effects of Bad Debt Expense Estimates and Write-Offs

LO2

For each transaction listed in E8-1, indicate the amount and direction (+ or −) of effects on the financial statement accounts and on the overall accounting equation.

Assets	=	Liabilities	+	Stockholders' Equity

E8-3 Recording, Reporting, and Evaluating a Bad Debt Estimate Using the Percentage of Credit Sales Method

LO2

During the year ended December 31, 2009, Kelly's Camera Shop had sales revenue of $170,000, of which $85,000 was on credit. At the start of 2009, Accounts Receivable showed a $10,000 debit balance, and the Allowance for Doubtful Accounts showed an $800 credit balance. Collections of accounts receivable during 2009 amounted to $68,000.

Data during 2009 follow:

a. On December 10, 2009, a customer balance of $1,500 from a prior year was determined to be uncollectible, so it was written off.
b. On December 31, 2009, a decision was made to continue the accounting policy of basing estimated bad debt losses on 2 percent of credit sales for the year.

Required:

1. Give the required journal entries for the two events in December 2009.
2. Show how the amounts related to Accounts Receivable and Bad Debt Expense would be reported on the balance sheet and income statement for 2009.
3. On the basis of the data available, does the 2 percent rate appear to be reasonable? Explain.

E8-4 Recording Write-Offs and Recoveries

LO2

Prior to recording the following, Elite Electronics, Incorporated, had a credit balance of $2,000 in its Allowance for Doubtful Accounts.

Required:

Prepare journal entries for each transaction.

a. On August 31, 2010, a customer balance for $300 from a prior year was determined to be uncollectible and was written off.
b. On December 15, 2010, the customer balance for $300 written off on August 31, 2010, was collected in full.

LO2   **E8-5 Determining Financial Statement Effects of Write-Offs and Recoveries**

For each transaction listed in E8-4, indicate the amount and direction (+ or −) of effects on the financial statement accounts and on the overall accounting equation.

Assets	=	Liabilities	+	Stockholders' Equity

LO2   **E8-6 Computing Bad Debt Expense Using Aging of Accounts Receivable Method**

Young and Old Corporation (YOC) uses two aging categories to estimate uncollectible accounts. Accounts less than 60 days are considered young and have a 5% uncollectible rate. Accounts more than 60 days are considered old and have a 35% uncollectible rate.

Required:

1. If YOC has $100,000 of young accounts and $400,000 of old accounts, how much should be reported in the Allowance for Doubtful Accounts?
2. If YOC's Allowance for Doubtful Accounts currently has an unadjusted credit balance of $40,000, how much should be credited to the account?
3. If YOC's Allowance for Doubtful Accounts has an unadjusted debit balance of $5,000, how much should be credited to the account?
4. Explain how YOC's Allowance for Doubtful Accounts could have a debit balance.

LO2   **E8-7 Computing Bad Debt Expense Using Aging of Accounts Receivable Method**

Brown Cow Dairy uses the aging approach to estimate Bad Debt Expense. The balance of each account receivable is aged on the basis of three time periods as follows: (1) 1–30 days old, $12,000; (2) 31–90 days old, $5,000; and (3) more than 90 days old, $3,000. Experience has shown that for each age group, the average loss rate on the amount of the receivable due to uncollectibility is (1) 3 percent, (2) 15 percent, and (3) 30 percent, respectively. At December 31, 2010 (end of the current year), the Allowance for Doubtful Accounts balance was $800 (credit) before the end-of-period adjusting entry is made.

Required:

1. Prepare a schedule to estimate an appropriate year-end balance for the Allowance for Doubtful Accounts.
2. What amount should be recorded as Bad Debt Expense for the current year?
3. If the unadjusted balance in the Allowance for Doubtful Accounts was a $600 debit balance, what would be the amount of Bad Debt Expense in 2010?

LO2   **E8-8 Recording and Reporting Allowance for Doubtful Accounts Using the Percentage of Credit Sales and Aging of Accounts Receivable Methods**

Innovative Tech Inc. (ITI) uses the percentage of credit sales method to estimate bad debts each month and then uses the aging method at year-end. During November 2010, ITI sold services on account for $100,000 and estimated that ½ of one percent of those sales would be uncollectible. At its December 31 year-end, total Accounts Receivable is $89,000, aged as follows: (1) 1–30 days old, $75,000; (2) 31–90 days old, $10,000; and (3) more than 90 days old, $4,000. Experience has shown that for each age group, the average rate of uncollectibility is (1) 1 percent, (2) 15 percent, and (3) 40 percent, respectively. Before the end-of-year adjusting entry is made, the Allowance for Doubtful Accounts has a $1,600 credit balance at December 31, 2010.

Required:

1. Prepare the November 2010 adjusting entry for bad debts.
2. Prepare a schedule to estimate an appropriate year-end balance for the Allowance for Doubtful Accounts.
3. Prepare the December 31, 2010, adjusting entry.
4. Show how the various accounts related to accounts receivable should be shown on the December 31, 2010, balance sheet.

LO2   **E8-9 Recording and Determining the Effects of Write-Offs, Recoveries, and Bad Debt Expense Estimates on the Balance Sheet and Income Statement**

Academic Dishonesty Investigations Ltd. operates a plagiarism detection service for universities and community colleges.

Required:

1. Prepare journal entries for each transaction below.

   a. On March 31, 10 customers were billed for detection services totaling $25,000.

   b. On October 31, a customer balance of $1,500 from a prior year was determined to be uncollectible and was written off.

   c. On December 15, a customer paid an old balance of $900, which had been written off in a prior year.

   d. On December 31, $500 of bad debts were estimated and recorded for the year.

2. Complete the following table, indicating the amount and effect (+ for increase, − for decrease, and NE for no effect) of each transaction. Ignore income taxes.

Transaction	Net Receivables	Net Sales	Income from Operations
a			
b			
c			
d			

E8-10 Recording Note Receivable Transactions, Including Accrual Adjustment for Interest   **LO3**

The following transactions took place for Smart Solutions Ltd.

2009

July 1   Loaned $70,000 to an employee of the company and received back a one-year, 10 percent note.

Dec. 31   Accrued interest on the note.

2010

July 1   Received interest and principal on the note. (No interest has been recorded since December 31.)

Required:

Prepare the journal entries that Smart Solutions Ltd. would record for the above transactions.

E8-11 Recording Note Receivable Transactions, Including Accrual Adjustment for Interest   **LO3**

The following transactions took place for Parker's Grocery.

Jan. 1   Loaned $50,000 to a cashier of the company and received back a one-year, 7 percent note.

June 30   Accrued interest on the note.

Dec. 31   Received interest and principal on the note. (No interest has been recorded since June 30.)

Required:

Prepare the journal entries that Parker's Grocery would record for the above transactions.

E8-12 Recording Note Receivable Transactions, Including Accrual Adjustment for Interest   **LO3**

To attract retailers to its shopping center, the Marketplace Mall will lend money to tenants under formal contracts, provided that they use it to renovate their store space. On November 1, 2010, the company loaned $100,000 to a new tenant on a one-year note with a stated annual interest rate of 6 percent. Interest is to be received by Marketplace Mall on April 30, 2011, and at maturity on October 31, 2011.

Required:

Prepare journal entries that Marketplace Mall would record related to this note on the following dates: (*a*) November 1, 2010; (*b*) December 31, 2010 (Marketplace Mall's fiscal year-end); (*c*) April 30, 2011; and (*d*) October 31, 2011.

LO2, 4
Microsoft Corporation

E8-13 Using Financial Statement Disclosures to Infer Write-Offs and Bad Debt Expense and to Calculate the Receivables Turnover Ratio

Microsoft Corporation develops, produces, and markets a wide range of computer software including the Windows operating system. Microsoft reported the following information about Net Sales Revenue and Accounts Receivable (all amounts in millions).

	June 30, 2008	June 30, 2007
Accounts Receivable, Net of Allowances of $153 and $117	$13,589	$11,338
Net Revenues	60,420	51,122

According to its Form 10-K, Microsoft recorded Bad Debt Expense of $88 and did not recover any previously written off accounts during the year ended June 30, 2008.

Required:

1. What amount of accounts receivable was written off during the year ended June 30, 2008?
2. What was Microsoft's receivables turnover ratio (to one decimal place) in the current year?

LO2

E8-14 Using Financial Statement Disclosures to Infer Bad Debt Expense

The 2009 annual report for Sears Holding Corporation contained the following information (in millions):

	2009	2008
Accounts Receivable	$881	$781
Allowance for Doubtful Accounts	42	37
Accounts Receivable, Net	$839	$744

A footnote to the financial statements disclosed that accounts receivable write-offs amounted to $13 during 2009 and $3 during 2008. Assume that Sears did not record any recoveries.

Required:

Determine the Bad Debt Expense for 2009 based on the above facts.

LO2, 4

E8-15 Determining the Effects of Uncollectible Accounts on the Receivables Turnover Ratio

Refer to the information about Sears given in E8-14.

Required:

Complete the following table indicating the direction of the effect (+ for increase, − for decrease, and NE for no effect) of each transaction during 2009:

Transaction	Net Credit Sales	Average Net Accounts Receivable	Receivables Turnover Ratio
a. Writing off $13,000,000 in uncollectible accounts.			
b. Recording bad debt expense.			

LO4
FedEx Corporation

E8-16 Analyzing and Interpreting Receivables Turnover Ratio and Days to Collect

A recent annual report for FedEx Corporation contained the following data (in millions):

	May 31	
	2008	2007
Accounts Receivable	$ 4,517	$ 4,078
Less: Allowance for Doubtful Accounts	158	136
Accounts Receivable, Net of Allowance	$ 4,359	$ 3,942
Net Sales (assume all on credit)	$37,953	$35,214

Required:

1. Determine the receivables turnover ratio and days to collect for 2008. Round your answers to one decimal place.
2. Explain the meaning of each number.

E8-17 Determining the Effects of Bad Debt Write-Offs on the Receivables Turnover Ratio

LO2, 4

During 2010, Jesse Enterprises Corporation recorded credit sales of $650,000. At the beginning of the year, Accounts Receivable, Net of Allowance was $50,000. At the end of the year, *after* the Bad Debt Expense adjustment was recorded but *before* any bad debts had been written off, Accounts Receivable, Net of Allowance was $49,000.

Required:

1. Assume that on December 31, 2010, accounts receivable totaling $6,000 for the year were determined to be uncollectible and written off. What was the receivables turnover ratio for 2010? Round to one decimal place.
2. Assume instead that on December 31, 2010, $7,000 of accounts receivable was determined to be uncollectible and written off. What was the receivables turnover ratio for 2010? Round to one decimal place.
3. Explain why the answers to requirements 1 and 2 differ or do not differ.

E8-18 (Supplement 8A) Recording Write-Offs and Reporting Accounts Receivable Using the Direct Write-Off Method

Trevorson Electronics is a small company privately owned by Jon Trevorson, an electrician who installs wiring in new homes. Because the company's financial statements are prepared only for tax purposes, Jon uses the direct write-off method. During 2009, its first year of operations, Trevorson Electronics sold $30,000 of services on account. The company collected $26,000 of these receivables during the year, and Jon believed that the remaining $4,000 was fully collectible. In 2010, Jon discovered that none of the $4,000 would be collected, so he wrote off the entire amount. To make matters worse, Jon sold only $5,000 of services during the year.

Required:

1. Prepare journal entries to record the transactions in 2009 and 2010.
2. Using only the information provided (ignore other operating expenses), prepare comparative income statements for 2009 and 2010. Was 2009 really as profitable as indicated by its income statement? Was 2010 quite as bad as indicated by its income statement? What should Jon do if he wants better information for assessing his company's ability to generate profit?

COACHED PROBLEMS

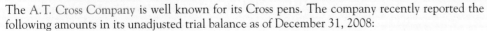

CP8-1 Recording Accounts Receivable Transactions Using Two Estimation Methods

|ACCOUNTING   LO2

The A.T. Cross Company is well known for its Cross pens. The company recently reported the following amounts in its unadjusted trial balance as of December 31, 2008:

A.T. Cross Company

	Debits	Credits
Accounts Receivable	$29,152,000	
Allowance for Doubtful Accounts		$ 849,000
Sales Revenue		38,974,000

(handwritten: 9,822,000 / 9,74,350)

Required:

1. Assume Cross uses ¼ of 1 percent of sales to estimate its bad debt expense for the year. Prepare the adjusting journal entry required at December 31, 2008, for recording Bad Debt Expense.

   TIP: The percentage of credit sales method directly calculates Bad Debt Expense.

2. Assume instead that Cross uses the aging of accounts receivable method and estimates that $1,007,000 of Accounts Receivable will be uncollectible. Prepare the adjusting journal entry required at December 31, 2008, for recording bad debt expense.

   TIP: The aging of accounts receivable method focuses on calculating what the adjusted Allowance for Doubtful Accounts balance should be. You need to consider the existing balance when determining the adjustment.

3. Repeat requirement 2, except this time assume the unadjusted balance in Cross's Allowance for Doubtful Accounts at December 31, 2008, was a debit balance of $10,050.

   TIP: See page 367 for advice on how to handle debit balances.

4. If one of Cross's main customers declared bankruptcy in 2009, what journal entry would be used to write off its $10,000 balance?

LO2, 3

Sonic Corp.

CP8-2 Interpreting Disclosure of Allowance for Doubtful Accounts

Sonic Corp. runs the largest chain of drive-in restaurants in the United States. It has an Allowance for Doubtful Accounts that relates to its accounts and notes receivable. In its 2008 10-K, Sonic reported the following changes in the Allowance for Doubtful Accounts (in thousands):

Balance at Beginning of Period	Charged to Bad Debt Expense	Amounts Written Off	Balance at End of Period
$711	$341	$335	$717

Required:

1. Create a T-account for the Allowance for Doubtful Accounts and enter into it the amounts from the above schedule. Then write the T-account in equation format to prove that the above items account for the changes in the account.

   TIP: The allowance increases when estimates are charged to Bad Debt Expense and when recoveries are reported. The allowance decreases when accounts are written off.

2. Record summary journal entries related to (a) estimating bad debt expense, and (b) write-offs of specific balances during the year.

   TIP: Use the generic account name "Receivables" to refer to the combined accounts receivable and notes receivable.

3. If Sonic had written off an additional $20,000 of accounts receivable during the period, how would Net Receivables have been affected? How would Net Income have been affected? Explain why.

LO3

CP8-3 Recording Notes Receivable Transactions

Jung & Newbicalm Advertising (JNA) recently hired a new creative director, Howard Rachell, for its Madison Avenue office in New York. To persuade Howard to move from San Francisco, JNA agreed to advance him $100,000 on April 30, 2009, on a one-year, 10 percent note, with interest payments required on October 31, 2009, and April 30, 2010. JNA issues quarterly financial statements on March 31, June 30, September 30, and December 31.

Required:

1. Prepare the journal entry that JNA will make to record the promissory note created on April 30, 2009.

   TIP: See demonstration case B for a similar problem.

2. Prepare the journal entries that JNA will make to record the interest accruals at each quarter end and interest payments at each payment date.

   TIP: Interest receivable will be accrued at the end of each quarter, and then will be reduced when the interest payment is received.

3. Prepare the journal entry that JNA will make to record the principal payment at the maturity date.

CP8-4 Accounting for Accounts and Notes Receivable Transactions   LO2, 3

Execusmart Consultants has provided business consulting services for several years. The company uses the percentage of credit sales method to estimate bad debts for internal monthly reporting purposes. At the end of each quarter, the company adjusts its records using the aging of accounts receivable method. The company entered into the following selected transactions during the first quarter of 2010.

a. During January, the company provided services for $200,000 on credit.
b. On January 31, the company estimated bad debts using 1 percent of credit sales.
c. On February 4, the company collected $100,000 of accounts receivable.
d. On February 15, the company wrote off a $500 account receivable.
e. During February, the company provided services for $150,000 on credit.
f. On February 28, the company estimated bad debts using 1 percent of credit sales.
g. On March 1, the company loaned $12,000 to an employee who signed a 10% note, due in 3 months.
h. On March 15, the company collected $500 on the account written off one month earlier.
i. On March 31, the company accrued interest earned on the note.
j. On March 31, the company adjusted for uncollectible accounts, based on the following aging analysis. Allowance for Doubtful Accounts has an unadjusted credit balance of $6,000.

| Customer | Total | Number of Days Unpaid | | | |
		0–30	31–60	61–90	Over 90
Arrow Ergonomics	$ 1,000	$ 500	$ 400	$ 100	
Asymmetry Architecture	2,000				$2,000
Others (not shown to save space)	85,000	34,000	42,000	5,000	4,000
Weight Whittlers	2,000	2,000			
Total Accounts Receivable	$90,000	$36,500	$42,400	$5,100	$6,000
Estimated Uncollectible (%)		2%	10%	20%	40%

Required:

1. For items a–j, analyze the amount and direction (+ or −) of effects on specific financial statement accounts and the overall accounting equation and prepare journal entries.
2. Show how the receivables related to these transactions would be reported in the current assets section of a classified balance sheet.
3. Name the accounts related to Accounts Receivable and Note Receivable that would be reported on the income statement and indicate whether they would appear before, or after, Income from Operations.

CP8-5 Analyzing Allowance for Doubtful Accounts, Receivables Turnover Ratio, and Days to Collect   LO4

Mattel and Hasbro are two of the largest and most successful toymakers in the world, in terms of the products they sell and their receivables management practices. To evaluate their ability to collect on credit sales, consider the following information reported in their annual reports (amounts in millions).

Mattel, Inc.

www.mhhe.com/phillips3e

| Fiscal Year Ended: | Mattel | | | Hasbro | | |
	2008	2007	2006	2008	2007	2006
Net Sales	$5,918	$5,970	$5,650	$4,022	$3,838	$3,151
Accounts Receivable	900	1,012	963	644	686	584
Allowance for Doubtful Accounts	26	21	19	32	31	28
Accounts Receivable, Net of Allowance	874	991	944	612	655	556

Required:

1. Calculate the receivables turnover ratios and days to collect for Mattel and Hasbro for 2008 and 2007. (Round your final answers to one decimal place.)
   TIP: In your calculations, use average Accounts Receivable, Net of Allowance.
2. Which of the companies was quicker to convert its receivables into cash in 2008? in 2007?

GROUP A PROBLEMS

LO2   **PA8-1 Recording Accounts Receivable Transactions Using the Aging Method**

Kraft Foods Inc.

Kraft Foods Inc. is the second-largest food and beverage company in the world. Assume the company recently reported the following amounts in its unadjusted trial balance as of December 31, 2008 (all amounts in millions):

	Debits	Credits
Accounts Receivable	$4,833	
Allowance for Doubtful Accounts		$ 129
Sales (assume all on credit)		42,201

Required:

1. Assume Kraft uses ½ of 1 percent of sales to estimate its Bad Debt Expense for the year. Prepare the adjusting journal entry required for the year, assuming no Bad Debt Expense has been recorded yet.

2. Assume instead that Kraft uses the aging of accounts receivable method and estimates that $233 of its Accounts Receivable will be uncollectible. Prepare the adjusting journal entry required at December 31, 2008, for recording Bad Debt Expense.

3. Repeat requirement 3, except this time assume the unadjusted balance in Kraft's Allowance for Doubtful Accounts at December 31, 2008, was a debit balance of $20.

4. If one of Kraft's main customers declared bankruptcy in 2009, what journal entry would be used to write off its $15 balance?

LO2   **PA8-2 Interpreting Disclosure of Allowance for Doubtful Accounts**

Heelys, Inc.

Heelys, Inc., designs and sells footwear with the wheel in the heel, worn by annoying kids at shopping malls. It recently disclosed the following information concerning the Allowance for Doubtful Accounts on its Form 10-K annual report.

		SCHEDULE II		
		Valuation and Qualifying Accounts		
		(dollars in thousands)		

Allowance for Doubtful Accounts	Balance at Beginning of Year	Additions Charged to Bad Debt Expense	Write Offs	Balance at End of Year
2008	$189	$ 0	$ 69	$120
2007	410	333	554	189
2006	130	435	?	410

Required:

1. Create a T-account for the Allowance for Doubtful Accounts and enter into it the 2008 amounts from the above schedule. Then write the T-account in equation format to prove that the above items account for the changes in the account.

2. Heelys reported sales of $70 million in 2008. Why might its Bad Debt Expense equal zero that year?

3. Record summary journal entries for 2007 related to (a) estimating Bad Debt Expense and (b) writing off specific balances.

4. Supply the missing dollar amount noted by ? for 2006.

5. If Heelys had written off an additional $20 of Accounts Receivable during 2008, how would Net Receivables have been affected? How would Net Income have been affected? Explain why.

LO3   **PA8-3 Recording Notes Receivable Transactions**

C&S Marketing (CSM) recently hired a new marketing director, Jeff Otos, for its downtown Minneapolis office. As part of the arrangement, CSM agreed on February 28, 2009, to advance Jeff $50,000 on a one-year, 8 percent note, with interest to be paid at maturity on February 28, 2010. CSM prepares financial statements on June 30 and December 31.

Required:

1. Prepare the journal entry that CSM will make when the note is established.
2. Prepare the journal entries that CSM will make to accrue interest on June 30 and December 31.
3. Prepare the journal entry that CSM will make to record the interest and principal payments on February 28, 2010.

PA8-4 Accounting for Accounts and Notes Receivable Transactions   LO2, 3

Web Wizard, Inc., has provided information technology services for several years. The company uses the percentage of credit sales method to estimate bad debts for internal monthly reporting purposes. At the end of each quarter, the company adjusts its records using the aging of accounts receivable method. The company entered into the following selected transactions during the first quarter of 2010.

a. During January, the company provided services for $40,000 on credit.
b. On January 31, the company estimated bad debts using 1 percent of credit sales.
c. On February 4, the company collected $20,000 of accounts receivable.
d. On February 15, the company wrote off a $100 account receivable.
e. During February, the company provided services for $30,000 on credit.
f. On February 28, the company estimated bad debts using 1 percent of credit sales.
g. On March 1, the company loaned $2,400 to an employee who signed a 6% note, due in 6 months.
h. On March 15, the company collected $100 on the account written off one month earlier.
i. On March 31, the company adjusted for uncollectible accounts, based on an aging analysis (below). Allowance for Doubtful Accounts has an unadjusted credit balance of $1,200.
j. On March 31, the company accrued interest earned on the note.

Customer	Total	Number of Days Unpaid			
		0–30	31–60	61–90	Over 90
Alabama Tourism	$ 200	$ 100	$ 80	$ 20	
Bayside Bungalows	400				$ 400
Others (not shown to save space)	17,000	6,800	8,400	1,000	800
Xciting Xcursions	400	400			
Total Accounts Receivable	**$18,000**	**$7,300**	**$8,480**	**$1,020**	**$1,200**
Estimated uncollectible (%)		**2%**	**10%**	**20%**	**40%**

(handwritten annotations: 1200, 478, 1678; and below the table: 146, 848, 204, 480)

Required:

1. For items *a–j*, analyze the amount and direction (+ or −) of effects on specific financial statement accounts and the overall accounting equation and prepare journal entries.
2. Show how the receivables related to these transactions would be reported in the current assets section of a classified balance sheet.
3. Name the accounts related to Accounts Receivable and Note Receivable that would be reported on the income statement and indicate whether they would appear before, or after, Income from Operations.

PA8-5 Analyzing Allowance for Doubtful Accounts, Receivables Turnover Ratio, and Days to Collect

LO4
Coca-Cola
PepsiCo

Coca-Cola and PepsiCo are two of the largest and most successful beverage companies in the world in terms of the products that they sell and their receivables management practices. To evaluate their ability to collect on credit sales, consider the following information reported in their 2008, 2007, and 2006 annual reports (amounts in millions).

www.mhhe.com/phillips3e

	Coca-Cola			PepsiCo		
Fiscal Year Ended:	2008	2007	2006	2008	2007	2006
Net Sales	$31,944	$28,857	$24,088	$43,251	$39,474	$35,137
Accounts Receivable	3,141	3,373	2,650	3,784	3,670	3,147
Allowance for Doubtful Accounts	51	56	63	70	69	64
Accounts Receivable, Net of Allowance	3,090	3,317	2,587	3,714	3,601	3,083

Required:

1. Calculate the receivables turnover ratios and days to collect for Coca-Cola and PepsiCo for 2008 and 2007. (Round to one decimal place.)

2. Which of the companies is quicker to convert its receivables into cash?

GROUP B PROBLEMS

LO2

Intel Corporation

PB8-1 Recording Accounts Receivable Transactions Using the Allowance Method

Intel Corporation is a well-known supplier of computer chips, boards, systems, and software building blocks. Assume the company recently reported the following amounts in its unadjusted trial balance at its year-end of December 27, 2008 (all amounts in millions):

	Debits	Credits
Accounts Receivable	$1,729	
Allowance for Doubtful Accounts		$ 17
Sales (assume all on credit)		37,586

Required:

1. Assume Intel uses ¼ of 1 percent of sales to estimate its Bad Debt Expense for the year. Prepare the adjusting journal entry required for the year, assuming no Bad Debt Expense has been recorded yet.

2. Assume instead that Intel uses the aging of accounts receivable method and estimates that $40 of its Accounts Receivable will be uncollectible. Prepare the adjusting journal entry required at December 27, 2008, for recording Bad Debt Expense.

3. Repeat requirement 2, except this time assume the unadjusted balance in Intel's Allowance for Doubtful Accounts at December 27, 2008, was a debit balance of $20.

4. If one of Intel's main customers declared bankruptcy in 2009, what journal entry would be used to write off its $15 balance?

LO2

Xerox Corporation

PB8-2 Interpreting Disclosure of Allowance for Doubtful Accounts

Xerox Corporation is the company that made the photocopier popular, although it now describes itself as a technology and services enterprise that helps businesses deploy document management strategies and improve productivity. It recently disclosed the following information concerning the allowance for doubtful accounts on its Form 10-K annual report.

<table>
<tr><th colspan="5" style="text-align:center">SCHEDULE II
Valuation and Qualifying Accounts
(dollars in millions)</th></tr>
<tr><th>Allowance for
Doubtful Accounts</th><th>Balance at
Beginning of Year</th><th>Additions Charged to
Bad Debt Expense</th><th>Write-Offs</th><th>Balance at
End of Year</th></tr>
<tr><td>2008</td><td>$128</td><td>$72</td><td>$69</td><td>$131</td></tr>
<tr><td>2007</td><td>116</td><td>?</td><td>42</td><td>128</td></tr>
<tr><td>2006</td><td>136</td><td>27</td><td>?</td><td>116</td></tr>
</table>

Required:

1. Create a T-account for the Allowance for Doubtful Accounts and enter into it the 2008 amounts from the above schedule. Then, write the T-account in equation format to prove that the above items account for the changes in the account.

2. Record summary journal entries for 2008 related to (a) estimating bad debt expense and (b) writing off specific balances.

3. Supply the missing dollar amounts noted by ? for 2007 and 2006.

4. If Xerox had written off an additional $20 of accounts receivable during 2008, how would it have affected Net Accounts Receivable? How would the write-off have affected Net Income? Explain.

PB8-3 Recording Notes Receivable Transactions

LO3

Stinson Company recently agreed to loan an employee $100,000 for the purchase of a new house. The loan was executed on May 31, 2010, and is a one-year, 6 percent note, with interest payments required on November 30, 2010, and May 31, 2011. Stinson issues quarterly financial statements on March 31, June 30, September 30, and December 31.

Required:

1. Prepare the journal entry that Stinson will make when the note is established.
2. Prepare the journal entries that Stinson will make to record the interest accruals at each quarter end and interest payments at each payment date.
3. Prepare the journal entry that Stinson will make to record the principal payment at the maturity date.

PB8-4 Accounting for Accounts and Notes Receivable Transactions

LO2, 3

Elite Events Corporation has provided event planning services for several years. The company uses the percentage of credit sales method to estimate bad debts for internal monthly reporting purposes. At the end of each quarter, the company adjusts its records using the aging of accounts receivable method. The company entered into the following selected transactions during the first quarter of 2010.

a. During January, the company provided services for $300,000 on credit.
b. On January 31, the company estimated bad debts using 1 percent of credit sales.
c. On February 4, the company collected $250,000 of accounts receivable.
d. On February 15, the company wrote off a $3,000 account receivable.
e. During February, the company provided services for $250,000 on credit.
f. On February 28, the company estimated bad debts using 1 percent of credit sales.
g. On March 1, the company loaned $15,000 to an employee who signed a 4% note, due in 9 months.
h. On March 15, the company collected $3,000 on the account written off one month earlier.
i. On March 31, the company accrued interest earned on the note.
j. On March 31, the company adjusted for uncollectible accounts, based on the following aging analysis. Allowance for Doubtful Accounts has an unadjusted credit balance of $9,000.

Customer	Total	Number of Days Unpaid			
		0–30	31–60	61–90	Over 90
Aerosmith	$ 2,000	$ 1,000	$ 1,000		
Biggie Small	2,000			$ 1,000	$ 1,000
Others (not shown to save space)	99,000	39,000	42,000	9,000	9,000
ZZ Top	7,000	7,000			
Total Accounts Receivable	$110,000	$47,000	$43,000	$10,000	$10,000
Estimated uncollectible (%)		2%	10%	20%	40%

Required:

1. For items a–j, analyze the amount and direction (+ or −) of effects on specific financial statement accounts and the overall accounting equation and prepare journal entries.
2. Show how the receivables related to these transactions would be reported in the current assets section of a classified balance sheet.
3. Name the accounts related to Accounts Receivable and Note Receivable that would be reported on the income statement and indicate whether they would appear before, or after, Income from Operations.

PB8-5 Analyzing Allowance for Doubtful Accounts, Receivables Turnover Ratio, and Days to Collect

LO4

Wal-Mart and Target are two of the largest and most successful retail chains in the world. To evaluate their ability to collect on credit sales, consider the following information reported in their annual reports (amounts in millions).

Walmart

Target

Fiscal Year Ended January 31:	Wal-Mart			Target		
	2009	2008	2007	2009	2008	2007
Net Sales	$401,244	$374,307	$344,992	$62,894	$61,471	$57,878
Accounts Receivable, Net of Allowance	3,905	3,642	2,840	8,084	8,054	6,194

Required:

1. Calculate the receivables turnover ratios and days to collect for Wal-Mart and Target for the years ended January 31, 2009 and 2008. (Round to one decimal place.)
2. Which of the companies is quicker to convert its receivables into cash?
3. How did the economic difficulties in 2008–09 affect the accounts receivable collections?

COMPREHENSIVE PROBLEM

LO2

Walgreen's

C8-1 Recording and Reporting Credit Sales and Bad Debts Using the Aging of Accounts Receivable Method (Chapters 6 and 8)

Okay Optical, Inc., (OOI) began operations in January 2010, selling inexpensive sunglasses to large retailers like Walgreen's and other smaller stores. Assume the following transactions occurred during its first six months of operations.

January 1   Sold merchandise to Walgreen's for $20,000; the cost of these goods to OOI was $12,000.

February 12   Received payment in full from Walgreen's.

March 1   Sold merchandise to Tony's Pharmacy on account for $3,000; the cost of these goods to OOI was $1,400.

April 1   Sold merchandise to Travis Pharmaco on account for $8,000. The cost to OOI was $4,400.

May 1   Sold merchandise to Anjuli Stores on account for $2,000; the cost to OOI was $1,200.

June 17   Received $6,500 on account from Travis Pharmaco.

Required:

1. Complete the following aged listing of customer accounts at June 30.

		Unpaid Since			
Customer	Total Balance	June (one month)	May (two months)	April (three months)	March (greater than three months)
Anjuli Stores	$2,000		$2,000		
Tony's Pharmacy	3,000				$3,000
Travis Pharmaco					
Walgreen's					

2. Estimate the Allowance for Doubtful Accounts required at June 30, 2010, assuming the following uncollectible rates: one month, 1 percent; two months, 5 percent; three months, 20 percent; more than three months, 40 percent.
3. Show how OOI would report its accounts receivable on its June 30 balance sheet. What amounts would be reported on an income statement prepared for the six-month period ended June 30, 2010?
4. Bonus Question: In July 2010, OOI collected the balance due from Tony's Pharmacy but discovered that the balance due from Travis Pharmaco needed to be written off. Using this information, determine how accurate OOI was in estimating the Allowance for Doubtful Accounts needed for each of these two customers and in total.

SKILLS DEVELOPMENT CASES

S8-1 Finding Financial Information

LO2, 4

Refer to the financial statements of The Home Depot in Appendix A at the end of this book, or download the 2008 annual report from the *Cases* section of the text's Web site at www.mhhe.com/phillips3e.

1. Does the company report an Allowance for Doubtful Accounts on the balance sheet or in the notes? Explain why it does or does not. (*Hint:* The company refers to its Allowance for Doubtful Accounts as a "Valuation Reserve" related to Accounts Receivable.)
2. Compute the company's receivables turnover ratio and days to collect for the year ended February 1, 2009.

S8-2 Comparing Financial Information

LO2, 4

Lowe's

Refer to the financial statements of Lowe's in Appendix B at the end of this book, or download the annual report from the *Cases* section of the text's Web site at www.mhhe.com/phillips3e.

1. Does the company report Accounts Receivable or an Allowance for Doubtful Accounts in its financial statements? Explain why it does or does not.
2. Based on your observations for requirement 1, describe the usefulness of the receivables turnover ratio and days to collect analyses for companies that are involved in home improvement retail sales.

S8-3 Internet-Based Team Research: Examining an Annual Report

LO2, 4

As a team, select an industry to analyze. Using your Web browser, each team member should access the annual report or 10-K for one publicly traded company in the industry, with each member selecting a different company. (See S1-3 in Chapter 1 for a description of possible resources for these tasks.)

Required:

1. On an individual basis, each team member should write a short report that incorporates the following:
   a. Calculate the receivables turnover ratio for the current and prior year, and explain any change between the two years. (To obtain the beginning accounts receivable number for the prior year, you will need the prior year's annual report.)
   b. Look in the 10-K for the Schedule II analysis of "Valuation and Qualifying Accounts," which provides additional disclosures concerning the Allowance for Doubtful Accounts. From this schedule, determine the level of Bad Debt Expense, as a percentage of sales, for the current and prior year.
2. Then, as a team, write a short report comparing and contrasting your companies using these attributes. Discuss any patterns across the companies that you as a team observe. Provide potential explanations for any differences discovered.

S8-4 Ethical Decision Making: A Real-Life Example

LO2, 3

MCI

You work for a company named MCI and you have been assigned the job of adjusting the company's Allowance for Doubtful Accounts balance. You obtained the following aged listing of customer account balances for December.

Accounts Receivable Aged Listing—December 31						
Customer	Total	0–30 days	31–60 days	61–90 days	91–120 days	> 120 days
AfriTel	40,000	20,000	10,000	5,000	5,000	0
CT&T	0	0	0	0	0	0
GlobeCom	28,000	0	18,000	8,000	1,000	1,000
Hi-Rim	35,000	0	0	0	0	35,000
Level 8	162,000	63,000	44,000	29,000	13,000	13,000
NewTel	0	0	0	0	0	0
Telemedia	0	0	0	0	0	0
Others	485,000	257,000	188,000	28,000	11,000	1,000
TOTAL	**750,000**	**340,000**	**260,000**	**70,000**	**30,000**	**50,000**

Historically, bad debt loss rates for each aging category have been 1% (0–30 days), 5% (31–60 days), 8% (61–90 days), 10% (91–120 days), and 50% (> 120 days). Using these rates, you calculate a desired balance for the allowance. No entries have been made to the account since the end of November when the account had a credit balance of $46,820.

To check the reasonableness of the calculated balance, you obtain the aged listings for prior months (shown below). As you scan the listings, you notice an interesting pattern. Several account balances, which had grown quite large by the end of November, had disappeared in the final month of the year. You ask the accounts receivable manager, Walter Pavlo, what happened. He said the customers "obtained some financing . . . I guess out of nowhere" and they must have used it to pay off their account balances.

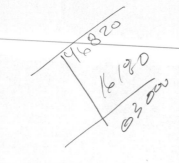

| | Total Accounts Receivable as of . . . | | | | | |
Customer	Q1 (March 31)	Q2 (June 30)	Q3 (September 30)	(October 31)	Q4 (November 30)	(December 31)
AfriTel	19,000	19,000	21,000	16,000	20,000	40,000
CT&T	0	30,000	100,000	100,000	100,000	0
GlobeCom	29,000	28,000	31,000	27,000	28,000	28,000
Hi-Rim	0	0	25,000	35,000	35,000	35,000
Level 8	229,000	229,000	198,000	174,000	190,000	162,000
NewTel	0	0	25,000	25,000	25,000	0
Telemedia	0	0	2,000	2,000	2,000	0
Others	524,000	489,000	375,000	503,000	463,000	485,000
TOTAL	**801,000**	**795,000**	**777,000**	**882,000**	**863,000**	**750,000**

Required:

1. Calculate the balance that should be reported in Allowance for Doubtful Accounts as of December 31.
2. Prepare the adjusting journal entry that is required on December 31.
3. Show how Accounts Receivable would be reported on the balance sheet at December 31.
4. If the balances for CT&T, NewTel, and Telemedia at the end of November continued to exist at the end of December (in the over 120 days category), what balance would you have estimated for the Allowance for Doubtful Accounts on December 31? Would this have changed MCI's net income in the current year? Explain.
5. A few days later, you overhear Mr. Pavlo talking about the account receivable from Hi-Rim. Apparently, MCI will soon loan Hi-Rim some money, creating a note receivable. Hi-Rim will use the money to pay off the Accounts Receivable balance it owes to MCI. You are aware that Mr. Pavlo receives a bonus based on MCI's net income. Should you investigate this matter further? Explain why or why not.

Epilogue: The events described above are based on an article in the June 10, 2002, issue of *Forbes* magazine that describes how, in the mid-1990s, Walter Pavlo was pressured to commit accounting fraud at MCI. Ironically, MCI was later taken over by WorldCom—the company that went on to commit the world's largest accounting fraud at the time.

LO2   S8-5 Ethical Decision Making: A Mini-Case

Having just graduated with a business degree, you're excited to begin working as a junior accountant at Clear Optics, Inc. The company supplies lenses, frames, and sunglasses to opticians and retailers throughout the country. Clear Optics is currently in the process of finalizing its third quarter (Q3) operating results. All Q3 adjusting entries have been made, except for bad debt expense. The preliminary income statement for Q3 is shown below, along with reported results for Q2 and Q1.

CLEAR OPTICS, INC.
Quarterly Income Statements
(amounts in thousands of U.S. dollars)

	Q3 (preliminary)	Q2 (as reported)	Q1 (as reported)
Net Sales	$135,800	$135,460	$130,100
Cost of Goods Sold	58,400	58,250	55,990
Gross Profit	77,400	77,210	74,110
Selling, General, and Administrative Expenses	56,560	53,975	53,690
Bad Debt Expense	—	6,050	4,200
Income before Income Tax Expense	20,840	17,185	16,220
Income Tax Expense	5,620	5,155	5,020
Net Income	$ 15,220	$ 12,030	$ 11,200

The corporate controller has asked you to examine the Allowance for Doubtful Accounts and use the aged listing of accounts receivable to determine the adjustment needed to record estimated bad debts for the quarter. The controller states that, "Although our customers are somewhat slower in paying this quarter, we can't afford to increase the Allowance for Doubtful Accounts. If anything, we need to decrease it—an adjusted balance of about $8,000 is what I'd like to see. Play around with our estimated bad debt loss rates until you get it to work."

You were somewhat confused by what the controller had told you, but you chalked it up to your lack of experience and decided to analyze the Allowance for Doubtful Accounts. You summarized the transactions recorded in the Allowance for Doubtful Accounts using the T-account below:

Allowance for Doubtful Accounts (xA)			
		7,900	January 1 bal. fwd.
Q1 Write-offs	4,110	4,200	Q1 Bad debts estimate
		7,990	March 31 adjusted
Q2 Write-offs	4,120	6,050	Q2 Bad debts estimate
		9,920	June 30 adjusted
Q3 Write-offs	4,030	—	
		5,890	September 30 unadjusted

Required:

1. What bad debts estimate for Q3 will produce the $8,000 balance that the controller would like to see?
2. Prepare the adjusting journal entry that would be required to record this estimate.
3. If the entry in requirement 2 is made, what does it do to the Q3 income and the trend in earnings? (Assume that Income Tax Expense does not change.)
4. Reconsider the statement the controller made to you. Is his suggestion a logical way to use the aging method to estimate bad debts?
5. What would be the Q3 net income if the Bad Debt Expense estimate was 3.8 percent of sales, as in Q2 and Q1? What would this do to the trend in net income across the three quarters? (Assume that Income Tax Expense does not change.)
6. Is there any evidence of unethical behavior in this case? Explain your answer.

S8-6 Critical Thinking: Analyzing

LO1, 4

Problem Solved Company has been operating for five years as a software consulting firm. During this period, it has experienced rapid growth in Sales Revenue and in Accounts Receivable.

To solve its growing receivables problem, the company hired you as its first corporate controller. You have put into place more stringent credit-granting and collection procedures that you expect will reduce receivables by approximately one-third by year-end. You have gathered the following data related to the changes (in thousands):

	(in thousands)	
	Beginning of Year	End of Year (projected)
Accounts Receivable	$1,000,608	$660,495
Less: Allowance for Doubtful Accounts	36,800	10,225
Accounts Receivable, Net	$ 963,808	$650,270
	Prior Year	Current Year (projected)
Net Sales (assume all on credit)	$7,515,444	$7,015,069

Required:

1. Compute, to one decimal place, the accounts receivable turnover ratio based on three different assumptions:
   a. The stringent credit policies reduce Accounts Receivable, Net and decrease Net Sales as projected in the table.
   b. The stringent credit policies reduce Accounts Receivable, Net as projected in the table but do not decrease Net Sales from the prior year.
   c. The stringent credit policies are not implemented, resulting in no change from the beginning of the year Accounts Receivable balance and no change in Net Sales from the prior year.

2. On the basis of your findings in requirement 1, write a brief memo to the chief financial officer explaining the potential benefits and drawbacks of more stringent credit policies and how they are likely to affect the accounts receivable turnover ratio.

LO2   **S8-7 Using an Aging Schedule to Estimate Bad Debts and Improve Collections from Customers**

www.mhhe.com/phillips3e

Assume you were recently hired by Caffe D'Amore, the company that formulated the world's first flavored instant cappuccino and now manufactures several lines of coffee flavored cappuccino mixes. Given the company's tremendous sales growth, Caffe D'Amore's receivables also have grown. Your job is to evaluate and improve collections of the company's receivables.

By analyzing collections of accounts receivable over the past five years, you were able to estimate bad debt loss rates for balances of varying ages. To estimate this year's uncollectible accounts, you jotted down the historical loss rates on the last page of a recent aged listing of outstanding customer balances (see below).

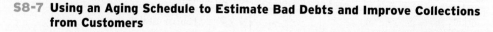

		Number of Days Unpaid				
Customer	Total	1–30	31–60	61–90	91–120	Over 120
Subtotal from previous page	$280,000	$150,000	$60,000	$40,000	$20,000	$10,000
Jumpy Jim's Coffee	1,000					1,000
Pasadena Coffee Company	24,500	14,500	8,000	2,000		
Phillips Blender House	17,000	12,000	4,000		1,000	
Pugsly's Trading Post	26,600	19,600	7,000			
Q-Coffee	12,400	8,400	3,000	1,000		
Special Sips	10,000	6,000	4,000			
Uneasy Isaac's	3,500	500				3,000
Total accounts receivable	375,000	211,000	86,000	43,000	21,000	14,000
Bad debt loss rates		1%	5%	10%	15%	30%

Required:

1. Enter the above totals in a spreadsheet and then insert formulas to calculate the total estimated uncollectible balance.

2. Prepare the year-end adjusting journal entry to adjust the Allowance for Doubtful Accounts to the balance you calculated above. Assume the allowance account has an unadjusted credit balance of $8,000.

3. Of the customer account balances shown above on the last page of the aged listing, which should be your highest priority for contacting and pursuing collection?

4. Assume Jumpy Jim's Coffee account is determined to be uncollectible. Prepare the journal entry to write off the entire account balance.

CONTINUING CASE

Mc Graw Hill **connect**

|ACCOUNTING

LO2, 4

CC8 Accounting for Receivables and Uncollectible Accounts

The following transactions occurred over the months of September to December 2011 at Nicole's Getaway Spa (NGS).

September	Sold spa merchandise to Ashley Welch Beauty for $1,800 on account; the cost of these goods to NGS was $900.
October	Sold merchandise to Kelly Fast Nail Gallery for $450 on account; the cost of these goods to NGS was $200.
November	Sold merchandise to Raea Gooding Wellness for $300 on account; the cost of these goods to NGS was $190.
December	Received $1,200 from Ashley Welch Beauty for payment on its account.

Required:

1. Prepare journal entries for each of the transactions. Assume a perpetual inventory system.

2. Estimate the Allowance for Doubtful Accounts required at December 31, 2011, assuming NGS uses the aging of accounts receivable method with the following uncollectible rates: one month, 2%; two months, 6%; three months, 20%; more than three months, 35%.

3. The Allowance for Doubtful Accounts balance was $50 (credit) before the end-of-period adjusting entry is made. Prepare the journal entry to account for the Bad Debt Expense.

4. Assume the end of the previous year showed net accounts receivable of $800, and net sales for the current year is $9,000. Calculate the accounts receivable turnover ratio (round to one decimal place).

5. Audrey's Mineral Spa has an accounts receivable turnover ratio of 9.0 times. How does NGS compare to this competitor?

CHAPTER 9

Reporting and Interpreting Long-Lived Tangible and Intangible Assets

YOUR LEARNING OBJECTIVES

Understand the business

LO1   Define, classify, and explain the nature of long-lived assets.

Study the accounting methods

LO2   Apply the cost principle to the acquisition of long-lived assets.

LO3   Apply various depreciation methods as economic benefits are used up over time.

LO4   Explain the effect of asset impairment on the financial statements.

LO5   Analyze the disposal of long-lived tangible assets.

LO6   Analyze the acquisition, use, and disposal of long-lived intangible assets.

Evaluate the results

LO7   Interpret the fixed asset turnover ratio.

LO8   Describe factors to consider when comparing companies' long-lived assets.

Review the chapter

THAT WAS
THEN

In the past few chapters, you learned about the sale of goods and services to customers.

Lecture Presentation-LP9
www.mhhe.com/phillips3e

FOCUS COMPANY: Cedar Fair

www.cedarfair.com

Cedar Fair. L.P.

Most people agonize over how much money to spend on a house or which car to buy. After all, they will own these expensive items for many years to come. The same concerns exist when companies acquire long-lived assets. One of the major challenges business managers face is determining the right amount to invest in long-lived assets.

The task is especially challenging for companies such as Disney, Six Flags, and Cedar Fair, which operate amusement parks. Unlike merchandising companies, an amusement park cannot build up an inventory of unused roller-coaster seats to be sold sometime in the future. If managers build more rides than needed to satisfy park-goers, some rides will run with empty seats. Although the company will still incur all the costs of running the rides, it will generate only a fraction of the potential revenue. On the other hand, amusement parks can also run into trouble if they have too few rides to satisfy patrons. Fortunately for managers, accounting reports provide information to evaluate a company's investment in long-lived assets.

In this chapter, by studying specific long-lived asset decisions at Cedar Fair, you will see the significant effect that long-lived assets can have on a company's financial statements. Although manufacturing companies, retailers, and even airlines must deal with the same issues as Cedar Fair, the impact on this amusement park company is particularly significant because it relies almost exclusively on long-lived assets. As of December 31, 2008, in fact, Cedar Fair's rides, hotels, and other long-lived assets accounted for more than 97 percent of its total assets.

THIS IS
NOW

This chapter focuses on the assets that enable companies to produce and sell goods and services.

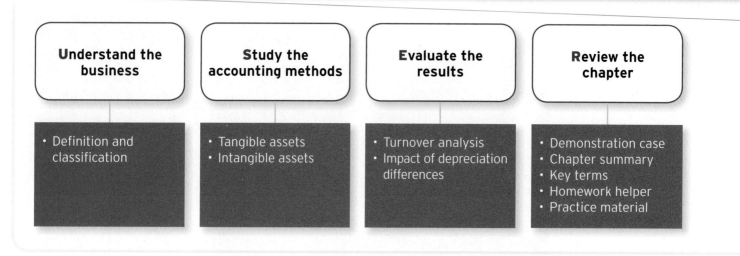

Understand the business	Study the accounting methods	Evaluate the results	Review the chapter
• Definition and classification	• Tangible assets • Intangible assets	• Turnover analysis • Impact of depreciation differences	• Demonstration case • Chapter summary • Key terms • Homework helper • Practice material

Understand the Business

Learning Objective 1
Define, classify, and explain the nature of long-lived assets.

DEFINITION AND CLASSIFICATION

Long-lived assets are business assets acquired for use over one or more years. These assets are not intended for resale. Instead, they are considered "productive" assets in the sense that they enable the business to produce the goods or services that the business then sells to customers. Examples include the ovens in which Pizza Aroma bakes pizza, the stores where Wal-Mart sells merchandise, and the legal rights that restrict use of the Skechers logo. So when you hear the term "long-lived assets," think more broadly than just rusty old equipment. This class of assets includes two major types: tangible and intangible.

YOU SHOULD KNOW

Long-lived assets: Resources owned by a business that enable it to produce the goods or services that are sold to customers.

1. **Tangible assets.** These are long-lived assets that have physical substance, which simply means that you can see, touch, or kick them. The most prominent examples of tangible assets are land, buildings, machinery, vehicles, office equipment, and furniture and fixtures. These assets are typically grouped into a single line item on the balance sheet called Property, Plant, and Equipment. Because many long-lived tangible assets are fixed in place, they are also known as **fixed assets.** Cedar Fair's tangible assets include roller coasters, hotels, and land in the western, midwestern, and northeastern United States.

2. **Intangible assets.** These long-lived assets have special rights but no physical substance. The existence of most intangible assets is indicated only by legal documents that describe their rights. Compared to the tangible assets that you see in daily life, such as store buildings and cash registers, intangible assets are probably less familiar to you. For this reason, we'll describe the various types of intangibles in detail later in this chapter. For now you can think of this category as including brand names, trademarks, and licensing rights such as the ones that allow Cedar Fair to use PEANUTS® characters throughout its amusement parks.

A third category of long-lived assets that are depleted over time, like an oil well or gold mine, is common in natural resource industries. Chapter Supplement 9A describes how these natural resource assets are accounted for.

| EXHIBIT 9.1 | Cedar Fair's Assets |  |

	AT DECEMBER 31	
(in millions)	2008	2007
Assets		
Current Assets	$ 70	$ 60
(details omitted to save space)		
Property and Equipment		
Land	320	350
Land Improvements	310	320
Buildings	570	580
Rides and Equipment	1,300	1,270
Construction in Progress	20	30
Property and Equipment, at cost	2,520	2,550
Less: Accumulated Depreciation	(720)	(610)
Property and Equipment, net	1,800	1,940
Goodwill and Other Intangible Assets	300	390
Other Assets	20	30
Total Assets	$2,190	$2,420

> **COACH'S TIP**
>
> Accumulated Depreciation is reported here as a total for the entire tangible assets category. Alternatively, it can be reported separately for each type of tangible asset.

Exhibit 9.1 shows how Cedar Fair reported long-lived assets on its 2008 balance sheet. From this exhibit, you can see how important tangible and intangible assets are to Cedar Fair. Of the nearly $2.2 billion in total assets at December 31, 2008, Cedar Fair owned long-lived assets totalling $2.1 billion ($1,800 + $300 = $2,100, in millions).

Study the Accounting Methods

In this section, you will study the accounting decisions that relate to long-lived assets. We'll start with tangible long-lived assets and consider key accounting decisions related to their (1) acquisition, (2) use, and (3) disposal. Accounting for intangible assets will be the focus of the last part of this section.

TANGIBLE ASSETS

Most companies own a variety of tangible assets. Earlier chapters introduced you to the most common examples: land, buildings, equipment, and automobiles. Other, less common examples include land improvements and construction in progress—both of which Cedar Fair reported on its balance sheet in Exhibit 9.1. **Land improvements** differ from land in that they deteriorate over time, whereas land is assumed to last forever. Land improvements include the sidewalks, pavement, landscaping, fencing, lighting, and sprinkler systems that are added to improve the usefulness of land. **Construction in progress** includes the costs of constructing new buildings and equipment. When construction is finished, these costs are moved from this account into the building or equipment account to which they relate.

> **Learning Objective 2**
> Apply the cost principle to the acquisition of long-lived assets.

Video 9.1
www.mhhe.com/phillips3e

Acquisition of Tangible Assets

YOU SHOULD KNOW

Capitalize: To record a cost as an asset, rather than an expense.

The general rule for tangible assets under the cost principle is that **all reasonable and necessary costs to acquire and prepare an asset for use should be recorded as a cost of the asset.** Accountants say costs have been **capitalized** when they are recorded as assets (rather than as expenses).

Deciding whether a cost is a reasonable and necessary cost to acquire or prepare tangible assets for use can involve a great deal of judgment. Because capitalizing costs has a significant impact on both the balance sheet (it increases assets) and the income statement (it decreases expenses), some dishonest accountants and managers have exploited the judgment involved in this decision by capitalizing costs that should have been expensed. A well-known example of this tactic is described in the following Spotlight on Ethics feature. As you read the feature and the next couple of pages, focus on distinguishing between what types of costs should be capitalized and what types should be expensed.

Spotlight On ETHICS

www.mhhe.com/phillips3e

Simple Violations, Serious Consequences

In the early 2000s, executives at WorldCom (now owned by Verizon) committed an $11 billion fraud by capitalizing costs that should have been expensed. Their decision caused WorldCom to report huge increases in assets (rather than expenses) when the costs were incurred. The result was a balance sheet that appeared stronger (more total assets) and an income statement that appeared more profitable (lower expenses) than would have been the case had the costs been expensed. Learn more about this fraud in Case S9-4 at the end of this chapter.

The illustration that follows shows the types of costs that should be capitalized when a tangible asset is acquired. All are necessary for acquiring and preparing tangible assets for use. Notice that they are not limited to the amounts paid to purchase or construct the assets. For example, the Land account at Cedar Fair would include legal fees for title searches, fees for land surveys, and commissions paid to brokers when purchasing the land on Ohio's Sandusky Bay shown in the photograph on the left. Take a moment right now to read the lists of costs that should be capitalized when buildings (middle) and equipment (right) are acquired.

Land

Purchase cost
Legal fees
Survey fees
Title search fees

Equipment

Purchase/construction cost
Sales taxes
Transportation costs
Installation costs

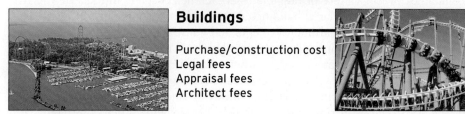

Buildings

Purchase/construction cost
Legal fees
Appraisal fees
Architect fees

If a company buys land, a building, or a piece of used equipment and incurs demolition, renovation, or repair costs before it can be used, these additional costs would be capitalized as a cost of the land, building, or equipment. These costs are capitalized because they are needed to prepare the asset for use.

In some cases, land, buildings, and equipment are purchased together. On June 30, 2006, Cedar Fair bought five amusement parks from Paramount Parks for $1.2 billion. When this type of "basket purchase" occurs, the total cost is split among the assets in proportion to the market value of the assets as a whole. For example, if Cedar Fair were to pay $10 million for a hotel and the land surrounding it, based on an appraisal that estimates that the land contributes 40 percent of the property's value and the building contributes 60 percent, Cedar Fair would record 40 percent of the total cost as land ($4 million) and the other 60 percent as buildings ($6 million). Splitting the total purchase price among individual assets is necessary because the cost of different asset types may be depreciated over different periods. **Land is not depreciated,** so any costs assigned to Land will remain in that account until Cedar Fair sells the land.

Spotlight On THE WORLD

Component Allocation

IFRS takes the idea of a basket purchase one step further. The cost of an individual asset's components is allocated among each significant component and then depreciated separately over that component's useful life. For example, British Airways separates the cost of an aircraft into its body, engines, and interior cabin space, and then depreciates the body, engines, and cabin interior over 25, 18, and 5 years, respectively.

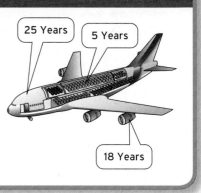

To illustrate how the costs of tangible assets are recorded, let's consider the Top Thrill Dragster that Cedar Fair purchased from Intamin, a Swiss roller-coaster manufacturer. When it was purchased, the Top Thrill Dragster was the biggest, fastest roller coaster in the world. Some of its specs are shown in the following graphic.

Top Thrill Dragster

Ride Height:	42 stories
Vertical Drop:	400 ft.
Track Length:	2,800 ft.
Ride Time:	17 seconds
Angle of Descent:	90 degrees
Angle of Twist:	270 degrees
Launch Speed:	120 mph in 4 seconds
Ride Capacity:	1,500 riders per hour

Assume the list price for the roller coaster (including sales tax) was $26 million but that Cedar Fair received a $1 million discount. In other words, the roller coaster's net purchase price to Cedar Fair was $25 million. Assume too that Cedar Fair paid $125,000 to have the roller coaster delivered and another $625,000 to have it assembled and prepared for use. Cedar Fair would calculate the costs to be capitalized for this asset as follows:

List price	$26,000,000
Less: Discount	1,000,000
Net invoice price	25,000,000
Add: Transportation costs paid by Cedar Fair	125,000
Installation costs paid by Cedar Fair	625,000
Total cost of the roller coaster	$25,750,000

The total $25,750,000 cost would be the amount Cedar Fair recorded in the Rides and Equipment account regardless of how the company paid for or financed the roller coaster. As you will see next, the method of payment or financing affects only whether the purchase reduces cash, increases liabilities, or both.

Cash Purchase   If Cedar Fair paid cash for the roller coaster and related transportation and installation costs, the effects of the transaction and the journal entry to record these effects would be:

1 Analyze

Assets		=	Liabilities	+	Stockholders' Equity
Cash	−25,750,000				
Rides and Equipment	+25,750,000				

2 Record

dr Rides and Equipment (+A)	25,750,000	
cr Cash (−A)		25,750,000

You might find it hard to believe that Cedar Fair would pay cash for assets that cost more than $25 million, but this isn't unusual. Companies often pay with cash generated from operations or with cash that has been borrowed. In addition, it's possible the seller may extend credit to the buyer, a situation we examine next.

Credit Purchase   If we assume Cedar Fair signed a note payable for the new roller coaster and paid cash for the transportation and installation costs, the accounting equation effects and journal entry would be:

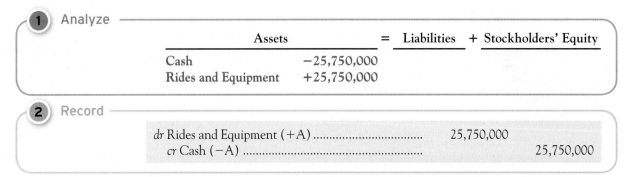

1 Analyze

Assets		=	Liabilities		+	Stockholders' Equity
Cash	−750,000		Note Payable	+25,000,000		
Rides and Equipment	+25,750,000					

2 Record

dr Rides and Equipment (+A)	25,750,000	
cr Cash (−A)		750,000
cr Note Payable (+L)		25,000,000

💡 How's it going?   Self-Study Practice

In a recent year, the New Bakery Company of Ohio opened a new baking plant that can make 200,000 buns per hour. The equipment cost $21 million. Assume New Bakery financed the equipment purchase using a promissory note and paid in cash $900,000 of sales tax, $60,000 of transportation costs, and $40,000 of installation costs before the equipment could be used. Indicate the effects of the purchase on the accounting equation and give the journal entry to record the purchase.

1 Analyze

Assets	=	Liabilities	+	Stockholders' Equity
2.2 mill		+ 21 mill		
– 1 mill				

2 Record 21

debit Rect Eqpt 22 mill
    Credit Cass 1 mill
    credit liabts 21 mll.

After you have finished, check your answers with the solution in the margin.

Solution to Self-Study Practice

1.	Assets	=	Liabilities	+	Stockholders' Equity
Equipment	+22,000,000				
Cash	–1,000,000	Note Payable	+21,000,000		
2.				22,000,000	
dr Equipment (+A)		22,000,000			
cr Cash (–A)			1,000,000		
cr Note Payable (+L)			21,000,000		

Before we leave this section, we should mention that not all fixed asset costs are capitalized. The cost of some fixed assets, like staplers or hole punches, is such a small dollar amount that it's not worth the trouble of recording them as fixed assets. Outback Steakhouse, for example, reports in its financial statement notes that it expenses all expenditures less than $1,000. Such policies are acceptable because immaterial (relatively small) amounts will not affect users' analysis of financial statements. **Other costs that are expensed when incurred include insurance for fixed assets, interest on loans to purchase fixed assets, and ordinary repairs and maintenance,** as discussed in the next section.

Use of Tangible Assets

Maintenance Costs Incurred during Use Most tangible assets require substantial expenditures over the course of their lives to maintain or enhance their operation. Maintenance is a big deal in the roller-coaster industry where safety is vital. Despite the tremendous stress created by frequent use and wicked-fast speeds, surprisingly few accidents occur. According to some estimates, the odds of a serious amusement park injury are 1 in 23 million. Companies achieve this level of safety by spending a lot of money on two types of maintenance: (1) ordinary repairs and maintenance and (2) extraordinary repairs and maintenance.

1. **Ordinary repairs and maintenance.** *Expense* **Ordinary repairs and maintenance** are expenditures for the routine maintenance and upkeep of long-lived assets. Just like an oil change for your car, these are recurring, relatively small expenditures that do not directly increase an asset's usefulness. Because these costs occur frequently to maintain the asset's productive capacity for a short time, they are recorded as expenses in the current period. Because these expenses are matched to revenues, ordinary repairs and maintenance are sometimes called **revenue expenditures.**

    In the case of Cedar Fair, ordinary repairs and maintenance would include greasing the tracks on the Steel Venom roller coaster at Valleyfair in Minnesota.

YOU SHOULD KNOW

Ordinary repairs and maintenance: Expenditures for routine operating upkeep of long-lived assets that are recorded as expenses.

It would also include replacing the lights on the eight-story Ferris wheel at Michigan's Adventure and tightening the seams on a water slide at Knott's Soak City in California.

2. **Extraordinary repairs, replacements, and additions.** In contrast to ordinary repairs and maintenance, **extraordinary repairs** occur infrequently, involve large expenditures, and increase an asset's economic usefulness through enhanced efficiency, capacity, or lifespan. Examples include additions, major overhauls, complete reconditioning, and major replacements and improvements, such as the complete replacement of the passenger train on a roller coaster. Because these costs increase the usefulness of tangible assets beyond their original condition, they are added to the appropriate long-lived asset accounts. And because doing so means capitalizing costs, these extraordinary repairs, replacements, and additions are called **capital expenditures.**

YOU SHOULD KNOW

Extraordinary repairs:
Expenditures that increase a tangible asset's economic usefulness in the future and are recorded as increases in asset accounts, not as expenses.

How's it going?   Self-Study Practice

As you know from living in a house, apartment, or dorm, buildings often require maintenance and repair. For each of the following expenditures, indicate whether it should be expensed in the current period or capitalized.

Expense or Capitalize?

1. Replacing electrical wiring throughout the building.
2. Repairing the hinge on the front door of the building.
3. Yearly cleaning of the building's air conditioning filters.
4. Making major structural improvements to a clubhouse.

After you have finished, check your answers with the solution in the margin.

Solution to Self-Study Practice
1. Capitalize—extends life.
2. Expense—does not increase usefulness.
3. Expense—does not increase usefulness.
4. Capitalize—extends life.

Depreciation Expense

In addition to repairs and maintenance expense, a company reports depreciation every period that a long-lived asset is used. Depreciation doesn't involve new payments for using the asset. Rather, **depreciation** is the allocation of existing costs that were already recorded as a long-lived asset. Think of the cost of a long-lived asset as a big prepayment for future benefits. As that asset is used, those prepaid benefits are used up, so the asset needs to be decreased each period. This decrease in the asset creates an expense, which is reported on the income statement to match the revenues generated by the asset.

As you learned in Chapter 4, depreciation affects one income statement account and one balance sheet account. The income statement account, Depreciation Expense, reports the depreciation of the current period. The balance sheet account, Accumulated Depreciation, contains the current period's depreciation as well as that of prior periods. It is an **accumulation** over several periods. The effects of $130 of depreciation on the accounting equation and the journal entry to record them follow:

YOU SHOULD KNOW

Depreciation: The allocation of the cost of long-lived tangible assets over their productive lives using a systematic and rational method.

① Analyze

Assets		= Liabilities +	Stockholders' Equity	
Accumulated Depreciation (+xA)	−130		Depreciation Expense (+E)	−130

② Record

dr Depreciation Expense (+E, −SE)	130	
cr Accumulated Depreciation (+xA, −A)		130

Exhibit 9.2 shows how Cedar Fair reported its depreciation in 2008. The income statement on the right shows the $130 million of Depreciation Expense in 2008. The balance sheet on the left shows that this $130 million, when combined with depreciation of prior years, brought the total Accumulated Depreciation to $720 million at December 31, 2008. The $1,800 difference between the Property and Equipment's $2,520 cost and $720 of Accumulated Depreciation is called the **book (or carrying) value**. Most companies report a breakdown of these totals by class of asset (e.g., buildings, equipment) in their financial statement notes.

> **YOU SHOULD KNOW**
>
> **Book (or carrying) value:** The acquisition cost of an asset less accumulated depreciation.

Cost − Acc. Dep = book value
Net book value
Carrying value

H
Market Value

EXHIBIT 9.2	Reporting Depreciation on the Balance Sheet and Income Statement

(in millions) **Balance Sheet**	**Dec. 31, 2008**
Assets	
Property and Equipment, at cost	$2,520
Less: Accumulated Depreciation	(720)
Property and Equipment, net	1,800

(in millions) **Income Statement**	**2008**
Net Revenues	$1,000
Operating Expenses:	
Food and Operating Expenses	500
Depreciation Expense	130
Selling, General, and Other	130
Loss on Disposal of Fixed Assets	10
Impairment Losses	90
Total Operating Expenses	860
Income from Operations	140

One way to interpret the information in Exhibit 9.2 is that the Property and Equipment's $2,520 million cost represents the assets' total economic benefits. Thus, $130 million of Depreciation Expense means Cedar Fair used up about 5 percent ($130 / $2,520 = 0.052) of the assets' benefits in 2008. As of December 31, 2008, nearly 29 percent ($720 / $2,520 = 0.286) of their total benefits had been used up.

To fully understand the depreciation numbers in Exhibit 9.2, you need to know how they are calculated. Depreciation calculations are based on the following three items:

1. **Asset cost.** This includes all the asset's capitalized costs, including the purchase cost, sales tax, legal fees, and other costs needed to acquire and prepare the asset for use.

2. **Residual value.** **Residual (or salvage) value** is an estimate of the amount the company will receive when it disposes of the asset. Cedar Fair will recover some of the initial cost of its roller coasters when it disposes of them by either selling them "as is" to local amusement companies or by dismantling them and selling their parts to other roller coaster or scrap metal companies.

Calculate Dep. cost

3. **Useful life.** **Useful life** is an estimate of the asset's useful economic life to the company (not its economic life to all potential users). It may be expressed in terms of years or units of capacity, such as the number of units it can produce or the number of miles it will travel. **Land is the only tangible asset that's assumed to have an unlimited (indefinite) useful life. Because of this, land is not depreciated.**

> **YOU SHOULD KNOW**
>
> **Residual (or salvage) value:** The estimated amount to be recovered at the end of the company's estimated useful life of an asset. **Useful life:** The expected service life of an asset to the present owner.

The basic idea of depreciation is to match the economic benefit that will be used up (asset cost minus residual value) to the periods the asset will be used to generate revenue (useful life). Residual value is considered when calculating depreciation because we want to leave a little of the asset's cost in the accounts after we have finished depreciating it. We do this because, when we dispose of the asset, we're likely to get back some of the money we initially paid for the asset. So the amount to be depreciated over the asset's life is the difference between its cost and residual value, an amount called the **depreciable cost.** A company should record depreciation each year of an asset's useful

> **YOU SHOULD KNOW**
>
> **Depreciable cost:** The portion of the asset's cost that will be used in generating revenue; calculated as asset cost minus residual value.

life until its total accumulated depreciation equals its depreciable cost. After that, the company should report no additional depreciation, even if the company continues to use the asset.

If every company used the same techniques for calculating depreciation, we'd stop right here. But they don't. Companies own different assets and use them differently, so they are allowed to choose from several alternative depreciation methods. These alternative depreciation methods produce different patterns of depreciation as represented by the depreciation amounts recorded each year. The depreciation method chosen for each type of property, plant, and equipment should reflect the pattern in which those assets' economic benefits are used up.

Learning Objective 3
Apply various depreciation methods as economic benefits are used up over time.

Depreciation Methods   We discuss the three most common depreciation methods:

1. **Straight-line**
2. **Units-of-production**
3. **Declining-balance**

To show how each method works, let's assume that Cedar Fair acquired a new go-cart ride on January 1, 2010. The relevant information is shown in Exhibit 9.3.

EXHIBIT 9.3	Information for Depreciation Computations

CEDAR FAIR—Acquisition of a New Go-Cart Ride	
Cost, purchased on January 1, 2010	$62,500
Estimated residual value	$2,500
Estimated useful life	3 years; 100,000 miles

Straight-Line Method   Managers choose the **straight-line depreciation method** if they want to report an equal amount of depreciation in each period of the asset's estimated useful life. The straight-line formula for estimating annual depreciation expense is:

YOU SHOULD KNOW

Straight-line depreciation method: Allocates the cost of an asset in equal periodic amounts over its useful life.

Straight-Line Formula
$$(\text{Cost} - \text{Residual Value}) \times \frac{1}{\text{Useful Life}} = \text{Depreciation Expense}$$

In the straight-line formula, Cost − Residual Value is the total amount to be depreciated (the depreciable cost). The depreciation rate is 1/Useful Life. Using the information in Exhibit 9.3, the depreciation expense for Cedar Fair's new ride is $20,000 per year, calculated in the following depreciation schedule:

Straight-line (Cost − Residual Value) × (1/Useful Life)		INCOME STATEMENT	BALANCE SHEET		
Year	Yearly Computation	Depreciation Expense	Cost	Accumulated Depreciation	Book Value
At acquisition			$62,500	$ 0	$62,500
2010	($62,500 − $2,500) × (1/3)	$20,000	62,500	20,000	42,500
2011	($62,500 − $2,500) × (1/3)	20,000	62,500	40,000	22,500
2012	($62,500 − $2,500) × (1/3)	20,000	62,500	60,000	2,500
	Total	$60,000			

Take a moment to study the straight-line depreciation schedule. Notice that as the name straight line suggests,

1. Depreciation Expense is a constant amount each year.
2. Accumulated Depreciation increases by an equal amount each year.
3. Book Value decreases by the same equal amount each year.

Notice too that at the end of the asset's life, accumulated depreciation ($60,000) equals the asset's depreciable cost ($62,500 − $2,500), and book value ($2,500) equals residual value.

As you will see with other depreciation methods, the amount of depreciation depends on estimates of an asset's useful life and residual value at the end of that life. A question people often ask is: **How do accountants estimate useful lives and residual values?** While some of this information can be obtained from the asset's supplier or from other sources such as reseller databases or insurance companies, the simple answer is that professional judgment is required. Because useful lives and residual values are difficult to estimate with precision, accountants are encouraged to update their calculations regularly (see Supplement 9B at the end of this chapter).

Straight-line (graph: Yearly Depreciation vs. Year)

Units-of-Production (graph: Yearly Depreciation vs. Year)

Units-of-Production Method

Choose the **units-of-production depreciation method** if the amount of asset production varies significantly from period to period. An asset's production can be defined in terms of miles, products, or machine-hours. The units-of-production formula for estimating depreciation expense is:

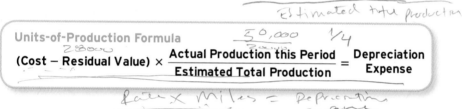

Units-of-Production Formula

$$(\text{Cost} - \text{Residual Value}) \times \frac{\text{Actual Production this Period}}{\text{Estimated Total Production}} = \frac{\text{Depreciation}}{\text{Expense}}$$

If the go-cart in Exhibit 9.3 was driven 30,000 miles in 2010, 50,000 miles in 2011, and 20,000 miles in 2012, the units-of-production method would calculate depreciation in each year of the asset's life as follows:

YOU SHOULD KNOW

Units-of-production depreciation method: Allocates the cost of an asset over its useful life based on the relationship of its periodic output to its total estimated output.

Units-of-production
(Cost − Residual Value) × (Actual/Estimated Total Production)

		INCOME STATEMENT	BALANCE SHEET		
Year	Yearly Computation	Depreciation Expense	Cost	Accumulated Depreciation	Book Value
At acquisition			$62,500	$ 0	$62,500
2010	($62,500 − $2,500) × (30,000/100,000 miles)	$18,000	62,500	18,000	44,500
2011	($62,500 − $2,500) × (50,000/100,000 miles)	30,000	62,500	48,000	14,500
2012	($62,500 − $2,500) × (20,000/100,000 miles)	12,000	62,500	60,000	2,500
	Total	$60,000			

Under the units-of-production method, the depreciation expense, accumulated depreciation, and book value vary from period to period, depending on the number of units produced.

Declining-Balance Method

Choose the **declining-balance depreciation method** if you want a higher amount of depreciation expense in the early years of an asset's life and a lower amount in later years. Because this method speeds up depreciation reporting, it is sometimes called an accelerated depreciation method. Although accelerated methods are used infrequently for financial reporting purposes in the United States, they are used commonly in financial reporting in other countries, such as Japan and Canada, as well as in tax reporting in the United States (a point we discuss in greater detail later).

YOU SHOULD KNOW

Declining-balance depreciation method: Assigns more depreciation to early years of an asset's life and less depreciation to later years.

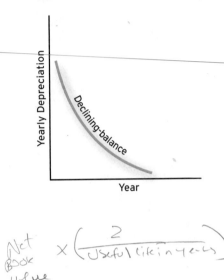

The declining-balance method applies a depreciation rate to the book value of the asset at the beginning of each accounting period. Notice that the following formula uses book value (Cost − Accumulated Depreciation) rather than depreciable cost (Cost − Residual Value). This slight difference in the formula produces declining amounts of depreciation as the asset ages. Because the 2/Useful Life rate used in the formula is double the straight-line rate, this particular version of the declining-balance method is called the **double-declining-balance depreciation method.**

> **Double-Declining-Balance Formula**
>
> $$\text{(Cost − Accumulated Depreciation)} \times \frac{2}{\text{Useful Life}} = \text{Depreciation Expense}$$

This formula uses the accumulated depreciation balance at the beginning of each year. In the first year of an asset's life, the beginning balance in Accumulated Depreciation is zero. However, with each passing year as additional depreciation is recorded, the Accumulated Depreciation balance increases, causing the amount of double-declining depreciation expense to decline over time.

Because **residual value is not included in the formula for the declining-balance method of computing depreciation expense,** you must take extra care to ensure that an asset's book value is not depreciated beyond its residual value. If the calculated amount of depreciation for the year would reduce the book value below the asset's residual value, you must record a lower amount of depreciation so that the book value will equal the residual value. The following depreciation schedule illustrates this point.

(handwritten annotations in margin:)

$\text{Net Book Value} \times \left(\dfrac{2}{\text{Useful Life in years}} \right)$

yr 1: $62{,}500 \times \left(\dfrac{2}{3\,yr} \right) = \$41{,}667$

yr 2: $20{,}833 \times \left(\dfrac{2}{3\,yr} \right) = 13{,}889$

yr 3: $6944 \times \left(\dfrac{2}{3\,yr} \right) = 4629$

Double-declining-balance (Cost − Accumulated Depreciation) × (2/Useful Life)		INCOME STATEMENT	BALANCE SHEET		
Year	Yearly Computation	Depreciation Expense	Cost	Accumulated Depreciation	Book Value
At acquisition			$62,500	$ 0	$62,500
2010	($62,500 − $0) × (2/3)	$41,667	62,500	41,667	20,833
2011	($62,500 − $41,667) × (2/3)	13,889	62,500	55,556	6,944
2012	($62,500 − $55,556) × (2/3)	4,629	62,500	60,185	2,315
		4,444	62,500	60,000	2,500
	Total	$60,000			

Notice that the calculated depreciation expense for 2012 ($4,629) would not be recorded because it would cause the asset's book value to fall below its residual value. Instead, in the final year of the asset's life, just enough depreciation ($4,444) is recorded to make the book value of the asset equal its residual value of $2,500.

Summary of Depreciation Methods   See Exhibit 9.4 for a summary of the depreciation expense that would be reported in each year of our example under the three alternative depreciation methods. Notice that the amount of depreciation expense recorded in each year of an asset's life depends on the method that is used. That means that the amount of net income that is reported can vary, depending on the depreciation method used. At the end of an asset's life, after it has been fully depreciated, the total amount of depreciation will equal the asset's depreciable cost regardless of the depreciation method used.

| EXHIBIT 9.4 | Differences in Depreciation Expense by Method |

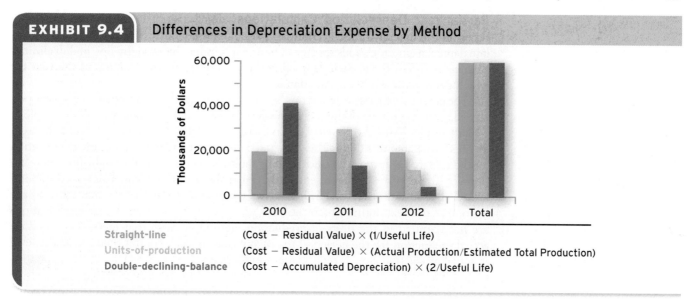

Straight-line	(Cost − Residual Value) × (1/Useful Life)
Units-of-production	(Cost − Residual Value) × (Actual Production/Estimated Total Production)
Double-declining-balance	(Cost − Accumulated Depreciation) × (2/Useful Life)

Different depreciation methods can be used for different classes of assets provided they are used consistently over time so that financial statement users can compare results across periods. The methods that companies use most frequently are shown in the margin. The straight-line method is the preferred choice because it is the easiest to use and understand, and it does a good job of matching depreciation expense to revenues when assets are used evenly over their useful lives. The units-of-production method is the typical choice when asset use fluctuates significantly from period to period. Declining-balance methods apply best to assets that are most productive when they are new but quickly lose their usefulness as they get older.

How's it going?   Self-Study Practice

Assume that Cedar Fair has acquired new equipment at a cost of $24,000. The equipment has an estimated life of six years, an estimated operating life of 5,000 hours, and an estimated residual value of $3,000. Determine depreciation expense for the **second year** under each of the following methods:

1. Straight-line method.

$(24,000 − 3000) × 1/6 = $ _3,500_

2. Double-declining-balance method.

Year 1 : $(24,000 − _0_) × 2/6 = $ _8000_

Year 2 : $(24,000 − _8000_) × 2/6 = $ _5 333_

3. Units-of-production method (assume the equipment ran for 800 hours in Year 2).

$(24000 − 300) × 800 /5,000 = $ _3 360_

After you have finished, check your answers with the solution in the margin.

Solution to Self-Study Practice
1. $(24,000 − 3,000) × 1/6 = $3,500
2. Year 1: $(24,000 − 0) × 2/6 = $8,000
   Year 2: $(24,000 − 8,000) × 2/6 = $5,333
3. $(24,000 − 3,000) × (800/5,000) = $3,360

Partial-Year Depreciation Calculations Purchases of long-lived assets seldom occur on the first day of the accounting period. Consequently, the need arises to calculate depreciation for periods shorter than a year. **Under the straight-line and declining-balance methods, the annual depreciation is multiplied by the fraction of the year for which depreciation is being calculated.**

For purposes of these calculations, accountants typically assume that assets were purchased at the beginning of the month nearest to the actual purchase date. For example, if Cedar Fair purchased the go-cart ride on October 7, 2010, it would have owned the asset for about three months during the year ended December 31, 2010. Thus, the depreciation for the ride in 2010 would be calculated by multiplying the annual straight-line depreciation of $20,000 by 3 ÷ 12, representing the 3 months of 12 that Cedar Fair owned it. Similarly, if an asset is disposed of during the year, the annual depreciation is multiplied by the fraction of the year during which the asset was owned. **These partial-year modifications are not required in the units-of-production method because that method is based on actual production for the period.** If the accounting period is shorter than a year, the level of actual production already reflects that shorter period.

Tax Depreciation Before we leave the topic of depreciation methods, we should note that most companies use one method of depreciation for reporting to stockholders and a different method for determining income taxes. Keeping two sets of accounting records like this is both ethical and legal because the primary objective of financial reporting differs from that of income tax reporting.

Financial Reporting	Income Tax Reporting
Objective: Provide economic information about a business that is useful in projecting its future cash flows.	Objective: Raise sufficient tax revenues to pay for the expenditures of the federal government and to encourage certain social and economic behaviors.

One of the behaviors the government wants to encourage is economic renewal and growth. Thus, the IRS allows companies to deduct larger amounts of tax depreciation in the early years of an asset's life than what GAAP allows.[1] The larger tax deduction reduces the company's income taxes significantly in the years immediately following the purchase of a long-lived asset.

Although the IRS allows super-sized deductions in the early years of an asset's life, it doesn't allow a company to depreciate more than an asset's depreciable cost over its life. So the tax savings enjoyed in the early years of an asset's life will eventually be returned to the government in later years of that asset's life. The tax payment that is put off (deferred) as a result of taking large tax deductions for depreciation is reported as a long-term liability called Deferred Income Tax. Although the deferral delays the payment of taxes only temporarily, it can be worth the effort of keeping two sets of records. The following companies report that they deferred significant tax obligations in recent years by choosing different depreciation methods for tax and financial reporting purposes.

Company	Deferred Income Tax Liabilities	Percentage Due to Applying Different Depreciation Methods
AT&T Corp.	$27,406 million	77%
Southwest Airlines	2,104 million	87
Revlon, Inc.	27 million	99

---

[1]Most corporations use the IRS-approved Modified Accelerated Cost Recovery System (MACRS) to calculate depreciation expense for their tax returns. MACRS is similar to the declining-balance method and is applied over relatively short asset lives set by the IRS to yield high tax deductions for depreciation expense in the early years.

The preceding table shows that, like most individuals, companies follow an economic rule called the **least and latest rule.** All taxpayers want to pay the least tax that is legally permitted, and at the latest possible date. If you had the choice of paying $1,000 to the federal government at the end of this year or at the end of next year, you would choose the end of next year. Doing so would allow you to invest the money for an extra year and earn a return on your investment.

Asset Impairment Losses

As a result of recording depreciation, an asset's book value declines as it ages. However, because **depreciation is not intended to report an asset at its current value,** an asset's book value could exceed its current value, particularly if the asset becomes impaired. **Impairment** occurs when events or changed circumstances cause the estimated future cash flows from a long-lived asset to fall below its book value. If an asset's estimated future cash flows are less than its book value, the book value should be written down to what the asset is worth (called fair value) with the amount of the write-down reported as an impairment loss. Impairment losses are classified as an operating expense on the income statement and reported above the Income from Operations subtotal, as shown in Exhibit 9.2 on page 409.

Cedar Fair recorded a write-down in 2002 after a rare engineering phenomenon called "vortex shedding" reportedly caused a steel support tower in one of its VertiGo slingshot rides to snap during the off-season. Even though only one of the rides was affected, Cedar Fair dismantled and removed its two VertiGo rides because few people are willing to go on a ride that snapped apart, even if it is fixable.[2] To see how this event would be accounted for, assume that the book value of Cedar Fair's VertiGo rides was $8 million. If the fair value of the rides was estimated to be $4.8 million—an amount that represents what other amusement park companies and scrap dealers might be expected to pay for the rides' parts—then the impairment loss would be calculated as $8 million minus $4.8 million. The effects of the resulting $3.2 million impairment and the journal entry to record it would be:

Learning Objective 4
Explain the effect of asset impairment on the financial statements.

YOU SHOULD KNOW

Impairment: Occurs when the cash to be generated by an asset is estimated to be less than the carrying value of that asset.

1 Analyze

Assets	=	Liabilities	+	Stockholders' Equity	
Rides and				Impairment	
Equipment −3,200,000				Loss (+E)	−3,200,000

2 Record

dr Impairment Loss (+E, −SE)...................................	3,200,000	
cr Rides and Equipment (−A)...................................		3,200,000

Disposal of Tangible Assets

In some cases, a business may voluntarily decide not to hold a long-term asset for its entire life. For example, your local gym might decide to replace its treadmills with elliptical trainers. Or, if a company discontinues a product, it may sell the equipment that was used to make the product. To get rid of used assets, companies do just what you do.

Learning Objective 5
Analyze the disposal of long-lived tangible assets.

[2]"Insurer Refuses Damage Payment to Sandusky, Ohio-Based Amusement Park Company," *Knight Ridder/Tribune Business News*, February 11, 2003.

They trade them in on a new asset, sell them on eBay, or "retire" them to a junkyard. Sometimes, assets are damaged or destroyed in storms, fires, or accidents, creating what are politely called involuntary disposals.

The disposal of a depreciable asset usually requires two accounting adjustments:

1. **Update the Depreciation Expense and Accumulated Depreciation accounts.** If a long-lived asset is disposed of during the year, it should be depreciated to the date of disposal using the partial-year calculations explained on page 414.

2. **Record the disposal.** All disposals of long-lived assets require that you account for (1) the book value of the items given up, (2) the value of the items received on disposal, and (3) any difference between the two amounts, which reflects a gain or loss on the disposal. Any gain or loss on the disposal is included on the income statement when calculating Income from Operations, as Cedar Fair did in 2008 (see Exhibit 9.2) on page 409.

Earlier in this chapter, you saw how to compute and record depreciation expense on a long-lived asset (step 1 above), so let's look instead at an example where we only have to record the disposal (step 2). Assume that, at the end of year 16, Cedar Fair sold one of its hotels for $3 million cash. The original $20 million cost of the hotel was depreciated using the straight-line method over 20 years with no residual value ($1 million depreciation expense per year). **The gain or loss on disposal is calculated as the difference between the asset's selling price and its book value (BV).** Based on the numbers for this example, the book value is

Original cost	$20,000,000
Less: Accumulated Depreciation ($1,000,000 × 16 years)	16,000,000
Book value (BV) at date of sale	$ 4,000,000

COACH'S TIP

Be sure to reduce both the asset and accumulated depreciation accounts for their full cost and accumulated depreciation (updated to the time of disposal).

The selling price ($3,000,000) is less than the book value ($4,000,000), so the difference ($1,000,000) is reported as a loss on sale. The effects of the loss and the hotel sale on Cedar Fair are shown below, along with the journal entry to record them.

1 Analyze

	Assets	= Liabilities +	Stockholders' Equity	
Buildings	−20,000,000		Loss on	
Accumulated			Disposal (+E)	−1,000,000
Depreciation (−xA)	+16,000,000			
Cash	+3,000,000			

2 Record

dr Cash (+A)	3,000,000	
dr Accumulated Depreciation (−xA, +A)	16,000,000	
dr Loss on Disposal (+E, −SE)	1,000,000	
cr Buildings (−A)		20,000,000

Loss on Disposal is recorded just like any other expense (with a debit). Had the selling price exceeded the book value, Cedar Fair would have recorded a gain on disposal (with a credit).

How's it going?   Self-Study Practice

Assume that Cedar Fair sold the hotel described above at the end of year 16 for $5,000,000 cash. Also assume that depreciation had been updated to that point in time, resulting in Accumulated Depreciation of $16,000,000 at the time of sale. Complete the accounting equation effects and the journal entry for this disposal below.

① Analyze

Assets		= Liabilities + Stockholders' Equity
Buildings	−20,000,000	+ 1,000,000
Accumulated Depreciation (−xA)	+16,000,000	
Cash	+5,000,000	

② Record

dr Cash (+A) +5,000,000
dr AD (−xA)+A
  Credit Building 20,000,000
  Credit SE 1,000,000

After you have finished, check your answers with the solution in the margin.

Solution to Self-Study Practice

1.	Assets	=	Liabilities	+	Stockholders' Equity
Buildings	−20,000,000				Gain on Disposal (+R, +SE) + 1,000,000
Acc. Depn.	+16,000,000				
Cash	+5,000,000				

2. dr Cash (+A)   5,000,000
   dr Accumulated Depreciation (−xA, +A)   16,000,000
     cr Buildings (−A)   20,000,000
     cr Gain on Disposal (+R, +SE)   1,000,000

INTANGIBLE ASSETS

Intangible assets are long-lived assets that lack physical substance. Their existence is indicated by legal documents of the types described below.

Learning Objective 6
Analyze the acquisition, use, and disposal of long-lived intangible assets.

- **Trademarks.** A **trademark** is a special name, image, or slogan identified with a product or company, like the name Kleenex or the image of McDonald's golden arches. The symbol ® signifies a trademark registered with the U.S. Patent and Trademark Office and ™ indicates unregistered trademarks. Both types of trademark are considered intangible assets.

- **Copyrights.** A **copyright** gives the owner the exclusive right to publish, use, and sell a literary, musical, artistic, or dramatic work for a period not exceeding 70 years after the author's death. The book you are reading is copyrighted. It is illegal, therefore, for an instructor to copy several chapters from this book and hand them out in class without first obtaining permission from the copyright owner.

- **Patents.** A **patent** is an exclusive right granted by the federal government for a period of 20 years, typically to whoever invents a new product or discovers a new process. The patent declares the owner to be the only one who can use, manufacture, or sell the patented item. This protection is intended to encourage people to be inventive because it prevents others from simply copying innovations until after the inventor has had time to profit from the new product or process. One of the first roller-coaster patents was granted in 1884 for what was then called a "gravity pleasure road."

- **Licensing rights.** **Licensing rights** are limited permissions to use something according to specific terms and conditions. Your university or college likely has obtained the licensing right to make computer programs available for use on your campus network. A licensing right also allows Cedar Fair to showcase Snoopy at its parks.

YOU SHOULD KNOW

Trademark: A special name, image, or slogan identified with a product or company. **Copyright:** A form of protection provided to the original authors of literary, musical, artistic, dramatic, and other works of authorship. **Patent:** A right to exclude others from making, using, selling, or importing an invention. **Licensing rights:** The limited permission to use property according to specific terms and conditions set out in a contract.

YOU SHOULD KNOW

Franchise: A contractual right to sell certain products or services, use certain trademarks, or perform activities in a certain geographical region. **Goodwill:** The premium a company pays to obtain the favorable reputation associated with another company.

- **Franchises.** A **franchise** is a contractual right to sell certain products or services, use certain trademarks, or perform activities in a geographical region. For example, a business can buy franchise rights that allow it to use the Krispy Kreme name, store format, recipes, and ingredients by paying an up-front fee ranging from $15,000 to $50,000 per store plus ongoing fees of 4.5 to 6.0 percent of store sales.[3]

- **Goodwill.** Goodwill tops the charts as the most frequently reported intangible asset. It encompasses lots of good stuff like a favorable location, an established customer base, a great reputation, and successful business operations. Although many companies have probably built up their own goodwill, GAAP do not allow it to be reported as an intangible asset on the balance sheet unless it has been purchased from another company. To understand the reasons behind this, keep reading. We explain them in the next section.

Acquisition, Use, and Disposal

Acquisition   The costs of intangible assets are recorded as assets only if they have been purchased. If an intangible asset is being self-constructed or internally developed, its costs generally are reported as **research and development** expenses. The primary reason that the cost of self-developed intangibles is reported as an expense rather than an asset is that it's easy for people to claim that they've developed a valuable (but invisible) intangible asset. But to believe what they are saying, you really need to see some evidence that it's actually worth what they say it's worth. And that only happens when someone gives up their hard-earned cash to buy it. At that time, the purchaser records the intangible asset at its acquisition cost. This general rule applies to trademarks, copyrights, patents, licensing rights, franchises, and goodwill.

YOU SHOULD KNOW

Research and development: Expenditures that may someday lead to patents, copyrights, or other intangible assets; the uncertainty about their future benefits requires that they be expensed.

Goodwill is a particularly interesting type of intangible asset because it represents the value paid for the unidentifiable assets of another business. You might wonder how you can put a value on something you can't identify, but it is possible. When one company buys another business, the purchase price often is greater than the appraised value of all of the **net assets** of the business. Why would a company pay more for a business as a whole than it would pay if it bought the assets individually? The answer is to obtain its goodwill.

YOU SHOULD KNOW

Net assets: The shorthand term used to refer to assets minus liabilities.

Spotlight On BUSINESS DECISIONS

Valuing Goodwill in a Business Acquisition

Most business acquisitions involve goodwill. For example, in 2006 Cedar Fair bought five theme parks from Paramount Parks. The total purchase price that Cedar Fair agreed to pay ($1.2 billion) exceeded the fair value of Paramount's net assets ($890 million). As shown below, Cedar Fair paid this extra $310 million to acquire the goodwill associated with the theme parks' businesses.

Cedar Fair Purchases Paramount Parks (in millions)		
Purchase price		$1,200
Assets purchased and liabilities assumed		
Current assets	$ 70	
Property and equipment	1,000	
Intangible assets	80	
Debt and other liabilities	(260)	
Net assets, at fair value		890
Goodwill		$ 310

[3]Krispy Kreme Form 10-K annual report for the year ended February 1, 2009.

Use   The accounting rules that apply to the use of intangible assets, after they have been purchased, depend on whether the intangible asset has a limited or unlimited life.

- **Limited life.** The cost of intangible assets with a limited life (copyrights, patents, licensing rights, and franchises) is spread on a straight-line basis over each period of useful life in a process called **amortization**, which is similar to depreciation. Most companies do not estimate a residual value for their intangible assets because, unlike tangible assets that can be sold as scrap, intangibles usually have no value at the end of their useful lives. Amortization is reported as an expense each period on the income statement and also is subtracted directly from the applicable intangible asset accounts on the balance sheet.[4]

  To illustrate, assume Cedar Fair purchased a patent for an uphill water-coaster for $800,000 and intends to use it for 20 years. Each year, the company would record $40,000 in Amortization Expense ($800,000 ÷ 20 years). The effect of this amortization and the journal entry to record it follow:

> **YOU SHOULD KNOW**
>
> **Amortization:** The name given to allocating the cost of intangible assets over their limited useful lives.

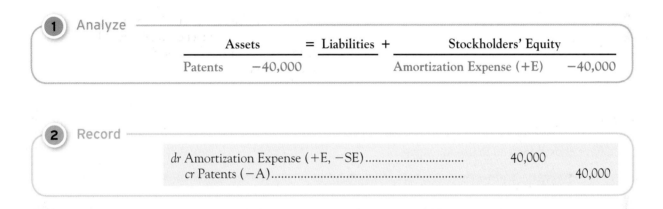

1 Analyze

	Assets	= Liabilities +	Stockholders' Equity	
Patents	−40,000		Amortization Expense (+E)	−40,000

2 Record

dr Amortization Expense (+E, −SE).............................. 40,000
    cr Patents (−A)... 40,000

- **Unlimited life.** Intangibles with unlimited or indefinite lives (trademarks and goodwill) are not amortized.

All intangible assets are tested at least annually for possible impairment, just like long-lived tangible assets. If an intangible asset is impaired, its book value is written down (reduced) to its fair value and the amount of the reduction is reported as an expense. For example, in 2008, Cedar Fair determined that declining economic conditions had impaired its Goodwill and Other Intangible Assets by approximately $90 million. These assets were written down on the balance sheet to their remaining fair value of $300 million (shown in Exhibit 9.1), with the $90 million reduction reported as an operating expense on the income statement (shown in Exhibit 9.2 on page 409).

Disposal   Just like long-lived tangible assets, disposals of intangible assets result in gains (or losses) if the amounts received on disposal are greater than (less than) their book values.

The accounting rules for long-lived tangible and intangible assets are summarized and compared in the Homework Helper section on page 429.

---

[4]Consistent with the procedure for recording accumulated depreciation, an Accumulated Amortization account may be used. In practice, however, most companies directly reduce the intangible asset account.

Spotlight On THE WORLD

Differences between GAAP and IFRS

IFRS differ from GAAP in many ways, particularly when accounting for tangible and intangible assets. Two of the most significant differences are summarized below. GAAP requires tangible and intangible assets to be recorded at cost and not revalued for later increases in asset values. In contrast, IFRS allows companies the option of reporting these assets at fair values (e.g., appraisals), provided they use the fair value method consistently each year. Another difference is that IFRS requires companies to capitalize costs of developing intangible assets, such as prototypes or models for making new products or tools. GAAP generally expenses such development costs because of the uncertainty of their ultimate value.

GAAP	IFRS
Cost versus Fair Value	**Cost versus Fair Value**
• Must record at cost	• Choose between either cost or fair value
• Adjust for depreciation and impairment	• Adjust for depreciation and impairment
• Do not record increases in value	• If using fair value, record increases in value
Research and Development	**Research and Development**
• Expense all costs of researching and developing intangible assets	• Expense research costs but capitalize measurable costs of developing intangible assets

Until the United States switches to IFRS, you should carefully read the financial statement notes of any non-U.S. company you analyze. Euro Disney and LEGO reported in 2008 that they chose to use historical costs just like Cedar Fair, but they could have chosen instead to use fair value.

Evaluate the Results

Learning Objective 7
Interpret the fixed asset turnover ratio.

TURNOVER ANALYSIS

A primary goal of financial analysts is to evaluate how well management uses long-lived tangible assets to generate revenues. The fixed asset turnover ratio provides a good measure of this aspect of managerial performance. It is calculated as shown in the table that follows. The denominator uses the value of **average** net fixed assets over the same period as the revenues in the numerator. You can calculate the average net fixed assets by summing the beginning and ending balances in fixed assets (net of accumulated depreciation) and dividing by 2.

Accounting Decision Tools

Name of Measure	Formula	What It Tells You
Fixed asset turnover ratio	$\dfrac{\text{Net Sales Revenue}}{\text{Average Net Fixed Assets}}$	• Indicates dollars of sales generated for each dollar invested in fixed assets (long-lived tangible assets) • A higher ratio implies greater efficiency

The fixed asset turnover ratio measures the sales dollars generated by each dollar invested in (tangible) fixed assets. Just as the number of miles per gallon provides a

EXHIBIT 9.5	Summary of Fixed Asset Turnover Ratio Analyses

Company	Relevant Information (in millions)			2008 Fixed Asset Turnover Calculation
		2008	**2007**	
Cedar Fair L.P.	Net sales	$1,000	$ 990	$\dfrac{\$1,000}{(\$1,800 + \$1,940)/2} = 0.53$
	Net fixed assets	1,800	1,940	
Six Flags	Net sales	$1,020	$ 970	$\dfrac{\$1,020}{(\$1,560 + \$1,640)/2} = 0.64$
	Net fixed assets	1,560	1,640	
YAHOO!	Net sales	$7,210	$6,970	$\dfrac{\$7,210}{(\$1,330 + \$1,210)/2} = 5.68$
	Net fixed assets	1,330	1,210	

measure of a car's fuel efficiency, the fixed asset turnover ratio provides a measure of fixed asset operating efficiency. Generally speaking, a high or increasing turnover ratio relative to others in the industry suggests better than average use of fixed assets in the sense that each dollar of fixed assets is generating higher than average sales.

Be aware that fixed asset turnover ratios can vary across industries because capital intensity—the need for tangible assets—varies widely. Compared to Cedar Fair, a company such as Yahoo! needs fewer fixed assets to generate revenues. So Yahoo! is likely to have a high turnover ratio compared to Cedar Fair or Six Flags, which must invest considerable money in fixed assets to attract customers. Exhibit 9.5 shows the fixed asset turnover ratios for the three companies in 2008. Practice computing this ratio and comparing it to prior periods by trying the Self-Study Practice that follows.

💡 How's it going?   Self-Study Practice

Cedar Fair reported net fixed assets of $1,990 (million) at December 31, 2006.

a. Use this information, along with that in Exhibit 9.5, to calculate Cedar Fair's fixed asset turnover ratio in 2007.

$$\frac{990}{(1990 + 1940)/2} = .5$$

b. Did Cedar Fair's fixed asset turnover improve or decline from 2007 (calculated in *a*) to 2008 (shown in Exhibit 9.5)?

After you have finished, check your answers with the solution in the margin.

Solution to Self-Study Practice

a. $\dfrac{\$990}{(\$1,940 + \$1,990)/2} = 0.50$

b. Cedar Fair's fixed asset turnover improved in 2008.

IMPACT OF DEPRECIATION DIFFERENCES

Just as differences in the nature of business operations affect financial analyses and the conclusions you draw from them, so too do differences in depreciation. Depreciation varies from one company to the next as a result of differences in depreciation methods, estimated useful lives, and estimated residual values. In this section, we present a

Learning Objective 8
Describe factors to consider when comparing companies' long-lived assets.

EXHIBIT 9.6   Straight-Line versus Double-Declining-Balance Depreciation Schedules

| CEDAR FAIR (STRAIGHT LINE) | | | | SIX FLAGS (DOUBLE-DECLINING BALANCE) | | |
Depreciation Expense	Accumulated Depreciation	Book Value	Year	Depreciation Expense	Accumulated Depreciation	Book Value
$2,000,000	$ 2,000,000	$13,500,000	1	$4,429,000	$ 4,429,000	$11,071,000
2,000,000	4,000,000	11,500,000	2	3,163,000	7,592,000	7,908,000
2,000,000	6,000,000	9,500,000	3	2,259,000	9,851,000	5,649,000
2,000,000	8,000,000	7,500,000	4	1,614,000	11,465,000	4,035,000
2,000,000	10,000,000	5,500,000	5	1,153,000	12,618,000	2,882,000
2,000,000	12,000,000	3,500,000	6	823,000	13,441,000	2,059,000
2,000,000	14,000,000	1,500,000	7	559,000	14,000,000	1,500,000

COACH'S TIP

For tips and practice involving the calculations in Exhibit 9.6, try S9-7 at the end of this chapter.

simple example to show how different depreciation methods can affect financial analysis throughout the life of a long-lived asset. Do not be fooled by the simplicity of the example. Differences in depreciation can have a significant impact in the real world.

Assume that Cedar Fair and Six Flags each acquired a new roller coaster at the beginning of the year for $15.5 million. The two companies estimate that the roller coasters will have residual values of $1.5 million at the end of their seven-year useful lives. Assume too that everything about the roller coasters is identical. However, Cedar Fair uses the straight-line depreciation method and Six Flags uses the double-declining-balance method. Exhibit 9.6 shows the yearly depreciation reported by the two companies. Notice that early in the asset's life, before year 4, the straight-line depreciation expense reported by Cedar Fair is less than the declining-balance depreciation expense reported by Six Flags. Thus, even if the two companies attract exactly the same number of customers and earn exactly the same total revenues, their reported net incomes will differ each year simply because they use two different (but equally acceptable) methods of depreciation. This example shows why a user of financial statements needs to understand the accounting methods companies use.

These differences in depreciation affect more than just depreciation expense, however. Taking this example one step further, assume that the two companies sell the roller coasters at the end of year 4 for $6,000,000. Because the disposal occurs on the last day of the year, the companies will record a full year of depreciation prior to the disposal. Thus, at the time of disposal, Cedar Fair's roller coaster will have a book value of $7,500,000, but Six Flags's roller coaster will have a book value of $4,035,000 (see the highlighted line in Exhibit 9.6). To account for the disposal at the end of year 4, the companies record what they received, remove what they gave up (the book value of the asset), and recognize a gain or loss for the difference between what was received and what was given up. Exhibit 9.7 shows the calculations for the two companies.

Based on the information in Exhibit 9.7, which company appears to be better managed? Someone who does not understand accounting is likely to say that Six Flags is better managed because it reported a gain on disposal whereas Cedar Fair reported a loss.

EXHIBIT 9.7   Calculation of Gain/Loss on Disposal

	Cedar Fair	Six Flags
Selling price	$ 6,000,000	$6,000,000
Book value (see Exhibit 9.6)	(7,500,000)	(4,035,000)
Gain (loss) on disposal	$(1,500,000)	$1,965,000

You know that cannot be right, however, because both companies experienced exactly the same events. They bought the same asset at the same cost ($15.5 million) and sold it for the same amount of money ($6 million). The only difference between them is that Cedar Fair reported less depreciation over the years leading up to the disposal, so its roller coaster had a larger book value at the time of disposal. Six Flags reported more depreciation, so its roller coaster had a smaller book value at the time of disposal. As a financial statement user, you should realize that any gain or loss on disposal that is reported on the income statement tells you as much about the method used to depreciate the asset as about management's apparent ability to successfully negotiate the sale of long-lived assets.

Although the previous example concerned different depreciation methods, the same effects can occur for two companies that use the same depreciation method but different estimated useful lives or residual values. Useful lives can vary for several reasons including differences in (1) the type of equipment each company uses, (2) the frequency of repairs and maintenance, (3) the frequency and duration of use, and (4) the degree of conservatism in management's estimates. How large can these differences be? Even within the same industry, sizable differences can occur. The notes to the financial statements of various companies in the airline industry, for example, reveal the following differences in the estimated useful lives of airplanes and other flight equipment:

Company	Estimated Life (in years)
US Airways	Up to 30
Southwest Airlines	Up to 25
Alaska Airlines	Up to 20
Singapore Airlines	Up to 15

Some analysts try to sidestep such differences in depreciation calculations by focusing on financial measures that exclude the effects of depreciation. One popular measure is called **EBITDA** (pronounced something like *'e bit, duh*), which stands for "earnings before interest, taxes, depreciation, and amortization." Analysts calculate EBITDA by starting with net income and then adding back depreciation and amortization expense (as well as nonoperating expenses such as interest and taxes). The idea is that this measure allows analysts to conduct financial analyses without having to deal with possible differences in depreciation and amortization.

SUPPLEMENT 9A: Natural Resources

Industries such as oil and gas, mining, and timber harvesting rely significantly on a third category of long-lived assets called *natural resources*. These natural resources, whether in the form of oil wells, mineral deposits, or timber tracts, provide the raw materials for products that are sold by companies like ExxonMobil and International Paper. When a company first acquires or develops a natural resource, the cost of the natural resource is recorded in conformity with the **cost principle.** As the natural resource is used up, its acquisition cost must be split among the periods in which revenues are earned in conformity with the **matching principle.** The term **depletion** describes the process of allocating a natural resource's cost over the period of its extraction or harvesting. The units-of-production method is often used to compute depletion.

Depletion is similar to the concepts of depreciation and amortization discussed earlier in the chapter for tangible and intangible assets, with one important exception. When a natural resource such as timberland is depleted, the company obtains inventory (logs). Because depletion of the natural resource is necessary to obtain the inventory, the depletion computed during a period is added to the cost of the inventory, not expensed in the period. For example, if a timber tract costing $530,000 is depleted over its estimated cutting period based on a "cutting" rate of approximately 20 percent per year, it would be depleted by $106,000 each year. Recording this depletion would have the following effects

YOU SHOULD KNOW

EBITDA: An abbreviation for "earnings before interest, taxes, depreciation, and amortization," which is a measure of operating performance that some managers and analysts use in place of net income.

YOU SHOULD KNOW

Depletion: The process of allocating a natural resource's cost over the period of its extraction or harvesting.

on the company's accounting equation, which would be recorded with the journal entry shown below.

1 Analyze

Assets		= Liabilities +	Stockholders' Equity
Timber Inventory	+106,000		
Timber Tract	−106,000		

2 Record

Timber Inventory (+A)	106,000	
Timber Tract (−A) (or Accumulated Depletion +xA, −A)		106,000

Timber Inventory remains as an asset on the balance sheet until it is sold, at which time its cost is removed from the balance sheet and reported on the income statement as an expense called Cost of Goods Sold.

SUPPLEMENT 9B: Changes in Depreciation Estimates

Depreciation is based on two estimates, useful life and residual value. These estimates are made at the time a depreciable asset is acquired. As you gain experience with the asset, one or both of these initial estimates may need to be revised. In addition, extraordinary repairs and additions may be added to the original acquisition cost at some time during the asset's use. When it is clear that either estimate should be revised to a significant degree or that the asset's capitalized cost has changed, depreciation is revised for the remaining years of the asset's estimated life.

To compute the new depreciation expense due to the changes described above, substitute the book value for the original acquisition cost, the new residual value for the original residual value, and the estimated remaining life for the original useful life. As an illustration, the formula using the straight-line method follows:

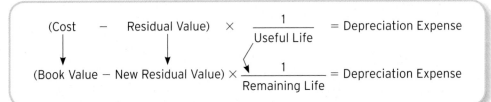

Assume Cedar Fair purchased the largest and fastest roller coaster in the universe for $60,000,000 with an estimated useful life of 20 years and estimated residual value of $3,000,000. Shortly after the start of year 5, Cedar Fair changed the initial estimated life to 25 years and lowered the estimated residual value to $2,400,000. At the end of year 5, the computation of the new amount for depreciation expense is as follows:

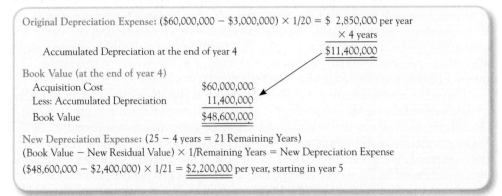

Companies may also change depreciation methods (for example, from declining-balance to straight-line), although such a change requires significantly more disclosure, as described in intermediate accounting textbooks. Under GAAP, changes in accounting estimates and depreciation methods should be made only when a new estimate or accounting method "better measures" the periodic income of the business.

REVIEW THE CHAPTER

DEMONSTRATION CASE

Diversified Industries (DI) started as a house construction company. In recent years, it has expanded into heavy construction, ready-mix concrete, sand and gravel, construction supplies, and earth-moving services. The company completed the following transactions during 2010. Amounts have been simplified.

www.mhhe.com/phillips3e

Jan. 1	The management decided to buy a 10-year-old building for $175,000 and the land on which it was situated for $130,000. DI paid $100,000 in cash and signed a note payable for the rest.
Jan. 3	DI paid $38,000 in cash for renovations to the building prior to its use.
July 10	DI paid $1,200 cash for ordinary repairs on the building.
Dec. 31	DI considered the following information to determine year-end adjustments:

a. The building will be depreciated on a straight-line basis over an estimated useful life of 30 years. The estimated residual value is $33,000.
b. DI purchased another company two years ago at $100,000 more than the fair values of the net assets acquired. The goodwill has an unlimited life.
c. At the beginning of the year, DI owned equipment with a cost of $650,000 and accumulated depreciation of $150,000. The equipment is being depreciated using the double-declining-balance method, with a useful life of 20 years and no residual value.
d. At year-end, DI tested its long-lived assets for possible impairment of their value. Included in its equipment was a piece of old excavation equipment with a cost of $156,000 and book value of $120,000, after making the adjustment for (c). Due to its smaller size and lack of safety features, the old equipment has limited use. The future cash flows and fair value are expected to be $35,000. Goodwill was found to be not impaired.

December 31, 2010, is the end of the annual accounting period.

Required:

1. Indicate the accounts affected and the amount and direction (+ for increase and − for decrease) of the effect of each of the preceding events and required adjustments on the financial statement categories at the end of the year. Use the following headings:

Date	Assets	=	Liabilities	+	Stockholders' Equity

2. Prepare the journal entries to record each event that occurred during the year and the adjusting journal entries required at December 31.
3. Which accounts would be reported on the income statement? Where?
4. Show how the December 31, 2010, balance sheet would report these long-lived tangible and intangible assets.
5. Assuming that the company had Net Sales of $1,000,000 for the year and a book value of $500,000 for fixed assets at the beginning of the year, compute the fixed asset turnover ratio. Explain its meaning and evaluate it relative to the prior year's ratio of 1.5.

Suggested Solution

1. Effects of events (with computations in notes below the table):

Date	Assets		=	Liabilities	+	Stockholders' Equity	
Jan. 1	Cash	−100,000		Note Payable +205,000			
	Land	+130,000					
	Building	+175,000					
Jan. 3 (Note 1)	Cash	−38,000					
	Building	+38,000					
July 10 (Note 2)	Cash	−1,200				Repairs and Maintenance Expense (+E)	−1,200
Dec. 31 (a) (Note 3)	Accumulated Depreciation (+xA)	−6,000				Depreciation Expense (+E)	−6,000
Dec. 31 (b) (Note 4)	No entry						
Dec. 31 (c) (Note 5)	Accumulated Depreciation (+xA)	−50,000				Depreciation Expense (+E)	−50,000
Dec. 31 (d) (Note 6)	Equipment	−85,000				Impairment Loss (+E)	−85,000

Notes

(1) Capitalize the $38,000 expenditure because it is necessary to prepare the asset for use.

(2) This is an ordinary repair and should be expensed.

(3)

Cost of building		Straight-line depreciation (building)
Initial payment	$175,000	($213,000 cost − $33,000 residual value) ×
Renovations prior to use	38,000	1/30 years = $6,000 annual depreciation
Acquisition cost	$213,000	

(4) Goodwill has an indefinite life and is therefore not amortized. Goodwill is tested for impairment but as described later in the case, was found to be not impaired.

(5) **Double-declining-balance depreciation (equipment)**
($650,000 cost − $150,000 accumulated depreciation) × 2/20 years = $50,000 depreciation for the year.

(6) **Asset impairment test**
The book value of the old equipment ($120,000) exceeds expected future cash flows ($35,000). The asset has become impaired, so it needs to be written down to its fair value.

Impairment loss:	
Book Value	$120,000
Fair Value	(35,000)
Impairment Loss	$ 85,000

2. Journal entries for events during the year:

Jan. 1, 2010	dr Land (+A)...	130,000	
	dr Building (+A)	175,000	
	cr Cash (−A)		100,000
	cr Note Payable (+L)		205,000
Jan. 3, 2010	dr Building (+A)	38,000	
	cr Cash (−A)..		38,000
July 10, 2010	dr Repairs and Maintenance Expense (+E, −SE)	1,200	
	cr Cash (−A)..		1,200

Adjusting journal entries at December 31, 2010:

a. *dr* Depreciation Expense (+E, −SE) 6,000

    cr Accumulated Depreciation—Building (+xA, −A)   6,000

b. No adjusting journal entry required because goodwill is assumed to have an unlimited (or indefinite) life.

c. *dr* Depreciation Expense (+E, −SE) 50,000

    cr Accumulated Depreciation—Equipment (+xA, −A)   50,000

d. *dr* Impairment Loss (+E, −SE) 85,000

    cr Equipment (−A)   85,000

3. The income statement would report <u>Depreciation Expense</u>, <u>Repairs and Maintenance Expense</u>, and <u>Impairment Loss</u> as operating expenses included in the computation of <u>Income from Operations</u>.

4. Partial balance sheet, December 31, 2010:

Assets	
Property, Plant, and Equipment	
Land	$130,000
Building	213,000
Equipment	565,000*
Property, Plant, and Equipment, at cost	908,000
Less: Accumulated Depreciation	(206,000)†
Property, Plant, and Equipment, net	702,000
Goodwill	100,000

    * $565,000 = $650,000 − $85,000

    † $206,000 = $6,000 + $150,000 + $50,000

5. Fixed asset turnover ratio:

$$\frac{\text{Net Sales}}{(\text{Beginning Net Fixed Asset Balance} + \text{Ending Net Fixed Asset Balance})/2} = \frac{\$1,000,000}{(\$500,000 + \$702,000)/2} = 1.66$$

The fixed asset turnover ratio measures the company's efficiency at using its investment in property, plant, and equipment to generate sales. Approximately $1.66 of sales were generated for each dollar of fixed assets, which is an improvement over last year's 1.5.

CHAPTER SUMMARY

Define, classify, and explain the nature of long-lived assets. p. 402   **LO1**

- Long-lived assets are those that a business retains for long periods of time for use in the course of normal operations rather than for sale. They may be divided into tangible assets (land, buildings, equipment) and intangible assets (including goodwill, patents, and franchises).

Apply the cost principle to the acquisition of long-lived assets. p. 403   **LO2**

- The acquisition cost of property, plant, and equipment is the cash-equivalent purchase price plus all reasonable and necessary expenditures made to acquire and prepare the asset for its intended use. Expenditures made after the asset is in use are either expensed or capitalized as a cost of the asset:
  a. Expenditures are expensed if they recur frequently, involve relatively small amounts, and do not directly lengthen the asset's useful life. These are considered ordinary repairs and maintenance expense.
  b. Expenditures are capitalized as a cost of the asset if they provide benefits for one or more accounting periods beyond the current period. This category includes extraordinary repairs, replacements, and additions.

LO3   Apply various depreciation methods as economic benefits are used up over time. p. 410

- In conformity with the matching principle, the cost of long-lived tangible assets (less any estimated residual value) is allocated to depreciation expense over each period benefited by the assets.

- Because of depreciation, the book value of an asset declines over time and net income is reduced by the amount of the expense.

- Common depreciation methods include straight-line (a constant amount over time), units-of-production (a variable amount over time), and double-declining-balance (a decreasing amount over time).

LO4   Explain the effect of asset impairment on the financial statements. p. 415

- When events or changes in circumstances reduce the estimated future cash flows of a long-lived asset below its book value, the book value of the asset should be written down, with the amount of the write-down reported as an impairment loss.

LO5   Analyze the disposal of long-lived tangible assets. p. 415

When assets are disposed of through sale or abandonment,

- Record additional depreciation arising since the last adjustment was made.

- Remove the cost of the old asset and its related accumulated depreciation.

- Recognize the cash proceeds (if any).

- Recognize any gains or losses when the asset's book value is not equal to the cash received.

LO6   Analyze the acquisition, use, and disposal of long-lived intangible assets. p. 417

- Intangible assets are recorded at cost, but only when purchased. The costs of most internally developed intangible assets are expensed as research and development when incurred.

- Intangibles are reported at book value on the balance sheet.

- Amortization is calculated for intangibles with limited useful lives, using the straight-line method.

- Intangibles with unlimited useful lives, including goodwill, are not amortized, but are reviewed for impairment.

LO7   Interpret the fixed asset turnover ratio. p. 420

- The fixed asset turnover ratio measures the company's efficiency at using its investment in property, plant, and equipment to generate sales. Higher turnover ratios imply greater efficiency.

LO8   Describe factors to consider when comparing companies' long-lived assets. p. 421

- Companies in different industries require different levels of investment in long-lived assets. Beyond that, you should consider whether differences exist in depreciation methods, estimated useful lives, and estimated residual values, which can affect the book value of long-lived assets as well as ratios calculated using these book values and any gains or losses reported at the time of asset disposal.

Accounting Decision Tools

Name of Measure	Formula	What It Tells You
Fixed asset turnover ratio	$\dfrac{\text{Net Sales Revenue}}{\text{Average Net Fixed Assets}}$	• Dollars of sales generated for each dollar invested in (tangible) fixed assets • A higher ratio implies greater efficiency

KEY TERMS

Amortization p. 419	EBITDA p. 423	Patent p. 417
Book (or Carrying) Value p. 409	Extraordinary Repairs p. 408	Research and Development p. 418
Capitalize p. 404	Franchise p. 418	Residual (or Salvage) Value p. 409
Copyright p. 417	Goodwill p. 418	Straight-Line Depreciation
Declining-Balance Depreciation	Impairment p. 415	Method p. 410
Method p. 411	Licensing Right p. 417	Trademark p. 417
Depletion p. 423	Long-Lived Assets p. 402	Units-of-Production Depreciation
Depreciable Cost p. 409	Net Assets p. 418	Method p. 411
Depreciation p. 408	Ordinary Repairs and Maintenance p. 407	Useful Life p. 409

See complete definitions in the glossary in the back of this text.

HOMEWORK HELPER

Stage	Subject	Tangible Assets	Intangible Assets
Acquire	*Purchased asset*	Capitalize all related costs	Capitalize all related costs
Use	*Repairs and maintenance*		
	Ordinary	Expense related costs	Not applicable
	Extraordinary	Capitalize related costs	Not applicable
	Depreciation/amortization		
	Limited life	One of several methods: • Straight-line • Units-of-production • Declining-balance	Straight-line method
	Unlimited life	Do not depreciate (e.g., land)	Do not amortize (e.g., goodwill)
	Impairment test	Write down if necessary	Write down if necessary
Dispose	*Report gain (loss) when . . .*	Receive more (less) on disposal than book value	Receive more (less) on disposal than book value

Alternative terms

- Declining-balance depreciation methods are also called accelerated methods.

Helpful reminders

- Costs that benefit future periods are capitalized as assets. Costs that benefit the current period are recorded as expenses.
- See Exhibit 9.2 for an income statement showing where to report Depreciation Expense, Impairment Losses, and Losses (Gains) on Disposal of Assets.
- Declining-balance depreciation methods subtract Accumulated Depreciation, not residual value, from the asset's cost. For this reason, take extra care to ensure that you stop depreciating the asset when its book value equals its residual value.

Frequent mistakes

- Depreciation does not represent a decline in the current value of an asset; declines in asset values are recorded as impairment losses, not depreciation. The purpose of depreciation is to allocate the cost of a long-lived asset to each period in which the asset is used to generate revenue.
- When recording an asset disposal, remove its cost and accumulated depreciation separately, rather than remove just its book value from the asset's account.

PRACTICE MATERIAL

QUESTIONS (⊜ Symbol indicates questions that require analysis from more than one perspective.)

1. Define long-lived assets. What are the two common categories of long-lived assets? Describe each.

2. Under the cost principle, what amounts should be recorded as a cost of a long-lived asset?

3. What is the term for recording costs as assets rather than as expenses? Describe how the decision to record costs as assets, rather than expenses, affects the balance sheet and income statement.

4. Waste Management, Inc., regularly incurs costs (e.g., salaries, legal fees, travel) to find new locations for landfill sites. What reasons support capitalizing these costs? What reasons support expensing these costs? ⊜

5. Distinguish between ordinary repairs and extraordinary repairs. How is each accounted for?

6. Describe the relationship between the matching principle and accounting for long-lived assets.

7. Why are different depreciation methods allowed?

8. In computing depreciation, three values must be known or estimated. Identify and describe each.

9. What type of depreciation expense pattern is used under each of the following methods and when is its use appropriate?

   a. The straight-line method.
   b. The units-of-production method.
   c. The double-declining-balance method.

10. After merging with Northwest Airlines, Delta Airlines increased the estimated useful life and increased the estimated residual value of its flight equipment. All else equal, how will each of these changes affect Delta's Depreciation Expense and Net Income? ⊜

11. A local politician claimed, "to reduce the government's deficit, it's time we require companies to start paying their deferred income tax liabilities." Explain to the politician what deferred income taxes represent and why they should not be viewed as accounts payable to the government. ⊜

12. What is an *asset impairment*? How is it accounted for?

13. What is book value? When equipment is sold for more than book value, how is the transaction recorded? How is it recorded when the selling price is less than book value?

14. Distinguish between depreciation and amortization.

15. Define *goodwill*. When is it appropriate to record goodwill as an intangible asset? When is its value decreased?

16. FedEx Corporation reports the cost of its aircraft in a single category called Flight Equipment. What impact will IFRS have on this aspect of FedEx's accounting? ⊜

17. How is the fixed asset turnover ratio computed? Explain its meaning.

18. Johnson & Johnson, the maker of Tylenol, uses GAAP. Bayer, the maker of Aspirin, uses IFRS. Explain what complications might arise when comparing the Property, Plant, and Equipment of these two companies. ⊜

19. (Supplement 9A) How does depletion affect the balance sheet and income statement? Why is depletion accounted for in a manner that differs from depreciation and amortization?

20. (Supplement 9B) Over what period should an addition to an existing long-lived asset be depreciated? Explain.

MULTIPLE CHOICE

1. Which of the following should be capitalized when a piece of production equipment is acquired for a factory?

   Quiz 9
   www.mhhe.com/phillips3e

   a. Sales tax.
   b. Transportation costs.
   c. Installation costs.
   d. All of the above.

2. When recording depreciation, which of the following statements is true?

   a. Total assets increase and stockholders' equity increases.
   b. Total assets decrease and total liabilities increase.
   c. Total assets decrease and stockholders' equity increases.
   d. None of the above are true.

3. Under what depreciation method(s) is an asset's book value used to calculate depreciation each year?

   a. Straight-line method.
   b. Units-of-production method.
   c. Declining-balance method.
   d. All of the above.

4. A company wishes to report the highest earnings possible according to GAAP. Therefore, when calculating depreciation for financial reporting purposes,

   a. It will follow the MACRS depreciation rates prescribed by the IRS.
   b. It will estimate the shortest lives possible for its assets.
   c. It will estimate the longest lives possible for its assets.
   d. It will estimate lower residual values for its assets.

$(c - 20,000) \times \frac{1}{20} = 20{,}000$

5. Barber, Inc., depreciates its building on a straight-line basis. A building was purchased on January 1, 2010, and it had an estimated useful life of 20 years and a residual value of $20,000. The company's Depreciation Expense for 2010 was $20,000 on the building. What was the original cost of the building?

   a. $360,000   c. $400,000
   b. $380,000   d. $420,000

6. Thornton Industries purchased a machine on July 1, 2010, for $45,000 and is depreciating it with the straight-line method over a life of 10 years, using a residual value of $3,000. Depreciation Expense for the machine for the year ended December 31, 2010, is .5(

   a. $2,100   c. $4,200
   b. $2,250   d. $4,500   1000 −

7. ACME, Inc., uses straight-line depreciation for all of its depreciable assets. ACME sold a used piece of machinery on December 31, 2010, that it purchased on January 1, 2009, for $10,000. The asset had a five-year life, zero residual value, and Accumulated Depreciation as of December 31, 2010, of $4,000. If the sales price of the used machine was $7,500, the resulting gain or loss on disposal was which of the following amounts?   6000

   a. Loss of $2,500   c. Loss of $1,500
   b. Gain of $3,500   d. Gain of $1,500

8. What assets should be amortized using the straight-line method?

   a. Land.
   b. Intangible assets with limited lives.
   c. Intangible assets with unlimited lives.
   d. All of the above.

9. How many of the following statements regarding goodwill are true?
   • Goodwill is not reported unless purchased in an exchange.
   • Goodwill must be reviewed annually for possible impairment.
   • Impairment of goodwill results in a decrease in net income.

   a. None   c. Two
   b. One   d. Three

10. The Simon Company and the Allen Company each bought a new delivery truck on January 1, 2009. Both companies paid exactly the same cost, $30,000, for their respective vehicles. As of December 31, 2010, the book value of Simon's truck was less than the Allen Company's book value for the same vehicle. Which of the following are acceptable explanations for the difference in book value?

    a. Both companies elected straight-line depreciation, but the Simon Company used a longer estimated life.
    b. The Simon Company estimated a lower residual value, but both estimated the same useful life and both elected straight-line depreciation.
    c. Because GAAP specifies rigid guidelines regarding the calculation of depreciation, this situation is not possible.
    d. None of the above explain the difference in book value.

For answers to the Multiple-Choice Questions **see page Q1** located in the last section of the book.

MINI-EXERCISES

|ACCOUNTING   LO1, 3, 6

M9-1 Classifying Long-Lived Assets and Related Cost Allocation Concepts

For each of the following long-lived assets, indicate its nature and related cost allocation concept. Use the abbreviations shown on the right:

Asset	Nature	Cost Allocation		Nature
1. Software license			L	Land
2. Property			B	Building
3. New engine			E	Equipment
4. Delivery vans			I	Intangible
5. Production plant				**Cost Allocation**
6. Warehouse				
7. Copyright			D	Depreciation
8. Trademark			A	Amortization
9. Computers			NO	No cost allocation

M9-2 Deciding Whether to Capitalize or Expense   LO2, 6

American Golf Corporation operates over 170 golf courses throughout the country. For each of the following items, enter the correct letter to show whether the cost should be capitalized (C) or expensed (E).

American Golf Corporation

Transactions
_____

_____ 1. Purchased a golf course in Orange County, California.

_____ 2. Paid a landscaping company to clear one hundred acres of land on which to build a new course.

_____ 3. Paid a landscaping company to apply fertilizer to the fairways on its Coyote Hills Golf Course.

_____ 4. Hired a building maintenance company to build a 2,000 square foot addition on a clubhouse.

_____ 5. Hired a building maintenance company to replace the locks on a clubhouse and equipment shed.

_____ 6. Paid an advertising company to create a campaign to build goodwill.

LO2, 6   **M9-3 Deciding Whether to Capitalize an Expense**

For each of the following items, enter the correct letter to show whether the expenditure should be capitalized (C) or expensed (E).

Transactions
_____

_____ 1. Paid $600 for ordinary repairs.

_____ 2. Paid $16,000 for extraordinary repairs.

_____ 3. Paid cash, $200,000, for addition to old building.

_____ 4. Paid $250 for routine maintenance.

_____ 5. Purchased a machine, $70,000; gave long-term note.

_____ 6. Purchased a patent, $45,300 cash.

_____ 7. Paid $20,000 for monthly salaries.

LO3   **M9-4 Computing Book Value (Straight-Line Depreciation)**

Calculate the book value of a two-year-old machine that cost $200,000, has an estimated residual value of $40,000, and has an estimated useful life of four years. The company uses straight-line depreciation.

LO3   **M9-5 Computing Book Value (Units-of-Production Depreciation)**

Calculate the book value of a two-year-old machine that cost $200,000, has an estimated residual value of $40,000, and has an estimated useful life of 20,000 machine hours. The company uses units-of-production depreciation and ran the machine 3,000 hours in year 1 and 8,000 hours in year 2.

LO3   **M9-6 Computing Book Value (Double-Declining-Balance Depreciation)**

Calculate the book value of a two-year-old machine that cost $200,000, has an estimated residual value of $40,000, and has an estimated useful life of four years. The company uses double-declining-balance depreciation. Round to the nearest dollar.

LO3   **M9-7 Calculating Partial-Year Depreciation**

Calculate the amount of depreciation to report during the year ended December 31, 2010, for equipment that was purchased at a cost of $33,000 on September 1, 2010. The equipment has an estimated residual value of $3,000 and an estimated useful life of five years or 20,000 hours. Assume the equipment was used for 1,000 hours from September 1 to December 31 and the company uses: (*a*) straight-line, (*b*) double-declining-balance, or (*c*) units-of-production depreciation.

LO4   **M9-8 Understanding the Significance of Asset Impairment Losses**

General Motors Corporation

For the year ended December 31, 2008, General Motors Corporation reported a Loss from Operations of $20 billion. The following asset impairment losses were included among its operating expenses.

Goodwill impairment	$ 610 million
HUMMER equipment impairment	290 million
Saab equipment impairment	500 million
Other impairment losses	1,100 million
Total impairment losses	$2,500 million

Do GM's asset impairment losses seem significant in terms of total dollar value? What percentage of the company's 2008 operating loss was explained by asset impairments? Why might GM write down its HUMMER and Saab production equipment, but not its Chevrolet production equipment?

M9-9 Recording the Disposal of a Long-Lived Asset

L05

Prepare journal entries to record these transactions: (*a*) Morrell Corporation disposed of two computers at the end of their useful lives. The computers had cost $4,800 and their Accumulated Depreciation was $4,800. No residual value was received. (*b*) Assume the same information as (*a*), except that Accumulated Depreciation, updated to the date of disposal, was $3,600.

M9-10 Reporting and Recording the Disposal of a Long-Lived Asset (Straight-Line Depreciation)

L05

As part of a major renovation at the beginning of the year, Hauser Pharmaceuticals, Inc., sold shelving units (store fixtures) that were 10 years old for $1,000 cash. The shelves originally cost $6,400 and had been depreciated on a straight-line basis over an estimated useful life of 10 years with an estimated residual value of $400. Assuming that depreciation has been recorded to the date of sale, show the effect of the disposal on the accounting equation. Prepare the journal entry to record the sale of the shelving units.

M9-11 Capitalizing versus Expensing Intangible Asset Costs

L06

Most highly visible companies spend significant amounts of money to protect their intellectual property, ensuring that no one uses this property without direct permission. For example, to include logos throughout this book, we had to obtain written permission from each company—a process that stretched over nearly a year and often resulted in requests being denied. Discuss whether companies should capitalize or expense the money paid to employees who evaluate requests for use of their logos and who search for instances where the companies' intellectual property has been used without permission. Draw an analogy to similar costs incurred for employees responsible for the use and upkeep of tangible assets.

M9-12 Computing Goodwill and Patents

L06

Taste-T Company has been in business for 30 years and has developed a large group of loyal restaurant customers. Down Home Foods made an offer to buy Taste-T Company for $6,000,000. The market value of Taste-T's recorded assets, net of liabilities, on the date of the offer is $5,600,000. Taste-T also holds a patent for a fluting machine that the company invented (the patent with a market value of $200,000 was never recorded by Taste-T because it was developed internally). How much has Down Home Foods included for intangibles in its offer of $6,000,000? Assuming Taste-T accepts this offer, which company will report Goodwill on its balance sheet?

M9-13 Computing and Evaluating the Fixed Asset Turnover Ratio

L07

The following information was reported by Amuse Yourself Parks (AYP) for 2008:

Net fixed assets (beginning of year)	$8,450,000
Net fixed assets (end of year)	8,250,000
Net sales for the year	4,175,000
Net income for the year	1,700,000

Compute the company's fixed asset turnover ratio for the year. What can you say about AYP's fixed asset turnover ratio when compared to Cedar Fair's 2008 ratio in Exhibit 9.5?

M9-14 (Supplement 9A) Recording Depletion for a Natural Resource

Saskatchewan Forestry Company purchased a timber tract for $600,000 and estimates that it will be depleted evenly over its 10-year useful life with no residual value. Show the journal entry that would be recorded if 10 percent of the total timber is cut and placed into inventory during the current year.

M9-15 (Supplement 9B) Computing Revised Depreciation after Change in Cost and Estimated Life

Thornton Industries purchased a machine for $45,000 and is depreciating it with the straight-line method over a life of 10 years, using a residual value of $3,000. At the beginning of the sixth year, an extraordinary repair was made costing $5,000, the estimated useful life was extended to 13 years, and no change was made to the estimated residual value. Calculate depreciation expense for year 6, rounded to the nearest dollar.

EXERCISES

L01, 7 **E9-1 Preparing a Classified Balance Sheet**

The following is a list of account titles and amounts (in millions) reported at December 28, 2008, by Hasbro, Inc., a leading manufacturer of games, toys, and interactive entertainment software for children and families:

Buildings and Improvements	$195	Goodwill	$475
Prepaids and Other Current Assets	171	Machinery and Equipment	413
Allowance for Doubtful Accounts	32	Accumulated Depreciation	403
Other Noncurrent Assets	200	Inventories	301
Cash and Cash Equivalents	630	Other Intangibles	568
Accounts Receivable	644	Land and Improvements	7

Required:

1. Prepare the asset section of a classified balance sheet for Hasbro, Inc.
2. Using Hasbro's 2008 Net Sales Revenue of $4,022 (million) and its Net Fixed Assets of $188 (million) at December 30, 2007, calculate the fixed asset turnover ratio for 2008. Has the company generated more or less revenue from each dollar of fixed assets than in 2007, when the ratio was 20.75?

L02, 3 **E9-2 Computing and Recording a Basket Purchase and Straight-Line Depreciation**

Bridge City Consulting bought a building and the land on which it is located for $182,000 cash. The land is estimated to represent 70 percent of the purchase price. The company paid $22,000 for building renovations before it was ready for use.

Required:

1. Explain how the renovation costs should be accounted for.
2. Give the journal entry to record all expenditures. Assume that all transactions were for cash and they occurred at the start of the year.
3. Compute straight-line depreciation on the building at the end of one year, assuming an estimated 12-year useful life and a $4,600 estimated residual value.
4. What should be the book value of the land and building at the end of year 2?

L02, 3 **E9-3 Determining Financial Statement Effects of an Asset Acquisition and Straight-Line Depreciation**

Conover Company ordered a machine on January 1, 2009, at a purchase price of $30,000. On the date of delivery, January 2, 2009, the company paid $8,000 on the machine and signed a note payable for the balance. On January 3, 2009, it paid $250 for freight on the machine. On January 5, Conover paid installation costs relating to the machine amounting to $1,500. On December 31, 2009 (the end of the accounting period), Conover recorded depreciation on the machine using the straight-line method with an estimated useful life of 10 years and an estimated residual value of $2,750.

Required:

1. Indicate the effects (accounts, amounts, and + or −) of each transaction (on January 1, 2, 3, and 5) on the accounting equation. Use the following schedule:

Date	Assets	=	Liabilities	+	Stockholders' Equity

2. Compute the acquisition cost of the machine.
3. Compute the depreciation expense to be reported for 2009.
4. What should be the book value of the machine at the end of 2010?

E9-4 **Recording Straight-Line Depreciation and Repairs**   LO2, 3

Wiater Company operates a small manufacturing facility. On January 1, 2010, an asset account for the company showed the following balances:

Manufacturing equipment	$160,000
Accumulated depreciation through 2009	110,000

During the first week of January 2010, the following expenditures were incurred for repairs and maintenance:

Routine maintenance and repairs on the equipment	$ 1,850
Major overhaul of the equipment that improved efficiency	21,000

The equipment is being depreciated on a straight-line basis over an estimated life of 15 years with a $10,000 estimated residual value. The annual accounting period ends on December 31.

Required:

Indicate the effects (accounts, amounts, and + or −) of the following two items on the accounting equation, using the headings shown below.

1. The adjustment for depreciation made at the end of 2009.
2. The two expenditures for repairs and maintenance during January 2010.

Item	Assets	=	Liabilities	+	Stockholders' Equity

E9-5 **Determining Financial Statement Effects of Straight-Line Depreciation and Repairs**   LO2, 3

Refer to the information in E9-4.

Required:

1. Give the adjusting journal entry that would have been made at the end of 2009 for depreciation on the manufacturing equipment.
2. Starting at the beginning of 2010, what is the remaining estimated life?
3. Give the journal entries to record the two expenditures for repairs and maintenance during 2010.

E9-6 **Computing Depreciation under Alternative Methods**   LO3

PlasticWorks Corporation bought a machine at the beginning of the year at a cost of $12,000. The estimated useful life was five years, and the residual value was $2,000. Assume that the estimated productive life of the machine is 10,000 units. Expected annual production was: year 1, 3,000 units; year 2, 3,000 units; year 3, 2,000 units; year 4, 1,000 units; and year 5, 1,000 units.

Required:

1. Complete a depreciation schedule for each of the alternative methods.
   a. Straight-line.
   b. Units-of-production.
   c. Double-declining-balance.

		Income Statement		Balance Sheet		
Year	Computation	Depreciation Expense	Cost	Accumulated Depreciation	Book Value
At acquisition						
1						

2. Which method will result in the highest net income in year 2? Does this higher net income mean the machine was used more efficiently under this depreciation method?

LO3

Sonic Corporation

E9-7 Computing Depreciation under Alternative Methods

Sonic Corporation purchased and installed electronic payment equipment at its drive-in restaurants in San Marcos, TX, at a cost of $27,000. The equipment has an estimated residual value of $1,500. The equipment is expected to process 255,000 payments over its three-year useful life. Per year, expected payment transactions are 61,200, year 1; 140,250, year 2; and 53,550, year 3.

Required:

Complete a depreciation schedule for each of the alternative methods.

1. Straight-line.
2. Units-of-production.
3. Double-declining-balance.

		Income Statement	Balance Sheet		
Year	Computation	Depreciation Expense	Cost	Accumulated Depreciation	Book Value
At acquisition					
1					

LO3

FedEx Corporation

E9-8 Interpreting Management's Choice of Different Depreciation Methods for Tax and Financial Reporting

The annual report for FedEx Corporation includes the following information:

> For financial reporting purposes, depreciation and amortization of property and equipment is provided on a straight-line basis over the asset's service life. For income tax purposes, depreciation is generally computed using accelerated methods.

Required:

Explain why FedEx uses different methods of depreciation for financial reporting and tax purposes.

LO3

E9-9 Inferring Asset Age from Straight-Line Depreciation

On January 1, 2010, the records of Tuff Turf Corporation (TTC) showed the following regarding production equipment:

Equipment (estimated residual value, $4,000)	$14,000
Accumulated Depreciation (straight-line, one year)	2,000

Required:

Based on the data given, compute the estimated useful life of the equipment.

LO4

E9-10 Exploring Financial Statement Effects of Asset Impairment

Refer to E9-9.

Required:

If TTC's management estimated that the equipment had future cash flows and a fair value of only $6,800 at December 31, 2010, how would this affect TTC's balance sheet and income statement? Explain.

LO5

FedEx Corporation

E9-11 Demonstrating the Effect of Book Value on Reporting an Asset Disposal

FedEx Corporation is the world's leading express-distribution company. In addition to the world's largest fleet of all-cargo aircraft, the company has more than 53,700 ground vehicles that pick up and deliver packages. Assume that FedEx sold a delivery truck for $16,000. FedEx had originally purchased the truck for $28,000, and had recorded depreciation for three years.

Required:

1. Calculate the amount of gain or loss on disposal, assuming that Accumulated Depreciation was: (*a*) $12,000, (*b*) $10,000, and (*c*) $15,000.

2. Using the following structure, indicate the effects (accounts, amounts, and + or −) for the disposal of the truck in each of the three preceding situations.

Assets	=	Liabilities	+	Stockholders' Equity

3. Based on the three preceding situations, explain how the amount of depreciation recorded up to the time of disposal affects the amount of gain or loss on disposal.

4. Prepare the journal entry to record the disposal of the truck for each situation in requirement 1.

E9-12 Computing and Reporting the Acquisition and Amortization of Three Different Intangible Assets   LO6

Kreiser Company had three intangible assets at the end of 2010 (end of the accounting year):

a. A patent purchased from J. Miller on January 1, 2010, for a cash cost of $5,640. When purchased, the patent had an estimated life of fifteen years.

b. A trademark was registered with the federal government for $10,000. Management estimated that the trademark could be worth as much as $200,000 because it has an indefinite life.

c. Computer licensing rights were purchased on January 1, 2010, for $60,000. The rights are expected to have a four-year useful life to the company.

Required:

1. Compute the acquisition cost of each intangible asset.

2. Compute the amortization of each intangible for the year ended December 31, 2010.

3. Show how these assets and any related expenses should be reported on the balance sheet and income statement for 2010.

E9-13 Recording the Purchase, Amortization, and Impairment of a Patent   LO4, 6

Nutek, Inc., holds a patent for the Full Service™ handi-plate, which the company described as "a patented plastic buffet plate that allows the user to hold both a plate and cup in one hand" and that "has a multitude of uses including social gatherings such as backyard barbecues, buffets, picnics, and parties of any kind." (No, we're not making this up.) Nutek also purchased a patent for $1,000,000 for "a specialty line of patented switch plate covers and outlet plate covers specifically designed to light up automatically when the power fails." Assume the switch plate patent was purchased January 1, 2009, and it is being amortized over a period of 10 years. Assume Nutek does not use an accumulated amortization account but instead charges amortization directly against the intangible asset account.

Nutek, Inc.

Required:

1. Describe the effects of the purchase and amortization of the switch plate patent on the 2009 balance sheet and income statement.

2. Give the journal entries to record the purchase and amortization of the switch plate patent in 2009.

3. After many months of unsuccessful attempts to manufacture the switch plate covers, Nutek determined the patent was significantly impaired and its book value on January 1, 2010, was written off. Describe the financial statement effects of accounting for the asset impairment and give the journal entry to record the impairment.

E9-14 Computing and Interpreting the Fixed Asset Turnover Ratio from a Financial Analyst's Perspective   LO7

The following data were included in a recent Apple Inc. annual report (in millions):

Apple Inc.

	2005	2006	2007	2008
Net sales	$13,931	$19,315	$24,006	$32,479
Net property, plant, and equipment	817	1,281	1,832	2,455

Required:

1. Compute Apple's fixed asset turnover ratio for 2006, 2007, and 2008. Round your answer to one decimal place.

2. Was Apple able to maintain its strong financial performance in recent years when the economy was beginning to falter?

LO3, 7   **E9-15** **Computing Depreciation and Book Value for Two Years Using Alternative Depreciation Methods and Interpreting the Impact on the Fixed Asset Turnover Ratio**

Torge Company bought a machine for $65,000 cash. The estimated useful life was five years, and the estimated residual value was $5,000. Assume that the estimated useful life in productive units is 150,000. Units actually produced were 40,000 in year 1 and 45,000 in year 2.

Required:

1. Determine the appropriate amounts to complete the following schedule. Show computations.

Method of Depreciation	Depreciation Expense for		Book Value at the End of	
	Year 1	Year 2	Year 1	Year 2
Straight-line				
Units-of-production				
Double-declining-balance				

2. Which method would result in the lowest net income for year 1? For year 2?
3. Which method would result in the lowest fixed asset turnover ratio for year 1? Why?

E9-16 **(Supplement 9A) Calculating and Reporting Depletion**

Louisiana Oil Company (LOC) paid $3,000,000 for an oil reserve estimated to hold 50,000 barrels of oil. Oil production is expected to be 10,000 barrels in year 1, 30,000 barrels in year 2, and 10,000 barrels in year 3. LOC expects to begin selling barrels from its oil inventory in year 2.

Required:

Assuming these estimates are accurate, describe the amounts, financial statements, and classifications that would be used for the oil reserves and oil inventory at the end of year 1.

E9-17 **(Supplement 9B) Determining Financial Statement Effects of a Change in Estimate**

Refer to E9-4.

Required:

1. Indicate the effects (accounts, amounts, and + or −) of the 2010 adjustment for depreciation of the manufacturing equipment, assuming no change in the estimated life or residual value. Show computations.

Date	Assets	=	Liabilities	+	Stockholders' Equity

2. Give the adjusting entry that should be made at the end of 2010 for depreciation.

COACHED PROBLEMS

LO2, 3   **CP9-1** **Computing Acquisition Cost and Recording Depreciation under Three Alternative Methods**

At the beginning of the year, McCoy Company bought three used machines from Colt, Inc. The machines immediately were overhauled, installed, and started operating. Because the machines were different, each was recorded separately in the accounts.

	Machine A	Machine B	Machine C
Amount paid for asset	$6,600	$25,600	$6,400
Installation costs	300	600	200
Renovation costs prior to use	1,500	400	1,000
Repairs after production began	400	350	325

By the end of the first year, each machine had been operating 8,000 hours.

Required:

1. Compute the cost of each machine. Explain the rationale for capitalizing or expensing the various costs.

2. Give the journal entry to record depreciation expense at the end of year 1, assuming the following:

Machine	Estimates		Depreciation Method
	Life	Residual Value	
A	5 years	$ 500	Straight-line
B	40,000 hours	1,000	Units-of-production
C	5 years	2,000	Double-declining-balance

TIP: Remember that the formula for double-declining-balance uses cost minus accumulated depreciation (not residual value).

CP9-2 Recording and Interpreting the Disposal of Long-Lived Assets   LO5

During 2010, Bhumika Company disposed of two different assets. On January 1, 2010, prior to their disposal, the accounts reflected the following:

Asset	Original Cost	Residual Value	Estimated Life	Accumulated Depreciation (straight line)
Machine A	$76,200	$4,200	15 years	$57,600 (12 years)
Machine B	20,000	3,000	8 years	12,750 (6 years)

The machines were disposed of in the following ways:

a. Machine A: Sold on January 2, 2010, for $8,200 cash.
b. Machine B: On January 2, 2010, this machine suffered irreparable damage from an accident and was removed immediately by a salvage company at no cost.

Required:

1. Give the journal entries related to the disposal of each machine at the beginning of 2010.
   TIP: When no cash is received on disposal, the loss on disposal will equal the book value of the asset at the time of disposal.

2. Explain the accounting rationale for the way that you recorded each disposal.

CP9-3 Analyzing and Recording Long-Lived Asset Transactions with Partial-Year   LO2, 3, 6
Depreciation

Palmer Cook Productions manages and operates two rock bands. The company entered into the following transactions during a recent year.

January 2	Purchased a tour bus for $80,000 by paying $20,000 cash and signing a $60,000 note.
January 8	The bus was painted with the logos of the two bands at a cost of $350, on account.
January 30	Wrote a check for the amount owed on account for the work completed on January 8.

February 1	Purchased new speakers and amplifiers and wrote a check for the full $12,000 cost.
February 8	Paid $250 cash to tune up the tour bus.
March 1	Paid $20,000 cash and signed a $190,000 note to purchase a small office building and land. An appraisal indicated that the building and land contributed equally to the total price.
March 31	Paid $90,000 cash to acquire the goodwill and certain tangible assets of Kris' Myth, Inc. The fair values of the tangible assets acquired were: $20,000 for band equipment and $60,000 for recording equipment.

Required:

1. Analyze the accounting equation effects and record journal entries for each of the transactions.
   TIP: Goodwill is recorded as the excess of the purchase price over the fair value of individual assets.

2. For the tangible and intangible assets acquired in the preceding transactions, determine the amount of depreciation and amortization that Palmer Cook Productions should report for the quarter ended March 31. For convenience, the equipment and vehicle are depreciated the same way, using the straight-line method with a useful life of five years and no residual value. The building is depreciated using the double-declining-balance method, with a 10-year useful life and residual value of $20,000.
   TIP: Calculate depreciation from the acquisition date to the end of the quarter.

3. Prepare a journal entry to record the depreciation calculated in requirement 3.

4. What advice would you offer the company in anticipation of switching to IFRS in the future?
   TIP: Consider whether the vehicle and different types of equipment should be grouped together.

GROUP A PROBLEMS

LO2, 3

www.mhhe.com/phillips3e

PA9-1 **Computing Acquisition Cost and Recording Depreciation under Three Alternative Methods**

At the beginning of the year, Chemical Control Corporation bought three used machines from Radial Compression Incorporated. The machines immediately were overhauled, installed, and started operating. Because the machines were different, each was recorded separately in the accounts.

	Machine A	Machine B	Machine C
Cost of the asset	$10,000	$31,500	$22,000
Installation costs	1,600	2,100	800
Renovation costs prior to use	600	1,400	1,600
Repairs after production began	500	400	700

By the end of the first year, each machine had been operating 7,000 hours.

Required:

1. Compute the cost of each machine. Explain the rationale for capitalizing or expensing the various costs.

2. Give the journal entry to record depreciation expense at the end of year 1, assuming the following:

	Estimates		
Machine	Life	Residual Value	Depreciation Method
A	4 years	$1,000	Straight-line
B	33,000 hours	2,000	Units-of-production
C	5 years	1,400	Double-declining-balance

PA9-2 Recording and Interpreting the Disposal of Long-Lived Assets   LO5

During 2010, Ly Company disposed of two different assets. On January 1, 2010, prior to their disposal, the accounts reflected the following:

Asset	Original Cost	Residual Value	Estimated Life	Accumulated Depreciation (straight line)
Machine A	$24,000	$2,000	5 years	$17,600 (4 years)
Machine B	59,200	3,200	14 years	48,000 (12 years)

The machines were disposed of in the following ways:

a. Machine A: Sold on January 1, 2010, for $5,750 cash.
b. Machine B: On January 1, 2010, this machine suffered irreparable damage from an accident and was removed immediately by a salvage company at no cost.

Required:

1. Give the journal entries related to the disposal of each machine at the beginning of 2010.
2. Explain the accounting rationale for the way that you recorded each disposal.

PA9-3 Analyzing and Recording Long-Lived Asset Transactions   LO2, 3, 6
with Partial-Year Depreciation

Casting Crown Construction entered into the following transactions during a recent year.

January 2	Purchased a bulldozer for $200,000 by paying $20,000 cash and signing a $180,000 note.
January 3	Replaced the steel tracks on the bulldozer at a cost of $20,000, purchased on account.
January 30	Wrote a check for the amount owed on account for the work completed on January 3.
February 1	Replaced the seat on the bulldozer and wrote a check for the full $600 cost.
March 1	Paid $2,400 cash for the rights to use computer software for a two-year period.

Required:

1. Analyze the accounting equation effects and record journal entries for each of the transactions.
2. For the tangible and intangible assets acquired in the preceding transactions, determine the amount of depreciation and amortization that Casting Crown Construction should report for the quarter ended March 31. The equipment is depreciated using the double-declining-balance method with a useful life of five years and $40,000 residual value.
3. Prepare a journal entry to record the depreciation calculated in requirement 2.
4. What advice would you offer the company in anticipation of switching to IFRS in the future?

PA9-4 Recording Transactions and Adjustments for Tangible and Intangible Assets   LO1, 2, 3, 4, 5, 6

The following transactions and adjusting entries were completed by a paper-packaging company called Gravure Graphics International. The company uses straight-line depreciation for trucks and other vehicles, double-declining-balance depreciation for buildings, and straight-line amortization for patents.

January 2, 2009	Paid $95,000 cash to purchase storage shed components.
January 3, 2009	Paid $5,000 cash to have the storage shed erected. The storage shed has an estimated life of 10 years, and a residual value of $10,000.
April 1, 2009	Paid $38,000 cash to purchase a pickup truck for use in the business. The truck has an estimated useful life of five years, and a residual value of $8,000.
May 13, 2009	Paid $250 cash for repairs to the pickup truck.
July 1, 2009	Paid $20,000 cash to purchase patent rights on a new paper bag manufacturing process. The patent is estimated to have a remaining useful life of five years.

December 31, 2009	Recorded depreciation and amortization on the pickup truck, storage shed, and patent.
June 30, 2010	Sold the pickup truck for $33,000 cash. (Record the depreciation on the truck prior to recording its disposal.)
December 31, 2010	Recorded depreciation on the storage shed. Determined that the patent was impaired and wrote off its remaining book value (i.e., wrote down the book value to zero).

Required:

Give the journal entries required on each of the above dates.

GROUP B PROBLEMS

LO2, 3   **PB9-1 Computing Acquisition Cost and Recording Depreciation under Three Alternative Methods**

At the beginning of the year, Oakmont Company bought three used machines from American Manufacturing, Inc. The machines immediately were overhauled, installed, and started operating. Because the machines were different, each was recorded separately in the accounts.

	Machine A	Machine B	Machine C
Amount paid for asset	$19,600	$10,100	$9,800
Installation costs	300	500	200
Renovation costs prior to use	100	300	600
Repairs after production began	220	900	480

By the end of the first year, each machine had been operating 4,000 hours.

Required:

1. Compute the cost of each machine. Explain the rationale for capitalizing or expensing the various costs.
2. Give the journal entry to record depreciation expense at the end of year 1, assuming the following:

Machine	Estimates Life	Residual Value	Depreciation Method
A	7 years	$1,100	Straight-line
B	40,000 hours	900	Units-of-production
C	4 years	2,000	Double-declining-balance

LO5   **PB9-2 Recording and Interpreting the Disposal of Long-Lived Assets**

During 2010, Rayon Corporation disposed of two different assets. On January 1, 2010, prior to their disposal, the accounts reflected the following:

Asset	Original Cost	Residual Value	Estimated Life	Accumulated Depreciation (straight line)
Machine A	$60,000	$11,000	7 years	$28,000 (4 years)
Machine B	14,200	1,925	5 years	7,365 (3 years)

The machines were disposed of in the following ways:

a. Machine A: Sold on January 2, 2010, for $33,500 cash.
b. Machine B: On January 2, 2010, this machine suffered irreparable damage from an accident and was removed immediately by a salvage company at no cost.

Required:

1. Give the journal entries related to the disposal of each machine at the beginning of 2010.
2. Explain the accounting rationale for the way that you recorded each disposal.

PB9-3 Analyzing and Recording Long-Lived Asset Transactions with Partial-Year Depreciation   LO2, 3, 6

Randy's Restaurant Company (RRC) entered into the following transactions during a recent year.

April 1	Purchased a new food locker for $5,000 by paying $1,000 cash and signing a $4,000 note.
April 2	Installed an air conditioning system in the food locker at a cost of $3,000, purchased on account.
April 30	Wrote a check for the amount owed on account for the work completed on April 2.
May 1	A local carpentry company repaired the restaurant's front door, for which RRC wrote a check for the full $120 cost.
June 1	Paid $9,120 cash for the rights to use the name and store concept created by a different restaurant that has been successful in the region. For the next four years, RRC will operate under the Mullet Restaurant name, with the slogan "business customers in the front, and partiers in the back."

Required:

1. Analyze the accounting equation effects and record journal entries for each of the transactions.
2. For the tangible and intangible assets acquired in the preceding transactions, determine the amount of depreciation and amortization that Randy's Restaurant Company should report for the quarter ended June 30. For convenience, the food locker and air-conditioning system are depreciated as a group using the straight-line method with a useful life of five years and no residual value.
3. Prepare a journal entry to record the depreciation calculated in requirement 2.
4. What advice would you offer the company in anticipation of switching to IFRS in the future?

PB9-4 Recording Transactions and Adjustments for Tangible and Intangible Assets   LO1, 2, 3, 4, 5, 6

The following transactions and adjusting entries were completed by a local delivery company called Super Swift. The company uses straight-line depreciation for delivery vehicles, double-declining-balance depreciation for buildings, and straight-line amortization for franchise rights.

January 2, 2010	Paid $75,000 cash to purchase a small warehouse building near the airport. The building has an estimated life of 20 years, and a residual value of $15,000.
July 1, 2010	Paid $40,000 cash to purchase a delivery van. The van has an estimated useful life of five years, and a residual value of $8,000.
October 2, 2010	Paid $400 cash to paint a small office in the warehouse building.
October 13, 2010	Paid $150 cash to get the oil changed in the delivery van.
December 1, 2010	Paid $60,000 cash to UPS to begin operating Super Swift business as a franchise using the name The UPS Store. This franchise right expires in five years.
December 31, 2010	Recorded depreciation and amortization on the delivery van, warehouse building, and franchise right.
June 30, 2011	Sold the warehouse building for $64,000 cash. (Record the depreciation on the building prior to recording its disposal.)
December 31, 2011	Recorded depreciation on the delivery van and amortization on the franchise right. Determined that the franchise right was not impaired in value.

Required:

Give the journal entries required on each of the above dates.

COMPREHENSIVE PROBLEM

LO2, 3   C9-1 Accounting for Operating Activities (Including Depreciation) and Preparing Financial Statements (Chapters 4, 8, and 9)

Grid Iron Prep Inc. (GIPI) is a service business incorporated in January 2010 to provide personal training for athletes aspiring to play college football. The following transactions occurred during the year ended December 31, 2010.

- a. GIPI issued stock in exchange for $90,000 cash.
- b. GIPI purchased a gymnasium building and gym equipment at the beginning of the year for $50,000, 80% of which related to the gymnasium and 20% to the equipment.
- c. GIPI paid $250 cash to have the gym equipment refurbished before it could be used.
- d. GIPI collected $36,000 cash in training fees during the year, of which $2,000 were customer deposits to be earned in 2010.
- e. GIPI paid $23,000 of wages and $7,000 in utilities.
- f. GIPI provided $3,000 in training during the final month of the year and expected collection in 2011.
- g. GIPI will depreciate the gymnasium building using the double-declining-balance method over 20 years. Gym equipment will be depreciated using the straight-line method, with an estimated residual value of $2,250 at the end of its four-year useful life.
- h. GIPI received a bill for $350 of advertising done during December. The bill has not been paid or recorded.
- i. GIPI will record an estimated 5 percent of its Accounts Receivable as not collectible.
- j. GIPI's income tax rate is 30%. Assume depreciation for tax is the same amount as depreciation for financial reporting purposes.

Required:

1. Prepare journal entries to record the transactions and adjustments listed in (a)–(j).
2. Prepare GIPI's annual income statement, statement of retained earnings, and classified balance sheet.

SKILLS DEVELOPMENT CASES

LO2, 3, 6, 7

S9-1 Finding Financial Information

Refer to the financial statements of The Home Depot in Appendix A at the end of this book, or download the annual report from the *Cases* section of the text's Web site at www.mhhe.com/phillips3e.

Required:

1. What method of depreciation does the company use?
2. What is the amount of Accumulated Depreciation at February 1, 2009? What percentage is this of the total cost of property and equipment?
3. For depreciation purposes, what is the range of estimated useful lives for the buildings?
4. What amount of Depreciation and Amortization Expense was reported for the year ended February 1, 2009? What percentage of net sales is it?
5. What is the fixed asset turnover ratio for the current year?
6. For each of the preceding questions, where did you locate the information?

LO2, 3, 6, 7, 8

Lowe's

S9-2 Comparing Financial Information

Refer to the financial statements of The Home Depot in Appendix A and Lowe's in Appendix B at the end of this book, or download the annual reports from the *Cases* section of the text's Web site at www.mhhe.com/phillips3e.

Required:

1. What method of depreciation does Lowe's use?
2. Refer to Note 4 in Lowe's annual report. What amount of Accumulated Depreciation did Lowe's report at January 30, 2009? What percentage is this of the total cost of property and equipment? Is this a larger (or smaller) percentage of the total cost of property and equipment than for The Home Depot (in S9-1)? What does it suggest to you about the length of time the assets have been depreciated?

3. Lowe's estimated useful life of buildings is shorter than that estimated by The Home Depot. How will this affect the fixed asset turnover ratios of the two companies?

4. What amount of Depreciation Expense was reported on Lowe's income statement for the year ended January 30, 2009? What percentage of net sales is it? Compare this percentage to that of The Home Depot and describe what this implies about the two companies' operations.

5. What is Lowe's fixed asset turnover ratio for the current year? Compare this ratio to that of The Home Depot and describe what it implies about the operations of the two companies.

S9-3 Internet-Based Team Research: Examining an Annual Report   LO1, 3, 6, 7

As a team, select an industry to analyze. Using your Web browser, each team member should access the annual report or 10-K for one publicly traded company in the industry, with each member selecting a different company. (See S1-3 in Chapter 1 for a description of possible resources for these tasks.)

Required:

1. On an individual basis, each team member should write a short report that incorporates the following:
   a. Describe the depreciation methods used.
   b. Compute the percentage of fixed asset cost that has been depreciated. What does this imply about the length of time the assets have been depreciated?
   c. Compute the fixed asset turnover ratios for the current and prior years. What does this tell you about the efficiency of the company's asset use?
   d. Describe the kinds of intangible assets, if any, that the company reports on the balance sheet.
2. Then, as a team, write a short report comparing and contrasting your companies using these attributes. Discuss any patterns across the companies that you as a team observe. Provide potential explanations for any differences discovered.

S9-4 Ethical Decision Making: A Real-Life Example   LO2, 7

Assume you work as a staff member in a large accounting department for a multinational public company. Your job requires you to review documents relating to the company's equipment purchases. Upon verifying that purchases are properly approved, you prepare journal entries to record the equipment purchases in the accounting system. Typically, you handle equipment purchases costing $100,000 or less.

This morning, you were contacted by the executive assistant to the chief financial officer (CFO). She says that the CFO has asked to see you immediately in his office. Although your boss's boss has attended a few meetings where the CFO was present, you have never met the CFO during your three years with the company. Needless to say, you are anxious about the meeting.

Upon entering the CFO's office, you are warmly greeted with a smile and friendly handshake. The CFO compliments you on the great work that you've been doing for the company. You soon feel a little more comfortable, particularly when the CFO mentions that he has a special project for you. He states that he and the CEO have negotiated significant new arrangements with the company's equipment suppliers, which require the company to make advance payments for equipment to be purchased in the future. The CFO says that, for various reasons that he didn't want to discuss, he will be processing the payments through the operating division of the company rather than the equipment accounting group. Given that the payments will be made through the operating division, they will initially be classified as operating expenses of the company. He indicates that clearly these advance payments for property and equipment should be recorded as assets, so he will be contacting you at the end of every quarter to make an adjusting journal entry to capitalize the amounts inappropriately classified as operating expenses. He advises you that a new account, called Prepaid Equipment, has been established for this purpose. He quickly wraps up the meeting by telling you that it is important that you not talk about the special project with anyone. You assume he doesn't want others to become jealous of your new important responsibility.

A few weeks later, at the end of the first quarter, you receive a voicemail from the CFO stating, "The adjustment that we discussed is $771,000,000 for this quarter." Before deleting the message, you replay it to make sure you heard it right. Your company generates over $8 billion in revenues and incurs $6 billion in operating expenses every quarter, but you've never made a journal entry for that much money. So, just to be sure there's not a mistake, you send an e-mail to the CFO confirming the amount. He phones you back immediately to abruptly inform you, "There's no mistake. That's the number." Feeling embarrassed that you may have annoyed the CFO, you quietly make the adjusting journal entry.

For each of the remaining three quarters in that year and for the first quarter in the following year, you continue to make these end-of-quarter adjustments. The "magic number," as the CFO liked to call it, was $560,000,000 for Q2, $742,745,000 for Q3, $941,000,000 for Q4, and

$818,204,000 for Q1 of the following year. During this time, you've had several meetings and lunches with the CFO where he provides you the magic number, sometimes supported with nothing more than a Post-it note with the number written on it. He frequently compliments you on your good work and promises that you'll soon be in line for a big promotion.

Despite the CFO's compliments and promises, you are growing increasingly uncomfortable with the journal entries that you've been making. Typically, whenever an ordinary equipment purchase involves an advance payment, the purchase is completed a few weeks later. At that time, the amount of the advance is removed from an Equipment Deposit account and transferred to the appropriate equipment account. This hasn't been the case with the CFO's special project. Instead, the Prepaid Equipment account has continued to grow, now standing at over $3.8 billion. There's been no discussion about how or when this balance will be reduced, and no depreciation has been recorded for it.

Just as you begin to reflect on the effect the adjustments have had on your company's fixed assets, operating expenses, and operating income, you receive a call from the vice president for internal audit. She needs to talk with you this afternoon about "a peculiar trend in the company's fixed asset turnover ratio and some suspicious journal entries that you've been making."

Required:

1. Complete the following table to determine what the company's accounting records would have looked like had you not made the journal entries as part of the CFO's special project. Comment on how the decision to capitalize amounts, which were initially recorded as operating expenses, has affected the level of income from operations in each quarter.

(amounts in millions of U.S. dollars)	Q1 Year 1 (March 31)		Q2 Year 1 (June 30)		Q3 Year 1 (September 30)		Q4 Year 1 (December 31)		Q1 Year 2 (March 31)	
	With the Entries	Without the Entries	With the Entries	Without the Entries	With the Entries	Without the Entries	With the Entries	Without the Entries	With the Entries	Without the Entries
Property and Equipment, Net	$38,614	$	$35,982	$	$38,151	$	$38,809	$	$39,155	$
Sales Revenues	8,825	8,825	8,910	8,910	8,966	8,966	8,478	8,478	8,120	8,120
Operating Expenses	7,628		8,526		7,786		7,725		7,277	
Income from Operations	1,197		384		1,180		753		843	

2. Using the publicly reported numbers (which include the special journal entries that you recorded), compute the fixed asset turnover ratio (rounded to two decimal places) for the periods ended Q2–Q4 of year 1 and Q1 of year 2. What does the trend in this ratio suggest to you? Is this consistent with the changes in operating income reported by the company?

3. Before your meeting with the vice president for internal audit, you think about the above computations and the variety of peculiar circumstances surrounding the "special project" for the CFO. What in particular might have raised your suspicion about the real nature of your work?

4. Your meeting with internal audit was short and unpleasant. The vice president indicated that she had discussed her findings with the CFO before meeting with you. The CFO claimed that he too had noticed the peculiar trend in the fixed assets turnover ratio, but that he hadn't had a chance to investigate it further. He urged internal audit to get to the bottom of things, suggesting that perhaps someone might be making unapproved journal entries. Internal audit had identified you as the source of the journal entries and had been unable to find any documents that approved or substantiated the entries. She ended the meeting by advising you to find a good lawyer. Given your current circumstances, describe how you would have acted earlier had you been able to foresee where it might lead you.

5. In the real case on which this one is based, the internal auditors agonized over the question of whether they had actually uncovered a fraud or whether they were jumping to the wrong conclusion. *The Wall Street Journal* mentioned this on October 30, 2002, by stating, "it was clear . . . that their findings would be devastating for the company. They worried about whether their revelations would result in layoffs. Plus, they feared that they would somehow end up being blamed for the mess." Beyond the personal consequences mentioned in this quote, describe other potential ways in which the findings of the internal auditors would likely be devastating for the publicly traded company and those associated with it.

Epilogue: This case is based on a fraud committed at WorldCom (now owned by Verizon). The case draws its numbers, the nature of the unsupported journal entries, and the CFO's role in carrying out the fraud from a report issued by WorldCom's bankruptcy examiner. Year 1 in this case was actually 2001 and year 2 was 2002. This case excludes other fraudulent activities that contributed to WorldCom's $11 billion fraud. The 63-year-old CEO was sentenced to 25 years in prison for planning and executing the biggest fraud in the history of American business. The CFO, who cooperated in the investigation of the CEO, was sentenced to five years in prison.

WorldCom
Verizon

S9-5 Ethical Decision Making: A Mini-Case

LO3

Assume you are one of three members of the accounting staff working for a small, private company. At the beginning of this year, the company expanded into a new industry by acquiring equipment that will be used to make several new lines of products. The owner and general manager of the company has indicated that, as one of the conditions for providing financing for the new equipment, the company's bank will receive a copy of the company's annual financial statements. Another condition of the loan is that the company's total assets cannot fall below $250,000. Violation of this condition gives the bank the option to demand immediate repayment of the loan. Before making the adjustment for this year's depreciation, the company's total assets are reported at $255,000. The owner has asked you to take a look at the facts regarding the new equipment and "work with the numbers to make sure everything stays onside with the bank."

A depreciation method has not yet been adopted for the new equipment. Equipment used in other parts of the company is depreciated using the double-declining-balance method. The cost of the new equipment was $35,000 and the manager estimates it will be worth "at least $7,000" at the end of its four-year useful life. Because the products made with the new equipment are only beginning to catch on with consumers, the company used the equipment to produce just 4,000 units this year. It is expected that, over all four years of its useful life, the new equipment will make a total of 28,000 units.

Required:

1. Calculate the depreciation that would be reported this year under each of the three methods shown in this chapter. Which of the methods would meet the owner's objective?

2. Evaluate whether it is ethical to recommend that the company use the method identified in requirement 1. What two parties are most directly affected by this recommendation? How would each party benefit from or be harmed by the recommendation? Does the recommendation violate any laws or applicable rules? Are there any other factors that you would consider before making a recommendation?

S9-6 Critical Thinking: Analyzing the Effects of Depreciation Policies on Income

LO3, 5, 8

As an aspiring financial analyst, you have applied to a major Wall Street firm for a summer job. To screen potential applicants, the firm provides you a short case study and asks you to evaluate the financial success of two hypothetical companies that started operations on January 1, 2009. Both companies operate in the same industry, use very similar assets, and have very similar customer bases. Among the additional information provided about the companies are the following comparative income statements.

	Fast Corporation		Slow Corporation	
	2010	2009	2010	2009
Net Sales	$60,000	$60,000	$60,000	$60,000
Cost of Goods Sold	20,000	20,000	20,000	20,000
Gross Profit	40,000	40,000	40,000	40,000
Selling, General, and Administrative Expenses	19,000	19,000	19,000	19,000
Depreciation Expense	3,555	10,667	5,000	5,000
Gains (Losses) on Disposal	2,222	—	(2,000)	—
Income from Operations	$19,667	$10,333	$14,000	$16,000

Required:

Prepare an analysis of the two companies with the goal of determining which company is better managed. If you could request two additional pieces of information from these companies' financial statements, describe specifically what they would be and explain how they would help you to make a decision.

LO3   **S9-7 Preparing Depreciation Schedules for Straight-Line and Double-Declining-Balance**

www.mhhe.com/phillips3e

To make some extra money, you've started preparing templates of business forms and schedules for others to download from the Internet (for a small fee). After relevant information is entered into each template, it automatically performs calculations using formulas you have entered into the template. For the depreciation template, you decide to produce two worksheets—one that calculates depreciation and book value under the straight-line method and another that calculates these amounts using the double-declining-balance method. The templates perform straightforward calculations of depreciation and book value, when given the cost of an asset, its estimated useful life, and its estimated residual value. These particular templates won't handle disposals or changes in estimates—you plan to create a deluxe version for those functions. To illustrate that your templates actually work, you enter the information used to produce the depreciation schedules shown in Exhibit 9.6, with Cedar Fair and Six Flags as examples.

Although you're confident you can use appropriate formulas in the spreadsheet to create a template for the straight-line method, you're a little uncertain about how to make the double-declining-balance method work. As usual, you e-mail your friend Owen for advice. Here's what he said:

From:	Owentheaccountant@yahoo.com
To:	Helpme@hotmail.com
Cc:	
Subject:	Excel Help

I wish I'd thought of charging money for showing how to do ordinary accounting activities. You'd have made me rich by now. ☺ Here's how to set up your worksheets. Begin by creating an "input values" section. This section will allow someone to enter the asset cost, residual value, and estimated life in an area removed from the actual depreciation schedule. You don't want someone accidentally entering amounts over formulas that you've entered into the schedule.

The cells from the input values section will be referenced by other cells in the depreciation schedule. You will want to enter formulas in the cells for the first year row, and then copy and paste them to rows for the other years. When doing this, you will need to use what is called an "absolute reference," which means that the cell reference does not change when one row is copied and pasted to a different row. Unlike an ordinary cell reference that has a format of A1, an absolute reference has the format of $A$1, which prevents the spreadsheet from changing either the column (A) or row (1) when copying the cell to other cells. You may find this useful when preparing both the straight-line and double-declining-balance schedules.

To create the depreciation schedules, use five columns labeled: (1) year, (2) beginning of year accumulated depreciation, (3) depreciation, (4) end of year accumulated depreciation, and (5) end of year book value.

Cell D8: =IF((C8+(($C$3-C8)*2/$C$5))>$C$3-$C$4,F7-$C$4,($C$3-C8)*2/$C$5)

	A	B	C	D	E	F
2		Input Values				
3		Cost	$ 15,500			
4		RV	$ 1,500			
5		Life	$ 7			
6						
7		Year	BOY-AD	Depn	EOY-AD	EOY-BV
8		1	0	$4,429	$4,429	$11,071
9		2	4,429	$3,163	$7,592	$7,908
10		3	7,592	$2,259	$9,851	$5,649
11		4	9,851	$1,614	$11,465	$4,035
12		5	11,465	$1,153	$12,618	$2,882
13		6	12,618	$823	$13,441	$2,059
14		7	13,441	$559	$14,000	$1,500

straight-line   double-declining

The double-declining-balance template will be the trickiest to create because you need to be concerned that the book value is not depreciated below the residual value in the last year of the asset's life. To force the template to automatically watch for this, you will need to use the IF function. I have included a screenshot of a template I created, using the IF function to properly calculate depreciation for all years of the asset's life. Notice the formula shown in the formula bar at the top.

Required:

Create the spreadsheet templates to calculate depreciation and book value using the straight-line and double-declining-balance methods. Demonstrate that the template works by reproducing the schedules in Exhibit 9.6.

TIP: To switch between displaying cell formulas and their values, press CTRL and ~ (tilde) at the same time. Also, use Excel's help feature to obtain further information about the IF function.

CONTINUING CASE

CC9 Accounting for the Use and Disposal of Long-Lived Assets   LO3, 5

Nicole's Getaway Spa (NGS) purchased a hydrotherapy tub system to add to the wellness programs at NGS. The machine was purchased at the beginning of 2011 at a cost of $5,000. The estimated useful life was five years, and the residual value was $500. Assume that the estimated productive life of the machine is 15,000 hours. Expected annual production was: year 1, 4,100 hours; year 2, 2,500 hours; year 3, 3,400 hours; year 4, 1,800 hours; and year 5, 3,200 hours.

Required:

1. Complete a depreciation schedule for each of the alternative methods.
    a. Straight-line.
    b. Units-of-production.
    c. Double-declining-balance.
2. Assume NGS sold the hydrotherapy tub system for $2,100 at the end of year 3. Prepare the journal entry to account for the disposal of this asset under the three different methods.
3. The following amounts were forecast for the year ended December 31, 2013: Sales Revenues $42,000; Cost of Goods Sold $33,000; Other Operating Expenses $4,000; and Interest Expense $800. Create an income statement for the year ended December 31, 2013 (end of year three) for each of the different depreciation methods, ending at Income before Income Tax Expense. (Don't forget to include a loss or gain on disposal for each method.)

CHAPTER 10

Reporting and Interpreting Liabilities

YOUR LEARNING OBJECTIVES

Understand the business

LO1   Explain the role of liabilities in financing a business.

Study the accounting methods

LO2   Explain how to account for common types of current liabilities.

LO3   Analyze and record bond liability transactions.

LO4   Describe how to account for contingent liabilities.

Evaluate the results

LO5   Calculate and interpret the quick ratio and the times interest earned ratio.

Review the chapter

THAT WAS
THEN

Previous chapters focused on items related to the assets section of the balance sheet.

Lecture Presentation-LP10
www.mhhe.com/phillips3e

FOCUS COMPANY: General Mills

www.generalmills.com

GENERAL MILLS

They've turned in the reports, and they're just waiting to hear their letter grade. They're expecting an A and would be devastated if it's a B. Sounds like some high-achieving students, right? It could be. But it's actually the Jolly Green Giant, Lucky the Leprechaun, Poppin' Fresh, and their corporate bosses at General Mills. That's right. This magically delicious company and all its characters receive a letter grade just like you and your friends. Their grading process differs a bit from yours, because their grade is assigned by credit rating agencies like Standard & Poor's, Fitch, and Moody's, indicating the company's ability to pay its liabilities on a timely basis. Another difference is that their grades can range from AAA to D. The AAA rating is given to companies in rock-solid financial condition, and the D goes to those likely to pay less than half of what they owe. In general, anything above BB is considered a good to high-quality credit rating, which is what General Mills typically earns.

In this chapter, you will learn about the accounting procedures and financial ratios used to report and interpret liabilities, and how they influence credit ratings. Although we focus on corporate reporting and analyses, this chapter also can help you to understand the kind of information others use to evaluate your own personal credit rating.

THIS IS
NOW

This chapter focuses on items related to the liabilities section of the balance sheet.

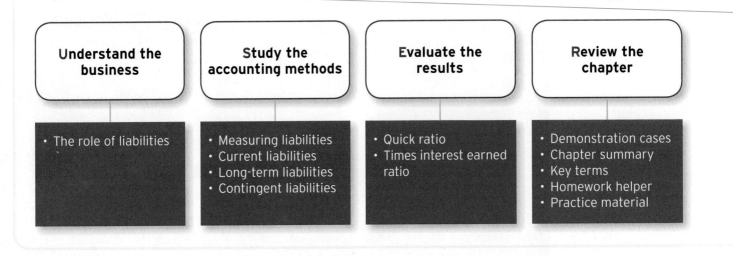

Understand the business	Study the accounting methods	Evaluate the results	Review the chapter
• The role of liabilities	• Measuring liabilities • Current liabilities • Long-term liabilities • Contingent liabilities	• Quick ratio • Times interest earned ratio	• Demonstration cases • Chapter summary • Key terms • Homework helper • Practice material

Understand the Business

THE ROLE OF LIABILITIES

Learning Objective 1
Explain the role of liabilities in financing a business.

Liabilities play a significant role in financing most business activities. Liabilities are created when a company buys goods and services on credit, obtains short-term loans to cover gaps in cash flows, and issues long-term debt to obtain money for expanding into new regions and markets. The importance of liabilities became most apparent during the financial crisis of 2008–2009. Soon after banks restricted their lending activities and suppliers tightened their credit terms, companies began to fail. Circuit City, for example, filed for bankruptcy protection just one week after its suppliers required the company to pay cash on delivery (C.O.D.). Less than two months later, when the company discovered it could not obtain alternative sources of financing, Circuit City terminated its 30,000 employees and shut down the business. Rap rocker Toby Mac said it best: "You never know what you got til it's gone."

General Mills survived the financial crisis because it was able to pay suppliers on time and its BBB+ credit rating helped it obtain short-term financing as needed. Also, just prior to the crisis, the company had arranged long-term debt financing that will not come due until the year 2037. With these critical sources of financing in place, the company was able to ride out the rough economic times.

To help financial statement users know when liabilities must be repaid, companies prepare a classified balance sheet, as shown in Exhibit 10.1. In Chapter 2, you learned that a classified balance sheet reports current liabilities separate from other liabilities. Technically, **current liabilities** are defined as short-term obligations that will be paid with current assets within the company's current operating cycle or within one year of the balance sheet date, whichever is longer. Practically, this definition can be simplified as liabilities that are due within one year (because most companies have operating cycles that are shorter than a year). This means that, as shown in Exhibit 10.1, General Mills will have to pay nearly $4.9 billion in the year following its 2008 fiscal year. An additional $7.7 billion will need to be paid in the longer term. Although these long-term obligations rarely get a separate subheading of their own, people often refer to them as noncurrent or long-term liabilities.

YOU SHOULD KNOW

Current liabilities: Short-term obligations that will be paid with current assets within the current operating cycle or one year, whichever is longer.

EXHIBIT 10.1	Excerpt from General Mills's Balance Sheet

(in millions)	2008	2007
Liabilities		
Current Liabilities		
Accounts Payable	$ 937	$ 778
Accrued Liabilities	1,268	2,079
Notes Payable	2,209	1,254
Current Portion of Long-term Debt	442	1,734
Total Current Liabilities	4,856	5,845
Long-term Debt	4,349	3,218
Deferred Income Taxes	1,455	1,433
Other Liabilities	1,924	1,230
Total Liabilities	12,584	11,726

Study the Accounting Methods

MEASURING LIABILITIES

As Exhibit 10.1 illustrates, General Mills owed various types of liabilities at the end of its 2008 fiscal year. In this section, we will describe each of these liabilities and how they are accounted for. In general, the amount reported for each liability is the result of three factors:

> **Learning Objective 2**
> Explain how to account for common types of current liabilities.

1. **The initial amount of the liability.** Initially, the company records each liability at its cash equivalent, which is the amount of cash a creditor would accept to settle the liability immediately after a transaction or event creates the liability.

2. **Additional amounts owed to the creditor.** The company increases liabilities whenever additional obligations arise, by purchasing goods and services or incurring interest charges over time.

3. **Payments or services provided to the creditor.** The company decreases liabilities whenever the company makes a payment or provides services to the creditor.

Notice that a liability is first recorded at a cash-equivalent amount, which excludes interest charges. **Interest arises only when time passes, so no interest is recorded on the day the company purchases an item on account or the day the company receives a loan.** This practice makes sense because if you borrowed $10 from a friend and paid it back a split-second later, you wouldn't have to pay interest.

CURRENT LIABILITIES

Let's look more closely at each current liability listed in Exhibit 10.1.

Accounts Payable

You've used this account in previous chapters, so we'll keep this discussion short. Accounts Payable is increased (credited) when a company receives goods or services on credit, and it is decreased (debited) when the company pays on its account. Accounts Payable is interest free unless it becomes overdue.

Accrued Liabilities

Chapter 4 showed how to use an adjusting journal entry at the end of the accounting period to record increases in both Wages Expense (debit) and Wages Payable (credit) when a company had incurred but not yet paid that period's wages. Similar adjustments

EXHIBIT 10.2	Examples of Accrued Liabilities	GENERAL MILLS

(in millions)	2008
Accrued Advertising	$ 446
Accrued Payroll	364
Accrued Taxes	95
Accrued Interest	147
Other	216
Total Accrued Liabilities	$1,268

YOU SHOULD KNOW

Accrued liabilities: Liabilities for expenses that have been incurred but not paid at the end of the accounting period.

were made for interest incurred but not paid, and income taxes incurred but not paid. Because these adjustments are called *accruals*, the liabilities (Wages Payable, Interest Payable, etc.) are generally referred to as *accrued liabilities*. **Accrued liabilities** relate to various unpaid expenses, including advertising, electricity, corporate income tax, interest, payroll tax, and warranties. General Mills itemizes its nearly $1.3 billion of Accrued Liabilities in a note to its financial statements, similar to Exhibit 10.2.

Accrued Payroll   In addition to Wages Payable, companies record liabilities for other aspects of payroll. Two significant payroll liabilities relate to payroll deductions and employer payroll taxes.

Payroll Deductions   Payroll deductions are amounts subtracted from employees' gross earnings to determine their net pay. **Gross earnings** are computed by multiplying the time worked by the pay rate promised by the employer (40 hours × $15 per hour = $600 gross earnings). From these gross earnings, certain **payroll deductions** are subtracted, for items such as income tax, FICA tax, and charitable donations. The tear-away portion of the paycheck shown in Exhibit 10.3 illustrates payroll deductions totaling $116.80. **Net pay** equals gross earnings less payroll deductions ($483.20 = $600.00 − $116.80).

You might think your employer keeps the deductions from your gross earnings, but that's not true. Your employer is obligated to remit those deductions to another organization or government agency on your behalf. As Exhibit 10.3 shows, **payroll deductions create liabilities for your employer.**

Payroll deductions are either required by law or voluntarily requested by employees. The law requires that employers deduct federal income tax (and possibly state, county, and city income tax) from each employee's gross earnings. The law also requires, through the Federal Insurance Contributions Act, that each employee support Medicare and Social Security

EXHIBIT 10.3	Accounting for Gross Earnings, Payroll Deductions, and Net Pay

GENERAL MILLS, INC.
Number One General Mills Blvd
Minneapolis, MN, 55426

Check No.   282

Date: January 7, 2010

PAY   FOUR HUNDRED EIGHTY-THREE AND 20/100   **DOLLARS**

To the Order of   ADAM PALMER
444 Forest Glen Circle
Murfreesboro, TN 37128

$483.20

For illustration only.

- - - - - - - - - - - DETACH AND RETAIN THIS PORTION FOR YOUR RECORDS - - - - - - - - - - -

GROSS EARNINGS			PAYROLL DEDUCTIONS				NET PAY
HOURS	HOURLY RATE	GROSS	FED. INC. TAX	FICA TAX	OTHER	TOTAL	NET PAY
40.00	$15.00	$600.00	$58.00	$48.80	$10.00	$116.80	483.20

Wages Expense   Current Liabilities   Cash Payment

through employee payroll deductions called **FICA taxes.** In 2009, employers were required to deduct 1.45 percent from each employee's earnings for Medicare and 6.2 percent (on earnings up to $106,800) for Social Security. Employers use these same methods to account for any other payroll deductions (including voluntary deductions for charitable donations, parking, union dues, retirement savings, etc.). The employer classifies payroll deductions as *current* liabilities because they must be paid no more than one month after the payroll date.

To illustrate how to record these items, let's assume (for simplicity) that General Mills has 1,000 employees just like the one in Exhibit 10.3. The accounting equation effects and journal entry would be as follows:

① Analyze

Assets	=	Liabilities		+	Stockholders' Equity
Cash −483,200		Withheld Income Tax Payable	+58,000		Wages Expense (+E) −600,000
		FICA Payable	+48,800		
		United Way Payable	+10,000		

② Record

dr Wages Expense (+E, −SE)	600,000	
cr Withheld Income Tax Payable (+L)		58,000
cr FICA Payable (+L)		48,800
cr United Way Payable (+L)		10,000
cr Cash (−A)		483,200

Employer Payroll Taxes   Beyond paying employees and remitting payroll deductions, employers have other responsibilities that lead to substantial additional labor costs. According to the U.S. Department of Labor, **in 2008, nearly 30 percent of labor costs were for costs other than salaries and wages.** In the remainder of this section, we consider two employer payroll taxes: FICA and unemployment taxes.

Like their employees, all employers are required to pay FICA taxes. The required contribution is 100% of total employee contributions (called a "matching" contribution). In addition, employers are required by the Federal Unemployment Tax Act (FUTA) and State Unemployment Tax Act (SUTA) to pay unemployment taxes. The rates for these taxes vary by industry, state, and employer history but can be substantial, as shown in the pie chart.

To illustrate how these payroll expenses affect the accounting records, let's assume General Mills was required to contribute $48,800 for FICA, $750 for federal unemployment tax, and $4,000 for state unemployment tax. These payroll taxes are extra costs the employer incurs beyond the costs of salaries and wages, so they are reported as an additional operating expense on the income statement. Until they have been paid, the liabilities for these taxes are recorded in current liability accounts, as follows:

Average hourly payroll costs

70%
10%
8%
8%
4%

- ■ Wages and salaries
- ■ Vacation, bonuses, etc.
- ■ Payroll taxes (FICA, FUTA, SUTA)
- ■ Health/life insurance
- ■ Retirement, savings

① Analyze

Assets	=	Liabilities		+	Stockholders' Equity
		FICA Payable	+48,800		Payroll Tax
		Federal Unemployment Tax Payable	+750		Expense (+E) −53,550
		State Unemployment Tax Payable	+4,000		

② Record

dr Payroll Tax Expense (+E, −SE)	53,550	
cr FICA Payable (+L)...		48,800
cr Federal Unemployment Tax Payable (+L).....................		750
cr State Unemployment Tax Payable (+L)........................		4,000

When the employer pays these taxes (and the payroll deductions shown at the top of this page), it decreases the liability accounts (with debits) and decreases its Cash account (with a credit).

The adjusting journal entry to accrue income taxes was presented in Chapter 4 on pages 158–159.

Accrued Income Taxes Corporations pay taxes not only on payroll but also on income they earn, just like you. The corporate tax return, which the IRS calls a Form 1120, is similar to the company's income statement, except that it calculates *taxable* income by subtracting tax-allowed expenses from revenues. This taxable income is then multiplied by a tax rate, which for most large corporations is about 35 percent. Corporate income taxes are due two and a half months after year-end, although most corporations are required to pay advance installments during the year.

Notes Payable

The next liability reported by General Mills in Exhibit 10.1 is Notes Payable. This liability represents the amount the company owes to others as a result of issuing promissory notes. It is the flipside of the notes receivable transactions that were explained in Chapter 8.

Four key events occur with any note payable: (1) establishing the note, (2) accruing interest incurred but not paid, (3) recording interest paid, and (4) recording principal paid. Financial effects are recorded for each of these four events. As an example, assume that on November 1, 2009, General Mills borrowed $100,000 cash on a one-year note that required General Mills to pay 6 percent interest and $100,000 principal, both on October 31, 2010.

1. **Establish the note payable.** The $100,000 loan that created the note payable has the following accounting equation effects, which General Mills would record using the following journal entry:

① Analyze

	Assets	=	Liabilities	+ Stockholders' Equity
Cash	+100,000	Note Payable	+100,000	

② Record

dr Cash (+A)...	100,000	
cr Note Payable (+L)..		100,000

2. **Accrue interest incurred but not paid.** Interest occurs as time passes. It is not owed the day the note is established, but rather it accumulates as each day passes. Under accrual accounting, interest must be recorded as it is incurred over time. The timeline in Exhibit 10.4 shows how General Mills should account for the interest incurred on the note over its one-year term. In reality, General Mills would record an adjustment each month or quarter for interest incurred in that period, but for simplicity, we have assumed it occurs only once, at the end of the year. From the date the note was established (November 1, 2009) to the end of the year (December 31, 2009), General Mills incurred two months of interest expense.

The amount of interest to record for two months is computed using the interest formula, as follows:

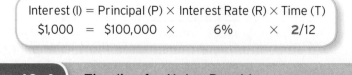

$$\text{Interest (I)} = \text{Principal (P)} \times \text{Interest Rate (R)} \times \text{Time (T)}$$
$$\$1,000 = \$100,000 \times 6\% \times 2/12$$

This example shows how to account for the note from the borrower's perspective. The same example is presented on pages 369–371 from the lender's perspective.

EXHIBIT 10.4 **Timeline for Notes Payable**

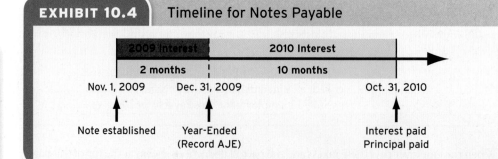

The effect of this adjustment, along with the adjusting journal entry to record the $1,000 of interest expense that is payable on December 31, 2009, is as follows:

1 Analyze

Assets	=	Liabilities	+	Stockholders' Equity
		Interest Payable +1,000		Interest Expense (+E) −1,000

2 Record

dr Interest Expense (+E, −SE)   1,000
   cr Interest Payable (+L)   1,000

3. **Record interest paid.** The timeline in Exhibit 10.4 indicates that on October 31, 2010, General Mills pays both the principal and the interest. Although the company is likely to pay both amounts with a single check, it is instructive to consider these payments separately. In this step, we analyze and record the interest payment. The interest payment is $6,000 (= $100,000 × 6% × 12/12). As shown in the following timeline, this $6,000 interest payment includes the $1,000 that was accrued as Interest Payable at December 31, 2009, plus $5,000 interest expense incurred during the 10 months between January 1 and October 31, 2010.

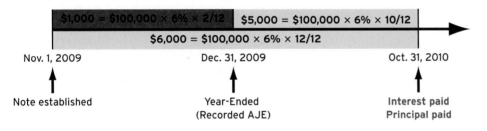

$1,000 = $100,000 × 6% × 2/12 $5,000 = $100,000 × 6% × 10/12

$6,000 = $100,000 × 6% × 12/12

Nov. 1, 2009	Dec. 31, 2009	Oct. 31, 2010
Note established	Year-Ended (Recorded AJE)	Interest paid Principal paid

The $6,000 interest payment is analyzed and recorded as follows:

1 Analyze

Assets	=	Liabilities	+	Stockholders' Equity
Cash −6,000		Interest Payable −1,000		Interest Expense (+E) −5,000

2 Record

dr Interest Payable (−L)   1,000
dr Interest Expense (+E, −SE)   5,000
   cr Cash (−A)   6,000

4. **Record principal paid.** The accounting equation effects and journal entry to record the $100,000 principal payment on October 31, 2010, are as follows.

1 Analyze

Assets	=	Liabilities	+ Stockholders' Equity
Cash −100,000		Note Payable −100,000	

2 Record

dr Note Payable (−L)   100,000
   cr Cash (−A)   100,000

Solution to Self-Study Practice

	Assets	=	Liabilities	+	Stockholders' Equity
Dec. 1	Cash +12,000		Note Payable +12,000		
Dec. 31			Interest Payable +50		Interest Expense (+E) −50 ($50 = $12,000 × 5% × 1/12)

How's it going?   Self-Study Practice

Assume Starbucks issues a 5 percent, $12,000 note on December 1. How would this transaction and the month-end interest adjustment affect the accounting equation?

1 Analyze

	Assets	=	Liabilities	+	Stockholders' Equity
December 1	Cash +12,000		+12000		
December 31			+50		+50 × E −50 SE

After you have finished, check your answers with the solution in the margin.

Current Portion of Long-term Debt

Remember when you were in grade 9 and it seemed as if it would be forever before you'd graduate from high school? At that time, graduation was something that would happen in the long term. Later, when you became a senior, graduation became a current event—one that was less than a year away. A similar progression occurs with long-term debt.

If a company borrows money with the promise to repay it in two years, the loan is classified as a long-term debt. The company reports only the accrued interest on the loan as a current liability in that year's balance sheet. After a year has passed, however, the loan becomes a current liability (just as your graduation became a current event when you reached your senior year). When that happens, the borrower must report the loan in the Current Liabilities section of the balance sheet. Rather than create a different account for this, accountants simply remove the amount of principal to be repaid in the upcoming year from the total long-term debt and report it as a current liability, Current Portion of Long-term Debt.

The final line item in the Current Liabilities section of the General Mills balance sheet provides an example (see Exhibit 10.1, page 453). Notice that in 2008, General Mills reported a current liability for the $442 million of long-term debt that was expected to be paid in 2009. This reclassification of long-term debt into current liabilities is needed so that the balance sheet accurately reports the dollar amount of existing liabilities that will be paid in the upcoming year.

Solution to Self-Study Practice

	At December 31	
	2010	2009
Current Liabilities		
Current Portion of Long-term Debt	$2,000	$1,000
Long-term Debt	7,000	9,000
Total Liabilities	$9,000	$10,000

How's it going?   Self-Study Practice

Assume that on December 31, 2009, Blockbuster borrowed $10,000, a portion of which is to be repaid each year on November 30. Specifically, Blockbuster will make the following principal payments: $1,000 in 2010, $2,000 in 2011, $3,000 in 2012, and $4,000 in 2013. Show how this loan will be reported on the balance sheets on December 31, 2010 and 2009, assuming that principal payments will be made when required.

	At December 31	
	2010	2009
Current Liabilities:		
Current Portion of Long-term Debt	$2,000	$1,000
Long-term Debt	7,000	9,000
Total Liabilities	$9,000	$10,000

After you have finished, check your answers with the solution in the margin.

Spotlight On THE WORLD

Violated Loan Covenants

Most lending agreements allow the lender to revise loan terms (e.g., interest rates, due dates) if a borrower's financial condition deteriorates significantly. These escape hatches, called **loan covenants**, are often based on financial statement ratios such as those you have learned in earlier chapters. Under GAAP, if a company violates loan covenants on long-term debt but renegotiates the loan prior to releasing its financial statements, the debt remains classified as long term. Under IFRS, the company must reclassify that long-term debt as a current liability.

Additional Current Liabilities

Because of the nature of General Mills's business, the company does not have some current liabilities that are common to other companies. This section covers two such liabilities.

Sales Tax Payable   Retail companies are required to charge a sales tax in all but five states (Alaska, Delaware, Montana, New Hampshire, and Oregon). Retailers collect sales tax from consumers at the time of sale and forward it to the state government. Just like payroll taxes, the tax collected by the company is reported as a current liability until it is forwarded to the government. Sales tax is not an expense to the retailer because it is simply collected and passed on to the government. So if Best Buy sold a television for $1,000 cash plus 5 percent sales tax, Best Buy would collect $1,050 cash, earn $1,000 in sales revenue, and recognize a $50 liability (= 5% × $1,000) for the sales tax collected. The financial effects of this sale are analyzed below and would be recorded with the journal entry that follows.

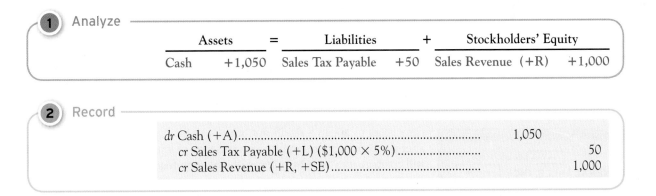

1 Analyze

	Assets	=	Liabilities	+	Stockholders' Equity	
Cash	+1,050		Sales Tax Payable +50		Sales Revenue (+R)	+1,000

2 Record

dr Cash (+A)...	1,050	
cr Sales Tax Payable (+L) ($1,000 × 5%).........................		50
cr Sales Revenue (+R, +SE)...		1,000

When Best Buy pays the sales tax to the state government, its accountants will reduce Sales Tax Payable (with a debit) and reduce Cash (with a credit).

Unearned Revenue   In Chapter 4, you learned that some companies receive cash before they provide goods or services to customers. Airlines are paid in advance of providing flights, retailers receive cash for gift cards that can be used for future purchases of goods and services, and other companies receive money for subscriptions before the subscriptions begin. IAC, the owner of Ticketmaster and Match.com, provides a great example of this type of liability. Consider what happens when IAC receives cash for subscription services to Match.com. Because IAC receives cash before providing subscription services, accountants initially record a liability in the account Unearned Revenue. As the subscription services are provided, IAC reduces this liability and reports the earned subscription fees as revenue.

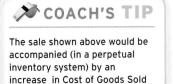

COACH'S TIP

The sale shown above would be accompanied (in a perpetual inventory system) by an increase in Cost of Goods Sold (recorded with a debit) and a decrease in Inventory (recorded with a credit).

Assume, for example, that on October 1 IAC received cash for a three-month subscription paid in advance at a rate of $10 per month (or $30 in total). The financial effects and related journal entries occur in two stages:

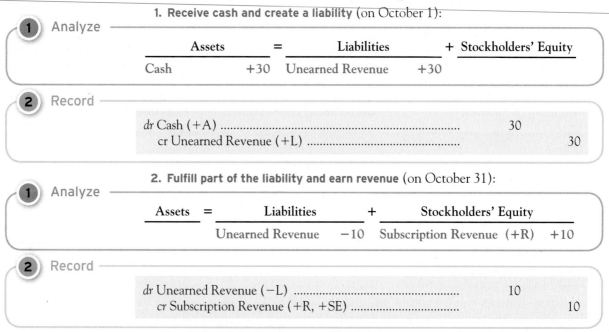

1. Receive cash and create a liability (on October 1):

① Analyze

Assets	=	Liabilities	+	Stockholders' Equity
Cash +30		Unearned Revenue +30		

② Record

dr Cash (+A) 30
   cr Unearned Revenue (+L) 30

2. Fulfill part of the liability and earn revenue (on October 31):

① Analyze

Assets	=	Liabilities	+	Stockholders' Equity
		Unearned Revenue −10		Subscription Revenue (+R) +10

② Record

dr Unearned Revenue (−L) 10
   cr Subscription Revenue (+R, +SE) 10

As each month passes, IAC would make another adjustment like the one in step 2 to show that it has continued to fulfill its obligation and to earn subscription revenues. Don't let the tiny amounts in our examples fool you. Unearned revenues can be huge. For IAC, they totaled over $50 million at December 31, 2008. That equaled the company's Accounts Payable.

LONG-TERM LIABILITIES

Learning Objective 3
Analyze and record bond liability transactions.

Like most companies, General Mills reports several long-term liabilities on its balance sheet (see Exhibit 10.1). Common long-term liabilities include long-term notes payable, deferred income taxes, and bonds payable. Long-term notes payable are accounted for in the same way as the short-term notes payable discussed in the previous section (except, of course, long-term notes are on the books for more than one year). Liabilities for deferred income taxes were explained in Chapter 9; they represent the amount of tax put off (deferred) by taking tax deductions on the corporation's income tax return that are greater than the expenses subtracted on the income statement. This section focuses on accounting for bonds that a company issues to obtain a significant amount of financing. Later, in Chapter 11, after you become more familiar with this form of long-term debt financing, we will compare it to alternative forms of long-term (equity) financing.

Bonds

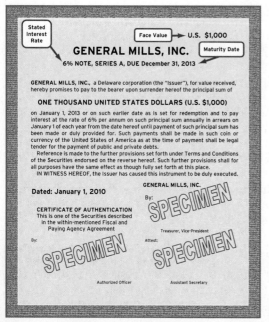

Occasionally, governments and very large companies such as General Mills need to borrow more money than any single lender can provide. In 2008, for example, General Mills needed to borrow $750 million. Because issuing a promissory note for such a large amount of money was impractical, the company instead issued bonds. A sample bond certificate is shown here.

Bonds are financial instruments that outline the future payments a company promises to make in exchange for receiving a sum of money now. From the company's perspective, the bond is a long-term liability. From the bondholder's perspective, the bond is an investment. After a company issues the bonds, they can be traded on established exchanges such as the New York Bond Exchange. The ability to sell a bond on the bond exchange is attractive to bondholders because it provides them liquidity, or the ability to receive cash for the bond whenever they wish to sell it. In return for this liquidity, bondholders will accept a lower interest rate, which benefits the company by lowering the cost of long-term borrowing.

As you can see from the sample bond certificate, three key elements of a bond are (1) the **maturity date**, (2) the amount payable on the maturity date (often called the **face value**), and (3) the **stated interest rate**. In most cases, the face value of each bond is $1,000. The stated interest rate is always expressed as an annual rate although many bonds require interest payments every six months (that is, semiannually). Each interest payment is computed by multiplying the face value times the stated interest rate (times the fraction of the year if payments are made semiannually). As you will see later, for good economic reasons, bonds may be priced at amounts above or below their face value. A bond's price does not affect the amount of each interest payment, however. For example, a 6 percent bond with a face value of $1,000 will always pay interest of $60 cash each year ($= \$1,000 \times 6\% \times 12/12$).

YOU SHOULD KNOW

Maturity date: The date on which the bonds are due to be paid in full. **Face value:** The payment made when the bond matures. **Stated interest rate:** The rate stated on the face of the bond, which is used to compute interest payments.

Bond Pricing

Neither the company nor its financial advisers determine the price at which bonds issue. Instead, investors in the market establish the issue price. The bond **issue price** represents the amount that investors are willing to pay on the issue date in exchange for the cash payments that the company promises to make over the life of the bond. Theoretically, this amount is based on a mathematical calculation called a **present value**, which is described in Appendix C at the end of this book. (Case C on page C.10 shows the calculations for the $1,000, 6 percent General Mills bond.)

YOU SHOULD KNOW

Issue price: The amount of money that a lender pays (and the company receives) when a bond is issued. **Present value:** A mathematical calculation that determines the amount that one or more payments made in the future are worth today.

Spotlight On FINANCIAL REPORTING

Bond Prices in the Financial Press

The financial press (and Yahoo!Finance bond center) reports bond prices each day based on transactions that occurred on the bond exchange. The following is typical of the information you will find:

Company Name	Maturity	INTEREST RATE Stated	INTEREST RATE Market	Bond Price
Costco	2017	5.50	4.10	109.25
General Mills	2013	6.00	4.00	107.26
Home Depot	2036	5.90	7.40	82.05

GENERAL MILLS

This listing reports that the General Mills bond will mature in the year 2013. It has a stated interest rate of 6.00 percent. At the present time, 4.00 is the typical interest rate earned by investors in the market when buying similar bonds. Because the 6.00 percent stated interest rate is better than the 4.00 percent market interest rate, investors are attracted to the General Mills bond. Consequently, they are willing to pay a higher bond price. The bond price is quoted as a percentage of face value. In this case, investors were willing to pay 107.26 percent of face value, or $1,072.60 for each $1,000 bond (107.26% $\times$ $1,000).

When companies issue bonds, they try to offer competitive interest rates. However, changing economic events can cause the bond's stated interest rate to differ from the market's desired rate, which affects the bond's attractiveness and its price. After a bond has issued, the market's desired rate fluctuates frequently, which affects the bond price in the market. **Daily fluctuations in the market do not directly involve the company, so they are not considered transactions of the company.** Except in rare situations, the company continues to account for its bonds using the bond price and interest rates that existed when the bonds were first issued to the market.

Accounting for a Bond Issue

Although it is useful to know how to determine bond prices, it is not a necessary step in accounting for a bond issue. Instead, what we need to know is the amount of cash the company receives from investors when the bonds are first issued. This amount may be equal to the face value, above the face value, or below the face value. A bond issued for more than its face value is said to have been issued at a **premium**, which is the excess of the bond's issue price over its face value. A bond issued for less than its face value is said to have been issued at a **discount**, which is the amount by which the issue price falls

YOU SHOULD KNOW

Premium: The amount by which a bond's issue price exceeds its face value. **Discount:** The amount by which a bond's issue price is less than its face value.

short of the bond's face value. The following sections show how to account for bonds issued at face value, at a premium, and at a discount.

Bonds Issued at Face Value   If General Mills receives $100,000 cash in exchange for issuing 100 bonds at their $1,000 face value, the transaction will be analyzed and recorded as follows:

1 Analyze

Assets	=	Liabilities	+ Stockholders' Equity
Cash +100,000		Bonds Payable +100,000	

2 Record

dr Cash (+A)	100,000
cr Bonds Payable (+L)	100,000

Bonds Issued at a Premium   If General Mills issues 100 of its $1,000 bonds at a price of 107.26, the company will receive $107,260 (= 100 × $1,000 × 1.0726). Thus, the cash-equivalent amount is $107,260, which represents the total liability on that date. The company's accountants will distinguish the $100,000 total face value from the $7,260 premium by recording them in separate liability accounts as follows:

1 Analyze

Assets	=	Liabilities	+ Stockholders' Equity
Cash +107,260		Bonds Payable +100,000	
		Premium on	
		Bonds Payable +7,260	

2 Record

dr Cash (+A)	107,260
cr Bonds Payable (+L)	100,000
cr Premium on Bonds Payable (+L)	7,260

Why would bondholders be willing to pay a premium? For the same reason that you might pay a premium to acquire tickets to a great concert or a big game. If a bond offers something attractive, such as a high interest rate, bondholders may be willing to pay a premium to acquire it.

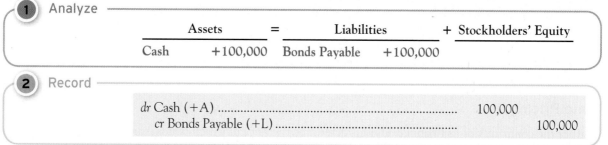

COACH'S TIP

Although Discount on Bonds Payable is recorded with a debit, it is not an asset—it is a contra-liability.

Bonds Issued at a Discount   If General Mills receives $93,376 for bonds with a total face value of $100,000, the cash-equivalent amount is $93,376, which represents the liability on that date. As shown in the analyze step below, the discount of $6,624 (= $100,000 − $93,376) offsets the face value, so accountants will record it in a contra-liability account, which we identify using "xL." A contra-liability account is recorded as a debit as in the journal entry that follows:

1 Analyze

Assets	=	Liabilities	+ Stockholders' Equity
Cash +93,376		Bonds Payable +100,000	
		Discount on Bonds	
		Payable (+xL) −6,624	

2 Record

dr Cash (+A)	93,376
dr Discount on Bonds Payable (+xL, −L)	6,624
cr Bonds Payable (+L)	100,000

Why would companies be willing to discount a bond? The answer is that they must if they want to issue it. If a bond promises to pay interest at a stated rate of 6 percent when other financial instruments offer 8 percent, no one will be willing to buy the bond unless the company discounts it. The discount reduces the initial bond price for investors without changing the interest payments and the face value paid to them. In effect, a discount increases the return that bondholders earn on their initial investment.

To illustrate, suppose you could buy a $1,000 bond that pays a stated interest rate of 6 percent and matures in one year. After one year, you would receive the stated interest of $60 ($1,000 × 6% × 12/12) plus the face value of $1,000. If you had paid $1,000 for the bond, you would receive 1.06 times as much as your initial investment [($60 + $1,000) ÷ $1,000]—a return of 6 percent. If instead the bond price were discounted $19, so that you paid only $981 for it, you would receive 1.08 times as much as your initial investment [($60 + $1,000) ÷ $981 = 1.08]— a return of 8 percent. This percentage represents both the bondholder's rate of return and the company's cost of borrowing. It is commonly referred to as the **market interest rate.**

> **YOU SHOULD KNOW**
>
> **Market interest rate:** The rate of interest that investors demand from a bond.

Reporting Bond Liabilities   The total face value of a bond plus any related premium or minus any related discount is reported in the liabilities section of the balance sheet as in Exhibit 10.5 for our three examples. The amount of the bond liability, after taking into account any premium or discount, is referred to as the bond's **carrying value.**

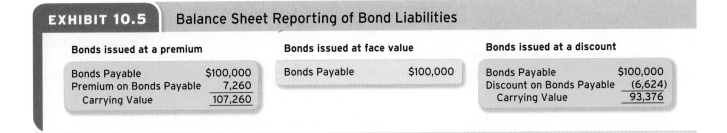

EXHIBIT 10.5   Balance Sheet Reporting of Bond Liabilities

Bonds issued at a premium

Bonds Payable	$100,000
Premium on Bonds Payable	7,260
Carrying Value	107,260

Bonds issued at face value

| Bonds Payable | $100,000 |

Bonds issued at a discount

Bonds Payable	$100,000
Discount on Bonds Payable	(6,624)
Carrying Value	93,376

To determine whether a bond will be issued at a premium, at face value, or at a discount, you need consider only the relationship between the stated interest rate on the bond (what the bond pays in cash) and the market interest rate (the return that bondholders require). Exhibit 10.6 illustrates this relationship.

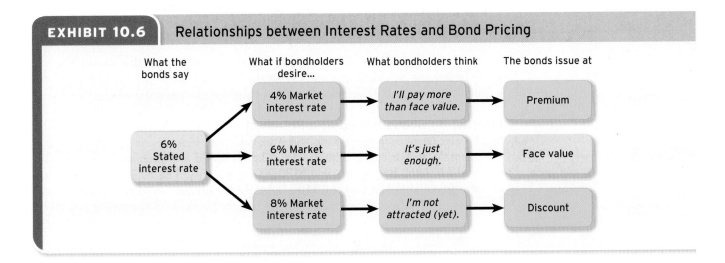

EXHIBIT 10.6   Relationships between Interest Rates and Bond Pricing

Solution to Self-Study Practice
1. Face value.
2. Discount—investors not attracted to lower stated rate.
3. Premium—investors pay more than face value.

Before you continue, try the following Self-Study Practice.

💡 How's it going?   Self-Study Practice

For each of the following independent situations, indicate whether the bonds were issued at a premium, at a discount, or at face value.

1. Stated interest rate = 7% and market interest rate = 7%. *face value*
2. Stated interest rate = 5% and market interest rate = 6%. *discount*
3. Bond issue price = $10,100 and bond face value = $10,000. *premium*

After you have finished, check your answers with the solution in the margin.

Interest Expense

As time passes, a bond liability creates interest expense, which is matched to each period in which the liability is owed. Because interest expense arises from a financing decision (not an operating decision), it is reported below the Income from Operations line on the company's income statement.

Interest on Bonds Issued at Face Value

When bonds have issued at face value, the process of calculating and recording interest on bonds is similar to that for Notes Payable. Assume, for example, that General Mills issues bonds on January 1, 2010, at their total face value of $100,000. If the bonds carry an annual stated interest rate of 6 percent payable in cash on December 31 of each year, General Mills will need to accrue an expense and liability for interest at the end of each accounting period. For the first month ended January 31, 2010, assuming no previous accrual of interest, General Mills would record interest of $500 ($= \$100,000 \times 6\% \times 1/12$) as follows:

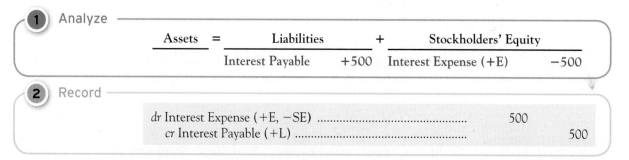

1 Analyze

Assets	=	Liabilities	+	Stockholders' Equity	
		Interest Payable +500		Interest Expense (+E)	−500

2 Record

dr Interest Expense (+E, −SE)	500	
cr Interest Payable (+L)		500

General Mills would continue to calculate and record interest this way each month until the interest is paid. When interest is paid, Interest Payable will be decreased (with a debit) and Cash will be decreased (with a credit) for the amount paid.

Interest on Bonds Issued at a Premium

When bonds issue at a premium, the bond issuer receives more cash on the issue date than it repays on the maturity date. For example, in our earlier illustration of bonds issued at a premium, General Mills received $107,260 but repays only $100,000 at maturity. The $7,260 difference isn't exactly "free money" for General Mills but rather is a reduction in the company's cost of borrowing. For accounting purposes, we match the reduced borrowing cost to the periods in which interest expense is recorded. This process, called **bond amortization**, makes the Interest Expense smaller than the actual interest payment and, at the same time, causes the balance in Premium on Bonds Payable to decline each period, as shown in Exhibit 10.7.

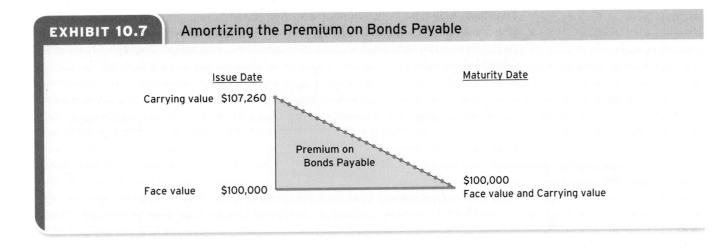

EXHIBIT 10.7 Amortizing the Premium on Bonds Payable

Procedures for amortizing bond premiums are explained in chapter supplements 10A, 10B, and 10C. If you have been assigned any of these supplements, don't jump to them yet. We'll tell you later when it's best to read them.

Interest on Bonds Issued at a Discount   When bonds issue at a discount, the bond issuer receives less cash on the issue date than it repays on the maturity date. For example, in our earlier illustration of bonds issued at a discount, General Mills receives $93,376 on the issue date but repays $100,000 at maturity. For General Mills, the $6,624 discount represents an extra cost of borrowing, over and above each interest payment. For accounting purposes, we match the extra borrowing cost to the periods in which interest is recorded. This amortization causes the Interest Expense to be more than the interest payment and, at the same time, causes Discount on Bonds Payable to decrease each period. As the Discount on Bonds Payable decreases, the carrying value of the liability increases until it reaches $100,000 on the maturity date, as illustrated in Exhibit 10.8.

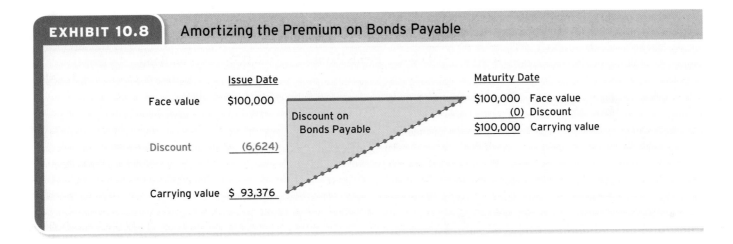

EXHIBIT 10.8 Amortizing the Premium on Bonds Payable

At this point, you should read any of the assigned chapter supplements, then come back here and continue with the remainder of this section. The chapter supplements begin on page 470.

Bond Retirements

Retirement at Maturity
Most bonds are retired (paid off) at maturity. If interest has been fully paid at the time of maturity, the only remaining account to settle will be Bonds Payable. Assuming the General Mills bonds in our example were retired with a payment equal to their $100,000 face value, the transaction would be analyzed and recorded as follows:

1 Analyze

	Assets	=	Liabilities	+ Stockholders' Equity
Cash	−100,000	Bonds Payable	−100,000	

2 Record

dr Bonds Payable (−L)	100,000	
cr Cash (−A)		100,000

Early Retirement
Rather than wait until the maturity date to retire bonds, a company may retire them early. Companies with a lot of cash often retire their bonds early to reduce future interest expense. Even companies that do not have extra cash may decide to retire their bonds early if interest rates have fallen since issuing the original bonds. In this case, the companies would issue new bonds at the lower interest rate and use the money they receive from the new bonds to retire the old ones before maturity. Again, this decision reduces future interest expense, which increases future earnings.

The early retirement of bonds has three financial effects. The company (1) pays cash, (2) eliminates the bond liability, and (3) reports either a gain or a loss. A gain arises if the cash paid to retire the bonds is less than the carrying value of the bond liability. A loss is incurred if the company pays more than the carrying value at the time of retirement.

To illustrate these effects, assume that in 2000, General Mills issued $100,000 of bonds at face value. Ten years later, in 2010, the company retired the bonds early. At the time, the bond price was 103, so General Mills made a payment of $103,000 (= $100,000 × 1.03) to retire the bonds. This transaction would be analyzed and recorded as follows:

1 Analyze

	Assets	=	Liabilities	+	Stockholders' Equity	
Cash	−103,000	Bonds Payable	−100,000		Loss on Bond Retirement (+E)	−3,000

2 Record

dr Bonds Payable (−L)	100,000	
dr Loss on Bond Retirement (+E, −SE)..................	3,000	
cr Cash (−A)....................................		103,000

Notice two features of this example. First, because the bond retirement is a financing decision, the loss would be reported after the Income from Operations line on the income statement. Second, this retirement example does not involve the removal of a bond discount or bond premium account because the bonds were issued at face value. If the bonds had been issued below or above face value, any premium or discount balance that existed at the time of retirement would need to be removed as well.

Types of Bonds

When you first start learning about bonds, it may seem the number of new terms that describe the bonds are limitless. These terms can generally be grouped into two categories: (1) those that describe the type of organization that issued the bonds and (2) those that describe specific features of the bond. In the first category are bonds issued by the U.S. Treasury Department ("treasuries"); municipal organizations such as states, cities, counties, and towns ("munis"); and corporations ("corporates"). In the second category are bonds that are backed by collateral ("secured") or not ("debentures"), that the issuing corporation can call in and exchange for cash ("callable") or convert into shares of its stock ("convertible"), and that mature in a series of installments ("serial bonds") or include no periodic interest payments ("zero-coupon bonds" and "strips"). The basic procedures shown in the previous sections for recording bond liabilities and interest expense apply equally to these various types of bonds.

CONTINGENT LIABILITIES

Contingent liabilities are potential liabilities that arise as a result of past transactions or events, but their ultimate resolution depends (is contingent) on a future event. Contingent liabilities differ from other liabilities discussed in this chapter because their dependence on a future event introduces a great deal of uncertainty. For example, consider the product warranties on watches and computers. These warranties obligate the company to repair defective products for a limited time, but the ultimate cost of those repairs depends on future events including the number of warranty claims, labor rates, and supply costs. Even more uncertainty is introduced when accounting for lawsuits against the company. Some suits may be defended successfully but others may result in huge fines or penalties. Given such uncertainties, accounting rules require the company to evaluate whether it is likely to be found liable and, if so, whether the amount of the liability is estimable (let's just pretend that's a word). As Exhibit 10.9 indicates, if a contingent liability is possible but not probable or its amount cannot be estimated, a liability is not recorded in the accounting records or reported on the balance sheet. Instead, the potential liability and related loss should be described in a note to the financial statements.

> **Learning Objective 4**
> Describe how to account for contingent liabilities.

> **YOU SHOULD KNOW**
>
> **Contingent liabilities:** Potential liabilities that have arisen as a result of a past transaction or event; their ultimate outcome will not be known until a future event occurs or fails to occur.

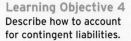

Video 10.1
www.mhhe.com/phillips3e

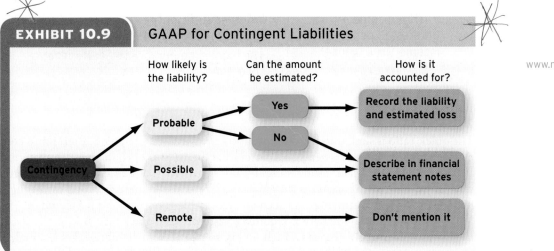

EXHIBIT 10.9 GAAP for Contingent Liabilities

Spotlight On THE WORLD

Just How Certain Are You?

Under GAAP, contingent liabilities (and corresponding losses) are recorded if the estimated loss is probable. Under IFRS, contingent liabilities (and corresponding losses) are recorded if the estimated loss is "more likely than not" to occur. The threshold under IFRS is lower than that under GAAP, which should cause more contingent liabilities to be reported on the balance sheet under IFRS than under GAAP.

Now that you have seen how liabilities are accounted for inside a company, let's consider them again from the outside. How do users judge whether liabilities are likely to be repaid in full?

Evaluate the Results

Learning Objective 5
Calculate and interpret the quick ratio and the times interest earned ratio.

In evaluating a company's ability to pay its liabilities, a good place to start is with the reports credit-rating agencies issue. These agencies do not report on all companies, however, particularly the smaller ones. Even if they did, their reports might not address your specific concerns. So, you need to know how to analyze a set of financial statements in the same way that a credit rater would.

Essentially, you want to assess whether the company has the assets available to pay what it currently owes, and whether the company is likely to generate the resources needed to pay future amounts that will be owed. Two financial ratios are commonly used to make these assessments: the quick ratio and the times interest earned ratio.

Accounting Decision Tools

Name of Measure	Formula	What It Tells You
Quick ratio	$$\frac{\text{(Cash + Short-term Investments + Accounts Receivable, Net)}}{\text{Current Liabilities}}$$	• Whether liquid assets are sufficient to pay current liabilities • The higher the number the better able to quickly pay
Times interest earned ratio	$$\frac{\text{(Net Income + Interest Expense + Income Tax Expense)}}{\text{Interest Expense}}$$	• Whether sufficient resources are generated to cover interest costs • The higher the number the better the coverage

QUICK RATIO

YOU SHOULD KNOW

Quick ratio: The ratio of liquid assets to current liabilities; liquid assets include cash and cash equivalents, short-term investments, and accounts receivable (net of doubtful accounts).

The **quick ratio** is similar to the current ratio introduced in Chapter 2. Both ratios compare a company's current assets to its current liabilities. Rather than consider all current assets, however, the quick ratio focuses on just the assets that can be quickly converted into cash. These liquid assets, as they are called, typically include cash and cash equivalents, short-term investments, and accounts receivable (net of doubtful accounts).

As with all ratios, judgment is required to interpret the quick ratio. Generally speaking, a high quick ratio suggests a high ability to pay current liabilities. For example, a quick ratio greater than 1.0 implies a company could pay all its current liabilities immediately if it were required to. However, lower ratios do not necessarily imply a company will be unable to pay its current liabilities. For example, at the end of its 2008 fiscal year, General Mills reported $661 million of cash and cash equivalents, no short-term investments, and $1,082 million of net accounts receivable. Using these numbers and the $4,856 million in total current liabilities shown in Exhibit 10.1, we can calculate the quick ratio for General Mills as follows:

$$\frac{\text{Cash} + \text{Short-term Investments} + \text{Accounts Receivable, Net}}{\text{Current Liabilities}} = \frac{\$661 + \$0 + \$1{,}082}{\$4{,}856} = 0.359$$

A quick ratio of 0.359 implies that General Mills would be able to pay only 35.9 percent of its current liabilities, if forced to pay them immediately. However, this interpretation overlooks a few important facts. First, not all current liabilities are to be paid immediately. The $2.2 billion of Notes Payable in Exhibit 10.1, for example, may not be payable until late in the following year and, at that time, could be refinanced over even longer periods. Second, General Mills generates nearly $5 million in cash from its operations each day. These huge future cash inflows aren't included in the existing cash balance. Third, the company has arranged a **line of credit**, as discussed in the following spotlight feature.

> **YOU SHOULD KNOW**
>
> **Line of credit:** A prearranged agreement that allows a company to borrow any amount of money at any time, up to a prearranged limit.

Spotlight On FINANCIAL REPORTING

Surviving a Financial Crunch

In difficult economic times, it is imperative for companies to have adequate financing in place. Prior to the economic downturn in 2008, General Mills had established a line of credit that provides up to $3 billion cash on an as-needed basis. Rather than hold extra cash, General Mills uses its line of credit to borrow only when money is needed. Not all companies are able to establish lines of credit, but those that do are able to survive with a quick ratio less than 1.0. To determine whether a company has a line of credit available, be sure to read the company's notes to the financial statements. General Mills reports its line of credit in its long-term debt note.

TIMES INTEREST EARNED RATIO

One way to judge a company's ability to pay interest is to ask whether it has generated enough income to cover its interest expense. The measure that most analysts use for this purpose is the **times interest earned ratio.**

The accounting decision tools feature (on page 468) showed the formula for the times interest earned ratio. It is reproduced after the following paragraph. Notice that in this ratio, interest and income tax expenses are added back into net income. The reason for this is simple: Analysts want to know whether a company generates enough income to cover its interest expense before the costs of financing and taxes. In general, a high times interest earned ratio is viewed more favorably than a low one. A high ratio indicates an extra margin of protection should the company's profitability decline in the future.

> **YOU SHOULD KNOW**
>
> **Times interest earned ratio:** Divides net income before interest and taxes by interest expense to determine the extent to which earnings before taxes and financing costs are sufficient to cover interest incurred on debt.

Using information from a recent income statement reported by General Mills, we can compute the times interest earned ratio as follows.

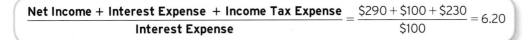

$$\frac{\text{Net Income} + \text{Interest Expense} + \text{Income Tax Expense}}{\text{Interest Expense}} = \frac{\$290 + \$100 + \$230}{\$100} = 6.20$$

This ratio means that General Mills generates $6.20 of income (before the costs of financing and taxes) for each dollar of interest expense. No doubt this ratio is part of the reason that General Mills has earned a favorable credit rating of BBB+.

Every now and then you will see a times interest earned ratio that is less than 1.0 or even negative. When the times interest earned ratio is less than 1.0, a company is not generating enough income to cover its interest expense. Most companies with a negative times interest earned ratio survive only a couple of years before declaring bankruptcy.

SUPPLEMENT 10A: Straight-Line Method of Amortization

YOU SHOULD KNOW

Straight-line method of amortization: Evenly allocates the amount of bond premium or discount over each period of a bond's life to adjust interest expense for differences between its stated interest rate and market interest rate.

Exhibits 10.7 and 10.8 illustrated how a bond premium or discount decreases each year, until it is completely eliminated on the bond's maturity date. This process is called amortizing the bond premium or discount. The **straight-line method of amortization** reduces the premium or discount by an equal amount each period. Because this method results in an equal amount each period, it is easy to apply. However, it distorts the financial results somewhat because it produces an equal Interest Expense each period, even though the bond's carrying value changes each period. For this reason, the straight-line method may be used only when it does not materially differ from the effective-interest method of amortization (presented in Supplement 10B).

Bond Premiums

In our earlier example of bonds issued at a premium, General Mills received $107,260 on the issue date (January 1, 2010) but repays only $100,000 at maturity (December 31, 2013). The $7,260 difference is considered a reduction in the company's borrowing cost over the four-year period the bond is owed. Under the straight-line method, this $7,260 is spread evenly as a reduction in interest expense over the four years ($7,260 ÷ 4 = $1,815 per year). So when General Mills makes its yearly $6,000 cash payment for interest, it will report Interest Expense of only $4,185 ($6,000 − $1,815). The remainder of the $6,000 cash payment is reported as a reduction in the bond liability, as follows:

1 Analyze

Assets	=	Liabilities	+	Stockholders' Equity
Cash −6,000		Premium on		Interest
		Bonds Payable −1,815		Expense (+E) −4,185

2 Record

dr Interest Expense (+E, −SE)	4,185
dr Premium on Bonds Payable (−L)	1,815
cr Cash (−A)	6,000

In effect, the $6,000 payment includes both an interest component ($4,185) and a repayment of the bond liability ($1,815). The same accounting equation effects and journal entry will be recorded each year on December 31 until the bonds mature. The following bond amortization schedule summarizes the journal entry effects each period (on the left) and the updated balance sheet account balances (on the right):

Bond Premium Amortization Schedule: Straight-Line Method

	Journal Entry Components			Balance Sheet Accounts		
	(A)	(B) Amortized Premium	(C) (= A − B) Interest Expense	(D) Bonds Payable	(E) Premium on Bonds Payable	(F) (= D + E) Carrying Value
Period Ended	Cash Paid					
01/01/2010				$100,000	$7,260	$107,260
12/31/2010	$6,000	$1,815	$4,185	100,000	5,445	105,445
12/31/2011	6,000	1,815	4,185	100,000	3,630	103,630
12/31/2012	6,000	1,815	4,185	100,000	1,815	101,815
12/31/2013	6,000	1,815	4,185	100,000	0	100,000

Bond Discounts

A discount arises when the bond issuer receives less cash than the issuer repays at maturity. In effect, a discount increases the company's cost of borrowing, so amortization of the discount causes interest expense to be higher than the interest payment each period. To report this effect, accountants record a decrease in Discount on Bonds Payable and an increase in Interest Expense.

In our earlier example, General Mills received $93,376 for four-year bonds with a total face value of $100,000, implying a discount of $6,624. Using the straight-line method, amortization of the discount in each of the four years that the bonds remain unpaid would be $1,656 (= $6,624 ÷ 4). This amount would be added to the interest to be paid ($6,000) to calculate the amount of Interest Expense ($7,656). The effects would be recorded as follows:

1 Analyze

Assets	=	Liabilities	+	Stockholders' Equity
Cash −6,000		Discount on Bonds Payable (−xL) +1,656		Interest Expense (+E) −7,656

2 Record

dr Interest Expense (+E, −SE) 7,656
dr Discount on Bonds Payable (−xL, +L).............................   1,656
   cr Cash (−A)   6,000

The same accounting equation effects and journal entry would be recorded each year on December 31 until the bonds mature. The following bond amortization schedule summarizes the effects that must be recorded each period (on the left), producing the end-of-year balance sheet account balances (on the right):

Bond Discount Amortization Schedule: Straight-Line Method

| | Journal Entry Components | | | | Balance Sheet Accounts | | |
| | (A) | (B) Amortized Discount | (C) (= A + B) Interest Expense | | (D) Bonds Payable | (E) Discount on Bonds Payable | (F) (= D − E) Carrying Value |
Period Ended	Cash Paid						
01/01/2010					$100,000	$6,624	$ 93,376
12/31/2010	$6,000	$1,656	$7,656		100,000	4,968	95,032
12/31/2011	6,000	1,656	7,656		100,000	3,312	96,688
12/31/2012	6,000	1,656	7,656		100,000	1,656	98,344
12/31/2013	6,000	1,656	7,656		100,000	0	100,000

SUPPLEMENT 10B: Effective-Interest Method of Amortization

The **effective-interest method of amortization** is considered a conceptually superior method of accounting for bonds because it correctly calculates interest expense by multiplying the true cost of borrowing times the amount of money actually owed to investors. The true cost of borrowing is the market interest rate that investors used to determine the bond issue price. The actual amount owed to investors is the carrying value of the bond, which equals the cash received when the bond was issued plus any interest that has been incurred but not yet paid.

To clearly understand the effective-interest method, it helps to see how a bond's issue price depends on the market interest rate. As we mentioned in the chapter, investors in the market decide how much to pay for a bond by using a mathematical calculation called a **present value.** You can read instructions about how to calculate present values in Appendix C at the end of this book, but for now just focus on understanding what a present value is. Present value is the idea that something is worth more if you get it today than if you get it some time in the future. For example, if someone offered to pay you $100,000 today

YOU SHOULD KNOW

Effective-interest method of amortization: Allocates the amount of bond premium or discount over each period of a bond's life in amounts corresponding to the bond's carrying value.

or $100,000 five years from now, you'd be better off taking it today. You could invest the money and earn interest for five years, making it worth more than $100,000. The same idea explains why you could be equally happy with receiving $100,000 in five years or some smaller amount today. To figure out how much this smaller amount is, you just calculate the present value of $100,000. The only pieces of information you need for this calculation are (1) the amounts to be received in the future, (2) the number of months between now and then, and (3) the interest rate you expect to earn during that time.

In the bond context, investors calculate the present value of the amounts received periodically (at the stated interest rate) and at maturity (the face value), using the interest rate that they want to earn. We have summarized this calculation in Exhibit 10B.1 for General Mills's 6 percent, four-year bond. We show three different scenarios, with each one involving different market interest rates but the same 6 percent stated interest rate. The first column calculates the amount of money that investors would be willing to give up if they needed to earn 4 percent on the amount they pay for the bond. The second column calculates the amount investors would pay if they wanted to earn an interest rate of 6 percent. The third column calculates the amount that investors would be willing to pay if they wanted to earn 8 percent on the amount they pay for the bond. (For detailed calculations underlying the amounts in Exhibit 10B.1, see Appendix C at the end of the book.)

EXHIBIT 10B.1	Computing the Present Value of Bond Payments		
	MARKET INTEREST RATES		
	4%	6%	8%
Present value of $100,000 face value (principal) paid four years from now	$ 85,480	$ 79,210	$73,503
Present value of $6,000 (6% stated interest rate) paid once a year for four years	21,780	20,790	19,873
Bond price	**$107,260**	**$100,000**	**$93,376**

Notice that when the bond pays interest at a rate that exactly matches the rate required by investors in the market (6 percent), they are willing to pay face value ($100,000) for it. If the 6 percent interest rate stated on the bond is more than investors require (4 percent), they will pay a premium for the bond (as shown in the first column). If the 6 percent interest promised is less than the market interest rate (8 percent), investors pay less than face value for the bond, resulting in a discounted bond price as indicated in the third column. Let's now look at what happens to a bond premium and discount under the effective-interest amortization method.

Bond Premiums

In our earlier example of a bond premium, General Mills promised to make cash interest payments each year at a stated rate of 6 percent. Investors found this stated interest rate attractive, so the bond issued at a $7,260 premium. When General Mills adds this $7,260 premium to the $100,000 face value, it reports a carrying value of $107,260 (= $100,000 + $7,260) on January 1, 2010. Exhibit 10B.1 indicates that the $107,260 total implies the market interest rate was 4 percent. General Mills uses this market interest rate to calculate its **Interest Expense** on the bond, using a variation of the interest formula. For example, General Mills calculates Interest Expense in the first year ended December 31, 2010, as follows:

$$
\begin{array}{llllll}
2010: & \text{Interest (I)} & = & \text{Principal (P)} & \times \text{Interest Rate (R)} & \times \text{Time (T)} \\
& \text{Interest Expense} & = & \text{Carrying Value} & \times \text{Market Interest Rate} & \times \text{n/12} \\
& \$4{,}290 & = & \$107{,}260 & \times \ 4\% & \times \ 12/12
\end{array}
$$

Use the information *stated* on the *face* of the bond to calculate the Cash interest payment:

Interest (I)	=	Principal (P)	×	Interest Rate (R)	×	Time (T)
Cash Payment	=	Face Value	×	Stated Interest Rate	×	n/12
$6,000	=	$100,000	×	6%	×	12/12

Because the $6,000 cash interest payment exceeds the $4,290 Interest Expense by $1,710 ($6,000 − $4,290 = $1,710), General Mills records a $1,710 reduction in its bond liability. In effect, the $6,000 cash payment includes both an interest component ($4,290) and a partial repayment of the bond liability ($1,710), as analyzed and recorded below:

① Analyze

Assets	=	Liabilities	+	Stockholders' Equity
Cash −6,000		Premium on		Interest
		Bonds Payable −1,710		Expense (+E) −4,290

② Record

dr Interest Expense (+E, −SE)	4,290
dr Premium on Bonds Payable (−L)	1,710
cr Cash (−A)	6,000

Similar calculations and accounting effects occur each period until the bonds mature. The only thing to watch out for is that **the carrying value of the bond liability decreases each year because the cash payment includes a partial repayment of the bond liability.** For example, after the above entry is recorded on December 31, 2010, the Premium on Bonds Payable decreases by $1,710, from $7,260 to $5,550. Thus, the Interest Expense for the second year of the bond (for the year ended December 31, 2011) is:

Premium on Bonds Payable (L)	
	7,260 1/1/2010
12/31/2010 1,710	
	5,550 12/31/2010

2011:	Interest (I)	=	Principal (P)	×	Interest Rate (R)	×	Time (T)
	Interest Expense	=	Carrying Value	×	Market Interest Rate	×	n/12
	$4,222	=	$105,550	×	4%	×	12/12

The following bond amortization schedule summarizes the effects that must be recorded each period (on the left), producing the end-of-year balance sheet account balances (on the right):

Essay question on Test

create this chart

Bond Premium Amortization Schedule: Effective-Interest Method

	Journal Entry Components			Balance Sheet Accounts		
	(A)	(B) Interest Expense	(C) (= A − B) Amortized Premium	(D) Bonds Payable	(E) Premium on Bonds Payable	(F) (= D + E) Carrying Value
Period Ended	Cash Paid					
01/01/2010				$100,000	$7,260	$107,260
12/31/2010	$6,000	$4,290	$1,710	100,000	5,550	105,550
12/31/2011	6,000	4,222	1,778	100,000	3,772	103,772
12/31/2012	6,000	4,151	1,849	100,000	1,923	101,923
12/31/2013	6,000	4,077	1,923	100,000	0	100,000

Bond Discounts

In our earlier example of a bond discount, General Mills promised to make cash interest payments each year at a stated rate of 6 percent. Investors did not find this stated interest rate attractive, so the bond issued at a $6,624 discount. When General Mills subtracts this $6,624 discount from the $100,000 face value, it reports a carrying value of $93,376 (= $100,000 − $6,624) on January 1, 2010. Exhibit 10B.1 indicates that the $93,376 implies the market interest rate was 8 percent. General Mills uses this market interest rate to calculate its Interest Expense on the bond, as we did in the case of a bond premium. The Interest Expense for the first year ended December 31, 2010, is calculated as:

2010 :	**Interest (I)**	=	**Principal (P)**	×	**Interest Rate (R)**	×	**Time (T)**
	Interest Expense	=	Carrying Value	×	Market Interest Rate	×	n/12
	$7,470	=	$93,376	×	8%		× 12/12

Use the information *stated* on the *face* of the bond to calculate the cash interest payment:

	Interest (I)	=	**Principal (P)**	×	**Interest Rate (R)**	×	**Time (T)**
Cash Payment		=	Face Value	×	Stated Interest Rate	×	n/12
$6,000		=	$100,000	×	6%		× 12/12

Because the $7,470 Interest Expense is more than the $6,000 cash paid, General Mills records the $1,470 difference ($7,470 − $6,000 = $1,470) as an increase in its bond liability. As illustrated in Exhibit 10.8 (on page 465), the increase in the bond liability is achieved by decreasing the contra-liability Discount on Bonds Payable. These effects are analyzed and recorded as follows:

1 Analyze

Assets	=	Liabilities	+	Stockholders' Equity
Cash −6,000		Discount on Bonds Payable (−xL) +1,470		Interest Expense (+E) −7,470

2 Record

dr Interest Expense (+E, −SE)	7,470	
cr Discount on Bonds Payable (−xL, +L).........................		1,470
cr Cash (−A)		6,000

Discount on Bonds Payable (xL)	
1/1/2010 6,624	
	1,470 12/31/2010
12/31/2010 5,154	

The T-account presented in the margin shows how the above journal entry reduces Discount on Bonds Payable. A reduction of this contra-liability account increases the carrying value of the long-term liability, as you can see by moving from left to right in Exhibit 10B.2.

EXHIBIT 10B.2 Sample Balance Sheet Reporting of Bond Discount GENERAL MILLS

GENERAL MILLS, INC.
Balance Sheet (excerpt)

	January 1, 2010	December 31, 2010
Long-Term Liabilities		
Bonds Payable	$100,000	$100,000
Discount on Bonds Payable	(6,624)	(5,154)
Carrying Value	93,376	94,846

Let's now consider the interest expense for 2011. As in 2010, the 2011 interest expense is calculated using the market interest rate. However, the carrying value of bonds owed at the end of 2010 increased, as shown in Exhibit 10B.2. Thus, interest expense also will increase in 2011, calculated as follows:

COACH'S TIP

The interest expense for 2011 is greater than that for 2010 because the carrying value was greater in 2011 than in 2010.

2011:

Interest (I)	**=**	**Principal (P)**	**× Interest Rate (R)**	**× Time (T)**
Interest Expense	=	Carrying Value	× Market Interest Rate	× n/12
$7,588	=	$94,846	× 8%	× 12/12

Because the Interest Expense ($7,588) is greater than the cash payment ($6,000), the bond liability is increased (by reducing the contra-liability). This is reflected in the accounting equation and recorded with the journal entry on December 31, 2011, as follows:

1 Analyze

Assets	=	Liabilities	+	Stockholders' Equity
Cash −6,000		Discount on		Interest
		Bonds Payable (−xL) +1,588		Expense (+E) −7,588

2 Record

dr Interest Expense (+E, −SE)	7,588	
cr Discount on Bonds Payable (−xL, +L)..........................		1,588
cr Cash (−A)		6,000

The following bond amortization schedule summarizes the effects that must be recorded each period (on the left), producing the end-of-year balance sheet account balances (on the right):

Bond Discount Amortization Schedule: Effective-Interest Method

	Journal Entry Components			Balance Sheet Accounts		
	(A)	(B) Interest	(C) (= B − A) Amortized	(D) Bonds	(E) Discount on	(F) (= D − E) Carrying
Period Ended	Cash Paid	Expense	Discount	Payable	Bonds Payable	Value
01/01/2010				$100,000	$6,624	$ 93,376
12/31/2010	$6,000	$7,470	$1,470	100,000	5,154	94,846
12/31/2011	6,000	7,588	1,588	100,000	3,566	96,434
12/31/2012	6,000	7,715	1,715	100,000	1,851	98,149
12/31/2013	6,000	7,851	1,851	100,000	0	100,000

SUPPLEMENT 10C: Simplified Effective-Interest Amortization

The approach shown in this supplement presents a simplified explanation of how to account for bond liabilities and interest expense. You should be aware that this approach involves taking a shortcut. While the shortcut will help you to focus on the line items that ultimately are reported on the financial statements, it requires that we ignore a few accounts that are typically used behind the scenes in real-world accounting systems. Be sure to check with your instructor (or course outline) to see whether you are expected to read this supplement.

If you're like most people, you probably have to concentrate really hard when reading about how a *reduction* in a contra-liability account causes an *increase* in the carrying value of a bond. You may even whisper this thought quietly to yourself a few times before it starts making sense. In this section, we present a shortcut when accounting for bonds that will allow you to avoid thinking in "double-negatives" like this. Hopefully it will also help you to stop whispering to yourself when you read.

Accounting for the Bond Issue

The shortcut involves simplifying only one aspect of what you studied earlier in this chapter. Rather than record a discount or premium in a separate account, we combine the discount or premium with the bond's face value in a single account that we will call Bonds Payable, Net. This name is used to remind you that we are focusing on what is ultimately reported in the financial statements rather than what is actually used behind the scenes. The following journal entries demonstrate how the shortcut is applied to bonds issued at a premium, at face value, and at a discount.

	Premium	Face Value	Discount
dr Cash (+A)	107,260	100,000	93,376
cr Bonds Payable, Net (+L)	107,260	100,000	93,376

As you can see, the structure of the journal entry does not vary from one case to the next; only the amount does.

Interest Expense

As time passes, the company incurs Interest Expense on its bond liability. Because the bond liability was recorded in a single account, the interest calculation is the same whether the bond has been issued at a premium or discount. The following version of the interest formula is used to compute Interest Expense.

$$\text{Interest (I)} = \text{Principal (P)} \quad \times \text{Interest Rate (R)} \quad \times \text{Time (T)}$$
$$\text{Interest Expense} = \text{Bonds Payable, Net} \times \text{Market Interest Rate} \times n/12$$

The market interest rate is determined by using present value techniques (discussed in Appendix C) that relate the bond's issue price to the payments promised over the life of the bond.

Bond Premiums

Our bond premium example indicated that General Mills received $107,260 on the issue date, which we would record in Bonds Payable, Net, using the journal entry shown above. The $107,260 issue price implies a 4 percent market interest rate. The bonds promise to pay the 6 percent stated interest rate on their total face value of $100,000. This information is used to compute Interest Expense and the annual cash payment as follows:

$$2010: \quad \text{Interest (I)} = \text{Principal (P)} \quad \times \text{Interest Rate (R)} \quad \times \text{Time (T)}$$
$$\text{Interest Expense} = \text{Bonds Payable, Net} \times \text{Market Interest Rate} \times n/12$$
$$\$4{,}290 = \$107{,}260 \quad \times 4\% \quad \times 12/12$$

$$\text{Interest (I)} = \text{Principal (P)} \times \text{Interest Rate (R)} \quad \times \text{Time (T)}$$
$$\text{Cash Payment} = \text{Face Value} \times \text{Stated Interest Rate} \times n/12$$
$$\$6{,}000 = \$100{,}000 \quad \times 6\% \quad \times 12/12$$

Because the $6,000 cash interest payment exceeds the $4,290 Interest Expense by $1,710 ($6,000 − $4,290 = $1,710), General Mills records a $1,710 reduction in

Bonds Payable, Net. In effect, the $6,000 cash payment includes both an interest component ($4,290) and a partial repayment of the bond liability ($1,710), as analyzed and recorded below:

1 Analyze

Assets	=	Liabilities	+	Stockholders' Equity
Cash −6,000		Bonds Payable, Net −1,710		Interest Expense (+E) −4,290

2 Record

dr Interest Expense (+E, −SE) 4,290
dr Bonds Payable, Net (−L) 1,710
   cr Cash (−A)   6,000

Similar calculations and accounting effects occur each period until the bonds mature. The only thing to watch out for is that Bonds Payable, Net decreases each year because the cash payment includes a partial repayment of the bond liability. For example, after the above entry is recorded on December 31, 2010, Bonds Payable, Net decreases by $1,710, from $107,260 to $105,550. This new balance is used to compute Interest Expense for the second year of the bond (for the year ended December 31, 2011):

Bonds Payable, Net (L)	
	107,260 1/1/2010
12/31/2010 1,710	
	105,550 12/31/2010

2011:   **Interest (I) = Principal (P)   × Interest Rate (R)   × Time (T)**
    Interest Expense = Bonds Payable, Net × Market Interest Rate × n/12
           $4,222 = $105,550   × 4%   × 12/12

Because the $6,000 annual cash payment exceeds the $4,222 Interest Expense by $1,778 ($6,000 − $4,222 = $1,778), General Mills records a $1,778 reduction in Bonds Payable, Net in 2011. In effect, the $6,000 cash payment includes both an interest component ($4,222) and a partial repayment of the bond liability ($1,778). As the following amortization schedule shows, the bond liability continues to decrease until, at maturity, it reaches the bonds' face value ($100,000).

	Beginning of Year	Changes During the Year			End of Year
Period	(A) Bonds Payable, Net	(B) Interest Expense	(C) Cash Paid	(D) = (C − B) Reduction in Bonds Payable, Net	(E) = (A − D) Bonds Payable, Net
1/1/10–12/31/10	$107,260	$4,290	$6,000	$1,710	$105,550
1/1/11–12/31/11	105,550	4,222	6,000	1,778	103,772
1/1/12–12/31/12	103,772	4,151	6,000	1,849	101,923
1/1/13–12/31/13	101,923	4,077	6,000	1,923	100,000

Bond Premium Amortization Schedule: Simplified Method

Bond Discounts

Our bond discount example indicated that General Mills received $93,376 on the issue date, which we would record in Bonds Payable, Net, using the journal entry shown on page 476. This issue price implies an 8 percent market interest rate. The bonds promise to pay the 6 percent stated interest rate on their total face value of $100,000. This information is used to compute Interest Expense and the annual cash payment as follows:

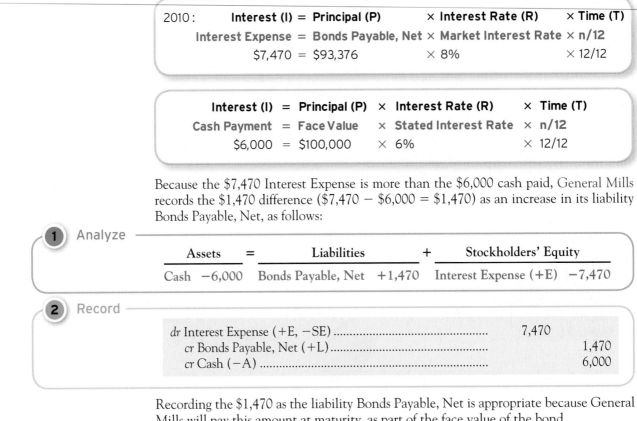

2010:	**Interest (I)**	=	**Principal (P)**	× **Interest Rate (R)**	× **Time (T)**
	Interest Expense	=	Bonds Payable, Net	× Market Interest Rate	× n/12
	$7,470	=	$93,376	× 8%	× 12/12

	Interest (I)	=	**Principal (P)**	× **Interest Rate (R)**	× **Time (T)**
	Cash Payment	=	Face Value	× Stated Interest Rate	× n/12
	$6,000	=	$100,000	× 6%	× 12/12

Because the $7,470 Interest Expense is more than the $6,000 cash paid, General Mills records the $1,470 difference ($7,470 − $6,000 = $1,470) as an increase in its liability Bonds Payable, Net, as follows:

1 Analyze

Assets	=	Liabilities	+	Stockholders' Equity
Cash −6,000		Bonds Payable, Net +1,470		Interest Expense (+E) −7,470

2 Record

dr Interest Expense (+E, −SE)	7,470	
cr Bonds Payable, Net (+L)..		1,470
cr Cash (−A)		6,000

Recording the $1,470 as the liability Bonds Payable, Net is appropriate because General Mills will pay this amount at maturity, as part of the face value of the bond.

Similar calculations and accounting effects occur each period until the bonds mature. The only thing to watch out for is that Bonds Payable, Net increases each year because the cash payment is less than the interest expense. For example, after the above entry is recorded on December 31, 2010, Bonds Payable, Net increases by $1,470, from $93,376 to $94,846. This new balance is used to compute Interest Expense for the second year of the bond (for the year ended December 31, 2011):

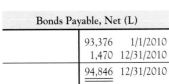

Bonds Payable, Net (L)	
	93,376 1/1/2010
	1,470 12/31/2010
	94,846 12/31/2010

2011:	**Interest (I)**	=	**Principal (P)**	× **Interest Rate (R)**	× **Time (T)**
	Interest Expense	=	Bonds Payable, Net	× Market Interest Rate	× n/12
	$7,588	=	$94,846	× 8%	× 12/12

Because the $7,588 Interest Expense exceeds the $6,000 annual cash payment by $1,588 ($7,588 − $6,000 = $1,588), General Mills records a $1,588 increase in Bonds Payable, Net in 2011. In effect, the $1,588 in unpaid interest will be paid at maturity. As the following amortization schedule shows, the bond liability continues to increase until, at maturity, it reaches the bonds' face value ($100,000).

	Bond Discount Amortization Schedule: Simplified Method				
	Beginning of Year	**Changes During the Year**			**End of Year**
Period	(A) Bonds Payable, Net	(B) Interest Expense	(C) Cash Paid	(D) = (B − C) Reduction in Bonds Payable, Net	(E) = (A + D) Bonds Payable, Net
1/1/10–12/31/10	$93,376	$7,470	$6,000	$1,470	$ 94,846
1/1/11–12/31/11	94,846	7,588	6,000	1,588	96,434
1/1/12–12/31/12	96,434	7,715	6,000	1,715	98,149
1/1/13–12/31/13	98,149	7,851	6,000	1,851	100,000

REVIEW THE CHAPTER

DEMONSTRATION CASE A: ACCRUED LIABILITIES AND UNEARNED REVENUE

Online Games, Inc., reported the following information in its accounting records on December 31, 2010.

Annual subscription payments received in December 2010 for 2011 services	$12,000
Gross salaries earned by employees (December 26–31, 2010)	3,600
Income taxes withheld from employees (December 26–31, 2010)	550
FICA taxes withheld from employees (December 26–31, 2010)	210
Net payment to employees (made on December 31, 2010)	2,840

The 2011 subscription payments will be earned equally throughout each month of 2011. The employees were paid $2,840 on December 31, 2010, but the withholdings have not yet been remitted nor have the matching employer FICA contributions.

Required:

1. Describe how the 2011 subscription payments should be reported in the balance sheet and income statement on (*a*) December 31, 2010, and (*b*) January 31, 2011.

2. Show the accounting equation effects and give the journal entries for (*a*) the receipt of annual subscription payments in December 2010, and (*b*) any required adjustments for the subscription payments on January 31, 2011.

3. Compute the total payroll costs relating to the period from December 26–31, 2010. (Assume $280 in total unemployment taxes.)

4. Show the accounting equation effects and give the journal entries on December 31, 2010, to adjust for payroll costs relating to December 26–31, 2010.

Suggested Solution

1. **a.** On December 31, 2010, the $12,000 of advance subscription payments would be reported on the balance sheet as a current liability called Unearned Revenue. No amounts relating to 2011 subscription services would be reported in the 2010 income statement.
    b. On January 31, 2011, one month of subscription services would be earned, so Unearned Revenue on the balance sheet would be reduced by $1,000 (= $12,000 × 1/12) and Subscription Revenue on the income statement would be increased by $1,000.

2. **a.** <u>December 2010 (receipt of 2011 subscription payments):</u>

Assets	=	Liabilities	+	Stockholders' Equity
Cash +12,000		Unearned Revenue +12,000		

dr Cash (+A) 12,000
   cr Unearned Revenue (+L) 12,000

   b. <u>January 31, 2011 (earned one month of 2011 subscriptions):</u>

Assets	=	Liabilities	+	Stockholders' Equity
		Unearned Revenue −1,000		Subscription Revenue (+R) +1,000

dr Unearned Revenue (−L) 1,000
   cr Subscription Revenue (+R, +SE) 1,000

3. <u>Computation of total payroll costs:</u>

Salaries and wages:	Net pay to employees	$2,840
	Income taxes withheld from employees	550
	FICA taxes withheld from employees	210
	Total cost of salaries and wages	3,600
Employer payroll taxes:	FICA taxes (matching contribution)	210
	Unemployment taxes	280
Total payroll costs		$4,090

4. <u>Salaries and wage costs:</u>

Assets	=	Liabilities	+	Stockholders' Equity
Cash −2,840		Withheld Income		Salaries and Wages Expense (+E) −3,600
		Taxes Payable +550		
		FICA Payable +210		

dr Salaries and Wages Expense (+E, −SE) 3,600
    cr Withheld Income Taxes Payable (+L) 550
    cr FICA Payable (+L) 210
    cr Cash (−A) 2,840

<u>Employer-related payroll costs:</u>

Assets	=	Liabilities	+	Stockholders' Equity
		FICA Payable +210		Payroll Tax Expense (+E) −490
		Unemployment		
		Tax Payable +280		

dr Payroll Tax Expense (+E, −SE) 490
    cr FICA Payable (+L).. 210
    cr Unemployment Tax Payable (+L) 280

DEMONSTRATION CASE B: NOTES PAYABLE AND ACCRUED INTEREST

Caterpillar, Inc.

www.mhhe.com/phillips3e

On December 31, 2008, Caterpillar, Inc., had $20.9 billion in Cash, Short-term Investments, and Accounts Receivable, Net and $26.1 billion in current liabilities. On December 3, 2008, Caterpillar had received $350 million when it issued promissory notes that will mature in 2013. The notes pay interest at the annual rate of 7.00 percent, which was comparable to other interest rates available in the market. Caterpillar's fiscal year ends on December 31.

Required:

1. Describe which sections of Caterpillar's classified balance sheet are affected by its issuance of promissory notes.

2. Give the journal entry on December 3, 2008, to record the issuance of the notes.

3. Give the journal entry on December 31, 2008, to record one month of interest expense, assuming none had been accrued prior to that date.

4. Compute Caterpillar's quick ratio at December 31, 2008. What proportion of its current liabilities could Caterpillar pay quickly if it were required to? What was the likely effect (increase or decrease) of the note issuance on the company's quick ratio?

Suggested Solution

1. The issuance of notes increases Caterpillar's Cash (a current asset) and its Notes Payable (a long-term liability) by $350 million.

2. December 3, 2008 (issuance date):

dr Cash (+A) 350,000,000
    cr Notes Payable (+L) 350,000,000

3. December 31, 2008 (accrual of interest expense for one month):

dr Interest Expense (+E, −SE) ($350,000,000 × 7.00% × 1/12) 2,041,667
    cr Interest Payable (+L) 2,041,667

4. December 31, 2008, quick ratio = (Cash + Short-term Investments
                        + Accounts Receivable, Net) ÷ Current Liabilities
                  = $20.9 ÷ $26.1 = 0.80

The quick ratio of 0.80 implies that Caterpillar could quickly pay 80 percent of its current liabilities if it were required to.

The issuance of the notes increases the quick ratio, because Cash increased by $350 million, but the only increase in current liabilities was a relatively small amount of Interest Payable. The $350 million in Notes Payable increased long-term liabilities.

DEMONSTRATION CASE C: BONDS PAYABLE

To raise funds to build a new plant, Reed Company issued bonds with the following terms:

> Face value of the bonds: $100,000.
> Dates: Issued January 1, 2010; due in 5 years on January 1, 2015.
> Interest rate: 6 percent per year, payable on December 31 each year.

The bonds were issued on January 1, 2010, at 104.3, implying a 5 percent market rate of interest. The annual accounting period for Reed Company ends on December 31.

Required:

1. How much cash did Reed Company receive from the issuance of the bonds? Show computations.
2. What was the amount of premium on the bonds payable? Over how many months should it be amortized?
3. Show the accounting equation effects and give the journal entry on January 1, 2010, for recording the issuance of the bonds.
4. (Supplement 10A) Show the accounting equation effects and give the journal entry required on December 31, 2010, relating to interest on the bond. Use the straight-line amortization method.
5. (Supplement 10B) Show the accounting equation effects and give the journal entry required on December 31, 2010, relating to interest on the bond. Use the effective-interest amortization method.
6. (Supplement 10C) Show the accounting equation effects and give the journal entries required on January 1, 2010, relating to the bond issuance and on December 31, 2010, relating to interest on the bond. Use the simplified effective-interest amortization method.

Suggested Solution

1. Issue price of the bonds: $100,000 \times 104.3\% = \$104,300$.
2. Premium on the bonds payable: $\$104,300 - \$100,000 = \$4,300$.

   Months amortized: From date of issue, January 1, 2010, to maturity date, January 1, 2015
   $= 5 \text{ years} \times 12 \text{ months per year} = 60 \text{ months}.$

3. January 1, 2010 (issuance date):

Assets	=	Liabilities	+	Stockholders' Equity
Cash +104,300		Bonds Payable +100,000		
		Premium on		
		Bonds Payable +4,300		

   dr Cash (+A) 104,300
       cr Premium on Bonds Payable (+L) 4,300
       cr Bonds Payable (+L) 100,000

4. December 31, 2010:

Assets	=	Liabilities	+	Stockholders' Equity
Cash −6,000		Premium on		Interest Expense (+E) −5,140
		Bonds Payable −860		

   dr Premium on Bonds Payable (−L) ($4,300 × 12/60 months) 860
   dr Interest Expense (+E, −SE) ($6,000 − $860) 5,140
       cr Cash (−A) ($100,000 × 6% × 12/12) 6,000

5. December 31, 2010:

Assets	=	Liabilities	+	Stockholders' Equity
Cash −6,000		Premium on Bonds Payable −785		Interest Expense (+E) −5,215

dr Interest Expense (+E, −SE) ($104,300 × 5% × 12/12)	5,215	
dr Premium on Bonds Payable (−L) ($6,000 − $5,215)	785	
cr Cash (−A) ($100,000 × 6% × 12/12)		6,000

6. January 1, 2010 (issuance date):

Assets	=	Liabilities	+	Stockholders' Equity
Cash +104,300		Bonds Payable, Net +104,300		

dr Cash (+A)	104,300	
cr Bonds Payable, Net (+L)		104,300

December 31, 2010 (interest accrual):

Assets	=	Liabilities	+	Stockholders' Equity
Cash −6,000		Bonds Payable, Net −785		Interest Expense (+E) −5,215

dr Interest Expense (+E, −SE) ($104,300 × 5% × 12/12)	5,215	
dr Bonds Payable, Net (−L) ($6,000 − $5,215)	785	
cr Cash (−A) ($100,000 × 6% × 12/12)		6,000

CHAPTER SUMMARY

LO1   Explain the role of liabilities in financing a business. p. 452

- Liabilities play a vital role in allowing a business to buy goods and services on credit, cover gaps in cash flows, and expand into new regions and markets.

- Liabilities are classified as current if due to be paid with current assets within the current operating cycle of the business or within one year of the balance sheet date (whichever is longer). All other liabilities are considered long term.

LO2   Explain how to account for common types of current liabilities. p. 453

- Liabilities are initially reported at their cash equivalent value, which is the amount of cash that a creditor would accept to settle the liability immediately after the transaction or event occurred.

- Liabilities are increased whenever additional obligations arise (including interest) and are reduced whenever the company makes payments or provides services to the creditor.

LO3   Analyze and record bond liability transactions. p. 460

- For most public issuances of debt (bonds), the amount borrowed by the company does not equal the amount repaid at maturity. The effect of a bond discount is to provide the borrower less money than the value stated on the face of the bond, which increases the cost of borrowing above the interest rate stated on the bond. The effect of a bond premium is to provide the borrower more money than the face value repaid at maturity, which decreases the cost of borrowing below the stated interest rate.

- Interest Expense reports the cost of borrowing, which equals the periodic interest payments plus (or minus) the amount of the bond discount (or premium) amortized in that interest period.

LO4   Describe how to account for contingent liabilities p. 467

- A contingent liability is a potential liability (and loss) that has arisen as a result of a past transaction or event. Its ultimate outcome will not be known until a future event occurs or fails to occur. Under GAAP, it is recorded when likely and estimable.

Calculate and interpret the quick ratio and the times interest earned ratio. p. 468   LO5

- The quick ratio measures the company's ability to pay its current liabilities using current assets that are quickly converted into cash.
- The times interest earned ratio measures a company's ability to meet its interest obligations with resources generated from its profit-making activities.

Accounting Decision Tools		
Name of Measure	Formula	What It Tells You
Quick ratio	$\dfrac{\text{(Cash + Short-term Investments + Accounts Receivable, Net)}}{\text{Current Liabilities}}$	• Whether current assets are sufficient to pay current liabilities • The higher the number the better able to quickly pay
Times interest earned ratio	$\dfrac{\text{(Net Income + Interest Expense + Income Tax Expense)}}{\text{Interest Expense}}$	• Whether sufficient resources are generated to cover interest costs • The higher the number the better the coverage

KEY TERMS

Accrued Liabilities p. 454

Contingent Liability p. 467

Current Liabilities p. 452

Discount p. 461

Effective-Interest Method of Amortization (Supplement 10B) p. 471

Face Value p. 461

Issue Price p. 461

Line of Credit p. 469

Market Interest Rate p. 463

Maturity Date p. 461

Premium p. 461

Present Value p. 461

Quick Ratio p. 468

Stated Interest Rate p. 461

Straight-Line Method of Amortization (Supplement 10A) p. 470

Times Interest Earned Ratio p. 469

See complete definitions in the glossary in the back of this book.

HOMEWORK HELPER

Alternative terms

- The stated interest rate on a bond is also called the coupon rate or contract rate. The market interest rate is also called the effective interest rate or yield rate.
- The word amortize comes from the root word "mort," which means to kill or eliminate; as bond discounts and premiums are amortized, they are gradually eliminated.
- The quick ratio is also called the acid test ratio.

Helpful reminders

- From the employer's perspective, payroll deductions create liabilities, not expenses. They are not expenses because they do not increase the employer's wages and salaries cost; they simply redirect part of the wages and salaries payments to a government agency or other organization, rather than to employees.
- Bonds issue above face value (at a premium) if their stated interest rate is attractive (more than the market interest rate). If bonds have issued at a premium, their periodic cash payments will be greater than the interest expense, causing a reduction in the bond liability's carrying value.
- Bonds issue below face value (at a discount) if their stated interest is unattractive (less than the market interest rate). If bonds have issued at a discount, their periodic cash payments will be less than the interest expense, causing an increase in the bond liability's carrying value.

Frequent mistakes

- Use the stated interest rate, not the market interest rate, to calculate the cash paid periodically on a bond. (The market interest rate is used to calculate Interest Expense when using the effective-interest method.)

PRACTICE MATERIAL

QUESTIONS (⊖ Symbol indicates questions that require analysis from more than one perspective.)

1. Describe three ways in which liabilities are used to finance business activities.

2. Define *liability*. What's the difference between a current liability and a long-term liability?

3. What three factors influence the dollar amount reported for liabilities?

4. Define *accrued liability*. Give an example of a typical accrued liability.

5. Why is Unearned Revenue considered a liability?

6. Why are payroll taxes and sales taxes considered liabilities?

7. Your company plans to hire an employee at a yearly salary of $70,000. Someone in your company says the actual cost will be lower because of payroll deductions. Someone else says it will be higher. Who is right? What is likely to be the total cost to the company? Explain. ⊖

8. If a company has a long-term loan that has only two years remaining until it matures, how is it reported on the balance sheet (a) this year, and (b) next year?

9. What are the reasons that some bonds are issued at a discount and others are issued at a premium?

10. What is the difference between the stated interest rate and the market interest rate on a bond?

11. Will the stated interest rate be higher than the market interest rate or will the market interest rate be higher than the stated interest rate when a bond is issued at (a) face value, (b) a discount, and (c) a premium?

12. What is the carrying value of a bond payable?

13. What is the quick ratio? How is it related to the classification of liabilities?

14. What is the difference between a secured bond and a debenture? Which type carries more risk for the lender?

15. What is a contingent liability? How is a contingent liability reported under GAAP? How does this differ under IFRS?

16. (Supplement 10A) How is interest expense calculated using the straight-line method of amortization for a bond issued at (a) a discount and (b) a premium?

17. (Supplement 10B) How is interest expense calculated using the effective-interest method of amortization for a bond issued at (a) a discount and (b) a premium?

18. (Supplement 10C) How is interest expense calculated using the simplified approach to the effective-interest method for a bond issued at (a) a discount and (b) a premium?

MULTIPLE CHOICE

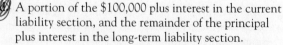

1. Which of the following best describes Accrued Liabilities?

   a. Long-term liabilities.

   b. Current amounts owed to suppliers of inventory.

   c. Expenses incurred, but not paid at the end of the accounting period.

   d. Revenues that have been collected, but not earned.

   Quiz 10
   www.mhhe.com/phillips3e

2. As of February 28, 2009, American Greetings Corporation had 9,000 full-time and 17,600 part-time employees. Assume that in the last pay period of the year, the company paid $8,000,000 to employees after deducting $2,000,000 for employee income taxes, $612,000 for FICA taxes, and $700,000 for other purposes. No payments have been made to the government relating to these taxes. Which of the following statements is true regarding this pay period?

   a. FICA Taxes Payable should be $612,000.

   b. FICA Taxes Payable should be $1,224,000.

   c. Salaries and Wages Expense should be $8,000,000.

   d. None of the above is true.

3. Assume that Warnaco Group Inc., the makers of Calvin Klein underwear, borrowed $100,000 from the bank to be repaid over the next five years, with principal payments beginning next month. Which of the following best describes the presentation of this debt in the balance sheet as of today (the date of borrowing)?

   a. $100,000 in the long-term liability section.

   b. $100,000 *plus* the interest to be paid over the five-year period in the long-term liability section.

   c. A portion of the $100,000 in the current liability section, and the remainder of the principal in the long-term liability section.

   d. A portion of the $100,000 plus interest in the current liability section, and the remainder of the principal plus interest in the long-term liability section.

4. Assume that Speedo International received $400,000 for long-term promissory notes that were issued on November 1. The notes pay interest on April 30 and October 31 at the annual rate of 6 percent, which was comparable to other interest rates in the market at that time. Which of the following journal entries would be required at December 31?

   a. *dr* Interest Expense 4,000
          cr Interest Payable 4,000

   b. *dr* Interest Expense 4,000
          cr Cash 4,000

c. *dr* Interest Expense 4,000
   dr Interest Payable 8,000
     cr Cash 12,000

d. *dr* Interest Expense 8,000
   dr Interest Payable 4,000
     cr Cash 12,000

5. Which of the following does not impact the calculation of the cash interest payments to be made to bondholders?

  a. Face value of the bond.
  b. Stated interest rate.
  c. Market interest rate.
  d. The length of time between payments.

6. Which of the following is false when a bond is issued at a premium?

  a. The bond will issue for an amount above its face value.
  b. Interest expense will exceed the cash interest payments.
  c. The market interest rate is lower than the stated interest rate.
  d. The issue price will be quoted at a number greater than 100.

7. To determine if a bond will be issued at a premium, discount, or at face value, one must know which of the following pairs of information?

  a. The face value and the stated interest rate on the date the bonds were issued.
  b. The face value and the market interest rate on the date the bonds were issued.
  c. The stated interest rate and the market interest rate on the date the bonds were issued.
  d. You can't tell without having more information.

8. A bond is issued at a price of 103 and retired early at a price of 97. Which of the following is true?

  a. A gain will be reported on the income statement when the bond is issued.
  b. A loss will be reported on the income statement when the bond is issued.
  c. A gain will be reported on the income statement when the bond is retired.
  d. A loss will be reported on the income statement when the bond is retired.

9. For the year ended December 31, 2008, Land O' Lakes, Inc., reported (in millions) Income from Operations of $206, Net Income of $160, Interest Expense of $63, and Income Tax Expense of $15. What was this dairy company's times interest earned ratio (rounded) for the year?

  a. 1.49   **c.** 3.27
  b. 2.53   **d.** 3.78

10. Big Hitter Corp. is facing a class-action lawsuit in the upcoming year. It is possible, but not probable, that the company will have to pay a settlement of approximately $2,000,000 in the upcoming year. How would this fact be reported, if at all, in the financial statements prepared at the end of the current month using GAAP?

  a. Report $2,000,000 as a current liability.
  b. Report $2,000,000 as a long-term liability.
  c. Describe the potential liability in the notes to the financial statements.
  d. Reporting is not required in this case.

> For answers to the Multiple-Choice Questions **see page Q1** located in the last section of the book.

MINI-EXERCISES

McGraw Hill connect | ACCOUNTING

M10-1 Recording Unearned Revenues

LO2

A local theater company sells 1,500 season ticket packages at a price of $250 per package. The first show in the five-show season starts this week. Show the accounting equation effects and prepare the journal entries related to (*a*) the sale of the season tickets before the first show and (*b*) the revenue earned after putting on the first show.

M10-2 Recording Sales and State Tax

LO2

Ahlers Clocks is a retailer of wall, mantle, and grandfather clocks and is located in the Empire Mall in Sioux Falls, South Dakota. Assume that a grandfather clock was sold for $5,000 cash plus 4 percent sales tax. The clock had originally cost Ahlers $3,000. Show the accounting equation effects and prepare the journal entries related to this transaction. Assume Ahlers uses a perpetual inventory system, as explained in Chapter 6.

Ahlers Clocks

M10-3 Calculating Payroll Tax Liabilities

LO2

Lightning Electronics is a midsize manufacturer of lithium batteries. The company's payroll records for the November 1–14 pay period show that employees earned wages totaling $100,000 but that employee income taxes totaling $14,000 and FICA taxes totaling $5,250 were withheld from this amount. The net pay was directly deposited into the employees' bank accounts. What was the amount of net pay? Assuming Lighting Electronics must pay $500 of unemployment taxes for this pay period, what amount would be reported as the total payroll costs?

M10-4 Reporting Payroll Tax Liabilities

LO2

Refer to M10-3. Prepare the journal entry or entries that Lightning would use to record the payroll. Include both employee and employer taxes.

LO2   **M10-5 Reporting Current and Noncurrent Portions of Long-term Debt**

Assume that on December 1, 2010, your company borrowed $14,000, a portion of which is to be repaid each year on November 30. Specifically, your company will make the following principal payments: 2011, $2,000; 2012, $3,000; 2013, $4,000; and 2014, $5,000. Show how this loan will be reported in the December 31, 2011 and 2010 balance sheets, assuming that principal payments will be made when required.

LO2   **M10-6 Recording a Note Payable**

Greener Pastures Corporation borrowed $1,000,000 on November 1, 2009. The note carried a 6 percent interest rate with the principal and interest payable on June 1, 2010. Show the accounting equation effects and prepare the journal entries for (a) the note issued on November 1 and (b) the interest accrual on December 31.

LO2   **M10-7 Reporting Interest and Long-term Debt, Including Current Portion**

Barton Chocolates used a promissory note to borrow $1,000,000 on July 1, 2009, at an annual interest rate of 6 percent. The note is to be repaid in yearly installments of $200,000, plus accrued interest, on June 30 of every year until the note is paid in full (on June 30, 2014). Show how the results of this transaction would be reported in a classified balance sheet prepared as of December 31, 2009.

LO3   **M10-8 Determining Bond Discount or Premium from Quoted Price**

Ford Motor Company

On May 25, 2009, finance.yahoo.com/bonds quoted a bond price of 60.0 for Ford Motor Company's 9.3 percent bonds maturing on March 1, 2030. Were the bonds selling at a discount or premium? Does this mean the market interest rate for comparable bonds was higher or lower than 9.3 percent?

LO3   **M10-9 Computing and Reporting a Bond Liability at an Issuance Price of 98**

E-Tech Initiatives Limited plans to issue $500,000, 10-year, 4 percent bonds. Interest is payable annually on December 31. All of the bonds will be issued on January 1, 2010. Show how the bonds would be reported on the January 2, 2010, balance sheet if they are issued at 98.

LO3   **M10-10 Computing and Reporting a Bond Liability at an Issuance Price of 103**

Repeat M10-9 assuming the bonds are issued at 103.

LO3   **M10-11 Recording Bonds Issued at Face Value**

Schlitterbahn Waterslide Company issued 25,000, 10-year, 6 percent, $100 bonds on January 1, 2010, at face value. Interest is payable each December 31. Show the accounting equation effects and prepare journal entries for (a) the issuance of these bonds on January 1, 2010, and (b) the interest payment on December 31, 2010.

LO3   **M10-12 Determining Financial Statement Effects of an Early Retirement of Debt**

If the market price of a bond increased after it was issued and the company decided to retire its debt early, would you expect the company to report a gain or loss on debt retirement? Describe the financial statement effects of a debt retirement under these circumstances.

LO4   **M10-13 Reporting a Contingent Liability**

Buzz Coffee Shops is famous for its large servings of hot coffee. After a famous case involving McDonald's, the lawyer for Buzz warned management (during 2009) that it could be sued if someone were to spill hot coffee and be burned. "With the temperature of your coffee, I can guarantee it's just a matter of time before you're sued for $1,000,000." Buzz felt the likelihood was remote. Unfortunately, in 2010, the lawyer's prediction came true when a customer filed suit. After consulting with his attorney, Buzz felt the loss was possible but not likely or probable. The case went to trial in 2011, and the jury awarded the customer $400,000 in damages, which the company immediately appealed. Buzz felt a loss was probable but believed a lower amount could be negotiated. During 2012, the customer and the company settled their dispute for $150,000. What is the proper reporting of this liability each year under GAAP? Would the reporting differ under IFRS?

LO5   **M10-14 Computing the Quick Ratio and the Times Interest Earned Ratio**

The balance sheet for Shaver Corporation reported the following: current assets $100,000; inventory $40,000; prepaids $10,000; current liabilities, $40,000; total stockholders' equity, $90,000; net income, $3,320; interest expense, $4,400; income before income taxes, $5,280. Compute

Shaver's quick ratio and times interest earned ratio. Based on these ratios, does it appear Shaver will be able to meet its obligations to pay current liabilities and future interest obligations as they become payable?

M10-15 Analyzing the Impact of Transactions on the Quick Ratio

LO5

BSO, Inc., has liquid assets of $600,000 and current liabilities of $500,000, resulting in a quick ratio of 1.2. For each of the following transactions, determine whether the quick ratio will increase, decrease, or remain the same.

a. Purchased $20,000 of new inventory on credit.
b. Paid accounts payable in the amount of $50,000.
c. Recorded accrued salaries in the amount of $100,000.
d. Borrowed $250,000 from a local bank, to be repaid in 90 days.

M10-16 (Supplement 10A) Recording Bond Issuance and Interest Payment (Straight-Line Amortization)

Simko Company issued $600,000, 10-year, 5 percent bonds on January 1, 2009. The bonds were issued for $580,000. Interest is payable annually on December 31. Using straight-line amortization, prepare journal entries to record (a) the bond issuance on January 1, 2009, and (b) the payment of interest on December 31, 2009.

M10-17 (Supplement 10B) Recording Bond Issuance and Interest Payment (Effective-Interest Amortization)

Clem Company issued $800,000, 10-year, 5 percent bonds on January 1, 2009. The bonds sold for $741,000. Interest is payable annually on December 31. Using effective-interest amortization, prepare journal entries to record (a) the bond issuance on January 1, 2009, and (b) the payment of interest on December 31, 2009. The market interest rate on the bonds is 6 percent.

M10-18 (Supplement 10C) Recording Interest Accrual and Interest Payment (Simplified Approach to Effective-Interest Amortization)

On January 1, 2009, Buchheit Enterprises reported $95,000 in a liability called "Bonds Payable, Net." This liability related to a $100,000 bond with a stated interest rate of 5 percent that was issued when the market interest rate was 6 percent. Assuming that interest is paid December 31 each year, prepare the journal entry to record interest paid on December 31, 2009, using the simplified effective-interest method shown in chapter supplement 10C.

EXERCISES

E10-1 Determining Financial Statement Effects of Transactions Involving Notes Payable

|ACCOUNTING   LO2

Target Corporation

Many businesses borrow money during periods of increased business activity to finance inventory and accounts receivable. Target Corporation is one of America's largest general merchandise retailers. Each Christmas, Target builds up its inventory to meet the needs of Christmas shoppers. A large portion of Christmas sales are on credit. As a result, Target often collects cash from the sales several months after Christmas. Assume that on November 1, 2010, Target borrowed $6 million cash from Metropolitan Bank and signed a promissory note that matures in six months. The interest rate was 7.5 percent payable at maturity. The accounting period ends December 31.

Required:

1. Indicate the accounts, amounts, and effects (+ for increase, − for decrease, and NE for no effect) of the (a) issuance of the note on November 1, (b) impact of the adjusting entry on December 31, 2010, and (c) the payment of the note and interest on April 30, 2011, on the accounting equation. Use the following structure for your answer:

   Date   Assets   =   Liabilities   +   Stockholders' Equity

2. If Target needs extra cash every Christmas season, should management borrow money on a long-term basis to avoid negotiating a new short-term loan each year? Explain your answer.

LO2   **E10-2 Recording a Note Payable through Its Time to Maturity**

Use the information in E10-1 to complete the following requirements.

Required:

1. Give the journal entry to record the note on November 1, 2010.
2. Give any adjusting entry required on December 31, 2010.
3. Give the journal entry to record payment of the note and interest on the maturity date, April 30, 2011, assuming that interest has not been recorded since December 31, 2010.

LO2   **E10-3 Recording Payroll Costs**

McLoyd Company completed the salary and wage payroll for March 2010. The payroll provided the following details:

Salaries and wages earned	$230,000
Employee income taxes withheld	50,200
FICA taxes withheld	16,445
Unemployment taxes	1,600

Required:

1. Considering both employee and employer payroll taxes, use the preceding information to calculate the total labor cost for the company.
2. Prepare the journal entry to record the payroll for March, including employee deductions (but excluding employer payroll taxes).
3. Prepare the journal entry to record the employer's FICA taxes and unemployment taxes.

LO2   **E10-4 Recording Payroll Costs with and without Withholdings**

Assume an employee of Rocco Rock Company earns $1,000 of gross wages during the current pay period, and is required to remit to the government $100 for income tax and $50 for FICA. Consider the following two procedures for paying the employee:

Procedure 1 (Withholdings)	Procedure 2 (No Withholdings)
Rocco Rock Company pays the employee net wages of $850 and will remit income taxes and FICA on behalf of the employee.	Rocco Rock Company pays the employee gross wages of $1,000 and the employee is responsible for remitting income taxes and FICA himself.

Required:

1. Ignoring employer payroll taxes, under each procedure calculate (*a*) the total labor cost for the company, and (*b*) the amount of cash the employee will have after satisfying all responsibilities to the government.
2. Explain why procedure 1 (withholdings) is the approach required by the government.
3. Considering that employers are responsible for matching employees' FICA contributions, explain why employers might also prefer procedure 1 over procedure 2.
4. Prepare the journal entries required by the employer under procedure 1, assuming that the employee is paid in cash, but the withholdings and matching employer FICA contribution have not yet been paid. (Assume no unemployment taxes.)

LO2, 5   **E10-5 Determining the Impact of Current Liability Transactions, Including Analysis of the Quick Ratio**

Bryant Company sells a wide range of inventories, which are initially purchased on account. Occasionally, a short-term note payable is used to obtain cash for current use. The following transactions were selected from those occurring during 2010:

a. On January 10, 2010, purchased merchandise on credit for $18,000. The company uses a perpetual inventory system.
b. On March 1, 2010, borrowed $40,000 cash from City Bank and signed a promissory note with a face amount of $40,000, due at the end of six months, accruing interest at an annual rate of 8 percent, payable at maturity.

Required:

1. For each of the transactions, indicate the accounts, amounts, and effects (+ for increase, − for decrease, and NE for no effect) on the accounting equation. Use the following structure:

Date	Assets	=	Liabilities	+	Stockholders' Equity

2. What amount of cash is paid on the maturity date of the note?
3. Discuss the impact of each transaction on the quick ratio. (Assume Bryant Company's quick ratio was 1.10 prior to each transaction.)

E10-6 Determining and Recording the Financial Statement Effects of Unearned Subscription Revenue

LO2

Reader's Digest Association is a publisher of magazines, books, and music collections. The following note is from its 2008 annual report:

> **Revenues**
>
> Sales of our magazine subscriptions are deferred (as unearned revenue) and recognized as revenues proportionately over the subscription period.

Assume that Reader's Digest (*a*) collected $394 million in 2009 for magazines that will be delivered later in 2009 and 2010, and (*b*) delivered $190 million worth of magazines on these subscriptions in 2009.

Required:

1. Using the information given, indicate the accounts, amounts, and accounting equation effects (+ for increase, − for decrease, and NE for no effect) of the transactions involving $394 million and $190 million.
2. Using the information given, prepare the journal entries that would be recorded in each year.

E10-7 Preparing Journal Entries to Record Issuance of Bonds and Payment of Interest

LO3

On January 1, 2010, Applied Technologies Corporation (ATC) issued $600,000 in bonds that mature in 10 years. The bonds have a stated interest rate of 10 percent. When the bonds were issued, the market interest rate was 10 percent. The bonds pay interest once per year on December 31.

Required:

1. Determine the price at which the bonds were issued and the amount that ATC received at issuance.
2. Prepare the journal entry to record the bond issuance.
3. Prepare the journal entry to record the interest payment on December 31, 2010, assuming no interest has been accrued earlier in the year.

E10-8 Preparing Journal Entries to Record Issuance of Bonds at Face Value, Payment of Interest, and Early Retirement

LO3

On January 1, 2010, Innovative Solutions, Inc., issued $200,000 in bonds at face value. The bonds have a stated interest rate of 6 percent. The bonds mature in 10 years and pay interest once per year on December 31.

Required:

1. Prepare the journal entry to record the bond issuance.
2. Prepare the journal entry to record the interest payment on December 31, 2010. Assume no interest has been accrued earlier in the year.
3. Assume the bonds were retired immediately after the first interest payment at a quoted price of 102. Prepare the journal entry to record the early retirement of the bonds.

LO3, 5   **E10-9   Describing the Effects of a Premium Bond Issue and Interest Payment on the Financial Statements, Quick Ratio, and Times Interest Earned Ratio**

Grocery Corporation received $300,328 for $250,000, 11 percent bonds issued on January 1, 2009, at a market interest rate of 8 percent. The bonds stated that interest would be paid each December 31 and that they mature on December 31, 2018.

Required:

1. Describe how the bond issuance affects the 2009 balance sheet and income statement, specifically identifying the account names and direction of effects (ignore amounts). Also, describe its impact, if any, on the quick ratio and times interest earned ratio.

2. Without doing calculations, describe how the balance sheet and income statement are affected by the recording of interest on December 31, 2009. Also, describe the impact, if any, of the December 31 interest payment on the quick ratio and times interest earned ratio.

LO5   **E10-10   Calculating and Interpreting the Quick Ratio and Times Interest Earned Ratio**

Kraft Foods Inc.

According to its Web site, Kraft Foods Inc. sells enough Kool-Aid® mix to make 1,000 gallons of the drink every minute during the summer and over 560 million gallons each year. At December 31, 2008, the company reported no short-term investments but did report the following amounts (in millions) in its financial statements:

	2008	2007
Cash and Cash Equivalents	$ 1,244	$ 567
Accounts Receivable, Net	4,704	5,197
Total Current Liabilities	11,044	17,086
Interest Expense	1,240	604
Income Tax Expense	728	1,002
Net Income	2,901	2,590

Required:

1. Compute the quick ratio and times interest earned ratio (to two decimal places) for 2008 and 2007.

2. Did Kraft appear to have increased or decreased its ability to pay current liabilities and future interest obligations as they become due? How can you explain the seemingly conflicting findings of your ratio analysis?

E10-11   (Supplement 10A) Recording the Effects of a Premium Bond Issue and First Interest Period (Straight-Line Amortization)

Refer to the information in E10-9 and assume Grocery Corporation uses the straight-line method to amortize the bond premium.

Required:

1. Prepare the journal entry to record the bond issuance.
2. Prepare the journal entry to record the interest payment on December 31, 2009.

E10-12   (Supplement 10B) Recording the Effects of a Premium Bond Issue and First Interest Period (Effective-Interest Amortization)

Refer to the information in E10-9 and assume Grocery Corporation uses the effective-interest method to amortize the bond premium.

Required:

1. Prepare the journal entry to record the bond issuance.
2. Prepare the journal entry to record the interest payment on December 31, 2009.

E10-13   (Supplement 10C) Recording the Effects of a Premium Bond Issue and First Interest Period (Simplified Effective-Interest Amortization)

Refer to the information in E10-9 and assume Grocery Corporation accounts for the bond using the shortcut approach shown in chapter supplement 10C.

Required:

1. Prepare the journal entry to record the bond issuance.
2. Prepare the journal entry to record the interest payment on December 31, 2009.

E10-14 (Supplement 10A) Recording the Effects of a Discount Bond Issue and First Interest Payment and Preparing a Discount Amortization Schedule (Straight-Line Amortization)

On January 1, 2010, when the market interest rate was 9 percent, Seton Corporation completed a $200,000, 8 percent bond issue for $187,163. The bonds were dated January 1, 2010, pay interest each December 31, and mature in 10 years on December 31, 2019. Seton amortizes the bond discount using the straight-line method.

Required:

1. Prepare the journal entry to record the bond issuance.
2. Prepare the journal entry to record the interest payment on December 31, 2010.
3. Prepare a bond discount amortization schedule for these bonds. Round calculations to the nearest dollar.

E10-15 (Supplement 10B) Recording the Effects of a Discount Bond Issue and First Interest Payment and Preparing a Discount Amortization Schedule (Effective-Interest Amortization)

Refer to the information in E10-14 and assume Seton Corporation uses the effective-interest method to amortize the bond discount.

Required:

1. Prepare the journal entry to record the bond issuance.
2. Prepare the journal entry to record the interest payment on December 31, 2010.
3. Prepare a bond discount amortization schedule for these bonds. Round calculations to the nearest dollar.

E10-16 (Supplement 10C) Recording the Effects of a Discount Bond Issue and First Interest Payment and Preparing a Discount Amortization Schedule (Simplified Effective-Interest Amortization)

Refer to the information in E10-14 and assume Seton Corporation accounts for the bond using the simplified effective-interest method shown in chapter supplement 10C.

Required:

1. Prepare the journal entry to record the bond issuance.
2. Prepare the journal entry to record the interest payment on December 31, 2010.
3. Prepare a bond discount amortization schedule for these bonds. Round calculations to the nearest dollar.

COACHED PROBLEMS

|ACCOUNTING   **LO2, 5**

CP10-1 Determining Financial Effects of Transactions Affecting Current Liabilities with Evaluation of Effects on the Quick Ratio

EZ Curb Company completed the following transactions during 2010. The annual accounting period ends December 31, 2010.

Jan.	8	Purchased merchandise on account at a cost of $14,000. (Assume a perpetual inventory system.)
	17	Paid for the January 8 purchase.
Apr.	1	Received $40,000 from National Bank after signing a 12-month, 6 percent, promissory note.
June	3	Purchased merchandise on account at a cost of $18,000.
July	5	Paid for the June 3 purchase.

Aug. 1	Rented out a small office in a building owned by EZ Curb Company and collected six months' rent in advance amounting to $6,000. (Use an account called Unearned Rent Revenue.)
Dec. 20	Received a $100 deposit from a customer as a guarantee to return a large trailer "borrowed" for 30 days.
	TIP: Consider whether EZ Curb Company has an obligation to return the money when the trailer is returned.
Dec. 31	Determined that wages of $6,500 were earned but not yet paid on December 31 (ignore payroll taxes).
Dec. 31	Adjusted the accounts at year-end, relating to interest.
Dec. 31	Adjusted the accounts at year-end, relating to rent.

Required:

1. For each listed transaction and related adjusting entry, indicate the accounts, amounts, and effects (+ for increase, − for decrease, and NE for no effect) on the accounting equation, using the following format:

Date	Assets	=	Liabilities	+	Stockholders' Equity

2. For each transaction and related adjusting entry, state whether the quick ratio is increased, decreased, or there is no change. (Assume EZ Curb Company's quick ratio has always been greater than 1.0.)

LO2, 5

www.mhhe.com/phillips3e

CP10-2 Recording and Reporting Current Liabilities with Evaluation of Effects on the Quick Ratio

Using data from CP10-1, complete the following requirements.

Required:

1. Prepare journal entries for each of the transactions.
2. Prepare any adjusting entries required on December 31, 2010.
3. Show how all of the liabilities arising from these items are reported on the balance sheet at December 31, 2010.
4. Complete requirement 2 of CP10-1, if you have not already done so.

LO2

CP10-3 Recording and Reporting Current Liabilities

During 2010, Riverside Company completed the following two transactions. The annual accounting period ends December 31.

a. On December 31, 2010, calculated the payroll, which indicates gross earnings for wages ($130,000), payroll deductions for income tax ($13,000), payroll deductions for FICA ($10,000), payroll deductions for United Way ($2,000), employer contributions for FICA (matching), state unemployment taxes ($1,100), and federal unemployment taxes ($200). Employees were paid in cash, but these payments and the corresponding payroll deductions and employer taxes have not yet been recorded.

b. Collected rent revenue of $3,600 on December 10, 2010, for office space that Riverside rented to another business. The rent collected was for 30 days from December 11, 2010, to January 10, 2011, and was credited in full to Unearned Rent Revenue.

Required:

1. Give the journal entries to record payroll on December 31, 2010.
2. Give (a) the journal entry for the collection of rent on December 10, 2010, and (b) the adjusting journal entry on December 31, 2010.
   TIP: Notice that the revenue recorded on December 10 includes revenue for 10 days (out of 30) that isn't earned until after December 31.
3. Show how any liabilities related to these items should be reported on the company's balance sheet at December 31, 2010.
4. Explain why the accrual basis of accounting provides more relevant information to financial analysts than the cash basis.

CP10-4 Comparing Bonds Issued at Par, Discount, and Premium

LO3

Sikes Corporation, whose annual accounting period ends on December 31, issued the following bonds:

> Date of bonds: January 1, 2009
> Maturity amount and date: $200,000 due in 10 years (December 31, 2018)
> Interest: 10 percent per year payable each December 31
> Date issued: January 1, 2009

Required:

1. Provide the following amounts to be reported on the January 1, 2009, financial statements immediately after the bonds are issued:

	Case A (issued at 100)	Case B (at 96)	Case C (at 102)
a. Bonds payable	$	$	$
b. Unamortized premium (or discount)			
c. Carrying value			

TIP: See Exhibit 10.5 for an illustration distinguishing Bonds Payable from their carrying value.

2. Assume that a retired person has written to you (an investment adviser) asking, "Why should I buy a bond at a premium when I can find one at a discount? Isn't that stupid? It's like paying list price for a car instead of negotiating a discount." Write a brief message in response to the question.

CP10-5 Comparing Carrying Value and Market Value and Recording Early Retirement of Debt

LO3

The Bilton Corporation annual report contained the following information concerning long-term debt:

> ### Long-Term Debt
>
> The estimated current market value of long-term debt is based on the quoted market price for the same or similar issues. The current carrying value for long-term debt is $1,132.5 (million) and the current market value is $1,173.5 (million).

Required:

1. Explain why there is a difference between the carrying value and the current market value of the long-term debt for Bilton.
   TIP: Think about whether changes in the market interest rate affect the carrying value and/ or current market value of bonds.
2. Assume that Bilton retired all of its long-term debt early (a very unlikely event) by buying the bonds in the bond market. This required a cash payment equal to the current market value. Prepare the journal entry to record the transaction.

CP10-6 Determining Financial Statement Reporting of Contingent Liabilities

LO4

⧼BRUNSWICK

Brunswick Corporation is a multinational company that manufactures and sells marine and recreational products. A prior annual report contained the following information:

> ### Litigation
>
> A jury awarded $44.4 million in damages in a suit brought by Independent Boat Builders, Inc., a buying group of boat manufacturers and its 22 members. Under the antitrust laws, the damage award has been tripled, and the plaintiffs will be entitled to their attorney's fees and interest. The Company has filed an appeal contending the verdict was erroneous as a matter of law, both as to liability and damages.

Required:

What are the alternative ways in which Brunswick could account for this litigation?
TIP: Consider the different possible outcomes that could arise from the appeal.

CP10-7 (Supplement 10A) Recording Bond Issuance and Interest Payments (Straight-Line Amortization)

Southwest Corporation issued bonds with the following details:

> Face value: $600,000
> Interest: 9 percent per year payable each December 31
> Terms: Bonds dated January 1, 2009, due five years from that date

The annual accounting period ends December 31. The bonds were issued at 104 on January 1, 2009, when the market interest rate was 8 percent. Assume straight-line amortization.

Required:

1. Compute the issue price of the bonds in dollars (show computations).
   TIP: The issue price typically is quoted at a percentage of face value.
2. Give the journal entry to record the issuance of the bonds.
3. Give the journal entries to record the payment of interest on December 31, 2009 and 2010.
4. How much interest expense would be reported on the income statements for 2009 and 2010? Show how the liability related to the bonds should be reported on the balance sheets at December 31, 2009 and 2010.

CP10-8 (Supplement 10B) Recording Bond Issuance and Interest Payments (Effective-Interest Amortization)

Complete the requirements of CP10-7, assuming Southwest Corporation uses effective-interest amortization.

CP10-9 (Supplement 10C) Recording Bond Issuance and Interest Payments (Simplified Approach to Effective-Interest Amortization)

Complete the requirements of CP10-7, assuming Southwest Corporation uses simplified effective-interest amortization shown in chapter supplement 10C.

CP10-10 (Supplement 10A) Completing an Amortization Schedule (Straight-Line Amortization)

The Peg Corporation (TPC) issued bonds and received cash in full for the issue price. The bonds were dated and issued on January 1, 2009. The stated interest rate was payable at the end of each year. The bonds mature at the end of four years. The following schedule has been prepared (amounts in thousands):

Date	Cash	Interest	Amortization	Balance
January 1, 2009				$6,101
End of year 2009	$450	$425	$25	?
End of year 2010	450	?	25	6,051
End of year 2011	450	?	25	6,026
End of year 2012	450	424	26	6,000

Required:

1. Complete the amortization schedule.
   TIP: The switch in amortization from $25 to $26 in 2012 is caused by rounding.
2. What was the maturity amount (face value) of the bonds?
3. How much cash was received at date of issuance of the bonds?
4. Was there a premium or a discount? If so, which and how much was it?
5. How much cash is paid for interest each period and will be paid in total for the full life of the bond issue?
6. What is the stated interest rate?
7. What is the market interest rate?
8. What amount of interest expense should be reported on the income statement each year?
9. Show how the bonds should be reported on the balance sheet at the end of 2010 and 2011.

CP10-11 (Supplements 10B or 10C) Completing an Amortization Schedule (Effective-Interest Amortization or Simplified Effective-Interest)

Hondor Corporation issued bonds and received cash in full for the issue price. The bonds were dated and issued on January 1, 2009. The stated interest rate was payable at the end of each year. The bonds mature at the end of four years. The following schedule has been completed (amounts in thousands):

Date	Cash	Interest	Amortization	Balance
January 1, 2009				$6,101
End of year 2009	$450	$427	$23	6,078
End of year 2010	450	426	24	6,054
End of year 2011	450	?	?	?
End of year 2012	450	?	28	6,000

Required:

1. Complete the amortization schedule.
2. What was the maturity amount (face value) of the bonds?
3. How much cash was received at date of issuance (sale) of the bonds?
4. Was there a premium or a discount? If so, which and how much was it?
5. How much cash is paid for interest each period and will be paid in total for the full life of the bond issue?
6. What is the stated interest rate?
   TIP: The stated interest rate can be calculated by comparing the cash payment to the face value of the bond.
7. What is the market interest rate?
8. What amount of interest expense should be reported on the income statement each year?
9. Show how the bonds should be reported on the balance sheet at the end of 2009 and 2010.

GROUP A PROBLEMS

PA10-1 Determining Financial Effects of Transactions Affecting Current Liabilities with Evaluation of Effects on the Quick Ratio

ACCOUNTING   LO2, 5

Jack Hammer Company completed the following transactions during 2010. The annual accounting period ends December 31, 2010.

Apr. 30	Received $550,000 from Commerce Bank after signing a 12-month, 6 percent, promissory note.
June 6	Purchased merchandise on account at a cost of $75,000. (Assume a perpetual inventory system.)
July 15	Paid for the June 6 purchase.
Aug. 31	Signed a contract to provide security service to a small apartment complex and collected six months' fees in advance amounting to $12,000. (Use an account called Unearned Service Revenue.)
Dec. 31	Determined salary and wages of $40,000 were earned but not yet paid as of December 31 (ignore payroll taxes).
Dec. 31	Adjusted the accounts at year-end, relating to interest.
Dec. 31	Adjusted the accounts at year-end, relating to security service.

Required:

1. For each listed transaction and related adjusting entry, indicate the accounts, amounts, and effects (+ for increase, − for decrease, and NE for no effect) on the accounting equation, using the following format:

Date	Assets	=	Liabilities	+	Stockholders' Equity

2. For each item, state whether the quick ratio is increased, decreased, or there is no change. (Assume Jack Hammer's quick ratio is greater than 1.0.)

LO2, 5

PA10-2 Recording and Reporting Current Liabilities with Evaluation of Effects on the Quick Ratio

www.mhhe.com/phillips3e

Using data from PA10-1, complete the following requirements.

Required:

1. Prepare journal entries for each of the transactions.
2. Prepare all adjusting entries required on December 31, 2010.
3. Show how all of the liabilities arising from these items are reported on the balance sheet at December 31, 2010.
4. Complete requirement 2 of PA10-1, if you have not already done so.

LO2

PA10-3 Recording and Reporting Current Liabilities

During 2010, Lakeview Company completed the following two transactions. The annual accounting period ends December 31.

a. On December 31, 2010, calculated the payroll, which indicates gross earnings for wages ($80,000), payroll deductions for income tax ($8,000), payroll deductions for FICA ($6,000), payroll deductions for American Cancer Society ($2,000), employer contributions for FICA (matching), state unemployment taxes ($500), and federal unemployment taxes ($100). Employees were paid in cash, but these payments and the corresponding payroll deductions and employer taxes have not yet been recorded.

b. Collected rent revenue of $3,000 on December 10, 2010, for office space that Lakeview rented to another business. The rent collected was for 30 days from December 11, 2010, to January 10, 2011, and was credited in full to Unearned Rent Revenue.

Required:

1. Give the journal entries to record payroll on December 31, 2010.
2. Give (*a*) the journal entry for the collection of rent on December 10, 2010, and (*b*) the adjusting journal entry on December 31, 2010.
3. Show how any liabilities related to these items should be reported on the company's balance sheet at December 31, 2010.
4. Explain why the accrual basis of accounting provides more relevant information to financial analysts than the cash basis.

LO3

PA10-4 Comparing Bonds Issued at Par, Discount, and Premium

Net Work Corporation, whose annual accounting period ends on December 31, issued the following bonds:

> Date of bonds: January 1, 2009
> Maturity amount and date: $200,000 due in 10 years (December 31, 2018)
> Interest: 10 percent per year payable each December 31
> Date issued: January 1, 2009

Required:

1. Provide the following amounts to be reported on the January 1, 2009, financial statements immediately after the bonds were issued:

	Case A (issued at 100)	Case B (at 97)	Case C (at 101)
a. Bonds payable	$	$	$
b. Unamortized premium (or discount)			
c. Carrying value			

2. Assume that you are an investment adviser and a retired person has written to you asking, "Why should I buy a bond at a premium when I can find one at a discount? Isn't that stupid? It's like paying list price for a car instead of negotiating a discount." Write a brief message in response to the question.

PA10-5 Comparing Carrying Value and Market Value and Recording Early Retirement of Debt

Quaker Oats is a well-known name at most breakfast tables. Before it was acquired by PepsiCo, Quaker Oats reported the following information about its long-term debt in its annual report:

Quaker Oats
PepsiCo

Long-Term Debt

The fair value of long-term debt was $779.7 million at the end of the current fiscal year, which was based on market prices for the same or similar issues or on the current rates offered to the Company for similar debt of the same maturities. The carrying value of long-term debt as of the same date was $759.5 million.

Required:

1. Explain what is meant by "fair value." Explain why there is a difference between the carrying value and the fair value of the long-term debt for Quaker Oats.

2. Assume that Quaker Oats retired all of its long-term debt early (a very unlikely event) by buying the bonds in the bond market. This required a cash payment equal to the current market value. Prepare the journal entry to record the transaction.

PA10-6 Determining Financial Statement Reporting of Contingent Liabilities

Macromedia, Inc., is the original maker of shockwave and flash technologies. One of its annual reports indicated that a lawsuit had been filed against the company and five of its former officers for securities fraud in connection with allegedly making false or misleading statements about its financial results. The lawsuit was settled on January 9, 2002, as described in the following note:

Macromedia, Inc.

Legal

The settlement amount was $48.0 million, of which approximately $19.5 million was paid by insurance. As a result, the Company recorded a $28.5 million charge as a component of other income (expense) in its consolidated statements of operations during fiscal year 2002.

Required:

Explain why Macromedia didn't record a contingent liability under GAAP when the lawsuit was first filed.

PA10-7 (Supplement 10A) Recording Bond Issue, Interest Payments (Straight-Line Amortization), and Early Bond Retirement

On January 1, 2009, Loop Raceway issued 600 bonds, each with a face value of $1,000, a stated interest rate of 5% paid annually on December 31, and a maturity date of December 31, 2011. On the issue date, the market interest rate was 6 percent, so the total proceeds from the bond issue were $583,950. Loop uses the straight-line bond amortization method.

Required:

1. Prepare a bond amortization schedule.
2. Give the journal entry to record the bond issue.
3. Give the journal entries to record the interest payments on December 31, 2009 and 2010.
4. Give the journal entry to record the interest and face value payment on December 31, 2011.
5. Assume the bonds are retired on January 1, 2011, at a price of 98. Give the journal entries to record the bond retirement.

PA10-8 (Supplement 10B) Recording Bond Issue, Interest Payments (Effective-Interest Amortization), and Early Bond Retirement

On January 1, 2009, Surreal Manufacturing issued 600 bonds, each with a face value of $1,000, a stated interest rate of 3 percent paid annually on December 31, and a maturity date of December 31, 2011. On the issue date, the market interest rate was 4 percent, so the total proceeds from the bond issue were $583,352. Surreal uses the effective-interest bond amortization method.

Required:

1. Prepare a bond amortization schedule.
2. Give the journal entry to record the bond issue.
3. Give the journal entries to record the interest payments on December 31, 2009 and 2010.
4. Give the journal entry to record the interest and face value payment on December 31, 2011.
5. Assume the bonds are retired on January 1, 2011, at a price of 101. Give the journal entry to record the bond retirement.

PA10-9 (Supplement 10C) Recording Bond Issue, Interest Payments (Simplified Effective-Interest Amortization), and Early Bond Retirement

Assume the same facts as PA10-8, except that Surreal uses the simplified effective-interest bond amortization method, as shown in supplement 10C.

Required:

1. Prepare a bond amortization schedule.
2. Give the journal entry to record the bond issue.
3. Give the journal entries to record the interest payments on December 31, 2009 and 2010.
4. Give the journal entry to record the interest and face value payment on December 31, 2011.
5. Assume the bonds are retired on January 1, 2011, at a price of 101. Give the journal entry to record the bond retirement.

GROUP B PROBLEMS

LO2, 5   **PB10-1 Determining Financial Effects of Transactions Affecting Current Liabilities with Evaluation of Effects on the Quick Ratio**

Tiger Company completed the following transactions during 2010. The annual accounting period ends December 31, 2010.

Jan.	3	Purchased merchandise on account at a cost of $24,000. (Assume a perpetual inventory system.)
	27	Paid for the January 3 purchase.
Apr.	1	Received $80,000 from Atlantic Bank after signing a 12-month, 5 percent, promissory note.
June	13	Purchased merchandise on account at a cost of $8,000.
July	25	Paid for the June 13 purchase.
Aug.	1	Rented out a small office in a building owned by Tiger Company and collected eight months' rent in advance amounting to $8,000. (Use an account called Unearned Rent Revenue.)
Dec.	31	Determined wages of $12,000 were earned but not yet paid on December 31 (ignore payroll taxes).
Dec.	31	Adjusted the accounts at year-end, relating to interest.
Dec.	31	Adjusted the accounts at year-end, relating to rent.

Required:

1. For each listed transaction and related adjusting entry, indicate the accounts, amounts, and effects (+ for increase, − for decrease, and NE for no effect) on the accounting equation, using the following format:

Date	Assets	=	Liabilities	+	Stockholders' Equity

2. For each item, state whether the quick ratio is increased, decreased, or there is no change. (Assume Tiger Company's quick ratio is greater than 1.0.)

LO2, 5   **PB10-2 Recording and Reporting Current Liabilities with Evaluation of Effects on the Quick Ratio**

Using data from PB10-1, complete the following requirements.

Required:

1. Prepare journal entries for each of the transactions.
2. Prepare any adjusting entries required on December 31, 2010.

3. Show how all of the liabilities arising from these items are reported on the balance sheet at December 31, 2010.
4. Complete requirement 2 of PB10-1, if you have not already done so.

PB10-3 Recording and Reporting Current Liabilities

LO2

During 2010, Sandler Company completed the following two transactions. The annual accounting period ends December 31.

a. On December 31, 2010, calculated the payroll, which indicates gross earnings for wages ($260,000), payroll deductions for income tax ($28,000), payroll deductions for FICA ($20,000), payroll deductions for United Way ($4,000), employer contributions for FICA (matching), state unemployment taxes ($1,700), and federal unemployment taxes ($300). Employees were paid in cash, but these payments and the corresponding payroll deductions and employer taxes have not yet been recorded.

b. Collected rent revenue of $1,500 on December 10, 2010, for office space that Sandler rented to another business. The rent collected was for 30 days from December 11, 2010, to January 10, 2011, and was credited in full to Unearned Rent Revenue.

Required:

1. Give the entries required on December 31, 2010, to record payroll.
2. Give (a) the journal entry for the collection of rent on December 10, 2010, and (b) the adjusting journal entry on December 31, 2010.
3. Show how any liabilities related to these items should be reported on the company's balance sheet at December 31, 2010.
4. Explain why the accrual basis of accounting provides more relevant information to financial analysts than the cash basis.

PB10-4 Comparing Bonds Issued at Par, Discount, and Premium

LO3

Marshalls Corporation sold a $500,000, 7 percent bond issue on January 1, 2010. The bonds pay interest each December 31 and mature 10 years from January 1, 2010.

Required:

1. Provide the following amounts to be reported on the January 1, 2010, financial statements immediately after the bonds were issued:

	Case A (issued at 100)	Case B (at 98)	Case C (at 102)
a. Bonds payable	$	$	$
b. Unamortized premium (or discount)			
c. Carrying value			

2. Assume that you are an investment adviser and a retired person has written to you asking, "Why should I buy a bond at a premium when I can find one at a discount? Isn't that stupid? It's like paying list price for a car instead of negotiating a discount." Write a brief message in response to the question.

PB10-5 Recording and Explaining the Early Retirement of Debt

LO3

AMC Entertainment, Inc.

AMC Entertainment, Inc., owns and operates 239 movie theaters worldwide, with 3,120 screens in 28 states. On August 12, 1992, the company sold 11 7/8 percent bonds in the amount of $52,720,000 and used the $52,720,000 cash proceeds to retire bonds with a coupon rate of 13.6 percent. At that time, the 13.6 percent bonds had a carrying value of $50,000,000.

Required:

1. Prepare the journal entries to record the issuance of the new bonds and the early retirement of the old bonds. Assume both the new and old bonds were issued at face value.
2. How should AMC report any gain or loss on this transaction?
3. Why might the company have issued new bonds to retire the old bonds?

PB10-6 (Supplement 10A) Recording Bond Issue, Interest Payments (Straight-Line Amortization), and Early Bond Retirement

On January 1, 2009, Methodical Manufacturing issued 100 bonds, each with a face value of $1,000, a stated interest rate of 5 percent paid annually on December 31, and a maturity date of December 31, 2011. On the issue date, the market interest rate was 4.25 percent, so the total proceeds from the bond issue was $102,070. Methodical uses the straight-line bond amortization method.

Required:

1. Prepare a bond amortization schedule.
2. Give the journal entry to record the bond issue.
3. Give the journal entries to record the interest payments on December 31, 2009 and 2010.
4. Give the journal entry to record the interest and face value payment on December 31, 2011.
5. Assume the bonds are retired on January 1, 2011, at a price of 102. Give the journal entries to record the bond retirement.

PB10-7 (Supplement 10B) Recording Bond Issue, Interest Payments (Effective-Interest Amortization), and Early Bond Retirement

Refer to PB10-6. Assume Methodical uses the effective-interest bond amortization method.

Required:

1. Prepare a bond amortization schedule.
2. Give the journal entry to record the bond issue.
3. Give the journal entries to record the interest payments on December 31, 2009 and 2010.
4. Give the journal entry to record the interest and face value payment on December 31, 2011.
5. Assume the bonds are retired on January 1, 2011, at a price of 101. Give the journal entry to record the bond retirement.

PB10-8 (Supplement 10C) Recording Bond Issue, Interest Payments (Simplified Effective-Interest Amortization), and Early Bond Retirement

Assume the same facts as PB10-6, but now assume that Methodical uses the simplified effective-interest bond amortization method, as shown in supplement 10C.

Required:

1. Prepare a bond amortization schedule.
2. Give the journal entry to record the bond issue.
3. Give the journal entries to record the interest payments on December 31, 2009 and 2010.
4. Give the journal entry to record the interest and face value payment on December 31, 2011.
5. Assume the bonds are retired on January 1, 2011, at a price of 101. Give the journal entry to record the bond retirement.

SKILLS DEVELOPMENT CASES

S10-1 Finding Financial Information

LO5

Refer to the financial statements of The Home Depot in Appendix A at the end of this book, or download the annual report from the *Cases* section of the text's Web site at www.mhhe.com/phillips3e.

Required:

1. Calculate, to two decimal places, the company's quick ratio using amounts reported in its financial statements for the years ended February 1, 2009, and February 3, 2008. What do the changes in this ratio suggest about the company's ability to quickly pay its liabilities?
2. Calculate, to two decimal places, the company's times interest earned ratio for the year ended February 1, 2009. Does this ratio cause you any concern about the company's ability to meet future interest obligations as they become due?

S10-2 Comparing Financial Information

LO5

Refer to the financial statements of The Home Depot in Appendix A and Lowe's in Appendix B at the end of this book, or download the annual reports from the *Cases* section of the text's Web site at www.mhhe.com/phillips3e.

Lowe's

Required:

1. Calculate, to two decimal places, the companies' quick ratios using amounts reported in the financial statements for the years ending in early 2009 and 2008. What do the changes in this ratio suggest about the companies' ability to quickly pay their liabilities? Does it appear that Lowe's or The Home Depot is in a less secure position?

2. Calculate, to two decimal places, the companies' times interest earned ratios for the years ending in early 2009. Does it appear that Lowe's or The Home Depot will be better able to meet future interest obligations as they become payable?

S10-3 Internet-Based Team Research: Examining an Annual Report

LO1, 2, 3, 4, 5

As a team, select an industry to analyze. Using your Web browser, each team member should access the annual report or 10-K for one publicly traded company in the industry, with each member selecting a different company. (See S1-3 in Chapter 1 for a description of possible resources for these tasks.)

Required:

1. On an individual basis, each team member should write a short report that incorporates the following:
   a. What are the most significant types of current liabilities owed by the company?
   b. Read the company's financial statement note regarding long-term debt and commitments and contingencies. Does the company have any significant amounts coming due in the next five years?
   c. Compute and analyze the quick ratio and times interest earned ratio.
2. Then, as a team, write a short report comparing and contrasting your companies using these attributes. Discuss any patterns across the companies that you as a team observe. Provide potential explanations for any differences discovered.

S10-4 Ethical Decision Making: A Real-Life Example

LO3

Many retired people invest a significant portion of their money in bonds of corporations because of their relatively low level of risk. During the 1980s, significant inflation caused some interest rates to rise to as high as 15 percent. Retired people who bought bonds that paid only 6 percent continued to earn at the lower rate. During the 1990s, inflation subsided and interest rates declined. Many corporations took advantage of the callability feature of these bonds and retired the bonds early. Many of these early retirements of high interest rate bonds were replaced with low interest rate bonds.

Required:

In your judgment, is it ethical for corporations to continue paying low interest rates when rates increase but to call bonds when rates decrease? Why or why not?

S10-5 Ethical Decision Making: A Mini-Case

LO3

Assume that you are a portfolio manager for a large insurance company. The majority of the money you manage is from retired school teachers who depend on the income you earn on their investments. You have invested a significant amount of money in the bonds of a large corporation and have just received news released by the company's president explaining that it is unable to meet its current interest obligations because of deteriorating business operations related to increased international competition. The president has a recovery plan that will take at least two years. During that time, the company will not be able to pay interest on the bonds and, she admits, if the plan does not work, bondholders will probably lose more than half of their money. As a creditor, you can force the company into immediate bankruptcy and probably get back at least 90 percent of the bondholders' money. You also know that your decision will cause at least 10,000 people to lose their jobs if the company ceases operations.

Required:

Given only these two options, what should you do? Consider who would be helped or harmed by the two options.

L05   **S10-6 Critical Thinking: Evaluating Effects on the Quick Ratio**

Assume you work as an assistant to the chief financial officer (CFO) of Fashions First, Inc. The CFO reminds you that the fiscal year-end is only two weeks away and that he is looking to you to ensure the company stays in compliance with its loan covenant to maintain a quick ratio of 1.25 or higher. A review of the general ledger indicates that cash and other liquid assets total $690,000 and current liabilities are $570,000. Your company has an excess of Cash ($300,000) and an equally large balance in Accounts Payable ($270,000), although none of its Accounts Payable are due until next month.

Required:

1. Determine whether the company is currently in compliance with its loan covenant.
2. Assuming the level of assets and liabilities remains unchanged until the last day of the fiscal year, evaluate whether Fashions First should pay down $90,000 of its Accounts Payable on the last day of the year, before the Accounts Payable become due.

S10-7 (Supplement 10A) Preparing a Bond Amortization Schedule (Straight-Line Amortization)

www.mhhe.com/phillips3e

Assume the authors of a popular introductory accounting text have hired you to create spreadsheets that will calculate bond discount amortization schedules like those shown in this chapter. As usual, you e-mail your friend Owen for some guidance. Much to your disappointment, you receive an auto-reply message from Owen indicating that he's gone skiing in New Zealand. After a bit of panicking, you realize you can refer to Owen's previous e-mail messages for spreadsheet advice that will help you complete this task. From his advice for Chapter 9, you decide to create a data input section for the stated interest rate, market interest rate, face value, issue price, and years to maturity. The spreadsheet file also will have a separate amortization schedule worksheet that contains only formulas, references to the cells in the data input section, and references to other cells in the amortization schedule. All amounts will be rounded to the nearest dollar (using the Round function in Excel), which means the discount amortization in the final year might be off a few dollars (unless you use the IF function in Excel to eliminate any remaining discount in the final year of the bond's life, in the same way that Owen showed in Chapter 9 for declining-balance depreciation).

Required:

Prepare a worksheet that uses formulas to reproduce the straight-line bond discount amortization schedule shown in chapter supplement 10A. Display both the completed spreadsheet and a "formulas revealed" (Ctrl ~) version of it.

S10-8 (Supplement 10B) Preparing a Bond Amortization Schedule (Effective-Interest Amortization)

www.mhhe.com/phillips3e

Refer to the information in S10-7 and prepare a worksheet that uses formulas to reproduce the effective-interest bond discount amortization schedule shown in chapter supplement 10B. Display both the completed spreadsheet and a "formulas revealed" (Ctrl ~) version of it.

S10-9 (Supplement 10C) Preparing a Bond Amortization Schedule (Simplified Effective-Interest Amortization)

www.mhhe.com/phillips3e

Refer to the information in S10-7 and prepare a worksheet that uses formulas to reproduce the bond discount amortization schedule shown for simplified effective-interest amortization in chapter supplement 10C. Display both the completed spreadsheet and a "formulas revealed" (Ctrl ~) version of it.

CONTINUING CASE

CC10 Accounting for Debt Financing

Nicole thinks that her business, Nicole's Getaway Spa (NGS), is doing really well and she is planning a large expansion. With such a large expansion, Nicole will need to finance some of it using debt. She signed a one-year note payable with the bank for $50,000 with a 6 percent interest rate. The note was issued October 1, 2011, interest is payable semiannually, and the end of Nicole's accounting period is December 31.

LO2

Required:

1. Prepare the journal entries required from the issuance of the note until its maturity on September 30, 2012, assuming that no entries are made other than at the end of the accounting period, when interest is payable and when the note reaches its maturity.

2. Is there any similarity between the way Notes Payable and Notes Receivable are accounted for? Explain.

CHAPTER 11

Reporting and Interpreting Stockholders' Equity

YOUR LEARNING OBJECTIVES

Understand the business

LO1   Explain the role of stock in financing a corporation.

Study the accounting methods

LO2   Explain and analyze common stock transactions.

LO3   Explain and analyze cash dividends, stock dividends, and stock split transactions.

LO4   Describe the characteristics of preferred stock and analyze transactions affecting preferred stock.

Evaluate the results

LO5   Analyze the earnings per share (EPS), return on equity (ROE), and price/earnings (P/E) ratios.

Review the chapter

THAT WAS
THEN

The last chapter focused on debt financing, as reported in the liabilities section of the balance sheet.

Lecture Presentation-LP11
www.mhhe.com/phillips3e

FOCUS COMPANY: National Beverage Corp.

www.nationalbeverage.com

News about shares of stock is everywhere. You've probably read it in *The Wall Street Journal*, listened to it on MSNBC, or searched for it at Yahoo!Finance. Behind this fascination with stock is a dream that many people share: taking a small amount of money and turning it into a fortune. That's what National Beverage Corp. has managed to do. National Beverage first started operations about 25 years ago, after acquiring Shasta Beverages from Sara Lee Corporation. The company went public in September 1991 and was issuing 100 shares of stock for $4,200. As the company grew larger, by acquiring and developing new brands such as Everfresh and LaCroix, its earnings and stock value began to grow. By 2001, the company's shares had doubled in value. And over this last decade alone, the shares have tripled in value. Those 100 shares are now worth over $22,000.

In this chapter, you will see how companies like National Beverage Corp. account for various stock transactions, including issuances, splits, and dividends. Soon you'll understand many of the stock terms used in the news.

THIS IS
NOW

This chapter focuses on equity financing, as reported in the stockholders' equity section of the balance sheet.

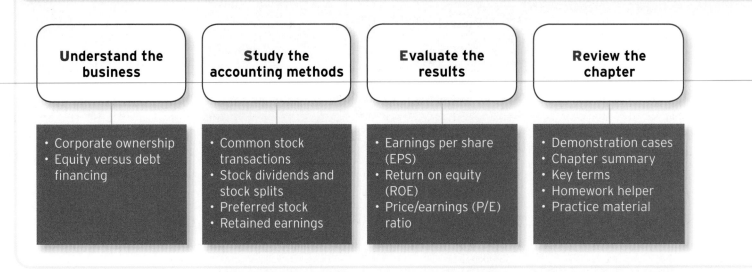

Understand the business	Study the accounting methods	Evaluate the results	Review the chapter
• Corporate ownership • Equity versus debt financing	• Common stock transactions • Stock dividends and stock splits • Preferred stock • Retained earnings	• Earnings per share (EPS) • Return on equity (ROE) • Price/earnings (P/E) ratio	• Demonstration cases • Chapter summary • Key terms • Homework helper • Practice material

Understand the Business

CORPORATE OWNERSHIP

Learning Objective 1
Explain the role of stock in financing a corporation.

Video 11.1
www.mhhe.com/phillips3e

If you were to write down the names of 50 familiar businesses, probably all of them would be corporations. This is understandable because, according to the U.S. Census Bureau, corporations account for about 90 percent of the total sales reported by U.S. businesses.[1] Many Americans own shares in corporations, either directly or indirectly through a mutual fund or pension program.

You probably recall from Chapter 1 that the act of creating a corporation is costly, so why is the corporate form so popular? One reason is that it limits the legal liability of its owners. Another reason is that corporations can raise large amounts of money because investors can easily participate in a corporation's ownership. This ease of participation is related to several factors.

- **Shares of stock can be purchased in small amounts.** According to Yahoo!Finance, you could have become one of National Beverage's owners in 2009 by buying a share of the company's stock for just $11.

- **Ownership interests are transferable.** The shares of public companies are regularly bought and sold on established markets such as the New York Stock Exchange. National Beverage's shares are traded on the NASDAQ under the ticker symbol FIZZ.

- **Stockholders are not liable for the corporation's debts.** Creditors have no legal claim on the personal assets of stockholders like they do on the personal assets belonging to owners of sole proprietorships and partnerships. So if you owned stock in Circuit City, which went bankrupt and was liquidated in 2009, you would lose what you paid to buy the stock but, unless you personally guaranteed the company's debt, you wouldn't have to pay the hundreds of millions the company owed.

The law recognizes a corporation as a separate legal entity. It may own assets, incur liabilities, expand and contract in size, sue others, be sued, and enter into contracts

---

[1]Chapter Supplement 11A discusses accounting for owners' equity in proprietorships, partnerships, and other business forms.

independently of its owners. A corporation exists separate and apart from its owners, which means it doesn't die when its owners die. Thomas Edison died in 1931, but the company he founded (General Electric) continues in existence today.

To protect everyone's rights, the creation and oversight of corporations are tightly regulated by law. Corporations are created by submitting an application to a state government (not the federal government). Because laws vary from state to state, you might decide to create a corporation in a state other than the one in which it operates. Although National Beverage has its headquarters in Fort Lauderdale, it was actually incorporated in Delaware. More than half of the largest corporations in America are incorporated in Delaware because it has some of the most favorable laws for establishing corporations. If the application to create a corporation is approved, the state issues a charter, also called the articles of incorporation, which spells out information about the corporation such as its name, address, nature of business, and ownership structure.

The ownership structure of a corporation can vary from one company to the next. In the most basic form, a corporation must have one type of stock, appropriately called **common stock**. Owners of common stock usually enjoy a number of benefits:

1. **Voting rights.** For each share you own, you get a set number of votes on major issues. Some classes of common stock can carry more votes than others, so watch for this if you care about voting on which accounting firm will be appointed as external auditors and who will serve on the board of directors. (In case you don't remember from Chapter 5, the board of directors is the group that appoints the corporation's officers and governs top management, as shown in Exhibit 11.1).

2. **Dividends.** Stockholders receive a share of the corporation's profits when distributed as dividends.

3. **Residual claim.** If the company ceases operations, stockholders share in any assets remaining after creditors have been paid.

4. **Preemptive rights.** Existing stockholders may be given the first chance to buy newly issued stock before it is offered to others.

> **YOU SHOULD KNOW**
>
> **Common stock:** The basic voting stock issued by a corporation to stockholders.

EQUITY VERSUS DEBT FINANCING

Whenever a company needs a large amount of long-term financing, its executives will have to decide whether to obtain it by issuing new stock to investors (called

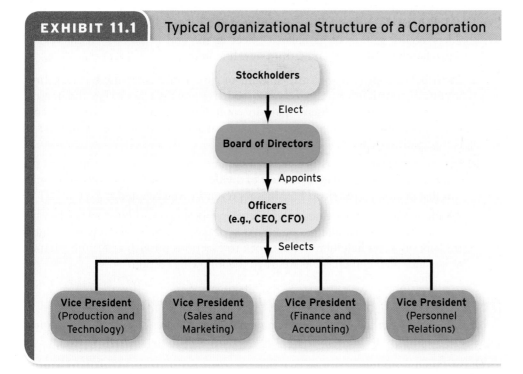

EXHIBIT 11.1 Typical Organizational Structure of a Corporation

EXHIBIT 11.2	Advantages of Equity and Debt Financing

Advantages of Equity Financing	Advantages of Debt Financing
1. **Equity does not have to be repaid.** Debt must be repaid or refinanced.	1. **Interest on debt is tax deductible.** Dividends on stock are not tax deductible.
2. **Dividends are optional.** Interest must be paid on debt.	2. **Debt does not change stockholder control.** In contrast, a stock issue gives new stockholders the right to vote and share in the earnings, diluting existing stockholders' control.

equity financing) or borrowing money from lenders (debt financing). Each form of financing has certain advantages over the other, as listed in Exhibit 11.2. These factors play a big role in determining whether equity or debt financing is most appropriate for each particular corporation. One company, for example, might be primarily concerned about the impact of financing on income taxes and decide to rely on debt financing because its interest payments are tax deductible. A different company might be so concerned about being able to pay its existing liabilities that it can't afford to take on additional debt. By using equity financing, which doesn't have to be repaid, the company could obtain the financing it needs. Ultimately, the decision to pursue additional equity or debt financing depends on the circumstances.

Study the Accounting Methods

The first point to note is that **all transactions between a company and its stockholders affect the company's balance sheet accounts only.** They do not affect the company's income statement.

COMMON STOCK TRANSACTIONS

Learning Objective 2
Explain and analyze common stock transactions.

Exhibit 11.3 shows the balance sheet accounts that National Beverage reported in the stockholders' equity section of its balance sheet at the end of its 2008 fiscal year. It includes two familiar line items and a third new line item:

1. **Contributed Capital** reports the amount of capital the company received from investors' contributions, in exchange for the company's stock. For this reason, contributed capital represents paid-in capital. As Exhibit 11.3 suggests, contributed capital can include several components, which we'll explain later in this section.

2. **Retained Earnings** reports the cumulative amount of net income earned by the company less the cumulative amount of dividends declared since the corporation was first organized. Retained Earnings represents earned capital.

3. **Treasury Stock** reports shares that were previously owned by stockholders but have been reacquired and are now held by the corporation. To fully understand treasury stock, it's helpful to follow stock transactions through from authorization to issuance and repurchase, as we do in the following section.

Authorization, Issuance, and Repurchase of Stock

A corporation's charter indicates the maximum number of shares of stock that the corporation is allowed to issue. Look closely at the Contributed Capital section of Exhibit 11.3

EXHIBIT 11.3	Explanation of National Beverage's Stockholders' Equity

NATIONAL BEVERAGE CORP.
Partial Balance Sheets

(in thousands, except share amounts)	2008	2007		Explanation
STOCKHOLDERS' EQUITY				
Contributed Capital				
Preferred Stock, 7% cumulative, $1 par value	$ 150	$ 150		Stock with special rights
Common Stock, $0.01 par value	500	496		Basic voting stock
Authorized: 75,000,000 shares				Maximum number of shares
Issued: 50,000,000 shares				Number of shares distributed
Additional Paid-in Capital	26,508	24,847		Amount in excess of par value
Total Contributed Capital	27,158	25,493		Total equity paid-in by investors
Retained Earnings	135,467	149,868		Total equity earned by the company
Treasury Stock (4,000,000 shares, at cost)	(18,000)	(18,000)		Stock reacquired by the company
Total Stockholders' Equity	144,625	157,361		

and you will see that National Beverage is **authorized** to issue 75 million common shares. The next line in Exhibit 11.3 tells us how many shares have actually been issued. At the end of 2008, 50 million common shares have been issued. **Issued shares** will be owned forever by one stockholder or another, unless the company has repurchased them. Shares that have been repurchased by the corporation are called **treasury stock.** During the time treasury stock is held by the corporation, the shares do not carry voting, dividend, or other stockholder rights. Shares that are owned by stockholders (not the corporation itself) are called **outstanding shares.**

National Beverage reports its treasury stock in the second-last line of Exhibit 11.3. It is shown as a negative amount because it represents shares that are no longer outstanding with investors. By the end of its 2008 fiscal year, National Beverage had repurchased 4 million of the 50 million shares previously issued. From this information, you should be able to compute the number of shares still outstanding, which is important for financial analysts who need to express certain dollar amounts on a per share basis. Earnings per share (EPS)—a key financial ratio that we discuss later in this chapter—is expressed in terms of the number of outstanding shares owned by investors. Be sure you can map the number of shares reported in Exhibit 11.3 into relationships among the number of authorized, issued, outstanding, and treasury stock, as diagrammed in Exhibit 11.4.

> **YOU SHOULD KNOW**
>
> **Authorized shares:** The maximum number of shares of capital stock of a corporation that can be issued, as specified in the charter. **Issued shares:** Shares of stock that have been distributed by the corporation. **Treasury stock:** Issued shares that have been reacquired by the company. **Outstanding shares:** Shares that are currently held by stockholders (not the corporation itself).

EXHIBIT 11.4	Authorized, Issued, Outstanding, and Treasury Stock

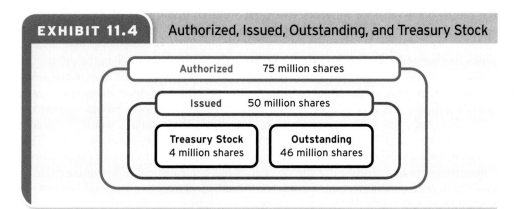

YOU SHOULD KNOW

Par value: An insignificant value per share of capital stock specified in the charter.

COACH'S TIP

Don't confuse par value as it relates to stock, with par value as it relates to bonds. They differ in meaning and how they are accounted for.

YOU SHOULD KNOW

No-par value stock: Capital stock that has no par value specified in the corporate charter.

Stock Authorization   Before stock can be issued, its specific rights and characteristics must be authorized and defined in the corporate charter. This authorization does not affect the accounting records, but it does establish certain characteristics that, later, will affect how the stock is accounted for. One characteristic of importance is the stock's **par value.** Oddly enough, par value has little meaning today. It is an old concept from long ago, originally introduced to prevent stockholders from removing contributed capital of businesses that were about to go bankrupt. Stronger laws and regulations exist today to prevent this from happening, so par value no longer has a business use. Yet, many states still require that corporations specify a par value for stock. Typically, par value is set at a token amount, such as $0.01 per share, as is the case with National Beverage's common stock in Exhibit 11.3. Some states have dropped the requirement to specify a par value and instead allow the issuance of no-par value stock. **No-par value stock** is similar to stock with par value, except it does not have a specified legal value per share. In any event, par value is a legal concept and is not related in any way to the market value of the company's stock.

Stock Issuance   A stock issuance ocurs when a corporation distributes its shares to existing or new stockholders, usually in exchange for cash. The very first issuance of a company's stock to the public is called an **initial public offering,** or IPO. This is what most people are referring to when they say a private company is going public. If a company has issued stock previously, additional issuances of new stock by the company are called **seasoned new issues.** Whether stock is issued as part of an IPO or as a seasoned new issue, a company accounts for it in the same way.

Most stock issuances are cash transactions. To illustrate the accounting for a stock issuance, assume that during the next fiscal year, National Beverage issues 100,000 shares of its $0.01 par value stock at the market price existing at the time of issuance of $10 per share. The accounting equation effects of this stock issuance and the journal entry to record them would be:

1 Analyze

	Assets	= Liabilities +	Stockholders' Equity	
Cash	+1,000,000		Common Stock	+1,000
			Additional Paid-In Capital	+999,000

2 Record

Based on Par value ⟵

dr Cash (+A) (100,000 × $10)	1,000,000	
cr Common Stock (+SE) (100,000 × $0.01)		1,000
cr Additional Paid-In Capital		
(+SE) ($1,000,000 − $1,000)		999,000

Notice that the increase in Common Stock is the number of shares sold times the par value per share (100,000 × $0.01), and the increase in Additional Paid-in Capital is the amount of cash received in excess of this amount. If the corporate charter does not specify a par value for the stock, the total proceeds from the stock issuance will be entered in the Common Stock account.

Stock Exchanged between Investors   When a company issues stock to the public, the transaction is between the issuing corporation and an investor. After this initial stock issuance, an investor can exchange shares for cash provided by other investors without directly affecting the corporation. For example, if investor Aaron Cadieux disposed of 1,000 shares of National Beverage stock to Tara Rink, the company would not record a journal entry on its books. Mr. Cadieux received cash for the shares, and Mrs. Rink received stock for the cash she paid. National Beverage did not receive or pay anything. These transactions involve only the owners of the company and not the corporation itself. It's like an auto dealer who records the initial sale of a car to a customer but doesn't later record another sale when the customer sells the car to someone else.

COACH'S TIP

Remember the separate entity assumption from Chapter 1, which states that owners' transactions are recorded only if they directly involve the corporation.

Stock Used to Compensate Employees   To encourage employees to work hard for a corporation, employee pay packages often include a combination of base pay, cash bonuses, and stock options. Stock options give employees the option of acquiring the company's stock at a predetermined price during a specified time period. The idea behind this arrangement is that if employees work hard and meet the corporation's goals, the company's stock price is likely to increase. If the stock price increases, employees can exercise their option to acquire the company's stock at the lower predetermined price and then turn around and dispose of it at the higher stock market price for a profit. If the stock price declines, employees haven't lost anything. Accounting rules require that, at the time the company grants stock options, an expense must be reported for the estimated cost associated with stock options. The specific accounting procedures for this will be discussed in an intermediate accounting course.

Spotlight On ETHICS

At Whose Expense?

Some critics claim that stock options, which are intended to give the senior executives of a company the same goals as stockholders, often come at the expense of existing stockholders. When senior executives exercise their stock options to acquire new stock, existing stockholders lose voting power because their percentage of ownership in the company is diluted. Furthermore, critics contend that stock options create an incentive for senior executives to over-state financial results in an attempt to falsely increase the company's stock price so they can exercise their options for huge personal gains.

Repurchase of Stock   A corporation may want to repurchase its stock from existing stockholders for a variety of reasons, including: (1) to distribute excess cash to stockholders, (2) to send a signal to investors that the company itself believes its own stock is worth acquiring, (3) to obtain shares that can be reissued as payment for purchases of other companies, and (4) to obtain shares to reissue to employees as part of employee stock option plans. Because of Securities and Exchange Commission regulations concerning newly issued shares, it is generally less costly for companies to give employees repurchased shares than to issue new ones.

Most companies record the purchase of treasury stock based on the cost of the shares when they are purchased by the company. This approach is called the cost method. Assume that during the next fiscal year, National Beverage repurchased 50,000 shares of its stock for $25 per share (50,000 shares × $25 = $1,250,000). Using the cost method, the effects of this repurchase on the accounting equation and the journal entry for it would be:

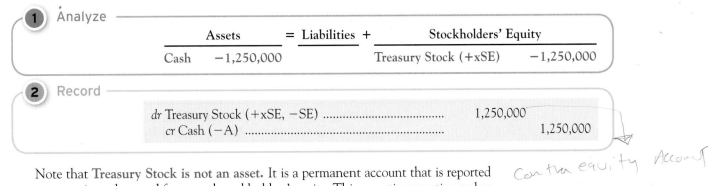

1 Analyze

	Assets	= Liabilities +	Stockholders' Equity
Cash	−1,250,000		Treasury Stock (+xSE) −1,250,000

2 Record

dr Treasury Stock (+xSE, −SE)	1,250,000	
cr Cash (−A)		1,250,000

Contra equity Account

Note that **Treasury Stock is not an asset.** It is a permanent account that is reported as contra-equity, subtracted from total stockholders' equity. This reporting practice makes sense because treasury stock is stock that is not outstanding and therefore should be removed from total stockholders' equity. Look at the second-last line of Exhibit 11.3 on page 509 to see how National Beverage reported its treasury stock at its 2008 fiscal year end.

How's it going?   Self-Study Practice

1. Assume that Aéropostale, Inc., issued 1,000 shares of its common stock, par value $0.01, for $21,900. Show the accounting equation effects and journal entry for this transaction.

① Analyze

Assets	= Liabilities +	Stockholders' Equity
Cash		+10
		Additional Paid-in Capital

② Record

dr

    cr

    cr

2. Assume that Aéropostale, Inc., repurchased 500 of its common shares in the stock market when it was selling for $20 per share. Show the journal entry to record this transaction at cost.

dr

    cr

After you have finished, check your answers with the solution in the margin.

Solution to Self-Study Practice

1.

Assets	=	Liabilities	+	Stockholders' Equity	
				Common Stock	+10
				APIC	+21,890
Cash +21,900					

dr Cash (+A) 21,900
  cr Common Stock (+SE) (1,000 × $0.01) 10
  cr Additional Paid-in Capital (+SE) 21,890

2. dr Treasury Stock (+xSE, −SE) 10,000
  cr Cash (−A) ($20 × 500) 10,000

Reissuance of Treasury Stock

When a company reissues shares of its treasury stock, it does not report a gain or loss on sale, even if it sells the shares for more or less than they cost when the company reacquired them. GAAP does not permit a corporation to report income or losses from investments in its own stock because transactions with the owners are not considered profit-making activities. Instead, this type of transaction affects only the balance sheet, just like other stock issuances. To illustrate, let's extend our previous example where National Beverage had repurchased its stock at a cost of $25 per share. If National Beverage reissues 5,000 shares of this treasury stock for $26 per share (5,000 × $26 = $130,000), the accounting equation effects and journal entry would be:

COACH'S TIP

Notice that the contra-account Treasury Stock is reduced only for the cost of each treasury share. Any amount received for treasury stock in excess of its cost is recorded as an increase in Additional Paid-in Capital, as shown below.

① Analyze

Assets	= Liabilities +	Stockholders' Equity	
Cash +130,000		Treasury Stock (−xSE)	+125,000
		Additional Paid-In Capital	+5,000

② Record

dr Cash (+A) (5,000 × $26) 130,000
  cr Treasury Stock (−xSE, +SE) (5,000 × $25) 125,000
  cr Additional Paid-In Capital (+SE) [5,000 × ($26 − $25)] 5,000

If treasury stock were reissued at a price below its repurchase price, the difference between the repurchase price ($25 per share) and the reissue price (say, $23 per share) is recorded as a reduction in Additional Paid-in Capital. The accounting equation effects and journal entry for reissuing at an amount less than its cost are:

1 Analyze

	Assets	= Liabilities +	Stockholders' Equity	
Cash	+115,000		Treasury Stock (−xSE)	+125,000
			Additional Paid-In Capital	−10,000

2 Record

dr Cash (+A) (5,000 × $23) 115,000
dr Additional Paid-In Capital (−SE) [5,000 × ($25 − $23)] 10,000
    cr Treasury Stock (−xSE, +SE) (5,000 × $25)   125,000

Dividends on Common Stock

Investors acquire common stock because they expect a return on their investment. This return can come in two forms: dividends and increases in stock price. Some investors prefer to buy stocks that pay little or no dividends (called a **growth investment**), because companies that reinvest the majority of their earnings tend to increase their future earnings potential, along with their stock price. Dell Corporation, for example, has never paid a dividend, yet if your parents had bought 100 Dell shares when they were first issued on June 22, 1988, for $850, the investment would be worth about $100,000 at the time this chapter was being written. Rather than wait for growth in stock value, other investors, such as retired people who need a steady income, prefer to receive their return in the form of dividends. These people often seek stocks that consistently pay dividends (called an **income investment**), such as Coca-Cola, which has paid cash dividends each year since 1920.

> **Learning Objective 3**
> Explain and analyze cash dividends, stock dividends, and stock split transactions.

Spotlight On BUSINESS DECISIONS

Dividend Cuts in Difficult Times

Under pressure to save cash during the global economic crisis, many big-name companies reversed or cut their policy to pay cash dividends in 2009. Although dividends are discretionary, companies are reluctant to cut them because doing so suggests the company is facing significant financial challenges. Huge percentage declines in 2009 dividends, as compared to prior years, were announced by:

General Electric	67%	CBS Corp.	81%
Motorola, Inc.	75%	Black & Decker	71%

A corporation does not have a legal obligation to pay dividends. It is a decision made by the board of directors, and it is made each time a dividend is to be paid. Once the board of directors formally declares a dividend, a liability is created. When National Beverage declared a dividend, its press release contained the following information:

FORT LAUDERDALE, Fla., June 15, 2007—National Beverage Corp. (NASDAQ: FIZZ)—"The Board today . . . (declared that) shareholders of record on July 20, 2007 shall be entitled to receive $0.80 per share payable on or before August 17, 2007."

Notice that this announcement contains three important dates: (1) the declaration date (June 15), (2) the date of record (July 20), and (3) the date of payment (August 17).

YOU SHOULD KNOW

Declaration date: The date on which the board of directors officially approves a dividend.

1. **Declaration Date–June 15.** The **declaration date** is the date on which the board of directors officially approves the dividend. As soon as the board makes the declaration, the company records an increase in its liabilities and a corresponding increase in the Dividends Declared account. Dividends Declared is a temporary account that summarizes dividends declared during the year and later is closed to Retained Earnings at year-end, causing a decrease in Retained Earnings. Remember, **dividends are distributions of a company's accumulated prior earnings,** so they are reported on the statement of retained earnings (or the more general statement of stockholders' equity shown in Chapter 5). Dividends declared by a company are not reported on its income statement because they are not expenses. With approximately 46 million common shares outstanding (see Exhibit 11.4), National Beverage's $0.80 dividend per share equals $36.8 million (46 million × $0.80 = $36.8 million). The accounting equation effects and journal entry to record them would be:

① Analyze

Assets	=	Liabilities	+	Stockholders' Equity
		Dividends Payable +36,800,000		Dividends Declared (+D) −36,800,000

② Record

dr Dividends Declared (+D, −SE) 36,800,000
    cr Dividends Payable (+L) 36,800,000

YOU SHOULD KNOW

Record date: The date on which the corporation prepares the list of current stockholders as shown on its records; dividends can be paid only to the stockholders who own stock on that date.
Payment date: The date on which a cash dividend is paid to the stockholders of record.

2. **Date of Record–July 20.** After a dividend is declared, the corporation needs some time to identify who will receive the dividend. The **record date** is the date on which the corporation finalizes its list of current stockholders. The dividend is payable only to those names listed on the record date. No journal entry is made on this date.

3. **Date of Payment–August 17.** The **payment date** is the date on which the cash is disbursed to pay the dividend liability. It follows the date of record, as described in the dividend announcement. Continuing our example above, when the dividend is paid and the liability satisfied on August 17, the accounting equation effects and journal entry are:

① Analyze

Assets	=	Liabilities	+	Stockholders' Equity
Cash −36,800,000		Dividends Payable −36,800,000		

② Record

dr Dividends Payable (−L) 36,800,000
    cr Cash (−A) 36,800,000

These three dates and the corresponding balance sheet effects are summarized in the timeline in Exhibit 11.5.

The declaration of a cash dividend reduces stockholders' equity because Dividends Declared is closed into Retained Earnings at the end of each fiscal year. The payment of a cash dividend similarly reduces Cash (by the same amount). These two observations

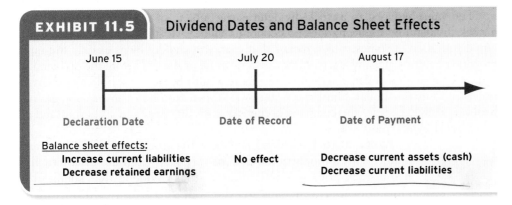

EXHIBIT 11.5 | Dividend Dates and Balance Sheet Effects

explain two key financial requirements that the board of directors must consider when declaring a cash dividend:

1. **Sufficient retained earnings.** The corporation must have accumulated a sufficient amount of Retained Earnings to cover the amount of the dividend. State laws often restrict dividends to the balance in Retained Earnings. A company may be further restricted by clauses in its loan agreements that require an even larger minimum balance in Retained Earnings. If the company were to violate such a loan covenant, a lender could require renegotiation of the loan and possibly demand its immediate repayment. **Because restrictions on Retained Earnings can severely limit the ability to pay dividends, accounting rules require that companies disclose any restrictions in their financial statement notes.** National Beverage reported in its 2008 financial statements that "$25 million of retained earnings were restricted from distribution."

2. **Sufficient cash.** The corporation must have sufficient cash to pay the dividend. Cash can be used in many ways, so the mere fact that Retained Earnings has a large credit balance does not mean that the company has sufficient cash to pay a dividend. Remember, retained earnings is not cash.

> **COACH'S TIP**
>
> A lender imposes dividend restrictions because it doesn't want to lend money to a corporation and then have the corporation pay it out in dividends to stockholders.

💡 How's it going?   Self-Study Practice

Answer the following questions concerning dividends:

1. On which dividend date is a liability created?

2. A cash outflow occurs on which dividend date?

3. What are the two fundamental requirements for the payment of a dividend?

After you have finished, check your answers with the solution in the margin.

Solution to Self-Study Practice
1. Declaration date.
2. Date of payment.
3. Dividends can be paid only if sufficient retained earnings and sufficient cash are both available.

STOCK DIVIDENDS AND STOCK SPLITS

Stock Dividends

The term *dividend*, when used alone with no adjectives, implies a cash dividend. However, some dividends are not paid in cash but in additional shares of stock. These dividends, called **stock dividends**, are distributed to a corporation's stockholders on a pro rata basis at no cost to the stockholder. The phrase *pro rata basis* means that each stockholder receives additional shares equal to the percentage of shares held. A stockholder who owns 10 percent of the outstanding shares would receive 10 percent of any additional shares issued as a stock dividend.

> **YOU SHOULD KNOW**
>
> **Stock dividend:** A dividend that distributes additional shares of a corporation's own stock.

Video 11.2
www.mhhe.com/phillips3e

The value assigned to a stock dividend is the subject of much debate. In reality, a stock dividend by itself provides no economic value. All stockholders receive a pro rata distribution of shares, which means that each stockholder owns exactly the same proportion of the company after a stock dividend as he or she did before the dividend. If you get change for a dollar, you do not have more wealth because you hold four quarters instead of only one dollar. Similarly, if you own 10 percent of a company, you are not wealthier simply because the company declares a stock dividend and gives you (and all other stockholders) more shares of stock.

When a stock dividend is issued, the stock market reacts immediately with a proportional decline in the stock price. Theoretically, if the stock price was $60 before a stock dividend that doubles the number of shares outstanding, the price per share would fall to $30. Thus, an investor who owns 100 shares before the stock dividend would own 200 shares after the stock dividend, but the total stock value before (100 × $60 = $6,000) would equal the value after (200 × $30 = $6,000). In reality, the fall in price is not exactly proportional to the number of new shares issued because the stock dividend makes the stock more attractive to investors who acquire stock in round lots (multiples of 100 shares). An investor with $10,000 might not buy a stock selling for $150, for instance, because she cannot afford to buy 100 shares. However, she might buy the stock if the price were less than $100 as the result of a stock dividend. Thus, **one of the main reasons for issuing a stock dividend is that it reduces the market price per share of stock.**

When a stock dividend occurs, the company must decrease Retained Earnings (to show that a dividend was declared) and increase Common Stock (to show that additional shares were issued). The amount recorded depends on whether the stock dividend is classified as large or small. Most stock dividends are classified as large. A large stock dividend involves the distribution of additional shares that amount to more than 20–25 percent of currently outstanding shares. A small stock dividend involves the distribution of shares that amount to less than 20–25 percent of the outstanding shares. Large stock dividends are recorded at the par value of the additional shares issued. Small stock dividends are recorded at the total market value of the shares issued, with the par value recorded in Common Stock and the excess in Additional Paid-in Capital.

On May 25, 2007, National Beverage declared a 20 percent stock dividend on the 38 million shares of $0.01 par value common stock outstanding at the time. The company accounted for it as a large stock dividend by moving $76,000 (=38 million × 20% × $0.01 par value) from Retained Earnings to Common Stock as follows:

① Analyze

Assets	=	Liabilities	+	Stockholders' Equity	
				Retained Earnings	−76,000
				Common Stock	+76,000

② Record

dr Retained Earnings (−SE)	76,000	
cr Common Stock (+SE)		76,000

Notice that the stock dividend does not change total stockholders' equity. It changes only the balances of some of the accounts that make up stockholders' equity.

Before we leave this section, we must caution you on a potential point of confusion. Some companies refer to 100 percent stock dividends as a "stock split effected as a stock dividend." Although they *say* stock split, they actually mean a stock dividend as described above. A true stock split is different, both in terms of how it is done and how it is accounted for, as we discuss in the following section.

Stock Splits

Stock splits are not dividends. While they are similar to a stock dividend, they are quite different in terms of how they occur and how they affect the stockholders' equity accounts. In a **stock split,** the total number of authorized shares is increased by a specified amount, such as 2-for-1. In this instance, each issued share is called in and two new shares are issued in its place. Cash is not affected when the company splits its stock, so the total resources of the company do not change. It's just like taking a four-piece pizza and cutting each piece into two smaller pieces.

Typically, a stock split involves revising the corporate charter to reduce the per-share par value of all authorized shares, so that the total par value across all shares is unchanged. For instance, if a company with 1 million shares outstanding executes a 2-for-1 stock split, it reduces the per-share par value of its stock from $0.01 to $0.005 and doubles the number of shares outstanding. The decrease in par value per share offsets the increase in the number of shares, so the financial position of the company is not affected and no journal entry is needed. By reading the following illustration from left to right, you can see these offsetting effects on the number of shares and par value per share.

YOU SHOULD KNOW

Stock split: An increase in the total number of authorized shares by a specified ratio; does not affect retained earnings.

Stockholders' Equity	Before a 2-for-1 Stock Split		After a 2-for-1 Stock Split	
Number of shares outstanding	1,000,000		2,000,000	
Par value per share	$ 0.01		$ 0.005	
Total par value outstanding	$ 10,000		$ 10,000	
Retained earnings	650,000		650,000	
Total stockholders' equity	$ 660,000		$ 660,000	

Exhibit 11.6 reviews the similarities and differences between large stock dividends and stock splits. Notice that although they have similar effects on the number of shares outstanding, they are accounted for differently.

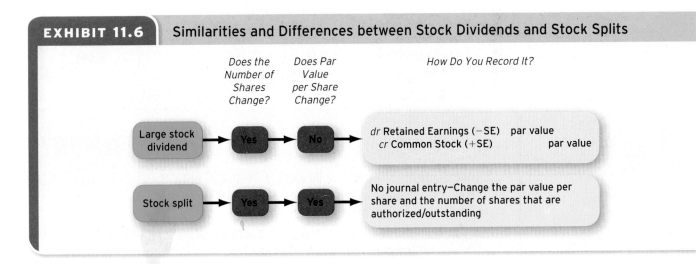

EXHIBIT 11.6	**Similarities and Differences between Stock Dividends and Stock Splits**

	Does the Number of Shares Change?	Does Par Value per Share Change?	How Do You Record It?
Large stock dividend	Yes	No	*dr* Retained Earnings (−SE) par value *cr* Common Stock (+SE) par value
Stock split	Yes	Yes	No journal entry—Change the par value per share and the number of shares that are authorized/outstanding

If you're like most new financial managers, you probably wonder how a company's board of directors chooses between stock dividends and stock splits. The following spotlight explains that accounting differences are a key factor in this decion.

Spotlight On BUSINESS DECISIONS

Choosing Between Stock Dividends and Stock Splits

Both stock dividends and stock splits increase the number of shares outstanding and decrease the per-share market price. A key difference between them is that a stock dividend causes a reduction in Retained Earnings, whereas a "true" stock split doesn't (see Exhibit 11.6). By itself, this accounting difference might not mean much. Remember, though, that to declare a cash dividend, a company must maintain an adequate balance in Retained Earnings. If you're managing a company that you expect will struggle financially in the future, you'll prefer a stock split because it doesn't reduce Retained Earnings, so it doesn't reduce your ability to declare cash dividends in the future. On the other hand, if you expect your company will be financially successful in the near future, you won't care that a stock dividend reduces Retained Earnings because future earnings will replenish that account to allow cash dividends to be declared. In fact, you'll probably *want* to declare a stock dividend to show how confident you are of your company's financial outlook. This reasoning suggests that **a company's board of directors may declare a stock dividend rather than a stock split to signal to financial statement users that the company expects significant future earnings** (which will replenish the reduction in Retained Earnings caused by the stock dividend).

Exhibit 11.7 shows the typical components of the stockholders' equity section of the balance sheet and highlights amounts (in blue) that are changed by a 2-for-1 stock split, a 100% stock dividend, and an equivalent ($10,000) cash dividend. Notice that the cash dividend is the only distribution that affects total stockholders' equity because it is the only one that distributes the company's resources to stockholders.

EXHIBIT 11.7	**Comparison of Distributions to Stockholders**			

			AFTER	
Stockholders' Equity	BEFORE	2-for-1 Stock Split	100% Stock Dividend	$10,000 Cash Dividend
Contributed Capital				
Number of common shares outstanding	1,000,000	2,000,000	2,000,000	1,000,000
Par value per common share	$ 0.01	$ 0.005	$ 0.01	$ 0.01
Common stock, at par	$ 10,000	$ 10,000	$ 20,000	$ 10,000
Additional paid-in capital	30,000	30,000	30,000	30,000
Retained Earnings	650,000	650,000	640,000	640,000
Total stockholders' equity	$ 690,000	$ 690,000	$ 690,000	$ 680,000

How's it going?   Self-Study Practice

Vandalay Industries wanted to reduce the market price of its stock, so it issued 100,000 new shares of common stock (par value $10) in a 100 percent stock dividend when the market value was $30 per share.

1. Prepare the journal entry that Vandalay would use to record this transaction.
2. What journal entry would be required if the transaction instead involved a 2-for-1 stock split? Theoretically, what would be the new stock price after the split?

After you have finished, check your answers with the solution in the margin.

Solution to Self-Study Practice
1. *dr* Retained Earnings (−SE)   1,000,000
      cr Common Stock (+SE)   1,000,000
2. No journal entry is required in the case of a stock split. Theoretically, the new price would be one-half of what it was before the 2-for-1 split ($30 × ½ = $15).

PREFERRED STOCK

In addition to common stock, some corporations issue **preferred stock** to a select group of investors. This special form of stock differs from common stock, typically in the following ways:

1. **Preferred stock generally does not grant voting rights.** As a result, preferred stock does not appeal to investors who want some control over the operations of a company. However, it does appeal to existing common stockholders because the company can issue preferred stock to raise funds without reducing common stockholders' voting control.

2. **Dividends on preferred stock, if any, may be paid at a fixed rate,** specified as either a dollar amount or a percentage per share. For example, if dividends are declared on National Beverage's "7%, $1 par value" preferred stock, the dividend will equal 7 cents per share ($0.07 = 7% × $1.00). A fixed dividend can be attractive to certain investors, such as company founders or retirees, who seek a stable income from their investments.

3. **Preferred stock carries priority over common stock.** Preferred stockholders have higher priority than common stockholders if a corporation distributes assets to its owners through dividends or at liquidation. That is, any dividends the corporation declares must be paid to preferred stockholders before they can be paid to common stockholders. Also, if the corporation goes out of business, its assets will be sold and used to pay creditors and then preferred stockholders. Common stockholders are paid last from whatever assets remain after paying preferred stockholders.

> **Learning Objective 4**
> Describe the characteristics of preferred stock and analyze transactions affecting preferred stock.

> **YOU SHOULD KNOW**
> **Preferred stock:** Stock that has specified rights over common stock.

Spotlight On THE WORLD

Under IFRS, preferred stock is typically classified as stockholders' equity. However, if the issuing company is contractually obligated to pay dividends or redeem the stock at a future date, then preferred stock is classified as a liability. This classification can dramatically affect financial ratios that use total stockholders' equity (e.g., return on equity, discussed later in this chapter) or total liabilities (e.g., debt-to-assets ratio in Chapter 5).

Preferred Stock Issuance

Just like a common stock issuance, a preferred stock issuance increases a company's cash and its stockholders' equity. To illustrate, assume that during the upcoming fiscal year, National Beverage issued 10,000 shares of its $1 par value preferred stock for $5 per share ($5 × 10,000 shares = $50,000 cash received). As shown below, the Preferred Stock account increases by its par value for each share issued ($1 × 10,000 = $10,000) and the amount of cash received in excess of par value is recorded as Additional Paid-In Capital—Preferred:

1 Analyze

Assets	=	Liabilities	+	Stockholders' Equity	
Cash +50,000				Preferred Stock	+10,000
				Additional Paid-In Capital—Preferred	+40,000

2 Record

dr Cash (+A) (10,000 × $5)	50,000	
cr Preferred Stock (+SE) (10,000 × $1)		10,000
cr Additional Paid-In Capital—Preferred (+SE)		40,000

Preferred Stock Dividends

Because investors who acquire preferred stock give up voting rights that are available to investors in common stock, preferred stock offers dividend preferences. The two most common dividend preferences are called current and cumulative.

YOU SHOULD KNOW

Current dividend preference: The feature of preferred stock that grants priority on preferred dividends over common dividends.

Current Dividend Preference   A **current dividend preference** requires that preferred dividends be paid before paying any dividends to holders of common stock. This preference is a feature of all preferred stock. After the current dividend preference has been met, and if no other preference exists, dividends may be paid to the common stockholders. To illustrate, consider the following example:

Flavoria Company
Preferred stock outstanding, 6%, par $20; 2,000 shares
Common stock outstanding, par $10; 5,000 shares

Assume the preferred stock carries only a current dividend preference and that the company declares dividends totaling $8,000 in 2009 and $10,000 in 2010. In each year, a fixed amount of the total dividends would first go to the preferred stockholders, and only the excess would go to the common stockholders.

Year	Total Dividends Declared	Dividends on 6% Preferred Stock*	Dividends on Common Stock†
2009	$ 8,000	$2,400	$5,600
2010	10,000	2,400	7,600

*Dividends on preferred stock = 2,000 shares × $20 par value × 6% dividend = $2,400
†Dividends on common stock = Total dividends declared − Dividends on preferred stock

Had Flavoria Company not declared dividends in 2009, preferred stockholders would have had preference to $2,400 of dividends only in 2010. The current dividend preference does not carry over to later years unless the preferred stock is designated as cumulative, as discussed next.

YOU SHOULD KNOW

Cumulative dividend preference: The preferred stock feature that requires current dividends not paid in full to accumulate for every year in which they are not paid. These cumulative unpaid amounts (called **dividends in arrears**) must be paid before any common dividends can be paid.

Cumulative Dividend Preference   A **Cumulative dividend preference** states that if all or a part of the current dividend is not paid in full, the cumulative unpaid amount, known as **dividends in arrears,** must be paid before any future common dividends can be paid. Of course, if the preferred stock is noncumulative, dividends can never be in arrears; any preferred dividends that are not declared are permanently lost. Because preferred stockholders are unwilling to accept this unfavorable feature, preferred stock is usually cumulative.

To illustrate the cumulative preference, assume that Flavoria Company has the same amount of stock outstanding as in the last example. In this case, however, assume that dividends are in arrears for 2007 and 2008. The following table shows that, in 2009, dividends in arrears are satisfied first, followed by the current dividend preference, and the excess goes to common stockholders. In 2010, preferred dividends include only the current preference of that year because dividends in arrears were fulfilled in 2009.

Year	Total Dividends Declared	DIVIDENDS ON 6% PREFERRED STOCK		Dividends on Common Stock‡
		In Arrears*	Current†	
2009	$ 8,000	$4,800	$2,400	$ 800
2010	10,000	—	2,400	7,600

*Dividends in arrears preference = 2,000 shares × $20 par value × 6% dividend × 2 years = $4,800
†Current dividend preference = 2,000 shares × $20 par value × 6% dividend = $2,400
‡Dividends on common stock = Total dividends declared − Total dividends on preferred stock

Because dividends are not an actual liability until the board of directors declares them, dividends in arrears are not reported on the balance sheet. Instead, they are disclosed in the notes to the financial statements.

RETAINED EARNINGS

As its name suggests, Retained Earnings represents the company's total earnings that have been retained in the business (rather than being distributed to stockholders). The balance in this account increases each year that the company reports net income on the income statement, and it decreases each year that the company reports a net loss (expenses greater than revenues) or declares cash or stock dividends to stockholders. **Think of retained earnings as the amount of equity that the company itself has generated for stockholders (through profitable operations) but not yet distributed to them.**

Should a company ever accumulate more net losses than net income over its life, it will report a negative (debit) balance in the Retained Earnings account. This amount is (*a*) shown in parentheses in the stockholders' equity section of the balance sheet, (*b*) deducted when computing total stockholders' equity, and (*c*) typically called an **Accumulated Deficit** rather than Retained Earnings. Exhibit 11.8 provides a recent example courtesy of Dr Pepper Snapple Group, Inc.

EXHIBIT 11.8	**Reporting Negative Retained Earnings (Accumulated Deficit)**

DR PEPPER SNAPPLE GROUP, INC.
Balance Sheet (Partial)
March 31, 2009
(in millions of dollars)

Stockholders' Equity:	
Common Stock	$ 3
Additional Paid-in Capital	3,143
Accumulated Deficit	(298)
Other	(112)
Total Stockholders' Equity	2,736

Evaluate the Results

Now that you know how dividends and other stockholders' equity transactions are accounted for inside a company, it's time to evaluate things from the outside. In this section, you will learn to use three ratios to evaluate how well a company appears to be using its capital to generate returns for the company and, ultimately, for its stockholders.

EARNINGS PER SHARE (EPS)

The most famous of all ratios, earnings per share (EPS), reports how much profit is earned for each share of common stock outstanding. The calculation of EPS can involve many details and intricacies, but in its basic form, it is computed by dividing "bottom line" net income by the average number of common shares outstanding. Most companies

> **Learning Objective 5**
> Analyze the earnings per share (EPS), return on equity (ROE), and price/earnings (P/E) ratios.

report EPS on the income statement immediately below Net Income or in the notes to the financial statements.[2]

You might be wondering why *earnings* per share is so popular when dividends and stock prices ultimately determine the return to stockholders. The reason is that current earnings can predict future dividends and stock prices. If a company generates increased earnings in the current year, it will be able to pay higher dividends in future years. In other words, current EPS influences expectations about future dividends, which investors factor into the current stock price. That's why National Beverage's stock price increased 8 percent on March 12, 2009, when the company announced that its EPS for the quarter was higher than in the previous year.

Another reason that EPS is so popular is that it allows you to easily compare results over time. For example, in the third quarter of 2009, National Beverage earned net income of $3.6 million, compared to $3.3 million for the same quarter in the previous year. It's hard to know whether the increase is good for stockholders, because it's possible that the increase in net income was accompanied by an increase in the number of shares outstanding. By considering earnings on a per-share basis, we adjust for the effect of additional stock issued, resulting in a clearer picture of what increases mean for each investor. The increase in net income from $3.3 million to $3.6 million actually did translate into EPS growth for the quarter from $0.07 to $0.08.

COACH'S TIP

Outstanding shares are issued shares minus treasury shares.

Accounting Decision Tools		
Name of Measure	**Formula**	**What It Tells You**
Earnings per share (EPS)	$$\dfrac{\text{Net Income}}{\substack{\text{Average Number of}\\ \text{Common Shares Outstanding}}}$$	• The amount of income generated for each share of common stock owned by stockholders • A higher ratio means greater profitability
Return on equity (ROE)	$$\dfrac{\text{Net Income}}{\text{Average Stockholders' Equity}}$$	• The amount of income earned for each dollar of stockholders' equity • A higher ratio means stockholders are likely to enjoy greater returns
Price/Earnings (P/E) ratio	$$\dfrac{\text{Current Stock Price (per share)}}{\text{Earnings per Share (annual)}}$$	• How many times more than the current year's earnings investors are willing to pay for a company's common stock • A higher number means investors anticipate an improvement in the company's future results

Exhibit 11.9 (on page 523) shows how to calculate EPS for National Beverage and its rival PepsiCo. We should caution you against comparing EPS across companies. The number of shares outstanding for one company can differ dramatically from the number outstanding for a different company, simply because one chooses to issue more shares of stock than the other. Also, as you have seen in earlier chapters, net income can be affected by differences in how two companies cost inventory (Chapter 7), estimate bad debts (Chapter 8), depreciate long-lived tangible assets (Chapter 9), and estimate losses from contingent liabilities (Chapter 10). So, **while EPS is an effective and widely used measure for comparing a company with itself over time, it is not appropriate for comparing across companies.**

---

[2]Although companies report their annual EPS numbers only at the end of their fiscal years, most analysts find it useful to update annual EPS as each quarter's results are reported. To do this, analysts will compute their own "trailing 12 months" EPS measure by summing the most recent four quarters of EPS. This way, they can get a timely measure of year-long EPS, without having to wait until the end of the fiscal year.

EXHIBIT 11.9	Summary of EPS, ROE, and P/E Ratio Analyses

National Beverage | | | | | **PepsiCo** | | | |
|---|---|---|---|---|---|---|---|

(in millions except stock price)	2008	2007	2006	(in billions except stock price)	2008	2007	2006
Net Income	$ 22.5	$ 24.7	$ 22.2	Net Income	$ 5.1	$ 5.7	$ 5.6
Average # shares	45.9	45.8	45.3	Average # shares	1.56	1.64	1.62
Stockholders' equity	$144.6	$157.4	$130.9	Stockholders' equity	$ 12.1	$ 17.2	$ 15.4
Stock price per share	$ 7.74	$12.44	$16.60	Stock price per share	$52.20	$71.73	$64.61

		2008	2007			2008	2007
EPS = $\dfrac{\text{Net income}}{\text{Avg. \# shares}}$		$\dfrac{\$22.5}{45.9}$	$\dfrac{\$24.7}{45.8}$	EPS = $\dfrac{\text{Net income}}{\text{Avg. \# shares}}$		$\dfrac{\$5.1}{1.56}$	$\dfrac{\$5.7}{1.64}$
		= $0.49	= $0.54			= $3.27	$3.48

		2008	2007			2008	2007
ROE = $\dfrac{\text{Net income}}{\text{Average SE}}$		$\dfrac{\$22.5}{(\$144.6 + \$157.4)/2}$	$\dfrac{\$24.7}{(\$157.4 + \$130.9)/2}$	ROE = $\dfrac{\text{Net income}}{\text{Average SE}}$		$\dfrac{\$5.1}{(\$12.1 + \$17.2)/2}$	$\dfrac{\$5.7}{(\$17.2 + \$15.4)/2}$
		= 0.149 or 14.9%	= 0.171 or 17.1%			0.348 or 34.8%	0.350 or 35.0%

		2008	2007			2008	2007
P/E = $\dfrac{\text{Stock price}}{\text{EPS}}$		$\dfrac{\$7.74}{\$0.49}$	$\dfrac{\$12.44}{\$0.54}$	P/E = $\dfrac{\text{Stock price}}{\text{EPS}}$		$\dfrac{\$52.20}{\$3.27}$	$\dfrac{\$71.73}{\$3.48}$
		= 15.8	= 23.0			= 16.0	= 20.6

RETURN ON EQUITY (ROE)

Like EPS, return on equity (ROE) reports a company's return to investors. However, rather than relate net income to the average *number* of shares outstanding, the return on equity (ROE) ratio relates net income to the average *dollars* of stockholder investment and earnings reinvested in the company.[3] Because ROE uses dollars contributed to and reinvested in the company, this ratio can be appropriately compared across companies.

The results reported in Exhibit 11.9 indicate that National Beverage's 2008 return to common stockholders was 14.9%, which is quite respectable. According to Yahoo!Finance, the average return on equity for the entire beverage industry was about 6.7%. In comparison, PepsiCo shows a startling ROE of 34.8% in 2008. PepsiCo's superior return demonstrates a strategy called **financial leverage.** Rather than rely on equity financing, PepsiCo relies heavily on debt. PepsiCo has been able to generate more profit from using these borrowed funds than it incurred for interest on that debt. As a result, PepsiCo was able to generate a superior return on equity for stockholders. Financial leverage isn't always the best strategy, though, as another industry competitor (Dr Pepper) discovered in 2008 when its Interest Expense on debt financing was greater than its Income from Operations.

PRICE/EARNINGS (P/E) RATIO

While EPS and ROE are useful for evaluating a company's return to stockholders, they don't help you determine what a reasonable price would be for the company's stock. Sophisticated techniques to value a company are taught in advanced courses in finance,

---

[3]If a company has preferred stock outstanding, the ROE ratio can be adjusted to focus on the common stockholders' perspective. Simply deduct any preferred dividends from net income and exclude any preferred stock accounts from the calculation of average stockholders' equity. This adjustment is not required in National Beverage's case because all its issued preferred stock is held as treasury stock, so it has already been excluded from average stockholders' equity.

but for this course, let's focus on a simple tool. The price/earnings ratio is the most basic way to determine the value investors place on a company's common stock. The P/E ratio, as most people call it, measures how many times more than current year's earnings investors are willing to pay for a company's stock. It is calculated as shown in Exhibit 11.9 by dividing a company's EPS for the year into the stock price at the time its EPS is reported.

Generally, a relatively high P/E ratio means investors expect the company to improve in the future and increase its profits, so they have factored in the future earnings when determining the current stock price. A relatively low P/E ratio typically means that they don't expect strong future performance. P/E ratios can vary significantly across industries, so you'll find them most meaningful when comparing a company over time with itself or with competitors in the same industry. Both National Beverage and PepsiCo showed P/E ratios in 2008 (15.8 and 16.0) that exceeded the industry average (5.9). This suggests that investors were anticipating good things to come from these companies.

💡 How's it going?   Self-Study Practice

National Beverage reported stockholders' equity of $143.3 (million) at its 2005 fiscal year-end.

(a) Use this information, along with that in Exhibit 11.9, to calculate National Beverage's earnings per share (EPS), return on equity (ROE), and price/earnings (P/E) ratios for 2006.

2006 EPS:	2006 ROE:	2006 P/E:
—— =	———————— =	—— =
	(+)/2	

(b) Did National Beverage's EPS and ROE improve or decline from 2006 (calculated in a) to 2007 (shown in Exhibit 11.9)? Does the 2006 P/E ratio suggest investors anticipated the changes that occurred in 2007 (assume the industry average was 8.0).

After you have finished, check your answers with the solution in the margin.

Solution to Self-Study Practice

a. EPS: $22.2 ÷ 45.3 = $0.49
   ROE: $22.2 ÷ [($130.9 + $143.3)/2] = 0.162
   P/E: $16.60 ÷ $0.49 = 33.9

b. National Beverage's EPS and ROE improved in 2007. Investors appeared to anticipate the improved performance because they were willing to pay 33.9 times earnings to buy a share, when the industry average was only 8.0 times earnings.

SUPPLEMENT 11A: Owners' Equity for Other Forms of Business

Owner's Equity for a Sole Proprietorship

A sole proprietorship is an unincorporated business owned by one person. Only two owner's equity accounts are needed: (1) a capital account for the proprietor (H. Simpson, Capital) and (2) a drawing (or withdrawal) account for the proprietor (H. Simpson, Drawings).

The capital account of a sole proprietorship serves two purposes: to record investments by the owner and to accumulate periodic income or loss. The drawing account is used to record the owner's withdrawals of cash or other assets from the business, similar to recording dividends declared by corporations. The drawing account is closed to the capital account at the end of each accounting period. Thus, after the drawing account is closed, the capital account reflects the cumulative total of all investments by the owner and all earnings of the business less all withdrawals from the entity by the owner.

In most respects, the accounting for a sole proprietorship is the same as for a corporation. Exhibit 11A.1 presents the recording of selected transactions of Homer's Dough Store and a statement of owner's equity, which replaces the statement of retained earnings.

🔨 **COACH'S TIP**

The capital account is like all the permanent stockholders' equity accounts for a corporation combined into a single account. The drawing account is like the temporary dividends declared account for a corporation.

EXHIBIT 11A.1	Accounting for Owner's Equity for a Sole Proprietorship

COACH'S TIP

Because a sole proprietorship does not issue stock, its equity is called owner's equity rather than stockholders' equity. We use OE to designate an owner's equity account.

Selected Entries during 2010

January 1, 2010

H. Simpson started a sole proprietorship by placing $150,000 cash in a bank account opened for the business. The accounting equation effects and journal entry follow:

Assets	=	Liabilities	+	Owner's Equity	
Cash +150,000				H. Simpson, Capital	+150,000

dr Cash (+A) 150,000
   cr H. Simpson, Capital (+OE) 150,000

During 2010

Each month during the year, Simpson withdrew $1,000 cash from the business for personal living costs. Accordingly, each month the financial effects and required journal entry are:

Assets	=	Liabilities	+	Owner's Equity	
Cash −1,000				H. Simpson, Drawings (+D)	−1,000

dr H. Simpson, Drawings (+D, −OE) 1,000
   cr Cash (−A) 1,000

Note: At December 31, 2010, after the last withdrawal, the drawings account reflected a debit balance of $12,000.

December 31, 2010

The usual journal entries for the year, including adjusting and closing entries for the revenue and expense accounts, resulted in revenue of $48,000 and expenses of $30,000. The net income of $18,000 was closed to the capital account as follows:

Assets	=	Liabilities	+	Owner's Equity	
				Revenues (−R)	−48,000
				Expenses (−E)	+30,000
				H. Simpson, Capital	+18,000

dr Individual Revenue Accounts (−R, −OE) 48,000
   cr Individual Expense Accounts (−E, +OE) 30,000
   cr H. Simpson, Capital (+OE) 18,000

December 31, 2010

The drawings account was closed as follows:

Assets	=	Liabilities	+	Owner's Equity	
				H. Simpson, Capital	−12,000
				H. Simpson, Drawings (−D)	+12,000

dr H. Simpson, Capital (−OE) 12,000
   cr H. Simpson, Drawings (−D, +OE) 12,000

HOMER'S DOUGH STORE
Statement of Owner's Equity
For the Year Ended December 31, 2010

H. Simpson, Capital, January 1, 2010	$ 0
Add: Capital contribution	150,000
Add: Net income for 2010	18,000
Total	168,000
Less: Withdrawals for 2010	(12,000)
H. Simpson, Capital, December 31, 2010	$156,000

Because a sole proprietorship does not pay income taxes, its financial statements do not report Income Tax Expense or Income Tax Payable. Instead, the net income of a sole proprietorship is taxed when it is included on the owner's personal income tax return. Likewise, the owner's salary is not recognized as an expense in a sole proprietorship because an employer/employee contractual relationship cannot exist with only one party involved. The owner's salary is therefore accounted for as a distribution of profits—a withdrawal—instead of salary expense, as it would be in a corporation.

Owner's Equity for a Partnership

The Uniform Partnership Act, which most states have adopted, defines a partnership as "an association of two or more persons to carry on as co-owners of a business for profit." Small businesses and professionals such as accountants, doctors, and lawyers often use the partnership form of business.

A partnership is formed by two or more persons reaching mutual agreement about the terms of the relationship. The law does not require an application for a charter as in the case of a corporation. Instead, the agreement between the partners constitutes a partnership contract. This agreement should specify matters such as division of income, management responsibilities, transfer or sale of partnership interests, disposition of assets upon liquidation, and procedures to be followed in case of the death of a partner. If the partnership agreement does not specify these matters, the laws of the resident state are binding.

In comparison to a corporation, the primary advantages of a partnership are (1) ease of formation, (2) complete control by the partners, and (3) lack of income taxes on the business itself. The primary disadvantage is the unlimited liability of each partner for the partnership's debts. If the partnership does not have sufficient assets to satisfy outstanding debt, creditors of the partnership can seize each partner's personal assets. In some cases, this can even result in one partner being held responsible for another partner's share of the partnership's debt.

As with a sole proprietorship, accounting for a partnership follows the same underlying principles as any other form of business organization, except for those entries that directly affect owners' equity. Accounting for partners' equity follows the same pattern as for a sole proprietorship, except that separate capital and drawings accounts must be established for each partner. Investments by each partner are credited to that partner's Capital account and withdrawals are debited to the respective Drawings account. The net income of a partnership is divided among the partners in accordance with the partnership agreement and credited to each account. The respective Drawings accounts are closed to the partner Capital accounts. After the closing process, each partner's Capital account reflects the cumulative total of all that partner's investments plus that partner's share of the partnership earnings less all that partner's withdrawals.

Exhibit 11A.2 presents selected journal entries and partial financial statements for AB Partnership to illustrate the accounting for the distribution of income and partners' equity.

Other Business Forms

In addition to sole proprietorships, partnerships, and corporations, other forms of business exist. These forms blend features of the "pure" organizational forms described earlier in this chapter to create hybrid business forms such as S corporations, limited liability partnerships (LLPs), and limited liability companies (LLCs). The LLC in particular is an increasingly common form of business that combines legal characteristics of corporations (such as a separate legal identity and limited liability) with the tax treatment of partnerships (where tax is paid by the individual owners rather than by the business entity itself). Accounting for these hybrid entities generally follows the methods shown earlier in this chapter.

The financial statements of an LLC follow the same format as those for a partnership, which differs from a corporation in the following ways: (1) the financial statements include an additional section entitled Distribution of Net Income; (2) the owners' equity section of the balance sheet is detailed for each owner; (3) the income statement does not report income tax expense because these forms of business do not pay income tax (owners must report their share of the entity's profits on their individual tax returns); and (4) unless other contractual arrangements exist, amounts paid to the owners are not recorded as expenses but instead are accounted for as withdrawals of capital.

EXHIBIT 11A.2 | **Accounting for Partners' Equity**

Selected Entries during 2010

January 1, 2010

A. Able and B. Baker organized AB Partnership on this date. Able contributed $60,000 cash and Baker contributed $40,000 cash to the partnership and they agreed to divide net income (and net loss) 60 percent and 40 percent, respectively. The financial effects of this investment on the business and the journal entry to record them are:

Assets	=	Liabilities	+	Partners' Equity	
Cash +100,000				A. Able, Capital	+60,000
				B. Baker, Capital	+40,000

dr Cash (+A) 100,000
   cr A. Able, Capital (+OE) 60,000
   cr B. Baker, Capital (+OE) 40,000

During 2010

The partners agreed that Able would withdraw $1,000 and Baker $650 per month in cash. Accordingly, each month the following financial effects were recorded with the journal entry that appears below:

Assets	=	Liabilities	+	Partners' Equity	
Cash −1,650				A. Able, Drawings (+D)	−1,000
				B. Baker, Drawings (+D)	−650

dr A. Able, Drawings (+D, −OE) 1,000
dr B. Baker, Drawings (+D, −OE) 650
   cr Cash (−A) 1,650

Note: At December 31, 2010, after the last withdrawals, the Drawings account for Able had a debit balance of $12,000 and the Drawings account for Baker had a debit balance of $7,800.

December 31, 2010

Assume that the normal closing entries for the revenue and expense accounts resulted in revenue of $78,000, expenses of $48,000, and net income of $30,000. The partnership agreement specified Able would receive 60 percent of net income ($18,000 = 60% × $30,000) and Baker would get 40 percent ($12,000 = 40% × $30,000). The financial effects and related closing entry follow:

Assets	=	Liabilities	+	Partners' Equity	
				Revenues (−R)	−78,000
				Expenses (−E)	+48,000
				A. Able, Capital	+18,000
				B. Baker, Capital	+12,000

dr Individual Revenue Accounts (−R, −OE) 78,000
   cr Individual Expense Accounts (−E, +OE) 48,000
   cr A. Able, Capital (+OE) (60% × $30,000) 18,000
   cr B. Baker, Capital (+OE) (40% × $30,000) 12,000

December 31, 2010

The financial effects of closing the drawings accounts and the related closing journal entry are:

Assets	=	Liabilities	+	Partners' Equity	
				A. Able, Capital	−12,000
				B. Baker, Capital	−7,800
				A. Able, Drawings (−D)	+12,000
				B. Baker, Drawings (−D)	+7,800

dr A. Able, Capital (−OE) 12,000
dr B. Baker, Capital (−OE) 7,800
   cr A. Able, Drawings (−D, +OE) 12,000
   cr B. Baker, Drawings (−D, +OE) 7,800

A separate statement of partners' capital, similar to a corporation's statement of stockholders' equity, is customarily prepared to supplement the balance sheet, as shown next:

EXHIBIT 11A.2 **Accounting for Partners' Equity (Continued)**

AB PARTNERSHIP
Statement of Partners' Equity
For the Year Ended December 31, 2010

	A. Able	B. Baker	Total
Partners' equity, January 1, 2010	$ 0	$ 0	$ 0
Add: Additional contributions during the year	60,000	40,000	100,000
Add: Net income for the year	18,000	12,000	30,000
Totals	78,000	52,000	130,000
Less: Drawings during the year	(12,000)	(7,800)	(19,800)
Partners' equity, December 31, 2010	$66,000	$44,200	$110,200

REVIEW THE CHAPTER

DEMONSTRATION CASE A: STOCK ISSUANCE AND REPURCHASES

This case focuses on selected transactions from the first year of operations of Zoogle Corporation, which became a public company on January 1, 2010, for the purpose of operating a lost-pet search business. The charter authorized the following stock:

> Common stock, $0.10 par value, 20,000 shares
> Preferred stock, 5 percent noncumulative, $100 par value, 5,000 shares

The following summarized transactions, selected from 2010, were completed on the dates indicated:

a. Jan. 1   Issued a total of 8,000 shares of $0.10 par value common stock for cash at $50 per share.

b. Feb. 1   Sold 2,000 shares of preferred stock at $102 per share; cash collected in full.

c. July 1   Purchased 400 shares of common stock that had been issued earlier. Zoogle Corporation paid the stockholder $54 per share for the stock, which is currently held in treasury.

d. Aug. 1   Sold 30 shares of the common treasury stock at $56 per share.

e. Dec. 31   The board decided not to declare any dividends for the current year.

Required:

1. Give the appropriate journal entries, and show calculations for each transaction.
2. Prepare the stockholders' equity section of the balance sheet for Zoogle Corporation at December 31, 2010. Assume that Retained Earnings is $31,000.

Suggested Solution

1. Journal entries:

a. Jan. 1, 2010   dr Cash (+A) ($50 × 8,000 shares) 400,000
            cr Common Stock (+SE) ($0.10 × 8,000 shares)   800
            cr Additional Paid-In Capital: Common (+SE)   399,200

b. Feb. 1, 2010   dr Cash (+A) ($102 × 2,000 shares) 204,000
            cr Preferred Stock (+SE) ($100 par × 2,000 shares)   200,000
            cr Additional Paid-In Capital: Preferred (+SE)   4,000
            [($102 − $100) × 2,000 shares]

c. July 1, 2010 *dr* Treasury Stock (+xSE, −SE) 21,600
   cr Cash (−A) ($54 × 400 shares) 21,600

d. Aug. 1, 2010 *dr* Cash (+A) ($56 × 30 shares) 1,680
   cr Treasury Stock (−xSE, +SE) ($54 × 30 shares) ... 1,620
   cr Additional Paid-In Capital: Common (+SE) 60

e. Dec. 31, 2010 No journal entry is required.

2. Stockholders' equity section of the balance sheet:

ZOOGLE CORPORATION
Partial Balance Sheet
At December 31, 2010

Stockholders' Equity

Contributed Capital

Preferred Stock, 5% (par value $100; 5,000 authorized
shares, 2,000 issued and outstanding shares) $200,000

Additional Paid-in Capital, Preferred Stock 4,000

Common Stock ($.10 par value; authorized 20,000
shares, issued 8,000 shares of which 370 shares are
held as treasury stock) 800

Additional Paid-in Capital, Common Stock 399,260

Total Contributed Capital $604,060

Retained Earnings 31,000

Treasury Stock, at cost, 370 common shares (19,980)

Total Stockholders' Equity 615,080

DEMONSTRATION CASE B: CASH AND STOCK DIVIDENDS

This case extends Demonstration Case A by focusing on dividend transactions occurring during Zoogle Corporation's second year. The following summarized transactions, selected from 2011, were completed on the dates indicated:

1. Nov. 1 To make the company's stock more affordable, the board declared and issued a 100 percent stock dividend on the outstanding common stock.
2. Dec. 1 The board declared a cash dividend on the preferred stock, payable on December 22, 2011, to stockholders of record as of December 15, 2011.
3. Dec. 31 The temporary Dividends Declared account was closed.

Required:

Give the appropriate journal entries, and show calculations for each transaction.

Suggested Solution

1. Nov. 1, 2011 *dr* Retained Earnings (−SE) 763
   cr Common Stock (+SE) 763
   [(8,000 common shares issued − 370 in treasury) × $0.10]

2. Dec. 1, 2011 *dr* Dividends Declared (+D, −SE) 10,000
   cr Dividends Payable (+L) 10,000
   (2,000 preferred shares × $100 par × 5% dividend rate)

   Dec. 15, 2011 No journal entry is required.

   Dec. 22, 2011 *dr* Dividends Payable (−L) 10,000
   cr Cash (−A) 10,000

3. Dec. 31, 2011 *dr* Retained Earnings (−SE) 10,000
   cr Dividends Declared (−D, +SE) 10,000

CHAPTER SUMMARY

LO1   **Explain the role of stock in financing a corporation. p. 506**

- The law recognizes corporations as separate legal entities. Owners invest in a corporation and receive capital stock that can be bought from and sold to other investors. Stock provides a number of rights, including the rights to vote, to receive dividends, and share in residual assets at liquidation.

LO2   **Explain and analyze common stock transactions. p. 508**

- A number of key transactions involve common stock: (1) initial issuance of stock, (2) repurchase of stock into treasury, and (3) reissuance of treasury stock. Each is illustrated in this chapter. Note that these transactions have only balance sheet effects; corporations do not report income arising from gains or losses on transactions involving their own stock.

LO3   **Explain and analyze cash dividends, stock dividends, and stock split transactions. p. 513**

- Cash dividends reduce stockholders' equity (Retained Earnings) and create a liability (Dividends Payable) when they are declared by the board of directors (on the date of declaration). The liability is reduced when the dividends are paid (on the date of payment).

- Stock dividends are pro rata distributions of a company's stock to existing owners. The transaction typically is accounted for by transferring an amount out of Retained Earnings and into contributed capital accounts.

- A stock split also involves the distribution of additional shares to owners but no additional amount is transferred into the contributed capital accounts. Instead, the per-share par value of stock is reduced.

LO4   **Describe the characteristics of preferred stock and analyze transactions affecting preferred stock. p. 519**

- Preferred stock provides investors certain advantages including current dividend preferences and a preference on asset distributions in the event the corporation is liquidated.

- If preferred stock carries cumulative dividend rights, any part of a current dividend that is not paid (called *dividends in arrears*) must be paid in full before any additional dividends can be paid.

LO5   **Analyze the earnings per share (EPS), return on equity (ROE), and price/earnings (P/E) ratios. p. 521**

- The earnings per share (EPS) ratio is calculated by dividing net income by the average number of shares of common stock outstanding during the year. This ratio makes it easy to compare a company's earnings over time but it does not allow reliable comparisons across companies because it does not adjust for likely differences in the number of shares that each company has outstanding.

- The return on equity (ROE) ratio relates earnings to each dollar contributed to and retained by the company. Because it is calculated using dollar amounts contributed to and retained by a company, it allows comparisons to be made across companies.

- The price/earnings (P/E) ratio relates the company's current stock price to its most recent annual earnings per share, indicating the value investors place on the company's stock.

Accounting Decision Tools

Name of Measure	Formula	What It Tells You
Earnings per share (EPS)	$$\frac{\text{Net Income}}{\text{Average Number of Common Shares Outstanding}}$$	• The amount of income generated for each share of common stock owned by stockholders • A higher ratio means greater profitability
Return on equity (ROE)	$$\frac{\text{Net Income}}{\text{Average Stockholders' Equity}}$$	• The amount earned for each dollar invested by stockholders • A higher ratio means stockholders are likely to enjoy greater returns
Price/Earnings (P/E) ratio	$$\frac{\text{Current Stock Price (per share)}}{\text{Earnings per Share (annual)}}$$	• How many times more than the current year's earnings investors are willing to pay for a company's common stock • A higher number means investors anticipate an improvement in the company's future results

KEY TERMS

Authorized Shares p. 509

Common Stock p. 507

Cumulative Dividend
Preference p. 520

Current Dividend
Preference p. 520

Declaration Date p. 514

Dividends in Arrears p. 520

Issued Shares p. 509

No-Par Value Stock p. 510

Outstanding Shares p. 509

Par Value p. 510

Payment Date p. 514

Preferred Stock p. 519

Record Date p. 514

Stock Dividend p. 515

Stock Split p. 517

Treasury Stock p. 509

See complete definitions in the glossary in the back of this text.

HOMEWORK HELPER

Alternative terms

• Stockholders are also called shareholders.
• Additional Paid-In Capital is also called Capital in Excess of Par.

Helpful reminders

• Large stock dividends are recorded at par value; small stock dividends are recorded at the stock market price, with the excess of market over par accounted for as Additional Paid-In Capital.

Frequent mistakes

• Do not record a liability for dividends in arrears at the end of each year. They are recorded as a liability only when dividends are declared on the cumulative preferred stock.

PRACTICE MATERIAL

QUESTIONS (⊖ Symbol indicates questions that require analysis from more than one perspective.)

1. Identify the primary advantages of the corporate form of business.

2. What are the relative advantages of equity versus debt financing?

3. Just prior to filing for bankruptcy protection in 2009, General Motors asked its bondholders to exchange their investment in GM's bonds for GM stock. The bondholders rejected this proposal. Why might GM have proposed this exchange? Why might the bondholders have rejected it? ⊖

4. Explain each of the following terms: (*a*) authorized common stock, (*b*) issued common stock, and (*c*) outstanding common stock.

5. What are the differences between common stock and preferred stock?

6. What is the distinction between par value and no-par value capital stock?

7. What are the usual characteristics of preferred stock?

8. What are the two basic sources of stockholders' equity? Explain each.

9. What is treasury stock? Why do corporations acquire treasury stock?

10. How is treasury stock reported on the balance sheet? How is the "gain or loss" on reissued treasury stock reported on the financial statements?

11. What are the two financial requirements to support the declaration of a cash dividend? What are the effects of a cash dividend on assets and stockholders' equity?

12. What is the difference between cumulative and noncumulative preferred stock?

13. What is a stock dividend? How does a stock dividend differ from a cash dividend?

14. What are the primary reasons for issuing a stock dividend?

15. Your company has been very profitable and expects continued financial success. Its stock price has reached a point where the company needs to make it more affordable. Would you recommend a stock dividend or a stock split? Why? ⊖

16. Identify and explain the three important dates with respect to dividends.

17. Why is the EPS number so popular? What are its limitations?

18. How do stock repurchases affect the EPS and ROE ratios?

19. What is one interpretation of a high P/E ratio?

20. You work for a public company that has relied heavily on debt financing in the past and is now considering a preferred stock issuance to reduce its debt-to-assets ratio. Debt-to-assets is one of the key ratios in your company's loan covenants. Should the preferred stock have a fixed annual dividend rate, or a dividend that is determined yearly? In what way might this decision be affected by IFRS? ⊖

MULTIPLE CHOICE

1. Which feature is not applicable to common stock ownership?

   Quiz 11
   www.mhhe.com/phillips3e

   a. Right to receive dividends before preferred stock shareholders.
   b. Right to vote on appointment of external auditor.
   c. Right to receive residual assets of the company should it cease operations.
   d. All of the above are applicable to common stock ownership.

2. Which statement regarding treasury stock is false?

   a. Treasury stock is considered to be issued but not outstanding.
   b. Treasury stock has no voting, dividend, or liquidation rights.
   c. Treasury stock reduces total stockholders' equity on the balance sheet.
   d. None of the above are false.

3. Which of the following statements about stock dividends is true?

   a. Stock dividends are reported on the income statement.
   b. Stock dividends increase total stockholders' equity.

   c. Stock dividends decrease total stockholders' equity.
   d. None of the above.

4. Which of the following is ordered from the largest number of shares to the smallest number of shares?

   a. Shares authorized, shares issued, shares outstanding.
   b. Shares issued, shares outstanding, shares authorized.
   c. Shares outstanding, shares issued, shares authorized.
   d. Shares in treasury, shares outstanding, shares issued.

5. Which of the following statements about the relative advantages of equity and debt financing is false?

   a. An advantage of equity financing is that it does not have to be repaid.
   b. An advantage of equity financing is that dividends are optional.
   c. An advantage of equity financing is that new stockholders get to vote and share in the earnings of the company.
   d. An advantage of debt financing is that interest is tax deductible.

6. A journal entry is not recorded on what date?

   a. Date of declaration.
   b. Date of record.

c. Date of payment.

d. A journal entry is recorded on all of the above dates.

7. Which of the following transactions will increase the return on equity?

  a. Declare and issue a stock dividend.

  b. Split the stock 2-for-1.

  c. Repurchase the company's stock.

  d. None of the above.

8. Which statement regarding dividends is false?

  a. Dividends represent a sharing of corporate profits with owners.

  b. Both stock and cash dividends reduce retained earnings.

  c. Cash dividends paid to stockholders reduce net income.

  d. None of the above statements are false.

9. When treasury stock is purchased with cash, what is the impact on the balance sheet equation?

  a. No change—the reduction of the asset Cash is offset with the addition of the asset Treasury Stock.

  b. Assets decrease and stockholders' equity increases.

  c. Assets increase and stockholders' equity decreases.

  d. Assets decrease and stockholders' equity decreases.

10. In what situation does total stockholders' equity decrease?

  a. When a cash dividend is declared.

  b. When a stock dividend is declared.

  c. When a stock split is announced.

  d. None of the above.

> For answers to the Multiple-Choice Questions **see page Q1** located in the last section of the book.

MINI-EXERCISES

M11-1 Equity versus Debt Financing   LO1

Indicate whether each of the following relates to equity (E) or debt (D) financing, and whether it makes that form of financing more, or less, favorable.

D   1. Interest is tax deductible.

E   2. Dividends are optional.

D   3. It must be repaid.

E   4. Additional stock issuances dilute existing stockholders' control.

M11-2 Evaluating Stockholders' Rights   LO1

Name four rights of stockholders. Which of these seems most important? Why?

Voting, dividends, purchase shares, residual claim

M11-3 Computing the Number of Unissued Shares   LO1

The balance sheet for Crutcher Corporation reported 247,000 shares outstanding, 300,000 shares authorized, and 20,000 shares in treasury stock. Compute the maximum number of new shares that Crutcher could issue.

247,000 outst.
300,000 Auth
20,000 Treas.

M11-4 Analyzing and Recording the Issuance of Common Stock   LO2

To expand operations, Aragon Consulting issued 100,000 shares of previously unissued common stock with a par value of $1. The price for the stock was $75 per share. Analyze the accounting equation effects and record the journal entry for the stock issuance. Would your answer be different if the par value were $2 per share? If so, analyze the accounting equation effects and record the journal entry for the stock issuance with a par value of $2.

dt Cash 7,500,000
cr Common stock 100,000
cr. Additional Paid-In capital 7,400,000

M11-5 Analyzing and Recording the Issuance of No-Par Value Common Stock   LO2

Refer to M11-4. Assume the issued stock has no par value. Analyze the accounting equation effects and record the journal entry for the issuance of the no-par value stock at $75. Do the effects on total assets, total liabilities, and total stockholders' equity differ from those in M11-4?

Cash 7,500,000
Paid-In capital 7,500,000

M11-6 Comparing Common Stock and Preferred Stock   LO2, 4

Your parents have just retired and have asked you for some financial advice. They have decided to invest $100,000 in a company very similar to National Beverage Corp. The company has issued both common and preferred stock. Which type of stock would you recommend? What factors are relevant to this recommendation?

LO2   **M11-7 Determining the Effects of Stock Issuance and Treasury Stock Transactions**

Trans Union Corporation issued 5,000 shares for $50 per share in the current year, and it issued 10,000 shares for $37 per share in the following year. The year after that, the company reacquired 20,000 shares of its own stock for $45 per share. Determine the impact (increase, decrease, or no change) of each of these transactions on the following classifications:

1. Total assets.
2. Total liabilities.
3. Total stockholders' equity.
4. Net income.

LO3   **M11-8 Determining the Amount of a Dividend**

Netpass Company has 300,000 shares of common stock authorized, 270,000 shares issued, and 100,000 shares of treasury stock. The company's board of directors declares a dividend of 50 cents per share of common stock. What is the total amount of the dividend that will be paid?

LO3   **M11-9 Recording Dividends**

On April 15, 2010, the board of directors for Auction.com declared a cash dividend of 40 cents per share payable to stockholders of record on May 20. The dividends will be paid on June 14. The company has 500,000 shares of stock outstanding. Prepare any necessary journal entries for each date.

LO3   **M11-10 Determining the Impact of a Stock Dividend**

Sturdy Stone Tools, Inc., announced a 100 percent stock dividend. Determine the impact (increase, decrease, no change) of this dividend on the following:

1. Total assets.
2. Total liabilities.
3. Common stock.
4. Total stockholders' equity.
5. Market value per share of common stock.

LO3   **M11-11 Determining the Impact of a Stock Split**

Complete the requirements of M11-10 assuming that the company announced a 2-for-1 stock split.

LO3   **M11-12 Recording a Stock Dividend**

To reduce its stock price, Shriver Food Systems, Inc., declared and issued a 50 percent stock dividend. The company has 800,000 shares authorized and 200,000 shares outstanding. The par value of the stock is $1 per share and the market value is $100 per share. Prepare the journal entry to record this large stock dividend.

LO4   **M11-13 Determining the Amount of a Preferred Dividend**

Colliers, Inc., has 100,000 shares of cumulative preferred stock outstanding. The preferred stock pays dividends in the amount of $2 per share but because of cash flow problems, the company did not pay any dividends last year. The board of directors plans to pay dividends in the amount of $1 million this year. What amount will go to preferred stockholders? How much will be available for common stock dividends?

LO5   **M11-14 Calculating and Interpreting Earnings per Share (EPS) and Return on Equity (ROE)**

Academy Driving School reported the following amount in its financial statements:

	2010	2009
Number of common shares	11,500	11,500
Net income	$ 23,000	$ 18,000
Cash dividends paid on common stock	$ 3,000	$ 3,000
Total stockholders' equity	$240,000	$220,000

Calculate 2010 EPS and ROE. Another driving school in the same city reported a higher net income ($45,000) in 2010, yet its EPS and ROE ratios were lower than those for the Academy Driving School. Explain how this apparent inconsistency could occur.

M11-15 Determining the Impact of Transactions on Components of Earnings per Share (EPS) and Return on Equity (ROE)   LO2, 3, 5

Indicate the direction of effect (+ for increase, − for decrease, or NE for no effect) of each of the following transactions on the accounting equation in the table below. The first transaction is shown as an example.

		Assets	= Liabilities +	Stockholders' Equity
a.	(example) Purchased 50 shares into treasury for $5,000.	Cash −5,000		Treasury stock (+xSE) −5,000
b.	Declared and paid a cash dividend of $600.			
c.	Declared and issued a stock dividend valued at $10,000 on no-par preferred stock.			
d.	Sold inventory for $80 cash, when it had cost $55.			
e.	Issued common stock at par for $60,000 cash.			

M11-16 Determining the Impact of Transactions on Earnings per Share (EPS) and Return on Equity (ROE)   LO5

Indicate the direction of effect (+ for increase, − for decrease, or NE for no effect) of each of the transactions listed in M11-15 on EPS and ROE.

M11-17 Inferring Financial Information Using the P/E Ratio   LO5

In 2009, Rec Room Sports reported earnings per share of $8.50 when its stock price was $212.50. In 2010, its earnings increased by 20 percent. If the P/E ratio remains constant, what is the price of the stock? Explain.

M11-18 (Supplement 11A) Comparing Owner's Equity to Stockholders' Equity

On January 2, Daniel Harrison contributed $20,000 to start his business. At the end of the year, the business had generated $30,000 in sales revenues, incurred $18,000 in operating expenses, and distributed $5,000 for Daniel to use to pay some personal expenses. Prepare (a) a statement of owner's equity, assuming this is a sole proprietorship, (b) the owner's equity section of the balance sheet, assuming this is a sole proprietorship, and (c) the stockholder's equity section of the balance sheet, assuming this is a corporation with no-par value stock.

EXERCISES

E11-1 Computing Shares Outstanding   LO1

The 2008 annual report for Fortune Brands, the seller of Pinnacle golf balls and MasterLock padlocks, disclosed that 750 million shares of common stock have been authorized. At the end of 2007, 235 million shares had been issued and the number of shares in treasury stock was 81 million. During 2008, 1 million common shares were reissued from treasury, and 5 million common shares were purchased for treasury stock.

Required:

Determine the number of common shares (a) issued, (b) in treasury, and (c) outstanding at the end of 2008.

LO2, 3   **E11-2 Reporting Stockholders' Equity and Determining Dividend Policy**

Incentive Corporation was organized in 2009 to operate a financial consulting business. The charter authorized the following capital stock: common stock, par value $4 per share, 12,000 shares. During the first year, the following selected transactions were completed:

a. Issued 6,000 shares of common stock for cash at $20 per share.
b. Issued 2,000 shares of common stock for cash at $23 per share.

Required:

1. Show the effects of each transaction on the accounting equation.
2. Give the journal entry required for each of these transactions.
3. Prepare the stockholders' equity section as it should be reported on the 2009 year-end balance sheet. At year-end, the accounts reflected a profit of $100.
4. Incentive Corporation has $30,000 in the company's bank account. Should the company declare cash dividends at this time? Explain.

LO2, 4   **E11-3 Preparing the Stockholders' Equity Section of the Balance Sheet**

North Wind Aviation received its charter during January 2010. The charter authorized the following capital stock:

> Preferred stock: 8 percent, par $10, authorized 20,000 shares.
> Common stock: par $7, authorized 50,000 shares.

During 2010, the following transactions occurred in the order given:

a. Issued a total of 40,000 shares of the common stock to the company's founders for $11 per share.
b. Issued 5,000 shares of the preferred stock at $18 per share.
c. Issued 3,000 shares of the common stock at $14 per share and 1,000 shares of the preferred stock at $28.
d. Net income for the first year was $48,000.

Required:

Prepare the stockholders' equity section of the balance sheet at December 31, 2010.

LO2, 3, 4   **E11-4 Reporting the Stockholders' Equity Section of the Balance Sheet**

Shelby Corporation was organized in January 2010 by 10 stockholders to operate an air conditioning sales and service business. The charter issued by the state authorized the following capital stock:

> Common stock, $1 par value, 200,000 shares.
> Preferred stock, $8 par value, 6 percent, 50,000 shares.

During January and February 2010, the following stock transactions were completed:

a. Collected $40,000 cash from each of the 10 organizers and issued 2,000 shares of common stock to each of them.
b. Issued 15,000 shares of preferred stock at $25 per share; collected in cash.

Net income for 2010 was $40,000; cash dividends declared and paid at year-end were $10,000.

Required:

Prepare the stockholders' equity section of the balance sheet at December 31, 2010.

LO2, 4   **E11-5 Determining the Effects of the Issuance of Common and Preferred Stock**

Inside Incorporated was issued a charter on January 15, 2010, that authorized the following capital stock:

> Common stock, $6 par, 100,000 shares, one vote per share.
> Preferred stock, 7 percent, par value $10 per share, 5,000 shares, nonvoting.

During 2010, the following selected transactions were completed in the order given:

a. Issued 20,000 shares of the $6 par common stock at $18 cash per share.

b. Issued 3,000 shares of preferred stock at $22 cash per share.

c. At the end of 2010, the accounts showed net income of $38,000.

Required:

1. Prepare the stockholders' equity section of the balance sheet at December 31, 2010.

2. Assume that you are a common stockholder. If Inside Incorporated needed additional capital, would you prefer to have it issue additional common stock or additional preferred stock? Explain.

E11-6 Recording and Reporting Stockholders' Equity Transactions   LO2, 4

Ava School of Learning obtained a charter at the start of 2010 that authorized 50,000 shares of no-par common stock and 20,000 shares of preferred stock, par value $10. During 2010, the following selected transactions occurred:

a. Collected $40 cash per share from four individuals and issued 5,000 shares of common stock to each.

b. Issued 6,000 shares of common stock to an outside investor at $40 cash per share.

c. Issued 8,000 shares of preferred stock at $20 cash per share.

Required:

1. Give the journal entries indicated for each of these transactions.

2. Prepare the stockholders' equity section of the balance sheet at December 31, 2010. At the end of 2010, the accounts reflected net income of $36,000. No dividends were declared.

E11-7 Finding Amounts Missing from the Stockholders' Equity Section   LO2, 4

The stockholders' equity section on the December 31, 2009, balance sheet of Chemfast Corporation reported the following amounts:

Contributed Capital	
Preferred Stock (par $20; authorized 10,000 shares, ? issued,	
of which 500 shares are held as treasury stock)	$104,000
Additional Paid-in Capital, Preferred	14,300
Common Stock (no-par; authorized 20,000 shares, issued and	
outstanding 8,000 shares)	600,000
Retained Earnings	30,000
Preferred Treasury Stock, 500 shares at cost	(9,500)

Assume that no shares of treasury stock have been sold in the past.

Required:

Complete the following statements and show your computations.

1. The number of shares of preferred stock issued was _____.

2. The number of shares of preferred stock outstanding was _____.

3. The average issue price of the preferred stock was $_____ per share.

4. The average issue price of the common stock was $_____.

5. The treasury stock transaction increased (decreased) stockholders' equity by _____.

6. The treasury stock cost $_____ per share?

7. Total stockholders' equity is $_____.

E11-8 Recording Treasury Stock Transactions and Analyzing Their Impact   LO2, 3

During 2010, the following selected transactions affecting stockholders' equity occurred for Corner Corporation:

Feb.   1   Purchased 400 shares of the company's own common stock at $22 cash per share.

Jul.   15   Issued 100 of the shares purchased on February 1 for $24 cash per share.

Sept. 1   Issued 60 more of the shares purchased on February 1 for $20 cash per share.

Required:

1. Show the effects of each transaction on the accounting equation.
2. Give the indicated journal entries for each of the transactions.
3. What impact does the purchase of treasury stock have on dividends paid?
4. What impact does the reissuance of treasury stock for an amount higher than the purchase price have on net income?

LO2, 3 ~~E11-9~~ **Recording Stockholders' Equity Transactions**

The annual report for Malibu Beachwear reported the following transactions affecting stockholders' equity:

a. Purchased $3.5 million in treasury stock.
b. Declared and paid cash dividends in the amount of $254.2 million.
c. Issued 100 percent common stock dividend involving 222.5 million additional shares with a total par value of $556.3 million.

Required:

1. Indicate the effect (increase, decrease, or no effect) of each of these transactions on total assets, liabilities, and stockholders' equity.
2. Prepare journal entries to record each of these transactions.

LO3, 4 **E11-10** **Computing Dividends on Preferred Stock and Analyzing Differences**

The records of Hoffman Company reflected the following balances in the stockholders' equity accounts at December 31, 2009:

> Common stock, par $12 per share, 40,000 shares outstanding.
> Preferred stock, 8 percent, par $10 per share, 6,000 shares outstanding.
> Retained earnings, $220,000.

On January 1, 2010, the board of directors was considering the distribution of a $62,000 cash dividend. No dividends were paid during 2008 and 2009.

Required:

1. Determine the total and per-share amounts that would be paid to the common stockholders and to the preferred stockholders under two independent assumptions:
   a. The preferred stock is noncumulative.
   b. The preferred stock is cumulative.
2. Briefly explain why the dividends per share of common stock were less for the second assumption.
3. What factors would cause a more favorable dividend for the common stockholders?

LO2, 3 **E11-11** **Recording the Payment of Dividends and Preparing a Statement of Retained Earnings**

The 2009 annual report for Sneer Corporation disclosed that the company declared and paid preferred dividends in the amount of $119.9 million in 2009. It also declared and paid dividends on common stock in the amount of $2 per share. During 2009, Sneer had 1,000,000,000 shares of common authorized; 387,570,300 shares had been issued; and 41,670,300 shares were in treasury stock. The balance in Retained Earnings was $1,554 million on December 31, 2008, and 2009 Net Income was $858 million.

Required:

1. Prepare journal entries to record the declaration, and payment, of dividends on (a) preferred and (b) common stock.
2. Using the information given above, prepare a statement of retained earnings for the year ended December 31, 2009.

E11-12 Analyzing Stock Dividends   **LO3**

On December 31, 2010, the stockholders' equity section of the balance sheet of R & B Corporation reflected the following:

Common stock (par $10; authorized 60,000 shares, outstanding 25,000 shares)	$250,000
Additional paid-in capital	12,000
Retained earnings	75,000

On February 1, 2011, the board of directors declared a 12 percent stock dividend to be issued April 30, 2011. The market value of the stock on February 1, 2011, was $18 per share.

Required:

1. For comparative purposes, prepare the stockholders' equity section of the balance sheet (a) immediately before the stock dividend and (b) immediately after the stock dividend.
   TIP: Use two columns for the amounts in this requirement.
2. Explain the effects of this stock dividend on the assets, liabilities, and stockholders' equity.
3. How would your answers to requirements 1 and 2 change if the stock dividend were 100%?

E11-13 Accounting for Dividends during the Credit Crisis   **LO3**

Black & Decker is a leading global manufacturer and marketer of power tools, hardware, and home improvement products. A press release on April 30, 2009, contained the following announcement:

> The Black & Decker Corporation (NYSE: BDK) announced that its board of directors declared a quarterly cash dividend of $0.12 per share of the Corporation's outstanding common stock payable June 26, 2009, to stockholders of record at the close of business on June 12, 2009. This represents a reduction from the $0.42 quarterly dividend paid by the Corporation since 2007. Nolan D. Archibald, Chairman and Chief Executive Officer, commented, "In today's uncertain and challenging economic environment, however, we believe it is important to preserve liquidity. By lowering the dividend to $0.12 per quarter, we will reduce cash outflows by $54 million in 2009. This action will strengthen our balance sheet, improve our credit metrics and provide greater financial flexibility."

At the time of the press release, Black & Decker had 150,000,000 shares authorized and 60 million outstanding. The par value for the company's stock is $.50 per share.

Required:

1. Prepare journal entries as appropriate for each of the three dates mentioned above.
2. Explain how a dividend cut from $0.42 to $0.12 will strengthen the company's balance sheet.

E11-14 Comparing Stock Dividends and Splits   **LO3**

On July 1, 2010, Jones Corporation had the following capital structure:

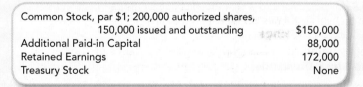

Common Stock, par $1; 200,000 authorized shares, 150,000 issued and outstanding	$150,000
Additional Paid-in Capital	88,000
Retained Earnings	172,000
Treasury Stock	None

Required:

Complete the following table based on three independent cases involving stock transactions:

Case 1: The board of directors declared and issued a 10 percent stock dividend when the stock price was $8 per share.

Case 2: The board of directors declared and issued a 100 percent stock dividend when the stock price was $8 per share.

Case 3: The board of directors voted a 2-for-1 stock split. The stock price prior to the split was $8 per share.

Items	Before Stock Transactions	Case 1 After 10% Stock Dividend	Case 2 After 100% Stock Dividend	Case 3 After Stock Split
Number of shares outstanding				
Par per share	$ 1	$ _____	$ _____	$ _____
Common stock account	$	$ _____	$ _____	$ _____
Additional paid-in capital	88,000			
Retained earnings	172,000			
Total stockholders' equity	$ _____	$ _____	$ _____	$ _____

L04   **E11-15 Analyzing Dividends in Arrears**

Mission Critical Software, Inc., was a leading provider of systems management software for Windows NT network and Internet infrastructure. Like many start-up companies, Mission Critical struggled with cash flows as it developed new business opportunities. A student found a financial statement for Mission Critical that stated that the increase in dividends in arrears on preferred stock this year was $264,000.

The student who read the note suggested that the Mission Critical preferred stock would be a good investment because of the large amount of dividend income that would be earned when the company started paying dividends again: "As the owner of the stock, I'll get dividends for the period I hold the stock plus some previous periods when I didn't even own the stock." Do you agree? Explain.

L03, 4   **E11-16 Determining the Impact of Cash and Stock Dividends**

Superior Corporation has the following capital stock outstanding:

> Preferred stock, 6 percent, par $15, outstanding shares, 8,000.
> Common stock, par $8, outstanding shares, 30,000.

On October 1, 2010, the board of directors declared dividends as follows:

> Preferred stock: Full cash preference amount, payable December 20, 2010.
> Common stock: 10 percent common stock dividend (i.e., one additional share for each 10 held), to be issued on December 20, 2010.

On December 20, 2010, the market prices were preferred stock, $40, and common stock, $32.

Required:

At each date indicated above, describe the overall effect of the cash and stock dividends on the assets, liabilities, and stockholders' equity of the company.

L03, 4   **E11-17 Determining the Financial Statement Effects of Cash and Stock Dividends**

Lynn Company has outstanding 60,000 shares of $10 par value common stock and 25,000 shares of $20 par value preferred stock (8 percent). On December 1, 2010, the board of directors voted an 8 percent cash dividend on the preferred stock and a 10 percent stock dividend on the common stock. At the date of declaration, the common stock price was $35 and the preferred stock price was $20 per share. The dividends are to be paid, or issued, on February 15, 2011. The annual accounting period ends December 31.

Required:

Explain the comparative effects of the two dividends on the assets, liabilities, and stockholders' equity (a) through December 31, 2010, (b) on February 15, 2011, and (c) in regard to the overall effects from December 1, 2010, through February 15, 2011. Use the following structure:

Item	Comparative Effects Explained	
	Cash Dividend on Preferred	Stock Dividend on Common
(a) Through December 31, 2010:		
Effect on Assets		
Effect on Liabilities		
Effect on Stockholders' Equity		

E11-18 Preparing a Statement of Retained Earnings and Partial Balance Sheet and Evaluating Dividend Policy   LO3, 5

The following account balances were selected from the records of beverage maker Blake Corporation at December 31, 2010, after all adjusting entries were completed:

Common stock (par $15; authorized 100,000 shares, issued 35,000 shares, of which 1,000 shares are held as treasury stock)	$525,000
Additional paid-in capital	180,000
Dividends declared and paid in 2010	28,000
Retained earnings, January 1, 2010	76,000
Treasury stock at cost (1,000 shares)	20,000

Net income for the year was $48,000.

Required:

1. Prepare the statement of retained earnings for the year ended December 31, 2010, and the stockholders' equity section of the balance sheet at December 31, 2010.
2. Determine the number of shares of stock that received dividends.
3. Compute the ROE ratio, assuming total stockholders' equity was $629,000 on December 31, 2009. How does it compare to the ratios shown in Exhibit 11.9?

E11-19 Analyzing Stock Repurchases and Stock Dividends   LO2, 3, 5

Winnebago is a familiar name on vehicles traveling U.S. highways. The company manufactures and sells large motor homes for vacation travel. These motor homes can be quickly recognized because of the company's "flying W" trademark. A July 2, 2007, press release contained the following information:

Winnebago Industries, Inc., (NYSE: WGO) today announced a new $60 million stock repurchase authorization. Winnebago Industries has repurchased approximately 24.4 million shares of common stock for approximately $356.8 million since December 31, 1997.

Required:

1. Determine the impact of this stock repurchase on the financial statements.
2. Why might the board have decided to repurchase the stock?
3. What impact will this purchase have on Winnebago's future dividend obligations?
4. Back on January 14, 2004, the company's board of directors declared a 2-for-1 stock split effected in the form of a 100 percent stock dividend distributed on March 5, 2004. Why would Winnebago choose a stock dividend rather than a stock split?
5. What impact would this stock dividend have had on Winnebago's financial statements? What impact would it have had on the EPS and ROE ratios?

LO2, 5   **E11-20 Determining the Effect of a Stock Repurchase on EPS and ROE**

Swimtech Pools Inc. (SPI) reported the following in its financial statements for the quarter ended March 31, 2010.

	December 31, 2009	March 31, 2010
Common Stock, $1 par, 50,000 shares outstanding	$ 50,000	$ 50,000
Additional Paid-In Capital	30,000	30,000
Retained Earnings	20,000	20,000
Total Stockholders' Equity	$100,000	$100,000

During the quarter ended March 31, 2010, SPI reported Net Income of $5,000 and declared and paid cash dividends totaling $5,000.

Required:

1. Calculate earnings per share (EPS) and return on equity (ROE) for the quarter ended March 31, 2010.
2. Assume SPI repurchases 10,000 of its common stock at a price of $2 per share on April 1, 2010. Also assume that during the quarter ended June 30, 2010, SPI reported Net Income of $5,000, and declared and paid cash dividends totaling $5,000. Calculate earnings per share (EPS) and return on equity (ROE) for the quarter ended June 30, 2010.
3. Based on your calculations in requirements 1 and 2, what can you conclude about the impact of a stock repurchase on EPS and ROE?

E11-21 (Supplement 11A) Comparing Stockholders' Equity Sections for Alternative Forms of Organization

Assume for each of the following independent cases that the annual accounting period ends on December 31, 2010, and that the total of all revenue accounts was $150,000 and the total of all expense accounts was $130,000.

Case A: Assume that the company is a *sole proprietorship* owned by Proprietor A. Prior to the closing entries, the Capital account reflected a credit balance of $50,000 and the Drawings account showed a balance of $8,000.

Case B: Assume that the company is a *partnership* owned by Partner A and Partner B. Prior to the closing entries, the owners' equity accounts reflected the following balances: A, Capital, $40,000; B, Capital, $38,000; A, Drawings, $5,000; and B, Drawings, $9,000. Profits and losses are divided equally.

Case C: Assume that the company is a *corporation*. Prior to the closing entries, the stockholders' equity accounts showed the following: Capital Stock, par $10, authorized 30,000 shares, outstanding 15,000 shares; Additional Paid-In Capital, $5,000; Retained Earnings, $65,000.

Required:

1. Give all the closing entries required at December 31, 2010, for each of the separate cases.
2. Show how the equity section of the balance sheet would appear at December 31, 2010, for each case. Show computations.

COACHED PROBLEMS

LO2   **CP11-1 Analyzing Accounting Equation Effects, Recording Journal Entries, and Preparing a Partial Balance Sheet Involving Stock Issuance, Purchase, and Reissuance Transactions**

Worldwide Company obtained a charter from the state in January 2010, which authorized 200,000 shares of common stock, $10 par value. During the first year, the company earned $38,200 and the following selected transactions occurred in the order given:

a.   Issued 60,000 shares of the common stock at $12 cash per share.
b.   Reacquired 2,000 shares at $15 cash per share from stockholders.
c.   Reissued 1,000 of the shares of the treasury stock purchased in transaction (b) two months later at $18 cash per share.

Required:

1. Indicate the effects of each transaction on the accounting equation.
2. Prepare journal entries to record each transaction.
3. Prepare the stockholders' equity section of the balance sheet at December 31, 2010.

   TIP: Because this is the first year of operations, Retained Earnings has a zero balance at the beginning of the year.

CP11-2 Recording Stock Dividends

LO3

Activision Blizzard, Inc., reported the following in the notes to its financial statements for the quarter ended September 30, 2008.

> *Stock Split* — In July 2008, the Board of Directors approved a two-for-one split of our outstanding common shares effected in the form of a stock dividend ("the split"). The split was paid September 5, 2008, to shareholders of record as of August 25, 2008. The par value of our common stock was maintained at the pre-split amount of $.000001 per share.

Required:

1. Describe the effects that this transaction would have had on the company's financial statements. Assume that 600 million shares were outstanding at the time of the transaction, trading at a stock price of $33.

   TIP: Although the financial statements refer to a stock split, the transaction actually involved a 100% stock dividend. Large stock dividends, such as a 100% dividend, are recorded at par value.

2. Why might the board of directors have decided to declare a stock dividend rather than a stock split?

CP11-3 Finding Missing Amounts

LO2, 3, 5

At December 31, 2010, the records of Nortech Corporation provided the following selected and incomplete data:

> Common stock (par $10; no changes during 2010).
> Shares authorized, 200,000.
> Shares issued, __?__; issue price $17 per share.
> Common stock account $1,250,000.
> Shares held as treasury stock, 3,000 shares, cost $20 per share.
> Net income for 2010, $118,000.
> Dividends declared and paid during 2010, $73,200.
> Retained earnings balance, January 1, 2010, $155,000.

Required:

1. Complete the following:
   Shares authorized _____.
   Shares issued _____.
   Shares outstanding _____.

   TIP: To determine the number of shares issued, divide the balance in the Common Stock account by the par value per share.

2. The balance in Additional Paid-in Capital would be $_____.
3. Earnings per share is $_____.
4. Dividends paid per share of common stock is $_____.
5. Treasury stock should be reported in the stockholders' equity section of the balance sheet in the amount of $_____.
6. Assume that the board of directors approved a 2-for-1 stock split. After the stock split, the par value per share will be $_____.
7. Disregard the stock split (assumed above). Assume instead that a 100 percent stock dividend was declared and issued after the treasury stock had been acquired, when the market price of the common stock was $21. Give any journal entry that should be made.

LO2, 3, 4

www.mhhe.com/phillips3e

CP11-4 Comparing Stock and Cash Dividends

Water Tower Company had the following stock outstanding and Retained Earnings at December 31, 2009:

Common Stock (par $8; outstanding, 30,000 shares)	$240,000
Preferred Stock, 7% (par $10; outstanding, 6,000 shares)	60,000
Retained Earnings	280,000

On December 31, 2009, the board of directors is considering the distribution of a cash dividend to the common and preferred stockholders. No dividends were declared during 2007 or 2008. Three independent cases are assumed:

Case A: The preferred stock is noncumulative; the total amount of 2009 dividends would be $30,000.

Case B: The preferred stock is cumulative; the total amount of 2009 dividends would be $12,600. Dividends were not in arrears prior to 2007.

Case C: Same as Case B, except the amount is $66,000.

Required:

1. Compute the amount of 2009 dividends, in total and per share, that would be payable to each class of stockholders for each case. Show computations.

   TIP: Preferred stockholders with cumulative dividends are paid dividends for any prior years (in arrears) *and* for the current year before common stockholders are paid.

2. Complete the following schedule, which compares case C to a 100 percent common stock dividend issued when the stock price is $24.

	Amount of Dollar Increase (Decrease)	
Item	Case C (Cash Dividend)	Stock Dividend
Assets	$	$
Liabilities	$	$
Stockholders' Equity	$	$

LO5

Aaron's, Inc.
Rent-A-Center, Inc.

CP11-5 Computing and Interpreting Return on Equity (ROE) and Price/Earnings (P/E) Ratios

Aaron's, Inc., and Rent-A-Center, Inc., are two publicly traded rental companies. They reported the following in their 2008 financial statements (in millions of dollars, except per share amounts and stock prices):

	Aaron's, Inc.		Rent-A-Center, Inc.	
	2008	2007	2008	2007
Net income	$ 90.2	$ 80.3	$ 139.6	$ 76.3
Total stockholders' equity	761.5	673.4	1,079.2	947.1
Earnings per share	1.69	1.48	2.10	1.11
Stock price when annual results reported	26.67	21.54	19.37	18.35

Required:

1. Compute the 2008 ROE for each company. Express ROE as a percentage rounded to one decimal place. Which company appears to generate greater returns on stockholders' equity in 2008?

   TIP: Remember that the bottom of the ROE ratio uses the *average* stockholders' equity.

2. Compute the 2008 P/E ratio for each company (rounded to one decimal place). Do investors appear to value one company more than the other? Explain.

GROUP A PROBLEMS

McGraw Hill connect™
|ACCOUNTING

PA11-1 Analyzing Accounting Equation Effects,   **LO2**
          Recording Journal Entries, and Preparing a Partial
          Balance Sheet Involving Stock Issuance and Purchase Transactions

Global Marine obtained a charter from the state in January 2010, which authorized 1,000,000 shares of common stock, $5 par value. During the first year, the company earned $429,000 and the following selected transactions occurred in the order given:

a. Issued 700,000 shares of the common stock at $54 cash per share.
b. Reacquired 25,000 shares at $50 cash per share to use as stock incentives for senior management.

Required:

1. Indicate the effects of each transaction on the accounting equation.
2. Prepare journal entries to record each transaction.
3. Prepare the stockholders' equity section of the balance sheet at December 31, 2010.

PA11-2 Recording Cash Dividends   **LO3**

National Chocolate Corp. produces chocolate bars and snacks under the brand names Blast and Soothe. A press release contained the following information:

> March 5, 2010—National Chocolate Corp. today announced that its Board of Directors has declared a special "one-time" cash dividend of $1.00 per share on its one million outstanding common shares. The dividend will be paid on April 30 to shareholders of record at the close of business on March 26.

Required:

1. Prepare any journal entries that National Chocolate Corp. should make as the result of information in the preceding report. Assume that the company has 1.0 million shares outstanding on March 5, the par value is $0.01 per share, and the stock price is $10 per share.
2. What two requirements would the board of directors have considered before making the dividend decisions?

PA11-3 Finding Missing Amounts   **LO2, 3, 5**

At December 31, 2010, the records of Kozmetsky Corporation provided the following selected and incomplete data:

> Common stock (par $1; no changes during 2010).
> Shares authorized, 5,000,000.
> Shares issued, _____?_____ ; issue price $80 per share.
> Shares held as treasury stock, 100,000 shares, cost $60 per share.
> Net income for 2010, $4,800,000.
> Common stock account $1,500,000.
> Dividends declared and paid during 2010, $2 per share.
> Retained earnings balance, January 1, 2010, $82,900,000.

Required:

1. Complete the following:
   Shares issued _____.
   Shares outstanding _____.
2. The balance in Additional Paid-in Capital would be $_____.
3. Earnings per share is $_____. Round your answer to two decimal places.
4. Total dividends paid on common stock during 2010 is $_____.
5. Treasury stock should be reported in the stockholders' equity section of the balance sheet in the amount of $_____.

6. Assume that the board of directors voted a 2-for-1 stock split. After the stock split, the par value per share will be $_____.

7. Disregard the stock split (assumed above). Assume instead that a 100 percent stock dividend was declared and issued after the treasury stock had been acquired, when the market price of the common stock was $21. Explain how stockholders' equity will change.

LO2, 3, 4   **PA11-4 Comparing Stock and Cash Dividends**

Ritz Company had the following stock outstanding and Retained Earnings at December 31, 2010:

Common stock (par $1; outstanding, 500,000 shares)	$500,000
Preferred stock, 8% (par $10; outstanding, 21,000 shares)	210,000
Retained earnings	900,000

On December 31, 2010, the board of directors is considering the distribution of a cash dividend to the common and preferred stockholders. No dividends were declared during 2008 or 2009. Three independent cases are assumed:

Case A: The preferred stock is noncumulative; the total amount of 2010 dividends would be $30,000.

Case B: The preferred stock is cumulative; the total amount of 2010 dividends would be $30,000. Dividends were not in arrears prior to 2008.

Case C: Same as Case B, except the amount is $75,000.

Required:

1. Compute the amount of dividends, in total and per share, payable to each class of stockholders for each case. Show computations. Round per-share amounts to two decimal places.

2. Complete the following schedule, which compares case C to a 100 percent stock dividend on the outstanding common shares when the stock price was $50.

	Amount of Dollar Increase (Decrease)	
Item	Case C (Cash Dividend)	Stock Dividend
Assets	$	$
Liabilities	$	$
Stockholders' Equity	$	$

LO5   **PA11-5 Computing and Interpreting Return on Equity (ROE) and Price/Earnings (P/E) Ratios**

eXcel

www.mhhe.com/phillips3e

Two magazine companies reported the following in their 2009 financial statements (in thousands of dollars, except per-share amounts and stock prices):

	BusinessWorld		Fun and Games	
	2009	2008	2009	2008
Net income	$ 55,000	$ 54,302	$ 91,420	$172,173
Total stockholders' equity	587,186	512,814	894,302	934,098
Earnings per share	3.20	3.19	2.10	3.98
Stock price when annual results reported	54.40	51.04	32.55	59.70

Required:

1. Compute the 2009 ROE for each company (express ROE as a percentage rounded to one decimal place). Which company appears to generate greater returns on stockholders' equity in 2009?

2. Compute the 2009 P/E ratio for each company. Do investors appear to value one company more than the other? Explain.

3. Fun and Games reacquired 32,804 (thousand) shares of common stock in 2009 at $4 per share. Recalculate the company's ROE for 2009 assuming that this stock repurchase did not occur. Does this new ROE change your interpretation of the ROE ratios calculated in requirement 1?

GROUP B PROBLEMS

PB11-1 Analyzing Accounting Equation Effects, Recording Journal Entries, and Preparing a Partial Balance Sheet Involving Stock Issuance and Purchase Transactions

LO2

Whyville Corporation obtained its charter from the state in January 2010, which authorized 500,000 shares of common stock, $1 par value. During the first year, the company earned $58,000 and the following selected transactions occurred in the order given:

a. Issued 200,000 shares of the common stock at $23 cash per share.
b. Reacquired 5,000 shares at $24 cash per share to use as stock incentives for senior management.

Required:

1. Indicate the effects of each transaction on the accounting equation.
2. Prepare journal entries to record each transaction.
3. Prepare the stockholders' equity section of the balance sheet at December 31, 2010.

PB11-2 Recording Cash and Stock Dividends

LO3

Yougi Corp. is an animation studio operating in South Florida. A recent press release contained the following information:

April 1, 2009—Yougi Corp. today announced that its Board of Directors has declared a cash dividend of $0.50 per share on 605,000 outstanding preferred shares. The dividend will be paid on or before May 31, 2009, to preferred shareholders of record at the close of business on May 26, 2009. The Board of Directors also announced a 100% common stock dividend will occur on May 31, 2009, on its 1,900,000 outstanding $0.01 par common stock for stockholders of record on May 26, 2009.

Required:

1. Prepare any journal entries that Yougi Corp. should make as the result of information in the preceding report.
2. What two requirements would the board of directors have considered before making the dividend decision?

PB11-3 Finding Missing Amounts

LO2, 3, 5

At December 31, 2010, the records of Seacrest Enterprises provided the following selected and incomplete data:

Common stock (par $0.50; no changes during 2010).
Shares authorized, 10,000,000.
Shares issued, _____?_____; issue price $10 per share.
Shares held as treasury stock, 50,000 shares, cost $11 per share.
Net income for 2010, $2,400,000.
Common stock account $750,000.
Dividends declared and paid during 2010, $1 per share.
Retained earnings balance, January 1, 2010, $36,400,000.

Required:

1. Complete the following:
    Shares issued _____.
    Shares outstanding _____.
2. The balance in Additional Paid-in Capital would be $_____.
3. Earnings per share is $_____. Round your answer to two decimal places.
4. Total dividends paid on common stock during 2010 is $_____.
5. Treasury stock should be reported in the stockholders' equity section of the balance sheet in the amount of $_____.

6. Assume that the board of directors voted a 2-for-1 stock split. After the stock split, the par value per share will be $_____.

7. Disregard the stock split (assumed above). Assume instead that a 100 percent stock dividend was declared and issued after the treasury stock had been acquired, when the stock price of the common stock was $21. Explain how stockholders' equity will change.

LO2, 3, 4 **PB11-4 Comparing Stock and Cash Dividends**

Carlos Company had the following stock outstanding and Retained Earnings at December 31, 2010:

Common Stock (par $1; outstanding, 490,000 shares)	$490,000
Preferred Stock, 8% (par $10; outstanding, 19,000 shares)	190,000
Retained Earnings	966,000

On December 31, 2010, the board of directors is considering the distribution of a cash dividend to the common and preferred stockholders. No dividends were declared during 2008 or 2009. Three independent cases are assumed:

Case A: The preferred stock is noncumulative; the total amount of 2010 dividends would be $24,000.

Case B: The preferred stock is cumulative; the total amount of 2010 dividends would be $24,000. Dividends were not in arrears prior to 2008.

Case C: Same as Case B, except the amount is $67,000.

Required:

1. Compute the amount of 2010 dividends, in total and per share, payable to each class of stockholders for each case. Show computations. Round per-share amounts to two decimal places.

2. Complete the following schedule, which compares case C to a 100 percent stock dividend on the outstanding common shares when the stock price was $45.

	Amount of Dollar Increase (Decrease)	
Item	Case C (Cash Dividend)	Stock Dividend
Assets	$	$
Liabilities	$	$
Stockholders' Equity	$	$

LO5 **PB11-5 Computing and Interpreting Return on Equity (ROE)**

Two music companies reported the following in their 2009 financial statements (in thousands of dollars, except per-share amounts and stock prices):

	Urban Youth		Sound Jonx	
	2009	2008	2009	2008
Net income	$ 27,500	$ 24,302	$ 41,500	$ 36,739
Total stockholders' equity	387,101	300,399	516,302	521,198
Earnings per share	1.10	1.00	0.95	0.85
Stock price when annual results reported	20.35	18.50	16.15	14.45

Required:

1. Compute the 2009 ROE for each company (express ROE as a percentage rounded to one decimal place). Which company appears to generate greater returns on stockholders' equity in 2009?

2. Compute the 2009 P/E ratio for each company. Do investors appear to value one company more than the other? Explain.

3. Sound Jonx reacquired 5,000 (thousand) shares of common stock in 2009 at $13 per share. Recalculate the company's ROE for 2009 assuming that this stock repurchase did not occur. Does this new ROE change your interpretation of the ROE ratios calculated in requirement 1?

COMPREHENSIVE PROBLEM

C11-1 Financial Reporting of Bond Issuance and Common Stock Issuance, Purchase, Reissuance, and Cash Dividends (Chapters 10 and 11)

LO2, 3

American Laser, Inc., reported the following stockholders' equity account balances on January 1, 2010.

Notes Payable (due 2013)	$10,000	Bonds Payable	$ 0
Common Stock, 10,000 shares of $1 par	10,000	Retained Earnings	120,000
Additional Paid-in Capital	90,000	Treasury Stock	0

The company entered into the following transactions during 2010.

Jan. 15	Issued 5,000 shares of $1 par common stock for $50,000 cash.
Feb. 15	Reacquired 3,000 shares of $1 par common stock into treasury for $33,000 cash.
Mar. 15	Reissued 2,000 shares of treasury stock for $24,000 cash.
Aug. 15	Reissued 600 shares of treasury stock for $4,600 cash.
Sept. 15	Declared (but did not yet pay) a $1 cash dividend on each outstanding share of common stock.
Oct. 1	Issued 100, 10-year, $1,000 bonds, at a quoted bond price of 101.

Required:

1. Analyze the effects of each transaction on total assets, liabilities, and stockholders' equity.
2. Prepare journal entries to record each transaction.
3. Prepare the noncurrent liabilities and stockholders' equity sections of the balance sheet at December 31, 2010. At the end of 2010, the accounts reflected net income of $20,000.

SKILLS DEVELOPMENT CASES

S11-1 Finding Financial Information

LO2, 3, 5

Refer to the financial statements of The Home Depot in Appendix A at the end of this book, or download the annual report from the *Cases* section of the text's Web site at www.mhhe.com/phillips3e.

Required:

1. As of February 1, 2009, how many shares of common stock were authorized? How many shares were issued? How many shares were held in treasury? What does this suggest to you about the number of shares outstanding?
2. According to the Retained Earnings column in the Statement of Stockholders' Equity, what was the total dollar amount of cash dividends declared during the year ended February 1, 2009?
3. According to the income statement, how has The Home Depot's net earnings changed over the past three years? Has the company's basic earnings per share changed over the past three years? Are these patterns consistent?

S11-2 Comparing Financial Information

LO2, 3, 5

Refer to the financial statements of The Home Depot in Appendix A and Lowe's in Appendix B at the end of this book, or download the annual reports from the *Cases* section of the text's Web site at www.mhhe.com/phillips3e.

Lowe's

Required:

1. Did Lowe's have more or fewer authorized shares of common stock than The Home Depot at the beginning of February 2009?
2. From the Retained Earnings column in the statement of stockholders' equity, what total amount of cash dividends did Lowe's declare during the year ended January 30, 2009? Compared to The Home Depot, is Lowe's policy on dividends better, worse, or just different?
3. How have Lowe's net earnings changed over the past three years? How has the company's basic earnings per share changed over the past three years? According to financial statement note 11, were the changes in EPS caused only by changes in Lowe's net earnings?

LO3, 5   **S11-3 Internet-Based Team Research: Examining an Annual Report**

As a team, select an industry to analyze. Using your Web browser, each team member should access the annual report or 10-K for one publicly traded company in the industry, with each member selecting a different company. (See S1-3 in Chapter 1 for a description of possible resources for these tasks.)

Required:

1. On an individual basis, each team member should write a short report that incorporates the following:
   a. Has the company declared cash or stock dividends during the past three years?
   b. What is the trend in the company's EPS over the past three years?
   c. Compute and analyze the return on equity ratio over the past two years.
2. Then, as a team, write a short report comparing and contrasting your companies using these attributes. Discuss any patterns across the companies that you as a team observe. Provide potential explanations for any differences discovered.

LO1, 2   **S11-4 Ethical Decision Making: A Real-Life Example**

ACTIVISION

Activision became a public company with an initial public offering of stock on June 9, 1983, at $12 per share. In June 2002, Activision issued 7.5 million additional shares to the public at approximately $33 per share in a seasoned new issue. In October 2002, when its stock was trading at about $22 per share, Activision executives announced that the company would spend up to $150 million to reacquire stock from investors. On January 8, 2003, *The Wall Street Journal* reported that several analysts were criticizing Activision's executives because the company had issued the shares to the public at a high price ($33) and then were offering to reacquire them at the going stock market price, which was considerably lower than the issue price in 2002.

Required:

1. Do you think it was inappropriate for Activision to offer to reacquire the stock at a lower stock price in October 2002?
2. Would your answer to question 1 be different if Activision had not issued additional stock in June 2002?
3. The above *Wall Street Journal* article also reported that, in December 2002, Activision executives had purchased, for their own personal investment portfolios, 530,000 shares of stock in the company at the then-current price of $13.32 per share. If you were an investor, how would you feel about executives buying stock in their own company?
4. Would your answer to question 3 be different if you also learned that the executives had disposed of nearly 2.5 million shares of Activision stock earlier in the year, when the price was at least $26.08 per share?

LO3   **S11-5 Ethical Decision Making: A Mini-Case**

You are the president of a very successful Internet company that has had a remarkably profitable year. You have determined that the company has more than $10 million in cash generated by operating activities not needed in the business. You are thinking about paying it out to stockholders as a special dividend. You discuss the idea with your vice president, who reacts angrily to your suggestion:

> Our stock price has gone up by 200 percent in the last year alone. What more do we have to do for the owners? The people who really earned that money are the employees who have been working 12 hours a day, six or seven days a week to make the company successful. Most of them didn't even take vacations last year. I say we have to pay out bonuses and nothing extra for the stockholders.

As president, you know that you are hired by the board of directors, which is elected by the stockholders.

Required:

What is your responsibility to both groups? To which group would you give the $10 million? Why?

S11-6 Critical Thinking: Making a Decision as an Investor

LO3

You have retired after a long and successful career as a business executive and now spend a good portion of your time managing your retirement portfolio. You are considering three basic investment alternatives. You can invest in (1) corporate bonds paying 7 percent interest, (2) conservative stocks that pay substantial dividends (typically 5 percent of the stock price every year), and (3) growth-oriented technology stocks that pay no dividends.

Required:

Analyze each of these alternatives and select one. Justify your selection.

S11-7 Charting Stock Price Movement around Important Announcement Dates

LO1, 3

Using a Web search engine such as Google, find either an earnings or dividend announcement for two different companies. Using a source such as bigcharts.com, determine the closing stock price for each company for each day during the five business days before and after the announcement. Using a separate worksheet for each company, prepare a line chart of its stock price movement.

Required:

Examine the charts for each company. Does the stock price appear to change as a consequence of their announcements? Explain why or why not.

CONTINUING CASE

CC11 Accounting for Equity Financing

LO1, 2, 3, 4, 5

Nicole has been financing Nicole's Getaway Spa (NGS) using equity financing. Currently NGS has authorized 100,000, $0.30 no-par preferred shares, and 200,000, $1 par common shares. Outstanding shares include 50,000 preferred shares and 40,000 common shares.

Recently the following transactions have taken place.

a. NGS repurchases 1,000 common shares for $10 a share.
b. NGS issues 1,000 preferred shares for $12 a share.
c. On November 12, 2011, the board of directors declared a cash dividend on each outstanding preferred share.
d. The dividend is paid December 20, 2011.

Required:

1. Prepare the journal entries needed for each of the transactions.
2. If you were a common shareholder concerned about your voting rights, would you prefer Nicole to issue additional common shares or additional preferred shares? Why?
3. Describe the overall effect of each transaction on the assets, liabilities, and shareholders' equity of the company. (Use + for increase, − for decrease, and NE for no effect.)
4. How would each transaction affect the ROE ratio?

CHAPTER 12

Reporting and Interpreting the Statement of Cash Flows

YOUR LEARNING OBJECTIVES

Understand the business

LO1   Identify cash flows arising from operating, investing, and financing activities.

Study the accounting methods

LO2   Report cash flows from operating activities, using the indirect method.

LO3   Report cash flows from investing activities.

LO4   Report cash flows from financing activities.

Evaluate the results

LO5   Interpret cash flows from operating, investing, and financing activities.

LO6   Report and interpret cash flows from operating activities, using the direct method

Review the chapter

THAT WAS
THEN

In the previous chapters, you learned about the income statement, statement of retained earnings, and balance sheet.

Lecture Presentation-LP12
www.mhhe.com/phillips3e

▶ UA PROTO EVADE™ II TRAINER

FOCUS COMPANY: Under Armour

www.underarmour.com

UNDER ARMOUR

Have you ever studied your bank statements to see how much money you bring in and pay out during a typical month? You don't have to be a financial genius to know that if you are spending more than you earn, your savings will quickly disappear, and you will need to get a loan or some other source of financing to see you through.

Most businesses face the same issues you do. In 2007, for example, Under Armour Inc.—famous for its frictionless sportswear—reported a net cash outflow from day-to-day operating activities. To ensure the company's long-term survival, managers had to stay on top of this change in the cash situation. Fortunately, the company had saved a great deal of cash in prior years. Managers were also able to negotiate some new loans to keep the business from running out of cash. By 2008, the company had turned things around and was again experiencing a positive net cash inflow from its operations.

Just like Under Armour's managers, investors and creditors also monitor the company's cash inflows and outflows. Investors want to know whether Under Armour is likely to pay dividends and creditors want to know whether Under Armour is likely to pay them the amounts they are owed. They find information for making such predictions in the statement of cash flows. Similar to your personal bank statement, the statement of cash flows reports changes in a company's cash situation.

THIS IS
N O W

This chapter focuses on the fourth main financial statement—the statement of cash flows.

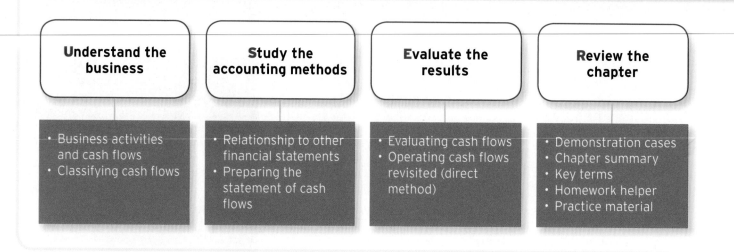

Understand the business
- Business activities and cash flows
- Classifying cash flows

Study the accounting methods
- Relationship to other financial statements
- Preparing the statement of cash flows

Evaluate the results
- Evaluating cash flows
- Operating cash flows revisited (direct method)

Review the chapter
- Demonstration cases
- Chapter summary
- Key terms
- Homework helper
- Practice material

Understand the Business

BUSINESS ACTIVITIES AND CASH FLOWS

Learning Objective 1
Identify cash flows arising from operating, investing, and financing activities.

Video 12.1
www.mhhe.com/phillips3e

To this point in the course, we've analyzed business activities to identify their financial effects on assets, liabilities, stockholders' equity, revenues, and expenses. We've emphasized that business activities have financial effects even when they don't involve cash. That's why accrual accounting exists. When accurately reported, accrual-based net income is the best measure of a company's profitability during the period.

Despite its importance, net income is not what companies use when they pay wages, dividends, or loans. These activities require cash, so financial statement users need information about the company's cash and changes in its cash. Neither the balance sheet nor the income statement provide this information. The balance sheet shows a company's cash balance at a point in time, but it doesn't explain the activities that caused changes in its cash. Cash may have been generated by the company's day-to-day operations, by the sale of the company's buildings, or by the negotiation of new loans. The income statement doesn't explain changes in cash because it focuses on just the operating results of the business, excluding cash that is received or paid when taking out or paying down loans, issuing or buying the company's own stock, and selling or investing in long-lived assets. Also, the timing of cash receipts and payments may differ from the accrual-based income statement, which reports revenues when they are earned and expenses when they are incurred. Under Armour, for example, reported a hefty amount of net income in each quarter of 2008, yet its related cash flows were negative in two of those four quarters. Such differences between net income and cash flows are the reason that GAAP requires every company to report a statement of cash flows.

The statement of cash flows shows each major type of business activity that caused a company's cash to increase or decrease during the accounting period. For purposes of this statement, cash is defined to include cash and cash equivalents. As explained in Chapter 6, cash equivalents are short-term, highly liquid investments purchased within three months of maturity. They are considered equivalent to cash because they are both (1) readily convertible to known amounts of cash, and (2) so near to maturity that their value is unlikely to change.

Spotlight On ETHICS

Cash Isn't Estimated

Critics of accrual-based net income claim it can be manipulated because it relies on many estimates (of bad debts, inventory market values, assets' useful lives), but cash flows do not involve estimates so they are not easily manipulated. A cash balance changes only when cash has been received or paid. One particularly dramatic illustration of the subjectivity of net income, but not cash, involved the bankruptcy of a department store chain operated by the W. T. Grant Company. Through biased estimates, the company reported net income for nine consecutive years but then shocked everyone when it declared bankruptcy and shut down the following year. At the time, a statement of cash flows wasn't required. Had it been required, the company would have reported negative operating cash flows in seven of the ten years.

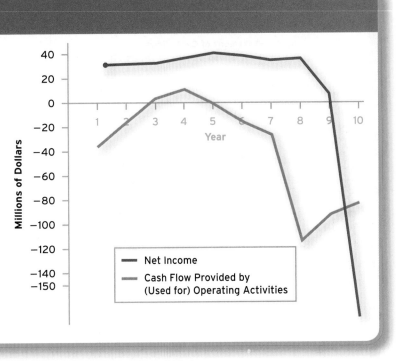

James A. Largay, III, and Clyde P. Stickney, "Cash Flows, Ratio Analysis and the W. T. Grant Company Bankruptcy," *Financial Analysts Journal* 36, no. 4: 51–54, July/August 1980.

CLASSIFYING CASH FLOWS

The statement of cash flows requires that all cash inflows and outflows be classified as relating to the company's operating, investing, or financing activities. This classification of cash flows is useful because most companies experience different cash flow patterns as they develop and mature. Think back to Chapter 2 when Pizza Aroma had just started. The first thing the owner needed to get his idea off the ground was **financing,** which he could then use to **invest** in assets that later would be needed to **operate** his business. At this early stage, financing and investing cash flows were crucial for Pizza Aroma. For an established business, like Activision in Chapter 5, operating activities often are the focus. Financial statement users are interested in a company's ability to generate operating cash flows that will allow it to continue investing in additional assets and repay the financing it originally obtained. Creditors and investors will tolerate poor operating cash flows for only so long before they stop lending to or investing in the company. For any company to survive in the long run, the amount of cash generated through daily operating activities has to exceed the amount spent on them.

A condensed version of Under Armour's statement of cash flows is presented in Exhibit 12.1. Don't worry about the details in the three cash flow categories yet. For now, focus on the categories' totals. Notice that each category can result in net cash inflows (represented by a positive number) or net cash outflows (represented by a negative number by using brackets). The sum of these three categories ($79 − $38 + $21 = $62) represents the overall change in cash on the balance sheet between the beginning and end of the period ($62 + $40 = $102).

Under Armour's 2008 cash flows in Exhibit 12.1 suggest the company is financially healthy. The company generated $79 million cash from its day-to-day operations. This money allowed Under Armour to invest $38 million in additional long-term assets and, combined with $21 million of net cash inflow from financing activities, build its cash balance at the end of the year. To learn the specific causes of these cash flows, you would consider the details of each category, as we will do now.

EXHIBIT 12.1	Under Armour's Condensed Statement of Cash Flows

UNDER ARMOUR, INC. Statement of Cash Flows For the Year Ended December 31, 2008		Explanations
(in millions)		
Cash Flows from Operating Activities		Cash flows related to day-to-day activities
Net income	$ 38	Assume net income (NI) generates cash inflow
Depreciation	16	Depreciation decreased NI but didn't decrease cash
Changes in current assets and current liabilities	25	Differences in the timing of net income and cash flows
Net cash provided by operating activities	79	Indicates overall cash impact of operating activities
Cash Flows Used in Investing Activities		Cash flows related to long-term assets
Purchase of equipment	(36)	Cash was used to purchase equipment
Purchase of intangible and other assets	(2)	Cash was used to purchase intangibles
Net cash used in investing activities	(38)	Indicates overall cash impact of investing activities
Cash Flows from Financing Activities		Cash flows from transactions with lenders, investors
Additional borrowings of long-term debt	16	Cash received from borrowing
Payments on long-term debt	(7)	Cash used to repay amounts previously borrowed
Proceeds from stock issuance	12	Cash received from issuing stock
Net cash provided by financing activities	21	Indicates overall cash impact of financing activities
Net Change in Cash and Cash Equivalents	62	$79 + $(38) + $21 = $62
Cash and cash equivalents, beginning of year	40	Cash balance at beginning of the period
Cash and cash equivalents, end of year	$102	Cash balance at end of the period (on balance sheet)

Operating Activities

YOU SHOULD KNOW

Cash flows from operating activities (cash flows from operations): Cash inflows and outflows related to components of net income.

Cash flows from operating activities (or cash flows from operations) are the cash inflows and outflows related directly to the revenues and expenses reported on the income statement. Operating activities involve day-to-day business activities with customers, suppliers, employees, landlords, and others. Typical cash flows from operating activities include:

Inflows	Outflows
Cash provided by	*Cash used for*
Collecting from customers	Purchasing services (electricity, etc.) and goods for resale
Receiving dividends	Paying salaries and wages
Receiving interest	Paying income taxes
	Paying interest

The difference between these cash inflows and outflows is reported on the statement of cash flows as a subtotal, Net Cash Provided by (Used for) Operating Activities.

Investing Activities

YOU SHOULD KNOW

Cash flows from investing activities: Cash inflows and outflows related to the sale or purchase of investments and long-lived assets.

Cash flows from investing activities are the cash inflows and outflows related to the purchase and disposal of investments and long-lived assets. Typical cash flows from investing activities include:

Inflows	Outflows
Cash provided by	*Cash used for*
Sale or disposal of property, plant, and equipment	Purchase of property, plant, and equipment
Sale or maturity of investments in securities	Purchase of investments in securities

The difference between these cash inflows and outflows is reported on the statement of cash flows as a subtotal, Net Cash Provided by (Used in) Investing Activities.

Financing Activities

Cash flows from financing activities include exchanges of cash with stockholders and cash exchanges with lenders (for principal on loans). Common cash flows from financing activities include:

> **YOU SHOULD KNOW**
>
> **Cash flows from financing activities:** Cash inflows and outflows related to financing sources external to the company (owners and lenders).

Inflows	Outflows
Cash provided by	*Cash used for*
Borrowing from lenders through formal debt contracts	Repaying principal to lenders
Issuing stock to owners	Repurchasing stock from owners
	Paying cash dividends to owners

The difference between these cash inflows and outflows is reported on the statement of cash flows as a subtotal, Net Cash Provided by (Used in) Financing Activities.

One way to classify cash flows into operating, investing, and financing categories is to think about the balance sheet accounts to which the cash flows relate. Although exceptions exist, a general rule is that operating cash flows cause changes in current assets and current liabilities, investing cash flows affect noncurrent assets, and financing cash flows affect noncurrent liabilities or stockholders' equity accounts.[1] Exhibit 12.2 shows how this general rule relates the three sections of the statement of cash flows (SCF) to each of the main sections of a classified balance sheet.

Cash - actually liquid short term inv. within 3 months of maturity. low risk

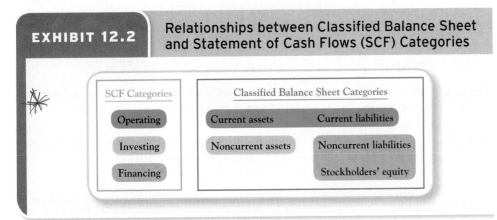

EXHIBIT 12.2 Relationships between Classified Balance Sheet and Statement of Cash Flows (SCF) Categories

---

> How's it going? Self-Study Practice
>
> Brunswick Corporation produces the Life Fitness line of gym equipment. A listing of some of its cash flows follows. Indicate whether each item is disclosed in the operating activities (O), investing activities (I), or financing activities (F) section of the statement of cash flows.
>
> [F] *a.* Stock issued to stockholders.   [I] *d.* Purchase of plant and equipment.
>
> [O] *b.* Collections from customers.   [I] *e.* Purchase of investment securities.
>
> [O] *c.* Interest paid on debt.   [F] *f.* Cash dividends paid.
>
> *After you have finished, check your answers with the solution in the margin.*

Solution to Self-Study Practice
a. F, *b.* O, *c.* O, *d.* I, *e.* I, *f.* F

---

[1]Intermediate accounting courses discuss in detail exceptions to this general rule. Exceptions include investing activities that affect current assets (for example, short-term investments) and financing activities that affect current liabilities (for example, dividends payable and short-term notes payable).

Spotlight On THE WORLD

Classification Choices under IFRS

To create consistency across companies, GAAP restricts interest and dividend classifications to a single category. IFRS, on the other hand, allows managers to choose between categories, as follows.

	COMPANY PAYS		COMPANY RECEIVES	
	Dividends	Interest	Dividends	Interest
GAAP	F	O	O	O
IFRS	O, F	O, F	O, I	O, I

GAAP classifies dividends paid as financing because they are transactions with stockholders. IFRS allows dividends paid to be classified as operating to assist users in determining the company's ability to pay dividends out of operating cash flows. GAAP requires the other three items to be classified as operating because they enter into the determination of net income. IFRS allows interest paid to be classified as financing because it is a cost of obtaining financial resources. IFRS allows interest and dividends received to be classified as investing because they are returns on investments.

Study the Accounting Methods

RELATIONSHIP TO OTHER FINANCIAL STATEMENTS

The statement of cash flows is intended to provide a cash-based view of a company's business activities during the accounting period. It uses the same transactions that have been reported in the income statement and balance sheet but converts them from the accrual basis to a cash basis. This conversion involves analyzing the income statement and the changes in balance sheet accounts, and relating these changes to the three cash flow categories. To prepare a statement of cash flows, you need the following:

1. **Comparative balance sheets,** showing beginning and ending balances, used in calculating the cash flows from all activities (operating, investing, and financing).

2. **A complete income statement,** used primarily in calculating cash flows from operating activities.

3. **Additional data** concerning selected accounts that increase and decrease as a result of investing and/or financing activities.

The approach to preparing the cash flow statement focuses on changes in the balance sheet accounts. It relies on a simple rearrangement of the balance sheet equation:

$$\text{Assets} = \text{Liabilities} + \text{Stockholders' Equity}$$

First, assets can be split into cash and all other assets, which we'll call **noncash assets:**

$$\text{Cash} + \text{Noncash Assets} = \text{Liabilities} + \text{Stockholders' Equity}$$

If we move the noncash assets to the right side of the equation, we get

$$\text{Cash} = \text{Liabilities} + \text{Stockholders' Equity} - \text{Noncash Assets}$$

Given this relationship, the **changes** in cash between the beginning and end of the period must equal the **changes** in the amounts on the right side of the equation between the beginning and end of the period:

> Change in Cash = Change in (Liabilities + Stockholders' Equity − Noncash Assets)

This equation says that **changes in cash must be accompanied by and can be accounted for by the changes in liabilities, stockholders' equity, and noncash assets.**

PREPARING THE STATEMENT OF CASH FLOWS

Based on the idea that the change in cash equals the sum of the changes in all other balance sheet accounts, we use the following steps to prepare the statement of cash flows:

1. **Determine the change in each balance sheet account.** From this year's ending balance, subtract this year's beginning balance (i.e., last year's ending balance).

2. **Identify the cash flow category or categories to which each account relates.** Use Exhibit 12.2 as a guide, but be aware that some accounts may include two categories of cash flows. Retained Earnings, for example, can include both financing cash flows (paying dividends) and operating cash flows (generating net income). Similarly, Accumulated Depreciation can be affected by operating activities (depreciation for using equipment in daily operations) as well as investing activities (disposing of equipment).

3. **Create schedules that summarize operating, investing, and financing cash flows.**

   We will follow these three steps to prepare a statement of cash flows for Under Armour for the year ended December 31, 2008. Step 1 requires that we subtract each account's beginning balance from its ending balance, as we have done in the right side of Exhibit 12.3. Next, for step 2, we indicated whether each account's cash flows relate to operating (O), investing (I), and/or financing (F) activities. Notice that Cash is not classified as O, I, or F, because Cash is not reported in these three sections but instead appears at the bottom of the statement of cash flows, as shown earlier in Exhibit 12.1. Step 3 in preparing a statement of cash flows is explained in the following sections.

Direct and Indirect Reporting of Operating Cash Flows

Two alternative methods may be used when presenting the operating activities section of the statement of cash flows:

1. The **direct method** reports the total cash inflow or outflow from each main type of transaction (that is, transactions with customers, suppliers, employees, etc.). The difference between these cash inflows and outflows equals the Net Cash Provided by (Used in) Operating Activities.

2. The **indirect method** starts with net income from the income statement and adjusts it by eliminating the effects of items that do not involve cash (for example, depreciation) and including items that do have cash effects. Adjusting net income for these items yields the amount of Net Cash Provided by (Used in) Operating Activities.

> **YOU SHOULD KNOW**
>
> **Direct method:** Reports the components of cash flows from operating activities as gross receipts and gross payments.
> **Indirect method:** Presents the operating activities section of the cash flow statement by adjusting net income to compute cash flows from operating activities.

Direct Method		Indirect Method	
Cash collected from customers	$ 738	Net income	$38
Cash paid to suppliers of inventory	(369)	Depreciation	16
Cash paid to employees and suppliers of services	(251)		
Cash paid for interest	(7)	Changes in current assets and current liabilities	25
Cash paid for income tax	(32)		
Net cash provided by (used in) operating activities	$ 79	Net cash provided by (used in) operating activities	$79

EXHIBIT 12.3 | **Information for Preparing a Statement of Cash Flows**

UNDER ARMOUR, INC.
Balance Sheet*

			Step ①	Step ②
(in millions)	December 31, 2008*	December 31, 2007*	*Change*	*Related Cash Flow Section*
Assets				
Current Assets:				
Cash and Cash Equivalents	$102	$ 40	+62	Cash
Accounts Receivable	81	94	−13	O
Inventories	182	166	+16	O
Prepaid Expenses	31	22	+9	O
Total Current Assets	396	322		
Equipment	120	84	+36	I
Less: Accumulated Depreciation	(47)	(31)	−16	O (no I; see note 2 below)
Intangible and Other Assets	18	16	+2	I
Total Assets	$487	$391		
Liabilities and Stockholders' Equity				
Current Liabilities:				
Accounts Payable	$ 72	$ 55	+17	O
Accrued Liabilities	61	41	+20	O
Total Current Liabilities	133	96		
Long-term Debt	23	14	+9	F
Total Liabilities	156	110		
Stockholders' Equity:				
Contributed Capital	175	163	+12	F
Retained Earnings	156	118	+38	O (no F; see note 1 below)
Total Stockholders' Equity	331	281		
Total Liabilities and Stockholders' Equity	$487	$391		

UNDER ARMOUR, INC.
Income Statement*
For the Year Ended December 31, 2008

(in millions)	
Net Sales	$725
Cost of Goods Sold	370
Gross Profit	355
Operating Expenses:	
Selling, General, and Administrative Expenses	262
Depreciation Expense	16
Total Operating Expenses	278
Income from Operations	77
Interest Expense	7
Net Income before Income Tax Expense	70
Income Tax Expense	32
Net Income	$ 38

Additional data

1. No dividends were declared or paid.

2. No disposals or impairments of equipment or intangibles occurred.

3. Equipment costing $36 million and intangibles costing $2 million were purchased with cash.

4. Long-term debt of $7 million was paid and $16 million in new loans was issued.

5. Shares of stock were issued for $12 million.

*Certain balances have been adjusted to simplify the presentation.

The point to remember about the direct and indirect methods is that they are simply different ways to arrive at the same number. **Net cash flows provided by (used in) operating activities is always the same under the direct and indirect methods.** Also, the choice between the two methods affects only the operating activities section of the statement of cash flows, not the investing and financing sections.

Spotlight On THE WORLD

Direct vs. Indirect Method Presentation

GAAP and IFRS currently allow companies to use either the direct or indirect method. The FASB and IASB have recently proposed removing this choice and allowing only the direct method. If adopted, this proposal would significantly change the way companies report their statement of cash flows. Currently, about 99 percent of large U.S. companies, including Under Armour, use the indirect method.

We focus on the indirect method in the following section because it is currently the most commonly used method in the United States. The direct method, which may be required by GAAP and IFRS in the future, is presented in the last section of this chapter.

> **Learning Objective 2**
> Report cash flows from operating activities, using the indirect method.

Determining Operating Cash Flows Using the Indirect Method

When using the indirect method, the schedule of operating activities has the following format. We explain each of these items below and then, on pages 563–565, we demonstrate how to use Under Armour's information in Exhibit 12.3 to create such a schedule.

> Net income
> Items included in net income that do not involve cash
>   + Depreciation
> Changes in current assets and current liabilities
>   + Decreases in current assets
>   − Increases in current assets
>   − Decreases in current liabilities
>   + Increases in current liabilities
> _____
> Net cash flow provided by (used in) operating activities

Net income. When preparing a schedule to determine operating cash flows using the indirect method, start with net income as reported on the last line of the company's income statement. By starting with net income, it's as if we are assuming all revenues resulted in cash inflows and all expenses resulted in cash outflows. But we know this is not true, however, so we adjust net income to eliminate items that are included in net income but do not involve cash and to include items that were excluded from net income but do involve cash.

+Depreciation. When initially recording depreciation in the accounting system, we increase Depreciation Expense (with a debit) and increase Accumulated Depreciation (with a credit). Notice that depreciation does not involve cash. To **eliminate** the effect of having deducted Depreciation Expense in the income statement, we add it back in the statement of cash flows.

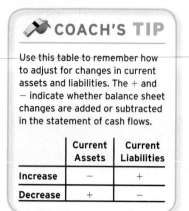

COACH'S TIP

Use this table to remember how to adjust for changes in current assets and liabilities. The + and − indicate whether balance sheet changes are added or subtracted in the statement of cash flows.

	Current Assets	Current Liabilities
Increase	−	+
Decrease	+	−

+ Decreases in current assets. Adding decreases in current assets serves two purposes. First, it **eliminates** the effects of some transactions that decreased net income but did not affect cash in the current period. For example, when Supplies are used, net income decreases but cash is not affected. To eliminate these noncash effects from our cash flow computations, we must add back decreases in Supplies and other current assets. Second, adding decreases in current assets allows us to **include** the cash effects of other transactions that did not affect net income in the current period but did increase cash. For example, Cash increases when Accounts Receivable are collected. These cash inflows are captured by adding the amount by which this current asset had decreased.

− Increases in current assets. Subtracting increases in current assets similarly serves two purposes. First, it **eliminates** the effects of transactions that increased net income but did not affect cash in the current period. For example, net income increases when a company provides services on account, but cash is not affected. We eliminate these noncash effects by subtracting increases in current assets. Second, subtracting increases in current assets allows us to **include** the cash effects of other transactions that did not affect net income in the current period but did decrease cash. For example, Cash decreases when a company prepays its insurance or rent, but net income isn't affected until these assets are used up. The cash outflows can be captured by subtracting the increase in these current assets.

− Decreases in current liabilities. Subtracting decreases in current liabilities serves two purposes. First, it **eliminates** the effects of transactions that increased net income but did not affect cash. For example, a company decreases Unearned Revenue and increases net income in the current period when it fulfills its prior obligations to provide services, but cash is not affected. To eliminate these noncash effects, we subtract decreases in current liabilities. Second, subtracting decreases in current liabilities allows us to **include** the cash effects of other transactions that did not affect net income in the current period but did decrease cash. For example, Cash decreases when a company pays wages that were incurred and expensed in a previous period. These cash outflows are captured by subtracting decreases in current liabilities.

+ Increases in current liabilities. Adding increases in current liabilities serves two purposes. First, it **eliminates** the effects of transactions that decreased net income but did not affect cash. For example, when interest is accrued, a company decreases net income but its cash is not affected. To eliminate these noncash effects, we add back increases in current liabilities. Second, adding increases in current liabilities allows us to **include** the cash effects of other transactions that did not affect net income in the current period but did increase cash. For example, Cash and Unearned Revenue increase when the company receives cash in advance of providing services. Adding the increase in current liabilities captures these cash inflows.

Under Armour's Operating Cash Flows—Indirect Method

The preceding approach to preparing an operating cash flow schedule can be applied to Under Armour's information in Exhibit 12.3. By taking the amount of the change in each account marked by an O in Exhibit 12.3, we have prepared an operating cash flow schedule for Under Armour in Exhibit 12.4. Understanding the causes of increases or decreases in each current asset and current liability is the key to understanding the logic behind the items in the schedule. Take your time reading the following explanations and make sure you understand the reasons for each item.

EXHIBIT 12.4	Under Armour's Schedule of Operating Cash Flows	

Items	Amount (in millions)	
Net income	$38	Starting point, fro...
Items included in net income that do not involve cash		
+ Depreciation	16	Depreciation is a noncash expe...
Changes in current assets and current liabilities		
+ Decrease in Accounts Receivable	13	Cash collections greater than sales on accoun...
− Increase in Inventories	(16)	Purchases greater than cost of goods sold
− Increase in Prepaid Expenses	(9)	Prepayments greater than related expenses
+ Increase in Accounts Payable	17	Purchases greater than payments to suppliers
+ Increase in Accrued Liabilities	20	Cash payments less than accrued expenses
Net cash flow provided by (used in) operating activities	$79	Overall increase in cash from operations

Net Income + Depreciation

Net income and depreciation are always the first two lines to appear in a statement of cash flows prepared using the indirect method. They begin the process of converting net income to operating cash flows. They also begin the process of explaining the change in Cash by accounting for changes in the other balance sheet accounts. In the case of Under Armour, the $38 million of net income fully accounts for the change in Retained Earnings (the company had no dividends). Similarly, the $16 million of depreciation accounts for the change in Accumulated Depreciation (the company had no disposals).[2]

Decrease in Accounts Receivable

Accounts Receivable increases when sales are made on account and it decreases when cash is collected from customers. An overall decrease in this account, then, implies that cash collections were greater than sales on account. To convert from the lower sales number that is included in net income to the higher cash collected from customers, we add the difference ($13 million).

   Another way to remember whether to add or subtract the difference is to think about whether the overall change in the account balance is explained by a debit or credit. If the change in the account is explained by a debit, the adjustment in the cash flow schedule is reported like a corresponding credit to cash (subtracted). In Under Armour's case, the decrease in Accounts Receivable is explained by a credit, so the adjustment in the cash flow schedule is reported like a debit to cash (an increase), as follows.

> **COACH'S TIP**
>
> The depreciation addback is not intended to suggest that depreciation creates an increase in cash. Rather, it's just showing that depreciation does not cause a decrease in cash. This is a subtle, but very important, difference in interpretation.

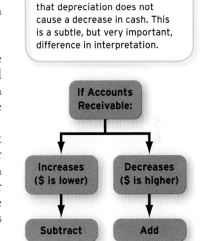

CASH FLOWS FROM OPERATING ACTIVITIES	
Net income	38
+ Accounts receivable decrease	13
. . .	. . .
Net cash inflow	——

Accounts Receivable (A)			
Beg. bal.	94		
		13	Decrease
End. bal.	81		

Increase in Inventory

The income statement reports the cost of merchandise sold during the period, but cash flow from operating activities must report cash purchases of

---

[2]Amortization and impairment losses (discussed in Chapter 9) are handled in exactly the same way as depreciation. Gains and losses on fixed asset disposals also are dealt with in a similar manner and are discussed in chapter supplement 12A.

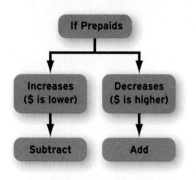

inventory. As shown in the T-account on the left, purchases of goods increase the balance in inventory, and recording merchandise sold decreases the balance in inventory.

Inventories (A)	
Beg. bal.	
Purchases	Cost of goods sold
End. bal.	

Inventories (A)	
Beg. bal.	166
Increase	16
End. bal.	182

Under Armour's $16 million inventory increase means that the amount of purchases is more than the cost of goods sold. The increase (the extra purchases) must be subtracted from net income to convert to cash flow from operating activities in Exhibit 12.4. (A decrease would be added.)

Increase in Prepaid Expenses   The income statement reports expenses of the period, but cash flow from operating activities must reflect the cash payments. Cash prepayments increase the balance in prepaid expenses, and recording of expenses decreases the balance in prepaid expenses.

Prepaid Expenses (A)	
Beg. bal.	
Cash prepayments	Used-up / expensed
End. bal.	

Prepaid Expenses (A)	
Beg. bal.	22
Increase	9
End. bal.	31

Under Armour's $9 million increase in Prepaid Expenses means that cash prepayments this period were more than expenses. These extra cash prepayments must be subtracted in Exhibit 12.4. (A decrease would be added.)

Increase in Accounts Payable   Cash flow from operations must reflect cash purchases, but not all purchases are for cash. Purchases on account increase Accounts Payable and cash paid to suppliers decreases Accounts Payable.

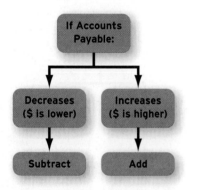

Accounts Payable (L)	
	Beg. bal.
Cash payments	Purchases on account
	End. bal.

Accounts Payable (L)	
	Beg. bal.	55
	Increase	17
	End. bal.	72

Accounts Payable increased by $17 million, which means that cash payments to suppliers were less than purchases on account. This increase in Accounts Payable (cash payments are less than purchases) must be added in Exhibit 12.4. (A decrease would be subtracted.)

Increase in Accrued Liabilities   The income statement reports all accrued expenses, but the cash flow statement must reflect only the actual payments for expenses. Recording accrued expenses increases the balance in Accrued Liabilities and cash payments for the expenses decreases Accrued Liabilities.

Accrued Liabilities (L)	
	Beg. bal.
Cash payments	Accrued expenses
	End. bal.

Accrued Liabilities (L)	
	Beg. bal.	41
	Increase	20
	End. bal.	61

Under Armour's Accrued Liabilities increased by $20 million, which indicates that more expenses were accrued than paid. Consequently, this difference (representing less cash paid) must be added back in Exhibit 12.4. (A decrease would be subtracted.)

By scanning Exhibit 12.3 on page 560, you can see that you have now considered the changes in all balance sheet accounts that relate to operating activities (marked by the letter O). The last step in determining the net cash flow provided by (used in) operating activities is to calculate a total. As shown in Exhibit 12.4, the combined effects of all operating cash flows is a net inflow of $79 million.

Now that you have seen how to compute operating cash flows using the indirect method, take a moment to complete the following Self-Study Practice.

How's it going?   Self-Study Practice

Indicate whether the following items taken from Brunswick Corporation's cash flow statement would be added (+), subtracted (−), or not included (0) in the reconciliation of net income to cash flow from operations.

+	a. Decrease in inventories.		d. Increase in accounts receivable.
+	b. Increase in accounts payable.	+	e. Increase in accrued liabilities.
−	c. Depreciation expense.		f. Increase in prepaid expenses.

After you have finished, check your answers with the solution in the margin.

Solution to Self-Study Practice

a. +, b. +, c. +, d. −, e. +, f. −

Under Armour's Investing Cash Flow Calculations

Learning Objective 3
Report cash flows from investing activities.

To prepare the investing section of the statement of cash flows, you must analyze accounts related to long-lived tangible and intangible assets.[3] Unlike the analysis of operating activities, where you were concerned only with the *net* change in selected balance sheet accounts, an analysis of investing (and financing) activities requires that you identify and separately report the causes of *both* increases and decreases in account balances. The following relationships are the ones that you will encounter most frequently:

Related Balance Sheet Accounts	Investing Activity	Cash Flow Effect
Property, Plant, and Equipment	Purchase of property, plant, and equipment for cash	Outflow
	Sale of property, plant, and equipment for cash	Inflow
Intangible Assets	Purchase of intangible assets	Outflow
	Sale of intangible assets	Inflow

Under Armour's balance sheet (Exhibit 12.3) shows two investing assets (noted with an I) that changed during the year: Equipment and Intangible and Other Assets.

Equipment   To determine the cause of the change in the Equipment account, accountants would examine the detailed accounting records for equipment. Purchases of equipment increase the account, and disposals of equipment decrease it. The additional data in Exhibit 12.3 indicates that Under Armour purchased equipment for $36 million cash. This purchase is a cash outflow, which we subtract in the schedule of investing activities in Exhibit 12.5. In our example, this purchase fully accounts for the change in the Equipment balance, as shown in the Equipment T-account. Thus, we can assume that Under Armour did not dispose of any equipment during the year. Chapter Supplement 12A explains how disposals of property, plant, and equipment affect the statement of cash flows.

Equipment (A)			
Beg. bal.	84		
Purchases	36	Disposals	0
End. bal.	120		

---

[3]Investing activities also affect other assets described in Appendix D (investments in other companies). Although not shown here, the cash flows for investments are similar to those shown in this section for equipment and intangible assets.

EXHIBIT 12.5	Under Armour's Schedule of Investing Cash Flows

Items	Amount (in millions)	Explanations
Purchase of equipment	$(36)	Payment of cash for equipment
Purchase of intangible and other assets	(2)	Payment of cash for intangibles
Net cash provided by (used in) investing activities	(38)	Subtotal for the statement of cash flows

Intangible and Other Assets   A similar approach is used to determine cash flows associated with intangible assets. Analysis of Under Armour's detailed records indicate that the company did not have any reductions in its intangible assets as a result of disposals, impairments, or amortization during the year. However, Under Armour did purchase intangible assets for $2 million cash, as noted in the additional data in Exhibit 12.3. This cash outflow is subtracted in the schedule of investing activities in Exhibit 12.5.

Under Armour's Financing Cash Flow Calculations

Learning Objective 4
Report cash flows from
financing activities.

This section of the cash flow statement includes changes in liabilities owed to owners (Dividends Payable) and financial institutions (Notes Payable and other types of debt), as well as changes in stockholders' equity accounts. Interest is considered an operating activity so it is excluded from financing cash flows. The following relationships are the ones that you will encounter most often:

COACH'S TIP

Dividends paid are financing
cash flows. Dividends received,
however, are operating cash flows.

Related Balance Sheet Accounts	Financing Activity	Cash Flow Effect
Notes Payable	Borrowing cash from bank or other financial institutions	Inflow
	Repayment of loan principal	Outflow
Bonds Payable	Issuance of bonds for cash	Inflow
	Repayment of bond face value	Outflow
Contributed Capital	Issuance of stock for cash	Inflow
	Repurchase of stock with cash	Outflow
Retained Earnings	Payment of cash dividends	Outflow

To compute cash flows from financing activities, you should review changes in all debt and stockholders' equity accounts. Increases and decreases must be identified and reported separately. Under Armour's balance sheet in Exhibit 12.3 indicates that Long-term Debt and Contributed Capital changed during the period as a result of financing cash flows (noted with an F).

Long-term Debt   The additional data in Exhibit 12.3 indicates that Long-term Debt was affected by both cash inflows and outflows, as shown in the T-account below. These cash flows are reported separately in the schedule of financing activities shown in Exhibit 12.6.

Long-term Debt (L)			
		Beg. bal.	14
Repayments	7	Borrowings	16
		End. bal.	23

Contributed Capital   Under Armour did not repurchase stock during the year, but it did issue stock for $12 million cash. This stock issuance fully accounts for

EXHIBIT 12.6	Under Armour's Schedule of Financing Cash Flows

Items	Amount (in millions)	Explanations
Additional borrowings of long-term debt	$16	Cash received when new loan obtained
Payments on long-term debt	(7)	Cash paid on loan principal
Proceeds from stock issuance	12	Cash received from stockholders for new stock
Net cash provided by financing activities	21	Subtotal for the statement of cash flows

the change in Contributed Capital, as shown in the following T-account. This cash inflow is listed in the schedule of financing activities in Exhibit 12.6.

Contributed Capital (SE)

		Beg. bal.	163
		Stock issued	12
		End. bal.	175

Retained Earnings Net income increases Retained Earnings and any dividends decrease Retained Earnings. Net income has already been accounted for as an operating cash flow. In Under Armour's case, no dividends were declared or paid in 2008 (see the additional data in Exhibit 12.3). As shown in the following T-account, dividends would have decreased Retained Earnings, had they been declared; their payment would have been reported as a cash outflow in the financing section of the statement of cash flows.

Retained Earnings (SE)

		Beg. bal.	118
Dividends	0	Net income	38
		End. bal.	156

Under Armour's Statement of Cash Flows

Now that you have determined the cash flows for the three main types of business activities in Exhibits 12.4, 12.5, and 12.6, you can prepare the statement of cash flows in a proper format. Exhibit 12.7 shows the statement of cash flows for Under Armour using the indirect method. Notice that the net increase (decrease) subtotal combines cash flows from operating, investing, and financing activities to produce an overall net change in cash. This net change is added to the beginning cash balance to arrive at the ending cash balance, which is the same cash balance as reported on the balance sheet.

Supplemental Disclosures In addition to their cash flows, all companies are required to report material investing and financing transactions that did not have cash flow effects (called **noncash investing and financing activities**). For example, the purchase of a $10,000 piece of equipment with a $10,000 note payable to the supplier does not cause either an inflow or an outflow of cash. As a result, these activities are not listed in the three main sections of the statement of cash flows. This important information is normally presented for users in a supplementary schedule to the statement of cash flows or in the financial statement notes. Supplementary information must also disclose (for companies using the indirect method) the amount of cash paid for interest and for income taxes. An example of this disclosure is shown at the bottom of Exhibit 12.7.

COACH'S TIP

When doing homework problems, assume that all changes in noncurrent account balances are caused by cash transactions (unless the problem also describes changes caused by noncash investing and financing activities).

EXHIBIT 12.7	Under Armour's Statement of Cash Flows (Indirect Method)

UNDER ARMOUR, INC.
Statement of Cash Flows*
For the Year Ended December 31, 2008

(in millions)

Cash Flows from Operating Activities	
Net income	$ 38
Adjustments to reconcile net income to net cash provided by operating activities:	
Depreciation	16
Changes in current assets and current liabilities	
Accounts Receivable	13
Inventories	(16)
Prepaid Expenses	(9)
Accounts Payable	17
Accrued Liabilities	20
Net cash provided by (used in) operating activities	79
Cash Flows from Investing Activities	
Purchase of equipment	(36)
Purchase of intangible and other assets	(2)
Net cash provided by (used in) investing activities	(38)
Cash Flows from Financing Activities	
Additional borrowings of long-term debt	16
Payments on long-term debt	(7)
Proceeds from stock issuance	12
Net cash provided by (used in) financing activities	21
Net increase (decrease) in cash and cash equivalents	62
Cash and cash equivalents at beginning of period	40
Cash and cash equivalents at end of period	$102
Supplemental Disclosures	
Cash paid for interest	$ 7
Cash paid for income tax	32

*Certain amounts have been adjusted to simplify the presentation.

COACH'S TIP

If you have difficulty remembering the order in which to report operating (O), investing (I), and financing (F) cash flows, say to yourself, "O, IF only I could remember!"

Evaluate the Results

Learning Objective 5
Interpret cash flows from operating, investing, and financing activities.

Unlike the income statement, which summarizes its detailed information in one number (net income), the statement of cash flows does not provide a summary measure of cash flow performance. Instead, it must be evaluated in terms of the cash flow pattern suggested by the subtotals of each of the three main sections. As we discussed at the beginning of this chapter, expect different patterns of cash flows from operating, investing, and financing activities depending on how well established a company is. An established, healthy company will show positive cash flows from operations, which are sufficiently large to pay for replacing existing property, plant, and equipment and to pay dividends to stockholders. Any additional cash (called **free cash flow**) can (a) be used to expand the business through additional investing activities, (b) be used for other financing activities, or (c) simply build up the company's cash balance. After considering where the company stands in relation to this big picture, you should then look at the details within each of the three sections.

EVALUATING CASH FLOWS

The operating activities section indicates how well a company is able to generate cash internally through its operations and management of current assets and current liabilities. Most analysts believe this is the most important section of the statement because, in the long run, operations are the only continuing source of cash. Investors will not invest in a company if they do not believe that cash generated from operations will be available to pay dividends or expand the company. Similarly, creditors will not lend money or extend credit if they believe that cash generated from operations will be insufficient to repay them.

When evaluating the operating activities section of the statement of cash flows, consider the absolute amount of cash flow (is it positive or negative?), keeping in mind that operating cash flows have to be positive over the long run for a company to be successful. Also, look at the relationship between operating cash flows and net income, using a ratio called the Quality of Income Ratio.

Accounting Decision Tools		
Name of Measure	Formula	What It Tells You
Quality of income ratio	$\dfrac{\text{Net Cash Flow from Operating Activities}}{\text{Net Income}}$	• Whether operating cash flows and net income are in sync • A ratio near 1.0 means operating cash flows and net income are in sync

The quality of income ratio measures the portion of income that was generated in cash. All other things equal, a quality of income ratio near 1.0 indicates a high likelihood that revenues are realized in cash and that expenses are associated with cash outflows. This ratio is most useful when compared to industry competitors or to prior periods. Any major deviations (say below 0.5 or above 1.5) should be investigated. In some cases, a deviation may be nothing to worry about, but in others, it could be the first sign of big problems to come. Four potential causes of deviations to consider include:

1. **Seasonality.** As in Under Armour's case, seasonal variations in sales and inventory levels can cause the ratio to fluctuate from one quarter to the next. Usually, this isn't a cause for alarm.

2. **The corporate life cycle (growth in sales).** New companies often experience rapid sales growth. When sales are increasing, accounts receivable and inventory normally increase faster than the cash flows being collected from sales. This often reduces operating cash flows below net income, which, in turn, reduces the ratio. This isn't a big deal, provided that the company can obtain cash from financing activities until operating activities begin to generate more positive cash flows.

3. **Changes in revenue and expense recognition.** Most cases of fraudulent financial reporting involve aggressive revenue recognition (recording revenues before they are earned) or delayed expense recognition (failing to report expenses when they are incurred). Both of these tactics cause net income to increase in the current period, making it seem as though the company has improved its performance. Neither of these tactics, though, affects cash flows from operating activities. As a result, if revenue and expense recognition policies are changed to boost net income, the quality of income ratio will drop, providing one of the first clues that the financial statements might contain errors or fraud.

4. **Changes in working capital management.** Working capital is a measure of the amount by which current assets exceed current liabilities. If a company's current assets (such as accounts receivable and inventories) are allowed to grow out of control, its operating cash flows and quality of income ratio will decrease. More efficient management will have the opposite effect. To investigate this potential cause more closely, use the inventory and accounts receivable turnover ratios covered in Chapters 7 and 8.

Spotlight On BUSINESS DECISIONS

Quality of Income Deteriorates Prior to Bankruptcy

Lehman Brothers Holdings, Inc., was one of the largest and most profitable financial services companies in the world. But cash flow and working capital management problems led to the company's bankruptcy only a month before the stock market crash of 2008. The following comparison of Lehman's net income and net operating cash flows reveals the company's problems:

(in billions)	2006	2007	2008
Net income	$ 3.3	$ 4.0	$ 4.2
Net cash provided by (used in) operating activities	(12.2)	(36.4)	(45.6)

Another key issue that analysts assess using the statement of cash flows is the company's ability to generate enough cash internally to purchase new long-term assets. The capital acquisitions ratio is commonly used to determine the extent to which purchases of Property, Plant, and Equipment (PPE) were financed from operating activities (without the need for outside debt or equity financing or the sale of investments or other long-term assets). A ratio greater than 1.0 indicates that, all else equal, outside financing was not needed to replace equipment in the current period. Assuming this continues in the future, the higher a company's capital acquisitions ratio, the less likely that external financing will be needed to fund future expansion.

Accounting Decision Tools

Name of Measure	Formula	What It Tells You
Capital acquisitions ratio	$\dfrac{\text{Net Cash from Operations}}{\text{Cash Paid for PPE}}$	• Whether operating cash flows are sufficient to pay for PPE purchases • A higher ratio means less need for external financing

The cash paid for property, plant, and equipment (used in the bottom part of the ratio) is reported in the investing activities section of the statement of cash flows. These expenditures can vary greatly from year to year, so the ratio typically is calculated as an average over a longer period, for instance, three years. When calculating the ratio, enter these expenditures as positive amounts (without brackets).

In Exhibit 12.8, we present the three-year average capital acquisitions ratio for Under Armour. The ratio shows that, over the past three years, Under Armour has financed about 79% of its purchases of property, plant, and equipment with cash generated from operating activities.

EXHIBIT 12.8 | Capital Acquisitions Ratio Computation

(in millions)	Relevant Information				Average 2006–08 Ratio Calculation
	2008	2007	2006	Average	$\dfrac{\$22}{28} = 0.79$ or 79%
Net operating cash	$79	$(25)	$11	$22	
Cash for PPE	36	34	15	28	

How's it going?   Self-Study Practice

The relevant cash flows for NIKE, Inc., are shown below. Calculate the capital acquisitions ratio for NIKE and compare it to Under Armour's ratio in Exhibit 12.8.

(in billions)	2008	2007	2006	Average	Ratio
Cash flow from operating activities	$1.9	$1.9	$1.7	$ ___	___
Purchases of property, plant, and equipment	0.4	0.3	0.3	0.3	

After you have finished, check your answers with the solution in the margin.

Solution to Self-Study Practice

$1.8 ÷ $0.3 = 6.0 or 600%

NIKE's operations generated six times more cash than was spent on Property, Plant, and Equipment. This suggests NIKE has more free cash flow than Under Armour to use for other purposes, such as paying dividends and repaying loans.

Because equipment needs differ dramatically across industries (for example, consider Under Armour versus Google), a particular company's ratio should be compared only with its prior years' figures or with other companies in the same industry. Also, while a high ratio can indicate strong cash flows, it also might suggest a failure to update plant and equipment, which can limit a company's ability to compete in the future. The main point is that you have to interpret the ratio in relation to the company's other activities and business strategy.

OPERATING CASH FLOWS REVISITED (DIRECT METHOD)   *Not on test*

> **Learning Objective 6**
> Report and interpret cash flows from operating activities, using the direct method.

Earlier in this chapter, we discussed the indirect method of presenting a company's statement of cash flows. This method computes operating cash flows indirectly, by adding and subtracting items from Net Income. Because these items, by themselves, don't mean a lot, analyses of operating cash flows are limited to using just the overall Net Cash Provided by (Used for) Operating Activities. In contrast, the direct method of presentation provides more detailed information on each input into overall operating cash flows, which allows analysts to conduct more detailed analyses.

Exhibit 12.9 presents Under Armour's statement of cash flows using the direct method. Because this method lists each operating cash flow component, it allows more detailed analyses of operating cash flows. For example, the direct method would allow Under Armour's managers to determine that a 10 percent increase in product costs in 2008 would have required an additional cash outflow to inventory suppliers of $36.9 million (= 10% × $369 million). To cover these additional cash outflows, Under Armour could raise prices by 5 percent, which would generate a $36.9 million (= 5% × $738 million) cash inflow from customer collections.

The direct method also provides financial statement users with more information to identify potential relationships between cash inflows and outflows. An increase in some activities, such as sales, generally leads to an increase in cash inflows from customers and cash outflows to inventory suppliers. However, an increase in sales activity only loosely affects other cash outflows, such as interest paid on loans. Knowing the detailed components of operating cash flows allows analysts to more reliably predict a company's future cash flows.[4]

In the remainder of this section, we describe how to prepare the statement of cash flows using the direct method. We focus on preparing just the operating activities section. For instructions on preparing the investing and financing activities sections, which are identical under both the direct and indirect methods, see pages 565—568.

Reporting Operating Cash Flows with the Direct Method

The direct method presents a summary of all operating transactions that result in either a debit or a credit to cash. It is prepared by adjusting each revenue and expense on the income statement from the accrual basis to the cash basis. We will complete this process

---

[4]Steven F. Orpurt and Yoonseok Zang, "Do Direct Cash Flow Disclosures Help Predict Future Operating Cash Flows and Earnings?" *The Accounting Review* 84, no. 3, 893–936 (May 2009).

| **EXHIBIT 12.9** | Under Armour's Statement of Cash Flows (Direct Method) |

UNDER ARMOUR, INC.
Statement of Cash Flows
For the Year Ended December 31, 2008

Explanations

(in millions)

Cash Flows from Operating Activities		Cash flows related to day-to-day activities
Cash collected from customers	$738	Cash collected on account and from any cash sales
Cash paid to suppliers of inventory	(369)	Cash paid in the current period to acquire inventory
Cash paid to employees and suppliers of services	(251)	Cash paid for salaries, wages, utilities, rent, etc.
Cash paid for interest	(7)	Separate reporting of these items fulfills the role of
Cash paid for income tax	(32)	the supplemental disclosures in Exhibit 12.7
Net cash provided by (used in) operating activities	79	Indicates overall cash impact of operating activities
Cash Flows from Investing Activities		Cash flows related to long-term assets
Purchase of equipment	(36)	Cash was used to purchase equipment
Purchase of intangible and other assets	(2)	Cash was used to purchase intangibles
Net cash provided by (used in) investing activities	(38)	Indicates overall cash impact of investing activities
Cash Flows from Financing Activities		Cash flows from transactions with lenders, investors
Proceeds from long-term debt	16	Cash received from borrowing
Payments on long-term debt	(7)	Cash used to repay amounts previously borrowed
Proceeds from stock issuances	12	Cash received from issuing stock
Net cash provided by (used in) financing activities	21	Indicates overall cash impact of financing activities
Net Change in Cash and Cash Equivalents	62	$79 + $(38) + $21 = $62
Cash and cash equivalents, beginning of year	40	Cash balance at beginning of the period
Cash and cash equivalents, end of year	$102	Cash balance at end of the period (on balance sheet)

for all of the revenues and expenses reported in the Under Armour income statement in Exhibit 12.3 to show the calculations underlying the operating cash flows in Exhibit 12.9. Notice that, with the direct method, we work directly with each revenue and expense listed on the income statement and ignore any totals or subtotals (such as net income).

Converting Sales Revenues to Cash Inflows   When sales are recorded, Accounts Receivable increases, and when cash is collected, Accounts Receivable decreases. This means that if Accounts Receivable decreases by $13 million, then cash collections were $13 million more than sales on account. To convert sales revenue to the cash collected, we need to add $13 million to Sales Revenue. The following flowchart shows this visually:

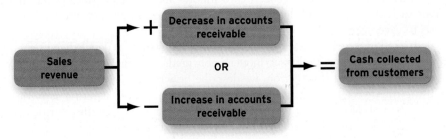

Using information from Under Armour's income statement and balance sheet presented in Exhibit 12.3, we compute cash collected from customers as follows:

Accounts Receivable (A)	
Beg. bal. 94	
	Decrease 13
End. bal. 81	

Net Sales	$725
+ Decrease in Accounts Receivable	13
Cash collected from customers	$738

Converting Cost of Goods Sold to Cash Paid to Suppliers

Cost of Goods Sold represents the cost of merchandise sold during the accounting period, which may be more or less than the amount of cash paid to suppliers during the period. In Under Armour's case, Inventory increased during the year, implying the company bought more merchandise than it sold. If the company paid cash to suppliers of inventory, it would have paid more cash to suppliers than the amount of Cost of Goods Sold. So, the increase in Inventory must be added to Cost of Goods Sold to compute cash paid to suppliers.

Typically, companies buy inventory on account from suppliers (as indicated by an Accounts Payable balance on the balance sheet). Consequently, we need to consider more than just the change in Inventory to convert Cost of Goods Sold to cash paid to suppliers. The credit purchases and payments that are recorded in Accounts Payable must also be considered. Credit purchases increase Accounts Payable, and cash payments decrease it. The overall increase in Accounts Payable reported by Under Armour in Exhibit 12.3 indicates that cash payments were less than credit purchases, so the difference must be subtracted in the computation of total cash payments to suppliers.

In summary, to fully convert Cost of Goods Sold to a cash basis, you must consider changes in both Inventory and Accounts Payable as follows:

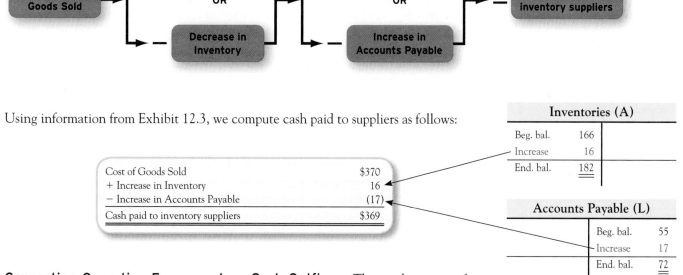

Using information from Exhibit 12.3, we compute cash paid to suppliers as follows:

Cost of Goods Sold	$370
+ Increase in Inventory	16
− Increase in Accounts Payable	(17)
Cash paid to inventory suppliers	$369

Inventories (A)

Beg. bal.	166
Increase	16
End. bal.	182

Accounts Payable (L)

Beg. bal.	55
Increase	17
End. bal.	72

Converting Operating Expenses to a Cash Outflow

The total amount of an expense on the income statement may differ from the cash outflow associated with that activity. Some amounts, like prepaid rent, are paid before they are recognized as expenses. When prepayments are made, the balance in the asset Prepaid Expenses increases. When expenses are recorded, Prepaid Expenses decreases. When we see Under Armour's prepaids increase by $9 million during the year, it means the company paid more cash than it recorded as operating expenses. This amount must be added in computing cash paid to service suppliers for operating expenses.

Some other expenses, like wages, are paid for after they are incurred. In this case, when expenses are recorded, the balance in Accrued Liabilities increases. When payments are made, Accrued Liabilities decreases. When Under Armour's Accrued Liabilities increase by $20 million, it means the company paid that much less cash than it recorded as operating expenses. This amount must be subtracted when computing cash paid to employees and service suppliers for operating expenses.

Generally, operating expenses such as Selling, General, and Administrative Expenses can be converted from the accrual basis to the cash basis in the following manner:

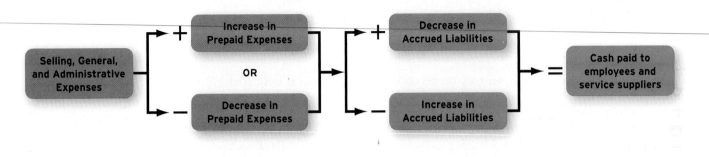

Using information from Exhibit 12.3, we can compute the total cash paid as follows:

Prepaid Expenses (A)	
Beg. bal.	22
Increase	9
End. bal.	31

Accrued Liabilities (L)	
Beg. bal.	41
Increase	20
End. bal.	61

Selling, General, and Administrative Expenses	$262
+ Increase in Prepaid Expenses	9
− Increase in Accrued Liabilities	(20)
Cash paid to employees and suppliers of services	$251

You don't have to convert Depreciation Expense on the income statement to the cash basis for the statement of cash flows because depreciation doesn't involve cash. It is merely reporting previously incurred costs as an expense in the current period. Noncash expenses like depreciation (or, similarly, revenues that don't affect cash) are omitted when the statement of cash flows is prepared using the direct method. Because of this, be sure to exclude any Depreciation Expense that might have been included in Selling, General, and Administrative Expenses.

The next account listed on the income statement in Exhibit 12.3 is Interest Expense of $7 million. Because the balance sheet does not report Interest Payable, we will assume all of the interest was paid in cash. Thus, interest expense equals interest paid.

Interest Expense	$7
No change in Interest Payable	0
Cash paid for interest	$7

The same logic can be applied to income taxes. Under Armour presents Income Tax Expense of $32 million. Exhibit 12.3 does not report an Income Tax Payable balance, so we assume income tax paid is equal to income tax expense.

Income Tax Expense	$32
No change in Income Tax Payable	0
Cash paid for income tax	$32

You have now seen, in this section, how to determine each amount reported in the operating activities section of a statement of cash flows prepared using the direct method. For a quick check on your understanding of this material, complete the following Self-Study Practice.

How's it going?
Self-Study Practice

Indicate whether the following items taken from a cash flow statement would be added (+), subtracted (−), or not included (0) when calculating cash flow from operations using the direct method.

_____ a. Cash paid to suppliers.

_____ b. Payment of dividends to stockholders.

_____ c. Cash collections from customers.

_____ d. Purchase of plant and equipment for cash.

_____ e. Payments of interest to lenders.

_____ f. Payment of taxes to the government.

After you have finished, check your answers with the solution in the margin.

Solution to Self-Study Practice
a. −, b. 0, c. +, d. 0, e. −, f. −

SUPPLEMENT 12A: Reporting Sales of Property, Plant, and Equipment (Indirect Method)

Whenever a company sells property, plant, and equipment (PPE), it records three things: (1) decreases in the PPE accounts for the assets sold, (2) an increase in the Cash account for the cash received on disposal, and (3) a gain if the cash received is more than the book value of the assets sold (or a loss if the cash received is less than the book value of the assets sold). The only part of this transaction that qualifies for the statement of cash flows is the cash received on disposal. This cash inflow is classified as an investing activity, just like the original equipment purchase.

Okay, that seems straightforward, so why do we have a separate chapter supplement for this kind of transaction? Well, there is one complicating factor. Gains and losses on disposal are included in the computation of net income, which is the starting point for the operating activities section when prepared using the indirect method. So, just as we had to add back the depreciation subtracted on the income statement, we also have to add back losses reported on disposals of PPE. As the following example shows, the flip side is true for gains on disposal (they are subtracted).

To illustrate, assume that Under Armour sold a piece of its manufacturing equipment for $7 million. The equipment originally cost $15 million and had $10 million of accumulated depreciation at the time of disposal. The disposal would have been analyzed and recorded as follows (in millions):

COACH'S TIP

If you're a little rusty on the journal entry to record this disposal, it would be worth your time to review the material on pages 415–416 of Chapter 9.

① Analyze

Assets		=	Liabilities	+	Stockholders' Equity	
Cash	+7				Gain on Disposal (+R)	+2
Accumulated Depreciation (−xA)	+10					
Equipment	−15					

② Record

dr Cash (+A)	7	
dr Accumulated Depreciation (−xA, +A)	10	
cr Equipment (−A)		15
cr Gain on Disposal (+R, +SE)		2

The $7 million inflow of cash would be reported as an investing activity. The $10 million and $15 million are taken into account when considering changes in the Accumulated Depreciation and Equipment account balances. Lastly, the $2 million Gain on Disposal was included in net income, so we must remove (subtract) it in the operating activities section of the statement. Thus, the disposal would affect two parts of the statement of cash flows:

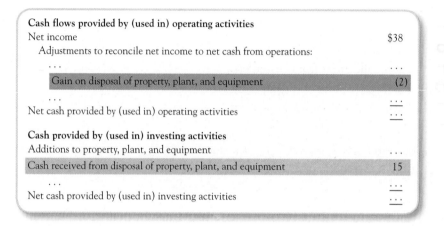

Cash flows provided by (used in) operating activities	
Net income	$38
Adjustments to reconcile net income to net cash from operations:	
. . .	. . .
Gain on disposal of property, plant, and equipment	(2)
. . .	
Net cash provided by (used in) operating activities	. . .
	. . .
Cash provided by (used in) investing activities	
Additions to property, plant, and equipment	. . .
Cash received from disposal of property, plant, and equipment	15
. . .	. . .
Net cash provided by (used in) investing activities	. . .

SUPPLEMENT 12B: Spreadsheet Approach (Indirect Method)

As situations become more complex, the analytical approach that we used to prepare the statement of cash flows for Under Armour becomes cumbersome and inefficient. In actual practice, many companies use a spreadsheet approach to prepare the statement of cash flows. The spreadsheet is based on the same logic that we used in the main body of the chapter. The spreadsheet's primary advantage is that it offers a more systematic way to keep track of information. You may find it useful even in simple situations.

Exhibit 12B.1 shows the Under Armour spreadsheet, which we created as follows:

1. Make four columns to record dollar amounts. The first column is for the beginning balances for items reported on the balance sheet, the next two columns reflect debit and credit changes to those balances, and the final column contains the ending balances for the balance sheet accounts.

2. Enter each account name from the balance sheet in the far left of the top half of the spreadsheet.

3. As you analyze changes in each balance sheet account, enter the explanation of each item to be reported on the statement of cash flows in the far left of the bottom half of the spreadsheet.

Changes in the various balance sheet accounts are analyzed in terms of debits and credits in the top half of the spreadsheet with the corresponding debits and credits being recorded in the bottom half of the spreadsheet in terms of their impact on cash flows. The changes in balance sheet accounts other than cash contribute to explaining the change in the Cash account.

Let's go through each of the entries on the spreadsheet for Under Armour shown in Exhibit 12B.1, starting with the first one shown in the bottom half of the spreadsheet (all amounts in millions).

a. Net income of $38 is shown as an inflow in the operating activities section, with the corresponding credit going to Retained Earnings in the top half of the spreadsheet (to show that net income increased Retained Earnings).

b. Depreciation Expense of $16 is added back to net income because this type of expense does not cause a cash outflow when it is recorded. The corresponding credit explains the increase in the Accumulated Depreciation account during the period.

COACH'S TIP

Think of the statement of cash flows (in the bottom half of the spreadsheet) as a big Cash T-account.

Spreadsheet to Prepare Statement of Cash Flows, Indirect Method

UNDER ARMOUR, INC.
Statement of Cash Flow Spreadsheet
For the Year Ended December 31, 2008

Analysis of Changes

(in millions)	Beginning Balances, December 31, 2007	Debit		Credit		Ending Balances, December 31, 2008
Items from Balance Sheet						
Cash and Cash Equivalents (A)	40	(m)	62			102
Accounts Receivable (A)	94			(c)	13	81
Inventories (A)	166	(d)	16			182
Prepaid Expenses (A)	22	(e)	9			31
Equipment (A)	84	(h)	36			120
Accumulated Depreciation (xA)	31			(b)	16	47
Intangible and Other Assets (A)	16	(i)	2			18
Accounts Payable (L)	55			(f)	17	72
Accrued Liabilities (L)	41			(g)	20	61
Long-term Debt (L)	14	(k)	7	(j)	16	23
Contributed Capital (SE)	163			(l)	12	175
Retained Earnings (SE)	118			(a)	38	156

Cash

	Inflows		Outflows		Subtotals
Statement of Cash Flows					
Cash flows from operating activities:					
Net income	(a)	38			
Adjustments to reconcile net income to cash provided by operating activities:					
Depreciation	(b)	16			
Changes in current assets and current liabilities					
Accounts Receivable	(c)	13			
Inventories			(d)	16	
Prepaid Expenses			(e)	9	
Accounts Payable	(f)	17			
Accrued Liabilities	(g)	20			
					79
Cash flows from investing activities:					
Purchase of equipment			(h)	36	
Purchase of intangible and other assets			(i)	2	
					(38)
Cash flows from financing activities:					
Additional borrowings of long-term debt	(j)	16			
Payments of long-term debt			(k)	7	
Proceeds from stock issuance	(l)	12			
					21
Net increase in Cash and Cash Equivalents			(m)	62	
		132		132	62

c.   The decrease in Accounts Receivable means that cash collections from customers were more than sales on account. Net income includes the sales number, so to adjust up to the actual cash collected, we add the extra amount. This appears in our spreadsheet as if it is a debit to Cash and a corresponding credit to Accounts Receivable.

d.   This entry reconciles the purchases of Inventory with Cost of Goods Sold. It is subtracted from net income because more inventory was purchased than was sold.

e.   This entry reconciles the prepayment of expenses with their expiration. It is subtracted from net income because cash payments for new prepayments are more than the amounts that were reported as expenses when they expired.

f.   This entry reconciles cash paid to suppliers with purchases on account. It is added because more was purchased on account than was paid in cash.

g.   This entry reconciles the accrual of liabilities for operating expenses with payments for these expenses. The increase in Accrued Liabilities is added because the cash paid for accrued liabilities was less than the expenses accrued. The debit to Cash corresponds to the net credit to Accrued Liabilities.

h.   This entry records the cash purchases of new equipment.

i.   This entry records the cash purchase of intangibles.

j.   This entry records cash provided by borrowing additional long-term debt.

k.   This entry records cash used to repay long-term debt.

l.   This entry records the cash received from issuing stock.

m.   This entry shows that the change in cash (in the top part of the spreadsheet) is accounted for by the net cash flows listed in the bottom part of the spreadsheet.

Check to see that Debits = Credits in your spreadsheet, because if they don't, you've missed something along the way. The bottom part of the spreadsheet can be used to prepare the formal statement of cash flows shown in Exhibit 12.7.

REVIEW THE CHAPTER

DEMONSTRATION CASE A: INDIRECT METHOD

BRUNSWICK

During a recent quarter (ended March 31), Brunswick Corporation reported net income of $3,800 (all numbers in thousands). The balance in cash and cash equivalents at the beginning of the quarter (on January 1) was $351,400, and at the end of the quarter (on March 31) it was $280,000. The company also reported the following activities:

a.   Borrowed $2,200 of debt.
b.   Accounts receivable increased by $40,300.
c.   Paid $31,800 in cash for purchase of property, plant, and equipment.
d.   Recorded depreciation of $35,600.
e.   Salaries payable increased by $10,210.
f.   Other accrued liabilities decreased by $35,000.
g.   Prepaid expenses decreased by $14,500.
h.   Inventories increased by $20,810.
i.   Accounts payable decreased by $10,200.
j.   Issued stock to employees for $400 in cash.

Required:

Based on this information, prepare the cash flow statement using the indirect method. Evaluate the cash flows reported in the statement.

Suggested Solution

BRUNSWICK CORPORATION
Statement of Cash Flows
For the Quarter Ended March 31

 BRUNSWICK

(in thousands)

Cash Flows from Operating Activities	
Net income	$ 3,800
Adjustments	
Depreciation	35,600
Change in Accounts Receivable	(40,300)
Change in Inventories	(20,810)
Change in Prepaid Expenses	14,500
Change in Accounts Payable	(10,200)
Change in Salaries Payable	10,210
Change in Other Accrued Liabilities	(35,000)
Net cash provided by (used in) operating activities	(42,200)
Cash Flows from Investing Activities	
Additions to property, plant, and equipment	(31,800)
Net cash provided by (used in) investing activities	(31,800)
Cash Flows from Financing Activities	
Proceeds from debt borrowings	2,200
Proceeds from issuance of stock to employees	400
Net cash provided by (used in) financing activities	2,600
Increase (decrease) in Cash and Cash Equivalents	(71,400)
Cash and Cash Equivalents, January 1	351,400
Cash and Cash Equivalents, March 31	$280,000

Despite reporting profits this quarter, the company has negative cash flows from operations. This is caused primarily by build-ups of accounts receivable and inventories, with no corresponding reduction in spending for accounts payable and other accrued liabilities. This is potentially troublesome because it suggests the company may be encountering difficulties in selling its products and collecting on past sales. In addition to the drain on cash for operating activities, the company also spent over $30 million for additional property, plant, and equipment. Financing activities had relatively little effect on cash flows during the period. The company entered this quarter with lots of cash (over $350 million) and, despite the shortfall in cash flow, still has lots remaining to finance future activities.

DEMONSTRATION CASE B: DIRECT METHOD

During a recent quarter (ended March 29), Cybex International reported that its cash and cash equivalents had increased from $216 on December 31 to $469 on March 29 (all amounts in thousands). The company also indicated the following:

CYBEX

a. Paid $13,229 to suppliers for inventory purchases.
b. Borrowed $2,400 from one of the company's main stockholders.
c. Paid $554 in cash for purchase of property, plant, and equipment.
d. Reported sales on account of $20,608. The company reported Accounts Receivable of $13,628 at the beginning of the quarter and $12,386 at the end of the quarter.
e. Paid operating expenses to employees and suppliers of services totaling $6,188.
f. Cash payments for interest totaled $1,060.
g. Made payments of $2,625 for principal owed on long-term debt.
h. Paid $284 cash for other financing activities.
i. Paid $57 cash for income taxes.

Required:

Based on this information, prepare the cash flow statement using the direct method. Evaluate the cash flows reported in the statement.

Suggested Solution

CYBEX INTERNATIONAL
Statement of Cash Flows
For the Quarter Ended March 29

(in thousands)

Cash Flows from Operating Activities	
Cash collected from customers ($13,628 + $20,608 − $12,386)	$21,850
Cash paid to suppliers of inventory	(13,229)
Cash paid to employees and suppliers of services	(6,188)
Cash paid for interest	(1,060)
Cash paid for income taxes	(57)
Net cash flow provided by operating activities	1,316
Cash Flows from Investing Activities	
Additions to property, plant, and equipment	(554)
Net cash flow provided by (used in) investing activities	(554)
Cash Flows from Financing Activities	
Proceeds from borrowing from a related party (stockholder)	2,400
Repayment of long-term debt principal	(2,625)
Payments for other financing activities	(284)
Net cash flow provided by (used in) financing activities	(509)
Increase (decrease) in Cash and Cash Equivalents	253
Cash and Cash Equivalents, December 31	216
Cash and Cash Equivalents, March 29	$ 469

Cybex reported a net inflow of $1,316 cash from operating activities during the quarter. These cash flows were more than enough to pay for the property, plant, and equipment purchased this quarter, as indicated by its capital acquisitions ratio of 2.38 ($1,316 ÷ $554). Some of the extra cash from operations that was not used to purchase property, plant, and equipment (also called free cash flow) could be used to pay down debt or to increase the company's cash balance. The financing activities section suggests that the company paid down a significant amount of long-term debt ($2,625), in part by borrowing funds from a related party ($2,400). Borrowing from a related party (particularly a major stockholder) is unusual, which would prompt analysts to investigate further. The company's quarterly report explains that its lenders had demanded immediate repayment of their loans because the company had violated its debt covenants. A major stockholder loaned money to the company so that it could make this repayment.

CHAPTER SUMMARY

LO1   **Identify cash flows arising from operating, investing, and financing activities. p. 554**

- The statement has three main sections: Cash flows from operating activities, which are related to earning income from normal operations; Cash flows from investing activities, which are related to the acquisition and sale of productive assets; and Cash flows from financing activities, which are related to external financing of the enterprise.

- The net cash inflow or outflow for the period is the same amount as the increase or decrease in cash and cash equivalents for the period on the balance sheet. Cash equivalents are highly liquid investments purchased within three months of maturity.

Report cash flows from operating activities, using the indirect method. p. 561   **LO2**

- The indirect method for reporting cash flows from operating activities reports a conversion of net income to net cash flow from operating activities.
- The conversion involves additions and subtractions for (1) noncash expenses (such as depreciation expense) and revenues that do not affect current assets or current liabilities, and (2) changes in each of the individual current assets (other than cash) and current liabilities (other than debt to financial institutions, which relates to financing).

Report cash flows from investing activities. p. 565   **LO3**

- Investing activities reported on the cash flow statement include cash payments to acquire fixed assets and investments and cash proceeds from the sale of fixed assets and investments.

Report cash flows from financing activities. p. 566   **LO4**

- Cash inflows from financing activities include cash proceeds from issuance of debt and common stock. Cash outflows include cash principal payments on debt, cash paid for the repurchase of the company's stock, and cash dividend payments. Cash payments associated with interest are a cash flow from operating activities.

Interpret cash flows from operating, investing, and financing activities. p. 568   **LO5**

- A healthy company will generate positive cash flows from operations, some of which will be used to pay for purchases of property, plant, and equipment. Any additional cash (called free cash flow) can be used to further expand the business, pay down some of the company's debt, or simply build up the cash balance. A company is in trouble if it is unable to generate positive cash flows from operations in the long-run because eventually creditors will stop lending to the company and stockholders will stop investing in it.
- Two common ratios for assessing cash flows are the quality of income ratio and the capital acquisitions ratio.

Accounting Decision Tools

Name of Measure	Formula	What It Tells You
Quality of income ratio	Net Cash Flow from Operating Activities / Net Income	• Whether operating cash flows and net income are in sync • A ratio near 1.0 means operating cash flows and net income are in sync
Capital acquisitions ratio	Net Cash Flow from Operating Activities / Cash Paid for PPE	• Whether operating cash flows are sufficient to pay for PPE purchases • A higher ratio means less need for external financing

Report and interpret cash flows from operating activities, using the direct method. p. 571   **LO6**

- The direct method for reporting cash flows from operating activities accumulates all of the operating transactions that result in either a debit or a credit to cash into categories. The most common inflows are cash received from customers and dividends and interest on investments. The most common outflows are cash paid for purchase of services and goods for resale, salaries and wages, income taxes, and interest on liabilities. It is prepared by adjusting each item on the income statement from an accrual basis to a cash basis.

KEY TERMS

Cash Flows from Financing Activities p. 557
Cash Flows from Investing Activities p. 556

Cash Flows from Operating Activities (Cash Flows from Operations) p. 556

Direct Method p. 559
Indirect Method p. 559

See complete definitions in the glossary in the back of this text.

HOMEWORK HELPER

Helpful reminders

- Although some exceptions exist, operating activities typically affect current assets and current liabilities; investing activities typically affect noncurrent assets; and financing activities typically affect noncurrent liabilities and stockholders' equity accounts.

- The typical additions and subtractions that are required when using the indirect method to reconcile net income with cash flow from operating activities are as follows:

COACH'S TIP

Notice in this table that, to reconcile net income to cash flows from operations, you:
- add the change when the current asset decreases or current liability increases
- subtract the change when the current asset increases or current liability decreases

Item	Additions and Subtractions to Reconcile Net Income to Cash Flow From Operating Activities*	
	When Item Increases	When Item Decreases
Depreciation	+	n/a
Accounts Receivable	−	+
Inventory	−	+
Prepaid Expenses	−	+
Accounts Payable	+	−
Accrued Liabilities	+	−

*This summary excludes additions and subtractions for losses and gains arising on disposal of certain assets, which are discussed in Supplement 12A.

- The following adjustments are commonly made to convert income statement items to the related operating cash flow amounts for the direct method:

Income Statement Account	+/− Change in Balance Sheet Account(s)	= Operating Cash Flow
Sales Revenue	+ Decrease in Accounts Receivable (A) − Increase in Accounts Receivable (A)	= Cash collected from customers
Cost of Goods Sold	+ Increase in Inventory (A) − Decrease in Inventory (A) − Increase in Accounts Payable (L) + Decrease in Accounts Payable (L)	= Cash paid to suppliers of inventory
Other Expenses	+ Increase in Prepaid Expenses (A) − Decrease in Prepaid Expenses (A) − Increase in Accrued Expenses (L) + Decrease in Accrued Expenses (L)	= Cash paid to employees and suppliers of services (e.g., wages, rent, utilities)
Interest Expense	− Increase in Interest Payable (L) + Decrease in Interest Payable (L)	= Cash paid for interest
Income Tax Expense	− Increase in Income Taxes Payable (Deferred Taxes) (L) + Decrease in Income Taxes Payable (Deferred Taxes) (L)	= Cash paid for income tax

Frequent mistakes

- Do not merely report the net change in all balance sheet accounts. Some accounts (typically those affected by investing and financing activities) include both inflows and outflows of cash, which must be reported separately.

PRACTICE MATERIAL

QUESTIONS (⊕ Symbol indicates questions that require analysis from more than one perspective.)

1. Compare the purposes of the income statement, the balance sheet, and the statement of cash flows.

2. What information does the statement of cash flows report that is not reported on the other required financial statements?

3. What are cash equivalents? How are they reported on the statement of cash flows?

4. What are the major categories of business activities reported on the statement of cash flows? Define each of these activities.

5. What are the typical cash inflows from operating activities? What are the typical cash outflows from operating activities?

6. Describe the types of items used to compute cash flows from operating activities under the two alternative methods of reporting.

7. Under the indirect method, depreciation expense is added to net income to report cash flows from operating activities. Does depreciation cause an inflow of cash?

8. Explain why cash outflows during the period for purchases and salaries are not specifically reported on a statement of cash flows prepared using the indirect method.

9. Explain why a $50,000 increase in inventory during the year must be included in computing cash flows from operating activities under both the direct and indirect methods.

10. Loan covenants require that E-Gadget Corporation (EGC) generate $200,000 cash from operating activities each year. Without intervening during the last month of the current year, EGC will generate only $180,000 cash from operations. What are the pros and cons of each of the following possible interventions: (*a*) pressuring customers to pay overdue accounts, (*b*) delaying payment of amounts owing to suppliers, and (*c*) purchasing additional equipment to increase depreciation? ●

11. As a junior analyst, you are evaluating the financial performance of Digilog Corporation. Impressed by this year's growth in sales (20% increase), receivables (40% increase), and inventories (50% increase), you plan to report a favorable evaluation of the company. Your supervisor cautions you that those increases may signal difficulties rather than successes. When you ask what she means, she just says you should look at the company's statement of cash flows. What do you think you will find there? What are the cash flow effects when a company's receivables and inventories increase faster than its sales? ●

12. What are the typical cash inflows from investing activities? What are the typical cash outflows from investing activities?

13. What are the typical cash inflows from financing activities? What are the typical cash outflows from financing activities?

14. What are noncash investing and financing activities? Give one example. How are noncash investing and financing activities reported on the statement of cash flows?

15. (Supplement 12A) How is the sale of equipment reported on the statement of cash flows using the indirect method?

MULTIPLE CHOICE

Quiz 12
www.mhhe.com/phillips3e

1. Where is the overall change in cash shown in the statement of cash flows?
   a. In the top part, before the operating activities section.
   b. In one of the operating, investing, or financing activities sections.
   c. In the bottom part, following the financing activities section.
   d. None of the above.

2. In what order do the three sections of the statement of cash flows appear when reading from top to bottom?
   a. Financing, investing, operating.
   b. Investing, operating, financing.
   c. Operating, financing, investing.
   d. Operating, investing, financing.

3. Total cash inflow in the operating section of the statement of cash flows should include which of the following?
   a. Cash received from customers at the point of sale.
   b. Cash collections from customer accounts receivable.
   c. Cash received in advance of revenue recognition (unearned revenue).
   d. All of the above.

4. If the balance in Prepaid Expenses increased during the year, what action should be taken on the statement of cash flows when following the indirect method, *and why?*
   a. The change in the account balance should be subtracted from net income, because the net increase in Prepaid Expenses did not impact net income but did reduce the cash balance.
   b. The change in the account balance should be added to net income, because the net increase in Prepaid Expenses did not impact net income but did increase the cash balance.

   c. The net change in Prepaid Expenses should be subtracted from net income, to reverse the income statement effect that had no impact on cash.
   d. The net change in Prepaid Expenses should be added to net income, to reverse the income statement effect that had no impact on cash.

5. Which of the following would not appear in the investing section of the statement of cash flows?
   a. Purchase of inventory.
   b. Sale of investments.
   c. Purchase of land.
   d. All of the above would appear in the investing section of the statement of cash flows.

6. Which of the following items would not appear in the financing section of the statement of cash flows?
   a. The issuance of the company's own stock.
   b. The repayment of debt.
   c. The payment of dividends.
   d. All of the above would appear in the financing section of the statement of cash flows.

7. Which of the following is not added when computing cash flows from operations using the indirect method?
   a. The net increase in accounts payable.
   b. The net decrease in accounts receivable.
   c. The net decrease in inventory.
   d. All of the above should be added.

8. If a company engages in a material noncash transaction, which of the following is required?
   a. The company must include an explanatory narrative or schedule accompanying the statement of cash flows.
   b. No disclosure is necessary.

c. The company must include an explanatory narrative or schedule accompanying the balance sheet.

d. It must be reported in the investing and financing sections of the statement of cash flows.

9. The *total* change in cash as shown near the bottom of the statement of cash flows for the year should agree with which of the following?

a. The difference in Retained Earnings when reviewing the comparative balance sheet.

b. Net income or net loss as found on the income statement.

c. The difference in cash when reviewing the comparative balance sheet.

d. None of the above.

10. Which of the following is a ratio used to assess the extent to which operating cash flows are sufficient to cover replacement of property, plant, and equipment?

a. Free cash flow.
b. Capital acquisitions ratio.
c. Current ratio.
d. Quality of income ratio.

> For answers to the Multiple-Choice Questions **see page Q1** located in the last section of the book.

MINI-EXERCISES

LO1, 5   **M12-1** **Identifying Companies from Cash Flow Patterns**

Based on the cash flows shown, classify each of the following cases as a growing start-up company (S), a healthy established company (E), or an established company facing financial difficulties (F).

	Case 1	Case 2	Case 3
Cash provided by (used for) operating activities	$ 3,000	$(120,000)	$80,000
Cash provided by (used for) investing activities	(70,000)	10,000	(40,000)
Cash provided by (used for) financing activities	75,000	75,000	(30,000)
Net change in cash	8,000	(35,000)	10,000
Cash position at beginning of year	2,000	40,000	30,000
Cash position at end of year	$10,000	$ 5,000	$40,000

LO1, 2   **M12-2** **Matching Items Reported to Cash Flow Statement Categories (Indirect Method)**

The Buckle, Inc.

The Buckle, Inc., operates 387 stores in 39 states, selling brand name apparel like Lucky jeans and Fossil belts and watches. Some of the items included in its 2008 statement of cash flows presented using the indirect method are listed here. Indicate whether each item is disclosed in the operating activities (O), investing activities (I), or financing activities (F) section of the statement or use (NA) if the item does not appear on the statement.

_____ 1. Purchase of investments.

_____ 2. Proceeds from issuance of stock.

_____ 3. Purchase of property and equipment.

_____ 4. Depreciation.

_____ 5. Accounts payable (decrease).

_____ 6. Inventories (increase).

LO2   **M12-3** **Determining the Effects of Account Changes on Cash Flows from Operating Activities (Indirect Method)**

Indicate whether each item would be added (+) or subtracted (−) in the computation of cash flow from operating activities using the indirect method.

_____ 1. Depreciation.

_____ 2. Inventories decrease.

_____ 3. Accounts payable decrease.

_____ 4. Accounts receivable increase.

_____ 5. Accrued liabilities increase.

LO2   **M12-4** **Computing Cash Flows from Operating Activities (Indirect Method)**

For each of the following independent cases, compute cash flows from operating activities. Assume the list below includes all balance sheet accounts related to operating activities.

	Case A	Case B	Case C
Net income	$200,000	$ 20,000	$360,000
Depreciation expense	40,000	150,000	80,000
Accounts receivable increase (decrease)	100,000	(200,000)	(20,000)
Inventory increase (decrease)	(50,000)	(100,000)	50,000
Accounts payable increase (decrease)	(110,000)	120,000	70,000
Accrued liabilities increase (decrease)	60,000	(220,000)	(80,000)

M12-5 Computing Cash Flows from Operating Activities (Indirect Method)   LO2

For the following two independent cases, show the cash flows from operating activities section of the 2010 statement of cash flows using the indirect method.

	Case A		Case B	
	2010	2009	2010	2009
Sales Revenue	$10,000	$9,000	$21,000	$18,000
Cost of Goods Sold	6,000	5,500	12,000	11,000
Gross Profit	4,000	3,500	9,000	7,000
Depreciation Expense	1,000	1,000	2,000	1,500
Salaries Expense	2,500	2,000	5,000	5,000
Net Income	500	500	2,000	500
Accounts Receivable	300	400	750	600
Inventories	600	500	790	800
Accounts Payable	800	700	800	850
Salaries Payable	1,000	1,200	200	250

M12-6 Computing Cash Flows from Investing Activities   LO3

Based on the following information, compute cash flows from investing activities under GAAP.

Cash collections from customers	$800	Sale of investments	300
Purchase of used equipment	350	Dividends received	100
Depreciation expense	200	Interest received	200

M12-7 Computing Cash Flows from Financing Activities   LO4

Based on the following information, compute cash flows from financing activities under GAAP.

Purchase of investments	$ 250
Dividends paid	800
Interest paid	400
Additional borrowing from bank	2,000

M12-8 Computing Cash Flows Under IFRS   LO1

Refer to M12-6 and M12-7. Calculate the maximum investing and financing cash inflows that could be reported under IFRS.

M12-9 Reporting Noncash Investing and Financing Activities   LO3, 4

Which of the following transactions would be considered noncash investing and financing activities?

____ 1. Additional borrowing from bank.

____ 2. Purchase of equipment with investments.

____ 3. Dividends paid in cash.

____ 4. Purchase of a building with a promissory note.

M12-10 Interpreting Cash Flows from Operating, Investing, and Financing Activities   LO5

Quantum Dots, Inc., is a nanotechnology company that manufactures "quantum dots," which are tiny pieces of silicon consisting of 100 or more molecules. Quantum dots can be used to illuminate very small objects, enabling scientists to see the blood vessels beneath a mouse's skin ripple with each heartbeat, at the rate of 100 times per second. Evaluate this research-intensive company's cash flows, assuming the following was reported in its statement of cash flows.

	Current Year	Previous Year
Cash Flows from Operating Activities		
Net cash provided by (used for) operating activities	$ (50,790)	$(46,730)
Cash Flows from Investing Activities		
Purchases of research equipment	(250,770)	(480,145)
Proceeds from selling all short-term investments	35,000	—
Net cash provided by (used for) investing activities	(215,770)	(480,145)
Cash Flows from Financing Activities		
Additional long-term debt borrowed	100,000	200,000
Proceeds from stock issuance	140,000	200,000
Cash dividends paid	—	(10,000)
Net cash provided by (used for) financing activities	240,000	390,000
Net increase (decrease) in cash	(26,560)	(136,875)
Cash at beginning of period	29,025	165,900
Cash at end of period	$ 2,465	$ 29,025

LO5 **M12-11 Calculating and Interpreting the Capital Acquisitions Ratio**

Capital Corporation reported the following information in its statement of cash flows:

	2008	2009	2010
Net cash flow from operating activities	$35,000	$32,000	$23,000
Purchases of property, plant, and equipment	31,818	22,857	20,325

Calculate, to one decimal place, the average capital acquisitions ratio for the period covering 2008–2010 and the capital acquisitions ratio for *each* year during the period. What does this analysis tell you about the company's need for using external financing to replace property, plant, and equipment?

LO5 **M12-12 Calculating and Interpreting the Quality of Income Ratio**

Dan's Products, Inc., reported net income of $80,000, depreciation expense of $2,000, and cash flow from operations of $60,000. Compute the quality of income ratio. What does the ratio tell you about the company's accrual of revenues and/or deferral of expenses?

LO1, 6 **M12-13 Matching Items Reported to Cash Flow Statement Categories (Direct Method)**

Prestige Manufacturing Corporation reports the following items in its 2010 statement of cash flows presented using the direct method. Indicate whether each item is disclosed in the operating activities (O), investing activities (I), or financing activities (F) section of the statement under GAAP or use (NA) if the item does not appear on the statement.

_____ 1. Payment for equipment purchase.

_____ 2. Repayments of bank loan.

_____ 3. Dividends paid.

_____ 4. Proceeds from issuance of stock.

_____ 5. Interest paid.

_____ 6. Receipts from customers.

LO6 **M12-14 Computing Cash Flows from Operating Activities (Direct Method)**

For each of the following independent cases, compute cash flows from operating activities using the direct method. Assume the list below includes all items relevant to operating activities.

	Case A	Case B	Case C
Sales revenue	$70,000	$55,000	$95,000
Cost of goods sold	35,000	32,000	65,000
Depreciation expense	10,000	2,000	10,000
Other operating expenses	5,000	13,000	8,000
Net income	20,000	8,000	12,000
Accounts receivable increase (decrease)	(1,000)	4,000	3,000
Inventory increase (decrease)	2,000	0	(4,000)
Accounts payable increase (decrease)	0	3,000	(2,000)
Accrued liabilities increase (decrease)	1,000	(2,000)	1,000

M12-15 Computing Cash Flows from Operating Activities (Direct Method)   LO6

Refer to the two cases presented in M12-5, and show the cash flow from operating activities section of the 2010 statement of cash flows using the direct method.

EXERCISES

E12-1 Matching Items Reported to Cash Flow Statement Categories (Indirect Method)   LO1, 2

NIKE, Inc., is the best-known sports shoe, apparel, and equipment company in the world because of its association with sports stars such as LeBron James. Some of the items included in its recent statement of cash flows presented using the indirect method are listed here.

NIKE, Inc.

Indicate whether each item is disclosed in the operating activities (O), investing activities (I), or financing activities (F) section of the statement or use (NA) if the item does not appear on the statement.

____ 1. Additions to long-term debt.

____ 2. Depreciation.

____ 3. Additions to property, plant, and equipment.

____ 4. Increase (decrease) in notes payable. (The amount is owed to financial institutions.)

____ 5. (Increase) decrease in other current assets.

____ 6. Cash received from disposal of property, plant, and equipment.

____ 7. Reductions in long-term debt.

____ 8. Issuance of stock.

____ 9. (Increase) decrease in inventory.

____ 10. Net income.

E12-2 Understanding the Computation of Cash Flows from Operating Activities (Indirect Method)   LO2

Suppose your company sells services of $150 in exchange for $100 cash and $50 on account.

Required:

1. Show the journal entry to record this transaction.
2. Identify the amount that should be reported as net cash flow from operating activities.
3. Identify the amount that would be included in net income.
4. Show how the indirect method would convert net income (requirement 3) to net cash flow from operating activities (requirement 2).
5. What general rule about converting net income to operating cash flows is revealed by your answer to requirement 4?

E12-3 Understanding the Computation of Cash Flows from Operating Activities (Indirect Method)   LO2

Suppose your company sells services for $300 cash this month. Your company also pays $100 in wages, which includes $20 that was payable at the end of the previous month and $80 for wages of this month.

Required:

1. Show the journal entries to record these transactions.
2. Calculate the amount that should be reported as net cash flow from operating activities.
3. Calculate the amount that should be reported as net income.
4. Show how the indirect method would convert net income (requirement 3) to net cash flow from operating activities (requirement 2).
5. What general rule about converting net income to operating cash flows is revealed by your answer to requirement 4?

LO2   **E12-4 Understanding the Computation of Cash Flows from Operating Activities (Indirect Method)**

Suppose your company sells services of $150 in exchange for $100 cash and $50 on account. Depreciation of $40 also is recorded.

Required:

1. Show the journal entries to record these transactions.
2. Calculate the amount that should be reported as net cash flow from operating activities.
3. Calculate the amount that should be reported as net income.
4. Show how the indirect method would convert net income (requirement 3) to net cash flow from operating activities (requirement 2).
5. What general rule about converting net income to operating cash flows is revealed by your answer to requirement 4?

LO2   **E12-5 Understanding the Computation of Cash Flows from Operating Activities (Indirect Method)**

Suppose your company sells goods for $300, of which $200 is received in cash and $100 is on account. The goods cost your company $125 in a previous period. Your company also recorded wages of $70, of which only $30 has been paid in cash.

Required:

1. Show the journal entries to record these transactions.
2. Calculate the amount that should be reported as net cash flow from operating activities.
3. Calculate the amount that should be reported as net income.
4. Show how the indirect method would convert net income (requirement 3) to net cash flow from operating activities (requirement 2).
5. What general rule about converting net income to operating cash flows is revealed by your answer to requirement 4?

LO2, 5   **E12-6 Preparing and Evaluating a Simple Statement of Cash Flows (Indirect Method)**

Suppose your company's income statement reports $105 of net income, and its comparative balance sheet indicates the following.

	Beginning	Ending	
Cash	$ 35	$205	170
Accounts Receivable	75	175	100
Inventory	260	135	(125)
Total	$370	$515	
Wages Payable	$ 10	$ 50	40
Retained Earnings	360	465	105
Total	$370	$515	

Required:

1. Prepare the operating activities section of the statement of cash flows, using the indirect method.
2. Identify the most important cause of the difference between the company's net income and net cash flow from operating activities.

E12-7 Preparing and Evaluating a Simple Statement of Cash Flows (Indirect Method)

LO1, 2, 5

Suppose the income statement for Goggle Company reports $70 of net income, after deducting depreciation of $35. The company bought equipment costing $60 and obtained a long-term bank loan for $60. The company's comparative balance sheet, at December 31, indicates the following.

	2009	2010	Change
Cash	$ 35	$205	170 O
Accounts Receivable	75	175	160 O
Inventory	260	135	(125) O
Equipment	500	560	60 F
Accumulated Depreciation	(45)	(80)	(35) O
Total	$825	$995	
Wages Payable	$ 10	$ 50	40 O
Long-term Debt	445	505	60
Contributed Capital	10	10	O
Retained Earnings	360	430	70 O
Total	$825	$995	

Required:

1. Calculate the change in each balance sheet account, and indicate whether each account relates to operating, investing, and/or financing activities.
2. Prepare a statement of cash flows using the indirect method.
3. In one sentence, explain why an increase in accounts receivable is subtracted.
4. In one sentence, explain why a decrease in inventory is added.
5. In one sentence, explain why an increase in wages payable is added.
6. Are the cash flows typical of a start-up, healthy, or troubled company? Explain.

E12-8 Reporting Cash Flows from Operating Activities (Indirect Method)

LO2

The following information pertains to Guy's Gear Company:

Sales		$80,000
Expenses:		
Cost of Goods Sold	$50,000	
Depreciation Expense	6,000	
Salaries Expense	12,000	68,000
Net Income		$12,000
Accounts Receivable decrease	$ 5,000	
Merchandise Inventory increase	8,000	
Salaries Payable increase	500	

Required:

Present the operating activities section of the statement of cash flows for Guy's Gear Company using the indirect method.

E12-9 Reporting and Interpreting Cash Flows from Operating Activities from an Analyst's Perspective (Indirect Method)

LO2, 5

New Vision Company completed its income statement and balance sheet for 2010 and provided the following information:

Service Revenue		$66,000
Expenses:		
Salaries	$42,000	
Depreciation	7,300	
Utilities	7,000	
Other	1,700	58,000
Net Income		$ 8,000
Decrease in Accounts Receivable	$12,000	
Bought a small service machine	5,000	
Increase in Salaries Payable	9,000	
Decrease in Other Accrued Liabilities	4,000	

Required:

1. Present the operating activities section of the statement of cash flows for New Vision Company using the indirect method.

2. Of the potential causes of differences between cash flow from operations and net income, which are the most important to financial analysts?

LO2, 5 **E12-10 Reporting and Interpreting Cash Flows from Operating Activities from an Analyst's Perspective (Indirect Method)**

Pizza International, Inc., operates 700 family restaurants around the world. The company's annual report contained the following information (in thousands):

Operating Activities			
Net loss	$(9,482)	Decrease in accounts payable	2,282
Depreciation	33,305	Decrease in accrued liabilities	719
Increase in receivables	170	Increase in income taxes payable	1,861
Decrease in inventories	643	Reduction of long-term debt	12,691
Increase in prepaid expenses	664	Additions to equipment	29,073

Required:

1. Based on this information, compute cash flow from operating activities using the indirect method.

2. What were the major reasons that Pizza International was able to report positive cash flow from operations despite having a net loss?

3. Of the potential causes of differences between cash flow from operations and net income, which are the most important to financial analysts?

LO2 **E12-11 Inferring Balance Sheet Changes from the Cash Flow Statement (Indirect Method)**

Colgate-Palmolive

Colgate-Palmolive was founded in 1806. Its statement of cash flows reported the following information (in millions) for the year ended December 31, 2008:

Operating Activities	
Net Income	$1,957
Depreciation	348
Cash effect of changes in	
Accounts Receivable	(70)
Inventories	(135)
Accounts Payable	125
Other	13
Net Cash Provided by Operations	$2,238

Required:

Based on the information reported in the operating activities section of the statement of cash flows for Colgate-Palmolive, determine whether the following accounts increased or decreased during the period: Accounts Receivable, Inventories, and Accounts Payable.

LO2 **E12-12 Inferring Balance Sheet Changes from the Cash Flow Statement (Indirect Method)**

Apple Inc.

The statement of cash flows for Apple Inc. contained the following information (in millions) for the year ended September 27, 2008:

Operating Activities	
Net Income	$4,834
Depreciation	473
Changes in current assets and current liabilities	
Accounts Receivable	(785)
Inventories	(163)
Accounts Payable	596
Unearned Revenue	5,642
Other adjustments	(1,001)
Net Cash Provided by Operations	$9,596

Required:

For each of the four current asset and liability accounts listed in the operating activities section of the statement of cash flows, determine whether the account balances increased or decreased during the period.

E12-13 Preparing and Evaluating a Statement of Cash Flows (Indirect Method)   LO1, 2, 3, 4, 5
from Comparative Balance Sheets and Income Statements

Consultex, Inc., was founded in 2007 as a small financial consulting business. The company had done reasonably well in 2007–2009, but started noticing its cash dwindle early in 2010. In January 2010, Consultex had paid $16,000 to purchase land and repaid $2,000 principal on an existing promissory note. In March 2010, the company paid $2,000 cash for dividends and $1,000 to repurchase Consultex stock that had previously been issued for $1,000. To improve its cash position, Consultex borrowed $5,000 by signing a new promissory note in May 2010 and also issued stock to a new private investor for $12,000 cash. Comparative balance sheets and income statements for the most recent fiscal year are presented below.

CONSULTEX, INC.
Balance Sheet
October 31

	2010	2009
Assets		
Cash	$11,000	$14,000
Accounts Receivable	14,000	12,000
Prepaid Rent	2,000	3,000
Land	26,000	10,000
Total Assets	$53,000	$39,000
Liabilities and Stockholders' Equity		
Wages Payable	$ 2,000	$ 3,000
Income Taxes Payable	1,000	1,000
Notes Payable (long-term)	15,000	12,000
Contributed Capital	20,000	9,000
Retained Earnings	15,000	14,000
Total Liabilities and Stockholders' Equity	$53,000	$39,000

CONSULTEX, INC.
Income Statement
For the Year Ended October 31

	2010	2009
Sales Revenue	$158,000	$161,000
Wages Expense	98,000	97,000
Rent Expense	36,000	30,000
Other Operating Expenses	19,700	20,000
Income before Income Tax Expense	4,300	14,000
Income Tax Expense	1,300	4,200
Net Income	$ 3,000	$ 9,800

Requirements:

1. Prepare a properly formatted Statement of Cash Flows for Consultex, Inc., for the year ended October 31, 2010 (using the indirect method).

2. What one thing can Consultex reasonably change in 2011 to avoid depleting its cash?

LO2, 5   **E12-14 Analyzing Cash Flows from Operating Activities (Indirect Method) and Calculating and Interpreting the Quality of Income Ratio**

PepsiCo   The 2008 annual report for PepsiCo contained the following information for the period (in millions):

Net income	$5,142	Increase in prepaid expense	68
Cash dividends paid	2,541	Increase in accounts payable	718
Depreciation	1,543	Decrease in taxes payable	180
Increase in accounts receivable	549	Increase in other liabilities related to operations	738
Increase in inventory	345		

Required:

1. Compute cash flows from operating activities for PepsiCo using the indirect method.
2. Compute the quality of income ratio to one decimal place.
3. What was the main reason that PepsiCo's quality of income ratio did not equal 1.0?

LO2   **E12-15 Calculating and Understanding Operating Cash Flows Relating to Inventory Purchases (Indirect Method)**

The following information was reported by three companies. When completing the requirements, assume that any and all purchases on account are for inventory.

	Aztec Corporation	Bikes Unlimited	Campus Cycles
Cost of goods sold	$175	$175	$350
Inventory purchases from suppliers made using cash	200	0	200
Inventory purchases from suppliers made on account	0	200	200
Cash payments to suppliers on account	0	160	160
Beginning inventory	100	100	200
Ending inventory	125	125	250
Beginning accounts payable	0	80	80
Ending accounts payable	0	120	120

Required:

1. What amount did each company deduct on the income statement related to inventory?
2. What total amount did each company pay out in cash during the period related to inventory purchased with cash and on account?
3. By what amount do your answers in 1 and 2 differ for each company?
4. By what amount did each company's inventory increase (decrease)? By what amount did each company's accounts payable increase (decrease)?
5. Using the indirect method of presentation, what amount(s) must each company add (deduct) from net income to convert from accrual to cash basis?
6. Describe any similarities between your answers to requirements 3 and 5. Are these answers the same? Why or why not?

LO3, 4   **E12-16 Reporting Cash Flows from Investing and Financing Activities**

Rowe Furniture Corporation is a Virginia-based manufacturer of furniture. In a recent quarter, it reported the following activities:

Net income	$ 4,135	Payments to reduce long-term debt	46
Purchase of property, plant, and equipment	871	Sale of investments	134
Borrowings under line of credit (bank)	1,417	Proceeds from sale of property and equipment	6,594
Proceeds from issuance of stock	11	Dividends paid	277
Cash received from customers	29,164	Interest paid	90

Required:

Based on this information, present the cash flows from investing and financing activities sections of the cash flow statement.

E12-17 Reporting and Interpreting Cash Flows from Investing and Financing Activities with Discussion of Management Strategy

LO3, 4, 5

Gibraltar Industries, Inc., is a manufacturer of steel products for customers such as Home Depot, Lowe's, Chrysler, Ford, and General Motors. In the year ended December 31, 2008, it reported the following activities:

Gibraltar Industries, Inc.

Net income	$24,068	Proceeds from sale of property, plant, and equipment	28,669
Purchase of property, plant, and equipment	21,595	Decrease in accounts receivable	12,273
Payments on notes payable (bank)	184,937	Proceeds from notes payable (bank)	53,439
Net proceeds from stock issuance	250	Payment of dividends	5,985
Depreciation	33,907	Other financing cash outflows	1,694

Required:

1. Based on this information, present the cash flows from the investing and financing activities sections of the cash flow statement.
2. Referring to your response to requirement 1, comment on whether you think Gibraltar's cash flows are typical of a healthy or struggling company.

E12-18 Analyzing and Interpreting the Capital Acquisitions Ratio

LO5

Sportsnet Corporation reported the following data for the three most recent years:

	(in thousands)		
	2010	2009	2008
Cash flows from operating activities	$ 801	$1,480	$619
Cash flows from investing activities	(1,504)	(1,415)	(662)
Cash flows from financing activities	42,960	775	360

Required:

1. Assuming that all investing activities involved acquisition of new plant and equipment, compute the capital acquisitions ratio for the three-year period in total.
2. During the three-year period, what portion of Sportsnet's investing activities was financed from cash flows from operating activities? What portion was financed from external sources or preexisting cash balances during the three-year period?
3. What are two plausible explanations for the dramatic increase in cash flow from financing activities during the period?

E12-19 Calculating and Interpreting the Capital Acquisitions Ratio

LO5

The Walt Disney Company reported the following in its 2008 annual report (in millions).

Walt Disney Company

	2008	2007	2006
Net income	$4,427	$4,687	$3,374
Net cash provided by operating activities	5,446	5,398	5,960
Purchase of parks, resorts, and other property	(1,578)	(1,566)	(1,292)

Required:

1. Calculate, to two decimal places, the average capital acquisitions ratio for the period covering 2006–2008.
2. Interpret the results of your calculations in requirement 1. What do they suggest about the company's need for external financing to acquire property and equipment?

LO5

Walt Disney Company

E12-20 Calculating and Interpreting the Quality of Income Ratio

Refer to the information about the Walt Disney Company in E12-19.

Required:

1. Calculate, to one decimal place, the quality of income ratio for each year.
2. Interpret the results of your calculations in requirement 1. Given what you know about the Walt Disney Company from your own personal observations, provide one reason that could explain the sizable difference between net income and net cash provided by operating activities.

LO2, 6

E12-21 Comparing the Direct and Indirect Methods

To compare statement of cash flows reporting under the direct and indirect methods, enter check marks to indicate which line items are reported on the statement of cash flows with each method.

Cash Flows (and Related Changes)	Statement of Cash Flows Method	
	Direct	Indirect
1. Net income		
2. Receipts from customers		
3. Accounts receivable increase or decrease		
4. Payments to suppliers		
5. Inventory increase or decrease		
6. Accounts payable increase or decrease		
7. Payments to employees		
8. Wages payable, increase or decrease		
9. Depreciation expense		
10. Cash flows from operating activities		
11. Cash flows from investing activities		
12. Cash flows from financing activities		
13. Net increase or decrease in cash during the period		

LO5, 6

E12-22 Reporting and Interpreting Cash Flows from Operating Activities from an Analyst's Perspective (Direct Method)

Refer to the information for New Vision Company in E12-9.

Required:

1. Present the operating activities section of the statement of cash flows for New Vision Company using the direct method. Assume that Other Accrued Liabilities relate to Other Expenses on the income statement.
2. Of the potential causes of differences between cash flow from operations and net income, which are the most important to financial analysts?

LO5, 6

E12-23 Reporting and Interpreting Cash Flows from Operating Activities from an Analyst's Perspective (Direct Method)

Refer back to the information given for E12-10, plus the following summarized income statement for Pizza International, Inc. (in millions):

Revenues	$136,500
Cost of Sales	45,500
Gross Profit	91,000
Salary Expense	56,835
Depreciation	33,305
Other Expenses	7,781
Net Loss before Income Tax Expense	(6,921)
Income Tax Expense	2,561
Net Loss	$ (9,482)

Required:

1. Based on this information, compute cash flow from operating activities using the direct method. Assume that Prepaid Expenses and Accrued Liabilities relate to other expenses.
2. What were the major reasons that Pizza International was able to report positive cash flow from operations despite having a net loss?
3. Of the potential causes of differences between cash flow from operations and net income, which are the most important to financial analysts?

E12-24 (Supplement 12A) Determining Cash Flows from the Sale of Property

AMC Entertainment operates 307 movie theaters in the United States, Canada, and Europe. During fiscal 2008, the company sold its Fandango assets for $20,360,000 cash and recorded a gain on disposal of $18,360,000, which was included in the company's net income of $43,445,000.

AMC Entertainment

Required:

1. Show how the disposal would be reported on the statement of cash flows, using the following format (which assumes the indirect method):

(in thousands)	
Cash flows from operating activities	
Net income	$43,445
Gain on sale of property	
Cash flows from investing activities	
Proceeds from disposition of property	

2. Compute the book value of the Fandango assets that were sold.

E12-25 (Supplement 12A) Determining Cash Flows from the Sale of Equipment

During the period, Teen's Trends sold some excess equipment at a loss. The following information was collected from the company's accounting records:

From the income statement	
Depreciation expense	$ 700
Loss on sale of equipment	4,000
From the balance sheet	
Beginning equipment	12,500
Ending equipment	7,000
Beginning accumulated depreciation	2,000
Ending accumulated depreciation	2,200

No new equipment was bought during the period.

Required:

For the equipment that was sold, determine its original cost, its accumulated depreciation, and the cash received from the sale.

E12-26 (Supplement 12B) Preparing a Statement of Cash Flows, Indirect Method: Complete Spreadsheet

To prepare a statement of cash flows for Golf Champion Store, you examined the company's accounts, noting the following:

Purchased equipment, $20,000, and issued a promissory note in full payment.
Purchased a long-term investment for cash, $15,000.
Paid cash dividend, $12,000.
Sold equipment for $6,000 cash (cost, $21,000, accumulated depreciation, $15,000).
Issued shares of no-par stock, 500 shares at $12 per share cash.
Net income was $20,200.
Depreciation expense was $3,000.

You also created the following spreadsheet to use when preparing the statement of cash flows.

	Beginning Balances, December 31, 2009	Analysis of Changes		Ending Balances, December 31, 2010
		Debit	Credit	
Balance Sheet Items				
Cash	$ 20,500			$ 19,200
Accounts Receivable	22,000			22,000
Merchandise Inventory	68,000			75,000
Investments	0			15,000
Equipment	114,500			113,500
Accumulated Depreciation	32,000			20,000
Accounts Payable	17,000			14,000
Wages Payable	2,500			1,500
Income Taxes Payable	3,000			4,500
Notes Payable	54,000			74,000
Contributed Capital	100,000			106,000
Retained Earnings	16,500			24,700
		Inflows	Outflows	
Statement of Cash Flows				
Cash flows from operating activities				
Cash flows from investing activities				
Cash flows from financing activities				
Net increase (decrease) in cash				
Totals				

Required:

1. Complete the spreadsheet.
2. Prepare the 2010 statement of cash flows using the indirect method.

COACHED PROBLEMS

LO1   **CP12-1 Determining Cash Flow Statement Effects of Transactions**

For each of the following transactions, indicate whether operating (O), investing (I), or financing activities (F) are affected and whether the effect is a cash inflow (+) or outflow (−), or (NE) if the transaction has no effect on cash.

TIP: Think about the journal entry recorded for the transaction. The transaction affects net cash flows if and only if the account Cash is affected.

_____ 1. Purchased new equipment by signing a promissory note.

_____ 2. Recorded and paid income taxes to the federal government.

_____ 3. Issued shares of stock for cash.

_____ 4. Prepaid rent for the following period.

_____ 5. Recorded an adjusting entry for expiration of a prepaid expense.

_____ 6. Paid cash to purchase new equipment.

_____ 7. Issued long-term debt for cash.

_____ 8. Collected payments on account from customers.

_____ 9. Recorded and paid salaries to employees.

LO2   **CP12-2 Computing Cash Flows from Operating Activities (Indirect Method)**

The income statement and selected balance sheet information for Hamburger Heaven for the year ended December 31, 2010, are presented below.

Income Statement	
Sales Revenue	$2,060
Expenses:	
Cost of Goods Sold	900
Depreciation Expense	200
Salaries Expense	500
Rent Expense	250
Insurance Expense	80
Interest Expense	60
Utilities Expense	50
Net Income	$ 20

Selected Balance Sheet Accounts		
	2010	2009
Merchandise Inventory	$ 82	$ 60
Accounts Receivable	380	450
Accounts Payable	240	210
Salaries Payable	29	20
Utilities Payable	20	60
Prepaid Rent	2	7
Prepaid Insurance	14	5

TIP: Prepaid Rent decreased in 2010 because the amount taken out of Prepaid Rent (and subtracted from net income as Rent Expense) was more than the amount paid for rent in cash during 2010.

Required:

Prepare the cash flows from operating activities section of the 2010 statement of cash flows using the indirect method.

CP12-3 Preparing a Statement of Cash Flows (Indirect Method)

LO2, 3, 4, 5

Hunter Company is developing its annual financial statements at December 31, 2010. The statements are complete except for the statement of cash flows. The completed comparative balance sheets and income statement are summarized:

www.mhhe.com/phillips3e

	2010	2009
Balance Sheet at December 31		
Cash	$ 44,000	$ 18,000
Accounts Receivable	27,000	29,000
Merchandise Inventory	30,000	36,000
Property and Equipment	111,000	102,000
Less: Accumulated Depreciation	(36,000)	(30,000)
	$176,000	$155,000
Accounts Payable	$ 25,000	$ 22,000
Wages Payable	800	1,000
Note Payable, Long-Term	38,000	48,000
Contributed Capital	80,000	60,000
Retained Earnings	32,200	24,000
	$176,000	$155,000
Income Statement for 2010		
Sales	$100,000	
Cost of Goods Sold	61,000	
Other Expenses	27,000	
Net Income	$ 12,000	

Additional Data:

a. Bought equipment for cash, $9,000.
b. Paid $10,000 on the long-term note payable.
c. Issued new shares of stock for $20,000 cash.
d. Declared and paid a $3,800 cash dividend.
e. Other expenses included depreciation, $6,000; wages, $10,000; taxes, $3,000; other, $8,000.
f. Accounts Payable includes only inventory purchases made on credit. Because there are no liability accounts relating to taxes or other expenses, assume that these expenses were fully paid in cash.

Required:

1. Prepare the statement of cash flows for the year ended December 31, 2010, using the indirect method.
2. Use the statement of cash flows to evaluate Hunter's cash flows.
    TIP: The demonstration cases provide good examples of information to consider when evaluating cash flows.

LO2, 3, 4, 5   **CP12-4 Preparing and Interpreting a Statement of Cash Flows (Indirect Method)**

Soft Touch Company was started several years ago by two golf instructors. The company's comparative balance sheets and income statement are presented below, along with additional information.

	2010	2009
Balance Sheet at December 31		
Cash	$12,000	$ 8,000
Accounts Receivable	2,000	3,500
Equipment	11,000	10,000
Less: Accumulated Depreciation	(3,000)	(2,500)
	$22,000	$19,000
Accounts Payable	$ 1,000	$ 2,000
Wages Payable	1,000	1,500
Long-term Bank Loan Payable	3,000	1,000
Contributed Capital	10,000	10,000
Retained Earnings	7,000	4,500
	$22,000	$19,000
Income Statement for 2010		
Lessons Revenue	$75,000	
Wages Expense	70,000	
Depreciation Expense	500	
Income Tax Expense	2,000	
Net Income	$ 2,500	

Additional Data:

a. Bought new golf clubs using cash, $1,000.
b. Borrowed $2,000 cash from the bank during the year.
c. Accounts Payable includes only purchases of services made on credit for operating purposes. Because there are no liability accounts relating to income tax, assume that this expense was fully paid in cash.

Required:

1. Prepare the statement of cash flows for the year ended December 31, 2010, using the indirect method.
2. Use the statement of cash flows to evaluate the company's cash flows.
    TIP: The demonstration cases provide good examples of information to consider when evaluating cash flows.

LO6   **CP12-5 Computing Cash Flows from Operating Activities (Direct Method)**

Refer to the information in CP12-2.

Required:

Prepare the cash flows from operating activities section of the 2010 statement of cash flows using the direct method.
TIP: Convert the cost of goods sold to cash paid to suppliers by adding the increase in inventory and subtracting the increase in accounts payable.

LO3, 4, 5, 6   **CP12-6 Preparing and Interpreting a Statement of Cash Flows (Direct Method)**

Refer to CP12-4.

Required:

Complete requirements 1 and 2 using the direct method.
TIP: Remember to exclude depreciation expense when converting to the cash basis.

CP12-7 (Supplement 12A) Preparing and Interpreting a Statement of Cash Flows with Loss on Disposal (Indirect Method)

Assume the same facts as CP12-4, except for additional data item (a) and the income statement. Instead of item (a) from CP12-4, assume that the company bought new golf clubs for $3,000 cash and sold existing clubs for $1,000 cash. The clubs that were sold cost $2,000 and had Accumulated Depreciation of $500 at the time of sale. The income statement follows.

Income Statement for 2010	
Lessons Revenue	$75,000
Wages Expense	70,000
Depreciation Expense	1,000
Loss on Disposal of Equipment	500
Income Tax Expense	1,000
Net Income	$ 2,500

Required:

1. Prepare the statement of cash flows for the year ended December 31, 2010, using the indirect method.

2. Use the statement of cash flows to evaluate the company's cash flows.

GROUP A PROBLEMS

PA12-1 Determining Cash Flow Statement Effects of Transactions   LO1

Motif Furniture is an Austin-based furniture company. For each of the following first-quarter transactions, indicate whether operating (O), investing (I), or financing activities (F) are affected and whether the effect is a cash inflow (+) or outflow (−), or (NE) if the transaction has no effect on cash.

____ 1. Bought used equipment for cash.

____ 2. Paid cash to purchase new equipment.

____ 3. Declared and paid cash dividends to stockholders.

____ 4. Collected payments on account from customers.

____ 5. Recorded an adjusting entry to record accrued salaries expense.

____ 6. Recorded and paid interest on debt to creditors.

____ 7. Repaid principal on loan from bank.

____ 8. Prepaid rent for the following period.

____ 9. Made payment to suppliers on account.

PA12-2 Computing Cash Flows from Operating Activities (Indirect Method)   LO2

The income statement and selected balance sheet information for Direct Products Company for the year ended December 31, 2010, is presented below.

Income Statement	
Sales Revenue	$48,600
Expenses:	
Cost of Goods Sold	21,000
Depreciation Expense	2,000
Salaries Expense	9,000
Rent Expense	4,500
Insurance Expense	1,900
Interest Expense	1,800
Utilities Expense	1,400
Net Income	$ 7,000

Selected Balance Sheet Accounts		
	2010	2009
Accounts Receivable	$560	$580
Merchandise Inventory	990	770
Accounts Payable	440	460
Prepaid Rent	25	20
Prepaid Insurance	25	28
Salaries Payable	100	70
Utilities Payable	20	15

Required:

Prepare the cash flows from operating activities section of the 2010 statement of cash flows using the indirect method.

LO2, 3, 4, 5

www.mhhe.com/phillips3e

PA12-3 Preparing a Statement of Cash Flows (Indirect Method)

XS Supply Company is developing its annual financial statements at December 31, 2010. The statements are complete except for the statement of cash flows. The completed comparative balance sheets and income statement are summarized:

	2010	2009
Balance Sheet at December 31		
Cash	$ 34,000	$ 29,000
Accounts Receivable	35,000	28,000
Merchandise Inventory	41,000	38,000
Property and Equipment	121,000	100,000
Less: Accumulated Depreciation	(30,000)	(25,000)
	$201,000	$170,000
Accounts Payable	$ 36,000	$ 27,000
Wages Payable	1,200	1,400
Note Payable, Long-Term	38,000	44,000
Contributed Capital	88,600	72,600
Retained Earnings	37,200	25,000
	$201,000	$170,000
Income Statement for 2010		
Sales	$120,000	
Cost of Goods Sold	70,000	
Other Expenses	37,800	
Net Income	$ 12,200	

Additional Data:

a. Bought equipment for cash, $21,000.
b. Paid $6,000 on the long-term note payable.
c. Issued new shares of stock for $16,000 cash.
d. No dividends were declared or paid.
e. Other expenses included depreciation, $5,000; wages, $20,000; taxes, $6,000; other, $6,800.
f. Accounts Payable includes only inventory purchases made on credit. Because there are no liability accounts relating to taxes or other expenses, assume that these expenses were fully paid in cash.

Required:

1. Prepare the statement of cash flows for the year ended December 31, 2010, using the indirect method.
2. Evaluate the statement of cash flows.

LO2, 3, 4, 5

PA12-4 Preparing and Interpreting a Statement of Cash Flows (Indirect Method)

Heads Up Company was started several years ago by two hockey instructors. The company's comparative balance sheets and income statement follow, along with additional information.

	2010	2009
Balance Sheet at December 31		
Cash	$ 6,000	$4,000
Accounts Receivable	1,000	1,750
Equipment	5,500	5,000
Less: Accumulated Depreciation	(1,500)	(1,250)
	$11,000	$9,500
Accounts Payable	$ 500	$1,000
Wages Payable	500	750
Long-Term Bank Loan Payable	1,500	500
Contributed Capital	5,000	5,000
Retained Earnings	3,500	2,250
	$11,000	$9,500
Income Statement for 2010		
Lessons Revenue	$37,500	
Wages Expense	35,000	
Depreciation Expense	250	
Income Tax Expense	1,000	
Net Income	$ 1,250	

Additional Data:

a. Bought new hockey equipment for cash, $500.
b. Borrowed $1,000 cash from the bank during the year.
c. Accounts Payable includes only purchases of services made on credit for operating purposes. Because there are no liability accounts relating to income tax, assume that this expense was fully paid in cash.

Required:

1. Prepare the statement of cash flows for the year ended December 31, 2010, using the indirect method.
2. Use the statement of cash flows to evaluate the company's cash flows.

PA12-5 Computing Cash Flows from Operating Activities (Direct Method)   LO6

Refer to the information in PA12-2.

Required:

Prepare the cash flows from operating activities section of the 2010 statement of cash flows using the direct method.

PA12-6 Preparing and Interpreting a Statement of Cash Flows   LO3, 4, 5, 6
(Direct Method)

Refer to PA12-4.

Required:

Complete requirements 1 and 2 using the direct method.

PA12-7 (Supplement 12A) Preparing and Interpreting a Statement of Cash Flows with Loss on Disposal (Indirect Method)

Assume the same facts as PA12-4, except for the income statement and additional data item (a). The new income statement is shown on the following page. Instead of item (a) from PA12-4, assume that the company bought new equipment for $1,500 cash and sold existing equipment for $500 cash. The equipment that was sold had cost $1,000 and had Accumulated Depreciation of $250 at the time of sale.

Income Statement for 2010	
Lessons Revenue	$37,500
Wages Expense	35,000
Depreciation Expense	500
Loss on Disposal of Equipment	250
Income Tax Expense	500
Net Income	$ 1,250

Required:

1. Prepare the statement of cash flows for the year ended December 31, 2010, using the indirect method.
2. Use the statement of cash flows to evaluate the company's cash flows.

GROUP B PROBLEMS

LO1   **PB12-1 Determining Cash Flow Statement Effects of Transactions**

For each of the following transactions, indicate whether operating (O), investing (I), or financing activities (F) are affected and whether the effect is a cash inflow (+) or outflow (−), or (NE) if the transaction has no effect on cash.

_____ 1. Received deposits from customers for products to be delivered the following period.

_____ 2. Principal repayments on loan.

_____ 3. Paid cash to purchase new equipment.

_____ 4. Received proceeds from loan.

_____ 5. Collected payments on account from customers.

_____ 6. Recorded and paid salaries to employees.

_____ 7. Paid cash for building construction.

_____ 8. Recorded and paid interest to debt holders.

LO2   **PB12-2 Computing Cash Flows from Operating Activities (Indirect Method)**

The income statement and selected balance sheet information for Calendars Incorporated for the year ended December 31, 2010, is presented below.

Income Statement	
Sales Revenue	$78,000
Expenses:	
Cost of Goods Sold	36,000
Depreciation Expense	16,000
Salaries Expense	10,000
Rent Expense	2,500
Insurance Expense	1,300
Interest Expense	1,200
Utilities Expense	1,000
Net Income	$10,000

Selected Balance Sheet Accounts	2010	2009
Merchandise Inventory	$ 430	$ 490
Accounts Receivable	1,800	1,500
Accounts Payable	1,200	1,300
Salaries Payable	450	300
Utilities Payable	100	0
Prepaid Rent	50	100
Prepaid Insurance	70	90

Required:

Prepare the cash flows from operating activities section of the 2010 statement of cash flows using the indirect method.

PB12-3 Preparing a Statement of Cash Flows (Indirect Method)   LO2, 3, 4, 5

Audio City, Inc., is developing its annual financial statements at December 31, 2010. The statements are complete except for the statement of cash flows. The completed comparative balance sheets and income statement are summarized below:

	2010	2009
Balance Sheet at December 31		
Cash	$ 63,000	$ 65,000
Accounts Receivable	15,000	20,000
Merchandise Inventory	22,000	20,000
Property and Equipment	210,000	150,000
Less: Accumulated Depreciation	(60,000)	(45,000)
	$250,000	$210,000
Accounts Payable	$ 8,000	$ 19,000
Wages Payable	2,000	1,000
Note Payable, Long-Term	60,000	75,000
Contributed Capital	100,000	70,000
Retained Earnings	80,000	45,000
	$250,000	$210,000
Income Statement for 2010		
Sales	$190,000	
Cost of Goods Sold	90,000	
Other Expenses	60,000	
Net Income	$ 40,000	

Additional Data:

a. Bought equipment for cash, $60,000.
b. Paid $15,000 on the long-term note payable.
c. Issued new shares of stock for $30,000 cash.
d. Dividends of $5,000 were paid in cash.
e. Other expenses included depreciation, $15,000; wages, $20,000; taxes, $25,000.
f. Accounts Payable includes only inventory purchases made on credit. Because a liability relating to taxes does not exist, assume that they were fully paid in cash.

Required:

1. Prepare the statement of cash flows for the year ended December 31, 2010, using the indirect method.
2. Evaluate the statement of cash flows.

PB12-4 Preparing and Interpreting a Statement of Cash Flows (Indirect Method)   LO2, 3, 4, 5

Dive In Company was started several years ago by two diving instructors. The company's comparative balance sheets and income statement are presented below. Additional information is presented on the following page.

	2010	2009
Balance Sheet at December 31		
Cash	$ 3,200	$4,000
Accounts Receivable	1,000	500
Prepaid Expenses	100	50
	$ 4,300	$4,550
Wages Payable	$ 350	$1,100
Contributed Capital	1,200	1,000
Retained Earnings	2,750	2,450
	$ 4,300	$4,550
Income Statement for 2010		
Lessons Revenue	$33,950	
Wages Expense	30,000	
Other Operating Expenses	3,650	
Net Income	$ 300	

Additional Data:

a. Prepaid Expenses relate to rent paid in advance.
b. Other Operating Expenses were paid in cash.
c. An owner contributed capital by paying $200 cash in exchange for the company's stock.

Required:

1. Prepare the statement of cash flows for the year ended December 31, 2010, using the indirect method.
2. Use the statement of cash flows to evaluate the company's cash flows.

LO6   PB12-5 Computing Cash Flows from Operating Activities (Direct Method)

Refer to the information in PB12-2.

Required:

Prepare the cash flows from operating activities section of the 2010 statement of cash flows using the direct method.

LO3, 4, 5, 6   PB12-6 Preparing and Interpreting a Statement of Cash Flows (Direct Method)

Refer to PB12-4.

Required:

Complete requirements 1 and 2 using the direct method.

SKILLS DEVELOPMENT CASES

LO1, 5   S12-1 Finding Financial Information

Refer to the financial statements of The Home Depot in Appendix A at the end of this book, or download the annual report from the *Cases* section of the text's Web site at www.mhhe.com/phillips3e.

Required:

1. Which of the two basic reporting approaches for the cash flows from operating activities did The Home Depot use?
2. What amount of tax payments did The Home Depot make during the year ended February 1, 2009? Where did you find this information?
3. In the 2008–09 fiscal year, The Home Depot generated $5,528 million from operating activities. Where did The Home Depot spend this money? List the two largest cash outflows.

LO1, 5   S12-2 Comparing Financial Information

Lowe's

Refer to the financial statements of The Home Depot in Appendix A and Lowe's in Appendix B at the end of this book, or download the annual reports from the *Cases* section of the text's Web site at www.mhhe.com/phillips3e.

Required:

1. Which of the two basic reporting approaches for the cash flows from operating activities did Lowe's use? Is this the same as what The Home Depot used?
2. What amount of cash did Lowe's receive from issuing long-term debt during the year ended January 30, 2009?
3. In the 2008–09 fiscal year, Lowe's generated $4,122 million from operating activities. Where did Lowe's spend this money? List the two largest cash outflows reported in the investing or financing activities sections. Do Lowe's uses differ significantly from The Home Depot's?

S12-3 Internet-Based Team Research: Examining an Annual Report

LO5

As a team, select an industry to analyze. Using your Web browser, each team member should access the annual report or 10-K for one publicly traded company in the industry, with each member selecting a different company. (See S1-3 in Chapter 1 for a description of possible resources for these tasks.)

Required:

1. On an individual basis, each team member should write a short report that incorporates the following:
   a. Has the company generated positive or negative operating cash flows during the past three years?
   b. Has the company been expanding over the period? If so, what appears to have been the source of financing for this expansion (operating cash flow, additional borrowing, issuance of stock)?
   c. Compute and analyze the capital acquisitions ratio averaged over the past three years.
   d. Compute and analyze the quality of income ratio in each of the past three years.
2. Then, as a team, write a short report comparing and contrasting your companies using these attributes. Discuss any patterns across the companies that you as a team observe. Provide potential explanations for any differences discovered.

S12-4 Ethical Decision Making: A Real-Life Example

LO1, 5

Enron

Merrill Lynch

In a February 19, 2004, press release, the Securities and Exchange Commission described a number of fraudulent transactions that Enron executives concocted in an effort to meet the company's financial targets. One particularly well-known scheme is called the "Nigerian barge" transaction. According to court documents, Enron arranged to sell three electricity-generating power barges moored off the coast of Nigeria. The "buyer" was the investment banking firm of Merrill Lynch. Although Enron reported this transaction as a sale in its income statement, it turns out this was no ordinary sale. Merrill Lynch didn't really want the barges and had only agreed to buy them because Enron guaranteed, in a secret side-deal, that it would arrange for the barges to be bought back from Merrill Lynch within six months of the initial transaction. In addition, Enron promised to pay Merrill Lynch a hefty fee for doing the deal. In an interview on National Public Radio on August 17, 2002, Michigan Senator Carl Levin declared, the "case of the Nigerian barge transaction was, by any definition, a loan."

Required:

1. Discuss whether the Nigerian barge transaction should have been considered a loan rather than a sale. As part of your discussion, consider the following questions. Doesn't the Merrill Lynch payment to Enron at the time of the initial transaction automatically make it a sale, not a loan? What aspects of the transaction are similar to a loan? Which aspects suggest revenue has not been earned by Enron?
2. The income statement effect of recording the transaction as a sale rather than a loan is fairly clear: Enron was able to boost its revenues and net income. What is somewhat less obvious, but nearly as important, are the effects on the statement of cash flows. Describe how including the transaction with sales of other Enron products, rather than as a loan, would change the statement of cash flows.
3. How would the difference in the statement of cash flows (described in your response to requirement 2) affect financial statement users?

S12-5 Ethical Decision Making: A Mini-Case

LO1, 5

Assume you serve on the board of a local golf and country club. In preparation for renegotiating the club's bank loans, the president indicates that the club needs to increase its operating cash flows before the end of the current year. The club's treasurer reassures the president and other board members that he knows a couple of ways to boost the club's operating cash flows. First, he says, the club can sell some of its accounts receivable to a collections company that is willing to pay the club $97,000 up front for the right to collect $100,000 of the overdue accounts. That will immediately boost operating cash flows. Second, he indicates that the club paid about $200,000 last month to relocate the 18th fairway and green closer to the clubhouse. The treasurer indicates that although these costs have been reported as expenses in the club's own monthly financial statements, he feels an argument can be made for reporting them as part of land and land improvements (a long-lived asset) in the year-end financial statements that would be provided to the bank. He explains that, by recording these payments as an addition to a long-lived asset, they will not be shown as a reduction in operating cash flows.

Required:

1. Does the sale of accounts receivable to generate immediate cash harm or mislead anyone? Would you consider it an ethical business activity?
2. What category in the statement of cash flows is used when reporting cash spent on long-lived assets, such as land improvements? What category is used when cash is spent on expenses, such as costs for regular upkeep of the grounds?
3. What facts are relevant to deciding whether the costs of the 18th hole relocation should be reported as an asset or as an expense? Is it appropriate to make this decision based on the impact it could have on operating cash flows?
4. As a member of the board, how would you ensure that an ethical decision is made?

LO2   **S12-6**   **Critical Thinking: Interpreting Adjustments Reported on the Statement of Cash Flows from a Management Perspective (Indirect Method)**

QuickServe, a chain of convenience stores, was experiencing some serious cash flow difficulties because of rapid growth. The company did not generate sufficient cash from operating activities to finance its new stores, and creditors were not willing to lend money because the company had not produced any income for the previous three years. The new controller for QuickServe proposed a reduction in the estimated life of store equipment to increase depreciation expense; thus, "we can improve cash flows from operating activities because depreciation expense is added back on the statement of cash flows." Other executives were not sure that this was a good idea because the increase in depreciation would make it more difficult to report positive earnings: "Without income, the bank will never lend us money."

Required:

What action would you recommend for QuickServe? Why?

LO2   **S12-7**   **Using a Spreadsheet that Calculates Cash Flows from Operating Activities (Indirect Method)**

www.mhhe.com/phillips3e

You've recently been hired by B2B Consultants to provide financial advisory services to small business managers. B2B's clients often need advice on how to improve their operating cash flows and, given your accounting background, you're frequently called upon to show them how operating cash flows would change if they were to speed up their sales of inventory and their collections of accounts receivable or delay their payment of accounts payable. Each time you're asked to show the effects of these business decisions on the cash flows from operating activities, you get the uneasy feeling that you might inadvertently miscalculate their effects. To deal with this once and for all, you e-mail your friend Owen and ask him to prepare a template that automatically calculates the net operating cash flows from a simple comparative balance sheet. You received his reply today.

From: Owentheaccountant@yahoo.com
To: Helpme@hotmail.com
Cc:
Subject: Excel Help

Hey pal. I like your idea of working smarter, not harder. Too bad it involved me doing the thinking. Anyhow, I've created a spreadsheet file that contains four worksheets. The first two tabs (labeled BS and IS) are the input sheets where you would enter the numbers from each client's comparative balance sheets and income statement. Your clients are small, so this template allows for only the usual accounts. Also, I've assumed that depreciation is the only reason for a change in accumulated depreciation. If your clients' business activities differ from these, you'll need to contact me for more complex templates. The third worksheet calculates the operating cash flows using the indirect method and the fourth does this calculation using the direct method. I'll attach the screenshots of each of the worksheets so you can create your own. To answer "what if" questions, all you'll need to do is change selected amounts in the balance sheet and income statement.

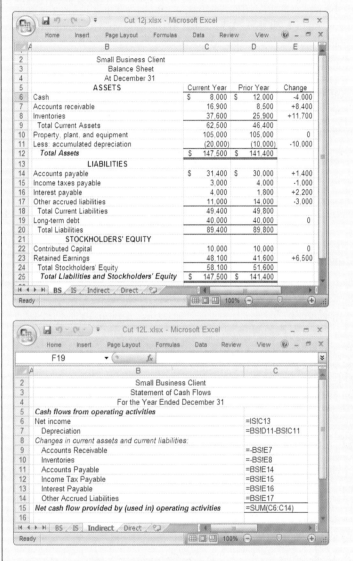

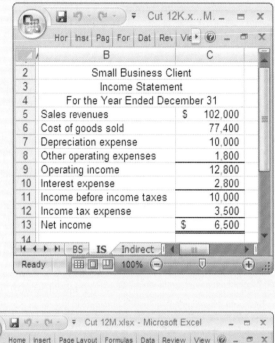

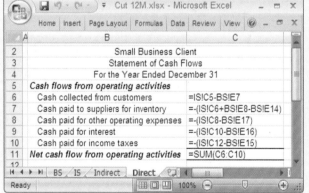

Required:

Copy the account balances from the worksheets for the balance sheet and income statement into a spreadsheet file. Enter formulas into the balance sheet worksheet to compute the change in each account balance, and then enter the formulas for the statement of cash flows (indirect method only) into a third worksheet. From this third worksheet, report the net cash flow provided by (used in) operating activities.

LO6   **S12-8 Using a Spreadsheet that Calculates Cash Flows from Operating Activities (Direct Method)**

www.mhhe.com/phillips3e

Refer to the information presented in S12-7.

Required:

Complete the same requirements, except use the direct method only.

LO5   **S12-9 Using a Spreadsheet to Answer "What If" Management Decisions (Indirect or Direct Method)**

www.mhhe.com/phillips3e

Change the amounts for selected balance sheet accounts in the spreadsheets created for either S12-7 or S12-8 to calculate the net cash flows from operating activities if, just before the current year-end, the company's management took the actions listed in the following requirements. Consider each question independently, unless indicated otherwise.

Required:

1. What if the company collected $10,000 of the accounts receivable?
2. What if the company had paid down its interest payable by an extra $2,000?
3. What if the company waited an additional month before paying $6,000 of its accounts payable?
4. What if the company had reported $5,000 more depreciation expense?
5. What if all four of the above events had taken place at the same time?

CONTINUING CASE

LO2, 3, 4, 5   **CC12 Accounting for Cash Flows**

During a recent year (ended December 31, 2011), Nicole's Getaway Spa (NGS) reported net income of $2,300. The company reported the following activities:

a. Increase in inventories of $400.
b. Depreciation of $3,000.
c. Increase of $2,170 in prepaid expenses.
d. Payments of $4,600 on long-term debt.
e. Purchased new spa equipment for $7,582.
f. Payments on accounts payable exceeded purchases by $320.
g. Collections on accounts receivable exceeded credit sales by $859.
h. Issued $10,000 of common stock.

Required:

1. Based on this information, prepare a statement of cash flows for the year ended December 31, 2011, using the indirect method. Assume the cash balance at December 31, 2010, was $7,000.
2. Calculate the capital acquisitions ratio (round to two decimal places). What does this tell you about NGS's ability to finance expansion with operating cash flows?

CHAPTER 13

Measuring and Evaluating Financial Performance

YOUR LEARNING OBJECTIVES

Understand the business

> **LO1** Describe the purposes and uses of horizontal, vertical, and ratio analyses.

Study the accounting methods

> **LO2** Use horizontal (trend) analyses to recognize financial changes that unfold over time.
>
> **LO3** Use vertical (common size) analyses to understand important relationships within financial statements.
>
> **LO4** Calculate financial ratios to assess profitability, liquidity, and solvency.

Evaluate the results

> **LO5** Interpret the results of financial analyses.
>
> **LO6** Describe how analyses depend on key accounting decisions and concepts.

Review the chapter

THAT WAS
THEN

In the previous chapters, you learned how to report and interpret the financial effects of various business activities.

Lecture Presentation-LP13
www.mhhe.com/phillips3e

FOCUS COMPANY: Lowe's

www.lowes.com

Measuring and evaluating financial performance is like judging gymnastics or figure skating at the Olympics. You have to know three things: (1) the general categories to evaluate for each event, (2) the particular elements to consider within each category, and (3) how to measure performance for each element. On the financial side, analysts follow the same process. They evaluate general categories such as profitability, liquidity, and solvency, which are separated into particular elements such as gross profit margin and net profit margin. For each of these elements, analysts measure performance by computing various percentages and ratios, which themselves are based on information reported in the financial statements.

In this chapter, we focus on Lowe's, the second largest home improvement retailer in the world. Lowe's is a giant with nearly 1,650 stores and 230,000 employees. Yet the company's continued success still requires innovations to increase sales in existing markets and to successfully enter new markets. At the same time, Lowe's must control costs while maintaining a high level of customer service in its stores. Finally, Lowe's management must anticipate the actions of its larger rival, The Home Depot, and deal with changes in overall demand for building products over which it has no control.

How do managers, analysts, investors, and creditors assess Lowe's success in meeting these challenges? This is the purpose of financial statement analysis. Our discussion begins with an explanation of how to analyze financial statements to understand the financial results of a company's business activities. We conclude the chapter with a review of the key accounting decisions analysts consider when evaluating financial statements.

**THIS IS
NOW**

This chapter synthesizes previous chapters, by evaluating the financial statements and accounting decisions of a publicly traded company.

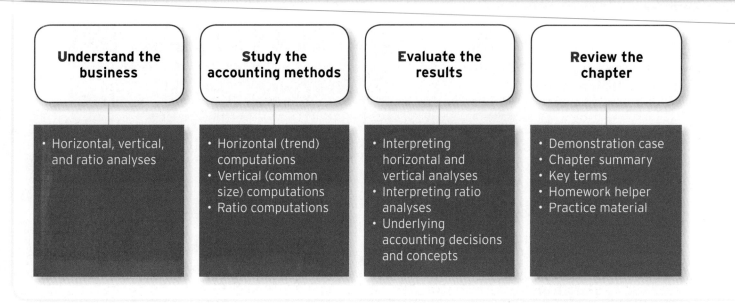

Understand the business	Study the accounting methods	Evaluate the results	Review the chapter
• Horizontal, vertical, and ratio analyses	• Horizontal (trend) computations • Vertical (common size) computations • Ratio computations	• Interpreting horizontal and vertical analyses • Interpreting ratio analyses • Underlying accounting decisions and concepts	• Demonstration case • Chapter summary • Key terms • Homework helper • Practice material

Understand the Business

Learning Objective 1
Describe the purposes and uses of horizontal, vertical, and ratio analyses.

As you first learned in Chapter 1, the goal of accounting is to provide information that allows decision makers to understand and evaluate the results of business activities. Throughout the course, you have learned how financial statements are used in a variety of decisions. Creditors use financial statements to assess compliance with loan covenants. Managers analyze financial statements to evaluate past financial performance and make future decisions. And, of course, analysts use financial statements to generate advice for investors and others. You have learned that no single number fully captures the results of all business activities nor does it predict a company's success or failure. Instead, to understand and evaluate the results of business activities, you need to look at a business from many different angles. An understanding of whether a business is successful will emerge only after you have learned to combine all of your evaluations into a complete picture or story that depicts the company's performance. Our goal for this chapter is to demonstrate how you can do this, relying on horizontal, vertical, and ratio analyses to develop the "story" of how well a company has performed.

HORIZONTAL, VERTICAL, AND RATIO ANALYSES

Most good stories have a plot, which the reader comes to understand as it unfolds over time or as one event relates to another. This is the same way that financial analyses work. **Horizontal (trend) analyses are conducted to help financial statement users recognize important financial changes that unfold over time.** Horizontal analyses compare individual financial statement line items horizontally (from one period to the next), with the general goal of identifying significant sustained changes (trends). These changes are typically described in terms of dollar amounts and year-over-year percentages. For example, trend analyses could be used to determine the dollar amount and percentage by which Cost of Goods Sold increased this year, relative to prior years. **Vertical analyses focus on important relationships between items on the same financial statement.** These items are compared vertically (one account balance versus another) and are typically expressed as percentages to reveal the relative contributions made by each financial statement item. For example, vertical analyses could show that operating expenses consume one quarter of a company's net sales revenue. **Ratio analyses are conducted to understand relationships among various items reported in one or more of the financial statements.** Ratio analyses allow you to evaluate how well a company has performed given the level of other company resources. For example, while vertical analyses can show that Cost of Goods Sold consumes 65 percent of Net Sales and horizontal analyses can show that this percentage has increased over time, ratio analyses can relate these amounts to inventory levels to evaluate inventory management decisions.

Before we show you how to calculate horizontal, vertical, and ratio analyses (in the next section), we must emphasize that **no analysis is complete unless it leads to an interpretation that helps financial statement users understand and evaluate a company's financial results.** Without interpretation, these computations can appear as nothing more than a list of disconnected numbers.

Study the Accounting Methods

HORIZONTAL (TREND) COMPUTATIONS

Horizontal (trend) analyses help financial statement users to recognize financial changes that unfold over time. This approach compares individual financial statement items from year to year with the general goal of identifying significant sustained changes or trends. For example, trend analysis can be used to determine the dollar and percentage changes in the cost of goods sold this year relative to prior years. Because this type of analysis compares the results on each line of the financial statements across several years, trend analysis is also known as horizontal analysis. Because it compares results over a series of periods, it is sometimes called **time-series analysis.**

Regardless of the name, trend analyses are usually calculated in terms of year-to-year dollar and percentage changes. A year-to-year percentage change expresses the current year's dollar change as a percentage of the prior year's total by using the following calculation:

Learning Objective 2
Use horizontal (trend) analyses to recognize financial changes that unfold over time.

YOU SHOULD KNOW

Horizontal (trend) analyses: Comparing results across time, often expressing changes in account balances as a percentage of prior year balances.

$$\text{Year-to-Year Change (\%)} = \frac{\text{Change This Year}}{\text{Prior Year's Total}} \times 100 = \frac{(\text{Current Year's Total} - \text{Prior Year's Total})}{\text{Prior Year's Total}} \times 100$$

To demonstrate how to calculate a trend, we analyze Lowe's financial statements. Summaries of Lowe's balance sheets and income statements from two recent years appear in Exhibits 13.1 and 13.2. Dollar and percentage changes from fiscal year 2007 to 2008[1] are shown to the right of the balance sheet and income statement. The dollar changes were calculated by subtracting the fiscal 2007 balances from the fiscal 2008 balances. The percentage changes were calculated by dividing those differences by the fiscal 2007 balances. For example, according to Exhibit 13.1, Cash decreased by \$36 (= \$245 − \$281) in fiscal 2008 relative to fiscal 2007 (all numbers in millions). That dollar amount represented a decrease of 12.8% [= (\$36 ÷ \$281) × 100].

Video 13.1
www.mhhe.com/phillips3e

---

[1]Like many retail companies, Lowe's fiscal year ends at the end of January.

EXHIBIT 13.1   Horizontal (Trend) Analysis of Lowe's Summarized Balance Sheets   **Lowe's**

LOWE'S
Balance Sheets
(in millions)

	January 30, 2009 (Fiscal 2008)	February 1, 2008 (Fiscal 2007)	Increase (Decrease) Amount	Increase (Decrease) Percent*
Assets				
Current Assets				
Cash	$ 245	$ 281	$ (36)	(12.8)%
Short-term Investments	416	249	167	67.1
Accounts Receivable	—	—	—	0.0
Inventories	8,209	7,611	598	7.9
Other Current Assets	381	545	(164)	(30.1)
Total Current Assets	9,251	8,686	565	6.5
Property and Equipment, Net	22,722	21,361	1,361	6.4
Other Assets	713	822	(109)	(13.3)
Total Assets	$32,686	$30,869	$1,817	5.9
Liabilities and Stockholders' Equity				
Current Liabilities	$ 8,022	$ 7,751	$ 271	3.5
Long-term Liabilities	6,609	7,020	(411)	(5.9)
Total Liabilities	14,631	14,771	(140)	(0.9)
Stockholders' Equity	18,055	16,098	1,957	12.2
Total Liabilities and Stockholders' Equity	$32,686	$30,869	$1,817	5.9

*Amount of Increase (Decrease) ÷ Fiscal 2007 × 100

EXHIBIT 13.2   Horizontal (Trend) Analysis of Lowe's Summarized Income Statements   **Lowe's**

LOWE'S
Income Statements
(in millions)

Year Ended:	January 30, 2009 (Fiscal 2008)	February 1, 2008 (Fiscal 2007)	Increase (Decrease) Amount	Increase (Decrease) Percent[†]
Net Sales Revenue	$48,230	$48,283	$ (53)	(0.1)%
Cost of Sales	31,729	31,556	173	0.5
Gross Profit	16,501	16,727	(226)	(1.4)
Operating and Other Expenses	12,715	12,022	693	5.8
Interest Expense	280	194	86	44.3
Income Tax Expense	1,311	1,702	(391)	(23.0)
Net Income	$ 2,195	$ 2,809	$ (614)	(21.9)
Earnings per Share	$ 1.51	$ 1.90	$(0.39)	(20.5)

[†]Amount of Increase (Decrease) ÷ Fiscal 2007 × 100

In a later section, we will explain and evaluate the underlying causes of significant changes in account balances. But before we leave this topic, we must note that not all large percentage changes will be significant. For example, the 67.1 percent increase in Short-term Investments is the largest percentage change on the balance sheet (Exhibit 13.1) but the dollar amount is relatively small when compared to other changes, such as the $598 increase in Inventories. To avoid focusing on unimportant changes, use the percentage changes to identify potentially significant changes but then check the dollar change to make sure that it too is significant.

VERTICAL (COMMON SIZE) COMPUTATIONS

A second type of analysis, **vertical (common size) analysis,** focuses on important relationships within a financial statement. When a company is growing or shrinking overall, it is difficult to tell from the dollar amounts whether the proportions within each statement category are changing. Common size financial statements provide this information by expressing each financial statement amount as a percentage of another amount on that statement. The usefulness of common size statements is illustrated by the fact that Lowe's presents its balance sheet and income statements in the common size format illustrated in Exhibits 13.3 and 13.4.

In a common size balance sheet, each asset appears as a percent of total assets, and each liability or stockholders' equity item appears as a percent of total liabilities and stockholders' equity. For example, in Exhibit 13.3, which presents Lowe's common size

> **Learning Objective 3**
> Use vertical (common size) analyses to understand important relationships within financial statements.

> **YOU SHOULD KNOW**
> **Vertical (common size) analyses:** Expressing each financial statement amount as a percentage of another amount on the same financial statement.

| **EXHIBIT 13.3** | Vertical (Common Size) Analysis of Lowe's Summarized Balance Sheets | Lowe's |

LOWE'S
Balance Sheets
(in millions)

	Fiscal 2008		Fiscal 2007	
	Amount	Percent	Amount	Percent
Assets				
Current Assets				
Cash	$ 245	0.7%	$ 281	0.9%
Short-term Investments	416	1.3	249	0.8
Inventories	8,209	25.1	7,611	24.6
Other Current Assets	381	1.2	545	1.8
Property and Equipment, Net	22,722	69.5	21,361	69.2
Other Assets	713	2.2	822	2.7
Total Assets	$32,686	100.0%	$30,869	100.0%
Liabilities and Stockholders' Equity				
Current Liabilities	$ 8,022	24.5%	$ 7,751	25.1%
Long-term Liabilities	6,609	20.3	7,020	22.8
Stockholders' Equity	18,055	55.2	16,098	52.1
Total Liabilities and Stockholders' Equity	$32,686	100.0%	$30,869	100.0%

EXHIBIT 13.4 Vertical (Common Size) Analysis of Lowe's Summarized Income Statements Lowe's

LOWE'S
Income Statements
(in millions)

	Fiscal 2008		Fiscal 2007	
	Amount	Percent	Amount	Percent
Net Sales Revenue	$48,230	100.0%	$48,283	100.0%
Cost of Sales	31,729	65.8	31,556	65.4
Gross Profit	16,501	34.2	16,727	34.6
Operating and Other Expenses	12,715	26.3	12,022	24.9
Interest Expense	280	0.6	194	0.4
Income Tax Expense	1,311	2.7	1,702	3.5
Net Income	$ 2,195	4.6%	$ 2,809	5.8%

balance sheets, cash was 0.7 percent of total assets [= ($245 ÷ $32,686) × 100] at the end of fiscal 2008.

The common size income statement reports each income statement item as a percentage of sales. For example, in Exhibit 13.4, which presents common size income statements for Lowe's for fiscal 2008 and 2007, cost of sales was equal to 65.8 percent of net sales revenue in 2008 [= ($31,729 ÷ $48,230) × 100].

RATIO COMPUTATIONS

Learning Objective 4
Calculate financial ratios to assess profitability, liquidity, and solvency.

Ratio analyses help financial statement users to understand relationships among various items reported in the financial statements. These analyses compare the amounts for one or more line items to the amounts for other line items in the same year. Ratio analyses are useful because they consider differences in the size of the amounts being compared, similar to common size statements. In fact, some of the most popular ratios, such as net profit margin and the debt-to-assets ratio, are taken directly from the common size statements. Ratios allow users to evaluate how well a company has performed given the level of its other resources.

Most analysts classify ratios into three categories:

YOU SHOULD KNOW

Profitability: The extent to which a company generates income.
Liquidity: The extent to which a company is able to pay its currently maturing obligations.
Solvency: The ability to survive long enough to repay lenders when debt matures.

1. **Profitability** ratios, which relate to the company's performance in the current period—in particular, the company's ability to generate income.

2. **Liquidity** ratios, which relate to the company's short-term survival—in particular, the company's ability to use current assets to repay liabilities as they become due.

3. **Solvency** ratios, which relate to the company's long-run survival—in particular, the company's ability to repay lenders when debt matures and to make the required interest payments prior to the date of maturity.

Exhibit 13.5 organizes the ratios introduced in previous chapters according to these three categories, and demonstrates their calculations for fiscal 2008 using data from Exhibits 13.1 and 13.2.

EXHIBIT 13.5 | **Common Ratios Used in Financial Statement Analysis**

Profitability Ratios

Fiscal 2008

(1) Net Profit Margin $= \dfrac{\text{Net Income}}{\text{Net Sales Revenue}} \times 100$
(Ch. 5, p. 226)

$\dfrac{\$2,195}{\$48,230} \times 100 = 4.6\%$

(2) Gross Profit Percentage $= \dfrac{\text{Net Sales Revenue} - \text{Cost of Goods Sold}}{\text{Net Sales Revenue}} \times 100$
(Ch. 6, p. 275)

$\dfrac{\$16,501}{\$48,230} \times 100 = 34.2\%$

(3) Asset Turnover $= \dfrac{\text{Net Sales Revenue}}{\text{Average Total Assets}}$
(Ch. 5, p. 226)

$\dfrac{\$48,230}{(\$32,686 + \$30,869)/2} = 1.52$

(4) Fixed Asset Turnover $= \dfrac{\text{Net Sales Revenue}}{\text{Average Net Fixed Assets}}$
(Ch. 9, p. 420)

$\dfrac{\$48,230}{(\$22,722 + \$21,361)/2} = 2.19$

(5) Return on Equity (ROE) $= \dfrac{\text{Net Income}}{\text{Average Stockholders' Equity}} \times 100$
(Ch. 11, p. 522)

$\dfrac{\$2,195}{(\$18,055 + \$16,098)/2} \times 100 = 12.9\%$

(6) Earnings per Share (EPS) $= \dfrac{\text{Net Income*}}{\text{Average Number of Common Shares Outstanding}}$
(Ch. 11, p. 522)

$\dfrac{\$2,195}{1,454} = \$1.51$

(7) Quality of Income $= \dfrac{\text{Net Cash from Operations}}{\text{Net Income}}$
(Ch. 12, p. 569)

$\dfrac{\$4,122}{\$2,195} = 1.88$

(8) Price/Earnings Ratio $= \dfrac{\text{Stock Price}}{\text{EPS}}$
(Ch. 11, p. 522)

$\dfrac{\$18.25}{\$1.51} = 12.1$

Liquidity Ratios

(9) Receivables Turnover $= \dfrac{\text{Net Sales Revenue}}{\text{Average Net Receivables}}$
(Ch. 8, p. 372)

n/a

Days to Collect $= \dfrac{365}{\text{Receivables Turnover Ratio}}$
(Ch. 8, p. 372)

n/a

(10) Inventory Turnover $= \dfrac{\text{Cost of Goods Sold}}{\text{Average Inventory}}$
(Ch. 7, p. 323)

$\dfrac{\$31,729}{(\$8,209 + \$7,611)/2} = 4.0$

Days to Sell $= \dfrac{365}{\text{Inventory Turnover Ratio}}$
(Ch. 7, p. 323)

$\dfrac{365}{4.0} = 91.3$

(11) Current Ratio $= \dfrac{\text{Current Assets}}{\text{Current Liabilities}}$
(Ch. 2, p. 65)

$\dfrac{\$9,251}{\$8,022} = 1.15$

(12) Quick Ratio $= \dfrac{\text{Cash} + \text{Short-term Investments} + \text{Accounts Receivable, Net}}{\text{Current Liabilities}}$
(Ch. 10, p. 468)

$\dfrac{\$245 + \$416 + \$0}{\$8,022} = 0.08$

Solvency Ratios

(13) Debt to Assets $= \dfrac{\text{Total Liabilities}}{\text{Total Assets}}$
(Ch. 5, p. 226)

$\dfrac{\$14,631}{\$32,686} = 0.45$

(14) Times Interest Earned $= \dfrac{\text{Net Income} + \text{Interest Expense} + \text{Income Tax Expense}}{\text{Interest Expense}}$
(Ch. 10, p. 468)

$\dfrac{\$2,195 + \$280 + \$1,311}{\$280} = 13.5$

(15) Capital Acquisitions Ratio $= \dfrac{\text{Net Cash from Operations}}{\text{Cash Paid for PPE}}$
(Ch. 12, p. 570)

$\dfrac{\$4,122}{\$3,266} = 1.26$

*If a company has preferred stock outstanding, preferred dividends are subtracted from net income in the numerator to assess the earnings for each share of common stock.

Solution to Self-Study Practice

Gross Profit Percentage = ($71.3 − $47.3)/$71.3 × 100
= 33.7%

Net Profit Margin = $2.2/$71.3 × 100 = 3.1%

Sales Decrease (Percentage) = ($71.3 − $77.3)/$77.3 × 100
= 7.8%

How's it going?   Self-Study Practice

For the year ended February 1, 2009, The Home Depot reported net income of $2.2 billion on sales of $71.3 billion. If the company's cost of sales that year was $47.3 billion, what was the company's gross profit percentage and net profit margin? If sales were $77.3 billion in the prior year, what was the year-over-year percentage decrease in the most recent year?

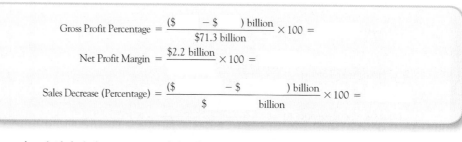

$$\text{Gross Profit Percentage} = \frac{(\$\_\_\_\_ - \$\_\_\_\_) \text{ billion}}{\$71.3 \text{ billion}} \times 100 = $$

$$\text{Net Profit Margin} = \frac{\$2.2 \text{ billion}}{\_\_\_\_} \times 100 = $$

$$\text{Sales Decrease (Percentage)} = \frac{(\$\_\_\_\_ - \$\_\_\_\_) \text{ billion}}{\$\_\_\_\_ \text{ billion}} \times 100 = $$

After you have finished, check your answers with the solution in the margin.

Evaluate the Results

Learning Objective 5
Interpret the results of financial analyses.

INTERPRETING HORIZONTAL AND VERTICAL ANALYSES

As noted in the previous section, financial statement analyses are not complete unless they lead to interpretations that help users understand and evaluate a company's financial results. When interpreting analyses, your goals should be to understand what each analysis is telling you and then combine your findings into a coherent "story" that explains the results of the company's business activities. We demonstrate how to do this, beginning with interpretations of each set of analyses shown in Exhibits 13.1–13.5 and later concluding with an overall summary of Lowe's results.

Trends Revealed in Horizontal Analyses

Horizontal (trend) analysis of Lowe's balance sheet in Exhibit 13.1 shows that the company grew in fiscal 2008. Overall, total assets increased approximately 5.9 percent. Lowe's explains the major driver of this increase in its Management's Discussion and Analysis (MD&A) section of the 2008 annual report. In fiscal 2008, Lowe's opened 60 new stores, resulting in significant increases in Inventories (7.9 percent) and Property and Equipment (6.4 percent). To finance this expansion, Lowe's relied on equity rather than debt (Stockholders' Equity increased 12.2 percent whereas Total Liabilities decreased 0.9 percent).

Horizontal analysis of Lowe's income statement in Exhibit 13.2 indicates that the company faced a challenging economic environment in fiscal 2008. Despite the increase in the number of stores, Net Sales Revenue fell slightly (0.1 percent). Lowe's MD&A explains that the company was forced to cut prices in 2008 to sell its seasonal inventory. Making matters worse, according to the MD&A, Lowe's experienced higher fuel costs, which contributed to an increase in its Cost of Sales (0.5 percent). The lower selling prices and higher cost of sales combined to decrease Gross Profit by 1.4 percent. Operating Expenses rose by 5.8 percent, largely as a result of having added the 60 new stores. The overall impact on Lowe's was a reduction in Net Income of $614 million (21.9 percent).

In summary, the story revealed by the trend analysis is that despite its asset growth in 2008, Lowe's was unable to increase profits. The weak economy led the company to cut selling prices and incur greater costs (for goods and operations).

Relationships Noted in Vertical Analyses

Vertical (common size) analysis of Lowe's balance sheet in Exhibit 13.3 highlights key elements of the company. Its most significant assets have always been Inventories and Property and Equipment, but with the additional store openings in 2008, these assets now represent 25.1 and 69.5 percent of Lowe's total assets. As noted in the horizontal analysis, the company's financing strategy shifted somewhat in 2008 from debt to equity. Compared to fiscal 2007, when debt and equity financing were nearly equally balanced (52.1 percent equity), Lowe's has turned more to equity in fiscal 2008 (55.2 percent).

Vertical analysis of Lowe's income statement in Exhibit 13.4 indicates that Cost of Sales and Operating Expenses are the most important determinants of the company's profitability. Cost of Sales consumed 65.8 percent of Sales in 2008 and Operating Expenses consumed an additional 26.3 percent. Much of the reduction in the company's Net Income (from 5.8 percent of Sales in 2007 to 4.6 in 2008) is explained by these two categories of expenses, as suggested by the horizontal analyses.

These findings from the vertical analyses serve to underscore findings from the horizontal analyses. The emerging story is that Lowe's success depends on its ability to use significant investments in Inventory and Property and Equipment to generate sales. Its expansion efforts in 2008 were not successful because a weak economy hampered sales, higher fuel costs cut into gross profit, and its larger labor force led to rising operating expenses, all of which combined to shrink Lowe's net income.

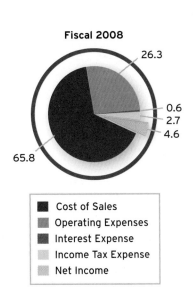

Fiscal 2008

- ■ Cost of Sales
- ■ Operating Expenses
- ■ Interest Expense
- ■ Income Tax Expense
- ■ Net Income

INTERPRETING RATIO ANALYSES

As shown throughout other chapters in this book, benchmarks help when interpreting a company's ratios. These benchmarks can include the company's prior year results, as well as the results of close competitors or the average for the industry. In a competitive economy, companies strive to outperform one another, so comparisons against other companies can provide clues about who is likely to survive and thrive in the long run.

In the following analyses, we compare Lowe's financial ratios to the prior year and in some cases to those for The Home Depot and the home improvement industry as a whole. (Both Lowe's and The Home Depot's annual reports for fiscal 2008 are printed in Appendix A and B at the end of this book.)

COACH'S TIP

Industry averages are reported in the *Annual Statement Studies*, which are published by the Risk Management Association. You can obtain industry averages also from reuters.com/finance or google.com/finance, which were available free of charge at the time this book was written.

Profitability Ratios

The analyses in this section focus on the level of profits the company generated during the period. We will analyze ratios (1) through (8) from Exhibit 13.5. The first two profitability ratios come right from the common size income statement in Exhibit 13.4.

(1) Net Profit Margin Net profit margin represents the percentage of sales revenues that ultimately make it into net income, after deducting expenses. Using the equation in Exhibit 13.5, the calculation of Lowe's net profit margin for each of the last two years yields:

Fiscal Year	2008	2007
$\text{Net profit margin} = \dfrac{\text{Net Income}}{\text{Net Sales Revenue}} \times 100$	4.6%	5.8%

As discussed in the previous sections, Lowe's faced a challenging economic environment in 2008. Weak sales and higher product costs and operating expenses hampered the company's attempts to generate net income through store expansion. Lowe's declining net profit margin from 5.8 percent in 2007 to 4.6 percent in 2008 is a downer because, when considered in light of over $48 billion in sales, this drop of 1.2 percent $(4.6 - 5.8)$ equates to a profit decline of about $576 million.

(2) Gross Profit Percentage   Our earlier analysis indicated that Lowe's gross profit from 2007 to 2008 decreased in terms of total dollars, but it did not indicate whether that decrease was caused by less total sales or less profit per sale. The gross profit percentage is particularly helpful in this kind of analysis because it indicates how much profit was made, on average, on each dollar of sales after deducting the cost of goods sold. Lowe's gross profit percentage for the last two years was:

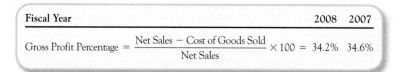

Fiscal Year		2008	2007
Gross Profit Percentage $= \dfrac{\text{Net Sales} - \text{Cost of Goods Sold}}{\text{Net Sales}} \times 100 =$		34.2%	34.6%

This analysis shows that in 2008, after deducting the cost of merchandise sold, 34.2 cents of each sales dollar were left to cover other costs, such as employee wages, advertising, and utilities and to provide profits to the stockholders. The decrease in the gross profit percentage from 2007 to 2008 (34.2% − 34.6%) means that Lowe's made 0.4¢ less gross profit on each dollar of sales in 2008 than in 2007. There are two potential explanations for this decrease: (1) Lowe's charged lower selling prices without experiencing a corresponding decrease in the cost of merchandise and (2) Lowe's obtained merchandise at a higher unit cost. The MD&A section of Lowe's annual report explains that the decrease in gross profit percentage came from both a cut in selling prices and an increase in product costs (primarily higher freight-in).

(3) Asset Turnover   The asset turnover ratio indicates the amount of sales revenue generated for each dollar invested in assets during the period. Lowe's ratios for the two years were:

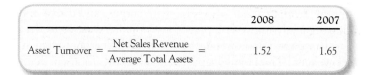

		2008	2007
Asset Turnover $= \dfrac{\text{Net Sales Revenue}}{\text{Average Total Assets}} =$		1.52	1.65

The asset turnover ratio suggests that Lowe's assets did not generate sales as efficiently in 2008 as in the prior year. To understand why, it is helpful to focus on the key assets used to generate sales. For a retailer such as Lowe's, the key asset is store properties, which we can compare to sales using the fixed asset turnover ratio, discussed next.

(4) Fixed Asset Turnover   The fixed asset turnover ratio indicates how much revenue the company generates in sales for each dollar invested in fixed assets, such as store buildings and the property they sit on. Lowe's fixed asset turnover ratios for the two years were:

		2008	2007
Fixed Asset Turnover $= \dfrac{\text{Net Sales Revenue}}{\text{Average Net Fixed Assets}} =$		2.19	2.39

This analysis shows that Lowe's had $2.19 of sales in 2008 for each dollar invested in fixed assets. Although the decline from 2007 was not good, it is understandable because 2008 was a difficult year for retailers, as consumers struggled to keep their jobs and pay their mortgages, let alone work on major home improvement projects. Lowe's 2008 fixed asset turnover also suffered because the company added stores during the year. Those stores will likely need some time to establish a strong customer base and begin generating sales at full capacity. Moreover, as additional stores are opened, they are likely to be located in areas of greater competition. Still, Lowe's fixed asset turnover ratio is low compared to that of its main competitor, The Home Depot, whose fixed asset turnover ratio was 2.65 in 2008. In terms of using fixed assets to generate sales revenue, The Home Depot has a competitive advantage over Lowe's. In other words, Lowe's is operating less efficiently than its major competitor.

(5) Return on Equity (ROE)

The return on equity ratio compares the amount of net income to average stockholders' equity. Like the interest rate on your bank account, ROE reports the net amount earned during the period as a percentage of each dollar contributed by stockholders and retained in the business. Lowe's ROE ratios for the past two years were:

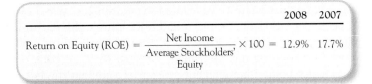

	2008	2007
Return on Equity (ROE) = $\dfrac{\text{Net Income}}{\text{Average Stockholders' Equity}} \times 100 =$	12.9%	17.7%

Lowe's ROE decline from 17.7 to 12.9 percent was inevitable, given our previous analyses. Specifically, horizontal analysis indicated that the company had increased its stockholders' equity to finance store expansion. But store expansion failed to increase sales in 2008, as indicated by the asset turnover ratio, and each dollar of sales generated less profit, as indicated by the net profit margin. Taken together, these results imply that net income as a percentage of average stockholders' equity was sure to fall in 2008. And fall it did. The only good news for Lowe's is that its 12.9 percent ROE was marginally better than The Home Depot's fiscal 2008 ROE of 12.7 percent.

(6) Earnings per Share (EPS)

Earnings per share (EPS) indicates the amount of earnings generated for each share of outstanding common stock. Consistent with the decline in ROE, the EPS ratio decreased from $1.90 in 2007 to $1.51 in 2008, as shown below. This represents a decline of $0.39 per share ($1.51 − $1.90).

Fiscal Year	2008	2007
Earnings per Share (EPS) = $\dfrac{\text{Net Income}}{\text{Average Number of Common Shares Outstanding}}$	$1.51	$1.90

(7) Quality of Income

The quality of income ratio relates operating cash flows (from the statement of cash flows) to net income, as follows:

Fiscal Year	2008	2007
Quality of Income = $\dfrac{\text{Net Cash from Operations}}{\text{Net Income}}$	1.88	1.55

The ratio of 1.88 in 2008 indicates that Lowe's generated $1.88 of operating cash flow for every dollar of net income. Because this ratio is much greater than 1.0, it is interpreted as "high quality," meaning that operations are producing even more positive results (cash flows from operating activities) than what is suggested by the net income number. Most cash-based businesses, like home improvement stores, have high quality of income ratios because their sales are collected in cash immediately, and they report substantial noncash expenses like depreciation. Consistent with this expectation, we see a high quality of income ratio for The Home Depot (2.45) for fiscal 2008.

(8) Price/Earnings (P/E) Ratio   The P/E ratio relates the company's stock price to its EPS, as follows:

Fiscal Year		2008	2007
Price/Earnings Ratio $= \dfrac{\text{Stock Price}}{\text{EPS}}$		12.1	12.1

Using the going price for Lowe's stock when its 2008 and 2007 earnings were announced, the P/E ratio was 12.1 in both years. This means investors were willing to pay 12.1 times earnings to buy a share of Lowe's stock. The Home Depot's P/E ratio at that time was around 18.5, suggesting that investors were less willing to buy stock in Lowe's than in The Home Depot.

Let's pause to summarize what we've learned so far. In fiscal 2008, Lowe's continued to expand by opening 60 new stores. Unfortunately for Lowe's, this expansion took place at the same time as a general economic crisis. Consumers were faced with rising interest and fuel costs and swelling unemployment rates, so they cut back on unnecessary spending such as major home improvement projects. To combat the fall in demand for its products and services, Lowe's cut prices. At the same time, Lowe's incurred higher product costs, which caused a decline in the company's gross profit. Adding to these problems, Lowe's operating expenses grew in 2008 as a result of the store expansion program. The company's net income fell by 21.9 percent, or $0.39 per share. Investors seemed to anticipate these results because they were just as willing to buy Lowe's stock in 2008 as they were in 2007 (at a price of 12.1 times earnings in each year). The bottom line is that Lowe's fared reasonably well during the 2008 economic crisis, although the company trails its main competitor, The Home Depot, on several key ratios.

Liquidity Ratios

The analyses in this section focus on the company's ability to survive in the short term, by converting assets to cash that can be used to pay current liabilities as they come due. We interpret ratios (9) through (12) from Exhibit 13.5.

(9) Receivables Turnover   Most home improvement retailers have low levels of accounts receivable relative to sales revenue because they collect the majority of their sales immediately in cash. Although the formula calls for net **credit** sales in the top of the ratio, companies rarely report their credit sales and cash sales separately. Consequently, financial statement users typically use total net sales revenue in the formula, which results in a receivables turnover ratio that is not terribly meaningful for businesses that make few sales on account. The formula is presented in Exhibit 13.5 simply to remind you of how it's calculated.

(10) Inventory Turnover   The inventory turnover ratio indicates how frequently inventory is bought and sold during the year. The measure "days to sell" converts the inventory turnover ratio into the average number of days needed to sell each purchase of inventory.

Fiscal Year		2008	2007
Inventory Turnover $= \dfrac{\text{Cost of Goods Sold}}{\text{Average Inventory}}$		4.0	4.3
Days to Sell $= \dfrac{365}{\text{Inventory Turnover Ratio}}$		91.3	85.3

Consistent with the weaker economy in 2008, Lowe's inventory turned over less frequently. On average, its inventory took an additional 6.0 days to sell (91.3 − 85.3).

These results are troubling because almost every retailer's success depends on its ability to offer customers the right product when they need it at a price that beats the competition. Although most retailers experienced a decline in inventory turnover in 2008, Lowe's decline was disappointing because it prevented the company from catching up to The Home Depot (where inventory takes an average of 87 days to sell). The Home Depot enjoys a faster inventory turnover because it carries fewer big-ticket items than Lowe's. According to their 2008 annual reports, the average ticket price was $65.15 at Lowe's and $55.61 at The Home Depot.

Turnover ratios vary significantly from one industry to the next. Companies in the food industry (restaurants and grocery stores) have high inventory turnover ratios because their inventory is subject to spoilage. Companies that sell expensive merchandise (automobiles and high-fashion clothes) have much slower turnover because sales of those items are infrequent, but these companies must carry lots of inventory so that customers have a wide selection to choose from when they do buy.

(11) Current Ratio The current ratio compares current assets to current liabilities, as follows:

Fiscal Year		2008	2007
Current Ratio $= \dfrac{\text{Current Assets}}{\text{Current Liabilities}}$		1.15	1.12

The current ratio measures the company's ability to pay its current liabilities. Lowe's ratio increased slightly from 2007 to 2008, ending the year with a ratio of 1.15. In this industry, a current ratio greater than 1.0 is deemed acceptable. Most analysts would judge Lowe's ratio to be very strong, especially considering the company's ability to generate cash.

(12) Quick Ratio The quick ratio compares the sum of cash, short-term investments, and accounts receivable to current liabilities as follows:

Fiscal Year		2008	2007
Quick Ratio $= \dfrac{\text{Cash + Short-term Investments + Accounts Receivable, Net}}{\text{Current Liabilities}}$		0.08	0.07

The quick ratio is a much more stringent test of short-term liquidity than is the current ratio. Lowe's quick ratio increased slightly in 2008, just as its current ratio did. The low quick ratio shown here is typical for industries where most customers buy with cash or credit card. These forms of payment result in very low levels of accounts receivable and the cash received from sales is often used immediately in other business activities. In industries where credit sales are common, the quick ratio may be much higher. For example, the average quick ratio in 2008 for the homebuilding industry was 0.66.

Solvency Ratios

The analyses in this section focus on Lowe's ability to survive over the long term—that is, its ability to repay debt when it matures, pay interest until that time, and finance the replacement and/or expansion of long-term assets. We interpret ratios (13) through (15) from Exhibit 13.5.

(13) Debt to Assets The debt-to-assets ratio indicates the proportion of total assets that creditors finance. Remember that creditors must be paid regardless of how difficult

COACH'S TIP

Instead of the debt-to-assets ratio, analysts might use a debt-to-equity ratio, which gives the same basic information as debt-to-assets. Debt-to-equity typically is calculated as total liabilities ÷ total stockholders' equity. As with debt-to-assets, the higher the debt-to-equity ratio, the more the company relies on debt (rather than equity) financing.

COACH'S TIP

If the company reports a net loss, rather than net income, include the loss as a negative number in the formula. A negative ratio indicates that the operating results (before the costs of financing and taxes) are insufficient to cover interest costs.

a year the company may have had. The higher this ratio, the riskier is the company's financing strategy. Lowe's ratio for the two years was:

		2008	2007
Debt to Assets $= \dfrac{\text{Total Liabilities}}{\text{Total Assets}} =$		0.45	0.48

Lowe's ratio of 0.45 in 2008 indicates that creditors contributed 45 percent of the company's financing, implying that stockholders' equity was the company's main source of financing at 55 percent (100 percent − 45 percent). The debt-to-assets ratio decreased slightly from 2007 to 2008, suggesting that Lowe's relies less on creditors and more on stockholders when financing its acquisition of assets. The Home Depot, which had a debt-to-assets ratio of 57 percent in 2008, relies much more on debt financing.

(14) Times Interest Earned The times interest earned ratio indicates how many times the company's interest expense was covered by its operating results. This ratio is calculated using accrual-based interest expense and net income before interest and income taxes, as follows:

		2008	2007
Times Interest Earned $= \dfrac{\text{Net Income + Interest Expense + Income Tax Expense}}{\text{Interest Expense}} =$		13.5	24.3

A times interest earned ratio above 1.0 indicates that net income (before the costs of financing and taxes) is sufficient to cover the company's interest expense. Lowe's ratio of 13.5 indicates the company is generating more than enough profit to cover its interest expense.

(15) Capital Acquisitions Ratio The capital acquisitions ratio compares cash flows from operations with cash paid for property and equipment. The ratio for the two recent years follows:

Fiscal Year		2008	2007
Capital Acquisitions $= \dfrac{\text{Net Cash from Operations}}{\text{Cash Paid for PPE}}$		1.26	1.08

The 1.26 capital acquisitions ratio in 2008 indicates that Lowe's was able to pay for all its store expansion using cash generated from operating activities.

In sum, these solvency ratios suggest that Lowe's is financially well-positioned, even though the economy has sputtered. In fiscal 2008, the company reduced its reliance on debt and was able to comfortably cover the interest expense incurred on that debt. Further, the company has been able to expand without taking on more debt because its cash flow from operating activities exceeded the cost of its new property and equipment.

How's it going? Self-Study Practice

Show the computations for the following two ratios for Lowe's for fiscal 2007. Use the information in Exhibits 13.1 and 13.2.

a. Times interest earned ratio
b. Current ratio

After you have finished, check your answers with the solution in the margin.

UNDERLYING ACCOUNTING DECISIONS AND CONCEPTS

Accounting Decisions

> **Learning Objective 6**
> Describe how analyses depend on key accounting decisions and concepts.

In the analyses just presented, we compared Lowe's results with those of The Home Depot. When appropriate, we discussed how differences in the two companies' strategies (for example, relying on debt versus equity financing) and business operations (for example, carrying big-ticket versus less expensive items) affected their financial ratios. We should also consider whether differences between the two companies' financial ratios might be caused by differences in their accounting decisions.

Information about a company's accounting decisions is presented in a note to the financial statements. Exhibit 13.6 shows the policies that three home improvement retailers follow in accounting for inventory and depreciation—two line items that can have a noticeable impact on a retailer's results. Take a moment to study the exhibit.

EXHIBIT 13.6	Comparison of Accounting Methods		
	Lowe's	The Home Depot	Builder's FirstSource
Inventory	FIFO	FIFO	Weighted Average Cost
Depreciation	Straight line Buildings: 10-40 yrs Equipment: 3-15 yrs	Straight line Buildings: 10-45 yrs Equipment: 3-20 yrs	Straight line Buildings: 20-40 yrs Equipment: 3-10 yrs

As you can see, the three companies follow similar but not identical policies. Lowe's and The Home Depot use the FIFO method of accounting for inventory and cost of goods sold; Builder's FirstSource uses the weighted average method. Although these two methods result in different numbers, the overall impact on the companies' financial ratios should be minor because inventory costs did not rise rapidly in 2008.

All three companies calculate depreciation using the straight-line method with a similar range of estimated useful lives for buildings and equipment. Because buildings and equipment make up such a large portion of each company's assets, these similarities go a long way toward making their financial results comparable. In conclusion, although the companies' accounting policies have some differences, they are unlikely to have a major impact on our comparisons.

Spotlight On THE WORLD

Lowe's and The Home Depot dominate the North American home improvement industry, but Kingfisher is Europe's largest home improvement retailer, with market-leading positions in the UK, France, Poland, Turkey, and China. For the year ended January 31, 2009, Kingfisher's gross profit percentage of 34.9 percent appeared better than Lowe's 34.2 percent, despite Kingfisher's inventory write-down of €21 million. Direct comparisons such as this should be made with caution, however, because Kingfisher follows IFRS and Lowe's follows GAAP. Under IFRS, Kingfisher would be allowed to reverse its inventory write-down if market conditions improve in the future. As discussed in Chapter 7, GAAP prohibits Lowe's from making this kind of adjustment.

Accounting Concepts

Before wrapping up this chapter, it's worth revisiting the accounting concepts that were introduced in previous chapters. At this stage of the course, you should have developed a fairly good understanding of the rules of accounting and be better able to appreciate

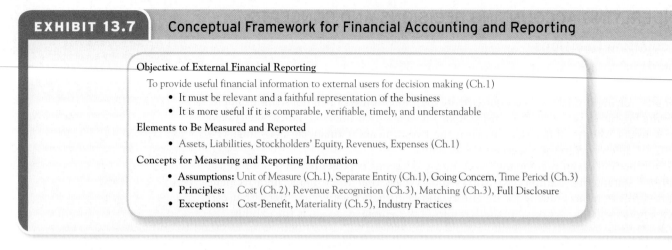

EXHIBIT 13.7 Conceptual Framework for Financial Accounting and Reporting

<u>Objective of External Financial Reporting</u>

To provide useful financial information to external users for decision making (Ch.1)
  • It must be relevant and a faithful representation of the business
  • It is more useful if it is comparable, verifiable, timely, and understandable

Elements to Be Measured and Reported

  • Assets, Liabilities, Stockholders' Equity, Revenues, Expenses (Ch.1)

Concepts for Measuring and Reporting Information

  • **Assumptions:** Unit of Measure (Ch.1), Separate Entity (Ch.1), Going Concern, Time Period (Ch.3)
  • **Principles:** Cost (Ch.2), Revenue Recognition (Ch.3), Matching (Ch.3), Full Disclosure
  • **Exceptions:** Cost-Benefit, Materiality (Ch.5), Industry Practices

why accounting relies on these particular concepts. Exhibit 13.7 presents the conceptual framework for financial accounting and reporting that was first introduced in Chapter 1. The concepts that you have already learned about in prior chapters are highlighted in red in Exhibit 13.7.

As shown in Exhibit 13.7, the primary objective of financial accounting and reporting is to provide useful financial information for people external to a company to use in making decisions about the company. To be useful, this information must be relevant and faithfully represent the underlying business.

As Exhibit 13.7 indicates, only four accounting concepts have not been introduced in previous chapters, so we will explain them here. The **going concern** (also called *continuity*) **assumption** quietly underlies accounting rules. It is the belief that any business will be capable of continuing its operations long enough to realize its recorded assets and meet its obligations in the normal course of business. If a company runs into severe financial difficulty (such as bankruptcy), this assumption may no longer be appropriate, leading to what is called a **going-concern problem**. If ever a company encounters a going-concern problem, it may need to adjust the amount and classification of items in its financial statements, which would be explained in the financial statement notes and to which the auditor's report would draw attention. Some of the factors that commonly contribute to going-concern problems are listed in Exhibit 13.8. Notice that some of the analyses presented earlier in this chapter are key inputs into determining whether a company has a going-concern problem.

One of the principles of accounting that was not previously explained is full disclosure. Simply put, according to the **full disclosure principle**, financial reports should present all information that is needed to properly interpret the results of the company's business activities. This doesn't mean that every single transaction needs to be explained in detail, but rather that adequate information needs to be presented to

YOU SHOULD KNOW

Going-concern assumption: A business is assumed to be capable of continuing its operations long enough to meet its obligations.

YOU SHOULD KNOW

Full disclosure principle: The financial statements should present information needed to understand the financial results of the company's business activities.

EXHIBIT 13.8 Factors Contributing to Going-Concern Problems

Revealed by Financial Analyses	Revealed by Other Analyses
• Declining sales	• Overdependence on one customer
• Declining gross profit	• Insufficient product innovation/quality
• Significant one-time expenses	• Significant barriers to expansion
• Fluctuating net income	• Loss of key personnel without replacement
• Insufficient current assets	• Inability to negotiate favorable purchases
• Excessive reliance on debt financing	• Inadequate maintenance of long-lived assets
• Adverse financial commitments	• Loss of a key patent

allow financial statement users to fairly interpret reports about the company's income, financial position, and cash flows.

Despite the best efforts to make accounting rules applicable in as many situations as possible, there are limits on how broadly they can be applied. These limits, or constraints, are listed in Exhibit 13.7. Two constraints not introduced in previous chapters relate to industry practices and cost-benefit trade-offs. The **industry practices constraint** is that companies in some industries, such as financial services, oil and gas, and agricultural production, have such unique circumstances that they need to use accounting rules that differ somewhat from what companies in most other industries use. The **cost-benefit constraint** recognizes that it is costly for companies to gather all the financial information that could possibly be reported. Accounting rules need to be implemented only to the extent that the informational benefits outweigh the costs of doing so.

Before closing the book on this topic (and possibly this course), take a moment to complete the following Self-Study Practice. It'll give you a good idea of whether you need a detailed review of the concepts introduced in earlier chapters or whether you're ready to move on to review and practice key aspects of this chapter.

YOU SHOULD KNOW

Industry practices constraint: Companies in certain industries may follow accounting rules peculiar to that industry. **Cost-benefit constraint:** Companies should follow accounting rules to the extent that the benefits outweigh the costs of doing so.

How's it going?   Self-Study Practice

Match each statement below to the assumption, principle, or constraint to which it most closely relates.

1. Everything comes down to dollars and cents.
2. That's not our issue. It's for somebody else to report.
3. Don't sweat it. It's not big enough to worry about.
4. We'll make an exception, but only because you're special.
5. If it relates to this period, you'd better report it.
6. I've told you everything you could possibly want to know.
7. At that rate, you may not survive past the end of the year.
8. I know it's a long time, but let's look at it in stages.
9. You can reach a point where it's just not worth all the trouble.

   (a) Separate entity
   (b) Matching
   (c) Going concern
   (d) Unit of measure
   (e) Time period
   (f) Cost-benefit
   (g) Materiality
   (h) Industry practices
   (i) Full disclosure

After you have finished, check your answers with the solution in the margin.

Solution to Self-Study Practice
1. (d) 2. (a) 3. (g) 4. (h) 5. (b)
6. (i) 7. (c) 8. (e) 9. (f)

You have now seen enough to interpret most basic financial statements. When analyzing real-world financial statements, you will probably encounter nonrecurring or other special items reported in the income statement. These items are discussed in chapter supplement 13A.

SUPPLEMENT 13A: Nonrecurring and Other Special Items

Nonrecurring Items

Until 2005, three different types of nonrecurring items were reported in income statements: discontinued operations, extraordinary items, and the cumulative effects of changes in accounting methods. Recently, however, **new accounting standards have nearly** eliminated income statement reporting of extraordinary items and the cumulative effects of changes in accounting methods. In fact, the definition of **extraordinary** has become so restricted that few events—not even the losses that arose from Hurricane Katrina—qualify as extraordinary. The cumulative effects of changes in accounting methods are reported as adjustments to Retained Earnings rather than as part of the income statement in the period when the change is made. (The technical procedures used to make these adjustments are discussed in intermediate accounting courses.) That leaves only one remaining nonrecurring item, discontinued operations.

Discontinued operations result from abandoning or selling a major business component. Because an abandoned or sold business unit will not affect financial results in future years, its results for the current year are reported on a separate line of the income statement following Income Tax Expense. This discontinued operations line includes any gain or loss on disposal of the discontinued operation as well as any operating income generated before its disposal. Because this appears below the Income Tax Expense line, any related tax effects are netted against (included with) the gains or losses on discontinued operations. Exhibit 13A.1 shows how The Home Depot reported discontinued operations in a recent year.

YOU SHOULD KNOW

Discontinued operations:
Result from the disposal of
a major component of the
business and are reported net
of income tax effects.

EXHIBIT 13A.1	Nonrecurring Items Reported Net of Tax on the Income Statement

THE HOME DEPOT, INC.
Condensed Income Statements
For the Year Ended February 1, 2009
(in millions)

Net Sales	$71,288
Cost of Sales	47,298
Gross Profit	23,990
Selling, General, and Administrative Expenses	17,846
Depreciation and Amortization Expense	1,785
Income from Operations	4,359
Interest and Other Expenses, Net	769
Income from Continuing Operations before Income Tax Expense	3,590
Income Tax Expense	1,278
Net Income from Continuing Operations	2,312
Loss from Discontinued Operations, Net of Tax	52
Net Income	$ 2,260

Other Special Items

In some cases, you may see that companies include additional items on their income statements after the net income line. These items may be added to or subtracted from net income to arrive at the amount of **Comprehensive Income**. As you can learn in detail in intermediate financial accounting courses, these items represent gains or losses relating to changes in the value of certain balance sheet accounts. While most gains and losses are included in the computation of net income, some (relating to changes in foreign currency exchange rates and the value of certain investments, for example) are excluded from net income and included only in comprehensive income. The main reason for excluding these gains and losses from net income is that the changes in value that created them may well disappear before they are ever realized (when the company sells the related assets or liabilities). For this reason, most analysts will take a moment to consider the size of these special items in relation to net income. If the amount is not large, they will exclude the items in calculating profitability ratios.

SUPPLEMENT 13B: Reviewing and Contrasting IFRS and GAAP

In this supplement, we review and contrast IFRS and GAAP, as they relate to topics raised in earlier chapters of the text. We begin with a theoretical discussion of similarities and differences between IFRS and GAAP that potentially affect the accounting rules for specific topics. We then follow with a summary of specific topic discussions.

Overview

Generally speaking, IFRS and GAAP are similar. Both aim to guide businesses in reporting financial information that is relevant and that faithfully represents the underlying activities of businesses. At a basic level, these accounting rules describe (1) when an item should be recognized in the accounting system, (2) how that item should be classified (e.g., asset or expense, revenue or liability), and (3) the amount at which each item should be measured.

Although some exceptions exist, both IFRS and GAAP require that items be recorded only after an exchange between the company and another party. Initially, these items are recorded at the value they enter the company (called the *entry price* or *historical cost*). Later, this value may be revised (upwards or downwards) as a result of events or changes in circumstances. The new value may be (*a*) the entry price adjusted for items such as interest, depreciation, and amortization, (*b*) a current market price, or (*c*) another computed amount (such as the *fair value* or *exit price* that the company would receive or pay in the future for that item).

Many differences between IFRS and GAAP that we have noted in this book relate to cases where IFRS requires or allows companies to report items using values that differ from those required or allowed by GAAP. For example, in Chapter 7, we noted that IFRS allows (and GAAP prohibits) the reversal of write-downs in inventory value. Similarly, in Chapter 9, we noted that IFRS allows companies to report fixed assets at fair values. Intermediate accounting courses will expand on these situations and add others. For now, though, just focus on gaining a general awareness of the ways in which accounting rules may differ, as discussed in the following specific cases introduced in previous chapters.

Specific Topics Integrated in Earlier Chapters

Chapter 1
- **Page 18.** Discusses the joint work of the Financial Accounting Standards Board and the International Accounting Standards Board to establish accounting rules and a unified conceptual framework.

Chapter 2
- **Page 60.** Discusses differences in level of detail in GAAP versus IFRS materials, and the increased role for transaction analysis skills and judgment in accounting.

Chapter 5
- **Pages 220–223.** Outlines financial statement presentation differences, including financial statement titles, ordering of accounts, and grouping of items. Illustrates a European company's statement of financial position and presents a glimpse into future possible directions for financial statement formatting. Applies ratio analysis to two U.S. companies and one European company.

Chapter 7

- **Page 318.** Explains that IFRS prohibits LIFO and discusses the potential tax impact of switching to IFRS.
- **Page 319.** Discusses how IFRS allows (and GAAP prohibits) reversals of write-downs when inventory recovers in value.

Chapter 9

- **Page 405.** Discusses IFRS's accounting for component costs.
- **Page 420.** Discusses IFRS's accounting for R&D and revaluation at fair value.

Chapter 10

- **Page 459.** Discusses IFRS's current classification of long-term debt involving violated loan covenants.
- **Page 468.** Discusses IFRS's threshold for accruing contingent liabilities.

Chapter 11

- **Page 519.** Discusses classification of some preferred stock as a liability.

Chapter 12

- **Page 558.** Illustrates differences in classification of dividends and interest received and paid, under IFRS and GAAP.

Chapter 13

- **Page 625.** Discusses the potential impact of accounting differences on ratio analyses.

REVIEW THE CHAPTER

DEMONSTRATION CASE

The following information was taken from The Home Depot's fiscal 2006 annual report.

(in millions of dollars)	Year Ended January 28, 2007 (Fiscal 2006)	
Net Sales Revenue	$90,837	
Cost of Goods Sold	61,054	
Net Income	5,761	
	January 28, 2007 (Fiscal 2006)	January 29, 2006 (Fiscal 2005)
Inventory	$12,822	$11,401
Current Assets	18,000	15,269
Property and Equipment, Net	26,605	24,901
Total Assets	52,263	44,405
Current Liabilities	12,931	12,706
Total Liabilities	27,233	17,496

Required:

1. Compute the following ratios for The Home Depot for the year ended January 28, 2007.

   Fixed Asset Turnover
   Return on Equity
   Days to Sell
   Current Ratio
   Debt to Assets

2. Interpret the meaning of the ratios you calculated in requirement 1.

Suggested Solution

1. Calculating ratios:

Fixed Asset Turnover	= Net Sales Revenue/Average Net Fixed Assets
	= $90,837 ÷ [($26,605 + $24,901) ÷ 2]
	= 3.53
Return on Equity	= Net Income/Average Stockholders' Equity
	= $5,761 ÷ [($25,030 + $26,909) ÷ 2]
	= 0.2218, or 22.2%
Days to Sell	= 365 ÷ Inventory Turnover Ratio
	= 365 ÷ (Cost of Goods Sold/Average Inventory)
	= 365 ÷ [$61,054 ÷ [($12,822 + $11,401) ÷ 2]]
	= 72
Current Ratio	= Current Assets/Current Liabilities
	= $18,000 ÷ $12,931
	= 1.39
Debt to Assets	= Total Liabilities/Total Assets
	= $27,233 ÷ $52,263
	= 0.52

2. Interpreting ratios

- The fixed asset turnover ratio of 3.53 means that, on average, The Home Depot generated $3.53 of sales for each dollar of fixed assets.

- The return on equity of 22.2 percent means that The Home Depot's net income for the year was 22.2 percent of the amount investors contributed to and left in the company.

- The days to sell ratio of 72 means that, on average, 72 days elapsed between the time The Home Depot acquired the inventory and the time the company sold it.

- The current ratio of 1.39 means that at year-end, The Home Depot had $1.39 of current assets for each dollar of current liabilities.

- The debt-to-assets ratio of 0.52 means that The Home Depot relied on short-term and long-term debt to finance 52 percent of its assets, implying that stockholders' equity financed 48 percent (=100 − 52) of its total assets.

CHAPTER SUMMARY

Describe the purposes and uses of horizontal, vertical, and ratio analyses. p. 612   **LO1**

- Horizontal analyses (also called trend analyses) compare financial statement items to comparable amounts in prior periods with the goal of identifying sustained changes, or trends.

- Vertical analyses create common size financial statements that express each line of the income statement (or balance sheet) as a percentage of total sales (or total assets).

- Ratio analyses compare one or more financial statement items to an amount for other items for the same year. Ratios take into account differences in the size of amounts to allow for evaluations of performance given existing levels of other company resources.

Use horizontal (trend) analyses to recognize financial changes that unfold over time. p. 613   **LO2**

- Trend analyses involve computing the dollar amount by which each account changes from one period to the next and expressing that change as a percentage of the balance for the prior period.

Use vertical (common size) analyses to understand important relationships within financial statements. p. 615   **LO3**

- Vertical (common size) analyses indicate the proportions within each financial statement category.

LO4 **Calculate financial ratios to assess profitability, liquidity, and solvency. p. 616**

- Financial ratios are commonly classified with relation to profitability, liquidity, or solvency. Exhibit 13.5 lists common ratios in these three categories and shows how to compute them.

- Profitability ratios focus on measuring the adequacy of a company's income by comparing it to other items reported on the financial statements.

- Liquidity ratios measure a company's ability to meet its current debt obligations.

- Solvency ratios measure a company's ability to meet its long-term debt obligations.

LO5 **Interpret the results of financial analyses. p. 618**

- Financial analyses are not complete unless they lead to an interpretation that helps financial statement users understand and evaluate a company's financial results.

- An understanding of whether a business is successful emerges only after you have learned to combine analyses into a complete picture or story that depicts the company's performance.

- To assist in developing this picture or story, most analysts compare to benchmarks such as the company's performance in prior years or to competitors' performance in the current year.

LO6 **Describe how analyses depend on key accounting decisions and concepts. p. 625**

- Before comparing across companies or time periods, users should determine the extent to which differences in accounting decisions (e.g., methods used to account for inventory, depreciation, contingent liabilities, etc.) might reduce comparability or consistency of the financial information being compared.

- Many accounting concepts were presented throughout earlier chapters, all of which aim to make accounting information more useful for creditors and investors. Four new concepts were explained in this chapter:

  - Going-concern (continuity) assumption—a business is assumed to continue to operate into the foreseeable future.

  - Full disclosure principle—a company's financial statements should provide all information that is important to users' decisions.

  - Industry practices constraint—general purpose accounting rules may not apply equally to all industries, recognizing that some industries may use industry-specific measurements and reporting practices.

  - Cost-benefit constraint—accounting rules should be followed to the extent that the benefits to users outweigh the costs of providing the required information.

Accounting Decision Tools

See Exhibit 13.5 on page 617 for a summary

KEY TERMS

See complete definitions in the glossary in the back of this text.

HOMEWORK HELPER

Helpful reminders

- Ratios that include both income statement and balance sheet accounts require you to calculate an average for the balance sheet accounts rather than just use the end-of-period balance. An average ensures the balance sheet data cover the same period as the income statement data.
- To calculate averages for the current and prior years, you will need three years of balance sheet data. (The statement of stockholders' equity reports three years of stockholders' equity data. To calculate averages for other balance sheet accounts, you will need comparative balance sheets from at least two annual reports.)
- The pronoun for referring to a specific company is "its" not "their."

Frequent mistakes

- In calculating year-over-year percentages, divide the change in the account balance by its balance from the prior year, not the current year.

PRACTICE MATERIAL

QUESTIONS (⊖ Symbol indicates questions that require analysis from more than one perspective.)

1. What is the general goal of trend analysis?

2. How is a year-over-year percentage calculated?

3. What is ratio analysis? Why is it useful?

4. What benchmarks are commonly used for interpreting ratios?

5. Into what three categories of performance are most financial ratios reported? To what in particular do each of these categories relate?

6. Why are some analyses called *horizontal* and others called *vertical*?

7. Slow Cellar's current ratio increased from 1.2 to 1.5. What is one favorable interpretation of this change? What is one unfavorable interpretation of this change? ⊖

8. From 2009 to 2010, Colossal Company's current ratio increased and its quick ratio decreased. What does this imply about the level of inventory and prepaids? ⊖

9. From 2009 to 2010, Shamwow reported that its Net Sales increased from $300,000 to $400,000, and its Gross Profit increased from $90,000 to $130,000. Was the Gross Profit increase caused by (a) an increase in sales volume only, (b) an increase in gross profit per sale only, or (c) a combination of both? Explain your answer. ⊖

10. Explain whether the following situations, taken independently, would be favorable or unfavorable: (a) increase in gross profit percentage, (b) decrease in inventory turnover ratio, (c) increase in earnings per share, (d) decrease in days to collect, (e) increase in net profit margin, and (f) decrease in quick ratio.

11. What are the two essential characteristics of useful financial information? What other characteristics enhance the usefulness of financial information?

12. What is the primary objective of financial reporting?

13. What is the full disclosure principle?

14. What is the going-concern assumption? What is a going-concern problem? What factors can contribute to such a problem?

15. How do industry practices and cost-benefit constraints impact financial reporting?

16. Techgear is an electronics company in the United States. It uses the LIFO inventory method. You plan to compare its ratios to Eurotext, but you are concerned because Eurotext uses IFRS. What accounting policy difference is certain to exist between the two companies? Of the ratios in Exhibit 13.5, name five that will be affected by this difference. ⊖

17. (Supplement 13A) Name the most commonly reported nonrecurring item, and explain where and how it is reported on the income statement.

MULTIPLE CHOICE

Quiz 13
www.mhhe.com/phillips3e

1. Which of the following ratios is *not* used to analyze profitability?

   a. Quality of income ratio.
   b. Gross profit percentage.
   c. Current ratio.
   d. Return on equity.

2. Which of the following would *not* directly change the receivables turnover ratio for a company?

   a. Increases in the selling prices of your inventory.
   b. A change in your credit policy.
   c. Increases in the cost you incur to purchase inventory.
   d. All of the above would directly change the receivables turnover ratio.

3. Which of the following ratios is used to analyze liquidity?

   a. Earnings per share.
   b. Debt-to-assets.
   c. Current ratio.
   d. Both *b* and *c*.

4. Analysts use ratios to

   a. Compare different companies in the same industry.
   b. Track a company's performance over time.
   c. Compare a company's performance to industry averages.
   d. All of the above describe ways that analysts use ratios.

5. Which of the following ratios incorporates cash flows from operations?

   a. Inventory turnover.
   b. Earnings per share.
   c. Quality of income.
   d. All of the above.

6. Given the following ratios for four companies, which company is least likely to experience problems paying its current liabilities promptly?

	Current Ratio	Receivables Turnover Ratio
a.	1.2	7.0
b.	1.2	6.0
c.	1.0	6.0
d.	0.5	7.0

7. A decrease in Selling and Administrative Expenses would directly impact what ratio?

   a. Fixed asset turnover ratio.   c. Current ratio.
   b. Times interest earned.   d. Gross profit percentage.

8. A bank is least likely to use which of the following ratios when analyzing the likelihood that a borrower will pay interest and principal on its loans?

   a. Current ratio.   c. Times interest earned ratio.
   b. Debt-to-assets ratio.   d. Price/earnings ratio.

9. Which of the following accounting concepts do accountants and auditors assess by using financial analyses?

   a. Cost benefit.   c. Industry practices.
   b. Materiality.   d. Going-concern assumption.

10. (Supplement 13A) Which of the following items is reported net of related income taxes?

    a. Gain or loss from discontinued operations.
    b. Gain or loss from disposal of property, plant, and equipment.
    c. Interest on long-term debt.
    d. Gain or loss from early extinguishment of debt.

> For answers to the Multiple-Choice Questions **see page Q1** located in the last section of the book.

MINI-EXERCISES

LO2   **M13-1 Calculations for Horizontal Analyses**

Using the following income statements, perform the calculations needed for horizontal analyses. Round percentages to one decimal place.

LOCKEY FENCING CORPORATION
Income Statements
For the Years Ended December 31

	2010	2009
Net Sales	$100,000	$75,000
Cost of Goods Sold	58,000	45,000
Gross Profit	42,000	30,000
Selling, General, and Administrative Expenses	9,000	4,500
Income from Operations	33,000	25,500
Interest Expense	3,000	3,750
Income before Income Tax	30,000	21,750
Income Tax Expense	9,000	6,525
Net Income	$ 21,000	$15,225

M13-2 Calculations for Vertical Analyses
LO3

Refer to M13-1. Perform the calculations needed for vertical analyses. Round percentages to one decimal place.

M13-3 Interpreting Horizontal Analyses
LO5

Refer to the calculations from M13-1. What are the two most significant year-over-year changes in terms of dollars and in terms of percentages? Give one potential cause of each of these changes.

M13-4 Interpreting Vertical Analyses
LO5

Refer to the calculations from M13-1. Which of the ratios from Exhibit 13.5 have been included in these calculations? Have these two ratios improved or deteriorated in 2010 compared to 2009?

M13-5 Inferring Financial Information Using Gross Profit Percentage
LO4

Your campus computer store reported Sales Revenue of $168,000. The company's gross profit percentage was 60.0 percent. What amount of Cost of Goods Sold did the company report?

M13-6 Inferring Financial Information Using Gross Profit Percentage and Year-over-Year Comparisons
LO2, 3, 4

A consumer products company reported a 25 percent increase in sales from 2009 to 2010. Sales in 2009 were $200,000. In 2010, the company reported Cost of Goods Sold in the amount of $150,000. What was the gross profit percentage in 2010? Round to one decimal place.

M13-7 Computing the Return on Equity Ratio
LO4

Given the following data, compute the 2010 return on equity ratio (expressed as a percentage with one decimal place).

	2010	2009
Net income	$ 1,850,000	$ 1,600,000
Stockholders' equity	10,000,000	13,125,000
Total assets	24,000,000	26,000,000
Interest expense	400,000	300,000

M13-8 Analyzing the Inventory Turnover Ratio
LO4, 5

A manufacturer reported an inventory turnover ratio of 8.6 during 2009. During 2010, management introduced a new inventory control system that was expected to reduce average inventory levels by 25 percent without affecting sales volume. Given these circumstances, would you expect the inventory turnover ratio to increase or decrease during 2010? Explain.

M13-9 Inferring Financial Information Using the Current Ratio
LO4

Mystic Laboratories reported total assets of $11,200,000 and noncurrent assets of $1,480,000. The company also reported a current ratio of 1.5. What amount of current liabilities did the company report?

M13-10 Inferring Financial Information Using the P/E Ratio
LO4

In 2009, Big W Company reported earnings per share of $2.50 when its stock was selling for $50.00. If its 2010 earnings increase by 10 percent and the P/E ratio remains constant, what will be the price of its stock? Explain.

M13-11 Identifying Relevant Ratios
LO4, 5

Identify the ratio that is relevant to answering each of the following questions.

a. How much net income does the company earn from each dollar of sales? *net profit margin*
b. Is the company financed primarily by debt or equity? *debt to asset ratio*
c. How many dollars of sales were generated for each dollar invested in fixed assets? *fixed asset turnover*
d. How many days, on average, does it take the company to collect on credit sales made to customers? *Receivables turnover*
e. How much net income does the company earn for each dollar owners have invested in it? *ROE*
f. Does the company's net income convert into more or less cash flow from operating activities? *quality of earnings*
g. Does the company have sufficient assets to convert into cash for paying liabilities as they come due in the upcoming year? *quick ratio or current ratio*

LO4, 5   **M13-12 Interpreting Ratios**

Generally speaking, do the following indicate good or bad news?

a.   Increase in times interest earned ratio.
b.   Decrease in days to sell.
c.   Increase in gross profit percentage.
d.   Decrease in EPS.
e.   Increase in asset turnover ratio.

LO6   **M13-13 Analyzing the Impact of Accounting Alternatives**

Nevis Corporation operates in an industry where costs are falling. The company is considering changing its inventory method from FIFO to LIFO and wants to determine the impact that the change would have on selected accounting ratios in future years. In general, what impact would you expect on the following ratios: net profit margin, fixed asset turnover, and current ratio?

LO6   **M13-14 Describing the Effect of Accounting Decisions on Ratios**

For each of the following three accounting choices, indicate the decision that will yield (a) a higher net profit margin and (b) a lower current ratio. If the decision does not affect the ratio, indicate "no effect."

1.   Straight-line versus accelerated depreciation (in the first year of the asset's life).
2.   FIFO versus LIFO (in periods of constantly rising costs and rising inventory levels).
3.   Straight-line depreciation with a four-year useful life versus a seven-year useful life (no residual value).

EXERCISES

LO2, 3, 5   **E13-1 Preparing and Interpreting a Schedule for Horizontal and Vertical Analyses**

Chevron Corporation

The average price of a gallon of gas in 2008 jumped $0.45 (16 percent) from $2.81 in 2007 (to $3.26 in 2008). Let's see whether these changes are reflected in the income statement of Chevron Corporation for the year ended December 31, 2008 (amounts in billions).

	2008	2007
Total Revenues	$273	$221
Costs of Crude Oil and Products	171	133
Other Operating Costs	59	56
Income before Income Tax Expense	43	32
Income Tax Expense	19	13
Net Income	$ 24	$ 19

Required:

1.   Conduct a horizontal analysis by calculating the year-over-year changes in each line item, expressed in dollars and in percentages (rounded to one decimal place). How did the change in gas prices compare to the changes in Chevron's total revenues and costs of crude oil and products?

2.   Conduct a vertical analysis by expressing each line as a percentage of total revenues (round to one decimal place). Excluding income tax and other operating costs, did Chevron earn more profit per dollar of revenue in 2008 compared to 2007?

LO4, 5   **E13-2 Computing and Interpreting Profitability Ratios**

Chevron Corporation   Use the information for Chevron Corporation in E13-1 to complete the following requirements.

Required:

1. Compute the gross profit percentage for each year (one decimal place). Assuming that the change for 2007 to 2008 is the beginning of a sustained trend, is Chevron likely to earn more or less gross profit from each dollar of sales in 2009?

2. Compute the net profit margin for each year (expressed as a percentage with one decimal place). Given your calculations here and in requirement 1, explain whether Chevron did a better or worse job of controlling expenses other than the costs of crude oil and products in 2008 relative to 2007.

3. Chevron reported average net fixed assets of $85 billion in 2008 and $74 billion in 2007. Compute the fixed asset turnover ratios for both years (round to two decimal places). Did the company better utilize its investment in fixed assets to generate revenues in 2008 or 2007?

4. Chevron reported average stockholders' equity of $82 billion in 2008 and $73 billion in 2007. Compute the return on equity ratios for both years (expressed as a percentage with one decimal place). Did the company generate greater returns for stockholders in 2008 or 2007?

E13-3 Preparing and Interpreting a Schedule for Horizontal and Vertical Analyses   LO2, 3, 5

According to the producer price index database maintained by the Bureau of Labor Statistics, the average cost of computer equipment fell 20.9 percent between 2007 and 2008. Let's see whether these changes are reflected in the income statement of Computer Tycoon Inc. for the year ended December 31, 2008.

	2008	2007
Sales Revenues	$98,913	$121,761
Cost of Goods Sold	59,249	71,583
Gross Profit	39,664	50,178
Selling, General, and Administrative Expenses	36,943	36,934
Interest Expense	565	474
Income before Income Tax Expense	2,156	12,770
Income Tax Expense	1,024	5,540
Net Income	$ 1,132	$ 7,230

Required:

1. Conduct a horizontal analysis by calculating the year-over-year changes in each line item, expressed in dollars and in percentages (rounded to one decimal place). How did the change in computer prices compare to the changes in Computer Tycoon's sales revenues?

2. Conduct a vertical analysis by expressing each line as a percentage of total revenues (round to one decimal place). Excluding income tax, interest, and operating expenses, did Computer Tycoon earn more profit per dollar of sales in 2008 compared to 2007?

E13-4 Computing Profitability Ratios   LO4, 5

Use the information in E13-3 to complete the following requirements.

Required:

1. Compute the gross profit percentage for each year (one decimal place). Assuming that the change for 2007 to 2008 is the beginning of a sustained trend, is Computer Tycoon likely to earn more or less gross profit from each dollar of sales in 2009?

2. Compute the net profit margin for each year (expressed as a percentage with one decimal place). Given your calculations here and in requirement 1, explain whether Computer Tycoon did a better or worse job of controlling operating expenses in 2008 relative to 2007.

3. Computer Tycoon reported average net fixed assets of $54,200 in 2008 and $45,100 in 2007. Compute the fixed asset turnover ratios for both years (round to two decimal places). Did the company better utilize its investment in fixed assets to generate revenues in 2008 or 2007?

4. Computer Tycoon reported average stockholders' equity of $54,000 in 2008 and $40,800 in 2007. Compute the return on equity ratios for both years (expressed as a percentage with one decimal place). Did the company generate greater returns for stockholders in 2008 than in 2007?

LO4, 5   **E13-5 Computing a Commonly Used Solvency Ratio**

Use the information in E13-3 to complete the following requirement.

Required:

Compute the times interest earned ratios for 2008 and 2007. In your opinion, does Computer Tycoon generate sufficient net income (before taxes and interest) to cover the cost of debt financing?

LO4   **E13-6 Matching Each Ratio with Its Computational Formula**

Match each ratio or percentage with its formula by entering the appropriate letter for each numbered item.

Ratios or Percentages	Formula
____ 1. Current ratio	A. Net income ÷ Net sales revenue
____ 2. Net profit margin	B. (Net sales revenue − Cost of goods sold) ÷ Net sales revenue
____ 3. Inventory turnover ratio	C. Current assets ÷ Current liabilities
____ 4. Gross profit percentage	D. Cost of goods sold ÷ Average inventory
____ 5. Fixed asset turnover	E. Net credit sales revenue ÷ Average net receivables
____ 6. Capital acquisitions ratio	F. Net cash flows from operating activities ÷ Net income
____ 7. Return on equity	G. Net income ÷ Average number of common shares outstanding
____ 8. Times interest earned	H. Total liabilities ÷ Total assets
____ 9. Debt-to-assets ratio	I. (Net income + Interest expense + Income tax expense) ÷ Interest expense
____ 10. Price/earnings ratio	J. Net cash flows from operating activities ÷ Cash paid for property, plant, and equipment
____ 11. Receivables turnover ratio	K. Current market price per share ÷ Earnings per share
____ 12. Earnings per share	L. Net income ÷ Average total stockholders' equity
____ 13. Quality of income ratio	M. Net sales revenue ÷ Average net fixed assets

LO4, 5   **E13-7 Computing and Interpreting Selected Liquidity Ratios**

Double West Suppliers (DWS) reported sales for the year of $300,000, all on credit. The average gross profit percentage was 40 percent on sales. Account balances follow:

	Beginning	Ending
Accounts receivable (net)	$45,000	$55,000
Inventory	60,000	40,000

Required:

1. Compute the turnover ratios for accounts receivable and inventory (round to one decimal place).
2. By dividing 365 by your ratios from requirement 1, calculate the average days to collect receivables and the average days to sell inventory (round to one decimal place).
3. Explain what each of these ratios and measures mean for DWS.

LO4, 5   **E13-8 Computing and Interpreting Liquidity Ratios**

Cintas Corporation

Cintas Corporation is the largest uniform supplier in North America, providing products and services to approximately 800,000 businesses of all types. Selected information from its 2008 annual report follows. For the 2008 fiscal year, the company reported sales revenue of $2.8 billion and Cost of Goods Sold of $1.6 billion.

Fiscal Year	2008	2007
Balance Sheet (amounts in millions)		
Cash	$ 70	$ 35
Accounts Receivable, less allowance of $15 and $15	430	410
Inventories	240	230
Prepaid Expenses	10	15
Other Current Assets	410	345
Accounts Payable	95	65
Wages Payable	50	60
Income Tax Payable	10	70
Other Current Liabilities	210	205

Required:

Assuming that all sales are on credit, compute the current ratio (two decimal places), inventory turnover ratio (one decimal place), and accounts receivable turnover ratio (one decimal place) for 2008. Explain what each ratio means for Cintas.

E13-9 Computing the Accounts Receivable and Inventory Turnover Ratios

LO4, 5

Procter & Gamble is a multinational corporation that manufactures and markets many products that you use every day. In 2008, sales for the company were $83,503 (all amounts in millions). The annual report did not report the amount of credit sales, so we will assume that all sales were on credit. The average gross profit percentage was 51.3 percent. Account balances follow:

	Beginning	Ending
Accounts receivable (net)	$6,761	$6,629
Inventory	8,416	6,819

Required:

1. Rounded to one decimal place, compute the turnover ratios for accounts receivable and inventory.
2. By dividing 365 by your ratios from requirement 1, calculate the average days to collect receivables and the average days to sell inventory.
3. Interpret what these ratios and measures mean for P&G.

E13-10 Inferring Financial Information from Profitability and Liquidity Ratios

LO4, 5

Dollar General Corporation

Dollar General Corporation operates approximately 8,400 general merchandise stores that feature quality merchandise at low prices to meet the needs of middle-, low-, and fixed-income families in southern, eastern, and midwestern states. For the year ended January 30, 2009, the company reported average inventories of $1,352 (in millions) and an inventory turnover of 5.47. Average total fixed assets were $1,272 (million), and the fixed asset turnover ratio was 8.22.

Required:

1. Calculate Dollar General's gross profit percentage (expressed as a percentage with one decimal place). What does this imply about the amount of gross profit made from each dollar of sales?

    TIP: Work backward from the fixed asset turnover and inventory turnover ratios to compute the amounts needed for the gross profit percentage.
2. Is this an improvement from the gross profit percentage of 28.2 percent earned during the previous year?

E13-11 Analyzing the Impact of Selected Transactions on the Current Ratio

LO4, 5

In its most recent annual report, Appalachian Beverages reported current assets of $54,000 and a current ratio of 1.80. Assume that the following transactions were completed: (1) purchased merchandise for $6,000 on account, and (2) purchased a delivery truck for $10,000, paying $1,000 cash and signing a two-year promissory note for the balance.

Required:

Compute the updated current ratio, rounded to two decimal places, after each transaction.

LO4, 5   **E13-12 Analyzing the Impact of Selected Transactions on the Current Ratio**

In its most recent annual report, Sunrise Enterprises reported current assets of $1,090,000 and current liabilities of $602,000.

Required:

Determine for each of the following transactions whether the current ratio, and each of its two components, for Sunrise will increase, decrease, or have no change: (1) sold long-term assets for cash, (2) accrued severance pay for terminated employees, (3) wrote down the carrying value of certain inventory items that were deemed to be obsolete, and (4) acquired new inventory by signing an 18-month promissory note (the supplier was not willing to provide normal credit terms).

LO4, 5   **E13-13 Analyzing the Impact of Selected Transactions on the Current Ratio**

The Sports Authority, Inc.

The Sports Authority, Inc., is the country's largest private full-line sporting goods retailer. Stores are operated under four brand names: Sports Authority, Gart Sports, Oshman's, and Sportmart. Assume one of the Sports Authority stores reported current assets of $88,000 and its current ratio was 1.75. Assume that the following transactions were completed: (1) paid $6,000 on accounts payable, (2) purchased a delivery truck for $10,000 cash, (3) wrote off a bad account receivable for $2,000, and (4) paid previously declared dividends in the amount of $25,000.

Required:

Compute the updated current ratio, rounded to two decimal places, after each transaction.

LO4, 5   **E13-14 Analyzing the Impact of Selected Transactions on the Current Ratio**

A company has current assets that total $500,000, a current ratio of 2.00, and uses the perpetual inventory method. Assume that the following transactions are completed: (1) sold $12,000 in merchandise on short-term credit for $15,000, (2) declared but did not pay dividends of $50,000, (3) paid prepaid rent in the amount of $12,000, (4) paid previously declared dividends in the amount of $50,000, (5) collected an account receivable in the amount of $12,000, and (6) reclassified $40,000 of long-term debt as a current liability.

Required:

Compute the updated current ratio, rounded to two decimal places, after each transaction.

LO6   **E13-15 Analyzing the Impact of Alternative Inventory Methods on Selected Ratios**

Company A uses the FIFO method to cost inventory, and Company B uses the LIFO method. The two companies are exactly alike except for the difference in inventory costing methods. Costs of inventory items for both companies have been falling steadily in recent years, and each company has increased its inventory each year. Ignore income tax effects.

Required:

Identify which company will report the higher amount for each of the following ratios. If it is not possible to identify which will report the higher amount, explain why.

1. Current ratio.
2. Debt-to-assets ratio.
3. Earnings per share.

COACHED PROBLEMS

CP13-1 **Analyzing Comparative Financial Statements Using Horizontal Analyses**

LO2, 5

The comparative financial statements prepared at December 31, 2010, for Golden Corporation showed the following summarized data:

www.mhhe.com/phillips3e

	2010	2009	Increase (Decrease) 2010 over 2009	
			Amount	Percentage
Income Statement				
Sales revenue	$180,000	$165,000		
Cost of goods sold	110,000	100,000		
Gross profit	70,000	65,000		
Operating expenses	53,300	50,400		
Interest expense	2,700	2,600		
Income before income taxes	14,000	12,000		
Income tax expense	4,000	3,000		
Net income	$ 10,000	$ 9,000		
Balance Sheet				
Cash	$ 4,000	$ 8,000		
Accounts receivable (net)	19,000	23,000		
Inventory	40,000	35,000		
Property and equipment (net)	45,000	38,000		
	$108,000	$104,000		
Current liabilities (no interest)	$ 16,000	$ 19,000		
Long-term liabilities (6% interest)	45,000	45,000		
Common stock (par $5)	30,000	30,000		
Additional paid-in capital	5,000	5,000		
Retained earnings	12,000	5,000		
	$108,000	$104,000		

Required:

1. Complete the two final columns shown beside each item in Golden Corporation's comparative financial statements. Round the percentages to one decimal place.

    TIP: Calculate the increase (decrease) by subtracting 2009 from 2010. Calculate the percentage by dividing the amount of increase (decrease) by the 2009 balance.

2. Does anything significant jump out at you from the horizontal (trend) analyses?

CP13-2 **Analyzing Comparative Financial Statements Using Selected Ratios**

LO4, 5

Use the data given in CP13-1 for Golden Corporation.

www.mhhe.com/phillips3e

Required:

1. Compute the gross profit percentage for 2010 and 2009. Round the percentages to one decimal place. Is the trend going in the right direction?

2. Compute the net profit margin for 2010 and 2009. Round the percentages to one decimal place. Is the trend going in the right direction?

3. Compute the earnings per share for 2010 and 2009. Does the trend look good or bad? Explain.

   TIP: To calculate EPS, use the balance in Common Stock to determine the number of shares outstanding. Common Stock equals the par value per share times the number of shares.

4. Stockholders' equity totaled $30,000 at the end of 2008. Compute the return on equity (ROE) ratios for 2009 and 2010. Express the ROE as percentages rounded to one decimal place. Is the trend going in the right direction?

5. Net property and equipment totaled $35,000 at the end of 2008. Compute the fixed asset turnover ratios for 2010 and 2009. Round the ratios to two decimal places. Is the trend going in the right direction?

6. Compute the debt-to-assets ratios for 2010 and 2009. Round the ratios to two decimal places. Is debt providing financing for a larger or smaller proportion of the company's asset growth? Explain.

7. Compute the times interest earned ratios for 2010 and 2009. Round the ratios to one decimal place. Do they look good or bad? Explain.

8. After Golden released its 2010 financial statements, the company's stock was trading at $30. After the release of its 2009 financial statements, the company's stock price was $21 per share. Compute the P/E ratios for both years, rounded to one decimal place. Does it appear that investors have become more (or less) optimistic about Golden's future success?

LO3, 5   **CP13-3 Vertical Analysis of a Balance Sheet**

Electronic Arts   Electronic Arts is a video game company that competes with Activision. A condensed balance sheet for Electronic Arts and a partially completed vertical analysis are presented below.

ELECTRONIC ARTS, INC.
Balance Sheet (summarized)
March 31, 2009
(in millions of U.S. dollars)

Cash and Short-term Investments	$2,520	54%	Accounts Payable	$ 152	3%
Accounts Receivable	116	2	Accrued Liabilities	984	d
Inventories	217	5	Long-term Debt	408	9
Other Current Assets	267	a	Total Liabilities	1,544	e
Intangibles	1,028	b	Contributed Capital	2,145	46
Property and Equipment	354	c	Retained Earnings	989	21
Other Assets	176	3	Total Stockholders' Equity	3,134	67
Total Assets	$4,678	100%	Total Liabilities & Stockholders' Equity	$4,678	100%

Required:

1. Complete the vertical analysis by computing each line item (a)–(e) as a percentage of total assets. Round to the nearest whole percentage.

   TIP: Inventories were 5 percent of total assets, computed as ($217 ÷ $4,678) × 100.

2. What percentages of Electronic Arts's assets relate to intangibles versus property and equipment? What business reasons would explain this relative emphasis?

LO3, 5   **CP13-4 Vertical Analysis of an Income Statement**

Electronic Arts   A condensed income statement for Electronic Arts and a partially completed vertical analysis follow.

ELECTRONIC ARTS, INC.
Income Statement (summarized)
For the Year Ended March 31
(in millions of U.S. dollars)

	2009		2008	
Net Revenues	$ 4,212	100%	$3,665	100%
Cost of Goods Sold	2,127	a	1,805	49
Research and Development Expense	1,359	b	1,145	31
Sales and Marketing Expense	691	c	588	16
General and Administrative Expense	862	21	614	17
Income (Loss) from Operations	(827)	(19)	(487)	(13)
Other Revenue (Expenses)	(28)	(1)	(20)	(1)
Income (Loss) before Income Tax	(855)	(20)	(507)	(14)
Income Tax Recovery (Expense)	(233)	(6)	53	2
Net Income (Loss)	$(1,088)	d%	$ (454)	(12)%

Required:

1. Complete the vertical analysis by computing each line item (a)–(d) as a percentage of net revenues. Round to the nearest whole percentage.

   TIP: Research and Development was 31 percent of net revenues in 2008, which was computed as ($1,145 ÷ $3,665) × 100.

2. Does Electronic Arts's 2009 Cost of Goods Sold, as a percentage of Net Revenues, represent better or worse performance as compared to 2008?

CP13-5 Interpreting Profitability, Liquidity, Solvency, and P/E Ratios

LO4, 5

Kohl's Corporation is a national retail department store. The company's total revenues for the year ended January 31, 2009, were $16 billion. J.C. Penney is a similar size department store company with $19 billion of revenues. The following ratios for the two companies were obtained for that fiscal year from reuters.com/finance:

Kohl's Corporation
J.C. Penney

Ratio	Kohl's	J.C. Penney
Gross profit percentage	37.1%	37.5%
Net profit margin	5.3%	2.6%
Return on equity	13.4%	10.2%
EPS	$2.89	$2.58
Inventory turnover ratio	3.67	3.29
Current ratio	2.10	2.01
Debt to assets	0.23	0.45
P/E ratio	16.1	13.2

Required:

1. Which company appears more profitable? Describe the ratio(s) that you used to reach this decision.

2. Which company appears more liquid? Describe the ratio(s) that you used to reach this decision.

3. Which company appears more solvent? Describe the ratio(s) that you used to reach this decision.

4. Are the conclusions from your analyses in requirements 1–3 consistent with the value of the two companies, as suggested by their P/E ratios? If not, offer one explanation for any apparent inconsistency.

   TIP: Remember that the stock price in the top of the P/E ratio represents investors' expectations about future financial performance whereas the bottom number reports past financial performance.

LO4, 5, 6   **CP13-6 Using Ratios to Compare Alternative Investment Opportunities**

The 2010 financial statements for Armstrong and Blair companies are summarized here:

	Armstrong Company	Blair Company
Balance Sheet		
Cash	$ 35,000	$ 22,000
Accounts Receivable, Net	40,000	30,000
Inventory	100,000	40,000
Property and Equipment, Net	180,000	300,000
Other Assets	45,000	408,000
Total Assets	$400,000	$800,000
Current Liabilities	$100,000	$ 50,000
Long-term Debt	60,000	370,000
Total Liabilities	160,000	420,000
Common Stock (par $10)	150,000	200,000
Additional Paid-in Capital	30,000	110,000
Retained Earnings	60,000	70,000
Total Liabilities and Stockholders' Equity	$400,000	$800,000
Income Statement		
Sales Revenue (1/3 on credit)	$450,000	$810,000
Cost of Goods Sold	(245,000)	(405,000)
Expenses (including interest and income tax)	(160,000)	(315,000)
Net Income	$ 45,000	$ 90,000
Selected Data from 2009 Statements		
Accounts Receivable, Net	$ 20,000	$ 38,000
Inventory	92,000	45,000
Property and Equipment, Net	180,000	300,000
Long-term Debt	60,000	70,000
Total Stockholders' Equity	231,000	440,000
Other Data		
Estimated value of each share at end of 2010	$ 18	$ 27

The companies are in the same line of business and are direct competitors in a large metropolitan area. Both have been in business approximately 10 years, and each has had steady growth. One-third of both companies' sales are on credit. Despite these similarities, the management of each has a different viewpoint in many respects. Blair is more conservative, and as its president said, "We avoid what we consider to be undue risk." Both companies use straight-line depreciation, but Blair estimates slightly shorter useful lives than Armstrong. No shares were issued in 2010, and neither company is publicly held. Blair Company has an annual audit by a CPA but Armstrong Company does not.

Required:

1. Calculate the ratios in Exhibit 13.5 for which sufficient information is available. Round all calculations to two decimal places.

   TIP: To calculate EPS, use the balance in Common Stock to determine the number of shares outstanding. Common Stock equals the par value per share times the number of shares.

2. A client of yours has decided to buy shares in one of the two companies. Based on the data given, prepare a comparative written evaluation of the ratio analyses (and any other available information) and conclude with your recommended choice.

   TIP: Comment on how accounting differences affect your evaluations, if at all.

LO5   **CP13-7 Analyzing an Investment by Comparing Selected Ratios**

You have the opportunity to invest $10,000 in one of two companies from a single industry. The only information you have follows. The word *high* refers to the top third of the industry; *average* is the middle third; *low* is the bottom third.

Ratio	Company A	Company B
Current	High	Average
Inventory turnover	Low	Average
Debt to assets	High	Average
Times interest earned	Low	Average
Price/earnings	Low	Average

Required:

Which company would you select? Write a brief explanation for your recommendation.

TIP: When interpreting ratios, think about how they are related to one another. For example, the current ratio and the inventory turnover ratio both include the Inventory balance. This means that the low inventory turnover ratio can help you to interpret the high current ratio.

GROUP A PROBLEMS

PA13-1 **Analyzing Financial Statements Using Horizontal Analyses**   LO2, 5

The comparative financial statements prepared at December 31, 2010, for Pinnacle Plus showed the following summarized data:

	2010	2009	Increase (Decrease) 2010 over 2009 Amount	Percentage
Income Statement				
Sales Revenue*	$110,000	$ 99,000		
Cost of Goods Sold	52,000	48,000		
Gross Profit	58,000	51,000		
Operating Expenses	36,000	33,000		
Interest Expense	4,000	4,000		
Income before Income Tax Expense	18,000	14,000		
Income Tax Expense (30%)	5,400	4,200		
Net Income	$ 12,600	$ 9,800		
Balance Sheet				
Cash	$ 49,500	$ 18,000		
Accounts Receivable, Net	37,000	32,000		
Inventory	25,000	38,000		
Property and Equipment, Net	95,000	105,000		
Total Assets	$206,500	$193,000		
Accounts Payable	$ 42,000	$ 35,000		
Income Tax Payable	1,000	500		
Note Payable, Long-term	40,000	40,000		
Total Liabilities	83,000	75,500		
Common Stock (par $10)	90,000	90,000		
Retained Earnings†	33,500	27,500		
Total Liabilities and Stockholders' Equity	$206,500	$193,000		

*One-half of all sales are on credit.
†During 2010, cash dividends amounting to $6,600 were declared and paid.

Required:

1. Complete the two final columns shown beside each item in Pinnacle Plus's comparative financial statements. Round the percentages to one decimal place.
2. Does anything significant jump out at you from the horizontal analyses?

LO4, 5   **PA13-2 Analyzing Comparative Financial Statements Using Selected Ratios**

Use the data given in PA13-1 for Pinnacle Plus.

Required:

1. Compute the gross profit percentage in 2010 and 2009. Round the percentages to one decimal place. Is the trend going in the right direction?
2. Compute the net profit margin for 2010 and 2009. Round the percentages to one decimal place. Is the trend going in the right direction?
3. Compute the earnings per share for 2010 and 2009. Does the trend look good or bad? Explain.
4. Stockholders' equity totaled $100,000 at the end of 2008. Compute the return on equity (ROE) ratios for 2010 and 2009. Express the ROE as percentages rounded to one decimal place. Is the trend going in the right direction?
5. Net property and equipment totaled $110,000 at the end of 2008. Compute the fixed asset turnover ratios for 2010 and 2009. Round the ratios to two decimal places. Is the trend going in the right direction?
6. Compute the debt-to-assets ratios for 2010 and 2009. Round the ratios to two decimal places. Is debt providing financing for a larger or smaller proportion of the company's asset growth? Explain.
7. Compute the times interest earned ratios for 2010 and 2009. Round the ratios to one decimal place. Do they look good or bad? Explain.
8. After Pinnacle Plus released its 2010 financial statements, the company's stock was trading at $18. After the release of its 2009 financial statements, the company's stock price was $15 per share. Compute the P/E ratios for both years, rounded to one decimal place. Does it appear that investors have become more (or less) optimistic about Pinnacle's future success?

LO3, 5   **PA13-3 Vertical Analysis of a Balance Sheet**

A condensed balance sheet for Simultech Corporation and a partially completed vertical analysis are presented below.

SIMULTECH CORPORATION **Balance Sheet (summarized)** **January 31, 2010** **(in millions of U.S. dollars)**					
Cash and Short-term Investments	$ 433	29%	Current Liabilities	$ 409	27%
Accounts Receivable	294	19	Long-term Liabilities	495	33
Inventories	206	14	Total Liabilities	904	b
Other Current Assets	109	a	Contributed Capital	118	c
Property and Equipment	27	2	Retained Earnings	492	32
Other Assets	445	29	Total Stockholders' Equity	610	d
Total Assets	$1,514	100%	Total Liabilities & Stockholders' Equity	$1,514	100%

Required:

1. Complete the vertical analysis by computing each line item (a)–(d) as a percentage of total assets. Round to the nearest whole percentage.
2. What percentages of Simultech's assets relate to inventories versus property and equipment? What does this tell you about the relative significance of these two assets to Simultech's business?
3. What percentage of Simultech's assets is financed by total stockholder's equity? By total liabilities?

PA13-4 Vertical Analysis of an Income Statement

LO3, 5

A condensed income statement for Simultech Corporation and a partially completed vertical analysis are presented below.

SIMULTECH CORPORATION
Income Statement (summarized)
(in millions of U.S. dollars)

	For the Years Ended			
	January 31, 2010		January 31, 2009	
Sales Revenues	$2,062	100%	$2,200	100%
Cost of Goods Sold	1,637	79	1,721	d
Selling, General, and Administrative Expenses	333	a	346	16
Other Operating Expenses	53	3	12	1
Interest Expense	22	b	26	1
Income before Income Tax Expense	17	1	95	e
Income Tax Expense	6	0	33	1
Net Income	$ 11	c%	$ 62	f%

Required:

1. Complete the vertical analysis by computing each line item (a)–(f) as a percentage of sales revenues. Round to the nearest whole percentage.

2. Does Simultech's Cost of Goods Sold for the year ended January 31, 2010, as a percentage of revenues, represent better or worse performance as compared to that for the year ended January 31, 2009?

3. Do the percentages for (c) and (f) that you calculated in 1 indicate whether Simultech's net profit margin has changed over the two years?

PA13-5 Interpreting Profitability, Liquidity, Solvency, and P/E Ratios

LO4, 5

Coke and Pepsi are well-known international brands. Coca-Cola sells nearly $32 billion worth of beverages each year while annual sales of Pepsi products exceed $43 billion. Compare the two companies as a potential investment based on the following ratios:

Coca-Cola Company
PepsiCo

Ratio	Coca-Cola	PepsiCo
Gross profit percentage	64.3%	53.1%
Net profit margin	17.9%	11.9%
Return on equity	25.9%	35.8%
EPS	$ 2.51	$ 3.26
Receivables turnover ratio	9.6	9.2
Inventory turnover ratio	4.8	8.0
Current ratio	1.12	1.36
Debt to assets	0.37	0.45
P/E ratio	20.0	16.4

Required:

1. Which company appears more profitable? Describe the ratio(s) that you used to reach this decision.

2. Which company appears more liquid? Describe the ratio(s) that you used to reach this decision.

3. Which company appears more solvent? Describe the ratio(s) that you used to reach this decision.

4. Are the conclusions from your analyses in requirements 1–3 consistent with the value of the two companies, as suggested by their P/E ratios? If not, offer one explanation for any apparent inconsistency.

LO4, 5, 6   PA13-6 Using Ratios to Compare Loan Requests from Two Companies

The 2010 financial statements for Royale and Cavalier companies are summarized here:

	Royale Company	Cavalier Company
Balance Sheet		
Cash	$ 25,000	$ 45,000
Accounts Receivable, Net	55,000	5,000
Inventory	110,000	25,000
Property and Equipment, Net	550,000	160,000
Other Assets	140,000	57,000
Total Assets	$880,000	$292,000
Current Liabilities	$120,000	$ 15,000
Long-term Debt	190,000	55,000
Capital Stock (par $20)	480,000	210,000
Additional Paid-in Capital	50,000	4,000
Retained Earnings	40,000	8,000
Total Liabilities and Stockholders' Equity	$880,000	$292,000
Income Statement		
Sales Revenue	$800,000	$280,000
Cost of Goods Sold	(480,000)	(150,000)
Expenses (including interest and income tax)	(240,000)	(95,000)
Net Income	$ 80,000	$ 35,000
Selected Data from 2009 Statements		
Accounts Receivable, Net	$ 47,000	$ 11,000
Long-term Debt	190,000	55,000
Property and Equipment, Net	550,000	160,000
Inventory	95,000	38,000
Total Stockholders' Equity	570,000	202,000
Other Data		
Per share price at end of 2010	$ 14.00	$ 11.00

These two companies are in the same business and state but different cities. One-half of Royale's sales and one-quarter of Cavalier's sales are on credit. Each company has been in operation for about 10 years. Both companies received an unqualified audit opinion on the financial statements. Royale Company wants to borrow $75,000 cash, and Cavalier Company is asking for $30,000. The loans will be for a two-year period. Both companies estimate bad debts based on an aging analysis, but Cavalier has estimated slightly higher uncollectible rates than Royale. Neither company issued stock in 2010.

Required:

1. Calculate the ratios in Exhibit 13.5 for which sufficient information is available. Round all calculations to two decimal places.

2. Assume that you work in the loan department of a local bank. You have been asked to analyze the situation and recommend which loan is preferable. Based on the data given, your analysis prepared in requirement 1, and any other information (e.g., accounting policies and decisions), give your choice and the supporting explanation.

LO5   PA13-7 Analyzing an Investment by Comparing Selected Ratios

You have the opportunity to invest $10,000 in one of two companies from a single industry. The only information you have is shown here. The word *high* refers to the top third of the industry; *average* is the middle third; *low* is the bottom third.

Ratio	Company A	Company B
Current	Low	High
Inventory turnover	High	Low
Debt to assets	Low	Average
Times interest earned	High	Average
Price/earnings	High	Average

Required:

Which company would you select? Write a brief explanation for your recommendation.

GROUP B PROBLEMS

PB13-1 Analyzing Financial Statements Using Horizontal and Ratio Analyses   LO2, 4, 5

The comparative financial statements prepared at December 31, 2010, for Tiger Audio showed the following summarized data:

	2010	2009	Increase (Decrease) 2010 over 2009 Amount	Percentage
Income Statement				
Sales Revenue	$222,000	$185,000		
Cost of Goods Sold	127,650	111,000		
Gross Profit	94,350	74,000		
Operating Expenses	39,600	33,730		
Interest Expense	4,000	3,270		
Income before Income Tax Expense	50,750	37,000		
Income Tax Expense (30%)	15,225	11,100		
Net Income	$ 35,525	$ 25,900		
Balance Sheet				
Cash	$ 40,000	$ 38,000		
Accounts Receivable, Net	18,500	16,000		
Inventory	25,000	22,000		
Property and Equipment, Net	127,000	119,000		
Total Assets	$210,500	$195,000		
Accounts Payable	$ 27,000	$ 25,000		
Income Tax Payable	3,000	2,800		
Note Payable, Long-term	75,500	92,200		
Total Liabilities	105,500	120,000		
Capital Stock (par $1)	25,000	25,000		
Retained Earnings	80,000	50,000		
Total Liabilities and Stockholders' Equity	$210,500	$195,000		

Required:

1. Complete the two final columns shown beside each item in Tiger Audio's comparative financial statements. Round the percentages to one decimal place.
2. Does anything significant jump out at you from the year-over-year analyses?

PB13-2 Analyzing Comparative Financial Statements Using Selected Ratios   LO4, 5

Use the data given in PB13-1 for Tiger Audio.

Required:

1. Compute the gross profit percentage in 2010 and 2009. Is the trend going in the right direction?
2. Compute the net profit margin for 2010 and 2009. Is the trend going in the right direction?
3. Compute the earnings per share for 2010 and 2009. Does the trend look good or bad? Explain.
4. Stockholders' equity totaled $65,000 at the end of 2008. Compute the return on equity ratios for 2010 and 2009. Is the trend going in the right direction?
5. Net property and equipment totaled $115,000 at the end of 2008. Compute the fixed asset turnover ratios for 2010 and 2009. Is the trend going in the right direction?
6. Compute the debt-to-assets ratios for 2010 and 2009. Is debt providing financing for a larger or smaller proportion of the company's asset growth? Explain.

7. Compute the times interest earned ratios for 2010 and 2009. Do they look good or bad? Explain.

8. After Tiger released its 2010 financial statements, the company's stock was trading at $17. After the release of its 2009 financial statements, the company's stock price was $12 per share. Compute the P/E ratios for both years. Does it appear that investors have become more (or less) optimistic about Tiger's future success?

LO3, 5

SOUTHWEST

PB13-3 Vertical Analysis of a Balance Sheet

A condensed balance sheet for Southwest Airlines and a partially completed vertical analysis are presented below.

SOUTHWEST AIRLINES
Balance Sheet (summarized)
December 31, 2008
(in millions of U.S. dollars)

Cash	$ 1,803	13%	Current Liabilities	$ 2,806	b%
Accounts Receivable	209	1	Long-term Liabilities	6,549	45
Inventory of Parts and Supplies	203	1	Total Liabilities	9,355	65
Other Current Assets	678	5	Contributed Capital	1,018	7
Property and Equipment, Net	11,040	a	Retained Earnings	3,935	28
Other Assets	375	3	Total Stockholders' Equity	4,953	c
Total Assets	$14,308	100%	Total Liabilities & Stockholders' Equity	$14,308	100%

Required:

1. Complete the vertical analysis by computing each line item (a)–(c) as a percentage of total assets. Round to the nearest whole percentage.

2. What percentages of Southwest's assets relate to inventory of parts and supplies versus property and equipment? What does this tell you about the relative significance of these two assets to Southwest's business?

3. What percentage of Southwest's assets is financed by total stockholders' equity? By total liabilities?

LO3, 5

SOUTHWEST

PB13-4 Vertical Analysis of an Income Statement

A condensed income statement for Southwest Airlines and a partially completed vertical analysis are presented below.

SOUTHWEST AIRLINES
Income Statement (summarized)
For the Year Ended December 31
(in millions of U.S. dollars)

	2008		2007	
Sales Revenues	$11,023	100%	$9,861	100%
Salaries, Wages, and Benefits	3,340	30	3,213	d
Fuel, Oil, Repairs, and Maintenance	4,434	a	3,306	33
Other Operating Expenses	2,800	b	2,551	26
Other Expenses (Revenues)	171	2	(267)	(3)
Income before Income Tax Expense	278	3	1,058	e
Income Tax Expense	100	1	413	4
Net Income	$ 178	c%	$ 645	f%

Required:

1. Complete the vertical analysis by computing each line item (a)–(f) as a percentage of sales revenues. Round to the nearest whole percentage.

2. Does the percentage that you calculated in 1(a) suggest that Southwest tried to increase its profit by cutting repairs and maintenance costs in 2008 compared to 2007?

3. Refer to the percentages that you calculated in 1(c) and (f). Is Southwest's net profit margin improving or declining?

PB13-5 Interpreting Profitability, Liquidity, Solvency, and P/E Ratios

LO4, 5

Mattel and Hasbro are the two biggest makers of games and toys in the world. Mattel sells nearly $6 billion of products each year while annual sales of Hasbro products exceed $4 billion. Compare the two companies as a potential investment based on the following ratios:

Mattel, Inc.

Ratio	Mattel	Hasbro
Gross profit percentage	45.5%	57.7%
Net profit margin	6.5%	7.3%
Return on equity	17.1%	21.8%
EPS	$ 1.05	$ 2.18
Receivables turnover ratio	8.9	10.5
Inventory turnover ratio	6.2	5.7
Current ratio	2.38	2.54
Debt to assets	0.31	0.35
P/E ratio	15.9	13.8

Required:

1. Which company appears more profitable? Describe the ratio(s) that you used to reach this decision.
2. Which company appears more liquid? Describe the ratio(s) that you used to reach this decision.
3. Which company appears more solvent? Describe the ratio(s) that you used to reach this decision.
4. Are the conclusions from your analyses in requirements 1–3 consistent with the value of the two companies, as suggested by their P/E ratios? If not, offer one explanation for any apparent inconsistency.

PB13-6 Using Ratios to Compare Loan Requests from Two Companies

LO4, 5, 6

The 2010 financial statements for Thor and Gunnar Companies are summarized here:

	Thor Company	Gunnar Company
Balance Sheet		
Cash	$ 35,000	$ 54,000
Accounts Receivable, Net	77,000	6,000
Inventory	154,000	30,000
Property and Equipment, Net	770,000	192,000
Other Assets	196,000	68,400
Total Assets	$1,232,000	$350,400
Current Liabilities	$ 168,000	$ 18,000
Long-term Debt (12% interest rate)	266,000	66,000
Capital Stock (par $20)	672,000	252,000
Additional Paid-in Capital	70,000	4,800
Retained Earnings	56,000	9,600
Total Liabilities and Stockholders' Equity	$1,232,000	$350,400
Income Statement		
Sales Revenue	$1,120,000	$336,000
Cost of Goods Sold	(672,000)	(180,000)
Expenses (including interest and income tax)	(336,000)	(114,000)
Net Income	$ 112,000	$ 42,000
Selected Data from 2009 Statements		
Accounts Receivable, Net	$ 65,800	$ 13,200
Inventory	133,000	45,600
Property and Equipment, Net	770,000	192,000
Long-term Debt (12% interest rate)	266,000	66,000
Total Stockholders' Equity	798,000	266,400
Other Data		
Per share price at end of 2010	$ 13.20	$ 19.60

These two companies are in the same business and state but different cities. One-half of Thor's sales and one-quarter of Gunnar's sales are on credit. Each company has been in operation for about 10 years. Both companies received an unqualified audit opinion on the financial statements. Thor Company wants to borrow $105,000, and Gunnar Company is asking for $36,000. The loans will be for a two-year period. Neither company issued stock in 2010.

Required:

1. Calculate the ratios in Exhibit 13.5 for which sufficient information is available. Round all calculations to two decimal places.

2. Assume that you work in the loan department of a local bank. You have been asked to analyze the situation and recommend which loan is preferable. Based on the data given, your analysis prepared in requirement 1, and any other information, give your choice and the supporting explanation.

LO5 **PB13-7 Analyzing an Investment by Comparing Selected Ratios**

You have the opportunity to invest $10,000 in one of two companies from a single industry. The only information you have is shown here. The word *high* refers to the top third of the industry; *average* is the middle third; *low* is the bottom third.

Ratio	Company A	Company B
EPS	High	High
Return on equity	High	Average
Debt to assets	High	Low
Current	Low	Average
Price/earnings	Low	High

Required:

Which company would you select? Write a brief explanation for your recommendation.

SKILLS DEVELOPMENT CASES

LO4 **S13-1 Computing Ratios**

Lowe's
The Home Depot

To benchmark Lowe's financial results, we reported the following ratios for The Home Depot's fiscal year ended February 1, 2009: fixed asset turnover (2.65), return on equity (12.7%), quality of income (2.45), days to sell (87), and debt to assets (0.57). Show that you can compute these ratios using the financial statements of The Home Depot in Appendix A at the end of this book, or downloaded from the *Cases* section of the text's Web site at www.mhhe.com/phillips3e.

LO5 **S13-2 Evaluating Financial Information**

Lumber Liquidators, Inc.
Lowe's

Lumber Liquidators, Inc., competes with Lowe's in product lines such as hardwood flooring, moldings, and noise-reducing underlay. The two companies reported the following financial results in fiscal 2008:

	Lumber Liquidators	Lowe's
Gross profit percentage	35.0%	34.2%
Net profit margin	4.7%	4.6%
Return on equity	21.1%	12.9%
Earnings per share	$ 0.83	$ 1.51

Required:

1. Explain how Lumber Liquidators could have a substantially higher gross profit percentage than Lowe's but a nearly identical net profit margin. What does this suggest about the relative ability of the two companies to control operating expenses?

2. Explain how Lumber Liquidators could have a higher return on equity but lower earnings per share. What does this suggest about the companies' relative number of outstanding shares? What other explanations could account for this seemingly contradictory pattern?

S13-3 Internet-Based Team Research: Examining an Annual Report

LO1, 2, 3, 4, 5, 6

As a team, select an industry to analyze. Using your Web browser, each team member should access the annual report or 10-K for one publicly traded company in the industry, with each member selecting a different company. (See S1-3 in Chapter 1 for a description of possible resources for these tasks.)

Required:

1. On an individual basis, each team member should write a short report that incorporates horizontal and vertical analyses and as many of the ratios from the chapter as are applicable given the nature of the selected company.

2. Then, as a team, write a short report comparing and contrasting your companies using these attributes. Discuss any patterns across the companies that you as a team observe. Provide potential explanations for any differences discovered. Consider the impact of differences in accounting policies.

S13-4 Ethical Decision Making: A Real-Life Example

LO6

During its deliberations on the Sarbanes-Oxley Act, the U.S. Senate considered numerous reports evaluating the quality of work done by external auditors. One study by Weiss Ratings, Inc., focused on auditors' ability to predict bankruptcy. The study criticized auditors for failing to identify and report going-concern problems for audit clients that later went bankrupt. Based on a sample of 45 bankrupt companies, the Weiss study concluded that had auditors noted unusual levels for just two of seven typical financial ratios, they would have identified 89 percent of the sample companies that later went bankrupt. A follow-up to the Weiss study found that had the criteria in the Weiss study been applied to a larger sample of nonbankrupt companies, 46.9 percent of nonbankrupt companies would have been predicted to go bankrupt.* In other words, the Weiss criteria would have incorrectly predicted bankruptcy for nearly half of the companies in the follow-up study and would have led the auditors to report that these clients had substantial going-concern problems when, in fact, they did not. Discuss the negative consequences that arise when auditors fail to identify and report going-concern problems. Who is harmed by these failures? Discuss the negative consequences that arise when auditors incorrectly report going-concern problems when they do not exist. Who is harmed by these errors? In your opinion, which of the potential consequences is worse?

S13-5 Ethical Decision Making: A Mini-Case

LO4, 5

Capital Investments Corporation (CIC) requested a sizable loan from First Federal Bank to acquire a large piece of land for future expansion. CIC reported current assets of $1,900,000 (including $430,000 in cash) and current liabilities of $1,075,000. First Federal denied the loan request for a number of reasons, including the fact that the current ratio was below 2:1. When CIC was informed of the loan denial, the controller of the company immediately paid $420,000 that was owed to several trade creditors. The controller then asked First Federal to reconsider the loan application. Based on these abbreviated facts, would you recommend that First Federal approve the loan request? Why? Are the controller's actions ethical?

S13-6 Critical Thinking: Analyzing the Impact of Alternative Depreciation Methods on Ratio Analysis

LO4, 5, 6

Speedy Company uses the double-declining-balance method to depreciate its property, plant, and equipment, and Turtle Company uses the straight-line method. The two companies are exactly alike except for the difference in depreciation methods.

Required:

1. Identify the financial ratios discussed in this chapter that are likely to be affected by the difference in depreciation methods.

2. Which company will report the higher amount for each ratio that you have identified in response to requirement 1? If you cannot be certain, explain why.

---

*Michael D. Akers, Meredith A. Maher, and Don E. Giacomino, "Going-Concern Opinions: Broadening the Expectations Gap," *CPA Journal*, October 2003. Retrieved June 12, 2009 from www.nysscpa.org/cpajournal/2003/1003/features/f103803.htm.

LO2, 3

www.mhhe.com/phillips3e

S13-7 Using a Spreadsheet to Calculate Financial Statement Ratios

Enter the account names and dollar amounts from the comparative balance sheets in Exhibit 13.1 into a worksheet in a spreadsheet file. Create a second copy of the worksheet in the same spreadsheet file.

Required:

1. To the right of the comparative numbers in the first worksheet, enter the necessary formulas to compute the amount and percent change as shown in Exhibit 13.1.

2. To the right of each column in the second worksheet, enter the necessary formulas to create common size statements similar to those shown in Exhibit 13.3.

CONTINUING CASE

Mc Graw Hill connect™
|ACCOUNTING

LO4, 5   **CC13 Evaluating Profitability, Liquidity, and Solvency**

Looking back over the last few years it is clear that Nicole Mackisey has accomplished a lot running her business Nicole's Getaway Spa (NGS). Nicole is curious about her company's performance as she compares its financial statements.

	2012	2011	2010
Balance Sheet			
Cash	$ 6,700	$ 4,200	$ 3,800
Accounts Receivable, Net	2,000	2,500	1,800
Inventory	1,200	3,000	1,600
Prepaid Expenses	750	1,050	200
Other Current Assets	300	350	200
Total Current Assets	10,950	11,100	7,600
Property and Equipment	64,000	79,000	27,000
Total Assets	$74,950	$90,100	$34,600
Current Liabilities	$ 8,000	$ 8,000	$ 9,000
Long-term Liabilities	35,000	50,000	14,000
Total Liabilities	43,000	58,000	23,000
Contributed Capital	25,000	30,000	10,900
Retained Earnings	6,950	2,100	700
Total Stockholders' Equity	31,950	32,100	11,600
Total Liabilities and Stockholders' Equity	$74,950	$90,100	$34,600
Income Statement			
Sales Revenue	$80,000	$56,000	$44,000
Cost of Goods Sold	65,000	48,000	35,000
Gross Profit	15,000	8,000	9,000
Operating Expenses	4,000	2,000	7,000
Income from Operations	11,000	6,000	2,000
Interest Expense	1,000	3,100	800
Income before Income Tax Expense	10,000	2,900	1,200
Income Tax Expense	3,050	800	500
Net Income	$ 6,950	$ 2,100	$ 700

• Net Cash Flows from Operating Activities:
  2012: $3,000; 2011: $2,500; and 2010: $2,300

Required:

1. Was NGS more profitable in 2011 or 2012? Use the gross profit percentage, quality of income ratio, return on equity, and asset turnover ratio to help in making a decision (round each ratio to two decimal places).

2. Was NGS more liquid in 2011 or 2012? Use the current ratio and quick ratio to help in making a decision (round each ratio to two decimal places).

3. Was NGS more solvent in 2011 or 2012? Use the debt-to-assets ratio and times interest earned ratio to help in making a decision (round each ratio to two decimal places).

APPENDIX A

Excerpts from the Fiscal 2008 Annual Report of The Home Depot, Inc.

Note: The materials in Appendix A are selected from the full Annual Report of The Home Depot, Inc., for fiscal year 2008, which ended February 1, 2009. The complete annual report is available from the textbook Web site at www.mhhe.com/phillips3e or from http://www.homedepotar.com/.

Management's Responsibility for Financial Statements

The financial statements presented in this Annual Report have been prepared with integrity and objectivity and are the responsibility of the management of The Home Depot, Inc. These financial statements have been prepared in conformity with U.S. generally accepted accounting principles and properly reflect certain estimates and judgments based upon the best available information.

The financial statements of the Company have been audited by KPMG LLP, an independent registered public accounting firm. Their accompanying report is based upon an audit conducted in accordance with the standards of the Public Company Accounting Oversight Board (United States).

The Audit Committee of the Board of Directors, consisting solely of outside directors, meets five times a year with the independent registered public accounting firm, the internal auditors, and representatives of management to discuss auditing and financial reporting matters. In addition, a telephonic meeting is held prior to each quarterly earnings release. The Audit Committee retains the independent registered public accounting firm and regularly reviews the internal accounting controls, the activities of the independent registered public accounting firm and internal auditors, and the financial condition of the Company. Both the Company's independent registered public accounting firm and the internal auditors have free access to the Audit Committee.

Management's Report on Internal Control over Financial Reporting

Our management is responsible for establishing and maintaining adequate internal control over financial reporting, as such term is defined in Rules 13a-15(f) promulgated under the Securities Exchange Act of 1934, as amended. Under the supervision and with the participation of our management, including our chief executive officer and chief financial officer, we conducted an evaluation of the effectiveness of our internal control over financial reporting as of February 1, 2009, based on the framework in *Internal Control—Integrated Framework* issued by the Committee of Sponsoring Organizations of the Treadway Commission (COSO). Based on our evaluation, our management concluded that our internal control over financial reporting was effective as of February 1, 2009, in providing reasonable assurance regarding the reliability of financial reporting and the preparation of financial statements for external purposes in accordance with generally accepted accounting principles. The effectiveness of our internal control over financial reporting as of February 1, 2009, has been audited by KPMG LLP, an independent registered public accounting firm, as stated in their report which is included on the following page.

/s/ FRANCIS S. BLAKE

Francis S. Blake
Chairman &
Chief Executive Officer

/s/ CAROL B. TOMÉ

Carol B. Tomé
Chief Financial Officer &
Executive Vice President — Corporate Services

Report of Independent Registered Public Accounting Firm

The Board of Directors and Stockholders
The Home Depot, Inc.:

We have audited The Home Depot, Inc.'s internal control over financial reporting as of February 1, 2009, based on criteria established in *Internal Control—Integrated Framework* issued by the Committee of Sponsoring Organizations of the Treadway Commission (COSO). The Home Depot, Inc.'s management is responsible for maintaining effective internal control over financial reporting and for its assessment of the effectiveness of internal control over financial reporting, included in the accompanying Management's Report on Internal Control Over Financial Reporting. Our responsibility is to express an opinion on the Company's internal control over financial reporting based on our audit.

We conducted our audit in accordance with the standards of the Public Company Accounting Oversight Board (United States). Those standards require that we plan and perform the audit to obtain reasonable assurance about whether effective internal control over financial reporting was maintained in all material respects. Our audit included obtaining an understanding of internal control over financial reporting, assessing the risk that a material weakness exists, and testing and evaluating the design and operating effectiveness of internal control based on the assessed risk. Our audit also included performing such other procedures as we considered necessary in the circumstances. We believe that our audit provides a reasonable basis for our opinion.

A company's internal control over financial reporting is a process designed to provide reasonable assurance regarding the reliability of financial reporting and the preparation of financial statements for external purposes in accordance with generally accepted accounting principles. A company's internal control over financial reporting includes those policies and procedures that (1) pertain to the maintenance of records that, in reasonable detail, accurately and fairly reflect the transactions and dispositions of the assets of the company; (2) provide reasonable assurance that transactions are recorded as necessary to permit preparation of financial statements in accordance with generally accepted accounting principles, and that receipts and expenditures of the company are being made only in accordance with authorizations of management and directors of the company; and (3) provide reasonable assurance regarding prevention or timely detection of unauthorized acquisition, use, or disposition of the company's assets that could have a material effect on the financial statements.

Because of its inherent limitations, internal control over financial reporting may not prevent or detect misstatements. Also, projections of any evaluation of effectiveness to future periods are subject to the risk that controls may become inadequate because of changes in conditions, or that the degree of compliance with the policies or procedures may deteriorate.

In our opinion, The Home Depot, Inc., maintained, in all material respects, effective internal control over financial reporting as of February 1, 2009, based on criteria established in *Internal Control—Integrated Framework* issued by the Committee of Sponsoring Organizations of the Treadway Commission.

We also have audited, in accordance with the standards of the Public Company Accounting Oversight Board (United States), the Consolidated Balance Sheets of The Home Depot, Inc., and subsidiaries as of February 1, 2009, and February 3, 2008, and the related Consolidated Statements of Earnings, Stockholders' Equity and Comprehensive Income, and Cash Flows for each of the fiscal years in the three-year period ended February 1, 2009, and our report dated March 26, 2009, expressed an unqualified opinion on those consolidated financial statements.

/s/ KPMG LLP

Atlanta, Georgia
March 26, 2009

Report of Independent Registered Public Accounting Firm

The Board of Directors and Stockholders
The Home Depot, Inc.:

We have audited the accompanying Consolidated Balance Sheets of The Home Depot, Inc., and subsidiaries as of February 1, 2009, and February 3, 2008, and the related Consolidated Statements of Earnings, Stockholders' Equity and Comprehensive Income, and Cash Flows for each of the fiscal years in the three-year period ended February 1, 2009. These Consolidated Financial Statements are the responsibility of the Company's management. Our responsibility is to express an opinion on these Consolidated Financial Statements based on our audits.

We conducted our audits in accordance with the standards of the Public Company Accounting Oversight Board (United States). Those standards require that we plan and perform the audit to obtain reasonable assurance about whether the financial statements are free of material misstatement. An audit includes examining, on a test basis, evidence supporting the amounts and disclosures in the financial statements. An audit also includes assessing the accounting principles used and significant estimates made by management, as well as evaluating the overall financial statement presentation. We believe that our audits provide a reasonable basis for our opinion.

In our opinion, the Consolidated Financial Statements referred to above present fairly, in all material respects, the financial position of The Home Depot, Inc., and subsidiaries as of February 1, 2009, and February 3, 2008, and the results of their operations and their cash flows for each of the fiscal years in the three-year period ended February 1, 2009, in conformity with U.S. generally accepted accounting principles.

As discussed in Note 7 to the consolidated financial statements, effective January 29, 2007, the beginning of the fiscal year ended February 3, 2008, the Company adopted Financial Accounting Standards Board Interpretation No. 48, *Accounting for Uncertainty in Income Taxes*.

We also have audited, in accordance with the standards of the Public Company Accounting Oversight Board (United States), The Home Depot, Inc.'s internal control over financial reporting as of February 1, 2009, based on criteria established in *Internal Control—Integrated Framework* issued by the Committee of Sponsoring Organizations of the Treadway Commission (COSO), and our report dated March 26, 2009, expressed an unqualified opinion on the effectiveness of the Company's internal control over financial reporting.

/s/ KPMG LLP

Atlanta, Georgia
March 26, 2009

THE HOME DEPOT, INC., AND SUBSIDIARIES
Consolidated Statements of Earnings

	Fiscal Year Ended[1]		
amounts in millions, except per share data	February 1, 2009	February 3, 2008	January 28, 2007
NET SALES	$71,288	$77,349	$79,022
Cost of Sales	47,298	51,352	52,476
GROSS PROFIT	23,990	25,997	26,546
Operating Expenses:			
Selling, General and Administrative	17,846	17,053	16,106
Depreciation and Amortization	1,785	1,702	1,574
Total Operating Expenses	19,631	18,755	17,680
OPERATING INCOME	4,359	7,242	8,866
Interest and Other (Income) Expense:			
Interest and Investment Income	(18)	(74)	(27)
Interest Expense	624	696	391
Other	163	—	—
Interest and Other, Net	769	622	364
EARNINGS FROM CONTINUING OPERATIONS BEFORE PROVISION FOR INCOME TAXES	3,590	6,620	8,502
Provision for Income Taxes	1,278	2,410	3,236
EARNINGS FROM CONTINUING OPERATIONS	2,312	4,210	5,266
EARNINGS (LOSS) FROM DISCONTINUED OPERATIONS, NET OF TAX	(52)	185	495
NET EARNINGS	$ 2,260	$ 4,395	$ 5,761
Weighted Average Common Shares	1,682	1,849	2,054
BASIC EARNINGS PER SHARE FROM CONTINUING OPERATIONS	$ 1.37	$ 2.28	$ 2.56
BASIC EARNINGS (LOSS) PER SHARE FROM DISCONTINUED OPERATIONS	$ (0.03)	$ 0.10	$ 0.24
BASIC EARNINGS PER SHARE	$ 1.34	$ 2.38	$ 2.80
Diluted Weighted Average Common Shares	1,686	1,856	2,062
DILUTED EARNINGS PER SHARE FROM CONTINUING OPERATIONS	$ 1.37	$ 2.27	$ 2.55
DILUTED EARNINGS (LOSS) PER SHARE FROM DISCONTINUED OPERATIONS	$ (0.03)	$ 0.10	$ 0.24
DILUTED EARNINGS PER SHARE	$ 1.34	$ 2.37	$ 2.79

(1) *Fiscal years ended February 1, 2009, and January 28, 2007, include 52 weeks. Fiscal year ended February 3, 2008, includes 53 weeks.*

See accompanying Notes to Consolidated Financial Statements.

THE HOME DEPOT, INC., AND SUBSIDIARIES
Consolidated Balance Sheets

amounts in millions, except share and per share data	February 1, 2009	February 3, 2008
ASSETS		
Current Assets:		
Cash and Cash Equivalents	$ 519	$ 445
Short-term Investments	6	12
Receivables, Net	972	1,259
Merchandise Inventories	10,673	11,731
Other Current Assets	1,192	1,227
Total Current Assets	13,362	14,674
Property and Equipment, at cost:		
Land	8,301	8,398
Buildings	16,961	16,642
Furniture, Fixtures and Equipment	8,741	8,050
Leasehold Improvements	1,359	1,390
Construction in Progress	625	1,435
Capital Leases	490	497
	36,477	36,412
Less Accumulated Depreciation and Amortization	10,243	8,936
Net Property and Equipment	26,234	27,476
Notes Receivable	36	342
Goodwill	1,134	1,209
Other Assets	398	623
Total Assets	$41,164	$44,324
LIABILITIES AND STOCKHOLDERS' EQUITY		
Current Liabilities:		
Short-term Debt	$ —	$ 1,747
Accounts Payable	4,822	5,732
Accrued Salaries and Related Expenses	1,129	1,094
Sales Taxes Payable	337	445
Deferred Revenue	1,165	1,474
Income Taxes Payable	289	60
Current Installments of Long-term Debt	1,767	300
Other Accrued Expenses	1,644	1,854
Total Current Liabilities	11,153	12,706
Long-term Debt, excluding current installments	9,667	11,383
Other Long-term Liabilities	2,198	1,833
Deferred Income Taxes	369	688
Total Liabilities	23,387	26,610
STOCKHOLDERS' EQUITY		
Common Stock, par value $0.05; authorized: 10 billion shares; issued 1.707 billion shares at February 1, 2009, and 1.698 billion shares at February 3, 2008; outstanding 1.696 billion shares at February 1, 2009, and 1.690 billion shares at February 3, 2008	85	85
Paid-In Capital	6,048	5,800
Retained Earnings	12,093	11,388
Accumulated Other Comprehensive Income (Loss)	(77)	755
Treasury Stock, at cost, 11 million shares at February 1, 2009, and 8 million shares at February 3, 2008	(372)	(314)
Total Stockholders' Equity	17,777	17,714
Total Liabilities and Stockholders' Equity	$41,164	$44,324

See accompanying Notes to Consolidated Financial Statements.

THE HOME DEPOT, INC., AND SUBSIDIARIES
Consolidated Statements of Stockholders' Equity and Comprehensive Income

amounts in millions, except per share data	Common Stock Shares	Amount	Paid-In Capital	Retained Earnings	Accumulated Other Comprehensive Income (Loss)	Treasury Stock Shares	Amount	Stockholders' Equity	Total Comprehensive Income
BALANCE, JANUARY 29, 2006	2,401	$120	$7,149	$28,943	$409	(277) $	(9,712)	$26,909	
Cumulative Effect of Adjustment Resulting from the Adoption of SAB 108, net of tax	—	—	201	(257)	—	—	—	(56)	
ADJUSTED BALANCE, JANUARY 29, 2006	2,401	$120	$7,350	$28,686	$409	(277) $	(9,712)	$26,853	
Net Earnings	—	—	—	5,761	—	—	—	5,761	$5,761
Shares Issued Under Employee Stock Plans	20	1	351	—	—	—	—	352	
Tax Effect of Sale of Option Shares by Employees	—	—	18	—	—	—	—	18	
Translation Adjustments	—	—	—	—	(77)	—	—	(77)	(77)
Cash Flow Hedges	—	—	—	—	(22)	—	—	(22)	(22)
Stock Options, Awards and Amortization of Restricted Stock	—	—	296	—	—	—	—	296	
Repurchase of Common Stock	—	—	—	—	—	(174)	(6,671)	(6,671)	
Cash Dividends ($0.675 per share)	—	—	—	(1,395)	—	—	—	(1,395)	
Other	—	—	(85)	—	—	—	—	(85)	
Comprehensive Income									$5,662
BALANCE, JANUARY 28, 2007	2,421	$121	$7,930	$33,052	$310	(451) $	(16,383)	$25,030	
Cumulative Effect of the Adoption of FIN 48	—	—	—	(111)	—	—	—	(111)	
Net Earnings	—	—	—	4,395	—	—	—	4,395	$4,395
Shares Issued Under Employee Stock Plans	12	1	239	—	—	—	—	240	
Tax Effect of Sale of Option Shares by Employees	—	—	4	—	—	—	—	4	
Translation Adjustments	—	—	—	—	455	—	—	455	455
Cash Flow Hedges	—	—	—	—	(10)	—	—	(10)	(10)
Stock Options, Awards and Amortization of Restricted Stock	—	—	206	—	—	—	—	206	
Repurchase of Common Stock	—	—	—	—	—	(292)	(10,815)	(10,815)	
Retirement of Treasury Stock	(735)	(37)	(2,608)	(24,239)	—	735	26,884	—	
Cash Dividends ($0.90 per share)	—	—	—	(1,709)	—	—	—	(1,709)	
Other	—	—	29	—	—	—	—	29	
Comprehensive Income									$4,840
BALANCE, FEBRUARY 3, 2008	1,698	$ 85	$5,800	$11,388	$755	(8) $	(314)	$17,714	
Net Earnings	—	—	—	2,260	—	—	—	2,260	$2,260
Shares Issued Under Employee Stock Plans	9	—	68	—	—	—	—	68	
Tax Effect of Sale of Option Shares by Employees	—	—	7	—	—	—	—	7	
Translation Adjustments	—	—	—	—	(831)	—	—	(831)	(831)
Cash Flow Hedges	—	—	—	—	(1)	—	—	(1)	(1)
Stock Options, Awards and Amortization of Restricted Stock	—	—	176	—	—	—	—	176	
Repurchase of Common Stock	—	—	—	—	—	(3)	(70)	(70)	
Cash Dividends ($0.90 per share)	—	—	—	(1,521)	—	—	—	(1,521)	
Other	—	—	(3)	(34)	—	—	12	(25)	
Comprehensive Income									$1,428
BALANCE, FEBRUARY 1, 2009	1,707	$ 85	$6,048	$12,093	$ (77)	(11) $	(372)	$17,777	

See accompanying Notes to Consolidated Financial Statements.

THE HOME DEPOT, INC., AND SUBSIDIARIES
Consolidated Statements Of Cash Flows

amounts in millions	February 1, 2009	February 3, 2008	January 28, 2007
CASH FLOWS FROM OPERATING ACTIVITIES:			
Net Earnings	$2,260	$ 4,395	$5,761
Reconciliation of Net Earnings to Net Cash Provided by Operating Activities:			
Depreciation and Amortization	1,902	1,906	1,886
Impairment Related to Rationalization Charges	580	—	—
Impairment of Investment	163	—	—
Stock-Based Compensation Expense	176	207	297
Changes in Assets and Liabilities, net of the effects of acquisitions and disposition:			
Decrease in Receivables, Net	121	116	96
Decrease (Increase) in Merchandise Inventories	743	(491)	(563)
(Increase) Decrease in Other Current Assets	(7)	109	(225)
(Decrease) Increase in Accounts Payable and Accrued Liabilities	(646)	(465)	531
Decrease in Deferred Revenue	(292)	(159)	(123)
Increase (Decrease) in Income Taxes Payable	262	—	(172)
(Decrease) Increase in Deferred Income Taxes	(282)	(348)	46
Increase (Decrease) in Other Long-term Liabilities	306	186	(51)
Other	242	271	178
Net Cash Provided by Operating Activities	5,528	5,727	7,661
CASH FLOWS FROM INVESTING ACTIVITIES:			
Capital Expenditures, net of $37, $19, and $49 of non-cash capital expenditures in fiscal 2008, 2007, and 2006, respectively	(1,847)	(3,558)	(3,542)
Proceeds from Sale of Business, Net	—	8,337	—
Payments for Businesses Acquired, Net	—	(13)	(4,268)
Proceeds from Sales of Property and Equipment	147	318	138
Purchases of Investments	(168)	(11,225)	(5,409)
Proceeds from Sales and Maturities of Investments	139	10,899	5,434
Net Cash (Used in) Provided by Investing Activities	(1,729)	4,758	(7,647)
CASH FLOWS FROM FINANCING ACTIVITIES:			
(Repayments of) Proceeds from Short-term Borrowings, Net	(1,732)	1,734	(900)
Proceeds from Long-term Borrowings, Net of discount	—	—	8,935
Repayments of Long-term Debt	(313)	(20)	(509)
Repurchases of Common Stock	(70)	(10,815)	(6,684)
Proceeds from Sale of Common Stock	84	276	381
Cash Dividends Paid to Stockholders	(1,521)	(1,709)	(1,395)
Other Financing Activities	(128)	(105)	(31)
Net Cash Used in Financing Activities	(3,680)	(10,639)	(203)
Increase (Decrease) in Cash and Cash Equivalents	119	(154)	(189)
Effect of Exchange Rate Changes on Cash and Cash Equivalents	(45)	(1)	(4)
Cash and Cash Equivalents at Beginning of Year	445	600	793
Cash and Cash Equivalents at End of Year	$ 519	$ 445	$ 600
SUPPLEMENTAL DISCLOSURE OF CASH PAYMENTS MADE FOR:			
Interest, net of interest capitalized	$ 622	$ 672	$ 270
Income Taxes	$1,265	$ 2,524	$3,963

(1) Fiscal years ended February 1, 2009, and January 28, 2007, include 52 weeks. Fiscal year ended February 3, 2008, includes 53 weeks.

See accompanying Notes to Consolidated Financial Statements.

EXCERPT FROM NOTES TO CONSOLIDATED FINANCIAL STATEMENTS

1. Summary of Significant Accounting Policies (excerpts)

Business, Consolidation and Presentation   The Home Depot, Inc., and its subsidiaries (the "Company") operate The Home Depot stores, which are full-service, warehouse-style stores averaging approximately 105,000 square feet in size. The stores stock approximately 30,000 to 40,000 different kinds of building materials, home improvement supplies, and lawn and garden products that are sold to do-it-yourself customers, do-it-for-me customers, home improvement contractors, tradespeople, and building maintenance professionals. At the end of fiscal 2008, the Company was operating 2,274 stores, which included 1,971 The Home Depot stores, 34 EXPO stores, five Yardbirds stores, and two THD Design Center stores in the United States, including the Commonwealth of Puerto Rico and the territories of the U.S. Virgin Islands and Guam ("U.S."), 176 The Home Depot stores in Canada, 74 The Home Depot stores in Mexico, and 12 The Home Depot stores in China. On January 26, 2009, the Company announced plans to close the EXPO, THD Design Center, and Yardbirds stores as part of the Company's focus on its core business. The Consolidated Financial Statements include the accounts of the Company and its wholly-owned subsidiaries. All significant intercompany transactions have been eliminated in consolidation.

Fiscal Year   The Company's fiscal year is a 52- or 53-week period ending on the Sunday nearest to January 31. Fiscal year ended February 1, 2009 ("fiscal 2008") includes 52 weeks, fiscal year ended February 3, 2008 ("fiscal 2007") includes 53 weeks, and fiscal year ended January 28, 2007 ("fiscal 2006") includes 52 weeks.

Use of Estimates   Management of the Company has made a number of estimates and assumptions relating to the reporting of assets and liabilities, the disclosure of contingent assets and liabilities, and reported amounts of revenues and expenses in preparing these financial statements in conformity with accounting principles generally accepted in the U.S. Actual results could differ from these estimates.

Fair Value of Financial Instruments   The carrying amounts of Cash and Cash Equivalents, Receivables, Short-Term Debt, and Accounts Payable approximate fair value due to the short-term maturities of these financial instruments. The fair value of the Company's investments is discussed under the caption "Short-term Investments" in this Note 1. The fair value of the Company's Long-term Debt is discussed in Note 6.

Cash Equivalents   The Company considers all highly liquid investments purchased with original maturities of three months or less to be cash equivalents. The Company's Cash Equivalents are carried at fair market value and consist primarily of high-grade commercial paper, money market funds, and U.S. government agency securities.

Short-term Investments   Short-term Investments are recorded at fair value based on current market rates and are classified as available-for-sale.

Accounts Receivable   The Company has an agreement with a third-party service provider who directly extends credit to customers, manages the Company's private label credit card program, and owns the related receivables. We evaluated the third-party entities holding the receivables under the program and concluded that they should not be consolidated by the Company in accordance with the provisions of Financial Accounting Standards Board ("FASB") Interpretation No. 46(R), "Consolidation of Variable Interest Entities." The agreement with the third-party service provider expires in 2018, with the Company having the option, but no obligation, to purchase the receivables at the end of the agreement. The deferred interest charges incurred by the Company for its deferred financing programs offered to its customers are included in Cost of Sales. The interchange fees charged to the Company for the customers' use of the cards and the profit sharing with the third-party administrator are included in Selling, General and Administrative expenses ("SG&A"). The sum of the three is referred to by the Company as "the cost of credit" of the private label credit card program.

In addition, certain subsidiaries of the Company extend credit directly to customers in the ordinary course of business. The receivables due from customers were $37 million and $57 million as of February 1, 2009, and February 3, 2008, respectively. The Company's valuation reserve related to accounts receivable was not material to the Consolidated Financial Statements of the Company as of the end of fiscal 2008 or 2007.

Merchandise Inventories   The majority of the Company's Merchandise Inventories are stated at the lower of cost (first-in, first-out) or market, as determined by the retail inventory method. As the inventory retail value is adjusted regularly to reflect market conditions, the inventory valued using the retail method approximates the lower of cost or market. Certain subsidiaries, including retail operations in Canada, Mexico, and China, and distribution centers record Merchandise Inventories at the lower of cost or market, as determined by a cost method. These Merchandise Inventories represent approximately 18% of the total Merchandise Inventories balance. The Company evaluates the inventory valued using a cost method at the end of each quarter to ensure that it is carried at the lower of cost or market. The valuation allowance for Merchandise Inventories valued under a cost method was not material to the Consolidated Financial Statements of the Company as of the end of fiscal 2008 or 2007.

Independent physical inventory counts or cycle counts are taken on a regular basis in each store and distribution center to ensure that amounts reflected in the accompanying Consolidated Financial Statements for Merchandise Inventories are properly stated. During the period between physical inventory counts in stores, the Company accrues for estimated losses related to shrink on a store-by-store basis based on historical shrink results and current trends in the business. Shrink (or in the case of excess inventory, "swell") is the difference between the recorded amount of inventory and the physical inventory. Shrink may occur due to theft, loss, inaccurate records for the receipt of inventory, or deterioration of goods, among other things.

Income Taxes   The Company provides for federal, state, and foreign income taxes currently payable, as well as for those deferred due to timing differences between reporting income and expenses for financial statement purposes versus tax purposes. Federal, state, and foreign tax benefits are recorded as a reduction of income taxes. Deferred tax assets and liabilities are recognized for the future tax consequences attributable to temporary differences between the financial statement carrying amounts of existing assets and liabilities and their respective tax bases. Deferred tax assets and liabilities are measured using enacted income tax rates expected to apply to taxable income in the years in which those temporary differences are expected to be recovered or settled. The effect of a change in income tax rates is recognized as income or expense in the period that includes the enactment date.

Depreciation and Amortization   The Company's Buildings, Furniture, Fixtures and Equipment are recorded at cost and depreciated using the straight-line method over the estimated useful lives of the assets. Leasehold Improvements are amortized using the straight-line method over the original term of the lease or the useful life of the improvement, whichever is shorter. The Company's Property and Equipment is depreciated using the following estimated useful lives:

	Life
Buildings	5–45 years
Furniture, Fixtures and Equipment	3–20 years
Leasehold Improvements	5–45 years

Capitalized Software Costs   The Company capitalizes certain costs related to the acquisition and development of software and amortizes these costs using the straight-line method over the estimated useful life of the software, which is three to six years. These costs are included in Furniture, Fixtures and Equipment in the accompanying Consolidated Balance Sheets. Certain development costs not meeting the criteria for capitalization are expensed as incurred.

Revenues   The Company recognizes revenue, net of estimated returns and sales tax, at the time the customer takes possession of merchandise or receives services. The liability for sales returns is estimated based on historical return levels. When the Company receives payment from customers before the customer has taken possession of the merchandise or the service has been performed, the amount received is recorded as Deferred Revenue in the accompanying Consolidated Balance Sheets until the sale or service is complete. The Company also records Deferred Revenue for the sale of gift cards and recognizes this revenue upon the redemption of gift cards in Net Sales. Gift card breakage income is recognized based upon historical redemption patterns and represents the balance of gift cards for which the Company believes the likelihood of redemption by the customer is remote. During fiscal 2008, 2007, and 2006, the Company recognized $37 million, $36 million, and $33 million, respectively, of gift card breakage income. This income is recorded as Other Income and is included in the accompanying Consolidated Statements of Earnings as a reduction in SG&A.

Services Revenue   Net Sales include services revenue generated through a variety of installation, home maintenance, and professional service programs. In these programs, the customer selects and purchases material for a project and the Company provides or arranges professional installation. These programs are offered through the Company's stores. Under certain programs, when the Company provides or arranges the installation of a project and the subcontractor provides material as part of the installation, both the material and labor are included in services revenue. The Company recognizes this revenue when the service for the customer is complete.

All payments received prior to the completion of services are recorded in Deferred Revenue in the accompanying Consolidated Balance Sheets. Services revenue was $3.1 billion, $3.5 billion, and $3.8 billion for fiscal 2008, 2007, and 2006, respectively.

Self-Insurance   The Company is self-insured for certain losses related to general liability, product liability, automobile, workers' compensation, and medical claims. The expected ultimate cost for claims incurred as of the balance sheet date is not discounted and is recognized as a liability. The expected ultimate cost of claims is estimated based upon analysis of historical data and actuarial estimates.

Prepaid Advertising   Television and radio advertising production costs, along with media placement costs, are expensed when the advertisement first appears. Included in Other Current Assets in the accompanying Consolidated Balance Sheets are $18 million and $31 million, respectively, at the end of fiscal 2008 and 2007 relating to prepayments of production costs for print and broadcast advertising as well as sponsorship promotions.

Vendor Allowances   Vendor allowances primarily consist of volume rebates that are earned as a result of attaining certain purchase levels and advertising co-op allowances for the promotion of vendors' products that are typically based on guaranteed minimum amounts with additional amounts being earned for attaining certain purchase levels. These vendor allowances are accrued as earned, with those allowances received as a result of attaining certain purchase levels accrued over the incentive period based on estimates of purchases.

Volume rebates and certain advertising co-op allowances earned are initially recorded as a reduction in Merchandise Inventories and a subsequent reduction in Cost of Sales when the related product is sold. Certain advertising co-op allowances that are reimbursements of specific, incremental, and identifiable costs incurred to promote vendors' products are recorded as an offset against advertising expense. In fiscal 2008, 2007, and 2006, gross advertising expense was $1.0 billion, $1.2 billion, and $1.2 billion, respectively, which was recorded in SG&A. Specific, incremental, and identifiable advertising co-op allowances were $107 million, $120 million, and $83 million for fiscal 2008, 2007, and 2006, respectively, and were recorded as an offset to advertising expense in SG&A.

Cost of Sales   Cost of Sales includes the actual cost of merchandise sold and services performed, the cost of transportation of merchandise from vendors to the Company's stores, locations or customers, the operating cost of the Company's sourcing and distribution network, and the cost of deferred interest programs offered through the Company's private label credit card program.

The cost of handling and shipping merchandise from the Company's stores, locations, or distribution centers to the customer is classified as SG&A. The cost of shipping and handling, including internal costs and payments to third parties, classified as SG&A was $501 million, $571 million, and $545 million in fiscal 2008, 2007, and 2006, respectively.

Goodwill and Other Intangible Assets   Goodwill represents the excess of purchase price over the fair value of net assets acquired. The Company does not amortize goodwill, but does assess the recoverability of goodwill in the third quarter of each fiscal year by determining whether the fair value of each reporting unit supports its carrying value. The fair values of the Company's identified reporting units were estimated using the present value of expected future discounted cash flows.

The Company amortizes the cost of other intangible assets over their estimated useful lives, which range from 1 to 20 years, unless such lives are deemed indefinite. Intangible assets with indefinite lives are tested in the third quarter of each fiscal year for impairment. The Company recorded no impairment charges for goodwill or other intangible assets for fiscal 2008, 2007, or 2006.

Impairment of Long-Lived Assets   The Company evaluates the carrying value of long-lived assets when management makes the decision to relocate or close a store or other location, or when circumstances indicate the carrying amount of an asset may not be recoverable. A store's assets are evaluated for impairment by comparing its undiscounted cash flows with its carrying value. If the carrying value is greater than the undiscounted cash flows, a provision is made to write down the related assets to fair value if the carrying value is greater than the fair value. Impairment losses are recorded as a component of SG&A in the accompanying Consolidated Statements of Earnings. When a location closes, the Company also recognizes in SG&A the net present value of future lease obligations, less estimated sublease income.

In fiscal 2008, the Company recorded $580 million of asset impairments and $252 million of lease obligation costs as part of its Rationalization Charges. See Note 2 for more details on the Rationalization Charges. The Company also recorded impairments on the other closings and relocations in the ordinary course of business, which were not material to the Consolidated Financial Statements in fiscal 2008, 2007, and 2006.

Comprehensive Income   Comprehensive Income includes Net Earnings adjusted for certain revenues, expenses, gains, and losses that are excluded from Net Earnings under accounting principles generally accepted in the U.S. Adjustments to Net Earnings and Accumulated Other Comprehensive Income consist primarily of foreign currency translation adjustments.

Foreign Currency Translation   Assets and Liabilities denominated in a foreign currency are translated into U.S. dollars at the current rate of exchange on the last day of the reporting period. Revenues and Expenses are generally translated using average exchange rates for the period and equity transactions are translated using the actual rate on the day of the transaction.

Segment Information   The Company operates within a single reportable segment primarily within North America. Net Sales for the Company outside of the U.S. were $7.4 billion for fiscal 2008 and 2007 and were $6.3 billion for fiscal 2006. Long-lived assets outside of the U.S. totaled $2.8 billion and $3.1 billion as of February 1, 2009, and February 3, 2008, respectively.

Other notes to the financial statements can be downloaded from the Web sites indicated on page A.1.

APPENDIX B

Excerpts from the Fiscal 2008 Annual Report of Lowe's Companies, Inc.

Note: The materials in Appendix B are selected from the full Annual Report of Lowe's Companies, Inc., for fiscal year 2008, which ended January 30, 2009. The complete annual report is available from the textbook Web site at www.mhhe.com/phillips3e or from http://investor.shareholder.com/lowes/annual.cfm.

MANAGEMENT'S REPORT ON INTERNAL CONTROL OVER FINANCIAL REPORTING

Management of Lowe's Companies, Inc., and its subsidiaries is responsible for establishing and maintaining adequate internal control over financial reporting (Internal Control) as defined in Rule 13a-15(f) under the Securities Exchange Act of 1934, as amended. Our Internal Control was designed to provide reasonable assurance to our management and the Board of Directors regarding the reliability of financial reporting and the preparation and fair presentation of published financial statements.

All internal control systems, no matter how well designed, have inherent limitations, including the possibility of human error and the circumvention or overriding of controls. Therefore, even those systems determined to be effective can provide only reasonable assurance with respect to the reliability of financial reporting and financial statement preparation and presentation. Further, because of changes in conditions, the effectiveness may vary over time.

Our management, with the participation of the Chief Executive Officer and Chief Financial Officer, evaluated the effectiveness of our Internal Control as of January 30, 2009. In evaluating our Internal Control, we used the criteria set forth by the Committee of Sponsoring Organizations of the Treadway Commission (COSO) in *Internal Control— Integrated Framework*. Based on our management's assessment, we have concluded that, as of January 30, 2009, our Internal Control is effective.

Deloitte & Touche LLP, the independent registered public accounting firm that audited the financial statements contained in this report, was engaged to audit our Internal Control. Their report follows.

REPORT OF INDEPENDENT REGISTERED PUBLIC ACCOUNTING FIRM

To the Board of Directors and Shareholders of Lowe's Companies, Inc.
Mooresville, North Carolina

We have audited the accompanying consolidated balance sheets of Lowe's Companies, Inc., and subsidiaries (the "Company") as of January 30, 2009, and February 1, 2008, and the related consolidated statements of earnings, shareholders' equity, and cash flows for each of the three fiscal years in the period ended January 30, 2009. These financial statements are the responsibility of the Company's management. Our responsibility is to express an opinion on these financial statements based on our audits.

We conducted our audits in accordance with the standards of the Public Company Accounting Oversight Board (United States). Those standards require that we plan and perform the audit to obtain reasonable assurance about whether the financial statements are free of material misstatement. An audit includes examining, on a test basis, evidence supporting the amounts and disclosures in the financial statements. An audit also includes assessing the accounting principles used and significant estimates made by management, as well as evaluating the overall financial statement presentation. We believe that our audits provide a reasonable basis for our opinion.

In our opinion, such consolidated financial statements present fairly, in all material respects, the financial position of the Company at January 30, 2009, and February 1, 2008, and the results of its operations and its cash flows for each of the three fiscal years in the period ended January 30, 2009, in conformity with accounting principles generally accepted in the United States of America.

We have also audited, in accordance with the standards of the Public Company Accounting Oversight Board (United States), the Company's internal control over financial reporting as of January 30, 2009, based on the criteria established in *Internal Control—Integrated Framework* issued by the Committee of Sponsoring Organizations of the Treadway Commission and our report dated March 31, 2009, expressed an unqualified opinion on the Company's internal control over financial reporting.

/s/ Deloitte & Touche LLP

Charlotte, North Carolina
March 31, 2009

REPORT OF INDEPENDENT REGISTERED PUBLIC ACCOUNTING FIRM

To the Board of Directors and Shareholders of Lowe's Companies, Inc., Mooresville, North Carolina

We have audited the internal control over financial reporting of Lowe's Companies, Inc., and subsidiaries (the "Company") as of January 30, 2009, based on criteria established in *Internal Control—Integrated Framework* issued by the Committee of Sponsoring Organizations of the Treadway Commission. The Company's management is responsible for maintaining effective internal control over financial reporting and for its assessment of the effectiveness of internal control over financial reporting, included in the accompanying Management's Report on Internal Control Over Financial Reporting. Our responsibility is to express an opinion on the Company's internal control over financial reporting based on our audit.

We conducted our audit in accordance with the standards of the Public Company Accounting Oversight Board (United States). Those standards require that we plan and perform the audit to obtain reasonable assurance about whether effective internal control over financial reporting was maintained in all material respects. Our audit included obtaining an understanding of internal control over financial reporting, assessing the risk that a material weakness exists, testing and evaluating the design and operating effectiveness of internal control based on the assessed risk, and performing such other procedures as we considered necessary in the circumstances. We believe that our audit provides a reasonable basis for our opinion.

A company's internal control over financial reporting is a process designed by, or under the supervision of, the company's principal executive and principal financial officers, or persons performing similar functions, and effected by the company's board of directors, management, and other personnel to provide reasonable assurance regarding the reliability of financial reporting and the preparation of financial statements for external purposes in accordance with generally accepted accounting principles. A company's internal control over financial reporting includes those policies and procedures that (1) pertain to the maintenance of records that, in reasonable detail, accurately and fairly reflect the transactions and dispositions of the assets of the company; (2) provide reasonable assurance that transactions are recorded as necessary to permit preparation of financial statements in accordance with generally accepted accounting principles, and that receipts and expenditures of the company are being made only in accordance with authorizations of management and directors of the company; and (3) provide reasonable assurance regarding prevention or timely detection of unauthorized acquisition, use, or disposition of the company's assets that could have a material effect on the financial statements.

Because of the inherent limitations of internal control over financial reporting, including the possibility of collusion or improper management override of controls, material misstatements due to error or fraud may not be prevented or detected on a timely basis. Also, projections of any evaluation of the effectiveness of the internal control over financial reporting to future periods are subject to the risk that the controls may become inadequate because of changes in conditions, or that the degree of compliance with the policies or procedures may deteriorate.

In our opinion, the Company maintained, in all material respects, effective internal control over financial reporting as of January 30, 2009, based on the criteria established in *Internal Control—Integrated Framework* issued by the Committee of Sponsoring Organizations of the Treadway Commission.

We have also audited, in accordance with the standards of the Public Company Accounting Oversight Board (United States), the consolidated financial statements as of and for the fiscal year ended January 30, 2009, of the Company and our report dated March 31, 2009, expressed an unqualified opinion on those financial statements.

/s/ Deloitte & Touche LLP

Charlotte, North Carolina
March 31, 2009

LOWE'S COMPANIES, INC.
Consolidated Statements of Earnings

(in millions, except per share and percentage data)

Fiscal years ended on	January 30, 2009	% Sales	February 1, 2008	% Sales	February 2, 2007	% Sales
Net Sales (Note 1)	$48,230	100.00%	$48,283	100.00%	$46,927	100.00%
Cost of Sales (Note 1)	31,729	65.79	31,556	65.36	30,729	65.48
Gross Margin	16,501	34.21	16,727	34.64	16,198	34.52
Expenses:						
Selling, General and Administrative	11,074	22.96	10,515	21.78	9,738	20.75
Store Opening Costs (Note 1)	102	0.21	141	0.29	146	0.31
Depreciation (Notes 1 and 4)	1,539	3.19	1,366	2.83	1,162	2.48
Interest, Net (Notes 10 and 15)	280	0.58	194	0.40	154	0.33
Total Expenses	12,995	26.94	12,216	25.30	11,200	23.87
Pre-tax Earnings	3,506	7.27	4,511	9.34	4,998	10.65
Income Tax Provision (Note 10)	1,311	2.72	1,702	3.52	1,893	4.03
Net Earnings	$ 2,195	4.55%	$ 2,809	5.82%	$ 3,105	6.62%
Basic earnings per share (Note 11)	$ 1.51		$ 1.90		$ 2.02	
Diluted earnings per share (Note 11)	$ 1.49		$ 1.86		$ 1.99	
Cash dividends per share	$ 0.335		$ 0.290		$ 0.180	

See accompanying notes to consolidated financial statements.

LOWE'S COMPANIES, INC.
Consolidated Balance Sheets

(in millions, except par value and percentage data)	January 30, 2009	% Total	February 1, 2008	% Total
Assets				
Current Assets:				
Cash and Cash Equivalents (Note 1)	$ 245	0.7%	$ 281	0.9%
Short-term Investments (Notes 1, 2 and 3)	416	1.3	249	0.8
Merchandise Inventory, Net (Note 1)	8,209	25.1	7,611	24.6
Deferred Income Taxes, Net (Notes 1 and 10)	166	0.5	247	0.8
Other Current Assets (Note 1)	215	0.7	298	1.0
Total Current Assets	9,251	28.3	8,686	28.1
Property, less Accumulated Depreciation (Notes 1 and 4)	22,722	69.5	21,361	69.2
Long-term Investments (Notes 1, 2 and 3)	253	0.8	509	1.7
Other Assets (Note 1)	460	1.4	313	1.0
Total Assets	$32,686	100.0%	$30,869	100.0%
Liabilities and Shareholders' Equity				
Current Liabilities:				
Short-term Borrowings (Note 5)	$ 987	3.0%	$ 1,064	3.5%
Current Maturities of Long-term Debt (Note 6)	34	0.1	40	0.1
Accounts Payable (Note 1)	4,109	12.6	3,713	12.0
Accrued Compensation and Employee Benefits	434	1.3	467	1.5
Self-insurance Liabilities (Note 1)	751	2.3	671	2.2
Deferred Revenue (Note 1)	674	2.1	717	2.3
Other Current Liabilities (Note 1)	1,033	3.1	1,079	3.5
Total Current liabilities	8,022	24.5	7,751	25.1
Long-term Debt, Excluding Current Maturities (Notes 3, 6 and 12)	5,039	15.4	5,576	18.1
Deferred Income Taxes, Net (Notes 1 and 10)	660	2.0	670	2.2
Other Liabilities (Note 1)	910	2.9	774	2.5
Total Liabilities	14,631	44.8	14,771	47.9
Commitments and Contingencies (Note 13)				
Shareholders' Equity (Note 7):				
Preferred Stock — $5 par value, none issued	—	—	—	—
Common Stock — $.50 par value;				
Shares issued and outstanding				
January 30, 2009: 1,470				
February 1, 2008: 1,458	735	2.2	729	2.3
Capital in Excess of Par Value	277	0.8	16	0.1
Retained Earnings	17,049	52.2	15,345	49.7
Accumulated Other Comprehensive (Loss) Income (Note 1)	(6)	—	8	—
Total Shareholders' Equity	18,055	55.2	16,098	52.1
Total Liabilities and Shareholders' Equity	$32,686	100.0%	$30,869	100.0%

See accompanying notes to consolidated financial statements.

LOWE'S COMPANIES, INC.
Consolidated Statements of Shareholders' Equity

(in millions)	Common Stock Shares	Common Stock Amount	Capital in Excess of Par Value	Retained Earnings	Accumulated Other Comprehensive (Loss) Income	Total Shareholders' Equity
Balance February 3, 2006	1,568	$784	$1,320	$12,191	$ 1	$14,296
Comprehensive income (Note 1):						
Net earnings				3,105		
Foreign currency translation					(2)	
Net unrealized investment gains (Note 3)					2	
Total comprehensive income						3,105
Tax effect of non-qualified stock options			21			21
Cash dividends				(276)		(276)
Share-based payment expense (Note 8)			59			59
Repurchase of common stock (Note 7)	(57)	(28)	(1,549)	(160)		(1,737)
Conversion of debt to common stock (Note 6)	4	2	80			82
Employee stock options exercised and restricted stock issued (Note 8)	7	3	96			99
Employee stock purchase plan (Note 8)	3	1	75			76
Balance February 2, 2007	1,525	$762	$ 102	$14,860	$ 1	$15,725
Cumulative effect adjustment (Note 10)				(8)		(8)
Comprehensive income (Note 1):						
Net earnings				2,809		
Foreign currency translation					7	
Total comprehensive income						2,816
Tax effect of non-qualified stock options			12			12
Cash dividends				(428)		(428)
Share-based payment expense (Note 8)			99			99
Repurchase of common stock (Note 7)	(76)	(38)	(349)	(1,888)		(2,275)
Conversion of debt to common stock (Note 6)	1	—	13			13
Employee stock options exercised and restricted stock issued (Note 8)	5	3	61			64
Employee stock purchase plan (Note 8)	3	2	78			80
Balance February 1, 2008	1,458	$729	$ 16	$15,345	$ 8	$16,098
Comprehensive income (Note 1):						
Net earnings				2,195		
Foreign currency translation					(13)	
Net unrealized investment losses (Note 3)					(1)	
Total comprehensive income						2,181
Tax effect of non-qualified stock options			5			5
Cash dividends				(491)		(491)
Share-based payment expense (Note 8)			95			95
Repurchase of common stock	—	—	(8)			(8)
Conversion of debt to common stock (Note 6)	—	—	1			1
Employee stock options exercised						
Employee stock options exercised and restricted stock issued (Note 8)	8	4	94			98
Employee stock purchase plan (Note 8)	4	2	74			76
Balance January 30, 2009	1,470	$735	$ 277	$17,049	$ (6)	$18,055

See accompanying notes to consolidated financial statements.

LOWE'S COMPANIES, INC.
Consolidated Statements of Cash Flows

(in millions) Fiscal years ended on	January 30, 2009	February 1, 2008	February 2, 2007
Cash flows from operating activities:			
Net earnings	$2,195	$2,809	$3,105
Adjustments to reconcile net earnings to net cash provided by operating activities:			
Depreciation and amortization	1,667	1,464	1,237
Deferred income taxes	69	2	(6)
Loss on property and other assets	89	51	23
Loss on redemption of long-term debt	8	—	—
Transaction loss from exchange rate changes	3	—	—
Share-based payment expense	95	99	62
Changes in operating assets and liabilities:			
Merchandise inventory—net	(611)	(464)	(509)
Other operating assets	31	(64)	(135)
Accounts payable	402	185	692
Other operating liabilities	174	265	33
Net cash provided by operating activities	**4,122**	**4,347**	**4,502**
Cash flows from investing activities:			
Purchases of short-term investments	(210)	(920)	(284)
Proceeds from sale/maturity of short-term investments	431	1,183	572
Purchases of long-term investments	(1,148)	(1,588)	(558)
Proceeds from sale/maturity of long-term investments	994	1,162	415
Increase in other long-term assets	(56)	(7)	(16)
Property acquired	(3,266)	(4,010)	(3,916)
Proceeds from sale of property and other long-term assets	293	57	72
Net cash used in investing activities	**(3,226)**	**(4,123)**	**(3,715)**
Cash flows from financing activities:			
Net (decrease) increase in short-term borrowings	(57)	1,041	23
Proceeds from issuance of long-term debt	15	1,296	989
Repayment of long-term debt	(573)	(96)	(33)
Proceeds from issuance of common stock under employee stock purchase plan	76	80	76
Proceeds from issuance of common stock from stock options exercised	98	69	100
Cash dividend payments	(491)	(428)	(276)
Repurchase of common stock	(8)	(2,275)	(1,737)
Excess tax benefits of share-based payments	1	6	12
Net cash used in financing activities	**(939)**	**(307)**	**(846)**
Effect of exchange rate changes on cash	**7**	**—**	**—**
Net decrease in cash and cash equivalents	(36)	(83)	(59)
Cash and cash equivalents, beginning of year	281	364	423
Cash and cash equivalents, end of year	**$ 245**	**$ 281**	**$ 364**

See accompanying notes to consolidated financial statements.

EXCERPTS FROM NOTES TO CONSOLIDATED FINANCIAL STATEMENTS

NOTE 1: Summary of Significant Accounting Policies (excerpts)

Lowe's Companies, Inc., and subsidiaries (the Company) is the world's second-largest home improvement retailer and operated 1,649 stores in the United States and Canada at January 30, 2009. Below are those accounting policies considered by the Company to be significant.

Fiscal Year   The Company's fiscal year ends on the Friday nearest the end of January. Each of the fiscal years presented contained 52 weeks. All references herein for the years 2008, 2007, and 2006 represent the fiscal years ended January 30, 2009, February 1, 2008, and February 2, 2007, respectively.

Principles of Consolidation   The consolidated financial statements include the accounts of the Company and its wholly-owned or controlled operating subsidiaries. All material intercompany accounts and transactions have been eliminated.

Foreign Currency   The functional currencies of the Company's international subsidiaries are primarily the local currencies of the countries in which the subsidiaries are located. Foreign currency denominated assets and liabilities are translated into U.S. dollars using the exchange rates in effect at the consolidated balance sheet date. Results of operations and cash flows are translated using the average exchange rates throughout the period. The effect of exchange rate fluctuations on translation of assets and liabilities is included as a component of shareholders' equity in accumulated other comprehensive (loss) income. Gains and losses from foreign currency transactions, which are included in selling, general and administrative (SG&A) expense, have not been significant.

Use of Estimates   The preparation of the Company's financial statements in accordance with accounting principles generally accepted in the United States of America requires management to make estimates that affect the reported amounts of assets, liabilities, sales and expenses, and related disclosures of contingent assets and liabilities. The Company bases these estimates on historical results and various other assumptions believed to be reasonable, all of which form the basis for making estimates concerning the carrying values of assets and liabilities that are not readily available from other sources. Actual results may differ from these estimates.

Cash and Cash Equivalents   Cash and cash equivalents include cash on hand, demand deposits, and short-term investments with original maturities of three months or less when purchased. The majority of payments due from financial institutions for the settlement of credit card and debit card transactions process within two business days and are, therefore, classified as cash and cash equivalents.

Investments   The Company has a cash management program which provides for the investment of cash balances not expected to be used in current operations in financial instruments that have maturities of up to 10 years.

Investments, exclusive of cash equivalents, with a stated maturity date of one year or less from the balance sheet date or that are expected to be used in current operations, are classified as short-term investments. The Company's trading securities are also classified as short-term investments. All other investments are classified as long-term. As of January 30, 2009, investments consisted primarily of money market funds, certificates of deposit, municipal obligations, and mutual funds. Restricted balances pledged as collateral for letters of credit for the Company's extended warranty program and for a portion of the Company's casualty insurance and Installed Sales program liabilities are also classified as investments.

The Company maintains investment securities in conjunction with certain employee benefit plans that are classified as trading securities. These securities are carried at fair market value with unrealized gains and losses included in SG&A expense. All other investment securities are classified as available-for-sale and are carried at fair market value with unrealized gains and losses included in accumulated other comprehensive (loss) income in shareholders' equity.

Merchandise Inventory   Inventory is stated at the lower of cost or market using the first-in, first-out method of inventory accounting. The cost of inventory also includes certain costs associated with the preparation of inventory for resale, including distribution center costs, and is net of vendor funds.

The Company records an inventory reserve for the anticipated loss associated with selling inventories below cost. This reserve is based on management's current knowledge with respect to inventory levels, sales trends, and historical experience. Management does not believe the Company's merchandise inventories are subject to significant risk of obsolescence in the near term, and management has the ability to adjust purchasing practices based on anticipated sales trends and general economic conditions. However, changes in consumer purchasing patterns could result in the need for additional reserves. The Company also records an inventory reserve for the estimated shrinkage between physical inventories. This reserve is based primarily on actual shrink results from previous physical inventories. Changes in the estimated shrink reserve may be necessary based on the timing and results of physical inventories. Management believes it has sufficient current and historical knowledge to record reasonable estimates for both of these inventory reserves.

Credit Programs   The majority of the Company's accounts receivable arises from sales of goods and services to Commercial Business Customers. The Company has an agreement with General Electric Company and its subsidiaries (GE) under which GE purchases at face value new commercial business accounts receivable originated by the Company and services these accounts. Sales generated through the Company's proprietary credit cards are not reflected in receivables. Under an agreement with GE, credit is extended directly to customers by GE. All credit-program-related services are performed and controlled directly by GE. The total portfolio of receivables held by GE, including both receivables originated by GE from the Company's proprietary credit cards and commercial business accounts receivable originated by the Company and sold to GE, approximated $6.8 billion at January 30, 2009, and $6.6 billion at February 1, 2008.

Property and Depreciation   Property is recorded at cost. Costs associated with major additions are capitalized and depreciated. Capital assets are expected to yield future benefits and have useful lives which exceed one year. The total cost of a capital asset generally includes all applicable sales taxes, delivery costs, installation costs, and other appropriate costs incurred by the Company in the case of self-constructed assets. Upon disposal, the cost of properties and related accumulated depreciation are removed from the accounts, with gains and losses reflected in SG&A expense on the consolidated statements of earnings.

Depreciation is provided over the estimated useful lives of the depreciable assets. Assets are depreciated using the straight-line method. Leasehold improvements are depreciated over the shorter of their estimated useful lives or the term of the related lease, which may include one or more option renewal periods where failure to exercise such options would result in an economic penalty in such amount that renewal appears, at the inception of the lease, to be reasonably assured. During the term of a lease, if a substantial additional investment is made in a leased location, the Company reevaluates its definition of lease term to determine whether the investment, together with any penalties related to non-renewal, would constitute an economic penalty in such amount that renewal appears, at the time of the reevaluation, to be reasonably assured.

Long-Lived Asset Impairment/Exit Activities   The carrying amounts of long-lived assets are reviewed whenever events or changes in circumstances indicate that the carrying amount may not be recoverable.

For long-lived assets held-for-use, a potential impairment has occurred if projected future undiscounted cash flows expected to result from the use and eventual disposition of the assets are less than the carrying value of the assets. An impairment loss is recognized when the carrying amount of the long-lived asset is not recoverable and exceeds its fair value. The Company estimates fair value based on projected future discounted cash flows from the use and eventual disposition of the assets.

For long-lived assets to be abandoned, the Company considers the asset to be disposed of when it ceases to be used. Until it ceases to be used, the Company continues to classify the assets as held-for-use and tests for potential impairment accordingly. If the Company commits to a plan to abandon a long-lived asset before the end of its previously estimated useful life, depreciation estimates are revised.

For long-lived assets held-for-sale, an impairment charge is recorded if the carrying amount of the asset exceeds its fair value less cost to sell. Fair value is based on a market appraisal or a valuation technique that considers various factors, including local market conditions. A long-lived asset is not depreciated while it is classified as held-for-sale.

The charge for impairment is included in SG&A expense. The Company recorded long-lived asset impairment charges of $21 million during 2008, including $16 million for operating stores and $5 million for relocated stores, closed stores, and other excess properties. The Company recorded long-lived asset impairment charges of $28 million and $5 million for relocated stores, closed stores, and other excess properties in 2007 and 2006, respectively.

The net carrying value for relocated stores, closed stores, and other excess properties that are expected to be sold within the next 12 months is classified as held-for-sale and included in other current assets on the consolidated balance sheets. Assets held-for-sale totaled $6 million at January 30, 2009, and $28 million at February 1, 2008. The net carrying value for relocated stores, closed stores, and other excess properties that do not meet the held-for-sale criteria is included in other assets (non-current) on the consolidated balance sheets and totaled $174 million and $91 million at January 30, 2009, and February 1, 2008, respectively.

Leases   For lease agreements that provide for escalating rent payments or free-rent occupancy periods, the Company recognizes rent expense on a straight-line basis over the non-cancelable lease term and option renewal periods where failure to exercise such options would result in an economic penalty in such amount that renewal appears, at the inception of the lease, to be reasonably assured. The lease term commences on the date that the Company takes possession of or controls the physical use of the property. Deferred rent is included in other liabilities (non-current) on the consolidated balance sheets.

Assets under capital lease are amortized in accordance with the Company's normal depreciation policy for owned assets or, if shorter, over the non-cancelable lease term and any option renewal period where failure to exercise such option would result in an economic penalty in such amount that renewal appears, at the inception of the lease, to be reasonably assured. The amortization of the assets is included in depreciation expense on the consolidated financial statements. During the term of a lease, if a substantial additional investment is made in a leased location, the Company reevaluates its definition of lease term.

Accounts Payable   In June 2007, the Company entered into a customer-managed services agreement with a third party to provide an accounts payable tracking system which facilitates participating suppliers' ability to finance payment obligations from the Company with designated third-party financial institutions. Participating suppliers may, at their sole discretion, make offers to finance one or more payment obligations of the Company prior to their scheduled due dates at a discounted price to participating financial institutions. The Company's goal in entering into this arrangement is to capture overall supply chain savings, in the form of pricing, payment terms, or vendor funding, created by facilitating suppliers' ability to finance payment obligations at more favorable discount rates, while providing them with greater working capital flexibility.

Self-Insurance   The Company is self-insured for certain losses relating to workers' compensation, automobile, property, and general and product liability claims. The Company has stop-loss coverage to limit the exposure arising from these claims. The Company is also self-insured for certain losses relating to extended warranty and medical and dental claims. Self-insurance claims filed and claims incurred but not reported are accrued based upon management's estimates of the discounted ultimate cost for self-insured claims incurred using actuarial assumptions followed in the insurance industry and historical experience.

Income Taxes   The Company establishes deferred income tax assets and liabilities for temporary differences between the tax and financial accounting bases of assets and liabilities. The tax effects of such differences are reflected in the balance sheet at the enacted tax rates expected to be in effect when the differences reverse. A valuation allowance is recorded to reduce the carrying amount of deferred tax assets if it is more likely than not that all or a portion of the asset will not be realized. The tax balances and income tax expense recognized by the Company are based on management's interpretation of the tax statutes of multiple jurisdictions.

The Company establishes a reserve for tax positions for which there is uncertainty as to whether or not the position will be ultimately sustained. The Company includes interest related to tax issues as part of net interest on the consolidated financial statements. The Company records any applicable penalties related to tax issues within the income tax provision.

Revenue Recognition   The Company recognizes revenues, net of sales tax, when sales transactions occur and customers take possession of the merchandise. A provision for anticipated merchandise returns is provided through a reduction of sales and cost of sales in the period that the related sales are recorded. Revenues from product installation services are recognized when the installation is completed. Deferred revenues associated with amounts received for which customers have not yet taken possession of merchandise or for which installation has not yet been completed were $328 million and $332 million at January 30, 2009, and February 1, 2008, respectively.

Revenues from stored value cards, which include gift cards and returned merchandise credits, are deferred and recognized when the cards are redeemed. The liability associated with outstanding stored value cards was $346 million and $385 million at January 30, 2009, and February 1, 2008, respectively, and these amounts are included in deferred revenue on the consolidated balance sheets. The Company recognizes income from unredeemed stored value cards at the point at which redemption becomes remote. The Company's stored value cards have no expiration date or dormancy fees. Therefore, to determine when redemption is remote, the Company analyzes an aging of the unredeemed cards based on the date of last stored value card use.

Extended Warranties   Lowe's sells separately-priced extended warranty contracts under a Lowe's-branded program for which the Company is ultimately self-insured. The Company recognizes revenue from extended warranty sales on a straight-line basis over the respective contract term. Extended warranty contract terms primarily range from one to four years from the date of purchase or the end of the manufacturer's warranty, as applicable. The Company's extended warranty deferred revenue is included in other liabilities (non-current) on the consolidated balance sheets.

Advertising   Costs associated with advertising are charged to expense as incurred. Advertising expenses were $789 million, $788 million, and $873 million in 2008, 2007, and 2006, respectively.

Shipping and Handling Costs The Company includes shipping and handling costs relating to the delivery of products directly from vendors to customers by third parties in cost of sales. Shipping and handling costs, which include salaries and vehicle operations expenses relating to the delivery of products from stores to customers, are classified as SG&A expense. Shipping and handling costs included in SG&A expense were $305 million, $307 million, and $310 million in 2008, 2007, and 2006, respectively.

Store Opening Costs Costs of opening new or relocated retail stores, which include payroll and supply costs incurred prior to store opening and grand opening advertising costs, are charged to operations as incurred.

Comprehensive Income The Company reports comprehensive income on its consolidated statements of shareholders' equity. Comprehensive income represents changes in shareholders' equity from non-owner sources and is comprised primarily of net earnings plus or minus unrealized gains or losses on available-for-sale securities, as well as foreign currency translation adjustments. Unrealized gains, net of tax, on available-for-sale securities classified in accumulated other comprehensive (loss) income on the consolidated balance sheets were $2 million at both January 30, 2009, and February 1, 2008. Foreign currency translation losses, net of tax, classified in accumulated other comprehensive (loss) income were $8 million at January 30, 2009, and foreign currency translation gains, net of tax, were $6 million at February 1, 2008. The reclassification adjustments for gains/losses included in net earnings were not significant for any of the periods presented.

Segment Information The Company's operating segments, representing the Company's home improvement retail stores, are aggregated within one reportable segment based on the way the Company manages its business. The Company's home improvement retail stores exhibit similar long-term economic characteristics, sell similar products and services, use similar processes to sell those products and services, and sell their products and services to similar classes of customers. The amounts of long-lived assets and net sales outside the U.S. were not significant for any of the periods presented.

Reclassifications Certain prior period amounts have been reclassified to conform to current classifications. The previous accrued salaries and wages caption was replaced with a new caption, accrued compensation and employee benefits, on the consolidated balance sheets. As part of this, certain prior period amounts were reclassified from other current liabilities into accrued compensation and employee benefits.

Other notes to the financial statements can be downloaded from the Web sites indicated on page B.1.

Present and Future Value Concepts

The concepts of present value (PV) and future value (FV) are based on the time value of money. The **time value of money** is the idea that, quite simply, money received today is worth more than money to be received one year from today (or at any other future date), because it can be used to earn interest. If you invest $1,000 today at 10 percent, you will have $1,100 in one year. So $1,000 in one year is worth $100 less than $1,000 today because you lose the opportunity to earn the $100 in interest.

In some business situations, you will know the dollar amount of a cash flow that occurs in the future and will need to determine its value now. This type of situation is known as a **present value** problem. The opposite situation occurs when you know the dollar amount of a cash flow that occurs today and need to determine its value at some point in the future. These situations are called **future value** problems. The value of money changes over time because money can earn interest. The following table illustrates the basic difference between present value and future value problems:

	Now	Future
Present value	?	$1,000
Future value	$1,000	?

Present and future value problems may involve two types of cash flow: a single payment or an annuity (which is the fancy word for a series of equal cash payments). Combining two types of time value of money problems with two types of cash flows yields four different situations:

1. Future value of a single payment
2. Present value of a single payment
3. Future value of an annuity
4. Present value of an annuity

Most inexpensive handheld calculators and any spreadsheet program can perform the detailed arithmetic computations required to solve future value and present value problems. In later courses and in all business situations, you will probably use a calculator or computer to solve these problems. At this stage, we encourage you to solve problems using Tables C.1 through C.4 at the end of this appendix. We believe that using the tables will give you a better understanding of how and why present and future value concepts apply to business problems. The tables give the value of

YOU SHOULD KNOW

Time value of money: The idea that money received today is worth more than the same amount received in the future because it can be invested today to earn interest over time.

YOU SHOULD KNOW

Present value: The current value of an amount to be received in the future. It is calculated by discounting a future amount for compound interest. **Future value:** The amount to which an amount will increase as the result of compound interest.

a $1 cash flow (single payment or annuity) for different periods (n) and at different interest rates (i). If a problem involves payments other than $1, multiply the value from the table by the amount of the payment.[1] In the final section of this appendix, we explain how to use Excel to compute present values.

Computing Future and Present Values of a Single Amount

FUTURE VALUE OF A SINGLE AMOUNT

In future value of a single amount problems, you will be asked to calculate how much money you will have in the future as the result of investing a certain amount in the present. If you were to receive a gift of $10,000, for instance, you might decide to put it in a savings account and use the money as a down payment on a house after you graduate. The future value computation would tell you how much money will be available when you graduate.

To solve a future value problem, you need to know three items:

1. Amount to be invested.
2. Interest rate (i) the amount will earn.
3. Number of periods (n) in which the amount will earn interest.

The future value concept is based on compound interest, which simply means that interest is calculated on top of interest. Thus, the amount of interest for each period is calculated using the principal plus any interest not paid out in prior periods. Graphically, the calculation of the future value of $1 for three periods at an interest rate of 10 percent may be represented as follows:

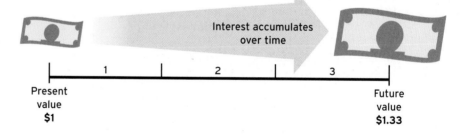

Assume that on January 1, 2010, you deposit $1,000 in a savings account at 10 percent annual interest, compounded annually. At the end of three years, the $1,000 will have increased to $1,331 as follows:

Year	Amount at Start of Year	+	Interest During the Year	=	Amount at End of Year
1	$1,000	+	$1,000 × 10% = $100	=	$1,100
2	1,100	+	1,100 × 10% = 110	=	1,210
3	1,210	+	1,210 × 10% = 121	=	1,331

---

[1]Present value and future value problems involve cash flows. The basic concepts are the same for cash inflows (receipts) and cash outflows (payments). No fundamental differences exist between present value and future value calculations for cash payments versus cash receipts.

We can avoid the detailed arithmetic by referring to Table C.1, Future Value of $1, on page C.14. For $i = 10\%$, $n = 3$, we find the value 1.3310. We then compute the balance at the end of year 3 as follows:

> From Table C.1,
> Interest rate = 10%
> $n = 3$

$$\$1,000 \times 1.3310 = \$1,331$$

Note that the increase of $331 is due to the time value of money. It is interest revenue to the owner of the savings account and interest expense to the bank.

PRESENT VALUE OF A SINGLE AMOUNT

The present value of a single amount is the worth to you today of receiving that amount some time in the future. For instance, you might be offered an opportunity to invest in a financial instrument that would pay you $1,000 in 3 years. Before you decided whether to invest, you would want to determine the present value of the instrument.

To compute the present value of an amount to be received in the future, we must discount (a procedure that is the opposite of compounding) at i interest rate for n periods. In discounting, the interest is subtracted rather than added, as it is in compounding. Graphically, the present value of $1 due at the end of the third period with an interest rate of 10 percent can be represented as follows:

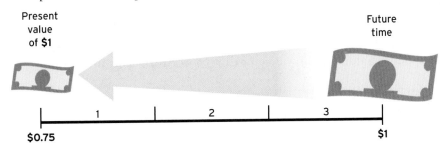

Assume that today is January 1, 2010, and you have the opportunity to receive $1,000 cash on December 31, 2012. At an interest rate of 10 percent per year, how much is the $1,000 payment worth to you on January 1, 2010? You could discount the amount year by year,[2] but it is easier to use Table C.2, Present Value of $1, on page C.15. For $i = 10\%$, $n = 3$, we find that the present value of $1 is 0.7513. The present value of $1,000 to be received at the end of three years can be computed as follows:

> From Table C.2,
> Interest rate = 10%
> $n = 3$

$$\$1,000 \times 0.7513 = \$751.30$$

It's important to learn not only how to compute a present value but also to understand what it means. The $751.30 is the amount you would pay now to have the right to receive $1,000 at the end of three years, assuming an interest rate of 10 percent. Conceptually, you should be indifferent between having $751.30 today and receiving $1,000 in three years. If you had $751.30 today but wanted $1,000 in three years, you would deposit the money in a savings account that pays 10% interest and it would grow to $1,000 in three years. Alternatively, if you had a contract that promised you $1,000 in three years, you could sell

---

[2]The detailed discounting is as follows:

Periods	Interest for the Year	Present Value*
1	$1,000 − ($1,000 × 1/1.10) = $90.91	$1,000 − $90.91 = $909.09
2	$909.09 − ($909.09 × 1/1.10) = $82.65	$909.09 − $82.65 = $826.44
3	$826.44 − ($826.44 × 1/1.10) = $75.14[†]	$826.44 − $75.14 = $751.30

*Verifiable in Table C.2.
[†]Adjusted for rounding

it to an investor for $751.30 in cash today because it would permit the investor to earn the difference in interest.

What if you could only earn 6 percent during the three-year period from January 1, 2010, to December 31, 2012? What would be the present value on January 1, 2010, of receiving $1,000 on December 31, 2012? To answer this we would take the same approach, using Table C.2, except that the interest rate would change to $i = 6\%$. Referring to Table C.2, we see the present value factor for $i = 6\%$, $n = 3$, is 0.8396. Thus, the present value of $1,000 to be received at the end of three years, assuming a 6 percent interest rate, would be computed as $1,000 × 0.8396 = $839.60. Notice that when we assume a 6 percent interest rate the present value is greater than when we assumed a 10 percent interest rate. The reason for this difference is that, to reach $1,000 three years from now, you'd need to deposit more money in a savings account now if it earns 6 percent interest than if it earns 10 percent interest.

Solution to Self-Study Practice
1. The present value will decrease.
2. $10,000 × 0.6139 = $6,139.
3. $10,000 × 1.6289 = $16,289.

How's it going?   Self-Study Practice

1. If the interest rate in a present value problem increases from 8 percent to 10 percent, will the present value increase or decrease?
2. What is the present value of $10,000 to be received 10 years from now if the interest rate is 5 percent, compounded annually?
3. If $10,000 is deposited now in a savings account that earns 5 percent interest compounded annually, how much will it be worth 10 years from now?

After you have finished, check your answers with the solution in the margin.

The Power of Compounding

Compound interest is a remarkably powerful economic force. In fact, the ability to earn interest on interest is the key to building economic wealth. If you save $1,000 per year for the first 10 years of your career, you will have more money when you retire than you would if you had saved $15,000 per year for the last 10 years of your career. This surprising outcome occurs because the money you save early in your career will earn more interest than the money you save at the end of your career. If you start saving money now, the majority of your wealth will not be the money you saved but the interest your money was able to earn.

The table in the margin shows how a single investment of $1,000 today grows over time, at the investment community's historic average growth rate of 10 percent. Two important lessons are revealed in the table: (1) **you can earn a lot of interest through the effects of compounding** (in just 10 years, you will earn $1,600 interest on a $1,000 investment), and (2) **start early** (notice that the balance more than doubles every 10 years, so letting your investment sit an extra decade could make you twice as rich).

Period	Value
Now	$ 1,000
10 years	$ 2,600
20 years	$ 6,700
30 years	$ 17,400
40 years	$ 45,300
50 years	$117,400
60 years	$304,500
70 years	$789,700

Computing Future and Present Values of an Annuity

Instead of a single payment, many business problems involve multiple cash payments over a number of periods. An **annuity** is a series of consecutive payments characterized by

1. An equal dollar amount each interest period.
2. Interest periods of equal length (year, half a year, quarter, or month).
3. An equal interest rate each interest period.

YOU SHOULD KNOW

Annuity: A series of periodic cash receipts or payments that are equal in amount each interest period.

Examples of annuities include monthly payments on a car or house, yearly contributions to a savings account, and monthly pension benefits.

FUTURE VALUE OF AN ANNUITY

If you are saving money for some purpose, such as a new car or a trip to Europe, you might decide to deposit a fixed amount of money in a savings account each month. The future value of an annuity computation will tell you how much money will be in your savings account at some point in the future.

The future value of an annuity includes compound interest on each payment from the date of payment to the end of the term of the annuity. Each new payment accumulates less interest than prior payments, only because the number of periods remaining in which to accumulate interest decreases. The future value of an annuity of $1 for three periods at 10 percent may be represented graphically as

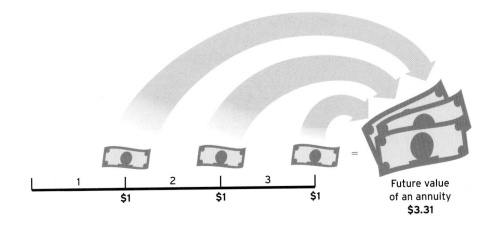

Future value
of an annuity
$3.31

Assume that each year for three years, you deposit $1,000 cash in a savings account at 10 percent interest per year. You make the first $1,000 deposit on December 31, 2010, the second one on December 31, 2011, and the third and last one on December 31, 2012. The first $1,000 deposit earns compound interest for two years (for a total principal and interest of $1,210); the second deposit earns interest for one year (for a total principal and interest of $1,100). The third deposit earns no interest because it was made on the day that the balance is computed. Thus, the total amount in the savings account at the end of three years is $3,310 ($1,210 + $1,100 + $1,000).

To calculate the future value of this annuity, we could compute the interest on each deposit, similar to what's described above. However, a faster way is to refer to Table C.3, Future Value of Annuity of $1, on page C.16. For i = 10%, n = 3, we find the value 3.3100. The future value of your three deposits of $1,000 each can be computed as follows:

From Table C.3,
Interest rate = 10%
n = 3

$1,000 × 3.3100 = $3,310

PRESENT VALUE OF AN ANNUITY

The present value of an annuity is the value now of a series of equal amounts to be received (or paid out) for some specified number of periods in the future. It is computed by discounting each of the equal periodic amounts. A good example of this type of problem is a retirement program that offers employees a monthly income after retirement. The present value of an annuity of $1 for three periods at 10 percent may be represented graphically as

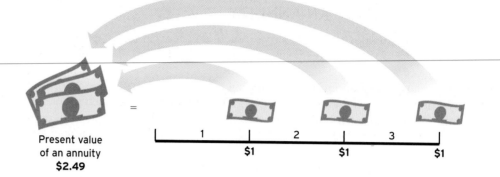

Present value
of an annuity
$2.49

Assume you are to receive $1,000 cash on each December 31, 2010, 2011, and 2012. How much would the sum of these three $1,000 future amounts be worth on January 1, 2010, assuming an interest rate of 10 percent per year? One way to determine this is to use Table C.2 to calculate the present value of each single amount as follows:

			FACTOR FROM TABLE C.2		
Year	Amount		$i = 10\%$		Present Value
1	$1,000	×	0.9091 ($n = 1$)	=	$ 909.10
2	$1,000	×	0.8264 ($n = 2$)	=	826.40
3	$1,000	×	0.7513 ($n = 3$)	=	751.30
			Total present value	=	$2,486.80

Alternatively, we can compute the present value of this annuity more easily by using Table C.4, Present Value of Annuity of $1 (on page C.17), as follows:

From Table C.4,
Interest rate = 10%
$n = 3$

$1,000 × 2.4869 = $2,487 (rounded)

INTEREST RATES AND INTEREST PERIODS

The preceding illustrations assumed annual periods for compounding and discounting. Although interest rates are almost always quoted on an annual basis, many compounding periods encountered in business are less than one year. When interest periods are less than a year, the values of n and i must be restated to be consistent with the length of the interest compounding period.

To illustrate, 12 percent interest compounded annually for five years requires the use of $n = 5$ and $i = 12\%$. If compounding is quarterly, however, there will be four interest periods per year (20 interest periods in five years), and the quarterly interest rate is one quarter of the annual rate (3 percent per quarter). Therefore, 12 percent interest compounded quarterly for five years requires use of $n = 20$ and $i = 3\%$.

Accounting Applications of Present Values

Many business transactions require the use of future and present value concepts. In finance classes, you will see how to apply future value concepts. In this section, we apply present value concepts to three common accounting cases.

Case A—Present Value of a Single Amount

On January 1, 2010, General Mills bought some new delivery trucks. The company signed a note and agreed to pay $200,000 on December 31, 2011, an amount representing the cash equivalent price of the trucks plus interest for two years. The market interest rate for this note was 12 percent.

1. How should the accountant record the purchase?

Answer   This case requires the computation of the present value of a single amount. In conformity with the cost principle, the cost of the trucks is their current cash equivalent price, which is the present value of the future payment. The problem can be shown graphically as follows:

The present value of the $200,000 is computed as follows:

$$\$200{,}000 \times 0.7972 = \$159{,}440$$

From Table C.2,
Interest rate = 12%
n = 2

This transaction has the following financial effects, and would be recorded with the journal entry shown below.

Assets	=	Liabilities	+ Stockholders' Equity
Delivery Trucks +159,440		Note Payable +159,440	

dr Delivery Trucks (+A)	159,440	
cr Note Payable (+L)		159,440

2. How should the effects of interest be reported at the end of 2010 and 2011?

Answer   Interest expense would be calculated, reported, and recorded as follows:

December 31, 2010

Interest = Principal × Rate × Time
= $159,440 × 12% × 12/12 = $19,132 (rounded)

Assets	=	Liabilities	+	Stockholders' Equity
		Note Payable +19,132		Interest Expense (+E) −19,132

dr Interest Expense (+E, −SE)	19,132	
cr Note Payable (+L)		19,132

 **COACH'S TIP**

The interest is recorded in the Note Payable account because it would be paid as part of the note at maturity.

December 31, 2011

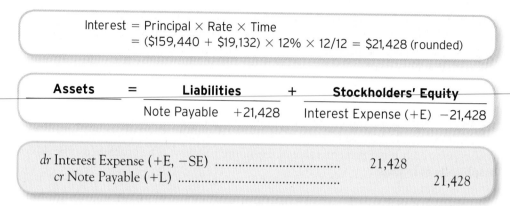

Interest = Principal × Rate × Time
= ($159,440 + $19,132) × 12% × 12/12 = $21,428 (rounded)

Assets	=	Liabilities	+	Stockholders' Equity
		Note Payable +21,428		Interest Expense (+E) −21,428

dr Interest Expense (+E, −SE) 21,428
  cr Note Payable (+L)   21,428

Note Payable (L)		
	159,440	Jan. 1, 2010
	19,132	Interest 2010
	21,428	Interest 2011
200,000		Dec. 31, 2011

3. What is the effect of the $200,000 debt payment made on December 31, 2011?

Answer   At this date the amount to be paid is the balance in Note Payable, after it has been updated for interest pertaining to 2011, as shown in the T-account in the margin. Notice that, just prior to its repayment, the balance for the note on December 31, 2011, is the same as the maturity amount on the due date.

  The debt payment has the following financial effects, and would be recorded with the journal entry shown below.

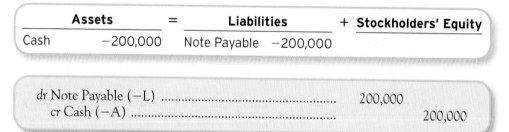

Assets		=	Liabilities		+	Stockholders' Equity
Cash	−200,000		Note Payable	−200,000		

dr Note Payable (−L) 200,000
  cr Cash (−A)   200,000

Case B—Present Value of an Annuity

On January 1, 2010, General Mills bought new milling equipment. The company elected to finance the purchase with a note payable to be paid off in three years in annual installments of $163,686. Each installment includes principal plus interest on the unpaid balance at 11 percent per year. The annual installments are due on December 31, 2010, 2011, and 2012. This problem can be shown graphically as follows:

January 1, 2010	December 31, 2010	December 31, 2011	December 31, 2012
?	$163,686	$163,686	$163,686

1. What is the amount of the note?

Answer   The note is the present value of each installment payment, $i = 11\%$ and $n = 3$. This is an annuity because the note repayment is made in three equal installments. The amount of the note is computed as follows:

From Table C.4,
Interest rate = 11%
n = 3

$163,686 × 2.4437 = $400,000

The acquisition on January 1, 2010, would be accounted for as follows:

Assets	=	Liabilities	+ Stockholders' Equity
Milling Equipment +400,000		Note Payable +400,000	

```
dr Milling Equipment (+A) ........................................... 400,000
   cr Note Payable (+L) ................................................       400,000
```

2. How should the payments made at the end of each year be accounted for?

Answer:

December 31, 2010
Each payment includes both interest and principal. The interest part of the first payment is calculated as:

$$\text{Interest} = \text{Principal} \times \text{Rate} \times \text{Time}$$
$$= \$400,000 \times 11\% \times 12/12 = \$44,000$$

Now that we know the interest component, the principal portion of the first payment of $163,686 can be calculated ($163,686 − $44,000 = $119,686). Thus, the first payment on December 31, 2010, would be accounted for as:

Assets	=	Liabilities	+	Stockholders' Equity
Cash −163,686		Note Payable −119,686		Interest Expense (+E) −44,000

```
dr Interest Expense (+E, −SE) ........................................ 44,000
dr Note Payable (−L) ($163,686 − $44,000) ............... 119,686
   cr Cash (−A) ..............................................................       163,686
```

December 31, 2011
The interest portion of the second and third payments would be calculated in the same way, although notice that the principal balance in the Note Payable account changes after each payment.

$$\text{Interest} = \text{Principal} \times \text{Rate} \times \text{Time}$$
$$= [(\$400,000 − \$119,686) \times 11\% \times 12/12] = \$30,835$$
$$\text{Principal} = \text{Payment} − \text{Interest}$$
$$= \$163,686 − \$30,835 = \$132,851$$

Assets	=	Liabilities	+	Stockholders' Equity
Cash −163,686		Note Payable −132,851		Interest Expense (+E) −30,835

```
dr Interest Expense (+E, −SE) ........................................ 30,835
dr Note Payable (−L) ....................................................... 132,851
   cr Cash (−A) ..............................................................       163,686
```

December 31, 2012

$$\begin{aligned} \text{Interest} &= \text{Principal} \times \text{Rate} \times \text{Time} \\ &= [(\$400{,}000 - \$119{,}686 - \$132{,}851) \times 11\% \times 12/12] \\ &= \$16{,}223 \text{ (adjusted to accommodate rounding)} \\ \text{Principal} &= \text{Payment} - \text{Interest} \\ &= \$163{,}686 - \$16{,}223 = \$147{,}463 \end{aligned}$$

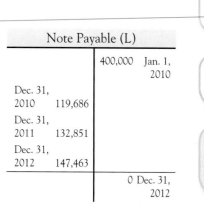

Note Payable (L)			
		400,000	Jan. 1, 2010
Dec. 31, 2010	119,686		
Dec. 31, 2011	132,851		
Dec. 31, 2012	147,463		
		0	Dec. 31, 2012

Assets	=	Liabilities	+	Stockholders' Equity
Cash −163,686		Note Payable −147,463		Interest Expense (+E) −16,223

dr Interest Expense (+E, −SE)	16,223	
dr Note Payable (−L)	147,463	
cr Cash (−A)		163,686

Case C—Present Value of a Single Amount and an Annuity

On January 1, 2010, General Mills issued 100 four-year, $1,000 bonds. The bonds pay interest annually at a rate of 6 percent of face value. What total amount would investors be willing to pay for the bonds if they require an annual return of: (*a*) 4 percent, (*b*) 6 percent, or (*c*) 8 percent?

Answer   This case requires the computation of the present value of a single amount (the $100,000 face value paid at maturity) plus the present value of an annuity (the annual interest payments of $6,000). The problem can be shown graphically as follows:

COACH'S TIP

Each interest payment of $6,000 is calculated as: $100,000 × 6% × 12/12.

(a) 4 Percent Market Interest Rate

The present value of the $100,000 face value is computed as follows:

From Table C.2, Interest rate = 4% *n* = 4

$$\$100{,}000 \times 0.8548 = \$85{,}480$$

The present value of the $6,000 annuity is computed as follows:

From Table C.4, Interest rate = 4% *n* = 4

$$\$6{,}000 \times 3.6299 = \$21{,}780^*$$

*Adjusted to accommodate rounding in the present value factor.

The present value of the total bond payments, computed using the discount rate of 4 percent, is $107,260 (= $85,480 + $21,780).

(b) 6 Percent Market Interest Rate

The present value of the $100,000 face value is computed as follows:

> From Table C.2,
> Interest rate = 6%
> $n = 4$

$$\$100,000 \times 0.7921 = \$79,210$$

The present value of the $6,000 annuity is computed as follows:

> From Table C.4,
> Interest rate = 6%
> $n = 4$

$$\$6,000 \times 3.4651 = \$20,790*$$

*Adjusted to accommodate rounding in the present value factor.

The present value of the total bond payments, computed using the discount rate of 6%, is $100,000 (= $79,210 + $20,790).

(c) 8 Percent Market Interest Rate

The present value of the $100,000 face value is computed as follows:

> From Table C.2,
> Interest rate = 8%
> $n = 4$

$$\$100,000 \times 0.7350 = \$73,503*$$

*Adjusted to accommodate rounding in the present value factor.

The present value of the $6,000 annuity is computed as follows:

> From Table C.4,
> Interest rate = 8%
> $n = 4$

$$\$6,000 \times 3.3121 = \$19,873$$

COACH'S TIP

The present values in *a*, *b*, and *c* demonstrate the calculation of the bond issue prices used in Chapter 10.

The present value of the total bond payments, computed using the discount rate of 8%, is $93,376 (= $73,503 + $19,873).

The following table summarizes these calculations:

	MARKET INTEREST RATES		
	4%	6%	8%
Present value of $100,000 face value (principal) paid four years from now	$ 85,480	$ 79,210	$ 73,503
Present value of $6,000 (interest) paid once a year for four years	21,780	20,790	19,873
Bond price	$107,260	$100,000	$93,376

Of course, these calculations are just the starting point for understanding how bond liabilities are determined and reported. You'll need to read Chapter 10 for information about how bond liabilities are accounted for.

PRESENT VALUE COMPUTATIONS USING EXCEL

While the present value tables are useful for educational purposes, most present value problems in business are solved with calculators or Excel spreadsheets. Because of the widespread availability of Excel, we will show you how to solve present value problems using Excel. Slightly different versions of Excel are available. The illustrations in this text are based on Microsoft Office 2007.

Present Value of a Single Payment

The calculation of a present value amount is based on a fairly simple mathematical formula:

$$PV = \text{Payment}/(1+i)^n$$

In this formula, *payment* is the cash payment made at some point in the future, i is the interest rate each period, and n is the number of periods in the problem. We could use this formula to solve all problems involving the present value of a single payment. It is, of course, easier to use a present value table (like the one at the end of this appendix) which is derived by solving the present value formula for various interest rates and numbers of periods. Unfortunately, a table that included all interest rates and numbers of periods actually encountered in business would be too large to work with. As a result, most accountants and analysts use Excel to compute a present value.

To compute the present value of a single payment in Excel, you enter the present value formula in a cell, using the format required by Excel. You should select a cell and enter the following formula:

$$= \text{Payment}/(1+i)\hat{\ }n$$

To illustrate, if you want to solve for the present value of a $100,000 payment to be made in five years with an interest rate of 10%, you would enter the following in the function field:

$$= 100,000/(1.10)\hat{\ }5$$

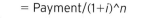

Based on this entry, Excel would compute the present value of $62,092.13. This answer is slightly different from the answer you would have if you used the present value tables at the end of this appendix. The tables are rounded based on four digits. Excel does not round and, therefore, provides a more accurate computation.

Present Value of an Annuity

The formula for computing the present value of an annuity is a little more complicated than the present value of a single payment. As a result, Excel has been programmed to include the formula so that you do not have to enter it yourself.

To compute the present value of an annuity in Excel, select a cell, click on the Formulas tab, and then click on the function button (f_x). The following dropdown box will appear:

Under the Select Category heading, you should pick "Financial," scroll down under "Select a Function," and click on PV. Then, click on "OK" and a new dropdown box will appear:

In this box, you should enter the interest rate, 10% in this example, under Rate. Notice that the rate must be entered as a decimal (i.e., 0.10). Enter the number of periods (20) under Nper. Excel has an unusual convention associated with the payment. It must be entered as a negative amount ($-15,000$) under Pmt. Do not include a comma or brackets with the amount you enter. When you click on OK, Excel will enter the present value in the cell you selected. In this example, the value determined by Excel is $127,703.46.

TABLE C.1 — Future Value of $1

Periods	2%	3%	3.75%	4%	4.25%	5%	6%	7%	8%
0	1.	1.	1.	1.	1.	1.	1.	1.	1.
1	1.02	1.03	1.0375	1.04	1.0425	1.05	1.06	1.07	1.08
2	1.0404	1.0609	1.0764	1.0816	1.0868	1.1025	1.1236	1.1449	1.1664
3	1.0612	1.0927	1.1168	1.1249	1.1330	1.1576	1.1910	1.2250	1.2597
4	1.0824	1.1255	1.1587	1.1699	1.1811	1.2155	1.2625	1.3108	1.3605
5	1.1041	1.1593	1.2021	1.2167	1.2313	1.2763	1.3382	1.4026	1.4693
6	1.1262	1.1941	1.2472	1.2653	1.2837	1.3401	1.4185	1.5007	1.5869
7	1.1487	1.2299	1.2939	1.3159	1.3382	1.4071	1.5036	1.6058	1.7138
8	1.1717	1.2668	1.3425	1.3686	1.3951	1.4775	1.5938	1.7182	1.8509
9	1.1951	1.3048	1.3928	1.4233	1.4544	1.5513	1.6895	1.8385	1.9990
10	1.2190	1.3439	1.4450	1.4802	1.5162	1.6289	1.7908	1.9672	2.1589
20	1.4859	1.8061	2.0882	2.1911	2.2989	2.6533	3.2071	3.8697	4.6610

Periods	9%	10%	11%	12%	13%	14%	15%	20%	25%
0	1.	1.	1.	1.	1.	1.	1.	1.	1.
1	1.09	1.10	1.11	1.12	1.13	1.14	1.15	1.20	1.25
2	1.1881	1.2100	1.2321	1.2544	1.2769	1.2996	1.3225	1.4400	1.5625
3	1.2950	1.3310	1.3676	1.4049	1.4429	1.4815	1.5209	1.7280	1.9531
4	1.4116	1.4641	1.5181	1.5735	1.6305	1.6890	1.7490	2.0736	2.4414
5	1.5386	1.6105	1.6851	1.7623	1.8424	1.9254	2.0114	2.4883	3.0518
6	1.6771	1.7716	1.8704	1.9738	2.0820	2.1950	2.3131	2.9860	3.8147
7	1.8280	1.9487	2.0762	2.2107	2.3526	2.5023	2.6600	3.5832	4.7684
8	1.9926	2.1436	2.3045	2.4760	2.6584	2.8526	3.0590	4.2998	5.9605
9	2.1719	2.3579	2.5580	2.7731	3.0040	3.2519	3.5179	5.1598	7.4506
10	2.3674	2.5937	2.8394	3.1058	3.3946	3.7072	4.0456	6.1917	9.3132
20	5.6044	6.7275	8.0623	9.6463	11.5231	13.7435	16.3665	38.3376	86.7362

TABLE C.2   Present Value of $1

Periods	2%	3%	3.75%	4%	4.25%	5%	6%	7%	8%
1	0.9804	0.9709	0.9639	0.9615	0.9592	0.9524	0.9434	0.9346	0.9259
2	0.9612	0.9426	0.9290	0.9246	0.9201	0.9070	0.8900	0.8734	0.8573
3	0.9423	0.9151	0.8954	0.8890	0.8826	0.8638	0.8396	0.8163	0.7938
4	0.9238	0.8885	0.8631	0.8548	0.8466	0.8227	0.7921	0.7629	0.7350
5	0.9057	0.8626	0.8319	0.8219	0.8121	0.7835	0.7473	0.7130	0.6806
6	0.8880	0.8375	0.8018	0.7903	0.7790	0.7462	0.7050	0.6663	0.6302
7	0.8706	0.8131	0.7728	0.7599	0.7473	0.7107	0.6651	0.6227	0.5835
8	0.8535	0.7894	0.7449	0.7307	0.7168	0.6768	0.6274	0.5820	0.5403
9	0.8368	0.7664	0.7180	0.7026	0.6876	0.6446	0.5919	0.5439	0.5002
10	0.8203	0.7441	0.6920	0.6756	0.6595	0.6139	0.5584	0.5083	0.4632
20	0.6730	0.5537	0.4789	0.4564	0.4350	0.3769	0.3118	0.2584	0.2145

Periods	9%	10%	11%	12%	13%	14%	15%	20%	25%
1	0.9174	0.9091	0.9009	0.8929	0.8850	0.8772	0.8696	0.8333	0.8000
2	0.8417	0.8264	0.8116	0.7972	0.7831	0.7695	0.7561	0.6944	0.6400
3	0.7722	0.7513	0.7312	0.7118	0.6931	0.6750	0.6575	0.5787	0.5120
4	0.7084	0.6830	0.6587	0.6355	0.6133	0.5921	0.5718	0.4823	0.4096
5	0.6499	0.6209	0.5935	0.5674	0.5428	0.5194	0.4972	0.4019	0.3277
6	0.5963	0.5645	0.5346	0.5066	0.4803	0.4556	0.4323	0.3349	0.2621
7	0.5470	0.5132	0.4817	0.4523	0.4251	0.3996	0.3759	0.2791	0.2097
8	0.5019	0.4665	0.4339	0.4039	0.3762	0.3506	0.3269	0.2326	0.1678
9	0.4604	0.4241	0.3909	0.3606	0.3329	0.3075	0.2843	0.1938	0.1342
10	0.4224	0.3855	0.3522	0.3220	0.2946	0.2697	0.2472	0.1615	0.1074
20	0.1784	0.1486	0.1240	0.1037	0.0868	0.0728	0.0611	0.0261	0.0115

TABLE C.3 | Future Value of Annuity of $1

Periods*	2%	3%	3.75%	4%	4.25%	5%	6%	7%	8%
1	1.	1.	1.	1.	1.	1.	1.	1.	1.
2	2.02	2.03	2.0375	2.04	2.0425	2.05	2.06	2.07	2.08
3	3.0604	3.0909	3.1139	3.1216	3.1293	3.1525	3.1836	3.2149	3.2464
4	4.1216	4.1836	4.2307	4.2465	4.2623	4.3101	4.3746	4.4399	4.5061
5	5.2040	5.3091	5.3893	5.4163	5.4434	5.5256	5.6371	5.7507	5.8666
6	6.3081	6.4684	6.5914	6.6330	6.6748	6.8019	6.9753	7.1533	7.3359
7	7.4343	7.6625	7.8386	7.8983	7.9585	8.1420	8.3938	8.6540	8.9228
8	8.5830	8.8923	9.1326	9.2142	9.2967	9.5491	9.8975	10.2598	10.6366
9	9.7546	10.1591	10.4750	10.5828	10.6918	11.0266	11.4913	11.9780	12.4876
10	10.9497	11.4639	11.8678	12.0061	12.1462	12.5779	13.1808	13.8164	14.4866
20	24.2974	26.8704	29.0174	29.7781	30.5625	33.0660	36.7856	40.9955	45.7620

Periods*	9%	10%	11%	12%	13%	14%	15%	20%	25%
1	1.	1.	1.	1.	1.	1.	1.	1.	1.
2	2.09	2.10	2.11	2.12	2.13	2.14	2.15	2.20	2.25
3	3.2781	3.3100	3.3421	3.3744	3.4069	3.4396	3.4725	3.6400	3.8125
4	4.5731	4.6410	4.7097	4.7793	4.8498	4.9211	4.9934	5.3680	5.7656
5	5.9847	6.1051	6.2278	6.3528	6.4803	6.6101	6.7424	7.4416	8.2070
6	7.5233	7.7156	7.9129	8.1152	8.3227	8.5355	8.7537	9.9299	11.2588
7	9.2004	9.4872	9.7833	10.0890	10.4047	10.7305	11.0668	12.9159	15.0735
8	11.0285	11.4359	11.8594	12.2997	12.7573	13.2328	13.7268	16.4991	19.8419
9	13.0210	13.5975	14.1640	14.7757	15.4157	16.0853	16.7858	20.7989	25.8023
10	15.1929	15.9374	16.7220	17.5487	18.4197	19.3373	20.3037	25.9587	33.2529
20	51.1601	57.2750	64.2028	72.0524	80.9468	91.0249	102.4436	186.6880	342.9447

*There is one payment each period.

TABLE C.4   Present Value of Annuity of $1

Periods*	2%	3%	3.75%	4%	4.25%	5%	6%	7%	8%
1	0.9804	0.9709	0.9639	0.9615	0.9592	0.9524	0.9434	0.9346	0.9259
2	1.9416	1.9135	1.8929	1.8861	1.8794	1.8594	1.8334	1.8080	1.7833
3	2.8839	2.8286	2.7883	2.7751	2.7620	2.7232	2.6730	2.6243	2.5771
4	3.8077	3.7171	3.6514	3.6299	3.6086	3.5460	3.4651	3.3872	3.3121
5	4.7135	4.5797	4.4833	4.4518	4.4207	4.3295	4.2124	4.1002	3.9927
6	5.6014	5.4172	5.2851	5.2421	5.1997	5.0757	4.9173	4.7665	4.6229
7	6.4720	6.2303	6.0579	6.0021	5.9470	5.7864	5.5824	5.3893	5.2064
8	7.3255	7.0197	6.8028	6.7327	6.6638	6.4632	6.2098	5.9713	5.7466
9	8.1622	7.7861	7.5208	7.4353	7.3513	7.1078	6.8017	6.5152	6.2469
10	8.9826	8.5302	8.2128	8.1109	8.0109	7.7217	7.3601	7.0236	6.7101
20	16.3514	14.8775	13.8962	13.5903	13.2944	12.4622	11.4699	10.5940	9.8181

Periods*	9%	10%	11%	12%	13%	14%	15%	20%	25%
1	0.9174	0.9091	0.9009	0.8929	0.8550	0.8772	0.8696	0.8333	0.8000
2	1.7591	1.7355	1.7125	1.6901	1.6681	1.6467	1.6257	1.5278	1.4400
3	2.5313	2.4869	2.4437	2.4018	2.3612	2.3216	2.2832	2.1065	1.9520
4	3.2397	3.1699	3.1024	3.0373	2.9745	2.9137	2.8550	2.5887	2.3616
5	3.8897	3.7908	3.6959	3.6048	3.5172	3.4331	3.3522	2.9906	2.6893
6	4.4859	4.3553	4.2305	4.1114	3.9975	3.8887	3.7845	3.3255	2.9514
7	5.0330	4.8684	4.7122	4.5638	4.4226	4.2883	4.1604	3.6046	3.1611
8	5.5348	5.3349	5.1461	4.9676	4.7988	4.6389	4.4873	3.8372	3.3289
9	5.9952	5.7590	5.5370	5.3282	5.1317	4.9464	4.7716	4.0310	3.4631
10	6.4177	6.1446	5.8892	5.6502	5.4262	5.2161	5.0188	4.1925	3.5705
20	9.1285	8.5136	7.9633	7.4694	7.0248	6.6231	6.2593	4.8696	3.9539

*There is one payment each period.

KEY TERMS

Annuity p. C.4   Present Value p. C.1   Time Value of Money p. C.1
Future Value p. C.1

See complete definitions in the glossary in the back of this text.

PRACTICE MATERIAL

QUESTIONS

1. Explain the concept of the time value of money.

2. Explain the basic difference between future value and present value.

3. If you deposited $10,000 in a savings account that earns 10 percent, how much would you have at the end of 10 years? Use a convenient format to display your computations.

4. If you hold a valid contract that will pay you $8,000 cash 10 years from now and the going rate of interest is 10 percent, what is its present value? Use a convenient format to display your computations.

5. What is an annuity?

6. Use tables C.1 to C.4 to complete the following schedule:

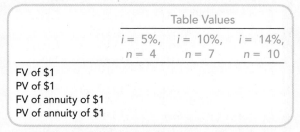

	Table Values		
	$i = 5\%$, $n = 4$	$i = 10\%$, $n = 7$	$i = 14\%$, $n = 10$
FV of $1			
PV of $1			
FV of annuity of $1			
PV of annuity of $1			

7. If you deposit $1,000 at the end of each period for 10 interest periods and you earn 8 percent interest, how much would you have at the end of period 10? Use a convenient format to display your computations.

MULTIPLE CHOICE

1. You are saving up for a Mercedes-Benz SLR McLaren, which currently sells for nearly half a million dollars. Your plan is to deposit $15,000 at the end of each year for the next 10 years. You expect to earn 5 percent each year. How much will you have saved after 10 years, rounded to the nearest 10 dollars?

   a. $150,000.
   b. $188,670.
   c. $495,990.
   d. None of the above.

2. Which of the following is a characteristic of an annuity?

   a. An equal dollar amount each interest period.
   b. Interest periods of equal length.
   c. An equal interest rate each interest period.
   d. All of the above are characteristics of an annuity.

3. Which of the following is most likely to be an annuity?

   a. Monthly payments on a credit card bill.
   b. Monthly interest earned on a checking account.
   c. Monthly payments on a home mortgage.
   d. Monthly utility bill payments.

4. Assume you bought a state of the art entertainment system, with no payments to be made until two years from now, when you must pay $6,000. If the going rate of interest on most loans is 5 percent, which table in this appendix would you use to calculate the system's equivalent cost if you were to pay for it today?

   a. Table C.1 (Future Value of $1)
   b. Table C.2 (Present Value of $1)
   c. Table C.3 (Future Value of Annuity of $1)
   d. Table C.4 (Present Value of Annuity of $1)

5. Assuming the facts in question 4, what is the system's equivalent cost if you were to pay for it today?

   a. $5,442   c. $11,100
   b. $6,615   d. $12,300

6. Assume you bought a car using a loan that requires payments of $3,000 to be made at the end of every year for the next three years. The loan agreement indicates the annual interest rate is 6 percent. Which table in this appendix would you use to calculate the car's equivalent cost if you were to pay for it in full today?

   a. Table C.1 (Future Value of $1)
   b. Table C.2 (Present Value of $1)
   c. Table C.3 (Future Value of Annuity of $1)
   d. Table C.4 (Present Value of Annuity of $1)

7. Assuming the facts in question 6, what is the car's equivalent cost if you were to pay for it today? Round to the nearest hundred dollars.

   a. $2,600   c. $8,000
   b. $3,600   d. $9,600

8. Which of the following statements is true?

   a. When the interest rate increases, the present value of a single amount decreases.
   b. When the number of interest periods increases, the present value of a single amount increases.
   c. When the interest rate increases, the present value of an annuity increases.
   d. None of the above are true.

9. Which of the following describes how to calculate a bond's issue price?

	Face Value	Interest Payments
a.	Present value of single amount	Future value of annuity
b.	Future value of single amount	Present value of annuity
c.	Present value of single amount	Present value of annuity
d.	Future value of single amount	Future value of annuity

10. If interest is compounded quarterly, rather than yearly, how do you adjust the number of years and annual interest rate when using the present value tables?

	Number of years	Annual interest rate
a.	Divide by 4	Divide by 4
b.	Divide by 4	Multiply by 4
c.	Multiply by 4	Divide by 4
d.	Multiply by 4	Multiply by 4

Solutions to Multiple-Choice Questions can be found on page Q1.

MINI-EXERCISES

MC-1 Computing the Present Value of a Single Payment

What is the present value of $500,000 to be paid in 10 years, with an interest rate of 8 percent?

MC-2 Computing the Present Value of an Annuity

What is the present value of 10 equal payments of $15,000, with an interest rate of 10 percent?

MC-3 Computing the Present Value of a Complex Contract

As a result of a slowdown in operations, Mercantile Stores is offering to employees who have been terminated a severance package of $100,000 cash; another $100,000 to be paid in one year; and an annuity of $30,000 to be paid each year for 20 years. What is the present value of the package, assuming an interest rate of 8 percent?

MC-4 Computing the Future Value of an Annuity

You plan to retire in 20 years. Calculate whether it is better for you to save $25,000 a year for the last 10 years before retirement or $15,000 for each of the 20 years. Assume you are able to earn 10 percent interest on your investments.

EXERCISES

EC-1 Computing Growth in a Savings Account: A Single Amount

On January 1, 2010, you deposited $6,000 in a savings account. The account will earn 10 percent annual compound interest, which will be added to the fund balance at the end of each year.

Required (round to the nearest dollar):

1. What will be the balance in the savings account at the end of 10 years?
2. What is the interest for the 10 years?
3. How much interest revenue did the fund earn in 2010? 2011?

EC-2 Computing Deposit Required and Accounting for a Single-Sum Savings Account

On January 1, 2010, Alan King decided to transfer an amount from his checking account into a savings account that later will provide $80,000 to send his son to college (four years from now). The savings account will earn 8 percent, which will be added to the fund each year-end.

Required (show computations and round to the nearest dollar):

1. How much must Alan deposit on January 1, 2010?
2. Give the journal entry that Alan should make on January 1, 2010, to record the transfer.
3. What is the interest for the four years?
4. Give the journal entry that Alan should make on (a) December 31, 2010, and (b) December 31, 2011.

EC-3 Recording Growth in a Savings Account with Equal Periodic Payments

On each December 31, you plan to transfer $2,000 from your checking account into a savings account. The savings account will earn 9 percent annual interest, which will be added to the savings account balance at each year-end. The first deposit will be made December 31, 2010 (at the end of the period).

Required (show computations and round to the nearest dollar):

1. Give the required journal entry on December 31, 2010.
2. What will be the balance in the savings account at the end of the 10th year (i.e., 10 deposits)?

3. What is the total amount of interest earned on the 10 deposits?
4. How much interest revenue did the fund earn in 2011? 2012?
5. Give all required journal entries at the end of 2011 and 2012.

EC-4 Computing Growth for a Savings Fund with Periodic Deposits

On January 1, 2010, you plan to take a trip around the world upon graduation four years from now. Your grandmother wants to deposit sufficient funds for this trip in a savings account for you. On the basis of a budget, you estimate that the trip currently would cost $15,000. Being the generous and sweet lady she is, your grandmother decided to deposit $3,500 in the fund at the end of each of the next four years, starting on December 31, 2010. The savings account will earn 6 percent annual interest, which will be added to the savings account at each year-end.

Required (show computations and round to the nearest dollar):

1. How much money will you have for the trip at the end of year 4 (i.e., after four deposits)?
2. What is the total amount of interest earned over the four years?
3. How much interest revenue did the fund earn in 2010, 2011, 2012, and 2013?

EC-5 Computing Value of an Asset Based on Present Value

You have the chance to purchase an oil well. Your best estimate is that the oil well's net royalty income will average $25,000 per year for five years. There will be no residual value at that time. Assume that the cash inflow occurs at each year-end and that considering the uncertainty in your estimates, you expect to earn 15 percent per year on the investment. What should you be willing to pay for this investment right now?

COACHED PROBLEM

CPC-1 Comparing Options Using Present Value Concepts

After hearing a knock at your front door, you are surprised to see the Prize Patrol from a large, well-known magazine subscription company. It has arrived with the good news that you are the big winner, having won "$20 million." You discover that you have three options: (1) you can receive $1 million per year for the next 20 years, (2) you can have $8 million today, or (3) you can have $2 million today and receive $700,000 for each of the next 20 years. Your financial adviser tells you that it is reasonable to expect to earn 10 percent on investments. Which option do you prefer? What factors influence your decision?

TIP: All three scenarios require you to determine today's value of the various payment options. These are present value problems.

GROUP A PROBLEM

PAC-1 Comparing Options Using Present Value Concepts

After completing a long and successful career as senior vice president for a large bank, you are preparing for retirement. After visiting the human resources office, you have found that you have several retirement options: (1) you can receive an immediate cash payment of $1 million, (2) you can receive $60,000 per year for life (your remaining life expectancy is 20 years), or (3) you can receive $50,000 per year for 10 years and then $70,000 per year for life (this option is intended to give you some protection against inflation). You have determined that you can earn 8 percent on your investments. Which option do you prefer and why?

GROUP B PROBLEM

PBC-1 Comparing Options Using Present Value Concepts

After incurring a serious injury caused by a manufacturing defect, your friend has sued the manufacturer for damages. Your friend received three offers from the manufacturer to settle the lawsuit: (1) receive an immediate cash payment of $100,000, (2) receive $6,000 per year for life (your friend's remaining life expectancy is 20 years), or (3) receive $5,000 per year for 10 years and then $7,000 per year for life (this option is intended to compensate your friend for increased aggravation of the injury over time). Your friend can earn 8 percent interest and has asked you for advice. Which option would you recommend and why?

Reporting and Interpreting Investments in Other Corporations

Online at www.mhhe.com/phillips3e

Appendix Introduction

Along with financial hardship, the 2008 stock market crash generated a great deal of criticism of accounting rules applied to Investments in Other Corporations. As you will read in Appendix D (online), these rules use fair values when accounting for certain types of investments. Critics complained that use of fair values ("mark-to-market accounting") had forced companies to report losses simply because the economic crisis had caused reductions in their investment values. Critics argued that these losses did not accurately reflect reality and that each reported loss caused further reductions in investment value, like the downward spiral of a toilet flush. Supporters of the accounting rules countered that the accounting rules did not cause the economic crisis. Rather, the accounting rules merely exposed the underlying economic problems that existed.

To download a copy of Appendix D, go to www.mhhe.com/phillips3e. The following topics are discussed in the appendix.

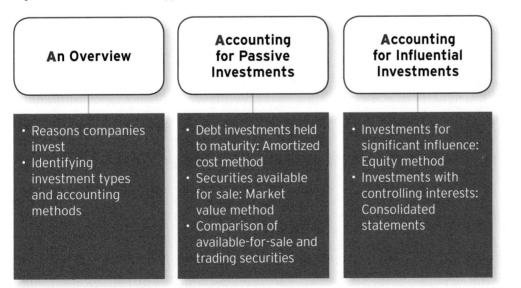

An Overview
- Reasons companies invest
- Identifying investment types and accounting methods

Accounting for Passive Investments
- Debt investments held to maturity: Amortized cost method
- Securities available for sale: Market value method
- Comparison of available-for-sale and trading securities

Accounting for Influential Investments
- Investments for significant influence: Equity method
- Investments with controlling interests: Consolidated statements

Solutions to Multiple-Choice Questions

Chapter 1
1. b 2. a 3. c 4. c 5. a 6. c 7. c 8. d 9. b 10. d

Chapter 2
1. d 2. a 3. d 4. a 5. d 6. c 7. a 8. d 9. d 10. b

Chapter 3
1. b 2. b 3. d 4. b 5. a 6. c 7. c 8. a 9. b 10. c

Chapter 4
1. b 2. a 3. d 4. c 5. d 6. d 7. a 8. c 9. c 10. a

Chapter 5
1. b 2. b 3. c 4. a 5. b 6. a 7. b 8. d 9. c 10. d

Chapter 6
1. b 2. d 3. d 4. c 5. c 6. a 7. b 8. c 9. c 10. b

Chapter 7
1. c 2. d 3. d 4. b 5. d 6. d 7. c 8. c 9. c 10. b

Chapter 8
1. d 2. b 3. b 4. d 5. c 6. d 7. c 8. b 9. d 10. d

Chapter 9
1. d 2. d 3. c 4. c 5. d 6. a 7. d 8. b 9. d 10. b

Chapter 10
1. c 2. b 3. c 4. a 5. c 6. b 7. c 8. c 9. d 10. c

Chapter 11
1. a 2. d 3. d 4. a 5. c 6. b 7. c 8. c 9. d 10. a

Chapter 12
1. c 2. d 3. d 4. a 5. a 6. d 7. d 8. a 9. c 10. b

Chapter 13
1. c 2. c 3. c 4. d 5. c 6. a 7. b 8. d 9. d 10. a

Appendix C
1. b 2. d 3. c 4. b 5. a 6. d 7. c 8. a 9. c 10. c

Appendix D
Included in the online appendix

A

Account A standardized format that organizations use to accumulate the dollar effects of transactions on each financial statement item. (10)

Accounting A system of analyzing, recording, and summarizing the results of a business's operating, investing, and financing activities and then reporting them to decision makers. (5)

Accounting Period The time period covered by the financial statements.

Accounting Process The process used by businesses to analyze, record, and summarize transactions and adjustments, prepare financial statements, and prepare the records for the next cycle.

Accounts Payable Amounts owed by the business to suppliers for past transactions.

Accounts Receivable (Trade Receivables, Receivables) Amounts owed to the business by customers for past transactions. (361)

Accrual Basis Accounting Recording revenues when earned and expenses when incurred, regardless of the timing of cash receipts or payments. (100)

Accrued Expenses See *Accrued Liabilities*.

Accrued Liabilities Previously unrecorded expenses that need to be adjusted at the end of the accounting period to reflect the amount incurred and its related liability account. (454)

Accrued Revenues Previously unrecorded revenues that need to be adjusted at the end of the accounting period to reflect the amount earned and its related receivable account.

Acquisition Cost Cash equivalent amount paid or to be paid for an asset.

Adjusted Trial Balance A list of all accounts and their adjusted balances to check on the equality of recorded debits and credits. (161)

Adjusting Journal Entries Entries necessary at the end of each accounting period to measure all revenues and expenses of that period. (150)

Adjustments See *Adjusting Journal Entries*. (148)

Aging of Accounts Receivable Method Using the age of each accounts receivable to estimate uncollectible amounts. (365)

Allowance for Doubtful Accounts (Allowance for Bad Debts, Allowance for Uncollectible Accounts, Reserve for Bad Debts) Contra-asset account containing the estimated dollar value of uncollectible accounts receivable.

Allowance Method Bases bad debt expense on an estimate of uncollectible accounts. (362)

Amortization (1) For intangible assets, this is the systematic and rational allocation of the cost of an intangible asset over its useful life. (2) For bonds payable, this involves allocating any premium or discount over the life of the bond. (419)

Annuity A series of periodic cash receipts or payments that are equal in amount each interest period. (C.4)

Assets Probable future economic benefits owned by the business as a result of past transactions. (46)

Asset Turnover Ratio Indicates how well assets are being used to generate revenues. (227)

Audit An examination of a company's financial statements (and management's report on internal control effectiveness) with the goal of detecting misstatements.

Audit Report Describes the auditors' opinion of the fairness of the financial statement presentations and management's assessment of internal control effectiveness.

Authorized Shares Maximum number of shares of a corporation's capital stock that can be issued. (509)

Average Cost Method See *Weighted Average Cost Method*. (314)

B

Bad Debt Expense (Doubtful Accounts Expenses, Uncollectible Accounts Expense, Provision for Uncollectible Accounts) Expense associated with estimated uncollectible accounts receivable. (362)

Balance When used as a noun, balance is the dollar amount recorded in an account; when used as a verb, balance is the act of ensuring total assets equal total liabilities plus stockholders' equity.

Balance Sheet (Statement of Financial Position) Reports the amount of assets, liabilities, and stockholders' equity of an accounting entity at a point in time. (12)

Bank Reconciliation Process of using both the bank statement and the cash accounts of a business to determine the appropriate amount of cash in a bank account, after taking into consideration delays or errors in processing cash transactions. (263)

Bank Statement Monthly report from a bank that shows deposits recorded, checks cleared, other debits and credits, and a running bank balance.

Basic Accounting Equation (Balance Sheet Equation) Assets = Liabilities + Stockholders' Equity. (8)

Board of Directors A group of people elected by the stockholders of a company to oversee the decisions made by officers and managers of the company.

Bond Certificate The bond document that each bondholder receives.

Bond Discount The difference between issue price and face value when a bond is sold for less than face value.

Bond Premium The difference between issue price and face value when a bond is sold for more than face value.

Bond Principal The amount (1) payable at the maturity of the bond and (2) on which the periodic cash interest payments are computed.

Book Value See *Carrying Value, Net Book Value.* (409)

C

Callable Bonds Bonds that may be called for early repayment at the option of the company that issued the bond.

Capitalize To record a cost as an asset rather than an expense. (404)

Carrying Value See *Book Value, Net Book Value.* (155, 409)

Cash Money or any instrument that banks will accept for deposit and immediate credit to the company's account, such as a check, money order, or bank draft. (268)

Cash Basis Accounting Recording revenues when cash is received and expenses when cash is paid. (99)

Cash Equivalents Short-term, highly liquid investments purchased within three months of maturity. (268)

Cash Flows from Financing Activities Cash inflows and outflows related to external sources of financing (owners and lenders). (557)

Cash Flows from Investing Activities Cash inflows and outflows related to the purchase or sale of long-lived productive assets. (556)

Cash Flows from Operating Activities (Cash Flows from Operations) Cash inflows and outflows directly related to earnings from normal operations. (556)

Certificate of Deposit A savings certificate, generally issued by commercial banks, entitling the holder to receive interest after a specified maturity date.

Chart of Accounts A summary of all account names and corresponding account numbers used to record financial results in the accounting system. (49)

Classified Balance Sheet A balance sheet that classifies assets and liabilities into current and other (long-term) categories. (63)

Closing Entries Made at the end of the accounting period to transfer balances in temporary accounts to *Retained Earnings* and to establish a zero balance in each of the temporary accounts.

Closing Journal Entries See *Closing Entries.*

Common Stock The basic voting stock issued by a corporation. (507)

Comparable Information Information that can be compared across businesses because similar accounting methods have been applied.

Comparative Financial Statements Report numbers for two or more time periods to make it easy for users to compare account balances from one period to the next. (214)

Comprehensive Income Includes net income plus net unrealized gains or losses on securities available for sale and other adjustments (related to pensions and foreign currency translation) which are directly credited or debited to the stockholders' equity accounts.

Conservatism An accounting concept that suggests care should be taken not to overstate assets and revenues or understate liabilities and expenses. (66)

Consistent Information Information that can be compared over time because similar accounting methods have been applied.

Consolidated Financial Statements The financial statements of two or more companies that have been combined into a single set of financial statements as if the companies were one. (D.16)

Contingent Liability Potential liability that has arisen as the result of a past event; not a liability until some future event occurs. (467)

Continuity Assumption See *Going-Concern Assumption.* (626)

Contra-Account An account that is an offset to, or reduction of, another account. (155)

Contract Rate See *Stated Interest Rate.* (461)

Contributed Capital The result of owners providing to the business cash (and sometimes other assets).

Convertible Bonds Bonds that may be converted to other securities of the issuer (usually common stock).

Copyright A form of protection provided to the original authors of literary, musical, artistic, dramatic, and other works of authorship. (417)

Corporation A business organized as a legal entity separate and distinct from its owners under state law.

Cost The amount of resources that a company sacrifices to obtain goods or services; often said to be incurred when the company pays cash or uses credit to acquire the item.

Cost-Benefit Constraint Suggests that the benefits of accounting for and reporting information should outweigh the costs. (627)

Cost of Goods Sold (CGS) Equation $BI + P - EI = CGS$; beginning inventory plus purchases minus ending inventory. (312)

Cost Principle Requires assets to be recorded at the historical cash-equivalent cost, which is the amount paid or payable on the date of the transaction. (47)

Coupon Rate See *Stated Interest Rate.* (461)

Credit When used as a noun, credit is the right side of an account; when used as a verb, credit is the act of recording the credit portion of a journal entry to a particular account. (56)

Creditor Any business or individual to whom the company owes money.

Cross-Sectional Analysis Compares one company's financial results to that of other companies competing in the same industry. (224)

Cumulative Dividend Preference Preferred stock feature that requires specified current dividends not paid in full to accumulate for every year in which they are not paid. These cumulative preferred dividends must be paid before any common dividends can be paid. (520)

Cumulative Effects of Changes in Accounting Methods Amounts reflected on the income statement for adjustments made to balance sheet accounts when applying new accounting principles.

Current Assets Assets that will be used up or turned into cash within 12 months or the next operating cycle, whichever is longer. (64)

Current Dividend Preference The feature of preferred stock that grants priority to preferred dividends over common dividends. (520)

Current Liabilities Short-term obligations that will be paid in cash (or fulfilled with other current assets) within 12 months or the next operating cycle, whichever is longer. (64, 452)

Current Ratio Ratio of current assets to current liabilities, used to evaluate liquidity.

D

Days to Collect Measure of the average number of days from the time a sale is made on account to the time it is collected. (372)

Days to Sell Measure of the average number of days from the time inventory is bought to the time it is sold. (323)

Debit When used as a noun, debit is the left side of an account; when used as a verb, debit is the act of recording the debit portion of a journal entry to a particular account. (56)

Debt Covenants See *Loan Covenants*. (209)

Debt-to-Assets Ratio Measures the proportion of total assets financed by debt, computed as total liabilities divided by total assets. (227)

Declaration Date The date on which the board of directors officially approves a dividend. (514)

Declining-Balance Depreciation Method Allocates the cost of an asset over its useful life based on a multiple of (often two times) the straight-line rate. (411)

Deferred Expenses Previously acquired assets that need to be adjusted at the end of the accounting period to reflect the amount of expense incurred in using the asset to generate revenue.

Deferred Revenues Previously recorded liabilities that need to be adjusted at the end of the period to reflect the amount of revenue earned.

Deferred Tax Items Caused by reporting revenues and expenses according to GAAP on a company's income statement at a time that differs from their reporting on the tax return.

Depletion Process of allocating a natural resource's cost over the periods of its extraction or harvesting. (423)

Depreciable Cost The portion of the asset's cost that will be used up during its life. It is calculated as asset cost minus residual value, and it is allocated to depreciation expense throughout the asset's life. (409)

Depreciation Process of allocating the cost of buildings and equipment over their productive lives using a systematic and rational method of allocation. (155, 408)

Direct Method A method of presenting the operating activities section of the statement of cash flows, in which each line of the income statement is reported in terms of gross cash receipts and payments. (559)

Direct Write-Off Method Records bad debt expense only when accounts are written-off; not allowed under GAAP. (375)

Discontinued Operations Financial results from the disposal of a major component of the business. (628)

Discount For bonds, occurs when the issue price is less than the face value. Alternatively used in the context of sales discounts and purchase discounts. (461)

Discount Rate The interest rate used to compute present values.

Dividends Payments a company periodically makes to its stockholders as a return on their investment.

Dividends in Arrears Dividends on cumulative preferred stock that have not been declared in prior years. (520)

E

Earnings Forecasts Predictions of earnings for future accounting periods.

Earned To have done what is necessary to obtain the right to receive payment.

EBITDA Abbreviation for "earnings before interest, taxes, depreciation, and amortization," which is a measure of operating performance that some managers and analysts use in place of net income. (423)

Effective-Interest Method of Amortization Amortizes a bond discount or premium on the basis of the market interest rate. (471)

Effective Interest Rate Another name for the market rate of interest on a bond.

Electronic Funds Transfer Funds transferred into or out of your account.

Equity Method Used when an investor can exert significant influence over an investee. It requires the investor to record its share of net income and dividends reported by the investee.

Estimated Useful Life Expected service life of a long-lived asset to the present owner.

Expenditures Outflows of cash for any purpose.

Expenses Decreases in assets or increases in liabilities from ongoing operations, incurred to generate revenues during the current period. (97)

Extraordinary Items Gains and losses that are both unusual in nature and infrequent in occurrence.

Extraordinary Repairs Infrequent expenditures that increase an asset's economic usefulness in the future, and that are capitalized. (408)

F

Face Value (Par Value) The amount of a bond payable at its maturity; used to compute interest payments. (461)

Factoring An arrangement where receivables are sold to another company (called a *factor*) for immediate cash (minus a factoring fee). (374)

Financial Accounting Standards Board (FASB) The private sector body given the primary responsibility to work out the concepts and detailed rules that become generally accepted accounting principles.

Financial Statements Reports that summarize the financial results of business activities. (6)

Financial Statement Users People who base their decisions, in part, on information reported in a company's financial statements.

Financing Activities Related to exchanging money with lenders or owners.

Finished Goods Inventory Manufactured goods that are completed and ready for sale.

First-In, First-Out (FIFO) Method Assumes that the first goods purchased (the first in) are the first goods sold. (314)

Fiscal Any matters relating to money; typically used to describe a specified period of time used for financial reporting.

Fixed Assets Tangible assets that are fixed in place, such as land, buildings, and production equipment.

FOB Destination Term of sale indicating that goods are owned by the seller until delivered to the customer. (270)

FOB Shipping Point Term of sale indicating that goods are owned by the customer the moment they leave the seller's premises. (270)

Form 10-K The annual report that publicly traded companies must file with the SEC.

Form 10-Q The quarterly report that publicly traded companies must file with the SEC.

Franchise A contractual right to sell certain products or services, use certain trademarks, or perform activities in a certain geographical region. (418)

Free Cash Flow Computed as Cash Flows from Operating Activities–Dividends–Capital Expenditures.

Full Disclosure Principle States that relevant information should be disclosed in either the main financial statements or the notes to the financial statements. (626)

Future Value The sum to which an amount will increase as the result of compound interest. (C.2)

G

Generally Accepted Accounting Principles (GAAP) The rules used in the United States to calculate and report information in the financial statements. (18)

Going-Concern Assumption States that businesses are assumed to continue to operate into the foreseeable future. (626)

Goods Available for Sale The sum of beginning inventory and purchases for the period. (312)

Goodwill (Cost in Excess of Net Assets Acquired) For accounting purposes, the excess of the purchase price of a business over the market value of the business's assets and liabilities. (418)

Gross Profit (Gross Margin, Margin) Net sales less cost of goods sold. (274)

Gross Profit Percentage Indicates how much above cost a company sells its products; calculated as Gross Profit divided by Net Sales. (275)

H

Historical Cost Principle See *Cost Principle*. (47)

Horizontal Analysis Trend comparisons across time, often expressing changes in account balances as a percentage of prior year balances. (613)

I

Impairment Occurs when the cash to be generated by an asset is estimated to be less than the carrying value of that asset and requires that the carrying value of the asset be written down. (415)

Imprest System A process that controls the amount paid to others by limiting the total amount of money available for making payments to others. (263)

Income from Operations (Operating Income) Equals net sales less cost of goods sold and other operating expenses.

Income Statement (Statement of Income, Statement of Profit and Loss, Statement of Operations) Reports the revenues less the expenses of the accounting period. (10)

Incur To make oneself subject to; typically refers to expenses, which are incurred by using up the economic benefits of assets or becoming obligated for liabilities, resulting in a decrease in the company's resources in the current period.

Indirect Method A method of presenting the operating activities section of the statement of cash flows, in which net income is adjusted to compute cash flows from operating activities. (559)

Industry Practices Constraint A constraint that recognizes that companies in certain industries must follow accounting rules peculiar to that industry. (627)

Intangible Assets Assets that have special rights but not physical substance.

Interest Formula $I = P \times R \times T$, where I = interest calculated; P = principal; R = annual interest rate; and T = time period covered in the interest calculation (number of months out of 12). (368)

Internal Controls Processes by which a company provides reasonable assurance regarding the reliability of the company's financial reporting, the effectiveness and efficiency of its operations, and its compliance with applicable laws and regulations. (254)

International Financial Reporting Standards (IFRS) The rules used internationally to calculate and report information in the financial statements. (18, 220)

Inventory Tangible property held for sale in the normal course of business or used in producing goods or services for sale.

Inventory Turnover The process of buying and selling inventory. (323)

Investing Activities Involve buying or selling long-lived items such as land, buildings, and equipment.

Investments in Associated (or Affiliated) Companies Investments in stock held for the purpose of influencing the operating and financing strategies for the long term.

Issue Price The amount of money that a lender pays (and the company receives) when a bond is issued. (461)

Issued Shares Total number of shares of stock that have been sold; equals shares outstanding plus treasury shares held. (509)

J

Journal A record of each day's transactions. (56)

Journal Entry An accounting method for expressing the effects of a transaction on accounts in a debits-equal-credits format. (56)

Journalize The process of noting a transaction in the journal in the debits-equal-credits journal entry format.

L

Last-In, First-Out (LIFO) Method Assumes that the most recently purchased units (the last in) are sold first. (314)

Ledger A collection of records that summarizes the effects of transactions entered in the journal. (56)

Lender A creditor that has loaned money to the company.

Liabilities Probable debts or obligations of the entity that result from past transactions, which will be fulfilled by providing assets or services. (46)

Licensing Right The limited permission to use property according to specific terms and conditions set out in a contract. (417)

LIFO Reserve A contra-asset for the excess of FIFO over LIFO inventory.

Line Item An account name or title reported in the body of a financial statement; can represent a single account or the total of several accounts.

Line of Credit A prearranged agreement that allows a company to borrow any amount of money at any time, up to a prearranged limit. (469)

Liquidity The ability to pay current obligations. (616)

Loan Covenants Terms of a loan agreement that, if broken, entitle the lender to renegotiate terms of the loan, including its due date. (209)

Long-Lived Assets Tangible and intangible resources owned by a business and used in its operations over several years. (402)

Long-Term Assets Resources that will be used up or turned into cash more than 12 months after the balance sheet date.

Long-Term Liabilities All of the entity's obligations that are not classified as current liabilities.

Lower of Cost or Market (LCM) Valuation method departing from the cost principle; recognizes a loss when asset value drops below cost. (318)

M

Manufacturing Company A company that sells goods that it has made itself. (254)

Market Interest Rate The current rate of interest that exists when a debt is incurred. Also called *yield, discount rate,* or *effective interest rate*. (463)

Market Value Method Reports securities at their current market value.

Matching Principle Requires that expenses be recorded when incurred in earning revenue. (102)

Material Misstatements Amounts that are large enough to influence a user's decision. (218)

Maturity Date The date on which a bond is due to be paid in full. (461)

Merchandise Inventory Goods held for resale in the ordinary course of business.

Merchandising Company A company that sells goods which have been obtained from a supplier. (254)

Multistep Income Statement Reports alternative measures of income by calculating subtotals for core and peripheral business activities. (274)

N

Net To combine by subtracting one or more amounts from another.

Net Assets Shorthand term used to refer to assets minus liabilities. (418)

Net Book Value (Book Value, Carrying Value) The amount at which an asset or liability is reported after deducting any contra-accounts.

Net Income Equal to revenues minus expenses. (98)

Net Income before Income Taxes Revenues and gains minus losses and all expenses except income tax expense.

Net Profit Margin Ratio Indicates how well expenses are controlled, by dividing net income by revenue. (227)

Net Sales Total sales revenue minus Sales Returns and Allowances and Sales Discounts.

Noncash Investing and Financing Activities Transactions that do not have direct cash flow effects; reported as a supplement to the statement of cash flows in narrative or schedule form.

Noncumulative Preferred Stock Preferred stock that does not have cumulative dividend rights, such that dividend rights do not carry over from one year to the next.

Noncurrent long-term; assets and liabilities that do not meet the definition of current. (64)

No-Par Value Stock Capital stock that has no specified par value. (510)

Notes (Footnotes) Provide supplemental information about the financial condition of a company, without which the financial statements cannot be fully understood.

Notes Receivable Written promises that require another party to pay the business under specified conditions (amount, time, interest). (361)

NSF Checks (Not Sufficient Funds) Checks written for an amount greater than the funds available to cover them. (265)

O

Obsolescence The process of becoming out of date or falling into disuse.

Operating Activities The day-to-day events involved in running a business.

Operating Cycle (Cash-to-Cash Cycle) The time and activities needed for a company to sell goods and services to customers, collect cash from customers, and pay cash to suppliers.

Ordinary Repairs and Maintenance Expenditures for the normal operating upkeep of long-lived assets, recorded as expenses. (407)

Outstanding Shares Total number of shares of stock that are owned by stockholders on any particular date. (509)

P

Paid-In Capital (Additional Paid-In Capital, Contributed Capital in Excess of Par) The amount of contributed capital less the par value of the stock.

Par Value (1) For shares of stock, this is a legal amount per share established by the board of directors; it establishes the minimum amount a stockholder must contribute and has no relationship to the market price of the stock. (2) For bonds, see *Face Value*. (510)

Parent Company The entity that gains a controlling influence over another company (the subsidiary). (D16)

Partnerships Business organizations owned by two or more people. Each partner often is personally liable for debts that the partnership cannot pay.

Patent A right to exclude others from making, using, selling, or importing an invention. (417)

Payment Date The date on which a cash dividend is paid to the stockholders of record. (514)

Percentage of Credit Sales Method Bases bad debt expense on the historical percentage of credit sales that result in bad debts. (365)

Periodic Inventory System A system in which ending inventory and cost of goods sold are determined only at the end of the accounting period based on a physical inventory count. (269)

Permanent Accounts The balance sheet accounts that carry their ending balances into the next accounting period. (165)

Perpetual Inventory System A system in which a detailed inventory record is maintained by recording each purchase and sale of inventory during the accounting period. (269)

Post-Closing Trial Balance Prepared as the last step in the accounting cycle to check that debits equal credits and that all temporary accounts have been closed. (167)

Preferred Stock Stock that has specified rights over common stock. (519)

Premium For bonds, occurs when the issue price is greater than the face value. (461)

Prepaid Expenses A general account name used to describe payments made in advance of receiving future services; typically includes prepaid rent, prepaid insurance, and other specific types of prepayments.

Present Value The current value of an amount to be received in the future; a future amount discounted for compound interest. (461, C.1)

Press Release A written public news announcement normally distributed to major news services.

Private Company A company that has its stock bought and sold privately.

Profit An alternative term for net income.

Profitability Extent to which a company generates income. (616)

Public Company A company that has its stock bought and sold on public stock exchanges.

Public Company Accounting Oversight Board Makes the rules used by auditors of public companies.

Purchase Discount Cash discount received for prompt payment of an account. (321)

Purchase Returns and Allowances A reduction in the cost of purchases associated with unsatisfactory goods. (321)

Q

Qualified Audit Opinion Indicates that either the financial statements do not follow GAAP or the auditors were not able to complete the tests needed to determine whether the financial statements follow GAAP. (218)

Quick Ratio The ratio of liquid assets to current liabilities. Liquid assets include cash and cash equivalents, short-term investments, and accounts receivable (net of doubtful accounts). (468)

R

Ratio (Percentage) Analysis An analytical tool that measures the proportional relationship between two financial statement amounts.

Raw Materials Inventory Items acquired for the purpose of processing into finished goods.

Receivables Turnover The process of selling and collecting on an account. The receivables turnover ratio determines how many times this process occurs during the period on average. (372)

Record Date The date on which the corporation prepares the list of current stockholders as shown on its records. Dividends are paid only to the stockholders who own stock on that date. (514)

Relevant Information Information that can influence a decision. It is timely and has predictive and/or feedback value.

Reliable Information Information that is accurate, unbiased, and verifiable.

Research and Development Costs Expenditures that may someday lead to patents, copyrights, or other intangible assets, but the uncertainty about their future benefits requires that they be expensed. (418)

Residual (or Salvage) Value Estimated amount to be recovered, less disposal costs, at the end of the company's estimated useful life of an asset. (409)

Retained Earnings Cumulative earnings of a company that are not distributed to the owners; profits from the current year and all prior years that are reinvested ("retained") in the business.

Revenue Principle Revenues are recorded when goods or services are delivered, there is evidence of an arrangement for customer payment, the price is fixed or determinable, and collection is reasonably assured. (100)

Revenue Recognition Policy An accounting policy that describes when a company reports revenue from providing services or goods to customers.

Revenues Increases in assets or settlements of liabilities arising from ongoing operations. (97)

S

Sales (or Cash) Discount Cash discount offered to customers to encourage prompt payment of an account receivable. (272)

Sales Returns and Allowances Reduction of sales revenues for return of or allowances for unsatisfactory goods. (271)

Sarbanes-Oxley Act (SOX) A set of laws established to strengthen corporate reporting in the United States. (19, 211)

Securities and Exchange Commission (SEC) The U.S. government agency that determines the financial statements that public companies must provide to stockholders and the rules that they must use in producing those statements.

Securities Available for Sale All passive investments other than trading securities (classified as either short term or long term). (D.5)

Segregation of Duties An internal control that involves separating employees' duties so that the work of one person can be used to check the work of another person. (256)

Separate-Entity Assumption States that business transactions are separate from and should exclude the personal transactions of the owners. (8)

Service Company A company that sells services rather than physical goods. (254)

Single-Step Income Statement Reports net income by subtracting a single group of expenses from a single group of revenues. (214)

Sole Proprietorship A business organization owned by one person who is liable for debts the business cannot pay.

Solvency Ability to survive long enough to repay lenders when debt matures. (616)

Specific Identification Method A method of assigning costs to inventory, which identifies the cost of each specific item purchased and sold. (313)

Stated Interest Rate The rate of cash interest per period specified in a bond contract. Also called *coupon rate* or *contract rate*. (461)

Statement of Cash Flows Reports inflows and outflows of cash during the accounting period in the categories of operating, investing, and financing. (13)

Statement of Retained Earnings Reports the way that net income and the distribution of dividends affected the financial position of the company during the accounting period. (11)

Stock Dividend Declared by the board of directors to distribute to existing stockholders additional shares of a corporation's own stock. (515)

Stock Split An increase in the total number of authorized shares by a specified ratio; does not decrease retained earnings. (517)

Stockholders' Equity (Owners' Equity or Shareholders' Equity) The financing provided by the owners and the operations of the business. (46)

Straight-Line Method of Amortization Method of amortizing a bond discount or premium that allocates an equal dollar amount to each interest period. (470)

Straight-Line Depreciation Method Allocates the cost of an asset in equal periodic amounts over its useful life. (410)

Subsidiary Company A business that is controlled by another company (the parent). (D.16)

T

10-K See *Form 10-K.*

10-Q See *Form 10-Q.*

T-Account A simplified version of a ledger account used for summarizing transaction effects and determining balances for each account. (58)

Tangible Assets Assets that have physical substance.

Temporary Accounts Income statement accounts that are closed to *Retained Earnings* at the end of the accounting period. (165)

Tests of Liquidity Ratios that measure a company's ability to meet its currently maturing obligations.

Tests of Profitability Ratios that compare income with one or more primary activities.

Tests of Solvency Ratios that measure a company's ability to meet its long-term obligations.

Ticker Symbol The one- to four-letter abbreviation used to identify a company on a public securities exchange.

Time Period Assumption The assumption that allows the long life of a company to be reported in shorter time periods. (98)

Time-Series Analysis Compares a company's results for one period to its own results over a series of time periods. (223)

Times Interest Earned Ratio Determines the extent to which earnings before taxes and financing costs are sufficient to cover interest expense incurred on debt. (469)

Time Value of Money The idea that money received today is worth more than the same amount received in the future because money received today can be invested to earn interest over time. (C.1)

Trademark An exclusive legal right to use a special name, image, or slogan. (417)

Trading Securities All investments in stocks or bonds that are held primarily for the purpose of active trading (buying and selling) in the near future (classified as short term). (D5)

Transaction An exchange or an event that has a direct economic effect on the assets, liabilities, or stockholders' equity of a business. (48)

Transaction Analysis The process of studying a transaction to determine its economic effect on the business in terms of the accounting equation.

Treasury Stock A corporation's own stock that has been issued but was subsequently reacquired by and is still being held by the corporation. (509)

Trial Balance A list of all accounts with their balances to provide a check on the equality of the debits and credits. (110)

U

Unearned Revenue A liability representing a company's obligation to provide goods or services to customers in the future. (101)

Unit of Measure Assumption States that accounting information should be measured and reported in the national monetary unit. (10)

Units-of-Production Depreciation Method Allocates the cost of an asset over its useful life based on its periodic output in relation to its total estimated output. (411)

Unqualified Audit Opinion Auditors' statements that the financial statements are fair presentations in all material respects in conformity with GAAP. (218)

Unrealized Holding Gains and Losses Amounts associated with price changes of securities that are currently held.

Useful Life The expected service life of an asset to the present owner. (409)

V

Vertical (Common Size) Analysis Expresses each financial statement amount as a percentage of another amount on the same financial statement. (615)

Voucher System A process for approving and documenting all purchases and payments on account. (262)

W

Weighted Average Cost Method Uses the weighted average unit cost of goods available for sale for calculations of both the cost of goods sold and ending inventory. (314)

Work in Process Inventory Goods in the process of being manufactured.

Write-Off The removal from an uncollectable account and its corresponding allowance from the accounting records. (363)

Y

Yield See *Market Interest Rate.* (463)

Chapter 1

Chapter 1 Opener: © Funkyfood London—Paul Williams/Alamy; p. 4 (top and bottom): © The McGraw-Hill Companies, Inc./Brian Moeskau, photographer. p. 18: Map from http://www.iasb.org/About+Us/About+the+IASB/IFRSs+around+the+world.htm. Under Armour logo: © Under Armour, Inc., 2006. Used with permission. Tootsie Roll logo: © Tootsie Roll Industries, Inc.

Chapter 2

Chapter 2 Opener: © Photofusion Picture Library/Alamy; Exhibit 2.1 (top, left): © Comstock/PunchStock; Exhibit 2.1 (top, right): © David A. Tietz/Editorial Image, LLC; Exhibit 2.2 (top, right): Coutresy of Toastmaster; Exhibit 2.2 (top, left): © David A. Tietz/Editorial Image, LLC; Exhibit 2.2 (bottom, left): © Jaimie Duplass/Alamy; Exhibit 2.2 (bottom, right): © Studio 101/Alamy; p. 51: © Creatrixcordis/iStock; p. 53: © Studio 101/Alamy; p. 54: © Corbis Premium RF/Alamy; p. 67: © Geostock/Getty Images. Half-Price books logo: © Half-Price Books, 2006. Used with permission. Trump Entertainment logo: Courtesy of Trump Entertainment Resorts, Inc.

Chapter 3

Chapter 3 Opener: © Ted Pink/Alamy; Exhibit 3.3: AP Photo/Douglas C. Pizac.

Chapter 4

Chapter 4 Opener: © Yellow Dog Productions/Taxi/Getty; p. 151: © Bernd Euler/VISUM/The Image Works; p. 169: AP Photo/Steve Helber.

Chapter 5

Chapter 5 Opener: © Charley Gallay/Getty; p. 219: © Thomas Lohnes/AFP/Getty. Mad Catz and the Mad Catz logo are trademarks or registered trademarks of Mad Catz, Inc., its subsidiaries and affiliates.

Chapter 6

Chapter 6 Opener: © Justin Sullivan/Getty; p. 257 (top): © Royalty-Free/Corbis; p. 257 (bottom): © Jill Battaglia/iStock Photo; p. 259 (top): © C Squared Studios/Getty Images; p. 259 (bottom): © PhotoDisc/Getty Images; p. 271: © Justin Sullivan/Getty. Walmart logo: Courtesy of Walmart Stores, Inc.

Chapter 7

Chapter 7 Opener: © Tim Boyle/Getty.

Chapter 8

Chapter 8 Opener: © Najlah Feanny/Corbis.

Chapter 9

Chapter 9 Opener: © Image State Royalty Free/Alamy Images; p. 404 (top and bottom left): Courtesy of Cedar Point; P. 404 (bottom right): © Jupiterimages/Thinkstock/Getty; p. 407: © Glowimages/Getty Images. Yahoo logo: Reproduced with permission of Yahoo! Inc. ©2009 Yahoo! Inc. YAHOO! and the YAHOO! logo are registered trademarks of Yahoo! Inc.

Chapter 10

Chapter 10 Opener: © Laura Dwight/PhotoEdit. American Greetings logo: Reproduced by permission. American Greetings Corporation. © AGC, Inc.

Chapter 11

Chapter 11 Opener: Courtesy of National Beverage Corporation; p. 516: © The McGraw-Hill Companies, Inc./David Tietz, photographer. Black & Decker logo: © Black & Decker, 2006. Used with permission.

Chapter 12

Chapter 12 Opener: Courtesy of Under Armour, Inc.

Chapter 13

Chapter 13 Opener: © Justin Sullivan/Getty; Appendix D1: © AP Photo/Pablo Martinez Monsivais; Appendix D2: © PRNewsFoto/Newsweek. Fortune logo: Courtesy Fortune Brands, Inc.

Subject Index